PSYCHOLOGY

IN THE NEW MILLENNIUM

SIXTH EDITION

PSYCHOLOGY
IN THE NEW MILLENNIUM

SIXTH EDITION

SPENCER A. RATHUS
ST. JOHN'S UNIVERSITY

HARCOURT BRACE COLLEGE PUBLISHERS

Fort Worth   Philadelphia   San Diego   New York   Orlando   Austin   San Antonio
Toronto   Montreal   London   Sydney   Tokyo

Publisher	Ted Buchholz
Editor in Chief	Christopher P. Klein
Senior Developmental Editor	Meera Dash
Project Editor	Jeff Beckham
Production Manager	Cynthia Young
Art Director	Peggy Young
Picture Editor	Sandra Lord
Photo Research	Marty Levick
Permissions Editor	Sheila Shutter

Cover Photo: © Barry Rosenthal/ FPG International (also page v and page ix)

Requests for permission to make copies of any part of the work should be mailed to: Permissions Department, Harcourt Brace & Company, 6277 Sea Harbor Drive, Orlando, Florida 32887-6777.

Address for Editorial Correspondence: Harcourt Brace College Publishers, 301 Commerce Street, Suite 3700, Fort Worth, TX 76102.

Address for Orders: Harcourt Brace & Company, 6277 Sea Harbor Drive, Orlando, FL 32887. 1-800-782-4479, or 1-800-433-0001 (in Florida).

(Copyright Acknowledgments begin on page A12, which constitutes a continuation of this copyright page.)

Printed in the United States of America

ISBN: 0-15-501699-7

Library of Congress Catalog Card Number: 94-79633

6 7 8 9 0 1 2   032   10 9 8 7 6 5 4 3 2

For Lois —
Number 1 on my
Wish List for the
New Millennium

About the Cover

*Will you, won't you, will you, won't you, will you join
the dance?*

LEWIS CARROLL, *ALICE IN WONDERLAND*

A dancer leaps symbolically into the new millennium. She is fearless, open to new experience. Psychology, too, is leaping into the new millennium—creating some of the substance of change and helping us adjust to change.

Each chapter of *Psychology in the New Millennium* opens with a photograph of dance. Why dance? Dance suggests the nature and drama of psychology.

Nearly all people are intricately involved in being within and controlling their bodies. Sensing ourselves within ourselves and within the world—this is part of the substance of psychology.

But dancers sense and control their movements more finely than most of us; they are more deeply in touch with the poetry in their bodies. Some of us are naturally more graceful, more attuned to dancing's rigors and beauties—which brings us to a core question of psychology: How do our inborn natures and our experiences lead us to dancing? To the ingenuity of the written word? To games like chess? To the building of computers and coliseums? To charity and brutality? To romantic love?

Dancing is an art form suggestive of human creativity and intelligence. As we see in the photo that opens Chapter 6, dancing is learned. We learn to dance; we remember how to dance. All these — creativity, intelligence, learning, memory — are also matters of psychology.

Some of us are more charged by dance than others. Some of us must dance; others feel no such inner edict — differences which bring us into the psychological domains of motivation, emotion, and personality.

We dance with others. We dance alone. Psychology is concerned with the dignity of the individual, and with the behavior of the individual within the group.

Psychology is leaping into the new millennium. . . . "Will you, won't you, will you, won't you, will you join the dance?"

S. A. RATHUS

Brief Contents

To the Instructor
xiii

To the Student
xxiii

Contents
xxxiii

Chapter 1
What Is Psychology?
2

Chapter 2
Research Methods
in Psychology
40

Chapter 3
Biology and Behavior
78

Chapter 4
Sensation and Perception
122

Chapter 5
States of Consciousness
172

Chapter 6
Learning
210

Chapter 7
Memory
248

Chapter 8
Thinking and Language
288

Chapter 9
Intelligence
328

Chapter 10
Motivation and Emotion
354

Chapter 11
Developmental Psychology
394

Chapter 12
Personality: Theories
and Measurement
438

Chapter 13
Psychological Disorders
480

Chapter 14
Methods of Therapy
520

Chapter 15
Health Psychology
562

Chapter 16
Social Psychology
608

Chapter 17
Applied Psychology
654

Appendix A
Statistics
A1

Appendix B
Answer Keys for Questionnaires
A10

Credits
A12

Glossary
G1

References
R1

Name Index
IN1

Subject Index
IN9

To the Instructor

"Blending the traditional and the familiar with the promise and the shock of the new . . ."

What will psychology be like in the new millennium? What will psychology have to offer? Will psychology's traversing of the literal edge of time place psychology on the cutting edge of technological advancement?

As psychology proceeds from the present into the future, what shall guide us? How will your textbook, *Psychology in the New Millennium,* guide the adventure? Perhaps by blending the traditional and the familiar with the promise and shock of the new.

The Tradition: The Adventure Continues

Much in your textbook is traditional and familiar. This edition continues to recount psychology's rich history, the philosophical and methodological roots that can be traced beyond the sages of the ancient Greeks. A century ago, William James wrote "I wished, by treating Psychology like a natural science, to help her become one." Psychology is very much that science of which he spoke. Your textbook explores psychology's tradition as an empirical science. It explores the research methods innovated in nineteenth-century Germany and brought to the shores of the New World in the twentieth. It also provides comprehensive coverage of the traditional areas of subject matter in psychology.

The writing style of *Psychology in the New Millennium* continues to communicate the excitement of psychology. The text was deliberately written to be user-friendly—to meet the needs of students. It uses personal anecdotes and humor to motivate students and help them understand the subject matter. The goal of the style is lofty: to engage and motivate students without descending into frivolity and condescension. The personal approach is exemplified in the way that the text walks students through the Milgram studies on obedience to authority in Chapter 2. Students vicariously experience Milgram's methods, and as a result, they enhance their motivation, comprehension, and retention.

You will also find many of the signature Rathus features and learning aids that have contributed to the success of earlier editions:

- "Truth or Fiction?" items stimulate students to delve into the subject matter by challenging folklore and common sense (which is often "common *non-sense*")

- Running glossary items provide ready access to the meanings of key terms so that students can maintain their concentration on the flow of the material in the chapter

- "Psychology in a World of Diversity" features help students perceive why people of different cultures and genders behave and think in different ways, and how the science of psychology in enriched by addressing those differences

- Questionnaires stimulate student interest by helping them satisfy their curiosities about themselves and make the text more user-friendly by enhancing its relevance to students' lives

- "Psychology and Modern Life" features highlight the relevance of psychology to contemporary issues and apply psychological knowledge to help students cope with the challenges in their own lives

However, *Psychology in the New Millennium* is also a new story that brings our science to the next generation.

Into the New Millennium: The Next Generation

The promise of the new truly places our tale of psychology on the cutting edge. On the edge of the new millennium, the very "language" of psychology has changed to be consistent with psychology's emphasis on the dignity of the individual. A new pedagogical package makes the textbook a more effective tool for teaching and learning than it has ever been.

The current edition of *Psychology in the New Millennium* includes two new chapters, full integration of the sociocultural perspective, full integration of gender, a new look at the very language of psychology, "Reflections" sections, increased emphasis on critical thinking, and "Psychology in the New Millennium" features.

NEW CHAPTERS

The new chapters cover "Research Methods in Psychology" and "Thinking and Language."

Chapter 2: Research Methods in Psychology. Research methods are at the core of psychology as a science. *Psychology in the New Millennium* thus devotes full chapter coverage to the topic. Yet in keeping with our tradition of presenting rigorous subject matter in an accessible manner, Chapter 2 walks students through essential research issues in a way that is both stimulating and user-friendly.

Chapter 8: Thinking and Language. In keeping with *Psychology in the New Millennium's* enhanced emphasis on critical thinking, there is now full chapter coverage of the interrelated topics of thinking and language. Increased coverage of problem solving, creativity, reasoning, and judgment

and decision making heighten the rigor of the book. Again, however, the increase in rigor is accompanied by a user-friendly approach. Relevant examples and humor motivate students and help them grasp new concepts.

FULL INTEGRATION OF THE SOCIOCULTURAL PERSPECTIVE

As we head toward the year 2000, our population is becoming an ever richer mix of cultural traditions. The sociocultural perspective brings those various traditions within the province of psychology. It enables us to consider how best to apply psychology's research findings to people from different backgrounds. In keeping with psychology's history, it also helps us focus more precisely on our understanding of the individual.

The sociocultural perspective is integrated throughout the book because it is relevant to all areas of psychology. Consider the following examples: Chapter 1 introduces "The Sociocultural Perspective" and "Human Diversity and Psychology." Other chapters include sections on "Samples and Populations: Representing Human Diversity," "Bilingualism and Bilingual Education," "Sex: A Sociocultural Perspective," "The Sociocultural Perspective: The Individual in the New Multicultural United States," "Psychotherapy in the New Multicultural United States," and "Human Diversity and Health: Nations within the Nation."

FULL INTEGRATION OF GENDER

A focus on gender helps us appreciate differences among individuals and helps us to see through to a common human core. Issues of gender bear on the subject matter in diverse areas of psychology and are thus integrated throughout *Psychology in the New Millennium*.

Chapter 1 devotes a section to "Gender" in the discussion of "Human Diversity and Psychology," and Chapter 2 discusses the need for more focus on research issues of importance to women, in the section

"Samples and Populations: Representing Human Diversity." Other chapters discuss such issues as gender differences in alcoholism and smoking; creativity and language development; the effects of sex hormones; gender differences in use of health care; and gender issues in level of moral judgment, formation of adolescent identity, and patterns of adult development. Gender is also addressed in major features, including "Individuality Versus Relatedness: The Rust Pile for Iron John?", "Gender Differences: Vive la Différence or Vive la Similarité?", and "Women and Psychotherapy."

A NEW LOOK AT THE LANGUAGE OF PSYCHOLOGY

Every line of *Psychology in the New Millennium* reflects sensitivity to the dignity of the individual. The book has always been sensitive to issues of gender and ethnicity in our language. Consider gender. We do not refer to a person of unspecified gender as "he." We say, rather, "she or he" or "they." However, the new edition of the *Publication Manual of the American Psychological Association* also finds that traditional use of terms such as *subjects, receiving treatments, schizophrenics,* and *the elderly* denies individuals their dignity and their active participation in research.

Psychology in the New Millennium, therefore, speaks of *individuals, people,* and *participants*—not of *subjects.* Your textbook speaks of individuals as active in research—as *partaking* in research, or as *obtaining* treatments, not as *receiving* treatments. Your textbook speaks of *people with schizophrenia* or of *people diagnosed with schizophrenia,* not of *schizophrenics.* Your textbook speaks of *older people,* not of *the elderly.* In *Psychology in the New Millennium,* the person always comes first. It is the person that defines the individual. The modifier, whether it refers to age, psychological disorders, or other matters, is secondary. This is not verbal gameplaying. People are people and deserve to be treated with dignity regardless of age, psychological disorder, or participation in research. Our descriptors expand or limit the nature of other human beings, and psychology teaches us that people deserve our very careful consideration.

"REFLECTIONS" SECTIONS

New "Reflections" sections serve a dual function: They help students learn the subject matter and they stimulate critical thinking.

Psychologists and educators have shown that students learn effectively when they *reflect* on what they are learning. Reflecting on a subject means *relating* it to things they already know, including their own life experiences and other academic subjects. Relating the material to things known makes the information meaningful and easier to remember. Relating also makes it more likely that students will be able to *use* the new information in their own lives.

A Reflections section appears at the end of every major section. These sections ask students to pause before proceeding so that they may relate what they have read to their life experiences and academic knowledge.

Many of the questions in the Reflections sections are also exercises in the workbook, *Thinking and Writing About Psychology in the New Millennium.* These exercises are especially constructed to stimulate critical thinking and are recognizable by blue typeface in the textbook.

"PSYCHOLOGY IN THE NEW MILLENNIUM" FEATURES

As we look into the new millennium, we feel very much of the edge of major technological advances and changes in lifestyle. The "Psychology in the New Millennium" features in every chapter explore these fascinating connections to psychology. In some cases we explore the future of psychological knowledge or applications. In other cases, we explore the effect of other kinds of advances or changes on people's behavior and mental processes. Examples include "And Now—Brainman?", "Sonic Device May Help Blind People Navigate," "Learning at the Feet of the . . . Information Superhighway?", "Goals 2000: Helping Our

Children Learn to Solve the Problems of the New Millennium," "Will Music Provide Our Children with the Sweet Sounds of Success?", "Will Your Problems Be Diagnosed by a Computer?", and "Beyond Wellness: Are Biological Treatments for Personality Improvement in the Offing?".

FIGURE 5.1

Spotlight on Levels of Consciousness, According to Sigmund Freud

EMPHASIZED TOPICS

As part and parcel of an enhanced pedagogical format, the current edition spotlights topics that many instructors find hard to teach and many students find hard to learn. The explanations of these topics are featured through clear illustrations and emphasized by a lead-in to the figure title called "Spotlight on . . . " This treatment will facilitate mastery of the most difficult topics.

There are from one to four spotlighted topics per chapter. Examples include "Contemporary Perspectives at a Glance" (Chapter 1), "Correlational Relationships, Causes and Effects" (Chapter 2), "Types of Conditioning" and "Positive Versus Negative Reinforcers" (Chapter 6).

CD-ROM MULTIMEDIA INTERFACES

MINILECTURE: A BRIEF HISTORY OF PSYCHOLOGY

A CD-ROM for psychology students contains interactive multimedia features including "minilectures" on core concepts in psychology. The availability of minilectures is indicated by a CD-ROM icon in the margin of the text. The topic of the minilecture is printed near the icon. Thus, the icon tells the student that more information about the topic is available in the CD-ROM. The CD-ROM brings a new generation of learning devices to the tradition of psychology.

In short, *Psychology in the New Millennium*—the book you are now holding in your hands—combines the traditional and the familiar with the promise and the shock of the new. As we move into the new millennium, psychology remains as vital and exciting as ever. Psychology's meaningful tradition and its innovations keep our science at the forefront of human endeavor.

The Package: Bringing Psychology to the Next Generation

The needs of a new generation of instructors and students demand a full and broad array of ancillary materials to make learning and teaching more effective. *Psychology in the New Millennium* is accompanied by a complete, convenient, and carefully conceived multimedia package. The ancillaries are available to qualified adopters. Interested instructors should contact their Harcourt Brace representative for more information.

THINKING AND WRITING ABOUT PSYCHOLOGY IN THE NEW MILLENNIUM

by Spencer A. Rathus,
St. John's University

As its name implies, *Thinking and Writing About Psychology in the New Millennium* is designed to promote two aspects of contemporary college education: critical thinking and writing across the curriculum. To this end, the ancillary contains a discussion of what critical thinking is, a comprehensive guide to writing about psychology using the APA's latest recommendation, and dozens of writing exercises. Writing exercises may be assigned as a way of encouraging the development of thinking and writing skills, as a way of providing an opportunity for class participation, and perhaps, as a way of earning part of the grade for the course.

ISBN: 0-15-503220-8

SELF-SCORING STUDENT STUDY GUIDE

by Spencer A. Rathus, St. John's University
and Joyce Bishop, Golden West College
Spence Rathus wrote the Student Study Guide to ensure that its quality matched that of the textbook. Its format is equally useful for traditional or individualized (PSI) settings. The guide features a section on "How to Do Well in College," addressing how to cope with test anxiety and how to plan a career in psychology. Each chapter

includes a pretest, an overview, learning objectives, key terms, exercises, a programmed chapter review, and a posttest. A special section, "ESL—Bridging the Gap," helps students of diverse cultures understand the language of psychology, while giving English-speaking students an understanding of the challenges faced by non-native speakers.

Joyce Bishop designed a new and unique layout for the guide that is more visually appealing and more student-oriented. Each of the chapter outlines provides space for notetaking. Graphics from the textbook have been reproduced in the study guide and can be removed from the book and placed on 3 × 5 notecards to enhance the students' learning of difficult psychological concepts. Likewise, flashcards allow students to study key terms more easily.
ISBN: 0-15-503218-6

INSTRUCTOR'S MANUAL WITH VIDEO INSTRUCTOR'S GUIDE

by Jim Tremain, Midland Lutheran College; *Lawrence Weinstein,* Cameron University; *and Gary King,* Rose State College

The Instructor's Manual has been expanded to be especially useful to the first-time teacher of psychology as well as a first-time teacher of the textbook, *Psychology in the New Millennium.* The opening section gives detailed guidelines for organizing and preparing the introductory psychology course. Each chapter features an outline of the material in the manual, an outline of the corresponding chapter in the textbook, a listing of teaching objectives that correspond to the learning objectives in the Student Study Guide, practical and effective lecture suggestions for each major topic in the chapter, references to resources that are appropriate for use with each topic (i.e., CD-ROM, films, transparencies, videodiscs, etc.), creative classroom demonstrations, innovative critical thinking exercises, suggestions for in-class and out-of-class activities, and student quiz handouts.

A *Video Instructor's Guide* has been combined with the manual to provide instructors with a complete resource teaching package. The guide references the Harcourt Brace psychology video and videodisc library, with more specific teaching suggestions for using the segments from the *Discovering Psychology* Teaching Modules. The guide is abundant with activities and discussions, and is customized to correspond with material covered in *Psychology in the New Millennium* (includes textbook page references).
ISBN: 0-15-503217-8

TEST BANK

by Harry Tiemann and Mara Merlino, both of Mesa State College

To provide instructors with a supply of test items that meets their particular needs and expectations, we surveyed a panel of experienced introductory psychology teachers and designed a test bank according to their combined preferences. A special thanks to Tom Billimek, *San Antonio College;* Colleen Gift, *Highland Community College;* Gloria Lewis, *Tennessee State University;* and Rosemary Price, *Rancho Santiago College,* for their contribution to the development of the sixth edition test bank.

The test bank maintains 125 to 200 multiple-choice items for each chapter, 40 of which are taken directly from the Student Study Guide, plus 65 test items for Appendix A: Statistics. Test items appear in the order of the presentation in the textbook, are keyed to teaching/learning objectives, and are coded in terms of correct answer, question type, difficulty level, cognitive type, textbook page reference, whether the item appears in the Student Study Guide, and whether the item tests material from a textbook feature (i.e., "Psychology in the New Millennium," "Psychology in a World of Diversity," and "Psychology and Modern Life").

Approximately 60 percent of the test items are designated as "recall", testing knowledge of factual material. The remaining 40 percent are designated as "applied", measuring students' abilities to understand and apply material in real-life situations. The breakdown of question difficulty is approximately 20 percent "easy", 60 percent "moderate", and 20 percent "difficult".
ISBN: 0-15-503219-4

EXAMASTER+™ COMPUTERIZED TEST BANK

Offers easy-to-use options for test creation: *EasyTest* creates a test from a single screen in just a few easy steps. Instructors choose parameters, then select questions from the data base or let *EasyTest* randomly select them.

FullTest offers a range of options that includes selecting, editing, adding, or linking questions or graphics; random selection of questions from a wide range of criteria; creating criteria; blocking questions; and printing up to 99 different versions of the same test and answer sheet.

On-Line Testing allows instructors to create a test in *EXAMaster+*™, save it to the OLT subdirectory or diskette, and administer the test on-line. The results of the test can then be imported to *ESAGrade*.

ESAGrade can be used to set up new classes, to record grades from tests or assignments utilizing scantron, and to analyze grades and produce class and individual statistics. *ESAGrade* comes packaged with *EXAMaster+*™.

IBM® 3.5″ ISBN: 0-15-503221-6
Macintosh® ISBN: 0-15-503222-4
MS Windows™ ISBN: 0-15-503223-2

RequesTest is a service for instructors without access to a computer. A software specialist will compile questions according to the instructor's criteria and mail or fax the test master within 48 hours! Call 1-800-447-9457.

The Software Support Hotline is available to answer questions Monday through Friday, 9 A.M. to 4 P.M. Central Time at 1-800-447-9457.

PSYCHOLOGY: THE CORE ON CD-ROM

by John Mitterer, Brock University
The CD-ROM is an innovative learning tool that allows students to explore and understand the realm of psychology in an interactive, multimedia environment. Mini-lectures, covering the key concepts in every chapter, include video footage, animation,

and experiments, and are linked directly to the full text, which also appears on the CD-ROM. In addition, the CD-ROM allows students to test their mastery of the material via a series of test questions hyperlinked to the relevant sections of *Psychology in the New Millennium,* Sixth Edition.

John Mitterer, who has been praised for his authorship of Harcourt Brace's videodisc, *Dynamic Concepts in Psychology,* has coordinated the creation of the CD-ROM with the additional content expertise of such experienced lecturers as Tom Brothen, *University of Minnesota;* Bill Buskist, *Auburn University;* Paula Goolkasian, *University of North Carolina at Charlotte;* Carolyn Meyer, *Lake Sumter Community College;* David Murphy, *Waubonsee Community College;* and Robert Patterson, *Washington State University*

INTERACTIVE SOFTWARE

Personal Discovery (IBM and Macintosh®): Eric Sandburg developed this interactive software program that provides a computerized series of self-description, self-exploration, and extended personal planning activities to help the student apply psychological principles to life.

IBM® 5.25″ ISBN: 0-15-501704-7
IBM® 3.5″ ISBN: 0-15-501703-9
Macintosh® ISBN: 0-15-501705-5

Other interactive software is available to psychology students. Contact your local Harcourt Brace representative for details.

THE WHOLE PSYCHOLOGY CATALOG (REVISED FOR 1996

Instructors can easily supplement their lectures with this manual's experiential exercises, questionnaires, and visual aids. Revised to integrate contemporary issues from the introductory psychology course, the manual is printed on perforated pages to facilitate use of individual handouts in the classroom or as homework.

DYNAMIC CONCEPTS IN PSYCHOLOGY OVERHEAD TRANSPARENCIES

This set of 130 full-color acetates is derived from Harcourt Brace's unique videodisc and covers the full range of topics typical to an introductory psychology course.

ISBN: 0-15-502082-X

DYNAMIC CONCEPTS IN PSYCHOLOGY VIDEODISC, SECOND EDITION

Revised and expanded with new media, this videodisc program keeps classrooms on the forefront of introductory psychology. Numerous animated sequences, film and video footage, still images, and demonstrations vividly illustrate each topic. Easy-to-use features and modular format allow instructors to customize the program to their course.

HARCOURT BRACE QUARTERLY: A VIDEO NEWS MAGAZINE

In conjunction with CBS Television, Harcourt Brace brings current psychological applications, straight from today's headlines, to your classroom. Harcourt Brace periodically selects the most applicable issues from *CBS Nightly News, CBS This Morning, 48 Hours,* and *Street Stories with Ed Bradley.* Pertinent segments are compiled and provide over an hour of the most contemporary video applications for the study of psychology. Accompanying *Instructor's Notes* provide a synopsis of each segment, page references to major Harcourt Brace psychology texts, and numerous additional questions and activities.

DISCOVERING PSYCHOLOGY

Hosted by Philip Zimbardo, this video series is an introductory psychology television course. It is divided into 26 half-hour segments, covering the full range of topics common to the introductory psychology course.

DISCOVERING PSYCHOLOGY TEACHING MODULES

This edited version of the *Discovering Psychology* series provides brief segments designed for easy classroom use. A *Video Instructor's Guide* comes with this package to provide descriptions and teaching suggestions for the 15 modules (84 total segments). Available on videodisc and videocassette.

DISCOVERING PSYCHOLOGY TELECOURSE FACULTY GUIDE

Revised by Bernardo Carducci of Indiana University, the telecourse faculty guide contains the telecourse study guide plus faculty notes. Special efforts have been made to ensure the accuracy of these guides.

DISCOVERING PSYCHOLOGY TELECOURSE STUDY GUIDE

The telecourse study guide helps students to bridge their understanding of the Discovering Psychology telcourse and the sixth edition of the Rathus textbook. Acitvities, questions, readings, and illustrations help reinforce the impact of psychology on daily life.

INFINITE VOYAGE, PRISONERS OF THE BRAIN, AND FIRES OF THE MIND

WQED of Boston produced this video series, which incorporates on-location, interview, laboratory, and candid footage to provide compelling coverage of high-interest topics in psychology. Available on videodisc and videocassette.

THE BRAIN

This series of videos offers key segments of the PBS television series *The Brain* in 30 video modules of about 6 minutes each.

THE MIND

Developed in cooperation with WNET of New York, this series of videos offers selections from the PBS series *The Mind* to illustrate important concepts in introductory psychology.

Acknowledgments

The discipline of psychology owes its progress and its scientific standing to experts who conduct research in many different areas. Similarly, the textbook *Psychology in the New Millennium* and its ancillaries owe a great deal of their substance and form to my colleagues who provided expert suggestions and insights at various stages of their development. My sincere thanks to the following individuals who contributed to the development of the sixth edition:

Melita Baumann, Glendale Community College; Tom Billimek, San Antonio College; Joyce Bishop, Golden West College; Robert Cameron, Fairmont State College; Michael Connor, Long Beach Community College; William Rick Fry, Youngstown State University; Peter Gram, Pensacola Junior College; Beverly Greene, St. John's University; Kevin Keating, Broward Community College; Gary King, Rose State College; Daniel Lapsley, University of Notre Dame; Joseph McNair, Miami–Dade Community College; Joel Morgovsky, Brookdale Community College; Peggy Nash, Broward Community College; Jeffrey S. Nevid, St. John's University; Nora Noel, University of North Carolina at Wilmington; Gregory Pezzetti, Rancho Santiago College; Rosemary Price, Rancho Santiago College; Beth Rienzi, California State University, Bakersfield; Ross Robak, Pace University; Gloria Scheff, Broward Community College; Joseph Shaver, Fairmont State College; Larry J. Siegel, University of Lowell; Pamela Simon, Baker College; Catherine Wambach, University of Minnesota.

My sincere thanks also to the reviewers of earlier editions:
Mark H. Ashcraft, Cleveland State University; Gladys J. Baez–Dickreiter, St. Phillip's College; Patricia Barker, Schenectady County Community College; Barbara Basden, California State University; James Beaird, Western Oregon State University; Thomas L. Bennett, Colorado State University; John Benson, Texarkana College; Otto Berliner, SUNY—Alfred; Richard A. Block, Montana State University; C. Robert Boresen, Wichita State University; Theodore N. Bosack, Providence College; Betty Bowers, North Central Technical Institute; Peter J. Brady, Clark Technical College; Jack Brennecke, Mount San Antonio College; Donald Buckley, Cumberland Community College; Garvin Chastain, Boise State University; John Childers, East Carolina University; Lauren Coodley, Napa Valley College; Richard Day, Manchester Community College; Donald L. Daoust, Southern Oregon State College; Carl L. Denti, Dutchess County Community College; Carol Doolin, Henderson County Junior College; Wendy L. Dunn, Coe College; John Foust, Parkland College; Morton P. Friedman, University of California at Los Angeles; Marian Gibney, Phoenix College; Bernard Gorman, Nassau County Community College; Richard Gottwald, Indiana University at South Bend; Gloria Griffith, Tennessee Technological University; Richard Griggs, University of Florida; Sandra L. Groeltz, DeVry Institute of Technology at Chicago; Arthur Gutman, Florida Institute of Technology; Jim Hail, McClennan Community College; Robert W. Hayes, Boston University; George Herrick, SUNY—Alfred; Sidney Hochman, Nassau Community College; Morton Hoffman, Metropolitan State College; Betsy Howton, Western Kentucky University; John H. Hummel, University of Houston; Sam L. Hutchinson, Radford University; Jarvel Jackson, McClellan Community College; Rafael Art. Javier, St. John's University; Robert L. Johnson, Umpqua Community College; Timothy Johnston, University of North Carolina at Greensboro; Eve Jones, Los Angeles City College; Karen Jones, University of the Ozarks; Kenneth Kallio, SUNY—Geneseo; Charles Karis, Northwestern University; Mary Louise-Kean, University of California at Irvine; Richard Kellogg, SUNY—Alfred; Dan Kimble, University of Oregon; Richard A. King, University of North Carolina at Chapel Hill; Mike Knight, Central State University; Wolanyo Kpo, Chicago State University; Velton Lacefield, Prairie State College; Alan Lanning, College of DuPage; Patsy Lawson, Volunteer State Community College; John D. Lawry, Marymount College; Charles Levinthal, Hofstra University; William Levy, Manchester Community College;

Robert G. Lowder, Bradley University; Robert MacAleese, Spring Hill College; Daniel Madsen, University of Minnesota—Duluth; John Malone, University of Tennessee; Marc Marshark, University of North Carolina at Greensboro; George Martin, Mount San Antonio College; S. R. Mathews, Converse College; Juan Mercado, McClellan Community College; Richard McCarbery, Lorain College; Leroy Metze, Western Kentucky University; Joseph Miele, East Stroudsberg University; Richard E. Miller, Navarro College; Thomas Minor, SUNY—Stony Brook; Thomas Moeschl, Broward Community College; Christopher F. Monte, Manhattanville College; Walena C. Morse, West Chester University; Basil Najjar, College of DuPage; John W. Nichols, Tulsa Junior College; Joseph Palladino, Indiana State University at Evansville; Carol Pandey, Los Angeles Pierce College; Fred Patrizi, East Central University; John Pennachio, Adirondack Community College; Terry Pettijohn, Ohio State University—Marion; Walter Pieper, Georgia State University; Donis Price, Mesa Community College; Gerald Pudelko, Olympic College; Richard A. Rare, University of Maine; Valda Robinson, Hillsborough Community College; Laurie Rotando, Westchester Community College; Patrick J. Ryan, Tompkins–Cortland Community College; H. R. Schiffman, Rutgers University; Paul Silverstein, Los Angeles Pierce College; William Sproull, Texas Christian University South; Jacob Steinberg, Fairleigh Dickinson University; Valierie Stratton, Pennsylvania State University—Altoona; Elizabeth Street, Central Washington University; Ann Swint, North Harris County College; Sherrill Tabing, Los Angeles Harbor College; Robert S. Tacker, East Carolina University; Francis Terrell, North Texas State University; Harry A. Tiemann, Mesa State College; Linda Truesdale, Midland Technical College; Frank. J. Vattano, Colorado State University; Douglas Wallen, Mankato State University; Glen Weaver, Calvin College; Charles Weichert, San Antonio College; Paul Wellman, Texas A&M University; Richard Whinery, Ohio University—Chillicothe; Kenneth Wildman, Ohio Northern University; Robert Williams, William Jewel College; Keith A. Wollen, Washington State University; Walter Zimmerman, New Hampshire College.

It is a continuing privilege to work with the fine publishing professionals at Harcourt Brace College Publishers. Ted Buchholz, Chris Klein, and Eve Howard provided me with editorial support. I value Ted for his knowledge and courage and, most of all, his friendship. Meera Dash made invaluable suggestions for developing the sixth edition. The project editor, Jeff Beckham, managed the myriad day-to-day activities that transformed my manuscript into a bound book. (Jeff's family graces page 113.) Cindy Young served as production manager. Art Director Peggy Young ably converted my design concepts into the elegant layout of the sixth edition. Amy Hester coordinated the development of the ancillaries, and Betsy Cummings and George Smyser produced the ancillaries. Sandra Lord, Marty Levick, and my wife, Lois Fichner–Rathus, scoured the four corners of the photo research houses of the earth to help secure and select the sixth edition's dynamic photo program.

SPENCER A. RATHUS
Short Hills, New Jersey
SRathus@aol.com
74673.2251@CompuServe.com

To the Student

This is your book. I wrote it with you in mind.

I included a number of features to help you learn about psychology, and about yourself. This section, "To the Student," shows you how to take full advantage of those features to truly make this book your own.

Make the investment. Spend a few minutes. By doing so, you will find ways in which you can better understand the subject matter and retain it longer. You may also find ways to keep psychology as an integral part of your life as we enter the new millennium.

Let me also confess that I envy you. I experienced the excitement of learning about psychology for the first time years ago. That excitement is now yours. Go to it!

SPENCER A. RATHUS, PH.D.
Short Hills, New Jersey
SRathus@aol.com
74673.2251@CompuServe.com

Each chapter opens with **Truth-or-Fiction?** items. Many students enter the course assuming that they already know a good deal about psychology—after all, by the time they enter college, they have observed people for many years. Complete these items before reading the chapter to learn how much you already know.

8

Thinking and Language

Truth or Fiction?

____ It may be boring, but using the "tried and true" formula is the most efficient way to solve a problem.

____ Only people are capable of solving problems by means of insight.

____ The best way to solve a frustrating problem is to keep plugging away at it.

____ Highly intelligent people are creative.

____ We are more creative when we are paid to be creative.

____ If A are B, and some B are C, then some A are C.

____ If a couple has five sons, the sixth child is likely to be a daughter.

____ An ice cream that is 97% fat free has less fat than an ice cream whose fat content makes up 10% of its calories.

____ People change their opinions when they are shown to be wrong.

____ The majority of people around the world speak at least two languages.

A chapter **Outline** appears on the first page within each chapter. Use this outline to give yourself an overview of the topics in the chapter. If you are using the PQ4R method of learning (see pages 38–39 in Chapter 1), you may want to transform the heads into questions that you answer as you read the chapter.

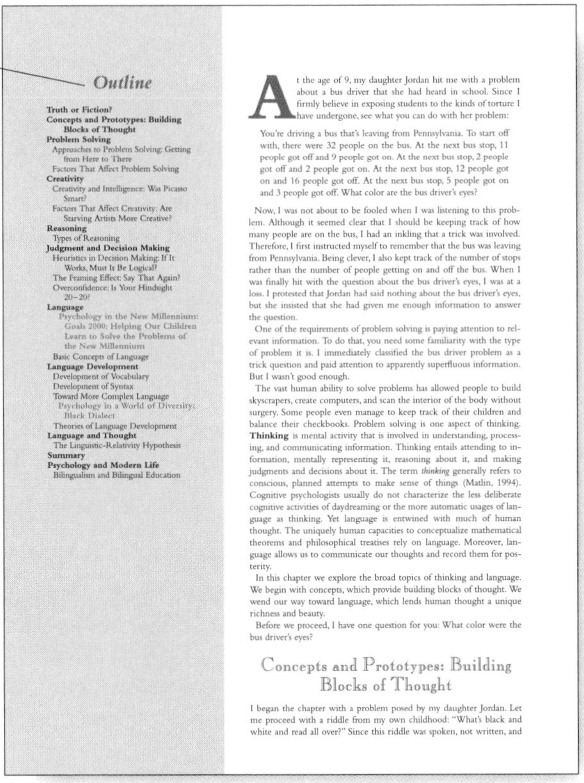

Outline

Truth or Fiction?
Concepts and Prototypes: Building Blocks of Thought
Problem Solving
Approaches to Problem Solving: Getting from Here to There
Factors That Affect Problem Solving
Creativity
Creativity and Intelligence: Was Picasso Smart?
Factors That Affect Creativity: Are Starving Artists More Creative?
Reasoning
Types of Reasoning
Judgment and Decision Making
Heuristics in Decision Making: If It Works, Must It Be Logical?
The Framing Effect: Say That Again?
Overconfidence: Is Your Hindsight 20–20?
Language
Psychology in the New Millennium: Goals 2000: Helping Our Children Learn to Solve the Problems of the New Millennium
Basic Concepts of Language
Language Development
Development of Vocabulary
Development of Syntax
Toward More Complex Language
Psychology in a World of Diversity: Black Dialect
Theories of Language Development
Language and Thought
The Linguistic-Relativity Hypothesis
Summary
Psychology and Modern Life
Bilingualism and Bilingual Education

At the age of 9, my daughter Jordan hit me with a problem about a bus driver that she had heard in school. Since I firmly believe in exposing students to the kinds of torture I have undergone, see what you can do with her problem:

> You're driving a bus that's leaving from Pennsylvania. To start off with, there were 32 people on the bus. At the next bus stop, 11 people got off and 9 people got on. At the next bus stop, 2 people got off and 2 people got on. At the next bus stop, 12 people got on and 16 people got off. At the next bus stop, 5 people got on and 3 people got off. What color are the bus driver's eyes?

Now, I was not about to be fooled when I was listening to this problem. Although it seemed clear that I should be keeping track of how many people are on the bus, I had an inkling that a trick was involved. Therefore, I first instructed myself to remember that the bus was leaving from Pennsylvania. Being clever, I also kept track of the number of stops rather than the number of people getting on and off the bus. When I was finally hit with the question about the bus driver's eyes, I was at a loss. I protested that Jordan had said nothing about the bus driver's eyes, but she insisted that she had given me enough information to answer the question.

One of the requirements of problem solving is paying attention to relevant information. To do that, you need some familiarity with the type of problem it is. I immediately classified the bus driver problem as a trick question and paid attention to apparently superfluous information. But I wasn't good enough.

The vast human ability to solve problems has allowed people to build skyscrapers, create computers, and scan the interior of the body without surgery. Some people even manage to keep track of their children and balance their checkbooks. Problem solving is one aspect of thinking. **Thinking** is mental activity that is involved in understanding, processing, and communicating information. Thinking entails attending to information, mentally representing it, reasoning about it, and making judgments and decisions about it. The term *thinking* generally refers to conscious, planned attempts to make sense of things (Matlin, 1994). Cognitive psychologists usually do not characterize the less deliberate cognitive activities of daydreaming or the more automatic usages of language as thinking. Yet language is entwined with much of human thought. The uniquely human capacities to conceptualize mathematical theorems and philosophical treatises rely on language. Moreover, language allows us to communicate our thoughts and record them for posterity.

In this chapter we explore the broad topics of thinking and language. We begin with concepts, which provide building blocks of thought. We wend our way toward language, which lends human thought a unique richness and beauty.

Before we proceed, I have one question for you: What color were the bus driver's eyes?

Concepts and Prototypes: Building Blocks of Thought

I began the chapter with a problem posed by my daughter Jordan. Let me proceed with a riddle from my own childhood: "What's black and white and read all over?" Since this riddle was spoken, not written, and

Truth or Fiction Revisited paragraphs answer the Truth-or-Fiction? questions to which you responded before beginning the chapter. Compare the answers with your own. Did research findings support your expectations? Why or why not?

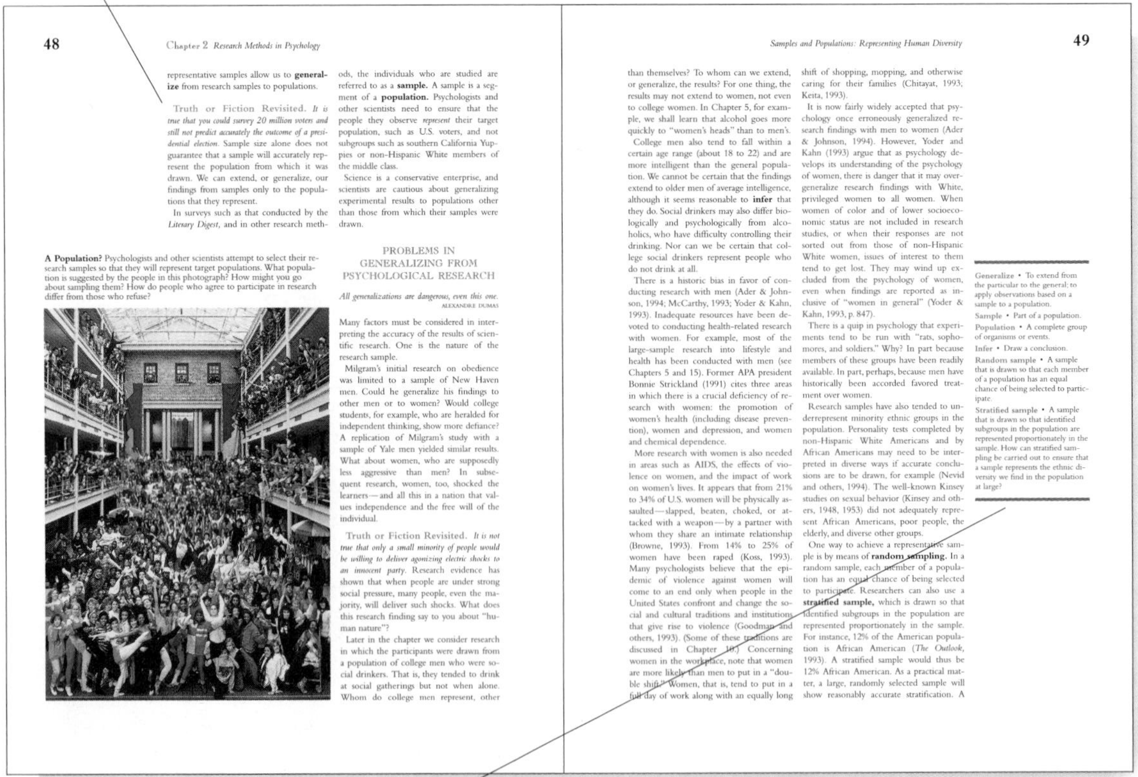

48 Chapter 2 *Research Methods in Psychology*

representative samples allow us to **generalize** from research samples to populations.

Truth or Fiction Revisited. *It is true that you could survey 20 million voters and still not predict accurately the outcome of a presidential election.* Sample size alone does not guarantee that a sample will accurately represent the population from which it was drawn. We can extend, or generalize, our findings from samples only to the populations that they represent.

In surveys such as that conducted by the *Literary Digest*, and in other research methods, the individuals who are studied are referred to as a **sample.** A sample is a segment of a **population.** Psychologists and other scientists need to ensure that the people they observe *represent* their target population, such as U.S. voters, and not subgroups such as southern California Yuppies or non-Hispanic White members of the middle class.

Science is a conservative enterprise, and scientists are cautious about generalizing experimental results to populations other than those from which their samples were drawn.

A Population? Psychologists and other scientists attempt to select their research samples so that they will represent target populations. What population is suggested by the people in this photograph? How might you go about sampling them? How do people who agree to participate in research differ from those who refuse?

PROBLEMS IN GENERALIZING FROM PSYCHOLOGICAL RESEARCH

All generalizations are dangerous, even this one.
ALEXANDRE DUMAS

Many factors must be considered in interpreting the accuracy of the results of scientific research. One is the nature of the research sample.

Milgram's initial research on obedience was limited to a sample of New Haven men. Could he generalize his findings to other men or to women? Would college students, for example, who are heralded for independent thinking, show more defiance? A replication of Milgram's study with a sample of Yale men yielded similar results. What about women, who are supposedly less aggressive than men? In subsequent research, women, too, shocked the learners—and all this in a nation that values independence and the free will of the individual.

Truth or Fiction Revisited. *It is not true that only a small minority of people would be willing to deliver agonizing electric shocks to an innocent party.* Research evidence has shown that when people are under strong social pressure, many people, even the majority, will deliver such shocks. What does this research finding say to you about "human nature"?

Later in the chapter we consider research in which the participants were drawn from a population of college men who were social drinkers. That is, they tended to drink at social gatherings but not when alone. Whom do college men represent, other than themselves? To whom can we extend, or generalize, the results? For one thing, the results may not extend to women, not even to college women. In Chapter 5, for example, we shall learn that alcohol goes more quickly to "women's heads" than to men's.

Samples and Populations: Representing Human Diversity 49

College men also tend to fall within a certain age range (about 18 to 22) and are more intelligent than the general population. We cannot be certain that the findings extend to older men of average intelligence, although it seems reasonable to **infer** that they do. Social drinkers may also differ biologically and psychologically from alcoholics, who have difficulty controlling their drinking. Nor can we be certain that college social drinkers represent people who do not drink at all.

There is a historic bias in favor of conducting research with men (Ader & Johnson, 1994; McCarthy, 1993; Yoder & Kahn, 1993). Inadequate resources have been devoted to conducting health-related research with women. For example, most of the large-sample research into lifestyle and health has been conducted with men (see Chapters 5 and 15). Former APA president Bonnie Strickland (1991) cites three areas in which there is a crucial deficiency of research with women: the promotion of women's health (including disease prevention), women and depression, and women and chemical dependence.

More research with women is also needed in areas such as AIDS, the effects of violence on women, and the impact of work on women's lives. It appears that from 21% to 34% of U.S. women will be physically assaulted—slapped, beaten, choked, or attacked with a weapon—by a partner with whom they share an intimate relationship (Browne, 1993). From 14% to 25% of women have been raped (Koss, 1993). Many psychologists believe that the epidemic of violence against women will come to an end only when people in the United States confront and change the social and cultural traditions and institutions that give rise to violence (Goodman and others, 1993). (Some of these traditions are discussed in Chapter 10.) Concerning women in the workplace, note that women are more likely than men to put in a "double shift." Women, that is, tend to put in a full day of work along with an equally long shift of shopping, mopping, and otherwise caring for their families (Chitayat, 1993; Keita, 1993).

It is now fairly widely accepted that psychology once erroneously generalized research findings with men to women (Ader & Johnson, 1994). However, Yoder and Kahn (1993) argue that as psychology develops its understanding of the psychology of women, there is danger that it may overgeneralize research findings with White, privileged women to all women. When women of color and of lower socioeconomic status are not included in research studies, or when their responses are not sorted out from those of non-Hispanic White women, issues of interest to them tend to get lost. They may wind up excluded from the psychology of women, even when findings are reported as inclusive of "women in general" (Yoder & Kahn, 1993, p. 847).

There is a quip in psychology that experiments tend to be run with "rats, sophomores, and soldiers." Why? In part because members of these groups have been readily available. In part, perhaps, because men have historically been accorded favored treatment over women.

Research samples have also tended to underrepresent minority ethnic groups in the population. Personality tests completed by non-Hispanic White Americans and by African Americans may need to be interpreted in diverse ways if accurate conclusions are to be drawn, for example (Nevid and others, 1994). The well-known Kinsey studies on sexual behavior (Kinsey and others, 1948, 1953) did not adequately represent African Americans, poor people, the elderly, and diverse other groups.

One way to achieve a representative sample is by means of **random sampling.** In a random sample, each member of a population has an equal chance of being selected to participate. Researchers can also use a **stratified sample,** which is drawn so that identified subgroups in the population are represented proportionately in the sample. For instance, 12% of the American population is African American (*The Outlook*, 1993). A stratified sample would thus be 12% African American. As a practical matter, a large, randomly selected sample will show reasonably accurate stratification. A

Generalize • To extend from the particular to the general; to apply observations based on a sample to a population.

Sample • Part of a population.

Population • A complete group of organisms or events.

Infer • Draw a conclusion.

Random sample • A sample that is drawn so that each member of a population has an equal chance of being selected to participate.

Stratified sample • A sample that is drawn so that identified subgroups in the population are represented proportionately in the sample. How can stratified sampling be carried out to ensure that a sample represents the ethnic diversity we find in the population at large?

The **Running Glossary** lets you learn and review terms at your own pace, without flipping back and forth between the page you are reading and an end-of-book glossary. It includes a pronunciation guide for difficult terms and word origins.

When you reach the end of a major section, a set of **Reflections** helps you learn the subject matter and also stimulates critical thinking. Respond to each question in your own thoughts and words. Draw upon your own experience as well as what you have read in the book. Notice that one or more items may appear in blue type. The blue type means that the question also appears in your workbook, *Thinking and Writing About Psychology in the New Millennium.*

6 Chapter 1 *What Is Psychology?*

lower animals, to normal-weight and overweight people, and to people who have been deprived of food for differing lengths of time. If our observations cannot be adequately explained by, or predicted from, a given theory, we should consider revising or replacing that theory.

In psychology, many theories have been found to be incapable of explaining or predicting new observations. As a result, they have been discarded or revised. For example, the theory that hunger results from stomach contractions may be partially correct for normal-weight individuals, but it is inadequate as an explanation for feelings of hunger among the overweight. In Chapter 10 we shall see that stomach contractions are only one of many factors, or **variables,** involved in hunger. Contemporary theories also focus on biological variables (such as the body's muscle-to-fat ratio) and situational variables (such as the presence of other people who are eating and the time of day).

The notion of controlling behavior and mental processes is controversial. Some people erroneously think that psychologists seek ways to make people do their bidding—like puppets on strings. This is not so. Psychologists are committed to a belief in the dignity of human beings, and human dignity demands that people be free to make their own decisions and choose their own behavior. Psychologists are learning more all the time about the various influences on human behavior, but they implement this knowledge only upon request and in order to help an individual or organization.

Truth or Fiction Revisited. *It is true that psychologists attempt to control behavior.* In practice, however, "controlling behavior" means helping clients engage in behavior that will help them meet their own goals.

Variable • A condition that is measured or controlled in a scientific study. A variable can vary in a measurable manner.
Pure research • Research conducted without concern for immediate applications.
Applied research • Research conducted in an effort to find solutions to particular problems.
Consultation • The provision of professional advice or services.
Psychotherapy • (sigh-coe-THER-uh-pea). The systematic application of psychological knowledge to the treatment of problem behavior.
Behavior therapy • Application of principles of learning to the direct modification of problem behavior.

Reflections

The research shows that if students are going to remember something, they have to think about it. They need to put it in their own heads in their own words, not just sit back passively and absorb it.

WILBERT MCKEACHIE, 1994, p. 39

Psychologists and educators have shown that you learn more effectively when you *reflect* on what you are learning. Reflecting on a subject means *relating* it to things you already know about (Willoughby and others, 1994). Trying to relate the material to things you already know about makes it meaningful and easier to remember (DeAngelis, 1994a; Woloshyn and others, 1994). Relating the material to things you already know also makes it more likely that you will be able to use the new information in your own life (Kintsch, 1994).

Things you already know include your own life experiences and other academic subjects. As you read through this book, you will notice that I tell you many things about my family (including many things my family would rather keep to themselves). My reasons for doing so are to arouse your interest (attention also promotes learning) and to hand you some of my life experiences to which you can relate the subject matter. The "Reflections" sections that you will find at the end of every major section further stimulate you to relate the subject matter to your life experiences and academic knowledge. They ask you to pause before going on to the following section and to consider some questions.

For example, now that you have read the section on "Psychology as a Science," reflect on the following questions:

- How would you have defined psychology before you began this course or opened your book? How does the true scientific nature of psychology differ from your expectations?
- What is a theory? Do you have theories as to why people act and think as they do? What are your theories? What is the evidence for them?
- Do you believe that it is possible to understand people from a scientific perspective? Why or why not?

The remainder of this chapter provides an overview of psychology and psychologists. You will see that psychologists have diverse interests and fields of specialization. We shall discuss the history of psychology and the major perspectives from which today's psychologists view behavior. Finally, we explore the impacts of human diversity and critical thinking on the science of psychology.

Psychology in the New Millennium sections explore the fascinating connections between technological advances, psychology, and our styles of life. Here, such a section explores the connections between training in music and the development of spatial reasoning in children.

348 Chapter 9 *Intelligence*

SES. High SES is also connected with above-average income and levels of education, a history of stimulating occupational pursuits, and the maintenance of intact families.

2. *Stimulating activities.* People who maintain their levels of intellectual functioning also tend to attend cultural events, travel, participate in professional organizations, and read extensively.
3. *Marriage to a spouse with a high level of intellectual functioning.* The spouse whose level of intellectual functioning is lower at the beginning of a marriage tends to narrow the gap as time elapses. Perhaps they are continually challenged.
4. *Flexible personality.*

We saw that Head Start programs have been effective in enhancing the intellectual development of children. It also turns out that training in reasoning and visual-spatial skills improves the cognitive functioning of older people (Schaie, 1994). The benefits of such training extend to performance on the practical tasks of daily living (Willis and others, 1992).

All in all, intellectual functioning at any age appears to reflect the interaction of a complex web of genetic, physical, personal, and sociocultural factors, as suggested by Figure 9.7.

ON ETHNICITY AND INTELLIGENCE: A CONCLUDING NOTE

Many psychologists believe that heredity and environment interact to influence intelligence. Forty-five percent of Snyderman

The Determinants of Intelligence: Where Does Intelligence Come From? 349

and Rothman's (1987, 1990) sample of 1,020 psychologists and educational specialists believe that African American-White differences in IQ are a "product of both genetic and environmental variation, compared to only 15% who feel the difference is entirely due to environmental variation [see Figure 9.8]. Twenty-four percent of experts do not believe there are sufficient data to support any reasonable opinion, [and 1%] indicate a belief in an entirely genetic determination" (1987, p. 141).

Diana Baumrind (1993) and Jacquelyne Jackson (1993) of the University of California Institute of Human Development argue that a strong belief in the predominance of genetic factors can undermine parental and educational efforts to enhance children's intellectual development. Jackson notes that such a view can be particularly harmful to African American children. Baumrind notes that parents are most effective when they believe their efforts will improve their children's functioning. Since parents cannot change their children's genetic codes, it is better for parents to assume that good parenting can make a difference.

Perhaps we need not be so concerned with whether we can sort out exactly "how much" of a person's IQ is due to heredity and how much is due to environmental influences. The largest number of psychologists and educators believe that IQ reflects the complex interaction of heredity, early childhood experiences, sociocultural factors and expectations, and even the atmosphere within which intelligence tests are conducted. Psychology has traditionally supported the dignity of the individual. It might be more appropriate for us to try to

PSYCHOLOGY IN THE NEW MILLENNIUM

Will Music Provide Our Children with the Sweet Sounds of Success?

We can expect that technological innovations will overleap themselves in the new millennium. Parents will doubtlessly be concerned about what they can do to help their children grasp the new technologies. Whatever environmental factors are found to enhance children's intellectual functioning may well be music to parents' ears. But it may also turn out that music will be spatial reasoning to the children's ears.

Research in the 1990s suggests that listening to music and studying music may enhance one aspect of intellectual functioning—spatial reasoning. In October of 1993, the research team of Frances Rauscher, Gordon Shaw, and Katherine Ky—all of the University of California at Irvine—published an intriguing article in *Nature* on the effects of listening to Mozart. According to that study, listening to 10 minutes of Mozart's Piano Sonata K 448 on a number of occasions enhanced college students' scores on spatial reasoning tasks of the kind found on intelligence tests.

The research team of Rauscher, Shaw, Linda Levine, Ky, and Eric Wright reported the results of a follow-up study with preschoolers at the 1994 meeting of the American Psychological Association: "Music and spatial task performance: A causal relationship." They recruited 19 preschool children aged from 3 years to 4 years 9 months and gave them 8 months of music lessons, including singing and use of a keyboard. They then found that the children's scores on an object assembly task—like that of the object assembly subtest of the Wechsler Intelligence Scale for Children—significantly exceed those of 15 preschoolers who did not obtain the musical training.

How might listening to music or training in music affect spatial reasoning? Shaw, Wright, and a third researcher, Xiaodan Leng, theorize that musical activity and a number of other cognitive functions—such as spatial reasoning—share overlapping neural pathways (Martin, 1994). Musical training thus develops the neural firing patterns used in spatial reasoning, which may eventually help children solve geometry problems, design skyscrapers, navigate ships, even fit suitcases into the trunk of a car (Martin, 1994).

Note the implications for Howard Gardner's theory of multiple intelligences. If the Rauscher team's research withstands the test of time and replication, it may be that musical talent and spatial skills represent one kind of intelligence and not two.

The researchers caution that their findings should be considered preliminary. It is not known, for example, whether the training effects endure or whether they will extend to older children, whose cerebral cortexes are more mature.

But perhaps the findings are enticing enough to encourage school administrators to maintain music programs, which are often among the first to go when school districts tighten the purse strings. Music, after all, may contribute to the sweet sounds of success.

The Sweet Sounds of Success? Research suggests that training in music advances children's spatial reasoning. Do musical activities and spatial reasoning share common neural pathways?

Here, another section discusses the use of computers in the diagnosis of psychological disorders.

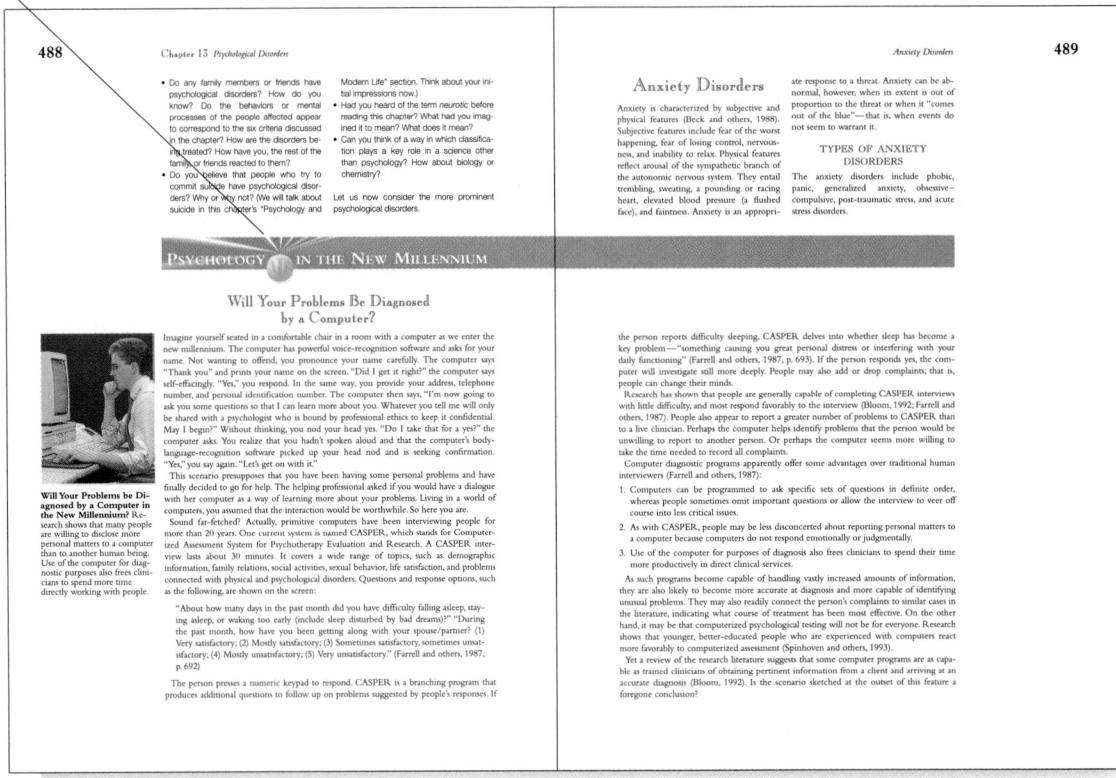

Psychology in a World of Diversity sections focus on meaningful similarities and differences among people of different genders and from various cultural backgrounds. For example, this reexamination of Erikson's theory of development reveals that women's development of identity formation is more similar to men's than Erikson himself had allowed. However, adolescents in minority groups are often faced with two conflicting sets of cultural values in their identity formation: the values espoused by their ethnic group and those of the dominant culture.

"Know thyself," said the ancient Greek philosopher Socrates. The **Questionnaires** found throughout the text truly help you to know yourself. They also help you satisfy your curiosity about your own motives, attitudes, and personality traits. Here, the Social Readjustment Rating Scale enables you to measure your stress level on the basis of the life changes you have experienced in the past year. Scoring keys for questionnaires are found in Appendix B of the book.

Key Illustrations make complex topics easier to grasp. When you see this dancer in the spotlight, you will find an illustration that has been carefully prepared to help illustrate the subject matter. Here, for example, a pair of diagrams help to illustrate the difference between positive correlations, such as the correlation between intelligence and academic achievement, and negative correlations, such as the correlation between stress and health.

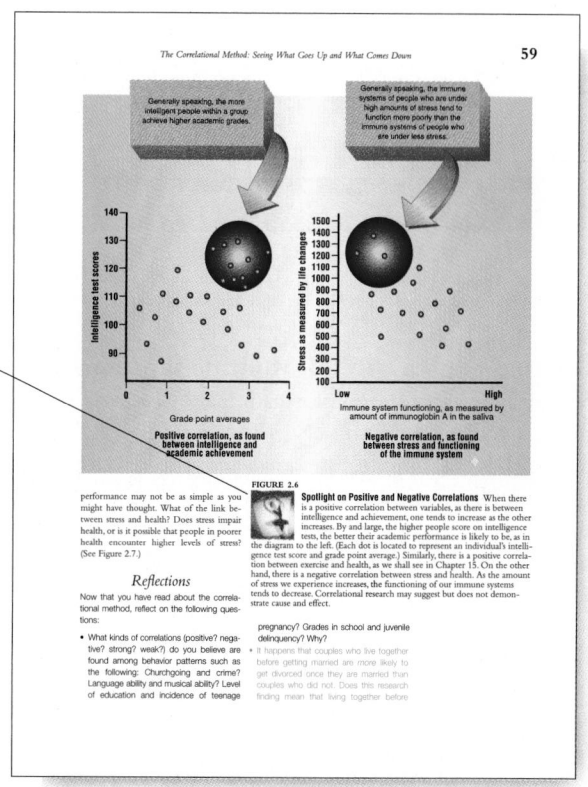

In another spotlighted topic, a drawing illustrates the differences between three stages of memory—sensory memory, short-term memory, and long-term memory. We use the example of attempting to remember other people's names, and we show how forgetting occurs in different ways in each stage.

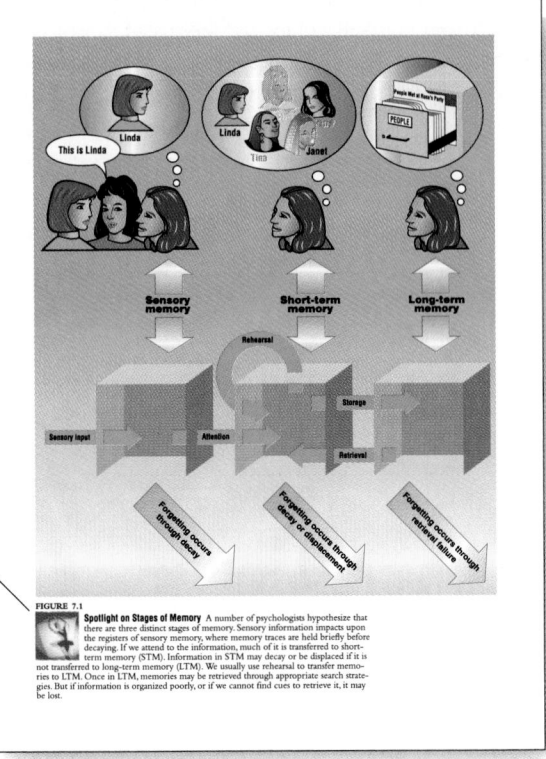

FIGURE 7.1

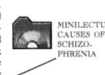 **Spotlight on Stages of Memory** A number of psychologists hypothesize that there are three distinct stages of memory. Sensory information impacts upon the registers of sensory memory, where memory traces are held briefly before decaying. If we attend to the information, much of it is transferred to short-term memory (STM). Information in STM may decay or be displaced if it is not transferred to long-term memory (LTM). We usually use rehearsal to transfer memories to LTM. Once in LTM, memories may be retrieved through appropriate search strategies. But if information is organized poorly, or if we cannot find cues to retrieve it, it may be lost.

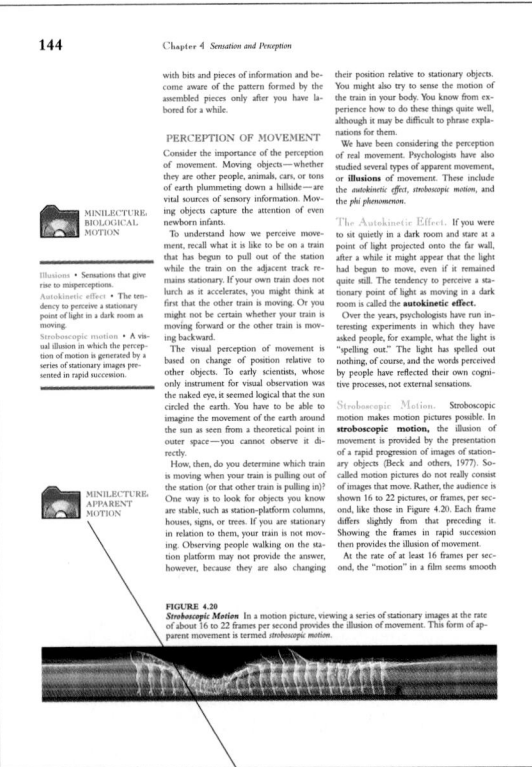

In the margins, **CD-ROM Multimedia Interfaces** let you know that more information about a particular topic is available in *Psychology: The Core on CD-ROM*. The CD-ROM minilectures enable you to develop deeper understandings of these topics and reinforce the information in the text. This example tells you that the CD-ROM includes "minilectures" on biological or real motion, and on apparent motion.

Here the CD-ROM interface informs you that the CD-ROM contains a minilecture on the causes of the psychological disorder of schizophrenia.

A **Chapter Summary** prompts you to review the information presented in the chapter. It is more than a list of terms and principles, however. The unique question-and-answer format stimulates active learning by posing questions that you can answer from your reading. As a matter of fact, many students read the summaries before reading the chapters so that they can read in order to answer the questions in the summaries.

After the summary of each chapter, a **Psychology and Modern Life** feature highlights the relevance of the material in the chapter to contemporary issues and your own life. For example, language and language development are major topics in the chapter on Thinking and Language. Because English is a second language for about 32 million people in the United States, that chapter's Psychology and Modern Life feature addresses bilingualism and bilingual education.

Similarly, stress is a major topic within the Health Psychology chapter. In this example, the Psychology and Modern Life feature in that chapter offers concrete advice for coping with stress. You learn how to cope with the stress in your own life by controlling stress-producing thoughts, relaxing, modifying Type A behavior, and exercising.

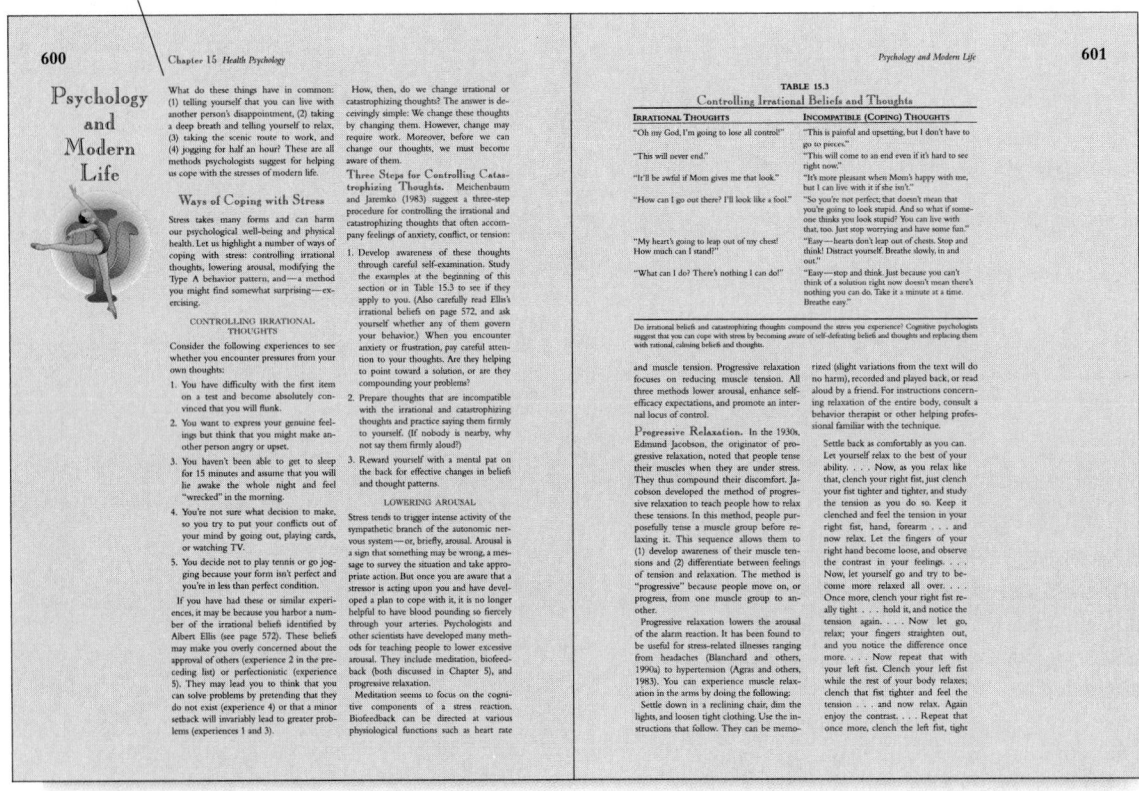

STUDY AIDS

The accompanying workbook, *Thinking and Writing About Psychology in the New Millennium,* gives you the means to record your responses to key Reflections in the textbook.

The **Study Guide** reflects the themes of the textbook and provides concentrated exercises for you to understand both the broader concepts and the narrower details of each chapter.

Harcourt Interactive, *Psychology: The Core on CD-ROM* lets you explore psychology through dozens of useful minilectures featuring videos, animation, and experiments. This multimedia product also lets you test your mastery of the material.

Chapter 1

What Is Psychology?　　2

Truth or Fiction?　　2
Psychology as a Science　　5
What Psychologists Do　　7
　Clinical and Counseling Psychologists　　7
　School and Educational Psychologists　　8
　Developmental Psychologists　　8
　Personality, Social, and Environmental
　　Psychologists　　8
　Experimental Psychologists　　9
　Psychologists in Industry　　9
　Emerging Fields　　10
**Where Psychology Comes From: A Brief
　History**　　10
　Structuralism　　11
　Functionalism　　12
　Behaviorism　　12
　Gestalt Psychology　　14
　Psychoanalysis　　15
**How Today's Psychologists View
　Behavior**　　17
　The Biological Perspective　　17
　The Cognitive Perspective　　18
　The Humanistic-Existential Perspective　　19
　The Psychodynamic Perspective　　19
　Learning Perspectives　　20
　The Sociocultural Perspective　　20
Human Diversity and Psychology　　22
　Ethnic Diversity: A Social Mosaic　　22
　Gender　　25

Other Kinds of Diversity　　26
　Psychology in a World of Diversity:
　　On Increasing Diversity in
　　American Higher Education　　27
　The Diversity of Contributors to the
　　Development of Psychology　　27
Critical Thinking and Psychology　　29
　Principles of Critical Thinking　　30
　Recognizing Common Fallacies in
　　Arguments　　31
　Psychology in the New Millennium:
　　A Partial Wish List　　32
Summary　　34
Psychology and Modern Life
　The Psychology of Studying Psychology　　36

Chapter 2

Research Methods in Psychology　　40

Truth or Fiction?　　40
**The Milgram Studies: Shocking Stuff at
　Yale**　　42
**The Scientific Method: Putting Ideas to
　the Test**　　45
**Samples and Populations: Representing
　Human Diversity**　　47
　Problems in Generalizing from Psychological
　　Research　　48

Psychology in a World of Diversity:
    The Wyatt Survey of African
    American and White Women in
    Los Angeles County   50
**Methods of Observation: The Better to
    See You With**   51
The Case-Study Method   51
The Survey Method   52
The Testing Method   55
The Naturalistic-Observation Method   55
The Laboratory-Observation Method   56
**The Correlational Method: Seeing What
    Comes Up and What Comes
    Down**   57
**The Experimental Method: Trying
    Things Out**   60
Independent and Dependent Variables   61
Experimental and Control Groups   62
Blinds and Double Blinds   62
    Psychology in the New Millennium:
        In the Global Research Lab   64
**Methods of Studying Your Crowning
    Glory—The Brain**   65
**Ethical Issues in Psychological Research
    and Practice**   68
Research with People   68
Research with Animals   70
Summary   71
Psychology and Modern Life
Science Versus Pseudoscience   72

Chapter 3
Biology and Behavior   78

Truth or Fiction?   78
Neurons: Into the Fabulous Forest   81
The Makeup of Neurons   81
The Neural Impulse: Let Us "Sing the
    Body Electric"   83
The Synapse   85
Neurotransmitters   85
The Nervous System   87
The Central Nervous System   88
The Peripheral Nervous System   93
The Cerebral Cortex   95
The Geography of the Cerebral Cortex   95
Thought, Language, and the Cortex   97
Left Brain, Right Brain?   98
Handedness: Is It Gauche to Be Left-Handed?   99
Split-Brain Experiments: When Hemi-
    spheres Stop Communicating   99
Electrical Stimulation of the Brain   101
    Psychology in the New Millennium:
        And Now—Brainman?   102
The Endocrine System   102
A Guided Tour of the Endocrine System   105
Heredity: The Nature of Nature   108
Genes and Chromosomes   108
    Psychology in the New Millennium:
        The Human Genome Project   110
Kinship Studies   112
Dominant and Recessive Traits   112
Experiments in Selective Breeding   113
Summary   115
Psychology and Modern Life
Alzheimer's Disease   117
Premenstrual Syndrome   119
    Psychology in a World of Diversity:
        Cross-Cultural Perspectives on
        Menstruation   120

Chapter 4

Sensation and Perception   122

Truth or Fiction?   122
Sensation and Perception: Your Ticket of Admission to the World Outside   126
Absolute Threshold: Is It There or Isn't It?   126
Difference Threshold: Is It the Same or Is It Different?   127
Signal-Detection Theory: Is Being Bright Enough?   128
Feature Detectors   128
Binding in the Brain: From Grandmother Cells to Convergence Zones   129
Sensory Adaptation: Where Did It Go?   130
Vision: Letting the Sun Shine In   130
Light: What Is This Stuff?   131
The Eye: The Better to See You With   132
Creating an Inner World of Color: Color Vision   135
Psychological Dimensions of Color   135
Theories of Color Vision   138
Color Blindness   139
Visual Perception   140
Perceptual Organization   140
Perception of Movement   144
Depth Perception   145
Problems in Visual Perception   148
Perceptual Constancies   148
Visual Illusions   151

Hearing   153
Pitch and Loudness   153
The Ear: The Better to Hear You With   155
Locating Sounds   157
Perception of Loudness and Pitch   157
Deafness   158
Psychology in the New Millennium: Sonic Device May Help Blind People Navigate   158
Psychology in a World of Diversity: The Signs of the Times Are Changing to Reflect New Sensibilities among the Deaf   160
Smell   161
Psychology in the New Millennium: Will We Be Using "a Sixth Sense for Sex" When the 21st Century Rolls In?   162
Taste   163
The Skin Senses   164
Touch and Pressure   164
Temperature   165
Pain: The Often Unwanted Message   166
Kinesthesis   167
The Vestibular Sense: On Being Upright   168
Summary   168
Psychology and Modern Life
Pain Management: More Than a Medical Issue   170

Chapter 5

States of Consciousness   172

Truth or Fiction?   172
A Minor Question: What *Is* Consciousness?   174
Sleep and Dreams   176
The Stages of Sleep   177
Functions of Sleep   179
Dreams: "Such Stuff as Dreams Are Made On"   179
Sleep Disorders   182
Altering Consciousness through Drugs   184
Substance Abuse and Dependence   184
Causal Factors in Substance Abuse and Dependence   185
Depressants   186
Alcohol   186
Psychology in a World of Diversity: On Alcoholism, Gender, Social Class, and Ethnicity   186
Opioids   188
Barbiturates and Methaqualone   190
Stimulants   190
Amphetamines   190
Cocaine   191
Cigarettes (Nicotine)   192
Hallucinogenics   194
Marijuana   194
LSD   195
Psychology in the New Millennium: Use and Abuse of Drugs: More Research Needed   196
Other Hallucinogenics   198
Altering Consciousness through Meditation: When Eastern Gods Meet Western Technology   198
Altering Consciousness through Biofeedback: Getting in Touch with the Untouchable   199
Altering Consciousness through Hypnosis: On Being Entranced   201
Hypnotic Inductions   201
Changes in Consciousness Brought About by Hypnosis   202
Theories of Hypnosis   203
Summary   204
Psychology and Modern Life
Coping with Insomnia: How *(and How Not)* to Get to Sleep at Night   206
Quitting and Cutting Down on Smoking   207

Chapter 6

Learning   210

Truth or Fiction?   210
Classical Conditioning   214
Ivan Pavlov Rings a Bell   214
Stimuli and Responses in Classical Conditioning: US, CS, UR, and CR   216
Types of Classical Conditioning   217
Taste Aversion   218
Extinction and Spontaneous Recovery   218
Generalization and Discrimination   220
Higher-Order Conditioning   221
Applications of Classical Conditioning   221
Operant Conditioning   224
Edward L. Thorndike and the Law of Effect   224
B. F. Skinner and Reinforcement   224
Types of Reinforcers   227
Extinction and Spontaneous Recovery in Operant Conditioning   228

Reinforcers versus Rewards and Punishments 229
Discriminative Stimuli 230
Schedules of Reinforcement 231
Applications of Operant Conditioning 233
Psychology in the New Millennium: Learning at the Feet of the . . . Information Superhighway? 236
Cognitive Factors in Learning 238
Contingency Theory: Contiguity or Contingency? What "Really" Happens during Classical Conditioning? 238
Latent Learning: When Learning Is Not Doing 239
Observational Learning: Monkey See, Monkey May Choose to Do 239
Psychology in a World of Diversity: Sociocultural Factors in Learning, or, Donald Duck Meets a Samurai 240
Summary 242
Psychology and Modern Life
The Effects of Media Violence 244

Chapter 7

Memory 248

Truth or Fiction? 248
Five Challenges to Memory 250
Three Kinds of Memory 251
Episodic Memory 251
Semantic Memory 251
Procedural Memory 251
Three Processes of Memory 252
Encoding 253
Storage 253
Retrieval 253

Three Stages of Memory 254
Sensory Memory 254
Short-Term Memory 258
Long-Term Memory 262
The Levels-of-Processing Model of Memory 271
Forgetting 272
Memory Tasks Used in Measuring Forgetting 272
Interference Theory 274
Repression 275
Infantile Amnesia 275
Anterograde and Retrograde Amnesia 276
The Biology of Memory: From Engrams to Adrenaline 277
Changes at the Neural Level 278
Changes at the Structural Level 278
Psychology in the New Millennium: Getting Organized to the Max: Adventures in Living with an Electronic Memory 280
A Final Challenge to Memory 282
Summary 282
Psychology and Modern Life
Methods for Improving Memory 284

Chapter 8

Thinking and Language 288

Truth or Fiction? 288
Concepts and Prototypes: Building Blocks of Thought 290
Problem Solving 292
Approaches to Problem Solving: Getting from Here to There 293
Factors That Affect Problem Solving 297

Creativity 301
 Creativity and Intelligence: Was Picasso
  Smart? 302
 Factors That Affect Creativity: Are Starving
  Artists More Creative? 302
Reasoning 304
 Types of Reasoning 305
Judgment and Decision Making 306
 Heuristics in Decision Making: If It Works,
  Must It Be Logical? 306
 The Framing Effect: Say That Again? 308
 Overconfidence: Is Your Hindsight 20–20? 308
Language 309
 Psychology in the New Millennium:
  Goals 2000: Helping Our Children
  Learn to Solve the Problems of
  the New Millennium 310
 Basic Concepts of Language 312
Language Development 314
 Development of Vocabulary 314
 Development of Syntax 315
 Toward More Complex Language 315
 Psychology in a World of Diversity:
  Black Dialect 316
 Theories of Language Development 318
Language and Thought 321
 The Linguistic-Relativity Hypothesis 321
Summary 322
Psychology and Modern Life
 Bilingualism and Bilingual Education 324

Chapter 9

Intelligence 328

Truth or Fiction? 328
Theories of Intelligence 330
 Factor Theories 330
 Gardner's Theory of Multiple Intelligences 333
 Sternberg's Triarchic Theory 333
Measurement of Intelligence 335
 Individual Intelligence Tests 335
 Psychology in the New Millennium:
  Artificial Intelligence 336
 Group Tests 339
 Psychology in a World of Diversity:
  Socioeconomic and Ethnic Differ-
  ences in Intelligence 340
The Testing Controversy: Just What Do
 Intelligence Tests Measure? 341
 Is It Possible to Develop Culture-Free
  Intelligence Tests? 342
The Determinants of Intelligence:
 Where Does Intelligence
 Come From? 343
 Genetic Influences on Intelligence 344
 Environmental Influences on Intelligence 345
 On Ethnicity and Intelligence: A Con-
  cluding Note 348
 Psychology in the New Millennium:
  Will Music Provide Our Children
  with the Sweet Sounds of Success? 348
Summary 350
Psychology and Modern Life
 Mental Retardation and Giftedness 351

Chapter 10

Motivation and Emotion 354

Truth or Fiction? 354
Coming to Terms with Motivation 357
**Theories of Motivation: The Whys
    of Why** 357
Instinct Theory: "Doing What Comes
    Naturally"? 358
Drive-Reductionism and Homeostasis:
    "Steady, Steady . . ." 358
Opponent-Process Theory: From Lambs to
    Lions 359
Humanistic Theory: "I've Got to Be Me"? 359
Cognitive Theory: "I Think, Therefore I
    Am Consistent"? 360
Sociocultural Theory 360
Evaluation: Which Whys Rise to the
    Occasion? 361
**Hunger: Do You Go by "Tummy-
    Time"?** 362
Sex: A Sociocultural Perspective 364
Organizing and Activating Effects of Sex
    Hormones 365
Psychology in the New Millennium:
    Sex Gets Interactive 366
Sexual Orientation 366
Psychology in a World of Diversity:
    Ethnicity and Sexual Orientation:
    A Matter of Belonging 369
Stimulus Motives 370
Sensory Stimulation and Activity 370
Exploration and Manipulation 372
**Cognitive Consistency: Making
    Things Fit** 373
Balance Theory 373
Cognitive-Dissonance Theory: "If I Did
    It, It Must Be Important"? 374

**The Three A's of Motivation: Achieve-
    ment, Affiliation, and Aggression** 375
Achievement 375
Affiliation: "People Who Need People" 376
Aggression: Some Facts of Life and Death 377
Emotion: Adding Color to Life 379
Arousal, Emotions, and Lie Detection 380
How Many Emotions Are There? Where
    Do They Come From? 381
The Expression of Emotions 382
The Facial-Feedback Hypothesis 383
Theories of Emotion: *Is* Feeling First? 383
Summary 387
Psychology and Modern Life
Obesity: Coping with a Serious and
    Pervasive Problem 389

Chapter 11

Developmental Psychology 394

Truth or Fiction? 394
**Controversies in Developmental
    Psychology** 397
Does Development Reflect Nature or
    Nurture? 397
Is Development Continuous or
    Discontinuous? 397
Psychology in the New Millennium:
    How Many of You Are There? How
    Many Will There Be? 398
Prenatal Development 399
Physical Development 402
Reflexes 402
Perceptual Development 404
Social Development 406
Attachment 406
Dimensions of Child Rearing 409

Cognitive Development   410
Jean Piaget's Cognitive-Developmental
Theory   410
Information-Processing Approaches to
Cognitive Development   417
Lawrence Kohlberg's Theory of Moral
Development   418
Psychology in a World of Diversity:
Are the Stages of Moral Develop-
ment Universal? Evidence for
Gender and Ethnocentric Biases   420
Adolescence   421
Physical Development   422
Social and Personality Development   423
Psychology in a World of Diversity:
Gender and Ethnic Factors in
Adolescent Identity Formation   424
Adult Development   425
Young Adulthood   425
Middle Adulthood   427
Late Adulthood   429
Summary   433
Psychology and Modern Life
Day Care   435
Child Abuse   436

Chapter 12

*Personality: Theories and
Measurement*   *438*

Truth or Fiction?   438
"Why Are They Sad and Glad and Bad?"
Introduction to Personality   440
The Psychodynamic Perspective   440
Sigmund Freud's Theory of Psychosexual
Development   441

Other Psychodynamic Theorists   445
Evaluation of the Psychodynamic
Perspective   447
Psychology in a World of Diversity:
Individuality Versus Relatedness:
The Rust Pile for Iron John?   449
The Trait Perspective   450
From Hippocrates to the Present Day   450
Hans Eysenck   451
The Big Five Factor Structure   452
Evaluation of the Trait Perspective   453
The Learning Perspective   454
Behaviorism   454
Social-Cognitive Theory   454
Evaluation of the Learning Perspective   458
The Humanistic-Existential Perspective   458
Abraham Maslow and the Challenge of
Self-Actualization   459
Carl Rogers' Self Theory   459
Evaluation of the Humanistic-Existential
Perspective   461
Psychology in the New Millennium:
The Sociocultural Perspective: The In-
dividual in the New Multicultural
United States   462
Measurement of Personality   466
Objective Tests   466
Projective Tests   469
Summary   470
Psychology and Modern Life
Gender Differences: Vive la Différence or
Vive la Similarité?   472
On Becoming a Woman or a Man: The
Development of Gender Differences   474

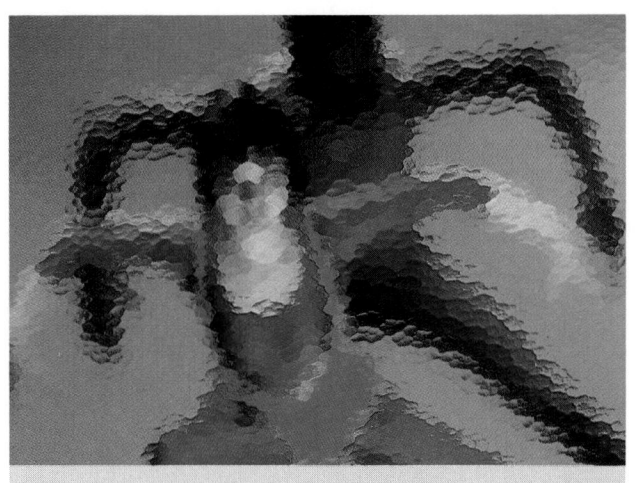

Chapter 13

Psychological Disorders 480

Truth or Fiction?	480
What Are Psychological Disorders?	483
Classifying Psychological Disorders	485
Psychology in the New Millennium:	
Will Your Problems Be Diagnosed by	
a Computer?	488
Anxiety Disorders	489
Types of Anxiety Disorders	489
Theoretical Views	492
Dissociative Disorders	494
Types of Dissociative Disorders	494
Theoretical Views	496
Somatoform Disorders	497
Types of Somatoform Disorders	497
Theoretical Views	498
Mood Disorders	498
Types of Mood Disorders	498
Theoretical Views	499
Schizophrenia	501
Types of Schizophrenia	503
Theoretical Views	504
Personality Disorders	506
Types of Personality Disorders	506
Theoretical Views	507
Eating Disorders	508
Types of Eating Disorders	509
Psychology in a World of Diversity:	
Eating Disorders: Why the	
Gender Gap?	510
Theoretical Views	511
Sexual Dysfunctions	512
Types of Sexual Dysfunctions	512
Theoretical Views	513
Summary	514
Psychology and Modern Life	
Suicide	516

Chapter 14

Methods of Therapy 520

Truth or Fiction?	520
What Is Therapy? In Search of That	
"Sweet Oblivious Antidote"	522
History of Therapies	523
Psychodynamic Therapies	525
Traditional Psychoanalysis: "Where Id Was,	
There Shall Ego Be"	526
Psychology in a World of Diversity:	
Women and Psychotherapy	528
Modern Psychodynamic Approaches	529
Humanistic-Existential Therapies	530
Person-Centered Therapy: Removing	
Roadblocks to Self-Actualization	530
Transactional Analysis: I'm OK—You're	
OK—We're All OK	531
Gestalt Therapy: Getting It Together	532
Cognitive Therapies	533
Rational-Emotive Therapy: Overcoming	
"Musts" and "Shoulds"	534
Cognitive Therapy: Correcting Cognitive	
Errors	534
Cognitive Restructuring: "No, No, Look at It	
This Way"	535
Behavior Therapy: Adjustment Is What	
You Do	536
Fear-Reduction Methods	537
Aversive Conditioning	538
Operant Conditioning Procedures	539
Self-Control Methods	540
Group Therapies	544
Encounter Groups	545
Couple Therapy	545
Family Therapy	546
Does Psychotherapy Work?	546
Problems in Conducting Research on	
Psychotherapy	546

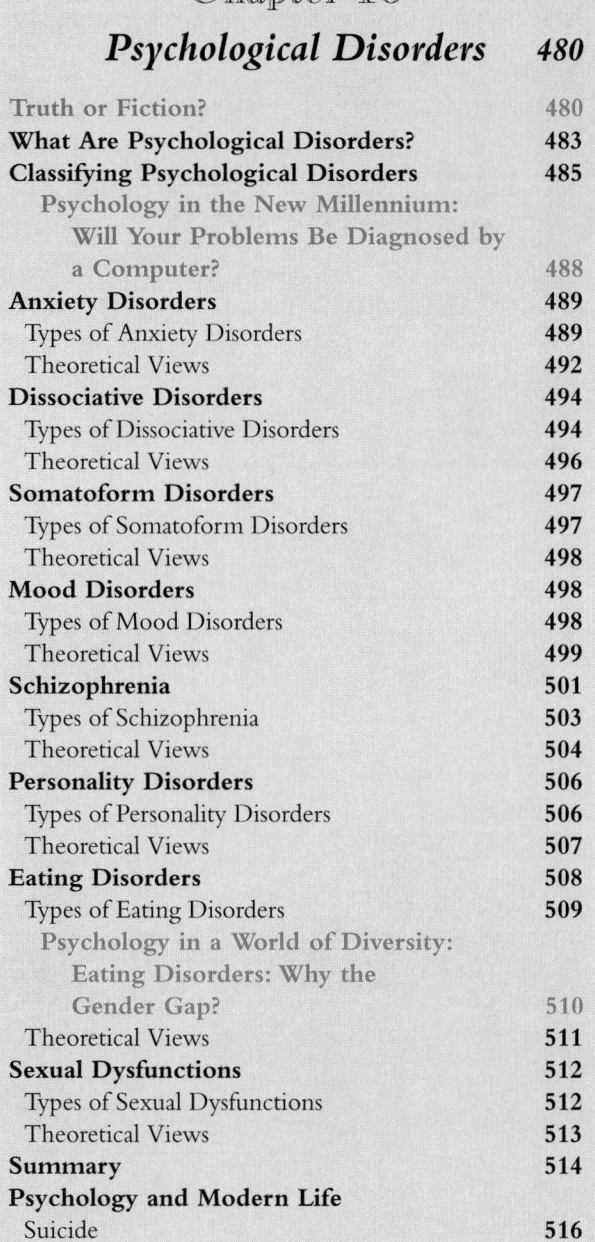

Analyses of Therapy Effectiveness	**548**
Biological Therapies	**549**
Drug Therapy	**549**
Psychology in the New Millennium:	
Beyond Wellness: Are Biological	
Treatments for Personality Im-	
provement in the Offing?	*550*
Electroconvulsive Therapy	**552**
Psychosurgery	**553**
Does Biological Therapy Work?	**554**
Summary	**555**
Psychology and Modern Life	
Psychotherapy in the New Multicultural	
United States	**557**
Psychology in a World of Diversity:	
Ethnic Matching of Clients and	
Therapists	*557*

Headaches	**587**
Coronary Heart Disease	**588**
Asthma	**590**
Cancer	**591**
Psychology in the New Millennium:	
Health Psychology in the 21st	
Century: The Shape of Things	
to Come	*594*
Compliance with Medical Advice	**596**
Encouraging Compliance by Enhancing	
Physician–Patient Interactions	**597**
Summary	**598**
Psychology and Modern Life	
Ways of Coping with Stress	**600**

Chapter 15
Health Psychology   **562**

Truth or Fiction?	562
Health Psychology	**564**
Stress: Presses, Pushes, and Pulls	**565**
Sources of Stress: Don't Hassle Me?	**566**
Psychological Moderators of Stress	**574**
The General Adaptation Syndrome	**579**
Effects of Stress on the Immune System	**582**
A Multifactorial Approach to Health	
and Illness	**584**
Human Diversity and Health: Nations within	
the Nation	**584**
Psychology in a World of Diversity:	
Health and Socioeconomic Status:	
The Rich Get Richer and the Poor	
Get . . . Sicker	*587*

Chapter 16
Social Psychology   **608**

Truth or Fiction?	608
Attitudes	**611**
The A–B Problem: Do We Do as We Think?	**612**
Origins of Attitudes	**612**
Changing Attitudes through Persuasion	**613**
Prejudice	**617**
Social Perception	**619**
Primacy and Recency Effects: The	
Importance of First Impressions	**619**
Attribution Theory: You're Free but I'm	
Caught in the Middle?	**620**
Body Language	**623**
Psychology in the New Millennium:	
Can Psychologists Usher in an Age	
of Peace?	*624*
Interpersonal Attraction: Liking and	
Loving	**626**
Physical Attractiveness: How Important Is	
Looking Good?	**626**

Similarity: Do "Opposites Attract" or Do
"Birds of a Feather Flock Together"? **632**
Reciprocity: If You Like Me, You Must
Have Excellent Judgment **632**
Love: Doing What Comes . . . Culturally? **635**
Social Influence
Obedience to Authority: Does Might Make
Right? **635**
Conformity: Do Many Make Right? **637**
Psychology in a World of Diversity:
Muslim Women Face Pressure to
Conform in the United States **639**
Group Behavior **640**
Social Facilitation: Monkey See, Monkey
Do Faster? **640**
Group Decision Making **641**
Polarization and the Risky Shift **642**
Groupthink **642**
Mob Behavior and Deindividuation **643**
Altruism and the Bystander Effect: Some
Watch While Others Die **644**
Summary **647**
Psychology and Modern Life
Gender Polarization: Gender Stereotypes
and Their Costs **649**
Psychology in a World of Diversity:
Machismo/Marianismo Stereo-
types and Hispanic Culture **649**

Chapter 17

Applied Psychology **654**

Truth or Fiction? **654**
Industrial/Organizational Psychology **656**
Currents in Industrial/Organizational
Psychology **657**
Recruitment and Placement **657**

Psychology in a World of Diversity:
"But You're Not in Hong Kong":
Asian Americans Fight a Stereotype
through Assertiveness Training **659**
Training and Instruction **660**
Appraisal of Workers' Performance **660**
Psychology in a World of Diversity:
Women Scientists Lagging in
Industry Jobs **661**
Organizational Theory **662**
Psychology in the New Millennium:
U.S. Corporations in the 21st Cen-
tury: Will Psychology Prevent the
Behemoths from Falling? **664**
Human Factors **666**
Criteria for Evaluating Person-Machine
Systems and Work Environments **666**
Criteria for Evaluating the Coding in
Displays **667**
Consumer Psychology **670**
Task Analysis of Consumer Behavior **670**
Marketing Research **670**
Environmental Psychology **671**
Environmental Activism **673**
Noise: Of Muzak, Rock 'n' Roll, and
Low-Flying Aircraft **673**
Temperature: Getting Hot under the Collar **674**
Of Aromas and Air Pollution: Facilitating,
Fussing, and Fuming **675**
Crowding and Personal Space: "Don't Burst
My Bubble, Please" **675**
Community Psychology **677**
Levels of Prevention **677**
Psychology in a World of Diversity:
"At the Heart of What Psychology
Should Be Doing in the Community" **678**
Forensic Psychology **679**
The Insanity Plea **679**
Sports Psychology **680**
Task Analysis of Athletic Performances **680**
How Sports Psychologists Help Athletes
Handle "Choking" **681**
Positive Visualization **682**
Peak Performance **682**
Educational Psychology **682**
Teaching Practices **683**
Classroom Management **683**
Planning and Teaching **684**
Teaching Exceptional Students **685**
Tests and Grades **685**
Summary **687**
Psychology and Modern Life
Primary Prevention of Rape **689**
Primary Prevention of AIDS **693**

Appendix A
Statistics   **A1**

Descriptive Statistics   **A1**
  The Frequency Distribution   **A2**
  Measures of Central Tendency   **A2**
  Measures of Variability   **A4**
The Normal Curve   **A5**
The Correlation Coefficient   **A6**
Inferential Statistics   **A7**
  Statistically Significant Differences   **A7**
  Samples and Populations   **A9**

Appendix B
Answer Keys for Questionnaires   **A10**

Credits   *A12*

Glossary   *G1*

References   *R1*

Name Index   *IN1*

Subject Index   *IN9*

PSYCHOLOGY

IN THE NEW MILLENNIUM

SIXTH EDITION

1

What Is Psychology?

Truth or Fiction?

_____ Psychologists attempt to control behavior.

_____ A book on psychology, whose contents are similar to those of the book you are now holding, was written by Aristotle more than 2,000 years ago.

_____ The ancient Greek philosopher Socrates suggested a research method that is still used in psychology.

_____ Some psychologists look upon our strategies for solving problems as "mental programs" operated by our very "personal computers"—our brains.

_____ The numbers of students from ethnic minority groups have increased dramatically on college campuses in the past decade.

_____ Women were not permitted to attend college in the United States until 1833.

_____ Men receive the majority of doctoral degrees in psychology.

Outline

Psychology as a Science
What Psychologists Do
  Clinical and Counseling Psychologists
  School and Educational Psychologists
  Developmental Psychologists
  Personality, Social, and Environmental
    Psychologists
  Experimental Psychologists
  Psychologists in Industry
  Emerging Fields
Where Psychology Comes From:
  A Brief History
  Structuralism
  Functionalism
  Behaviorism
  Gestalt Psychology
  Psychoanalysis
How Today's Psychologists View
  Behavior
  The Biological Perspective
  The Cognitive Perspective
  The Humanistic–Existential Perspective
  The Psychodynamic Perspective
  Learning Perspectives
  The Sociocultural Perspective
Human Diversity and Psychology
  Ethnic Diversity: A Social Mosaic
  Gender
  Other Kinds of Diversity
    Psychology in a World of Diversity:
    On Increasing Diversity in
    American Higher Education
  The Diversity of Contributors to the
    Development of Psychology
Critical Thinking and Psychology
  Principles of Critical Thinking
  Recognizing Common Fallacies in
    Arguments
    Psychology in the New Millennium:
    A Partial Wish List
Summary
Psychology and Modern Life
  The Psychology of Studying Psychology

"What a piece of work is man," wrote William Shakespeare. He was writing about you: "How noble in reason! How infinite in faculty! In form and moving how express and admirable! In action how like an angel! In apprehension how like a god! The beauty of the world! The paragon of animals!"

You probably had no trouble recognizing yourself in this portrait—"noble in reason," "admirable," godlike in understanding, head and shoulders above other animals. That's you to a *tee,* isn't it? Consider some of the noble and admirable features of human behavior:

- The human abilities to think and solve problems have allowed us to build cathedrals and computers and to scan the interior of the body without surgery. Yet what is thinking? How do we solve problems?

- The human ability to create led to the writing of great works of literature and the composition of glorious operas. Yet what is creativity?

- Human generosity and charity have encouraged us to care for older people, people who are ill, and people who are less advantaged than we are—even to sacrifice ourselves for those we love. Why do we care for others? What motivates us to care for our children and protect our families?

Human behavior varies greatly, however. Some of it is not noble or admirable. Some of it is downright puzzling. Consider these examples:

- Although people can be generous, most adults on crowded city streets will not stop to help a person lying on the sidewalk. Why?

- Most people who overeat or smoke cigarettes know they are jeopardizing their health. Yet they continue in their hazardous ways. Why?

- A person claims to have raped, killed, or mutilated a victim because of insanity. An "irresistible" impulse overcame the person, or "another personality" took control. What is insanity? What is an irresistible impulse? How we can know if someone is insane? Should people who are found to be insane be judged guilty or not guilty of their crimes?

Human behavior has always fascinated people. Sometimes we are even surprised at ourselves. We have thoughts or impulses that seem to be out of character, or we can't recall something on the "tip of the tongue." Most people try to satisfy their curiosities about behavior, if at all, in their spare time. Perhaps they ask a friend for an opinion or make some casual observations. Psychologists, like other people, are also intrigued by the mysteries of behavior, but they make the scientific study of behavior their life's work.

Psychology is the scientific study of behavior and mental processes. Topics of interest to psychologists have included the nervous system, sensation and perception, learning and memory, intelligence, language, thought, growth and development, personality, stress and health, **psychological disorders,** ways of treating psychological disorders, sexual behavior, and the behavior of people in social settings such as groups and organizations.

Psychology tests ideas with carefully designed methods of research such as the survey and the experiment. Although most psychologists are interested primarily in human behavior, many others focus on the behavior of animals ranging from sea snails and pigeons to rats and gorillas. Some psychologists believe that research findings with lower animals can be applied, or **generalized,** to humans. Other psychologists argue that people are so distinct that we can learn about people only by studying people. Each view holds some merit. For example, laboratory studies of the nerve cells of squids have afforded insight into the workings of human nerve cells. Experiments in teaching sign language to chimpanzees and gorillas have sparked innovations in teaching language to severely retarded people. Only by studying people, however, can we learn about human qualities such as morality, values, and romantic love. Still, many psychologists prefer to study lower animals. They need not justify their interests on the basis of applicability to people.

Psychology as a Science

Psychology, like other sciences, seeks to describe, explain, predict, and control the events it studies. Psychology thus seeks to describe, explain, predict, and control behavior and mental processes.

When possible, descriptive terms and concepts are interwoven into **theories.** Theo-

ries are formulations of apparent relationships among observed events. Psychological theories are based on assumptions about behavior and mental processes, contain statements about the principles and laws that may govern them, and allow us to derive explanations and predictions. Many psychological theories combine statements about behavior (such as eating or aggression), mental processes (such as attitudes and mental images), and anatomical structures or biological processes. For instance, many of our responses to drugs such as alcohol and marijuana can be measured as overt behavior, and they are presumed to reflect the biochemical actions of these drugs and our (mental) expectations about their effects.

A satisfactory psychological theory allows us to predict behavior and mental processes. For instance, a satisfactory theory of hunger will allow us to predict when people will or will not eat. A broadly satisfying, comprehensive theory should have a wide range of applicability. A broad theory of hunger might apply to human beings and

Psychology • (sigh-KOLL-oh-gee). The science that studies behavior and mental processes.
Psychological disorders • Patterns of behavior or mental processes that are connected with emotional distress or significant impairment in functioning.
Generalize • To go from the particular to the general; to extend.
Theory • A formulation of relationships underlying observed events.

"What a piece of work is man," wrote William Shakespeare. "How noble in reason! How infinite in faculty! In form and moving how express and admirable! In action how like an angel! In apprehension how like a god!" Psychologists are also fascinated by people's behavior and mental processes.

lower animals, to normal-weight and over-weight people, and to people who have been deprived of food for differing lengths of time. If our observations cannot be adequately explained by, or predicted from, a given theory, we should consider revising or replacing that theory.

In psychology, many theories have been found to be incapable of explaining or predicting new observations. As a result, they have been discarded or revised. For example, the theory that hunger results from stomach contractions may be partially correct for normal-weight individuals, but it is inadequate as an explanation for feelings of hunger among the overweight. In Chapter 10 we shall see that stomach contractions are only one of many factors, or **variables,** involved in hunger. Contemporary theories also focus on biological variables (such as the body's muscle-to-fat ratio) and situational variables (such as the presence of other people who are eating and the time of day).

The notion of controlling behavior and mental processes is controversial. Some people erroneously think that psychologists seek ways to make people do their bidding—like puppets on strings. This is not so. Psychologists are committed to a belief in the dignity of human beings, and human dignity demands that people be free to make their own decisions and choose their own behavior. Psychologists are learning more all the time about the various influences on human behavior, but they implement this knowledge only upon request and in order to help an individual or organization.

Truth or Fiction Revisited. *It is true that psychologists attempt to control behavior.* In practice, however, "controlling behavior" means helping clients engage in behavior that will help them meet their own goals.

Reflections

The research shows that if students are going to remember something, they have to think about it. They need to put it in their own heads in their own words, not just sit back passively and absorb it.
WILBERT MCKEACHIE, 1994, p. 39

Psychologists and educators have shown that you learn more effectively when you *re-*

flect on what you are learning. Reflecting on a subject means *relating* it to things you already know about (Willoughby and others, 1994). Trying to relate the material to things you already know about makes it meaningful and easier to remember (DeAngelis, 1994a; Woloshyn and others, 1994). Relating the material to things you already know also makes it more likely that you will be able to use the new information in your own life (Kintsch, 1994).

Things you already know include your own life experiences and other academic subjects. As you read through this book, you will notice that I tell you many things about my family (including many things my family would rather keep to themselves). My reasons for doing so are to arouse your interest (attention also promotes learning) and to hand you some of my life experiences to which you can relate the subject matter. The "Reflections" sections that you will find at the end of every major section further stimulate you to relate the subject matter to your life experiences and academic knowledge. They ask you to pause before going on to the following section and to consider some questions.

For example, now that you have read the section on "Psychology as a Science," reflect on the following questions:

- How would you have defined psychology before you began this course or opened your book? How does the true scientific nature of psychology differ from your expectations?
- What is a theory? Do you have theories as to why people act and think as they do? What are your theories? What is the evidence for them?
- Do you believe that it is possible to understand people from a scientific perspective? Why or why not?

The remainder of this chapter provides an overview of psychology and psychologists. You will see that psychologists have diverse interests and fields of specialization. We shall discuss the history of psychology and the major perspectives from which today's psychologists view behavior. Finally, we explore the impacts of human diversity and critical thinking on the science of psychology.

Variable • A condition that is measured or controlled in a scientific study. A variable can vary in a measurable manner.

Pure research • Research conducted without concern for immediate applications.

Applied research • Research conducted in an effort to find solutions to particular problems.

Consultation • The provision of professional advice or services.

Psychotherapy • (sigh-coe-THER-uh-pea). The systematic application of psychological knowledge to the treatment of problem behavior.

Behavior therapy • Application of principles of learning to the direct modification of problem behavior.

What Psychologists Do

Psychologists share a keen interest in behavior, but in other ways, they may differ markedly. Some psychologists engage primarily in basic research, or **pure research.** Pure research has no immediate application to personal or social problems and thus has been characterized as research for its own sake. Other psychologists engage in **applied research,** which is designed to find solutions to specific personal or social problems. Although pure research is spurred onward by curiosity and the desire to know and understand, today's pure research frequently enhances tomorrow's way of life. For example, pure research into learning and motivation with lower animals early in the century has found widespread applications in today's school systems. Pure research into the workings of the nervous system has enhanced knowledge of disorders such as epilepsy.

Many psychologists do not engage in research at all. Instead, they apply psychological knowledge to help people change their behavior so that they can meet their own goals more effectively. Numerous psychologists engage primarily in teaching. They disseminate psychological knowledge in classrooms, seminars, and workshops.

Many psychologists are involved in all of these activities: research, **consultation,** and teaching. For example, professors of psychology usually conduct pure or applied research and consult with individuals or industrial clients as well as teach. Full-time researchers may be called on to consult with industrial clients and to organize seminars or workshops to help clients develop skills. Practitioners, such as clinical and industrial psychologists, may also engage in research—which is usually applied—and teach in the classroom or workshop. Unfortunately for psychologists who teach, conduct research, and also carry on a practice, research into expanding the week to 250 hours does not look promising.

Let us now explore some of the specialties of psychologists. Although psychologists tend to wear more than one hat, most of them carry out their functions in the following fields.

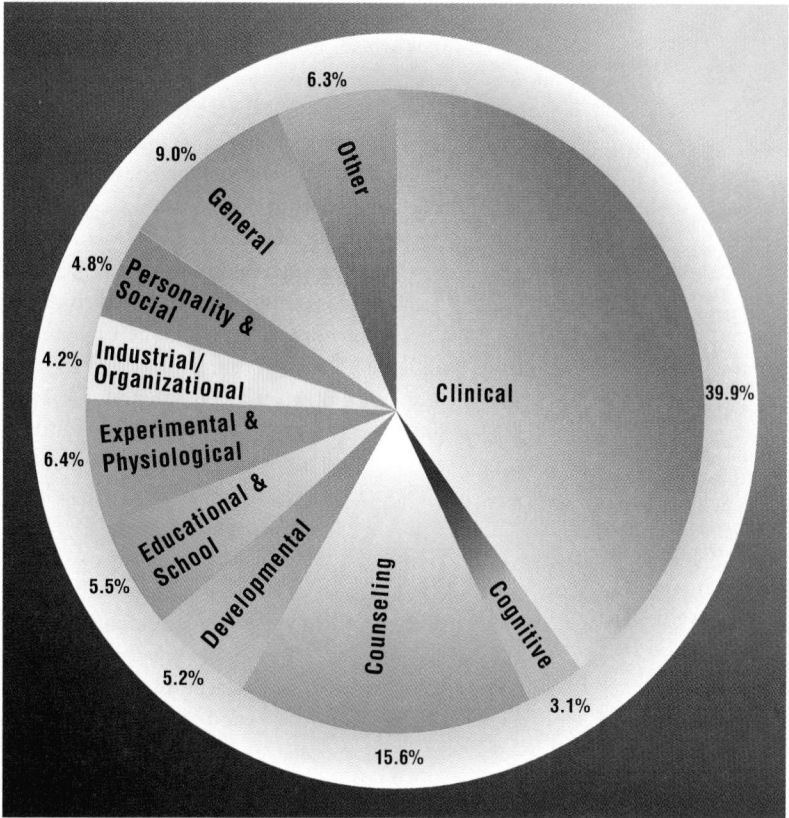

FIGURE 1.1
Recipients of Doctorates in the Various Subfields of Psychology In 1992, nearly 40% of the doctorates in psychology were awarded in clinical psychology. The next most popular subfield was counseling psychology. Source: *Summary Report Doctorate Recipients from United States Universities* (Table W04846), Office of Demographic, Employment, and Educational Research, 1994, Washington, DC: American Psychological Association.

CLINICAL AND COUNSELING PSYCHOLOGISTS

Clinical psychologists specialize in helping people with psychological problems adjust to the demands of life. Clients' problems may range from anxiety and depression to sexual dysfunctions to loss of goals. Clinical psychologists are trained to evaluate problems through structured interviews and psychological tests. They help their clients resolve their problems and change maladaptive behavior through techniques of **psychotherapy** and **behavior therapy.** Clinical psychologists may work in institutions for mentally ill or mentally retarded people, in outpatient clinics, in college and university clinics, or in private practices. Clinical psychologists are the largest subgroup of psychologists (see Figure 1.1). Most people therefore think of clinical psychologists whenever they hear the term *psychologist.* Many clinical psychologists divide their time among clinical practice, teaching, and research.

Clinical psychologists are not to be confused with psychiatrists. A psychiatrist is a medical doctor who specializes in the study and treatment of maladjustment and psychological disorders.

Counseling psychologists, like clinical psychologists, use interviews and tests to define their clients' problems. Clients of counseling psychologists typically have adjustment problems but not serious psychological disorders. Clients may encounter difficulty in making academic or vocational decisions or difficulty in making friends in college. They may experience marital or family conflicts, have physical handicaps, or have adjustment problems such as those encountered by a convict who is returning to the community. Counseling psychologists use various counseling methods to help clients clarify their goals and find ways of surmounting obstacles. Counseling psychologists are often employed in college and university counseling and testing centers. They are also found in rehabilitation agencies. As suggested by Figure 1.1, more than half of psychologists are clinical or counseling psychologists.

SCHOOL AND EDUCATIONAL PSYCHOLOGISTS

School psychologists are employed by school systems to help identify and assist students who encounter problems that interfere with learning. These range from social and family problems to emotional disturbances and specific learning disorders. School psychologists define students' problems through interviews with teachers, parents, and students; psychological tests such as intelligence and achievement tests; and classroom observation. They consult with teachers, school officials, parents, and other professionals to help students overcome obstacles to learning. They help make decisions about placement of students in special education and remediation programs.

Educational psychologists, like school psychologists, are concerned with optimizing classroom conditions to facilitate learning. They usually focus, however, on improvement of course planning and instructional methods for a school system rather than on

identification of, and assistance to, children with learning problems. Educational psychologists are concerned about theoretical issues relating to learning, measurement, and child development. Their research interests include the ways in which psychological factors such as motivation and intelligence, sociocultural factors such as poverty and acculturation, and teacher behavior affect learning. Some educational psychologists prepare standardized tests such as the SAT.

DEVELOPMENTAL PSYCHOLOGISTS

Developmental psychologists study the changes—physical, emotional, cognitive, and social—that occur throughout the life span. They attempt to sort out the relative influences of heredity (nature) and the environment (nurture) on development. Developmental psychologists conduct research on issues such as the effects of maternal use of drugs on an embryo, the outcomes of various patterns of child rearing, children's concepts of space and time, adolescent conflicts, and adjustment among older people.

PERSONALITY, SOCIAL, AND ENVIRONMENTAL PSYCHOLOGISTS

Personality psychologists attempt to define human traits; to determine influences on human thought processes, feelings, and behavior; and to explain psychological disorders. They are particularly concerned with human issues such as anxiety, aggression, and gender roles.

Social psychologists are primarily concerned with the nature and causes of individuals' thoughts, feelings, and overt behavior in social situations. Whereas personality psychologists tend to look within the person for explanations of behavior, social psychologists tend to focus on social or external influences. Behavior is influenced from within and without.

Social psychologists have historically focused on topics such as attitude formation and attitude change, interpersonal attraction and liking, **stereotypes,** obedience to authority, conformity to group norms, and

Stereotype • A fixed, conventional idea about a group.

Environmental Psychology. Environmental psychologists focus on the ways in which we affect and are affected by the physical environment. Among the concerns of environmental psychologists are the effects of crowding and "stimulus overload" on city dwellers.

group decision-making processes. Social psychologists, like personality psychologists, study gender roles and aggression.

Environmental psychologists focus on the ways in which behavior influences, and is influenced by, the physical environment. Environmental psychologists are concerned with the ways in which buildings and cities serve, or fail to serve, human needs. They investigate the effects of extremes of temperature, noise, and air pollution.

EXPERIMENTAL PSYCHOLOGISTS

Psychologists in all specialties may conduct experimental research. However, those called experimental psychologists conduct research into fundamental processes relevant to more applied specialties. These basic processes include the functions of the nervous system, sensation and perception, learning and memory, thought, motivation, and emotion. Experimental psychologists who focus on the relationships between biological changes and psychological events

are called physiological or biological psychologists.

Experimental psychologists are more likely than other psychologists to engage in basic or pure research. Their findings are often applied by other specialists in practice. Pure research in motivation, for example, has helped clinical and counseling psychologists devise strategies for helping people control weight. Pure research in learning and memory has helped school and educational psychologists enhance learning conditions in the schools.

PSYCHOLOGISTS IN INDUSTRY

Industrial and organizational psychology are closely related fields. Industrial psychologists focus on the relationships between people and work. Organizational psychologists study the behavior of people in organizations such as business firms. However, many psychologists are trained in both areas. Industrial and organizational psychologists are employed by business firms to improve working conditions, enhance productivity, and—if they have counseling skills—work with employees who encounter problems on the job. They assist in the processes of hiring, training, and promotion. They devise psychological tests to ascertain whether job applicants have the abilities, interests, and traits that predict successful performance of various jobs. They conduct research concerning job motivation, job satisfaction, the psychological and physical well-being of employees, and ways of making technical systems such as automobile dashboards and computer keyboards more user friendly.

Consumer psychologists study the behavior of shoppers in an effort to predict and influence their behavior. They advise store managers about how to lay out the aisles of a supermarket to boost impulse buying and how to arrange window displays to attract customers. They devise strategies for enhancing the persuasiveness of newspaper ads and television commercials.

EMERGING FIELDS

There are many other fields and subfields in psychology. The behavior problems that affect children can be very different from those encountered by adults. Clinical child psychologists assess these problems and work with parents and teachers, and the children themselves, to help children overcome or adjust to problems.

Forensic psychologists apply psychological expertise within the criminal-justice system. They may serve as expert witnesses in the courtroom, testifying about the competence of defendants to stand trial or describing mental disorders and how they may affect criminal behavior (DeAngelis, 1994c). Psychologists are employed by police departments to assist in the selection of stable applicants; to counsel officers on how to cope with stress; and to train police in the handling of suicide threats, hostage crises, and family disputes.

Health psychologists examine the ways in which behavior and mental processes such as attitudes are related to physical health (Wiggins, 1994). They study the effects of stress on health problems such as headaches, cardiovascular disease, and cancer. Health psychologists investigate the factors

MINILECTURE:
A BRIEF
HISTORY OF
PSYCHOLOGY

that contribute to patient compliance with medical advice. Health psychologists also guide clients to undertake more healthful behavior patterns such as exercising, quitting smoking, and eating a more healthful diet.

Psychologists are continually finding new areas in which to apply their knowledge and skills.

Reflections

Now that you have seen what psychologists do, reflect on the following questions:

- Which fields of psychology are most in keeping with your own interests?
- Which fields are most consistent with what you imagined psychologists did before you read this section? Which fields are most different? Why?
- What characteristics or interests are shared by all psychologists? What kinds of characteristics or interests set different kinds of psychologists apart?
- If a friend had a problem, would it be adequate to advise "Why don't you see a psychologist?"? Why or why not?

Where Psychology Comes From: A Brief History

Psychology is as old as history and as modern as today. Knowledge of the history of psychology allows us to appreciate psychology's theoretical conflicts, its place among the sciences, the evolution of its methods, and its social and political roles (McGovern and others, 1991).

Although research findings and theoretical developments seem to change the face of psychology every few years, the outline for this textbook could have been written by the Greek philosopher Aristotle (ca. 384– 322 B.C.). One of Aristotle's works is called *Peri Psyches,* which translates as "About the Psyche." *Peri Psyches,* like this book, begins with a history of psychological thought and historical perspectives on the nature of the mind and behavior. Given his scientific approach, Aristotle made the case that human behavior, like the movements of the stars and the seas, is subject to rules and laws. Then Aristotle delved into his subject matter topic by topic: personality, sensation and perception, thought, intelligence, needs and motives, feelings and emotion, and memory. This book reorganizes these topics, but each is here.

Truth or Fiction Revisited. *It is true that a book on psychology, whose contents are similar to those of the book you are now holding, was written by Aristotle more than 2,000 years ago.* The name of that book is *Peri Psyches.*

Aristotle also declared that people are basically motivated to seek pleasure and avoid pain, a view employed in modern psychodynamic and learning theories.

There are other contributors from ancient Greece. Democritus, for instance, suggested around 400 B.C. that we could think of behavior in terms of a body and a mind. (Contemporary psychologists still talk about the interaction of biological and cognitive processes.) Democritus also pointed out that our behavior is influenced by external stimulation, and he was one of the first to raise the issue of whether there is such a thing as free will or choice. After all, if we are influenced by external forces, can we be said to control our own behavior? Putting it another way, where do the influences of others end and our "real selves" begin? We shall return to this theme repeatedly.

Plato (ca. 427–347 B.C.), the disciple of Socrates, recorded Socrates' advice "Know thyself," which has remained one of the mottos of psychological thought ever since. Socrates claimed that we could not attain reliable self-knowledge through our senses because the senses do not exactly mirror reality. Today, we still differentiate between the stimuli that impact upon our sensory receptors and our frequently distorted perceptions and memories. Because the senses provide imperfect knowledge, Socrates suggested that we should rely on processes such as rational thought and **introspection** to achieve self-knowledge.

Truth or Fiction Revisited. *It is true that the ancient Greek philosopher Socrates suggested a research method that is still used in psychology.* The method is termed *introspection.*

Socrates also stressed the importance of social psychology. He pointed out that people are social creatures who influence one another profoundly.

Had we room enough and time, we could trace psychology's roots to thinkers more distant than the ancient Greeks, and we could trace its development through the great thinkers of the Renaissance. We could point to 19th-century influences such as theories about evolution, the movements of the atoms, transmission of neural messages in the brain, and the association of thoughts and memories. We could also describe the development of statistics, which is used by psychologists to help judge the results of their research.

As it is, we must move to the development of psychology as a laboratory science during the second half of the 19th century. Some historians set the marker date at 1860. It was then that Gustav Theodor Fechner (1801–1887) published his landmark book *Elements of Psychophysics,* which showed how physical events (such as lights and sounds) were related to psychological sensation and perception. Fechner also showed how we could scientifically measure the effect of these events. Most historians set the debut of modern psychology as a laboratory science in the year 1879, when Wilhelm Wundt (1832–1920) established the first psychological laboratory in Leipzig, Germany.

STRUCTURALISM

Wilhelm Wundt, like Aristotle, claimed that the mind was a natural event and could be studied scientifically, just like light, heat, and the flow of blood. Wundt used the method of introspection, recommended by Socrates, to try to discover the basic elements of experience. When presented with various sights and sounds, he and his colleagues tried to look inward as objectively as possible to describe their sensations and feelings.

Wundt and his students—among them Edward Bradford Titchener, who brought Wundt's methodology to Cornell University—founded the school of psychology known as **structuralism.** Structuralism attempted to define the makeup of conscious

Introspection • An objective approach to describing one's mental content.

Structuralism • The school of psychology that argues that the mind consists of three basic elements—sensations, feelings, and images—that combine to form experience.

Wilhelm Wundt

William James

Objective • Of known or perceived objects rather than existing only in the mind; real.

Subjective • Of the mind; personal; determined by thoughts and feelings rather than by external objects.

Functionalism • The school of psychology that emphasizes the uses or functions of the mind rather than the elements of experience.

Habit • A response to a stimulus that becomes automatic with repetition.

Behaviorism • The school of psychology that defines psychology as the study of observable behavior and studies relationships between stimuli and responses.

Response • A movement or other observable reaction to a stimulus.

Stimuli • (STIM-you-lie *or* STIM-you-lee). Plural of *stimulus.* (1) A feature in the environment that is detected by an organism or leads to a change in behavior (a response). (2) A form of physical energy such as light or sound that impinges on the sensory receptors.

Conditioning • A simple form of learning in which stimuli come to signal other stimuli by means of association.

Reinforcement • A stimulus that follows a response and increases the frequency of the response.

experience, breaking it down into **objective** sensations such as sight or taste, and **subjective** feelings such as emotional responses, will, and mental images (for example, memories or dreams). Structuralists believed that the mind functioned by creatively combining the elements of experience.

Another of Wundt's American students was G. Stanley Hall (1844–1924), whose main interests included the psychological developments of childhood, adolescence, and old age. Hall is usually credited with originating the discipline of child psychology, and he founded the American Psychological Association. The development of child psychology altered the widespread belief that children were miniature adults.

FUNCTIONALISM

I wished, by treating Psychology like a natural science, to help her become one.
                                    WILLIAM JAMES

Toward the end of the 19th century, William James (1842–1910), brother of the novelist Henry James, adopted a broader view of psychology that focused on the relation between conscious experience and behavior. James was a major figure in the development of psychology in the United States. He received an MD degree from Harvard University but never practiced medicine. He made his career in academia, teaching at Harvard—first in physiology, then in philosophy, and finally in psychology. He described his views in the first modern psychology textbook, *The Principles of Psychology,* which was published in 1890. James argued, for example, that the stream of consciousness is fluid and continuous. Introspection convinced him that experience cannot be broken down into units as the structuralists maintained.

James was also one of the founders of the school of **functionalism,** which dealt with overt behavior as well as consciousness. The American philosopher and educator John Dewey (1859–1952) also contributed to functionalist thought. Functionalism addressed the ways in which experience permits us to function more adaptively in our environments, and it used behavioral observation in the laboratory to supplement introspection. The structuralists tended to

ask, "What are the parts of psychological processes?" The functionalists tended to ask, "What are the purposes (functions) of overt behavior and mental processes? What difference do they make?"

Dewey and James were influenced by the English naturalist Charles Darwin's (1809–1882) theory of evolution. Earlier in the 19th century, Darwin had argued that organisms with adaptive features survive and reproduce, whereas those without such features are doomed to extinction. This doctrine is known as the "survival of the fittest." It suggests that as the generations pass, organisms whose behavior and physical traits (weight, speed, coloring, size, and so on) are best suited to their environments are most likely to survive until maturity and to transmit these traits to future generations.

Functionalists adapted Darwin's view to behavior and proposed that more adaptive behavior patterns are learned and maintained. Less adaptive behavior patterns tend to drop out, or to be discontinued, however. The "fittest" behavior patterns survive. Adaptive actions tend to be repeated and become **habits.** James wrote that "habit is the enormous flywheel of society." Habit maintains civilization from day to day.

The formation of habits is seen in acts such as lifting forks to our mouths and turning doorknobs. At first, these acts require full attention. If you are in doubt, stand by with paper towels and watch a baby's first efforts at self-feeding. Through repetition, the acts that make up self-feeding become automatic, or habitual. The multiple acts involved in learning to drive a car also become routine through repetition. We can then perform them without much attention, freeing ourselves to focus on other matters such as our clever conversation and the cultured sounds issuing from the radio. The idea of learning by repetition is also basic to the behavioral tradition.

BEHAVIORISM

Think of placing a hungry rat in a maze. It meanders down a pathway that comes to an end. It can then turn left or right. If you consistently reward the rat with food for turning right at this choice-point, it will learn to turn right when it arrives there, at least when it is hungry. But what does the rat *think* when it is learning to turn right? "Hmm, last time I was in this situation and turned to the right, I was given some food. Think I'll try that again"?

Does it seem absurd to try to place yourself in the "mind" of a rat? So it seemed to John Broadus Watson (1878–1958), the founder of American **behaviorism.** But Watson was asked to consider just such a question as one of the requirements for his doctoral degree, which he received from the University of Chicago in 1903. Functionalism was abroad in the land and dominant at the University of Chicago, and functionalists were concerned with the stream of consciousness as well as observable behavior. Watson bridled at the introspective struggles of the functionalists to study consciousness, especially the consciousness of lower animals. He asserted that if psychology was to be a natural science, like physics or chemistry, it must limit itself to observable, measurable events—that is, to behavior. Observable behavior includes activities such as pressing a lever; turning left or right; eating and mating; even involuntary body functions such as heart rate, dilation of the pupils of the eyes, blood pressure, and emission of brain waves. These behaviors are *public.* They can be measured by simple observation or by laboratory instruments. Even the emission of brain waves is made public by scientific instruments (see Chapters 3 and 5), and diverse observers would readily agree about their existence and features. Psychology must not concern itself with "elements of consciousness" that are accessible only to the organism perceiving them. (Behaviorists define psychology as the scientific study of *behavior,* not of *behavior and mental processes.*)

Watson agreed with the functionalist focus on the importance of learning, however, and suggested that psychology address the learning of measurable **responses** to environmental **stimuli.** He pointed to the laboratory experiments being conducted by Ivan Pavlov in Russia as a model. Pavlov had found that dogs will learn to salivate when a bell is rung if ringing the bell has been repeatedly associated with feeding. Pavlov explained the salivation in terms of the laboratory conditions, or **conditioning,** that led to it, not in terms of the imagined mental processes of the dogs.

Moreover, the response that Pavlov chose to study, salivation, was a public event that could be measured by laboratory instruments. It was absurd to try to determine what a dog, or person, was thinking.

Watson began teaching at Johns Hopkins University in 1908, where behaviorism took root and soon became firmly planted in American psychology. In 1920 Watson got a divorce so that he could marry a former student, and the scandal forced him to leave academic life. For a while Watson sold coffee and worked as a clerk in a department store. Then he undertook a second productive career in advertising, and he eventually became vice-president of a New York agency.

John B. Watson

Harvard University psychologist B. F. Skinner (1904–1990) took up the behaviorist call and introduced the concept of **reinforcement** to behaviorism. Organisms, Skinner maintained, learn to behave in certain ways because they have been reinforced for doing so. He demonstrated that laboratory animals will carry out various simple and complex behaviors because of reinforcement. They will peck buttons (Figure 1.2), turn in circles, climb ladders, and push toys across the floor. Many psychologists adopted the view that, in principle, one

FIGURE 1.2

A Couple of Examples of the Power of Reinforcement In the photo on the left, we see how our feathered gift to city life has earned its keep in many behavioral experiments on the effects of reinforcement. Here, the pigeon pecks the blue button because pecking this button has been followed (reinforced) by the dropping of a food pellet into the cage. In the photo on the right, "Air Raccoon" shoots a basket. Behaviorists teach animals complex behaviors such as shooting baskets by first reinforcing approximations to the goal (or target behavior). As time progresses, closer approximations are demanded before reinforcement is given.

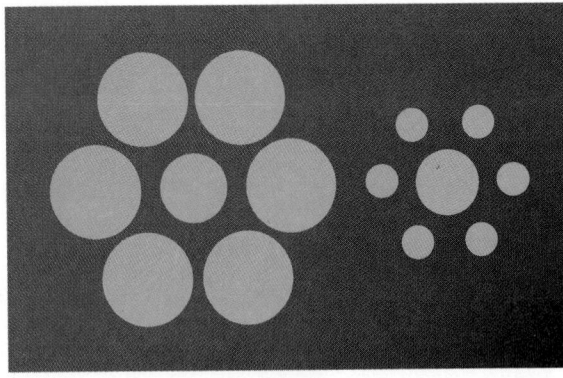

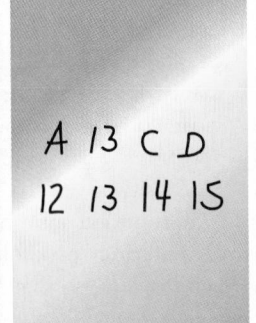

A. Are the circles in the center of the configurations the same size? Why not take a ruler and measure their diameters?

B. Is the second symbol in each line the letter B or the number 13?

C. Which one of the gray squares is brighter?

FIGURE 1.3

The Importance of Context Gestalt psychologists have shown that our perceptions depend not only on our sensory impressions but also on the context of our impressions. They argue that human perception cannot be explained in terms of basic units because we tend to interpret our perceptions of things as wholes, in terms of the contexts in which they occur. You will interpret a man running toward you very differently depending on whether you are on a deserted street at night or at a track in the morning.

could explain intricate human behavior as the summation of instances of learning through reinforcement. Nevertheless, as a practical matter, they recognized that trying to account for all of a person's behaviors by enumerating her or his complete history of reinforcement would be a hopeless task.

GESTALT PSYCHOLOGY

In the 1920s, another school of psychology—**Gestalt psychology**—was quite prominent in Germany. In the 1930s, the three founders of the school—Max Wertheimer (1880–1943), Kurt Koffka (1886–1941), and Wolfgang Köhler (1887–1967)—left Europe to escape the Nazi threat. They carried on their work in the United States, giving further impetus to American ascendance in psychology.

Wertheimer and his colleagues focused on perception and on how perception influences thinking and problem solving. In contrast to the behaviorists, Gestalt psychologists argued that one cannot hope to understand human nature by focusing only on clusters of overt behavior. In contrast to the structuralists, they claimed that one cannot explain human perceptions, emotions, or thought processes in terms of basic units. Perceptions were *more* than the sums of

their parts: Gestalt psychologists saw our perceptions as wholes that give meaning to parts.

Gestalt psychologists illustrated how we tend to perceive separate pieces of information as integrated wholes, including the contexts in which they occur. Consider Figure 1.3. The circles in the centers of the configurations at the left are the same size, yet we may perceive them as being of different sizes because of the contexts in which they appear. The second symbol in each line of the center figure is identical, but in the top row we may perceive it as a B and in the bottom row as the number 13. The symbol has not changed, only the context in which it appears. The inner squares in the figure at the right are equally bright, but they may look different because of their contrasting backgrounds. In *The Prince and the Pauper,* Mark Twain dressed a peasant boy as a prince, and the kingdom bowed to him. Do clothes sometimes make the man or woman?

Gestalt psychologists believed that learning could be active and purposeful, not merely responsive and mechanical as in Pavlov's experiments. Wolfgang Köhler and the others demonstrated that much learning, especially in learning to solve problems, is accomplished by **insight,** not by

Max Wertheimer

mechanical repetition. Köhler was marooned by World War I on one of the Canary Islands, where the Prussian Academy of Science kept a colony of apes, and his research on the island lent him, well, insight into the process of learning by insight.

Consider the chimpanzee in Figure 1.4. At first, the ape is unsuccessful in reaching for bananas suspended from the ceiling. Then it suddenly piles the boxes atop one another and climbs them to reach the bananas. It seems that the chimp has experienced a sudden reorganization of the mental elements that represent the problem—that is, it has had a "flash of insight." Köhler's findings suggest that we often manipulate the mentally represented elements of problems until we group them in such a way that we believe we will be able to reach a goal. The manipulations may take quite some time as mental trial and error proceeds. Once the proper grouping has been found, however, we seem to perceive it all at once.

Have you ever sat pondering a problem for quite a while and then, suddenly, the solution appeared? Did it seem to come out of nowhere? In a flash? Was it difficult at that point to understand how it could have taken so long?

Gestalt principles of perceptual organization are discussed in Chapter 4, and learning by insight is elaborated on in Chapter 8.

PSYCHOANALYSIS

Psychoanalysis, the school of psychology founded by Sigmund Freud, is very different from the other schools in its background and approach. Freud's theory, more than the others, has invaded the popular culture, and you may already be familiar with a number of its concepts. For example, an unstable person goes on a killing spree on at least one TV crime show each season. At the show's conclusion, a psychiatrist typically explains that the killer was

Gestalt psychology • (gesh-TALT). The school of psychology that emphasizes the tendency to organize perceptions into wholes and to integrate separate stimuli into meaningful patterns.

Insight • In Gestalt psychology, the sudden reorganization of perceptions, allowing the sudden solution of a problem.

Psychoanalysis • (sigh-coe-an-AL-uh-sis). The school of psychology that emphasizes the importance of unconscious motives and conflicts as determinants of human behavior.

FIGURE 1.4

Some Insight into the Role of Insight At first, the chimpanzee cannot reach the bananas hanging from the ceiling. After some time has passed, the chimp suddenly piles the boxes on top of one another to reach the fruit, behavior suggestive of a "flash of insight." Gestalt psychologists argue that behavior is often too complex to be explained in terms of learning mechanical responses to environmental stimulation.

Sigmund Freud

Psychodynamic • (sigh-coe-die-NAM-ick). Referring to Freud's theory, which proposes that the motion of underlying forces of personality determines our thoughts, feelings, and behavior. (From the Greek *dynamis*, meaning "power.")

Hormone • A chemical substance that promotes development of body structures and regulates various body functions.

Genes • (jeans). The basic building blocks of heredity.

"unconsciously" doing away with his own mother or father. Or perhaps a friend has tried to "interpret" a slip of the tongue you made or has asked you what you thought might be the symbolic meaning of a dream.

The notions that people are driven by hidden impulses and that verbal slips and dreams represent unconscious wishes largely reflect the influence of a Viennese physician who fled to England in the 1930s to escape the Nazi tyranny—Sigmund Freud (1856–1939). Academic psychologists conducted their research mainly in the laboratory. Freud, however, gained his understanding of people through clinical interviews with patients. He was astounded at how little insight his patients seemed to have into their motives. Some patients justified, or rationalized, the most abominable behavior with absurd explanations. Others seized the opportunity to blame themselves for nearly every misfortune that had befallen the human species.

Freud came to believe that unconscious processes, especially primitive sexual and aggressive impulses, were more influential than conscious thought in determining human behavior. Freud thought that most of the mind was unconscious, consisting of a seething cauldron of conflicting impulses, urges, and wishes. People were motivated to gratify these impulses, ugly as some of them were. But at the same time, people were motivated to judge themselves as being decent. Thus, they would often delude themselves about their real motives. Because of the assumed motion of underlying forces in personality, Freud's theory is referred to as **psychodynamic.**

Freud devised a method of psychotherapy called psychoanalysis. Psychoanalysis aims to help patients gain insight into many of their deep-seated conflicts and find socially acceptable ways of expressing wishes and gratifying needs. Psychoanalytic therapy is a process that can extend for years. We describe psychoanalysis at length (but not for years) in Chapter 14.

Now let's turn to the "top 10"—psychology's golden oldies. Table 1.1 ranks the top 10 ("most important") historic figures in psychology according to historians of psychology and chairpersons of psychology departments (Kern and others, 1991). The historians and chairpersons concur on 7 of their top 10.

TABLE 1.1

Historians' and Chairpersons' Rankings of the Importance of Figures in the History of Psychology

HISTORIANS			CHAIRPERSONS		
RANK	FIGURE	AREA OF CONTRIBUTION	RANK	FIGURE	AREA OF CONTRIBUTION
1.	Wilhelm Wundt	Structuralism	1.	B. F. Skinner	Operant Conditioning
2.	William James	Functionalism	2.	Sigmund Freud	Psychoanalysis
3.	Sigmund Freud	Psychoanalysis	3.	William James	Functionalism
4.	John B. Watson	Behaviorism	4.	Jean Piaget	Cognitive Development
5.	Ivan Pavlov	Conditioning	5.	G. Stanley Hall	Development
6.	Hermann Ebbinghaus	Memory	6.	Wilhelm Wundt	Structuralism
7.	Jean Piaget	Cognitive Development	7.	Carl Rogers	Self Theory, Person-Centered Therapy
8.	B. F. Skinner	Operant Conditioning	8.	John B. Watson	Behaviorism
9.	Alfred Binet	Assessment of Intelligence	9.	Ivan Pavlov	Conditioning
10.	Gustav Theodor Fechner	Psychophysics	10.	Edward L. Thorndike	Learning—Law of Effect

Rankings based on data from "Historians' and chairpersons' judgments of eminence among psychologists," by J. H. Kern, R. Davis and S. F. Davis, 1991, *American Psychologist, 46,* pp. 789–792.

Today we no longer find psychologists who describe themselves as structuralists or functionalists. Although the school of Gestalt psychology gave birth to current research approaches in perception and problem solving, few would consider themselves Gestalt psychologists. The numbers of orthodox behaviorists and psychoanalysts have also been declining. Many contemporary psychologists in the behaviorist tradition look on themselves as social-cognitive[1] theorists, and many psychoanalysts consider themselves neoanalysts rather than traditional Freudians. Still, the historical traditions of psychology find expression in many contemporary fields and schools of psychology.

Reflections

Now that you have surveyed the history of psychology, reflect on the following questions:

- Which school of psychology is most consistent with your own interests or your own views of people? Why?
- Why do behaviorists object to schools of psychology that use introspection to learn about people? Do you agree with the behaviorist point of view? Why or why not?
- Had you heard of Sigmund Freud before you began this course? What had you heard? Were your impressions accurate? Why or why not?
- Psychology's "top 10," as selected both by historians of psychology and chairpersons of psychology departments, consists completely of White males. Why do you think this is so?

How Today's Psychologists View Behavior

First a new theory is attacked as absurd; then it is admitted to be true, but obvious and insignificant; finally it is seen to be so important that its adversaries claim that they themselves discovered it.

WILLIAM JAMES

The history of psychological thought has taken many turns, and contemporary psychologists also differ in their approaches. Today, there are six broad, influential perspectives in psychology: the biological, cognitive, humanistic–existential, psychodynamic, learning, and sociocultural perspectives. Each perspective emphasizes different topics of investigation, and each tends to approach its topics in its own ways.

THE BIOLOGICAL PERSPECTIVE

Psychologists assume that our thoughts, fantasies, dreams, and mental images are made possible by the nervous system and especially by that pivotal part of the nervous system, the brain. Biologically oriented psychologists seek the links between events in the brain—such as the activity of brain cells—and mental processes. They use techniques such as CAT scans, PET scans, and electrical stimulation of sites in the brain to show that these sites are involved in thoughts, emotions, and behavior (see Chapter 3). Through biological psychology, we have discovered parts of the brain that are highly active when we listen to music, solve math problems, or experience certain psychological disorders. We have learned how the production of chemical substances in certain parts of the brain is essential to the storage of information—that is, the formation of memories. Among some lower animals, electrical stimulation of parts of the brain prompts the expression of innate, or built-in, sexual and aggressive behaviors.

Biological psychologists are also concerned about the influences of hormones and genes. In people, for instance, the **hormone** prolactin stimulates production of milk. In rats, however, prolactin also sparks maternal behavior. In lower animals, sex hormones determine whether mating behavior will follow stereotypical masculine or feminine behavior patterns. In people, hormones seem to play a subtler role, as we see in Chapters 3, 10, and 12.

Genes are the basic units of heredity. Psychologists are vitally interested in the extent of genetic influences on human traits such

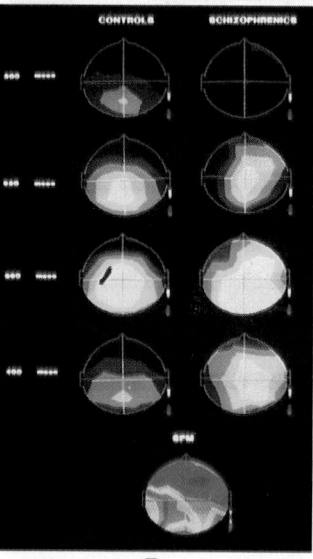

A

B

The Biological Perspective. Psychologists with a biological perspective study the connections between biological processes, behavior, and mental processes. They use methods such as Brain Electrical Activity Mapping, in which electrodes measure the electrical activity of parts of the brain (photo A). The left-hand column of photo B shows the average level of electrical activity of the brains of 10 normal people at four time intervals. The right-hand column shows the average activity of 10 people diagnosed with schizophrenia. (Schizophrenia is a severe psychological disorder.) The more intense the activity, the brighter the color (white is most intense). The bottom diagram summarizes similarities and differences between people not diagnosed with schizophrenia and people diagnosed with schizophrenia: areas in blue reflect smaller differences; white areas reflect larger differences.

[1] Social-cognitive theorists were formerly termed *social-learning theorists.*

Cognitive • Having to do with mental processes such as sensation and perception, memory, intelligence, language, thought, and problem solving.

Humanism • The philosophy and school of psychology that asserts that people are conscious, self-aware, and capable of free choice, self-fulfillment, and ethical behavior.

Existentialism • (egg-ziss-TEN-shall-izm). The view that people are completely free and responsible for their own behavior.

Neoanalysts • (knee-oh-AN-al-lists). Contemporary followers of Freud who focus less on the roles of unconscious impulses and more on conscious choice and self-direction.

as intelligence, psychological disorders, criminal behaviors, and even the tendency to become addicted to substances such as alcohol and narcotics. Identical twins (who share the same genetic endowment) are more likely than fraternal twins (who are no more closely related than other brothers and sisters) to share such broad personality traits as sociability, emotionality, and level of activity (see Chapter 3). In Chapter 9, we shall see that the relative influences of heredity (nature) or environmental influences (nurture) on intelligence is a hotly debated issue, with political implications. Generally speaking, genetic factors provide a broad "reaction range" for the expression of various traits. Environmental factors interact with genetic factors to determine the expression of traits.

THE COGNITIVE PERSPECTIVE

Cognitive psychologists believe that we must venture into the realm of mental processes to understand human nature (Sperry, 1993). They investigate the ways in which we perceive and mentally represent the world, how we go about solving problems, how we dream and daydream. Cognitive psychologists, in short, attempt to study those things we refer to as the *mind*.

The cognitive tradition has roots in Socrates' advice "Know thyself" and in Socrates' suggested method of looking inward (introspection) to find truth. We also find cognitive psychology's roots in structuralism, functionalism, and Gestalt psychology, each of which, in its own way, addressed issues of interest to cognitive psychologists.

Cognitive - Developmental Theory. Today, the cognitive perspective has many faces. One is the cognitive-developmental theory advanced by the Swiss biologist Jean Piaget (1896–1980). Piaget's innovative study of the intellectual or cognitive development of children has inspired thousands of research projects by developmental and educational psychologists (Beilin, 1992). The focus of this research is to learn how children and adults mentally represent and reason about the world.

According to Piaget and his intellectual descendants, the child's conception of the world grows more sophisticated as the child matures (see Chapter 11). Although experience is essential to children, their perception and understanding of the world around them unfolds as if guided by an inner clock.

Information Processing. Another face of the cognitive perspective is information processing. Psychological thought has been influenced by the status of the physical sciences of the day. For example, Freud's psychodynamic theory was related to the development of thermodynamics in the last century. Many of today's cognitive psychologists have been influenced by concepts of computer science. Computers process information to solve problems. Information is first fed into the computer (encoded so that it can be accepted by the computer as input). Then it is placed in memory—or working memory—while it is manipulated. You can also store the information more permanently in storage on a floppy disk, a hard disk, or another device. In Chapter 7, we shall see that many psychologists also speak of people as having working memories (short-term memories) and storage (long-term memories). If information has been placed in storage (or in long-term memory), it must be retrieved before we can work on it again. To retrieve information from computer storage, we must know the code or name for the data file and the rules for retrieving data files. Similarly, note psychologists, we must have appropriate cues to retrieve information from our own long-term memories or the information is lost to us. The data in a computer's storage is usually retrieved in a more exact state than human memories. Our memories tend to be colored by our biases and our expectations.

Many cognitive psychologists thus focus on information processing in people—the processes by which information is encoded (input), stored (in long-term memory), retrieved (placed in working memory), and manipulated to solve problems (output). Our strategies for solving problems are sometimes referred to as our "mental programs" or "software." In this computer metaphor, our brains are translated into the "hardware" that runs our mental programs. Our brains, that is, become *very* personal computers.

Truth or Fiction Revisited. *It is true that some psychologists look upon our strategies for solving problems as "mental programs" operated by our very "personal computers"—our brains.* These psychologists are cognitive psychologists, and they investigate the ways in which we process information.

When psychologists who study information processing contemplate the cognitive development of children, they are likely to talk in terms of the size of the child's working memory at a given age and of the number of programs a child can run simultaneously. Research suggests that these are indeed useful ways of talking about children (see Chapter 11). They allow us to explain and predict behavior quite well.

Psychologists in the behaviorist tradition argue that cognitions are not directly observable and that cognitive psychologists do not place adequate emphasis on the situational determinants of behavior. Cognitive psychologists counter that the richness of human behavior cannot be understood without reference to cognition.

THE HUMANISTIC–EXISTENTIAL PERSPECTIVE

The humanistic-existential perspective is related to Gestalt psychology and is cognitive in flavor. **Humanism** stresses the human capacity for self-fulfillment and the central roles of human consciousness, self-awareness, and the capacity to make choices. Consciousness is seen as the force that unifies our personalities. **Existentialism** views people as free to choose and responsible for choosing ethical conduct.

Humanistic psychology considers subjective or personal experience to be the most important event in psychology. Humanists believe that self-awareness, experience, and choice permit us, to a large extent, to "invent ourselves"—to fashion our growth and our ways of relating to the world—as we progress through life.

There is a debate in psychology about whether we are free to choose or whether our behavior is determined by external factors. John Watson's behaviorism was a deterministic stance that assumed that our behavior reflects the summation of the effects of the stimuli impinging upon us. The humanistic–existential approach of American psychologists such as Carl Rogers (1902–1987), Rollo May (born 1909), and Abraham Maslow (1916–1972) asserts that we are basically free to determine our own behavior. Humanistic–existential psychologists suggest that we are engaged in quests to discover our personal identities and the meanings of our lives.

The goals of humanistic–existential psychology have been more applied than academic. Humanistic–existential psychologists have devised ways to help people "get in touch" with their feelings and realize their potentials, for example. Humanistic–existential psychology reached the peak of its popularity in the 1970s with encounter groups, Gestalt therapy, meditation, and a number of other methods that have been stamped collectively as the Human Potential Movement. We shall discuss some of these techniques in Chapter 14.

Critics, including those in the behaviorist tradition, insist that psychology must be a natural science and address itself to observable events. They argue that our experiences are subjective events that are poorly suited to objective observation and measurement. Humanistic–existential psychologists such as Carl Rogers (1985) may agree that the observation methods of humanists have sometimes been less than scientific. They argue, however, that subjective human experience remains vital to the understanding of human nature. Rogers would have us improve the research methods used to study humanistic–existential concepts rather than remove them from serious scientific consideration.

THE PSYCHODYNAMIC PERSPECTIVE

In the 1940s and 1950s, psychodynamic theory dominated the practice of psychotherapy and was also widely influential in scientific psychology and the arts. Most psychotherapists were psychodynamically oriented, and many renowned artists and writers sought ways to liberate the expression of their unconscious ideas.

Today, the influence of psychoanalytic thought continues to be felt, although it no longer dominates psychology. Its influence has subsided in the humanities as well. Psychologists who follow Freud today are likely to consider themselves to be **neoanalysts.** Neoanalysts such as Karen Horney, Erich Fromm, and Erik Erikson tend to focus less on the roles of unconscious sexual and aggressive impulses in human behavior and more on deliberate choice and self-direction.

Many Freudian ideas are retained in a sort of watered-down form by the population at large. Sometimes we have ideas or inclinations that seem foreign to us. We may say, in the vernacular, that it seems as if something is trying to get the better of us. In the Middle Ages, such thoughts and impulses were usually attributed to the Devil or to demons. Dreams, likewise, were thought to enter us magically from the spirit world beyond. Today, largely because of Sigmund Freud, many people ascribe uncharacteristic ideas and dreams to unconscious processes.

Research and philosophical analysis have been somewhat hard on psychodynamic theory. Many psychoanalytic concepts cannot be confirmed by scientific means (see Chapter 12). On the other hand, reviews of psychoanalytic forms of psychotherapy have been generally positive (see Chapter 14).

LEARNING PERSPECTIVES

Many psychologists today study the effects of experience on behavior. Learning, to them, is the essential factor in describing, explaining, predicting, and controlling behavior. The term *learning* has different meanings to psychologists of different persuasions, however. Some students of learning find roles for consciousness and insight. Others do not. This distinction is found among those who adhere to the behavioral and social–cognitive perspectives.

The Behavioral Perspective. For John B. Watson, behaviorism was an approach to life as well as a broad guideline for psychological research. Not only did Watson despair of measuring consciousness and mental processes in the laboratory, he also applied behavioral analysis to virtually all situations in his daily life. He viewed people as doing things because of their learning histories, situational influences, and the rewards involved rather than because of conscious choice.

Learning, for Watson and his followers, is

exemplified by experiments in conditioning. The results of conditioning are explained in terms of external laboratory procedures, not in terms of changes that have occurred within the organism. Behaviorists do not attempt to find out what an organism has come to "know" through learning. Cognitive psychologists, in contrast, view conditioning as a process that alters the organism's mental representation of the environment—one that may encourage but does not compel changes in behavior (Rescorla, 1988).

The Social–Cognitive Perspective. Since the early 1960s, **social–cognitive theorists** (previously termed *social–learning theorists*) have gained influence in the areas of personality development, psychological disorders, and methods of therapy. Theorists such as Albert Bandura, Julian Rotter, and Walter Mischel see themselves as being within the behaviorist tradition because of their focus on the role of learning in human behavior. Yet they also return to their functionalist roots by theorizing a key role for cognition. Behaviorists emphasize the importance of environmental influences and focus on the learning of habits through repetition and reinforcement. Social–cognitive theorists, in contrast, suggest that people can modify or create their environments. People also engage in intentional learning by observing others. Through observational learning, we acquire a storehouse of responses to life's situations. Social–cognitive theorists are also humanistic in that they believe that our expectations and values help determine whether we shall *choose* to do what we have learned how to do.

THE SOCIOCULTURAL PERSPECTIVE

The **sociocultural perspective** fosters the consideration of matters of ethnicity, gender, culture, and socioeconomic status in psychology (Allen, 1993; Lewis-Fernández & Kleinman, 1994). For example, what is often seen as healthful, self-assertive, outspoken behavior by most U.S. women may be interpreted as brazen behavior within Hispanic American or Asian American communities (Lopez & Hernandez, 1986). Sociocultural theorists are vitally concerned with the experience of various

Social-cognitive theory • A school of psychology in the behaviorist tradition that includes cognitive factors in the explanation and prediction of behavior. Formerly termed *social-learning theory.*

Sociocultural perspective • The view that focuses on the roles of ethnicity, gender, culture, and socioeconomic status in behavior and mental processes.

Ethnic group • A group characterized by common features such as cultural heritage, history, race, and language.

TABLE 1.2

Contemporary Perspectives at a Glance

PERSPECTIVE	SUBJECT MATTER	KEY ASSUMPTIONS
Biological	Nervous system, endocrine system, genetic factors	Behavior and mental process can be explained in terms of biological processes
Cognitive	Mental imagery, information processing, thinking, language	People mentally represent the world and consciously attempt to understand it
Humanistic–existential	Subjective experience	People make free and conscious choices based on their unique experiences and frames of reference
Psychodynamic	Unconscious processes, early childhood experiences	Defensive processes prevent people from being aware of their underlying motives; people may be influenced for a lifetime by unconscious early childhood conflicts
Learning	Environmental influences on behavior; habitual behavior; observational learning	People are very similar at birth but unique histories of experience and reinforcement guide unique patterns of development of behavior and skills
Sociocultural	Effects of ethnicity, gender, culture, and socioeconomic status on behavior and mental processes	Individual differences are created by sociocultural factors as well as biological and psychological processes

ethnic groups in the United States. Some sociocultural theorists (e.g., Ogbu, 1993; Tharp, 1991) study differences between the children of voluntary immigrant groups, such as Asians and Europeans, and involuntary minorities, such as African Americans and Native Americans (Ogbu, 1993; Tharp, 1991). Involuntary minority children may perceive that education usually does not lead to economic advancement. Hostility and withdrawal may become the norm in school for many of them. Children of recent voluntary minority groups may also encounter stresses associated with being different. Yet they may be strongly devoted to schoolwork because of the perception that education pays off for their group (Gibson & Ogbu, 1991; Ogbu, 1993).

The sociocultural perspective also deals with matters such as the prevalence of psychological disorders among various ethnic groups within the United States. It asks whether the apparent prevalence of such disorders reflects true group differences or biases in the diagnostic process (see Chapter 13).

Contemporary psychologists continue to view behavior and mental processes from various perspectives (see Table 1.2). The influences of the cognitive and biological perspectives appear to be on the ascent (Boneau, 1992). Yet there is little or no falloff in interest in the behavioral and psychodynamic perspectives, as measured by the number of journal articles that address these views (Friman and others, 1993). Some psychologists believe that the future of psychology will see efforts to integrate diverse approaches. Many cognitive psychologists, for example, incorporate the discoveries of behaviorists by reinterpreting learning as an active, intentional process (Boneau, 1992). The behaviorist tradition, they assert, has served its historic purpose of highlighting some of the nonscientific excesses that had characterized early cognitive efforts to explore the stream of consciousness. But cognitive psychologists believe that no approach that diminishes the roles of mental representation of the world, of intentional learning, or of human values and personal choice can hope to explain the complexity and richness of human behavior. Behaviorist B. F. Skinner (1987), on the other hand, indicted cognitive psychology and humanistic psychology as two of the obstacles in the path of psychology's development as a true science of behavior.[2] Psychologists continue to exercise their rights to disagree.

---

[2] The third obstacle, according to Skinner, is psychotherapy, because psychotherapy addresses what clients think and feel as well as what they do.

Human Diversity. How can psychologists comprehend the aspirations and problems of individuals from an ethnic group without understanding the history and cultural heritage of that group? Not only does the study of human diversity help us to understand and appreciate the true scope of human behavior and mental processes, it is enriching for its own sake.

Biculturalism • Competence within two cultures without losing one's cultural identity or choosing one culture over another.

Reflections

Now that you have read about contemporary perspectives on psychology, reflect on the following questions:

- Which psychological perspectives seem to support the view that people are free to choose their own destinies? Which do not? Does it seem to you that people are free? Why or why not?
- In what ways do some psychologists see our mental processes as computerlike? Does the comparison of human mental processes to computer information processing seem reasonable to you? Why or why not?
- Does it seem possible to you to "believe in" more than one perspective? Why or why not?

Let us now consider two ways in which higher education is a broadening experience—by exposing us to human diversity and by fostering critical thinking.

Human Diversity and Psychology

The profession of psychology focuses mainly on individual people and is committed to the dignity of the individual. We cannot understand individuals without an awareness of the richness of human diversity, however (Betancourt & López, 1993; Goodchilds, 1991). Inclusion of human diversity makes psychology a stronger science and better serves the public interest (Denmark, 1994; Reid, 1994). People diverge, or differ, from one another in many ways.

ETHNIC DIVERSITY: A SOCIAL MOSAIC

One kind of diversity involves people's ethnic groups, which tend to unite them according to features such as their cultural heritage, their race, their language, and their common history.[3] Learning about the

---

[3] I use the term *ethnicity* to include the concept of race, but it should be noted that some authors limit ethnicity to refer to cultural heritage, language, and common history. The root of the word, the Greek *ethnos,* was first used to refer to the people of a nation or a tribe (Betancourt & López, 1993).

experiences of various ethnic groups in the United States highlights the influences of social forces on the individual. Students become aware of the impact of social, political, and economic factors on human behavior and development (Whitten, 1993).

The United States was once considered a "melting pot"—a crucible in which the ethnic identities of immigrants and various cultural groups were liquefied and blended into one. This view made sense to many at a time when nearly all immigrants were from Europe and physically interchangeable. Today, however, the population is becoming a richer mix, and multiple traditions and language are to be found around the nation. Many observers tend to see the United States of today and tomorrow as more of a "social mosaic" (Portes & Stepick, 1993). Moreover, many people in the United States show **biculturalism.** That is, they function competently within two cultures—the dominant culture in the United States and another culture within the home, without losing their cultural identity or choosing one culture over another (LaFromboise and others, 1993).

Consider the changing ethnic makeup of the United States. Figures 1.5 and 1.6 highlight the dramatic changes under way in the United States due to reproductive patterns and immigration. The U.S. Bureau of the Census projects, for example, that the nation's non-Hispanic White population will increase from 191 million in 1992 to 202 million in the year 2050, an increase of 11 million people (*The Outlook,* 1993; see Figure 1.5). Because, however, the populations of other ethnic groups in the United States are projected to increase relatively more rapidly, the *percentage* of non-Hispanic White Americans in the total population will *decrease* from 74–75% in 1992 to 53% in 2050 (see Figure 1.6). The fastest growing ethnic group consists of Asians and Pacific Islanders (to whom we refer as Asian Americans). In 1992 there were 9 million Asian Americans in the United States, and they are expected to increase to 41 million by 2050 (Figure 1.5), rising from 3% to 11% of the U.S. population (Figure 1.6). As shown in Figures 1.5 and 1.6, the numbers of African Americans and Hispanic Americans (who may be White, Black, or Native American Indian in racial origin) are also

growing more rapidly than those of non-Hispanic White Americans. The African American population is expected to grow from 32 million people (12% of the current population) in 1992 to 62 million people (16%) by the year 2050. The Hispanic American population is expected to increase from 24 million people (9% of the current population) to 81 million people (21% of the projected overall population) by the year 2050. The cultural heritages, languages, and histories of ethnic minority groups are thus likely to have increasing impacts on the cultural life of the United States.

Figure 1.7 reveals the ethnic diversity to be found in the United States' college

FIGURE 1.5

Projected Growth of Ethnic Groups in the United States, 1992–2050 Although non-Hispanic White Americans are more numerous than the other U.S. ethnic groups shown in this figure, their growth rate is projected to be lower.

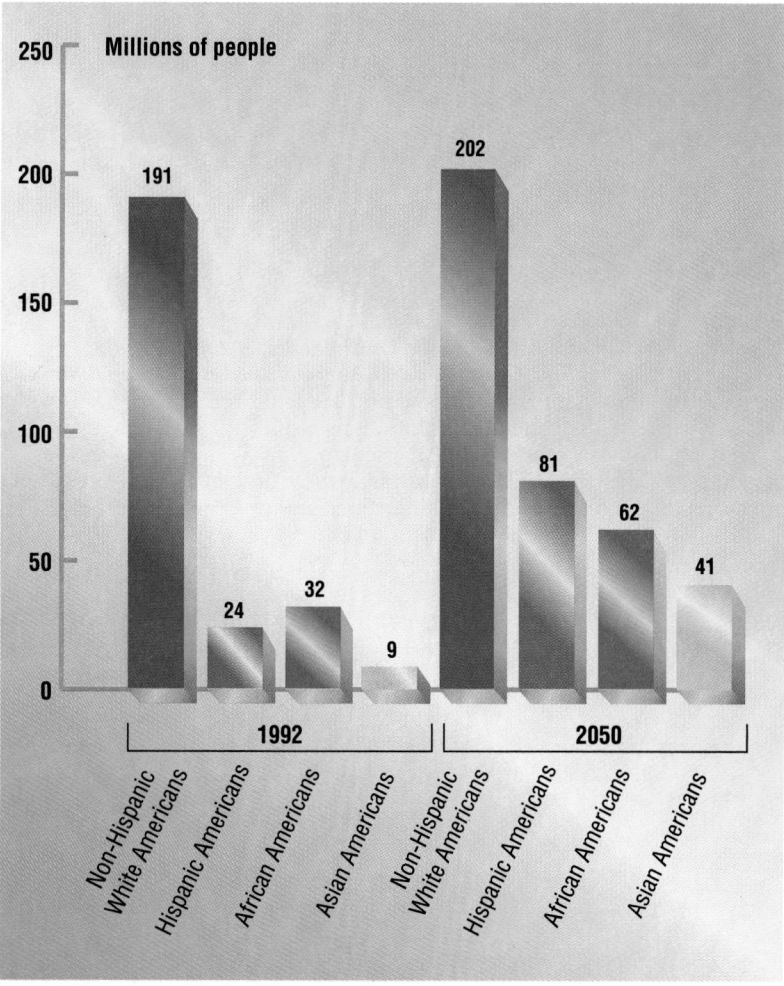

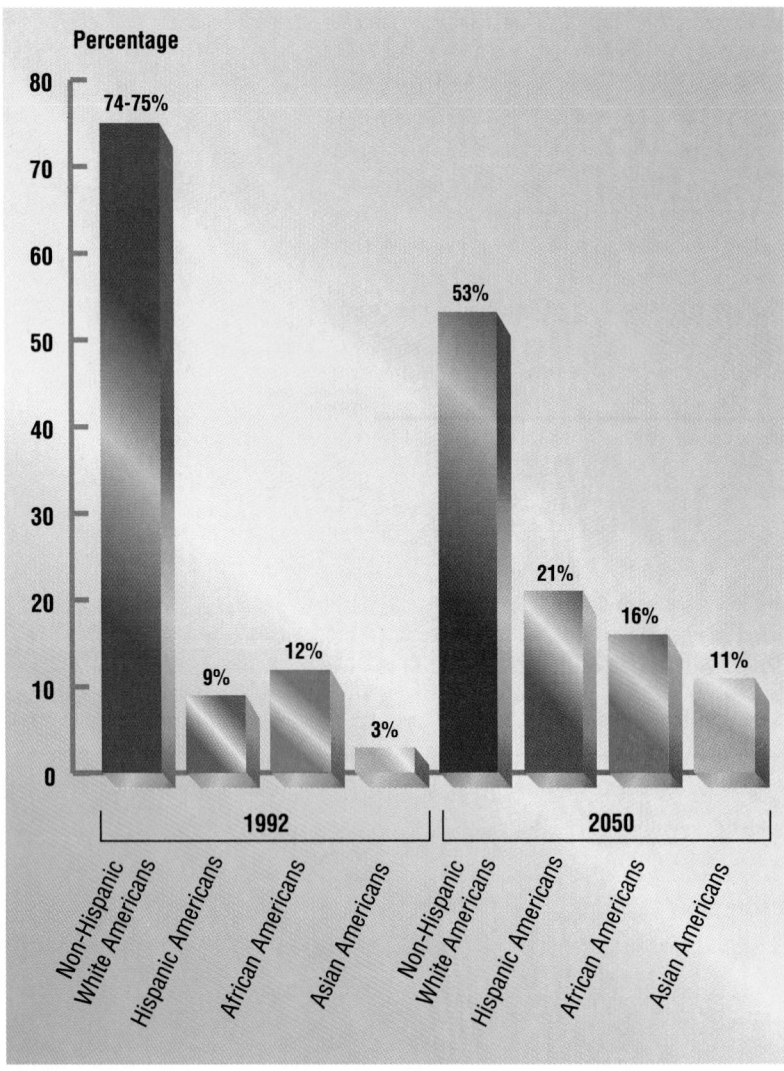

FIGURE 1.6
***Changes in the Ethnic Makeup of the United States, According to the
Numbers of Each Ethnic Group as a Percentage of the Overall Population,
1992–2050*** Although the numbers of non-Hispanic White Americans will
increase between 1992 and 2050, trends in reproduction and immigration
suggest that non-Hispanic White Americans will make up a much smaller
percentage of the overall U.S. population by the year 2050. Asian Americans
are currently the most rapidly growing ethnic group in the United States.

ble, and the percentage of non-Hispanic
White Americans declined (to 77.9% from
81.3%).

Truth or Fiction Revisited. *It is not
true that the numbers of students from ethnic minority groups have increased dramatically on college campuses in the past decade.* Actually, the
numbers of only Asian Americans and Hispanic Americans have increased dramatically on U.S. college campuses over the past
decade. The numbers of African Americans
and Native Americans have remained relatively stable.

The probing of human diversity enables
students to appreciate the cultural heritages
and historical problems of various ethnic
groups. Too often throughout our history,
the traditions, languages, and achievements
of ethnic minority groups have been judged
by majority standards or denigrated (Jones,
1991; Sue, 1991). Black dialect has been
considered inferior to standard English,
for example—an issue we discuss in
Chapter 8. Bilingualism has been erroneously considered to be inferior to being
reared to speak English only—another
issue we discuss in Chapter 8. Asian
Americans have been stereotyped as good
engineers but poor managers. There are
also significant differences *within* ethnic
groups, such as Hispanic Americans
(Greene, 1994). Many Puerto Ricans and
Mexican Americans are politically liberal,
for example. However, the majority of
Cuban Americans, who fled (or whose parents fled) from Fidel Castro's communist
takeover of Cuba, are politically conservative (Rieff, 1993).

Another reason for studying diversity concerns psychological intervention and consultation. Psychologists are called upon
to help people of all ethnic groups solve
personal problems, for example. How can
psychologists hope to understand the aspirations and problems of individuals from an
ethnic group without understanding the
history and cultural heritage of that group
(Jones, 1991; Sue, 1991)? How can psychologists understand African Americans or
Hispanic Americans, for example, without
sensitivity to the histories of prejudice
and conflict to which members of these
ethnic groups have been exposed? Moreover, should psychologists from the White
majority attempt to practice psychotherapy

population. The non-Hispanic White majority accounts for less than 80% of the
nation's more than 13 million college students overall. As noted in *The Chronicle of
Higher Education* (1992), the percentage of
Asian Americans increased by 67% between
1980 and 1990 (from 2.4% to 4%), and the
percentage of Hispanic Americans increased by nearly 40% (from 3.9% to 5.5%).
The percentages of African Americans
(8.9% versus 9.2%) and Native Americans
(0.8% versus 0.7%) remained relatively sta-

with people from ethnic minority groups? If so, what kinds of special education or training might they need to do so? What is meant by "culturally sensitive" forms of psychotherapy? We deal with issues such as these in Chapters 13, 14, and 15.

The study of ethnicity also contributes to our understanding of basic psychological processes (Betancourt & López, 1993). Both the diversity of human behavior and mental processes—and the commonalities—enhance our understanding of human nature.

Throughout the text we consider many issues that address ethnic minority groups and psychology. Consider a sampling:

- The representation of ethnic minority groups in psychological research studies
- Alcohol and substance abuse among adolescents from various ethnic minority groups
- The influence of ethnic stereotypes on our perceptions and memories
- Black dialect
- Bilingualism
- Ethnic differences in intelligence test scores—their implications and possible origins
- Ethnic differences in vulnerability to various physical problems and disorders, ranging from obesity to hypertension and cancer
- Ethnic differences in the utilization of health care
- Differential patterns of diagnosis of psychological disorders among various ethnic groups
- The prevalence of suicide among members of different ethnic minority groups
- Multicultural issues in the practice of psychotherapy
- Machismo/Marianismo stereotypes and Hispanic culture
- Prejudice

GENDER

Another way in which people differ concerns their **gender**—that is, the state of being male or being female. Gender is not simply a matter of anatomic sex; it involves a complex web of cultural expectations and

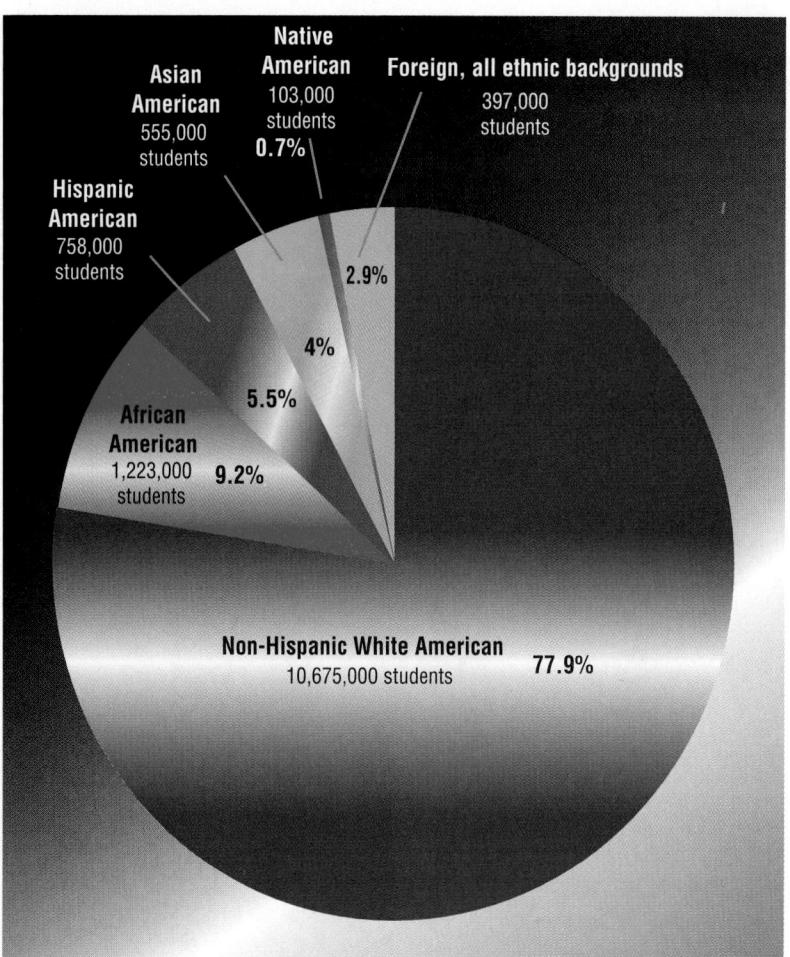

FIGURE 1.7
Ethnic Diversity in the U.S. College Population About 78% of the nation's more than 13 million postsecondary students are non-Hispanic White Americans. The percentages of Hispanic Americans and Asian Americans in higher education have been increasing rapidly in recent years. Source of data: *The Chronicle of Higher Education,* March 18, 1992, p. A35.

social roles that affects people's self-concepts and hopes and dreams, as well as their overt behavior. How can sciences such as psychology and medicine hope to understand the particular viewpoints, qualities, and problems of women if most research is conducted with men and by men (Hyde, 1993; Reid, 1993, 1994)?

Just as there have been historic prejudices against members of ethnic minority groups, so too have there been prejudices against women. Even much of the scientific research into gender roles and gender differences assumes that male behavior represents the norm (Ader & Johnson, 1994; Matlin, 1993; Walsh, 1993). The careers of women have been traditionally channeled into domestic chores, regardless of their wishes as

Gender • The state of being female or being male.

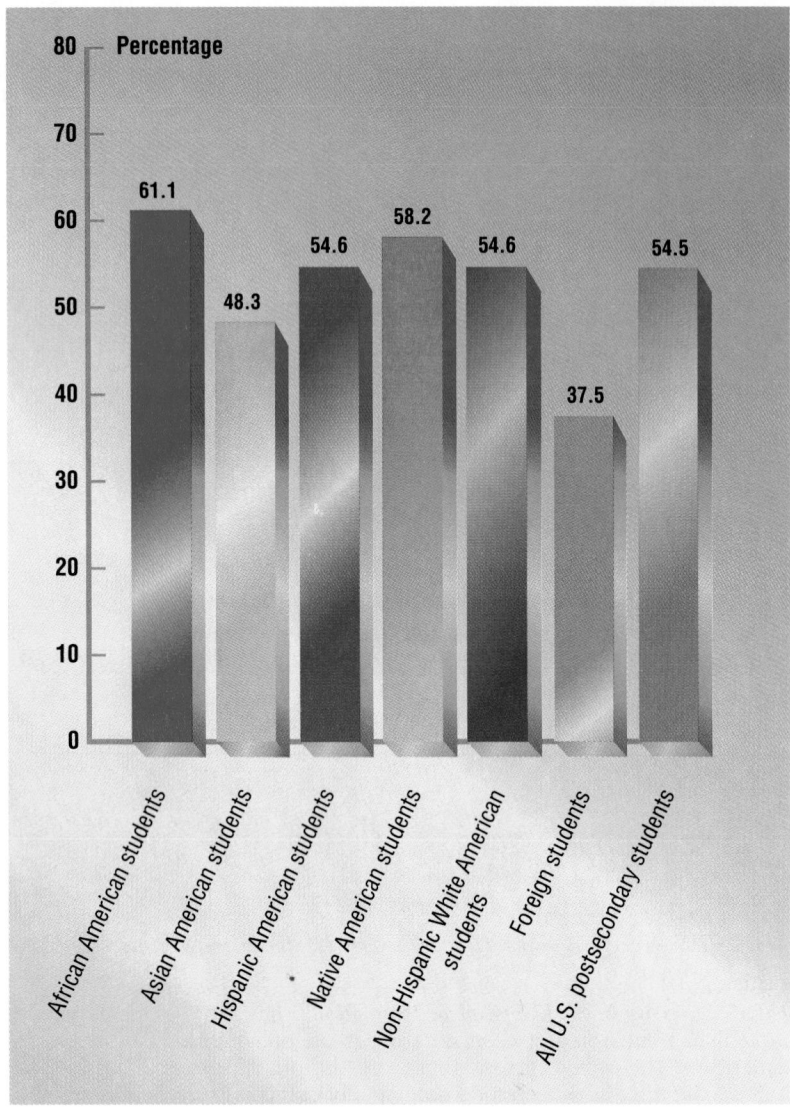

FIGURE 1.8
***The Percentages of Female Postsecondary Students in the United States,
According to Ethnic Group*** Note that the percentages of African American
and Native American women among postsecondary students are relatively
high, whereas the percentages of Asian American and foreign women are
relatively low. Why do you think this is so? Source of data: *The Chronicle of
Higher Education,* March 18, 1992, p. A35.

contribute relatively higher percentages of
women than other ethnic groups.

Truth or Fiction Revisited. *It is
true that women were not permitted to attend
college in the United States until 1833.* In that
year, Oberlin began to accept women students.

Contemporary women are also making
inroads into academic and vocational
spheres—such as medicine, law, and engineering—that were traditionally male preserves. Women now make up about 40% of
U.S. medical students, for example, although
fewer women physicians are currently in
practice. Women make up about 40% of
Harvard Law School's students and about
40% of new associates in the 250 largest
U.S. legal firms. Because women have only
recently increased their numbers in the legal profession, their numbers are lower
among lawyers in practice today (Goldstein,
1988). Women now make up nearly 15% of
engineering graduates. Although this figure
is relatively low, history provides some perspective. Only 20 years ago, women accounted for only about 4% of engineering
graduates (Adelson, 1988; Morrison & Von
Glinow, 1990)! Obvious trends are in
place—and overdue.

OTHER KINDS OF DIVERSITY

Human diversity also touches upon differences in age, ability, and sexual orientation.
Older people, people with disabilities, and
gay males and lesbians have all suffered from
discrimination, and the mainstream culture
has from time to time been loath to consider and profit from the particular sensitivities and perspectives afforded by individuals
from each of these groups. Society too often writes off older people and people with
disabilities (Bronstein & Quina, 1988).

Our focus on human diversity throughout the text will help us better understand
and fully appreciate the true extent of
human behavior and mental processes.
This broader view of psychology—and the
world—is enriching for its own sake and
heightens the accuracy and scope of our
presentation.

individuals. Not until relatively modern
times were women generally considered
suitable for higher education (and women
are still considered unsuited to education in
many parts of the world!). Women have
attended college in the United States
only since 1833, when Oberlin opened its
doors to women. Today, however, more
than half (54.5%) of U.S. postsecondary students are women. As noted in Figure 1.8,
African Americans and Native Americans

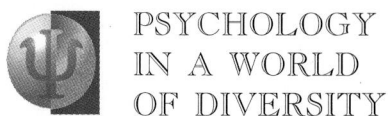

PSYCHOLOGY IN A WORLD OF DIVERSITY

ON INCREASING DIVERSITY IN AMERICAN HIGHER EDUCATION[4]

The increasing diversity of American higher education has been created not only by demographic changes in American society, but, just as importantly, by the rising awareness in the United States of various group identities and cultures. At one time, most American colleges and universities were relatively homogeneous. Even those that were not were able to persuade their students to leave their ethnicity and other cultural "baggage" at the campus gate. Today, that would no longer be realistic, even if it were desirable.

Students now enter college with their group identity intact, and they expect the institution to respond accordingly. Although that is a fairly new situation, it is rooted in events of the 1960s and 1970s, when African American students began demanding African American studies. Since then people have come to identify themselves not only according to race, gender, or ethnic identity, but also by class, sexual orientation, disability, and age.

This new reality suggests a need for students to learn about groups that were formerly ignored in the curriculum, not only so they may more fully appreciate the rich variety of cultures that make up our national community, but so they will better understand the complex ways in which cultural identity and personal identity interact. Today's multicultural world also requires critical inquiry into culture, not mere naive acceptance or celebration of it. And since the critical study and mastery of one's own culture is the best preparation for critical encounters with the cultures of others, the curriculum should not only teach students about those who are different, but help them discover themselves culturally as well.

Perhaps the most far-reaching result of the intercultural discourse beginning on today's campuses will be the introduction of *all* participants to unfamiliar cultures. Critical inquiry can open borders, introduce outside influences, and ultimately create new cultural values.

THE DIVERSITY OF CONTRIBUTORS TO THE DEVELOPMENT OF PSYCHOLOGY

Let us return to psychology's "golden oldies," as listed in Table 1.1 on page 16. Did you notice something they have in common? They are all White males. Critics assert that such lists create the erroneous impression that women and people of color have not made major contributions to the history of psychology (Russo, 1990a; Guthrie, 1990).

Consider some of the women. Christine Ladd-Franklin was born in 1847, during an era in American history in which women were expected to remain in the home and were excluded from careers in science (Furumoto, 1992). She nevertheless pursued a career in psychology, taught at Johns Hopkins and Columbia universities, and formulated a theory of color vision. Mary Whiton Calkins (born in 1863), a student of William James, pioneered research in memory. She introduced the method of paired associates and discovered the primacy and recency effects (see Chapters 6 and 16) (Madigan & O'Hara, 1992). She was also the first female president of the American Psychological Association in 1905. Margaret Floy Washburn (born in 1871) was the first woman to receive a PhD in psychology. Washburn also wrote *The Animal Mind,* a work that presaged behaviorism.

Then there are psychologists of different ethnic backgrounds. Back in 1901, African American Gilbert Haven Jones received his PhD in psychology in Germany. J. Henry Alston engaged in research in the perception of heat and cold and was the first

Margaret Floy Washburn

[4] This "World of Diversity" feature is adapted from "Campus Diversity: Facing New Realities," by Edgar F. Beckham, 1993, *The Ford Foundation Report, 23*(4), pp. 8–9.

Kenneth B. Clark

African American psychologist to be published in a key psychology journal (the year was 1920). A more contemporary African American psychologist, Kenneth B. Clark, studied ethnicity and influenced a key Supreme Court decision on desegregation (Kern and others, 1991).

Hispanic American and Asian American psychologists have also made their mark. Jorge Sanchez, for example, was among the first to show how intelligence tests are culturally biased—to the detriment of Mexican American children. Asian American psychologist Stanley Sue (see Chapter 9) has engaged in prominent research in racial differences in intelligence and academic achievement and has discussed these differences in terms of adaptation to discrimination, among other factors.

True—psychology was once the province of White males. Today, however, more than half (59%) of the PhDs in psychology are awarded to women (see Figure 1.9; ODEER, 1994). African Americans and Hispanic Americans each receive 3 to 4% of the PhDs awarded in psychology, however (ODEER, 1994). This percentage is far below their representation in the general population, unfortunately. In a recent year, only one-tenth of one percent of the 65,000 members of the American Psychological Association were Native Americans (DeAngelis, 1993a). Even so, fewer than two psychology PhDs in five are now received by White males. Psychology, like the world in which it is housed, is showing diversification.

Truth or Fiction Revisited. *It is not true that men receive the majority of doctoral degrees in psychology.* Women actually receive the majority of PhDs in psychology today.

Critical thinking • An approach to thinking characterized by skepticism and thoughtful analysis of statements and arguments—for example, probing arguments' premises and the definitions of terms.

FIGURE 1.9
Growth in the Percentage of Women Who Received Doctorates in the Various Subfields of Psychology, 1980 versus 1992 This growth of the percentage of women in psychology has been dramatic. In 1980, about two doctorate recipients in five were women, as compared to nearly three in five in 1992. Source: *Summary Report Doctorate Recipients from United States Universities.* (Table W04846), Office of Demographic, Employment, and Educational Research, 1994, Washington, DC: American Psychological Association.

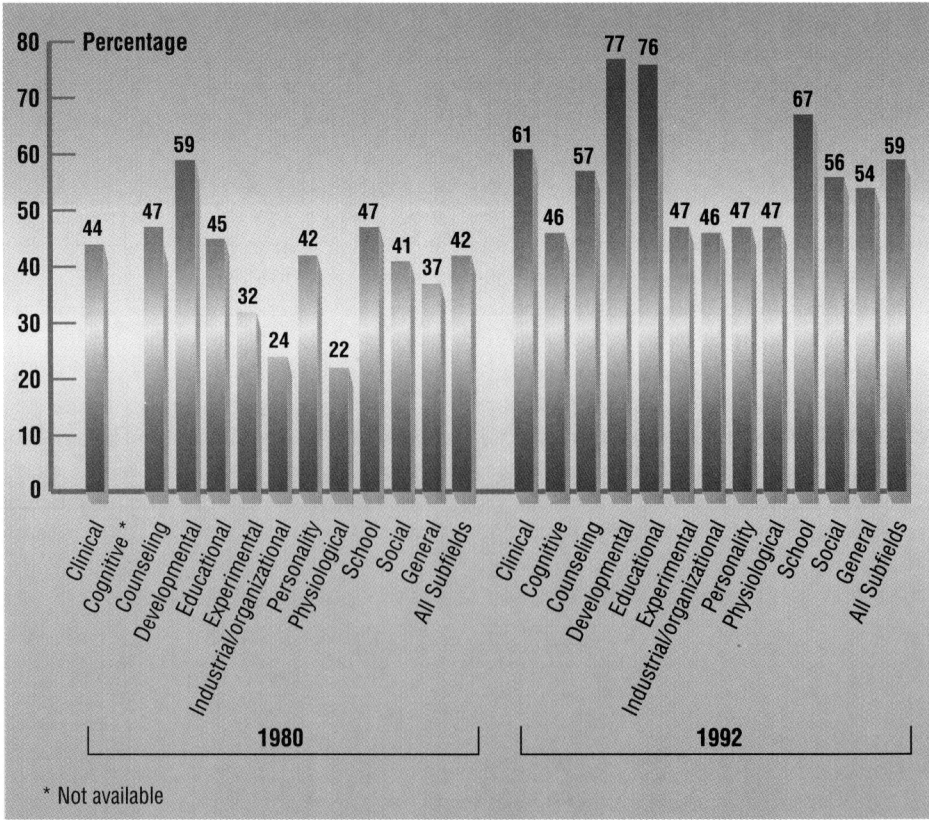

Put it another way: Psychology is for everyone.

Because it challenges narrow views of the world, the study of human diversity is also used by many postsecondary institutions to encourage critical thinking (Celis, 1993).

Reflections

Now that you have read about human diversity, reflect on the following questions:

- Where do you place yourself in the "social mosaic" that makes up the United States? How has your membership in an ethnic group affected your view of other people and of the nation at large? How has it affected the ways in which people from other ethnic backgrounds relate to you?
- How do you think your perceptions of other people and your expectations about the future might differ if you belonged to another ethnic group or if you were a member of the other gender? Why?
- Why is human diversity a key issue in the science of psychology? In what ways does knowledge of human diversity contribute to our understanding of behavior and mental processes?

Critical Thinking and Psychology

A great many people think they are thinking when they are merely rearranging their prejudices.
WILLIAM JAMES

Higher education is a broadening experience not only because of exposure to intellectual disciplines and human diversity, but also because it encourages students to learn to think critically. By thinking critically, people can challenge widely accepted but erroneous beliefs, including some of their own most cherished beliefs. **Critical thinking** helps make us into active, astute judges of other people and their points of view, rather than passive recipients of the latest intellectual fads and tyrannies.

Critical thinking fosters skepticism so that we no longer so readily take certain "truths" for granted. People largely assume that authority figures like doctors and government leaders usually provide us with factual information and are generally best equipped to make the decisions that affect our lives (Kimble, 1994). But when doctors disagree as to whether surgery is necessary to cure a health problem, how can they all be correct? When political leaders who all claim to have the "best interests" of the nation at heart fling accusations and epithets at one another, how can we know whom to trust? If we are to be conscientious, productive citizens of the nation and of the world, we need to learn to seek pertinent information to make our own decisions and to rely on our analytical abilities to judge the accuracy of this information. This textbook will help you learn to seek and analyze information that lies within the province of psychology, but the critical thinking skills you acquire will be broadly applicable in all of your courses and all of your adult undertakings.

Critical thinking helps students evaluate other people's claims and arguments. It encourages students to reconsider and, when necessary, dispute widely held beliefs (Mayer & Goodchild, 1990). Critical thinking has many meanings. On one level, critical thinking means taking nothing for granted. It means not believing things just because they are in print or because they were uttered by authority figures or celebrities. On another level, critical thinking refers to a process of thoughtfully analyzing and probing the questions, statements, and arguments of others. It means examining the definitions of terms, examining the premises or assumptions behind arguments, and scrutinizing the logic with which arguments are developed.

A psychology task force (McGovern, 1989) defined the goals of critical thinking as fostering the following thinking skills:

- Development of skepticism about explanations and conclusions
- The ability to inquire about causes and effects
- Refinement of curiosity about behavior
- Knowledge of research methods
- The ability to critically analyze arguments

Your college education is intended to do more than provide you with a data bank

Critical Thinking. Critical thinking means taking nothing for granted and refers to a process of thoughtfully analyzing and probing the questions, statements, and arguments of others. It means examining the definitions of terms, examining the premises or assumptions behind arguments, and scrutinizing the logic with which arguments are developed. Critical thinking skills provide the keys not only to a college education, but to a lifetime of self-education.

of useful knowledge. It is also meant to supply intellectual tools that allow you to analyze information independently. With these tools, you can continue to educate yourself for the rest of your life.

PRINCIPLES OF CRITICAL THINKING

Many of the "Truth or Fiction?" items presented in this textbook are intended to encourage you to apply principles of critical thinking to the subject matter of psychology. Some of them reflect "truisms," or beliefs, that are often taken for granted within our culture. Consider a sampling of "Truth or Fiction?" items from several chapters:

- Alcohol causes aggression.
- Onions and apples have the same taste.
- We tend to act out our forbidden fantasies in our dreams.
- We must make mistakes in order to learn.
- Some people have photographic memories.
- Head Start programs have raised children's IQs.
- We value things more when we have to work for them.
- Misery loves company.
- You can never be too rich or too thin.
- People who threaten suicide are only seeking attention.
- Beauty is in the eye of the beholder.

We won't give you the answers to the items—not yet. But we will provide hints and use them to illustrate some principles of critical thinking:

1. *Be skeptical.* Politicians and advertisers strive to convince you of their points of view. Even research reported in the media or in textbooks may take a certain slant. Extend this principle to yourself. You might discover that some of your own attitudes and beliefs are superficial or unfounded if you examine them critically. Accept nothing as true until you have personally examined the evidence.

2. *Examine definitions of terms.* Some statements are true when a term is defined in one way but not another. Consider the statement "Head Start programs have raised children's IQs." Although I won't drop the answer in your lap, I'll tell you that the correctness of the statement depends on the definition of "IQ." (In Chapter 9, you will see that the term *IQ* has a specific meaning and that it is not synonymous with *intelligence.*)

   One of the strengths of psychology is the use of *operational definitions* of concepts. Operational definitions are framed in terms of the ways in which we measure concepts. In interpreting research, pay attention to how concepts are defined. The truth of the following statement rests on the definitions of terms: "Onions and apples have the same taste." What does *taste* mean?

3. *Examine the assumptions or premises of arguments.* Consider the controversial abortion issue. The science of psychology cannot demonstrate the validity of either the pro-choice or pro-life positions (Kendler, 1993). However, critical thinking allows us to examine the assumptions that underlie assertions such as "Abortion is murder." Murder is a legal term that my dictionary defines as "the unlawful and malicious or premeditated killing of one human being by another." If one accepts this definition of murder as one's premise, then abortion may be murder if a fetus is considered a "human being." The question as to whether an embryo or fetus is a human being, or exactly when an embryo or fetus becomes a human being, sparks considerable controversy, of course.

   Also consider the view that one cannot learn about human beings by engaging in research with animals. One premise in the statement seems to be that human beings are not animals. We are, of course—thoroughly delightful animals, I might add. (Would you rather be a plant?)

4. *Be cautious in drawing conclusions from evidence.* Studies for many years had shown that most clients who receive psychotherapy improve. It was therefore generally assumed that psychotherapy worked. Some 40 years ago, however, a

psychologist named Hans Eysenck pointed out that most psychologically troubled people who did *not* receive psychotherapy also improved! The question thus becomes whether people receiving psychotherapy are *more* likely to improve than those who do not. Current research into the effectiveness of psychotherapy thus carefully compares the benefits of therapy techniques to those of other techniques or to those of no treatment at all. Be skeptical, moreover, when your friend swears by the effectiveness of megavitamin therapy for colds. What is the nature of the "evidence"? Is it convincing?

Correlational evidence is also inferior to experimental evidence as a way of determining cause and effect. Consider the statement "Alcohol causes aggression" in the following principle.

5. *Consider alternative interpretations of research evidence.* Does alcohol cause aggression? Is the assertion that it does so truth or fiction? Evidence certainly shows a clear *connection,* or "correlation," between alcohol and aggression. That is, many people who commit violent crimes have been drinking. Does the evidence show that this connection is *causal,* however? Tune in to Chapter 2's discussion of the differences between the correlational and experimental methods to find out. You will see that rival explanations can be employed to explain correlational evidence.

6. *Do not oversimplify.* As noted in the book's discussions of language, intelligence, and development, most behavior patterns involve complex interactions of genetic and environmental influences. Also consider the complex issue as to whether psychotherapy helps people with psychological problems. In Chapter 14 you will see that a broad answer to this question—a simple yes or no—might be oversimplifying and misleading. It is more worthwhile to ask, What *type* of psychotherapy, practiced by *whom,* is most helpful for *what kind of problem?*

7. *Do not overgeneralize.* Consider the statement, "Misery loves company." In Chapter 10 you will see that the statement is

accurate under certain circumstances. Again, consider the view that one cannot learn about human beings by engaging in research with animals. Is the truth of the matter an all-or-nothing issue? Are there certain kinds of information we can obtain about people from research with animals? What types of things about people might you be able to learn from animal research? What kinds of things are you likely to be able to learn only by conducting research with people?

8. *Apply critical thinking to all areas of life.* A skeptical attitude and a demand for evidence are not simply academic exercises that serve in introductory psychology and other college courses. They are of value in all areas of life. Be skeptical when you are bombarded by TV commercials, when political causes try to sweep you up, when you see the latest cover stories about Elvis and UFOs in the tabloids at the supermarket. How many times have you heard the claim "Studies have shown that . . ."? Perhaps such claims sound convincing, but ask yourself: Who ran the studies? Were the researchers neutral scientists or biased toward obtaining certain results? Did the studies possess the controls described in the discussion of experiments in Chapter 2?

As noted by the educator Robert M. Hutchins, "The object of education is to prepare the young to educate themselves throughout their lives." One of the primary ways of educating yourself is through critical thinking.

RECOGNIZING COMMON FALLACIES IN ARGUMENTS

Another aspect of critical thinking is learning to recognize the fallacies in other people's claims and arguments. Consider the following examples:

1. Arguments directed to the person *(argumentum ad hominem):* Psychological theories and research enterprises have met with historic upheavals. The views of Sigmund Freud, for example, the founder of psychodynamic theory, were assaulted almost as soon as they were

publicized both by members of his inner circle, such as Carl Jung, and by psychologists of other schools, such as behaviorists. Freud has been alternately referred to as an ingenious, compassionate scientist and as an elitist faker who spun his theories out of the fabric of the fantasy lives of bored, wealthy women. Both extremes are examples of *ad hominem* arguments. Freud's personality and motives are of historic interest, but neither of them addresses the accuracy of his views. Theories should be judged on evidence, not one's character.

2. Appeals to force *(argumentum ad baculum)*: Galileo invented the telescope in the 17th century and discovered that the Earth revolved around the sun, rather than vice versa. The Church had taught that the Earth was at the center of the universe, however. Galileo was condemned for heresy and warned that he would be burned to death if he did not confess the error of his ways. Galileo apparently agreed with Shakespeare's words in *King Henry IV, Part I* that "The better part of valour is discretion" and recanted his views, but the facts, of course, are as they are. Social approval and, at the opposite extreme, threats of violence do not make arguments correct or incorrect.

3. Appeals to authority *(argumentum ad verecundiam)*: You have heard arguments to

PSYCHOLOGY IN THE NEW MILLENNIUM

A Partial Wish List

How many people's lives have straddled two millennia?

Suddenly we are but a few years away from the new millennium—the year 2001. New years bring new hope, and we make resolutions to improve our lives. The thought of entering the new millennium brings yet greater hope and stirs yet greater resolve to enhance our lives and those of our children.

With the rapid pace of political change and the development of new technologies, we seem to be ever on the edge of major advances and changes in lifestyle. The "Psychology in the New Millennium" features in the text explore the connections between such advances, psychology, and our styles of life. In some cases we explore the future of psychological knowledge or applications. In other cases, we explore the effect of other kinds of advances or changes on people's behavior and mental processes.

The first of these features contains a wish list—a partial list of developments in psychology that may be ushered in with the refreshing breezes of the new millennium. Many of them seem to be right around the corner. Others appear to be more elusive. All of them are being researched as you read these pages:[5]

Development of psychological supertheories that integrate the strengths of existing theories and are shown to better fit specific areas of psychological functioning—such as the hunger drive and specific psychological disorders

Inclusion of members of diverse groups in research so that generalization is possible; research focus on issues of interest to diverse ethnic groups and women

Enhancement of knowledge about the links between biological processes and psychological processes so that we can better understand psychological processes and better cope with obstacles to psychological functioning

Application of research in developmental psychology, social psychology, and consumer psychology (advertising methods) to prevent drug abuse—including smoking cigarettes—among young people

---

[5] Some of these developments are discussed in "Psychologists forecast future of the profession," by Vicki Meade, 1994, *APA Monitor, 25*(5), pp. 14–15.

this effect many times: "Well, my mother/teacher/minister says this is true, and I think that he/she knows more about it than you do." Appeals to authority can be persuasive or infuriating, depending on whether or not you agree with them. It matters not *who* makes an assertion, however—even if that person is a psychological luminary like Sigmund Freud, William James, or John B. Watson. An argument is true or false on its own merits. Consider the evidence presented in arguments, not the person making the argument, no matter how exalted.

4. Appeals to popularity *(argumentum ad populum):* The appeal to popularity is cousin to the appeal to authority. The people making the pitches in TV commercials are usually very popular—either because they are good looking or because they are celebrities. Again, evaluate the evidence being presented and ignore the appeal of the person making the pitch.

The argument that you should do something or believe something because "everyone's doing it" is another type of appeal to popularity—one that gets some people involved in activities they later regret.

In sum, be skeptical of claims and arguments. Critically examine the evidence presented rather than focus on the authority, force, or appeal of the people making the

Development of effective methods for preventing violence against women and children

Application of research in learning, educational psychology, child development, and sociocultural factors to determine what works best in early childhood education and how to deliver it most effectively to children

Development of effective ways of educating all groups in the United States about AIDS and encouraging them to take preventive measures

Improvement of methods for determining the accuracy of childhood memories and eyewitness testimony; improvement of methods of eliciting testimony from children to foster accuracy and minimize harm

Teaching the public to think critically so that they will be more resistant to the claims of dictators, advertisers, and other tyrants of the mind

The finding of more effective ways of bringing psychological services to the homeless, one third to one half of whom are believed to have severe psychological disorders

Determination of which therapy methods work best for which kinds of psychological problems in which people; determination of how best to select and train psychologists to provide that kind of therapy

Public education as to the harmful nature of stereotypes, especially of stereotypes based on ethnicity, gender, and sexual orientation; teaching people how to recognize stereotypes and to think about them critically

Development of superior methods for determining the adequacy of the person-environment fit for specific jobs

Development of methods to effectively screen workers for sensitive positions, such as child care workers and police officers

Determination of which instructional methods work best for which kind of student; determination of how best to select and train teachers to provide that instruction

I would like to see much more, but because of space limitations, I end my list here. As you read through the text, what applications will you see for psychology in the new millennium?

On the Wish List. One of the goals for psychologists in the new millennium is to apply research findings in learning, educational psychology, child development, and sociocultural factors to determine what works best in early childhood education and how to deliver it most effectively to children.

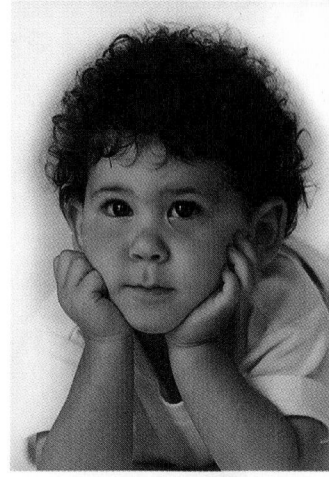

argument. Acquiring an education means more than memorizing data bases and learning how to solve problems in courses such as chemistry and calculus. It also means acquiring the tools to think critically, so that you can continue to educate yourself for a lifetime.

Reflections

Now that you have read the section on critical thinking, reflect on the following questions:

• As you reflect on your life to date, can you say that you have been a critical thinker? Why or why not? If not, are you going to do something about it? What?

• Have you been personally exposed to *ad hominem* arguments or to appeals to authority, force, or popularity? Did you recognize these arguments for what they were at the time? Are you satisfied with your response to them? Why or why not?

• Why is learning to think critically an essential part of higher education? How might critical thinking protect the individual from dictators, advertisers, and other tyrants of the mind?

We have concluded this chapter by urging students to examine the evidence before accepting the truth or falseness of other people's claims and arguments. In the following chapter, we explain how psychologists conduct research to gather evidence for their points of view.

Summary

1. **What is psychology?** Psychology is the scientific study of behavior and mental processes.

2. **What are the goals of psychology?** Psychology seeks to describe, explain, predict, and control behavior and mental processes. Psychologists do not attempt to control the behavior of other people against their wills. Instead, they help clients modify their behavior for their own benefit.

3. **What is the role of psychological theory?** Behavior and mental processes are explained through psychological theories, which are sets of statements that involve assumptions about behavior. Explanations and predictions are derived from theories. Theories are revised, as needed, to accommodate new observations. If necessary, they are discarded.

4. **What is the difference between pure and applied research?** Basic or pure research has no immediate applications. Applied research seeks solutions to specific problems.

5. **What do clinical and counseling psychologists do?** Clinical psychologists help people with psychological disorders adjust to the demands of life. Counseling psychologists usually work with individuals who have adjustment problems.

6. **What do school and educational psychologists do?** School psychologists assist students with problems that interfere with learning, whereas educational psychologists are more concerned with theoretical issues concerning human learning.

7. **What do developmental psychologists do?** Developmental psychologists study the changes that occur throughout the life span.

8. **What do personality and social psychologists do?** Personality psychologists study influences on our thought processes, feelings, and behavior, whereas social psychologists focus on the nature and causes of behavior in social situations.

9. **What do experimental psychologists do?** Experimental psychologists conduct research into basic psychological processes such as sensation and perception, learning and memory, and motivation and emotion.

10. **What do industrial and organizational psychologists do?** Industrial psychologists focus on the relationships between people and work, whereas organizational psychologists study the behavior of people in organizations.

11. **What contributions did the ancient Greek philosophers make to psychological thought?** The Greek

philosopher Aristotle was among the first to argue that human behavior is subject to rules and laws. Socrates proclaimed "Know thyself" and suggested the use of introspection to gain self-knowledge.

12. **Where did psychology begin as a laboratory science?** Wilhelm Wundt established the first psychological laboratory in Leipzig, Germany, in 1879.

13. **What is structuralism?** Structuralism is the school of psychology founded by Wundt that used introspection to study the objective and subjective elements of experience.

14. **What is functionalism?** Functionalism is the school of psychology founded by William James that dealt with observable behavior as well as conscious experience and focused on the importance of habit.

15. **What is behaviorism?** Behaviorism is the school of psychology founded by John B. Watson that argues that psychology must limit itself to observable behavior and forgo excursions into subjective consciousness. Behaviorism focuses on learning by conditioning, and B. F. Skinner introduced the concept of reinforcement as an explanation of how learning occurs.

16. **What is Gestalt psychology?** Gestalt psychology is the school of psychology founded by Wertheimer, Koffka, and Köhler that focuses on perception and argues that psychologists must focus on the wholeness of human experience.

17. **What is psychoanalysis?** Sigmund Freud founded the school of psychoanalysis, which asserts that people are driven by hidden impulses and that they distort reality to protect themselves from anxiety.

18. **What are the major contemporary perspectives in psychology?** They are the biological, cognitive, humanistic—existential, psychoanalytic, learning, and sociocultural perspectives. Biologically oriented psychologists study the links between behavior and biological events such as brain activity and the release of hormones. Cognitive psychologists study the ways in which we mentally represent the world and

process information. Humanistic—existential psychologists stress the importance of subjective experience and assert that people have the freedom to make choices. The sociocultural perspective focuses on the roles of matters of ethnicity, gender, culture, and socioeconomic status in behavior and mental processes.

19. **Why is knowledge of human diversity important to the study of psychology?** The profession of psychology is committed to the dignity of the individual, but we cannot understand individuals without an awareness of the richness of human diversity and the roles of cultural factors as determinants of behavior and mental processes.

20. **How have women and members of various ethnic groups contributed to the development of psychology?** As examples, Christine Ladd-Franklin formulated a theory of color vision. Mary Whiton Calkins introduced the method of paired associates and discovered the primacy and recency effects. Margaret Floy Washburn wrote *The Animal Mind*. African American psychologist J. Henry Alston engaged in research on the perception of heat and cold. Kenneth B. Clark influenced a key Supreme Court decision on desegregation. Jorge Sanchez was among the first to show how intelligence tests are culturally biased.

21. **What is critical thinking?** Critical thinking is intended to foster an attitude of skepticism and refers to thoughtfully analyzing the questions, statements, and arguments of others. It means examining the definitions of terms, examining the premises or assumptions behind arguments, and scrutinizing the logic with which arguments are developed.

22. **How is critical thinking applied to the science of psychology?** Critical thinking within the science of psychology also refers to the ability to inquire about causes and effects, and to knowledge of research methods. Critical thinkers are also cautious in drawing conclusions from evidence. Critical thinkers do not oversimplify.

Psychology and Modern Life

One of the wonderful things about psychology is that it is relevant to so many aspects of contemporary life. The "Psychology and Modern Life" sections provide examples of how this is so.

"Psychology and Modern Life" sections are usually related to the subject matter in the chapter. However, the first such section—the psychology of studying psychology—is an exception. The psychology of studying psychology might have more appropriately followed Chapters 6 and 7, on learning and memory. It seemed to make more sense, however, to place this section up front so that you could apply it at the beginning of the term and not a couple of weeks before final examinations. If you review this section after you have read Chapters 6 and 7, the rationales behind the suggestions will be reinforced.

The Psychology of Studying Psychology

When I first went off to college, I had little idea of what to expect. New faces, a new locale, responsibility for doing my own laundry, new courses—it added up to an overwhelming assortment of changes. Perhaps the most stunning change of all was the new-found freedom. Nobody told me what to read or when to study. It was up to me to plan ahead to do my coursework but somehow manage to leave time for socializing and playing bridge.

Another surprise was that it was no longer enough to enroll in a course and sit in class. I learned that I was not a sponge and would not passively soak up the knowledge. Active measures were required to take in the subject matter.

The problems of soaking up knowledge from this and other textbooks are not entirely dissimilar. Psychological theory and research have taught us that an active approach to learning results in better grades than a passive approach. It is better to look ahead and seek the answers to specific questions than to read the subject matter page by page "like a good student." We tend to remember material better when we attend to it and when it is meaningful. Reading in order to answer questions boosts our attention to it and renders it meaningful. It is also helpful not to try to do it all in one sitting, as in cramming before tests. *Learning takes time.*

PAY ATTENTION

Pay close attention to your professors in class and to your reading assignments. It is easier to remember things when you pay close attention to them in the first place (Scruggs & Mastropieri, 1992).

PLAN AHEAD

Modern college life makes conflicting demands on students' time. Classes, studying, writing papers, extracurricular activities, athletic events, and the desire to socialize all compete for the precious hours you devote to your coursework. Therefore, it is helpful to begin your active approach to studying by assessing the amount of material you must master during the term and relating it to your rate of learning. How long does it take you to learn the material in a chapter or in a book? How many hours do you spend studying each day? How much material is there? Does it add up right? Will you make it? It may be that you will not be able to determine the answers until you have gotten into the book for a week or two. Once you have, be honest with yourself about the mathematics of how you are doing. Be willing to revise initial estimates.

Once you have determined the amount of study time you will need, try to space it out fairly evenly. For most of us, spaced or distributed learning is more efficient than massed learning or cramming. Outline a study schedule that will provide nearly equal time periods each weekday. Leave weekends relatively open so that you can have some time for yourself and your friends as well as some extra hours to digest topics or assignments that are not going down so smoothly.

The following suggestions are derived from Rathus and Fichner-Rathus (1994):

1. Determine where and when the next test will be and what material will be covered.

2. Ask your instructor what will be most important for you to know, and check with students who have already taken the course to determine the sources of test questions—chapters in the text

book, lecture notes, student study guides, old exams, and so on.

3. Determine the number of chapters to be read between now and the test.

4. Plan to read a specific number of chapters each week and try to "psych out" your instructor by generating possible test questions from the chapters.

5. In generating possible test questions, keep in mind that good questions often start with phrases such as:

Give several examples of . . .

Which of the following is an example of . . .

Describe the functions of . . .

What is most important about . . .

List the major . . .

Compare and contrast . . .

Describe the structure of . . .

Explain how psychologists have determined that . . .

Why do psychologists advise clients to . . .

Identify the parts of . . .

6. Plan specific study periods each week during which you will generate questions from lecture notes, old exams, the student study guide, and so on.

7. Plan for weekly study periods during which you will compose and take practice tests.

8. Take the practice quizzes in the student study guide. Many instructors reinforce the use of the study guide by occasionally taking some exam questions directly from it.

9. Keep a diary or log in which you record your progress, including when, where, and how long you study and how well you perform on practice tests.

STUDY A VARIETY OF SUBJECTS EACH DAY

Variety is the spice of life: We are more responsive to novel stimulation. Don't study psychology all day Monday, physics all day Tuesday, and literature all day Wednesday. Study each for a little while each day so that you won't feel bored or dulled by too lengthy an immersion in one subject.[6]

ACCEPT YOUR CONCENTRATION SPAN

If you can't push yourself at first into studying enough each day, start at a more comfortable level and build toward the amount of study time you'll need by adding a few minutes every day. See what your concentration span is like for your subjects—how long you can continue to focus on coursework without your attention slipping away and, perhaps, lapsing into daydreaming. Plan to take brief study breaks before you reach your limit. Get up and stretch. Get a sip of water.

COPE WITH DISTRACTIONS

Find a study place that is comfortable and free from distractions. Environmental stimuli compete for our attention. A quiet place will help you screen out the background noise. To better understand how distractions work, consider the case of Schuyler:

All through high school, Schuyler withdrew to her bedroom to study—the one room where she had complete privacy—and studied in her bed. She assumed that it would be easy to do the same thing in college. But in college, she has two roommates, and they very often want to chat while Schuyler is hitting the books. Or, if they're not talking together, one of them may be on the phone. Or, if no one's on the phone, someone is likely to come knocking at the door. Schuyler has put a sign up on the door that says "No knocking between 7:00 and 10:00 P.M.—This means you!" Nevertheless, someone's always coming by and saying, "Oh, but I wanted to see if Nicky or Pam was in. I didn't mean to disturb you."

Pam, it happens, likes to study with the stereo on—soft, but on, nevertheless. Nicky eats in bed—incessantly. While Schuyler is trying to concentrate on the books, she's assailed by the chomping of potato chips or pretzels.

[6] Here, of course, I am referring to those other subjects. Obviously, you could study psychology endlessly without becoming bored.

Finally, Schuyler gets disgusted and gets up to go for a brief walk to clear her head. She passes the lounge and is intrigued by glimpses of a new hit series. A friend calls her over to pass the time. Before she knows it, it's 8:30 and she hasn't really begun to get to work. (Adapted from Rathus & Fichner-Rathus, 1994)

Avoid Schuyler's pitfalls by letting your spot for studying—your room, a study lounge, a place in the library—come to mean studying to you. Do nothing but study there—no leafing through magazines, no socializing, no snacking.

Here are some other ways of handling distractions:

Make Arrangements with Roommates. Arrange for certain times of the day to be quiet study periods.

Handle Internal Distractions. If you're hungry, get a small snack. If you're uncomfortable, move to another spot. If some important ideas come to you, jot them down so that you can think about them when you have some free time. Then let them go.

Place a "Do Not Disturb!" Sign on Your Door. You'd be surprised. Many people actually honor these signs. Of course, someone occasionally barges in and says, "Did you put up the sign now or leave it up from before?" or "Listen, I'll only take a minute of your time." (Be assertive!)

Just Say No. Say, "I'm in the middle of something and can't get distracted. You'll have to stop back later." It's better to give a specific time than to say "later," because people are more likely to follow concrete suggestions and instructions. If you have a hard time saying no, consider why. Are you afraid the intruder won't approve of your saying no or won't like you anymore? Psychologist Albert Ellis (see Chapter 15) notes that many of us hold the mistaken belief that we cannot survive unless other people approve of us all the time. *You don't need everybody's approval all the time!* Be polite but firm with intruders.

USE SELF-REWARD

Use rewards for meeting daily study goals. Rewards inspire repetition of desired behavior. Don't be a martyr and try to postpone all pleasures until the end of the term. Some students can do this, but it isn't necessary. And, if you have never spent much time in nonstop studying, you may be demanding too much of yourself.

PQ4R: PREVIEW, QUESTION, READ, REFLECT, RECITE, AND REVIEW

Don't question some of your instructors' assignments. Question all of them. By so doing, you can follow the active PQ4R study technique originated by educational psychologist Francis P. Robinson. In PQ4R, you phrase questions about your assignments and then you seek to answer them. There are six steps to PQ4R: previewing, questioning, reading, reflecting, reciting, and reviewing.

Preview. Skipping through the pages of a "whodunit" to identify the killer is a sure-fire way to destroy the impact of a mystery novel, but previewing can help you learn textbook material. In fact, many textbooks are written with devices that stimulate you to survey the material before reading it. This book has chapter outlines, "Truth-or-Fiction?" sections, major and minor section headings throughout each chapter, and chapter summaries. If drama and suspense are your goals, begin with the outlines, then read the chapters page by page. But if learning the facts is more important, it may be more effective first to examine the chapter outlines, skim the minor headings not covered in the outlines, and read the summaries—before you get to the meat of the chapters. Familiarity with the skeletons or advance organizers of the chapters will provide you with frameworks for learning the meat of the chapters as you ingest them page by page.

Question. Generating questions about textbook material has been shown to promote retention (R. J. Hamilton, 1985). Phrase questions for each heading in the chapter. Write them down in a notebook. Some questions can also be based on material within sections. For courses in which the textbooks do not have helpful major and minor headings, get into the material page by page and phrase questions as you proceed. With practice, you will develop questioning skills, and your questions will help you perceive the underlying structure of each chapter. The following questions are recastings of some of the major and minor headings in Chapter 15. Notice that they are indented according to the outlined chapter structure, providing an instant sense of how the material is organized:

A. What is stress?
  B. What are the sources of stress?
  B. What psychological factors moderate the effects of stress?
  B. What is the general adaptation syndrome?
  B. What are the effects of stress on the immune system?
A. What factors contribute to physical illness?
  B. How do patterns of health and illness vary among different ethnic groups?
  B. How are psychological factors related to headaches?
    C. What are muscle-tension headaches?
    C. What are migraine headaches?
  B. How are psychological factors related to cardiovascular disorders?

Read. Once you have phrased questions, read the subject matter with the purpose of answering them. This sense of purpose will help you focus on the essential points of the material. As you answer each question, write down in your notebook a few key words that will telegraph that answer to you when you recite and review later on. Many students find it helpful to keep two columns in their notebooks: questions in the column to the left and key words (to the answer) in the column to the right.

If the material you are reading happens to be fine literature, you may wish to read it once just to appreciate its poetic features. When you reread it, however, use PQ4R to tease out the essential information it contains.

Reflect. Reflecting on subject matter is a key way to understanding and remembering it (Simpson and others, 1994). As you are reading, think of examples or create mental images of the subject matter. One way of reflecting is to relate new information to old information. We can reflect on information about whales by relating whales to other mammals. Then we will better remember that whales are warm-blooded, breathe air rather than water, bear their young live (rather than lay eggs), and nurse their young. Another strategy for reflecting is to relate new information to events in our personal lives. The media (and sometimes our personal lives) are replete with stories about people with psychological disorders. To help learn about the psychological disorders outlined in Chapter 13, think of media portrayals of characters who had the problem. Or perhaps a friend or family member has one of the problems.

Recite. Once you have read a section and jotted down the key words to the answer, recite each answer aloud if possible. (Doing so may depend on where you are, who's around, and your level of concern over how you think they'll react to you.) Reciting answers aloud helps us to remember them and provides an immediate check on the accuracy of the key words.

Review. Review the material according to a reasonably regular schedule such as once weekly. Relearning material regularly is much easier than initial learning. Moreover, by reviewing material regularly, we foster retention.

Cover the answer column and read the questions as though they were a quiz. Recite your answers and check them against the key response words. Reread the subject matter when you forget an answer. Forgetting too many answers may mean that you haven't phrased the questions efficiently for your own use or that you haven't reviewed the material frequently enough. (Maybe you didn't learn it well enough in the first place.) By taking a more active approach to studying, you may find that you are earning higher grades and gaining more pleasure from the learning process.

2

Research Methods in Psychology

Truth or Fiction?

_____ You could survey 20 million voters and still not predict accurately the outcome of a presidential election.

_____ Only a small minority of people would be willing to deliver agonizing electric shocks to an innocent party.

_____ Only people use tools.

_____ In many experiments, neither the participants in the experiment nor the researchers who are running the experiment know which participants are taking the real treatment and which participants are taking a placebo ("sugar pill").

_____ Alcohol causes aggression.

_____ Psychologists would not be able to carry out certain kinds of research without deceiving participants as to the purposes and methods of the studies.

_____ A psychologist could write a believable personality report about you without interviewing you, testing you, or even knowing who you are.

_____ Some people can read other people's minds.

Outline

Truth or Fiction?
The Milgram Studies: Shocking Stuff at Yale
The Scientific Method: Putting Ideas to the Test
Samples and Populations: Representing Human Diversity
Problems in Generalizing from Psychological Research
Psychology in a World of Diversity: The Wyatt Survey of African American and White Women in Los Angeles County
Methods of Observation: The Better to See You With
The Case-Study Method
The Survey Method
The Testing Method
The Naturalistic-Observation Method
The Laboratory-Observation Method
The Correlational Method: Seeing What Goes Up and What Comes Down
The Experimental Method: Trying Things Out
Independent and Dependent Variables
Experimental and Control Groups
Blinds and Double Blinds
Psychology in the New Millennium: In the Global Research Lab
Methods of Studying Your Crowning Glory — The Brain
Ethical Issues in Psychological Research and Practice
Research with People
Research with Animals
Summary
Psychology and Modern Life
Science Versus Pseudoscience

Psychology is the scientific study of behavior and mental processes. Consider some questions of interest to psychologists: Do only people use tools? Does alcohol cause aggression? Why do some people hardly ever think of food, while others are obsessed with it and snack all day long? Why do some unhappy people attempt suicide, whereas others seek alternate ways of coping with their problems? Does having people of different ethnic backgrounds collaborate in their work serve to decrease or increase feelings of prejudice?

Many of us have expressed opinions on questions such as these at one time or another. Different psychological theories also suggest a number of possible answers. Psychology is an **empirical** science, however. Within an empirical science, assumptions about the behavior of cosmic rays, chemical compounds, cells, or people must be supported by evidence. Strong arguments, reference to authority figures, even tightly knit theories are not adequate as scientific evidence. As noted in Chapter 1's discussion of critical thinking, psychologists and other scientists make it their business — literally and figuratively — to be skeptical.

Psychologists use research to study behavior and mental processes empirically. To undertake our study of research methods, let us recount some famous research undertaken at Yale University more than 30 years ago.

The Milgram Studies: Shocking Stuff at Yale

People are capable of boundless generosity and of hideous atrocities. Throughout history, people have sacrificed themselves for the welfare of their families, friends, and nations. Throughout history, people have maimed and destroyed other people to vent their rage or to please their superiors.

Let us follow up on the negative. Soldiers have killed civilians and raped women in occupied areas to obey the orders of their superiors or to win the approval of their comrades. Millions of Native Americans, Armenians, and Jews have been slaughtered by people who were obeying the orders of their officers.

Obeying the orders of officers . . . How susceptible are people — how susceptible are you and I — to the demands of authority figures such as military officers? Is there something unusual or abnormal about people who follow orders and inflict pain and suffering on their fellow human beings? Are they very much unlike you and me? Or *are* they you and me?

It is easy to imagine that there must be something terribly wrong with people who would hurt strangers without provocation. There must be something abnormal about people who would slaughter innocents. But these are assumptions, and scientists are skeptical. Psychologist Stanley Milgram also wondered if normal people would acquiesce to authority figures who made immoral demands. But rather than speculate on the issue, he undertook a series of classic experiments at Yale University that have become known as the Milgram studies on obedience.

In an early phase of his work, Milgram (1963) placed ads in New Haven newspapers for participants[1] for studies on learning and memory. He enlisted 40 people ranging in age from 20 to 50—teachers, engineers, laborers, salespeople, people who had not completed elementary school, people with graduate degrees.

Let's suppose that you've answered the ad. You show up at the university for a reasonable fee ($4.50, which in the early '60s might easily fill your gas tank), for the sake of science, and for your own curiosity. You may be impressed. After all, Yale is a venerable institution that dominates the city. You are no less impressed by the elegant labs where you meet a distinguished behavioral scientist dressed in a white laboratory coat and another newspaper recruit like you. The scientist explains that the purpose of the experiment is to study the *effects of punishment on learning*. The experiment would require a "teacher" and a "learner." By chance, you are appointed the teacher and the other recruit the learner.

You, the scientist, and the learner enter a laboratory room where there is a rather threatening-looking chair with dangling straps. The scientist straps the learner in. The learner expresses some concern, but this is, after all, for the sake of science. And this is Yale University, is it not? What could happen to a person at Yale?

You follow the scientist to an adjacent room from which you are to do your "teaching." This teaching promises to have an impact. You are to punish the learner's errors by pressing levers marked from 15 to 450 volts on a fearsome-looking console (see Figure 2.1). Labels describe 28 of the 30 levers as running the gamut from "slight shock" to "danger: severe shock." The last two levers are simply labeled "XXX." Just in case you've no idea what electric shock feels like, the scientist gives you a sample 45-volt shock. It stings. You pity the person who might receive more.

Your learner is expected to learn word pairs. Pairs of words are to be read from a list. After hearing the list once, the learner

FIGURE 2.1
The "Aggression Machine" In the Milgram studies on obedience to authority, pressing levers on the "aggression machine" was the operational definition of aggression.

is to produce the word that pairs with the stimulus word by pressing a switch that signifies the choice from a list of four alternatives. The switch lights one of four panels in your room. If it is the correct panel, you proceed to the next stimulus word. If not, you are to deliver an electric shock. With each error, you are to increase the voltage of the shock (Figure 2.2).

You probably have some misgivings. Electrodes had been strapped to the learner's wrists, and the scientist has applied electrode paste "to avoid blisters and burns." You also are told that the shocks will cause "no permanent tissue damage," although they might be extremely painful. Still, the learner is going along, and after all, this is Yale.

The learner answers some items correctly and then makes some errors. With mild concern you press the levers up through 45 volts. You've tolerated that much yourself. Then a few more mistakes are made. You press the 60-volt lever, then 75. The learner makes another mistake. You pause and look

Empirical • Emphasizing or based on observation and experiment.

---

[1] Also termed *subjects*. The current (1994) edition of the *Publication Manual of the American Psychological Association* prefers usage of *participants* because it is more personal and acknowledges that individuals in research studies take an active role in the studies.

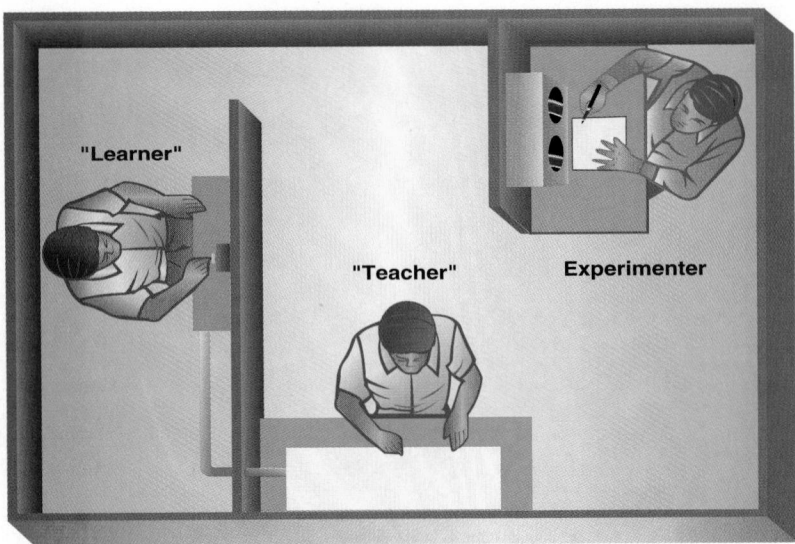

FIGURE 2.2
The Experimental Setup in the Milgram Studies When the "learner" makes an error, the experimenter prods the "teacher" to deliver a painful electric shock.

Scientific method • A method for obtaining scientific evidence in which research questions or hypotheses are formulated and tested.

Theory • A formulation of the relationships and principles that underlie observed events. Theories allow us to explain and predict behavior.

Hypothesis • In psychology, a specific statement about behavior or mental processes that is tested through research.

at the scientist, who is reassuring: "Although the shocks may be painful, there is no permanent tissue damage, so please go on." Further errors are made, and quickly you are up to a shock of 300 volts. But now the learner is pounding on the other side of the wall! Your chest tightens and you begin to perspire. Damn science and the $4.50! you think. You hesitate and the scientist says, "The experiment requires that you continue." After the delivery of the next stimulus word, the learner chooses no answer at all. What are you to do? "Wait for 5 to 10 seconds," the scientist instructs, "and then treat no answer as a wrong answer." But after the next shock, the pounding on the wall resumes! Now your heart is racing, and you are convinced that you are causing extreme pain and discomfort. Is it possible that no lasting damage is being done? Is the experiment that important, after all? What to do? You hesitate again. The scientist says, "It is absolutely essential that you continue." His voice is very convincing. "You have no other choice," he says, "you must go on." You can barely think straight, and for some unaccountable reason you feel laughter rising in your throat. Your finger shakes above the lever. What are you to do?

Milgram (1963, 1974) found out what

most people in his sample would do. The sample was a cross-section of the male population of New Haven, Connecticut. Of the 40 men in this phase of his research, only 5 refused to go beyond the 300-volt level, the level at which the learner first pounded the wall. Nine other "teachers" defied the scientist within the 300-volt range. But 65% of the participants complied with the scientist throughout the series, believing that they were delivering 450-volt, XXX-rated shocks.

Were these newspaper-ad recruits simply unfeeling? Not at all. Milgram was impressed by their signs of stress. They trembled, they stuttered, they bit their lips. They groaned, they sweated, they dug their fingernails into their flesh. Some had fits of laughter, though laughter was inappropriate. One salesperson's laughter was so convulsive that he could not continue with the experiment.

Let us not find much comfort in the fact that a minority of individuals refused to follow the experimenter's orders. *Not one teacher attempted to extricate the unfortunate learner from the experiment. Not one teacher barged into the administrative offices at Yale and demanded that they investigate and put an end to the experiment* (Ross, 1988).

We shall return to the Milgram studies later in the chapter. The Milgram studies are a rich mine. They not only have important implications about human nature, they are also useful for our discussions of research issues such as replication, the experimental method, and ethics.

Reflections

Now that you know what happened to "teachers" and "learners" in Milgram's research, reflect on the following questions:

- How would you have felt if you had been a "teacher" in the Milgram study? What would you have done? Would you have delivered a shock, or would you have refused? Are you sure?
- What would you do if you heard that such an experiment was being conducted at your own college or university? Why?

Now let us consider the underpinnings of psychological research, as found in the scientific method.

The Scientific Method: Putting Ideas to the Test

Although it is a science, psychology has a number of things in common with religion. Psychology and religion both seek to make sense out of a complex existence (Jones, 1994). Both try to understand and help correct human problems. Both inspire passionate devotion. Both seek truth. But religion tends to be based on faith in ancient revelations (Barbour, 1990). The scientific approach is accountable to daily experience and the testing of ideas (Jones, 1994).

The **scientific method** is an organized way of using experience and testing ideas to expand and refine knowledge. Psychologists do not necessarily place a list of steps of the scientific method on the counter and follow them as one might follow a cookbook. However, there are principles that generally guide scientists' research endeavors.

Psychologists usually begin by *formulating a research question.* Research questions can have many sources. Our daily experiences, psychological **theory,** even folklore all help to generate questions for research. Consider some questions that may arise from daily experience. Daily experience in using day-care centers may motivate us to conduct research into whether day care influences development of social skills or the bonds of attachment between children and their mothers.

Or consider questions that might arise from psychological theory (see Figure 2.3). Social-cognitive principles of observational learning may prompt research into the effects of TV violence. Sigmund Freud's psychoanalytic theory may prompt research into whether the verbal expression of feelings of anger helps relieve feelings of depression.

Research questions may also arise from common knowledge. Consider folklorist statements such as "Misery loves company," "Opposites attract," and "Beauty is in the eye of the beholder"—statements that we consider in Chapters 10 and 16. Psychologists may ask, *does* misery love company?

Do opposites attract? *Is* beauty in the eye of the beholder?

A research question may be studied in its question format, or it may be reworded into a **hypothesis** (see Figure 2.3). A hypothesis is a specific statement about behavior or mental processes that is tested through research. One hypothesis about day care might be that preschoolers placed in day care will acquire greater social skills in relating to peers than preschoolers cared for in the home. A hypothesis about TV violence might be that elementary school children who watch more violent TV shows

FIGURE 2.3

Spotlight on the Scientific Method The scientific method is a systematic way of organizing and expanding scientific knowledge. Daily experiences, cultural beliefs, and scientific observations all foster the development of scientific theory. Theory explains observations and leads to hypotheses about events—in the case of psychology, behavior and mental processes. Our observations of hypothesized events can confirm the theory, lead to the refinement of the theory, or disconfirm the theory and possibly suggest the formulation of a new theory.

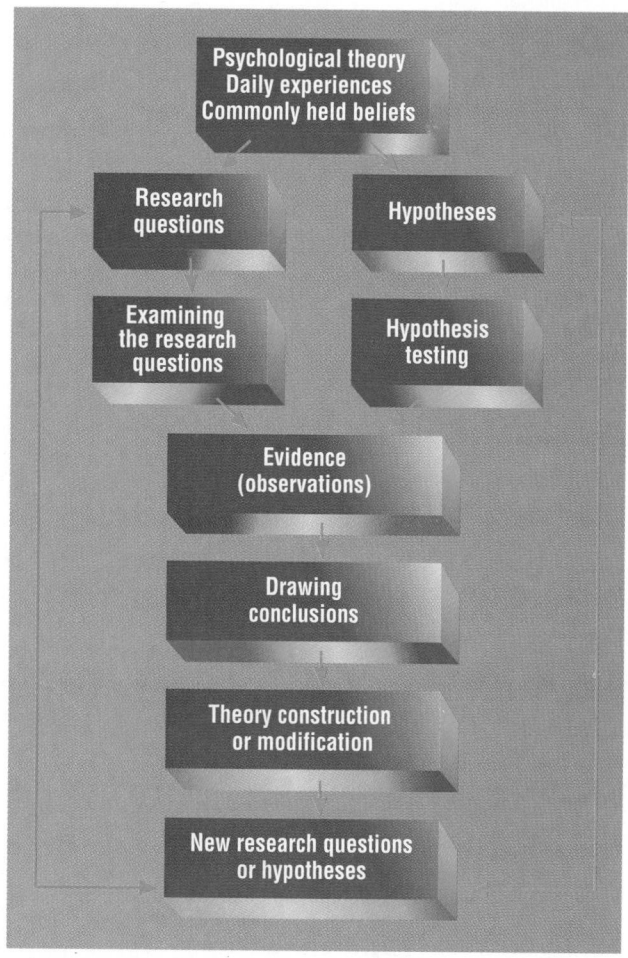

tend to behave more aggressively toward their peers. A hypothesis that addresses Freudian theory might be that the verbal expression of feelings of anger will decrease feelings of depression.

As a science, psychology is accountable to carefully examined human experience (Jones, 1994). Therefore, psychologists next examine the research question or *test the hypothesis* through controlled methods such as naturalistic or laboratory observation and the experiment. For example, we could introduce day-care and non-day-care children to a new child in a college child-research center and observe how each group fares with the new acquaintance.

To undertake research we must provide **operational definitions** for the variables under study. Concerning the effects of TV violence, we could have parents help us tally which TV shows their children watch and rate the shows for violent content. Each child could receive a composite "exposure-to-TV-violence score." We could also operationally define aggression in terms of teacher reports on how aggressively the children act toward their peers. Then we could determine whether more-aggressive children also watch more violence on television.

Testing the hypothesis that the verbal expression of feelings of anger decreases feelings of depression might be more complex. Researchers would have to decide, for example, whether they should use feelings of anger that people already have or use a standardized set of angry statements that addresses common areas of parent–child conflict. Would the people they study include people undergoing psychoanalysis or, say, introductory psychology students? What would be the operational definition of feelings of depression? Self-ratings of depression according to a numerical scale? Scores on psychological tests of depression? Reports of depressive behavior by informants such as spouses? Psychologists frequently use a combination of definitions to increase their chances of tapping into targeted behavior patterns and mental processes.

Psychologists draw conclusions about their research questions or the accuracy of their hypotheses on the basis of their research observations or findings. When their observations do not bear out their hypotheses, they may modify the theories from which the hypotheses were derived (see Figure 2.3). Research findings often suggest refinements to psychological theories and, consequently, new avenues of research.

In our research on day care, we would probably find that children in day care show somewhat greater social skills than children cared for in the home (Clarke-Stewart, 1991; Field, 1991). We would probably also find that more-aggressive children spend more time watching TV violence (see Chapter 6). Research into the effectiveness of psychoanalytic forms of therapy is usually based on case studies, as we shall see in Chapter 14.

As psychologists draw conclusions from research evidence, they are guided by principles of critical thinking. For example, they try not to confuse connections between the findings with cause and effect. Although more-aggressive children apparently spend more time watching TV violence, it may be erroneous to conclude from this kind of evidence that TV violence *causes* aggressive behavior. Perhaps there is a **selection factor** at work, for example, such that more-aggressive children are more likely than less-aggressive children to tune in to violent TV programs.

To better understand the potential effects of the selection factor, consider a study on the relationship between exercise and health. If we were to compare a group of people who exercised regularly to a group who did not, we might find that the exercisers were physically healthier than the couch potatoes. Could we conclude from this research approach that exercise is a causal factor in good health? Perhaps not. The selection factor—the fact that one group chose to exercise and the other did not—could also suggest that healthy people are more apt to choose to exercise.[2] Later we shall consider the kinds of research

Operational definition • A definition of a variable in terms of the methods used to create or measure that variable.

Selection factor • A source of bias that may occur in research findings when participants are allowed to determine for themselves whether or not they will partake of a certain treatment in a scientific study. Do you think, for example, that there are problems in studying the effects of a diet or of smoking cigarettes when we allow study participants to choose whether or not they will try the diet or smoke cigarettes? Why or why not?

Replicate • Repeat, reproduce, copy. What are some reasons that psychologists replicate the research conducted by other psychologists?

---

[2] I am not suggesting that exercise does not make a contribution to health. I am merely pointing out that research that compares people who have chosen to exercise with people who have not is subject to a source of bias termed the *selection factor*. That is, the groups of exercisers and nonexercisers are not comparable, because the exercisers have chosen to exercise whereas the nonexercisers have elected not to exercise.

studies that do permit us to draw conclusions about cause and effect.

As critical thinkers, psychologists similarly attempt to avoid oversimplifying or overgeneralizing their results. The effects of day care are apparently very complex, for example. Although children in day care usually exhibit better social skills than children who are not, there is also a tendency for them to be somewhat more aggressive. If we conducted our research into the benefits of expressing feelings of anger with clients in psychoanalysis, do you think that we would be justified in generalizing the results to the population at large? If we conducted that research with introductory psychology students, could we extend or generalize the results to people who sought psychotherapy to relieve feelings of depression? Why or why not?

Some psychologists include publication of research reports in professional journals as a crucial part of the scientific method. Psychologists and other scientists are obligated to provide enough details of their work that other scientists will be able to repeat or **replicate** it. Psychologists may attempt to replicate a study in all its details in order to corroborate the findings, especially when the findings are significant for people's health or general welfare. Sometimes psychologists replicate research methods with different kinds of participants to determine, for example, whether findings with women can be generalized to men, whether findings with non-Hispanic White Americans can be generalized to ethnic minority groups, or whether findings with people who have sought psychotherapy can be generalized to people at large.

Publication of data and researchers' interpretations of data also permits the scientific community at large to evaluate, and perhaps criticize, the methods and conclusions of other scientists. A bruised ego here and there is considered a reasonable price to pay for the advancement of scientific knowledge.

Reflections

Now that you have read about the scientific method, reflect on the following questions:

- Have you ever heard people say that "Misery loves company," "Opposites attract," or that "Beauty is in the eye of the beholder"? What was the nature of their evidence? Was it scientific? Why or why not?
- Can you compare and contrast religious and scientific approaches to understanding people? Do you see each of these approaches as offering something of value? Why or why not?
- If we can demonstrate that people who exercise are healthier than people who do not, have we shown that exercise is a causal factor in good health? Why or why not?

Let us now consider the research methods used by psychologists: methods of sampling, methods of observation, the use of correlation, and the queen of the empirical approach—the experiment.

Samples and Populations: Representing Human Diversity

Consider a piece of history that never quite happened: The Republican candidate Alf Landon defeated the incumbent president, Franklin D. Roosevelt, in 1936. Or at least Landon did so in a poll conducted by a popular magazine of the day, the *Literary Digest*. In the actual election, however, Roosevelt routed Landon in a landslide of 11 million votes. How, then, could the *Digest* predict a Landon victory? How was so great a discrepancy possible?

The *Digest,* you see, had surveyed voters by phone. Today, telephone sampling is a widely practiced and reasonably legitimate technique. But the *Digest* poll was taken during the Great Depression, when people who had telephones were much wealthier than those who did not. People at higher income levels are also more likely to vote Republican. No surprise, then, that the overwhelming majority of those sampled said they would vote for Landon.

The principle involved here is that samples must accurately represent the population they are intended to reflect. Only representative samples allow us to **generalize** from research samples to populations.

Truth or Fiction Revisited. *It is true that you could survey 20 million voters and still not predict accurately the outcome of a presidential election.* Sample size alone does not guarantee that a sample will accurately represent the population from which it was drawn. We can extend, or generalize, our findings from samples only to the populations that they represent.

In surveys such as that conducted by the *Literary Digest,* and in other research methods, the individuals who are studied are referred to as a **sample.** A sample is a segment of a **population.** Psychologists and other scientists need to ensure that the people they observe *represent* their target population, such as U.S. voters, and not subgroups such as southern California Yuppies or non-Hispanic White members of the middle class.

Science is a conservative enterprise, and scientists are cautious about generalizing experimental results to populations other than those from which their samples were drawn.

PROBLEMS IN GENERALIZING FROM PSYCHOLOGICAL RESEARCH

All generalizations are dangerous, even this one.
ALEXANDRE DUMAS

Many factors must be considered in interpreting the accuracy of the results of scientific research. One is the nature of the research sample.

Milgram's initial research on obedience was limited to a sample of New Haven men. Could he generalize his findings to other men or to women? Would college students, for example, who are heralded for independent thinking, show more defiance? A replication of Milgram's study with a sample of Yale men yielded similar results. What about women, who are supposedly less aggressive than men? In subsequent research, women, too, shocked the learners—and all this in a nation that values independence and the free will of the individual.

A Population? Psychologists and other scientists attempt to select their research samples so that they will represent target populations. What population is suggested by the people in this photograph? How might you go about sampling them? How do people who agree to participate in research differ from those who refuse?

Truth or Fiction Revisited. *It is not true that only a small minority of people would be willing to deliver agonizing electric shocks to an innocent party.* Research evidence has shown that when people are under strong social pressure, many people, even the majority, will deliver such shocks. What does this research finding say to you about "human nature"?

Later in the chapter we consider research in which the participants were drawn from a population of college men who were social drinkers. That is, they tended to drink at social gatherings but not when alone. Whom do college men represent, other than themselves? To whom can we extend, or generalize, the results? For one thing, the results may not extend to women, not even to college women. In Chapter 5, for example, we shall learn that alcohol goes more quickly to "women's heads" than to men's.

College men also tend to fall within a certain age range (about 18 to 22) and are more intelligent than the general population. We cannot be certain that the findings extend to older men of average intelligence, although it seems reasonable to **infer** that they do. Social drinkers may also differ biologically and psychologically from alcoholics, who have difficulty controlling their drinking. Nor can we be certain that college social drinkers represent people who do not drink at all.

There is a historic bias in favor of conducting research with men (Ader & Johnson, 1994; McCarthy, 1993; Yoder & Kahn, 1993). Inadequate resources have been devoted to conducting health-related research with women. For example, most of the large-sample research into lifestyle and health has been conducted with men (see Chapters 5 and 15). Former APA president Bonnie Strickland (1991) cites three areas in which there is a crucial deficiency of research with women: the promotion of women's health (including disease prevention), women and depression, and women and chemical dependence.

More research with women is also needed in areas such as AIDS, the effects of violence on women, and the impact of work on women's lives. It appears that from 21% to 34% of U.S. women will be physically assaulted—slapped, beaten, choked, or attacked with a weapon—by a partner with whom they share an intimate relationship (Browne, 1993). From 14% to 25% of women have been raped (Koss, 1993). Many psychologists believe that the epidemic of violence against women will come to an end only when people in the United States confront and change the social and cultural traditions and institutions that give rise to violence (Goodman and others, 1993). (Some of these traditions are discussed in Chapter 10.) Concerning women in the workplace, note that women are more likely than men to put in a "double shift." Women, that is, tend to put in a full day of work along with an equally long

shift of shopping, mopping, and otherwise caring for their families (Chitayat, 1993; Keita, 1993).

It is now fairly widely accepted that psychology once erroneously generalized research findings with men to women (Ader & Johnson, 1994). However, Yoder and Kahn (1993) argue that as psychology develops its understanding of the psychology of women, there is danger that it may overgeneralize research findings with White, privileged women to all women. When women of color and of lower socioeconomic status are not included in research studies, or when their responses are not sorted out from those of non-Hispanic White women, issues of interest to them tend to get lost. They may wind up excluded from the psychology of women, even when findings are reported as inclusive of "women in general" (Yoder & Kahn, 1993, p. 847).

There is a quip in psychology that experiments tend to be run with "rats, sophomores, and soldiers." Why? In part because members of these groups have been readily available. In part, perhaps, because men have historically been accorded favored treatment over women.

Research samples have also tended to underrepresent minority ethnic groups in the population. Personality tests completed by non-Hispanic White Americans and by African Americans may need to be interpreted in diverse ways if accurate conclusions are to be drawn, for example (Nevid and others, 1994). The well-known Kinsey studies on sexual behavior (Kinsey and others, 1948, 1953) did not adequately represent African Americans, poor people, the elderly, and diverse other groups.

One way to achieve a representative sample is by means of **random sampling.** In a random sample, each member of a population has an equal chance of being selected to participate. Researchers can also use a **stratified sample,** which is drawn so that identified subgroups in the population are represented proportionately in the sample. For instance, 12% of the American population is African American (*The Outlook*, 1993). A stratified sample would thus be 12% African American. As a practical matter, a large, randomly selected sample will show reasonably accurate stratification. A

Generalize • To extend from the particular to the general; to apply observations based on a sample to a population.

Sample • Part of a population.

Population • A complete group of organisms or events.

Infer • Draw a conclusion.

Random sample • A sample that is drawn so that each member of a population has an equal chance of being selected to participate.

Stratified sample • A sample that is drawn so that identified subgroups in the population are represented proportionately in the sample. How can stratified sampling be carried out to ensure that a sample represents the ethnic diversity we find in the population at large?

random sample of 1,500 people will represent the general U.S. population reasonably well. A haphazardly drawn sample of 20 million, however, might not.

Large-scale magazine surveys of sexual behavior have asked readers to fill out and return questionnaires. Although many thousands of readers completed the questionnaires and sent them in, did they represent the general U.S. population? Probably not. These studies and similar ones may have been influenced by **volunteer bias.** The concept behind volunteer bias is that people who offer to participate in research studies differ systematically from people who do not. In the case of research into sexual behavior, volunteers may represent subgroups of the population—or of readers of the magazines in question—who are willing to disclose intimate information (Rathus and others, 1993). Volunteers may also be more interested in research than nonvolunteers, as well as have more spare time. How might such volunteers differ

African American and White Women. Gail Wyatt and her colleagues at UCLA studied the sexual behavior of African American and White women in Los Angeles County. How did Wyatt achieve samples who were comparable according to socioeconomic status, marital status, and other demographic factors? How did Wyatt's findings differ from those of Kinsey and his colleagues, which were reported some 40 years earlier? How representative are Wyatt's samples of her target populations?

from the population at large? How might such differences slant or bias the research outcomes?

PSYCHOLOGY IN A WORLD OF DIVERSITY

THE WYATT SURVEY OF AFRICAN AMERICAN AND WHITE WOMEN IN LOS ANGELES COUNTY

Although Alfred Kinsey and his colleagues, the authors of the "Kinsey reports," gathered some data on the sexual behavior of African American people, they did not report it because African American people were significantly underrepresented in their samples. In more recent years, however, UCLA researcher Gail Wyatt and her colleagues (Wyatt, 1989, 1990; Wyatt and others, 1988a, 1988b, 1990) studied the sexual behavior of a sample of 122 White and 126 African American women aged 18 to 36 in Los Angeles County. She recruited study participants at random from telephone listings. Women who agreed to participate were selected to try to balance the sample in terms of demographic variables such as age, education, socioeconomic status, marital status, and number of children. One in three women called refused to cooperate, so a volunteer bias was clearly at work in Wyatt's final samples. The study participants were interviewed face-to-face.

Wyatt's work is important because it deals with changes in sexual behavior that have occurred in U.S. society since the years just following World War II, with prominent social issues such as childhood sexual abuse, and because it is one of the few studies of sexual behavior among African American women (Rathus and others, 1993). A striking difference between the Kinsey data and Wyatt's is that contemporary women—both African American and White—reported engaging in initial sexual intercourse at earlier ages than women in Kinsey's sample reported. Only about one woman in five in Kinsey's sample reported engaging in premarital intercourse by the age of 20 (Kinsey and others, 1953, p. 286). By contrast, 98% of the women in Wyatt's research (African American and White) reported engaging in premarital intercourse by the age of 20 (Wyatt, 1989). When social class differences were mathematically considered, the ages of initial intercourse for the African American and White women in Wyatt's sample were very much alike.

What of it? Can we conclude that in our liberated times, 98% of single women throughout the United States engage in premarital intercourse by the age of 20? Clearly not. Wyatt's research was limited to the Los Angeles area. One out of three women contacted by Wyatt refused to participate, introducing a volunteer bias. Moreover, to balance her White and African American samples for factors such as socioeconomic status, marital status, and level of education, Wyatt limited her pool of participants to women who were comparable according to these factors. Her final sample of African American women matched the population of African American women in Los Angeles County, but her final sample of White women did not match the population of White women in Los Angeles County. Her sample contained a disproportionate number of White women of lower socioeconomic status, for example.

Wyatt's samples thus did not fully represent the targeted populations. Remember, however, that when factors such as socioeconomic status, marital status, and level of education were held constant, the African American and White women in her samples exhibited highly similar patterns of sexual behavior. May we conclude, then, that sexual behavior is influenced more by such demographic factors than it is by race per se? What do you think?

═══════════════

Reflections

Now that you have read about samples and populations, reflect on the following questions:

• Were you surprised to find out that women in the Milgram studies obeyed orders and shocked "learners" just as men in the study did? Why or why not?
• From your own life experiences, why do you think that there has been a historic bias toward conducting research with men?

• If scientists conducted research with a "random sample" of students from your own school, would their sample represent the general U.S. population? Why or why not?

Methods of Observation: The Better to See You With

Many people consider themselves experts on behavior and mental processes on the basis of their life experiences. How many times have grandparents, for example, told us what they have seen in their lives and what it means about human nature?

We see much indeed during our lifetimes. Our personal observations tend to be fleeting and uncontrolled, however. We sift through experience for the minutiae that interest us. We often ignore the obvious because it does not fit our preexisting ideas (or "schemes") of the ways that things ought to be.

Scientists, however, have devised more controlled ways of observing others. Let us consider the case-study, survey, testing, naturalistic-observation, and laboratory-observation methods (see Figure 2.4).

THE CASE-STUDY METHOD

We begin with the case-study method because our own informal ideas about human nature tend to be based on **case studies,** or information we collect about individuals and small groups. But most of us gather our information haphazardly. Often, we see what we want to see. Unscientific accounts of people's behavior are referred to as *anecdotes.* Psychologists attempt to gather information about individuals more carefully.

Sigmund Freud developed psychodynamic theory largely on the basis of case studies. Freud studied his patients in great depth, seeking factors that seemed to contribute to notable patterns of behavior. He followed some patients for many years, meeting with them several times a week.

However, there are gaps and factual inaccuracies in autobiographical memory

Volunteer bias • A source of bias or error in research that reflects the prospect that people who offer to participate in research studies differ systematically from people who do not.
Case study • A carefully drawn biography that may be obtained through interviews, questionnaires, and psychological tests.

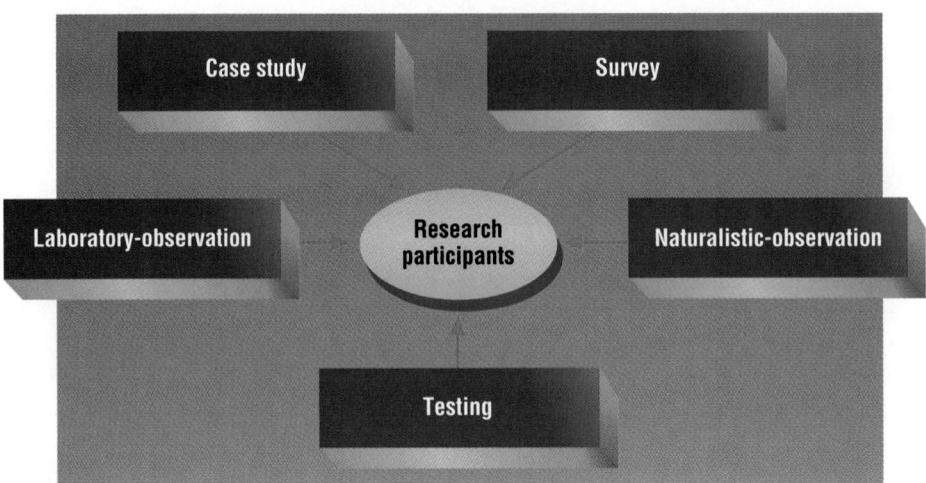

FIGURE 2.4
Methods of Observation in Psychology

(Brewin and others, 1993). People may also distort their pasts because of social desirability or the desire to remember things in certain ways. Interviewers may also have certain expectations and subtly encourage study participants to fill in gaps in ways that are consistent with the researchers' theoretical perspectives. Bandura (1986) notes, for example, that psychoanalysts have been criticized for guiding their patients into viewing their own lives from the psychodynamic perspective. No wonder, then, that many patients provide "evidence" that is consistent with psychodynamic theory. However, interviewers and other kinds of researchers who hold any theoretical viewpoint run the risk of indirectly prodding their studies' participants into producing what they want to hear.

Case studies are often used to investigate rare occurrences, as in the cases of "Eve" and "Genie." "Eve" (in real life, Chris Sizemore) was an example of a person with dissociative identity disorder (see Chapter 13). "Eve White," as we shall see, was a mousy, well-intentioned woman who had two other "personalities" living inside her. One was "Eve Black," a promiscuous personality who now and then emerged to take control of her behavior.

"Genie's" father locked her in a small room at the age of 20 months and kept her there until she was discovered at the age of 13½ (Rymer, 1993). Her social contacts were limited to her nearly blind mother, who entered the room only to feed her, and

to beatings at the hands of her father. No one spoke to her throughout this period. After her rescue, Genie's language development followed the normal sequence outlined in Chapter 8, suggesting the universality of this sequence. Genie did not reach normal proficiency in her use of language, however. Perhaps there is a "sensitive period" for learning language in early childhood.

The case study is also used in psychological consultation. Psychologists learn whatever they can about individuals, agencies, and business firms so that they can suggest ways in which these clients can more effectively meet their challenges. Psychologists base their suggestions on laboratory research whenever possible, but psychological practice is also sometimes an art in which psychologist and client agree that a suggestion or a treatment has been helpful on the basis of the client's self-report.

THE SURVEY METHOD

In the good old days, one had to wait until the wee hours of the morning to learn the results of local and national elections. Throughout the evening and early morning hours, suspense would build as ballots from distant neighborhoods and states were tallied. Nowadays, one is barely settled with an after-dinner cup of coffee on election night when the news-show computer cheerfully announces (computers do not, of course, have emotions or make "cheerful" announcements, but they do seem rather smug at times) that it has examined the ballots of a "scientifically selected sample" and then predicts the next president of the United States. All this may occur with less than 1% of the vote tallied. Preelection polls also do their share of eroding wonderment and doubt—so much so that some supporters of projected winners must be encouraged to actually vote on Election Day so that predictions will be borne out.

Just as computers and pollsters predict election results and report national opinion on the basis of scientifically selected samples, psychologists conduct **surveys** to learn about behavior and mental processes that cannot be observed in the natural setting or studied experimentally. Psychologists making surveys may employ questionnaires and interviews or examine public records. By distributing questionnaires and analyzing answers with a computer, psychologists can survey many thousands of people at a time.

We alluded to the "Kinsey reports," in which Alfred Kinsey of Indiana University and his colleagues published two surveys of sexual behavior, based on interviews, that shocked the nation: these were *Sexual Behavior in the Human Male* (1948) and *Sexual Behavior in the Human Female* (1953). Kinsey reported that masturbation was virtually universal in his sample of men at a time when masturbation was still widely thought to impair physical or mental health. He also reported that about one woman in three still single at age 25 had engaged in premarital intercourse. In addition to compiling self-reports of behavior, surveys are also used to learn about people's mental processes, including their opinions, attitudes, and values.

Interviews and questionnaires are not foolproof, of course. People may inaccurately recall their behavior or purposefully misrepresent it. Some people try to ingratiate themselves with their interviewers by answering in what they perceive to be the socially desirable direction. The Kinsey studies all relied on male interviewers, for example. It has been speculated that female interviewees might have been more open and honest with female interviewers. Similar problems may occur when interviewers and those surveyed are from different ethnic or socioeconomic backgrounds. Other people may falsify attitudes and exaggerate problems to draw attention to themselves or just to try to foul up the results.

Humphrey Taylor (1993), president of Louis Harris & Associates (the company that takes the Harris polls), recounts two fascinating examples of survey measurement errors caused by inaccurate self-reports of behavior. In one survey, many people sampled reported that they read *Collier's* magazine—5 years after it was no longer published. The other example is this: If people brushed their teeth as often as they claimed, and used the amount of toothpaste they indicated, three times as much toothpaste would be sold in the United States as is actually sold. People also appear to overreport their church attendance and to underreport abortions (Espenshade, 1993).

Although errors in measurement are clearly possible, let us consider the results of a recent survey of 210,739 first-year students entering 2- and 4-year postsecondary institutions. The students were asked to identify themselves as either far left, liberal, middle of the road, conservative, or far right in their political views. As you can see in Table 2.1, about one student in four

Survey • A method of scientific investigation in which a large sample of people answer questions about their attitudes or behavior.

TABLE 2.1
Political Views of First-Year Students

Far left	2.1%
Liberal	23.6
Middle of the road	54.0
Conservative	19.1
Far right	1.2

Source of data: "The American Freshman: National Norms for Fall 1991," by A. W. Astin. Published by The American Council on Education and University of California at Los Angeles. Reprinted from *The Chronicle of Higher Education,* August 26, 1992, p. 13.

TABLE 2.2

Percentage of First-Year Students Who Agree Strongly
or Somewhat That—

Government is not doing enough to protect the consumer from faulty goods and services.	69.1%
Government is not doing enough to control pollution.	85.5
Taxes should be raised to reduce the federal deficit.	25.5
There is too much concern in courts for the rights of criminals.	65.3
Military spending should be increased.	26.0
Abortion should be legal.	63.0
The death penalty should be abolished.	21.1
It is right for two people who really like each other to have sex even if they've known each other for a very short time.	50.1
Married women's activities are best confined to home and family.	26.0
Marijuana should be legalized.	20.9
Busing to achieve racial balance in schools is all right.	54.7
It is important to have laws prohibiting homosexual relationships.	42.2
The chief benefit of college is that it increases one's earning power.	71.0
Employers should be allowed to require employees or job applicants to take drug tests.	80.8
The best way to control AIDS is through widespread, mandatory testing.	66.4
Just because a man thinks that a woman has "led him on" does not entitle him to have sex with her.	87.1
The government should do more to control the sale of handguns.	78.1
A national health-care plan is needed to cover everybody's medical costs.	75.8
Nuclear disarmament is attainable.	63.7
Racial discrimination is no longer a major problem in America.	20.3
The federal government should do more to discourage energy consumption.	78.5
Realistically, an individual can do little to bring about changes in our society.	31.3

Source of data: "The American Freshman: National Norms for Fall 1991," by A. W. Astin. Published by The American Council on Education and University of California at Los Angeles. Reprinted from *The Chronicle of Higher Education*, August 26, 1992, p. 13.

Reliability • Consistency.

Test–retest reliability • A method for determining the reliability of a test by comparing (correlating) test takers' scores from separate occasions.

Aptitude • An ability or talent to succeed in an area in which one has not yet been trained.

Validity • The degree to which a test measures what it is supposed to measure.

Validity scales • Groups of test items that suggest whether the test results are valid (measure what they are supposed to measure).

Naturalistic observation • A scientific method in which organisms are observed in their natural environments.

(25.7%) rated herself or himself as liberal or very liberal ("far left"); about one student in five (20.3%), as conservative or very conservative ("far right"); and slightly more than half (54%) rated themselves as middle of the road.

Table 2.2 shows the results of a survey of the political views of the same students on specific issues. The students were asked to respond to the statements shown, and others, according to a commonly used 5-point scale:

Agree strongly
Agree
No opinion
Disagree
Disagree strongly

One could say that the students neared a consensus on the statements that "Just because a man thinks that a woman has led him on does not entitle him to have sex

with her," and "Government is not doing enough to control pollution." Only about one student in four agreed with the traditionalist stance that "Married women's activities are best confined to home and family." Although nearly four students out of five rated themselves as middle of the road or liberal, consider their responses to statements that could be considered liberal: Only about one student in five agreed that "Marijuana should be legalized," and only about one student in four agreed that "Taxes should be raised to reduce the federal deficit." The death penalty is supported by a clear majority of students (only about one student in five would like to see it abolished), although one might consider support of the death penalty to represent a conservative political view. Only one student in five, moreover, agreed that "Racial discrimination is no longer a major problem in America." Ethnic diversity is unfortunately still connected with a great deal of prejudice and social friction. Fortunately, fewer than one third of the students surveyed (31.3%) agreed with the statement that "Realistically, an individual can do little to bring about changes in our society." If the majority of students believe in their capacity to bring about meaningful social changes, perhaps they will apply themselves to doing so.

I noted that this survey was conducted with 210,739 students. This vast number allowed the investigators to obtain information that allows them to compare and contrast the views and opinions of first-year students at many colleges and universities across the United States. If their sole intention had been to obtain a sample that represented the entire entering first-year class of 1991, however, a random sample of 1,500 or so first-year students would have sufficed.

THE TESTING METHOD

Psychologists also use psychological tests—such as intelligence, aptitude, and personality tests—to measure various traits and characteristics among a population. There is a wide range of psychological tests, and they measure traits ranging from verbal ability and achievement to anxiety, depression, the need for social dominance, musical aptitude, and vocational interests.

Because important decisions are made on the basis of psychological tests, they must be *reliable* and *valid*. The **reliability** of a measure is its consistency. A measure of height would not be reliable if a person appeared to be taller or shorter every time a measurement was taken. A reliable measure of personality or intelligence, like a good tape measure, must yield similar results on different testing occasions.

There are different ways of showing a test's reliability. One of the most commonly used is **test–retest reliability,** which is shown by comparing scores of tests taken on different occasions. The measurement of test–retest reliability may be confused in tests of intelligence and **aptitude** by the fact that people often improve their scores from one occasion to the next because of familiarity with the test items and the testing procedure.

The **validity** of a test is the degree to which it measures what it is supposed to measure. To determine whether a test is valid, we see whether it actually predicts an outside standard, or external criterion. A proper standard, or criterion, for determining the validity of a test of musical aptitude is the ability to learn to play a musical instrument. Tests of musical aptitude, therefore, should predict ability to learn to play a musical instrument. Most psychologists assume that intelligence is one of the factors responsible for academic prowess. Thus, intelligence test scores should predict school grades. They do moderately well (Sattler, 1988). Intelligence test scores received after the age of 7 also predict one's adult occupational status reasonably well (McCall, 1977).

Psychological test results, like the results of surveys, can be distorted by respondents who answer in a socially desirable direction or attempt to exaggerate problems. For these reasons, some commonly used psychological tests have items built into them called **validity scales.** Validity scales are sensitive to misrepresentations and alert the psychologist when test results may be deceptive.

THE NATURALISTIC-OBSERVATION METHOD

You use **naturalistic observation** every day of your life. That is, you observe people in their natural habitats.

So do psychologists. The next time you opt for a fast-food burger lunch, look around. Pick out slender people and overweight people and observe whether they eat their burgers and fries differently. Do the overweight eat more rapidly? Chew less frequently? Leave less food on their plates? This is precisely the type of research that psychologists have recently used to study the eating habits of normal-weight and overweight people. In fact, if you notice some mysterious people at McDonald's peering out over sunglasses and occasionally tapping the head of a partly concealed microphone, perhaps they are recording their observations of other people's eating habits, even as you watch.

In naturalistic observation, psychologists and other scientists observe behavior in the

The Naturalistic-Observation Method. In the naturalistic–observation method, psychologists study behavior in the field, "where it happens." For example, psychologists have recorded eating behavior in fast-food restaurants to learn whether or not obese people eat more rapidly or take larger bites than other people.

Unobtrusive • Not interfering.

Laboratory • A place in which theories, techniques, and methods are tested and demonstrated.

Correlational method • A scientific method that studies the relationships between variables.

Correlation coefficient • A number between +1.00 to −1.00 that expresses the strength and direction (positive or negative) of the relationship between two variables.

Positive correlation • A relationship between variables in which one variable increases as the other also increases.

field, or "where it happens." They try to avoid interfering with the behaviors they are observing by using **unobtrusive** measures. Jane Goodall has observed the behavior of chimpanzees in their natural environment to learn about their social behavior, sexual behavior, use of tools, and other facts of chimp life (see Figure 2.5). Her observations have shown us that (1) we were incorrect to think that only people use tools; and (2) kissing, as a greeting, is used by chimpanzees as well as people.

Truth or Fiction Revisited. *It is not true that only people use tools.* The naturalistic-observation method has taught us that other animals also use tools. Apes are an example. (Did you also know that otters use rocks to open the shells of mollusks?)

THE LABORATORY-OBSERVATION METHOD

I first became acquainted with the laboratory-observation method when, as a child, I was given tropical fish. My parents spent a small fortune to keep my new dependents

in sound health. My laboratory for observation—my tank—was an artificial sea world. I filtered impurities out of the water with an electric pump. I warmed the water with a heater with an angry orange eye. I regularly assessed and regulated the acidity (pH) of the water. All this enabled me to while away the hours watching the fish swim in and out of protecting leaves, establish and defend territories, and, sometimes, court mates and breed. I even noted how the fish became conditioned to swim to the surface of the water when the light was turned on in the room. They apparently came to associate the light with the appearance of food.

By bringing the fish into my home, I did not have to voyage to the reefs of the Caribbean or the mouth of the Amazon to make my observations. I also created just the conditions I wished, and I observed how my subjects reacted to them.

Somewhat like wondering children, psychologists at times place lower animals and people into controlled laboratory environments where they can be readily observed and where the effects of specific conditions can be discerned. Figure 1.2 on page 13 shows one such environment, which is constructed so that pigeons receive reinforcers for pecking buttons.

With people, the **laboratory** takes many forms. Do not confine your imagination to rows of Bunsen burners and the smell of sulfur or to rats and pigeons in wire cages being reinforced with food pellets from heaven.

Figure 2.2 (see p. 46), for example, diagrams the laboratory setup in the Milgram studies at Yale University, where human participants (the "teacher" in the diagram) were urged to deliver electric shock to other people (so-called learners) as a way of signaling them that they had made errors on a learning task. This study was inspired by the atrocities committed by apparently typical German citizens during World War II, and its true purpose was to determine how easy it would be to induce normal people to hurt others. In studies on sensation and perception, human participants may be placed in dark or quiet rooms in order to learn how bright or loud a stimulus must be before it can be detected.

FIGURE 2.5
The Naturalistic–Observation Method Jane van Lawick Goodall has used the naturalistic–observation method with chimpanzees, quietly observing them for many years in their natural environments. In using this method, scientists try to avoid interfering with the animals or people they observe, even though this sometimes means allowing an animal to be mistreated by other animals or to die from a curable illness. We learn from Goodall that tools are used by primates other than human beings. The chimp in the left-hand photo is using a stick as a tool to poke around in a termite hill for food. Goodall's observations have also taught us that not only humans use kissing as a social greeting (see right-hand photo). Male chimps have even been observed greeting females by kissing their hands. Very European?

Reflections

Now that you have read the section on methods of observation, reflect on the following questions:

• What methods of observation do your family and friends use when they make assertions about human behavior? How do their methods overlap with those presented in this section? How scientific are they?

• From your own experiences, why do you think that people tend to overreport how often they brush their teeth and go to church?

The Correlational Method: Seeing What Goes Up and What Comes Down

Are people with higher intelligence more likely to do well in school? Are people with a stronger need for achievement likely to climb higher up the corporate ladder? What is the relationship between stress and health?

Correlation follows observation. By using the **correlational method,** psychologists investigate whether observed behavior or a measured trait is related to, or correlated with, another. Consider the variables of intelligence and academic performance. The variables of intelligence and academic performance are assigned numbers such as intelligence test scores and academic averages. Then the numbers or scores are mathematically related and expressed as a **correlation coefficient.** A correlation coefficient is a number that varies between +1.00 and −1.00. Psychologists use the correlation coefficient to determine the reliability and validity of psychological tests.

Studies report **positive correlations** between intelligence and achievement. For a test to be considered reliable, correlations between a group's test results on separate

 MINILECTURE: CORRELATIONS

Intelligence and Achievement. Correlations between intelligence test scores and academic achievement—as measured by school grades and achievement tests—tend to be positive and strong. Does the correlational method allow us to say that intelligence *causes* or *is responsible for* academic achievements? Why, or why not?

Negative correlation • A relationship between two variables in which one variable increases as the other decreases.

+0.70 is generally considered to be adequate for purposes of test validity. However, such a correlation does not approach a perfect positive relationship. This finding suggests that factors *other* than performance on intelligence tests contribute to academic and occupational success. Motivation to do well and one's general level of personal adjustment are two of them (Anastasi, 1983; Collier, 1994; Scarr, 1981).

What of the need for achievement and getting ahead? The need for achievement can be assessed by rating stories told by study participants for the presence of this need (see Chapter 10). Getting ahead can be assessed in many ways—salary and the prestige of one's occupation or level within the corporation are just two of them.

There is a **negative correlation** between stress and health. As the amount of stress affecting us increases, the functioning of our immune systems decreases (see Chapter 15). Under high levels of stress, many people show poorer health.

Correlational research may suggest but does not show cause and effect. For instance, it may seem logical to assume that high intelligence makes it possible for children to profit from education. Research has also shown, however, that education contributes to higher scores on intelligence tests. Preschoolers placed in stimulating Head Start programs later attain higher scores on intelligence tests than agemates who did not have this experience. The relationship between intelligence and academic

occasions should be positive and high— about +0.90 (see Table 2.3). People's scores on intelligence tests are also positively correlated with their grades. Generally speaking, the higher people score on intelligence tests, the better their academic performance is likely to be. The scores attained on intelligence tests tend to be positively correlated (about +0.60 to +0.70) with academic achievement (see Figure 2.6). As noted in Table 2.3, a correlation of about +0.60 to

TABLE 2.3

Interpretations of Correlation Coefficients

CORRELATION COEFFICIENT	INTERPRETATION
+1.00	Perfect positive correlation, as between temperature in Fahrenheit and centigrade
+0.90	High positive correlation, adequate for test reliability
+0.60 to +0.70	Moderate positive correlation, usually considered adequate for test validity
+0.30	Weak positive correlation, unacceptable for test reliability or validity
0.00	No correlation between variables (no association indicated)
−0.30	Weak negative correlation
−0.60 to −0.70	Moderate negative correlation
−0.90	High negative correlation
−1.00	A perfect negative correlation

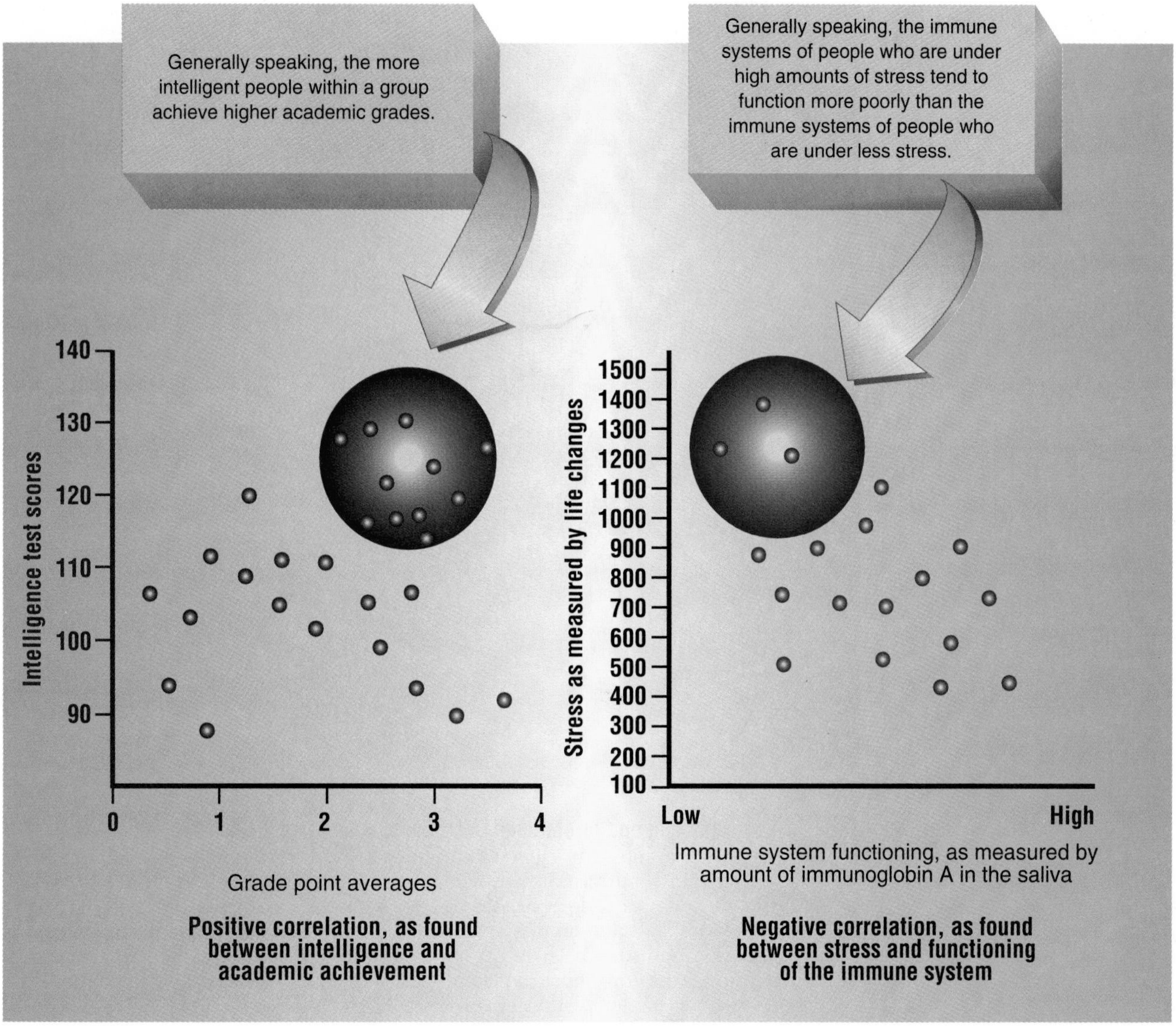

Generally speaking, the more intelligent people within a group achieve higher academic grades.

Generally speaking, the immune systems of people who are under high amounts of stress tend to function more poorly than the immune systems of people who are under less stress.

Intelligence test scores (y-axis: 90, 100, 110, 120, 130, 140)

Grade point averages (x-axis: 0, 1, 2, 3, 4)

Positive correlation, as found between intelligence and academic achievement

Stress as measured by life changes (y-axis: 100–1500)

Immune system functioning, as measured by amount of immunoglobin A in the saliva (Low — High)

Negative correlation, as found between stress and functioning of the immune system

FIGURE 2.6

Spotlight on Positive and Negative Correlations When there is a positive correlation between variables, as there is between intelligence and achievement, one tends to increase as the other increases. By and large, the higher people score on intelligence tests, the better their academic performance is likely to be, as in the diagram to the left. (Each dot is located to represent an individual's intelligence test score and grade point average.) Similarly, there is a positive correlation between exercise and health, as we shall see in Chapter 15. On the other hand, there is a negative correlation between stress and health. As the amount of stress we experience increases, the functioning of our immune systems tends to decrease. Correlational research may suggest but does not demonstrate cause and effect.

performance may not be as simple as you might have thought. What of the link between stress and health? Does stress impair health, or is it possible that people in poorer health encounter higher levels of stress? (See Figure 2.7.)

Reflections

Now that you have read about the correlational method, reflect on the following questions:

- What kinds of correlations (positive? negative? strong? weak?) do you believe are found among behavior patterns such as the following: Churchgoing and crime? Language ability and musical ability? Level of education and incidence of teenage pregnancy? Grades in school and juvenile delinquency? Why?

- It happens that couples who live together before getting married are *more* likely to get divorced once they are married than couples who did not. Does this research finding mean that living together before

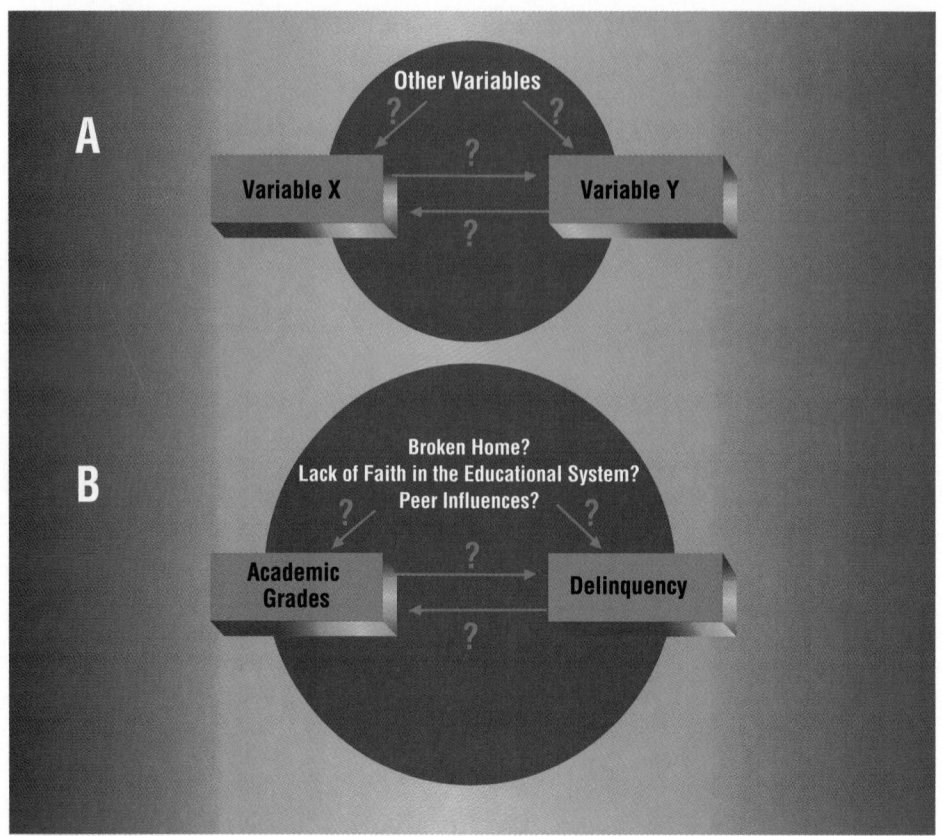

FIGURE 2.7

Spotlight on Correlational Relationships and Cause and Effect Correlational relationships may suggest but cannot demonstrate cause and effect. In part A, there is a correlation between variables *X* and *Y*. Does this mean that variable *X* causes variable *Y*, or that variable *Y* causes variable *X*? Not necessarily. Consider the examples of academic grades (variable *X*) and juvenile delinquency (variable *Y*) in part B. There is a negative correlation between the two. Does this mean that poor grades contribute to delinquency? Perhaps. Does it mean that delinquency contributes to poor grades? Again, perhaps. But there could also be other variables—such as a broken home, lack of faith in the educational system, or peer influences—that contribute both to poor grades and delinquency. Psychologists often find complex interactions among many variables when they study behavior and mental processes. In this case, for example, poor grades could make youth more susceptible to negative peer influences, leading to delinquent behavior. What other possibilities are there?

getting married *causes* marital instability? Why or why not? Can you think of rival explanations for the connection between living together and marital instability?

The Experimental Method: Trying Things Out

MINILECTURE: THE EXPERIMENTAL METHOD

The people who signed up for the Milgram studies participated in an elaborate **experiment.** The participants in an experiment

obtain a treatment. Milgram's participants partook of a most intricate **treatment**—one that involved a well-equipped research laboratory at Yale University or nearby. It also involved deception. Milgram had even foreseen participants' objections to the procedure. He had therefore conceived standardized statements that his assistants would use when participants balked—for example: "Although the shocks may be painful, there is no permanent tissue damage, so please go on." "The experiment requires that you continue." "It is absolutely essential that you continue." "You have no other choice, you *must* go on." These statements, the bogus "aggression machine," the use of the "learner" (who was actually a confederate of the experimenter)—all these things were part of the experimental treatment.

Although we can raise many questions about the Milgram studies, most psychologists agree that the preferred method for answering questions concerning cause and effect is the experiment. In an experiment, a group of participants obtains a treatment, such as a dose of alcohol, a change in room temperature, perhaps an injection of a drug. The participants are then observed carefully to determine whether the treatment makes a difference in their behavior. Does alcohol affect participants' ability to take tests, for example? Environmental psychologists have varied room temperatures and the background levels of noise to see whether these treatments have an effect on participants' behavior.

Experiments are used whenever possible in contemporary psychological research because they allow psychologists to control directly the experiences of animals and people and to draw conclusions about cause and effect.

A psychologist may theorize that alcohol leads to aggression because it reduces fear of consequences or because it generally energizes the activity levels of drinkers. She or he may then hypothesize that the treatment of a specified dosage of alcohol will lead to increases in aggression. Let us follow the example of the effects of alcohol on aggression to further our understanding of the experimental method.

INDEPENDENT AND DEPENDENT VARIABLES

In an experiment to determine whether alcohol causes aggression, experimental participants would be given an amount of alcohol, and its effects would be measured. In this case, alcohol is an **independent variable.** The presence of an independent variable is manipulated by the experimenters so that its effects may be determined. The independent variable of alcohol may be administered at different levels, or doses, from none or very little to enough to cause intoxication, or drunkenness.

The measured results, or outcomes, in an experiment are called **dependent variables.** The presence of dependent variable presumably depends on the independent variables. In an experiment to determine whether alcohol influences

Experiment • A scientific method that seeks to confirm cause-and-effect relationships by introducing independent variables and observing their effects on dependent variables.

Treatment • In experiments, a condition received by participants so that its effects may be observed.

Independent variable • A condition in a scientific study that is manipulated so that its effects may be observed.

Dependent variable • A measure of an assumed effect of an independent variable.

What Are the Effects of Alcohol? Psychologists have undertaken research to determine alcohol's effects on behavior. Questions have been raised about the soundness of research in which subjects *know* they have drunk alcohol. Why?

aggression, aggressive behavior would be a dependent variable. Other dependent variables of interest in an experiment on the effects of alcohol might include sexual arousal, visual-motor coordination, and performance on intellectual tasks such as defining words or doing numerical computations.

In an experiment on the relationships between temperature and aggression, temperature would be an independent variable and aggressive behavior would be a dependent variable. We could use temperature settings ranging from below freezing to blistering hot and study the effects of each. We could also use a second independent variable such as social provocation. That is, we could insult some study participants but not others. This method would allow us to study the interaction between temperature and social provocation as they affect aggression.

Experiments can be complex, with several independent and dependent variables. Psychologists often use complex experimental designs and sophisticated statistical techniques to determine the effect of each independent variable, as that variable acts alone and in combination with others, on each dependent variable.

EXPERIMENTAL AND CONTROL GROUPS

Ideal experiments use experimental and control groups. Experimental participants partake of the treatment, whereas members of control groups do not. Every effort is made to ensure that all other conditions are held constant for both experimental and control groups. This method enhances researchers' abilities to draw conclusions about cause and effect. Controls heighten researchers' confidence that experimental outcomes are caused by the treatments and not by chance factors or chance fluctuations in behavior.

In an experiment concerning the effects of alcohol on aggression, members of the experimental group would ingest alcohol and members of the control group would not. In a complex experiment, different experimental groups might ingest different dosages of alcohol and be exposed to different types of social provocations.

BLINDS AND DOUBLE BLINDS

One experiment on the effects of alcohol on aggression (Boyatzis, 1974) reported that men at parties where beer and liquor were served acted more aggressively than control groups at parties where only soft drinks were served. But we must be cautious in interpreting these findings because those in the experimental group *knew* that they had drunk alcohol, and those in the control group *knew* that they had not. Aggression that appeared to result from alcohol might not have reflected drinking per se; instead, it might have reflected the individuals' expectations about the effects of alcohol. People tend to act in stereotypical ways when they believe that they have been drinking alcohol. For instance, men tend to become less anxious in social situations, more aggressive, and more sexually aroused.

A **placebo,** or "sugar pill," often results in the behavior that people expect. Physicians now and then give sugar pills to demanding, but healthy, people; and many people who receive placebos report that they feel better. When people in psychological experiments are given placebos—such as tonic water—but think that they have drunk alcohol, we can conclude that changes in behavior stem from their beliefs about alcohol, not the alcohol itself.

Well-designed experiments control for the effects of expectations by creating conditions under which participants are unaware of, or **blind** to, the treatment. Yet researchers may also have expectations. They may, in effect, be "rooting for" a certain treatment. For instance, tobacco-company executives may wish to show that cigarette smoking is harmless. It is thus useful if the people measuring the experimental outcomes are also unaware of who has partaken of the treatment. Studies in which both participants and experimenters are unaware of who has partaken of the treatment are called **double-blind studies.**

Double-blind studies are required by the Food and Drug Administration before it will allow the marketing of new drugs (Carroll and others, 1994). The drug and the placebo look and taste alike. Experimenters assign the drug or placebo at random to participants. Neither the participants nor the people who measure their progress know who is taking the drug and

---

Placebo • A bogus treatment that has the appearance of being genuine.

Blind • In experimental terminology, unaware of whether or not one has partaken of a treatment.

Double-blind study • A study in which neither the participants nor the persons measuring results know who has received the treatment.

who is taking the placebo. After the final measurements are made, an impartial panel judges whether the effects of the drug differed from those of the placebo.

Truth or Fiction Revisited. *It is true that in many experiments, neither the participants nor the researchers know which participants are taking the real treatment and which participants are taking a placebo ("sugar pill").* Such experiments are referred to as *double-blind studies,* and they are designed to control for the effects of participants' and researchers' expectations. If you were running such an experiment, how would you keep track of which individuals had taken which treatments?

In one double-blind study on the effects of alcohol, Alan Lang and his colleagues (1975) pretested a highball of vodka and tonic water to determine that it could not be discriminated by taste from tonic water alone. They recruited as study participants college men who described themselves as social drinkers. Some participants drank vodka and tonic water, whereas others drank tonic water only. Of the individuals who drank vodka, half were misled into believing that they had drunk tonic water only (Figure 2.8). Of those drinking tonic water only, half were misled into believing that their drink contained vodka. Thus, half the participants were blind to their treatment. Experimenters who measured aggressive responses were also blind concerning which individuals had drunk vodka.

The research team found that men who believed that they had drunk vodka responded more aggressively to a provocation than men who believed that they had drunk tonic water only. The actual content of the drink was immaterial. That is, men who had actually drunk alcohol acted no more aggressively than men who had drunk tonic water only. The results of the Lang study differ dramatically from those reported by Boyatzis, perhaps because the Boyatzis study did not control for the effects of expectations or beliefs about alcohol.

Note that in the Lang study on alcohol and aggression, alcohol was operationally defined as a certain dose of vodka. Other types of drinks and other dosages of vodka might have had different effects. Aggression

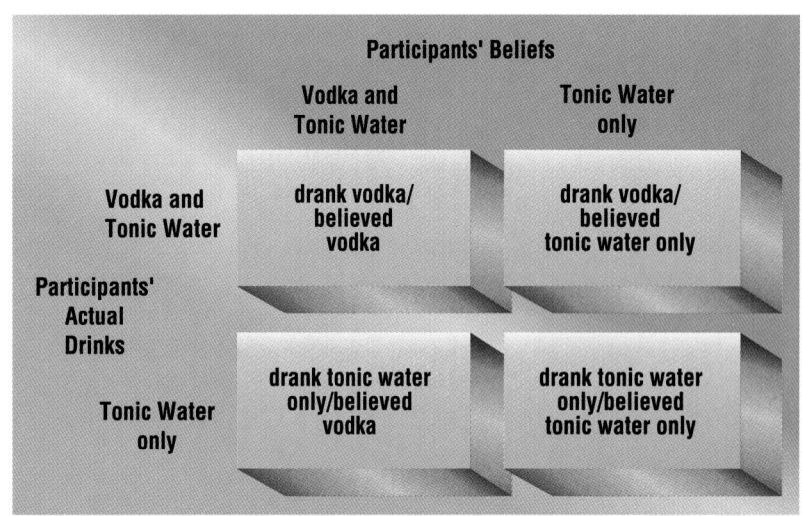

FIGURE 2.8
The Experimental Conditions in the Lang Study The taste of vodka cannot be discerned when vodka is mixed with tonic water. For this reason, it was possible for participants in the Lang study on the effects of alcohol to remain "blind" to whether they had actually drunk alcohol. Blind studies allow psychologists to control for the effects of participant expectations.

was operationally defined in the same way as it was in the Milgram studies on obedience: as selecting a certain amount of electric shock and administering it to another participant in a psychological experiment. College men might behave differently when they drink in other situations—for example, when they are insulted by a supporter of an opposing football team or are threatened outside a bar.

Is it possible, as the results of the Lang study suggest, that alcohol does not cause aggression, that centuries of folklore have been in error? Yes, quite possible. Other studies (replications) that control for the effects of expectations suggest that drinking alcohol increases aggressive behavior only when drinkers believe that aggression is the appropriate response for them (Jeavons & Taylor, 1985; Taylor & Sears, 1988).

Truth or Fiction Revisited. *It has not been shown that alcohol causes aggression.* Although alcohol is frequently *linked* to aggression, there is no scientific evidence that alcohol *causes* aggression. Correlation does not demonstrate cause and effect. Put on your critical thinking cap: If an older person should say to you, "Listen, my friends and I have had a little more life experience than you have, and we know that alcohol causes aggression," what type of argument are they making? If you describe the Lang study and the response is, "Well, I'm talking about real life, not some scientist's laboratory," what might you say?

Psychology is an empirical science. Centuries of folklore may stimulate research into certain topics, but folklore is not acceptable evidence within science.

What, then, do we make of these findings? Why does belief that one has drunk alcohol increase aggression, whereas alcohol itself may not? Perhaps alcohol gives one a certain social role to play in our culture—the role of the uninhibited social mover. Perhaps alcohol also provides an excuse for aggressive or other antisocial behavior. After all, the drinker can always claim, "It wasn't me; it was the alcohol." What will you think the next time someone says, "It was the alcohol"?

Reflections

Now that you have read the section on the experimental method, reflect on the following questions:

- Can you devise a method whereby researchers can use placebos and double blinds to investigate the effects of a new drug on the urge to smoke cigarettes? Can you think of various ways in which the researchers can measure the "urge" to smoke?
- Before reading this section, what were your beliefs concerning the effects of alcohol? Have your beliefs changed as a result of reading this section? Why or why not?

PSYCHOLOGY Ψ IN THE NEW MILLENNIUM

In the Global Research Lab

Imagine that you are a psychologist in Australia with complex data from twins on the subject of, say, sexual orientation. A question arises and you would like to confer with a colleague in, say, Chicago. Using a high-speed, long-distance telephone line and a technique called file transfer protocol (FTP), the data is tranferred from your computer to your colleague's within minutes. Your colleague then analyzes the data for herself or himself and the two of you compare results.

Sound farfetched? This technique is already used every day. The example I described refers to an exchange of information between Nick Martin at the Queensland Institute of Medical Research in Australia and J. Michael Bailey at Northwestern University (Azar, 1994d).

Electronic developments are in the process of linking the world's researchers. Psychologist Gary Olson and his colleagues at the University of Michigan are studying the ways in which electronic equipment can be used to match the ways in which researchers do their work (Azar, 1994c). One fascinating finding is that researchers are frequently inspired to strike out in new directions as they observe other researchers thousands of miles away. Researcher B may access Researcher A's data, analyze it, and suggest modifications to Researcher A's study before Researcher A has completed the first phase of her or his own work!

Graduate students and veterans alike stand to profit from the new global computer linkages. Graduate students are, in effect, apprentices who can learn by observing the interactions of other scientists (Azar, 1994c). Graduate students can also participate in research that is under way, providing fresh insights. Electronic interactions tend to be more candid and democratic than face-to-face interactions. Thus, the barriers between revered, established researchers and novices may be brought tumbling down—all to the betterment of psychological knowledge.

Methods of Studying Your Crowning Glory — The Brain

The brain is wider than the sky,
For, put them side by side,
The one the other will include
With ease, and you beside.

EMILY DICKINSON

Just where is that elusive piece of business you think of as your "mind"? Thousands of years ago, it was not generally thought that the mind had a place to hang its hat within the body. It was common to assume that the body was inhabited by demons or souls that could not be explained in terms of substance. After all, if you look inside a human being, the biological structures you find do not look all that different in quality from those of many lower animals. Thus, it seemed to make sense that those qualities that made us distinctly human—such as abstract thought, poetry, science, and the composition of music—were unrelated to substances that you could see, feel, and weigh on a scale.

Ancient Egyptians attributed control of the human being to a little person, or **homunculus,** who dwelled within the skull and regulated our behavior. The Greek philosopher Aristotle thought that the soul had set up living quarters in the heart. After all, serious injury to the heart could be said to cause the soul to take flight from the body.

Today, however, we recognize that the mind, or consciousness, dwells essentially

MINILECTURE: METHODS IN NEUROSCIENCE RESEARCH

Homunculus • (hoe-MONK-you-luss). Latin for "little man." A homunculus within the brain was once thought to govern human behavior.

In the Global Research Lab. Electronic developments are in the process of linking the world's researchers. Researchers are frequently inspired to strike out in new directions as they observe other researchers thousands of miles away. Researcher B may access Researcher A's data, analyze it, and suggest modifications to Researcher A's study before Researcher A has completed the first phase of her or his own work!

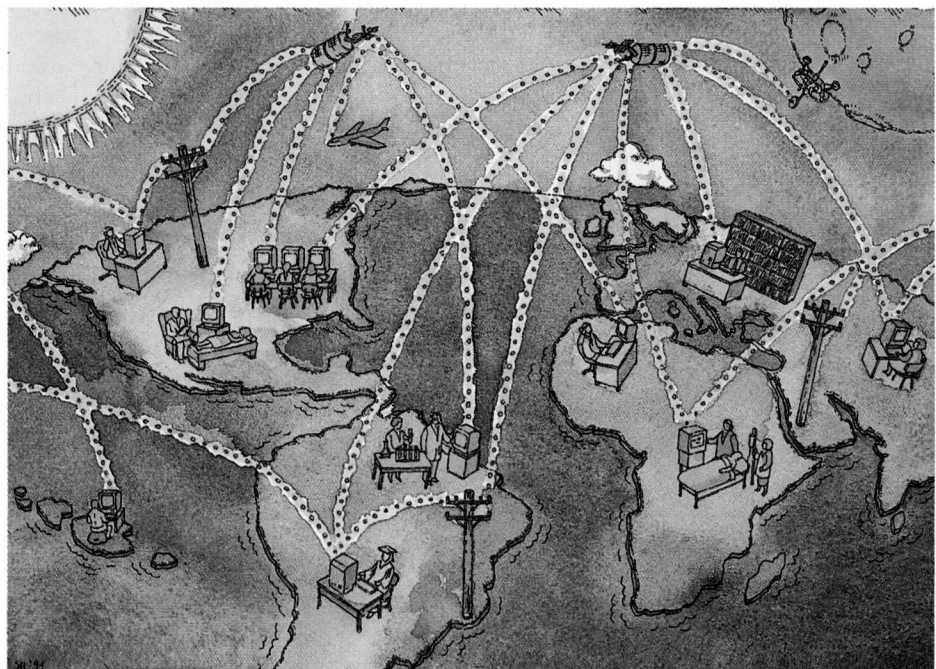

FIGURE 2.9
The Electroencephalograph In this method of research, brain waves are detected by placing electrodes on the scalp and measuring the current that passes between them.

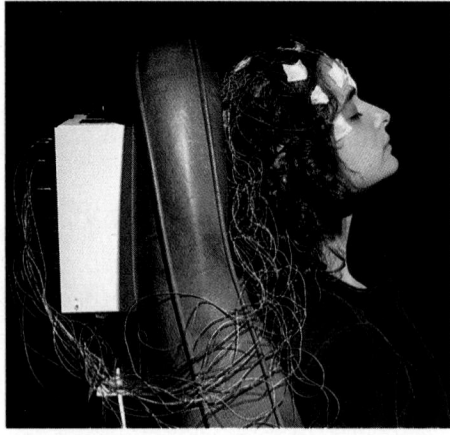

Lesion • (LEE-shun). An injury that results in impaired behavior or loss of a function.

Electroencephalograph • (el-eck-trow-en-SEFF-uh-lo-graf). An instrument that measures electrical activity of the brain. Abbreviated *EEG*. ("Cephalo-" derives from the Greek *kephale,* meaning "head.")

within the brain (Sperry, 1993). Our knowledge of the brain is based on both a variety of accidents and research methods that are designed to allow us to discover the links between the psychological and the biological. Some of these methods are purely methods of observation. Others involve experimentation.

Accidents. Consider the accidents that have taught us about the brain. From injuries to the head—some of them minimal, some horrendous—we have learned that brain damage can impair consciousness and

FIGURE 2.10
The Computerized Axial Tomograph (CAT) Scan In the CAT scan, a narrow X-ray beam is passed through the head and the amount of radiation that passes through is measured simultaneously from various angles. The computer enables us to integrate these measurements into a view of the brain.

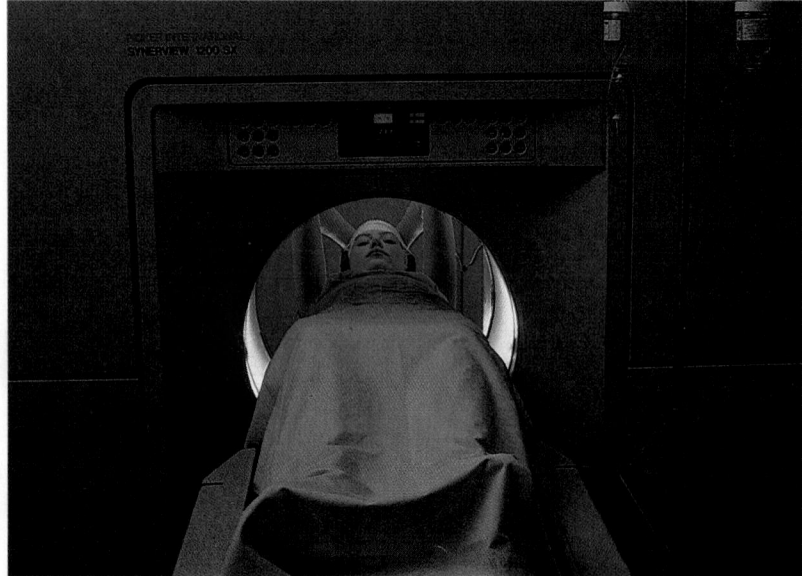

awareness. Brain damage can result in loss of vision and hearing, confusion, or loss of memory. In some cases, the loss of large portions of the brain may result in little loss of function. Ironically, the loss of sensitively located smaller portions can result in language problems, memory loss, or death.

Electrical Stimulation of the Brain (ESB). Experiments in electrical stimulation of areas in animal and human brains have shown that portions of the surface of the brain are associated with specific types of sensations (such as sensation of light or of a touch on the torso) or motor activities (such as movement of a leg). ESB has shown that a tiny group of structures near the center of the brain (the hypothalamus) is involved in sexual and aggressive behavior patterns. ESB has shown that a rectangular structure that rises from the back part of the brain into the forebrain (the reticular activating system) is involved in wakefulness and sleep.

Lesions. Whereas accidents have shown us how destruction of certain parts of the brain is related to behavioral changes in humans, intentional **lesions** in the brains of laboratory animals have led to more specific knowledge. For example, lesioning one part of the limbic system causes rats and monkeys to behave gently. Destruction of another part of the limbic system causes monkeys to rage at the slightest provocation. Destruction of yet another area of the limbic system prevents animals from forming new memories.

The Electroencephalograph. The **electroencephalograph** (EEG) records the electrical activity of the brain. When I was an undergraduate psychology student, I first heard that psychologists studied sleep by "connecting" people to the EEG. I had a gruesome image of people somehow being plugged in. Not so. As suggested in Figure 2.9, electrodes are simply attached to the scalp with tape or paste. Later, once the brain activity under study has been duly recorded, the electrodes are removed. A bit of soap and water and you're as good as new.

The EEG detects minute amounts of electrical activity—called brain waves—that pass between the electrodes (Wong,

1991). Certain brain waves are associated with feelings of relaxation and with various stages of sleep (see Chapter 5). Researchers and physicians use the EEG to locate the areas of the brain that respond to certain stimuli, such as lights or sounds, and to diagnose some kinds of abnormal behavior. The EEG also helps locate tumors.

The CAT Scan. The computer's capacity to generate images of the parts of the brain from various sources of radiation has sparked the development of imaging techniques that have been useful to researchers and physicians (Pollack, 1991; Posner & Raichle, 1994).

In one technique, **computerized axial tomography** (the CAT scan), a narrow X-ray beam is passed through the head. The amount of radiation that passes through is measured simultaneously from multiple angles (see Figure 2.10). The computer integrates these measurements into a three-dimensional view of the brain. As a result, brain damage and other abnormalities that years ago could be detected only by surgery can be displayed on a video monitor.

The PET Scan. A second method, **positron emission tomography** (the PET scan), forms a computer-generated image of the activity of parts of the brain by tracing the amount of glucose used (or metabolized) by these parts. More glucose is metabolized in the parts of the brain in which activity is greater. To trace the metabolism of glucose, a harmless amount of a radioactive compound, called a *tracer,* is mixed with glucose and injected into the bloodstream. When the glucose reaches the brain, the patterns of activity are revealed by measurement of the positrons—positively charged particles—that are given off by the tracer. The PET scan has been used by researchers to see which parts of the brain are most active when we are, for example, listening to music, working out a math problem, using language, or playing chess ("Pinpointing Chess Moves," 1994; Raichle, 1994). As shown in Figure 2.11, patterns of activity also appear to differ in the brains of people who are and are not diagnosed with schizophrenia. Researchers are exploring the meanings and potential applications of these differences.

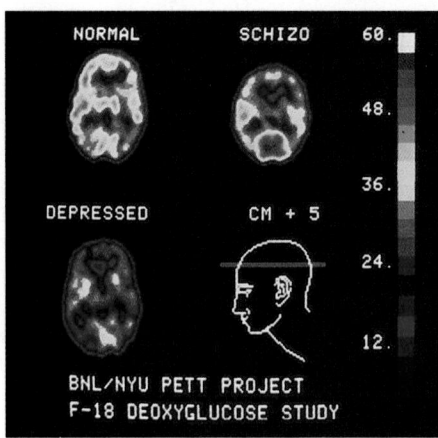

BNL/NYU PETT PROJECT
F-18 DEOXYGLUCOSE STUDY

MRI. A third imaging technique is **magnetic resonance imaging** (MRI). In MRI, the person lies in a powerful magnetic field and is exposed to radio waves that cause parts of the brain to emit signals that are measured from multiple angles. The PET scan assesses brain activity in terms of metabolism of glucose. MRI relies on subtle shifts in blood flow. (More blood flows to more active parts of the brain, supplying them with oxygen.) As with the CAT scan, the signals are integrated into an anatomic image (see Figure 2.12).

In *functional* or *fast MRI,* special hardware speeds the imaging process, and computer programs, in effect, turn static images into movies. Fast MRI yields sharper pictures than the PET scan (Raichle, 1994). Researchers are using fast MRI to pinpoint parts of the brain that are active when subjects engage in activities such as viewing objects of various shapes (for example, moving dots or colored stripes), pressing a lever when the name of a dangerous animal is mentioned, or reporting the first verb

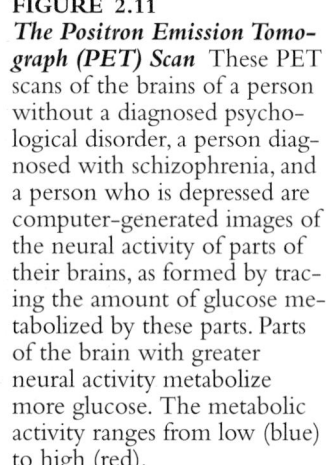

FIGURE 2.11
The Positron Emission Tomograph (PET) Scan These PET scans of the brains of a person without a diagnosed psychological disorder, a person diagnosed with schizophrenia, and a person who is depressed are computer-generated images of the neural activity of parts of their brains, as formed by tracing the amount of glucose metabolized by these parts. Parts of the brain with greater neural activity metabolize more glucose. The metabolic activity ranges from low (blue) to high (red).

Computerized axial tomography • (AX-ee-al toe-MOG-raf-fee). Formation of a computer-generated image of the anatomical details of the brain by passing a narrow X-ray beam through the head and measuring from different angles the amount of radiation that passes through. Abbreviated *CAT scan.*

Positron emission tomography • (POZZ-i-tron). Formation of a computer-generated image of the neural activity of parts of the brain by tracing the amount of glucose used by the various parts. Abbreviated *PET scan.*

Magnetic resonance imaging • (REZZ-oh-nants). Formation of a computer-generated image of the anatomy of the brain by measuring the signals emitted when the head is placed in a strong magnetic field.

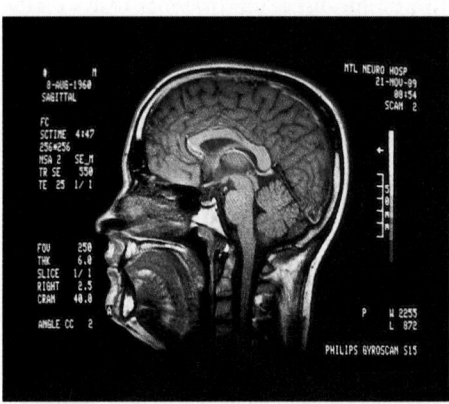

FIGURE 2.12
Magnetic Resonance Imaging (MRI) An image of the brain, as produced by MRI.

that comes to mind when researchers say a noun (Raichle, 1994).

All these methods make it clear that the mind is a manifestation of the brain. Without the brain, there is no mind. Within the brain lies the potential for self-awareness and purposeful activity. Somehow, the brain gives rise to the mind. Today, it is generally agreed that for every mental event such as a thought or a feeling there are accompanying, underlying biological events.

Reflections

Now that you have read about methods for studying the functions of the brain, reflect on the following questions:

- Before reading this section, had you believed that your mind, or sense of consciousness, dwelled within your brain? Why or why not?
- Are you aware of anyone who has had her or his brain, or another part of the body, scanned by one of the techniques discussed in this section? How was the procedure described to you? Was the discussion of these methods in this section consistent with what you had heard?

The use of some research methods, such as lesioning, raise ethical issues. To properly study behavior, psychologists must not only be skilled in the uses and limitations of research methods, they must also treat research subjects ethically.

Ethical Issues in Psychological Research and Practice

It is in our discussion of ethics that we raise the most serious questions about the Milgram studies. The participants experienced severe psychological anguish. The Milgram studies on obedience made key contributions to our understanding of the limits of human nature. In fact, it is difficult for professional psychologists to imagine a history of psychology bereft of the knowledge provided by such studies. But were the Milgram studies **ethical?**

Psychologists adhere to a number of ethical standards that are intended to promote the dignity of the individual, foster human welfare, and maintain scientific integrity (McGovern and others, 1991). They also ensure that psychologists do not undertake research methods or treatments that are harmful to study participants or clients (American Psychological Association, 1992a).

RESEARCH WITH PEOPLE

We described how Lang and his colleagues (1975) gave small doses of alcohol to college students who were social drinkers. Other researchers, however, have paid alcoholics—people who have difficulties limiting their alcohol consumption—to drink in the laboratory so that they could study their reactions and those of family members (e.g., Jacob and others, 1991). Practices such as these raise more complex ethical questions (Beutler & Kendall, 1991; Stricker, 1991). For example, paying the alcoholics to drink in the laboratory, and providing the alcohol, could be construed as encouraging them to engage in self-destructive behavior (Koocher, 1991).

Recall the signs of stress shown by the participants in the Milgram studies on obedience. They trembled, stuttered, groaned, sweated, bit their lips and dug their fingernails into their flesh. In fact, if Milgram had attempted to run his experiments in the 1990s rather than the 1960s, he might have been denied permission to do so by a university ethics review committee. In virtually all institutional settings, including colleges, hospitals, and research foundations, **ethics review committees** help researchers consider the potential harm of their methods and review proposed studies according to ethical guidelines. When such committees find that proposed research might be unacceptably harmful to participants, they may advise the researcher as to how to modify the research design to comply with ethical standards and withhold approval until the proposal has been made acceptable. Ethics review committees also weigh the potential benefits of research against the potential harm.

Today, to help avoid harming study participants, individuals must also provide **informed consent** before they participate in research programs. Having a general overview of the research and the

---

Ethical • Moral; referring to one's system of deriving standards for determining what is moral.

Ethics review committee • A group found in an institutional setting that helps researchers consider the potential harm of their methods and reviews proposed studies according to ethical guidelines.

Informed consent • The term used by psychologists to indicate that a person has agreed to participate in research after receiving information about the purposes of the study and the nature of the treatments.

Confidential • Secret; not to be disclosed.

opportunity to choose not to participate apparently gives individuals a sense of control and decreases the stress of participating (Dill and others, 1982). Is there a way in which participants in the Milgram studies could have provided informed consent? What do you think?

Psychologists treat the records of research participants and clients as **confidential.** This is because psychologists respect people's privacy and also because people are more likely to express their true thoughts and feelings when researchers or therapists keep their disclosures confidential (Blanck and others, 1992). Sometimes conflicts of interest arise, however, as when a client threatens a third party and the psychologist feels an obligation to warn the third party (Nevid and others, 1994).

Ethical standards tend to limit the types of research that psychologists may conduct. For example, how can we determine whether early separation from one's mother impairs social development? One research direction is to observe the development of children who have been separated from their mothers from an early age. It is difficult to draw conclusions from such research, however, because the same factors that led to the separation—such as family tragedy or irresponsible parents—instead of the separation itself, may have led to the observed outcomes. Scientifically, it would be more sound to run experiments in which children are purposefully separated from their mothers at an early age and compared with children who are not. Psychologists would not seriously consider such research because of ethical standards. However, experiments in which infants are purposefully separated from mothers have been run with lower animals.

The Use of Deception. Many psychological experiments cannot be run without deceiving their human participants. However, the use of deception raises ethical issues. Let us revisit the Milgram studies on obedience. You are probably skeptical enough to wonder whether the "teachers" in the Milgram study actually shocked the "learners" when the teachers pressed the levers on the console. They didn't. The only real shock in this experiment was the 45-volt sample given to the teachers. Its purpose was to lend credibility to the procedure.

The learners in the experiment were actually confederates of the experimenter. They had not answered the newspaper ads but were in on the truth from the start. "Teachers" were the only real study participants. They were led to believe that they were chosen at random for the teacher role, but the choosing was rigged so that newspaper-ad recruits would always become teachers.

As you can imagine, many psychologists have debated the ethics of deceiving participants in the Milgram studies (Fisher & Fyrberg, 1994). According to the American Psychological Association's (1992a) *Ethical Principles of Psychologists and Code of Conduct,* psychologists may use deception only when they believe that the benefits of the research outweigh its potential harm, when they believe that the individuals might have been willing to participate if they had understood the benefits of the research, and when participants receive an explanation afterward. Regardless of the propriety of Milgram's research, we must acknowledge that it has highlighted some hard truths about human nature.

Return to the Lang (Lang and others, 1975) study on alcohol and aggression. In this study, the researchers (1) misinformed participants about the beverage they were drinking and (2) misled individuals into believing that they were giving other participants electric shock when they, like the participants in the Milgram studies, were actually only pressing switches on a dead control board. (Pressing these switches was the operational definition of aggression in the study.) In the Lang study, students who believed they had drunk vodka were "more aggressive"—that is, selected higher levels of shock—than students who believed they had not. The actual content of the beverages was immaterial.

The Lang study, like the Milgram studies, could not have been run without deception. Foiling participants' expectations was crucial to the experiment. One can debate whether the potential benefits of the research outweigh the possible harm of deception.

Yet some psychologists oppose using deception—period. Diana Baumrind (1985)

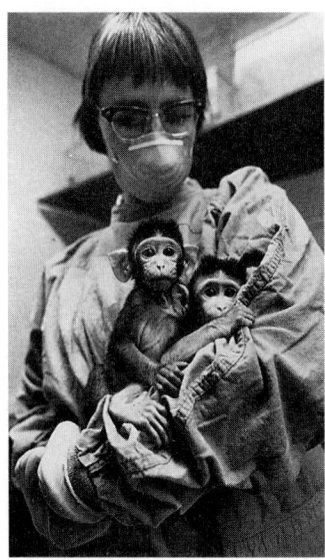

The Ethics of Animal Research. Now and then, psychologists and other scientists harm animals to answer research questions that may yield important benefits for people. Justifying such harm poses a major ethical dilemma.

Debrief • To elicit information about a just-completed procedure.
Breathalyzer • A device that measures the quantity of alcohol in the body by analyzing the breath.

argues, for example, that deception-based research can harm not only research participants but also the reputation of the profession of psychology. In a study that supports Baumrind's views, one group of students participated in experiments in which they were deceived. Afterward, they regarded psychologists as being less trustworthy than did students who were not deceived (Smith & Richardson, 1983). Baumrind argues that deception might eventually cause the public to lose trust in psychologists and other professionals.

In any event, many studies continue to employ deception (Adair and others, 1985). Psychological ethics require that research participants who are deceived be **debriefed** afterward. Debriefing helps to eliminate misconceptions and anxieties about the research and to leave participants with their dignity intact (Blanck and others, 1992). After the Lang study was completed, for example, the participants were informed of the deceptions and of the rationale for them. Participants who had actually drunk alcohol were given coffee and a **breathalyzer** test so that the researchers could be sure they were not leaving the laboratory while intoxicated.

Truth or Fiction Revisited. *It is true that psychologists would not be able to carry out certain kinds of research without deceiving participants as to the purposes and methods of the studies.* Deception may be required to prevent participants from purposefully distorting the outcomes of the research. Psychological ethics require that psychologists weigh the potential value of research findings against the possible harm that may be done by deceiving participants.

Psychologists use deception in research only when the research could not be run without it and when they believe that the benefits will outweigh the harm.

RESEARCH WITH ANIMALS

Psychologists and other scientists frequently turn to animals to conduct research that cannot be carried out with humans (Segal, 1993). For example, experiments on the effects of early separation from the mother have been done with monkeys and other animals. Such research has helped psychologists investigate the for-

mation of parent–child bonds of attachment (see Chapter 11).

Experiments with infant monkeys highlight some of the dilemmas faced by psychologists and other scientists who contemplate potentially harmful research. Psychologists and biologists who study the workings of the brain destroy sections of the brains of laboratory animals to learn how they influence behavior. For instance, a lesion in one part of a brain structure will cause a rat to overeat (see Chapter 10). A lesion elsewhere will cause the rat to go on a crash diet. Psychologists generalize to people from experiments such as these in the hope that we may find solutions to persistent human problems such as eating disorders. Proponents of the use of animals in research argue that major advances in medicine and psychology could not have taken place without them (Fowler, 1992; Martinez, 1992; Pardes and others, 1991).

Psychologists must still face the ethical dilemma of harming animals. As with humans, psychologists follow the principle that animals should be harmed only when there is no alternative and they believe that the benefits of the research will justify the harm (American Psychological Association, 1992a).

Reflections

Now that you have read about psychological ethics, reflect on the following questions:

- The Milgram studies were conducted prior to the advent of ethics review committees. (In fact, studies like Milgram's contributed to the social pressure to establish such committees.) If you were on an ethics review committee evaluating Milgram's proposed research, would you approve of his methods? Why or why not? If you were chairing an ethics review committee and Milgram presented his plans for research to you, what kinds of questions would you have asked him? Why? Would you have insisted on some changes in his methods? What changes? Would you ultimately have allowed him to conduct his studies? Why or why not?

- If a client in therapy were to tell his psychologist that he was thinking of hurting you, should the psychologist break the confidence and tell you about it? Why or why not?

- Do you believe that it is ethical to harm lower animals in conducting research when the results may be beneficial to people? Why or why not? Do you think that there are limits to the amount of harm to which animals should be exposed? What are they?

Summary

1. **What is the scientific method?** The scientific method is an organized way of going about expanding and refining knowledge. Psychologists usually begin by formulating a research question, which may be reworded as a hypothesis. Psychologists draw conclusions about their research questions or the accuracy of their hypotheses on the basis of their research observations or findings.

2. **How do psychologists use samples to represent populations?** Samples must accurately represent the population they are intended to reflect. The individuals who are studied are referred to as a sample. A sample is a segment of a population. Women's groups and health professionals argue that there is a historic bias in favor of conducting research with men. Research samples have also tended to underrepresent minority ethnic groups in the population.

3. **What kinds of sampling are undertaken to ensure that samples represent populations?** In a random sample, each member of a population has an equal chance of being selected to participate. Researchers can also use a stratified sample, which is drawn so that identified subgroups in the population are represented proportionately in the sample.

4. **What is volunteer bias?** The concept behind volunteer bias is that people who offer to participate in research studies differ systematically from people who do not.

5. **What methods of observation are used by psychologists?** These include the case-study, survey, testing, naturalistic-observation, and laboratory-observation methods. Case studies gather information about the lives of individuals or small groups. The survey method uses interviews, questionnaires, or public records to gather information about behavior that cannot be observed directly. Psychological tests are used to measure various traits and characteristics among a population. Useful tests must be reliable and valid. Reliability is a test's consistency. Validity is the degree to which a test measures what it is supposed to measure. The naturalistic-observation method observes behavior where it happens—in the "field." The laboratory-observation method observes behavior in a controlled environment.

6. **What is correlational research?** Correlational research reveals relationships between variables, but it does not determine cause and effect. In a positive correlation, variables increase simultaneously. A correlation coefficient of about $+0.90$ is considered adequate for test reliability. A correlation coefficient of about $+0.60$ to $+0.70$ is considered adequate for test validity. In a negative correlation, one variable increases while the other decreases.

7. **What is the experimental method?** Experiments are used to seek cause and effect—that is, the effects of independent variables on dependent variables. Experimental groups partake of a treatment, while control groups do not. Blinds and double blinds may be used to control for the effects of the expectations of the participants and the researchers themselves. Results can be generalized only to populations that have been adequately represented in the research samples.

8. **What are the ethical standards of psychologists?** Ethical standards are intended to prevent mistreatment of humans and animals in the course of research. Limits are set on the discomfort that may be imposed on animals. Records of human behavior are kept confidential. Human study participants are required to give informed consent prior to participating in research.

Psychology and Modern Life

Science Versus Pseudoscience

This chapter explores the methods used by psychologists. We have considered the scientific method. We have seen that psychologists are skeptical critical thinkers and that they insist upon evidence before they will accept people's claims and arguments as to what is truth and what is fiction.

The "Psychology and Modern Life" section considers a number of approaches to understanding and influencing behavior that are less than scientific. Why bother? you ask. The answer is that pseudoscience beckons us from the magazines and tabloids at nearly every checkout counter in every supermarket. Each week, there are 10 new sightings of Elvis and 10 new encounters with extraterrestrials. There are 10 new "absolutely proven effective" ways to take off weight and 10 new ways to beat stress and depression. There are 10 new ways to tell if your partner has been cheating and, of course, 10 new predictions by astrologers and psychics.

In this section we shall focus on the astrologers and the psychics. But before reading about these pseudoscientific approaches to behavior, take the following brief personality test. Indicate whether each item is mostly true or false for you. Then read the report that follows to learn everything you always wanted to know about your personality but were too intelligent to ask.

T	F	1. I can't unclasp my hands.
T	F	2. I often mistake my hands for food.
T	F	3. I never like room temperature.
T	F	4. My throat is closer than it seems.
T	F	5. Likes and dislikes are among my favorites.
T	F	6. I've lost all sensation in my throat.
T	F	7. I try to swallow at least three times a day.
T	F	8. My squirrels don't know where I am tonight.
T	F	9. Walls impede my progress.
T	F	10. My toes are numbered.
T	F	11. My beaver won't go near the water.

Total number of items marked true (T): _____

If your total number of items marked true was between 0 and 11, the following personality report applies to you:

> The personality test you have taken has been found to predict inner potential for change. . . . In the past it has been shown that people with similar personality scores . . . have a strong capacity for change. . . . You have a great deal of unused potential you have not yet turned to your advantage. . . .
>
> The test also suggests that you display ability for personal integration and many latent strengths, as well as the ability to maintain a balance between your inner impulses and the demands of outer reality. Therefore, your personality is such that you have a strong potential for improvement. (Halperin & Snyder, 1979, pp. 142–143)

That's you all right, isn't it? I shouldn't be surprised if you thought it sounded familiar. Psychologists Keith Halperin and C. R. Snyder (1979) administered a phony 50-item personality questionnaire to women in an introductory psychology course at the University of Kansas. The items weren't as silly as the ones you answered, which were thrown together by Daniel Wegner (1979) and some friends during their graduate school days. Still, the test was meaningless. The students then rated the same personality report, which included the paragraphs just cited, for accuracy. The average rating was "quite accurate"!

Truth or Fiction Revisited. *It is true that a psychologist could write a believable personality report about you without interviewing you, testing you, or even knowing who you are.* Such reports are rather generalized, however; that is, they have "something for everyone." The tendency to believe them has been termed the *Barnum effect.*

Women who had read the phony report and women who had not then participated in a therapy program conducted by the researchers. Believe it or not, women who had obtained the report, which underscored their capacity for change, showed greater improvement from the treatment than women who had not. When you believe that you have the capacity to improve your lot—when your self-efficacy expectations are raised—you are apparently more likely to succeed.

THE BARNUM EFFECT

The tendency to believe a generalized (but phony) personality report has been labeled the Barnum effect after circus magnate P. T. Barnum, who once declared that a good circus had a "little something for everybody." It is probably the Barnum effect—the tendency for general personality reports to have a "little something for everybody"—that allows fortune-tellers to make a living. That is, most of us have enough characteristics in common so that a fortune-teller's "revelations" about our personalities may have the ring of truth.

ON READING TEA LEAVES, BIRD DROPPINGS, PALMS, AND THE STARS

Most of us have personality traits in common. But what do tea leaves, bird droppings, palms (within your hands, not on the tropical sands), and the stars have in common? Let us see.

P. T. Barnum also once declared, "There's a sucker born every minute." The tendency to believe generalized personality reports has made people vulnerable to fakers and phonies throughout history. It enriches the pocketbooks of people who offer to "read their personalities" and predict their futures based on patterns of tea leaves or of bird droppings (check Shakespeare's play, *Julius Caesar*). These particular bogus methods of "personality measurement" and forecasting are not particularly fashionable in the United States today, but reading palms, consulting ghosts through "spiritualists," and studying the configurations of the stars and planets through astrology are. Now and then we also hear of "psychics" who are recruited by police departments to help find missing persons or criminals (no, we don't usually hear that they have successfully located them). Some psychics claim to be in contact with the "spirit world," as in the film *Ghost* (see Figure 2.13). The film *Ghost,* of course, was an exercise in wish fulfillment, not in science.

FIGURE 2.13
A Scene from **Ghost** In the film, Whoopi Goldberg portrayed a "psychic" who helped deceased Patrick Swayze get in touch with his girlfriend, Demi Moore. Despite its appeal, and Whoopi Goldberg's fine Academy Award-winning performance, the movie was an exercise in wish fulfillment, not in science.

Astrology has been popular for centuries (Maher & Maher, 1994). Gallup and Newport (1991) report that one person out of four in the United States believes in astrology. Another one in four to five is not sure. Put it this way: In an age in which science has proved itself capable of making significant contributions to people's daily lives and health, more people may be likely to check their horoscope than to seek scientific information when they have a decision to make.

Astrology is based on the notion that the positions of the sun, the moon, and the stars affect human temperament and human affairs (Maher & Maher, 1994). For example, personality types based on astrology include the jovial, the saturnine, and the martial. People born under the sign of Jupiter are believed to be jovial, or full of playful good humor. People born under Saturn are thought to be gloomy and morose (saturnine). And people born under Mars are believed to be warlike (martial). One can supposedly also foretell the future by studying the positions of these bodies. Astrologers maintain that the positions of these heavenly bodies at the time of our births determined our personalities and our destinies. They prepare forecasts called *horoscopes* that are based on the month during which we were born and which indicate whether it is safe for us to undertake various activities on various days. If you get involved with someone who asks for your "sign" (for example, Aquarius or Taurus), he or she is inquiring about your birth date in astrological terms. Astrologers claim that your sign, which reflects the month during which you were born, indicates whom you will be compatible with. You may have been wondering whether you should date someone of another religion. If you start to follow astrology, you may also be wondering whether it is safe for a Sagittarius to be dating a Pisces or a Gemini.

Psychologists consider astrology to be a pseudoscience ("false science"), not a genuine science. Yet astrology has many millions of adherents. How do we account for the allure of astrology and other pseudosciences? What can we tell people who believe in them?

Supporters of astrology tend to provide arguments such as the following:

- Astrology has been practiced for many centuries and is a time-honored aspect of human history, tradition, and culture (Crowe, 1990).

- Astrology seems to provide a path to the core of meaning in the universe for people who are uneducated, and for a fortunate few with limited means, a road to riches.

- People in high positions in government have followed the advice of astrologers. (Nancy Reagan, wife of former president Ronald Reagan, is reported to have consulted an astrologer in arranging her husband's schedule.)

- The tides, which are caused by just one heavenly body (the moon), are powerful enough to sway the swells of the seas. The pulls of heavenly bodies are therefore easily capable of affecting people's destinies (Crowe, 1990).

- Astrology is a special art and not a science. Therefore, it is inappropriate to subject astrology to the rigors of scientific testing (Crowe, 1990).

- Astrology has been shown to work (Crowe, 1990).

Refer to the principles of critical thinking that we elaborated in Chapter 1 as you consider each of the claims of astrologers. For example, does the fact that there may be a long-standing tradition in astrology affect its accuracy or scientific credibility? Does Nancy Reagan's (or anyone else's) possible belief in astrology affect its accuracy or scientific credibility? Are the tides of the seas comparable to human personality and human destiny?

Remember that psychology is an *empirical* science. We noted that within an empirical science, beliefs about the behavior of cosmic rays, chemical compounds, cells, people—or about the import of bird droppings or the configuration of the stars—must be supported by evidence. Persuasive arguments and reference to authority figures are not deemed adequate as scientific evidence (Kimble, 1994). Psychologists and other scientists are skeptical, critical thinkers.

Astrologers have made specific forecasts of events, and their accuracy—or lack of accuracy—has provided researchers with a means of evaluating astrology. It turns out that astrological predictions are no more likely to occur than predictions based on pure chance (Crowe, 1990; Dean, 1987; Kelly and others, 1989). That is scientific fact, but let me ask you a question: Will followers of astrology be dissuaded by facts? Perhaps some will. Perhaps a majority would if they were repeatedly required to explain why they still believed in astrology despite the inaccuracy of astrological forecasts. But cognitive dissonance theory (which is discussed in Chapter 10) suggests that the faith of some adherents to astrology will be *strengthened* when predictions are not borne out. (Perhaps your instructor will permit you to glance ahead for an explanation.)

Let us now put astrology aside. (Have you put astrology aside?) Let us turn to the fascinating realm of extrasensory perception (ESP), which has had a mixed reception among psychologists. Most psychologists consider the notion of ESP to be as false and misleading as any pseudoscience. Some psychologists, however, believe that there may be something to it. One thing that all psychologists will agree upon is that a key journal that publishes findings in ESP is the *Journal of Parapsychology*. Note that the term *para*psychology means "at the side of" or "alongside" psychology. That is, whether parapsychology has a place within psychology is a highly controversial issue. Let us see why that is so.

EXTRASENSORY PERCEPTION

Imagine the wealth you could amass if you had precognition, that is, if you were able to perceive future events. Perhaps you would check next month's stock market reports and know what to buy or sell. Or you could bet on the races and other sporting events with confidence.

Or think of the power you would have if you were capable of psychokinesis, that is, of mentally manipulating or moving objects. You may have gotten a glimpse of the types of things that could happen with psychokinesis in films like *Carrie* and *The Fury*.

Precognition and psychokinesis are two concepts associated with extrasensory perception (ESP) or psi communication. ESP by definition refers to the perception of objects or events through means other than

sensory organs. Psi communication refers to the transfer of information through an irregular or unusual process—not the usual senses. Two other theoretical forms of ESP are telepathy, or the direct transmission of thoughts or ideas from person to person, and clairvoyance, or the perception of objects that do not stimulate the sensory organs. An example of clairvoyance is "seeing" what card is to be dealt next, although it is still in the deck and unseen even by the dealer.

ESP, in short, seems to tap the same core of pseudoscientific belief that is tapped by astrology and similar endeavors. Only one psychologist in three believes that psi communication is likely to exist (Bem & Honorton, 1994). Yet more than half of college professors who teach other social sciences, natural sciences, or the arts allow that there might be something to it (Bem & Honorton, 1994). Many psychologists are skeptical because ESP smacks of the supernatural, even the occult. Some connect ESP with the nightclub act in which a blindfolded "clairvoyant" calls out the contents of an audience member's pocketbook. Other psychologists, however, believe that there is nothing wrong with investigating ESP. The issue for them is not whether ESP (or any "pseudoscience") is sensationalistic, but whether it can be demonstrated in the laboratory.

Perhaps the best known of the respected ESP researchers was the late Joseph Banks Rhine of Duke University. Rhine studied ESP for several decades, beginning in the late 1920s. In a typical experiment in clairvoyance, Rhine would use a pack of 25 Zener cards, which contained 5 sets of the 5 cards shown in Figure 2.14. Pigeons pecking patterns at random to indicate

FIGURE 2.14
Zener Cards Zener cards have been used in research on clairvoyance. Study participants are asked to predict which card will be turned up.

which was about to be turned up would select the correct one 20% of the time. Rhine found that some people guessed correctly significantly more often than the 20% chance rate and concluded that they may have had some degree of ESP.

A preferred contemporary method for studying telepathy is the Ganzfeld procedure. In this method, one participant acts as a "sender," and the other, a "receiver." The sender views randomly selected visual stimuli such as photographs or videotapes, while the receiver, whose eyes and ears are covered, in another room, tries to mentally tune in to the sender. After a session, the receiver is shown four visual stimuli and asked to select the one that was transmitted by the sender. A person guessing which stimulus was "transmitted" would be correct 25% of the time (one time in four) by chance alone. An analysis of 28 experiments using the Ganzfeld procedure, however, found that receivers correctly identified the visual stimulus 38% of the time (Honorton, 1985), a percentage highly unlikely to be due to chance. A series of 11 more-recent studies by Honorton and his colleagues that use the Ganzfeld procedure found comparable results (Bem & Honorton, 1994; Honorton and others, 1990).

Overall, however, there are many reasons for skepticism of ESP. One is the "file-drawer problem." Just as buyers of those supermarket magazines tend to forget "psy-chics'" predictions that fail (they "file" them away), ESP researchers are less likely to report results that fail (or to get them published!). Therefore, we would expect unusual findings (like an individual with a high success rate at psi-communication tasks over a period of several days) to surface in the literature. In other words, if you flip a coin indefinitely, eventually you will flip 10 heads in a row. The odds against this are high, but if you report your eventual success and do not report the weeks of failure, you give the impression that you have unique coin-flipping ability. (You may even fool yourself.)

Second, it has not been easy to replicate experiments in ESP. Hyman (1994) acknowledges that the studies reported by Honorton (Bem & Honorton, 1994; Hon-

orton and others, 1990) are the most tightly controlled studies to date. However, he argues that the studies need to be replicated by other researchers before they are granted credibility. People who have "shown" ESP with one researcher have failed to do so with another or have refused to participate in a study with another. Let's make this point a bit more strongly: From all of these studies, *not one person has emerged who can reliably show psi communication from one occasion to another, and with any researcher.* Science, in other words, has not identified one indisputable telepath or clairvoyant.

Third, the history of research into ESP has been plagued by poor methodology (Bem & Honorton, 1994; Hyman, 1994). There are also instances of out-and-out fraud, as in tampering with data or equipment.

For these and other reasons, most psychologists still do not grant ESP research much credibility. Although some psychologists attempt to study ESP scientifically, many critics consider the area to be another pseudoscience. To be fair, science has shown, again and again, that "there are more things in heaven and earth" than there were once thought to be. But science has not yet shown that ESP is one of them.

Truth or Fiction Revisited. *It is not true that some people can read other people's minds.* Of course, we can make educated guesses about the feelings of the people whom we know well. We may also be able to interpret other people's smiles and frowns. But it has not been shown that we can directly read other people's minds.

Reflections

Now that you have read the section on science versus pseudoscience, reflect on the following questions:

- Do you know people who believe in astrology or ghosts? How do their beliefs affect their lives? How do they seem to differ from people who are more scientifically oriented?
- Has your reading of the section on science versus pseudoscience affected your personal beliefs? If so, in what way?

NOTES

3

Biology and Behavior

Truth or Fiction?

_____ Some cells in your body stretch all the way down your back to your big toe.

_____ Messages travel in the brain by means of electricity.

_____ Our bodies produce natural painkillers that are more powerful than morphine.

_____ The human brain is larger than that of any other animal.

_____ Fear can give you indigestion.

_____ If a surgeon were to stimulate a certain part of your brain electrically, you might swear in court that someone had stroked your leg.

_____ Rats will learn to do things that result in a "reward" of a burst of electricity in the brain.

_____ Zookeepers who want to have baby girls or boys (crocodiles, that is) need only control the temperature at which the eggs develop.

_____ A child can have blue eyes even when both parents have brown eyes.

_____ Alzheimer's disease is a normal part of growing old.

_____ PMS impairs the academic, occupational, or social functioning of the majority of college women.

_____ Women can do little about menstrual discomfort other than "tough it out."

Outline

Truth or Fiction?
Neurons: Into the Fabulous Forest
The Makeup of Neurons
The Neural Impulse: Let Us "Sing the
  Body Electric"
The Synapse
Neurotransmitters
The Nervous System
The Central Nervous System
The Peripheral Nervous System
The Cerebral Cortex
The Geography of the Cerebral Cortex
Thought, Language, and the Cortex
Left Brain, Right Brain?
Handedness: Is It Gauche to Be Left-
  Handed?
Split-Brain Experiments: When
  Hemispheres Stop Communicating
Electrical Stimulation of the Brain
  Psychology in the New Millennium:
    And Now—Brainman?
The Endocrine System
A Guided Tour of the Endocrine System
Heredity: The Nature of Nature
Genes and Chromosomes
  Psychology in the New Millennium:
    The Human Genome Project
Kinship Studies
Dominant and Recessive Traits
Experiments in Selective Breeding
Summary
Psychology and Modern Life
Alzheimer's Disease
Premenstrual Syndrome
  Psychology in a World of Diversity:
    Cross-Cultural Perspectives on
    Menstruation

According to the big-bang theory, our universe began with an enormous explosion that sent countless particles hurtling into every corner of space. For billions of years, these particles have been forming immense gas clouds. Galaxies and solar systems have been condensing from the clouds, sparkling for some eons, then winking out. Human beings have only recently come into existence on an unremarkable rock circling an average star in a standard spiral galaxy.

Since the beginning of time, the universe has been in flux. Change has brought life and death and countless challenges. Some creatures have adapted successfully to these challenges. Others have not met the challenges and have become extinct, falling back into the distant mists of time. Some have left fossil records. Others have disappeared without a trace.

At first, human survival on planet Earth required a greater struggle than it does today. We fought predators like the leopard. We foraged across parched lands for food. We might have warred with creatures very much like ourselves—creatures who have since become extinct. We prevailed. The human species has survived and continues to transmit its unique traits through the generations by means of genetic material whose chemical codes are only now being cracked.

Yet, what is handed down through the generations? The answer is biological, or physiological, structures. There is no evidence that we inherit thoughts or ideas or images or plans. We do inherit physiological structures. They serve as the material base for our observable behaviors, emotions, and cognitions (our thoughts, images, and plans).

Biological psychologists (or psychobiologists) work at the interfaces of psychology and biology (Dewsbury, 1991). They study the ways in which our mental processes and observable behaviors are linked to physiological structures and biological processes. In recent years, biological psychologists have been unlocking the mysteries of:

1. *Neurons.* Neurons are the building blocks of the nervous system. There are billions upon billions of neurons in the body—perhaps as many as there are stars in the Milky Way galaxy.

2. *The nervous system.* Neurons combine to form the structures of the nervous system. The nervous system has branches that are responsible for muscle movement, perception, automatic functions such as breathing and the secretion of hormones, and psychological phenomena such as thoughts and feelings.

3. *The cerebral cortex.* The cerebral cortex is the large, wrinkled mass inside your head that you think of as your brain. Actually, it is only one part of the brain—the part that is the most characteristically human.

4. *The endocrine system.* Through secretion of hormones, the endocrine system controls functions ranging from growth in children to production of milk in nursing women.

5. *Heredity.* Within every cell of your body there are about 100,000 genes. These chemical substances determine just what type of creature you are, from the color of your hair to your body temperature to the fact that you have arms and legs rather than wings or fins.

Neurons: Into the Fabulous Forest

Let us begin our journey in a fabulous forest of nerve cells, or **neurons,** that can be visualized as having branches, trunks, and roots—something like trees. As in other forests, many nerve cells lie alongside one another like a thicket of trees. Neurons can also lie end to end, however, with their "roots" intertwined with the "branches" of neurons that lie below. Trees receive water and nutrients from the soil. Neurons receive "messages" from a number of sources such as other neurons, pressure on the skin, and light, and they can pass these messages along.

Neurons communicate by means of chemicals called **neurotransmitters.** Neurons release neurotransmitters that are taken up by other neurons, muscles, and glands. Neurotransmitters cause chemical changes in the receiving neuron so that the message can travel along its "trunk," be translated back into neurotransmitters in its "branches," and then travel through the small spaces between neurons to be received by the "roots" of yet other neurons.

Each neuron transmits and coordinates messages in the form of neural impulses. We are born with more than 100 billion neurons (Shatz, 1992), most of which are found in the brain. The nervous system also contains **glial cells.** Glial cells nourish and insulate neurons, direct their growth, and remove waste products from the nervous system. But neurons occupy center stage in the nervous system. The messages transmitted by neurons somehow account for phenomena ranging from perception of an itch from a mosquito bite to the coordination of a skier's vision and muscles to the composition of a concerto to the solution of an algebraic equation.

THE MAKEUP OF NEURONS

Neurons vary according to their functions and their location. Some in the brain are only a fraction of an inch in length, whereas others in the legs are several feet long. Every neuron is a single nerve cell with a cell body (or **soma**), dendrites, and

Pablo Picasso at Work. The great artist's nervous system was composed of neurons like those of other people. Biological psychologists delve into how our behavior and mental processes are linked to the functioning of the nervous system and other biological processes.

an axon (see Figure 3.1). The cell body contains the nucleus of the cell. The cell body uses oxygen and nutrients to generate energy to carry out the work of the cell. Anywhere from a few to several hundred short fibers, or **dendrites,** extend rootlike from the cell body to receive incoming messages from thousands of adjoining neurons. Each neuron has one **axon** that extends trunklike from the cell body. Axons are very thin, but those that carry messages from the toes to the spinal cord extend for several feet.

Truth or Fiction Revisited. *It is true that some cells in your body stretch all the way down your back to your big toe.* These cells are neurons. Question: How can cells that are this long be "microscopic"?

Like tree trunks, axons too can divide and extend in different directions. Axons end

Neuron • (NEW-ron). A nerve cell.

Neurotransmitters • (new-row-tranz-MIT-ters). Chemical substances involved in the transmission of neural impulses from one neuron to another.

Glial cells • (GLEE-al). Cells that nourish and insulate neurons, direct their growth, and remove waste products from the nervous system.

Soma • (SO-muh). A cell body.

Dendrites • Rootlike structures, attached to the soma of a neuron, that receive impulses from other neurons.

Axon • (AX-on). A long, thin part of a neuron that transmits impulses to other neurons from branching structures called *terminals.*

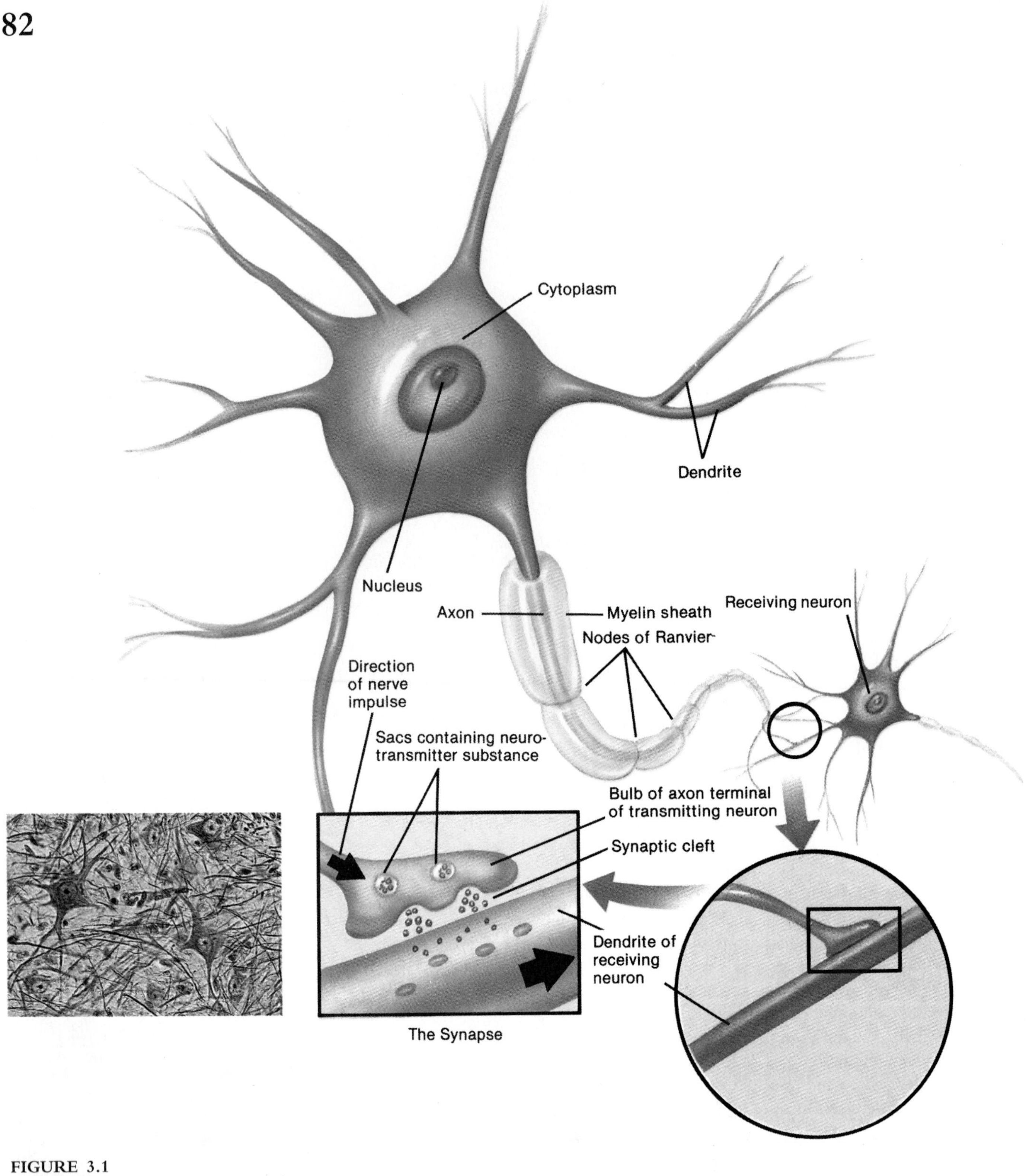

82

Cytoplasm

Dendrite

Nucleus

Axon — Myelin sheath

Nodes of Ranvier

Receiving neuron

Direction of nerve impulse

Sacs containing neuro-transmitter substance

Bulb of axon terminal of transmitting neuron

Synaptic cleft

Dendrite of receiving neuron

The Synapse

FIGURE 3.1

Spotlight on the Anatomy of a Neuron "Messages" enter neurons through dendrites, are transmitted along the trunklike axon, and then are sent through axon terminals to muscles, glands, and other neurons. A neuron relays its message to another neuron across a junction called a synapse, which consists of an axon terminal from the transmitting neuron, the membrane of the receiving neuron, and a small gap between the neurons referred to as the synaptic cleft. Axon terminals contain sacs of chemicals called neurotransmitters. Neurotransmitters are re-leased by the transmitting neuron into the synaptic cleft, and many of them are taken up by receptor sites on the dendrites of the receiving neuron. Some neurotransmitters (called "excitatory") influence receiving neurons in the direc-tion of firing; others (called "inhibitory") influence them in the direction of *not* firing. To date, a few dozen possible neuro-transmitters have been identified.

in smaller branching structures called **terminals.** At the tips of the axon terminals are swellings called **knobs.** Neurons carry messages in one direction only: from the dendrites or cell body through the axon to the axon terminals. The messages are then transmitted from the axon terminals to other neurons.

As a child matures, the axons of neurons grow in length, and the dendrites and axon terminals proliferate, creating vast interconnected networks for the transmission of complex messages. The number of glial cells also increases as the nervous system develops, contributing to its dense appearance.

Myelin. The axons of many neurons are wrapped tightly with white, fatty **myelin sheaths.** The fat insulates the axon from electrically charged atoms, or ions, found in the fluids that encase the nervous system. Myelin minimizes leakage of the electric current being carried along the axon, thus allowing messages to be conducted more efficiently. Myelin does not uniformly coat the surface of an axon. It is missing at points called **nodes of Ranvier,** where the axon is exposed. Because of the insulation provided by myelin, neural messages, or impulses, travel rapidly from node to node.

Myelination is part of the maturation process that leads to the abilities to crawl and walk during the first year. Babies are not physiologically "ready" to engage in visual–motor coordination and other activities until the coating process reaches certain levels. In the disease multiple sclerosis, myelin is replaced with a hard fibrous tissue that throws off the timing of nerve impulses and disrupts muscular control. Affliction of neurons that control breathing can result in suffocation.

Afferent and Efferent Neurons. If someone steps on your big toe, the sensation is registered by receptors or sensory neurons near the surface of your skin. Then it is transmitted to the spinal cord and brain through **afferent neurons,** which are perhaps 2 to 3 feet long. In the brain, subsequent messages might be buffeted about by associative neurons that are

only a few thousandths of an inch long. You experience the pain through this process and perhaps entertain some rather nasty thoughts about the perpetrator, who is now apologizing and begging for understanding. Long before you arrive at any logical conclusions, however, motor neurons **(efferent neurons)** send messages to your foot so that you withdraw it and begin an impressive hopping routine. Other efferent neurons stimulate glands so that your heart is now beating more rapidly, you are sweating, and the hair on the back of your arms has become erect! Being a sport, you say, "Oh, it's nothing." But considering all the neurons involved, it really is something, isn't it?

In case you think that afferent and efferent neurons will be hard to distinguish because they sound pretty much the SAME to you, remember that they *are* the "SAME." That is, *S*ensory = *A*fferent, and *M*otor = *E*fferent. But don't tell your professor I let you in on this **mnemonic** device.

THE NEURAL IMPULSE: LET US "SING THE BODY ELECTRIC"[1]

In the 18th century, Italian physiologist Luigi Galvani (1737–1798) conducted a shocking experiment in a rainstorm. While his neighbors had the sense to remain indoors, Galvani and his wife were out on the porch connecting lightning rods to the heads of dissected frogs whose legs were connected by wire to a well of water. When lightning blazed above, the frogs' muscles contracted repeatedly and violently. This is not a recommended way to prepare frogs' legs. Galvani was demonstrating that the messages **(neural impulses)** that travel along neurons are electrochemical in nature.

Neural impulses travel somewhere between 2 (in nonmyelinated neurons) and 225 miles an hour (in myelinated neurons). This speed is not impressive when compared with that of an electric current in a toaster oven or a lamp, which can travel at the speed of light—over 186,000 miles per second. Distances in the body are short,

MINILECTURE: THE NEURON

Terminals • Small structures at the tips of axons.

Knobs • Swellings at the ends of terminals. Also referred to as *bulbs* or *buttons.*

Myelin sheath • (MY-uh-lin). A fatty substance that encases and insulates axons, facilitating transmission of neural impulses.

Node of Ranvier • A noninsulated segment of a myelinated axon.

Afferent neurons • Neurons that transmit messages from sensory receptors to the spinal cord and brain. Also called *sensory neurons.*

Efferent neurons • Neurons that transmit messages from the brain or spinal cord to muscles and glands. Also called *motor neurons.*

Mnemonic • (neh-MON-nick). Aiding memory, usually by linking chunks of new information to well-known schemes.

Neural impulse • (NEW-ral). The electrochemical discharge of a nerve cell, or neuron.

---

[1] From "I Sing the Body Electric," a poem by Walt Whitman.

MINILECTURE:
GRADED
POTENTIALS
AND ACTION
POTENTIALS

Polarize • To ready a neuron for firing by creating an internal negative charge in relation to the body fluid outside the cell membrane.

Resting potential • The electrical potential across the neural membrane when it is not responding to other neurons.

Depolarize • To reduce the resting potential of a cell membrane from about − 70 millivolts toward zero.

Action potential • The electrical impulse that provides the basis for the conduction of a neural impulse along an axon of a neuron.

All-or-none principle • The fact that a neuron fires an impulse of the same strength whenever its action potential is triggered.

Absolute refractory period • A phase following firing during which a neuron's action potential cannot be triggered.

Relative refractory period • A phase following the absolute refractory period during which a neuron will fire in response to stronger-than-usual messages.

FIGURE 3.2
The Neural Impulse When a section of a neuron is stimulated by other neurons, the cell membrane becomes permeable to sodium ions so that an action potential of about +40 millivolts is induced. This action potential is transmitted along the axon. Eventually the neuron fires (or fails to fire) according to the all-or-none principle.

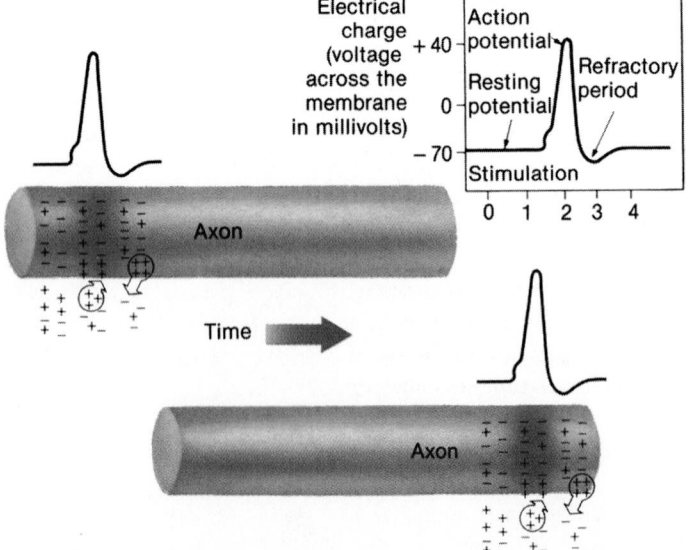

however, and a message will travel from a toe to the brain in perhaps 1/50th of a second.

An Electrochemical Process. The process by which neural impulses travel is electrochemical. Chemical changes take place within neurons that cause an electric charge to be transmitted along their lengths. In a resting state, when a neuron is not being stimulated by its neighbors, there are relatively greater numbers of positively charged sodium (Na+) ions and negatively charged chloride (Cl−) ions in the body fluid outside the neuron than in the fluid within the neuron. Positively charged potassium (K+) ions are more plentiful inside, but there are many other negative ions inside that are not balanced by negative ions on the outside, lending the inside an overall negative charge in relation to the outside. The difference in electrical charge **polarizes** the neuron with a negative **resting potential** of about −70 millivolts in relation to the body fluid outside the cell membrane.

When an area on the surface of the resting neuron is adequately stimulated by other neurons, the cell membrane in the area changes its permeability to allow sodium ions to enter. As a consequence,

the area of entry becomes positively charged, or **depolarized** with respect to the outside (Figure 3.2). The permeability of the cell membrane changes again, allowing no more sodium ions to enter.

The inside of the cell at the disturbed area has an **action potential** of 110 millivolts. This action potential, added to the −70 millivolts that characterize the resting potential, brings the membrane voltage to a positive charge of +40 millivolts. This inner change causes the next section of the cell to become permeable to sodium ions. At the same time, potassium ions are being pumped out of the area of the cell that was previously affected, which then returns to its resting potential. In this way, the neural impulse is transmitted continuously along an axon that is not myelinated. Because the impulse is created anew as it progresses, its strength does not change. Neural impulses are conducted more rapidly along myelinated axons because they jump from node to node.

Truth or Fiction Revisited. *It is true that messages travel in the brain by means of electricity.* However, this is not the whole story. Messages also travel from neurons to other neurons, muscles, or glands by means of chemical messengers termed *neurotransmitters.*

The conduction of the neural impulse along the length of a neuron is what is meant by "firing." Some neurons fire in less than 1/1,000th of a second. In firing, neurons "attempt" to transmit the message to other neurons, muscles, or glands. However, other neurons will not fire unless the incoming messages combine to reach an adequate threshold. A weak message may cause a temporary shift in electrical charge at some point along a neuron's cell membrane, but this charge will dissipate if the neuron is not stimulated to threshold.

A neuron may transmit several hundred such messages in a second. Yet, in accord with the **all-or-none principle,** each time a neuron fires, it transmits an impulse of the same strength. Neurons fire more frequently when they have been stimulated by larger numbers of other neurons; stronger stimuli result in firing with greater frequency.

For a thousandth of a second or so after firing, a neuron enters an **absolute refractory period,** during which it will not fire in response to stimulation from other neurons. Then, for another few thousandths of a second, the neuron is said to be in a **relative refractory period,** during which it will fire but only in response to messages that are stronger than usual. The refractory period is a time of recovery during which sodium is prevented from passing through the neuronal membrane. When we realize that such periods of recovery might take place hundreds of times per second, it seems a rapid recovery and a short rest indeed.

THE SYNAPSE

A neuron relays its message to another neuron across a junction called a **synapse.** A synapse consists of a "branch," or axon terminal from the transmitting neuron; a dendrite ("root"), or the soma of a receiving neuron; and a fluid-filled gap between the two that is called the *synaptic cleft* (see Figure 3.3). Although the neural impulse is electrical, it does not jump the synaptic cleft like a spark. Instead, when a nerve impulse reaches a synapse, axon terminals release chemicals into the synaptic cleft like myriad ships being cast off into the sea.

NEUROTRANSMITTERS

In the axon terminals are sacs, or synaptic vesicles, that contain chemicals called *neurotransmitters.* When a neural impulse reaches the axon terminal, the vesicles release varying amounts of these neurotransmitters into the synaptic cleft. From there, they influence the receiving neuron.

Dozens of neurotransmitters have been identified. Each neurotransmitter has its own chemical structure, and each can fit into a specifically tailored harbor, or **receptor site,** on the dendrite of the receiving cell. The analogy of a key fitting into a lock has been used. Once released, not all molecules of a neurotransmitter find their ways into receptor sites of other neurons. "Loose" neurotransmitters are usually either broken down or reabsorbed by the axon terminal (a process called *re-uptake*).

Some neurotransmitters act to excite other neurons—that is, to influence receiving neurons in the direction of firing. The synapses between axon terminals with excitatory neurotransmitters and receiving neurons are called **excitatory synapses.**

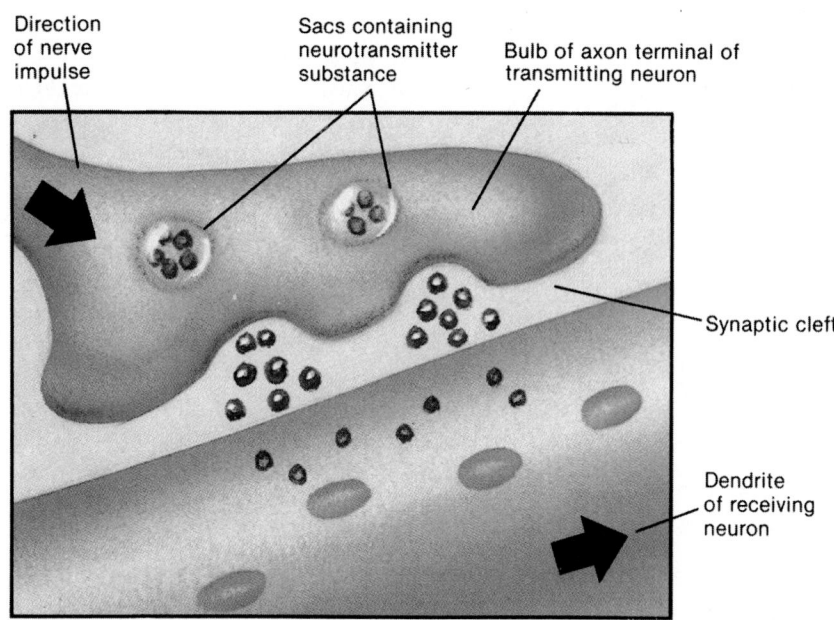

Direction of nerve impulse

Sacs containing neurotransmitter substance

Bulb of axon terminal of transmitting neuron

Synaptic cleft

Dendrite of receiving neuron

FIGURE 3.3

The Synapse Neurons relay their messages to other neurons across junctions called *synapses.* A synapse consists of an axon terminal from the transmitting neuron, the membrane of the receiving neuron, and a small gap between the two that is referred to as the *synaptic cleft.* Molecules of neurotransmitters are released into the synaptic cleft from vesicles within the axon terminal. Many molecules are taken up by receptor sites on the receiving neuron. Others are broken down or taken up again by the transmitting neuron.

Other neurotransmitters inhibit receiving neurons; that is, they influence them in the direction of not firing. The synapses between axon terminals with inhibitory neurotransmitters and receiving neurons are called **inhibitory synapses.** Neurons may be influenced by neurotransmitters that have been released by thousands of other neurons. The additive stimulation received from all these cells determines whether a particular neuron will also fire and which neurotransmitters will be released in the process.

Neurotransmitters are involved in processes ranging from muscle contraction to emotional response. Excesses or deficiencies of neurotransmitters have been linked to diseases and abnormal behavior.

Acetylcholine. Acetylcholine (ACh) is a neurotransmitter that controls muscle contractions. ACh is excitatory at synapses between nerves and muscles that involve voluntary movement but inhibitory at the heart and some other locations.

The effects of curare highlight the functioning of ACh. Curare is a poison that is extracted from plants by South American

MINILECTURE: NEUROTRANSMITTERS AND THE SYNAPSE

Synapse • (SIN-apps). A junction between the axon terminals of one neuron and the dendrites or soma of another neuron.

Receptor site • A location on a dendrite of a receiving neuron tailored to receive a neurotransmitter.

Excitatory synapse • (EX-it-uh-TORE-ee). A synapse that influences receiving neurons in the direction of firing by increasing depolarization of their cell membranes.

Inhibitory synapse • A synapse that influences receiving neurons in the direction of not firing by encouraging changes in their membrane permeability in the direction of the resting potential.

Acetylcholine • (uh-SEE-till-COE-lean). A neurotransmitter that controls muscle contractions. Abbreviated *ACh.*

Indians and used in hunting. If an arrow tipped with curare pierces the skin and the poison enters the body, it prevents ACh from lodging within receptor sites in neurons, resulting in paralysis. The victim is prevented from contracting the muscles used in breathing and dies from suffocation. Botulism, a disease that stems from food poisoning, prevents the release of ACh and has the same effect as curare.

ACh is also normally prevalent in a part of the brain called the **hippocampus,** a structure involved in the formation of memories. When the ACh available to the brain decreases, memory formation is impaired.

Dopamine. **Dopamine** is primarily an inhibitory neurotransmitter. Dopamine is involved in voluntary movements, learning and memory, and emotional arousal. Deficiencies of dopamine are linked to Parkinson's disease, a disorder in which people progressively lose control over their muscles. They develop muscle tremors and jerky, uncoordinated movements. The drug L-dopa, a substance that the brain converts to dopamine, helps slow the progress of Parkinson's disease.

The psychological disorder schizophrenia (see Chapter 13) has also been linked to dopamine. People with schizophrenia may have more receptor sites for dopamine in an area of the brain that is involved in emotional responding. For this reason, they may *overutilize* the dopamine that is available in the brain, which leads to hallucinations and disturbances of thought and emotion. The phenothiazines, a group of drugs used in the treatment of schizophrenia, block the action of dopamine by locking some dopamine out of these receptor sites (Carpenter & Buchanan, 1994). Not surprisingly, phenothiazines may have Parkinson's-like side effects, which are usually then treated by additional drugs, lowering the dose of phenothiazine, or switching to another drug.

Noradrenaline. **Noradrenaline** is produced largely by neurons in the brain stem. Noradrenaline acts both as a neurotransmitter and a hormone. It speeds up the heartbeat and other body processes and is involved in general arousal, learning and memory, and eating. Excesses and deficiencies of noradrenaline have been linked to mood disorders (see Chapter 13).

The stimulants cocaine and amphetamines ("speed") facilitate the release of dopamine and noradrenaline and also impede their reabsorption by the releasing synaptic vesicles—that is, their re-uptake. As a result, there are excesses of these neurotransmitters in the nervous system, vastly increasing the firing of neurons and leading to a persistent state of high arousal.

Serotonin. Also primarily an inhibitory transmitter, **serotonin** is involved in emotional arousal and sleep. Deficiencies of serotonin have been linked to anxiety, mood disorders, and insomnia. The drug LSD (see Chapter 5) decreases the action of serotonin and may also influence the utilization of dopamine. With LSD, "two no's make a yes." By inhibiting an inhibitor, brain activity increases, in this case frequently leading to hallucinations.

Endorphins. The word *endorphin* is the contraction of *endogenous morphine. Endogenous* means "developing from within." **Endorphins,** then, are similar to the narcotic morphine in their functions and effects and are produced by our own bodies. They occur naturally in the brain and in the bloodstream.

Endorphins are inhibitory neurotransmitters. They lock into receptor sites for chemicals that transmit pain messages to the brain. Once the endorphin "key" is in the "lock," pain-causing chemicals cannot transmit their (frequently unwelcome) messages. There are a number of endorphins. Beta-endorphin, for example, is many times more powerful than morphine, molecule for molecule, whether injected into the bloodstream or the brain (Snyder, 1977).

Truth or Fiction Revisited. *It is true that our bodies produce natural painkillers that are more powerful than morphine.* These chemicals are called *endorphins* and, ounce for ounce, they are more powerful than the narcotic morphine. Endorphins may also increase our sense of self-competence and may be connected with the "runner's high" reported by many long-distance runners.

There you have it—a fabulous forest of neurons in which billions upon billions of

Hippocampus • A part of the limbic system of the brain that is involved in memory formation.

Dopamine • (DOPE-uh-mean). A neurotransmitter that is involved in Parkinson's disease and that appears to play a role in schizophrenia.

Noradrenaline • (nor-uh-DRENN-uh-lin). A neurotransmitter whose action is similar to that of the hormone adrenaline and that may play a role in depression.

Serotonin • (ser-oh-TONE-in). A neurotransmitter, deficiencies of which have been linked to affective disorders, anxiety, and insomnia.

Endorphins • (en-DOOR-fins). Neurotransmitters that are composed of amino acids and that are functionally similar to morphine.

A View of the New York City Marathon. Why have thousands of people taken up long-distance running? Running, of course, promotes cardiovascular conditioning, firms the muscles, and helps us to control weight. But long-distance runners also report experiencing a "runner's high," which may be connected with the release of endorphins. Endorphins are naturally occurring substances similar in function to the narcotic morphine.

vesicles are pouring neurotransmitters into synaptic clefts at any given time: when you are involved in strenuous activity, now as you are reading this page, even as you are passively watching television. This microscopic picture is repeated several hundred times every second. The combined activity of all these neurotransmitters determines which messages will be transmitted and which will not. Your experience of sensations, your thoughts, and your psychological sense of control over your body are very different from the electrochemical processes we have described. Yet somehow, these many electrochemical events are responsible for your psychological sense of yourself and of the world.

Reflections

Now that you have read the section on neurons, reflect on the following questions:

• How does the text use the term *message* in referring to transmission from one neuron to another? How does the text's use of the term *message* correspond to your own sense of the meaning of the word?

How are messages "passed along" from one neuron to another?

• Had you heard that the brain works, or operates, by means of electricity? What electrochemical processes actually account for transmission of messages in the nervous system?

• Since psychology is the study of behavior and mental processes, why do you think that psychologists are interested in biological matters such as the nervous system, the endocrine system, and heredity?

The Nervous System

As a child, I did not think it a good thing to have a "nervous" system. After all, if your system were not so nervous, you might be less likely to jump at strange noises.

Later I learned that a nervous system is not a system that is nervous. It is a system of nerves involved in thought processes, heartbeat, visual–motor coordination, and so on. I also learned that the human nervous system is more complex than that of

MINILECTURE: ORGANIZATION OF THE NERVOUS SYSTEM

Nerve • A bundle of axons and dendrites from many neurons.

Nuclei • (NEW-klee-eye). Plural of *nucleus*. A group of neural cell bodies found in the brain or spinal cord.

Ganglia • (GANG-lee-uh). Plural of *ganglion*. A group of neural cell bodies found elsewhere in the body (other than the brain or spinal cord).

Central nervous system • The brain and spinal cord.

Peripheral nervous system • (pair-IF-uh-ral). The part of the nervous system consisting of the somatic nervous system and the autonomic nervous system.

Spinal cord • A column of nerves within the spine that transmits messages from sensory receptors to the brain and from the brain to muscles and glands throughout the body.

Spinal reflex • A simple, unlearned response to a stimulus that may involve only two neurons.

any other animal and that our brains are larger than those of any other animal. Now this last piece of business is not quite true. A human brain weighs about 3 pounds, but elephant and whale brains may be four times as heavy. Still, our brains compose a greater part of our body weight than do those of elephants or whales. Our brains weigh about 1/60th of our body weight. Elephant brains weigh about 1/1,000th of their total weight, and whale brains are a paltry 1/10,000th of their weight. So, if we wish, we can still find figures to make us proud.

Truth or Fiction Revisited. *It is not true that the human brain is larger than that of any other animal.* Elephants and whales have larger brains.

The brain is only one part of the nervous system. A **nerve** is a bundle of axons and dendrites. The cell bodies of these neurons are not considered to be part of the nerve. The cell bodies are gathered into clumps called **nuclei** in the brain and spinal cord and **ganglia** elsewhere.

The nervous system consists of the brain, the spinal cord, and the nerves linking them to receptors in the sensory organs and effectors in the muscles and glands. As shown in Figure 3.4, the brain and spinal cord make up what we refer to as the **central nervous system.** The sensory (afferent) neurons, which receive and transmit messages to the brain and spinal cord, and the motor (efferent) neurons, which transmit messages from the brain or spinal cord to the muscles and glands, make up the **peripheral nervous system.**

THE CENTRAL NERVOUS SYSTEM

The central nervous system consists of the spinal cord and the brain.

The Spinal Cord. The **spinal cord** is a column of nerves about as thick as a thumb. It transmits messages from receptors to the brain and from the brain to muscles and glands throughout the body (Figure 3.5). The spinal cord is also capable of

FIGURE 3.4

Spotlight on the Divisions of the Nervous System The nervous system contains two main divisions: the central nervous system and the peripheral nervous system. The central nervous system consists of the brain and spinal cord. The peripheral nervous system contains the somatic and autonomic systems. In turn, the autonomic nervous system is composed of sympathetic and parasympathetic divisions.

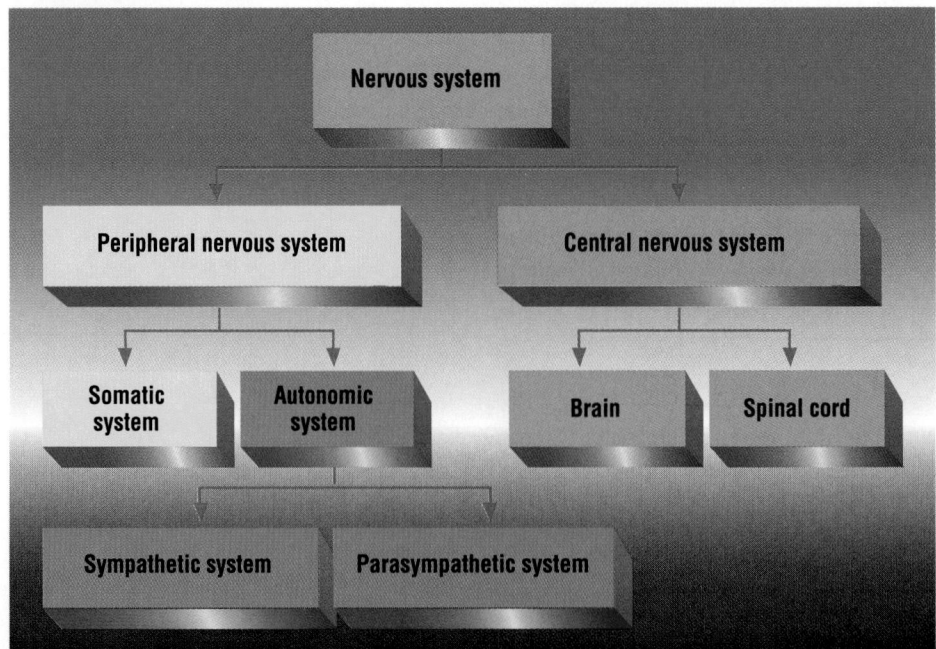

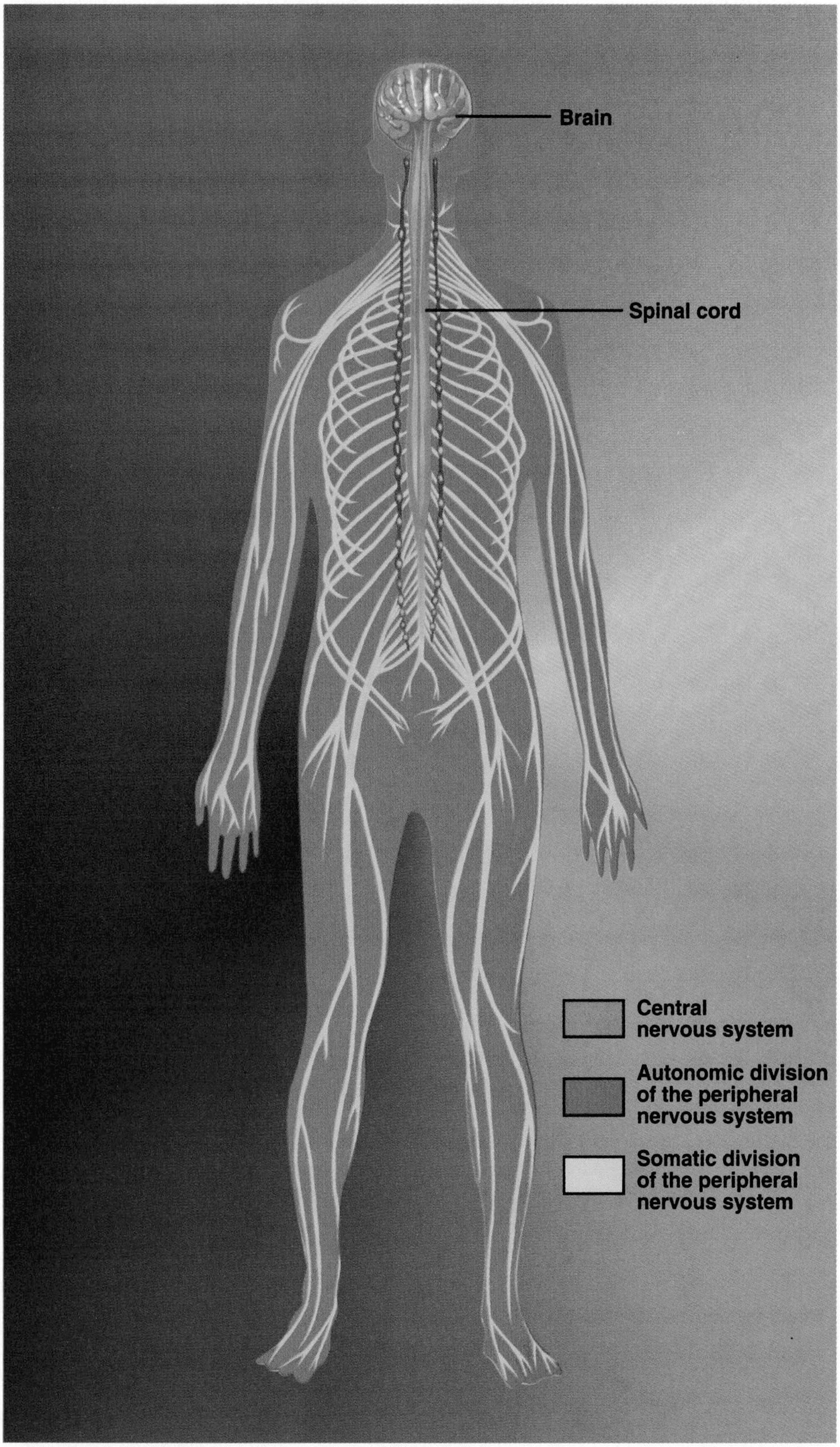

Brain

Spinal cord

Central
nervous system

Autonomic division
of the peripheral
nervous system

Somatic division
of the peripheral
nervous system

FIGURE 3.5

Spotlight on the Parts of the Nervous System
Note that the spinal cord is protected by a column of bones called vertebrae. The brain is protected by the skull.

some "local government" of responses to external stimulation through **spinal reflexes.** A spinal reflex is an unlearned re-sponse to a stimulus that may involve only two neurons—a sensory (afferent) neuron and a motor (efferent) neuron (Figure 3.6).

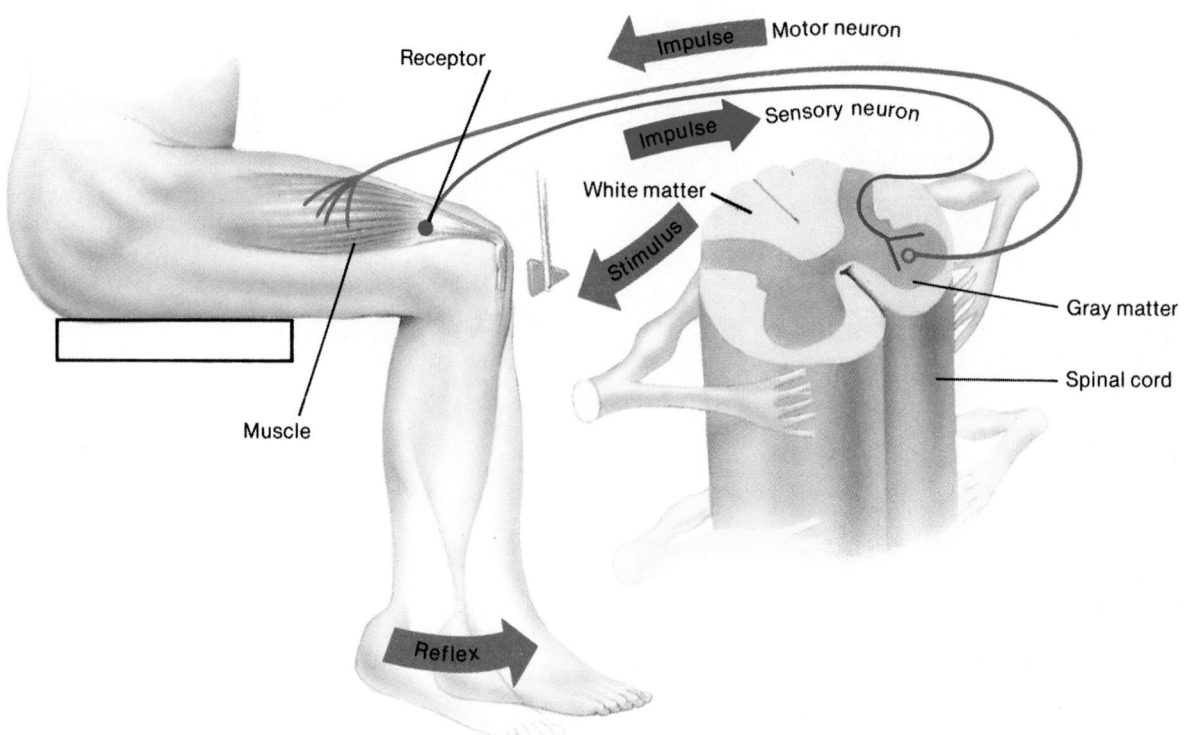

FIGURE 3.6
The Reflex Arc This cross section of the spinal cord shows a sensory neuron and a motor neuron, which are involved in the knee-jerk reflex. In some reflexes, interneurons link sensory and motor neurons.

Interneuron • A neuron that transmits a neural impulse from a sensory neuron to a motor neuron.

Gray matter • In the spinal cord, the grayish neurons and neural segments that are involved in spinal reflexes.

White matter • In the spinal cord, axon bundles that carry messages from and to the brain.

In some reflexes, a third neuron, called an **interneuron,** transmits the neural impulse from the sensory neuron through the spinal cord to the motor neuron.

The spinal cord (and the brain) consist of gray matter and white matter. The **gray matter** is composed of nonmyelinated neurons. Some of these nonmyelinated neurons are involved in spinal reflexes, whereas others send axons to the brain. The **white matter** is composed of bundles of longer, myelinated (and thus whitish) axons that carry messages to and from the brain. As you can see in Figure 3.6, a cross section of the spinal cord shows the gray matter, which includes cell bodies, to be distributed in a butterfly pattern.

We engage in many reflexes. We blink in response to a puff of air. We swallow when food accumulates in the mouth. A physician may tap the leg below the knee to elicit the knee-jerk reflex, a sign that the nervous system is operating adequately. Urinating and defecating are reflexes that occur in response to pressure in the bladder and the rectum. Parents typically spend a number of weeks or months toilet-training infants, or teaching them to involve their brains in the process of elimination. Learning to inhibit these reflexes makes civilization possible.

Sexual response also involves many reflexes. Adequate stimulation of the genital organs will lead to erection in the male, vaginal lubrication in the female (both are reflexes that make sexual intercourse possible), and the involuntary muscle contractions of orgasm. As reflexes, these processes need not involve the brain, but most often they do. Feelings of passion, memories of an enjoyable sexual encounter, and sexual fantasies usually contribute to sexual response by transmitting messages from the brain to the genitals through the spinal cord (Rathus and others, 1993).

The Brain. Every show has a star, and the brain is the undisputed star of the human nervous system. The size and shape of your brain are responsible for your large, delightfully rounded head. In all the animal kingdom, you (and about 6 billion other people) are unique because of the capaci-

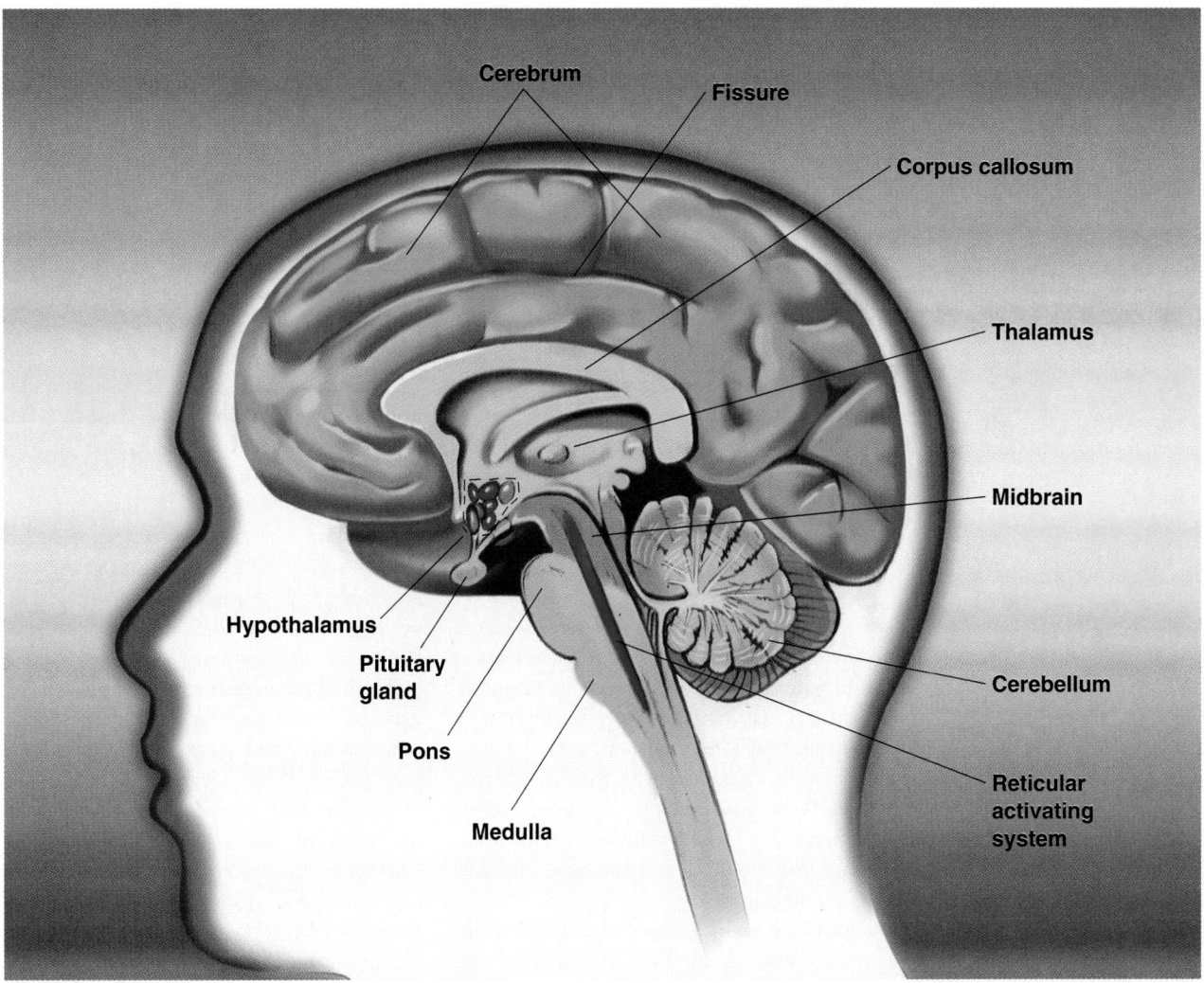

FIGURE 3.7
The Parts of the Human Brain This view of the brain, split top to bottom, labels some of the most important structures.

ties for learning and thought made possible by the human brain.

Let us look at the brain, as shown in Figure 3.7. We begin with the back of the head, where the spinal cord rises to meet the brain, and work our way forward. The lower part of the brain, or hindbrain, consists of three major structures: the medulla, the pons, and the cerebellum.

Many pathways that connect the spinal cord to higher levels of the brain pass through the **medulla.** The medulla regulates vital functions such as heart rate, blood pressure, and respiration. It also plays a role in sleep, sneezing, and coughing. The **pons** is a bulge in the hindbrain that lies forward of the medulla. *Pons* is the Latin word for "bridge," and the pons is so named because of the bundles of nerves that pass through it. The pons transmits information about body movement and is also involved in functions related to attention, sleep and alertness, and respiration.

Behind the pons lies the **cerebellum** ("little brain" in Latin). The two hemispheres of the cerebellum are involved in maintaining balance and in controlling motor (muscle) behavior. Injury to the cerebellum may lead to lack of motor coordination, stumbling, and loss of muscle tone.

The **reticular activating system** (RAS) begins in the hindbrain and ascends through the region of the midbrain into the

Medulla • (meh-DULL-ah). An oblong area of the hindbrain involved in regulation of heartbeat and respiration.

Pons • (ponz). A structure of the hindbrain involved in respiration, attention, and sleep and dreaming.

Cerebellum • (ser-uh-BELL-um). A part of the hindbrain involved in muscle coordination and balance.

Reticular activating system • (reh-TICK-you-lar). A part of the brain involved in attention, sleep, and arousal.

lower part of the forebrain. The RAS is vital in the functions of attention, sleep, and arousal. Injury to the RAS may leave an animal **comatose.** Stimulation of the RAS causes it to send messages to the cortex, making us more alert to sensory information. Electrical stimulation of the RAS awakens sleeping animals, and certain drugs—such as alcohol—called central-nervous-system depressants are thought to work, in part, by lowering RAS activity.

Sudden, loud noises stimulate the RAS and awaken a sleeping animal or person. But the RAS may become selective, or acquire the capacity to play a filtering role, through learning. It may allow some messages to filter through to higher brain levels and awareness while screening others out. For example, the parent who has primary responsibility for child care may be awakened by the stirring sounds of an infant, whereas louder sounds of traffic or street noise are filtered out. The other parent, in contrast, may usually sleep through even loud cries. If the first parent must be away for several days, however, the second parent's RAS may quickly acquire sensitivity to noises produced by the child. This sensitivity may rapidly fade again when the first parent returns.

Also located in the midbrain are areas involved in vision and hearing. These include the area that controls eye reflexes such as dilation of the pupils and eye movements.

Five major areas of the front-most part of the brain, or forebrain, are the thalamus, the hypothalamus, the limbic system, the basal ganglia, and the cerebrum.

The **thalamus** is located near the center of the brain. It consists of two joined egg- or football-shaped structures. The thalamus serves as a relay station for sensory stimulation. Nerve fibers from our sensory systems enter from below; the information carried by them is then transmitted to the cerebral cortex by way of fibers that exit from above. For instance, the thalamus relays sensory input from the eyes to the visual areas of the cerebral cortex. The thalamus is also involved in controlling sleep and attention in coordination with other brain structures, including the RAS.

The **hypothalamus** lies beneath the thalamus and above the pituitary gland. It weighs only 4 grams, yet it controls the au-

tonomic nervous system and the endocrine system. Thus, it is vital in the regulation of body temperature, the concentration of fluids, the storage of nutrients, and various aspects of motivation and emotion. Experimenters learn many of the functions of the hypothalamus by implanting electrodes in various parts of it and observing the behavioral effects when a current is switched on. In this way, it has been found that the hypothalamus is involved in hunger, thirst, sexual behavior, caring for offspring, and aggression. Among lower animals, stimulation of various areas of the hypothalamus can trigger stereotypical behaviors such as fighting, mating, or even nest building. The hypothalamus is just as important to people, but our behavior in response to messages from the hypothalamus is less stereotypical and relatively more influenced by cognitive functions such as thought, choice, and value systems.

The **limbic system** is made up of several structures, including the septum, amygdala, hippocampus, and parts of the hypothalamus (Figure 3.8) (Derryberry & Tucker, 1992). The limbic system lies along the inner edge of the cerebrum and is fully evolved in mammals only. It is involved in memory and emotion, and in the drives of hunger, sex, and aggression. People in whom operations have damaged the hippocampus can retrieve old memories but cannot permanently store new information. As a result, they may reread the same newspaper day in and day out without recalling that they have read it before. Or they may have to be perpetually reintroduced to people they have met just hours earlier (Squire, 1986). Destruction of an area within the **amygdala** leads monkeys and other mammals to show docile behavior. Destruction of the **septum** leads some mammals to respond aggressively, even with slight provocation.

The limbic system thus provides a system of "checks and balances." The amygdala and the septum appear to allow us to inhibit stereotypical behaviors that are prompted by the hypothalamus. We then have the chance to mull over situations and are less likely, when threatened, to automatically flee or attack.

The **basal ganglia** are buried beneath the cortex in front of the thalamus. The basal ganglia are involved in the control of postural movements and the coordination of the limbs. Most of the brain's dopamine is produced by neurons in the basal ganglia, and the degeneration of these neurons has been linked to Parkinson's disease (Rao and others, 1992). Researchers (e.g., Freed and others, 1992; Spencer and others, 1992; Widner and others, 1992) have recently implanted dopamine-producing neurons taken from the brains of aborted fetuses into the brains of people with Parkinson's disease. As a result, many of them regained greater control of motor functions and also showed less need of L-dopa (a drug that is converted into dopamine in the body and serves as the major form of treatment of Parkinson's disease).

The **cerebrum** is the crowning glory of the brain. Only in human beings does the cerebrum compose such a large proportion of the brain (Figure 3.7). The surface of the cerebrum is wrinkled, or convoluted, with ridges and valleys. This surface is the **cerebral cortex.** The convolutions allow a great deal of surface area to be packed into the brain.

Valleys in the cortex are called **fissures.** A most important fissure almost divides the cerebrum in half. The hemispheres of the cerebral cortex are connected by the **corpus callosum** (Latin for "thick body" or "hard body"), a thick fiber bundle.

THE PERIPHERAL NERVOUS SYSTEM

The peripheral nervous system consists of sensory and motor neurons that transmit messages to and from the central nervous system. Without the peripheral nervous system, our brains would be isolated from the world: They would not be able to perceive it, and they would not be able to act on it. The two main divisions of the peripheral nervous system are the somatic nervous system and the autonomic nervous system.

The Somatic Nervous System. The **somatic nervous system** contains sensory (afferent) and motor (efferent) neurons. It transmits messages about sights, sounds, smells, temperature, body positions, and so on, to the central nervous system. As a result, we can experience the beauties

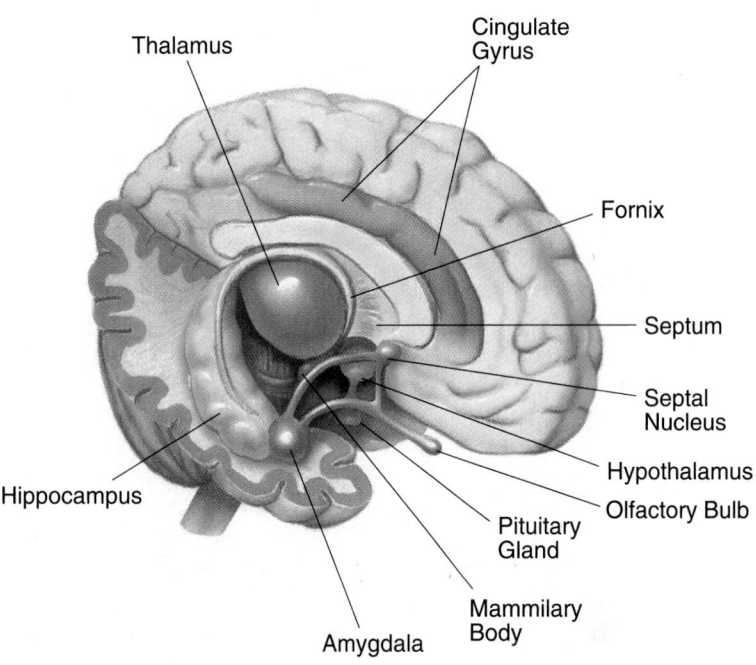

FIGURE 3.8
The Limbic System The limbic system consists of the amygdala, hippocampus, septum and septal nuclei, fornix, cingulate gyrus, and parts of the hypothalamus.

and the horrors of the world, its physical ecstasies and agonies. Messages from the brain and spinal cord to the somatic nervous system control purposeful body movements such as raising a hand, winking, or running; breathing; and movements that we hardly attend to—movements that maintain our posture and balance.

The Autonomic Nervous System. *Autonomic* means "automatic." The **autonomic nervous system** (ANS) regulates the glands and the muscles of internal organs. Thus, the ANS controls activities such as heartbeat, respiration, digestion, and dilation of the pupils of the eyes. These activities can occur automatically, as we are asleep. But some of them can be overridden by conscious control. You can breathe at a purposeful pace, for example. Methods like biofeedback and yoga also help people gain voluntary control of functions such as heart rate and blood pressure.

The ANS has two branches, or divisions: **sympathetic** and **parasympathetic.** These branches have largely opposing effects. Many organs and glands are stimulated by both branches of the ANS (Figure 3.9). When organs and glands are simultaneously stimulated by both

Somatic nervous system • (so-MAT-tick). The division of the peripheral nervous system that connects the central nervous system with sensory receptors, skeletal muscles, and the surface of the body.

Autonomic nervous system • (aw-toe-NOM-ick). The division of the peripheral nervous system that regulates glands and activities such as heartbeat, respiration, digestion, and dilation of the pupils. Abbreviated *ANS.*

Sympathetic • The branch of the ANS that is most active during emotional responses such as fear and anxiety that spend the body's reserves of energy.

Parasympathetic • The branch of the ANS that is most active during processes such as digestion that restore the body's reserves of energy.

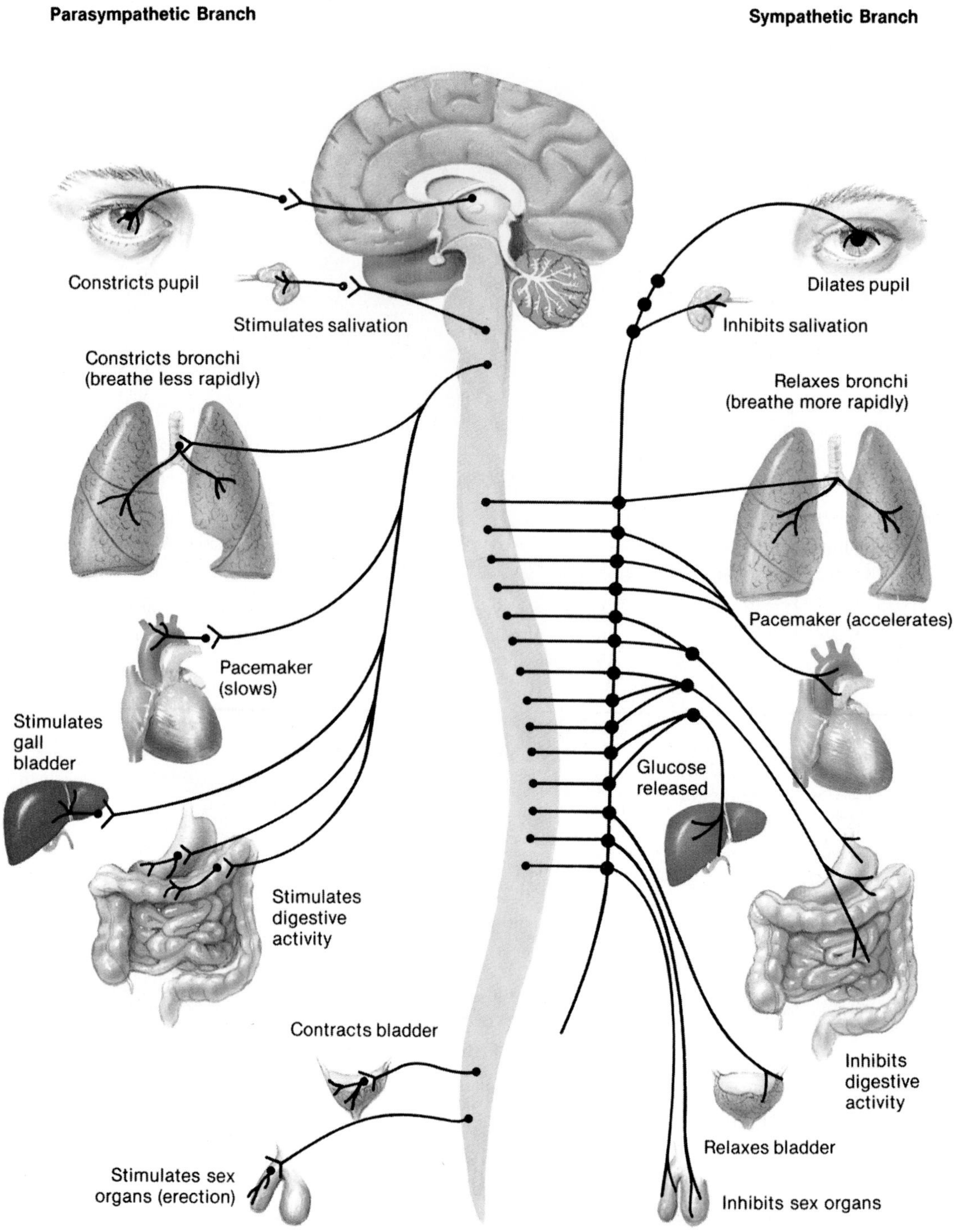

Parasympathetic Branch

Sympathetic Branch

Constricts pupil

Stimulates salivation

Constricts bronchi
(breathe less rapidly)

Pacemaker
(slows)

Stimulates
gall
bladder

Stimulates
digestive
activity

Contracts bladder

Stimulates sex
organs (erection)

Dilates pupil

Inhibits salivation

Relaxes bronchi
(breathe more rapidly)

Pacemaker (accelerates)

Glucose
released

Inhibits
digestive
activity

Relaxes bladder

Inhibits sex organs

FIGURE 3.9

Spotlight on the Activities of the Two Branches of the Autonomic Nervous System (ANS) The parasympathetic branch of the ANS generally acts to replenish stores of energy in the body. It is connected to organs by nerves that originate near the top and bottom of the spinal cord. The sympathetic branch is most active during activities that expend energy. Its neurons collect in clusters or chains of ganglia along the central portion of the spinal cord. The two branches of the ANS frequently have antagonistic effects on the organs they service.

divisions, their effects can average out to some degree. In general, the sympathetic division is most active during processes that involve the spending of body energy from stored reserves, such as in a fight-or-flight response to a predator or when you find out that your mortgage payment is going to be increased. The parasympathetic division is most active during processes that replenish reserves of energy, such as eating. When we are afraid, the sympathetic division of the ANS accelerates the heart rate. When we relax, it is the parasympathetic division that decelerates the heart rate. The parasympathetic division stimulates digestive processes, but the sympathetic branch inhibits digestion. Since the sympathetic division predominates when we feel fear or anxiety, fear or anxiety can cause indigestion.

Truth or Fiction Revisited. *It is true that fear can give you indigestion.* Fear predominantly involves sympathetic activity. Digestive processes involve parasympathetic activity. Since sympathetic activity can be incompatible with parasympathetic activity, fear can be incompatible with digestion.

The ANS is of particular interest to psychologists because its activities are linked to various emotions such as anxiety and love. Some people seem to have overly reactive sympathetic nervous systems. In the absence of external threats, their bodies still respond as though they were faced with danger (see Chapter 13).

Reflections

Now that you have read the section on the nervous system, reflect on the following questions:

- Does it seem possible that the sexual responses of the body are reflexive? How do you account for the fact that you can dwell on erotic ideas and thus cause sexual reflexes to occur?
- Before taking this course, you had doubtless heard of "nerves." How do the true definitions of *neurons* and *nerves* correspond to your earlier ideas?
- Dopamine-producing neurons have been taken from the brains of aborted fetuses and implanted in the brains of people with

Parkinson's disease, leading to greater control of motor functions. Do you believe that it is proper to use tissue from electively aborted fetuses in this way? Why or why not?
- Have you ever lost your appetite, been unable to eat, or thrown up because of anxiety or fear? What biological processes led fear to cause indigestion in you?

The Cerebral Cortex

Sensation and muscle activity involve many parts of the nervous system. The essential human activities of thought and language, however, involve the hemispheres of the cerebral cortex.

THE GEOGRAPHY OF THE CEREBRAL CORTEX

Each of the two hemispheres of the cerebral cortex is divided into four parts, or lobes, as shown in Figure 3.10. The **frontal lobe** lies in front of the central fissure, and the **parietal lobe** lies behind it. The **temporal lobe** lies below the side, or lateral, fissure, across from the frontal and parietal lobes. The **occipital lobe** lies behind the temporal lobe and behind and below the parietal lobe.

When light strikes the retinas of the eyes, neurons in the occipital lobe fire, and we "see." Direct artificial stimulation of the occipital lobe also produces visual sensations. You would "see" flashes of light if neurons in the occipital region of the cortex were stimulated with electricity, even if it were pitch black or your eyes were covered. The hearing or auditory area of the cortex lies in the temporal lobe along the lateral fissure. Sounds cause structures in the ear to vibrate (see Chapter 4). Messages are relayed to the auditory area of the cortex, and when you hear a noise, neurons in this area are firing.

Just behind the central fissure in the parietal lobe lies an area of **somatosensory cortex,** in which the messages received from skin senses all over the body are projected. These sensations include warmth and cold, touch, pain, and movement. Neurons in different parts of the sensory cortex fire, depending on whether you wiggle

Frontal lobe • The lobe of the cerebral cortex that lies to the front of the central fissure.
Parietal lobe • (par-EYE-uh-tal). The lobe that lies just behind the central fissure.
Temporal lobe • The lobe that lies below the lateral fissure, near the temples of the head.
Occipital lobe • (ox-SIP-it-all). The lobe that lies behind and below the parietal lobe and behind the temporal lobe.
Somatosensory cortex • (so-mat-toe-SENSE-or-ree). The section of cortex in which sensory stimulation is projected. It lies just behind the central fissure in the parietal lobe.

MINILECTURE: THE STRUCTURE OF THE BRAIN

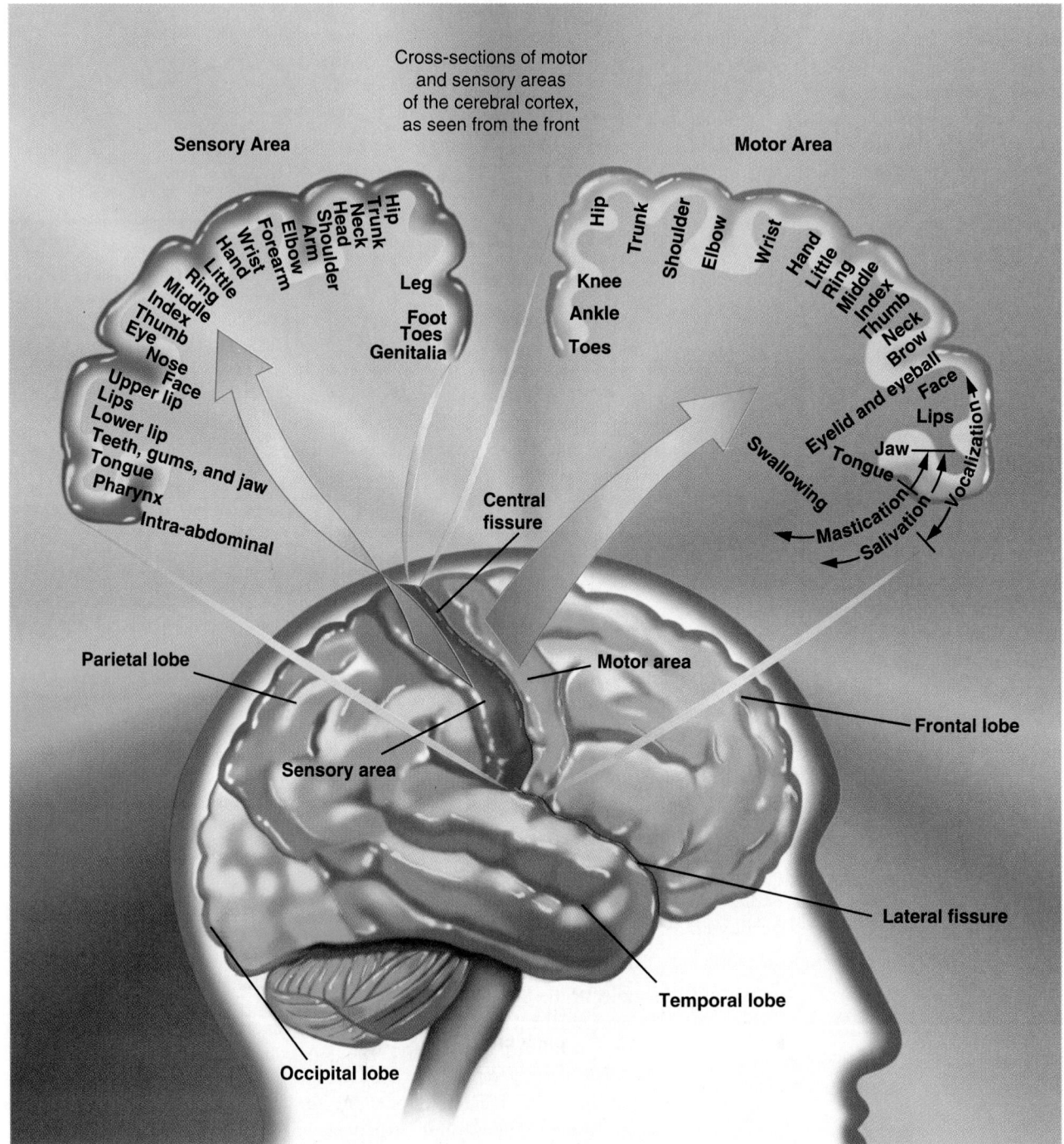

FIGURE 3.10
The Geography of the Cerebral Cortex The cortex is divided into four lobes: frontal, parietal, temporal, and occipital. The visual area of the cortex is located in the occipital lobe. The hearing, or auditory, cortex lies in the temporal lobe. The sensory and motor areas face each other across the central fissure. What happens when a surgeon stimulates areas of the sensory or motor cortex during an operation?

your finger or raise your leg. If a brain surgeon were to stimulate the proper area of your somatosensory cortex with a small probe known as a "pencil electrode," it might seem as if someone were touching your arm or leg.

Truth or Fiction Revisited. *It is true that if a surgeon were to stimulate a certain part of your brain electrically, you might swear in court that someone had stroked your leg.*

Figure 3.10 suggests how our faces and heads are overrepresented on this cortex as compared with, say, our trunks and legs. This overrepresentation is one of the reasons that our faces and heads are more sensitive to touch than other parts of the body.

Many years ago it was discovered that people with injuries to one hemisphere of the brain would show sensory or motor deficits on the opposite side of the body below the head. Experimentation since that time has made it clear that sensory and motor nerves cross in the brain and elsewhere. The left hemisphere controls functions on, and receives inputs from, the right side of the body. The right hemisphere controls functions on, and receives inputs from, the left side of the body.

The **motor cortex** lies in the frontal lobe, just across the valley of the central fissure from the somatosensory cortex. Neurons in the motor cortex fire when we move certain parts of our body. If a surgeon were to stimulate a certain area of the right hemisphere of the motor cortex with a pencil electrode, you would raise your left leg. Raising the leg would be sensed in the somatosensory cortex, and you might have a devil of a time trying to figure out whether you had "intended" to raise that leg!

THOUGHT, LANGUAGE, AND THE CORTEX

Areas of the cerebral cortex that are not primarily involved in sensation or motor activity are called **association areas.** They make possible the breadth and depth of human learning, thought, memory, and language. Association areas, for example, involve memory functions required for problem solving. Stimulation of many association areas with pencil electrodes during surgery leads some people to report visual/auditory experiences that seem like memories, and sometimes they seem to be attended by appropriate emotions (Penfield, 1969).

Some association areas are involved in the integration of sensory information. Certain neurons in the visual area of the occipital lobe fire in response to the visual presentation of vertical lines. Others fire in response to presentation of horizontal lines. Although one group of cells may respond to one aspect of the visual field and another group of cells may respond to another, association areas put it all together. As a result, you see a box or an automobile or a road map and not a confusing array of verticals and horizontals.

Language Functions. In some ways, the left and right hemispheres of the brain duplicate each other's functions. In other ways, they are very different. The left hemisphere contains language functions for nearly all (97%) right-handed people (Pinker, 1994a). For two of three left-handed people (68%), the left hemisphere also contains language functions. The right hemisphere contains language functions for about one left-handed person in five (19%).

Even at birth, the sounds of speech elicit greater electrical activity in the left hemisphere than in the right, as indicated by the activity of brain waves (Molfese & Molfese, 1979). Sensory pathways cross over in the brain. Thus, dominance of the left hemisphere is associated with dominance of the right ear, and vice versa.

Within the dominant (usually left) hemisphere of the cortex, two key language areas are Broca's area and Wernicke's area (see Figure 3.11). Damage to either area is likely to cause an **aphasia**—that is, a disruption of the ability to understand or produce language.

Wernicke's area lies in the temporal lobe near the auditory cortex. This area integrates auditory and visual information (Raichle, 1994). People with damage to Wernicke's area may show **Wernicke's aphasia,** which impairs their abilities to comprehend speech and to think of the proper words to express their own thoughts. Ironically, they usually speak freely and with proper syntax. Wernicke's area is thus essential to understanding the relationships between words and their meanings.

Broca's area is located in the frontal lobe, near the section of the motor cortex that controls the muscles of the tongue and throat and of other areas of the face that

Motor cortex • The section of cortex that lies in the frontal lobe, just across the central fissure from the sensory cortex. Neural impulses in the motor cortex are linked to muscular responses throughout the body.

Association areas • Areas of the cortex involved in learning, thought, memory, and language.

Aphasia • (uh-FAY-she-uh). Impaired ability to comprehend or express oneself through language.

Wernicke's aphasia • (WER-nick-key). A language disorder characterized by difficulty comprehending the meaning of spoken language.

FIGURE 3.11
Broca's and Wernicke's Areas of the Cerebral Cortex Areas of the dominant hemisphere most involved in speech are Broca's area and Wernicke's area. Damage to either area can produce a characteristic aphasia—that is, a predictable disruption of the ability to understand or produce language.

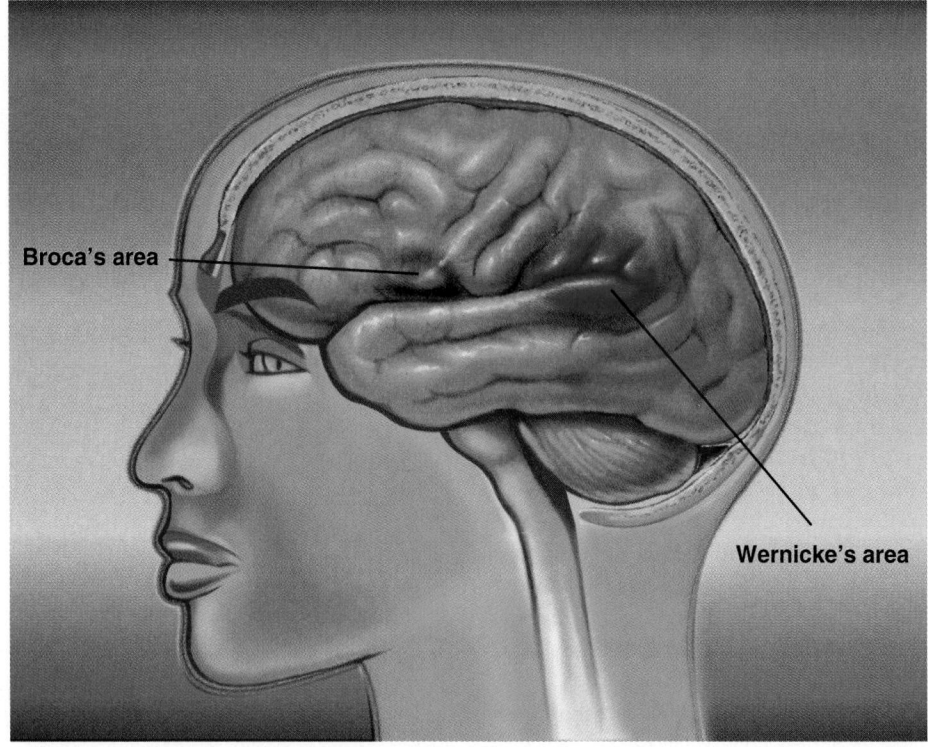

Broca's area

Wernicke's area

are used when speaking (Pinker, 1994a; Raichle, 1994). Broca's area and Wernicke's area are connected by nerve fibers. When Broca's area is damaged, people speak slowly and laboriously, with simple sen-

tences. The pattern is termed **Broca's aphasia.**

LEFT BRAIN, RIGHT BRAIN?

In recent years, it has become popular to speak of people as being "left-brained" or "right-brained." The notion is that the hemispheres of the brain are involved in very different kinds of intellectual and emotional functions and responses, along the lines suggested in Figure 3.12. According to this view, left-brained people would be primarily logical and intellectual. Right-brained people would be intuitive, creative, and emotional. Those of us fortunate enough to have our brains "in balance" would presumably have the best of it—the capacity for logic combined with emotional richness.

Like so many other popular ideas, the left-brain—right-brain notion is at best exaggerated. Research does suggest that in right-handed individuals, the left hemisphere is relatively more involved in intellectual undertakings that require logical analysis and problem solving, language, and mathematical computation (Borod, 1992; Hellige, 1990). The nondominant (usually right) hemisphere is relatively more concerned with spatial functions, aesthetic and

FIGURE 3.12
Some of the "Specializations" of the Left and Right Hemispheres of the Cerebral Cortex This cartoon, which appeared in a popular magazine, exaggerates the left brain—right brain notion. It seems to be true that the dominant (usually left) hemisphere is somewhat more involved in intellectual undertakings that require logic and problem solving, while the nondominant (usually right) hemisphere is relatively more concerned with decoding visual information, aesthetic and emotional responses, and imagination. However, each hemisphere has some involvement with logic and with creativity and intuition.

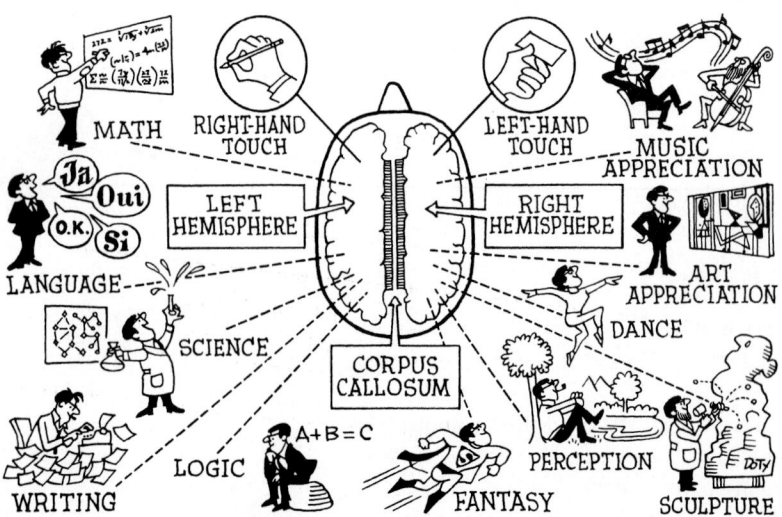

MATH
Ja
Oui
O.K. Si
LANGUAGE
SCIENCE
WRITING
LOGIC
RIGHT-HAND TOUCH
LEFT HEMISPHERE
CORPUS CALLOSUM
A+B=C
FANTASY
LEFT-HAND TOUCH
MUSIC APPRECIATION
RIGHT HEMISPHERE
ART APPRECIATION
DANCE
PERCEPTION
SCULPTURE

emotional responses, imagination, understanding metaphors, and creative mathematical reasoning.

Despite these differences, however, it would be erroneous to think that the hemispheres of the brain act independently—that some people are truly left-brained and others, right-brained (Hellige, 1990). The functions of the left and right hemispheres overlap to some degree, and the hemispheres tend to respond simultaneously as we focus our attention on one thing or another. The hemispheres are aided in their "cooperation" by myelination of the corpus callosum, the bundle of nerve fibers that connects them. Myelination of the corpus callosum proceeds rapidly during early and middle childhood and is largely complete by the age of 8. By that time, we apparently have greater ability to integrate logical and emotional functioning.

We can summarize left-brain and right-brain similarities and differences as follows (Hellige, 1990):

1. The hemispheres are similar enough that each can function quite well independently but not as well as they function in normal combined usage.

2. For the great majority of people, the left hemisphere plays a special role in language, whereas the right hemisphere seems to play a special role in emotional response.

3. Both hemispheres are involved in logic.

4. Creativity and intuition are not confined to the right hemisphere.

5. Both hemispheres are educated at the same time, even when instruction is intended to "appeal" to the right hemisphere (as in music) or the left (in a logic class).

HANDEDNESS: IS IT GAUCHE TO BE LEFT-HANDED?

What do Michelangelo, Leonardo da Vinci, Pablo Picasso, and Steve Young all have in common? No, they are not all artists. Only one is a football player. But they are all left-handed. Yet, being a lefty is often looked on as a deficiency. The language swarms with slurs on lefties. We speak of "left-handed compliments," of having "two left feet," of strange events as "coming out of left field." The word *sinister* means "left-hand or unlucky side" in Latin. *Gauche,* moreover, is a French word that literally means "left." Compare these usages to the positive phrases "being righteous" or "being on one's right side."

Yet, 10% of us are lefties. Left-handedness is more common in boys than girls. We are usually labeled right-handed or left-handed on the basis of our handwriting preferences, yet some people write with one hand and pass a football with the other. Some people even swing a tennis racket and pitch a baseball with different hands.

Because of the belief that left-handed children are relatively clumsy and more inclined toward reading disabilities and other academic problems, left-handed children were once encouraged to switch to writing with their right hands. Yet, research suggests that the stereotype of left-handed children may be off base.

One study (Tan, 1985), for example, examined the relationship between preschoolers' handedness and their motor coordination. Tan found no differences in motor skills between lefties and righties. She concluded that lefties may be regarded as less well-coordinated than righties because their movements *look* so different.

What of the academic competence of lefties? There are some reports of problems, but they are sketchy. Yet, 20% of groups of several hundred mathematically gifted 12- and 13-year-olds were lefties, as compared with 10% of the general population (Benbow & Stanley, 1980, 1983).

SPLIT-BRAIN EXPERIMENTS: WHEN HEMISPHERES STOP COMMUNICATING

A number of people with severe cases of **epilepsy** have undergone **split-brain operations** in which the corpus callosum is severed. The purpose of the operation is to try to confine epilepsy to one hemisphere of the cerebral cortex rather than allowing a reverberating neural tempest. These operations do seem to be of help. People who have undergone them can be thought of as winding up with two brains, yet under most circumstances their behavior remains ordinary enough. Still, some aspects of

Left-Handed Quarterback Steve Young Passes a Football. Is it gauche to be left-handed, or are lefties as competent (or incompetent) as righties?

Broca's aphasia • A language disorder characterized by slow, laborious speech.

Epilepsy • (EP-pea-lep-sea). Temporary disturbances of brain functions that involve sudden neural discharges.

Split-brain operation • An operation in which the corpus callosum is severed, usually in an effort to control epileptic seizures.

MINILECTURE: SPLIT-BRAIN PROCEDURE

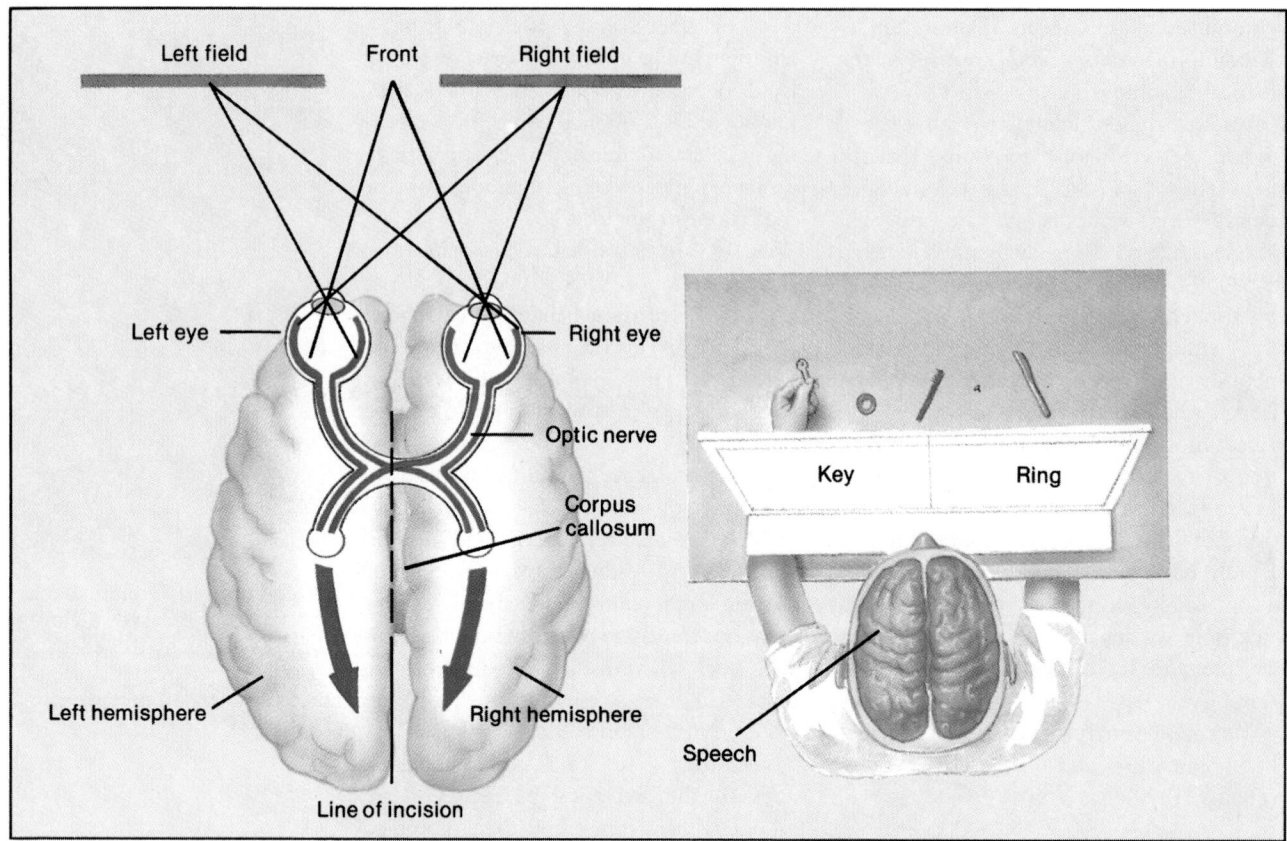

FIGURE 3.13
A Divided-Brain Experiment In the drawing on the left, we see that visual sensations from the left visual field are projected in the occipital cortex of the right hemisphere. Visual sensations from the right visual field are projected in the occipital cortex in the left hemisphere. In the divided-brain experiment diagrammed on the right, a person with a severed corpus callosum handles a key with his left hand and perceives the written word *key* with his left eye. The word *key* is projected in the right hemisphere. Speech, however, is usually a function of the left (dominant) hemisphere. The written word *ring,* perceived by the right eye, is projected in the left hemisphere. So, when asked what he is handling, the divided-brain person reports "ring," not "key."

Tactile • (TACK-tile). Of the sense of touch.

hemispheres that have stopped talking to one another are intriguing.

Gazzaniga (1992) showed that people with split brains whose eyes are closed may be able to verbally describe an object such as a key that they hold in one hand, but not when they hold the object in the other hand. As shown in Figure 3.13, if a person with a split brain handles a key with his left hand behind a screen, **tactile** impressions of the key are projected into the right hemisphere, which has little or no language ability. Thus, he will not be able to describe the key. If he holds it in his right hand, he will have no trouble describing it because sensory impressions are projected into the left hemisphere of the cortex,

which contains language functions. To further confound matters, if the word *ring* is projected into the dominant (left) hemisphere while he is asked what he is handling, he will say "ring," not "key."

However, this discrepancy between what is felt and what is said occurs only in people with split brains. As noted earlier, most of the time the hemispheres work together, even when we are playing the piano or are involved in scientific thought.

In case you have ever wondered whether other people could make us play the piano or engage in scientific thinking by "pressing the right buttons," let us consider some research into electrical stimulation of the brain.

FIGURE 3.14
The "Taming" of a Brave Bull by Electrical Stimulation of the Brain Brave bulls are dangerous animals that will attack an intruder in the arena. Even in full charge, however, a bull can be stopped abruptly by radio-triggered electrical stimulation of the brain. After several stimulations, there is a lasting inhibition of aggressive behavior.

ELECTRICAL STIMULATION OF THE BRAIN

Some years ago, José Delgado astounded the scientific world by stepping into a bull ring armed only with a radio transmitter, a cape, and, perhaps, crossed fingers (Figure 3.14). Describing his experiment in *Physical Control of the Mind* (1969), Delgado explained that he had implanted a radio-controlled electrode in the limbic system of a "brave bull"—a variety bred to respond with a raging charge when it sees any human being. When Delgado pressed a button on the transmitter, sending a signal to a battery-powered receiver attached to the bull's horns, an electrical impulse went into the bull's brain. The animal ceased its charge and circled to the right. After several repetitions, the bull no longer attempted to charge Delgado.

Another effect of electrical stimulation of the brain (ESB) was discovered accidentally (how many important discoveries are made by accident!) during the 1950s by James Olds and Peter Milner (Olds, 1969). Olds and Milner found that electrical stimulation of an area of the hypothalamus of a rat induced the animal to increase the frequency of whatever it was doing at the time (Figure 3.15). Rats also rapidly learned to engage in behavior such as pressing a lever that resulted in more stimulation. Rats, in fact, will stimulate themselves in this area repeatedly, up to 100 times a minute and over 1,900 times an hour. For this reason, Olds and Milner labeled this area of the hypothalamus a pleasure center.

Truth or Fiction Revisited. *It is true that rats will learn to do things that result in a "reward" of a burst of electricity in the brain.* An electrode is implanted that allows for stimulation of the "pleasure center" of the hypothalamus.

However, ESB is not perfectly reliable. ESB in the same site may produce different effects at different times. On one occasion, a rat may eat when receiving ESB. On another, it may drink. The sites for producing pleasant or unpleasant sensations in people may also vary from person to person and from day to day.

In our discussion of the makeup of the nervous system, we have described naturally occurring chemical substances that facilitate or inhibit the transmission of neural messages—neurotransmitters. Let us now turn our attention to other naturally occurring chemical substances that influence behavior—hormones. We shall see that some hormones also function as neurotransmitters.

Reflections

Now that you have read the section on the cerebral cortex, reflect on the following questions:

FIGURE 3.15
A "Pleasure Center" of the Brain A rat with an electrode implanted in a section of the hypothalamus that has been termed a *pleasure center* learns to press a lever to receive electrical stimulation.

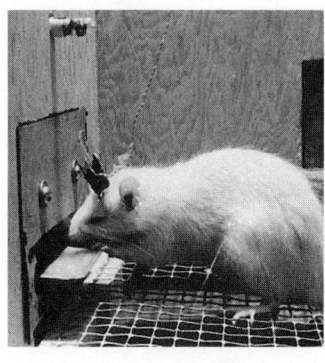

- As you read the words on this page, neurons in your brain are firing. Where are the neurons whose firing results in your seeing the words?
- Would you consider yourself to be more "left-brained" or "right-brained"? Why?
- Imagine that people could electrically stimulate the pleasure centers in their brains. Can you imagine the kinds of religious and political arguments that might arise as to whether people should be *allowed* to do so?

The Endocrine System

Here are some things you may have heard about hormones and behavior. Are they truth or fiction?

_____ Some overweight people actually eat very little, and their excess weight is caused by "glands."

_____ Injections of growth hormone have reversed some of the effects of aging in men in their 60s and 70s.

PSYCHOLOGY Ψ IN THE NEW MILLENNIUM

And Now—Brainman?

Just when you thought that dealing with real life might be taxing enough . . . enter *Brainman?*

The Walkman—a tiny, portable radio and cassette player—was a buzzword of the 1980s. The 1990s have seen the advent of Virtual Reality (VR)—electronic technology that brings you into a world of computer-generated imagery. People, for example, can "enter" videogames by means of the VR helmet, which surrounds the senses of vision and hearing with a computer-generated environment. Science fiction writer Arthur C. Clarke (1993) entertains the possibility of an advanced version for the year 2110, but is it really that far away?

The results produced by the early VR systems were almost as crude as the first television displays, yet they were impressive enough to be habit-forming, even addictive. Three-D, wide-angle images could grasp the attention of the subject so completely that their jerky, cartoonlike quality was ignored. As definition and animation steadily improved, the virtual world came closer and closer to the real one, but it could always be distinguished from it as long as it was presented through such clumsy contrivances as head-mounted displays and servo-operated gloves. To make the illusion perfect, and fool the brain completely, it would be necessary to bypass the external sense organs of eyes, ears, and muscles, and to feed information directly into the [brain].

The concept of the "dream machine" was at least a hundred years old before developments in brain scanning and nanosurgery made it possible. The first units, like the first computers, were massive racks of equipment occupying whole rooms—and, like computers, they were miniaturized with astonishing speed. However, their application was limited as long as they had to operate through electrodes implanted in the [brain].

Breakthrough. The real breakthrough came [when] the Brainman was perfected. A memory unit storing terabytes[2] of information was linked by a fiberoptic cable to a snugly fitting skullcap carrying literally billions of atom-size terminals, making painless contact with the skin of the cranium. The Brainman was so invaluable not only for entertainment but for education that within a single generation everyone who could afford it had acquired one. . . .

_____ A woman who becomes anxious and depressed just before menstruating is suffering from "raging hormones."

_____ Women who "pump iron" frequently use hormones to achieve the muscle definition that is needed to win bodybuilding contests.

_____ People who receive injections of adrenaline may report that they feel as if they are about to experience some emotion, but they're not sure which one.

Let us consider each of these items. Some overweight people do eat relatively little but are "sabotaged" in their weight-loss efforts by hormonal changes that lower the rates at which they metabolize food (Brownell & Wadden, 1992). A synthetic version of growth hormone, which is normally secreted by the **pituitary gland,** has helped many older people gain muscle, shed fat, and thicken the bone in their spines (Rudman and others, 1990). Women may become somewhat more anxious or depressed at the time of menstruation, but

Pituitary gland • (pit-TOO-it-tar-ree). The gland that secretes growth hormone, prolactin, antid-iuretic hormone, and other hormones.

Bringing Memories Closer to the Heart's Desire. Although the Brainman's potential for vicarious experience—especially erotic, thanks to the swiftly developing technology of hedonics—was recognized at once, its more serious applications were not neglected. Instant knowledge and skills became available through whole libraries of specialized "memory modules" or memnochips. Most appealing of all, however, was the "total diary" which allowed one to store and then relive precious moments of life—and even to re-edit them to bring them closer to the heart's desire (pp. 88–89).

Some questions to consider:

- If "Brainman" were to become available, would people travel through real space when they went on vacation, or would they just plug themselves in? Would VR make us voyeurs rather than actors? Would the ability to visit a virtual Tahiti or virtual Arthurian England promise risk-free experiences that are more exciting than anything real life has to offer (Heim, 1993)?

- Would we ever be motivated to unhook ourselves? (Consider how "addicted" some people are to television.) Would feeding our escapist tendencies loosen our connections to the demands of real life (Heim, 1993)?

- Would philosophers argue as to whether real reality or virtual reality was a more valuable or meaningful experience?

- Would editing memories to "bring them closer to the heart's desire" enhance the past or destroy it? Does it matter?

---

[2] What are *terabytes* of information? A trillion bytes, or a *million* megabytes. Most of today's personal computers store from 80 to 800 megabytes on their hard drives. Some newer personal computers can store gigabytes of information. The prefix *giga* derives from the Greek *gigas,* meaning "giant" and means 1 billion. One gigabyte equals 1,000 megabytes. If your PC stores 245 megabytes, that's about one fourth of a gigabyte. The prefix *tera* derives from the Greek *teras,* meaning "monster" and means 1 trillion. One terabyte equals 1,000 gigabytes.

the effects of hormones have been exaggerated. Moreover, women's response to menstruation reflects their attitudes as well as biological changes. Many top women (and men) bodybuilders do use steroids (hormones that are produced by the **adrenal cortex**) and growth hormone to achieve muscle mass and definition (Leerhsen & Abramson, 1985). Steroids and growth hormone promote resistance to stress and muscle growth in both genders. Finally, adrenaline, a hormone produced by the **adrenal medulla,** does generally

arouse people and heighten general emotional responsiveness. The emotion to which this arousal is attributed depends in part on the person's situation (see Chapter 10).

The body contains two types of glands: glands with **ducts** and glands without ducts. A duct is a passageway that carries substances to specific locations. Saliva, sweat, tears (the name of a new rock group?), and milk all reach their destinations by means of ducts. Psychologists are interested in the substances secreted by

Adrenal cortex • (ad-DREE-nal). The outer part of the adrenal glands located above the kidneys. It produces steroids.

Adrenal medulla • The inner part of the adrenal glands that produces adrenaline.

Duct • Passageway.

Endocrine system • (END-oh-krinn). Ductless glands that secrete hormones and release them directly into the bloodstream.

Hormone • A substance secreted by an endocrine gland that regulates various body functions.

TABLE 3.1

An Overview of Major Glands of the Endocrine System

GLAND	HORMONE	MAJOR EFFECTS
Hypothalamus	Growth-hormone releasing factor	Causes pituitary gland to secrete growth hormone
	Corticotrophin-releasing hormone	Causes pituitary gland to secrete adreno-corticotrophic hormone
	Thyrotropin-releasing hormone	Causes pituitary gland to secrete thyrotropin
	Gonadotropin-releasing hormone	Causes pituitary gland to secrete follicle-stimulating hormone and luteinizing hormone
Pituitary		
Anterior Lobe	Growth hormone	Causes growth of muscles, bones, and glands
	Adrenocorticotrophic hormone (ACTH)	Regulates adrenal cortex
	Thyrotrophin	Causes thyroid gland to secrete thyroxin
	Follicle-stimulating hormone	Causes formation of sperm and egg cells
	Luteinizing hormone	Causes ovulation, maturation of sperm and egg cells
	Prolactin	Stimulates production of milk
Posterior Lobe	Antidiuretic hormone (ADH)	Inhibits production of urine
	Oxytocin	Stimulates uterine contractions during delivery and ejection of milk during nursing
Pancreas	Insulin	Enables body to metabolize sugar; regulates storage of fats
Thyroid	Thyroxin	Increases metabolic rate
Adrenal		
Cortex	Steroids (e.g., cortisol)	Increase resistance to stress; regulate carbohydrate metabolism
Medulla	Adrenaline (epinephrine)	Increases metabolic activity (heart and respiration rates, blood sugar level, etc.)
	Noradrenaline (norepinephrine)	Raises blood pressure, acts as a neurotransmitter
Testes	Testosterone	Promotes growth of male sex characteristics
Ovaries	Estrogen	Regulates menstrual cycle
	Progesterone	Promotes growth of female reproductive tissues; maintains pregnancy
Uterus	(Several)	Maintain pregnancy

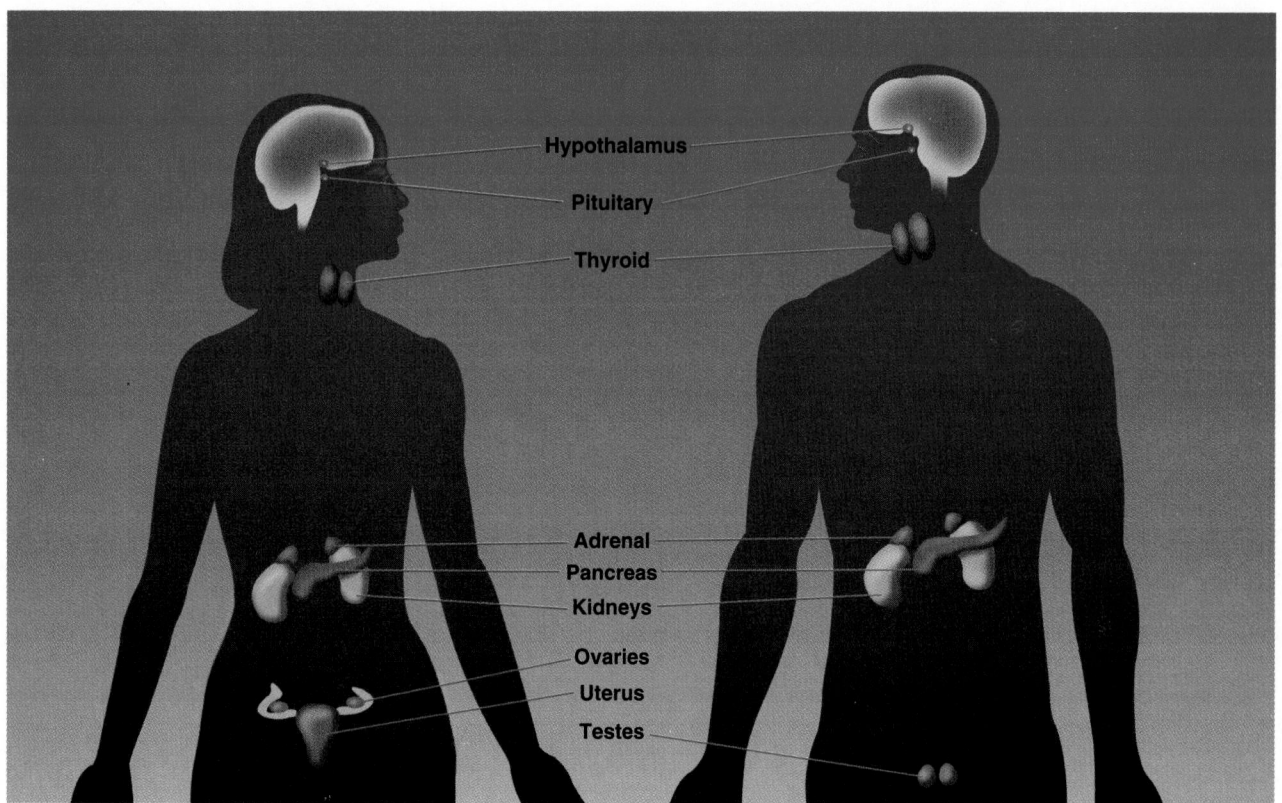

FIGURE 3.16
Major Glands of the Endocrine System The hypothalamus is a structure of the brain.
Since it secretes hormones, however, it is also an endocrine gland.

ductless glands because of their behavioral effects (see the summary in Table 3.1). The ductless glands constitute the **endocrine system** of the body, and they secrete **hormones** (from the Greek *horman*, meaning "to stimulate" or "to excite").

Hormones are released directly into the bloodstream. As is the case with neurotransmitters,[3] hormones have specific receptor sites. Although they are poured into the bloodstream and circulate throughout the body, they act only on hormone receptors in certain locations. Some hormones released by the hypothalamus influence only the pituitary gland. Some hormones released by the pituitary influence the adrenal cortex, others influence the testes and ovaries, and so on.

A GUIDED TOUR OF THE ENDOCRINE SYSTEM

Let us now consider the hormones produced by several glands.

The Hypothalamus. The hypothalamus secretes a number of releasing hormones, or factors, that influence the anterior (front) lobe of the pituitary gland to secrete corresponding hormones (Derryberry & Tucker, 1992). A dense network of blood vessels between the hypothalamus and the pituitary gland provides a direct route of influence.

The Pituitary Gland. The pituitary gland lies just below the hypothalamus (see Figure 3.16). It is about the size of a pea, but it is so central to the body's functioning that it has been referred to as the "master gland." Despite this designation, today we know that the hypothalamus regulates a good deal of pituitary activity.

Much hormonal action helps the body maintain steady states, as in fluid levels, blood sugar levels, and so on. Bodily mechanisms measure current levels and signal glands to release hormones when these levels deviate from optimal. The

---

[3] Recall that some hormones, such as noradrenaline, also function as neurotransmitters.

Negative feedback • Descriptive of a system in which information that a quantity (e.g., of a hormone) has reached a set point suspends action of the agency (e.g., a gland) that gives rise to that quantity.

Growth hormone • A pituitary hormone that regulates growth.

Prolactin • (pro-LACK-tin). A pituitary hormone that regulates production of milk and, in lower animals, maternal behavior.

Antidiuretic hormone • A pituitary hormone that conserves body fluids by increasing reabsorption of urine and is connected with paternal behavior in some mammals. Also called *vasopressin*.

Oxytocin • (OX-see-TOE-sin). A pituitary hormone that stimulates labor and lactation.

Pancreas • (PAN-kree-as). An organ behind the stomach; endocrine cells in the pancreas secrete hormones that influence the blood sugar level.

Insulin • (IN-sue-lin). A pancreatic hormone that stimulates the metabolism of sugar.

Hyperglycemia • (HIGH-purr-gly-SEEM-me-uh). A disorder caused by excess sugar in the blood.

Hypoglycemia • (HIGH-poe-gly-SEEM-me-uh). A disorder caused by too little sugar in the blood.

Syndrome • (SIN-drome). A cluster of symptoms characteristic of a disorder.

Thyroxin • (thigh-ROCKS-sin). The thyroid hormone that increases metabolic rate.

Metabolism • In organisms, a continuous process that converts food into energy.

Hypothyroidism • (HIGH-poe-THIGH-roid-izm). A condition caused by a deficiency of thyroxin and characterized by sluggish behavior and a low metabolic rate.

maintenance of steady states requires the feedback of bodily information to glands. This type of system is referred to as a **negative feedback** loop. That is, when enough of a hormone has been secreted, the gland is signaled to stop. With a negative feedback system in effect, even the master gland must serve a master—the hypothalamus. In turn, the hypothalamus responds to information from the body.

The anterior and posterior (back) lobes of the pituitary gland produce or secrete many hormones, some of which are listed in Table 3.1. **Growth hormone** regulates the growth of muscles, bones, and glands. Children who are naturally deficient in growth hormone may not grow taller than 3 or 4 feet unless they receive injections of the hormone. On the other hand, an excess of growth hormone can lead to acromegaly, a condition in which people may grow 2 to 3 feet taller than they normally would.

Children whose growth patterns seem abnormally slow often catch up to their agemates when growth hormone is administered by a physician. Growth-hormone releasing factor (hGRF) is produced by the hypothalamus and causes the pituitary to produce growth hormone.

Prolactin largely regulates maternal behavior in lower mammals such as rats and stimulates production of milk in women. As a water-conservation measure, **antidiuretic hormone** (ADH) inhibits production of urine when fluid levels in the body are low. ADH is also connected with stereotypical paternal behavior patterns in some mammals (Insel, 1993). For example, it transforms a naive male prairie vole (a mouselike rodent) into an affectionate and protective mate and father. **Oxytocin** stimulates labor in pregnant women and is connected with maternal behavior patterns (cuddling and caring for young) in some mammals (Carter, 1993). Obstetricians may induce labor or increase the strength of uterine contractions during labor by injecting pregnant women with oxytocin. During nursing, stimulation of nerve endings in and around the nipple sends messages to the brain that cause oxytocin to be secreted. Oxytocin then causes contractile cells in the breast to eject milk.

The Pancreas. Endocrine cells within the **pancreas** regulate the level of sugar

in the blood and the urine through **insulin** and other hormones. One form of diabetes (diabetes mellitus) is characterized by excess sugar in the blood—**hyperglycemia**—and in the urine, a condition that can lead to coma and death (Becker, 1990). Diabetes stems from inadequate secretion or utilization of insulin. People who do not secrete enough insulin of their own may need to inject this hormone daily to control diabetes.

The condition **hypoglycemia** is characterized by too little sugar in the blood. Symptoms of hypoglycemia include shakiness, dizziness, and lack of energy, a **syndrome** that is easily confused with anxiety. Many people have sought help for anxiety and learned through a series of blood tests that they are actually suffering from hypoglycemia. This disorder is generally controlled through dietary restrictions.

The Thyroid Gland. **Thyroxin** is produced by the thyroid gland. Thyroxin affects the body's **metabolism,** or rate of using oxygen and producing energy. Some people are overweight because of **hypothyroidism,** a condition which results from abnormally low secretions of thyroxin. Deficiency of thyroxin can lead to **cretinism** in children, which is symptomized by stunted growth and mental retardation. Adults who secrete too little thyroxin may feel tired and sluggish and may put on weight. People who produce excess amounts of thyroxin may develop **hyperthyroidism,** which is symptomized by excitability, insomnia, and weight loss (Becker, 1990).

The Adrenal Glands. The adrenal glands, located above the kidneys, have an outer layer, or cortex, and an inner core, or medulla. The adrenal cortex is regulated by pituitary ACTH. The cortex secretes as many as 20 different hormones known as **corticosteroids,** or cortical steroids. Cortical steroids (**cortisol** is one) increase resistance to stress; promote muscle development; and cause the liver to release stored sugar, making energy available for emergencies.

Anabolic steroids (synthetic versions of the male sex hormone testosterone) have been used, sometimes in tandem with growth hormone, to enhance athletic prowess. Steroids stoke the muscle mass, heighten resistance to stress, and increase the body's energy supply by signaling the liver to release sugar into the bloodstream. Steroids also spur the sex drive. On a psychological level, they boost self-esteem (Taylor, 1985). Steroids are generally outlawed in amateur and professional sports.

The lure of steroids is understandable. Sometimes the difference between an acceptable athletic performance and a great one is rather small. Thousands of athletes try to make it in the big leagues, and the "edge" offered by steroids—even if minor—can spell the difference between a fumbling attempt and success.

If steroids help, why the fuss? Some of it is related to the ethics of competition—the notion that all athletes should "play fair." Part of it is related to the fact that steroid use is linked to liver damage and other medical problems.

Adrenaline and noradrenaline are secreted by the adrenal medulla. **Adrenaline,** also known as epinephrine, is manufactured exclusively by the adrenal glands, but noradrenaline (norepinephrine) is also produced elsewhere in the body. The sympathetic branch of the autonomic nervous system causes the adrenal medulla to release a mixture of adrenaline and noradrenaline that helps arouse the body in preparation for coping with threats and stress. Adrenaline is of interest to psychologists because of its emotional, as well as physiological, effects. Adrenaline may intensify most emotions and is crucial to the experience of fear and anxiety. Noradrenaline raises the blood pressure, and in the nervous system, it acts as a neurotransmitter.

The Testes and the Ovaries. Did you know that if it were not for the secretion of the male sex hormone **testosterone** about 6 weeks after conception, we would all develop into females? Testosterone is produced by the testes and, in smaller amounts, by the ovaries and adrenal glands. A few weeks after conception, testosterone stimulates prenatal differentiation of male sex organs. (The quantities produced by the ovaries and adrenal glands are normally insufficient to foster development of male sex organs.)

During puberty, testosterone stokes the growth of muscle and bone and the development of primary and secondary sex characteristics. **Primary sex characteristics** such as the growth of the penis and the sperm-producing ability of the testes are directly involved in reproduction. **Secondary sex characteristics** such as growth of the beard and deepening of the voice differentiate males and females but are not directly involved in reproduction.

Testosterone levels are maintained at fairly even levels by the hypothalamus, pituitary gland, and testes. Low blood levels of testosterone signal the hypothalamus to produce gonadotropin-releasing hormone (GnRH). GnRH, in turn, signals the pituitary to secrete luteinizing hormone (LH), which stimulates the testes to secrete testosterone and follicle-stimulating hormone (FSH), which causes sperm cells to develop (Conn & Crowley, 1991). The negative feedback loop is completed as follows: High blood levels of testosterone signal the hypothalamus not to secrete GnRH so that production of LH, FSH, and testosterone is suspended.

The ovaries produce **estrogen** and **progesterone.** (Estrogen is also produced in smaller amounts by the testes.) Estrogen is a generic name for several female sex hormones that foster female reproductive capacity and secondary sex characteristics such as accumulation of fat in the breasts and hips. Progesterone also has multiple functions. It stimulates growth of the female reproductive organs and maintains pregnancy. As with testosterone, estrogen and progesterone levels influence and are also influenced by GnRH, LH, and FSH. In women, FSH causes ova (egg cells) within follicles in the ovaries to ripen.

Whereas testosterone levels remain fairly stable, estrogen and progesterone levels vary markedly and regulate the menstrual cycle. Following menstruation—the monthly sloughing off of the inner lining of the uterus—estrogen levels increase, leading to the development of an ovum (egg cell) and growth of the inner lining of the uterus. The ovum is released by the ovary when estrogens reach peak blood levels. Then, the inner lining of the uterus thickens in response to ecretion of progesterone, gaining the capacity to support an embryo if fertilization should occur. If the ovum is not fertilized, estrogen and progesterone levels drop suddenly, triggering menstruation once more. In this chapter's

Cretinism • (KREE-tin-izm). A condition caused by thyroid deficiency in childhood and characterized by mental retardation and stunted growth.

Hyperthyroidism • (HIGH-purr-THIGH-roid-izm). A condition caused by excess thyroxin and characterized by excitability, insomnia, and weight loss.

Corticosteroids • (CORE-tick-oh-STAIR-oids). Steroids produced by the adrenal cortex that regulate carbohydrate metabolism and increase resistance to stress by fighting inflammation and allergic reactions. Also called *cortical steroids.*

Cortisol • (CORE-tee-sol). A hormone (steroid) produced by the adrenal cortex that helps the body cope with stress by counteracting inflammation and allergic reactions.

Adrenaline • (ad-RENN-uh-lin). A hormone produced by the adrenal medulla that stimulates sympathetic ANS activity. Also called *epinephrine.*

Testosterone • (tess-TOSS-ter-own). A male sex hormone produced by the testes that promotes growth of male sexual characteristics and sperm.

Primary sex characteristics • Physical traits that distinguish males from females and are directly involved in reproduction.

Secondary sex characteristics • Physical traits that differentiate males from females but are not directly involved in reproduction.

Estrogen • (ESS-trow-jen). A generic term for several female sex hormones that promote growth of female sex characteristics and regulate the menstrual cycle.

Progesterone • (pro-JESS-ter-own). A female sex hormone that promotes growth of the sex organs and helps maintain pregnancy.

"Psychology and Modern Life" section, we see that cultural stereotypes about menstruation are scientifically unfounded and harmful to women.

Reflections

Now that you have read the section on the endocrine system, reflect on the following questions:

- Do you know of anyone with hormonal problems? What are they? Do they result from excesses of, or deficiencies in, any of the hormones discussed in this section?
- Have you heard of athletes who were using steroids? What were the effects of the hormones?
- What hormones are involved in reproductive behavior? Has someone you know of been given any of these hormones by a physician? For what reason?
- Why do you think that psychologists are particularly interested in adrenaline and noradrenaline?

Heredity: The Nature of Nature

Consider some of the facts of life:

- People cannot breathe underwater (without special equipment).
- People cannot fly (again, without rather special equipment).
- Fish cannot learn to speak French or do an Irish jig even if you raise them in enriched environments and send them to finishing school (which is why we look for tuna that tastes good, not for tuna with good taste).
- Chimpanzees and gorillas can use sign language but cannot speak.

People cannot breathe underwater or fly (without oxygen tanks, airplanes, or other devices) because of their **heredity**—that is, their basic nature, as defined by the biological structures and processes they have inherited. Fish are similarly limited by the natural traits and characteristics that have been passed down from one generation to another. Because of their heredity, fish cannot speak French or do a jig. Chimpanzees

and gorillas can understand many spoken words and express some concepts through nonverbal symbol systems such as American Sign Language. However, apes show no ability to speak, even though they can make sounds. They have probably failed to inherit the humanlike speech areas of the cerebral cortex. Their nature differs from ours.

Heredity plays a momentous role in the determination of human and nonhuman traits. The structures we inherit at the same time make our behaviors possible and place limits on them (Kimble, 1989). The field within the science of biology that studies heredity is called **genetics. Behavior genetics** is a specialty that bridges the sciences of psychology and biology. It is concerned with the transmission of structures and traits that give rise to patterns of behavior.

Genetics are fundamental in the transmission of physical traits such as height, hair texture, and eye color. Genetics also exerts a powerful influence on personality traits (Carey & DiLalla, 1994; Plomin and others, 1993). Examples include **extroversion** and **neuroticism** (McCartney and others, 1990; Lykken and others, 1992; Pederson and others, 1988; Tellegen and others, 1988), shyness (Plomin, 1989), social dominance, leadership (Lykken and others, 1992), effectiveness as a parent or a therapist (Lykken and others, 1992), aggressiveness (Goldsmith, 1993), even an interest in arts and crafts (Lykken and others, 1992). Genetic influences are also implicated in most psychological disorders (Carey & DiLalla, 1994), including anxiety and depression (Clark and others, 1994; Rothbart & Ahadi, 1994), schizophrenia (Gottesman, 1991), bipolar disorder (Vandenberg and others, 1986), alcoholism (Newlin & Thomson, 1990; Sher & Trull, 1994), even criminal behavior (DiLalla & Gottesman, 1991; Mednick and others, 1987).

GENES AND CHROMOSOMES

Genes are the basic building blocks of heredity. They are the biochemical materials that regulate the development of traits. Some traits, such as blood type, are controlled by a single pair of genes. (One gene is derived from each parent.) Other traits, referred to as **polygenic,** are determined

Heredity • The transmission of traits from one generation to another through genes.

Genetics • (jen-NET-ticks). The branch of biology that studies heredity.

Behavior genetics • The study of the genetic transmission of structures and traits that give rise to behavior.

Extroversion • A trait in which a person directs his or her interest to persons and things outside the self. Sociability.

Neuroticism • A trait in which a person is given to emotional instability, anxiety, feelings of foreboding, inhibition of impulses, and avoidance behavior.

Genes • (jeans). The basic building blocks of heredity, which consist of DNA.

Polygenic • (POLL-lee-JEN-nick). Determined by several genes.

Chromosomes • (CROW-moe-soams). Structures consisting of genes that are found in the nuclei of the body's cells.

Sex chromosomes • The 23rd pair of chromosomes, which determine whether the child will be male or female.

by combinations of genes. The inherited component of complex psychological traits, such as intelligence, is believed to be polygenic (Solomon and others, 1993). We have about 100,000 genes in every cell in our bodies. Genes are segments of chromosomes.

Chromosomes each consist of more than 1,000 genes. Chromosomes are large, complex molecules of deoxyribonucleic acid, which has several chemical components. You can breathe a sigh of relief, for this acid is usually referred to simply as DNA. The tightly wound structure of DNA was first demonstrated in the 1950s by James Watson and Francis Crick (1958). DNA takes the form of a double helix, a sort of twisting ladder (see Figure 3.17). In all living things, from one-celled animals, to fish, to people, the sides of the ladder consist of alternating segments of phosphate (P) and a simple sugar (S). The "rungs" of the ladder are attached to the sugars and consist of one of two pairs of bases, either *adenine* with *thymine* (A with T) or *cytosine* with *guanine* (C with G). A single gene can contain hundreds of thousands of base pairs. The sequence of the rungs is the genetic code that will cause the unfolding organism to grow arms or wings, skin or scales.

We receive 23 chromosomes from our fathers' sperm cells and 23 chromosomes from our mothers' egg cells (ova). When a sperm cell fertilizes an ovum, the chromosomes form 23 pairs (Figure 3.18). The 23rd pair consists of **sex chromosomes,** which determine whether we are female or male. We all receive an X sex chromosome (so called because of the "X" shape) from our mothers. If we also receive an X sex chromosome from our fathers, we develop into females. If we receive a Y sex chromosome (named after the "Y" shape) from our fathers, we develop into males.

Gender is not determined by sex chromosomes throughout the animal kingdom. Reptiles such as crocodiles do not have sex chromosomes, for example. The crocodile's gender is determined by the temperature at which the egg develops (Crews, 1994). Some like it hot. That is, hatchlings are usually male when the eggs develop in the

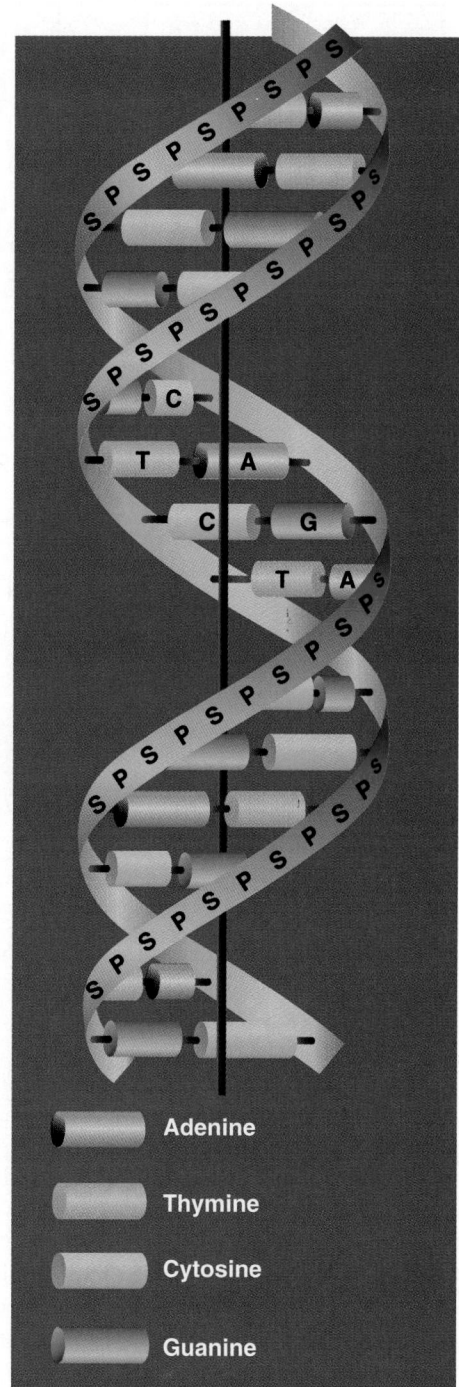

FIGURE 3.17
The Double Helix of DNA

mid-90s Fahrenheit or above. Some like it . . . well, not cold perhaps, but certainly cooler. When crocodile eggs develop below the mid-80s Fahrenheit, the hatchlings are usually female.[4]

---

[4] This does not mean that male crocodiles are hot-blooded. Reptiles are cold-blooded animals.

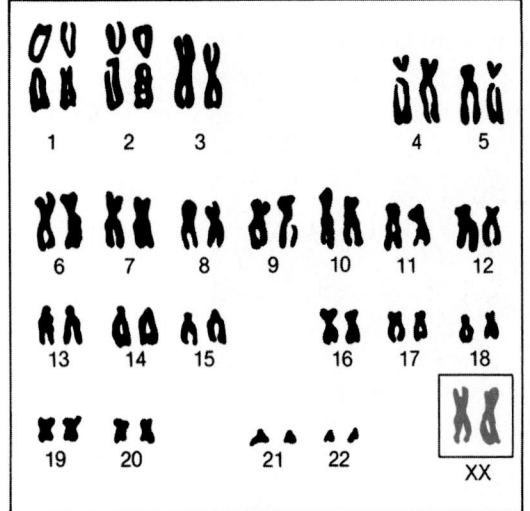

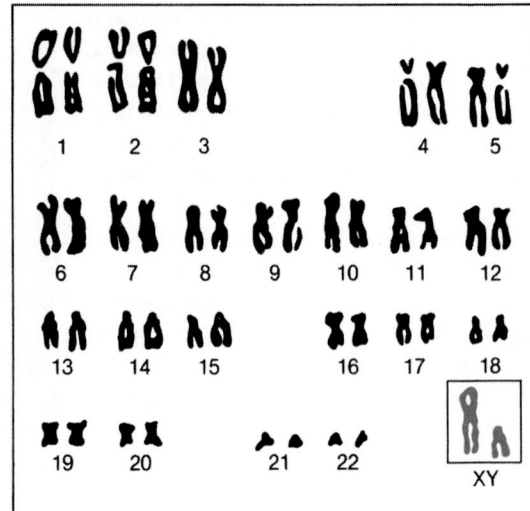

Female   Male

FIGURE 3.18
The 23 Pairs of Human Chromosomes People normally have 23 pairs of chromosomes. Whether one is female or male is determined by the 23rd pair of chromosomes. Females have two X sex chromosomes, whereas males have an X and a Y sex chromosome.

Nature • In behavior genetics, heredity.

Nurture • In behavior genetics, environmental influences on behavior, such as nutrition, culture, socioeconomic status, and learning.

Genome • (JEE-nome). All the DNA contained within the set of human chromosomes. The sum of the genetic material that controls the processes that define the human being.

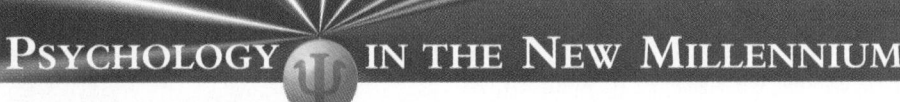

PSYCHOLOGY Ψ IN THE NEW MILLENNIUM

The Human Genome Project

If you had only four letters with which to work, how would you spell *human being?* In a sense, the answer to this question is a key quest of the Human Genome Project. (The Human Genome Project is a government-funded 15-year program that was begun in the late 1980s in the United States and elsewhere. It is expected to be completed early in the new millennium.) Using only *C, A, T,* and *G* (which stand for the bases *cytosine, adenine, thymine,* and *guanine*), one goal of the project is to sequence the 3 billion letters that compose human DNA.

Another goal of the project is to identify all the genes that make up the human **genome** (that is, all the DNA contained within the set of 23 pairs of human chromosomes). By so doing, researchers will be able to determine whether individuals have the genes that contribute to disorders ranging from physical disorders such as cancer to psychological disorders such as bipolar mood disorder and schizophrenia.

Health Implications. Part of the promise of the Human Genome Project is revealed in methods of genetic diagnosis and genetic engineering that are also under development today (Maxwell, 1994). Genetic engineering promises to provide couples with genetically abnormal embryos the possibility of correcting the problem in the uterus. In gene replacement therapy, for example, abnormal genes are replaced with normal genes.

Recent innovations include screening methods for the fatal hereditary diseases Huntington's chorea and cystic fibrosis. The following developments are in the offing or, in some form, here:

• Ways of detecting predispositions for physical disorders such as cancer, heart disease, and emphysema by studying a newborn's (or fetus's) genetic code.

• Ways of detecting predispositions for psychological disorders such as serious mood disorders and schizophrenia by studying a newborn's (or fetus's) genetic code.

Truth or Fiction Revisited. *It is true that zookeepers who want to have baby girls or boys (crocodiles, that is) need only control the temperature at which the eggs develop.*

A normal human cell contains 46 chromosomes, which are organized into 23 pairs. When we do not have the normal complement of 46 chromosomes, physical and behavioral abnormalities may result. The risk of these abnormalities rises with the age of the parents (Solomon and others, 1993).

Most persons with Down syndrome have an extra, or third, chromosome on the 21st pair. The extra chromosome is usually contributed by the mother and becomes increasingly likely as women age (Solomon and others, 1993). Persons with Down syndrome show a downward-sloping fold of skin at the inner corners of the eyes, creating a superficial resemblance to Asians.

Hence the old term *mongolism,* which is now recognized to be racist and no longer used. People with Down syndrome also show a characteristic round face, protruding tongue, and broad, flat nose. They are mentally retarded and may have respiratory problems and malformations of the heart. Most people with Down syndrome die by middle age.

Behavior geneticists are attempting to sort out the relative importance of **nature** (heredity) and **nurture** (environmental influences) in the origins of behavior. Psychologists are especially interested in the roles of nature and nurture in intelligence and psychological disorders.

Behavior in general reflects the influences of both nature and nurture. Organisms inherit structures that set the stage for certain behaviors. But none of us, as we appear, is the result of heredity alone. Environmental

MINILECTURE: GENETIC ABNORMAL- ITIES

- Ways of detecting predispositions for psychological traits such as activity level and shyness.
- Understanding how "spelling errors" in the genetic code cause hereditary diseases. For example, it is already known that a physical disorder prevalent among African Americans, sickle cell anemia, is connected with an abnormal sequence in the genetic code. The normal "spelling" in the key genetic site is CCTG**A**GG, but sickle cell anemia occurs when the base sequence is misspelled as CCTG**T**GG (Solomon and others, 1993).
- New vaccines for diseases like hepatitis and herpes.
- Modification of the genetic codes of unborn children through gene replacement therapy to prevent the individual from developing disease.
- Inserting healthy genes into white blood cells to enhance the cells' ability to combat cancer and other diseases.
- Inserting normal genes into fertilized egg cells, so that future generations within families at risk will not develop genetic disorders (Solomon and others, 1993). Such an approach would be a true genetic cure for such a disorder.
- Creation of wonder drugs from DNA.

On some day early in the new millennium, the genetic code that makes up the human being will be held in the memories of computers. Who knows what applications will occur when we have all the genetic information necessary to define a human being? Can you begin to speculate on the ethical and religious debates that are likely to take place? Can you sketch out a science fiction story in which researchers use this information to create super humans in the laboratory?

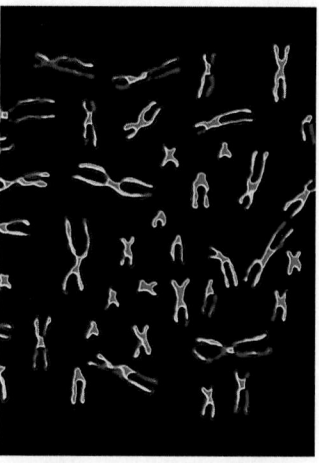

The Human Genome Project. The Human Genome Project is a government-funded program that is expected to be completed early in the new millennium. One goal of the project is to be able to determine whether individuals have the genes that contribute to disorders ranging from physical disorders such as cancer to psychological disorders such as bipolar mood disorder and schizophrenia.

factors such as nutrition, learning opportunities, cultural influences, exercise, and (unfortunately) accident and illness also determine whether genetically possible behaviors will be displayed. A potential Shakespeare reared in an impoverished environment and never taught to read or write will not create a *Hamlet.* Thus, behavior represents the interaction of nature and nurture.

KINSHIP STUDIES

Psychologists conduct kinship studies to help determine the role of genetic factors in behavior patterns and mental processes. They locate subjects who show the behavior pattern in question and then study the distribution of the behavior among relatives. The more closely people are related, the more genes they have in common. Parents and children have a 50% overlap in their genetic endowments, and so do siblings (brothers and sisters). Aunts and uncles related by blood have a 25% overlap with nieces and nephews; first cousins share 12.5% of their genetic endowment. If genes are implicated in a behavior pattern, people more closely related should be more likely to share the pattern.

Twin Studies. The fertilized egg cell (ovum) that carries genetic messages from both parents is called a **zygote.** Now and then, a zygote divides into two cells that separate so that each develops into an individual with the same genetic makeup. Such people are identical twins, or **monozygotic (MZ) twins.** If the woman releases two ova in the same month, and they are both fertilized, they develop into fraternal twins, or **dizygotic (DZ) twins.** DZ twins are related in the same way as other siblings and share 50% of their genes (Segal, 1993). MZ twins are important in the study of the relative influences of nature (heredity) and nurture (the environment) because differences between MZ twins are the result of nurture.

Physically speaking, MZ twins are more likely to look alike and be closer in height, even to have more similar blood levels of cholesterol, than DZ twins (Heller and others, 1993). Psychologically speaking, MZ twins resemble one another more strongly than DZ twins in traits such as shyness and activity levels (Emde, 1993), ir-

ritability (Goldsmith, 1993), sociability, and cognitive development (DeFries and others, 1987). MZ twins show more similarity than DZ twins in their early signs of attachment, such as smiling, cuddling, and expression of fear of strangers (Scarr & Kidd, 1983). Also, MZ twins are more likely than DZ twins to share psychological disorders such as **autism,** anxiety, substance dependence, and schizophrenia. In one study on autism, the **concordance** rate for MZ twins in one study was 96% (Ritvo and others, 1985). The concordance rate for DZ twins was only 24%.

Adoptee Studies. The interpretation of many kinship studies is confounded by the fact that relatives usually share common backgrounds as well as genes (Coon and others, 1990; Segal, 1993). This is especially true of identical twins, who are frequently dressed identically and encouraged to follow similar interests. Adoptee studies, in which children are separated from their parents at an early age (or in which identical twins are separated at an early age) and then reared apart provide special opportunities for sorting out nature and nurture. Psychologists look for the relative similarities between children and their adoptive and natural parents. When children who are reared by adoptive parents are nonetheless more similar to their natural parents in a trait, a powerful argument is made for a genetic role in the appearance of that trait.

DOMINANT AND RECESSIVE TRAITS

Traits are determined not by single genes but by pairs of genes. Each member of a pair is derived from the father or the mother.

Gregor Mendel (1822–1884), an Austrian monk, established a number of laws of heredity through his work with plants. Mid-19th-century science did not permit Mendel to learn of the biochemical nature of genes. Still, Mendel realized that some traits result from an averaging of the genetic instructions carried by the parents. Mendel also discovered the "law of dominance." For example, the offspring from the crossing of purebred tall peas and purebred dwarf peas were tall, suggesting that tallness is dominant over dwarfism. We now know

Zygote • (ZY-goat). A fertilized egg cell.

Monozygotic twins • (MON-oh-zy-GOT-tick). Identical, or MZ, twins. Twins who develop from a single zygote, thus carrying the same genetic instructions.

Dizygotic twins • (die-zy-GOT-tick). Fraternal, or DZ, twins. Twins who develop from separate zygotes.

Autism • A childhood disorder marked by problems such as failure to relate to others, lack of speech, and intolerance of change.

Concordance • Agreement.

Dominant trait • In genetics, a trait that is expressed.

Recessive trait • In genetics, a trait that is not expressed when the genes involved are paired with dominant genes. They are transmitted to future generations, however, and are expressed if they are paired with other recessive genes.

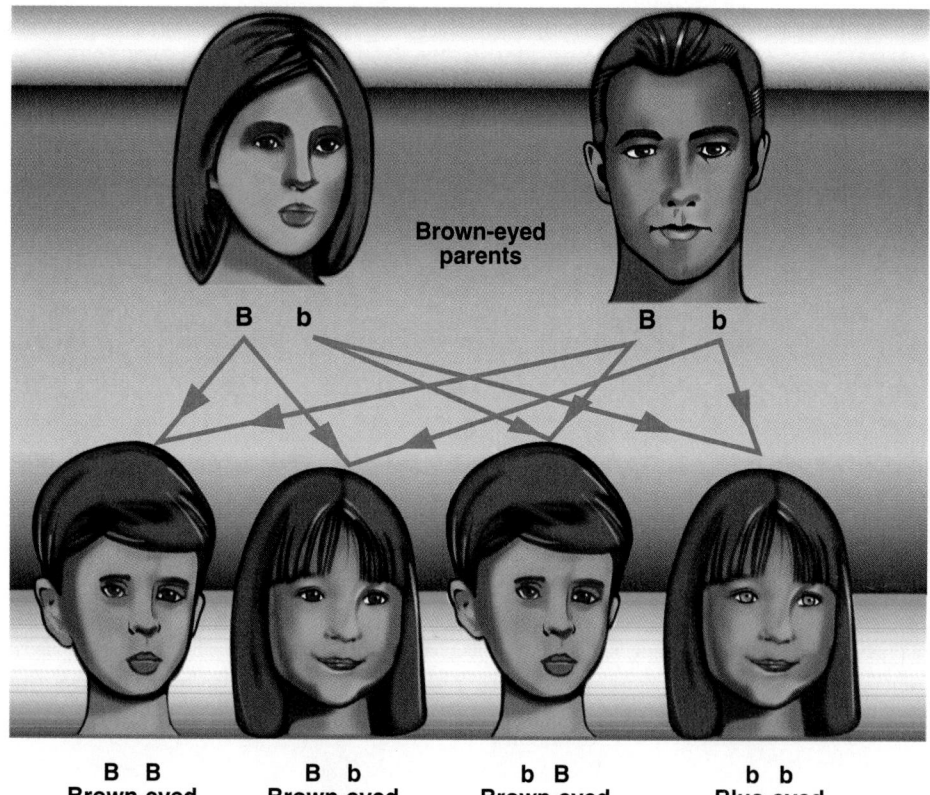

B B
Brown-eyed
child

B b
Brown-eyed
child

b B
Brown-eyed
child

b b
Blue-eyed
child

FIGURE 3.19
Transmission of Dominant and Recessive Traits Two brown-eyed parents each carry a recessive gene for blue eyes. Their children have an equal opportunity of receiving genes for brown eyes and blue eyes. In such cases, 25% of the children show the recessive trait—blue eyes. The other 75% show the dominant trait—brown eyes. But two of three who show brown eyes carry the recessive trait for transmittal to future generations.

that some genes carry **dominant traits** and others carry **recessive traits.** When a dominant gene is paired with a recessive gene, the dominant gene appears in the offspring.

Brown hair, for instance, is dominant over blond hair. Therefore, if one parent contributes genes that determine brown hair, and the other contributes genes that determine blond hair, the children will have brown hair.[5] Similarly, brown-haired parents may also carry recessive genes for blond hair.

If the recessive gene from one parent combines with the recessive gene from the other, the recessive trait will be shown. Brown eyes are dominant over blue eyes, but brown-eyed people may carry recessive genes for blue eyes. Approximately 25% of the offspring of parents who each carry a gene for brown and blue eye color will have blue eyes (see Figure 3.19). Mendel had found that 25% of the offspring of tall parent peas that carried recessive dwarfism would be dwarfs.

Truth or Fiction Revisited. *It is true that a child can have blue eyes even when both parents have brown eyes.* It is necessary, however, that the parents have recessive genes for blue eyes.

EXPERIMENTS IN SELECTIVE BREEDING

You need not be a psychologist to know that animals can be selectively bred to enhance desired traits. Compare wolves with their descendants—varieties as diverse as the Great Dane; the tiny, nervous Chihuahua; and the pug-nosed bulldog. We breed our cattle and chickens to be bigger and fatter so that they provide more food calories for less feed. We can also selectively breed animals to enhance traits that are of more interest to psychologists, such as aggressiveness and intelligence—though "intelligence" in lower animals may not correspond to human intelligence. As dogs go, poodles and Shih Tzus are relatively intelligent, bulldogs are loyal, golden

Can Brown-Haired Parents Have a Blond Child? As this photo shows, they certainly can, as long as they each carry recessive genes for blond hair. These parents are also brown-eyed, but the child has blue eyes.

[5] An exception would occur if the children also inherit a gene for albinism, in which case their hair and eyes would be colorless.

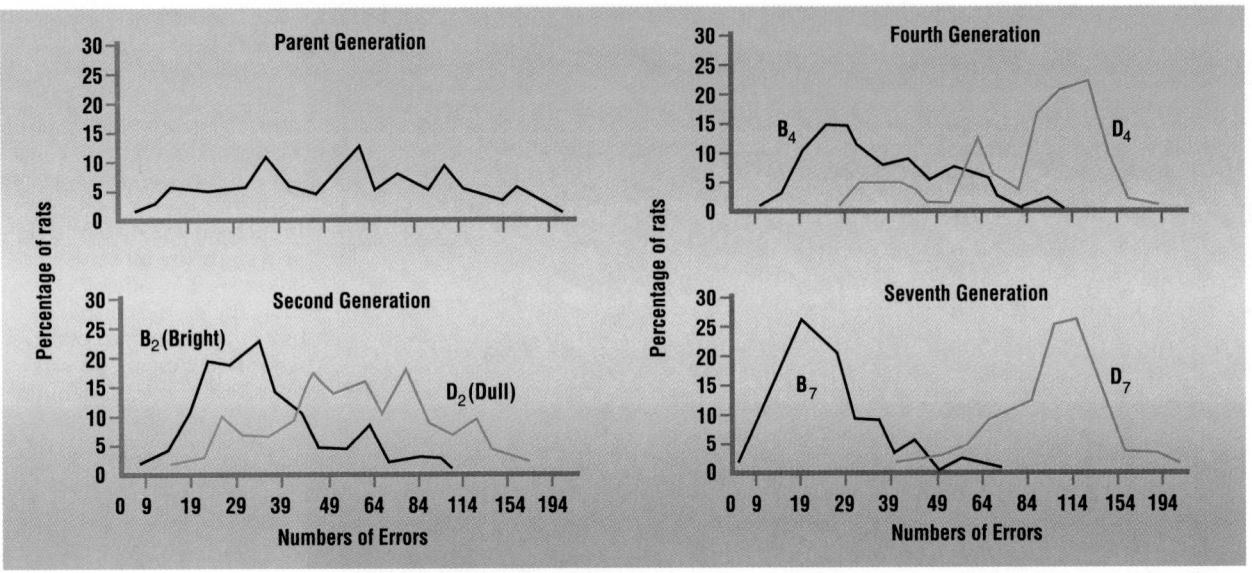

FIGURE 3.20
Selective Breeding for Maze-Learning Ability In the Tryon study, the offspring of maze-bright rats were inbred for six generations. So were the offspring of maze-dull rats. As the generations became further removed, there was progressively less overlap in the maze-learning ability of the offspring of the two groups, even though environmental influences were held as constant as possible for all offspring.

retrievers are docile and patient with children, and Border collies show a compulsive herding instinct (Rosenthal, 1991). Even as puppies, Border collies will attempt to corral people who are out on a lackadaisical stroll.

There is an extensive discussion in Chapter 9 of the roles of heredity (nature) and the environment (nurture) in human intelligence. Here, let us illustrate the concept of selective breeding for maze-learning ability with classic experiments with rats (Rosenzweig and others, 1972; Tryon, 1940).

In one study, an initial group of rats was tested for maze-learning ability as indicated by the number of mistakes they made in repeated efforts to find a food goal. Rats making the fewest mistakes were labeled B_1, signifying the first generation of "maze-bright" rats. "Maze-dull" rats were labeled D_1. The total distribution of errors, or blind-alley entrances, made by the first (parent) generation is shown in Figure 3.20. These errors were made over a series of 19 runs in the Tryon study.

Maze-bright rats from the first generation were then bred with other maze-bright rats, and maze-dull rats were similarly interbred. The second graph in Figure 3.20

shows how the offspring (B_2) of the maze-bright parents compared with the offspring (D_2) of the maze-dull parents in numbers of errors (blind-alley entrances). The offspring of the maze-bright rats, as a group, clearly made fewer errors than the offspring of the maze-dull, although there was considerable overlap between groups. The brightest offspring of the maze-bright were then interbred, as were the dullest of the maze-dull, for six consecutive generations. Fortunately for experimental psychologists, rat generations are measured in months, not decades. Throughout these generations, the environments of the rats were kept as constant as possible. Dull rats were often raised by bright mothers, and vice versa, so that a critic could not argue that the maze-learning ability of bright offspring could be attributed to an enriched environment provided by a bright mother.

After six generations, there was little overlap in maze-learning performance between maze-bright and maze-dull rats. The (spatial relations) superiority of the maze-bright rats did not generalize to all types of learning tasks. We also cannot emphasize too strongly that maze-learning ability in rats is not comparable to the complex groupings of behavior that define human intelligence.

Some breeds of dogs such as Doberman pinschers and German shepherds have been bred to be more aggressive than other varieties. Within breeds, however, dogs have been selectively bred to show high or low activity levels. Chickens have also been selectively bred for aggressiveness (consider the "sport" of cockfighting) and for level of sexual activity.

Reflections

Now that you have read about genetics and behavior genetics, reflect on the following questions:

- What is the role of heredity in the transmission of physical traits such as hair color and height? What are your assumptions concerning genetic factors in the development of psychological traits such as intelligence, social shyness, and depression? (Tune in to the rest of this book to check out your assumptions.)
- Which family members seem to be like you physically or psychologically? Which seem to be very different? To what do you attribute the similarities and differences? Why?
- Are you aware of any individuals who have genetic or chromosomal disorders? If a genetic disorder, is it a dominant or recessive trait?

Summary

1. **What are the parts of the nervous system?** The nervous system consists of neurons, which transmit information through neural impulses, and glial cells, which serve support functions. Neurons have a cell body (soma), dendrites, and axons. Neurotransmitters transmit messages across synapses to other neurons.

2. **What is myelin?** Many neurons have myelin sheaths that insulate axons but are missing at nodes of Ranvier. In myelinated neurons, neural impulses "jump" from node to node.

3. **What are afferent and efferent neurons?** Afferent neurons transmit sensory messages to the central nervous system. Efferent neurons conduct messages from the central nervous system that stimulate glands or cause muscles to contract.

4. **How are neural impulses transmitted?** Neural transmission is electrochemical. An electric charge is conducted along an axon through a process that allows sodium ions into the cell and then pumps them out. The neuron has a resting potential of -70 millivolts and an action potential of $+30$ to $+40$ millivolts.

5. **How do neurons fire?** Excitatory synapses stimulate neurons to fire; inhibitory neurons influence them not to. Neurons fire according to an all-or-none principle. Neurons may fire hundreds of times per second, and absolute and relative refractory (insensitive) periods follow each firing.

6. **What are some important neurotransmitters?** These include acetylcholine, which is involved in muscle contractions; dopamine, imbalances of which have been linked to Parkinson's disease and schizophrenia; and noradrenaline, which accelerates the heartbeat and other body processes. Endorphins are naturally occurring painkillers.

7. **What is the central nervous system?** The brain and spinal cord compose the central nervous system. Reflexes involve the spinal cord but not the brain. The somatic and autonomic systems compose the peripheral nervous system.

8. **What are the parts of the brain?** The hindbrain includes the medulla, pons, and cerebellum. The reticular activating system begins in the hindbrain and continues through the midbrain into the forebrain. Important structures of the forebrain include the thalamus, hypothalamus, limbic system, basal ganglia, and cerebrum.

The hypothalamus is involved in controlling body temperature and regulating motivation and emotion.

9. **What are the other parts of the nervous system?** The somatic nervous system transmits sensory information about skeletal muscles, skin, and joints to the central nervous system. It also controls skeletal muscular activity. The autonomic nervous system (ANS) regulates the glands and activities such as heartbeat, digestion, and dilation of the pupils.

10. **What are the parts of the cerebral cortex?** The cerebral cortex is divided into the frontal, parietal, temporal, and occipital lobes. The visual cortex is in the occipital lobe, and the auditory cortex is in the temporal lobe. The somatosensory cortex lies behind the central fissure in the parietal lobe, and the motor cortex lies in the frontal lobe, across the central fissure from the somatosensory cortex.

11. **What parts of the brain are involved in thought and language?** Association areas of the cortex are involved in thought and language. The language areas of the cortex lie near the intersection of the frontal, temporal, and parietal lobes in the dominant hemisphere. For right-handed people, the left hemisphere of the cortex is usually dominant. The notion that some people are left-brained whereas others are right-brained is exaggerated and largely inaccurate.

12. **How do people who have had split-brain operations behave?** For the most part, their behavior is perfectly normal. However, although they may be able to verbally describe a screened-off object such as a pencil that is held in the hand connected to the dominant hemisphere, they cannot do so when the object is held in the other hand.

13. **What is the endocrine system?** The endocrine system consists of ductless glands that secrete hormones.

14. **What are some pituitary hormones?** The pituitary gland secretes growth hormone; prolactin, which regulates maternal behavior in lower ani-

mals and stimulates production of milk in women; and oxytocin, which stimulates labor in pregnant women.

15. **What is the function of insulin?** Insulin enables the body to metabolize sugar. Diabetes, hyperglycemia, and hypoglycemia are all linked to imbalances in insulin.

16. **What hormones are produced by the adrenal glands?** The adrenal cortex produces steroids, which promote development of muscle mass and increase activity level. The adrenal medulla secretes adrenaline (epinephrine), which increases the metabolic rate and is involved in general emotional arousal.

17. **What hormones are secreted by the testes and ovaries?** These are sex hormones such as testosterone, progesterone, and estrogen. Sex hormones are responsible for prenatal sexual differentiation, and female sex hormones regulate the menstrual cycle.

18. **What is genetics?** Genetics is the branch of biology concerned with transmission of traits from generation to generation.

19. **What are genes and chromosomes?** Genes are the basic building blocks of heredity and consist of DNA. A thousand or more genes make up each chromosome. People normally have 46 chromosomes. They receive 23 from the father and 23 from the mother.

20. **What are kinship studies?** These are studies of the distribution of traits or behavior patterns among related people. When behaviors are more commonly shared by close relatives, such as identical twins, there may be genetic involvement in them. This is especially so when they are shared by close blood relatives (parents and children, or identical twins) who are separated early and reared apart.

21. **What are dominant and recessive traits?** Dominant traits are traits that are expressed, whereas recessive traits are those shown only if a recessive gene from one parent combines with a recessive gene from the other.

Psychology and Modern Life

MINILECTURE:
ALZHEIMER'S
DISEASE

This "Psychology and Modern Life" section concerns two crucial issues in the interfaces between psychology, brain structures, neurotransmitters, and hormones: Alzheimer's disease and premenstrual syndrome. The likelihood of encountering Alzheimer's disease increases dramatically with advanced age. Because people are living longer today, Alzheimer's has become a more widespread problem. Many women encounter premenstrual syndrome (PMS). Neither problem is fully understood. Alzheimer's involves brain structures and neurotransmitters, but the causal connections are clouded. PMS involves hormones, but here, too, our knowledge leaves much to be desired. In this section we review what is known about these problems, and ways of coping.

Alzheimer's Disease

Alzheimer's disease is a progressive form of mental deterioration that may affect as many as 4 million Americans (Angier, 1993; Growdon, 1992; Teri & Wagner, 1992). Studies in Massachusetts (see Figure 3.21) show that Alzheimer's affects about 10% of people over the age of 65, and the risk increases dramatically with advanced age (Evans and others, 1989; Selkoe, 1992). Although Alzheimer's is connected with aging, it is a disease and not part of a normal aging process (Kolata, 1991a).

Truth or Fiction Revisited. *Alzheimer's disease is thus not a normal part of growing old.*

Alzheimer's disease is characterized by progressive deterioration in mental processes such as memory, language, and problem solving (Crystal, 1988; Wilson & Kaszniak, 1986). Isolated memory losses (for example, forgetting where one put one's glasses) may be a normal feature of aging. Alzheimer's seriously impairs vocational and social functioning (Davies, 1988).

People with Alzheimer's disease may initially find it difficult to recall recent events or basic information such as telephone numbers, area codes, ZIP Codes, and the names of grandchildren. It becomes hard to manage finances and compute numbers. There may be subtle personality changes, such as signs of withdrawal in people who

had been outgoing or irritability in people who had been gentle (Davies, 1988). As the disease progresses, people require assistance to manage everyday tasks (Reisberg and others, 1986). They may be unable to select clothes, or recall their addresses or the names of family members. They eventually encounter difficulties in personal functioning, such as in using the bathroom and washing themselves. There are large gaps in memory for recent events. They may fail to recognize familiar people or forget their names (Mendez and others, 1992). They may not recognize themselves in mirrors. Memory for remote events is also affected. They are generally unable to recall the names of their schools, parents, or birthplaces. They may no longer be able to speak in full sentences and limit their verbal responses to a few words.

As time goes on, people with Alzheimer's may pace or fidget or display aggressive behavior—yelling, throwing, or hitting. They may wander off because of restlessness and be unable to find their way back. About one person in three shows evidence of hallucinations or delusions (Jeste and others, 1992). They may believe that someone is attempting to harm them or is stealing from them.

In the most severe cases, people become helpless. They become unable to communicate or walk and require help in toileting and feeding.

Alzheimer's disease was first described in 1907 by the German physician Alois Alzheimer (1864–1915). During an autopsy of a 56-year-old woman who had experienced severe dementia, he found two brain abnormalities that are now regarded as signs of the disease: plaques (portions of degenerative brain tissue) and tangles (twisted bundles of nerve cells). The plaques are believed to destroy the adjacent brain tissue, which leads to loss of memory function, confusion, and other symptoms of the disease. On a biochemical level, research finds that people with Alzheimer's have reduced levels of acetylcholine (ACh) in their brains (Davies, 1988). Lowered levels of ACh may reflect loss of brain cells in an area of the brain that manufactures ACh. A number of agents have been suspected in ACh reduction, including a virus that destroys the brain cells which produce

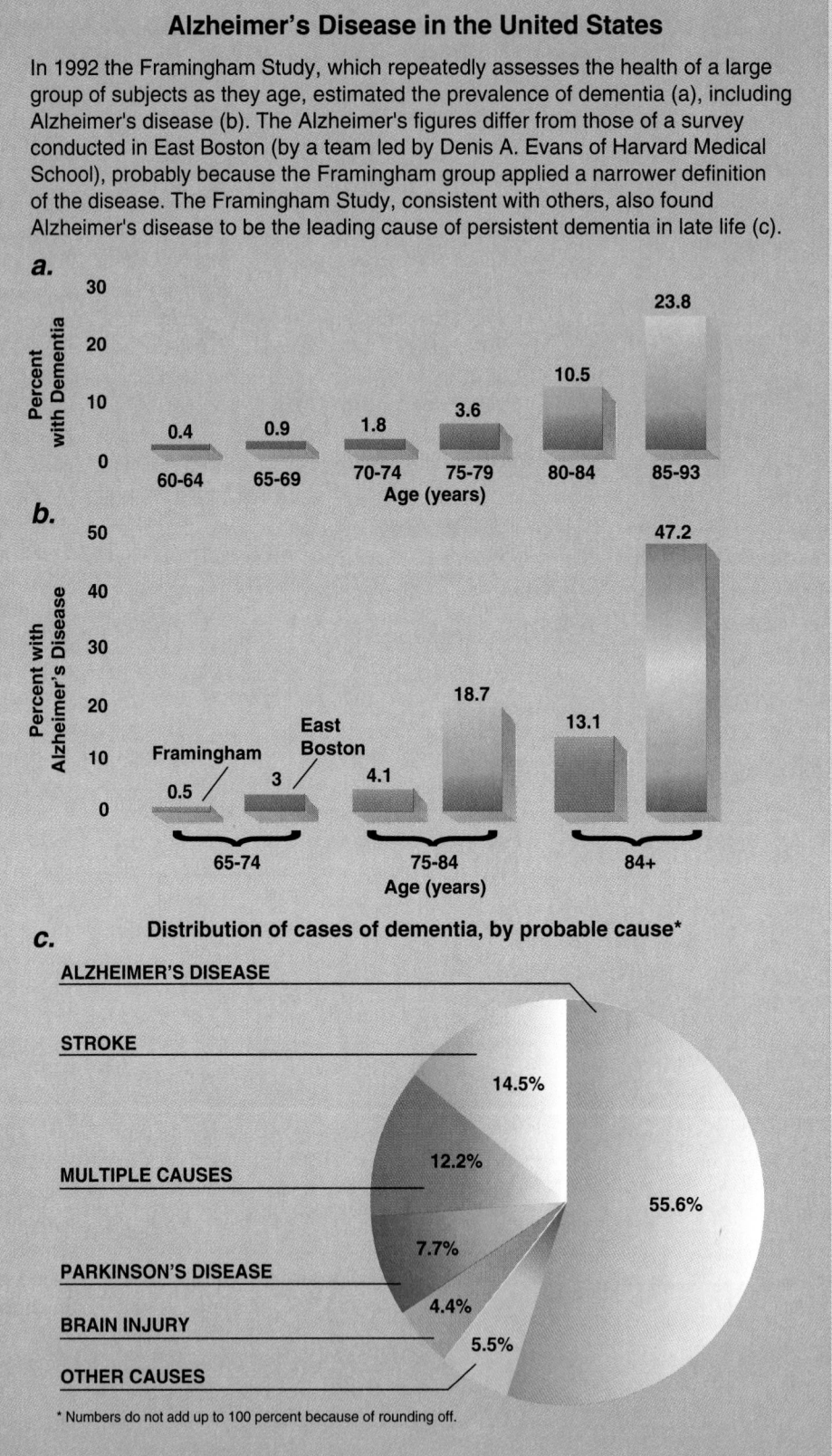

Alzheimer's Disease in the United States

In 1992 the Framingham Study, which repeatedly assesses the health of a large group of subjects as they age, estimated the prevalence of dementia (a), including Alzheimer's disease (b). The Alzheimer's figures differ from those of a survey conducted in East Boston (by a team led by Denis A. Evans of Harvard Medical School), probably because the Framingham group applied a narrower definition of the disease. The Framingham Study, consistent with others, also found Alzheimer's disease to be the leading cause of persistent dementia in late life (c).

a.

Percent with Dementia

30
20
10
0

0.4 — 60-64
0.9 — 65-69
1.8 — 70-74
3.6 — 75-79
10.5 — 80-84
23.8 — 85-93

Age (years)

b.

Percent with Alzheimer's Disease

50
40
30
20
10
0

Framingham   East Boston

0.5   3   — 65-74
4.1   18.7 — 75-84
13.1   47.2 — 84+

Age (years)

c.   **Distribution of cases of dementia, by probable cause***

ALZHEIMER'S DISEASE — 55.6%
STROKE — 14.5%
MULTIPLE CAUSES — 12.2%
PARKINSON'S DISEASE — 7.7%
BRAIN INJURY — 4.4%
OTHER CAUSES — 5.5%

* Numbers do not add up to 100 percent because of rounding off.

FIGURE 3.21
Alzheimer's Disease in the United States Source: Scientific American, September 1992.

ACh, brain traumas, and aluminum poisoning.

The PET scan can be used to measure glucose and oxygen consumption in areas of the brain that might be affected in Alzheimer's disease (Figure 3.22). People with the disease show evidence of generally reduced metabolic rates. Researchers have found a negative correlation between metabolic rate and cognitive performance: The greater the cognitive impairment, the lower the metabolic rate (de Leon and others, 1986).

There is evidence of genetic transmission of Alzheimer's disease. More than 90% of the people who inherit a key gene from both parents contract Alzheimer's disease by the age of 75, as compared with 60% of those who inherit the gene from only one parent and about 20% of those who do not inherit the gene (Angier, 1993).

Because the disease is connected with reductions in ACh, chemotherapy has aimed at heightening ACh levels. For example, the drug tacrine inhibits the breakdown of ACh by decreasing the action of an enzyme that metabolizes it. As of today, however, the effects of tacrine are considered modest at best (Growdon, 1992). Researchers are hopeful that genetic studies of Alzheimer's disease may lead to effective medications early in the new millennium (Roses, 1993).

Premenstrual Syndrome

Menstruation is a source of concern to psychologists because of stereotypes about menstruating women and because of physical discomfort experienced by numerous women. For several days prior to and during menstruation, the stereotype has been that "raging hormones" doom women to irritability and poor judgment—two facets of premenstrual syndrome (PMS). (The "Psychology in a World of Diversity" feature in this chapter shows how widespread misconceptions about menstruation may contribute to stereotypes of menstruating women.) This view has cost women opportunities to assume responsible positions in society.

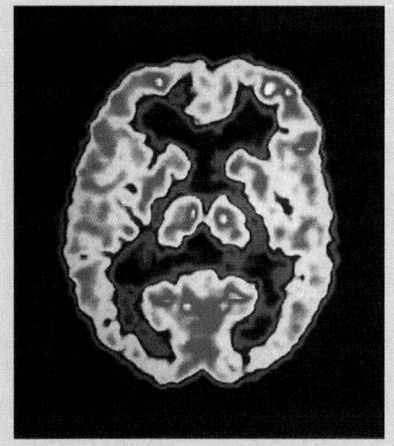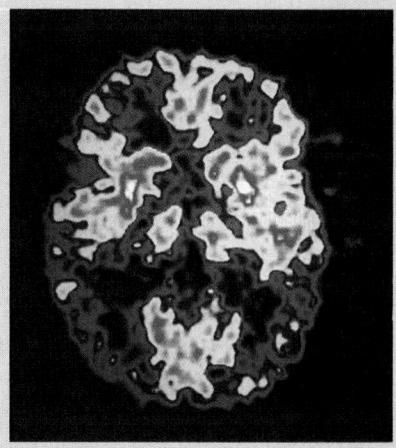

FIGURE 3.22
PET Scans of Brains from a Healthy Aged Adult (Left) and a Person with Alzheimer's Disease (Right)

Women have historically been assumed to be more likely to commit suicide or crimes, call in sick at work, and develop physical and emotional problems during the 8-day period prior to and during menstruation. Moreover, the ability of college women to focus on academic tasks during this period has been brought into question. However, recent research suggests that only 1 woman in 10 has symptoms severe enough to impair academic, occupational, or social functioning (Brody, 1989). Although nearly three out of four college women encounter PMS, the symptoms are usually mild to moderate (Wildman & White, 1986). Fewer than 1% of the women in another survey missed work because of menstrual problems (Gruber & Wildman, 1987).

Truth or Fiction Revisited. *It is not true that PMS impairs the academic, occupational, or social functioning of the majority of college women.* Although the majority of college women do encounter PMS, symptoms are most often mild to moderate. Only a small number are seriously impaired.

The symptoms of PMS are linked to hormone levels. Women's moods and performance on verbal and motor tasks tend to be most positive around time of ovulation, when estrogen peaks (Kimura, 1992). Paige (1971) studied women whose hormone levels were kept rather even by birth-control pills and women whose levels varied naturally throughout the cycle. Women whose hormone levels fluctuated appeared to show somewhat greater anxiety and hostility prior to and during menstruation. However, they did not commit crimes or wind up in mental wards.

Nevertheless, hormonal changes cause very real and painful problems for some women. For instance, prostaglandins cause uterine contractions. Most contractions go unnoticed, but strong, unrelieved contractions are uncomfortable in themselves and may temporarily deprive the uterus of oxygen, another source of pain (Ferin and others, 1993). In such cases, prostaglandin-inhibiting drugs such as ibuprofen and indomethacin help a number of women (Copeland and others, 1993). Other women report being helped by regular exercise and proper nutrition, including low-fat diets and dietary supplements, particularly B vitamins and minerals such as calcium and magnesium. Stress-management techniques such as relaxation training and social support are also sometimes helpful.

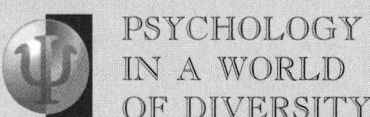

PSYCHOLOGY IN A WORLD OF DIVERSITY

CROSS-CULTURAL PERSPECTIVES ON MENSTRUATION

In Peru, they speak of a "visit from Uncle Pepe." In Samoa, menstruation is referred to as "the boogie man." One of the more common epithets given menstruation through the course of history is "the curse." The Fulani of Burkina Faso in Africa use a term for it that translates as "to see dirt." Nationalism also rises to the call, with some nations blaming "the curse" on their historic enemies. In earlier times, the French referred to menstruation as "the English" and to its onset as, "the English are coming." Iranians used to say "The Indians have attacked" to announce menstrual bleeding.

In preliterate societies, it is a common folk belief that menstrual blood is tainted (Rathus and others, 1993). Men thus avoid contact with menstruating women for fear of their lives. To avoid contamination, menstruating women are dispatched to special huts on the fringe of the village. In the traditional Navajo Indian culture, for instance, menstruating women would be consigned to huts that were set apart from other living quarters.

The Old Testament (Leviticus 15:19) warns against any physical contact with a menstruating woman, including of course, coitus:

> And if a woman have an issue, and her issue in her flesh be blood, she shall be put apart seven days; and whosoever toucheth her shall be unclean.

Orthodox Jews still abstain from coitus during menstruation and the week afterward. Prior to resuming sexual relations, the woman must attend a *mikvah*—a ritual cleansing.

Fears of contamination by menstruating women are nearly universal across cultures and remain quite current (Rathus and others, 1993). As late as the 1950s, women were not allowed in some European breweries for fear that the beer would turn sour. Some Indian castes still teach that a man who touches a woman during menses becomes contaminated and must be purified by a priest.

We might laugh off these misconceptions as folly if it were not for their profound effects on women. Women who suffer from premenstrual syndrome may be responding to negative cultural attitudes toward menstruation as well as to menstrual symptoms themselves. The traditional view of menstruation as a time of pollution may make women highly sensitive to internal sensations at certain times of the month as well as concerned about discreet disposal of the menstrual flow. Women who do not share highly traditional cultural attitudes—including attitudes about the debilitating nature of menstruation—are less likely to show mood changes throughout the different phases of the menstrual cycle (Paige, 1973).

Negative stereotypes about menstruation may heighten the biological problems some women face at this time of the month.

WHAT TO DO ABOUT MENSTRUAL DISCOMFORT

Most women experience some degree of menstrual discomfort. Women with persistent menstrual distress may profit from the suggestions listed below. Researchers are currently exploring the effectiveness of these techniques. For now, you may consider a personal experiment. Try some or all of the methods that sound right to you.

1. Do not blame yourself for your discomfort! Menstrual problems were once erroneously attributed to women's "hysterical" nature. Nonsense. Menstrual problems, as noted, largely reflect chemical changes during the menstrual cycle.

2. Keep a calendar to help track your menstrual symptoms and identify patterns. Then develop strategies to deal with days on which you are likely to experience the greatest distress. Such strategies include engaging in pleasurable activities and avoiding stressful activities. Try activities that may distract you from menstrual discomfort. See a movie or start that novel you've been meaning to read.

3. Examine whether you hold self-defeating attitudes toward menstruation that might be compounding your discomfort. Do your relatives or friends view menstruation as an illness or a "dirty thing"? Have you succumbed to these attitudes? For example, do you restrict your social activities during your period?

4. See a doctor about your concerns, especially if discomfort is severe. Deep pain may stem from medical disorders such as endometriosis and pelvic inflammatory disease (PID). Also ask your doctor about diuretics, ibuprofen and other analgesics, and vitamin supplements.

5. Cultivate nutritious eating habits. (Stick to them throughout your entire cycle—in other words, always). Consider whether your intake of alcohol, caffeine, fats, salt, and sweets is affecting your discomfort, especially during the days preceding menstruation.

6. Some women report that vigorous exercise—aerobic exercise, jogging, bicycling, swimming, dancing, fast walking, skating, or jump rope—helps relieve premenstrual and menstrual discomfort. Moreover, women who exercise are not taking menstruation discomfort "lying down"! They remain the masters of their physical fates.

7. Remember that menstrual problems are time-limited. Don't focus on getting through life or a career. Focus on getting through the next few days.

Truth or Fiction Revisited. *It is not true that women can do little about menstrual discomfort other than "tough it out."* Many measures may be of help. Explore those that may be of help to you.

Reflections

Now that you have read about genetics and behavior genetics, reflect on the following questions:

- Do you know any older people who have memory problems and appear to be disorganized? What are the possible origins of their problems? Are you assuming that the difficulties are basically biological? Could lack of motivation or feelings of depression play a role in their behavior? How can psychologists tell the difference?
- What attitudes toward menstruation were expressed in your family? Have these attitudes affected your own views? How so?
- If you are a female, do you experience menstrual discomfort? If so, have you investigated the reasons for it? How do you cope with the discomfort? Are you doing everything you can for yourself? (If not, why not?)

4

Sensation and Perception

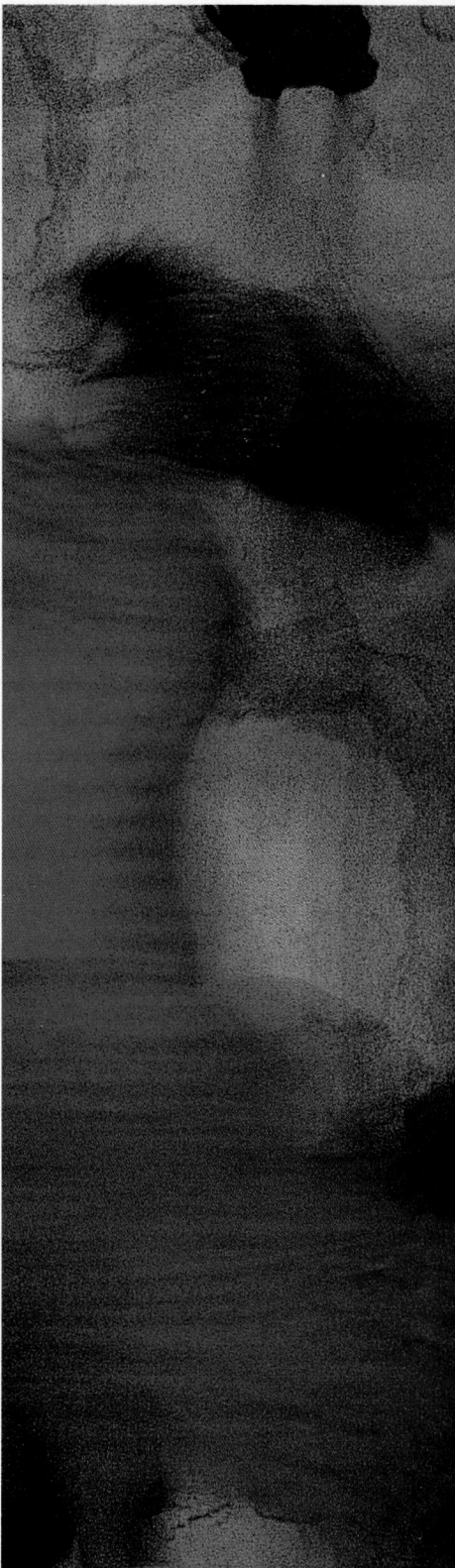

Truth or Fiction?

_____ People have five senses.

_____ On a clear, dark night you could probably see the light from a candle burning 30 miles away.

_____ If we could see lights of slightly longer wavelengths, warm-blooded animals would glow in the dark.

_____ White sunlight is actually composed of all the colors of the rainbow.

_____ When we mix blue light and yellow light, we attain green light.

_____ A $500 machine-made violin will produce the same musical notes as a $200,000 Stradivarius.

_____ Onions and apples have the same taste.

_____ Many amputees experience pain in limbs that have been removed.

_____ Rubbing or scratching a sore toe is often an effective way of relieving pain.

_____ We have a sense that keeps us upright.

Outline

Truth or Fiction?

Sensation and Perception: Your Ticket of Admission to the World Outside

Absolute Threshold: Is It There or Isn't It?

Difference Threshold: Is It the Same or Is It Different?

Signal-Detection Theory: Is Being Bright Enough?

Feature Detectors

Binding in the Brain: From Grandmother Cells to Convergence Zones

Sensory Adaptation: Where Did It Go?

Vision: Letting the Sun Shine In

Light: What Is This Stuff?

The Eye: The Better to See You With

Creating an Inner World of Color: Color Vision

Psychological Dimensions of Color

Theories of Color Vision

Color Blindness

Visual Perception

Perceptual Organization

Perception of Movement

Depth Perception

Problems in Visual Perception

Perceptual Constancies

Visual Illusions

Hearing

Pitch and Loudness

The Ear: The Better to Hear You With

Locating Sounds

Perception of Loudness and Pitch

Deafness

   Psychology in the New Millennium: Sonic Device May Help Blind People Navigate

   Psychology in a World of Diversity: The Signs of the Times Are Changing to Reflect New Sensibilities among the Deaf

Smell

   Psychology in the New Millennium: Will We Be Using "a Sixth Sense for Sex" When the 21st Century Rolls In?

Taste

The Skin Senses

Touch and Pressure

Temperature

Pain: The Often Unwanted Message

Kinesthesis

The Vestibular Sense: On Being Upright

Summary

Psychology and Modern Life

Pain Management: More Than a Medical Issue

Five thousand years ago in China, give or take a day or two, an arrow was shot into the air. Where did it land? Ancient records tell us precisely where: in the hand of a fierce warrior and master of the martial arts. As the story was told to me, the warrior had grown so fierce because of a chronic toothache. Incessant pain had ruined his disposition.

One fateful day, our hero watched as invading hordes assembled on surrounding hills. His troops were trembling in the face of their great numbers, and he raised his arms to boost their morale. A slender wooden shaft lifted into the air from a nearby rise, arced, and then descended—right into the warrior's palm. His troops cringed and muttered among themselves, but our hero said nothing. Although he saw the arrow through his palm, he did not scream. He did not run. He did not even complain.

He was astounded. His toothache had vanished. His whole jaw was numb.

Meanwhile the invaders looked on—horrified. They, too, muttered among themselves. What sort of warrior could regard an arrow through his hand with such indifference? Even with a smile? If this was the caliber of the local warrior, they'd be better off traveling west and looking for a brawl in ancient Sumer or in Egypt. They sounded the retreat and withdrew.

Our warrior received a hero's welcome back in town. A physician offered to remove the arrow without a fee—a tribute to bravery. But the warrior would have none of it. The arrow had done wonders for his toothache, and he would brook no meddling. He already had discovered that if the pain threatened to return, he need only twirl the arrow and it would recede once more.

All was not well on the home front, however. Yes, his wife was thrilled to find him jovial once more, but the arrow put a crimp in romance. When he put his arm around her, she was in danger of being stabbed. Finally, she gave him an ultimatum: It was she or the arrow.

Placed in deep conflict, our warrior consulted a psychologist, who then huddled with the physician and the village elders. After much to-do, they asked the warrior to participate in an experiment. They would remove the arrow and replace it with a pin that the warrior could twirl as needed. If the pin didn't do the trick, they could always fall back on the arrow, so to speak.

To the warrior's wife's relief, the pin worked. And here, in ancient China, lay the origins of the art of **acupuncture**—the use of needles to relieve pain and treat assorted ills.

I confess that this tale is not entirely accurate. To my knowledge, there were no psychologists in ancient China. (Their loss.) Moreover, the part about the warrior's wife is fictitious. It is claimed, however, that acupuncture as a means of dealing with pain originated in ancient China when a soldier was, in fact, wounded in the hand by an arrow and discovered that a chronic toothache had disappeared. The Chinese, historians say, then set out to map the body by sticking pins here and there to learn how they influenced the perception of pain.

Control of pain is just one of the many issues that interest psychologists who study the closely related concepts of sensation and perception. **Sensation** is the stimulation of sensory receptors and the transmission of sensory information to the central nervous system (the spinal cord or brain). Sensory receptors are located in sensory organs

Sensation and Perception on a Summer's Day. These children are beating the heat of a sweltering afternoon by frolicking in the water. How many senses are alive to their surroundings and activity? How do they perceive each other and the water? How do they avoid crashing into one another? Or intentionally jostling one another? How do they hear each other laugh? How do they acquire information about the temperatures of the air and the water? How do they gather information about their own movements?

such as the eyes and ears and, as we shall see, in the skin and elsewhere in the body. The stimulation of the senses is mechanical; it results from sources of energy like light and sound or from the presence of chemicals, as in smell and taste.

Perception is not mechanical. Perception is the process by which sensations are organized and interpreted, forming an inner representation of the world. Perception involves much more than sensation. It reflects learning and expectations and the ways in which we organize incoming information about the world. Perception is an active process through which we make sense of sensory stimulation. A human shape and a 12-inch ruler may stimulate paths of equal length among the sensory receptors in our eyes. Whether we interpret the human shape to be a foot-long doll or a full-grown person 15 to 20 feet away is a matter of perception.

In this chapter, you will see that your personal map of reality—your ticket of admission to a world of changing sights, sounds, and other sources of sensory input—depends largely on the so-called five senses: vision, hearing, smell, taste, and touch. We shall see, however, that touch is just one of several "skin senses," which also include pressure, warmth, cold, and pain. There are also senses that alert you to your own body position without your literally having to watch every step you take. As we explore the nature of each of these senses, we shall find that highly similar sensations may lead to quite different perceptions in different people—or within the same person in different situations.

Truth or Fiction Revisited. *It is not true that people have five senses.* People actually have many more than five senses, as we see in this chapter.

Acupuncture • The ancient Chinese practice of piercing parts of the body with needles to deaden pain and treat illness.

Sensation • The stimulation of sensory receptors and the transmission of sensory information to the central nervous system.

Perception • The process by which sensations are organized into an inner representation of the world.

Sensory Thresholds. How much stimulation is necessary before you can detect a stimulus? How bright must the beacon from the lighthouse be to enable you to see it through the fog from several miles offshore?

Sensation and Perception: Your Ticket of Admission to the World Outside

Before we begin our journey through the senses, let us consider a number of concepts that apply to all of them: absolute threshold, difference threshold, signal-detection theory, and sensory adaptation. In doing so, we shall learn why we might be able to dim the lights gradually to near darkness without people becoming aware of our mischief. We shall also learn why we might grow unaware of the most savory aromas of delightful dinners.

ABSOLUTE THRESHOLD: IS IT THERE OR ISN'T IT?

The weakest amount of a stimulus that can be told apart from no stimulus at all is called the **absolute threshold** for that stimulus. For example, the amount of physical energy required to activate the visual sensory system is the absolute threshold for light. Beneath this threshold, detection of light is impossible (Haber & Hershenson, 1980).

Psychophysicists experiment to determine the absolute thresholds of the senses by presenting stimuli of progressively greater intensity. In the **method of constant stimuli,** researchers use sets of stimuli with magnitudes close to the expected threshold. The order of the stimuli is randomized. Study participants say yes if they detect a stimulus and no if they do not. The stimuli are then repeatedly presented to the participants. An individual's absolute threshold for the stimulus is the lowest magnitude of the stimulus that he or she reports detecting 50% of the time. Weaker stimuli may be detected, but less than 50% of the time. Stronger stimuli, of course, will be detected more than 50% of the time.

The relationship between the intensity of a stimulus (a physical event) and its perception (a psychological event) is considered to be **psychophysical.** That is, it bridges psychological and physical events.

As you can see in Table 4.1, absolute thresholds have been determined for the senses of vision, hearing, taste, smell, and touch. Naturally, there are individual differences in absolute thresholds. Some people, that is, are more sensitive to sensory stimuli than others. The same person may also differ somewhat in sensitivity to sensory stimuli from day to day or from occasion to occasion. In the section on signal-detection theory, we shall see that sensitivity reflects psychological as well as physical and biological variables.

If the absolute thresholds for the human senses differed significantly, our daily

---

TABLE 4.1

Absolute Detection Thresholds and Other Characteristics of Human Sensory Systems

SENSE	STIMULUS	RECEPTORS	THRESHOLD
Vision	Electromagnetic energy	Rods and cones in the retina	A candle flame viewed from a distance of about 30 miles on a clear, dark night
Hearing	Sound pressure waves	Hair cells on the basilar membrane of the inner ear	The ticking of a watch from about 20 feet away in a quiet room
Taste	Chemical substances dissolved in saliva	Taste buds on the tongue in the mouth	About 1 teaspoon of sugar dissolved in 2 gallons of water
Smell	Chemical substances in the air	Receptor cells in the upper part of the nasal cavity (the nose)	About one drop of perfume diffused throughout a small house (1 part in 500 million)
Touch	Mechanical displacement or pressure on the skin	Nerve endings located in the skin	The wing of a fly falling on a cheek from a distance of about 0.4 inch

Source: Adapted from "Contemporary Psychophysics," by E. Galanter, 1962, in R. Brown and others (Eds.), *New Directions in Psychology,* New York: Holt, Rinehart and Winston.

TABLE 4.2
Weber's Constants for Various Sensory Discriminations

SENSE	TYPE OF DISCRIMINATION	WEBER'S CONSTANT
Vision	Brightness of a light	1/60
Hearing	Pitch (frequency) of a tone	1/333
	Loudness of a tone	1/10
Taste	Difference in saltiness	1/5
Smell	Amount of rubber smell	1/10
Touch	Pressure on the skin surface	1/7
	Deep pressure	1/77
	Difference in lifted weights	1/53

experiences would be unrecognizable. Our ears are particularly sensitive, especially to sounds low in **pitch.** If they were any more sensitive, we might hear the collisions among molecules of air. If our eyes were sensitive to lights of slightly longer wavelengths, we would perceive infrared light waves. As a result, animals that are warm-blooded and thus give off heat—including our mates—would literally glow in the dark.

Truth or Fiction Revisited. *It is true that on a clear, dark night you could probably see the light from a candle burning 30 miles away.* This figure is in keeping with the absolute threshold for light. *It is also true that if we could see lights of slightly longer wavelengths, warm-blooded animals would glow in the dark.*

DIFFERENCE THRESHOLD: IS IT THE SAME OR IS IT DIFFERENT?

How much of a difference in intensity between two lights is required before you will detect one as being brighter than the other? The minimum difference in the magnitude of two stimuli required to tell them apart is their **difference threshold.** As is the case with the absolute threshold, psychologists have agreed to the criterion of a difference in magnitudes that can be detected 50% of the time.

Psychophysicist Ernst Weber discovered through laboratory research that the difference threshold for perceiving differences in the intensity of light is about 2% (actually closer to 1/60th) of their intensity. This fraction, 1/60th, is known as **Weber's constant** for light. A closely related concept is

the **just noticeable difference** (jnd), or the minimal amount by which a source of energy must be increased or decreased so that a difference in intensity will be perceived. In the case of light, people can perceive a difference in intensity 50% of the time when the brightness of a light is increased or decreased by 1/60th. Weber's constant for light holds whether we are comparing two quite bright or rather dull lights. However, it becomes inaccurate when we compare extremely bright or extremely dull lights.

As you can see in Table 4.2, Weber's research in psychophysics touched on many senses. He derived difference thresholds for different types of sensory stimulation.

A little math will show you the practical importance of these jnd's. Consider weight lifting. Weber's constant for noticing differences in lifted weight is 1/53rd. (Round it off to 1/50th.) That means that one would probably have to increase the weight on a 100-pound barbell by about 2 pounds before the lifter would notice the difference. Now think of the 1-pound dumbbells used by many runners. Increasing the weight of each dumbbell by 2 pounds would be readily apparent to almost anyone because the increase would be threefold, not a small fraction. Yet the increase is still "only" 2 pounds. Return to our power lifter. When he is pressing 400 pounds, a 2-pound difference is less likely to be noticeable than when he is pressing 100 pounds. This is because our constant 2 pounds has become a difference of only 1/200th.

The same principle holds for the other senses: Small changes are more apt to be noticed when we begin our comparisons

Absolute threshold • The minimal amount of energy that can produce a sensation.

Psychophysicist • A person who studies the relationships between physical stimuli (such as light or sound) and their perception.

Method of constant stimuli • A psychophysical method for determining thresholds in which the researcher presents stimuli of various magnitudes and asks the person to report detection.

Psychophysical • Bridging the gap between the physical and psychological worlds.

Pitch • The highness or lowness of a sound, as determined by the frequency of the sound waves.

Difference threshold • The minimal difference in intensity required between two sources of energy so that they will be perceived as being different.

Weber's constant • The fraction of the intensity by which a source of physical energy must be increased or decreased so that a difference in intensity will be perceived.

Just noticeable difference • The minimal amount by which a source of energy must be increased or decreased so that a difference in intensity will be perceived.

with small stimuli. Some dieting programs suggest that dieters reduce calorie intake by "imperceptible" amounts on a daily or weekly basis. They will eventually reach sharply reduced calorie-intake goals, but they may not feel so deprived during the reduction process.

SIGNAL-DETECTION THEORY: IS BEING BRIGHT ENOUGH?

MINILECTURE: DETECTION

Our discussion so far has been rather "in-human." We have written about perception of sensory stimuli as if people are simply switched on by certain amounts of external stimulation. This is not fully accurate. Although people are sensory instruments, they are influenced by complex patterns of psychological stimulation as well as external changes (Macmillan & Creelman, 1991). **Signal-detection theory** considers the human aspects of sensation and perception.

The intensity of the signal is just one of the factors that determine whether people will perceive sensory stimuli (signals) or a difference between two signals. Another is the degree to which the signal can be distinguished from background **noise.** It is easier to hear a friend in a quiet room than in one where people are clinking silverware and glasses and engaging in competing conversations. The quality of a person's biological sensory system is still another factor. Here, we are concerned with the sharpness or acuteness of the individual's sensory system. We consider whether sensory capacity is fully developed or diminished because of illness or advanced years.

MINILECTURE: DISCRIMINATION

Signal-detection theory also considers psychological factors such as motivation, expectations, and learning. For example, the place in which you are reading this book may be abuzz with signals. If you are outside, perhaps there is a breeze against your face. Perhaps the shadows of passing clouds darken the scene now and then. If you are inside, perhaps there are the occasional clanks and hums of a heating system. Perhaps the odors of dinner are hanging in the air, or the voices from a TV set suggest a crowd in another room. Yet, you are focusing your attention on this page, I hope. Thus, the other signals recede into the backdrop of your consciousness. One psychological factor in signal detection is the

focusing or narrowing of attention to signals the person deems important.

Consider some examples. One parent may sleep through a baby's crying, whereas the other parent is awakened. This is not necessarily because one parent is innately more sensitive to the sounds of crying (although some men may conveniently assume that mothers are). Instead, it may be because one parent has been assigned the task of caring for the baby through the night and is thus more highly motivated to attend to the sounds. Because of training, an artist might notice the use of line or subtle colors that would go undetected by a layperson looking at the same painting. A book designer may notice subtle differences between typefaces among books, whereas a layperson would neither be motivated nor trained to attend to these differences.

Signal-detection theory emphasizes the psychological aspects of detecting and responding to signals. The relationship between a physical stimulus and a sensory response is more than mechanical or mathematical. People's ability to detect stimuli such as meaningful blips on a radar screen depends not only on the intensity of the blips themselves but also on their training (learning), motivation (their desire to perceive meaningful blips), and psychological states such as fatigue or alertness.

FEATURE DETECTORS

Imagine that you are standing by the curb of a busy street and a city bus is approaching (Blakeslee, 1992c). When neurons in your sensory organs—in this case, your eyes—are stimulated by the bus, they relay information to the sensory cortex in the brain. Nobel Prize winners David Hubel and Torsten Wiesel (1979) discovered that various neurons in the visual cortex fire in response to particular features of the visual input. Many cells, for example, fire in response to lines presented at various angles—vertical, horizontal, and in between. Other cells fire in response to specific colors. Because they respond to different aspects, or features, of a scene, these cells are termed **feature detectors.** In the example of the bus, visual feature detectors respond to the bus's edges, depth, contours, textures, shadows, speed, and kinds of motion

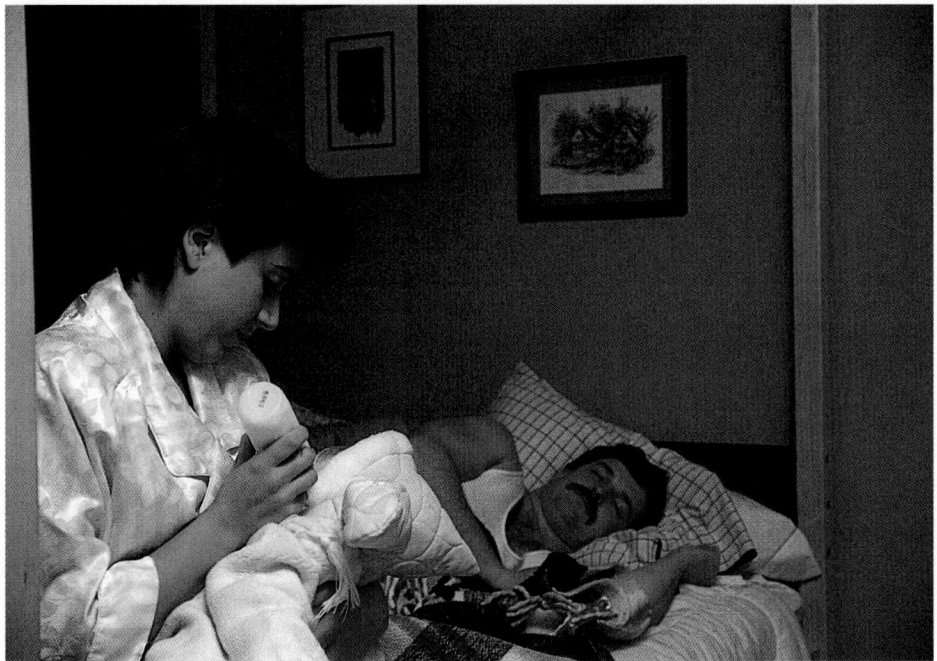

Signal Detection. He sleeps while she is awakened by the baby's crying. Detection of signals, such as a baby's crying, is determined not only by the physical characteristics of the signals but also by psychological factors, such as motivation and attention.

(up, down, forward, and back) (Blakeslee, 1992c). There are also feature detectors for other senses. Auditory feature detectors, for example, respond to the pitch, loudness, and other aspects of the sounds of the bus.

BINDING IN THE BRAIN: FROM GRANDMOTHER CELLS TO CONVERGENCE ZONES

Although feature detectors fire in response to sensory input, we do not merely perceive bits and pieces (features) of scenes. We perceive them in their entirety. Feature detectors transmit millions of pieces of visual information about the bus to higher brain centers, which somehow bind them together. When you consider that millions of feature detectors are involved in sensing the outer world, and that each fires many times per second to keep abreast of the changing scene, you can understand why mathematicians and computer scientists are in awe of the apparently effortless processes of sensation and perception.

How is the image of the bus bound, or pieced together, in the brain? How does it come together? Historically, philosophers and scientists have suggested the presence of a little man (homunculus) in the brain who interpreted sensory input. Some suggested that people have single neurons (such as a "grandmother" neuron) that would fire when we saw the faces of our grandmothers (Blakeslee, 1992c). Still others have suggested the presence of something akin to movie screens in the brain, where the separate streams of visual information are projected to form a unified picture.

The reassembly of sensory information is referred to as **binding.** Current views of how the brain binds input focus on the coordinated firing of millions of neurons. (There are no little men [or women], no grandmother cells, and no movie screens within the brain.) One theory, **synchrony theory,** holds that feature detectors—cells throughout the sensory cortex that respond to specific features of the city bus—fire repeatedly at the same frequency (Zeki, 1992). Neurons that are sensitive to the sounds and smells of the bus and other neurons that may be connected with memories of similar buses may join in to form an inner picture of the bus that is related to past experiences.

Signal-detection theory • The view that the perception of sensory stimuli involves the interaction of physical, biological, and psychological factors.

Noise • (1) In signal-detection theory, any unwanted signal that interferes with perception of the desired signal. (2) More generally, a combination of dissonant sounds.

Feature detectors • Neurons in the sensory cortex that fire in response to specific features of sensory information such as lines or edges of objects.

Binding • The reassembly of sensory information in the brain such that an image from the outer world is reconstituted.

Synchrony theory • A theory of binding that holds that feature detectors fire repeatedly at the same frequency and account for the reassembly of pieces of sensory information into a coherent image.

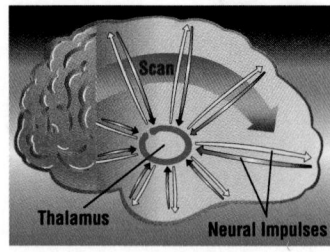

Neural Impulses from the Thalamus May Sweep the Cerebral Cortex to Stimulate Synchronized Firing in Sensory Areas of the Cortex. The cortex then sends information back to the thalamus so that the whole system "lights up" in synchronized fashion, leading to perception of the world outside.

 MINILECTURE: DARK ADAPTATION

Sensory neurons in the cerebral cortex apparently fire in a coordinated manner in response to sensory input. Each sense has a relay station in the thalamus and an area of the cerebral cortex (see Chapter 3). The thalamus sweeps the cerebral cortex with neural impulses nearly 90 times a second (Llinás, 1995). Each sweep leads to synchronized firing in so-called **convergence zones** of the cortex, which results in the binding of sensory information. We perceive the city bus when convergence zones send information back down to the thalamus so that the whole system "lights up" in synchronized fashion (Blakeslee, 1995; Damasio & Damasio, 1992; Zeki, 1992). The process is akin to a Christmas tree with billions of electric candles (Koch, 1992). Groups of "candles" flicker on and off simultaneously. As they fire, the image of the bus is formed within the brain.

SENSORY ADAPTATION: WHERE DID IT GO?

There is a saying that the only constant is change. Our sensory systems are admirably suited to a changing environment. **Sensory adaptation** refers to the processes by which we become more sensitive to stimuli of low magnitude and less sensitive to stimuli of relatively constant magnitude.

Most of us are familiar with the process by which the visual sense adapts to lower intensities of light. When we first walk into a darkened movie theater, we see little but the images on the screen. As time elapses, however, we become increasingly sensitive to the faces of those around us and the inner features of the theater. The process of becoming more sensitive to stimulation is referred to as **sensitization,** or positive adaptation.

On the other hand, we become less sensitive to ongoing stimulation. Sources of light appear to grow dimmer as we adapt to them. In fact, if you could keep an image completely stable on the retinas of your eyes—which is virtually impossible to accomplish without a still image and stabilizing equipment—the image would fade within a few seconds and be very difficult to see. Similarly, at the beach we soon become less aware of the lapping of the waves. When we live in the city, we become de-

sensitized to traffic sounds except for the occasional backfire or accident. As you may have noticed from experiences with freshly painted rooms, sensitivity to disagreeable odors fades quite rapidly. The process of becoming less sensitive to stimulation is referred to as **desensitization,** or negative adaptation.

Reflections

Now that you have read about some basic concepts in sensation and perception, reflect on the following questions:

- How sensitive are your vision and hearing? What is the dimmest light you can see? What is the softest sound you can hear? How do psychophysicists answer such questions?
- Can you think of an example of a just noticeable difference in your life? How much weight do you have to gain or lose to notice a difference? What percentage of your overall weight is that amount? How much harder would you have to work to make a noticeable difference in your grades?
- Have you ever been so involved in doing something that you didn't notice the heat or the cold? Have you gotten so used to sounds like those made by crickets or trains at night that you do not perceive them any more? How do these experiences relate to signal-detection theory?
- Have you had the experience of losing awareness of (getting used to) a disagreeable odor? How does this experience relate to the concepts of sensory adaptation and desensitization?

Let us now examine how each of the human sensory systems perceives signals from the outer (and inner) environments.

Vision: Letting the Sun Shine In

Our eyes are our "windows on the world." We consider information from vision to be more essential than that from hearing, smell, taste, and touch. Because vision is our dominant sense, we consider blindness our most debilitating sensory loss. An understanding of vision requires discussion of the

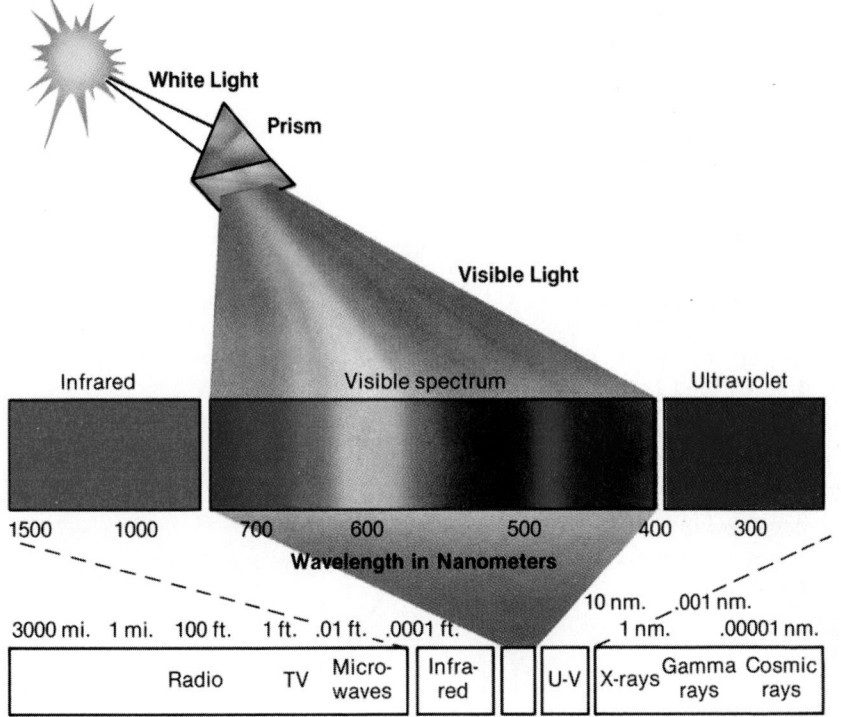

FIGURE 4.1

The Visible Spectrum By passing a source of white light, such as sunlight, through a prism, we break it down into the colors of the visible spectrum. The visible spectrum is just one part—and a narrow part indeed—of the electromagnetic spectrum. The electromagnetic spectrum also includes radio waves, microwaves, X-rays, cosmic rays, and many others. Different forms of electromagnetic energy have different wavelengths, which vary from a few trillionths of a meter to thousands of miles. Visible light varies in wavelength from about 400 to 700 nanometers. What is a nanometer? One *billionth* of a meter. (A meter = 39.37 inches.)

Convergence zones • Levels of processing sensory information in the brain which result in the formation of a coherent mental image from sensory input.

Sensory adaptation • The processes by which organisms become more sensitive to stimuli that are low in magnitude and less sensitive to stimuli that are constant or ongoing in magnitude.

Sensitization • The type of sensory adaptation in which we become more sensitive to stimuli that are low in magnitude. Also called *positive adaptation*.

Desensitization • The type of sensory adaptation in which we become less sensitive to constant stimuli. Also called *negative adaptation*.

Light • The part of the electromagnetic spectrum that stimulates the eye and produces visual sensations.

Visible light • See *light*.

Prism • A transparent triangular solid that breaks down visible light into the colors of the spectrum.

nature of light and of the master of the sensory organs, the eye.

LIGHT: WHAT IS THIS STUFF?

In almost all cultures, **light** is a symbol of goodness and knowledge. We describe capable people as being "bright" or "brilliant." If we are not being complimentary, we label them as "dull." People who aren't in the know are said to be "in the dark." Just what is this stuff called light?

Visible light is the stuff that triggers visual sensations. It is just one small part of a spectrum of electromagnetic energy (see Figure 4.1) that is described in terms of wavelengths. These wavelengths vary from those of cosmic rays, which are only a few trillionths of an inch long, to some radio

waves, which extend for many miles. Radar, microwaves, and X-rays are also forms of electromagnetic energy.

You have probably seen rainbows or light broken down into several colors as it filtered through your windows. Sir Isaac Newton, the British scientist, discovered that sunlight could be broken down into different colors by means of a triangular solid of glass called a **prism** (Figure 4.1). When I took introductory psychology, I was taught that I could remember the colors of the spectrum, from longest to shortest wavelengths, by using the mnemonic device *Roy G. Biv* (red, orange, yellow, green, blue, indigo, violet). I must have been a backward student because I found it easier to recall them in reverse order, using the meaningless acronym *vibgyor*.

MINILECTURE: LIGHT

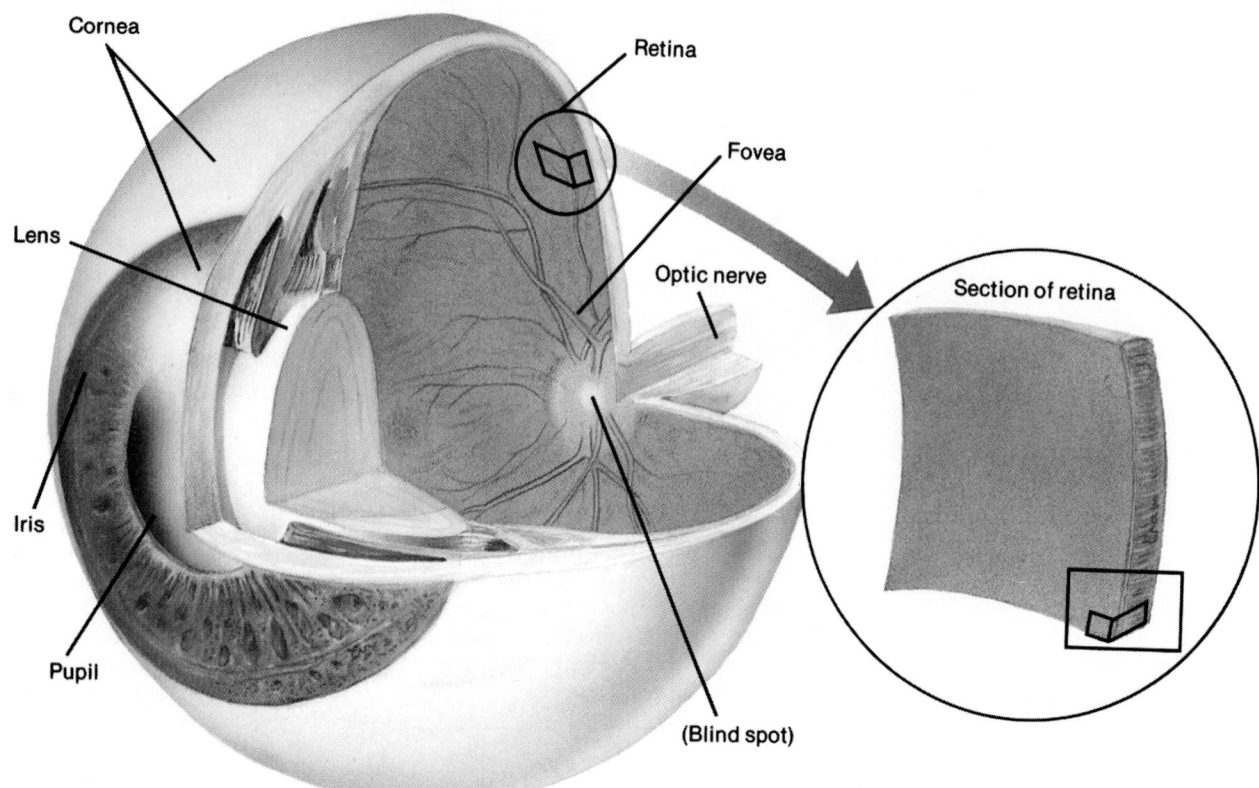

Cornea
Lens
Iris
Pupil
Retina
Fovea
Optic nerve
Section of retina
(Blind spot)

FIGURE 4.2

Spotlight on the Human Eye In both the eye and a camera, light enters through a narrow opening and is projected onto a sensitive surface. In the eye, the photosensitive surface is called the retina, and information concerning the changing images on the retina is transmitted to the brain. In a camera, the photosensitive surface is usually film, which captures a single image.

Hue • The color of light, as determined by its wavelength.

Cornea • Transparent tissue forming the outer surface of the eyeball.

Iris • A muscular membrane whose dilation regulates the amount of light that enters the eye.

MINILECTURE:
THE EYE

Truth or Fiction Revisited. *It is true that white sunlight is actually composed of all the colors of the rainbow.*

The wavelength of visible light determines its color, or **hue.** The wavelength for red is longer than that for orange, and so on through the spectrum.

THE EYE: THE BETTER TO SEE YOU WITH

Consider that magnificent invention called the camera, which records visual experiences. In the camera, light enters an opening and is focused onto a sensitive surface, or film. Chemicals on this surface create a lasting impression of the image that entered the camera.

The eye—our living camera—is no less remarkable. Consider its major parts (Figure 4.2). As with a film or TV camera, light en-

ters through a narrow opening and is projected onto a sensitive surface. Light first passes through the transparent **cornea,** which covers the front of the eye's surface. (The so-called white of the eye is composed of a hard protective tissue and is called the *sclera.*) The amount of light that passes through the cornea is determined by the size of the opening of the muscle called the **iris,** which is also the colored part of the eye. The opening in the iris is called the **pupil.** Pupil size adjusts automatically to the amount of light; you do not have to try purposefully to open the eye farther to see better under conditions of low lighting. The more intense the light, the smaller the opening. In a similar fashion, we adjust the amount of light allowed into a camera according to its brightness. Pupil size is also sensitive to emotional response: We can literally be "wide-eyed with fear."

Once light passes through the iris, it encounters the **lens.** The lens adjusts or accommodates to the image by changing its thickness. Changes in thickness permit projection of a clear image of the object onto the retina; that is, these changes focus the light according to the object's distance. If you hold a finger at arm's length, then slowly bring it toward your nose, you will feel tension in the eye as the thickness of the lens accommodates to keep the retinal image in focus (Haber & Hershenson, 1980). When people squint to bring an object into focus, they are adjusting the thickness of the lens. The lens in a camera does not accommodate to the distance of objects. Instead, to focus the light that is projected onto the film, the camera lens is moved farther away from or closer to the film.

The **retina** is like the film or image surface of the camera. Instead of being composed of film that is sensitive to light (photosensitive), however, the retina consists of photosensitive cells, or **photoreceptors,** called *rods* and *cones.* The retina (Figure 4.3) contains several layers of cells: the rods and cones, **bipolar cells,** and **ganglion cells.** All of these cells are neurons. Light travels past the ganglion cells and bipolar cells and stimulates the rods and cones. The rods and cones then send neural messages through the bipolar cells to the ganglion cells. The axons of the million or so ganglion cells in our retinae form the **optic nerve.** The optic nerve conducts sensory input to the brain, where it is relayed to the visual area of the occipital lobe. Other neurons in the retina—amacrine cells and horizontal cells—make sideways connections at a level near the receptor cells and at another level near the ganglion cells. As a result of these lateral connections, many rods and cones funnel visual information into one bipolar

Pupil • The apparently black opening in the center of the iris, through which light enters the eye.

Lens • A transparent body behind the iris that focuses an image on the retina.

Retina • The area of the inner surface of the eye that contains rods and cones.

Photoreceptors • Cells that respond to light.

Bipolar cells • Neurons that conduct neural impulses from rods and cones to ganglion cells.

Ganglion cells • Neurons whose axons form the optic nerve.

Optic nerve • The nerve that transmits sensory information from the eye to the brain.

FIGURE 4.3

 **Spotlight on the Retina** After light travels through the vitreous humor of the eye, it finds its way through ganglion neurons and bipolar neurons to the photosensitive rods and cones. These photoreceptors then transmit sensory input back through the bipolar neurons to the ganglion neurons. The axons of the ganglion neurons form the optic nerve, which transmits sensory stimulation through the brain to the visual cortex of the occipital lobe. Amacrine cells and horizontal cells make connections within layers that allow photoreceptors to funnel their information into the ganglion cells.

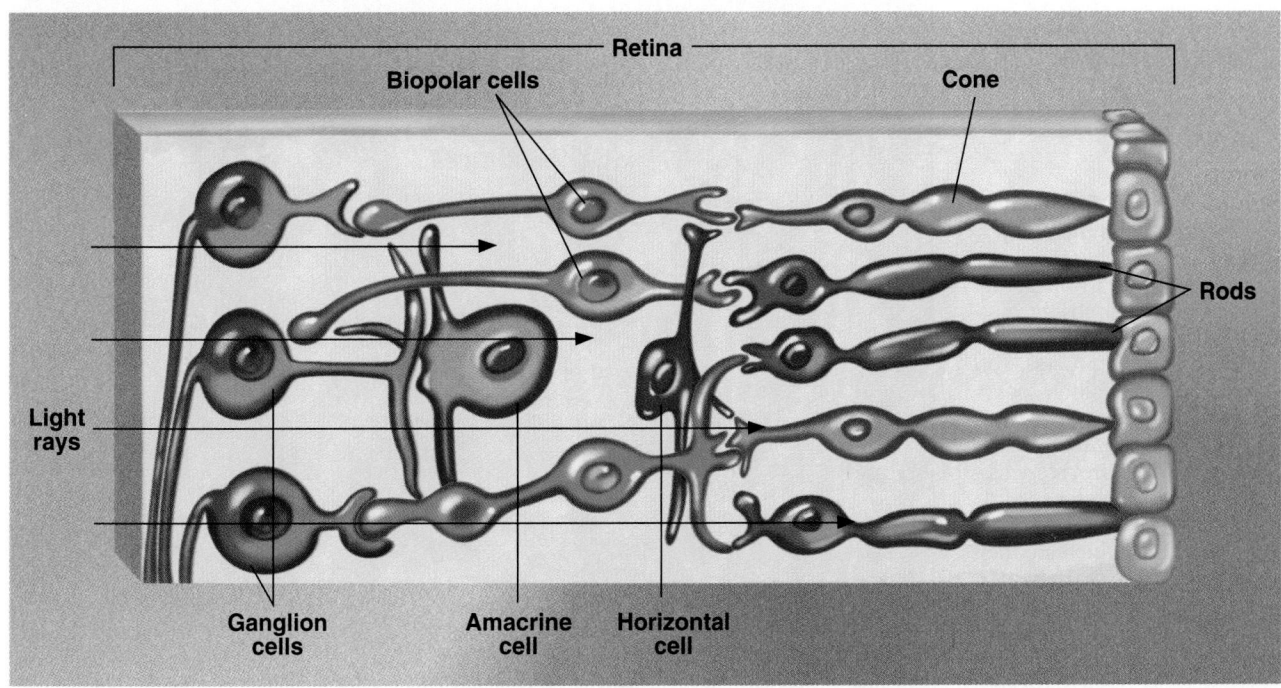

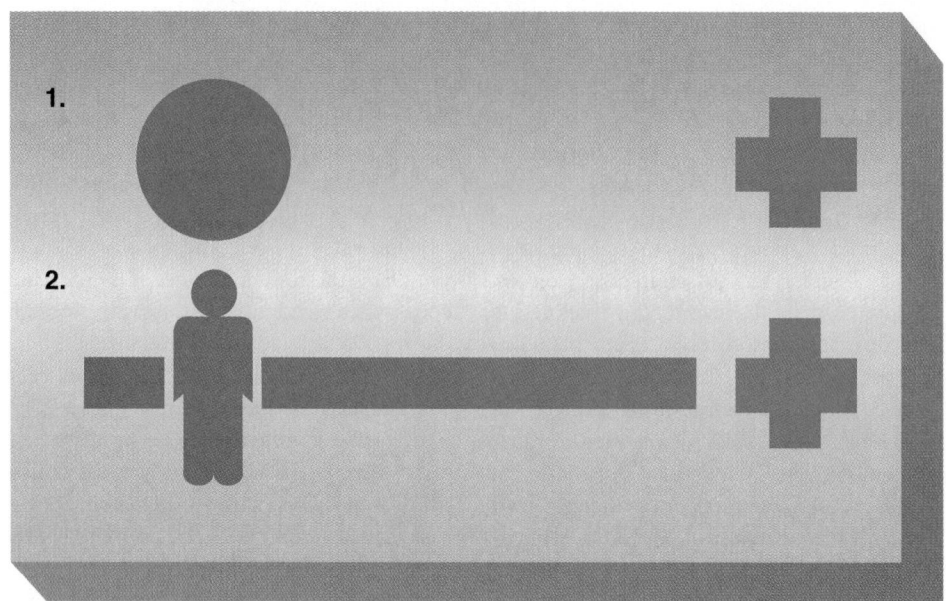

FIGURE 4.4
Locating the Blind Spots in Your Eyes To try a "disappearing act," first look at drawing 1. Close your right eye. Then move the book back and forth about 1 foot from your left eye while you stare at the plus sign. You will notice the circle disappear. When the circle disappears it is being projected onto the blind spot of your retina, the point at which the axons of ganglion neurons collect to form the optic nerve. Then close your left eye. Stare at the circle with your right eye and move the book back and forth. When the plus sign disappears, it is being projected onto the blind spot of your right eye. Now look at drawing 2. You can make this figure disappear and "see" the black line continue through the spot where it was by closing your right eye and staring at the plus sign with your left. When this figure is projected onto your blind spot, your brain "fills in" the line, which is one reason you're not usually aware that you have blind spots.

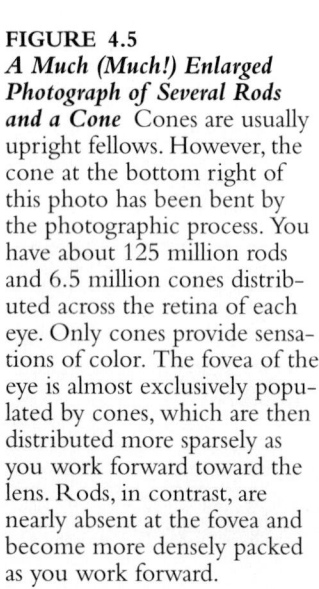

FIGURE 4.5
A Much (Much!) Enlarged Photograph of Several Rods and a Cone Cones are usually upright fellows. However, the cone at the bottom right of this photo has been bent by the photographic process. You have about 125 million rods and 6.5 million cones distributed across the retina of each eye. Only cones provide sensations of color. The fovea of the eye is almost exclusively populated by cones, which are then distributed more sparsely as you work forward toward the lens. Rods, in contrast, are nearly absent at the fovea and become more densely packed as you work forward.

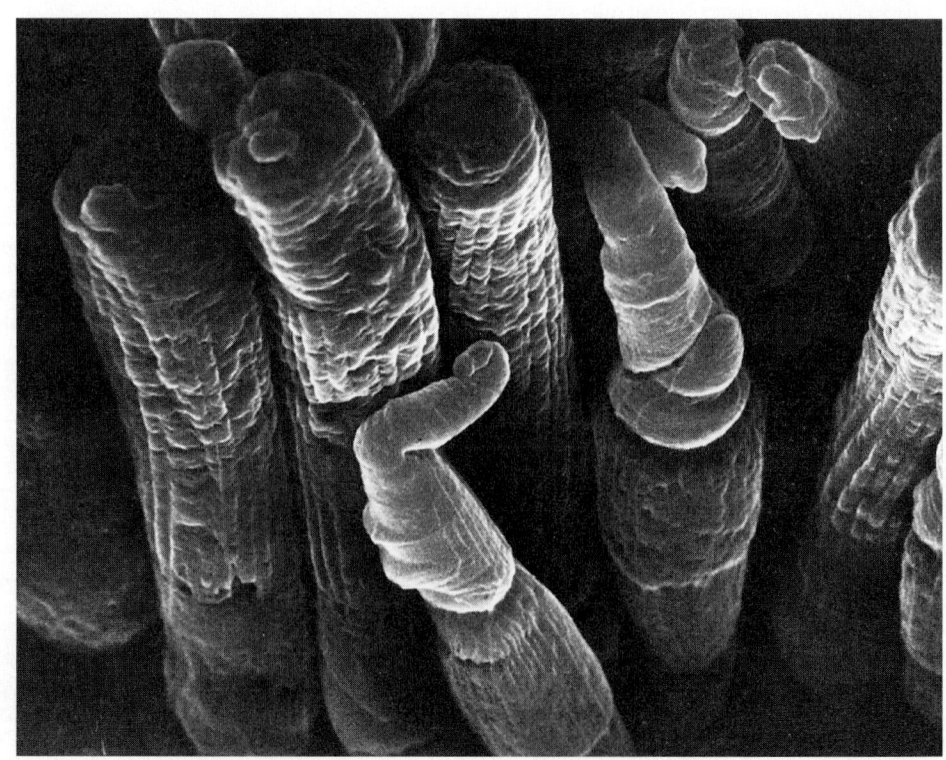

cell, and many bipolar cells funnel information to one ganglion cell. Receptors outnumber ganglion cells by more than 100 to 1.

The **fovea** is the most sensitive area of the retina (see Figure 4.2). Receptors there are more densely packed. The **blind spot,** in contrast, is insensitive to visual stimulation. It is the part of the retina where the axons of the ganglion cells congregate to form the optic nerve (Figure 4.4).

Rods and Cones. **Rods** and **cones** are the photoreceptors in the retina (Figure 4.5). About 125 million rods and 6.5 million cones are distributed across the retina (Solomon and others, 1993). The fovea is composed almost exclusively of cones. Cones then become more sparsely distributed as you work forward from the fovea toward the lens. Rods, in contrast, are nearly absent at the fovea but are distributed more densely as you approach the lens.

Rods are sensitive only to the intensity of light. They allow us to see in black and white. Cones provide color vision. If you are a camera buff, you know that under conditions of extreme low lighting, it is possible to photograph a clearer image with black-and-white film than with color film. Similarly, rods are more sensitive to light than cones. Therefore, as the illumination grows dim, as during the evening and nighttime hours, objects appear to lose their color well before their outlines fade from view.

Light Adaptation. A movie theater may at first seem too dark to allow us to find seats readily. But as time goes on, we come to see the seats and other people clearly. Adjusting to lower lighting is called **dark adaptation.**

Figure 4.6 shows the amount of light needed for detection as a function of the amount of time spent in the dark. The cones and rods adapt at different rates. The cones, which permit perception of color, reach their maximum adaptation to darkness in about 10 minutes. The rods, which allow perception of light and dark only, are more sensitive and continue to adapt to darkness for up to about 45 minutes.

Adaptation to brighter lighting conditions takes place much more rapidly. When you

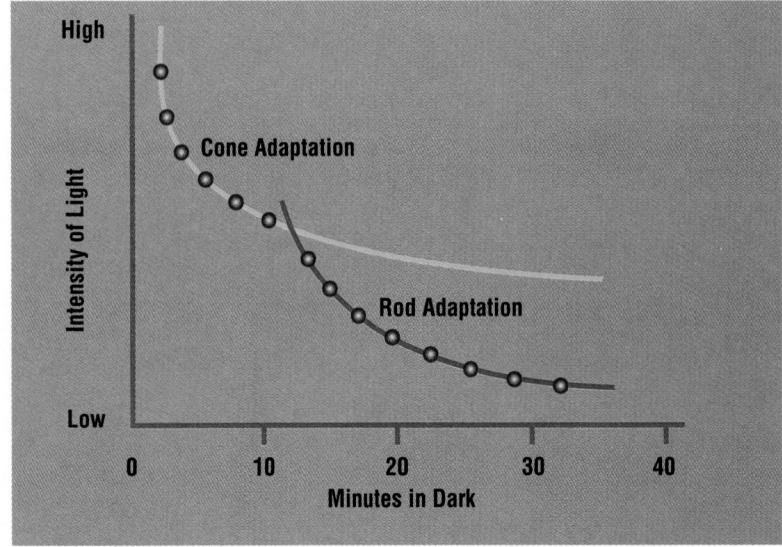

FIGURE 4.6
Dark Adaptation This illustration shows the amount of light necessary for detection as a function of the amount of time spent in the dark. Cones and rods adapt at different rates. Cones, which permit perception of color, reach maximum dark adaptation in about 10 minutes. Rods, which permit perception of dark and light only, are more sensitive than cones. Rods continue to adapt for up to about 45 minutes.

emerge from the theater into the brilliance of the afternoon, you may at first be painfully surprised by the featureless blaze around you. The visual experience is not unlike turning the brightness of the TV set to maximum, in which case the edges of objects dissolve into light. Within a minute or so of entering the street, however, the brightness of the scene will have dimmed and objects will have regained their edges.

CREATING AN INNER WORLD OF COLOR: COLOR VISION

For most of us, the world is a place of brilliant colors—the blue-greens of the ocean, the red-oranges of the lowering sun, the deepened greens of June, the glories of rhododendron and hibiscus. Color is an emotional and aesthetic part of our everyday lives. In this section, we explore psychological dimensions of color and then examine theories that concern how we manage to convert different wavelengths of light into perceptions of color.

PSYCHOLOGICAL DIMENSIONS OF COLOR

The wavelength of light determines its color, or hue. The brightness of a color is

MINILECTURE:
DARK
ADAPTATION

Fovea • An area near the center of the retina that is dense with cones and where vision is consequently most acute.

Blind spot • The area of the retina where axons from ganglion cells meet to form the optic nerve.

Rods • Rod-shaped photoreceptors that are sensitive only to the intensity of light.

Cones • Cone-shaped photoreceptors that transmit sensations of color.

Dark adaptation • The process of adjusting to conditions of lower lighting by increasing the sensitivity of rods and cones.

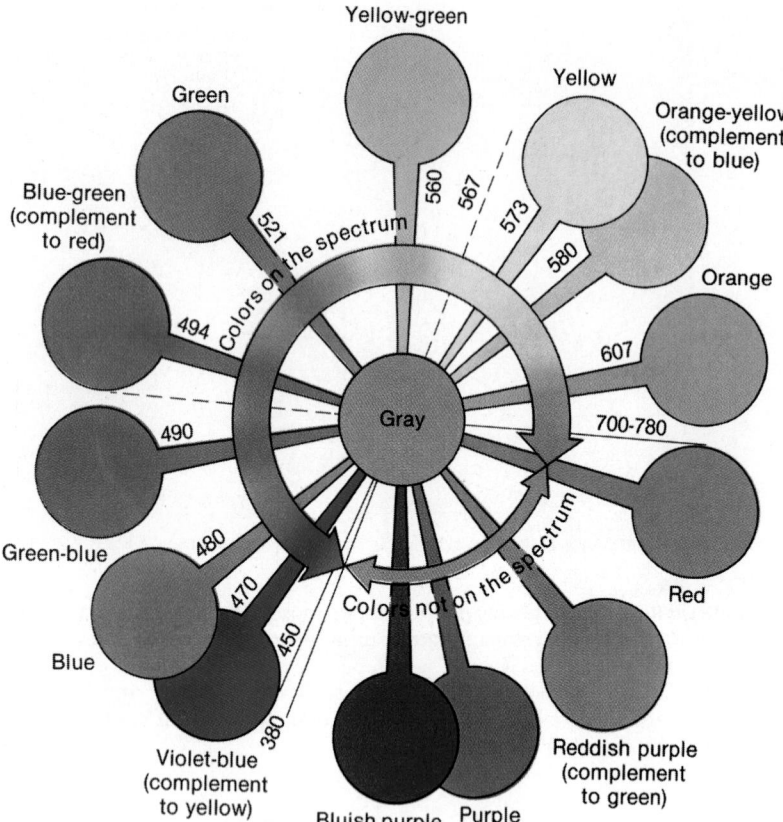

FIGURE 4.7
The Color Wheel A color wheel can be formed by bending the colors of the spectrum into a circle and placing complementary colors across from one another. (A few colors between violet and red that are not found on the spectrum must be added to complete the circle.) When lights of complementary colors such as yellow and violet-blue are mixed, they dissolve into neutral gray. The afterimage of a color is also the color's complement.

Saturation • The degree of purity of a color.

Complementary • Descriptive of colors of the spectrum that when combined produce white or nearly white light.

MINILECTURE: COLOR DEFICIENCY

its degree of lightness or darkness. The brighter the color, the lighter it is.

If we bend the colors of the spectrum into a circle, we create a color wheel, as shown in Figure 4.7. Yellow is the lightest color on the color wheel. As we work our way around from yellow to violet-blue, we encounter progressively darker colors.

Warm and Cool Colors. Psychologically, the colors on the green-blue side of the color wheel are considered to be cool in temperature, and the colors on the yellow-orange-red side are considered to be warm. Perhaps greens and blues suggest the coolness of the ocean and the sky, whereas things tend to burn red or orange. A room decorated in green or blue may seem more appealing on a hot day in July than a room decorated in red or orange.

When we look at a painting, warm colors seem to advance toward the viewer, which explains, in part, why the oranges and yellows of Mark Rothko's *Orange and Yellow* (Figure 4.8) seem to pulsate toward the observer. Cool colors seem to recede. Notice how the warm Sunoco sign in Allan d'Arcangelo's *Highway 1, No. 2* (Figure 4.9) leaps out toward the viewer. In contrast, the cool blue sky seems to recede into the distance.

The **saturation** of a color is its pureness. Pure hues have the greatest intensity, or brightness. The saturation, and thus the brightness, decreases when another hue or black, gray, or white is added. Artists produce shades of a given hue by adding black and produce tints by adding white.

Complementary Colors. The colors across from one another on the color wheel are labeled **complementary.** Red-green and blue-yellow are the major complementary pairs. If we mix complementary colors together, they dissolve into gray.

"But wait!" you say. "Blue and yellow cannot be complementary because by mixing pigments of blue and yellow we create green, not gray." True enough, but we have been talking about mixing *lights,* not *pigments.* Light is the source of all color. Pigments reflect and absorb different wavelengths of light selectively. The mixture of lights is an *additive* process. The mixture of pigments is *subtractive* (see Figure 4.10).

Truth or Fiction Revisited. *It is not true that we attain green light by mixing blue light and yellow light.* We attain a green *pigment* when we mix pigments of blue and yellow.

Pigments attain their colors by absorbing light from certain segments of the spectrum and reflecting the rest. For example, we see most plant life as green because the pigment in chlorophyll absorbs most of the red, blue, and violet wavelengths of light. The remaining green is reflected. A red pigment absorbs most of the spectrum but reflects red. White pigments reflect all colors equally. Black pigments reflect very little light.

Primary, Secondary, and Tertiary Colors. The pigments of red, blue, and yellow are the **primary colors**— those that cannot be produced by mixing

FIGURE 4.8
Orange and Yellow Warm colors such as orange and yellow seem to advance toward the viewer, while cool colors such as blue and green seem to recede. The oranges and yellows of Rothko's painting seem to pulsate toward the observer.

FIGURE 4.9
Highway 1, No. 2 The "warm" Sunoco sign in d'Arcangelo's painting leaps out toward the viewer, while the "cool" blue sky recedes into the distance. © 1996 Allan D'Arcangelo/Licensed by VAGA, New York, NY

pigments of other hues. **Secondary colors** are created by mixing pigments of the primary colors. The three secondary colors are orange (derived from mixing red and yellow), green (blue and yellow), and purple (red and blue). **Tertiary colors** are created by mixing pigments of primary and adjoining secondary colors, as in yellow-green and bluish-purple.

In his *Sunday Afternoon on the Island of La Grande Jatte* (Figure 4.11), French painter Georges Seurat molded his figures and forms from dabs of pure and complementary colors. Instead of mixing his pigments, he placed points of pure color next to one another. The sensations are of pure color when the painting is viewed from very close. But from a distance, the juxtaposition of pure colors creates the impression of mixtures of color.

Afterimages. Before reading on, why don't you try a brief experiment? Look at the strangely colored American flag in Figure 4.12 for at least half a minute. Then look at a sheet of white or gray paper. What has happened to the flag? If your color vision is working properly, and if you looked at the miscolored flag long enough, you should see a flag composed of the familiar red, white, and blue. The flag you perceive on the white sheet of paper is an **afterimage** of the first. (If you didn't look at the green, black, and yellow flag long

Primary colors • Colors that cannot be produced by mixing pigments of other hues.
Secondary colors • Colors derived by mixing primary colors.
Tertiary colors • Colors derived by mixing primary and adjoining secondary colors.
Afterimage • The lingering visual impression made by a stimulus that has been removed.

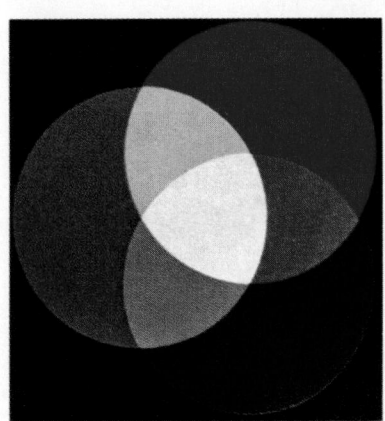

FIGURE 4.10
Additive Color Mixtures Produced by Lights of Three Colors: Red, Green, and Violet-Blue In the early 1800s, British scientist Thomas Young discovered that white light and all the colors of the spectrum could be produced by adding various combinations of lights of three colors and varying their intensities.

FIGURE 4.11
Sunday Afternoon on the Island of La Grande Jatte The French painter Seurat molded his figures and forms from dabs of pure and complementary colors. Up close, the dabs of pure color are visible. From afar, they create the impression of color mixtures.

enough the first time, you may wish to try it again. It will work any number of times.)

In afterimages, persistent sensations of color are followed by perception of the complementary color when the first color is removed. The same holds true for black and white; staring at one will create an afterimage of the others. Stare at d'Arcangelo's *Highway 1, No. 2* (Figure 4.9) for 30 seconds. Then look at a sheet of white paper. You are likely to perceive a black stripe down a white highway, along with a blue Sunoco sign and a yellow sky. The phenomenon of afterimages has contributed to one of the theories of color vision, as we shall soon see.

Analogous Colors. **Analogous** hues lie next to one another on the color wheel, forming families of colors like yellow and orange, orange and red, and green and blue. As we work our way around the wheel, the families intermarry, blue with violet, violet with red, and so on. Works of art that use closely related families of color seem harmonious. For example, Rothko's *Orange and Yellow* draws on the color family containing analogous oranges and yellows.

THEORIES OF COLOR VISION

Adults with normal color vision can discriminate hundreds of colors across the visible spectrum. Different colors have different wavelengths. Although we can vary the physical wavelengths of light in a continuous manner from shorter to longer, many changes in color are discontinuous. Our perception of a color shifts suddenly from blue to green, even though the change in wavelength may be smaller than that between two blues.

Our ability to perceive color depends on the eye's transmission of different messages

FIGURE 4.12
Three Cheers for the . . . Green, Black, and Yellow? Don't be concerned. We can readily restore Old Glory to its familiar hues. Place a sheet of white paper beneath the book, and stare at the center of the flag for 30 seconds. Then remove the book. You will see a more familiar image on the paper beneath. This is an afterimage.

to the brain when lights of different wavelengths stimulate the cones in the retina. In this section, we shall explore and evaluate two theories of how lights of different wavelengths are perceived as being of different colors: *trichromatic theory* and *opponent-process theory.*

Trichromatic Theory. **Trichromatic theory** is based on an experiment that was run by British scientist Thomas Young in the early 1800s. As in Figure 4.10, Young projected three lights of different colors onto a screen so that they partly overlapped. He found that he could create any color from the visible spectrum by simply varying the intensities of the lights. When all three lights fell on the same spot, they created white light, or the appearance of no color at all. The three lights manipulated by Young were red, green, and blue-violet.

German physiologist Hermann von Helmholtz saw in Young's discovery an explanation of color vision. Von Helmholtz suggested that the eye must have three different types of photoreceptors or cones. Some must be sensitive to red light, some to green, and some to blue. We see other colors when two different types of color receptors are stimulated. The perception of yellow, for example, would result from the simultaneous stimulation of receptors for red and green. Trichromatic theory is also known as the Young–Helmholtz theory, after Thomas Young and Hermann von Helmholtz.

Opponent-Process Theory. In 1870, Ewald Hering proposed the **opponent-process theory** of color vision. Opponent-process theory also holds that there are three types of color receptors, but not red, green, and blue. Hering suggested that afterimages (such as of the American flag shown in Figure 4.12) are made possible by three types of color receptors: red–green, blue–yellow, and a type that perceives differences in brightness from light to dark. A red–green cone could not transmit messages for red and green at the same time. According to Hering, staring at the green, black, and yellow flag for 30 seconds would disturb the balance of neural activity. The afterimage of red, white, and blue would represent the eye's attempt to reestablish a balance.

Evaluation. Both theories of color vision appear to be partially correct (Hurvich, 1981). Research with **microspectrophotometry** supports trichromatic theory. It shows that some cones are sensitive to blue, some to green, and some to red parts of the spectrum (Solomon and others, 1993).

But studies of the bipolar and ganglion neurons suggest that messages from cones are transmitted to the brain and relayed by the thalamus to the occipital lobe in an opponent-process fashion (DeValois & Jacobs, 1984). Some opponent-process cells that transmit messages to the visual centers in the brain are excited ("turned on") by green light but inhibited ("turned off") by red light. Others can be excited by red light but are inhibited by green light. A second set of opponent-process cells responds in an opposite manner to blue and yellow. A third set responds in an opposite manner to light and dark.

A neural rebound effect apparently helps explain afterimages. That is, a green-sensitive ganglion that had been excited by green light for half a minute or so might switch briefly to inhibitory activity when the light is shut off. The effect would be to perceive red, even though no red light was being shone (Haber & Hershenson, 1980).

These theoretical updates allow for the afterimage effects with the green, black, and yellow flag and are also consistent with Young's experiments in mixing lights of different colors.

COLOR BLINDNESS

If you can discriminate the colors of the visible spectrum, you have normal color vision and are labeled a **trichromat.** This means that you are sensitive to red–green, blue–yellow, and light–dark. People who are totally color blind are called **monochromats** and are sensitive to light–dark only. Total color blindness is quite rare. The fully color blind see the world as trichromats would on a black-and-white TV set or in a black-and-white movie.

Partial color blindness is more common than total color blindness. Partial color blindness is a gender- or sex-linked trait that strikes mostly males. The recessive genes for the disorder are found on the X

Analogous • Similar or comparable colors.

Trichromatic theory • The theory that color vision is made possible by three types of cones, some of which respond to red light, some to green, and some to blue. (From the Greek roots *treis,* meaning "three," and *chroma,* meaning "color.")

Opponent-process theory • The theory that color vision is made possible by three types of cones, some of which respond to red or green light, some to blue or yellow, and some only to the intensity of light.

Microspectrophotometry • A method for analyzing the sensitivity of single cones to lights of different wavelengths.

Trichromat • A person with normal color vision.

Monochromat • A person who is sensitive to black and white only and hence color blind.

MINILECTURE: COLOR BLINDNESS

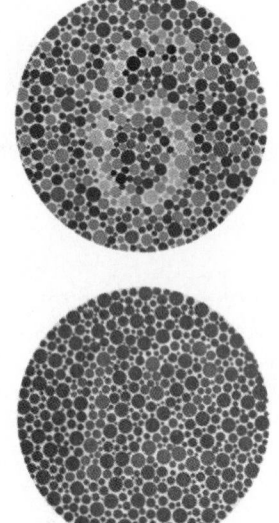

FIGURE 4.13
Plates from a Test for Color Blindness Can you see the numbers in these plates from a test for color blindness? A person with red–green color blindness would not be able to see the 6, and a person with blue–yellow color blindness would probably not discern the 12. (Caution: These reproductions cannot be used for actual testing of color blindness.)

Dichromat • A person who is sensitive to black–white and either red–green or blue–yellow and hence partially color blind.

Closure • The tendency to perceive a broken figure as being complete or whole.

Perceptual organization • The tendency to integrate perceptual elements into meaningful patterns.

Ambiguous • Having two or more possible meanings.

sex chromosome, and thus in males they are unopposed by dominant genes on a second X sex chromosome (Nathans and others, 1986). The partially color blind are called **dichromats.** Dichromats can discriminate only two colors—red and green, or blue and yellow—and the colors that are derived from mixing these colors. Figure 4.13 shows the types of tests that are used to diagnose color blindness. Also see Figure 4.14.

A dichromat might put on one red sock and one green sock but would not mix red and blue socks. Monochromats might put on socks of any color. They would not notice a difference as long as the socks' colors did not differ in intensity, or brightness.

When we selectively breed cats and dogs, we are interested in producing coats of certain colors. But if cats and dogs bred human beings, they would be less concerned about our color because their color vision is less well developed (Rosenzweig & Leiman, 1982). Cats, for example, can distinguish fewer colors and only on large surfaces.

Reflections

Now that you have read the section on vision, reflect on the following questions:

- Have you seen a rainbow? How do you account for the colors in a rainbow?
- Hold a finger at arm's length, then bring it slowly toward your eyes, maintaining a single image as you do so. What do you feel happening as the finger approaches? Why does it happen?
- Have you had the experience of entering a dark theater and then seeing gradually more and more as you adjust? What processes account for the adjustment? Do you first see the outlines of shapes or their colors? Why?
- What does color vision add to your own life? If you are color blind or partly color blind, how have you adjusted to society's use of color? For example, how do you know when to stop and when to go at a traffic light?

Visual Perception

Perception is the process by which we organize or make sense of our sensory impressions. Although visual sensations are caused by electromagnetic energy, visual perception also relies on our knowledge, expectations, and motivations. Whereas sensation may be thought of as a mechanical process, perception is an active process by which we interpret the world around us.

For example, just what do you see in Figure 4.15? Do you see random splotches of ink or a rider on horseback? If you perceive a horse and rider, it is not just because of the visual sensations provided by the drawing. Each of the blobs is meaningless in and of itself, and the pattern they form is also less than clear. Despite the lack of clarity, however, you may still perceive a horse and rider. Why? The answer has something to do with your general knowledge and your desire to fit incoming bits and pieces of information into familiar patterns.

In the case of the horse and rider, your integration of disconnected shards of information into a meaningful whole also reflects what Gestalt psychologists refer to as the principle of **closure,** or the tendency to perceive a complete or whole figure even when there are gaps in the sensory input. Put another way, in perception the whole can be very much more than the mere sum of the parts. Collecting parts alone can be meaningless; it is their configuration that matters.

PERCEPTUAL ORGANIZATION

Earlier in the century, Gestalt psychologists noted consistencies in our integration of bits and pieces of sensory stimulation into meaningful wholes and attempted to formulate rules that governed these processes. Max Wertheimer, in particular, discovered many such rules. As a group, these rules are referred to as the laws of **perceptual organization.** Let us examine a number of these rules, beginning with those concerning figure–ground perception. Then we consider top-down and bottom-up processing.

Figure–Ground Perception. If you look out your window, you may see people, buildings, cars, and streets, or perhaps grass, trees, birds, and clouds. All these objects tend to be perceived as figures against backgrounds. Cars against the background of the street are easier to pick out than cars piled

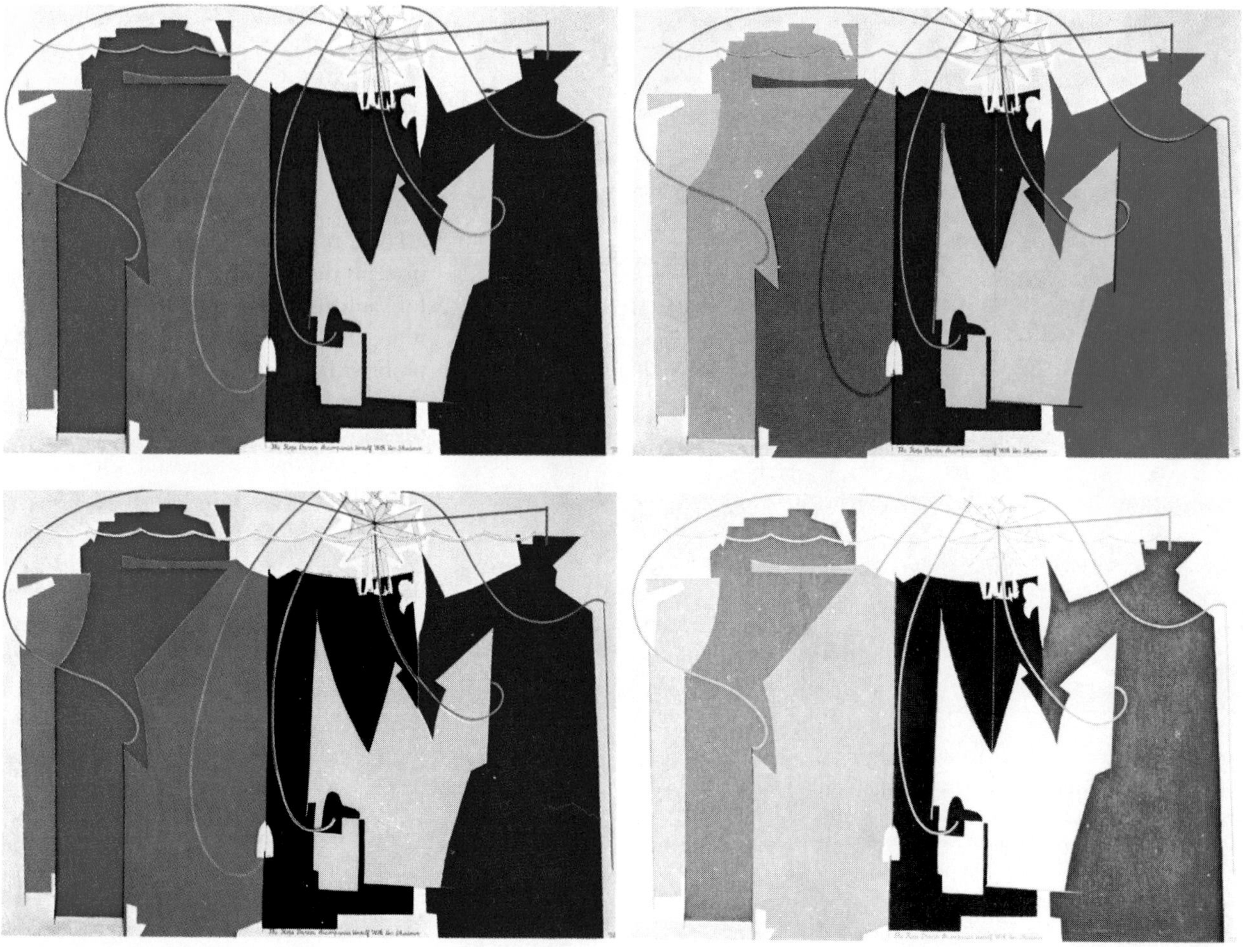

FIGURE 4.14
Color Blindness The painting in the upper left-hand panel—Man Ray's *The Rope Dancer Accompanies Herself with Her Shadows*—appears as it would to a person with normal color vision. If you had red–green color blindness, the picture would appear as it does in the upper right-hand panel. The lower left-hand and lower right-hand panels show how the picture would look to viewers with yellow–blue or total color blindness, respectively. (Man Ray: *The Rope Dancer Accompanies Herself with Her Shadows*. 1916. Museum of Modern Art, New York. Gift of G. David Thompson.)

on each other in a junkyard. Birds against the sky are more likely to be perceived than, as the saying goes, birds in the bush. Figures are closer to us than their grounds.

When figure–ground relationships are **ambiguous,** or capable of being interpreted in various ways, our perceptions tend to be unstable, to shift back and forth. As an example, take a look at Figure 4.16— a nice leisurely look. How many people, objects, and animals can you find in this Escher print? If your eye is drawn back and forth, so that sometimes you are perceiving light figures on a dark background and then dark figures on a light background, you are experiencing figure–ground reversals. In other words, a shift is occurring in your perception of what is figure and what is ground, or backdrop. Escher was able to

have some fun with us because of our tendency to try to isolate geometric patterns or figures from a background. However, in

MINILECTURE:
GESTALT
PRINCIPLES

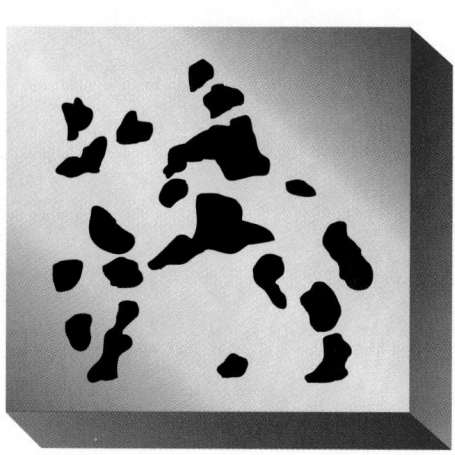

FIGURE 4.15
Closure Meaningless splotches of ink or a horse and rider? This figure illustrates the Gestalt principle of closure.

FIGURE 4.16
Figure and Ground How many animals and demons can you find in this Escher print? Do we have white figures on a black background or black figures on a white background? Figure–ground perception is the tendency to perceive geometric forms against a background.

Proximity • Nearness. The perceptual tendency to group together objects that are near one another.

Similarity • The perceptual tendency to group together objects that are similar in appearance.

Continuity • The tendency to perceive a series of points or lines as having unity.

this case the "background" is as meaningful and detailed as the "figure." Therefore, our perceptions shift back and forth.

The Rubin Vase. In Figure 4.17 we see a Rubin vase, one of psychologists' fa-

vorite illustrations of figure–ground relationships. The figure–ground relationship in part A of the figure is ambiguous. There are no cues that suggest which area must be the figure. For this reason, our perception may shift from seeing the vase as the figure and then seeing two profiles as the figure.

There is no such problem in part B. Since it seems that a purple vase has been brought forward against a colored ground, we are more likely to perceive the vase than the profiles. In part C, we are more likely to perceive the profiles than the vase because the profiles are whole, and the vase is broken against the background. Of course, we can still perceive the vase in part C, if we wish to, because experience has shown us where it is. Why not have fun with some friends by covering parts B and C and asking them what they see? (They'll catch on to you quickly if they can see all three drawings at once.)

The Necker Cube. The Necker cube (Figure 4.18) provides another example of how an ambiguous drawing can lead to perceptual shifts.

Hold this page at arm's length and stare at the center of the figure for 30 seconds or so. Try to allow your eye muscles to relax. (The feeling is of your eyes "glazing over.") After a while you will notice a dramatic shift in your perception of these "stacked boxes," so that what was once a front edge is now a back edge, and vice versa. Again,

FIGURE 4.17
The Rubin Vase A favorite drawing used by psychologists to demonstrate figure–ground perception. Part A is ambiguous, with neither the vase nor the profiles clearly the figure or the ground. In part B, the vase is the figure; in part C, the profiles are.

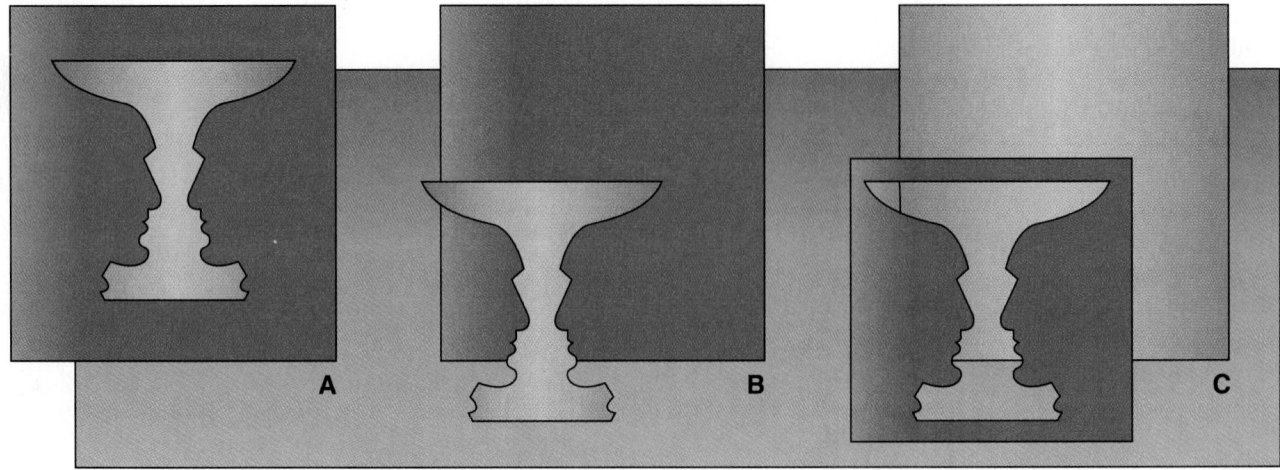

A   B   C

the dramatic perceptual shift is made possible by the fact that the outline of the drawing permits two interpretations.

Some Other Gestalt Rules for Organization. In addition to the law of closure, Gestalt psychologists have noted that our perceptions are guided by rules or laws of *proximity, similarity, continuity,* and *common fate.*

Verbally describe part A of Figure 4.19 without reading further. Did you say that part A consisted of six lines or of three groups of two parallel lines? If you said three sets of lines, you were influenced by the **proximity,** or nearness, of some of the lines. There is no other reason for perceiving them in pairs or subgroups: All lines are parallel and of equal length.

Now describe part B of the figure. Did you perceive the figure as a six-by-six grid, or as three columns of *x*'s and three columns of *o*'s? According to the law of **similarity,** we perceive similar objects as belonging together. For this reason, you may have been more likely to describe part B in terms of columns than rows or a grid.

What about part C? Is it a circle with two lines stemming from it, or is it a (broken) line that goes through a circle? If you saw it as a single (broken) line, you were probably organizing your perceptions according to the rule of **continuity.** That is, we perceive a series of points or a broken line as having unity.

According to the law of **common fate,** elements seen moving together are perceived as belonging together. A group of people running in the same direction appear unified in purpose. Birds that flock together seem to be of a feather. (Did I get that right?)

Part D of Figure 4.19 provides another example of the law of closure. The arcs tend to be perceived as a circle (or circle with gaps) rather than as just a series of arcs.

Top-Down versus Bottom-Up Processing in Pattern Perception. Imagine that you are trying to piece together a thousand-piece puzzle—a task that I usually avoid, despite the cajoling of my children. Now imagine that you are trying to accomplish it after someone has walked off with the box that contained the pieces—you know, the box with the picture formed by the completed puzzle.

When you have the box—when you know what the "big picture" or pattern looks like—cognitive psychologists refer to the task of assembling the pieces as **top-down processing.** The "top" of the visual system refers to the image of the pattern in the brain, and the top-down strategy for putting the puzzle together implies that you use the pattern to guide subordinate perceptual-motor tasks such as hunting for proper pieces. Without knowledge of the pattern, the assembly process is referred to as **bottom-up processing.** You begin

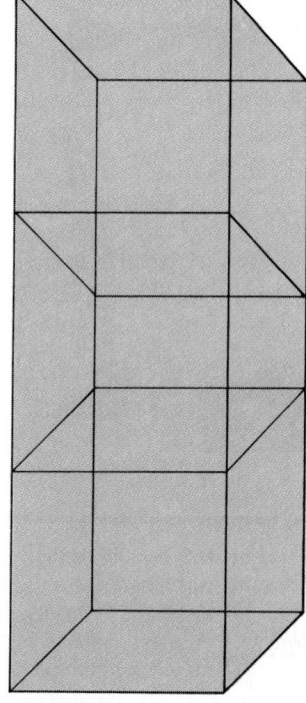

FIGURE 4.18
A Stack of Necker Cubes Ambiguity in the drawing of the cubes makes perceptual shifts possible.

Common fate • The tendency to perceive elements that move together as belonging together.

Top-down processing • The use of contextual information or knowledge of a pattern in order to organize parts of the pattern.

Bottom-up processing • The organization of the parts of a pattern to recognize, or form an image of, the pattern they compose.

FIGURE 4.19
Some Gestalt Laws of Perceptual Organization These drawings illustrate the Gestalt laws of proximity, similarity, continuity, and closure.

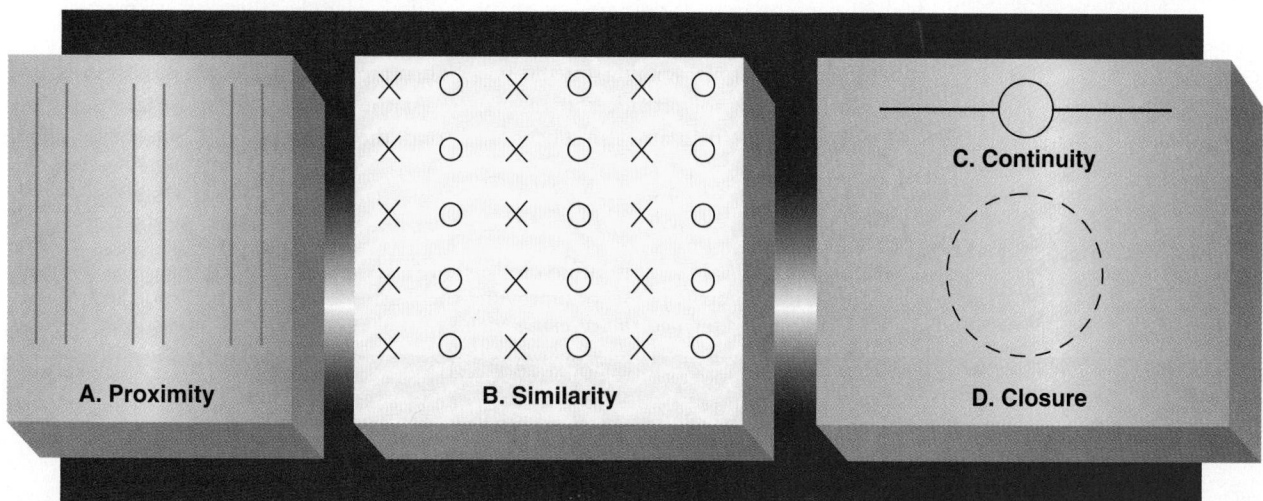

A. Proximity

B. Similarity

C. Continuity

D. Closure

with bits and pieces of information and become aware of the pattern formed by the assembled pieces only after you have labored for a while.

PERCEPTION OF MOVEMENT

Consider the importance of the perception of movement. Moving objects—whether they are other people, animals, cars, or tons of earth plummeting down a hillside—are vital sources of sensory information. Moving objects capture the attention of even newborn infants.

To understand how we perceive movement, recall what it is like to be on a train that has begun to pull out of the station while the train on the adjacent track remains stationary. If your own train does not lurch as it accelerates, you might think at first that the other train is moving. Or you might not be certain whether your train is moving forward or the other train is moving backward.

The visual perception of movement is based on change of position relative to other objects. To early scientists, whose only instrument for visual observation was the naked eye, it seemed logical that the sun circled the earth. You have to be able to imagine the movement of the earth around the sun as seen from a theoretical point in outer space—you cannot observe it directly.

How, then, do you determine which train is moving when your train is pulling out of the station (or that other train is pulling in)? One way is to look for objects you know are stable, such as station-platform columns, houses, signs, or trees. If you are stationary in relation to them, your train is not moving. Observing people walking on the station platform may not provide the answer, however, because they are also changing

their position relative to stationary objects. You might also try to sense the motion of the train in your body. You know from experience how to do these things quite well, although it may be difficult to phrase explanations for them.

We have been considering the perception of real movement. Psychologists have also studied several types of apparent movement, or **illusions** of movement. These include the *autokinetic effect, stroboscopic motion,* and the *phi phenomenon.*

The Autokinetic Effect. If you were to sit quietly in a dark room and stare at a point of light projected onto the far wall, after a while it might appear that the light had begun to move, even if it remained quite still. The tendency to perceive a stationary point of light as moving in a dark room is called the **autokinetic effect.**

Over the years, psychologists have run interesting experiments in which they have asked people, for example, what the light is "spelling out." The light has spelled out nothing, of course, and the words perceived by people have reflected their own cognitive processes, not external sensations.

Stroboscopic Motion. Stroboscopic motion makes motion pictures possible. In **stroboscopic motion,** the illusion of movement is provided by the presentation of a rapid progression of images of stationary objects (Beck and others, 1977). So-called motion pictures do not really consist of images that move. Rather, the audience is shown 16 to 22 pictures, or frames, per second, like those in Figure 4.20. Each frame differs slightly from that preceding it. Showing the frames in rapid succession then provides the illusion of movement.

At the rate of at least 16 frames per second, the "motion" in a film seems smooth

MINILECTURE:
BIOLOGICAL
MOTION

Illusions • Sensations that give rise to misperceptions.

Autokinetic effect • The tendency to perceive a stationary point of light in a dark room as moving.

Stroboscopic motion • A visual illusion in which the perception of motion is generated by a series of stationary images presented in rapid succession.

MINILECTURE:
STROBOSCOPIC
MOTION

FIGURE 4.20
Stroboscopic Motion In a motion picture, viewing a series of stationary images at the rate of about 16 to 22 frames per second provides the illusion of movement. This form of apparent movement is termed *stroboscopic motion.*

and natural. With fewer than 16 or so frames per second, the movement looks jumpy and unnatural. That is why slow motion is achieved through filming perhaps 100 or more frames per second. When they are played back at about 22 frames per second, movement seems slowed down, yet smooth and natural.

The Phi Phenomenon. Have you seen news headlines spelled out in lights that rapidly wrap around a building? Have you seen an electronic scoreboard in a baseball or football stadium? When the home team scores, some scoreboards suggest the explosions of fireworks. What actually happens is that a row of lights is switched on, then off. As the first row is switched off, the second row is switched on, and so on for dozens, perhaps hundreds of rows. When the switching occurs rapidly, the **phi phenomenon** occurs: The on–off process is perceived as movement.

Like stroboscopic motion, the phi phenomenon is an example of apparent motion. Both stroboscopic motion and the phi phenomenon appear to occur because of the law of continuity. We tend to perceive a series of points as having unity, so the series of lights (points) is perceived as moving lines.

DEPTH PERCEPTION

Think of the problems you might have if you could not judge depth or distance. You might bump into other people, thinking them to be farther away than they are. An outfielder might not be able to judge whether to run toward the infield or the fence to catch a fly ball. You might give your front bumper a workout in stop-and-go traffic. Fortunately, both *monocular and binocular cues* help us perceive the depth of objects. Let us examine a number of them.

Monocular Cues. Now that you have considered how difficult it would be to navigate through life without depth perception, ponder the problems of the artist who attempts to portray three-dimensional objects on a two-dimensional surface. Artists use **monocular cues,** or cues that can be perceived by one eye, to create an illusion of depth. These cues—including perspective, clearness, interposition, shadows, and

The Phi Phenomenon. The phi phenomenon is an illusion of movement that is produced by lights blinking on and off in sequence, as with this New York Stock Exchange electronic "ticker."

texture gradient—cause certain objects to appear to be more distant from the viewer than others.

Distant objects stimulate smaller areas on the retina than nearby objects. The amount of sensory input from them is smaller, even though they may be the same size. The distances between far-off objects also appear to be smaller than equivalent distances between nearby objects. For this reason, the phenomenon known as **perspective** occurs; that is, we tend to perceive parallel lines as coming closer, or converging, as they recede from us. However, as we shall see when we discuss *size constancy,* experience teaches us that distant objects that look small will be larger when they are close. In this way, their relative size also becomes a cue to their distance from us.

The two engravings in Figure 4.21 represent impossible scenes in which the artists use principles of perspective to fool the viewer. In the engraving to the left, *Waterfall,* note that the water appears to be flowing away from the viewer in a zigzag because the stream becomes gradually narrower (that is, lines that we assume to be parallel are shown to be converging) and the stone sides of the aqueduct appear to be stepping down. However, given that the water arrives at the top of the fall, it must actually somehow be flowing upward. However, the spot from which it falls is no farther from the viewer than the collection point from which it appears to (but does not) begin its flow backward.

Again, distant objects look smaller than nearby objects of the same size. The paradoxes in the engraving to the right, *False*

MINILECTURE: DEPTH PERCEPTION

FRONTISPIECE TO KERBY.

FIGURE 4.21
What Is Wrong with These Pictures? In *Waterfall,* to the left, how does Dutch artist M. C. Escher suggest that fallen water flows back upward, only to fall again? In *False Perspective,* to the right, how does English artist William Hogarth use monocular cues for depth perception to deceive the viewer?

Interposition • A monocular cue for depth based on the fact that a nearby object obscures a more distant object behind it.

Shadowing • A monocular cue for depth based on the fact that opaque objects block light and produce shadows.

Texture gradient • A monocular cue for depth based on the perception that closer objects appear to have rougher (more detailed) surfaces

Motion parallax • A monocular cue for depth based on the perception that nearby objects appear to move more rapidly in relation to our own motion.

Perspective, are made possible by the fact that more-distant objects are not necessarily depicted as being smaller than nearby objects. Thus, what at first seems to be background suddenly becomes foreground, and vice versa.

The clearness of an object also suggests its distance from us. Experience shows us that we sense more details of nearby objects. For this reason, artists can suggest that certain objects are closer to the viewer by depicting them in greater detail. Note that the "distant" hill in the Hogarth engraving (Figure 4.21) is given less detail than the nearby plants at the bottom of the picture. Our perceptions are mocked when a man "on" that distant hill in the background is shown conversing with a woman leaning out a window in the middle ground.

How does artist Victor Vasarely use monocular cues to provide the illusion of a

curving surface in his tapestry, *Vega-Tek* (Figure 4.22)?

We also learn that nearby objects can block our views of more-distant objects. Overlapping, or **interposition,** is the apparent placing of one object in front of another. Experience encourages us to perceive the partly covered objects as being farther away than the objects that hide parts of them from view (Figure 4.23). In the Hogarth engraving (Figure 4.21), which looks closer: the trees in the background (background?) or the moon sign hanging from the building (or is it buildings?) to the right? How does the artist use interposition to confound the viewer?

Additional information about depth is provided by **shadowing** and is based on the fact that opaque objects block light and produce shadows. Shadows and highlights give us information about objects' three-dimensional shapes and about their relationships to the source of light. The left part of Figure 4.24 is perceived as a two-dimensional circle, but the right part tends to be perceived as a three-dimensional sphere because of the highlight on its surface and the shadow underneath. In the "sphere," the highlighted central area is perceived as being closest to us, with the surface then receding to the edges.

Another monocular cue is **texture gradient.** A gradient is a progressive change, and closer objects are perceived as having progressively rougher textures. In the Hogarth engraving (Figure 4.21), the building just behind the large fisherman's head has a rougher texture and thus seems to be closer than the building with the window from which the woman is leaning. Our surprise is thus heightened when the moon sign is seen as hanging from both buildings.

Motion Cues. If you have ever driven in the country, you have probably noticed that distant objects such as mountains and stars appear to move along with you. Objects at an intermediate distance seem to be stationary, but nearby objects such as roadside markers, rocks, and trees seem to go by quite rapidly. The tendency of objects to seem to move backward or forward as a function of their distance is known as **motion parallax.** We learn to perceive objects that appear to move with us as being at greater distances.

Earlier we noted that nearby objects cause the lens of the eye to accommodate or

FIGURE 4.22
Creating the Illusion of Three Dimensions with Two How does Op artist Victor Vasarely use monocular cues for depth perception to lend this work a three-dimensional quality?

bend more to bring them into focus. The sensations of tension in the eye muscles also provide a monocular cue to depth, especially when we are within about 4 feet of the objects.

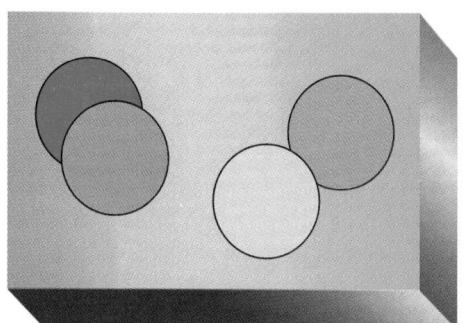

FIGURE 4.23
The Effects of Interposition The four circles are all the same size. Which circles seem closer: the complete circles or the circles with chunks bitten out of them?

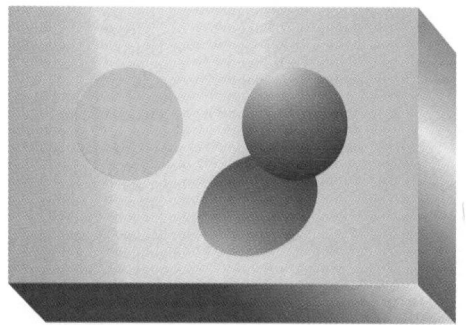

FIGURE 4.24
Shadowing as a Cue in the Perception of Depth Shadowing lends the circle on the right a sense of three-dimensionality.

FIGURE 4.25
Retinal Disparity and Convergence as Cues for Depth As an object nears your eyes, you begin to see two images of it because of retinal disparity. If you maintain perception of a single image, your eyes must converge on the object.

MINILECTURE:
BRIGHTNESS
CONTRAST AND
CONSTANCY

Binocular Cues. **Binocular cues,** or cues that involve both eyes, also help us perceive depth. Two binocular cues are *retinal disparity* and *convergence*.

Try an experiment. Hold your index finger at arm's length. Now, gradually bring it closer until it almost touches your nose. If you keep your eyes relaxed as you do so, you will see two fingers. An image of the finger will be projected onto the retina of each eye, and each image will be slightly different because the finger will be seen at different angles. The difference between the projected images is referred to as **retinal disparity** and serves as a binocular cue for depth perception (see Figure 4.25). Note that the closer your finger comes, the farther apart the "two fingers" appear to be. Closer objects have greater retinal disparity.

If we try to maintain a single image of the approaching finger, our eyes must turn inward, or converge on it, giving us a cross-eyed look. **Convergence** is associated with feelings of tension in the eye muscles and provides another binocular cue for depth. The binocular cues of retinal disparity and convergence are strongest at near distances.

PROBLEMS IN VISUAL PERCEPTION

Problems in Visual Acuity. **Visual acuity** refers to sharpness of vision, as defined by the ability to discriminate visual details. A familiar means of measuring visual acuity is the Snellen Chart, the "eye chart" used by many eye doctors. If you were to stand 20 feet from the Snellen Chart and could discriminate only the E, we would say that your vision is 20/200. This means that you can see from a distance of 20 feet what a person with normal vision can discriminate from a distance of 200 feet. In such a case, you would be quite **nearsighted.** You would have to be unusually close to an object to discriminate its details. A person who could read the smallest line on the chart from 20 feet would have 20/15 vision and be somewhat **farsighted.** Nearsightedness and farsightedness usually stem from problems in focusing on objects at various distances.

You may have noticed that older people often hold newspapers or books at a distance. As you reach middle age, the lenses

of the eyes become relatively brittle, making it more difficult to accommodate to, or focus on, objects. This condition is called **presbyopia,** from the Greek for "old man," although presbyopia usually begins at about the ages of 38 to 46. The lens structure of people with presbyopia differs from that of farsighted young people. Still, the effect of presbyopia is to make it difficult to perceive nearby visual stimuli. People who had normal visual acuity in their youth often require corrective lenses to read in old age. And people who were initially farsighted often have headaches linked to eyestrain.

Strabismus. In **strabismus,** the eye muscles do not work together, so people appear wall-eyed and seem to be looking at an object with one eye only. Strabismus is correctable by surgery. Binocular depth perception requires early experience in viewing objects simultaneously with both eyes.

Astigmatism. **Astigmatism** is a visual disorder in which vertical and horizontal contours cannot be focused on simultaneously. If astigmatism is not corrected early in childhood, the child will develop poor acuity for one of these types of contours.

PERCEPTUAL CONSTANCIES

The world is a constantly shifting display of visual sensations. What confusion would reign if we did not perceive a doorway to be the same doorway when seen from 6 feet as when seen from 4 feet. As we neared it, we might think that it was larger than the door we were seeking and become lost. Or consider the problems of the pet owner who recognizes his dog from the side but not from above, when the shapes differ. Fortunately, these problems tend not to occur—at least with familiar objects—because of perceptual constancies.

The image of a dog seen from 20 feet occupies about the same amount of space on your retina as an inch-long insect crawling in the palm of your hand. Yet, you do not perceive the dog to be as small as the insect. Through your experiences you have acquired **size constancy,** or the tendency to perceive the same object as being the same size, even though the size of its image on the retina varies as a function of its distance.

Experience teaches us about perspective, that the same object seen at a great distance will appear to be much smaller than when it is nearby.

Size Constancy. Westerners may say that people or cars look like ants from airplanes, but they know that they remain people and cars even if the details of their forms are lost in the distance. We can thus say that Westerners *perceive* them to be of the same size even from great distances, and even though the images they form on the retina and in the visual cortex are extremely small.

A cross-cultural case study suggests that a person from another culture might indeed perceive people and cars to be insects from the vantage point of an airplane. It also emphasizes the role of experience in the development of size constancy. Anthropologist Colin Turnbull (1961) found that an African Pygmy, Kenge, thought that buffalo perceived across an open field were some form of insect. Turnbull had to drive Kenge down to where the animals were grazing to convince him that they were not insects. During the drive, as the buffalo gradually grew in size, Kenge muttered to himself and moved closer to Turnbull in fear. Even after Kenge saw that these animals were, indeed, familiar buffalo, he still wondered how they could grow large so quickly. Kenge, you see, lived in a thick forest and normally did not view large animals from great distances. For this reason, he had not developed size constancy for distant objects. However, Kenge had no difficulty displaying size constancy with objects placed at various distances in his home.

Color Constancy. We also have **color constancy**—the tendency to perceive objects as retaining their color even though lighting conditions may alter their appearance. Your bright orange car may edge toward yellow-gray as the hours wend their way through twilight to nighttime. But when you finally locate it in the parking lot, you will still think of it as being orange. You expect an orange car and still judge it to be "more orange" than the (faded) blue and green cars to either side. However, it would be fiercely difficult to find it in a parking lot filled with yellow and red cars similar in size and shape.

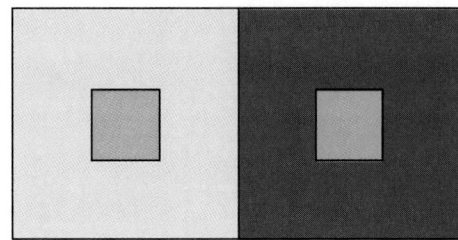

FIGURE 4.26
Color Constancy The orange squares within the blue squares are the same hue, yet the orange within the dark blue square is perceived as being purer. Why?

Consider Figure 4.26. The orange squares within the blue squares are the same hue. However, the orange within the dark blue square is perceived as being purer. Why? Again, experience teaches us that the pureness of colors fades as the background grows darker. Since the orange squares are equally pure, we assume that the one in the dark background must be more saturated. We would stand ready to perceive the orange squares as being equal in purity if the square within the darker blue field actually had a bit of black mixed in with it.

Brightness Constancy. Similar to color constancy is **brightness constancy.** The same gray square is perceived as brighter when placed within a black background than when placed within a white background (see Figure 1.3 on p. 14). Again, consider the role of experience. If it were nighttime, we would expect gray to fade to near blackness. The fact that the gray within the black square stimulates the eye with equal intensity suggests that it must be very much brighter than the gray within the white square.

Shape Constancy. We also perceive objects as maintaining their shapes, even if we perceive them from different angles so that the shape of the retinal image changes dramatically. This tendency is called **shape constancy.** You perceive the top of a coffee cup or a glass to be a circle even though it is a circle only when seen from above. When seen from an angle, it is an ellipse. When seen on edge, the retinal image of the cup or glass is the same as that of a straight line. So why do you still describe the rim of the cup or glass as being a circle?

Binocular cues • Stimuli suggestive of depth that involve simultaneous perception by both eyes.
Retinal disparity • A binocular cue for depth based on the difference in the image cast by an object on the retinas of the eyes as the object moves closer or farther away.
Convergence • A binocular cue for depth based on the inward movement of the eyes as they attempt to focus on an object that is drawing nearer.
Visual acuity • Sharpness of vision.
Nearsighted • Capable of seeing nearby objects with greater acuity than distant objects.
Farsighted • Capable of seeing distant objects with greater acuity than nearby objects.
Presbyopia • A condition characterized by brittleness of the lens.
Strabismus • A visual disorder in which both eyes cannot focus on the same point at the same time.
Astigmatism • A visual disorder caused by abnormal curvature of the lens, so that images are indistinct or distorted.
Size constancy • The tendency to perceive an object as being the same size even as the size of its retinal image changes according to the object's distance.
Color constancy • The tendency to perceive an object as being the same color even though lighting conditions change its appearance.
Brightness constancy • The tendency to perceive an object as being just as bright even though lighting conditions change its intensity.
Shape constancy • The tendency to perceive an object as being the same shape although the retinal image varies in shape as it rotates.

FIGURE 4.27
Shape Constancy When closed, this door is a rectangle. When open, the retinal image is trapezoidal. But because of shape constancy, we still perceive the door as being rectangular.

FIGURE 4.28
What Is Wrong with Each of These Four Drawings?

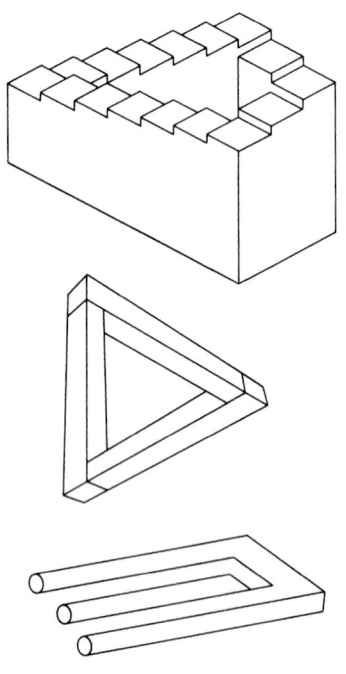

Perhaps for two reasons: One is that experience has taught you that the cup will look circular when seen from above. The second is that you may have labeled the cup circular or round. Experience and labels make the world a stable place. Can you imagine the chaos that would prevail if we described objects as they stimulated our sensory organs with each changing moment, rather than according to stable conditions?

In another example, a door is a rectangle only when viewed straight on (Figure 4.27). When we move to the side or open it, the left or right edge comes closer and appears to be larger, changing the retinal image to a trapezoid. Yet we continue to think of doors as being rectangles.

The principles of perceptual organization also make it possible to create fascinating "impossible" drawings. For example, what's wrong with each of the drawings in Figure 4.28? Each has firm lines. Each has interesting shapes. In fact, if you look at any one corner of a drawing, it makes perfect sense. But take a critical view of the endless staircase in M. C. Escher's *Relativity*. What would happen if you were walk up this staircase? Would you ever reach the top? Or what would happen if a ball rolled down and managed to turn all the corners? Would it ever reach bottom?

In each of these drawings, the artist, working in two dimensions, has used perceptual cues in such a way as to encourage us to perceive a three-dimensional figure. Any one segment of each of these drawings makes perfect sense. It's just when you put it all together that you realize that . . . well, you can't put it all together, can you? That would be impossible.

VISUAL ILLUSIONS

The principles of perceptual organization make it possible for our eyes to "play tricks on us." Psychologists, like magicians, enjoy pulling a rabbit out of the hat now and then, and I am pleased to be able to demonstrate how the perceptual constancies trick the eye through so-called visual illusions.

The Hering–Helmholtz and Müller–Lyer illusions (Figure 4.29, part A) are named after the people who originated them. In the Hering–Helmholtz illusion, the horizontal lines are straight and parallel. However, the radiating lines cause them to appear to be bent outward near the center. The two lines in the Müller–Lyer illusion are the same length, but the line on the left, with its reversed arrowheads, looks longer.

Let us try to explain these illusions. Because of experience and lifelong use of perceptual cues, we tend to perceive the Hering–Helmholtz drawing as being three-dimensional. Because of the tendency

MINILECTURE: VISUAL ILLUSIONS

FIGURE 4.29
The Hering–Helmholtz and Müller–Lyer Illusion In the Hering–Helmholtz illusion, are the horizontal lines straight or curved? In the Müller–Lyer illusion, are the vertical lines equal in length?

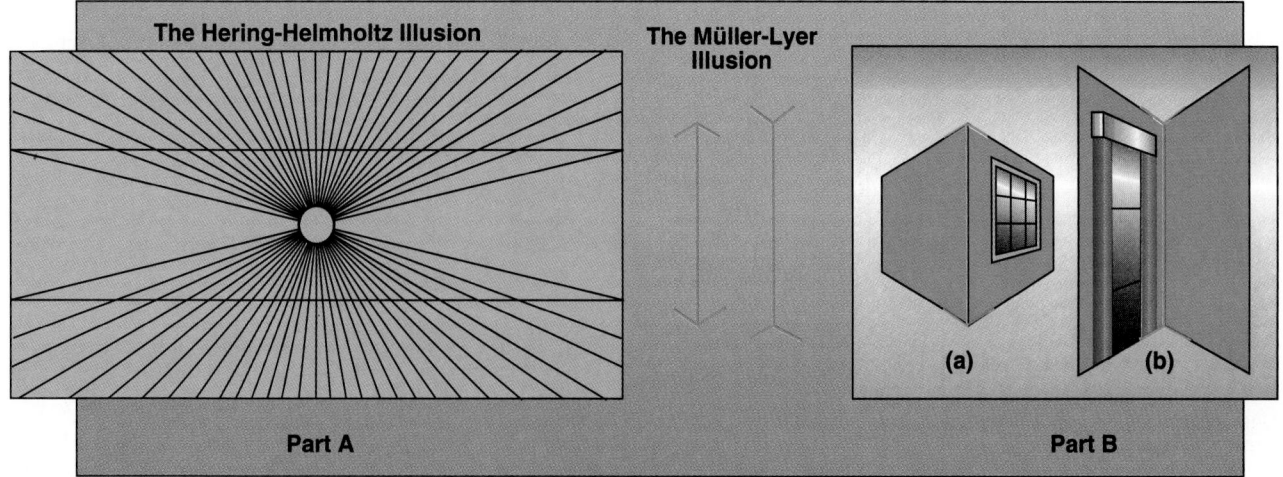

FIGURE 4.30
The Ponzo Illusion The two horizontal lines in this drawing are equal in length, but the top line is perceived as being longer. Can you use the principle of size constancy to explain why?

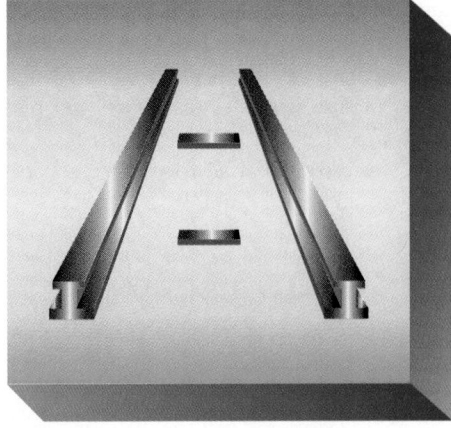

to perceive bits of sensory information as figures against grounds, we perceive the white area in the center as being a circle in front of a series of radiating lines, all of which lies in front of a white ground. Next, because of our experience with perspective, we perceive the radiating lines as being parallel. We perceive the two horizontal lines as intersecting the "receding" lines, and we know that they would have to appear bent out at the center if they were to be equidistant at all points from the center of the circle.

Experience probably compels us to perceive the vertical lines in the Müller–Lyer illusion as being the corners of a room as seen from inside a house, at left, and outside a house, at right (see Figure 4.29, part B). In

such an example, the reverse arrowheads to the left are lines where the walls meet the ceiling and the floor. We perceive such lines as extending toward us; they push the corner away from us. The arrowheads to the right are lines where exterior walls meet the roof and foundation. We perceive them as receding from us; they push the corner toward us. The vertical line to the left is thus perceived as being farther away. Since both vertical lines stimulate equal expanses across the retina, the principle of size constancy encourages us to perceive the line to the left as being longer.

Figure 4.30 is known as the Ponzo illusion. In this illusion, the two horizontal lines are the same length. However, do you perceive the top line as being longer? The rule of size constancy may also afford insight into this illusion. Perhaps the converging lines again strike us as being parallel lines receding into the distance, like train tracks. If so, we assume from experience that the horizontal line at the top is farther down the track—farther away from us. And again, the rule of size constancy tells us that if two objects appear to be the same size and one is farther away, the farther object must be larger. So we perceive the top line as being larger.

Now that you are an expert on these visual illusions, look at Figure 4.31. First take some bets from friends about whether the three cylinders are equal in height and width. Then get a ruler. Once you have made some money, however, try to explain why the cylinders to the right look progressively larger.

Reflections

Now that you have read the section on visual perception, reflect on the following questions:

- Why is it easier to spot your friend when she or he is walking alone than among a crowd?

- Have you ever seen two people walking next to one another and then been surprised to see them split up without saying anything to one another? How do you account for the assumption that they knew each other?

FIGURE 4.31
An Illusion Created by the Principle of Size Constancy
In this drawing, the three cylinders are the same size, yet they appear to grow larger toward the top of the picture. Can you use the principle of size constancy to explain why?

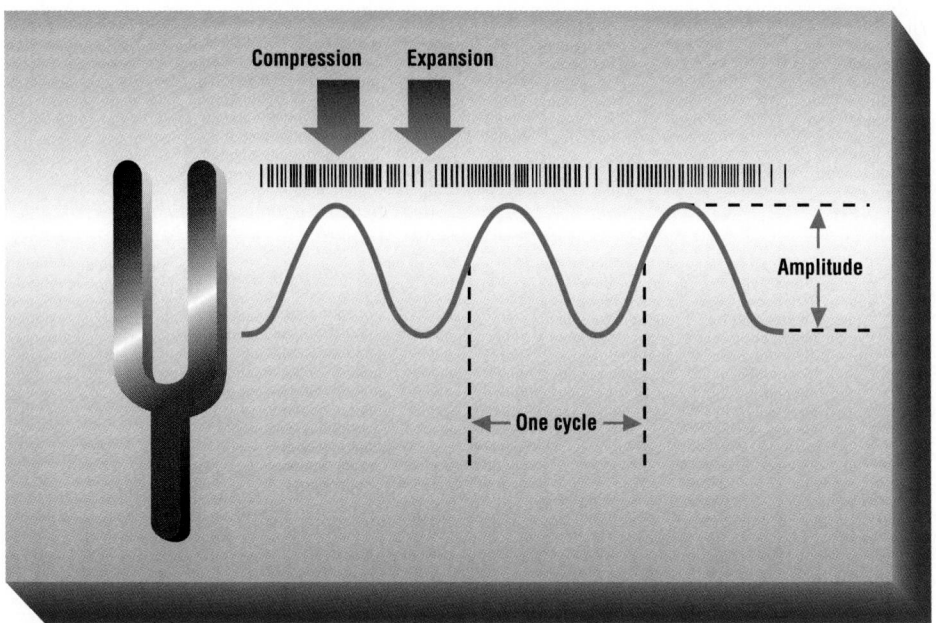

FIGURE 4.32
Creation of Sound Waves The vibration of the prongs of a tuning fork alternately compresses and expands air molecules, sending forth waves of sound.

- Did you enjoy looking over the two images in Figure 4.21? Or were you annoyed by them? What do you think that your response may suggest about your willingness to tolerate ambiguity?
- Have you had the experience of being in a train and not knowing whether your train or a train on the next track was moving? How do you explain the confusion?
- Can you think of some situations in your own life in which you have been confused or entertained by visual illusions?

Hearing

Consider the advertising slogan for the science fiction film *Alien*: "In space, no one can hear you scream." It's true. Space is an almost perfect vacuum, and hearing requires a medium such as air or water through which sound can travel.

Sound, or **auditory** stimulation, travels through the air like waves. Sound is caused by changes in air pressure that result from vibrations. These vibrations, in turn, can be created by a tuning fork, your vocal cords, guitar strings, or the clap of a book thrown down on a desk.

Figure 4.32 suggests the way in which a tuning fork creates sound waves. During a vibration back and forth, the right prong of the tuning fork moves to the right. In so doing, it pushes together, or compresses, the molecules of air immediately to the right. Then the prong moves back to the left, and the air molecules to the right expand. By vibrating back and forth, the tuning fork actually sends air waves in many directions. A cycle of compression and expansion is considered to be one wave of sound. Sound waves can occur many times in one second. The human ear is sensitive to sound waves that vary from frequencies of 20 to 20,000 cycles per second.

PITCH AND LOUDNESS

Pitch and loudness are two psychological dimensions of sound.

Pitch. The pitch of a sound is determined by its frequency, or the number of cycles per second as expressed in the unit **Hertz** (Hz). One cycle per second is one Hz. The greater the number of cycles per second (Hz), the higher the pitch of the sound. The pitch of women's voices is usually higher than those of men because

Auditory • Having to do with hearing.

Hertz • A unit expressing the frequency of sound waves. One Hertz, or *1 Hz,* equals one cycle per second.

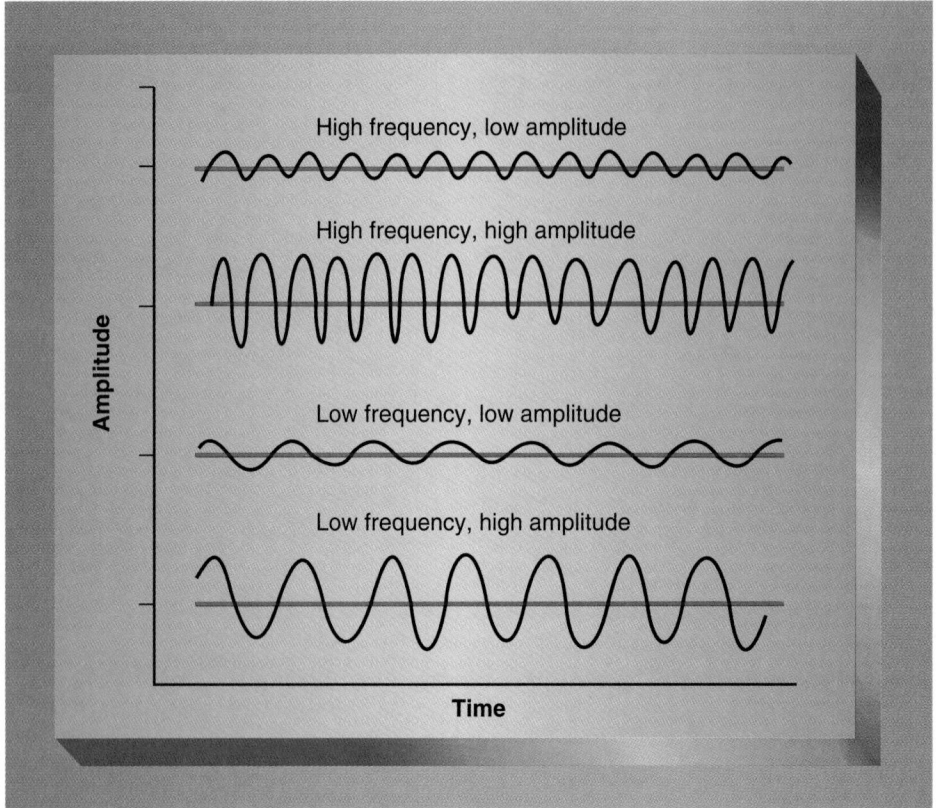

FIGURE 4.33
Sound Waves of Various Frequencies and Amplitudes Which sounds have the highest pitch? Which are loudest?

Amplitude • Height.

Decibel • A unit expressing the loudness of a sound. Abbreviated *dB.*

Consonant • In harmony.

Dissonant • Incompatible, not harmonious, discordant.

Overtones • Tones of a higher frequency than those played that result from vibrations throughout a musical instrument.

Timbre • The quality or richness of a sound.

White noise • Discordant sounds of many frequencies, often producing a lulling effect.

Eardrum • A thin membrane that vibrates in response to sound waves, transmitting the waves to the middle and inner ears.

Oval window • A membrane that transmits vibrations from the stirrup of the middle ear to the cochlea within the inner ear.

Cochlea • The inner ear; the bony tube that contains the basilar membrane and the organ of Corti.

women's vocal cords are usually shorter and thus vibrate at a greater frequency. The strings of a violin are shorter than those of a viola or bass viol. They vibrate at greater frequencies, and we perceive them to be higher in pitch.

Loudness. The loudness of a sound is determined by the height, or **amplitude,** of sound waves. The higher the amplitude of the wave, the louder the sound. Figure 4.33 shows records of sound waves that vary in frequency and amplitude. Frequency and amplitude are independent dimensions. Sounds both high and low in pitch can be either high or low in loudness.

The loudness of a sound is usually expressed in the unit **decibel,** abbreviated *dB,* which is named after the inventor of the telephone, Alexander Graham Bell. Zero dB is equivalent to the threshold of hearing. How loud is that? It's about as loud as the ticking of a watch 20 feet away in a very quiet room (see Table 4.1).

The decibel equivalents of many familiar sounds are shown in Figure 4.34. Twenty dB is equivalent in loudness to a whisper at 5 feet. Thirty dB is roughly the limit of loudness at which your librarian would like to keep your college library. You may suffer hearing damage if exposed protractedly to sounds of 85 to 90 dB.

When musical sounds (also called tones) of different frequency are played together, we also perceive a third tone that results from the difference in their frequencies. If the combination of tones is pleasant, we say that they are in harmony, or **consonant** (from Latin roots meaning "together" and "sound"). Unpleasant combinations of tones are labeled **dissonant** ("the opposite of" and "sound"). The expression that something "strikes a dissonant chord" means that we find it disagreeable.

Overtones and Timbre. In addition to producing the specified musical note, an instrument like the violin also produces a number of tones that are greater in frequency. These more highly pitched sounds are called **overtones.** Overtones result from vibrations elsewhere in the instrument and contribute to the quality or richness—the **timbre**—of a sound.

Truth or Fiction Revisited. *It is true that a $500 machine-made violin will produce the same musical notes as a $200,000 Stradivarius.* The Stradivarius has richer overtones, however, which lend the instrument its greater value.

Noise. In terms of the sense of hearing, noise is a combination of dissonant sounds.[1] When you place a spiral shell to your ear, you do not hear the roar of the ocean. Rather, you hear the reflected noise in your vicinity. **White noise** consists of many different frequencies of sound. Yet, this mixture can lull us to sleep if the loudness is not too great.

Now let us turn our attention to the marvelous instrument that senses all these different "vibes": the human ear.

THE EAR: THE BETTER TO HEAR YOU WITH

The human ear is good for lots of things—catching dust, combing your hair around, hanging jewelry from, and nibbling. It is also admirably suited for sensing sounds. The ear is shaped and structured to capture sound waves, to vibrate in sympathy with them, and to transmit all this business to centers in the brain. In this way, you not only hear something, you can also figure out what it is. You have an outer ear, a middle ear, and an inner ear (see Figure 4.35).

The Outer Ear. The outer ear is shaped to funnel sound waves to the **eardrum,** a thin membrane that vibrates in response to sound waves and thereby transmits them to the middle and inner ears.

The Middle Ear. The middle ear contains the eardrum and three small bones—the hammer, the anvil, and the stirrup—which also transmit sound by vibrating. These bones were given their names

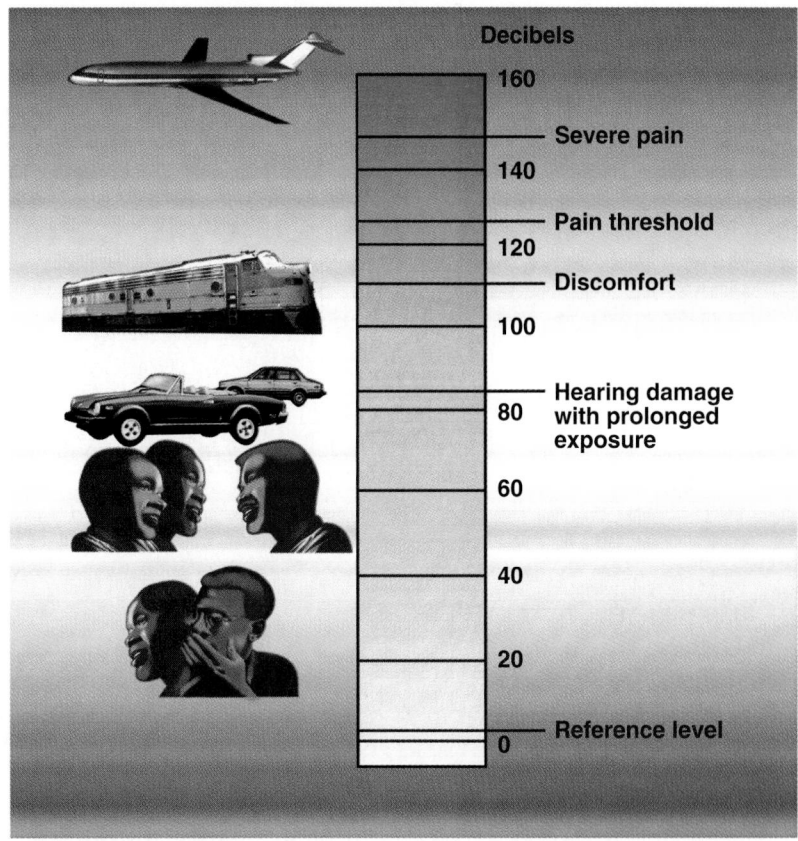

FIGURE 4.34

Spotlight on the Decibel Ratings of Some Familiar Sounds
Zero dB is the threshold of hearing. You may suffer hearing loss if you incur prolonged exposure to sounds of 85–90 dB.

(actually the Latin *malleus, incus,* and *stapes* [pronounced STAY-peas], which translate as hammer, anvil, and stirrup) because of their shapes. The middle ear functions as an amplifier: It increases the magnitude of the air pressure.

The stirrup is attached to another vibrating membrane, the **oval window.** The round window shown in Figure 4.35 balances the pressure in the inner ear. It pushes out when the oval window pushes in, and it is pulled in when the oval window vibrates outward.

The Inner Ear. The oval window transmits vibrations into the inner ear, the bony tube called the **cochlea** (from the

---

[1] Within the broader context of signal-detection theory, *noise* has a different meaning, discussed earlier in the chapter.

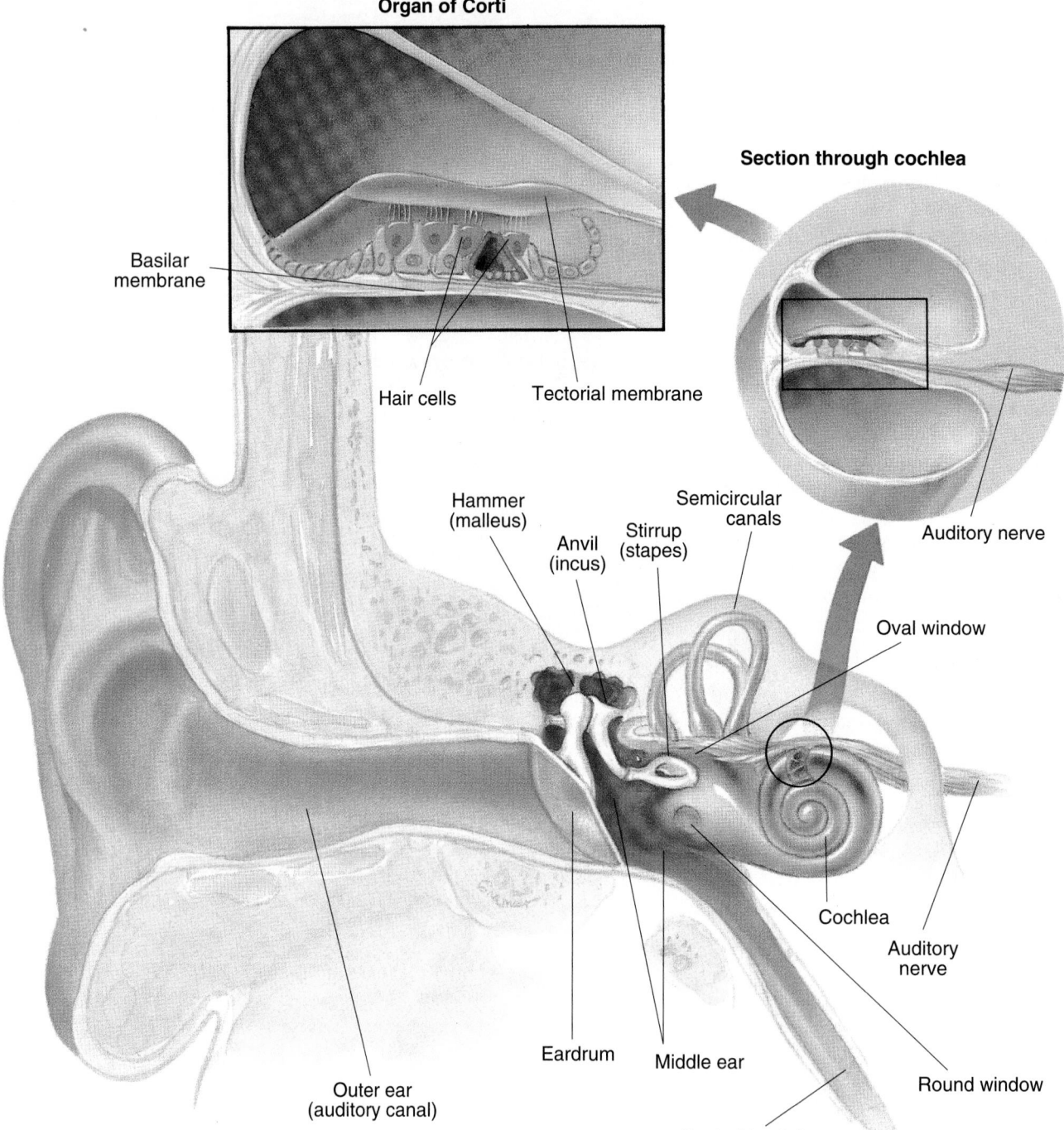

Organ of Corti

Section through cochlea

Basilar
membrane

Hair cells

Tectorial membrane

Auditory nerve

Hammer
(malleus)

Anvil
(incus)

Stirrup
(stapes)

Semicircular
canals

Oval window

Outer ear
(auditory canal)

Eardrum

Middle ear

Eustachian tube

Cochlea

Auditory
nerve

Round window

FIGURE 4.35

The Human Ear The outer ear funnels sound to the eardrum. Inside the eardrum, vibrations of the hammer, anvil, and stirrup transmit sound to the inner ear. Vibrations in the cochlea transmit the sound to the auditory nerve by way of the basilar membrane and the organ of Corti.

Greek for "snail"). The cochlea, which has the shape of a snail shell, contains two longitudinal membranes that divide it into three fluid-filled chambers. One of the membranes that lies coiled within the cochlea is called the **basilar membrane.** Vibrations in the fluids within the chambers of the inner ear press against the basilar membrane.

The **organ of Corti,** sometimes referred to as the "command post" of hearing, is attached to the basilar membrane. Thousands of hair cells (receptor cells that project like hair from the organ of Corti) "dance" in response to the vibrations of the basilar membrane (Brownell, 1992). This up-and-down movement generates neural impulses that are transmitted to the brain via the 31,000 neurons that form the **auditory nerve.** Within the brain, auditory input is projected onto the hearing areas of the temporal lobes of the cerebral cortex.

LOCATING SOUNDS

How do you balance the loudness of a stereo set? You sit between the speakers and adjust the volume until the sound seems to be equally loud in each ear. If the sound to the right is louder, the musical instruments will be perceived as being toward the right rather than straight ahead.

There is a resemblance between balancing a stereo set and locating sounds. A sound that is louder in the right ear is perceived as coming from the right. A sound from the right side also reaches the right ear first. Loudness and sequence of stimulating the ears both provide directional cues.

But it may not be easy to locate a sound that is directly in front, in back, or overhead. Such sounds are equally loud in and distant from each ear. So what do we do? Simple—usually we turn our heads slightly to determine in which ear the sound increases. If you turn your head a few degrees to the right and the loudness increases in your left ear, the sound must be in front of you. Of course we also use vision and general knowledge in locating the source of sounds. If you hear the roar of jet engines, most of the time you will make money by betting that the airplane is overhead.

PERCEPTION OF LOUDNESS AND PITCH

We know that sounds are heard because they cause vibration in parts of the ear, and information about these vibrations is transmitted to the brain. But what determines the loudness and pitch of our perceptions of these sounds?

The loudness and pitch of sounds appear to be related to the number of receptor neurons on the organ of Corti that fire and how often they fire. Psychologists generally agree that sounds are perceived as being louder when more of these sensory neurons fire. They are not so certain about the perception of pitch. Two of the theories that have been advanced to explain pitch discrimination are *place theory* and *frequency theory.*

Place Theory. According to **place theory,** the pitch of a sound is determined by the place along the basilar membrane that vibrates in response to it. In his classic research with guinea pigs and cadavers, von Békésy (1957) found that receptors at different sites along the membrane fire in response to tones of differing frequencies. By and large, the higher the pitch of a sound, the closer the responsive neurons lie to the oval window. However, the entire membrane appears to be responsive to tones that are low in frequency.

Frequency Theory. Place theory does not explain all the phenomena of hearing. For example, it has been found that impulses in the auditory nerve follow the pattern of the sound waves being detected. **Frequency theory** has been developed to account for such occurrences. In general, frequency theory proposes that pitch perception depends on the stimulation of neural impulses that match the frequency of the sound waves. However, frequency theory breaks down for perception of pitches higher than 1,000 Hz because neural impulses are not able to follow the forms of the sound waves at those levels.

Duplicity theory advances the view that pitch perception depends both on the place and frequency of neural response. A more

Basilar membrane • A membrane that lies coiled within the cochlea.

Organ of Corti • The receptor for hearing that lies on the basilar membrane in the cochlea.

Auditory nerve • The axon bundle that transmits neural impulses from the organ of Corti to the brain.

Place theory • The theory that the pitch of a sound is determined by the section of the basilar membrane that vibrates in response to the sound.

Frequency theory • The theory that the pitch of a sound is reflected in the frequency of the neural impulses that are generated in response to the sound.

Duplicity theory • A combination of the place and frequency theories of pitch discrimination.

comprehensive theory of pitch perception is needed to explain (1) why neurons at different sites on the basilar membrane fire in response to different pitches, (2) why impulses in the auditory nerve follow the patterns of sound waves at many frequencies, and (3) how we perceive pitches at above 1,000 Hz.

Unfortunately, not everyone perceives sound, and many of us do not perceive sounds of certain frequencies. Let us consider a number of kinds of hearing problems, or deafness.

DEAFNESS

An estimated 28 million Americans have impaired hearing. Two million of them are deaf (Nadol, 1993). They are thus deprived of a key source of information about the world outside. In recent years, however, society has made more of an effort to bring them into the mainstream of sensory experience. People are usually on hand to convert political and other speeches into hand signs (such as those of American Sign Language) for hearing-impaired members of the audience. Many television shows are

PSYCHOLOGY IN THE NEW MILLENNIUM

Sonic Device May Help Blind People Navigate[2]

The other day, Dr. Reginald Golledge, who is blind, took a remarkable stroll through the campus of the University of California at Santa Barbara. As Dr. Golledge walked along, places and impediments in his path seemed to call out their names to him—"library here, library here," "bench here, bench here"—guiding him through a Disney-esque landscape of talking objects.

Dr. Golledge was testing a prototype navigation system for the blind that announced the whereabouts of objects through stereo headphones mounted to a computer in his backpack, creating a virtual reality landscape (as in the figure on page 159). The information came not from some miniature radar but from the signals broadcast by the military's network of global positioning satellites. One day, its developers hope, miniaturized versions of this navigation device, which now weighs 28 pounds, will help the blind navigate unfamiliar neighborhoods.

"With this system you don't need to know a thing in advance about where you're going," said Dr. Roberta Klatzky (1994), a psychologist at Carnegie-Mellon University who is working with Dr. Golledge to develop the navigating device.

Dr. Michael Oberdorfer (1994) of the National Eye Institute said: "A blind person could walk down the street and know not just that he was at 80th and Broadway, but what stores are around, and that Zabar's delicatessen was up ahead. This navigation system tells you not just where there are obstacles, but your overall location geographically." It lets blind users construct a mental map of new surroundings and learn their way around.

The navigation system uses signals from a computerized map to create a "virtual acoustic display." This is a talking map in which large objects seem to announce themselves in the headphones with the precise timing and loudness that would be the case if the objects were actually making a sound. This allows the blind person to sense immediately his or her distance and direction, and use that information for guidance. While no one knows whether it is because blind people tend to develop a sharper sense of hearing, those who have tried the system say they quickly adapt to locating an object through the sounds.

"One of the crucial features of this system is that it takes advantage of sensory psychophysics—how the brain interprets signals from outside to make a map of your surroundings so you can navigate," Dr. Oberdorfer said.

[2] Adapted from Goleman, D. (1994, September 6). Sonic device for blind may help in navigation. *The New York Times*, pp. C1, C9.

now "closed captioned" so that they will be accessible to the hearing-impaired. Special decoders render the captions visible. Although people are more likely to encounter hearing loss as they age, educators have also grown more aware of the potential language-learning problems of hearing-impaired children.

There are two major types of hearing problems or deafness: *conductive deafness* and *sensorineural deafness*.

Conductive Deafness. **Conductive deafness** occurs because of damage to the structures of the middle ear—either to the eardrum or to the three bones that conduct (and amplify) sound waves from the outer ear to the inner ear (Nadol, 1993). People with conductive hearing loss have high absolute thresholds for detection of sounds at all frequencies. This is the type of hearing impairment frequently found among the elderly. People with conductive deafness often profit from hearing aids, which provide the amplification that the middle ear does not.

Conductive deafness • The forms of deafness in which there is loss of conduction of sound through the middle ear.

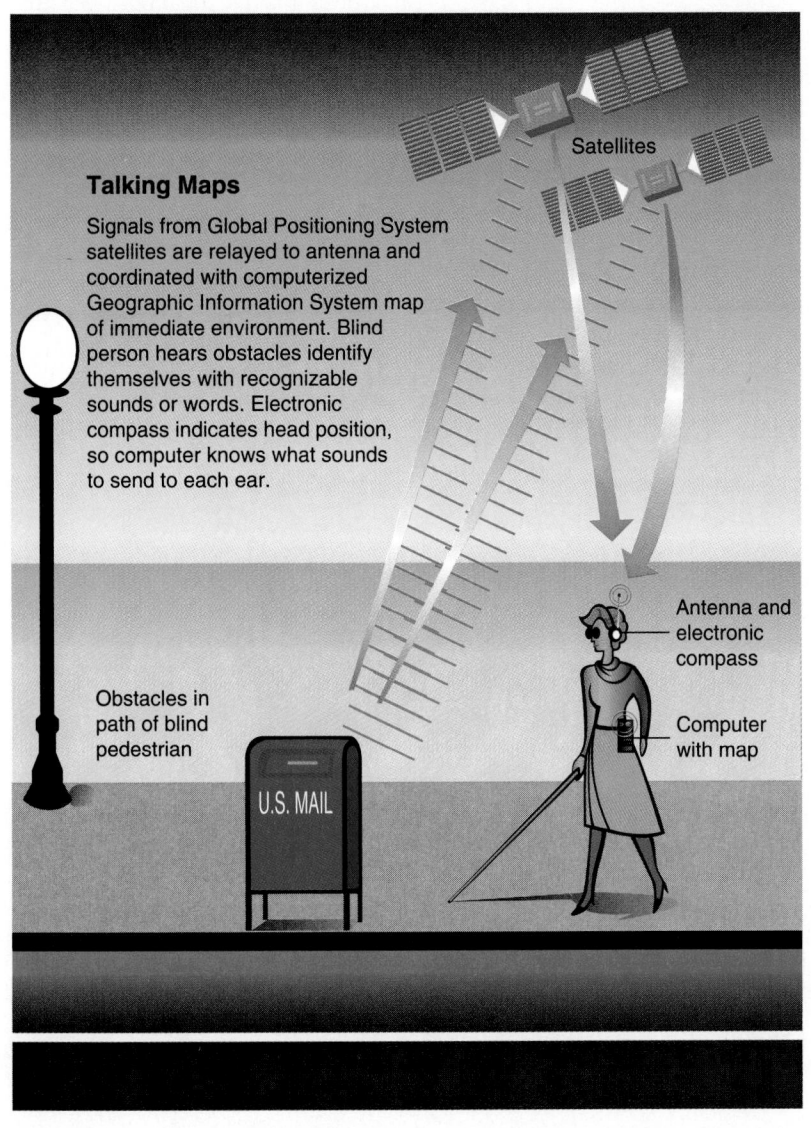

Talking Maps

Signals from Global Positioning System satellites are relayed to antenna and coordinated with computerized Geographic Information System map of immediate environment. Blind person hears obstacles identify themselves with recognizable sounds or words. Electronic compass indicates head position, so computer knows what sounds to send to each ear.

Satellites

Obstacles in path of blind pedestrian

U.S. MAIL

Antenna and electronic compass

Computer with map

Sensorineural Deafness. **Sensorineural deafness** usually stems from damage to the structures of the inner ear, most often the loss of hair cells, which will not regenerate. Sensorineural deafness can also stem from damage to the auditory nerve, for example, because of disease or because of acoustic trauma (exposure to loud sounds). In sensorineural deafness, people tend to be more sensitive to sounds of some pitches than others. In so-called Hunter's notch, hearing impairment is limited to particular frequencies—in this case, the frequencies of the sound waves generated by a gun firing. Prolonged exposure to 85 dB can cause hearing loss. People who attend high-volume rock concerts risk damaging their ears, as do workers who run pneumatic drills or drive high-volume transportation vehicles. The so-called ringing sensation that often follows exposure to loud sounds probably means that hair cells have been damaged. If you find yourself suddenly exposed to loud sounds, remember that your fingertips serve as good emergency ear protectors.

Experimental cochlear implants, or "artificial ears," contain microphones that sense sounds and electronic equipment that transmits sounds past damaged hair cells to stimulate the auditory nerve directly. Multi-channel implants apply the place theory of pitch perception to enable people with impaired hearing to discriminate sounds of high and low pitches. Such implants have

helped many people with sensorineural deafness. However, implants cannot assume the functions of damaged auditory nerves.

Reflections

Now that you have read the section on hearing, reflect on the following questions:

- Are you familiar with these four stringed instruments: violin, viola, cello, and bass fiddle? How do their sounds differ? What about the instruments accounts for their differences in sound?
- Have you ever been unsure of where a sound was coming from? How did you locate the sound?
- Do you know anyone who is hearing-impaired? What biological problem accounts for the impairment in hearing? How does the person cope with the impairment?

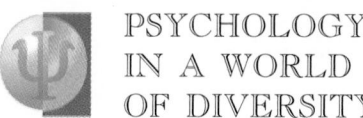

PSYCHOLOGY IN A WORLD OF DIVERSITY

THE SIGNS OF THE TIMES ARE CHANGING TO REFLECT NEW SENSIBILITIES AMONG THE DEAF

Perhaps as recently as 1990, a deaf person might make the sign that meant a Japanese person by twisting the little finger next to

Sensorineural deafness • The forms of deafness that result from damage to hair cells or the auditory nerve.

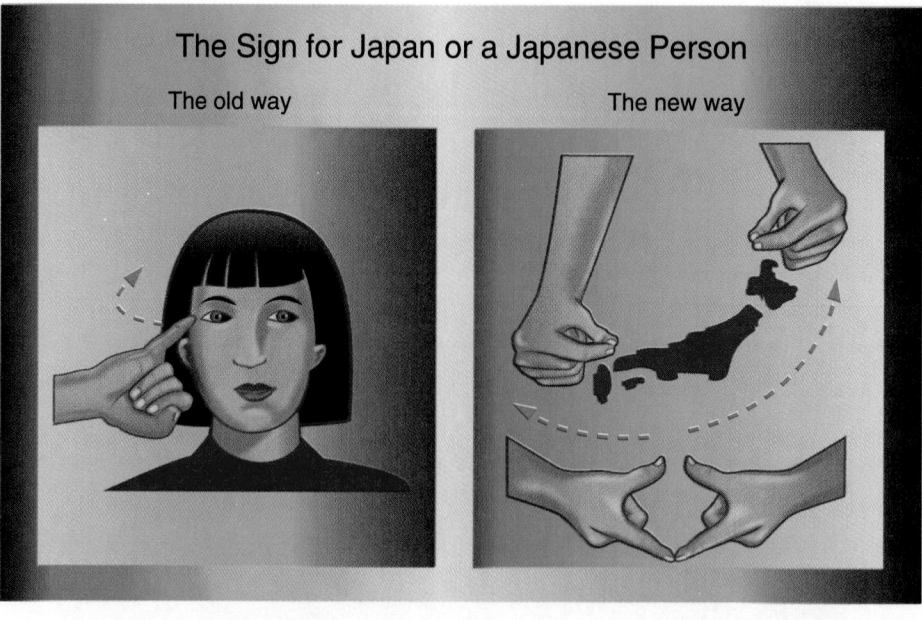

FIGURE 4.36
Old and New Signs for Japan or a Japanese Person in American Sign Language The old sign for Japanese is now considered offensive because it refers to the stereotypical physical feature of slanted eyes. The new sign involves simply outlining the island of Japan in the air.

the eye (see Figure 4.36). Today many of the people who use American Sign Language have discarded this sign because it refers to the stereotypical physical feature of slanted eyes. Instead, they are adopting Japanese people's own sign for themselves: They press the thumb and index finger of both hands together and then pull them apart to sculpt the outline of Japan in the air (Senior, 1994).

"In American Sign Language, politically incorrect terms are often a visual representation of the ugly metaphors we have about people," notes psycholinguist Elissa Newport (1994). As with the sign for *Japanese,* the signs for *Chinese* and *Korean,* which are made by forming the letters *C* and *K* around the eye, are also changing. There is a new sign for *African American.* It was once indicated by flattening the nose. It was then replaced by signs for the color black—the index finger either placed by the eyebrow or wiped across the forehead. The current sign for *African American* is still centered around the nose, however, and is thus being replaced by outlining Africa in the air (see Figure 4.37).

The old sign for a gay male was an offensive swish of the wrist. Now it is more widely acceptable to simply spell out words like *homosexual, gay male,* or *lesbian* with the hands.

A sign for *stingy* shows a clenched fist in connection with stroking an imaginary beard. Stroking an imaginary beard is the sign for *Jewish,* and so the fist and beard sign has sparked discussions among deaf Jews. Still, no new sign has replaced it as of this writing.

Politically correct changes in American Sign Language have thus far caught on mainly among highly educated deaf people in urban settings. It is taking longer for them to catch on in the wider deaf community and to appear in dictionaries of sign language. Nevertheless, the clear trend is for the deaf—who in many ways have been the victims of stereotyping themselves—to learn how not to stereotype others through sign language.

Smell

Smell and taste are the chemical senses. In the cases of vision and hearing, physical energy impacts on our sensory receptors. With smell and taste, we sample molecules of the substances being sensed.

You could say that we are underprivileged when it comes to the sense of smell. Dogs, for instance, devote about seven times as much area of the cerebral cortex to the sense of smell. Male dogs sniff to determine where the territories of other dogs leave off and to determine whether female dogs are sexually receptive. Dogs even make a living

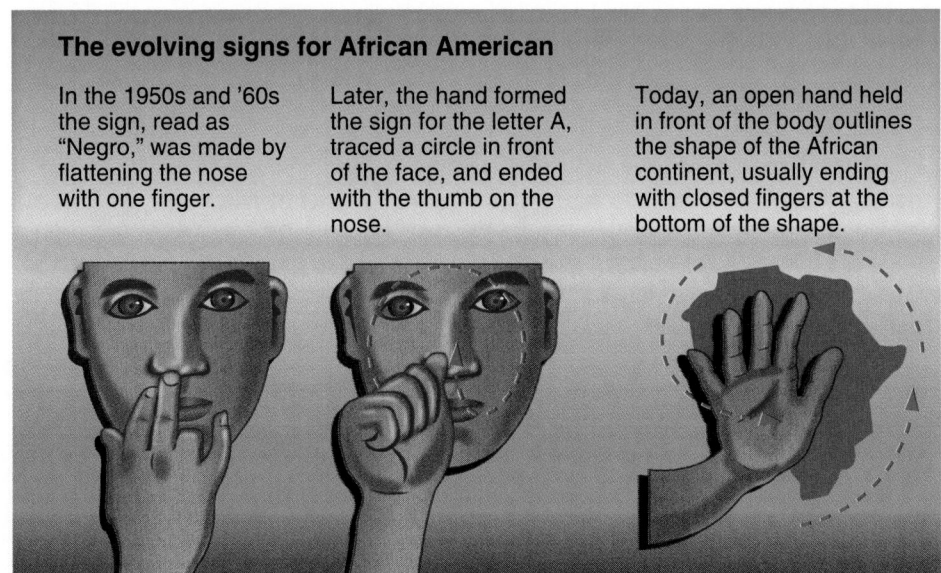

The evolving signs for African American

In the 1950s and '60s the sign, read as "Negro," was made by flattening the nose with one finger.

Later, the hand formed the sign for the letter A, traced a circle in front of the face, and ended with the thumb on the nose.

Today, an open hand held in front of the body outlines the shape of the African continent, usually ending with closed fingers at the bottom of the shape.

FIGURE 4.37
Old and New Signs for African Americans in American Sign Language The old signs for African Americans were considered offensive because they referred to the shape or location of the nose. The new sign involves outlining the African continent in the air.

sniffing out marijuana in closed packages and suitcases.

Still, smell has an important role in human behavior. Smell makes a crucial contribution to the flavor of foods, for example (Brody, 1992b). If you did not have a sense of smell, an onion and an apple would taste the same to you! People's senses of smell may be lacking when we compare them to those of a dog, but we can detect the odor of one one-millionth of a milligram of vanilla in a liter of air.

Truth or Fiction Revisited. *It is true that onions and apples have the same taste. Their flavors, however, which also reflect these foods' odors and other qualities, are very different.*

An **odor** is a sample of the substance being sensed. Odors are detected by sites on receptor neurons in the **olfactory** membrane high in each nostril. Receptor neu-

rons fire when a few molecules of the substance in gaseous form come into contact with them. Firing transmits information about odors to the brain via the **olfactory nerve.** That is how the substance is smelled.

It is unclear how many basic kinds of odors there are. In any event, olfactory receptors may respond to more than one kind of odor. Different odors may also activate different regions of olfactory receptors. Thus, the location of the receptor contributes to our olfactory perceptions (Kimble, 1992). Moreover, mixtures of smell sensations also help produce the broad range of odors that we can perceive (Solomon and others, 1993).

The sense of smell adapts rapidly to odors, even obnoxious ones (Solomon and others, 1993). This might be fortunate if you are using a locker room or an outhouse. It might not be so fortunate if you are being

Odor • The characteristic of a substance that makes it perceptible to the sense of smell.
Olfactory • Having to do with the sense of smell.
Olfactory nerve • The nerve that transmits information concerning odors from olfactory receptors to the brain.

PSYCHOLOGY IN THE NEW MILLENNIUM

Will We Be Using "a Sixth Sense for Sex" When the 21st Century Rolls In?

Pheromones are chemicals that drive the libido to do the lambada.

STEPHANIE STROM (1993)

For centuries, people have searched for a love potion—a magical formula that could make others fall in love with you or be strongly attracted to you (Strom, 1993). Some scientists, such as David Berliner (1993), suggest that such potions may indeed exist, in the form of chemical secretions known as *pheromones.*

Pheromones are odorless chemicals that in people would be detected through a "sixth sense"—the *vomeronasal organ.* This organ, located in the nose (hence, nasal) would detect these odorless chemicals and communicate information about them to the hypothalamus, where they might affect sexual response (Blakeslee, 1993). Researcher David Moran (1993) suggests that people may use pheromones in many ways. Infants, for example, may use them to recognize their mothers, and adults might respond to them in seeking a mate. Lower animals use pheromones to stimulate sexual response, organize food gathering, maintain pecking orders, sound alarms, and mark territories (Strom, 1993). Research has shown that pheromones induce mating behavior mechanically in insects. Male rodents show less sexual arousal when their senses of smell are blocked (Beauchamp, 1981), but the role of pheromones in sexual behavior becomes less vital as we rise through the ranks of the animal kingdom.

Gary K. Beauchamp (1993), director of Philadelphia's Monnell Chemical Senses Center, notes that only a few years ago, most researchers did not believe that pheromones played a role in human behavior. Today, however, that field of research has sprung into life. David

exposed to fumes from paints or second-hand smoke, since you may lose awareness of them while danger remains. One odor may also be masked by another, which is how air fresheners work.

Taste

Your cocker spaniel may jump at the chance to finish off your ice cream cone, but your Siamese cat may turn up her nose at the opportunity. Why? Dogs can perceive the taste quality of sweetness, as can pigs, but cats cannot.

There are four primary taste qualities: sweet, sour, salty, and bitter. The *flavor* of a food involves its taste but is more complex. Although apples and onions have the same taste—or the same mix of taste qualities—their flavors differ greatly. After all, you

A Taste of . . . Well, Certainly Not Honey. The flavors of foods are determined not only by taste but also by their odor, texture, and temperature.

wouldn't chomp into a nice cold onion on a warm day, would you? The flavor of a food depends on its odor, texture, and temperature as well as its taste. If it were not for

Berliner has jumped ahead of the research enterprise by forming two companies, Erox and Pherin, that are intended to commercialize the use of pheromones with people. As the new millennium rolls in, might people be using perfumes and colognes that have a double impact—one on the sense of smell and another on a "sixth sense for sex"?

Is It a Meeting of the Minds or Is It . . . Pheromones? Researchers suggest that infants may use odorless chemicals called pheromones to recognize their mothers, and that adults might respond to pheromones in seeking a mate. Pheromones would be detected through a "sixth sense"—the *vomeronasal organ*.

odor, heated tenderized shoe leather might pass for steak.

Taste is sensed through **taste cells**—receptor neurons that are located on **taste buds**. You have about 10,000 taste buds, most of which are located near the edges and back of your tongue. Taste buds tend to specialize a bit (see Figure 4.38). Some, for example, are more responsive to sweetness, whereas others react to several tastes. Receptors for sweetness lie at the tip of the tongue, and receptors for bitterness lie toward the back of the tongue. Sourness is sensed along the sides of the tongue, and saltiness overlaps the areas sensitive to sweetness and sourness (Figure 4.38). This is why people perceive a sour dish to "get them" at the sides of the tongue.

We live in different taste worlds. Some of us with a low sensitivity for the sweet taste may require twice the sugar to sweeten our food as others who are more sensitive to sweetness. Others of us who claim to enjoy very bitter foods may actually be taste-blind to them. Sensitivities to different tastes apparently have a strong genetic component.

By eating hot foods and scraping your tongue, you regularly kill off many taste cells. But you need not be alarmed at this inadvertent oral aggression. Taste cells are the rabbits of the sense receptors. They reproduce rapidly enough to completely renew themselves about once a week.

Although older people often complain that their food has little or no "taste," they are more likely to experience a decline in the sense of smell (Brody, 1992b). Because the flavor of a food represents its tastes and odors, or aromas, older people experience loss in the *flavor* of their food. Since the flavor of food supplies some of the motivation to eat, older people are also at risk of becoming malnourished. They are often encouraged to avert malnourishment by spicing their food to enhance its flavor (Brody, 1992b).

Taste cells • Receptor cells that are sensitive to taste.

Taste buds • The sensory organs for taste. They contain taste cells and are located on the tongue.

Two-point threshold • The least distance by which two rods touching the skin must be separated before the person will report that there are two rods, not one, on 50% of occasions.

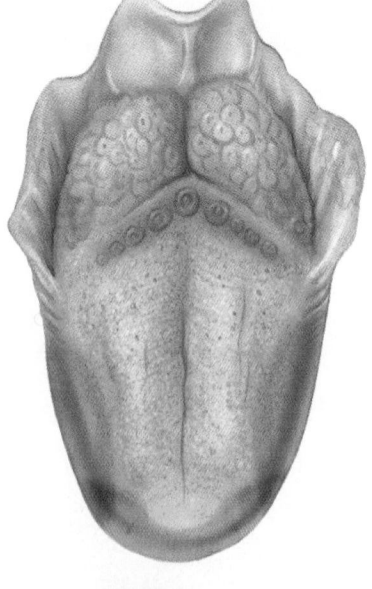

FIGURE 4.38
Location of Various Taste Buds on the Tongue Taste buds on different areas of the tongue are sensitive to different primary taste qualities.

Bitter

Sour

Salty

Sweet

The Skin Senses

The skin discriminates among many kinds of sensations—touch, pressure, warmth, cold, and pain (see Figure 4.39). We have distinct sensory receptors for pressure, temperature, and pain, but some nerve endings may receive more than one type of sensory input.

TOUCH AND PRESSURE

Sensory receptors located around the roots of hair cells appear to fire in response to touching the surface of the skin. You may have noticed that if you are trying to "get the feel of" a fabric or the texture of a friend's hair, you must move your hand over it (Loomis & Lederman, 1986). Otherwise, the sensations quickly fade. If you pass your hand over the skin and then hold it still, again sensations of touching will fade. This sort of "active touching" involves reception of information that concerns not only touch per se but also pressure, temperature, and feedback from the muscles that are involved in movements of our hands.

Other structures beneath the skin are apparently sensitive to pressure. All in all,

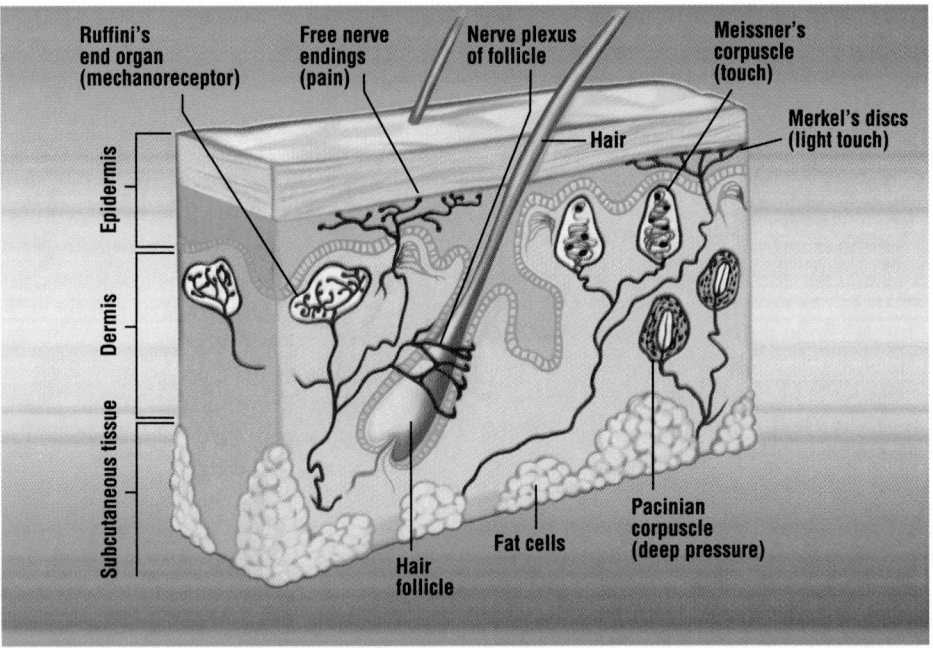

FIGURE 4.39
Skin—A Complex Organ Your skin may be more complex than you think. It contains several layers and various kinds of sensory receptors.

there are about half a million receptors for touch and pressure spaced throughout the body. Different parts of the body are more sensitive to touch and pressure than others. Psychophysicists use methods such as the **two-point threshold** to assess sensitivity to pressure. This method determines the smallest distance by which two rods touching the skin must be separated before the (blindfolded) individual will report that there are two rods, not one. As revealed by this method, our fingertips, lips, noses, and cheeks are much more sensitive than our shoulders, thighs, and calves. That is, the rods can be closer together when they touch the lips than the shoulders and still be perceived as distinct. Differential sensitivity occurs for at least two reasons: First, nerve endings are more densely packed in the fingertips and face than in other locations. Second, a greater amount of sensory cortex is devoted to the perception of sensations in the fingertips and face.

The sense of pressure, like the sense of touch, undergoes rather rapid adaptation. You may have undertaken several minutes of strategic movements to wind up with your hand on the arm or leg of your date, only to discover that adaptation to this de-lightful source of pressure saps the sensation.

TEMPERATURE

The receptors for temperature are neurons just beneath the skin. When skin temperature increases, receptors for warmth fire. Decreases in skin temperature cause receptors for cold to fire. Muscle changes connected with changes in temperature may also play a role in the sensing of temperature (Schiffman, 1990).

Sensations of temperature are relative. When we are at normal body temperature, we might perceive another person's skin as being warm. When we are feverish, though, the other person's skin might seem cool to the touch. We also adapt to differences in temperature. When we walk out of an air-conditioned house into the desert sun, we at first feel intense heat. Then the sensations of heat tend to fade (although we still may be made terribly uncomfortable by high humidity). Similarly, when we first enter a swimming pool, the water may seem cool or cold because it is below body temperature. Yet after a few moments, an 80-degree-Fahrenheit pool may seem quite warm. In fact, we may chide the tentative newcomer for being overly sensitive.

PAIN: THE OFTEN UNWANTED MESSAGE

Headaches, backaches, toothaches—these are only a few of the types of pain that most of us encounter from time to time. Some of us also suffer indescribable bouts of pain from arthritis, digestive disorders, cancer, and wounds.

Pain is a signal that something is wrong in the body. Pain is adaptive in the sense that it motivates us to do something about it. For some of us, however, chronic pain—pain that lasts even once injuries or illnesses have cleared up—saps our vitality and the pleasures of everyday life.

Pain originates at the point of contact, as with a stubbed toe (see Figure 4.40). The

pain message to the brain is initiated by the release of various chemicals including prostaglandins, bradykinin (perhaps the most painful known substance), and the mysterious chemical called *P* (yes, *P* stands for "pain"). Prostaglandins not only facilitate transmission of the pain message to the brain, they also heighten circulation to the injured area, causing the redness and swelling we call inflammation. Inflammation attracts infection-fighting blood cells to the area to protect against invading bacteria. **Analgesic** drugs such as aspirin and ibuprofen (Motrin, Medipren, Advil, and so on) work by inhibiting prostaglandin production.

The pain message is relayed from the spinal cord to the thalamus and then projected to the cerebral cortex, where the location and intensity of the damage become apparent.

Phantom Limb Pain. One of the more fascinating phenomena of psychology is found in the fact that many people experience pain in limbs that are no longer there. About two out of three combat veterans with amputated limbs report pain in missing, or "phantom," limbs (Kimble, 1992). In such cases, the pain occurs in the absence of (present) tissue damage, but the pain itself is real enough. It sometimes involves activation of nerves in the stump of the missing limb, but local anesthesia does not always eliminate the pain. Therefore, the pain must also reflect activation of the neural circuits that store memories connected with the missing limb (Melzack, 1990).

Truth or Fiction Revisited. *It is true that many amputees experience pain in limbs that have been removed.* The pain apparently reflects activation of the neural circuits that store memories connected with the limbs.

Gate Theory. Simple remedies like rubbing and scratching the injured toe frequently help relieve pain. Why? One possible answer lies in the gate theory of pain originated by Melzack (1980). From this perspective, only a limited amount of stimulation can be processed by the nervous system at a time. Rubbing or scratching the toe transmits sensations to the brain that, in

Analgesic • Giving rise to a state of not feeling pain though fully conscious.

Placebo • A bogus treatment that controls for the effect of expectations.

Kinesthesis • The sense that informs us about the positions and motion of parts of our bodies.

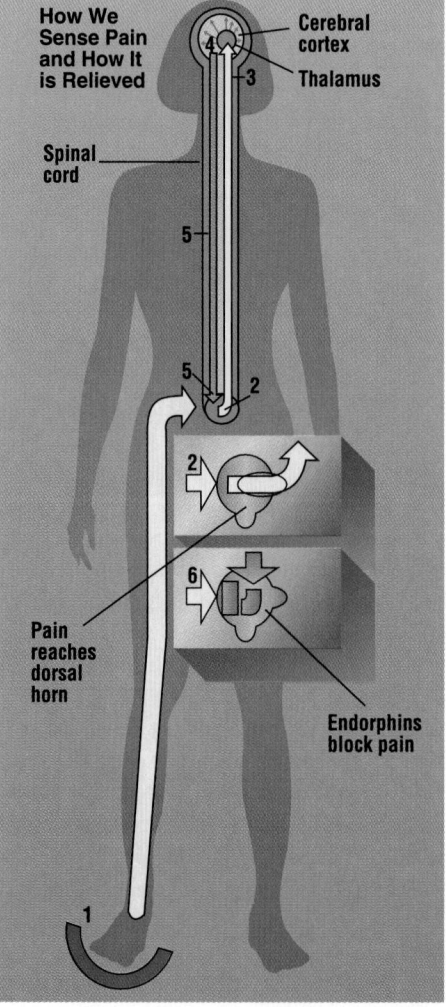

How We Sense Pain and How It is Relieved

Cerebral cortex

4 — 3 Thalamus

Spinal cord

5

5 — 2

2

6

Pain reaches dorsal horn

Endorphins block pain

1

FIGURE 4.40
Perception of Pain Pain originates at the point of contact, and the pain message to the brain is initiated by the release of prostaglandins, bradykinin, and substance *P*.

a sense, compete for neurons. Many nerves are thus prevented from transmitting pain messages to the brain. The mechanism is analogous to shutting down a "gate" in the spinal cord. It is as if too many calls are flooding a switchboard. The flooding prevents any calls from getting through.

Truth or Fiction Revisited. *It is true that rubbing or scratching a sore toe is often an effective way of relieving pain.* Rubbing or scratching may flood the nervous system with messages so that news of the pain does not get through to the brain.

Acupuncture. Thousands of years ago, the Chinese began mapping the body to learn where pins might be placed to deaden pain elsewhere. Much of the Chinese practice of acupuncture was unknown in the West, even though Western powers occupied much of China during the 1800s. But in the 1970s, *New York Times* columnist James Reston underwent an appendectomy in China, with acupuncture as his main anesthetic. He reported no discomfort. More recently, TV journalist Bill Moyers (1993) reported on current usage of acupuncture in China. For example, one woman underwent brain surgery to remove a tumor after receiving anesthesia that consisted of a mild sedative, a small dose of narcotics, and six needles placed in her forehead, calves, and ankles. The surgery itself and the use of a guiding CAT scan were consistent with contemporary U.S. practices.

Some of the effects of acupuncture may be due to the release of endorphins (Richardson & Vincent, 1986). There is supportive evidence. The drug *naloxone* is known to block the painkilling effects of morphine. The analgesic effects of acupuncture are also blocked by naloxone (Kimble, 1992). Therefore, it may well be that the analgesic effects of acupuncture can be linked to the morphinelike endorphins.

The Placebo Effect. Interestingly, some scientists have also attributed the so-called **placebo** effect—that is, the way in which expectation of relief sometimes leads to relief from pain and other problems—to release of endorphins.

The "Psychology and Modern Life" section in this chapter describes a number of ways in which psychologists help people manage pain.

Kinesthesis

Try a brief experiment. Close your eyes. Then touch your nose with your index finger. If you weren't right on target, I'm sure you came close. But how? You didn't see your hand moving, and you (probably) didn't hear your arm swishing through the air.

You were able to bring your finger to your nose through your kinesthetic sense. **Kinesthesis** derives from the Greek words for "motion" *(kinesis)* and "perception" *(aisthesis)*. When you "make a muscle" in your arm, the sensations of tightness and hardness are also provided by kinesthesis. Kinesthesis is the sense that informs you about the position and motion of parts of your body. In kinesthesis, sensory information is fed back to the brain from sensory organs in the joints, tendons, and muscles.

Imagine going for a walk without kinesthesis. You would have to watch the forward motion of each leg to be certain that you had raised it high enough to clear the curb. And if you had tried our brief experiment without the kinesthetic sense, you

Kinesthesis. This young acrobat at a Chinese academy receives information about the position and movement of the parts of his body through the sense of kinesthesis. Kinesthesis feeds sensory information to his brain from sensory organs in the joints, tendons, and muscles. He can follow his own movements intimately without visual self-observation.

would have had no sensory feedback until you felt the pressure of your finger against your nose (or cheek, or eye, or forehead), and you probably would have missed dozens of times.

Are you in the mood for another experiment? Close your eyes, again. Then "make a muscle" in your right arm. Could you sense the muscle without looking at it or feeling it with your left hand? Of course you could. Kinesthesis also provides information about muscle contractions.

The Vestibular Sense: On Being Upright

Your **vestibular sense** tells you whether you are upright—physically, not morally. Sensory organs located in the **semicircular canals** (Figure 4.35) and elsewhere in the ears monitor your body's motion and position in relation to gravity. They tell you whether you are falling and provide cues to whether your body is changing speeds such as when you are in an accelerating airplane or automobile.

Vestibular sense • The sense of equilibrium that informs us about our bodies' positions relative to gravity.

Semicircular canals • Structures of the inner ear that monitor body movement and position.

Truth or Fiction Revisited. *It is true that we have a sense that keeps us upright.* The sense—the vestibular sense—keeps us physically upright. It apparently takes more than the vestibular sense to keep us morally upright.

Reflections

Now that you have read the sections on smell, taste, the skin senses, and so forth, reflect on the following questions:

- Has food ever lost its flavor when you had a cold or an allergy attack? How do you account for the experience?
- Did a sour dish ever "get you" at the sides of the tongue? Why would it affect this area of the tongue?
- Why do older people often spice their food heavily?
- How can a drink that is 70 degrees Fahrenheit be either warming or cooling, depending on the weather?
- Has rubbing or scratching a painful area ever reduced the pain? How do you explain the experience?
- Can you touch your finger to your nose when your eyes are closed? How do you know where your finger is as you move it?

Summary

1. **What are sensation and perception?** Sensation refers to mechanical processes that involve the stimulation of sensory receptors (neurons) and the transmission of sensory information to the central nervous system. Perception is not mechanical. Perception is the active organization of sensations into a representation of the world, and it reflects learning and expectations.

2. **What are absolute and difference thresholds?** The absolute threshold for a stimulus, such as light, is the lowest intensity at which it can be detected. The minimum difference in intensity that can be discriminated is the difference threshold. Difference thresholds are expressed in Weber's constants.

3. **What is signal-detection theory?** Signal-detection theory explains the ways in which stimulus characteristics and psychological factors—for example, motivation, familiarity with a stimulus, and attention—interact to affect whether a stimulus will be detected.

4. **What is light?** Light is one part of the spectrum of electromagnetic energy.

5. **How does the eye detect light and transmit it to the brain?** The eye senses and transmits visual stimulation to the occipital lobe of the cerebral cortex. After passing through the cornea, pupil size determines the amount of light that can pass through the lens. The lens focuses light as it projects onto the retina, which is composed of photoreceptors called *rods* and *cones*. Neurons in the visual cortex of the brain (feature detectors) fire in response to specific features of visual information such as lines presented at particular angles and colors.

6. **What are rods and cones?** Cones are neurons in the retina that permit perception of color. Rods transmit

sensations of light and dark only. Rods are more sensitive than cones to lowered lighting and continue to adapt to darkness once cones have reached peak adaptation.

7. **What are the psychological dimensions of color?** These are hue, brightness, and saturation. The wavelength of light determines its color, or hue. The saturation of a color is its pureness.

8. **What are the theories of color vision?** There are two theories of color vision. According to trichromatic theory, there are three types of cones—some sensitive to red, others to blue, and still others to green light. Opponent-process theory proposes three types of color receptors: red–green, blue–yellow, and light–dark. Both theories appear to have some validity.

9. **What is perceptual organization?** Perceptual organization involves processing information about part–whole relationships and recognizing patterns. Gestalt rules of perceptual organization involve figure–ground relationships, proximity, similarity, continuity, common fate, and closure.

10. **How do we perceive movement?** We perceive movement when the light reflected by moving objects moves across the retina and also when objects shift in relation to one another. Distant objects appear to move more slowly than nearby objects, and middle-ground objects may give the illusion of moving backward.

11. **How do we perceive depth?** Depth perception involves monocular and binocular cues. Monocular cues include perspective, clearness, interposition, shadows, texture gradient, motion parallax, and accommodation. Binocular cues include retinal disparity and convergence.

12. **What are the perceptual constancies?** Through experience, we develop a number of perceptual constancies. For example, we learn to assume that objects retain their size, shape, brightness, and color despite their distance, their position, or changes in lighting.

13. **What is sound?** Sound is auditory stimulation, or sound waves. It requires a medium such as air or water to be transmitted. Sound waves alternately compress and expand molecules of the medium, creating vibrations.

14. **What is the range of sounds that can be sensed by the human ear?** The human ear can hear sounds varying in frequency from 20 to 20,000 cycles per second. The greater the frequency, the higher the sound's pitch.

15. **What is the loudness of a sound?** The loudness of a sound corresponds to the amplitude of sound waves as measured in decibels (dB). We can experience hearing loss if exposed to protracted sounds of 85–90 dB or more. Noise is a combination of dissonant sounds.

16. **How do we hear sound?** The eardrum, vibrating in sympathy to sound, transmits auditory stimulation through the bones of the middle ear to the cochlea of the inner ear. The basilar membrane of the cochlea transmits stimulation to the organ of Corti; from there, sound travels to the brain via the auditory nerve. Sounds seem louder when more neurons of the organ of Corti fire. Two competing theories account for the perception of pitch: place theory and frequency theory.

17. **How do we detect odors?** We detect odors through the olfactory membrane in each nostril. An odor is a sample of the substance being smelled.

18. **How do we detect tastes?** There are four primary taste qualities: sweet, sour, salty, and bitter. Flavor involves the odor, texture, and temperature of food, as well as its taste. Taste is sensed through taste cells, which are located in taste buds on the tongue.

19. **What are the skin senses?** Skin senses include touch, pressure, warmth, cold, and pain.

20. **What is kinesthesis?** Kinesthesis is the sensing of body position and movement, and it relies on sensory organs in the joints, tendons, and muscles. The vestibular sense is housed primarily in the semicircular canals of the ears and tells us whether we are upright.

Psychology and Modern Life

Pain Management: More Than a Medical Issue

In recent years, psychology has dramatically expanded our arsenal against an age-old enemy: pain. Pain management has traditionally been a medical issue, with the primary treatment being chemical, as in the use of analgesic drugs. In recent years, however, health professionals have become more interested in exploring psychological methods for managing pain (Flor and others, 1992). Let us review a number of them.

ACCURATE INFORMATION

One irony of pain management is that giving people accurate and thorough information about their conditions often helps them manage pain (Jacox and others, 1994). Most people try *not* to think about their symptoms (and their implications!) during the early phases of an illness (Moyers, 1993). Physicians, too, often neglect the "human" aspects of relating to their patients. That is, they try to do a competent job of diagnosing and treating the causes of pain, but often they fail to discuss with their patients the meaning of their pain or exactly what they can expect (McCrank, 1993).

Yet, when discomforting methods are used, such as cardiac catheterization or providing chemotherapy for cancer, knowledge of the details of the treatment, including how long it will last and how much pain will be entailed, can help people cope (Burish and others, 1991; Ludwick-Rosenthal & Neufeld, 1993). "If you explain things to people and take the time to tell them what to expect, they do a lot better than if you don't" (McCrank, 1993). Many people find that knowledge of medical procedures reduces stress by helping them to maintain control over their situations (Affleck and others, 1987; Martelli and others, 1987). Accurate information helps even children cope with painful procedures (Jay and others, 1983). Knowledge may permit us to brace ourselves and to realize that the pain will end—at least most of the time.

Some people, on the other hand, do not *want* information about painful procedures. Their attitude can be summed up as "Do what you have to do and get it over." Research suggests that it is most helpful to match the amount of information provided with the amount desired (Ludwick-Rosenthal & Neufeld, 1993).

DISTRACTION AND FANTASY: THE NINTENDO APPROACH TO PAIN MANAGEMENT?

Ignoring pain and diverting one's attention enhance the ability to cope with pain (Jensen & Karoly, 1991; Keefe and others, 1992). Though it is helpful for people to have accurate and detailed explanations of painful procedures, psychologists also study ways of minimizing discomfort once the procedures are under way. A number of methods involve the use of distraction or fantasy. For example, imagine that you've injured your leg and you're waiting to see the doctor in an emergency room. You can distract yourself from pain by focusing on environmental details such as by counting ceiling tiles or the hairs on the back of a finger or by describing the clothing of medical personnel or passers-by (McCaul & Haugvedt, 1982). People are also less sensitive to pain when they try to recall lists of meaningless words (Farthing and others, 1984; Spanos and others, 1984). Studies with children ranging in age from 9 into their teens have found that playing video games diminishes the pain and discomfort of the side effects of chemotherapy (Kolko & Rickard-Figueroa, 1985; Redd and others, 1987). While the children are receiving injections of nausea-producing chemicals, they are embroiled in battles on the video screen. Other distraction methods that help children in pain include combing one's hair and blowing on a noisemaker (Adler, 1990).

HYPNOSIS

In 1842 London physician W. S. Ward amputated a man's leg after using a rather strange anesthetic: hypnosis. According to reports, the individual experienced no discomfort. Several years later, operations were being performed routinely under hypnosis at the infirmary in London. Today hypnosis is often used to reduce chronic pain (Flor and others, 1992) and as an anesthetic in dentistry, childbirth, even some forms of surgery.

In using hypnosis to manage pain, the hypnotist usually instructs the person that he or she feels nothing or that the pain is distant and slight. Hypnosis can also augment the techniques of distraction and fantasy, as when the hypnotist instructs the person to imagine that he or she is lying on a warm, exotic shore.

RELAXATION TRAINING AND BIOFEEDBACK

When we are in pain, we often tense our muscles, which is uncomfortable in itself, heightens activity of the sympathetic nervous system, and centers our attention on our anguish and its source. Relaxation counters such self-defeating behavior patterns. Some psychological techniques that relax muscles and lower sympathetic activity focus on relaxing muscle groups. Some involve breathing exercises. Some focus on guided imagery, which distracts the person in pain as well as deepens feelings of relaxation. Still others use biofeedback to help clients relax targeted muscle groups. For example, relaxation training with biofeedback is at least as effective as most forms of medication for chronic pain in the lower back and jaw (Flor & Birbaumer, 1993).

COPING WITH IRRATIONAL BELIEFS

Irrational beliefs about pain have been shown to heighten pain. For example, telling oneself that the pain is unbearable and that it will never cease increases discomfort (Keefe and others, 1992). Some people feel obligated to focus their attention on things that distress them (Ellis, 1977). People who share this belief may be unwilling to allow themselves to be distracted from pain and discomfort. Thus, cognitive methods aimed at modifying irrational patient belief systems would also seem to be of promise (Jensen and others, 1994).

OTHER METHODS

Pain is a source of stress, and psychologists have uncovered many factors that seem to moderate the effects of stress (see Chapter 15). One is a sense of commitment. For example, if we are undergoing a painful medical procedure aimed at diagnosing or treating an illness, it might help for us to see ourselves as *choosing* to participate to get better instead of seeing ourselves as helpless victims. Thus, we see ourselves as being in control of the situation, and a sense of control also enhances our abilities to cope with pain (Affleck and others, 1987; Jensen & Karoly, 1991; Spinhoven and others, 1989).

A sense of humor also helps. There are often ironies and sillinesses in the most somber situations, and allowing ourselves to perceive them and even to laugh may be beneficial. Supportive social networks help as well. Having friends visit us—or our visiting ill friends—and encouraging a return to health is thus as consistent with psychological findings as with folklore (Rook & Dooley, 1985).

And don't forget gate theory. When there's pain in the toe, squeeze all your toes. When there's pain in the calf, rub the thighs. People around you may wonder, but you're entitled to experiment with "flooding the switchboard" so that some of the pain messages don't get through.

Driving to Distraction? Health psychologists have shown that children (and adults!) can be helped to cope with pain and discomfort through distraction. Child cancer patients, for example, have been helped to manage the discomfort of chemotherapy by playing video games during treatment.

Reflections

Now that you have read the section on pain management, reflect on the following questions:

- If you were to have to undergo a painful medical procedure, would you want to know all the details of what was going to happen to you, or would you just want to know when it's over? How does your choice help you cope with the pain and discomfort?
- Agree or disagree with the following statement and support your answer: "The best way to cope with pain is to ignore it."
- Have you ever been able to cope with pain or discomfort by thinking about something else or getting involved in doing something? How did your behavior help you?
- Has reading this section given you any information that you can apply to your own life?

5

States of Consciousness

Truth or Fiction?

_____ We act out our forbidden fantasies in our dreams.

_____ Many people have insomnia because they try too hard to get to sleep at night.

_____ It is dangerous to awaken a sleepwalker.

_____ Alcohol "goes to women's heads" more quickly than to men's.

_____ Heroin was once used as a cure for addiction to morphine.

_____ Coca-Cola once "added life" through a powerful but now illegal stimulant.

_____ The number of people who die from smoking-related causes is greater than the number lost to motor-vehicle accidents, abuse of alcohol and all other drugs, suicide, homicide, and AIDS combined.

_____ People have managed to bring high blood pressure under control through meditation.

_____ You can learn to increase or decrease your heart rate just by thinking about it.

_____ People who are easily hypnotized have positive attitudes toward hypnosis.

Outline

Truth or Fiction?
**A Minor Question: What *Is*
 Consciousness?**
Sleep and Dreams
 The Stages of Sleep
 Functions of Sleep
 Dreams: "Such Stuff as Dreams Are Made
  On"
 Sleep Disorders
Altering Consciousness through Drugs
 Substance Abuse and Dependence
 Causal Factors in Substance Abuse and
  Dependence
Depressants
 Alcohol
  *Psychology in a World of Diversity:
   On Alcoholism, Gender, Social
   Class, and Ethnicity*
 Opioids
 Barbiturates and Methaqualone
Stimulants
 Amphetamines
 Cocaine
 Cigarettes (Nicotine)
Hallucinogenics
 Marijuana
 LSD
  *Psychology in the New Millennium:
   Use and Abuse of Drugs: More
   Research Needed*
 Other Hallucinogenics
**Altering Consciousness through
 Meditation: When Eastern Gods
 Meet Western Technology**
**Altering Consciousness through
 Biofeedback: Getting in Touch
 with the Untouchable**
**Altering Consciousness through
 Hypnosis: On Being Entranced**
 Hypnotic Induction
 Changes in Consciousness Brought About
  by Hypnosis
 Theories of Hypnosis
Summary
Psychology and Modern Life
 Coping with Insomnia: How *(and How
  Not)* to Get to Sleep at Night
 Quitting and Cutting Down on Smoking

In 1904, William James wrote an intriguing article entitled "Does Consciousness Exist?" James did not think that consciousness was a proper area of study for psychologists, because no scientific method could be devised to directly observe or measure another person's consciousness.

John Watson, the "father of modern behaviorism," also insisted that only observable, measurable behavior was the proper province of psychology. In "Psychology as the Behaviorist Views It," published in 1913, Watson declared, "The time seems to have come when psychology must discard all references to consciousness" (p. 163). The following year, Watson was elected president of the American Psychological Association, which further cemented these ideas in the minds of many psychologists.

The titles of some recent articles—"The Problem of Consciousness" (Crick & Koch, 1992) and "Trouble in Mind" (Miller, 1992)—suggest that problems discussing consciousness remain into the 1990s. Researchers, that is, have not solved all problems in defining consciousness and in measuring consciousness. Nevertheless, we devote this chapter to the exploration of the meanings and varieties of this "most profound and puzzling facet of the mind" (Crick & Koch, 1992). Many psychologists, especially cognitive psychologists, believe that we cannot capture the richness of the human experience without referring to consciousness.

A Minor Question: What *Is* Consciousness?

Consciousness is one of those mental concepts that cannot be directly seen or touched, yet it is real enough to most people. Moreover, mental concepts such as consciousness acquire scientific status from being tied to behavior (Kimble, 1994). The concept of consciousness has several meanings. Consider a few of them.

Consciousness as Sensory Awareness. One meaning of consciousness is **sensory awareness** of the environment. The sense of vision permits us to be *conscious* of, or to see, the sun gleaming in the snow on the rooftops (Crick & Koch, 1992; Zeki, 1992). The sense of hearing allows us to be conscious of, or to hear, a concert.

Consciousness as the Selective Aspect of Attention. We are not always aware of sensory stimulation, however. We can be unaware, or unconscious of, sensory stimulation when we do not pay attention to it (Greenwald, 1992). The world is abuzz with signals, yet you are conscious of, or focusing on, the words on this page (I hope).

The focusing of one's consciousness on a particular stimulus is referred to as **selective attention.** The concept of selective attention is important to psychology and, indeed, to self-regulation. To pay attention in class, you must screen out the pleasant aroma of the cologne or perfume from the person in the next seat. To keep your car on the road, you must pay more attention to driving conditions than to your hunger pangs or your feelings about an argument with your family. If you are out in the woods at night, attending to rustling in the brush may be crucial to your very survival.

Part of our adaptation to our environments involves learning which stimuli must be attended to and which can be safely ignored. Selective attention markedly enhances our perceptual abilities (Johnston & Dark,

1986; Moran & Desimone, 1985), to the point where we can pick out the speech of a single person across a room at a cocktail party. (This phenomenon has been suitably termed the *cocktail party effect*.)

Although we to a large extent determine where and when we shall focus our attention, various kinds of stimuli also tend to capture attention. Such stimuli include:

- Sudden changes, as when a cool breeze enters a sweltering room, or we receive a particularly high or low grade on a returned exam
- Novel stimuli, as when a dog enters the classroom, or a person has an unusual hairdo
- Intense stimuli, such as bright colors, loud noises, or sharp pain
- Repetitive stimuli, as when the same TV commercial is played a dozen times throughout the course of a football game

Consciousness as Direct Inner Awareness. Close your eyes. Imagine spilling a can of bright red paint across a black tabletop. Watch it spread across the black, shiny surface, then spill onto the floor. Although this image may be vivid, you did not "see" it literally. Neither your eyes nor any other sensory organs were involved. You were *conscious* of the image through **direct inner awareness.**

We are conscious of—or have direct inner awareness of—thoughts, images, emotions, and memories. Although we may not be able to measure direct inner awareness scientifically, Miller argues that "It is detectable to anyone that has it" (1992, p. 180). These psychological processes are based on the firings of myriads of neurons—events that we do *not* experience consciously (Crick & Koch, 1992; Fischbach, 1992). Yet we are somehow conscious of, or know of, the cognitive parallels of these neural events.

Sigmund Freud, the founder of psychoanalysis, differentiated between thoughts and feelings of which we are conscious, or aware, and those that are preconscious and unconscious (see Figure 5.1). **Preconscious** material is not currently in awareness but is readily available. As you answer the following questions, you will summon up "preconscious" information: What did

you eat for dinner yesterday? About what time did you wake up this morning? What's happening outside the window or down the hall right now? What's your phone number? You can make these preconscious bits of information conscious simply by directing your inner awareness, or attention, to them.

According to Freud, still other mental events are **unconscious,** or unavailable to awareness under most circumstances. Freud believed that certain memories are painful, and certain impulses (primarily sexual and aggressive impulses) are unacceptable. Therefore, people place them out of awareness, or **repress** them, to escape feelings of anxiety, guilt, and shame.

Still, people do sometimes choose to stop thinking about distracting or unacceptable ideas. This conscious method of putting unwanted mental events out of awareness is termed **suppression.** We may suppress thoughts of a date when we need to study for a test. We may also try to suppress thoughts of an unpleasant test when we are on a date, so that the evening will not be ruined.

Some bodily processes such as the firings of individual neurons are **nonconscious.** They cannot be experienced through sensory awareness or direct inner awareness. The growing of hair and the carrying of oxygen in the blood are nonconscious. We can see that our hair has grown, but we have no sense receptors that provide sensations related to the process. We can feel the need to breathe but do not directly experience the exchange of carbon dioxide and oxygen.

Consciousness as Personal Unity: The Sense of Self. As we develop, we differentiate us from that which is not us. We develop a sense of being persons, individuals. There is a totality to our impressions, thoughts, and feelings that makes up our conscious existence—our continuing sense of **self** in a changing world. In this usage of the word, consciousness *is* self.

Consciousness as the Waking State. The word *conscious* also refers to the waking state as opposed, for example, to sleep. From this perspective, sleep, meditation, the hypnotic "trance," and the distorted perceptions

MINILECTURE: ATTENTION

Sensory awareness • Knowledge of the environment through perception of sensory stimulation—one definition of consciousness.

Selective attention • The focus of one's consciousness on a particular stimulus.

Direct inner awareness • Knowledge of one's own thoughts, feelings, and memories without use of sensory organs—another definition of consciousness.

Preconscious • In psychodynamic theory, descriptive of material that is not in awareness but can be brought into awareness by focusing one's attention. (The Latin root *prae-* means "before.")

Unconscious • In psychodynamic theory, descriptive of ideas and feelings that are not available to awareness.

Repress • In psychodynamic theory, to eject anxiety-provoking ideas, impulses, or images from awareness, without knowing that one is doing so.

Suppression • The deliberate, or conscious, placing of certain ideas, impulses, or images out of awareness.

Nonconscious • Descriptive of bodily processes such as the growing of hair, of which we cannot become conscious. We may "recognize" that our hair is growing but cannot directly experience the biological process.

Self • The totality of impressions, thoughts, and feelings. The sense of self is another definition of consciousness.

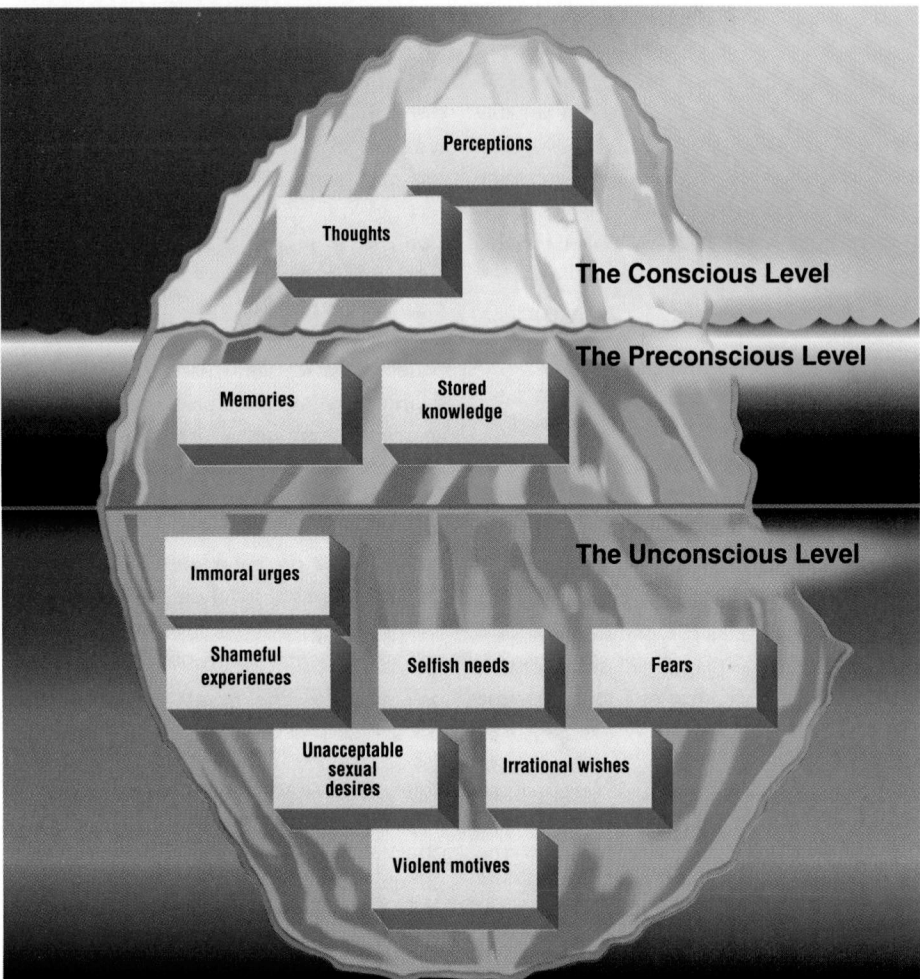

FIGURE 5.1

Spotlight on Levels of Consciousness, According to Sigmund Freud
According to Freud, many memories, impulses, and feelings exist below the level of conscious awareness. We could note that any film that draws an audience seems to derive its plot from items that populate the unconscious.

Altered states of consciousness • States other than the normal waking state, including sleep, meditation, the hypnotic trance, and the distorted perceptions produced by use of some drugs.

Circadian rhythm • (sir-KADE-ee-an). Referring to cycles that are connected with the 24-hour period of the earth's rotation. (A scientific term coined from the Latin roots *circa*, meaning "about," and *diem*, meaning "day.")

Electroencephalograph • An instrument that measures electrical activity of the brain. Abbreviated *EEG*.

that can accompany use of consciousness-altering drugs are considered **altered states of consciousness.**

For the remainder of this chapter, we explore these other states of consciousness and the agents that bring them about. They include sleep and dreams, the effects of drugs, meditation, biofeedback, and hypnosis.

Reflections

Now that you have read the section on the meanings of consciousness, reflect on the following questions:

• In what ways have you used the word *consciousness*? How does your usage of the word correspond to the usages described in the chapter?

• Can a person understand or study the consciousness of another person? Why or why not?

Sleep and Dreams

Sleep has always been a fascinating topic. After all, we spend about one third of our adult lives asleep. Most of us complain when we do not sleep at least 6 hours or so. Some people sleep for an hour or two a night, however, and apparently lead otherwise normal lives (Kimble, 1992).

Our alternating periods of wakefulness and sleep provide an example of an internally generated **circadian rhythm.** People normally associate their periods of wakefulness and sleep with the rotation of the earth, so that a full cycle is 24 hours. However, when people are removed from cues that signal day or night, a cycle tends to become extended to about 25 hours (Kimble, 1992). Why? We do not know.

Why do we sleep? Why do we dream? Why do some of us have trouble getting to sleep, and what can we do about it? Although we don't have all the answers to these questions, psychologists have learned much in the past couple of decades. In this section, we explore the stages and functions

of sleep, dreams, and sleep disorders, including insomnia and sleep terrors.

THE STAGES OF SLEEP

The **electroencephalograph,** or EEG, is one of the major tools of sleep researchers. The EEG measures the electrical activity of the brain, or brain waves. Figure 5.2 shows some scrawls produced by the EEG that reflect the frequency and strength of brain waves that occur during the waking state, when we are relaxed, and when we are in the various stages of sleep.

Brain waves, like other waves, are cyclical. During the various stages of sleep, our brains emit waves of different frequencies and amplitudes. The printouts in Figure 5.2 show what happens during a period of 15 seconds or so. Brain waves high in frequency are associated with wakefulness

FIGURE 5.2

The Stages of Sleep This figure illustrates typical EEG patterns for the stages of sleep. During REM sleep, EEG patterns resemble those of the lightest stage of sleep, stage 1 sleep. For this reason, REM sleep is often termed *paradoxical sleep.* As sleep progresses from stage 1 to stage 4, brain waves become slower and their amplitude increases. Dreams, including normal nightmares, are most vivid during REM sleep. More disturbing sleep terrors tend to occur during deep stage 4 sleep.

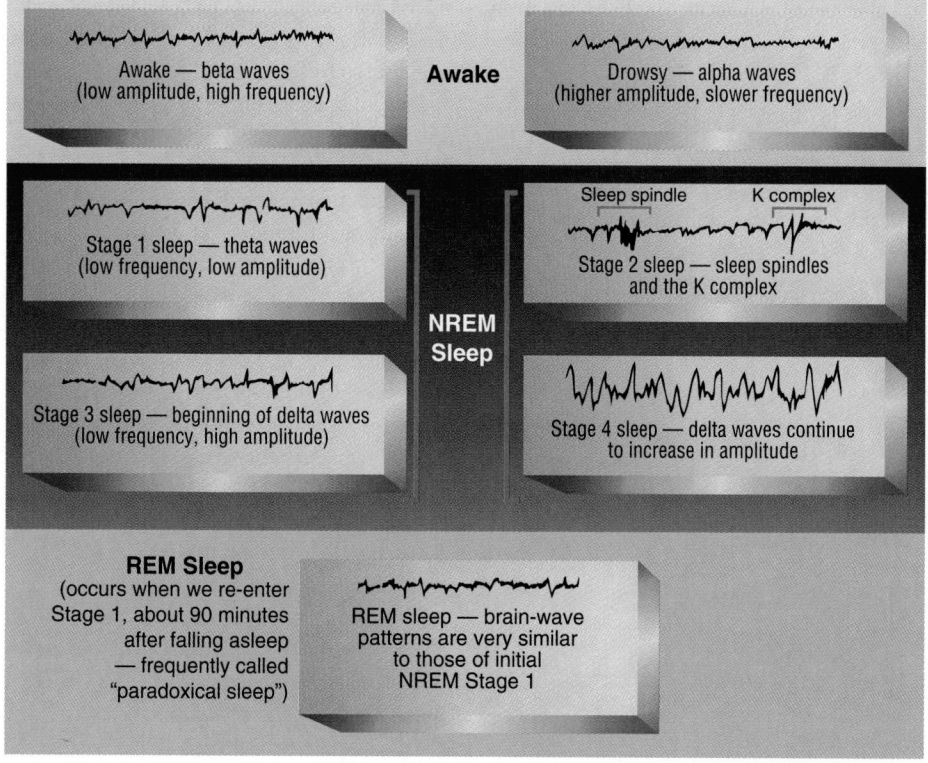

MINILECTURE:
STAGES OF
SLEEP

The amplitude of brain waves reflects their strength. The strength or energy of brain waves is expressed in the electric unit **volts.**

Figure 5.2 shows five stages of sleep: four stages of **non-rapid-eye-movement** (NREM) sleep, and one stage of **rapid-eye-movement** (REM) sleep. When we close our eyes and begin to relax before going to sleep, our brains emit many **alpha waves.** Alpha waves are low-amplitude brain waves of about 8 to 13 cycles per second.

As we enter stage 1 sleep, our brain waves slow down from the alpha rhythm and enter a pattern of **theta waves.** Theta waves, which have a frequency of about 6 to 8 cycles per second, are accompanied by slow, rolling eye movements. The transition from alpha waves to theta waves may be accompanied by a **hypnagogic state,** during which we may experience brief hallucinatory, dreamlike images that resemble vivid photographs. These images may be related to creativity. Stage 1 sleep is the lightest stage of sleep. If we are awakened from stage 1 sleep, we may feel that we have not slept at all.

After 30 to 40 minutes of stage 1 sleep, we undergo a rather steep descent into sleep stages 2, 3, and 4 (see Figure 5.3). During stage 2, brain waves are medium in amplitude and have a frequency of about 4 to 7

cycles per second, but these are punctuated by **sleep spindles.** Sleep spindles have a frequency of 12 to 16 cycles per second and represent brief bursts of rapid brain activity. During stage 2, we also experience instances of the so-called **K complex.** This complex occurs in response to external stimuli such as the sound of a book dropped in the room, or internal stimuli such as muscle tightness in the leg.

During deep-sleep stages 3 and 4, our brains produce slower **delta waves.** During stage 3, the delta waves are of about 1 to 3 cycles per second. Delta waves reach relatively great amplitude as compared with other brain waves. Stage 4 is the deepest stage of sleep, from which it is most difficult to be awakened. During stage 4 sleep, the delta waves slow to about 0.5 to 2 cycles per second, and their amplitude is greatest.

After perhaps half an hour of deep stage 4 sleep, we begin a relatively rapid journey back upward through the stages until we enter REM sleep (Figure 5.3). REM sleep derives its name from the *rapid eye movements,* observable beneath our closed lids, that characterize this stage. During REM sleep, we produce relatively rapid, low-amplitude brain waves that resemble those of light stage 1 sleep. REM sleep is also called *paradoxical sleep.* This is because the EEG patterns observed during REM sleep suggest a level of arousal similar to that of the waking state (Figure 5.2). However, we are difficult to awaken during REM sleep. When we are awakened during REM sleep, as is the practice in sleep research, about 80% of the time we report that we have been dreaming. (We also dream during NREM sleep, but less frequently. We report dreaming only about 20% of the time when awakened during NREM sleep.)

We tend to undergo five trips through the stages of sleep each night (see Figure 5.3). These trips include about five periods of REM sleep. Our first journey through stage 4 sleep is usually longest. Sleep tends to become lighter as the night wears on. Our periods of REM sleep tend to become longer, and, toward morning, our last period of REM sleep may last close to half an hour.

Now that we have some idea of what sleep is like, let us examine the issue of *why* we sleep.

FIGURE 5.3
Sleep Cycles This figure illustrates the alternation of REM and non-REM sleep for the typical sleeper. There are about five periods of REM sleep during an 8-hour night. Sleep is deeper earlier in the night, and REM sleep tends to become prolonged toward morning.

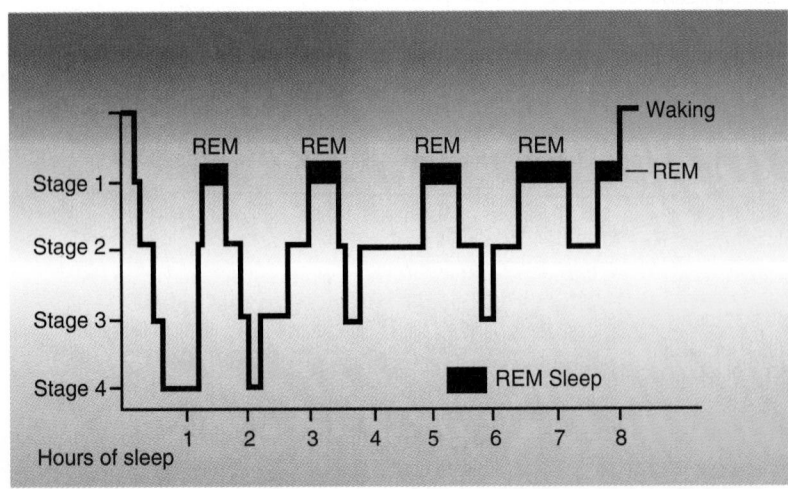

FUNCTIONS OF SLEEP

Strangely enough, researchers are not at all certain as to why we sleep (Kimble, 1992). One hypothesis is that sleep helps rejuvenate a tired body. Most of us have had the experience of going without sleep for a night and feeling "wrecked" or "punch drunk" the following day. Perhaps the next evening we went to bed early to "catch up on our sleep."

Sleep Deprivation. What will happen to you if you miss sleep for one night? For several nights?

Adler (1993b) compares people who are highly sleep-deprived with people who have been drinking heavily. Their abilities to concentrate and perform normal tasks may be seriously impaired, but they may be the last ones to recognize their limitations. Research shows that sleep deprivation mainly affects attention (Adler, 1993b). There are related psychological problems, however, including impaired memory formation, which in part may reflect lessened motivation to focus on details.

Sleep researcher Wilse Webb (1993) notes that most students can pull successful "all-nighters." That is, they can cram for a test through the night and then perform reasonably well on the test the following day. His rationale is that students will generally be highly motivated to pay attention to the details of the test. When we are sleep-deprived for several nights, aspects of psychological functioning such as attention, learning, and memory deteriorate notably. Webb (1993) also notes that many people sleep late or nap on their days off. Perhaps they suffer from mild sleep deprivation during the week and catch up on the weekend.

The amount of sleep we need seems to be in part genetically determined, like our heights (Webb, 1993). People also tend to need more sleep during periods of change and stress such as a change of jobs, an increase in work load, or an episode of depression. Perhaps sleep helps us recover from the stresses of life.

Deprivation of REM Sleep. In some studies, animals or people have been deprived of REM sleep. Animals and people deprived of REM sleep learn more slowly and forget what they have learned more rapidly (Adler, 1993b; Winson, 1992). Rats deprived of REM sleep for 10 days begin to eat voraciously but die of starvation (Hobson, 1992). REM sleep would appear to be essential to brain metabolism and body temperature regulation (Hobson, 1992).

In people, REM sleep may foster brain development during prenatal and infant development (McCarley, 1992). REM sleep may also help to maintain neurons in adults by "exercising" them at night (McCarley, 1992). REM-sleep deprivation is accomplished in people by monitoring EEG records and eye movements and waking them during REM sleep. There is too much individual variation to conclude that people deprived of REM sleep learn more poorly than they otherwise would. It does seem, though, that such deprivation interferes with memory—that is, the retrieval of information that has been learned previously (Winson, 1992). In any event, people and lower animals deprived of REM sleep tend to show *REM-rebound.* They spend more time in REM sleep during subsequent sleep periods. They catch up.

It is during REM sleep that we tend to dream. Let us now turn our attention to dreams, a mystery about which philosophers, poets, and scientists have theorized for centuries.

DREAMS: "SUCH STUFF AS DREAMS ARE MADE ON"

Just what is the stuff[1] of **dreams?** What are they "made on"? Like vivid memories and daytime fantasies, dreams involve imagery in the absence of external stimulation. Some dreams are so realistic and well organized that we feel they must be real—that we simply cannot be dreaming this time. You may have had such a dream on the night before a test. The dream would have been that you had taken the test and now it is all over. (Ah, what disappointment then prevailed when you woke up to realize that such was not the case!) Other dreams are disorganized and unformed.

Volt • A unit of electrical potential.

Non-rapid-eye-movement sleep • Stages of sleep 1 through 4. Abbreviated *NREM* sleep.

Rapid-eye-movement sleep • A stage of sleep characterized by rapid eye movements, which have been linked to dreaming. Abbreviated *REM* sleep.

Alpha waves • Rapid, low-amplitude brain waves that have been linked to feelings of relaxation.

Theta waves • Slow brain waves produced during the hypnagogic state.

Hypnagogic state • The drowsy interval between waking and sleeping, characterized by brief, hallucinatory, dreamlike experiences.

Sleep spindles • Short bursts of rapid brain waves that occur during stage 2 sleep.

K complex • Bursts of brain activity that occur during stage 2 sleep and reflect external stimulation.

Delta waves • Strong, slow brain waves usually emitted during stage 4 sleep.

Dreams • A sequence of images or thoughts that occur during sleep. Dreams may be vague and loosely plotted or vivid and intricate.

---

[1] The phrase "such stuff as dreams are made on" comes from Shakespeare's *The Tempest.*

Dream Images? In *Winter Night in Vitebsk,* Marc Chagall seems to depict images born in dreams.

MINILECTURE:
WHY WE DREAM

Dreams are most vivid during REM sleep. Then they are most likely to have clear imagery and coherent plots, even if some of the content is fantastic. Plots are vaguer and images more fleeting during NREM sleep.

You may well have a dream every time you are in REM sleep. Therefore, if you sleep for 8 hours and undergo five sleep cycles, you may have five dreams. Upon waking, you may think that time seemed to expand

TABLE 5.1
Dream Symbols in Psychodynamic Theory

SYMBOLS FOR THE MALE GENITAL ORGANS

airplanes	fish	neckties	tools	weapons
bullets	hands	poles	trains	
feet	hoses	snakes	trees	
fire	knives	sticks	umbrellas	

SYMBOLS FOR THE FEMALE GENITAL ORGANS

bottles	caves	doors	ovens	ships
boxes	chests	hats	pockets	tunnels
cases	closets	jars	pots	

SYMBOLS FOR SEXUAL INTERCOURSE

climbing a ladder	entering a room
climbing a staircase	flying in an airplane
crossing a bridge	riding a horse
driving an automobile	riding a roller coaster
riding an elevator	walking into a tunnel or down a hall

SYMBOLS FOR THE BREASTS

apples	peaches

Freud theorized that the content of dreams symbolizes urges, wishes, and objects of fantasy that we would censor in the waking state.

or contract during your dreams so that during 10 or 15 minutes, your dream content ranged over days or weeks. But dreams tend to take place in "real time": 15 minutes of events fills about 15 minutes of dreaming. Your dream theater is quite flexible: You can dream in black and white and in full color.

Theories of the Content of Dreams.

You may recall dreams involving fantastic adventures, but most dreams are simple extensions of the activities and problems of the day (Reiser, 1992). If we are preoccupied with illness or death, sexual or aggressive urges, or moral dilemmas, we are likely to dream about them. The characters in our dreams are more likely to be friends and neighbors than spies, monsters, and princes.

THE FREUDIAN VIEW.

"A dream is a wish your heart makes."

SONG TITLE FROM THE DISNEY FILM
CINDERELLA

Sigmund Freud theorized that dreams reflect unconscious wishes and urges. He argued that through dreams, we can express impulses that we would censor during the day. Moreover, he said that the content of dreams is symbolic of unconscious fantasized objects such as genital organs (see Table 5.1). In Chapter 14, we shall see that a major part of Freud's method of psychoanalysis involved interpretation of his clients' dreams. Freud also believed that dreams "protect sleep" by providing imagery that would help keep disturbing, repressed thoughts out of awareness.

The view that dreams protect sleep has been challenged by the observation that disturbing events of the day tend to be followed by related disturbing dreams—not protective imagery (Reiser, 1992). Our behavior in dreams is also generally consistent with our waking behavior. Most dreams, then, are unlikely candidates for the expression (even disguised) of repressed urges. The person who leads a moral life tends to dream moral dreams.

Truth or Fiction Revisited. *It is not true that we act out our forbidden fantasies in our dreams.* Most dreams are humdrum.

THE ACTIVATION-SYNTHESIS MODEL.
According to the **activation-synthesis model** proposed by J. Allan Hobson and Robert W. McCarley (1977), dreams primarily reflect biological, not psychological, activity. According to this view, an abundance of acetylcholine in the brain and a time-triggered mechanism in the pons stimulate a number of responses that lead to dreaming. One is *activation* of the reticular activating system (RAS), which arouses us but not to the point of waking. During the waking state, firing of these cells in the reticular formation is linked to movement, particularly the semiautomatic movements found in walking, running, and other physical acts. During REM sleep, however, neurotransmitters generally inhibit motor (muscular) activity, so we don't thrash about as we dream (Steriade, 1992). In this way, we save ourselves (and our bed partners) some wear and tear. The eye muscles are also stimulated, and they show the rapid eye movement associated with dreaming. In addition, the RAS stimulates neural activity in the parts of the cortex involved in vision, hearing, and memory. The cortex then automatically *synthesizes,* or puts together, these sources of stimulation to yield the substances of dreams.

The activation-synthesis model explains why there is a strong tendency to dream about events of the day: The most current neural activity of the cortex would be that which represented the events or concerns of the day. Even so, Hobson (1992) suggests that "There are many theories but little data" about the functions of REM sleep and dreams, although "everybody loves to speculate."

Nightmares.

Have you ever dreamed that something heavy was on your chest and watching as you breathed? Or that you were trying to run from a terrible threat but couldn't gain your footing or coordinate your leg muscles?

In the Middle Ages, such nightmares were thought to be the work of demons called *incubi* and *succubi* (singular: **incubus** and **succubus**). By and large, they were seen as a form of retribution. That is, they were sent to make you pay for your sins.

Nightmares, like most pleasant dreams, are generally products of REM sleep. College students keeping dream logs report an average of two nightmares a month (Wood &

Activation-synthesis model • The view that dreams reflect activation of cognitive activity by the reticular activating system and synthesis of this activity into a pattern by the cerebral cortex.
Incubus • (1) A spirit or demon thought in medieval times to lie on sleeping people, especially on women for sexual purposes. (2) A nightmare.
Succubus • A female demon thought in medieval times to have sexual intercourse with sleeping men.

The Scream. Norwegian artist Edvard Munch's well-known work of art contains the kind of imagery that we might find in a nightmare.

Bootzin, 1990). Traumatic events can spawn nightmares, as reported in a study of survivors of the San Francisco earthquake of 1989 (Wood and others, 1992). People who suffer frequent nightmares are more likely than other people to also suffer from anxieties, depression, and other kinds of psychological discomfort (Berquier & Ashton, 1992).

SLEEP DISORDERS

There are a number of sleep disorders. Some, like insomnia, are all too familiar. Others, like narcolepsy, seem somewhat exotic. In this section, we shall discuss insomnia, narcolepsy, apnea, and the deep-sleep disorders—sleep terrors, bed-wetting, and sleepwalking.

Insomnia. **Insomnia** refers to three types of sleeping problems: difficulty falling asleep (sleep-onset insomnia), difficulty remaining asleep through the night, and early morning awakening (Lacks & Morin, 1992). About one third of American adults are affected by insomnia in any given year (Gillin, 1991). Women complain of the disorder more frequently than men.

As a group, people who experience insomnia show greater restlessness and muscle tension than those who do not (Lacks & Morin, 1992). Those with insomnia also have greater "cognitive arousal" than those without. They are more likely to worry and have "racing thoughts" at bedtime (White & Nicassio, 1990). Insomnia comes and goes with many people, increasing during periods of anxiety and tension (Gillin, 1991).

People with insomnia tend to compound their sleep problems through their efforts to force themselves to get to sleep (Bootzin and others, 1991). Their concern heightens autonomic activity and muscle tension. You cannot force or will yourself to get to sleep. You can only set the stage for it by lying down and relaxing when you are tired. If you focus on sleep too closely, it will elude you. Yet, millions go to bed each night dreading the possibility of sleep-onset insomnia.

Truth or Fiction Revisited. *It is true that many people have insomnia because they try too hard to get to sleep at night.* Trying to get to sleep heightens tension and anxiety, both of which counteract the feelings of relaxation that help induce sleep. In the section on "Psychology and Modern Life," we examine ways in which psychologists help people cope with insomnia.

Narcolepsy. **Narcolepsy** (not to be confused with epilepsy) is, in a sense, the mirror image of insomnia. The person with narcolepsy falls suddenly, irresistibly asleep. Narcolepsy afflicts as many as 100,000 people in the United States and seems to run in families. The "sleep attack" may last about 15 minutes, after which the person awakens feeling refreshed. Despite being refreshing, these sleep episodes are dangerous and frightening. They can occur while a person is driving or engaged in work with sharp tools. They also may be accompanied by sudden collapse of muscle groups or even of the entire body (see Figure 5.4)—a condition called *sleep paralysis*. In sleep paralysis, the person cannot move during the transition from the waking state to sleep, and hallucinations such as of a person or object sitting on the chest occur.

Although the causes are unknown, narcolepsy is thought to be a disorder of REM-sleep functioning. Stimulants and antidepressant drugs have helped many people with narcolepsy.

Apnea. **Apnea** is a potentially dangerous sleep disorder in which the air passages are obstructed, causing those who have it to stop breathing periodically through the night, as many as 200 to 400 times (Phillipson, 1993). When obstruction occurs, sleepers may suddenly sit up, gasp to begin breathing again, then fall back asleep. They are stimulated nearly but not quite to waking by the buildup of carbon dioxide. Apnea afflicts about 4% of men and 2% of women and is strongly associated with obesity, habitual loud snoring, and drowsiness during the day (Young and others, 1993).

Causes of apnea include anatomical deformities that clog the air passageways, such as a thick palate, and problems in the breathing centers of the brain. Apnea is treated by such measures as weight loss, surgery, and nasal CPAP—a system that applies "continuous positive air pressure" through the nose to keep the airway open during sleep (Hellams, 1993).

Deep-Sleep Disorders: Sleep Terrors, Bed-Wetting, and Sleepwalking. Sleep terrors, bed-wetting, and sleepwalking all occur during deep (stage 3 or 4) sleep, are more common among children, and may reflect immaturity of the nervous system.

Sleep terrors are similar to, but more severe than, nightmares. Sleep terrors usually occur during deep sleep, whereas nightmares take place during REM sleep. Sleep terrors occur during the first couple of sleep cycles; nightmares more often occur later on (Hartmann, 1981). Experiencing a surge in the heart and respiration rates, the dreamer may suddenly sit up, talk incoherently, and move about wildly. The dreamer is never fully awake, returns to sleep, and may recall a brief image such as of someone pressing on the chest. In contrast to the

Insomnia • A term for three types of sleeping problems: (1) difficulty falling asleep, (2) difficulty remaining asleep, and (3) waking early. (From the Latin *in-*, meaning "not," and *somnus*, meaning "sleep.")

Narcolepsy • A sleep disorder characterized by uncontrollable seizures of sleep during the waking state. (From the Greek *narke,* meaning "sleep," and *lepsia,* meaning "an attack.")

Apnea • A temporary cessation of breathing while asleep. (From the Greek *a-,* meaning "without," and *pnoie,* meaning "wind.")

Sleep terrors • Frightening dreamlike experiences that occur during the deepest stage of NREM sleep. Nightmares, in contrast, occur during REM sleep.

FIGURE 5.4
Narcolepsy In a narcolepsy experiment, the dog barks, nods, then suddenly falls asleep. The causes of narcolepsy are unknown, but it is thought to be a disorder of REM sleep functioning.

 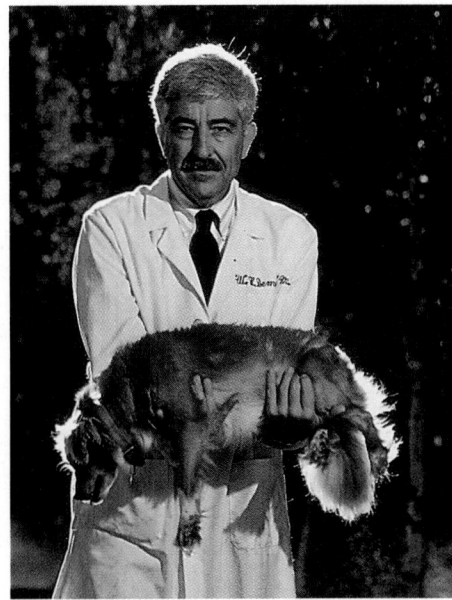

Tranquilizers • Drugs used to reduce anxiety and tension.

Psychoactive • Descriptive of drugs that have psychological effects such as stimulation or distortion of perceptions.

Depressant • A drug that lowers the rate of activity of the nervous system. (From the Latin *de-,* meaning "down," and *premere,* meaning "to press.")

Stimulant • A drug that increases activity of the nervous system.

Substance abuse • Persistent use of a substance even though it is causing or compounding problems in meeting the demands of life.

Tolerance • Habituation to a drug, with the result that increasingly higher doses of the drug are needed to achieve similar effects.

Abstinence syndrome • A characteristic cluster of symptoms that results from sudden decrease in an addictive drug's level of usage. (From the Latin *abstinere,* meaning "to hold back.")

Delirium tremens • A condition characterized by sweating, restlessness, disorientation, and hallucinations. The "DTs" occurs in some chronic alcohol users when there is a sudden decrease in usage.

Disorientation • Gross confusion. Loss of sense of time, place, and the identity of people.

Hallucinations • Perceptions in the absence of sensation. (From the Latin *hallucinari,* meaning "to wander mentally.")

nightmare, however, memories of the episode are not vivid. Sleep terrors are often decreased by a minor **tranquilizer** at bedtime, which reduces the amount of time spent in stage 4 sleep.

Bed-wetting is often seen as a stigma that reflects parental harshness or the child's attempt to punish the parents, but this disorder, too, may stem from immaturity of the nervous system. In most cases, bed-wetting resolves itself before adolescence, often by age 8. Behavior-therapy methods that condition children to awaken when about to urinate have been helpful. The drug imipramine often helps by increasing bladder capacity. Sometimes, all that is needed is reassurance that no one need be to blame for bed-wetting and that most children "outgrow" the disorder.

Perhaps half of all children occasionally talk in their sleep, and as many as 15% walk in their sleep (Mindell, 1993). Sleepwalkers may roam about almost nightly while their parents fret about the accidents that could befall them. Sleepwalkers typically do not remember their excursions, although they may respond to questions while they are up and about. Contrary to myth, there is no evidence that sleepwalkers become violent or grossly disturbed if they are awakened. Mild tranquilizers and maturity typically put an end to sleepwalking.

Truth or Fiction Revisited. *It is not true that it is dangerous to awaken a sleepwalker.* Sleepwalkers may be confused and startled when awakened, but they are not usually violent.

Reflections

Now that you have read the section on sleep and dreams, reflect on the following questions:

- How much sleep do you need? (How do you know?) How much sleep do you get? Did you ever "pull" an all-nighter? What were the effects?
- What do you tend to dream about? Is the stuff of your dreams consistent with any of the theories of dreams discussed in the chapter?

We have noted that drugs often play a role in the treatment of sleep disorders. But drugs are used recreationally or to "expand consciousness" as well as to treat problems. Let us now turn our attention to a number of such drugs.

Altering Consciousness through Drugs

The world is a supermarket of **psychoactive** substances, or drugs. The United States is flooded with drugs that distort perceptions and change mood—drugs that take you up, let you down, and move you across town. Some people use drugs because their friends do or because their parents tell them not to. Some are seeking pleasure; others are seeking inner truth.

Alcohol is the most popular drug on high school and college campuses (Johnston and others, 1993). Most college students have tried marijuana, and perhaps one in seven smokes it regularly. Many Americans take **depressants** to get to sleep at night and **stimulants** to get going in the morning. Karl Marx charged that "religion . . . is the opium of the people," but heroin is the real opium of the people. Cocaine was, until recently, the toy of the well-to-do, but price breaks have brought it into the lockers of high school students. Given laws, moral pronouncements, medical warnings, and an occasional horror story, drug use actually seems to have declined in recent years (Johnston and others, 1993). Table 5.2 shows a decade-long trend for college students, according to University of Michigan surveys. Overall, however, drugs remain a part of American life.

SUBSTANCE ABUSE AND DEPENDENCE

Where does drug use end and abuse begin? The borderline is not always clear. Even professionals can disagree on the definitions (Helzer & Schuckit, 1990). Yet many psychologists and other professionals define **substance abuse** as persistent use of a substance despite the fact that it is causing or compounding social, occupational, psychological, or physical problems. If you are

TABLE 5.2

Percentage of College Students Who Report Drug Use
"During the Last 30 Days," 1981–1992

DRUG	1981	1982	1983	1984	1985	1986	1987	1988	1989	1990	1991	1992
Alcohol	81.9	82.8	80.3	79.1	80.3	79.7	78.4	77.0	76.2	74.5	74.7	71.4
Cigarettes	25.9	24.4	24.7	21.5	22.4	22.4	24.0	22.6	21.1	21.5	23.2	23.5
Marijuana	33.2	26.8	26.2	23.0	23.6	22.3	20.3	16.8	16.3	14.0	14.1	14.6
Cocaine	7.3	7.9	6.5	7.6	6.9	7.0	4.6	4.2	2.8	1.2	1.0	1.0
(Crack)	NA*	NA	NA	NA	NA	NA	0.4	0.5	0.2	0.1	0.3	0.1
Stimulants	12.3	9.9	7.0	5.5	4.2	3.7	2.3	1.8	1.3	1.4	1.0	1.1
Sedatives	3.4	2.5	1.1	1.0	0.7	0.6	0.6	0.6	NA	NA	NA	NA
Barbiturates	NA	NA	NA	NA	NA	NA	NA	NA	0.2	0.2	0.2	0.7
Hallucinogens	2.3	2.6	1.8	1.8	1.3	2.2	2.0	1.7	2.3	1.4	1.2	2.3
Heroin	0.0	0.0	0.0	0.0	0.0	0.0	0.1	0.1	0.1	0.0	0.1	0.0

Source: Johnston and others (1993).
*NA = Not available.

missing school or work because you are drunk or "sleeping it off," you are abusing alcohol. The amount you drink is not as crucial as the fact that your pattern of use disrupts your life.

Dependence is more severe than abuse, although the borderline can be confusing here as well (Helzer & Schuckit, 1990; Schuckit, 1990). Dependence has behavioral and physiological aspects. Behaviorally, dependence is often characterized by loss of control over the substance, as in organizing one's life around getting it and using it. Physiologically, dependence is typified by tolerance, withdrawal symptoms, or both.[2] **Tolerance** is the body's habituation to a substance so that with regular usage, higher doses are required to achieve similar effects. There are characteristic withdrawal symptoms, or an **abstinence syndrome,** when the level of usage suddenly drops off. The abstinence syndrome for alcohol includes anxiety, tremors, restlessness, weakness, rapid pulse, and high blood pressure.

When doing without a drug, people who are *psychologically* dependent show signs of anxiety (shakiness, rapid pulse, and sweating are three) that overlap abstinence syndromes. Because of these signs, they may believe that they are physiologically dependent on a drug when they are psychologically dependent. Still, symptoms of abstinence from certain drugs are unmistak-

ably physiological. One is **delirium tremens** ("the DTs"), encountered by some chronic alcoholics when they suddenly lower intake. The DTs are characterized by heavy sweating, restlessness, general **disorientation,** and terrifying **hallucinations**—often of creepy, crawling animals.

CAUSAL FACTORS IN SUBSTANCE ABUSE AND DEPENDENCE

There are many reasons for substance abuse and dependence. A handful include curiosity, conformity to peer pressure, parental use, rebelliousness, and escape from boredom or pressure (Botvin and others, 1990; Johnson and others, 1990; Rhodes & Jason, 1990; Sher and others, 1991). Another reason is self-handicapping: By using alcohol or another drug when we are faced with a difficult task, we can blame failure on the alcohol, not ourselves. Similarly, alcohol and other drugs have been used as excuses for behaviors such as aggression, sexual forwardness, and forgetfulness.

Psychological and biological theories also account for substance abuse in the following ways.

Psychological Views. Psychodynamic explanations of substance abuse propose that drugs help people control or express

[2] The lay term *addiction* is usually used to connote physiological dependence, but here, too, there may be inconsistency. After all, some people speak of being "addicted" to work or to love.

unconscious needs and impulses. Alcoholism, for example, may reflect the need to remain dependent on an overprotective mother.

Social-cognitive theorists suggest that people commonly try tranquilizing agents such as Valium and alcohol on the basis of observing others or a recommendation. Cognitive psychologists note that expectancies about the effects of a substance are powerful predictors of its use (Darkes & Goldman, 1993; Schafer & Brown, 1991). Subsequent use may be reinforced by the drug's positive effects on mood and its reduction of unpleasant sensations such as anxiety, fear, and tension. For people who are physiologically dependent, avoidance of withdrawal symptoms is also reinforcing. Carrying the substance is reinforcing, because one need not worry about having to go without it. Some people, for example, will not leave the house without taking Valium along.

Parents who use drugs may increase their children's knowledge of drugs and, in effect, show them when to use them—for example, when they are seeking to reduce tension or to "lubricate" social interactions (Sher and others, 1991; Stacy and others, 1991).

Biological Views. There is some evidence that people may have a genetic predisposition toward physiological dependence on various substances, including alcohol (Goodwin, 1985; Schuckit, 1987) and nicotine (Pomerleau and others, 1993). For example, the biological children of alcoholics who are reared by adoptive parents seem more likely to develop alcohol-related problems than the natural children of the adoptive parents (Goodwin, 1985). An inherited tendency toward alcoholism may involve a combination of greater sensitivity to alcohol (enjoyment of it) and greater biological tolerance (Newlin & Thomson, 1990). For example, college-age children of alcoholics exhibit better muscular control and visual–motor coordination when they drink. They also feel less intoxicated when they drink (Pihl and others, 1990).

Let us now consider the effects of some frequently used depressants, stimulants, and hallucinogenics.

Sedative • A drug that soothes or quiets restlessness or agitation. (From the Latin *sedare,* meaning "to settle.")

Depressants

Depressant drugs generally act by slowing the activity of the central nervous system. There are also effects specific to each depressant drug. In this section we consider the effects of alcohol, opioids, barbiturates, and methaqualone.

ALCOHOL

No drug has meant so much to so many as alcohol. Alcohol is our dinnertime relaxant, our bedtime **sedative,** our cocktail-party social facilitator. We celebrate holy days, applaud our accomplishments, and express joyous wishes with alcohol. The young assert their maturity with alcohol. It is used at least occasionally by 85 to 88% of the high-school population (Johnston and others, 1993). The elderly use alcohol to stimulate circulation in peripheral areas of the body. Alcohol even kills germs on surface wounds.

Alcohol is the tranquilizer you can buy without prescription. It is the relief from anxiety you can swallow in public without criticism or stigma. A man who pops a Valium tablet may look weak. A man who chugalugs a bottle of beer may be perceived as "macho."

No drug has been so abused as alcohol. Ten million to 20 million Americans are alcoholics. In contrast, 500,000 use heroin regularly and 300,000 to 500,000 abuse sedatives. Excessive drinking has been linked to lower productivity, loss of employment, and downward movement in social status (Vaillant & Milofsky, 1982). Yet, half of all Americans use alcohol, and despite widespread marijuana use, it is the drug of choice among adolescents.

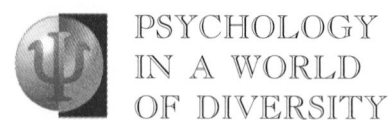 PSYCHOLOGY IN A WORLD OF DIVERSITY

ON ALCOHOLISM, GENDER, SOCIAL CLASS, AND ETHNICITY

Men are much more likely than women to become alcoholics. A cultural explanation is that tighter social constraints are usually placed on women. A biological explanation is that alcohol hits women harder. If, for example, you have the impression that alcohol "goes to women's heads" more quickly than to men's, you are probably correct. Women seem to be more affected by alcohol because they metabolize very little of it in the stomach. Thus, alcohol reaches women's bloodstreams and brains relatively intact. (Women have less of an enzyme that metabolizes alcohol in the stomach than men do [Lieber, 1990].) Women mainly metabolize alcohol in the liver. For women, reports one health professional, "drinking alcohol has the same effect as injecting it intravenously" (Lieber, 1990). Strong stuff, indeed.

Truth or Fiction Revisited. *It is true that alcohol goes to women's heads more quickly than to men's.* Women are less likely to metabolize alcohol before it affects psychological functioning. Despite their greater responsiveness to small quantities of alcohol, women who drink heavily are apparently as likely as men to become alcoholics.

Alcoholism is found at all socioeconomic levels. People low in socioeconomic status are apparently more vulnerable to the social problems connected with heavy drinking, such as incarceration and family instability. Yet, more-affluent people may be more likely to imbibe large quantities of alcohol and suffer the medical consequences of doing so, such as cirrhosis of the liver (Halldin, 1985). Rural versus urban residence is apparently not a factor in predicting alcoholism (Helzer, 1987).

Some ethnic factors are connected with alcohol abuse. Native Americans and Irish Americans have the highest rates of alcoholism in the United States (Lex, 1987; Moncher and others, 1990). Jewish Americans have relatively low rates of alcoholism, a fact for which a cultural explanation is usually offered. Jewish Americans tend to expose children to alcohol (wine) early in life, within a strong family or religious context. Wine is offered in small quantities, with consequent low blood alcohol levels. Alcohol is thus not connected with rebellion, aggression, or failure in Jewish culture.

There are also biological explanations for low levels of drinking among some ethnic groups such as Asian Americans. Asians are more likely than White people to show a "flushing response" to alcohol, as evidenced by rapid heart rate, dizziness, and headaches (Ellickson and others, 1992). Such sensitivity to alcohol may inhibit immoderate drinking among Asian Americans as it may among women.

Effects of Alcohol. Our response to a substance reflects the physiological effects of that substance and our interpretations of those effects. Our interpretations of the drug's effects are, in turn, influenced by our expectations.

What do people expect from alcohol? Adolescent and adult American samples tend to report the beliefs that alcohol reduces tension, diverts one from worrying, enhances pleasure, increases social ability, and transforms experiences for the better (Brown and others, 1985; Rohsenow, 1983). These are expectations. What *does* alcohol do?

The effects of alcohol vary with the dose and the duration of use. Low doses of alcohol may be stimulating. Higher doses of alcohol have a sedative effect (Niaura and others, 1988), which is why alcohol is classified as a depressant. Ironically, short-term use of alcohol may lessen feelings of depression, but regular use over a year or more may augment feelings of depression (Aneshensel & Huba, 1983). Alcohol relaxes and deadens minor aches and pains. Alcohol also intoxicates: It impairs cognitive functioning, slurs the speech, and reduces motor coordination. Alcohol is implicated in about half of U.S. automobile accidents.

Alcohol consumption is connected with a drop-off in sexual activity (Leigh, 1993). Yet some drinkers may do things they would not do if sober, such as engage in sexual activity that may lead to exposure to the AIDS virus (Cooper and others, 1994; Leigh & Stall, 1993). Why? Perhaps alcohol impairs the thought processes needed to inhibit impulses (Hull and others, 1983; Steele & Josephs, 1990). When intoxicated, people may be less able to foresee the consequences of their behavior. They may also be less likely to focus on their moral beliefs. Then, too, alcohol induces feelings of elation and **euphoria** that may wash away

Euphoria • Feelings of well-being, elation. (From the Greek *euphoros,* meaning "healthy.")

Cirrhosis of the liver • A disease caused by protein deficiency in which connective fibers replace active liver cells, impeding circulation of the blood. Alcohol does not contain protein; therefore, persons who drink excessively may be prone to this disease. (From the Greek *kirrhos,* meaning "tawny," referring to the yellow-orange color of the diseased liver.)

Wernicke–Korsakoff syndrome • A cluster of symptoms associated with chronic alcohol abuse and characterized by confusion, memory impairment, and filling in gaps in memory with false information (confabulation).

Opioids • A group of narcotics derived from the opium poppy, or similar in chemical structure, that provide a euphoric rush and depress the nervous system.

Narcotics • Drugs used to relieve pain and induce sleep. The term is usually reserved for opioids.

Analgesia • A state of not feeling pain although fully conscious.

Morphine • An opioid introduced at about the time of the U.S. Civil War.

Heroin • An opioid. Heroin, ironically, was used as a "cure" for morphine addiction when first introduced.

doubts. Moreover, alcohol is associated with a liberated social role in our culture. Drinkers may place the blame on the alcohol ("It's the alcohol, not me"), even though they choose to drink.

As a food, alcohol is fattening. Yet, chronic drinkers may be malnourished. Though high in calories, alcohol does not contain nutrients such as vitamins and proteins. Moreover, alcohol can interfere with the body's absorption of vitamins, particularly thiamine, a B vitamin. Thus, chronic drinking can lead to a number of disorders such as **cirrhosis of the liver,** which has been linked to protein deficiency, and **Wernicke–Korsakoff syndrome,** which has been linked to vitamin B deficiency.

When alcohol is metabolized, there are increases in levels of lactic and uric acids. Lactic acid has been correlated with anxiety attacks, although there is little reason to think that alcohol causes anxiety. Uric acid can cause gout. Although light to moderate drinking may increase levels of high-density lipoprotein (HDL, or "good" cholesterol; Gaziano and others, 1993), chronic drinking of high levels of alcohol has been linked

Shooting Up Heroin. Users of heroin claim that the drug is so pleasurable it can eradicate any thought of food or sex. Many users remain dependent on heroin because they are unwilling to undergo withdrawal symptoms or to contemplate a life devoid of drugs.

to cardiovascular disorders and cancer. Drinking by a pregnant woman may harm the embryo.

Drinking Your Troubles Away: Drinking as a Strategy for Coping with Stress and Failure. Adolescent involvement with alcohol has been linked repeatedly to poor school grades and other negative life events (Chassin and others, 1988; Mann and others, 1987; Wills, 1986). Drinking can, of course, contribute to poor grades and other problems, but people may drink to reduce academic and other stresses. Alcohol apparently disrupts people's ability to recognize and interpret stressful information (Sayette, 1993).

Regardless of how or why one starts drinking, regular drinking can lead to physiological dependence. Once one has become physiologically dependent on alcohol, one will be motivated to drink to avoid withdrawal symptoms. Still, even when alcoholics have "dried out"—withdrawn from alcohol—many return to drinking. Perhaps they still want to use alcohol as a way of coping with stress or as an excuse for failure.

The nearby questionnaire may offer some insight into your own reasons for drinking—if you do.

OPIOIDS

Opioids are a group of **narcotics.** Some opioids are derived from the opium poppy, from which they obtain their name. Others are similar in chemical structure but synthesized. The ancient Sumerians gave the opium poppy its name: It means "plant of joy." Opioids include morphine, heroin, codeine, Demerol, and similar drugs whose major medical application is **analgesia,** or pain relief (Rosenthal, 1993a).

Morphine was introduced at about the time of the Civil War in the United States and the Franco-Prussian War in Europe. It was used liberally to deaden pain from wounds. Physiological dependence on morphine became known as the "soldier's disease." There was little stigma attached to dependence until morphine became a restricted substance.

Heroin was so named because it made people feel "heroic" and was hailed as the

---

Questionnaire

WHY DO YOU DRINK?

Do you drink? If so, why? To enhance your pleasure? To cope with your problems? To help you in your social encounters? Half of all Americans use alcohol for a variety of reasons. Perhaps as many as 1 user in 10 is an alcoholic. College students who expect that alcohol will help them reduce tension are more likely than other students to encounter alcohol-related problems (Brown, 1985).

To gain insight into your reasons for using alcohol, respond to the following items by circling the *T* if an item is true or mostly true for you, or the *F* if an item is false or mostly false for you. Then turn to the answer key in Appendix B.

T F 1. I find it very unpleasant to do without alcohol for some time.

T F 2. Alcohol makes it easier for me to talk to other people.

T F 3. I drink to appear more grown-up and more sophisticated.

T F 4. When I drink, the future looks brighter to me.

T F 5. I like the taste of what I drink.

T F 6. If I go without a drink for some time, I am not bothered or uncomfortable.

T F 7. I feel more relaxed and less tense about things when I drink.

T F 8. I drink so that I will fit in better with the crowd.

T F 9. I worry less about things when I drink.

T F 10. I have a drink when I get together with the family.

T F 11. I have a drink as part of my religious ceremonies.

T F 12. I have a drink when a toothache or some other pain is disturbing me.

T F 13. I feel much more powerful when I have a drink.

T F 14. You really can't blame me for the things I do when I have been drinking.

T F 15. I have a drink before a big test, date, or interview when I'm afraid of how well I'll do.

T F 16. I find I have a drink for the taste alone.

T F 17. I've found a drink in my hand when I can't remember putting it there.

T F 18. I'll have a drink when I feel "blue" or want to take my mind off my cares and worries.

T F 19. I can do better socially and sexually after having a drink or two.

T F 20. Drinking makes me do stupid things.

T F 21. Sometimes when I have a few drinks, I can't get to work.

T F 22. I feel more caring and giving after having a drink or two.

T F 23. I drink because I like the look of a drinker.

T F 24. I like to drink more on festive occasions.

T F 25. When a friend or I have done something well, we're likely to have a drink or two.

T F 26. I have a drink when some problem is nagging away at me.

T F 27. I find drinking pleasurable.

T F 28. I like the "high" of drinking.

T F 29. Sometimes I pour a drink without realizing I still have one that is unfinished.

T F 30. I feel I can better get others to do what I want when I've had a drink or two.

T F 31. Having a drink keeps my mind off my problems at home, at school, or at work.

T F 32. I get a real gnawing hunger for a drink when I haven't had one for a while.

T F 33. A drink or two relaxes me.

T F 34. Things look better when I've had a drink or two.

T F 35. My mood is much better after I've been drinking.

T F 36. I see things more clearly when I've been drinking.

T F 37. A drink or two enhances the pleasure of sex and food.

T F 38. When I'm out of alcohol, I immediately buy more.

T F 39. I would have done much better on some things if it weren't for alcohol.

T F 40. When I have run out of alcohol, I find it almost unbearable until I can get some more.

"hero" that would cure physiological dependence on morphine.

Truth or Fiction Revisited. *It is true that heroin was once used as a cure for addiction to morphine.* Today, methadone is used to help addicts avert withdrawal symptoms from heroin.

Heroin is a powerful narcotic that can provide a euphoric rush. Users of heroin claim that it is so pleasurable it can eradicate any thought of food or sex.

Heroin is illegal. Because the penalties for possession or sale are high, it is also expensive. For this reason, many physiologically dependent people support their habits

Methadone • An artificial narcotic that is slower acting than, and does not provide the rush of, heroin. Methadone use allows heroin addicts to abstain from heroin without experiencing an abstinence syndrome.
Barbiturate • An addictive depressant used to relieve anxiety or induce sleep.
Methaqualone • An addictive depressant. Often called "ludes."
Amphetamines • Stimulants derived from *alpha-methyl-beta-phenyl-ethyl-amine*, a colorless liquid consisting of carbon, hydrogen, and nitrogen.

Snorting Cocaine. Cocaine is a powerful stimulant whose use has become widespread because of recent price breaks. Health professionals have become concerned about cocaine's stimulation of sudden rises in blood pressure, its constriction of blood vessels, and its acceleration of the heart rate. Several athletes have died from cocaine overdoses.

through dealing (selling heroin), prostitution, or selling stolen goods.

The word seems to have gotten out that the AIDS virus can be transmitted by sharing needles to inject ("shoot up") heroin and other drugs. More and more heroin users are thus "snorting" heroin (breathing it in through the nose in powder form) rather than injecting it in liquid form (Smolowe, 1993).

Although regular users develop tolerance for heroin, high doses can cause drowsiness, stupor, altered time perception, and impaired judgment.

Methadone is a synthetic opioid. Methadone has been used to treat physiological dependence on heroin in the same way that heroin was once used to treat physiological dependence on morphine. Methadone is slower acting than heroin and does not provide the thrilling rush. Most people treated with it simply swap dependence on one drug for dependence on another. Because they are unwilling to undergo withdrawal symptoms or to contemplate a lifestyle devoid of drugs, they must be maintained on methadone indefinitely.

Narcotics can have distressing abstinence syndromes, especially when used in high doses. Such syndromes may begin with flulike symptoms and progress through tremors, cramps, chills alternating with sweating, rapid pulse, high blood pressure, insomnia, vomiting, and diarrhea. However, these syndromes are somewhat variable from person to person.

BARBITURATES AND METHAQUALONE

Barbiturates such as amobarbital, phenobarbital, pentobarbital, and secobarbital are depressants with a number of medical uses, including relief of anxiety and tension, deadening of pain, and treatment of epilepsy, high blood pressure, and insomnia. Barbiturates lead rapidly to physiological and psychological dependence.

Methaqualone, sold under the brand names Quaalude and Sopor, is a depressant similar in effect to barbiturates. Methaqualone also leads to physiological dependence and is quite dangerous.

Psychologists generally oppose using barbiturates and methaqualone for anxiety, tension, and insomnia. These drugs lead rapidly to dependence and do nothing to teach the individual how to alter disturbing patterns of behavior.

Barbiturates and methaqualone are popular as street drugs because they relax the muscles and produce a mild euphoric state. High doses of barbiturates result in drowsiness, motor impairment, slurred speech, irritability, and poor judgment. A physiologically dependent person who is withdrawn abruptly from barbiturates may experience severe convulsions and die. High doses of methaqualone may cause internal bleeding, coma, and death. Because of additive effects, it is dangerous to mix alcohol and other depressants.

Stimulants

All stimulants increase the activity of the nervous system. Stimulants' other effects vary somewhat from drug to drug, and some seem to contribute to feelings of euphoria and self-confidence.

AMPHETAMINES

Amphetamines are a group of stimulants that were first used by soldiers during World War II to help them remain alert through the night. Truck drivers have used them to drive through the night. Amphetamines have become perhaps more widely known through students, who have used them for all-night cram sessions, and through dieters, who use them because they reduce hunger.

Called speed, uppers, bennies (for Benzedrine), and dexies (for Dexedrine), these drugs are often used for the euphoric rush they can produce, especially in high doses. (The so-called antidepressant drugs, discussed in Chapter 14, do not produce a euphoric rush.) Some people swallow amphetamines in pill form or inject liquid methedrine, the strongest form, into their veins. They may stay awake and "high" for days on end. Such highs must come to an end. People who have been on prolonged highs sometimes "crash," or fall into a deep sleep or depression. Some people commit suicide when crashing.

A related stimulant, methylphenidate (Ritalin), is widely used to treat **attention-deficit/hyperactivity disorder** in children (Wolraich and others, 1990). Ritalin has been shown to increase the attention span, decrease aggressive and disruptive behavior, and lead to academic gains (Klorman and others, 1994; Pelham and others, 1993). Why should Ritalin, a stimulant, calm children? The prevailing view is that hyperactivity is connected with immaturity of the cerebral cortex. Ritalin may spur the cortex to exercise control over more primitive centers in the lower brain.

People can become psychologically dependent on amphetamines, especially when they are used to cope with depression. Tolerance develops rapidly, but opinion is mixed as to whether they lead to physiological dependence. High doses may cause restlessness, insomnia, loss of appetite, hallucinations, paranoid delusions, and irritability. In the amphetamine psychosis, there are hallucinations and delusions that mimic the symptoms of paranoid schizophrenia (see Chapter 13).

COCAINE

Do you recall the commercials claiming that Coke adds life? Given its caffeine and sugar content, "Coke"—Coca-Cola, that is—should provide quite a lift. But Coca-Cola hasn't been "the real thing" since 1906. At that time, the manufacturers discontinued the use of cocaine in its formula. Cocaine is derived from coca leaves—the plant from which the soft drink took its name.

Truth or Fiction Revisited. *It is true that Coca-Cola once "added life" through a powerful but now illegal stimulant. That stimulant is cocaine.*

Coca leaves contain **cocaine,** a stimulant that produces a state of euphoria, reduces hunger, deadens pain, and bolsters self-confidence. Cocaine's popularity with college students seems to have peaked in the mid-1980s (see Table 5.2). Today, perhaps 1% use it regularly. The great majority of high-school seniors now believe that regular use of cocaine is harmful (Johnston and others, 1991).

A Vial of Crack. Crack "rocks" resemble white pebbles and produce a powerful rush when smoked. Crack is found only rarely on college campuses but appears to be more commonly used by youth in the inner cities.

Cocaine is brewed from coca leaves as a "tea," snorted in powder form, and injected in liquid form. Repeated snorting constricts blood vessels in the nose, drying the skin and, at times, exposing cartilage and perforating the nasal septum. These problems require cosmetic surgery. The potent derivatives "crack" and "bazooka" are inexpensive because they are unrefined.

Biologically speaking, cocaine stimulates sudden rises in blood pressure, constricts the coronary arteries (which decreases the oxygen supply to the heart), and quickens the heart rate. These events can occasionally cause respiratory and cardiovascular collapse (Moliterno and others, 1994), as with the sudden deaths of a number of athletes. Overdoses can lead to restlessness and insomnia, tremors, headaches, nausea, convulsions, hallucinations, and delusions. Use of crack has been connected with strokes (Levine and others, 1990).

Attention-deficit/hyperactivity disorder • A disorder that begins in childhood and is characterized by a persistent pattern of lack of attention, with or without hyperactivity and impulsive behavior.

Cocaine • A powerful stimulant.

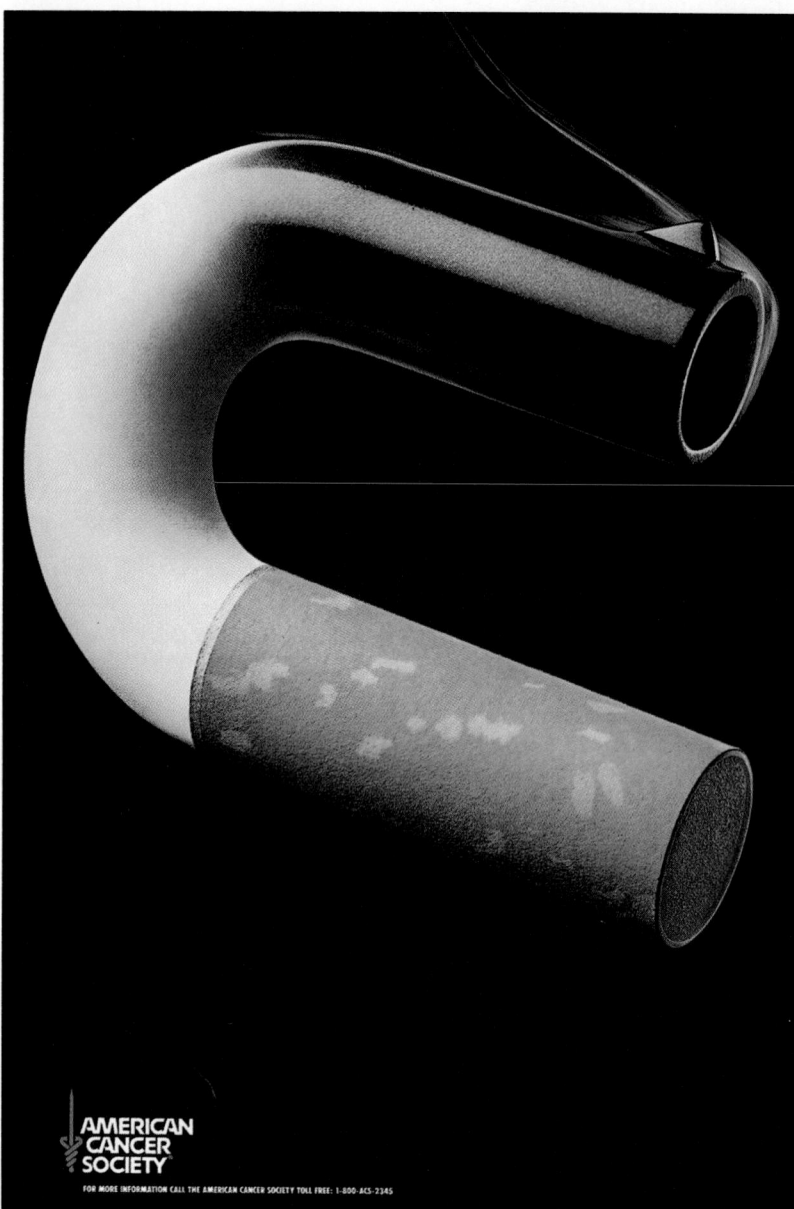

AMERICAN CANCER SOCIETY

FOR MORE INFORMATION CALL THE AMERICAN CANCER SOCIETY TOLL FREE: 1-800-ACS-2345

Cigarettes: Smoking Guns? The perils of cigarette smoking are widely known today. One Surgeon General declared that cigarette smoking is the chief preventable cause of death in the United States. The numbers of Americans who die from smoking are comparable to two jumbo jets crashing *every day.* If flying were that unsafe, would the government ground all flights? Would the public continue to book airline reservations?

Cocaine—also called *snow* and *coke,* like the slang term for the soft drink—has been used as a local anesthetic since the early 1800s. It came to the attention of one Viennese neurologist in 1884, a young chap named Sigmund Freud, who used it to fight his own depression and published an early supportive article, "Song of Praise." Freud's early ardor was soon tempered by awareness that cocaine was habit-forming and could cause hallucinations and delusions. Most authorities do believe that cocaine causes physiological dependence (Gold, 1993).

CIGARETTES (NICOTINE)

Smoking: a "custome lothesome to the Eye, hatefull to the Nose, harmefull to the Braine, dangerous to the Lungs."

KING JAMES I, 1604

The perils of smoking are no secret. All cigarette packs sold in the United States carry messages such as: "Warning: The Surgeon General Has Determined That Cigarette Smoking Is Dangerous to Your Health." Cigarette advertising has been banned on radio and television. Nearly 420,000 Americans die from smoking-related illnesses each year (CDC, 1993b). This is the equivalent of two jumbo jets colliding in midair each day with all passengers lost. This is more than the number who die from motor-vehicle accidents, abuse of alcohol and all other drugs, suicide, homicide, and AIDS *combined* (Rosenblatt, 1994).

Truth or Fiction Revisited. *It is true that the number of people who die from smoking-related causes is greater than the number lost to motor-vehicle accidents, abuse of alcohol and all other drugs, suicide, homicide, and AIDS.*

The percentage of American adults who smoke declined from 42.2% in 1966 to 25.7% in 1991 ("Decline in smoking," 1993), but there have been recent increases among women and African Americans ("Smoke rises," 1993). As shown in Table 5.3, the incidence of smoking is connected with gender, age, ethnicity, level of education, and socioeconomic status.

Every cigarette steals about 7 minutes of a person's life (CDC, 1993b). The carbon monoxide in cigarette smoke impairs the blood's ability to carry oxygen, causing shortness of breath. The **hydrocarbons** ("tars") in cigarette smoke cause several kinds of cancer in laboratory animals. Heavy smokers are about 10 times as likely as nonsmokers to die of lung cancer (Bishop, 1993). Cigarette smoking is linked to death from heart disease, chronic lung and respiratory diseases, and other illnesses (Bartecchi and others, 1994). Women who smoke show reduced bone density, significantly increasing the risk of fracture of the hip and back (Hopper & Seeman, 1994). Pregnant women who smoke risk miscarriage, premature birth, and birth defects.

Passive smoking is also connected with respiratory illnesses, asthma, and other diseases (USDHHS, 1993) and accounts for more than 50,000 deaths per year (Bartecchi and others, 1994). Prolonged childhood and adolescent exposure to tobacco smoke in the household is a risk factor for lung cancer (Janerich and others, 1990). Because of the noxious effects of secondhand smoke, smoking has been banished from many public places such as airplanes, restaurants, and elevators.

Why, then, do people smoke? For many reasons—such as the desires to look sophisticated (though smokers may be more likely to be judged foolish than sophisticated these days), to have something to do with their hands, and to take in nicotine.

Nicotine. **Nicotine** is the stimulant in cigarettes. Nicotine incites discharge of the hormone adrenaline. Adrenaline creates a burst of autonomic activity including rapid heart rate and release of sugar into the blood. As a stimulant, nicotine appears to enhance attention, improve performance on simple, repetitive tasks (Grunberg, 1993a; K. Perkins, 1993a), enhance the mood, and reduce stress (Hall and others, 1993). Nicotine does not appear to improve memory or functioning on complex cognitive tasks, such as solving math problems with many steps, however (Grunberg, 1993a; K. Perkins, 1993a). Some people smoke to control their weight (K. Perkins, 1993b). Nicotine both depresses the appetite and raises the metabolic rate (the rate at which the body processes food). People also tend to eat more when they stop smoking (Hatsukami and others, 1993; Ogden, 1994), which leads some people who have quit to return to smoking.

Cigarette smoking may be as addictive as the use of heroin or cocaine (MacKenzie and others, 1994). Nicotine is the agent that creates physiological dependence on cigarettes (Lichtenstein & Glasgow, 1992). Regular smokers adjust their smoking to maintain fairly even levels of nicotine in their bloodstream (Hall and others, 1993; Shiffman, 1993). Symptoms for withdrawal

Hydrocarbons • Chemical compounds consisting of hydrogen and carbon.

Passive smoking • Inhaling of smoke from the tobacco products and exhalations of other people; also called *secondhand smoking.*

Nicotine • A stimulant found in tobacco smoke. (From the French name for the tobacco plant, *nicotiane.*)

TABLE 5.3

Snapshot, U.S.A.: Human Diversity and Smoking

FACTOR	GROUP	PERCENT WHO SMOKE
Gender	Women	23.5
	Men	28.1
Age	18–24	22.9
	25–44	30.4
	45–64	26.9
	65–74	16.5
	75 and above	8.4
Ethnic Group	African American	29.2
	Asian American/Pacific Islander	16.0
	Hispanic American	20.2
	Native American	31.4
	Non-Hispanic White American	25.5
Level of Education	Fewer than 12 years	32.0
	12	30.0
	13–15	23.4
	16 and above	13.6
Socioeconomic Status (SES)	Below poverty level	33.3
	At poverty level or above	24.7

from nicotine include nervousness, drowsiness, energy loss, headaches, fatigue, irregular bowels, lightheadedness, insomnia, dizziness, cramps, palpitations, tremors, and sweating. Since many of these symptoms mimic anxiety, it was once thought that smoking might be a habit rather than an addiction.

The "Psychology and Modern Life" section in this chapter discusses ways of quitting and cutting down on smoking.

Hallucinogenics

Hallucinogenic drugs are so named because they produce hallucinations—that is, sensations and perceptions in the absence of external stimulation. But hallucinogenic drugs may also have additional effects such as relaxing the individual, creating a sense of euphoria, or, in some cases, causing panic. We shall focus on the effects of marijuana and LSD.

MARIJUANA

Marijuana is produced from the *Cannabis sativa* plant, which grows wild in many parts of the world. Marijuana helps some people relax and can elevate their mood. It also sometimes produces mild hallucinations, which is why marijuana is classified as a psychedelic, or hallucinogenic, drug. The major **psychedelic** substance in marijuana is **delta-9-tetrahydrocannabinol,** or THC. THC is found in the branches and leaves of male and female plants, but it is highly concentrated in the resin of the female plant. **Hashish,** or "hash," is derived from this sticky resin. Hashish is more potent than marijuana, although the effects are similar.

In the 19th century, marijuana was used almost as aspirin is used today for headaches and minor aches and pains. It could be bought without prescription in any drugstore. Today, marijuana use and possession are illegal in most states. As noted by the Institute of Medicine of the National Academy of Sciences, marijuana also carries a number of health risks (Maugh, 1982). For example, marijuana impairs motor coordination and perceptual functions used in the operation of machines, such as cars and trucks. It impairs short-term memory and

slows learning. Although it causes positive mood changes in many people, there are also disturbing instances of anxiety and confusion and occasional reports of psychotic reactions. Marijuana increases the heart rate up to 140–150 beats per minute and, in some people, raises blood pressure. This rise in workload poses a threat to persons with hypertension and cardiovascular disorders.

In the early 1990s, marijuana was used by about 14% of college students, down from nearly one third in 1981 (Johnston and others, 1993).

Psychoactive Effects of Marijuana. Marijuana smokers report different sensations at different levels of intoxication. The early stages of intoxication are frequently characterized by restlessness, which gives way to calmness. Fair to strong intoxication is linked to reports of heightened perceptions and increases in self-insight, creative thinking, and empathy for the feelings of others. Strong intoxication is linked to perceiving time as passing more slowly. A song, for example, might seem to last an hour rather than a few minutes. There is increased awareness of bodily sensations such as heartbeat. Smokers also report that strong intoxication heightens sexual sensations. Visual hallucinations are not uncommon. Strong intoxication may cause smokers to experience disorientation. If the smoker's mood is euphoric, loss of identity may be interpreted as harmony with the universe.

Yet, some smokers encounter negative experiences with strong intoxication. An accelerated heart rate and heightened awareness of bodily sensations lead some smokers to fear that their hearts will "run away" with them. Some smokers find disorientation threatening, and they fear failure to regain their identities. High levels of intoxication occasionally induce nausea and vomiting.

Some people report that marijuana helps them socialize at parties. However, the friendliness characteristic of early stages of intoxication may give way to self-absorption and social withdrawal as the smoker becomes higher.

People can become psychologically dependent on marijuana, as on any other

Hallucinogenic • Giving rise to hallucinations.

Marijuana • The dried vegetable matter of the *Cannabis sativa* plant. (A Mexican-Spanish word.)

Psychedelic • Causing hallucinations, delusions, or heightened perceptions.

Delta-9-tetrahydrocannabinol • The major active ingredient in marijuana. Abbreviated *THC.* Its name describes its chemical composition.

Hashish • A drug derived from the resin of *Cannabis sativa.* Often called "hash."

LSD • Lysergic acid diethylamide. A hallucinogenic drug.

Flashbacks • Distorted perceptions or hallucinations that occur days or weeks after LSD usage but mimic the LSD experience.

drug. However, many psychologists maintain that marijuana does not cause physiological dependence. Tolerance is a sign of physiological dependence. With marijuana, however, regular usage is often associated with the need for *less,* not *more,* of the substance to achieve the same effects. Some of the substances in marijuana smoke may take a long time to be metabolized by the body. Thus, the effects of new doses may be added to those of the chemicals remaining in the body.

Marijuana's entire story has not yet been told. Whereas certain horror stories about marijuana may have been exaggerated, one cannot assume that smoke containing 50% more carcinogenic hydrocarbon than tobacco smoke is completely harmless.

LSD

LSD is the abbreviation for lysergic acid diethylamide, a synthetic hallucinogenic drug. Users of "acid" claim that it "expands consciousness" and opens new worlds. Sometimes people believe they have achieved great insights while using LSD, but when it wears off they often cannot apply or recall these discoveries.

LSD and similar hallucinogenics are used by about 6% of the high school population (Johnston and others, 1991) and about 2% of the college population (see Table 5.2). As a powerful hallucinogenic, LSD produces vivid and colorful hallucinations.

Flashbacks. Some LSD users have **flashbacks**—distorted perceptions or hallucinations that occur days, weeks, or longer after usage but mimic the LSD trip. Some researchers have speculated that flashbacks stem from chemical changes in the brain produced by LSD. Heaton and Victor (1976) and Matefy (1980) offer a psychological explanation for flashbacks.

Heaton and Victor (1976) found that users who have flashbacks are more oriented toward fantasy and allowing their thoughts to wander. They are also more likely to focus on internal sensations. If they should experience sensations similar to a past trip, they may readily label them flashbacks and allow themselves to focus on them indefinitely, causing the experience to replay.

Matefy (1980) found that users who have flashbacks show greater capacity to become

An LSD Trip? This hallucinogenic drug can give rise to a vivid parade of colors and visual distortions. Some users claim to have arrived at great insights while "tripping," but afterward they have been typically unable to recall or apply them.

fully engrossed in role-playing and hypothesized that flashbacks may be nothing more than enacting the role of being on a trip. This does not necessarily mean that people who claim to have flashbacks are lying. They may be more willing to surrender personal control in response to internal sensations for the sake of altering their consciousness and having peak experiences. Users who do not have flashbacks prefer to

(text continues on page 198)

PSYCHOLOGY IN THE NEW MILLENNIUM

Use and Abuse of Drugs: More Research Needed

Drugs remain very much a part of U.S. society. Children and teenagers continue to become involved with drugs that impair their ability to learn at school and that are connected with reckless behavior (Cooper and others, 1994). There are also questions about the proper therapeutic use of drugs that are illicit under most circumstances. Such drugs include opioids, marijuana, and stimulants.

Let us consider a few key research questions about drugs—their use and abuse—that may be answered in the new millennium. The 20th century saw the chemical description of psychoactive drugs and the beginnings of knowledge about how these drugs act on the nervous system. Perhaps the 21st century will see developments in the following areas.

Substance Abuse in Teenagers. More research is needed into effective means of fighting substance abuse by children. Curiosity, peer pressure, parental use, rebelliousness, and the desire to escape from boredom or pressure are among the reasons children become involved with drugs. Inner-city youth are especially likely to become involved because of peer usage and the effort to escape a painful existence. Many means of fighting substance abuse have been tried with teenagers, including residential treatment centers, but their effectiveness has been shown to be modest at best (Nevid and others, 1994).

Efforts being made with younger children seem to hold somewhat more promise. For example, community psychologists are now experimenting with ways of tutoring youths to boost their self-esteem and success experiences in the schools (deGroot, 1994a, 1994b). In addition to boosting IQ scores, early childhood intervention programs also appear to decrease the likelihood of delinquent behavior, including substance abuse (Schweinhart & Weikart, 1993; Zigler and others, 1992). Perhaps these early approaches will succeed in helping children break away from poverty, a sense of lack of a future, and drug abuse.

Another positive note is that many teenagers now recognize that drugs such as crack cocaine are harmful (Johnston and others, 1993). A decade ago, teenagers were relatively

How Do We Fight Substance Abuse by Children? Curiosity, peer pressure, parental use, rebelliousness, and the desire to escape from boredom or pressure are among the reasons children become involved with drugs. Many means of fighting substance abuse have been tried with teenagers, but their effectiveness has been shown to be modest at best. Perhaps we will find more effective means in the new millennium.

more likely to attribute reports of drugs' harmfulness to horror stories concocted to scare them away from drugs. Perhaps the new millennium will also see more application of knowledge about the complex web of sociocultural factors that acts on youths from various ethnic groups.

Treatment of Alcoholism. More research is needed into effective ways of treating alcoholism. Alcoholics Anonymous (AA) is the most widely used program to treat alcoholism. Yet the majority of those who seek help from AA appear to drop out after a handful of meetings (Miller, 1982). AA urges complete abstinence from alcohol. AA teaches that even one drink can result in relapse. Belief that one has "fallen off the wagon" can be a self-fulfilling prophecy, of course, whether one is talking about drinking, smoking, or dieting. There is also some evidence that problem drinkers who are relatively less dependent on alcohol, and who believe that they can limit their drinking, have been able to adopt the alternate strategy of controlled drinking (Rosenberg, 1993).

More research into alcoholism is needed to help determine which alcoholics need to abstain from alcohol and which can learn to exercise control in drinking. More research into the cognitive behavioral methods that hold the most promise—aversion therapy, relaxation training, covert sensitization, instruction in social skills, and self-monitoring (Elkins, 1980; Monti and others, 1993; Sanchez-Craig and others, 1984)—would also be desirable.

Therapeutic Applications of Illicit Drugs. More research is needed into the therapeutic application of various illicit drugs. For example, many pain patients who use small to moderate doses of opioids for pain relief neither experience a euphoric rush nor become psychologically dependent on them (Lang & Patt, 1994; Taub, 1993). If pain patients no longer need the drugs but have become physiologically dependent, they can usually quit by gradually decreasing their dosage and suffer few, if any, side effects (Rosenthal, 1993a).

On the other hand, serious questions have been raised about using marijuana to decrease the nausea and vomiting often experienced by people with cancer who are taking chemotherapy. Supporters of marijuana argue that marijuana should be made widely available for medical purposes (Grinspoon & Bakalar, 1994). But detractors contend that carefully controlled studies on marijuana's medical benefits have not been conducted and that other drugs for nausea are available (Kolata, 1994a).

The therapeutic usages of opioids, marijuana, and other substances need further investigation. If drugs like opioids and marijuana are to be used therapeutically, researchers need to demonstrate that they provide necessary benefits that are unavailable from more socially acceptable substances.

Treatment of Children with Attention-Deficit/Hyperactivity Disorder (ADHD). More research is needed into the treatment of children with ADHD. The two major treatment methods have been stimulant medication (Ritalin) and cognitive behavior therapy. Some researchers have argued for the benefits of cognitive behavior therapy alone, whereas others argue for a combination of Ritalin and cognitive behavior therapy (Whalen & Henker, 1991). Although some research evidence suggests that Ritalin alone is as effective as a combination of Ritalin and cognitive behavior therapy (Pelham and others, 1993), Ritalin has side effects that are a cause of concern. Its use is connected with restlessness and loss of appetite. It may also suppress growth and give rise to tics and cardiovascular changes. These side effects are usually reversible with "drug holidays" or dosage decreases (Whalen & Henker, 1991). However, it would be highly desirable to develop effective drugs that have fewer side effects or to refine cognitive behavioral techniques so that drug therapy is not necessary.

As we gather new knowledge of the nervous system and the actions of drugs, perhaps we will develop more effective therapeutic drugs and find more effective ways of helping people discontinue harmful use of drugs.

be more in charge of their thought processes and have greater concern for meeting the demands of daily life.

OTHER HALLUCINOGENICS

Other hallucinogenic drugs include **mescaline** (derived from the peyote cactus) and **phencyclidine** (PCP). Regular use of hallucinogenics may lead to tolerance and psychological dependence. But hallucinogenics are not known to lead to physiological dependence. High doses may induce frightening hallucinations, impaired coordination, poor judgment, mood changes, and paranoid delusions.

Let us now consider a number of ways of altering consciousness that do not involve drugs.

Reflections

Now that you have read the sections on drugs, reflect on the following questions:

- Agree or disagree with the following statement and support your answer: "People cannot be held responsible for their behavior when they have been drinking."
- Agree or disagree with the following statement and support your answer: "Some people just can't hold their liquor."

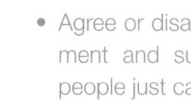

MINILECTURE:
MEDITATION:
TEACHING
STORIES

Meditation. People use many forms of meditation to try to expand inner awareness and experience inner harmony. The effects of meditation, like the effects of drugs, reflect both the bodily changes induced by meditation *and* the meditator's expectations.

- What had you heard about opioids such as heroin and morphine before reading this chapter? Is the information presented here consistent with what you had heard? How so, or how not?
- What have you heard about marijuana? Is the information presented here consistent with what you have heard? How so, or how not?
- Agree or disagree with the following statement and support your answer: "Cocaine and narcotics such as heroin are the most dangerous psychoactive drugs."

Altering Consciousness through Meditation: When Eastern Gods Meet Western Technology

There are many kinds of **meditation,** but they seem to share similar psychological threads: Through rituals, exercises, and passive observation, the normal person-environment relationship is altered. Problem solving, planning, worry, awareness of the events of the day are all suspended. In this way, consciousness—that is, the normal focuses of attention—is altered, and a state of relaxation is often induced. Scientifically speaking, it is reasonable to suggest that the effects of meditation, like the effects of drugs, reflect whatever bodily changes are induced by meditation *and* one's expectations about meditation. Many people believe that spiritual forces are also at work in meditation, but such beliefs are not scientifically verifiable.

Transcendental Meditation, or TM, is a simplified form of Far Eastern meditation that was brought to the United States by the Maharishi Mahesh Yogi in 1959. Hundreds of thousands of Americans practice TM by repeating and concentrating on **mantras**—words or sounds that are claimed to have the capacity to help one achieve an altered state of consciousness.

TM has a number of spiritual goals such as expanding consciousness, but there are also more worldly goals such as reducing anxiety and normalizing blood pressure. In early research, Herbert Benson (1975) found no scientific evidence that TM expands consciousness, despite the claims of many practitioners. However, TM did produce what Benson labeled a **relaxation response.** During TM, the body's metabolic rate dramatically decreased. The blood pressure of people with hypertension decreased (Benson and others, 1973). In fact, people who meditated twice daily tended to show normalized blood pressure through the day. Meditators produced more frequent alpha waves—brain waves associated with feelings of relaxation but infrequent during sleep. Participants in Benson's study also showed lower heart and respiration rates. More recent research supports the usefulness of meditation in reducing anxiety (Edwards, 1991).

Truth or Fiction Revisited. *It is true that people have managed to bring high blood pressure under control through meditation.* Meditation has been shown to normalize blood pressure.

Other researchers agree that TM lowers a person's level of arousal, but they argue that the same relaxing effects can be achieved in other ways, such as resting quietly for the same amount of time (Holmes, 1984). Holmes found no differences between experienced meditators and novice "resters" in heart rate, respiration rate, blood pressure, and sweat in the palms of the hands (that is, galvanic skin response, or GSR). The issue here is not whether meditation helps, but whether meditation has special effects as compared with a restful break from a tension-producing routine.

Note that formerly anxious and tense individuals who practice TM have also *chosen* to alter their stress-producing lifestyles by taking time out for themselves once or twice a day. Just taking time out for oneself may do the trick.

How to Meditate. If you wish to try meditation, the following instructions may be of help:

1. Begin by meditating once or twice daily for 10 to 20 minutes.

2. What you *don't* do is more important than what you do do. Adopt a passive, "what happens, happens" attitude.

3. Create a quiet, nondisruptive environment. For example, don't directly face a light.

4. Do not eat for an hour beforehand; avoid caffeine for at least two.

5. Assume a comfortable position. Change it as needed. It's okay to scratch or yawn.

6. For a concentrative device, you may focus on your breathing or seat yourself before a calming object such as a plant or burning incense. Benson suggests "perceiving" (rather than mentally saying) the word *one* on every outbreath. This means thinking the word, but "less actively" than usual (good luck). Others suggest thinking or perceiving the word *in* as you are inhaling and *out,* or *ah-h-h,* as you are exhaling.

7. If you are using a mantra, you can prepare for meditation and say the mantra out loud several times. Enjoy it. Then say it more and more softly. Close your eyes and think only the mantra. Allow yourself to perceive, rather than actively think, the mantra. Again, adopt a passive attitude. Continue to perceive the mantra. It may grow louder or softer, disappear for a while and then return.

8. If disruptive thoughts enter as you are meditating, you can allow them to "pass through." Don't get wrapped up in trying to squelch them, or you may raise your level of arousal.

9. Allow yourself to drift. (You won't go too far.) What happens, happens.

10. Above all, take what you get. You cannot force the relaxing effects of meditation. You can only set the stage for it and allow it to happen.

Mescaline • A hallucinogenic drug derived from the mescal (peyote) cactus. In religious ceremonies, Mexican Indians chew the buttonlike structures at the tops of the rounded stems of the plant.

Phencyclidine • Another hallucinogenic drug whose name is an acronym for its chemical structure. Abbreviated *PCP.*

Meditation • As a method for coping with stress, a systematic narrowing of attention that slows the metabolism and helps produce feelings of relaxation.

Transcendental meditation • The simplified form of meditation brought to the United States by the Maharishi Mahesh Yogi. Abbreviated *TM.*

Mantra • A word or sound that is repeated in TM. (A Sanskrit word that has the same origin as the word *mind.*)

Relaxation response • Benson's term for a group of responses that can be brought about by meditation. They involve lowered activity of the sympathetic branch of the autonomic nervous system.

Altering Consciousness through Biofeedback: Getting in Touch with the Untouchable

It seems there is little we can take for granted in life. A few decades ago, however, psychologists were reasonably secure with

Biofeedback. Biofeedback is a system that provides, or "feeds back," information about a bodily function to an organism. Through biofeedback training, people have learned to gain voluntary control over a number of functions that are normally involuntary.

Biofeedback training • The systematic feeding back to an organism information about a bodily function so that the organism can gain control of that function. Abbreviated *BFT.*

Electromyograph • An instrument that measures muscle tension. Abbreviated *EMG.* (From the Greek *mys,* meaning "mouse" and "muscle"—reflecting similarity between the movement of a mouse and the contraction of a muscle.)

Hypnosis • A condition in which people appear to be highly suggestible and behave as though they are in a trance. (From the Greek *hypnos,* meaning "sleep.")

the distinction between *voluntary* and *involuntary* functions. Voluntary functions, like lifting an arm or leg, were conscious. They could be directly willed. But other functions such as heart rate and blood pressure were involuntary or autonomic. They were beyond conscious control. We could no more consciously control blood pressure than, say, purposefully emit alpha waves.

Once in a while, to be sure, we heard tales of yogis (practitioners of yoga) or other exotics who could make their hair stand literally on end or "will" their cheeks to stop bleeding after a nail had been put through. But such episodes were viewed as horror stories or stage tricks. Serious scientists went back to serious research—except for a handful of pioneering psychologists like Neal E. Miller of Rockefeller University. In classic research of the 1960s, Miller trained laboratory rats to increase or decrease their heart rates voluntarily (Miller, 1969). His procedure was simple. There is a "pleasure center" in the hypothalamus of the rat. A small burst of electricity in this center is strongly reinforcing: Rats will do whatever they can to reap this bit of shock, such as learning to press a lever.

Miller implanted electrodes in the rats' pleasure centers. Then some rats were given electric shock whenever their heart rates

happened to increase. Other rats received shock when their heart rates went lower. In other words, one group of rats was consistently "rewarded" (that is, shocked) when the rats' heart rates showed an increase. The other group was consistently rewarded for a decrease. After a single 90-minute training session, rats learned to alter their heart rates by as much as 20% in the direction for which they had been rewarded.

Miller's research was an early example of **biofeedback training** (BFT). Biofeedback is simply a system that provides, or "feeds back," information about a bodily function to an organism. Miller used electrical stimulation of the brain to feed back information to rats when they had engaged in a targeted bodily response (in this case, raised or lowered their heart rates). Somehow the rats then used this information to raise or lower their heart rates voluntarily.

Similarly, people have learned to voluntarily change various bodily functions, including heart rate, that were once considered to be beyond their control.

Truth or Fiction Revisited. *It is true that you can learn to increase or decrease your heart rate just by thinking about it.* However, the "thinking about it" becomes more sophisticated through biofeedback training.

However, electrodes are not implanted in people's brains. Rather, people hear a "blip" or observe some other signal that informs them when the targeted response is being displayed.

There are many ways in which BFT helps people combat stress, tension, and anxiety (Budzynski & Stoyva, 1984). For example, people can learn to emit alpha waves (and feel somewhat more relaxed) through feedback from an EEG. A blip may increase in frequency whenever alpha waves are being emitted. The psychologist's instructions are simply to "make the blip go faster." An **electromyograph** (EMG), which monitors muscle tension, is commonly used to help people become more aware of muscle tension in the forehead and elsewhere and to learn to lower this tension. Through the use of other instruments, people have learned to lower their heart rates, their blood pressure, and the amount of sweat in the palm of the hand. All of these changes are relaxing. Biofeedback is widely used today by sports psychologists to teach athletes how to relax muscle groups that are unessential to the task at hand so that they can control anxiety and tension (Nelson, 1990).

People have also learned to elevate the temperature of a finger. Why bother, you ask? It happens that limbs become subjectively warmer when more blood flows into them. Increasing the temperature of a finger—that is, altering patterns of blood flow in the body—helps some people control migraine headaches, which may be caused by dysfunctional circulatory patterns.

Altering Consciousness through Hypnosis: On Being Entranced

Perhaps you have seen films in which Count Dracula hypnotized resistant victims into a stupor. Then he could get on with a bite in the neck with no further nonsense. Perhaps a fellow student labored to place a friend in a "trance" after reading a book on hypnosis. Or perhaps you have seen an audience member hypnotized in a nightclub act. If so, chances are this person acted as if he or she had returned to childhood, imagined that a snake was about to have a nip, or lay rigid between two chairs for a while.

Hypnosis, a term derived from the Greek word for sleep, has only recently become a respectable subject for psychological inquiry. Modern hypnosis seems to have begun with the ideas of Franz Mesmer in the 18th century. Mesmer asserted that the universe was connected by forms of magnetism—which may not be far from the mark. He claimed that people, too, could be drawn to one another by "animal magnetism."[3] (No bull's-eye here.) Mesmer used bizarre props to bring people under his "spell." He did manage a respectable cure rate for minor ailments. But we skeptics are more likely to attribute his successes to the placebo effect than to animal magnetism.

Hypnosis. Only recently has hypnosis become a respectable subject for psychological inquiry. Hypnotized subjects become passive and tend to deploy their attention according to the instructions of the hypnotist.

Today, hypnotism retains its popularity in nightclubs, but it is also used as an anesthetic in dentistry, childbirth, even surgery. Psychologists may use hypnosis to teach clients how to reduce anxiety, manage pain, or overcome fears (Crawford & Barabasz, 1993; Edwards, 1991). Police use hypnosis to prompt the memories of witnesses. But, as we see below, the accuracy of testimony by hypnotized people has been challenged.

HYPNOTIC INDUCTION

The state of consciousness called the *hypnotic trance* is traditionally induced by asking individuals to narrow their attention to a small light, a spot on the wall, an object held by the hypnotist, or just the hypnotist's voice. There are usually suggestions that the limbs are becoming warm, heavy, and relaxed. People may also be told that they are becoming sleepy or falling asleep. Hypnosis is *not* sleep, however, as shown by differences in EEG recordings for the hypnotic trance and the stages of sleep. But the word *sleep* is understood by subjects to suggest a hypnotic trance and has a track record of success.

---

[3] Hypnosis was first referred to as "magnetic sleep" (Crabtree, 1994).

Pseudomemories • Hypnotically induced false memories.

Hypermnesia • Greatly enhanced or heightened memory.

Age regression • In hypnosis, taking on the role of childhood, commonly accompanied by vivid recollections of one's past.

Regression • Return to a form of behavior characteristic of an earlier stage of development.

Role theory • A theory that explains hypnotic events in terms of the person's ability to act *as though* he or she were hypnotized. Role theory differs from faking in that subjects cooperate and focus on hypnotic suggestions instead of pretending to be hypnotized.

Neodissociation theory • A theory that explains hypnotic events in terms of the splitting of consciousness.

It is also possible to induce hypnosis through instructions that direct participants to remain active and alert (Clkurel & Gruzelier, 1990; Miller and others, 1991). So the effects of hypnosis probably cannot be attributed to relaxation.

People who are readily hypnotized are said to have *hypnotic suggestibility.* Part of hypnotic suggestibility is knowledge of what is expected during the "trance state." Generally speaking, suggestible people have positive attitudes and expectations about hypnosis and want to be hypnotized. Moreover, they can sustain their attention to the instructions of the hypnotist (Crawford and others, 1993). Liking and trusting the hypnotist also contribute to suggestibility (Gfeller and others, 1987).

Truth or Fiction Revisited. *It is true that people who are easily hypnotized have positive attitudes toward hypnosis.* Such people look forward to the experience and cooperate with the hypnotist.

CHANGES IN CONSCIOUSNESS BROUGHT ABOUT BY HYPNOSIS

Hypnotists and those who have been hypnotized report that hypnosis can bring about some or all of the following changes in consciousness. As you read them, bear in mind that changes in "consciousness" are inferred from changes in observable behavior and self-reports.

- *Passivity.* When being hypnotized, or in a trance, people await instructions and appear to suspend planning.

- *Narrowed Attention.* People may focus on the hypnotist's voice or a spot of light and avoid attending to background noise or intruding thoughts. It is claimed that individuals may not hear a loud noise behind the head if they are directed not to. (However, objective measures of hearing do suggest that people do not show any reduction in auditory sensitivity; rather, they report greater deafness [Spanos and others, 1982].)

- *Pseudomemories and Hypermnesia.* People may be instructed to report **pseudomemories** or **hypermnesia.** In police investigations, witnesses' memories are usually heightened by instructing them to

focus on selected details of a crime and then to reconstruct the entire scene. Studies suggest, however, that although people may report recalling more information when they are hypnotized, such information is often incorrect (Dwyan & Bowers, 1983; Nogrady and others, 1985; Weekes and others, 1992). But hypnotized people often report false information with conviction (Sheehan & Tilden, 1983; Weekes and others, 1992). Police investigators or juries may thus be misled.

- *Suggestibility.* People may respond to suggestions that an arm is becoming lighter and will rise or that the eyelids are becoming heavier and must close. They may act as though they cannot unlock hands clasped by the hypnotist or bend an arm "made rigid" by the hypnotist. Hypnotized individuals serving as witnesses are also highly open to the suggestions of their interviewers. They may incorporate ideas and images presented by interviewers into their "memories" and report them as facts (Laurence & Perry, 1983).

- *Playing Unusual Roles.* Most people expect to play sleepy, relaxed roles, but they may also be able to play roles calling for increased strength or alertness, such as riding a bicycle with less fatigue than usual (Banyai & Hilgard, 1976). In **age regression,** people may play themselves as infants or children. Research shows that many supposed childhood memories and characteristics are played inaccurately. Nonetheless, some people show excellent recall of such details as hair style or speech pattern. A person may speak a language forgotten since childhood.

- *Perceptual Distortions.* Hypnotized people may act as though hypnotically induced hallucinations and delusions are real. In the "thirst hallucination," for example, people act as if they are parched, even if they have just had a drink. People may behave as though they cannot hear loud noises, smell odors (Zamansky & Bartis, 1985), or sense pain (Miller & Bowers, 1993).

- *Posthypnotic Amnesia.* Many people apparently cannot recall events that take place under hypnosis (Davidson & Bowers, 1991), or even that they were hypnotized at all, if so directed. However, they can usually recall what occurred if they are hypnotized again and instructed by the hypnotist to do so (Kihlstrom and others, 1985).

The results of at least one experiment suggest that it may be advisable to take the phenomenon of posthypnotic amnesia with a grain of salt. People are more likely to report recalling events while "under a trance" when they are subjected to a lie-detector test and led to believe that they will be found out if they are faking (Coe & Yashinski, 1985).

• *Posthypnotic Suggestion.* People may follow instructions according to prearranged cues of which they are supposedly unaware. For instance, a subject may be directed to fall again into a deep trance upon the single command "Sleep!" Smokers frequently seek the help of hypnotists to break their habits, and they are frequently given the suggestion that upon "waking," cigarette smoke will become aversive. They may also be instructed to forget that this idea originated with the hypnotist.

THEORIES OF HYPNOSIS

Hypnotism is no longer explained in terms of animal magnetism, but psychodynamic theory and learning theory have offered explanations. According to Freud, the hypnotic trance represents **regression**. Hypnotized adults suspend "ego functioning," or conscious control of their behavior. They permit themselves to return to childish modes of responding that emphasize fantasy and impulse rather than fact and logic.

Role Theory. Theodore Sarbin (1972) offers a **role theory** view of hypnosis (Sarbin & Coe, 1972). He points out that the changes in behavior that are attributed to the hypnotic trance can be successfully imitated when people are instructed to behave *as though* they were hypnotized. For example, people can lie rigid between two chairs whether or not they are hypnotized. Also, people cannot be hypnotized unless they are familiar with the hypnotic "role"—the behavior that constitutes the trance. Sarbin is not saying that participants in hypnosis fake the hypnotic role. Research evidence suggests that most people

who are hypnotized are not faking (Kinnunen and others, 1994). Sarbin is suggesting, instead, that people allow themselves to enact this role under the hypnotist's directions.

Research findings that "suggestible" people are motivated to enact the hypnotic role, are good role players, and have vivid and absorbing imaginations would all seem to support role theory. The fact that the behaviors shown by hypnotized people can be mimicked by role players means that we need not resort to the concept of the "hypnotic trance"—an unusual and mystifying altered state of awareness—to explain hypnotic events.

Dissociation. Runners frequently get through the pain and tedium of long-distance races by *dissociating*—by imagining themselves elsewhere, doing other things. My students inform me that they manage the pain and tedium of *other* instructors' classes in the same way. Ernest Hilgard (1977) similarly explains hypnotic phenomena through **neodissociation theory.** This is the view that we can selectively focus our attention on one thing (like hypnotic suggestions) and dissociate ourselves from the things going on around us.

In one experiment related to neodissociation theory, participants were hypnotized and instructed to submerse their arms in ice water—causing "cold pressor pain" (Miller and others, 1991). Participants were given suggestions to the effect that they were not in pain, however. Highly hypnotizable people reported dissociative experiences that allowed them to avoid the perception of pain, such as imagining that they were at the beach or imagining that their limbs were floating in air above the ice water.

Though hypnotized people may be focusing on the hypnotist's suggestions and perhaps imagining themselves to be somewhere else, they still tend to perceive their actual surroundings peripherally. In a sense, we do this all the time. We are not fully conscious, or aware, of everything going on about us. Rather, at any moment we selectively focus on events such as tests, dates, or television shows that seem important or relevant. Yet while taking a test, we may be peripherally aware of the color of the wall or of the sound of rain.

Consider posthypnotic amnesia. When told to forget that they were hypnotized, people may focus on other matters. But the experience of hypnosis can be focused on afterward. Let us assume a person in a "trance" is given the posthypnotic suggestion to fall into a trance again upon hearing "sleep" but not to recall the fact that he or she was given this command. Upon "waking," the person does not focus on the posthypnotic suggestion. However, hearing the command "Sleep!" leads to rapid refocusing of attention and return to the trance. These thoughts are all, in a sense, separated or dissociated from each other. Yet, the person's attention can focus rapidly on one, then another.

Role theory and neodissociation theory do not suggest that the phenomena of hypnosis are phony. Instead, they suggest that we do not need to explain these events through an altered state of awareness called a trance. Hypnosis may not be special at all. Rather, it is *we* who are special—through our great imaginations, our role-playing ability, and our capacity to divide our consciousness—concentrating now on one event we deem important, concentrating later on another.

Reflections

Now that you have read the sections on meditation, biofeedback, and hypnosis, reflect on the following questions:

- Agree or disagree with the following statement and support your answer: "Through meditation, people have been able to transcend the boundaries of everyday experience."
- Agree or disagree with the following statement and support your answer: "Research into biofeedback training has altered the traditional distinction between *voluntary* and *involuntary* body functions."
- Had you heard of hypnosis or a hypnotic trance before taking this course? How does the information presented on hypnosis correspond to what you had heard?
- Agree or disagree with the following statement and support your answer: "You can only be hypnotized if you want to be hypnotized."

Summary

1. **What is consciousness?** The term *consciousness* has several meanings, including (1) sensory awareness, (2) direct inner awareness of cognitive processes, (3) personal unity or the sense of self, and (4) the waking state.

2. **What are the stages of sleep?** Electroencephalograph (EEG) records show different stages of sleep as characterized by different brain waves. There are four stages of non-rapid-eye-movement (NREM) sleep and one stage of REM sleep. Stage 1 sleep is lightest, and stage 4 is deepest.

3. **What are the functions of sleep?** Sleep apparently serves a restorative function, but we do not know exactly how sleep restores us or how much sleep we need.

4. **What are dreams?** Dreams are forms of cognitive activity that occur mostly while we are sleeping, and most take place during REM sleep. The content of most dreams is an extension of the events of the day. Nightmares are also dreams that occur during REM sleep.

5. **What are the sleep disorders?** Sleep disorders include insomnia, which is most often encountered by people who are anxious and tense, narcolepsy, apnea, sleep terrors, bed-wetting, and sleepwalking. Sleep terrors usually occur during deep sleep.

6. **What are substance abuse and dependence?** Substance abuse is use that persists despite impairing one's functioning. Dependence has behavioral and physiological aspects, as characterized by organizing one's life around getting and using the substance and by tolerance, withdrawal symptoms, or both.

7. **Why do people abuse drugs?** People usually try drugs because of curiosity, but usage can be reinforced by anxiety reduction, feelings of euphoria, and other sensations. People are also motivated to avoid withdrawal

symptoms once they become physiologically dependent. Some people may have genetic predispositions to become physiologically dependent on certain substances.

8. **What are depressants?** The group of substances called depressants acts by slowing the activity of the central nervous system.

9. **What are the effects of alcohol?** Alcohol is an intoxicating depressant that can lead to physiological dependence. Alcohol provides people with an excuse for failure or for antisocial behavior, but it has not been shown to induce antisocial behavior directly.

10. **What are the effects of opioids?** The opioids morphine and heroin are depressants that reduce pain, but they are also bought on the street because of the euphoric rush they provide. Opioids can lead to physiological dependence.

11. **What are the effects of barbiturates?** Barbiturates are depressants used to treat epilepsy, high blood pressure, anxiety, and insomnia. They lead rapidly to physiological dependence.

12. **What are stimulants?** Stimulants are substances that act by increasing the activity of the nervous system.

13. **What are the effects of amphetamines?** Amphetamines are stimulants that produce feelings of euphoria when taken in high doses. But high doses may also cause restlessness, insomnia, psychotic symptoms, and a "crash" upon withdrawal. Amphetamines and a related stimulant, Ritalin, are commonly used to treat hyperactive children.

14. **What are the effects of cocaine?** As a psychoactive substance, cocaine provides feelings of euphoria and bolsters self-confidence. Cocaine causes sudden rises in blood pressure and constricts blood vessels. Overdoses can lead to restlessness, insomnia, psychotic reactions, and cardiorespiratory collapse.

15. **What are the effects of smoking cigarettes?** Cigarette smoke contains carbon monoxide, hydrocarbons, and the stimulant nicotine. Regular smokers adjust their smoking to maintain a consistent blood level of nicotine, suggestive of physiological dependence. Cigarette smoking has been linked to death from heart disease, cancer, and many other disorders.

16. **What are hallucinogenics?** Hallucinogenic substances produce hallucinations—sensations and perceptions in the absence of external stimulation.

17. **What are the effects of marijuana?** Marijuana is a hallucinogenic substance whose active ingredients, including THC, often produce heightened and distorted perceptions, relaxation, feelings of empathy, and reports of new insights. Hallucinations are possible. The long-term effects of marijuana usage are not fully known, although it appears that marijuana smoke is in itself harmful.

18. **What are the effects of LSD?** LSD is a hallucinogenic drug that produces vivid hallucinations.

19. **What is meditation?** In meditation, one focuses "passively" on an object or a mantra to alter the normal person–environment relationship. In this way, consciousness (that is, the normal focuses of attention) is altered, and relaxation is often induced. TM and other forms of meditation appear to reduce high blood pressure as well as produce relaxation.

20. **What is biofeedback?** Biofeedback is a method for increasing consciousness of bodily functions, in which an organism is continuously provided with information about a targeted biological response such as heart rate or emission of alpha waves. Through biofeedback training, people and lower animals can learn to control some autonomic functions.

21. **What is hypnosis?** Hypnosis is an altered state of consciousness in which people show passivity, narrowed attention, hypermnesia (heightened memory), suggestibility, assumption of unusual roles, perceptual distortions, posthypnotic amnesia, and posthypnotic suggestion. Current theories of hypnosis emphasize our abilities to role-play the "trance" and to divide our consciousness as directed by the hypnotist.

Psychology and Modern Life

Insomnia and cigarette smoking are two of the banes of modern life. Insomnia is worsened by anxieties and the sources of stress that characterize modern life. Despite knowledge that cigarette smoking is, as former Surgeon General C. Everett Koop put it, "the chief preventable cause of death," millions of us smoke. We also tend to smoke more when we are under stress.

In this section, we outline psychology's contributions in helping people sleep and cut down on and quit smoking.

Coping with Insomnia: How (and *How Not*) to Get to Sleep at Night

In this section, we shall consider methods innovated by psychologists to help people get to sleep. First, though, let us take a side trip and discuss sleeping pills.

No question about it: The most common medical method for fighting insomnia in the United States is popping pills (Lacks & Morin, 1992). Sleeping pills may be effective—for a while. They generally work by reducing arousal. At first, lowered arousal may be effective in itself. Focusing on changes in arousal may also distract you from your efforts to *get* to sleep. Expectation of success may also help.

But there are problems with sleeping pills. First, because you attribute your success to the pill and not to yourself, you create dependency on the pill rather than self-reliance. Second, you develop tolerance for sleeping pills (Gillin, 1991). With regular use, you come to need higher doses to achieve the same effects. Third, high doses of these chemicals can be dangerous, especially if mixed with an alcoholic beverage or two. Sleeping pills and alcohol both depress the activity of the central nervous system, and their effects are additive.

Similarly, people use tranquilizers and alcohol to help them get to sleep. However, these chemical methods have problems similar to, and often more severe than, those posed by sleeping pills.

RELAXING

Psychological methods for coping with insomnia have also been developed. Some of these methods reduce tension directly, as in the case of muscle-relaxation exercises. Psychological methods also divert us from the "task" of trying somehow to *get* to sleep, which, of course, is one of the ways in which we keep ourselves awake. Instead, we need only recline when we are tired and allow sleep to happen.

Focusing on releasing muscle tension has been shown to reduce the amount of time needed to fall asleep and the incidence of waking during the night. It increases the number of hours slept and leaves us feeling more rested in the morning (Gillin

Insomnia. "You know I can't sleep at night," goes the 1960s song by the Mamas and the Papas. How many people can't sleep at night? Why? What can they do about it?

TABLE 5.4
Beliefs that Contribute to Insomnia and Alternatives

BELIEF THAT CONTRIBUTES TO INSOMNIA	ALTERNATIVE BELIEF
If I don't get to sleep, I'll feel wrecked tomorrow.	Not necessarily. If I'm tired, I can go to bed early tomorrow night.
It's unhealthy for me not to get more sleep.	Not necessarily. Some people do very well on only a few hours of sleep.
I'll wreck my sleeping schedule for the whole week if I don't get to sleep very soon.	Not at all. If I'm tired, I'll just go to bed a bit earlier. I'll get up about the same time with no problem.
If I don't get to sleep, I won't be able to concentrate on that big test/conference tomorrow.	Possibly, but my fears may be exaggerated. I may just as well relax or get up and do something enjoyable for a while.

& Byerley, 1990). A common method for easing muscle tension is progressive relaxation (see Chapter 15). Biofeedback training (BFT) has also been used successfully (Gillin & Byerly, 1990; Haynes and others, 1977). BFT for falling asleep usually focuses on reducing muscle tensions in the forehead or in the arms, but there has also been some success in teaching people to produce the kinds of brain waves that are associated with relaxation and sleep. These methods also provide one with something on which to focus other than trying to fall asleep.

COPING WITH EXAGGERATED FEARS

You need not be a sleep expert to realize that convincing yourself that the day will be ruined unless you get to sleep *right now* may increase, rather than decrease, bedtime tensions. As noted earlier, sleep does seem to restore us, especially after physical exertion. But we often exaggerate the problems that will befall us if we do not sleep (Morin and others, 1993). Table 5.4 shows some beliefs that contribute to insomnia and some alternatives.

AVOIDING RUMINATING IN BED

Don't plan or worry about tomorrow in bed (Bootzin and others, 1991; Morin and others, 1993). When you lie down for sleep, you may organize thoughts for the day for a few minutes, but then allow yourself to relax or engage in fantasy. If an important idea comes to you, jot it down on a handy pad so that you won't lose it. If thoughts persist, however, get up and follow them elsewhere. Let your bed be a place for relaxation and sleep—not your study. A bed—even a waterbed—is not a think tank.

ESTABLISHING A REGULAR ROUTINE

Sleeping late can encourage sleep-onset insomnia. Set your alarm for the same time each morning and get up, regardless of how many hours you have slept (Morin and others, 1993). By sticking to a regular time for rising, you'll be indirectly encouraging yourself to get to sleep at a regular time as well.

USING FANTASY

Fantasies or daydreams are almost universal and may occur naturally as we fall asleep. You can allow yourself to "go with" fantasies that occur at bedtime, or purposefully use fantasies to get to sleep. You may be able to ease yourself to sleep by focusing on a sun-drenched beach with waves lapping on the shore or on a walk through a mountain meadow on a summer day. You can construct your own "mind trips" and paint their details finely. With mind trips, you conserve fuel and avoid lines at airports.

Quitting and Cutting Down on Smoking

We have outlined the health hazards of smoking, so let us begin this section with some good news: Nearly as many Americans (44 million) have successfully quit smoking as smoke (46 million) (CDC, 1993b). Former smokers have mortality rates that approximate those of people who have never smoked (LaCroix and others, 1991). Moreover, by the age of 75, the death rate from lung cancer among "typical" ex-smokers is only 7 to 10% of that of people who continue to smoke (Bishop, 1993). ("Typical ex-smokers" begin to

A Smoke-Ending Vacation. Why not plan quitting smoking to coincide with a vacation when you can get away from all the cues connected with the habit? Ah, freedom!

smoke in their late teens and quit in their 30s.) So, rather than focusing on the damage we have already done ourselves, those of us who smoke can look forward to reasonably normal life expectancies if we quit.

Some smokers find it more effective to quit all at once (to go "cold turkey"). Others find cutting down gradually to be more effective. Although it is most healthful to quit smoking completely, some smokers who have not been able to quit have learned to reduce their cigarette consump-

tion by at least 50% (Glasgow and others, 1985).

STRATEGIES FOR QUITTING

Given the determination to quit, you or your friends may find it helpful to try some of the following suggestions:

- Tell your family and friends that you're quitting—make a public commitment.
- Think of specific things to tell yourself when you feel the urge to smoke: how you'll be stronger, free of fear of cancer, ready for the marathon, and so on.
- Tell yourself that the first few days are the hardest—after that, withdrawal symptoms weaken dramatically.
- Start when you wake up, at which time you've already gone 8 hours without nicotine.
- Go on a smoke-ending vacation to get away from places and situations in which you're used to smoking.
- Throw out ashtrays and don't allow smokers to visit you at home for a while.
- Don't carry matches or light other people's cigarettes.
- Sit in nonsmokers' sections of restaurants and trains.
- Fill your days with novel activities— things that won't remind you of smoking.
- Use sugar-free mints, cinnamon sticks, gum, or nicotine skin patches as substitutes for cigarettes. (Don't light them up.)
- Buy yourself presents with all that cash you're socking away.

STRATEGIES FOR CUTTING DOWN

- Count your cigarettes to establish your smoking baseline.
- Set concrete goals for controlled smoking. For example, plan to cut down baseline consumption by at least 50%.
- Gradually restrict the settings in which you allow yourself to smoke (see Chapter 14).
- Get involved in activities where smoking isn't allowed or practical.
- Switch to a brand you don't like. Hold your cigarettes with your nondominant hand only.
- Keep only enough cigarettes to meet the

(reduced) daily goal. Never buy more than a pack at a time.

- Use sugar-free candies or gum as a substitute for a few cigarettes each day.

- Jog instead of having a cigarette. Or go for a walk or swim.

- Pause before lighting up. Put the cigarette in an ashtray between puffs. Ask yourself before each puff if you really want more. If not, throw the cigarette away.

- Put the cigarette out before you reach the end. (No more eating the filter.)

- Gradually lengthen the amount of time between cigarettes.

- Imagine living a prolonged, noncoughing life. Ah, freedom!

- As you smoke, picture blackened lungs, coughing fits, the possibilities of cancer and other lung diseases.

Using strategies such as these, many have gradually cut down their cigarette consumption and eventually quit. Nicotine gums and skin patches also help some people (Cepeda-Benito, 1993; Hughes, 1993), but many people find it difficult to wean themselves from nicotine replacement methods (Grunberg, 1993b). There is also a high relapse rate for people who quit smoking. Be on guard: We are most likely to relapse—that is, return to smoking—when we feel highly anxious, angry, or depressed (Shiffman, 1984). If you are tempted, you can decrease the chances of relapsing by using almost any of the strategies described here (Hall and others, 1984; Shiffman, 1984), such as reminding yourself of reasons for quitting, having a mint, or going for a walk.

And those of you who are seeking an "instant cure" for smoking may be interested in the following information. However, you will see that the "magic" lies in our changing the way in which we interpret or structure our experiences—a method that is used by cognitive therapists.

COGNITIVE RESTRUCTURING: AN INSTANT CURE FOR SMOKING?

Let us assume that you are convinced that smoking is bad for your health and that you would like to quit if you could. Unfortunately, like many others, you question whether you have the willpower.

Well, then, what if there were an instant cure for smoking? A cure that was guaranteed to help you through the abstinence syndrome . . . with just one hitch?

The hitch? Some side effects. For 2 to 3 days after taking the cure, some people complain of nervousness and drowsiness, some of headaches, insomnia, or constipation. But these side effects are usually gone within a week. Considering the alternatives—fear of cancer and heart disease, the cost of cigarettes, the humiliation of being unable to quit—wouldn't "the cure" be worth it?

The instant cure exists and is readily available. It's called stopping smoking. I've simply described some common withdrawal symptoms. We need not look upon these symptoms as being awful. They are, after all, signs that the body is recovering from the effects of smoking.

Cognitive psychologists suggest that our interpretation of bodily sensations is central in coping with abstinence from any drug. Reinterpretation of sensations of hunger is also helpful in curbing overeating. We can cognitively restructure temporary, unpleasant sensations as signs that we are *winning,* not as disasters that must be avoided at all costs. After all, we wouldn't be experiencing them if we had not marshalled our willpower to take action that we believed was good for us.

Reflections

Now that you have read the "Psychology and Modern Life" section, reflect on the following questions:

- Is it easy or difficult for you to get to sleep? Is it more difficult at some times than others? Why?

- What kinds of things make it difficult for you to get to sleep?

- What methods have you or people you know tried to stop smoking? What, if anything, has worked? Why?

- Psychologist Gregory Kimble (1994) writes that many concepts in psychology have their origins in common sense. Which suggestions for coping with insomnia or quitting cigarettes seem like common sense to you? Why? Which seem to run counter to common sense? Why?

6

Learning

Truth or Fiction?

_____ One nauseating meal can give rise to a food aversion that persists for years.

_____ Dogs can be trained to salivate when a bell is sounded.

_____ Psychologists helped a young boy overcome fear of rabbits by having him eat cookies while a rabbit was brought nearer.

_____ During World War II, a psychologist devised a plan for training pigeons to guide missiles to their targets.

_____ Punishment does not work.

_____ Rats can be trained to climb a ramp, cross a bridge, climb a ladder, pedal a toy car, and do several other tasks—all in proper sequence.

_____ Psychologists successfully fashioned a method to teach an emaciated 9-month-old infant to stop throwing up.

_____ We must make mistakes if we are to learn.

_____ Despite all the media hoopla, no scientific connection has been established between TV violence and aggression in real life.

Outline

Truth or Fiction?
Classical Conditioning
  Ivan Pavlov Rings a Bell
  Stimuli and Responses in Classical
    Conditioning: US, CS, UR, and CR
  Types of Classical Conditioning
  Taste Aversion
  Extinction and Spontaneous Recovery
  Generalization and Discrimination
  Higher-Order Conditioning
  Applications of Classical Conditioning
Operant Conditioning
  Edward L. Thorndike and the Law of
    Effect
  B. F. Skinner and Reinforcement
  Types of Reinforcers
  Extinction and Spontaneous Recovery in
    Operant Conditioning
  Reinforcers versus Rewards and
    Punishments
  Discriminative Stimuli
  Schedules of Reinforcement
  Applications of Operant Conditioning
    Psychology in the New Millennium:
    Learning at the Feet of the . . .
    Information Superhighway?
Cognitive Factors in Learning
  Contingency Theory: Contiguity or
    Contingency? What "Really" Happens
    during Classical Conditioning?
  Latent Learning: When Learning Is Not
    Doing
  Observational Learning: Monkey See,
    Monkey May Choose to Do
    Psychology in a World of Diversity:
    Sociocultural Factors in Learning,
    or, Donald Duck Meets a Samurai
Summary
Psychology and Modern Life
  The Effects of Media Violence

When I was a child in The Bronx, my friends and I would go to the movies on Saturday mornings. There would be a serial ("Rocketman" was my favorite) followed by a feature film, and admission was a quarter. We would also eat candy (I loved Nonpareils and Raisinets) and popcorn. One morning, my friends dared me to eat two large containers of buttered popcorn by myself. For reasons that I label "youth," I rose to the challenge. Down went an enormous container of buttered popcorn. More slowly—much more slowly—I stuffed down the second. Predictably, I felt bloated and nauseated. The taste of the butter, corn, and salt lingered in my mouth and nose, and my head spun with the repulsive sensations. It was obvious to me that I would have no more popcorn that day. However, I was surprised that I could not face buttered popcorn again for a year.

Years later, I learned that psychologists refer to my response to buttered popcorn as a *taste aversion*. Although I could not analyze my reaction in a sophisticated fashion at the time, I recognized that there was something strange about it. As I thought of it then, my "head" was telling me one thing about the popcorn while my "stomach" was telling me another. On a cognitive level, I recognized that my feelings stemmed from eating too much buttered popcorn and that smaller amounts would be safe. But something had also apparently been learned on a "gut level" that overrode my belief that I should be able to eat and enjoy reasonable amounts of buttered popcorn.

Now I know that a **taste aversion** is an example of classical conditioning. Classical conditioning leads organisms to anticipate events. An "overdose" of buttered popcorn had made me queasy. Afterward, the sight and odor of buttered popcorn—even the thought of it—was sufficient to make me anticipate nausea. In fact, they induced sensations of nausea in my throat and stomach. My aversion seemed silly at the time, but it is adaptive for organisms to develop taste aversions readily. Often when foods make us ill, it is because they are poisoned or unhealthful for other reasons. A taste aversion serves the adaptive function of keeping us away from them.

After I had acquired my taste aversion, I stayed away from buttered popcorn. My avoidance could be explained in terms of another kind of learning, operant conditioning, in which organisms learn to do things—and not to do other things—because of the consequences of their behavior. I stayed away from buttered popcorn to avoid anticipated nausea. But we also seek fluids when thirsty, sex when aroused, and an ambient temperature of 68 to 70 degrees Fahrenheit because we anticipate pleasant consequences. Put briefly, classical conditioning focuses on how organisms form anticipations about their environments. Operant conditioning focuses on what they do about them.

By the way, more than 30 years have now passed—how many more is my business. But I still prefer my popcorn *un*buttered.

Truth or Fiction Revisited. *It is true that one nauseating meal can give rise to a food aversion that persists for years.*

Classical and operant conditioning are two forms of learning, which is the subject of this chapter. In lower organisms, much behavior is instinctive, or inborn. Fish are born "knowing" how to swim. Salmon instinctively return to spawn in the streams of their birth after they have matured and spent years roaming the deep seas. Robins instinctively know how to sing the songs of their species and to build nests. Rats

instinctively mate and rear their young. Among people, however, the variety and complexity of behavior patterns are largely learned through experience. Experience is essential in our learning to walk and in our acquisition of the languages of our parents and communities. We learn to read, to do mathematical computations, and to symbolically rotate geometric figures. We learn to seek out the foods valued in our cultures when we are hungry. We get into the habit of starting our days with coffee, tea, or other beverages. We learn which behavior patterns are deemed socially acceptable and which are considered wrong. And, of course, our families and communities use verbal guidance, set examples, and apply rewards and punishments in an effort to teach us to stick to the straight and narrow.

Sometimes our learning experiences are direct, as was my taste aversion for buttered popcorn. But we can also learn from the experiences of others. For example, I warn my children against the perils of jumping from high places and running wild in the house. (Occasionally they heed me.) We learn about the past, about other peoples, and about how to put things together from books and visual media. And we learn as we invent ways of doing things that have never been done before.

Having noted these various ways of learning, let me admit that the very definition of **learning** stirs controversy in psychology. *Learning* may be defined in different ways.

From the behaviorist perspective, learning is defined as a relatively permanent change in behavior that arises from experience. Changes in behavior also arise from maturation and physical changes, but they are not considered to reflect learning. The behaviorist definition is operational. Learning is defined in terms of the measurable events or changes in behavior by which it is known. From the behaviorist perspective, buttered popcorn came to evoke nausea because it was temporally associated with nausea. I also learned to avoid popcorn because of the temporal consequences of consuming it—simple and not-so-sweet.

From the cognitive perspective, learning involves processes by which experience contributes to relatively permanent changes in the way organisms mentally represent the environment. Changes in representation may influence, but do not cause, changes in behavior. From this perspective, learning is *made evident* by behavioral change, but learning is defined as an internal and not directly observable process. From the cognitive perspective, my gorging on buttered popcorn taught me to regard, or mentally

Taste aversion • A kind of classical conditioning in which a previously desirable or neutral food becomes repugnant because it is associated with aversive stimulation.

Learning • (1) According to behaviorists, a relatively permanent change in behavior that results from experience. (2) According to cognitive theorists, the process by which organisms make relatively permanent changes in the way they represent the environment because of experience. These changes influence the organism's behavior but do not fully determine it.

represent, buttered popcorn in a different way. My altered image of buttered popcorn then encouraged me to avoid it for a while. But my avoidance was not mechanical or compulsory.

Behaviorists do not concern themselves with the ways in which I mentally represent buttered popcorn. (And who can fault them?) They argue that there is no direct way of measuring my mental imagery, only my overt behavior. So why try to embrace imagery in a scientific theory?

Reflections

Now that you have read the beginning of the chapter, reflect on the following questions:

- Do you have a taste aversion to any kind of food? Can you recall an incident that led to the development of the taste aversion?
- How would you have defined learning before beginning this chapter? Are either of the approaches discussed above consistent with your definition? How, or how not? Are you more in sympathy with the behavioral or cognitive perspective on learning? Why?

Let us now focus on some of the particulars of a number of kinds of learning, beginning with classical conditioning.

Classical Conditioning

Classical conditioning involves some of the ways in which we learn to associate events. Consider: We have a distinct preference for having instructors grade our papers with A's rather than F's. We are also (usually) more likely to stop our cars for red than green traffic lights. Why? We are not born with instinctive attitudes toward the letters *A* and *F*. Nor are we born knowing that red means stop and green means go. We learn the meanings of these symbols because they are associated with other events. A's are associated with instructor approval and the likelihood of getting into graduate school. Red lights are associated with avoiding accidents and traffic citations.

IVAN PAVLOV RINGS A BELL

Lower animals also learn relationships among events, as Russian physiologist Ivan Pavlov (1849–1936) discovered in research with laboratory dogs. Pavlov was attempting to identify neural receptors in the mouth that triggered a response from the salivary glands. But his efforts were hampered by the dogs' salivating at undesired times, such as when a laboratory assistant inadvertently clanged a food tray.

Because of its biological makeup, a dog will salivate if meat powder is placed on its

Ivan Pavlov. Pavlov, his assistants, and a professional salivator (the dog) at a Russian academy early in the century.

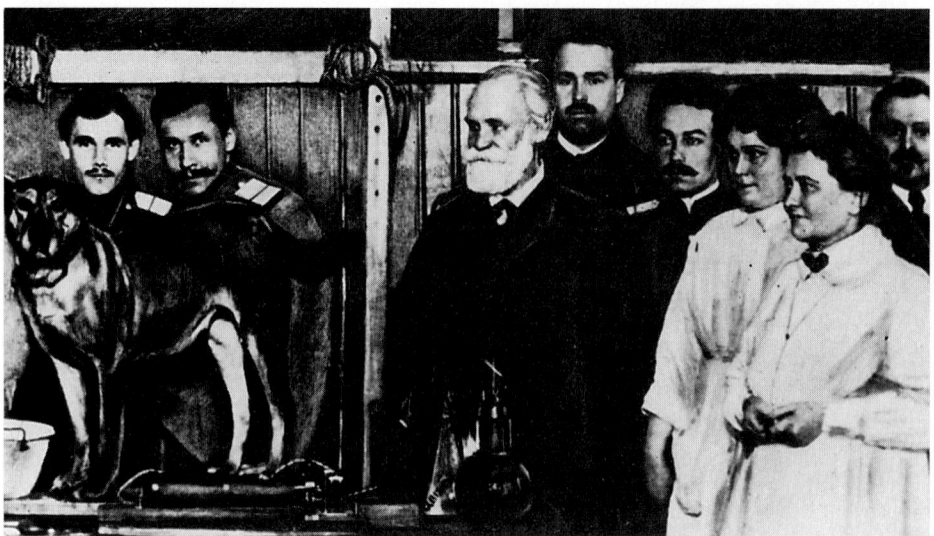

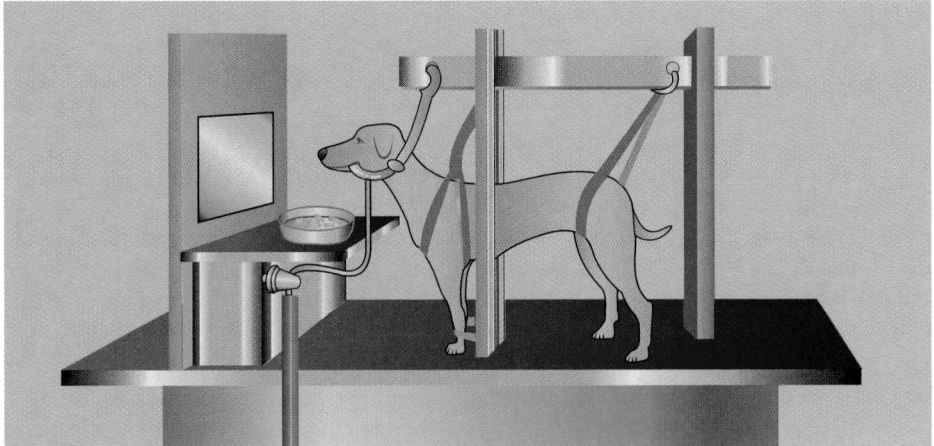

FIGURE 6.1

Pavlov's Demonstration of Conditioned Reflexes in Laboratory Dogs From behind the two-way mirror at the left, a laboratory assistant rings a bell and then places meat powder on the dog's tongue. After several pairings, the dog salivates in response to the bell alone. A tube collects saliva and passes it to a vial. The quantity of saliva is taken as a measure of the strength of the animal's response.

tongue. Salivation in response to meat powder is unlearned, a **reflex.** Reflexes are elicited by a certain range of stimuli. A **stimulus** is an environmental condition that evokes a response from an organism, such as meat powder on the tongue or a traffic light's changing colors. Reflexes are simple unlearned responses to stimuli. Pavlov discovered that reflexes can also be learned, or conditioned, through association. His dogs began salivating in response to clinking food trays because this noise, in the past, had been paired repeatedly with the arrival of food. The dogs would also salivate when an assistant entered the laboratory. Why? In the past, the assistant had brought food.

When we are faced with novel events, we sometimes have no immediate way of knowing whether they are important. When we are striving for concrete goals, we often ignore the unexpected, even when the unexpected is just as important, or more important, than the goal. So it was that Pavlov at first saw this uncalled-for canine salivation as an annoyance, a hindrance to his research. But in 1901, he decided that his "problem" was worth looking into. He then set about to show that he could train, or condition, his dogs to salivate when he wished and in response to any stimulus.

Pavlov termed these trained salivary responses "conditional reflexes." They were

conditional upon the repeated pairing of a previously neutral stimulus (such as the clinking of a food tray) and a stimulus (in this case, food) that predictably evoked the target response (in this case, salivation). Today, conditional reflexes are more generally referred to as **conditioned responses** (CRs). They are responses to previously neutral stimuli that are learned, or conditioned.

Pavlov demonstrated conditioned responses by strapping a dog into a harness such as the one in Figure 6.1. When meat powder was placed on the dog's tongue, the dog salivated. Pavlov repeated the process several times, with one difference. He preceded the meat powder by half a second or so with the sounding of a bell on each occasion. After several pairings of meat powder and bell, Pavlov sounded the bell but did not follow the bell with the meat powder. Still the dog salivated. It had learned to salivate in response to the bell.

Truth or Fiction Revisited. *It is true that dogs can be trained to salivate when a bell is sounded.*

Behaviorists explain the outcome of **classical conditioning** in terms of the publicly observable conditions of learning. They define classical conditioning as a simple form of learning in which one stimulus comes to evoke the response usually evoked

Reflex • A simple unlearned response to a stimulus.

Stimulus • An environmental condition that elicits a response.

Conditioned response (CR) • In classical conditioning, a learned response to a conditioned stimulus.

Classical conditioning • (1) According to behaviorists, a form of learning in which one stimulus comes to evoke the response usually evoked by a second stimulus by being paired repeatedly with the second stimulus. (2) According to cognitive theorists, the learning of relationships among events so as to allow an organism to represent its environment. Also referred to as *respondent conditioning* or *Pavlovian conditioning*.

MINILECTURE:
PAVLOV'S
STUDY

MINILECTURE:
THE
IMPORTANCE
OF TEMPORAL
CONTIGUITY

Contiguous • Next to one another.

Unconditioned stimulus (US) • A stimulus that elicits a response from an organism prior to conditioning.

Unconditioned response (UR) • An unlearned response to an unconditioned stimulus.

Orienting reflex • An unlearned response in which an organism attends to a stimulus.

Conditioned stimulus (CS) • A previously neutral stimulus that elicits a conditioned response because it has been paired repeatedly with a stimulus that already elicited that response.

Delayed conditioning • A classical-conditioning procedure in which the CS is presented before the US and remains in place until the response occurs.

Simultaneous conditioning • A classical-conditioning procedure in which the CS and US are presented at the same time.

Trace conditioning • A classical-conditioning procedure in which the CS is presented and then removed before the US is presented.

by a second stimulus by being paired repeatedly with the second stimulus. In Pavlov's demonstration, the dog learned to salivate in response to the bell *because* the sounding of the bell had been paired with meat powder. That is, in classical conditioning, the organism forms associations between stimuli because the stimuli are **contiguous.** Behaviorists do *not* say that the dog "knew" that food was on the way. They argue that we cannot speak meaningfully about what a dog "knows." We can only outline the conditions under which targeted behaviors will reliably occur. The behaviorist focus is on the mechanical acquisition of the conditioned response.

Cognitive psychologists view classical conditioning as the learning of relationships among events. The relationships allow organisms to mentally represent their environments and make predictions (Holyoak and others, 1989; Rescorla, 1988). In Pavlov's demonstration, the dog salivated in response to the bell because the bell—from the cognitive perspective—became mentally connected with the meat powder. The cognitive focus is on the information gained by organisms. Organisms are viewed as seekers of information who generate and test rules about the relationships among events (Weiner, 1991).

Behaviorists might counter that organisms can learn to engage in conditioned responses without any evidence that they are aware of what they are learning. There are any number of classic experiments in which people learn conditioned responses that are presumably too small to perceive. In one example, people learned to engage in apparently imperceptible thumb contractions that involved only 25–30 microvolts of energy (Hefferline & Keenan, 1963). Learners, in other words, are not necessarily privy to all of their changes in behavior.

STIMULI AND RESPONSES IN CLASSICAL CONDITIONING: US, CS, UR, AND CR

In the demonstration just described, the meat powder is an unlearned or **unconditioned stimulus** (US). Salivation in response to the meat powder is an unlearned or **unconditioned response** (UR). The bell was at first a meaningless or neutral stimulus. It might have produced an

FIGURE 6.2

Spotlight on Classical Conditioning Prior to conditioning, food elicits salivation. The bell, a neutral stimulus, elicits either no response or an orienting response. During conditioning, the bell is rung just before meat powder is placed on the dog's tongue. After several repetitions, the bell, now a CS, elicits salivation, the CR.

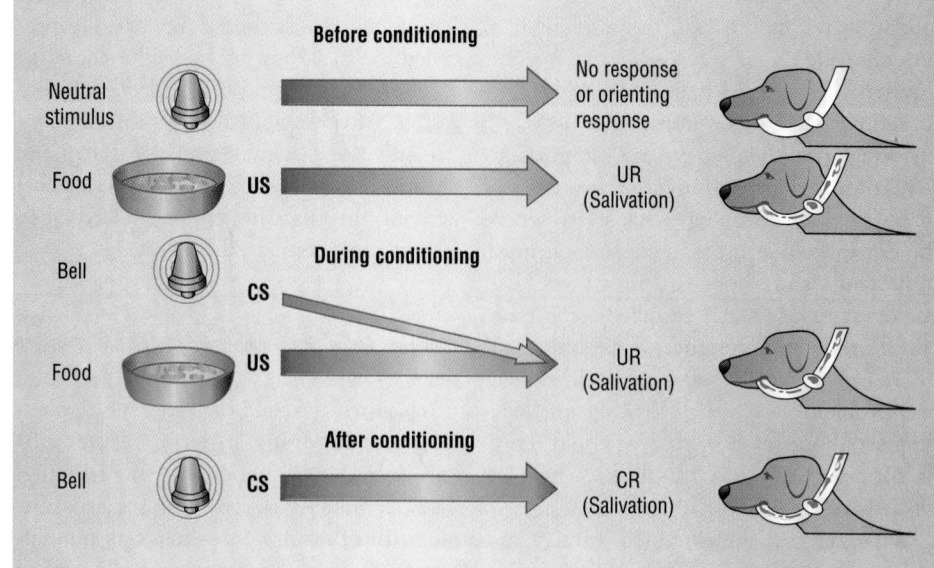

| Part A | CS | |
| Delayed Conditioning | US | |

| Part B | CS | |
| Simultaneous Conditioning | US | |

| Part C | CS | |
| Trace Conditioning | US | |

| Part D | CS | |
| Backward Conditioning | US | |

FIGURE 6.3

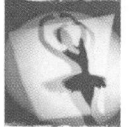

Spotlight on Kinds of Classical Conditioning In delayed conditioning (part A), the CS is presented before the US. In simultaneous conditioning (part B), the CS and US are presented together. In trace conditioning (part C), the CS is presented and then removed prior to the US. Thus, only the memory trace of the CS remains when the US is presented. In backward conditioning (part D), the US is presented before the CS. Delayed conditioning is most efficient, perhaps because it allows organisms to make predictions about their environments.

orienting reflex in the dog because of its distinctness. But it was not yet associated with food. Then, through repeated association with the meat powder, the bell became a learned or **conditioned stimulus** (CS) for the salivation response. Salivation in response to the *bell* (or CS) is a learned or conditioned response (CR). A CR is a response similar to a UR, but the response elicited by the CS is by definition a CR, not a UR (see Figure 6.2).

TYPES OF CLASSICAL CONDITIONING

Classical conditioning tends to occur most efficiently when the conditioned stimulus (CS) is presented about 0.5 second before the unconditioned stimulus (US) and is continued until the learner responds to the

US. This is an example of **delayed conditioning,** in which the CS (for example, a light) can be presented anywhere from a fraction of a second to several seconds before the US (in this case, meat powder) and is left on until the response (salivation) is shown (see Figure 6.3). Conditioning can also take place via **simultaneous conditioning,** in which a CS such as a light is presented along with a US such as meat powder. In **trace conditioning,** the CS (for example, a light) is presented and then removed (or turned off) prior to presentation of the US (meat powder). Therefore, only the memory trace of the CS (light) remains to be conditioned to the US.

Conditioning occurs most effectively in delayed conditioning, perhaps because it is the most adaptive procedure. That is, in delayed conditioning, the CS signals the consequent

MINILECTURE:
PHASES OF
CLASSICAL
CONDITIONING

appearance of the US. As a result, organisms can learn to make predictions about their environments. Predictability is adaptive because it allows organisms to prepare for future events. Learning is inefficient and may not take place at all when the US is presented before the CS (Hall, 1989), a sequence referred to as **backward conditioning.** Backward conditioning may not permit organisms to make useful predictions about their environments.

TASTE AVERSION

Taste aversions serve the adaptive function of motivating organisms to avoid potentially harmful foods. Although taste aversions are acquired by association, they differ from other kinds of classical conditioning in a couple of ways. First, only one association may be required. I did not have to go back for seconds at the movies to develop my aversion for buttered popcorn! Second, whereas most kinds of classical conditioning require that the US and CS be contiguous, in taste aversion the US (nausea) can occur hours after the CS (flavor of food).

Research in taste aversion also challenges the behaviorist view that organisms learn to associate any stimuli that are contiguous. Not all stimuli are created equal. Instead, it seems that organisms are biologically predisposed to develop aversions that are adaptive in their environmental settings (Garcia and others, 1989). In a classic study, Garcia and Koelling (1966) conditioned two groups of rats. Each group was exposed to the same three-part CS: a taste of sweetened water, a light, and a clicker. Afterward, one group was presented a US of nausea (induced by poison or radiation), and the other group was presented a US of electric shock.

After conditioning, the rats that had been nauseated showed an aversion for sweetened water but not to the light or clicker. Although all three stimuli had been presented at the same time, *they had acquired only the taste aversion.* After conditioning, the rats that had been shocked avoided both the light and the clicker, *but they did not show a taste aversion to the sweetened water.* For each group of rats, the conditioning that took place was adaptive. In the natural scheme of things, nausea is more likely to stem from poisoned food than from lights or sounds.

And so, for nauseated rats, acquiring the taste aversion was appropriate. Sharp pain, in contrast, is more likely to stem from natural events involving lights (fire, lightning) and sharp sounds (twigs snapping, things falling). Therefore, it was more appropriate for the shocked animals to develop an aversion to the light and the clicker than to the sweetened water.

This finding fits my experience as well. My nausea led to a taste aversion to buttered popcorn—but not to an aversion to the "Rocketman" serial (which, in retrospect, was more deserving of nausea) or the movie theater. I returned every Saturday morning to see what would happen next. Yet, the serial and the theater, as much as the buttered popcorn, had been associated (contiguous) with my nausea.

EXTINCTION AND SPONTANEOUS RECOVERY

Extinction and spontaneous recovery are aspects of conditioning that help organisms adapt by updating their expectations or revising their representations of the changing environment. A dog may learn to associate a new scent (CS) with the appearance of a dangerous animal. It can then take evasive action when it whiffs the scent. A child may learn to connect hearing a car pull into the driveway (CS) with the arrival of his or her parents (US). Thus, the child may come to squeal with delight (CR) when the car is heard.

But times can change. The once dangerous animal may no longer be a threat. (What a puppy perceives to be a threat may lose its power to menace once the dog matures.) After moving to a new house, the child's parents may commute by means of public transportation. The sounds of a car in a nearby driveway may signal a neighbor's, not a parent's, homecoming. When conditioned stimuli (such as the scent or the sound of a car) are no longer followed by unconditioned stimuli (a dangerous animal, a parent's homecoming), they lose their ability to elicit conditioned responses. In this way, the organism adapts to a changing environment.

Extinction. In classical conditioning, **extinction** is the process by which conditioned stimuli (CSs) lose the ability to elicit

Formation of a Taste Aversion? Taste aversions may be acquired by just one association of the US and the CS. Most kinds of classical conditioning require that the US and CS be contiguous, but in a taste aversion, the US (nausea) can occur hours after the CS (flavor of food).

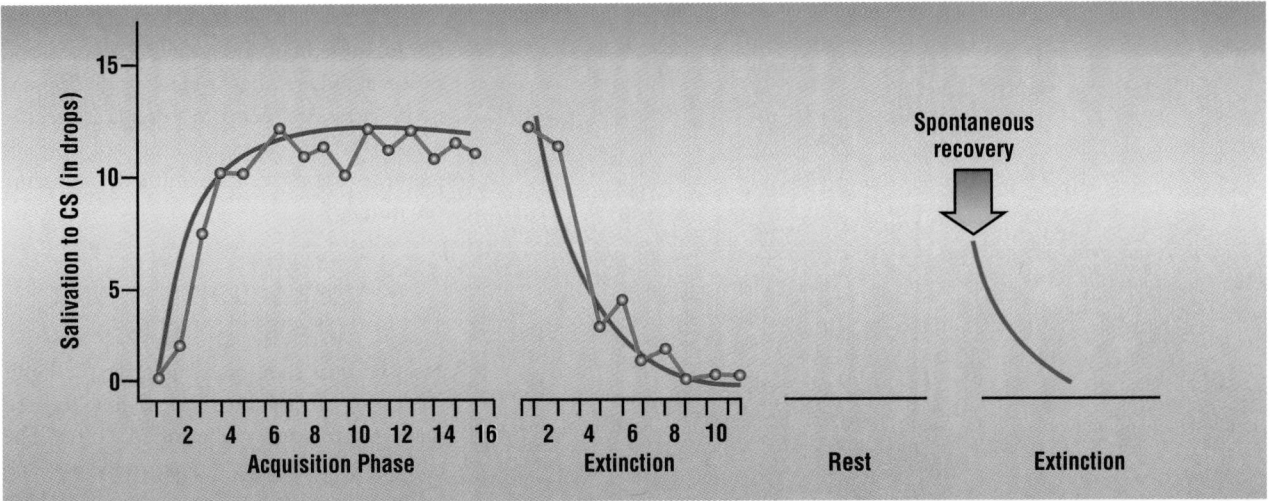

FIGURE 6.4

Learning and Extinction Curves Actual data from Pavlov (1927) compose the jagged line, and the curved lines are idealized. In the acquisition phase, a dog salivates (shows a CR) in response to a bell (CS) after only a few trials in which the bell is paired with meat powder (the US). Afterward, the CR is extinguished in about 10 trials in which the CS is not followed by the US. After a rest period, the CR recovers spontaneously. A second series of extinction trials then leads to more rapid extinction of the CR.

conditioned responses (CRs) because the CSs are no longer associated with unconditioned stimuli (USs). From the cognitive perspective, extinction teaches the organism to modify its representation of the environment because the CS no longer serves its predictive function.

In experiments in the extinction of CRs, Pavlov found that repeated presentations of the CS (or bell) without the US (meat powder) led to extinction of the CR (salivation in response to the bell). Figure 6.4 shows that a dog conditioned by Pavlov began to salivate (show a CR) in response to a bell (CS) after only a couple of pairings—referred to as **acquisition trials**—of the bell with meat powder (the US). Continued pairings of the stimuli led to increased salivation as measured in number of drops of saliva. After seven or eight trials, salivation leveled off at 11 to 12 drops.

Then, salivation to the bell (CR) was extinguished through several trials—referred to as **extinction trials**—in which the CS (bell) was presented without the meat powder (US). After about 10 extinction trials, the CR (salivation in response to the bell) was no longer shown.

What would happen if we were to allow a day or two to pass after we had extinguished the CR (salivation response to a

bell) in a laboratory dog, and then we again presented the CS (bell)? Where would you place your money? Would the dog salivate or not?

If you bet that the dog would again show the CR (salivate in response to the bell), you were correct. Organisms tend to show **spontaneous recovery** of extinguished CRs merely as a function of the passage of time. For this reason, the term *extinction* may be a bit misleading. When a species of animal becomes extinct, all members of that species capable of reproducing have died. The species vanishes permanently. But the experimental extinction of CRs does not lead to the permanent eradication of CRs. Rather, it seems that they inhibit that response. The response does remain available for future performance.

Consider Figure 6.4 again. When spontaneous recovery of the CR does occur, the strength of the response (in this case, the number of drops of saliva) is not as great as it was at the end of the series of acquisition trials. A second set of extinction trials will also extinguish the CR more rapidly than the first series of extinction trials. Although the CR is at first weaker the second time around, pairing the CS with the US once more will build response strength rapidly.

Backward conditioning • A classical-conditioning procedure in which the unconditioned stimulus is presented prior to the conditioned stimulus.

Extinction • An experimental procedure in which stimuli lose their ability to evoke learned responses because the events that had followed the stimuli no longer occur. (The learned responses are said to be *extinguished*.)

Acquisition trial • In conditioning, a presentation of stimuli such that a new response is learned and strengthened.

Extinction trial • In conditioning, a performance of a learned response in the absence of its predicted consequences so that the learned response becomes inhibited.

Spontaneous recovery • The recurrence of an extinguished response as a function of the passage of time.

Generalization at the Crossroads. Chances are that you have never seen this particular traffic light in this particular setting. Because of generalization, however, we can safely bet that you would know what to do if you were to drive up to it.

Spontaneous recovery, like extinction, is adaptive. What would happen if the child heard no car in the driveway for several months? It could be that the next time a car entered the driveway, the child would associate the sounds with a parent's homecoming (rather than the arrival of a neighbor). This expectation could be appropriate. After all, *something* had systematically changed in the neighborhood when no car had entered the nearby driveway for so long. In the wilds, a waterhole may contain water for only a couple of months during the year. But it is useful for animals to associate the waterhole with the thirst drive from time to time so that they will return to it at the appropriate time.

As time passes and the seasons change, things sometimes follow circular paths and arrive at where they were before. Spontaneous recovery seems to provide a mechanism whereby organisms are capable of rapidly adapting to intermittently recurring situations.

GENERALIZATION AND DISCRIMINATION

No two things are quite alike. Traffic lights are hung at slightly different heights, and shades of red and green differ a little. The barking of two dogs differs, and the sound of the same animal differs slightly from bark to bark. Adaptation requires that we respond similarly to stimuli that are equivalent in function and that we respond differently to stimuli that are not.

Generalization. Pavlov noted that responding to different stimuli as though they are functionally equivalent is adaptive for animals. Rustling sounds in the undergrowth differ, but rabbits and deer do well to flee when they perceive any of many varieties of rustling. Sirens differ, but people do well to become vigilant or to pull their cars to the side of the road when any siren is heard.

In a demonstration of **generalization,** Pavlov first conditioned a dog to salivate when a circle was presented. During each acquisition trial, the dog was shown a circle (CS), then given meat powder (US). After several trials, the dog exhibited the CR of salivating when presented with the circle alone. Pavlov demonstrated that the dog also exhibited the CR (salivation) in response to closed geometric figures such as ellipses, pentagons, and even squares. The more closely the figure resembled a circle, the greater the strength of the response (the more drops of saliva that flowed).

Discrimination. Organisms must also learn (1) that many stimuli perceived as being similar are functionally different and (2) to respond adaptively to each. During the first couple of months of life, babies can discriminate the voices of their mothers from those of others. They will often stop crying when they hear Mother but not when they hear a stranger's voice.

Pavlov showed that a dog conditioned to salivate in response to circles could be trained not to salivate in response to ellipses. The type of conditioning that trains an organism to show a CR in response to a narrow range of stimuli (in this case, circular rather than elliptical geometric figures) is termed **discrimination training.** Pavlov trained the dog by presenting it with circles and ellipses but associating the meat powder (US) with circles only. After a while, the dog no longer showed the CR (salivation) in response to the ellipses. Instead, the animal showed **discrimination.** It displayed the CR in response to circles only.

Pavlov then discovered that he could make the dog behave as though it were tormented by increasing the difficulty of the discrimination task. After the dog exhibited stimulus discrimination, Pavlov showed the animal progressively rounder ellipses. Eventually, the dog could no longer discriminate them from circles. The animal then put on an infantile show. It urinated, defecated, barked profusely, and snapped at laboratory personnel.

How do we explain the dog's belligerent behavior? In a classic work written half a century ago, *Frustration and Aggression,* a group of behaviorally oriented psychologists suggested that frustration induces aggression (Dollard and others, 1939). Why is failure to discriminate circles from ellipses frustrating? For one thing, in such experiments, rewards—such as meat powder—are usually made contingent on correct discrimination. That is, if the dog errs, it foregoes the meat. Cognitive theorists, however, propose that organisms are motivated to construct realistic maps of the world. In building their overall images of the world, organisms—including dogs—adjust their representations to reduce discrepancies and accommodate new information (Rescorla, 1988). In the Pavlovian experiment, the dog lost the ability to meaningfully adjust its representation of the environment as the ellipses grew more circular, and so it was frustrated.

Daily living requires appropriate generalization and discrimination. No two hotels are alike, but when traveling from one city to another, it is adaptive to expect to stay in some hotel. It is encouraging that green lights in Washington have the same meaning as green lights in Honolulu. But returning home in the evening requires the ability to discriminate between our homes or apartments and those of others. If we could not readily tell our spouses apart from those of others, we might land in divorce court.

HIGHER-ORDER CONDITIONING

In **higher-order conditioning,** a previously neutral stimulus comes to serve as a CS after being paired repeatedly with a stimulus that has already become a CS. Pavlov demonstrated higher-order conditioning by first conditioning a dog to salivate (show a CR) in response to a bell (a CS). He then paired the shining of a light repeatedly with the bell. After several pairings, shining the light (the higher-order CS) came to elicit the response (salivation) that had been elicited by the bell (the first-order CS).

Consider children who learn that their parents are about to arrive when they hear a car in the driveway. It may be the case that a certain TV cartoon show starts a few minutes before the car enters the driveway. The TV show can begin to elicit the expectation that the parents are coming by being paired repeatedly with the car's entering the driveway. In another example, a boy may burn himself by touching a hot stove. After this experience, the sight of the stove may serve as a CS for eliciting a fear response. And because hearing the word *stove* may evoke a cognitive image of the stove, hearing the word alone may also elicit a fear response.

APPLICATIONS OF CLASSICAL CONDITIONING

Classical conditioning is a major avenue of learning in our daily lives. It is how stimuli come to serve as signals for other stimuli. It is why we come to expect that someone will be waiting outside when the doorbell is rung or why we expect a certain friend to appear when we hear a characteristic knock.

The Bell-and-Pad Method for Bedwetting. By the ages of 5 or 6, children normally awaken in response to the sensations of a full bladder. They inhibit urination, which is an automatic or reflexive response to bladder tension, and go to the

Generalization • In conditioning, the tendency for a conditioned response to be evoked by stimuli that are similar to the stimulus to which the response was conditioned.

Discrimination training • Teaching an organism to show a learned response in the presence of only one of a series of similar stimuli, accomplished by alternating the stimuli but following only the one stimulus with the unconditioned stimulus.

Discrimination • In conditioning, the tendency for an organism to distinguish between a conditioned stimulus and similar stimuli that do not forecast an unconditioned stimulus.

Higher-order conditioning • According to behaviorists, a classical-conditioning procedure in which a previously neutral stimulus comes to elicit the response brought forth by a conditioned stimulus by being paired repeatedly with that *conditioned* stimulus.

MINILECTURE: BEDWETTING

Flooding • A behavioral fear-reduction technique based on principles of classical conditioning. Fear-evoking stimuli (CSs) are presented continuously in the absence of actual harm so that fear responses (CRs) are extinguished.

Systematic desensitization • A behavioral fear-reduction technique in which a hierarchy of fear-evoking stimuli is presented while the person remains relaxed.

Counterconditioning • A fear-reduction technique in which pleasant stimuli are associated with fear-evoking stimuli so that the fear-evoking stimuli lose their aversive qualities.

bathroom. But bed wetters tend not to respond to sensations of a full bladder while asleep. And so they remain asleep and frequently wet their beds.

By means of the bell-and-pad method, children are taught to wake up in response to bladder tension. They sleep on a special sheet or pad that has been placed on the bed. When the child starts to urinate, the water content of the urine causes an electrical circuit in the pad to be closed. Closing of the circuit triggers a bell or buzzer, and the child is awakened. In terms of principles of classical conditioning, the bell is a US that wakes the child (waking up is the UR). By means of repeated pairings, stimuli that precede the bell become associated with the bell and also gain the capacity to awaken the child. What stimuli are these? The sensations of a full bladder. In this way, bladder tension (the CS) gains the capacity to awaken the child *even though the child is asleep during the classical conditioning procedure.*

The bell-and-pad method provides a superb example of why behaviorists prefer to explain the effects of classical conditioning in terms of the pairing of stimuli and not in terms of what the learner knows. The behaviorist may argue that we cannot assume that a sleeping child "knows" that wetting the bed will cause the bell to ring. We can only note that by repeatedly pairing bladder tension with the bell, the child eventually *learns* to wake up in response to bladder tension alone. *Learning* is demonstrated by the change in the child's behavior. What the child *knows* about the learning process is a private matter and one on which others can only speculate.

Similar buzzer circuits have also been built into training pants as an aid to toilet training.

The Story of Little Albert: A Case Study in the Classical Conditioning of Emotional Responses.

In 1920, John B. Watson and his future wife, Rosalie Rayner, published an article describing their demonstration that emotional reactions such as fears can be acquired through principles of classical conditioning. The subject of their demonstration was a lad known in psychological literature by the name of Little Albert. Albert was a phleg-

matic fellow at the age of 11 months, not given to ready displays of emotion. But he did enjoy playing with a laboratory rat. Such are the playmates to be found in psychologists' laboratories.

Using a method that some psychologists have criticized as unethical, Watson startled Little Albert by clanging steel bars behind his head when the infant played with the rat. After seven pairings, Albert showed fear of the rat even though clanging was suspended. Albert's fear was also generalized to objects similar in appearance to the rat, such as a rabbit and the fur collar on a woman's coat. Albert's conditioned fear of rats may never have become extinguished. Extinction would have required perceiving rats (the conditioned stimuli) without painful consequences (in the absence of the unconditioned stimuli). Fear, however, might have prevented Albert from facing rats. And, as we shall see in the section on operant conditioning, avoiding rats might have been *reinforced* by reduction of fear.

Flooding and Systematic Desensitization.

Two behavior-therapy methods for reducing fears are based on the classical-conditioning principle of extinction. In one called **flooding,** the client is exposed to the fear-evoking stimulus until fear responses are extinguished (Turner and others, 1994). Albert, for example, might have been placed in close contact with a rat until his fears had become fully extinguished. In extinction, the CS (in this case, the rat) is presented repeatedly in the absence of the US (the clanging of the steel bars) until the CR (fear) is no longer evoked.

Although flooding is usually effective, it is unpleasant. (When you are fearful of rats, being placed in a small room with one is not a holiday.) For this reason, behavior therapists frequently prefer to use **systematic desensitization,** in which the client is exposed gradually to fear-evoking stimuli under circumstances in which he or she remains relaxed. For example, while feeling relaxed, Little Albert might have been given the opportunity to look at photos of rats or to see live rats from a distance before they were brought closer. Systematic desensitization is described fully in Chapter 14. Here let us note that systematic desensitization, like flooding, is highly effective. It takes longer to work than flooding, but the trade-off is that it is not as unpleasant.

Counterconditioning. Early in the century, University of California professors Harold Jones and Mary Cover Jones (Jones, 1924) reasoned that if fears could be conditioned by painful experiences, it should be possible to *countercondition* them by pleasant experiences. In **counterconditioning,** a pleasant stimulus is paired repeatedly with a fear-evoking object, in this way counteracting the fear response.

Two-year-old Peter feared rabbits intensely. The Joneses arranged for a rabbit to be gradually brought closer to Peter while he engaged in some of his favorite activities such as munching merrily away on candy and cookies. As opposed to flooding, the rabbit was not plopped in Peter's lap. Had they done so, the cookies on the plate and those already eaten might have decorated the walls. At first, they placed the rabbit in a far corner of the room while Peter munched and crunched. Peter, to be sure, cast a wary eye, but he continued to consume the treat. Gradually the animal was brought closer. Eventually, Peter ate treats and touched the rabbit at the same time. The Joneses theorized that the pleasure of eating was incompatible with fear and thus counterconditioned the fear.

Truth or Fiction Revisited. *It is true that psychologists helped a young boy overcome fear of rabbits by having him eat cookies while a rabbit was brought nearer.* It was theorized that the joy of cookies would "countercondition" fear.

Reflections

Now that you have read the section on classical conditioning, reflect on the following questions:

- Had you ever heard the expression "That rings a bell"? To what historic psychological events does the expression refer?
- How would you explain the process of classical conditioning? How do behaviorists explain it? Does your explanation differ from theirs? If so, how?
- How would you explain the difference between the psychological concept of *extinction* and the lay term *forgetting*?

Can Chocolate Chip Cookies Countercondition Fears? Yes, they taste good, but do they have the capacity to countercondition fears? At Berkeley in the 1920s, the Joneses helped a boy overcome his fear of rabbits by having him munch away as the animal was brought closer. Are contemporary behavior therapists just "keeping up with the Joneses"?

- Do you consider Watson and Rayner's experiment with "Little Albert" ethical? Why or why not?
- Can you think of examples of classical conditioning in your own life?

Through classical conditioning, we learn to associate stimuli so that a simple, usually passive, response made to one is then made in response to the other. In the case of Little Albert, clanging noises were associated with a rat, so the rat came to elicit the fear response brought forth by the noise. However, classical conditioning is only one kind of learning that occurs in these situations. According to O. Hobart Mowrer's two-factor theory of learning, classical conditioning in the study with Little Albert suffices to explain the acquisition of the fear response. But then the boy's voluntary behavior changed. He avoided the rat as a way of reducing his fear. Thus, Little Albert engaged in another kind of learning—operant conditioning.

In operant conditioning, as we see in the next section, organisms learn to engage in certain behaviors because of their effects. The sight of a hypodermic syringe, for example, may elicit a fear response because a person once had a painful injection. The subsequent avoidance of injections is *operant behavior.* It has the effect of reducing fear. In other cases, we engage in operant behavior to attain rewards, not to avoid unpleasant outcomes.

Operant Conditioning

In **operant conditioning**—also referred to as **instrumental conditioning**—an organism learns to engage in certain behavior because of the effects of that behavior. We begin this section with the historic work of psychologist Edward L. Thorndike. Then we shall examine the more recent work of B. F. Skinner.

EDWARD L. THORNDIKE AND THE LAW OF EFFECT

In the 1890s, stray cats were mysteriously disappearing from the streets and alleyways of Harlem. Many of them, it turned out, were being brought to the quarters of Columbia University doctoral student Edward Thorndike. Thorndike was using them as subjects in experiments in learning by trial and error.

Thorndike placed the cats in so-called puzzle boxes. If the animals managed to pull a dangling string, a latch would be released, allowing them to jump out and reach a bowl of food.

B. F. Skinner at the Harvard University laboratory.

When first placed in a puzzle box, a cat would try to squeeze through any opening and would claw and bite at the confining bars and wire. It would claw at any feature it could reach. Through such **random trial-and-error behavior,** it might take 3 to 4 minutes before the cat would chance on the response of pulling the string. Pulling the string would open the cage and allow the cat to reach the food. When placed back in the cage, it might again take several minutes for the animal to pull the string. But as these trials were repeated, it would take progressively less time for the cat to pull the string. After seven or eight trials, it might pull the string immediately when placed back in the box.

The Law of Effect. Thorndike explained the cat's learning to pull the string in terms of his **law of effect.** According to this law, a response (such as string pulling) is "stamped in" or strengthened in a particular situation (such as being inside a puzzle box) by a reward (escaping from the box and eating). Rewards, that is, stamp in S-R (stimulus-response) connections. Punishments, in contrast, "stamp out" stimulus-response connections. Organisms would learn *not* to engage in punished responses. Later we shall see that the effects of punishment on learning are not so certain.

B. F. SKINNER AND REINFORCEMENT

"What did you do in the war, Daddy?" is a question familiar to many who served during America's conflicts. Some stories involve heroism, others involve the unusual. When it comes to unusual war stories, few will top that of Harvard University psychologist B. F. Skinner. For, as he relates the tale in his autobiography, *The Shaping of a Behaviorist* (1979), one of Skinner's wartime efforts was "Project Pigeon."

During World War, II Skinner proposed that pigeons be trained to guide missiles to their targets. In their training, the pigeons would be **reinforced** with food pellets for pecking at targets projected onto a screen (see Figure 6.5). Once trained, the pigeons would be placed in missiles. Pecking at similar targets displayed on a screen within the missile would correct the flight path of the

---

Operant conditioning • A simple form of learning in which an organism learns to engage in behavior because it is reinforced.

Instrumental conditioning • A term similar to *operant conditioning,* reflecting the fact that the learned behavior is *instrumental* in achieving certain effects.

Random trial-and-error behavior • Behavior that occurs in a novel situation prior to the reception of rewards or reinforcements.

Law of effect • Thorndike's principle that responses are "stamped in" by rewards and "stamped out" by punishments.

Reinforce • To follow a response with a stimulus that increases the frequency of the response.

Operant behavior • Voluntary responses that are reinforced.

Operant • The same as an operant behavior.

MINILECTURE: THORNDIKE AND SKINNER

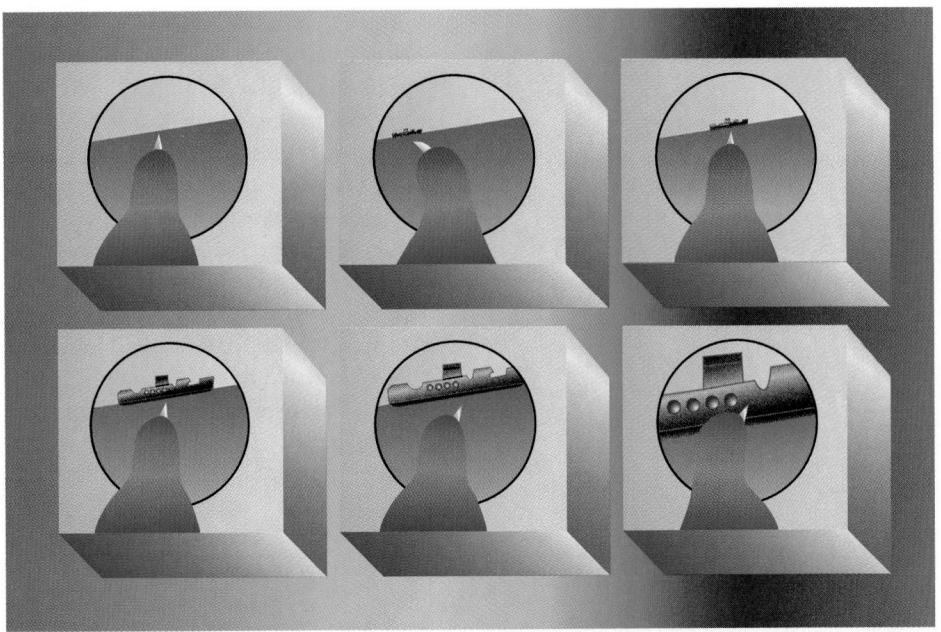

FIGURE 6.5
Project Pigeon During World War II, B. F. Skinner suggested training pigeons to guide missiles to their targets. In an operant conditioning procedure, the pigeons would be reinforced for pecking at targets projected on a screen. Afterward, in combat, pecking at the on-screen target would keep the missile on course.

missile, resulting in a "hit" and a sacrificed pigeon. However, plans for building the necessary missile—for some reason called the *Pelican* and not the *Pigeon*—were scrapped. The pigeon equipment was too bulky, and as Skinner lamented, his suggestion was not taken seriously. Apparently the Defense Department concluded that Project Pigeon was for the birds.

Truth or Fiction Revisited. *It is true that during World War II, a psychologist devised a plan for training pigeons to guide missiles to their targets.* That psychologist was B. F. Skinner, who employed principles of operant conditioning.

Project Pigeon may have been scrapped, but the principles of learning Skinner applied to the project have found wide applications in operant conditioning. In classical conditioning, an organism learns about the relationships among events. In other words, it learns to associate stimuli. As a laboratory procedure, one previously neutral stimulus (the CS) comes to elicit the response brought forth by another stimulus (the US) because they have been paired repeatedly. In operant conditioning, an organism learns

to *do* something because of its effects or consequences.

This is **operant behavior,** behavior that operates on, or manipulates, the environment. In classical conditioning, involuntary responses such as salivation or eyeblinks are often conditioned. In operant conditioning, *voluntary* responses such as pecking at a target, pressing a lever, or many of the athletic skills required in playing tennis are acquired, or conditioned.

In operant conditioning, organisms engage in operant behaviors, also known simply as **operants,** that result in presumably desirable consequences such as food, a hug, an A on a test, attention, or social approval. Some children learn to conform their behavior to social codes and rules to earn the attention and approval of their parents and teachers. Other children, ironically, may learn to "misbehave," since misbehavior also results in attention from other people. Children may especially learn to be "bad" when their "good" behavior is routinely ignored.

Units of Behavior, "Skinner Boxes," and Cumulative Recorders. In his most influential work, *The Behavior of*

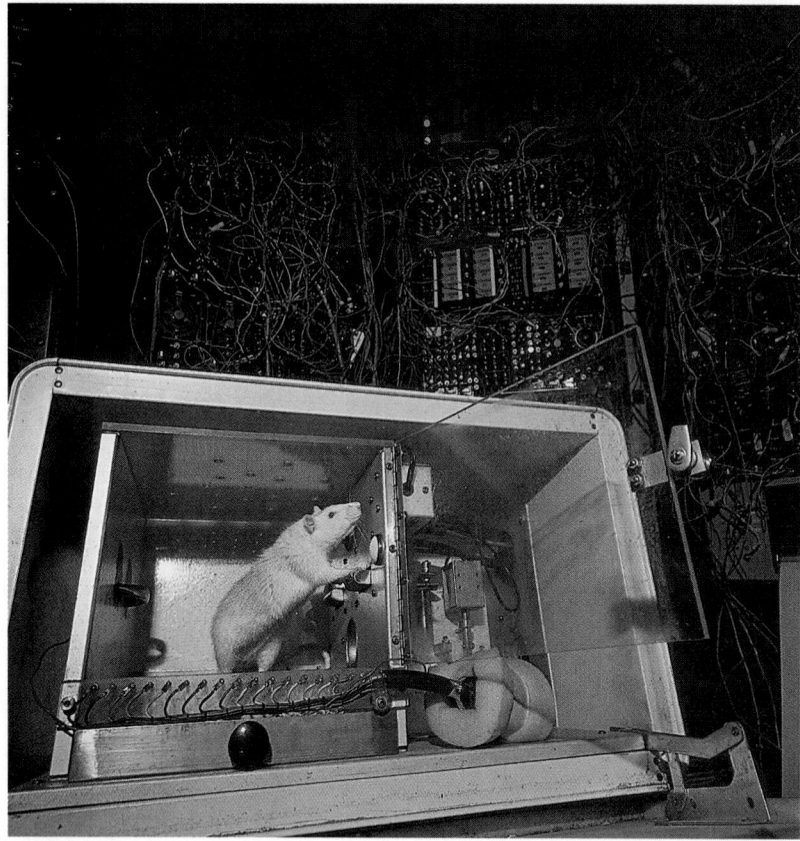

FIGURE 6.6
The Effects of Reinforcement One of the luminaries of modern psychology, an albino laboratory rat, earns its keep in a Skinner box. The animal presses a lever because of reinforcement—in the form of food pellets—delivered through the spout of the feeder. The habit strength of this operant can be measured as the frequency of lever pressing.

Organisms, Skinner (1938) made many theoretical and technological innovations. Among them was his focus on discrete behaviors such as lever pressing as the unit, or type, of behavior to be studied (Glenn and others, 1992). Whereas other psychologists might focus on how organisms think or "feel," Skinner focused on measurable things that they do. Many psychologists have found Skinner's kinds of behaviors inconsequential, especially when it comes to explaining and predicting human behavior. But Skinner's supporters point out that focusing on discrete behavior creates the potential for helpful behavior changes. For example, in helping people combat depression, one psychologist might focus on their "feelings." The Skinnerian would focus on cataloguing (and modifying) the types of

things that people who complain of depression *do.* Directly modifying depressive behavior might also brighten clients' self-reports about their "feelings of depression," of course.

To study operant behavior efficiently, Skinner also devised an animal cage (or "operant chamber") that was dubbed the *Skinner box* by psychologist Clark Hull, whose theory of drive-reductionism is discussed in Chapter 10. (Skinner himself repeatedly requested that his operant chamber *not* be called a Skinner box. History has thus far failed to honor his wishes, however.[1]) Such a box is shown in Figure 6.6. The cage is ideal for laboratory experimentation because experimental conditions (treatments) can be carefully introduced and removed, and the results on laboratory animals (defined as changes in the rate of lever pressing) can be carefully observed. The operant chamber (or Skinner box) is also energy-efficient in terms of the energy of the experimenter. In contrast to Thorndike's puzzle box, a "correct" response does not allow the animal to escape and thus have to be recaptured and placed back in the box. According to psychologist John Garcia, Skinner's "great contribution to the study of behavior was the marvelously efficient operant methodology" (1993, p. 1158).

The rat in Figure 6.6 was deprived of food and placed in a Skinner box with a lever at one end. At first it sniffed its way around the cage and engaged in random behavior. When organisms are behaving in a random manner, responses that meet with favorable consequences tend to occur more frequently. Responses that do not meet with favorable consequences tend to be performed less frequently.

The rat's first pressing of the lever was inadvertent. However, because of this action, a food pellet dropped into the cage. The food pellet increased the probability that the rat would press the lever again. The pellet is thus said to have served as a reinforcement for the lever pressing.

Skinner further mechanized his laboratory procedure by making use of a turning drum, or **cumulative recorder,** that had

---

[1] Of course, my using the term *Skinner box* does not exactly help Skinner's cause, either.

previously been used by physiologists. (See Figure 6.7.) The cumulative recorder provides a precise measure of operant behavior. The experimenter need not even be present to record correct responses. In the example used, the lever in the Skinner box is connected to the recorder so that the recording pen moves upward with each correct response. The paper moves continuously to the left at a slow but regular pace. In the sample record shown in Figure 6.7, lever pressings (which record correct responses) were at first few and far between. But after several reinforced responses, lever pressing came fast and furious. When the rat is no longer hungry, the lever pressing will drop off and then stop.

The First "Correct" Response. In operant conditioning, it matters little how the first response that is reinforced comes to be made. The organism can happen on it by chance, as in random learning. The organism can also be physically guided into the response. You may command your dog to "Sit!" and then press its backside down until it is in a sitting position. Finally, you reinforce sitting with food or a pat on the head and a kind word.

Animal trainers use physical guiding or coaxing to bring about the first "correct" response. Can you imagine how long it would take to train your dog if you waited for it to sit or roll over and then seized the opportunity to command it to sit or roll over? You would both age significantly in the process.

People, of course, can be verbally guided into desired responses when they are learning tasks such as running a machine, spelling, or adding numbers. But they then need to be informed when they have made the correct response. Knowledge of results is often all the reinforcement that motivated people need to learn new skills.

TYPES OF REINFORCERS

Any stimulus that increases the probability that responses preceding it will be repeated serves as a reinforcer. Reinforcers include food pellets when an organism has been deprived of food, water when it has been deprived of liquid, the opportunity to mate, and the sound of a bell that has been previously associated with eating.

Positive and Negative Reinforcers. Skinner distinguished between positive and negative reinforcers. **Positive reinforcers** increase the probability that an operant will occur when they are applied. Food and approval usually serve as positive reinforcers. **Negative reinforcers** increase the probability that an operant will occur when they are *removed* (see Figure 6.8). People often

Cumulative recorder • An instrument that records the frequency of an organism's operants (or "correct" responses) as a function of the passage of time.
Positive reinforcer • A reinforcer that when *presented* increases the frequency of an operant.
Negative reinforcer • A reinforcer that when *removed* increases the frequency of an operant.

FIGURE 6.7
The Cumulative Recorder In the cumulative recorder, paper moves continuously to the left while a pen automatically records each targeted response by moving upward. When the pen reaches the top of the paper, it is automatically reset to the bottom.

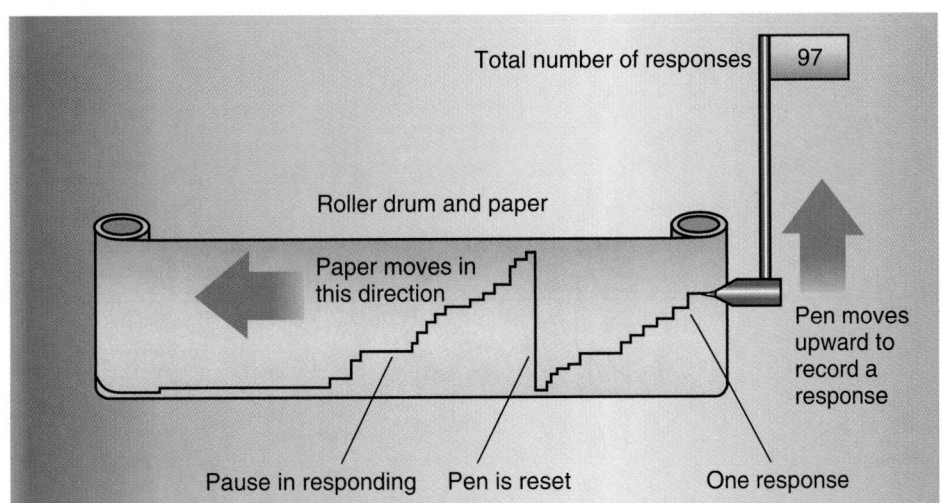

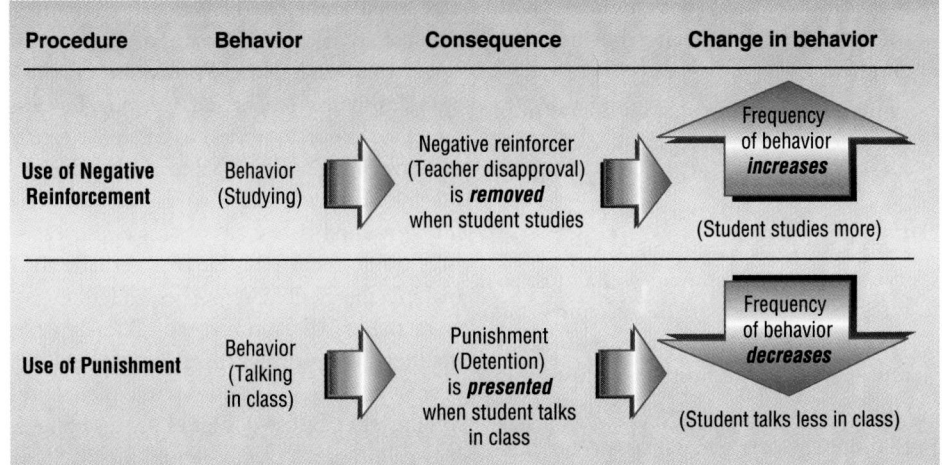

Procedure	Behavior	Consequence	Change in behavior
Use of Negative Reinforcement	Behavior (Studying)	Negative reinforcer (Teacher disapproval) is **removed** when student studies	Frequency of behavior **increases** (Student studies more)
Use of Punishment	Behavior (Talking in class)	Punishment (Detention) is **presented** when student talks in class	Frequency of behavior **decreases** (Student talks less in class)

FIGURE 6.9

Negative Reinforcers versus Punishments Negative reinforcers and punishments both tend to be aversive stimuli. However, reinforcers increase the frequency of behavior, whereas punishments decrease the frequency of behavior. Negative reinforcers increase the frequency of behavior when they are removed. Punishments decrease or suppress the frequency of behavior when they are applied. Can you think of situations in which punishing students might have effects other than those desired by the teacher?

without reinforcement. After a number of trials, the operant behavior is no longer shown.

When some time is allowed to pass after the extinction process, an organism will usually perform the operant again when placed in a situation in which the operant had been reinforced previously. Spontaneous recovery of learned responses occurs in operant conditioning as well as in classical conditioning. If the operant is reinforced at this time, it quickly regains its former strength. Spontaneous recovery of extinguished operants suggests that they are inhibited or suppressed by the extinction process and not lost permanently.

REINFORCERS VERSUS REWARDS AND PUNISHMENTS

Rewards, like reinforcers, are stimuli that increase the frequency of behavior. But rewards are also considered pleasant events. Skinner preferred the concept of reinforcement to that of reward because reinforcement does not suggest trying to "get inside the head" of an organism (person or lower animal) to guess what it would find pleasant or unpleasant. A list of reinforcers is arrived at **empirically,** by observing what sorts of stimuli will increase the frequency of the behavior. However, it should be noted that some psychologists consider the term *reward* synonymous with positive reinforcement.

Punishments are aversive events that suppress or decrease the frequency of the behavior they follow (see Figure 6.9).[2] Punishment can rapidly suppress undesirable behavior and may be warranted in "emergencies" such as when a child tries to run out into the street.

Despite the fact that punishment works, many learning theorists agree that punishment is usually undesirable, especially in rearing children, for reasons such as the following:

1. Punishment does not in itself suggest an alternative acceptable form of behavior.

2. Punishment tends to suppress undesirable behavior only under circumstances in which its delivery is guaranteed. It does not take children long to learn that

---

[2] Recall that *negative reinforcers* are defined in terms of *increasing* the frequency of behavior, although the increase occurs when the negative reinforcer is *removed.* A punishment *decreases* the frequency of a behavior when it is *applied.*

they can "get away with murder" with one parent, or one teacher, but not with another.

3. Punished organisms may withdraw from the situation. Severely punished children may run away, cut class, or drop out of school.

4. Punishment can create anger and hostility. Adequate punishment will almost always suppress unwanted behavior—but at what cost? A child may express accumulated feelings of hostility against other children.

5. Punishment may generalize too far. The child who is punished severely for bad table manners may stop eating altogether. Overgeneralization is more likely to occur when children do not know exactly why they are being punished and when they have not been shown alternative acceptable behaviors.

6. Punishment may be modeled as a way of solving problems or coping with stress. We shall see that one way that children learn is by observing others. Even though children may not immediately perform the behavior they observe, they may perform it later on, even as adults, when their circumstances are similar to those of the **model.**

7. Finally, children learn responses that are punished. Whether or not children choose to perform punished responses, punishment draws their attention to them.

It is usually preferable to focus on rewarding children for desirable behavior than on punishing them for unwanted behavior. By ignoring their misbehavior, or by using **time out** from positive reinforcement, we can consistently avoid reinforcing children for misbehavior.

Truth or Fiction Revisited. *Actually, punishment does work.* Strong punishment generally suppresses the behavior it follows. The issues pertaining to punishment concern its limitations and its side effects.

To reward or positively reinforce children for desired behavior takes time and care. Simply never using punishment is not enough. First, we must pay attention to children when they are behaving well. If we

take their desirable behavior for granted, and act as if we are aware of them only when they misbehave, we may be encouraging misbehavior. Second, we must be certain that children are aware of, and capable of performing, desired behavior. It is harmful and fruitless merely to punish children for unwanted behavior. We must also carefully guide them physically or verbally into making the desired responses and then reward them. We cannot teach children table manners by waiting for them to exhibit proper responses at random and then reinforcing them. If we waited by holding a half-gallon of ice cream behind our backs as a reward, we would have slippery dining room floors long before we had children with table manners.

DISCRIMINATIVE STIMULI

B. F. Skinner might not have been able to get his pigeons into the drivers' seats of missiles during the war, but he had no problem training them to respond to traffic lights. Try the following experiment for yourself.

Find a pigeon. Or sit on a park bench, close your eyes, and one will find you. Place it in a Skinner box with a button on the wall. Drop a food pellet into the cage whenever the pigeon pecks the button. (Soon it will learn to peck the button whenever it has not eaten for a while.) Now place a small green light in the cage. Turn it on and off intermittently throughout the day. Reinforce button pecking with food whenever the green light is on but not when the light is off. It will not take long for this clever city pigeon to learn that it will gain as much by grooming itself or squawking and flapping around as it will by pecking the button when the light is off.

The green light will have become a **discriminative stimulus.** Discriminative stimuli act as cues. They provide information about when an operant (in this case, pecking a button) will be reinforced (in this case, by a food pellet being dropped into the cage).

Operants that are not reinforced tend to become extinguished. For the pigeon in our experiment, pecking the button *when the light is off* becomes extinguished.

A Discriminative Stimulus. You might not think that pigeons are very discriminating, yet this gift to city life readily learns that pecking will not bring food in the presence of a discriminative stimulus such as a red light.

A moment's reflection will suggest many ways in which discriminative stimuli influence our behavior. Would you rather ask your boss for a raise when she is smiling or when she is frowning? Wouldn't you rather answer the telephone when it is ringing? Do you think it is wise to try to get smoochy when your date is blowing smoke in your face or chugalugging a bottle of antacid tablets? One of the factors involved in gaining social skills is learning to interpret social discriminative stimuli (smiles, tones of voice, body language) accurately.

SCHEDULES OF REINFORCEMENT

In operant conditioning, some responses are maintained by **continuous reinforcement.** You probably become warmer every time you put on heavy clothing. You probably become less thirsty every time you drink water. Yet, if you have ever watched people throwing money down the maws of slot machines, or "one-armed bandits," you know that behavior can also be maintained by **partial reinforcement.**

Some folklore about gambling is based on solid learning theory. You can get a person "hooked" on gambling by fixing the game to allow heavy winnings at first. Then you gradually space out the gambling behaviors that are reinforced until the gambling is maintained by infrequent winning—or even no winning at all. Partial reinforcement schedules can maintain behavior for a great deal of time, even though it goes unreinforced. Consider a critical-thinking question: Can you describe how behaviorists and cognitive psychologists might each explain the effects of a partial-reinforcement schedule on gamblers?

New operants or behaviors are acquired most rapidly through continuous reinforcement or, in some cases, through "one-trial learning" that meets with great reinforcement. So-called **pathological gamblers** often had big wins at the racetrack or casino or in the lottery in their late teens or early 20s (Greene, 1982). But once the operant has been acquired, it can be maintained by tapering off to a schedule of partial reinforcement.

There are four basic schedules of reinforcement. They are determined by changing either the *interval* of time that must elapse between correct responses before reinforcement is made available or the *ratio* of correct responses to reinforcements. If the interval that must elapse between correct responses, before reinforcement becomes available, is zero seconds, the reinforcement schedule is continuous. A larger interval of time, such as 1 or 30 seconds, is a partial-reinforcement schedule. A one-to-one (1 : 1) ratio of correct responses to reinforcements is a continuous-reinforcement schedule. A higher ratio such as 2 : 1 or 5 : 1 would be a partial-reinforcement schedule.

The four basic types of schedules of reinforcement are *fixed-interval, variable-interval, fixed-ratio,* and *variable-ratio* schedules.

In a **fixed-interval schedule,** a fixed amount of time—say, one minute—must elapse between the previous and subsequent times that reinforcement is made available for correct responses. In a **variable-interval schedule,** varying amounts of time are allowed to elapse between making reinforcement available. In a 3-minute variable-interval schedule, the mean amount of time that would elapse between reinforcement opportunities would be 3 minutes. Each interval might vary, however, from 1 to 5 minutes.

With a fixed-interval schedule, an organism's response rate falls off after each reinforcement, then picks up as it nears the time when reinforcement will be dispensed. For example, in a 1-minute fixed-interval schedule, a rat will be reinforced with, say, a food pellet for the first operant—for example, the first pressing of a lever—that occurs after a minute has elapsed. After each reinforcement, the rat's rate of lever pressing slows down, but as the end of the 1-minute interval draws near, lever pressing increases in frequency, as suggested by Figure 6.10. It is as if the rat has learned that it must wait a while before reinforcement will be made available. The resultant record on the cumulative recorder (Figure 6.10) shows a series of characteristic upward-moving waves, or scallops, which is referred to as a *fixed-interval scallop.*

Car sales executives are employing a fixed-interval reinforcement schedule when they offer incentives for buying up the remainder of the year's line every summer and fall. In a sense, they are suppressing

MINILECTURE: MEASURING SCHEDULES OF REINFORCEMENT

Model • An organism that engages in a response that is then imitated by another organism.

Time out • Removal of an organism from a situation in which reinforcement is available when unwanted behavior is shown.

Discriminative stimulus • In operant conditioning, a stimulus that indicates that reinforcement is available.

Continuous reinforcement • A schedule of reinforcement in which every correct response is reinforced.

Partial reinforcement • One of several reinforcement schedules in which not every correct response is reinforced.

Pathological gambler • A person who gambles habitually despite consistent losses.

Fixed-interval schedule • A schedule in which a fixed amount of time must elapse between the previous and subsequent times that reinforcement is available.

Variable-interval schedule • A schedule in which a variable amount of time must elapse between the previous and subsequent times that reinforcement is available.

FIGURE 6.10
The "Fixed–Interval Scallop"
Organisms that are reinforced on a fixed-interval schedule tend to slack off in responding after each reinforcement. The rate of response then picks up as they near the time when reinforcement will again become available. The results on the cumulative recorder look like an upward-moving series of waves, or scallops.

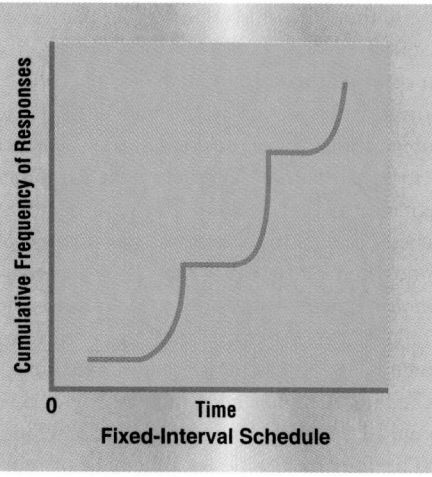

Fixed-ratio schedule • A schedule in which reinforcement is provided after a fixed number of correct responses.

Variable-ratio schedule • A schedule in which reinforcement is provided after a variable number of correct responses.

Shaping • A procedure for teaching complex behaviors that at first reinforces approximations of the target behavior.

Successive approximations • Behaviors that are progressively closer to a target behavior.

Socialization • Guidance of people into socially desirable behavior by means of verbal messages, the systematic use of rewards and punishments, and other methods of teaching.

buying at other times, except for those consumers whose current cars are in their death throes or those who cannot exercise self-control.

In the case of the more unpredictable variable-interval schedule, the response rate is steadier but lower. If the boss calls us in for a weekly report, we will probably work hard to pull the pieces together just before the report is to be given, just as we might cram the night before a weekly quiz. But if we know that the boss might call us in for a report on the progress of a project at any time (variable-interval schedule), we are likely to keep things in a state of reasonable readiness at all times. However, our efforts are unlikely to have the intensity they would in a fixed-interval (for example, weekly) schedule. Similarly, we are less likely to cram for a series of unpredictable "pop quizzes" than for regularly scheduled quizzes. But we are likely to do at least some studying on a regular basis.

In a **fixed-ratio schedule,** reinforcement is provided after a fixed number of correct responses has been made. In a **variable-ratio schedule,** reinforcement is provided after a variable number of correct responses has been made. In a 10 : 1 variable-ratio schedule, the mean number of correct responses that would have to be made before a subsequent correct response would be reinforced is 10, but the ratio of correct responses to reinforcements might be allowed to vary from, say, 1 : 1 to 20 : 1 on a random basis.

Fixed-ratio and variable-ratio schedules maintain a high response rate. With a fixed-ratio schedule, it is as if the organism learns

that it must make several responses before being reinforced. It then "gets them out of the way" as rapidly as possible. Consider the example of piecework. If a worker must sew five shirts to receive $10, he or she is on a fixed-ratio (5 : 1) schedule and is likely to sew at a uniformly high rate, although there might be a brief pause following each reinforcement. With a variable-ratio schedule, reinforcement can come at any time. This unpredictability also maintains a high response rate. Slot machines tend to pay off on variable-ratio schedules, and players can be seen popping coins into their maws and pulling their "arms" with barely a pause. I have seen players who do not even stop to pick up their winnings. Instead, they continue to smoothly pop in the coins, whether from their original stack or from the winnings tray.

Shaping. If you are teaching break dancing to people who have never danced, do not wait until they have performed a perfect moon walk before telling them they're on the right track. The foxtrot will be back in style before they have learned a thing.

We can teach complex behaviors by **shaping,** or at first reinforcing small steps toward the behavioral goals. In the beginning it may be wise to smile and say "Good" when a reluctant newcomer gathers the courage to get out on the dance floor, even if your feet get flattened by his initial clumsiness. If you are teaching someone to drive a car with a standard shift, at first generously reinforce the learner simply for shifting without stalling.

But as training proceeds, we come to expect more before dispensing reinforcement. We reinforce **successive approximations** of the goal. If you want to train a rat to climb a ladder, first reinforce it (with a food pellet) when it turns toward the ladder. Then wait until it approaches the ladder before using reinforcement. Then do not drop a food pellet into the cage until the rat touches the ladder. In this way, the rat will reach the top of the ladder more quickly than if you had waited until the target behavior had first occurred at random.

Truth or Fiction Revisited. *It is true that rats can be trained to climb a ramp, cross a bridge, climb a ladder, pedal a toy car, and do* *several other tasks—all in proper sequence.* The operant-conditioning procedure used to do so is called *shaping*.

Learning to drive a new standard-shift automobile to a new job also involves a complex sequence of operant behaviors. At first, we actively seek out all the discriminative stimuli or landmarks that cue us when to turn—signs, buildings, hills, and valleys. We also focus on shifting to a lower gear as we slow down so that the car won't stall. After many repetitions, though, these responses, these chains of behavior, become "habitual" and we need to pay very little attention to them.

Have you ever driven home from school or work and been suddenly unsettled as you got out of your car because you couldn't recall exactly how you had returned home? Your entire trip may seem "lost." Were you in great danger? How could you allow such a thing to happen? Actually, it may be that your responses to the demands of the route and to driving your car had become so habitual that you did not have to focus much awareness on them. You were able to think about dinner, a problem at work, or the weekend as you drove. But if something unusual such as hesitation in your engine or a severe rainstorm had occurred on the way, you would have deployed as much attention as was needed to arrive home. Your trip was probably quite safe, after all.

APPLICATIONS OF OPERANT CONDITIONING

Habit is the enormous flywheel of society.

Could the young but realize how soon they will become mere walking bundles of habit, they would give more heed to their conduct while in the plastic state.

WILLIAM JAMES

Operant conditioning, like classical conditioning, is not just an exotic laboratory procedure. We use operant conditioning every day in our efforts to influence other people. Parents and peers incline children to acquire "gender-appropriate" behavior patterns through the elaborate use of rewards and punishments (see Chapter 12). Parents also tend to praise their children for sharing with others and to punish them for being too aggressive. Peers participate in the **so-cialization** process by playing with children who are generous and nonaggressive and, often, by avoiding those who are not (Etaugh & Rathus, 1995).

Operant conditioning may also play a role in attitude formation (see Chapter 16). Parents tend to reward their children for expressing attitudes that coincide with their own and to punish or ignore them for expressing attitudes that deviate.

Let us now consider some specific applications of operant conditioning.

Biofeedback Training. Biofeedback training (BFT) is based on principles of operant conditioning. Through BFT, people and lower animals have learned to control autonomic responses to attain reinforcement. BFT has been an important innovation in the treatment of health-related problems during the past few decades.

Organisms can gain control of other autonomic functions such as blood pressure. They also can learn to improve their control over functions such as muscle tension that are within the grasp of voluntary manipulation. When people receive BFT, reinforcement is in the form of *information*. Perhaps a "bleep" sound changes in pitch or frequency of occurrence to signal that they have modified the autonomic function in the desired direction. People, for example,

Taking the Pledge. Operant conditioning appears to play a role in the socialization of children. Parents and teachers tend to reward children for expressing attitudes that coincide with their own and to punish or ignore them when they express deviant attitudes.

can learn to emit alpha waves (and feel somewhat more relaxed) through feedback from an electroencephalograph. Through the use of other instruments, people have learned to lower muscle tension, their heart rates, even their blood pressure.

BFT is also used with people who have had accidents who have lost neuromuscular control of parts of the body. A "bleep" informs them when they have contracted a muscle or sent an impulse down a neural pathway. By concentrating on changing the bleeps, these people also gradually regain voluntary control over the damaged function.

Token Economies. Behavior therapists apply operant conditioning in a mental hospital to foster desired responses such as social skills and to extinguish unwanted behaviors such as social withdrawal. Several techniques such as the use of the **token economy** are outlined in Chapter 14. In token economies, psychologists give hospital residents or prison inmates tokens such as poker chips for desired behavior. The tokens reinforce desired behavior because they can be exchanged for television time, desserts, and other desired commodities.

Principles of operant conditioning have also permitted psychologists and educators to develop many beneficial innovations such as interventions with young children, behavior modification in the classroom, and programmed learning.

Using Avoidance Learning to Save a Baby's Life. Operant conditioning techniques are sometimes used with children who are too young or distressed to respond to verbal forms of therapy. In one example, reported by Lang and Melamed (1969), a 9-month-old infant vomited regularly within 10 to 15 minutes after eating. Diagnostic workups found no medical basis for the problem, and medical treatments were to no avail. When the case was brought to the attention of Lang and Melamed, the infant weighed only 9 pounds and was in critical condition, being fed by a pump.

The psychologists monitored the infant for the first physical indications (local muscle tension) that vomiting was to occur. When the child tensed prior to vomiting, a tone was sounded and followed by painful but (presumably) harmless electric shock. After two 1-hour treatment sessions, the infant's muscle tensions ceased in response to the tone alone, and vomiting soon ceased altogether. At a 1-year follow-up, the infant was still not vomiting and had caught up in weight.

Truth or Fiction Revisited. *It is true that psychologists successfully fashioned a method to teach an emaciated 9-month-old infant to stop throwing up.* They derived the method from principles of conditioning. Conditioning allowed the psychologists to focus on what the child *did* and not on what the child knew or understood.

How do we explain this remarkable procedure through principles of conditioning? It appears to be an example of two-factor learning, as theorized by Mowrer (1947). The first factor was classical conditioning. Through repeated pairings, the tone (CS) came to elicit expectation of electric shock (US), so the psychologists could use the painful shock sparingly.

The second factor was operant conditioning. The electric shock and, after classical conditioning, the tone were aversive stimuli. The infant soon learned to suppress the behaviors (muscle tensions) that were followed with aversive stimulation. By so doing, the aversive stimuli were removed. And so, the aversive stimuli served as negative reinforcers.

This learning occurred at an age long before any sort of verbal intervention could have been understood, and it apparently saved the infant's life. Similar procedures have been used to teach very young autistic children to avoid mutilating and otherwise injuring themselves.

Classroom Discipline. Remember that reinforcers are defined as stimuli that increase the frequency of behavior—not as pleasant events. Ironically, adults frequently reinforce undesirable behavior in children by attending to them, or punishing them, when they misbehave but by ignoring them when they behave in desirable ways. Similarly, teachers who raise their voices when children misbehave may be unintentionally conferring hero status on their pupils in the eyes of their peers (Wentzel, 1994). Some

Token economy • An environmental setting that fosters desired behavior by reinforcing it with tokens (secondary reinforcers) that can be exchanged for other reinforcers.

Programmed learning • A method of learning in which complex tasks are broken down into simple steps, each of which is reinforced. Errors are not reinforced.

MINILECTURE: TREATING MALADAPTIVE VOMITING

children may go out of their way to earn teacher disapproval, frequently to the teacher's surprise.

Teacher-preparation programs and in-service programs now usually show teachers how to use behavior modification in the classroom to reverse these response patterns. Teachers are taught to pay attention to children when they are behaving appropriately and, when possible, to ignore (avoid reinforcing) their misbehavior (Abramowitz & O'Leary, 1991). The younger the schoolchild, the more powerful teacher attention and approval seem to be.

Among older children and adolescents, peer approval is often a more powerful reinforcer than teacher approval. Peer approval may maintain misbehavior, and ignoring misbehavior may only allow peers to become more disruptive. In such cases, it may be necessary to separate troublesome children.

Teachers also frequently use time out from positive reinforcement to discourage misbehavior. In this method, children are placed in drab, restrictive environments for a specified time period, usually about 10 minutes, when they behave disruptively. When isolated, they cannot earn the attention of peers or teachers, and no reinforcing activities are present.

Programmed Learning. B. F. Skinner developed an educational practice called **programmed learning** that is based on operant conditioning. Programmed learning assumes that any complex task involving conceptual learning as well as motor skills can be broken down into a number of small steps. These steps can be shaped individually and combined in sequence to form the correct behavioral chain.

Programmed learning does not punish errors. Instead, correct responses are reinforced. All children earn "100," but at their own pace. Programmed learning also assumes that it is the task of the teacher (or program) to structure the learning experience in such a way that errors will not be made.

Truth or Fiction Revisited. *It is not true that we must make mistakes if we are to learn.* The idea that we must make mistakes derives from folklore to the effect that we

Praise. Teacher praise reinforces desirable behavior in most children. Behavior modification in the classroom applies principles of operant conditioning.

learn from (bad) experience. However, we also learn from good (positively reinforced) experiences and from the experiences of others.

Reflections

Now that you have read the section on operant conditioning, reflect on the following questions:

- What kinds of effects have rewards and punishments had on your behavior over the years? Do you now work for rewards or to avert punishments? What kinds of rewards and punishments influence your behavior? Are the rewards and punishments that influence you less influential on other people? How so?
- Pianists' fingers fly over the keys faster than they can read notes or even think notes. What kinds of learning are at work in learning to play the piano or in learning to perfectly execute a piece with rapid notes?
- What role does habit play in your life? Do you have both "good habits" and "bad habits"? What are they? How did they develop?
- Do you learn from your mistakes? Why or why not? Provide some examples.
- Agree or disagree with the following statement and support your answer: "Apparently complex human behavior can be explained as the summation of so many instances of conditioning."

PSYCHOLOGY IN THE NEW MILLENNIUM

Learning at the Feet of the . . . Information Superhighway?

What mental images are conjured up when you reflect on learning? Do you picture children reading and writing in neat rows of school desks while a benevolent teacher looks on? Do you envision an adult in an apprenticeship in a factory or an operating room? Do you fancy a dynamic teacher dramatizing an obscure point in mathematics or physics? Do you imagine a solitary student studying at her or his desk in the wee hours of the morning? Or do you create a classical image of students sitting at the feet of a robed philosopher in ancient Greece?

Perhaps in the new millennium some of the robed philosophers will be electronic. Experiments are already under way on an innovation termed the *Virtual Classroom* (Hiltz, 1993). Although there will continue to be a need for charming, erudite human professors to guide your learning in the new millennium,[3] some of your learning may be at the "feet" of the information superhighway.

The *what?* In brief, the information superhighway is a much-ballyhooed innovation that will be a part of our daily lives in the new millennium. It will employ powerful computers (file servers) that provide multimedia programs on demand. (Today, you can play TV or radio programs only when they are broadcast to the public at large.). It will employ fiber-optic cables that can carry a vast array of information and may be installed by your local phone company. The cable, like today's coaxial cable, will likely be connected to a Smart Box that sits atop your TV set like the cable decoders of today. Your TV set will also be part of the system. Unlike today's TV fare, however, the information superhighway will be interactive. That means that our TV sets will become two-way streets. We may compete for prizes with *Jeopardy!* players in the studio (Sims, 1993). Rather than visit the video store, file servers will allow us to order movies on demand through our TV sets—whenever it is convenient for us to watch them. Smart Boxes will also provide another way for us to interact with file servers (and other people) to get the programming we want, to work together with people thousands of miles away on our computer files, and to check out and order specialty merchandise from boutiques across the country.

So what about learning? You will still use a printed textbook like the one in your hands (Proulx, 1994). After all, what device can be more user friendly than one that allows you to search "files" of information by flipping the pages?[4] But perhaps your textbook will have been planned to relate to multimedia programs that are being continuously updated. At this moment, you are reading a feature on learning and the information superhighway. In the next millennium, there may be a code number printed next to this sort of feature. When you read that number aloud—or punch it in—to your Smart Box, your TV set may play the latest version of a multimedia program about the information superhighway. If the feature is about the effects of media violence (like the "Psychology and Modern Life" feature at the end of this chapter), reading or punching in the number next to the feature may provide you with the latest research on media violence.

Or perhaps while reading this chapter on learning, you find it difficult to discriminate between concepts such as *reinforcements* and *rewards,* or between *negative reinforcements* and *punishments.* Each of these is a glossary item in the textbook. Perhaps in the next millennium there will be a number or code next to each glossary item. When you read or punch in the code to the Smart Box, you receive an interactive multimedia program that explains the fine points of the glossary item and related terms. Now what if you come

---

[3] Did I escape that trap?

[4] Your author certainly would not want the reader to think that he is in any way prejudiced in favor of printed textbooks. After all, he has no personal stake in their continued popularity.

Learning at the Feet of the . . . Information Superhighway? Learning in the new millennium is likely to involve the information superhighway. The information superhighway will employ powerful computers to provide multimedia programs on demand. Fiber-optic cables that carry a vast array of information may be connected to a Smart Box that sits atop your TV set like the cable decoders of today. The information superhighway will also be interactive, however. That means that our TV sets will become two-way streets.

across a difficult word that is not in the glossary? Simple. You face your Smart Box and say "Define *multimedia.*" Because you used the key word *define,* the dictionary function of a file server a thousand miles away immediately responds: "Multimedia means a combination of media, such as films, tape recordings, slides, and special lighting effects that are usually used for education or for entertainment. Do you wish me to elaborate?" You respond "yes" or "no," of course.

Or what if you have summoned up the canned program on negative reinforcement and you still have questions? Simple. You read two codes into your Smart Box. The first code defines the topic and the second code requests an interaction (video conference) with a living, breathing expert on the topic. A computer connects you to the first available tutor provided by your textbook company or a college consortium learning center (CCLC).

Want to find out how well you're doing in a subject? Easy. Inform your Smart Box of the self-test codes connected with the subject matter in your textbook. Your TV set will present you with options for multiple choice tests, essay tests, verbal tests, and so forth. Your strengths and weaknesses will be immediately analyzed, and multimedia programs for enhancing your knowledge and skills in weak areas will be offered. Your college may even subscribe to one of the many tutoring and grading services that will be available to help you learn and evaluate your performance.

Now who will pay for all this? Perhaps your textbook company will defray some of the cost. (Don't tell Harcourt Brace College Publishers about my suggestion. They may accuse me of giving away the store.) Perhaps your college's learning center will make a contribution. Or perhaps the charges will simply appear on your phone bill. Or your parents' phone bill. (Whoops! Make that your Interactive Multimedia Bill—that is, your IMB, not your IBM.)

There are some dangers to all this, of course. One is that your curiosity may draw you along avenues of information and you may find yourself learning for the sake of learning. What a tragedy. Another is that the information superhighway may also make it possible for you to play bridge with partners across the country and to access personality tests that will automatically connect you with compatible dates within your area code (or around the world). But then, students have always been tempted by distractions.

Cognitive Factors in Learning

Classical and operant conditioning were originally conceived as relatively simple forms of learning. Much of conditioning's appeal has been that it can be said to meet the behaviorist objective of explaining behavior in terms of public, observable events—in this case, laboratory conditions. Building on this theoretical base, some psychologists have suggested that the most complex human behavior involves the summation of so many instances of conditioning. However, many psychologists believe that the conditioning model is too mechanical to explain all instances of learned behavior, even in laboratory rats (Glover and others, 1990; Hayes, 1989; Weiner, 1991). They turn to cognitive factors to describe and explain additional findings in the psychology of learning.

In addition to concepts such as *association* and *reinforcement,* cognitive psychologists use concepts such as *mental structures, schemas, templates,* and *information processing.* Cognitive psychologists see people as searching for information, weighing evidence, and making decisions. Let us consider some classic research in learning that points to cognitive factors in learning, as opposed to mechanical associationism. These cognitive factors are not necessarily limited to humans, although people, of course, are the only species that can talk about them.

CONTINGENCY THEORY: CONTIGUITY OR CONTINGENCY? WHAT "REALLY" HAPPENS DURING CLASSICAL CONDITIONING?

Behaviorists and cognitive psychologists interpret the events of the conditioning process in different ways. Behaviorists explain the outcomes of classical conditioning in terms of the contiguous presentation of stimuli. Cognitive psychologists explain classical conditioning in terms of the ways in which stimuli provide information that allows organisms to form and revise mental representations of their environments.

In classical-conditioning experiments with dogs, Robert Rescorla (1967) obtained some results that are difficult to explain without reference to cognitive concepts. Each phase of his work paired a tone (CS) with electric shock (US) but in different ways. With one group of animals, the shock was presented consistently after the tone. That is, the US followed on the heels of the CS as in Pavlov's studies. The dogs in this group learned to show a fear response when the tone was presented.

A second group of dogs heard an equal number of tones and received an equal number of electric shocks, but the shock never immediately followed the tone. In other words, the tone and shock were unpaired. Now, from the behavioral perspective, the dogs should not have learned to associate the tone and the shock, since one did not presage the other. Actually, the dogs learned quite a lot: They learned that they had nothing to fear when the tone was sounded! The dogs showed vigilance and fear when the laboratory was quiet—for apparently the shock could come at any time—but they were calm in the presence of the tone.

The third group of dogs also received equal numbers of tones and shocks, but these were presented at purely random intervals. Occasionally they were paired, but most often they were not. According to Rescorla, behaviorists might argue that intermittent pairing of the tones and shocks should have brought about some learning. Yet it did not. The animals showed no fear in response to the tone. Rescorla suggests that the animals in this group learned nothing because the tones provided no information about the prospect of being shocked.

Rescorla concluded that contiguity—that is, the co-appearance of two events (the US and the CS)—cannot in itself explain classical conditioning. Instead, learning occurs only when the conditioned stimulus (in this case, the tone) provides information about the unconditioned stimulus (in this case, the shock). According to so-called **contingency theory,** learning occurs because a conditioned stimulus indicates that the unconditioned stimulus is likely to ensue.

Behaviorists might counter, of course, that for the second group of dogs, the *absence* of the tone became the signal for the shock. Shock may be a powerful enough event that the fear response becomes conditioned

Contingency theory • The view that learning occurs when stimuli provide information about the likelihood of the occurrence of other stimuli.

Latent • Hidden or concealed.

Observational learning • The acquisition of knowledge and skills through the observation of others (who are called *models*) rather than by means of direct experience.

to the laboratory environment. For the third group of dogs, the shock was as likely in the presence of the neutral stimulus as in its absence. Therefore, many behaviorists would expect no learning to occur.

Behaviorists and cognitive psychologists will thus probably interpret Rescorla's research in different ways.

LATENT LEARNING: WHEN LEARNING IS NOT DOING

I'm all grown up. I know the whole [shopping] mall.

THE AUTHOR'S DAUGHTER JORDAN, AT AGE 7

Many behaviorists argue that organisms acquire only those responses, or operants, for which they are reinforced. E. C. Tolman, however, showed that rats also learn about their environments in the absence of reinforcement.

Tolman trained some rats to run through mazes for standard food goals. Other rats were permitted to explore the same mazes for several days without food goals or other rewards.

After the unrewarded rats had been allowed to explore the mazes for 10 days, food rewards were placed in a box at the far end of the maze. The previously unrewarded explorers reached the food box as quickly as the rewarded rats after only one or two reinforced trials (Tolman & Honzik, 1950).

Tolman concluded that rats learned about mazes in which they roamed even when they were unrewarded for doing so. He distinguished between learning and performance. Rats would acquire a cognitive map of a maze, and even though they would not be motivated to follow an efficient route to the far end, they would learn rapid routes from end to end just by roaming about within the maze. Yet this learning might remain hidden, or **latent,** until they were motivated to follow the rapid routes for food goals.

OBSERVATIONAL LEARNING: MONKEY SEE, MONKEY MAY CHOOSE TO DO

How many things have you learned from watching other people in real life, in films, and on television? From films and televi-

Observational Learning. People acquire a variety of skills by means of observational learning. Here, students observe a model "throwing" a pot.

sion, you may have gathered vague ideas about how to sky dive, ride surfboards, climb sheer cliffs, run a pattern to catch a touchdown pass in the Super Bowl, and dust for fingerprints, even if you have never tried these activities.

In his studies on social learning, Albert Bandura has run experiments (e.g., Bandura and others, 1963) that show that we can acquire operants by observing the behavior of others. We may need some practice to refine the operants, but we can learn them by observation alone. We may also choose to allow these operants or skills to lie latent. For example, we may not imitate aggressive behavior unless we are provoked and believe that we are more likely to be rewarded than punished for it.

Observational learning may account for most human learning. It occurs when, as children, we observe parents cook, clean, or repair a broken appliance. There is evidence that observational learning for simple tasks such as opening the halves of a toy barrel to look at a smaller barrel within occurs as early as age 1 (Abravanel & Gingold, 1985). Observational learning takes place when we watch teachers solve problems on the blackboard or hear them speak in a foreign language. Observational learning is not mechanically acquired through reinforcement. We can learn by observation without engaging in overt responses at all. It appears sufficient to pay attention to the behavior of others.

In the terminology of observational learning, a person who engages in a response to be imitated is a *model*. When observers see a model being reinforced for displaying an operant, the observers are said to be *vicariously* reinforced. Display of the operant thus becomes more likely for the observer as well as the model.

Thus, there are many different kinds of learning. We have touched on a number of them in this chapter. We have seen that psychologists disagree about what learning is, what is learned, and whether organisms are basically active or passive as they participate in the processes of learning. Nonetheless, most psychologists agree that the capacity to learn is at the heart of organisms' abilities to adapt to their environments. Some psychologists also believe that organisms, especially humans, can learn to fashion their environments in ways that enable them to meet their needs better.

Reflections

Now that you have read the section on cognitive factors in learning, reflect on the following questions:

- What basic assumptions do cognitive theorists hold about human nature? How do their views correspond with your own?
- What is your own feeling as to what "really" happens during classical conditioning? How does the research evidence support or contradict your views?
- Have you ever studied an atlas, a road map, a cookbook, or a computer manual for the pleasure of doing so? In what way does the kind of learning involved in these activities reflect latent learning?
- In your own experiences, how much can you learn by observing others? What kinds of things do you have to practice for yourself in order to learn? What kinds of learnings are taking place in your classroom? As you consider these words?

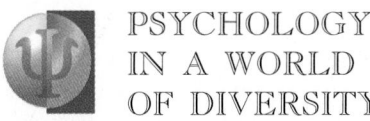

PSYCHOLOGY IN A WORLD OF DIVERSITY

SOCIOCULTURAL FACTORS IN LEARNING, *OR,* DONALD DUCK MEETS A SAMURAI

The psychology of learning addresses the core of personality. Even though what people learn is very different, it is assumed that people from different cultures learn in the same ways. People may have very different attitudes, but conditioning probably plays a role in the acquisition of attitudes. For example, classic laboratory experiments have shown that attitudes toward ethnic groups can be influenced by associating them with positive words (such as *gift* or *happy*) or negative words (such as *ugly* and *failure*) (Lohr & Staats, 1973). Parents usually positively reinforce their children for saying and doing things that are consistent with their own attitudes. Children in the United States may be shown approval for waving our flag, while children in hostile nations may be smiled upon for burning our flag.

Children also acquire many attitudes, including prejudices, by means of observational learning. Children tend to imitate their parents, and parents reinforce their children for doing so (Duckitt, 1992). Prejudices can thus be transmitted from generation to generation via learning.

People from diverse cultures share drives such as hunger and thirst, but the foods and drinks they prefer to satisfy those drives are based on learning within a given sociocultural setting. African and Swedish Americans may both like chicken, but African Americans in the South may prefer their chicken prepared in a different way than Swedish Americans from Minnesota do. Once upon a time we may have written that Mexican Americans prefer enchiladas and burritos, whereas Japanese Americans prefer sushi and Italian Americans prefer pasta. Today, however, "ethnic foods" have become so popular that most Americans have some familiarity with them and eat them from time to time. There are also many acquired individual preferences within the same ethnic group. Many White Americans like eating raw oysters, for example, whereas other White Americans are revolted by them.

FIGURE 6.11
Roger Shimomura. Untitled (1984) Acrylic on canvas. 60″ × 72″. Courtesy of Steinbaum Krauss Gallery, New York.

Our learning experiences also affect our cognition, including the nature of the very images that swim within our consciousness. Consider, for example, a painting by Japanese American artist Roger Shimomura (Figure 6.11). Shimomura is bicultural and blends popular Western imagery with the imagery found in traditional Japanese prints. At first glance, the painting suggests an amusing clash of American and Japanese popular cultures. American cartoon characters like Donald Duck, Pinocchio, Dick Tracy, and a combination Batman–Superman vie for space on the canvas with Japanese Samurai warriors and a contemporary Japanese. The battle of imagery from East and West may reflect the tensions within the artist regarding his ancestral roots and his chosen country.

It would be of little use to discuss how we learn if we were not capable of remembering what we learn from second to second, from day to day, or, in many cases, for a lifetime. In the next chapter, we turn our attention to the subject of memory. And, in Chapters 8 and 9, we shall see how learning is intertwined with thinking, language, and a concept that many people think of as learning ability: intelligence.

Summary

1. **What is learning?** Learning is the process by which experience leads to modified representations of the environment and relatively permanent changes in behavior.

2. **What is classical conditioning?** In classical conditioning as a laboratory procedure, a previously neutral stimulus (the conditioned stimulus, or CS) comes to elicit the response evoked by a second stimulus (the unconditioned stimulus, or US) as a result of being paired repeatedly with the second stimulus.

3. **What kinds of classical conditioning procedures are there?** In the most efficient classical conditioning procedure, the CS is presented about 0.5 seconds before the US. Other classical conditioning procedures include trace conditioning, simultaneous conditioning, and backward conditioning in which the US is presented first.

4. **How do extinction and spontaneous recovery occur in classical conditioning?** After a US–CS association has been learned, repeated presentation of the CS (for example, a bell) without the US (meat powder) will extinguish the CR (salivation). But extinguished responses may show spontaneous recovery as a function of the time that has elapsed since the end of the extinction process.

5. **What are generalization and discrimination?** In generalization, organisms show a CR in response to a range of stimuli similar to the CS. In discrimination, organisms learn to show a CR in response to a more limited range of stimuli by pairing only the limited stimulus with the US.

6. **What is the law of effect?** Edward L. Thorndike originated the law of effect, which holds that responses are "stamped in" by rewards and "stamped out" by punishments.

7. **What is operant conditioning?** In operant conditioning, organisms learn to engage in behavior that is reinforced. Initial "correct" responses may be performed at random or by physical or verbal guiding. Reinforced responses occur more frequently.

8. **What kinds of reinforcers are there?** Positive reinforcers increase the probability that operants will occur when they are applied. Negative reinforcers increase the probability that operants will occur when the reinforcers are removed. Primary reinforcers have their value because of the organism's biological makeup. Secondary reinforcers such as money and approval acquire their value through association with established reinforcers.

9. **How do extinction and spontaneous recovery occur in operant conditioning?** In operant conditioning, learned responses are extinguished as a result of repeated performance in the absence of reinforcement. As in classical conditioning, spontaneous recovery occurs as a function of the passage of time.

10. **What are rewards and punishments?** Rewards, like reinforcers, increase the frequency of behavior. But rewards differ from reinforcers in that they are pleasant stimuli. Punishments are aversive stimuli that suppress the frequency of behavior.

11. **Why do many learning theorists advise against using punishment in child rearing?** Many learning theorists prefer treating children's misbehavior by ignoring it or using time out from positive reinforcement for several reasons. Punishment fails to teach desirable responses, suppresses behavior only when it is guaranteed, creates hostility, can lead to overgeneralization, and serves as a model for aggression.

12. **What is a discriminative stimulus?** A discriminative stimulus indicates when an operant will be reinforced.

13. **What kinds of schedules of reinforcement are there?** Continuous reinforcement leads to the most rapid acquisition of new responses, but operants are maintained most economically through partial reinforcement. There

are four basic schedules of reinforcement. In a fixed-interval schedule, a specific amount of time must elapse after a previous correct response before reinforcement again becomes available. In a variable-interval schedule, the amount of time is allowed to vary. In a fixed-ratio schedule, a fixed number of correct responses must be performed before one is reinforced. In a variable-ratio schedule, this number is allowed to vary.

14. **What is shaping?** In shaping, successive approximations of the target response are reinforced.

15. **What is contingency theory?** This is the view that organisms learn associations between stimuli only when

stimuli provide new information about one another.

16. **What is latent learning?** In latent learning, as demonstrated by Tolman's classic research with rats, organisms can learn (modify their cognitive maps of the environment) in the absence of reinforcement.

17. **What is observational learning?** Bandura has shown that people can learn by observing others without emitting reinforced responses of their own. They may then choose to perform the behaviors they have observed when "the time is ripe"—that is, when they believe that the learned behavior is appropriate or likely to be rewarded.

Psychology and Modern Life

Much of human learning occurs by observation. Observational learning extends to observing parents and peers, classroom learning, reading books, and—in one of the more controversial aspects of modern life—learning from media such as television and films (American Psychological Association, 1992b). Nearly all of us have been exposed to television, videotapes, and films in the classroom. Children in day-care centers often watch *Sesame Street.* There are filmed and videotaped versions of great works of literature such as Orson Welles' *Macbeth* or Laurence Olivier's *Hamlet.* Nearly every school shows films of laboratory experiments. Sometimes we view "canned lectures" by master teachers.

But what of our viewing *outside* of the classroom? Television is also one of our major sources of informal observational learning. According to psychologist Leonard Eron (1993), if a child watches 2 to 4 hours of television a day, she or he will have seen 8,000 murders and another 100,000 acts of violence—*by the time she or he has finished elementary school.*

Why? Simple: Violence sells.

People are drawn to violence in films, TV dramas, books, professional wrestling and boxing, and reports of crime and warfare. Does violence do more than sell, however?

Do media portrayals of violence beget violence in the streets and in the home?

The Effects of Media Violence

It seems clear enough that there are *connections* between violence in the media and real violence. In the 1990s, for example, audiences at films about violent urban youth such as *Colors, Boyz N the Hood,* and *Juice* have gotten into fights, shot one another, and gone on rampages after the showings. The MTV cartoon characters Beavis and Butt-head, who comment on rock videos and burn and destroy things, may have been connected with the death of a 2-year-old. According to the local fire chief ("Mom Blames Beavis," 1993), the victim's 5-year-old brother, who set the blaze that killed the 2-year-old, had begun playing with fire after he observed Beavis and Butt-head to say that fire is fun.

Children are routinely exposed to murders, beatings, and sexual assaults—just by turning on the TV set (Huesmann & Miller, 1994). The public is wary of it, of course. According to a joint USA Today/CNN/Gallup poll, 80% of U.S. adults say that there is too much violence on TV (Gable, 1993). Although there are warning labels on violent shows, 61% say that the labels are not enough. In a country that values freedom of expression, 54% of the public nevertheless think that the government should do more to regulate TV shows. Rating systems already warn of violence in some video games such as *Mortal Kombat,* in which the player can decapitate the loser or rip out his heart.

Psychologists, educators, and parent groups have also raised many questions about the effects of media violence. For example, does media violence *cause* real violence? If there are causal connections between media violence and real violence, what can parents and educators do to prevent the fictional from spilling over into the real world?

In study after study, children and adults who view violence in the media later show higher levels of aggressive behavior than people who are not exposed to media violence (DeAngelis, 1993; Liebert and others, 1989). Aggressive video games apparently serve a similar purpose. In one study, 5- to

What Are the Effects of Media Violence? U.S. preschoolers watch TV an average of four hours a day. Schoolchildren spend more hours at the TV set than in the classroom. With so many shows brimming with violence, psychologists, educators, and parent groups have expressed concern about the possible effects of media violence.

FIGURE 6.12
A Classic Experiment in the Imitation of Aggressive Models Research by Albert Bandura
and his colleagues has shown that children frequently imitate the aggressive behavior that
they observe. In the top row, an adult model strikes a clown doll. The lower rows show a
boy and a girl imitating the aggressive behavior.

7-year-olds played one of two video games
(Schutte and others, 1988)—one *(Karateka)*
in which villains were destroyed by being
hit or kicked; the other *(Jungle Hunt)* in
which the character swung nonviolently
from vine to vine to cross a jungle.
Afterward the children were observed
in a playroom. Those who had played
Karateka—both boys and girls—were significantly more likely to hit their playmates
and an inflated doll. Most psychologists thus
agree that media violence *contributes* to aggression (Huesmann, 1993; NIMH, 1982).
Consider a number of ways in which depictions of violence make this contribution.

Observational Learning. Children
learn from observing the behavior of their
parents and other adults (Bandura, 1973,
1986; DeAngelis, 1993). TV violence supplies *models* of aggressive "skills." Acquisition
of these skills, in turn, enhances children's
aggressive *competencies*. In fact, children are
more likely to imitate what their parents do

than to heed what they say. If adults say
they disapprove of aggression but smash
furniture or slap each other when frustrated, children are likely to develop the notion that aggression is the way to handle
frustration. Classic experiments have shown
that children tend to imitate the aggressive
behavior they see on television, whether
the models are cartoons or real people (Bandura and others, 1963) (see Figure 6.12).

Disinhibition. The expression of operants or skills may be inhibited by punishment or by the expectation of punishment. Conversely, media violence may disinhibit
the expression of aggressive impulses that
would otherwise have been controlled, especially when media characters "get away"
with violence or are rewarded for it.

Bandura's research has shown that the
probability of aggression increases when the
models are similar to the observers and
when the models are rewarded for aggression. Viewers have been theorized to be

246

FIGURE 6.13
What Are the Connections Between Media Violence and Aggressive Behavior? Does media violence lead to aggression? Does aggressive behavior lead to a preference for viewing violence? Or does a third factor, such as a predisposition toward aggressive behavior, contribute to both? Might such a predisposition be, at least in part, genetic?

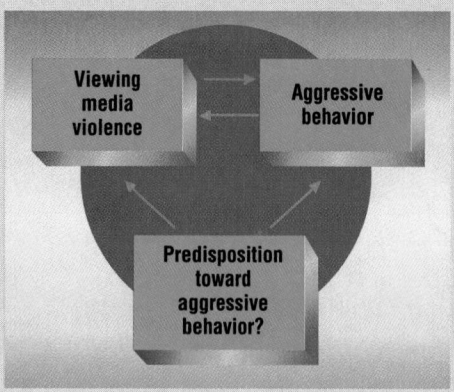

vicariously reinforced when they observe another person being reinforced for engaging in operants. And perhaps observers of rewarded aggressors are more likely to come to believe that aggression may be appropriate for them as well.

Increased Arousal. Media violence and aggressive video games increase viewers' levels of arousal. In the vernacular, television "works them up." We are more likely to engage in dominant forms of behavior, including aggressive behavior, under high levels of arousal.

Priming of Aggressive Thoughts and Memories. Media violence has cognitive effects that parallel those of biological arousal. It primes or arouses aggressive ideas and memories (Berkowitz, 1988). Media violence also provides viewers with aggressive *scripts*—that is, ideas on how to behave in situations that seem to parallel those they have observed (Huesmann & Miller, 1994).

Habituation. We become used to, or habituated to, many stimuli that impinge on us repeatedly. Repeated exposure to TV violence may therefore decrease viewers'

emotional response to real violence (Huesmann, 1993). If children come to perceive violence as the norm, their own attitudes toward violence may become less condemnatory and they may place less value on constraining aggressive urges (Eron, 1993; Huesmann, 1993).

Truth or Fiction Revisited. *Actually, a scientific connection has been established between TV violence and aggression in real life.* Now put on your critical-thinking cap and consider definitions: Is it necessary that we establish that media violence *cause* aggression for there to be a *connection* between the two? What are some of the relationships between media violence and aggression (see Figure 6.13)?

The Selection Factor. Though media violence encourages aggression in viewers, it has its greatest impact on children who are *already* considered the most aggressive by their teachers (Josephson, 1987). There also seems to be a circular relationship between viewing media violence and aggressive behavior (DeAngelis, 1993; Eron, 1982). Yes, TV violence contributes to aggressive behavior, but aggressive children are also more likely to tune in and stay tuned to it (see Figure 6.13). The viewers of films such as *Colors* and *Juice* who later went on sprees were often violent gang members to begin with. In fact, the audiences often packed in gangs that were hostile toward one another.

Aggressive children are frequently rejected by their nonaggressive peers—at least within the middle-class culture (Eron, 1982; Patterson, 1993). Aggressive children may watch more television because their peer relationships are less fulfilling and because the high incidence of TV violence tends to confirm their view that aggressive behavior is normal (Eron, 1982). Media violence also interacts with other contributors to violence. For example, parental rejection and use of physical punishment further increase the likelihood of aggression in children (Eron, 1982). Harsh home life may further confirm the TV viewer's vision of the world as a violent place and further encourage reliance on television for companionship.

What to Do. The question repeatedly arises as to whether media violence should be curtailed in an effort to stem community violence. Because of constitutional guarantees of free expression, current restraints on media depictions of violence are voluntary. Films, perhaps, are more violent than they have ever been, but TV stations now and then attempt to tone down the violence in shows intended for children.

Still, our children are going to be exposed to a great deal of media violence—if not in Saturday morning cartoon shows, then in evening dramas and in the news. Or they'll hear about violence from friends, watch children get into fights, or read about violence in the newspapers. Even if all those sources of violence were somehow hidden from view, they would learn of violence in *Hamlet, Macbeth,* and even in the Bible. Thus, the notion of preventing children from being exposed to violent models is impractical. We might also want our children to learn some aggressive skills so that they can defend themselves against bullies and rapists!

What, then, should be done? First of all, consider whether we are overestimating the threat. Although media violence contributes to aggressive behavior, it does not automatically trigger aggressive behavior (Eron, 1987). Many other factors, including the quality of the home environment, are involved. A loving, comfortable home life is not likely to feed into aggressive tendencies.

Second, Huesmann and his colleagues (1983) have shown that we as parents and educators can do many things to mitigate the impact of media violence. For example, children who watch violent shows are rated by peers as being significantly less aggressive when they are informed of the following:

1. The violent behavior they observe in the media does *not* represent the behavior of most people.

2. The apparently aggressive behaviors they watch are not real. They reflect camera tricks, special effects, and stunts.

3. Most people resolve conflicts by nonviolent means.

In observational learning, the emphasis is on the cognitive. If children consider violence inappropriate for them, they will probably not act aggressively, even if they have acquired aggressive skills.

Reflections

Now that you have read about the effects of media violence, reflect on the following questions:

- How much violence have you witnessed on television, in films, on the streets? How has observation of this violence affected your behavior? Your attitudes toward violence? For example, do you see violence as a natural or normal part of life, or do you see it as an oddity?
- Some people you know cut corners, cheat, or engage in criminal behavior. Other people you know—perhaps people with similar life experiences—do not. How do you account for the difference?

7

Memory

Truth or Fiction?

_____ Some people have photographic memories.

_____ It may be easier for you to recall the name of your first-grade teacher than of someone you just met at a party.

_____ All of our experiences are permanently imprinted on the brain so that proper stimulation can cause us to remember them exactly.

_____ There is no practical limit to the amount of information you can store in your memory.

_____ Learning must be meaningful if we are to remember it.

_____ We can remember important events that take place during the first 2 years of life.

_____ You can use tricks to improve your memory.

Outline

Truth or Fiction?
Five Challenges to Memory
Three Kinds of Memory
  Episodic Memory
  Semantic Memory
  Procedural Memory
Three Processes of Memory
  Encoding
  Storage
  Retrieval
Three Stages of Memory
  Sensory Memory
  Short-Term Memory
  Long-Term Memory
The Levels-of-Processing Model of
    Memory
Forgetting
  Memory Tasks Used in Measuring
    Forgetting
  Interference Theory
  Repression
  Infantile Amnesia
  Anterograde and Retrograde Amnesia
The Biology of Memory: From
    Engrams to Adrenaline
  Changes at the Neural Level
  Changes at the Structural Level
  Psychology in the New Millennium:
    Getting Organized to the Max:
    Adventures in Living with an
    Electronic Memory
A Final Challenge to Memory
Summary
Psychology and Modern Life
  Methods for Improving Memory

My oldest daughter Jill was talking about how she had run into a friend from elementary school and how they had had a splendid time recalling the goofy things they had done. Her sister Allyn, age 6 at the time, was not to be outdone. "I can remember when I was born," she put in.

The family's ears perked up. Being a psychologist, I knew exactly what to say. "You can remember when you were born?" I said.

"Oh, yes," she insisted. "Mommy was there."

So far she could not be faulted. I cheered her on, and she elaborated a remarkably meticulous account of how it had been snowing in the wee hours of a bitter December morning when Mommy had to go to the hospital. You see, she said, her memory was so good that she could also summon up what it had been like *before* she was born. She wove a wonderful patchwork quilt, integrating details we had given her with her own recollections of the events surrounding the delivery of her younger sister, Jordan. All in all, she seemed quite satisfied that she had pieced together a faithful portrait of her arrival on the world stage.

Later in the chapter, we shall see that children usually cannot recall events prior to the age of 2 years, much less those of the first hours. But Allyn's tale dramatized the way in which we "remember" many of the things that have happened to us. When it comes to long-term memories, truth can take a back seat to drama and embellishment. Very often, our memories are like the bride's apparel—there's something old, something new, something borrowed, and, from time to time, something blue.

Memory is what this chapter is about. Without memory, there is no past. Without memory, experience is trivial and learning cannot abide. We shall soon contemplate what psychologists have learned about the ways in which we remember things, but first try to meet the following challenges to your memory.

Five Challenges to Memory

Before we go any further, let's test your memory. If you want to participate, find four sheets of blank paper and number them 1 through 4. Then follow the directions given below.

1. Following are 10 letters. Look at them for 15 seconds. Later in the chapter, I shall ask you if you can write them on sheet number 1. (No cheating! Don't do it now.)

    THUNSTOFAM

2. Look at these nine figures for 30 seconds. Then try to draw them in the proper sequence on sheet number 2. (Yes, right after you've finished looking at them. We'll talk about your drawings later.)

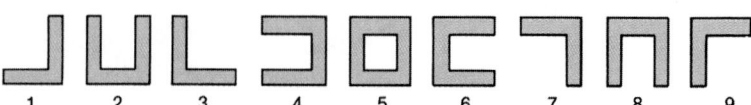

3. Okay, here's another list of letters, 17 this time. Look at the list for 60 seconds and then see whether you can reproduce it on sheet number 3. (I'm being generous this time—a full minute.)

    GMC-BSI-BMA-TTC-IAF-BI

4. Which of these pennies is an accurate reproduction of the Lincoln penny you see every day? This time there's nothing to draw on another sheet; just circle or put a checkmark by the penny you think resembles the ones you throw in the back of the drawer.

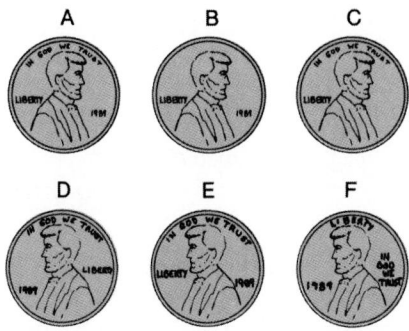

5. Examine the following drawings for 1 minute. Then copy the names of the figures on sheet number 4. When you're finished, just keep reading. Soon I'll be asking you to draw those figures.

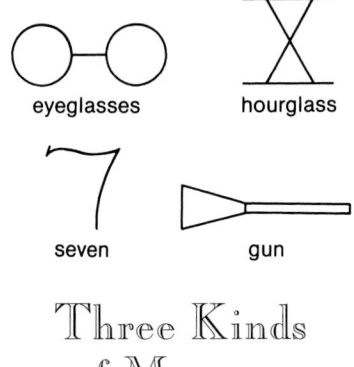

Three Kinds of Memory

Memories contain different kinds of information. Endel Tulving (1985, 1991) classifies memories according to the kind of material they hold. Return to Allyn's "recollection." Of course Allyn could not really remember her own birth. That is, she could not recall the particular event in which she had participated.

EPISODIC MEMORY

Memories of the events that happen to a person or take place in the person's presence are referred to as **episodic memory.** Your memory of what you ate for breakfast and of what your professor said in class this afternoon are examples of episodic memory.

What Allyn did recount is more accurately characterized as generalized knowledge than as visions of that important event in her young life. From listening to her parents, and from her personal experience with the events surrounding Jordan's birth, Allyn had gained extensive knowledge of what happens during childbirth. She had erroneously represented this knowledge as a precise portrayal of her birth.

SEMANTIC MEMORY

Generalized knowledge is referred to as **semantic memory.** *Semantics* concerns meanings, and Allyn was reporting her understanding of the meaning of childbirth rather than an episode in her own life. You "remember" that the United States has 50 states without necessarily visiting all of them and personally adding them up. You "remember" who authored *Hamlet,* although you were not looking over Shakespeare's shoulder as he did so. These, too, are examples of semantic memory.

Your future recollection that there are three kinds of memory is more likely to be semantic than episodic. In other words, you are more likely to "know" that there are three types of memory than to recall the date on which you learned about them, exactly where you were and how you were sitting, and whether or not you were also thinking about dinner at the time. We tend to use the phrase "I remember . . ." when we are referring to episodic memories, as in "I *remember* the blizzard of 1988." But we are more likely to say "I know . . ." in reference to semantic memories, as in "I *know* about—" (or, "I heard about—") "—the blizzard of 1888." Put it another way: You may *remember* that you wrote your mother, but you *know* that Shakespeare wrote *Hamlet.*

PROCEDURAL MEMORY

The third type of memory is **procedural memory,** also referred to as *skill memory.* Procedural memory involves knowledge of how to do things. You have learned and "remember" how to ride a bicycle, how to swim or swing a bat, how to type (or in the case of my hunting and pecking, the approximate location of the keyboard keys), how to turn the lights on and off, and how to drive a car. Procedural memories tend to

Episodic memory • Memories of events experienced by a person or that take place in the person's presence.
Semantic memory • General knowledge as opposed to episodic memory.
Procedural memory • Knowledge of ways of doing things; skill memory.

Procedural Memory. Procedural memory—also referred to as skill memory—involves knowledge of how to do things. Memories of how to ride a bicycle, how to type, how to turn on and off the lights, and how to drive a car are procedural memories. Procedural memories tend to persevere even when we have not used them for many years. Here, an elderly Jean Piaget, the famed cognitive-developmental theorist discussed in Chapter 11, demonstrates that we may never forget how to ride a bicycle.

MINILECTURE: ENCODING, STORAGE, AND RETRIEVAL

persevere even when we have not used them for many, many years. For example, it is said that we never forget how to ride a bicycle. On the other hand, procedural memories may concern skills that we cannot readily describe in words. Would you be able to explain to another person just how you manage to keep from falling when you ride a bike? When you're teaching someone how to use a manual shift, do you stick to words, or do you move your arm both to remember and to illustrate the technique?

Do you think it would help for a person to have "ESP" to remember the three types of memory? That is, E = episodic, S = semantic, and P = procedural. As we proceed, we shall see that a good deal of information about memory comes in threes. We shall also learn more about **mnemonic devices,** such as "ESP." By the way, is your use of the **acronym** *ESP* to help remember the kinds of memory an instance of episodic, semantic, or procedural memory?

Reflections

Now that you have read about different kinds of memory, reflect on the following questions:

- You remember that classes have professors, and you remember your professor's name (I hope). Which of these is an episodic memory? Which is a semantic memory? Can you explain the difference between the two?
- What kinds of procedural memories do you have? Do you remember how to hold a pen or pencil, how to type on a keyboard, how to drive a car? Can you provide other examples?

Before proceeding to the next section, why don't you turn to that piece of paper on which you wrote the names of the four figures—that is, sheet number 4—and draw them from memory as exactly as you can. Then hold on to the drawings, and we'll talk about them a bit later.

Three Processes of Memory

Psychologists and computer scientists both speak in terms of the processing of information. Think of using a minicomputer to write a term paper. Once the system is operating, you begin to type in information. You place information into the computer's memory by typing letters on a keyboard. If you were to practice grisly surgery on your computer (which I am often tempted to do) and open up its memory, however, you wouldn't find these letters inside. This is because the computer is programmed to change the letters, the information you have typed, into a form that can be placed in its electronic memory. Similarly, when we perceive information, we must convert it into a form that can be remembered if we are to place it in memory.

ENCODING

The first stage of information processing, or changing information so that we can place it in memory, is called **encoding.** Information about the world outside reaches our senses as physical and chemical stimulation. When we encode this information, we convert it into psychological formats that can be mentally represented. To do so, we commonly use visual, auditory, and semantic codes.

Let us illustrate the uses of coding by referring to the list of letters you first saw in the box on challenges to memory. Try to write the letters down now on sheet number 1, and then we'll talk about them. Go on, take a minute, and then come back.

Okay, now: If you had used a **visual code** to try to remember the list, you would have mentally represented it as a picture. That is, you would have maintained—or attempted to maintain—a mental image of the letters. Some artists and art historians seem to maintain marvelous visual mental representations of works of art, so that they recognize at once whether a work is authentic.

You may also have decided to read the list of letters to yourself—that is, to silently say them in sequence: "t," "h," "u," and so on. By so doing, you would have been using an **acoustic code,** or representing the stimuli as a sequence of sounds. You may also have read the list as a three-syllable word, "thun-sto-fam." This is an acoustic code, but it also involves the "meaning" of the letters, in the sense that you are interpreting the list as a word. And so this approach has elements of a semantic code.

Semantic codes represent stimuli in terms of their meaning. How can you use a semantic code to help remember the three colors blue, yellow, and gray? You may recall from Chapter 4 that blue and yellow are complementary, and when we mix lights of complementary colors we attain gray. Using this relationship among the colors to remember them lends the grouping meaning and, for this reason, is an example of a semantic code.

Our 10 letters were meaningless in and of themselves. However, they can also serve as an acronym for the familiar phrase "THe UNited STates OF AMerica," an observation that lends them meaning.

STORAGE

The second process of memory is **storage,** or the maintenance of information over time. If you were given the task of storing the list of letters (told to remember it), how would you attempt to place it in storage? One way would be by **maintenance rehearsal**—by mentally repeating the list, or saying it to yourself. Our awareness of the functioning of our memory, referred to by psychologists as **metamemory,** becomes more sophisticated as we develop.

You could also have condensed the amount of information you were rehearsing by reading the list as a three-syllable word; that is, you could have rehearsed three syllables rather than 10 letters. In either case, repetition would have been the key to memory. (We'll talk more about such condensing, or "chunking," very soon.) However, if you had encoded the list semantically, as an acronym for "The United States of America," storage might have been instantaneous and permanent, as we shall see.

RETRIEVAL

The third memory process is **retrieval,** or locating stored information and returning it to consciousness. With well-known information such as our names and occupations, retrieval is effortless and, for all practical purposes, immediate. But when we are trying to remember massive quantities of information, or information that is not perfectly understood, retrieval can be tedious and not always successful. To retrieve stored information in a computer, we need to know the name of the file. Similarly, retrieval of information from our memories requires knowledge of the proper cues.

If you had encoded THUNSTOFAM as a three-syllable word, your retrieval strategy would involve recollection of the word and rules of decoding. In other words, you would say the "word" *thun-sto-fam* and then decode it by spelling it out. You might err

Mnemonic devices • Systems for remembering in which items are related to easily recalled sets of symbols such as acronyms, phrases, or jingles.

Acronym • A word that is composed of the first letters of the elements of a phrase.

Encoding • Modifying information so that it can be placed in memory. The first stage of information processing.

Visual code • Mental representation of information as a picture.

Acoustic code • Mental representation of information as a sequence of sounds.

Semantic code • Mental representation of information according to its meaning.

Storage • The maintenance of information over time. The second stage of information processing.

Maintenance rehearsal • Mental repetition of information in order to keep it in memory.

Metamemory • Self-awareness of the ways in which memory functions, allowing the person to encode, store, and retrieve information effectively.

Retrieval • The location of stored information and its return to consciousness. The third stage of information processing.

in that "thun" sounds like "thumb" and "sto" could also be spelled "stow." Using the semantic code, or recognition of the acronym for "The United States of America," could lead to flawless recollection, however.

I stuck my neck out by predicting that you would immediately and permanently store the list if you recognized it as an acronym. Here, too, there would be recollection (of the name of our country) and decoding rules. That is, to "remember" the 10 letters, you would have to envision the phrase and read off the first two letters of each word. Since using this semantic code is more complex than simply seeing the entire list (using a visual code), it may take a while to recall (actually, to reconstruct) the list of 10 letters. But by using the phrase, you are likely to remember the list of letters perpetually and flawlessly.

Now, what if you were not able to remember the list of 10 letters? What would have gone wrong? In terms of the three processes of memory, it could be that you had (1) not encoded the list in a useful way, (2) not entered the encoded information into storage, or (3) stored the information but lacked the proper cues for remembering it—such as the phrase "The United States of America" or the rule for decoding the phrase.

You may have noticed, now that we have been drawn well into the chapter, that I have discussed three kinds of memory and three processes of memory, but I have not yet *defined* memory. No apologies—we weren't ready. Now that we have explored some basic concepts, let us have a try: **Memory** is defined as the processes by which information is encoded, stored, and retrieved.

Memory • The processes by which information is encoded, stored, and retrieved.

Reflections

Now that you have read about processes of memory, reflect on the following questions:

- Consider this list of letters: THUNSTO-FAM. Can you think of two strategies for storing the list? What are the different strategies called?

- Consider the two words *receive* and *retrieve*. How do you remember how to spell them? (That is, how do you retrieve the proper sequences of letters from your memory?)

Now let us turn our attention to two psychological models of memory—memory as stages and memory as levels of processing information.

Three Stages of Memory

Before the turn of the century, William James was intrigued by the fact that some memories were unreliable, "going in one ear and out the other," whereas others could be recalled for a lifetime:

The stream of thought flows on, but most of its elements fall into the bottomless pit of oblivion. Of some, no element survives the instant of their passage. Of others, it is confined to a few moments, hours, or days. Others, again, leave vestiges which are indestructible, and by means of which they may be recalled as long as life endures.
WILLIAM JAMES

Yes, the world is a constant display of sights and sounds and other sources of sensory stimulation, but only some of these things are remembered. James observed correctly that we remember various "elements of thought" for different lengths of time and many not at all. Atkinson and Shiffrin (1968) propose that there are three stages of information processing and that the progress of information through these stages determines whether (and how long) it will be retained (see Figure 7.1). These stages are *sensory memory*, *short-term memory* (STM), and *long-term memory* (LTM). Let us try to make *sense* of the *short* and the *long* of memory.

SENSORY MEMORY

Consciousness . . . does not appear to itself chopped up in bits. A "river" or a "stream" are the metaphors by which it is most naturally described. In talking of it hereafter, let us call it the stream of thought, of consciousness, or of subjective life.
WILLIAM JAMES

So William James wrote of the stream of thought, or of consciousness. When we look at a visual stimulus, our impressions may seem fluid enough. Actually, they consist of a series of eye fixations referred to as

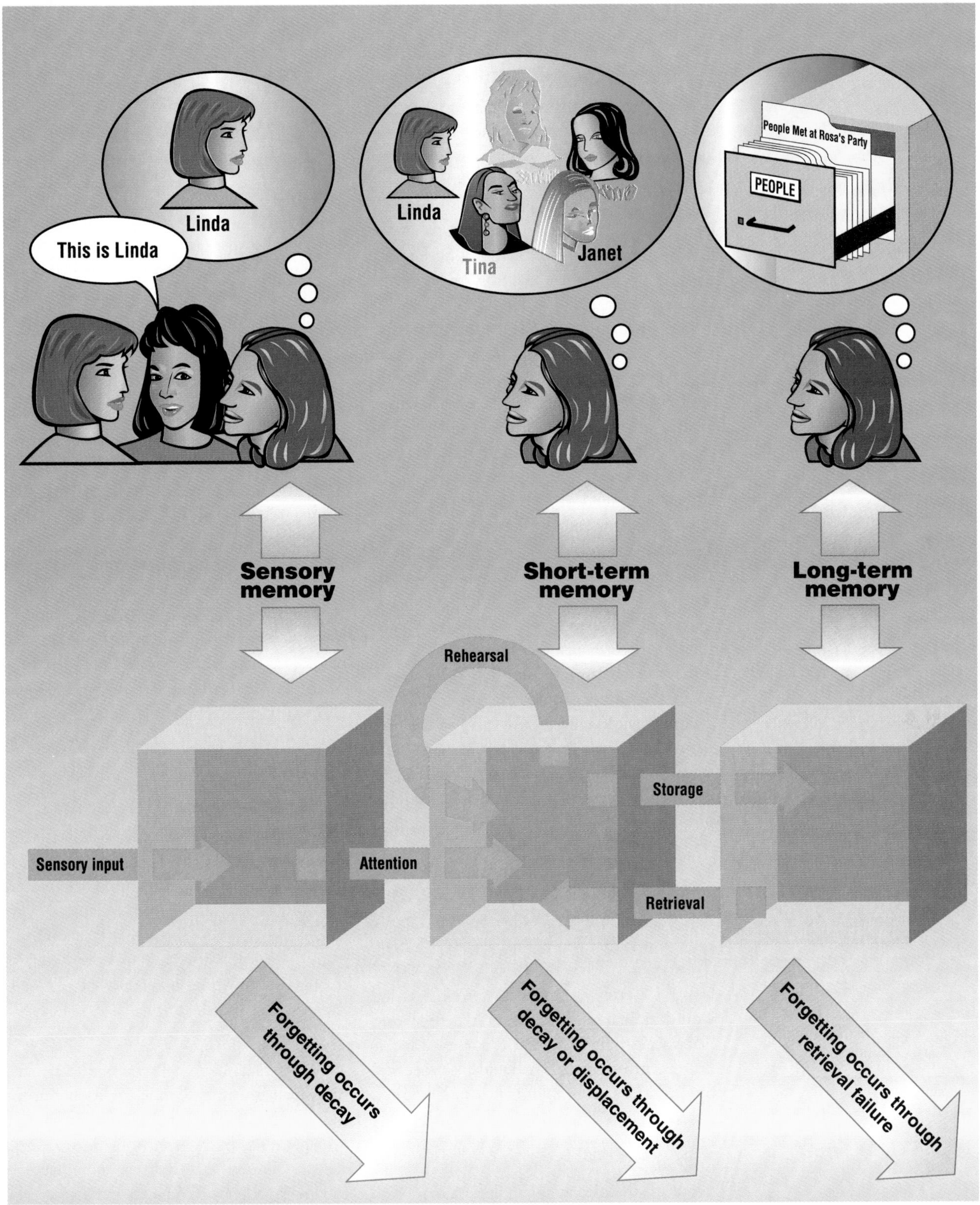

This is Linda

Linda

Linda   Tina   Janet

People Met at Rosa's Party

PEOPLE

Sensory memory

Short-term memory

Long-term memory

Rehearsal

Storage

Sensory input

Attention

Retrieval

Forgetting occurs through decay

Forgetting occurs through decay or displacement

Forgetting occurs through retrieval failure

FIGURE 7.1

Spotlight on Stages of Memory A number of psychologists hypothesize that there are three distinct stages of memory. Sensory information impacts upon the registers of sensory memory, where memory traces are held briefly before decaying. If we attend to the information, much of it is transferred to short-term memory (STM). Information in STM may decay or be displaced if it is not transferred to long-term memory (LTM). We usually use rehearsal to transfer memories to LTM. Once in LTM, memories may be retrieved through appropriate search strategies. But if information is organized poorly, or if we cannot find cues to retrieve it, it may be lost.

MINILECTURE:
SACCADIC EYE
MOVEMENTS

Saccadic eye movement •
The rapid jumps made by a person's eyes as they fixate on different points.

Sensory memory • The type or stage of memory first encountered by a stimulus. Sensory memory holds impressions briefly, but long enough so that series of perceptions are psychologically continuous.

Memory trace • An assumed change in the nervous system that reflects the impression made by a stimulus. Memory traces are said to be "held" in sensory registers.

Sensory register • A system of memory that holds information briefly, but long enough so that it can be processed further. There may be a sensory register for every sense.

Icon • A mental representation of a visual stimulus that is held briefly in sensory memory.

Iconic memory • The sensory register that briefly holds mental representations of visual stimuli.

Eidetic imagery • The maintenance of detailed visual memories over several minutes.

MINILECTURE:
SPERLING'S
EXPERIMENTS

saccadic eye movement. These movements jump from one point to another about four times each second. Yet, the visual sensations seem continuous, or stream-like, because of **sensory memory.** Sensory memory is the type or stage of memory first encountered by a stimulus. Although it holds impressions briefly, it is long enough so that series of perceptions seem to be connected.

Return to our example of the list of letters: THUNSTOFAM. If the list were flashed on a screen for a fraction of a second, the visual impression, or **memory trace,** of the stimulus would also last for only a fraction of a second afterward. Psychologists speak of the memory trace of the list as being held in a visual **sensory register.** Sensory memory, in other words, consists of registers that can briefly hold information that is entered by means of our senses.

If the letters had been flashed on a screen for, say, 1/10th of a second, your ability to remember them on the basis of sensory memory alone would be meager. Your memory would be based on a single eye fixation, and the trace of the image would vanish before a single second had passed. At the turn of the century, the social psychologist William McDougall (1904) engaged in research in which he presented subjects 1 to 12 letters arranged in rows—just long enough to allow a single eye fixation. Under these conditions, subjects could typically remember only four or five letters. Thus, recollection of THUNSTOFAM, a list of 10 letters arranged into a single row, would probably depend on whether one had successfully transformed or encoded it into a form in which it could be processed by further stages of memory.

George Sperling (1960) modified McDougall's experimental method and showed that there is a difference between what people can see and what they can report. McDougall had used a *whole-report procedure,* in which subjects were asked to report every letter seen in the array. Sperling used a modified *partial-report procedure,* in which subjects were asked to report the contents of one of three rows of letters. In a typical procedure, Sperling flashed three rows of letters like those that follow on a screen for 50 milliseconds (1/20th of a second):

A G R E
V L S B
N K B T

Using the whole-report procedure, subjects could report an average of four letters from the entire display (one out of three). But if Sperling pointed an arrow immediately after presentation at a row he wanted viewers to report, they usually reported most of the letters in the row successfully.

If Sperling presented six letters arrayed in two rows, subjects could usually report either row without error. If subjects were flashed 3 rows of 4 letters each—a total of 12—they reported correctly an average of 3 of 4 of the designated row, suggesting that about 9 letters of the 12 had been perceived.

Sperling found that the amount of time that elapsed before indicating the row to be reported was crucial. If he delayed pointing the arrow for a few fractions of a second after the display, subjects were much less successful in reporting the target row. If he allowed a full second to elapse, the arrow did not aid recall at all. From these data, Sperling concluded that the memory trace of visual stimuli *decays* within a second in the visual sensory register (see Figure 7.1). With a single eye fixation, subjects can *see* most of a display of 12 letters clearly, as shown by their ability to immediately read off most of the letters in a designated row. Yet, as the fractions of a single second are elapsing, the memory trace of the letters is fading. By the time a second has elapsed, the trace has vanished.

Iconic Memory. Psychologists believe there is a sensory register for each one of our senses. The mental representations of visual stimuli are referred to as **icons.** The sensory register that holds icons is labeled **iconic memory.** Iconic memories are accurate, photographic memories. So those of us who can see—who mentally represent visual stimuli—have "photographic memories." However, they are very brief. What most of us normally think of as a photographic memory—the ability to retain exact mental representations of visual stimuli over long periods of time—is referred to by psychologists as *eidetic imagery.*

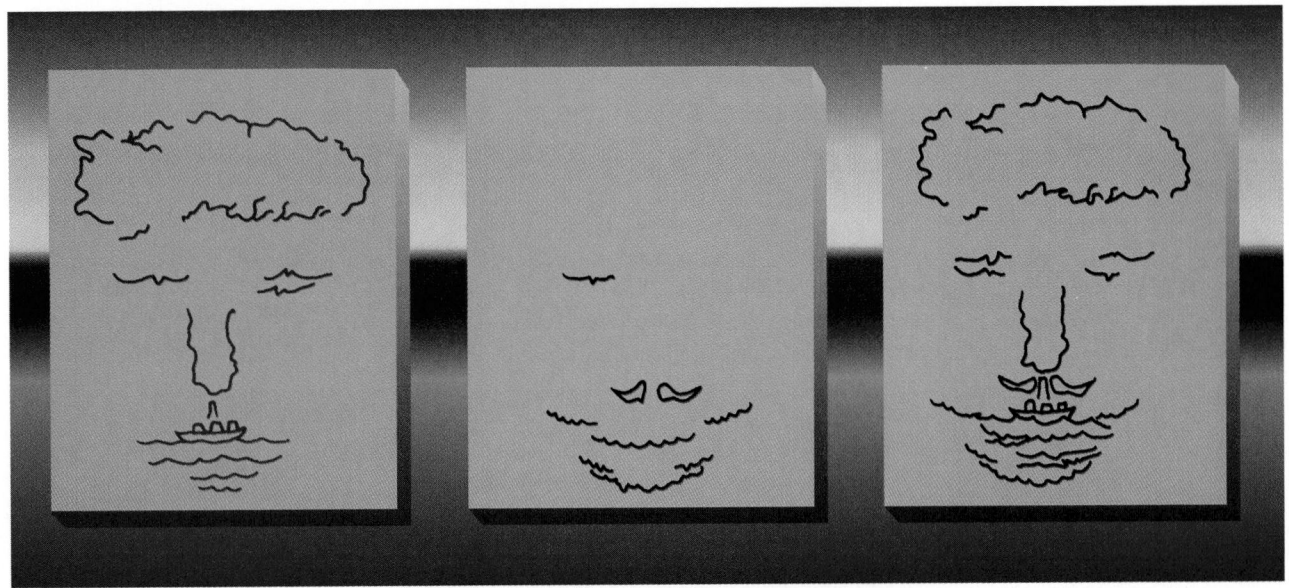

FIGURE 7.2
A Research Strategy for Assessing Eidetic Imagery Children look at the first drawing for 20
to 30 seconds, after which it is removed. Next, the children look at a neutral background
for several minutes. They are then shown the second drawing. When asked what they see,
children with the capacity for eidetic imagery report seeing a face. The face is seen only by
children who retain the first image and fuse it with the second, thus perceiving the third
image.

Eidetic Imagery.   Visual stimuli, or
icons, persist for remarkably long periods of
time among a few individuals. About 5% of
children can look at a detailed picture, turn
away, and several minutes later recall the
particulars of the picture with exceptional
clarity—as if they were still viewing it.
This extraordinary visual memory is referred to as **eidetic imagery** (Haber,
1980). Among the minority of children
who have this ability, it declines with age,
all but disappearing by adolescence.

Figure 7.2 provides an example of a test of
eidetic imagery. Children are asked to look
at the first drawing in the series for 20 to
30 seconds, after which it is removed. The
children then continue to gaze at a neutral
background. Several minutes later, the
drawing in the center is placed on the
backdrop. When asked what they see, many
report "a face." A face would be seen only
if the children had retained a clear image of
the first picture and fused it with the second so that they are, in effect, perceiving
the third picture in Figure 7.2 (Haber,
1980).

Eidetic imagery appears remarkably clear
and detailed. It seems to be essentially a

perceptual phenomenon in which coding is
not a factor.

Truth or Fiction Revisited. *It is
true that some people have photographic memories.* Those of us who can see have what is
actually defined as *photographic,* or *iconic,*
memories. However, only a few of us have
eidetic imagery, which is closer to what lay
people think of as "photographic memory."
Although eidetic imagery is rare, iconic
memory, as we see in the following section,
universally transforms visual perceptions
into smoothly unfolding impressions of the
world.

**Iconic Memory and Saccadic Eye
Movements: Smoothing Out the
Bumps in the Visual Ride.** Saccadic
eye movements occur about four times
every second. Iconic memory, however,
holds icons for up to a second. As a consequence, the flow of visual information
seems smooth and continuous. Your impression that the words you are reading flow
across the page, rather than jump across in
spurts, is a product of your iconic memory.
Similarly, you may recall from Chapter 4

that motion pictures present 16 to 22 separate frames, or still images, each second. Iconic memory allows you to perceive the imagery as being seamless (Loftus, 1983).

Echoic Memory. The mental representations of sounds, or auditory stimuli, are called **echoes.** The sensory register that holds echoes is referred to as **echoic memory.**

The memory traces of auditory stimuli (that is, echoes) can last for several seconds, many times longer than the traces of visual stimuli (icons). The difference in the duration of traces is probably based on biological differences between the eye and ear. This difference is one of the reasons that acoustic codes aid in the retention of information that has been presented visually—or why saying the letters or syllables of THUN-STOFAM makes the list easier to remember.

Yet echoes, like icons, will fade with the passage of time. If they are to be retained, we must pay attention to them. By selectively attending to certain stimuli, we sort them out from the background noise. For example, in studies on the development of patterns of processing information, young children have been shown photographs of rooms full of toys and then have been asked to recall as many as they can. One such

study found that 2-year-old boys are more likely to attend to and remember toys such as cars, puzzles, and trains, whereas 2-year-old girls are more likely to attend to and remember dolls, dishes, and teddy bears (Renninger & Wozniak, 1985). Even by this early age, children's patterns of attention have frequently fallen into stereotypical configurations.

SHORT-TERM MEMORY

We have . . . not memory so much as memories. . . . We can set our memory as it were to retain things for a certain time, and then let them depart.
WILLIAM JAMES

If you focus attention on a stimulus in the sensory register, you will tend to retain it in **short-term memory**—also referred to as **working memory**—for a minute or so after the trace of the stimulus decays (Baddeley, 1994). When you are given a phone number by the information operator and then write it down or dial the number, you are retaining the number in your short-term memory. When you are told the name of someone at a party and then use that name immediately in addressing the person, you are retaining the name in short-term memory. In short-term memory, the image tends to fade significantly after 10 to 12 seconds if it is not repeated or rehearsed. It is possible to focus on maintaining a visual image in the short-term memory, but it is more common to encode visual stimuli as sounds, or auditory stimulation. Then the sounds can be rehearsed, or repeated.

As noted, most of us know that a way of retaining information in short-term memory—and possibly storing it permanently—is to rehearse it. When an information operator tells me a phone number, I usually rehearse it continuously while I am dialing it or running around frantically searching for a pencil and a scrap of paper. Most of us also know that the more times we rehearse information, the more likely we are to remember it. We have the capacity (if not the will or the time) to rehearse information and thereby keep it in short-term memory indefinitely.

Encoding. Let us now return to the task of remembering the first list of letters in my challenges to memory. If you had coded the

Echoic Memory. The mental representations of auditory stimuli are called echoes, and the sensory register that holds echoes is referred to as echoic memory. By encoding visual information as echoes and rehearsing the echoes, we commit them to memory. The drama student is memorizing the script by encoding typed words as echoes (placing them in echoic memory) and rehearsing them.

letters as the three-syllable word THUN-STO-FAM, you would probably have recalled them by mentally rehearsing (saying to yourself) the three-syllable "word" and then spelling it out from the sounds. A few minutes later, if someone asked whether the letters had been uppercase (THUNSTO-FAM) or lowercase (thunstofam), you might not have been confident of an answer. You had used an acoustic code to help recall the list, and uppercase and lowercase letters sound alike.

Because it can be pronounced, THUN-STOFAM is not too difficult to retain in short-term memory. But what if the list of letters had been TBXLFNTSDK? This list of letters cannot be pronounced as it is. You would have had to find a complex acronym to code these letters, and within a fraction of a second—most likely an impossible task. To aid recall, you would probably have chosen to try to repeat or rehearse the letters rapidly—to read each one as many times as possible before the memory trace faded. You might have visualized each letter as you said it and tried to get back to it (that is, to run through the entire list) before it decayed.

Let us assume that you encoded the letters as sounds and then rehearsed the sounds. When asked to report the list, you might mistakenly say T-V-X-L-F-N-T-S-T-K. This would be an understandable error because the incorrect *V* and *T* sounds are similar, respectively, to the correct *B* and *D* sounds.

The Serial-Position Effect.

Note that you would also be likely to recall the first and last letters in the series, *T* and *K*, more accurately than the others. Why? The tendency to recall more accurately the first and last items in a series is known as the **serial-position effect.** This effect may occur because we pay more attention to the first and last stimuli in a series. They serve as the visual or auditory boundaries for the other stimuli. It may also be that the first items are likely to be rehearsed more frequently (repeated more times) than other items. The last items are likely to have been rehearsed most recently and so are most likely to be retained in short-term memory.

According to cognitive psychologists, the tendency to recall the initial items in a list

is referred to as the **primacy effect.** In Chapter 16, we shall see that social psychologists also note a powerful primacy effect in our formation of impressions of other people. In other words, first impressions tend to last. The tendency to recall the last items in a list is referred to as the **recency effect.** As noted, if we are asked to recall the last items in a list soon after we have been shown the list, they may still be in short-term memory. As a result, they can be "read off." Earlier items, in contrast, may have to be retrieved from long-term memory.

Chunks of Information: Is Seven a Magic Number or Did the Phone Company Get Lucky?

Rapidly rehearsing 10 meaningless letters is not an easy task. With TBXLFNTSDK there are 10 discrete elements, or **chunks,** of information that must be kept in short-term memory. When we encode THUNSTO-FAM as three syllables, there are only three chunks to swallow at once—a memory task that is much easier on the digestion.

Psychologist George Miller noted that the average person is comfortable with digesting about seven integers at a time, the number of integers in a telephone number. In an article appearing in *Psychological Review,* he wrote:

> My problem is that I have been persecuted by an integer. For seven years this number has followed me around, has intruded in my most private data, and has assaulted me from the pages of our most public journals (1956).

In public, yet. Most people have little trouble recalling five chunks of information, as in a ZIP Code. Some can remember nine, which is, for all but a few, an upper limit. So seven chunks, plus or minus one or two, is the "magic" number.

So how, you ask, do we successfully include the area codes in our recollections of telephone numbers, hence making them 10 digits long? The truth of the matter is that we usually don't. We tend to recall the area code as a single chunk of information derived from our general knowledge of where a person lives. So we are more likely to remember (or "know") the 10-digit numbers of acquaintances who reside in locales with area codes we use frequently.

Echo • A mental representation of an auditory stimulus (sound) that is held briefly in sensory memory.

Echoic memory • The sensory register that briefly holds mental representations of auditory stimuli.

Short-term memory • The type or stage of memory that can hold information for up to a minute or so after the trace of the stimulus decays. Also called *working memory.*

Working memory • Same as *short-term memory.*

Serial-position effect • The tendency to recall more accurately the first and last items in a series.

Primacy effect • The tendency to recall the initial items in a series of items.

Recency effect • The tendency to recall the last items in a series of items.

Chunk • A stimulus or group of stimuli that are perceived as a discrete piece of information.

Businesses pay the phone company hefty premiums so that they can attain numbers with two or three zeroes—for example, 592-2000 or 614-3300. These numbers have fewer chunks of information and hence are easier to remember. Customer recollection of business phone numbers increases sales. One financial services company uses the toll-free number CALL-IRA, which reduces the task to two chunks of information that also happen to be meaningfully related (semantically coded) to the nature of the business. Similarly, a clinic in my area that helps people quit smoking arranged for a telephone number that can be reached by dialing the letters NO SMOKE.

Return for a moment to the third challenge to memory presented on page 250. Were you able to remember the six groups of letters? Would your task have been simpler if you had grouped them differently? How about moving the dashes to the left by a letter, so that they read GM-CBS-IBM-ATT-CIA-FBI? We have exactly the same list of letters, but we suddenly have six chunks of information that can be coded semantically. You may have also been able to generate the list by remembering a rule, such as "big corporations and government agencies."

If we can recall seven or perhaps nine chunks of information, how, then, do children remember the alphabet? The alphabet contains 26 discrete pieces of information. How do children learn to encode the letters of the alphabet, presented visually, as spoken sounds? The 26 letters of the alphabet cannot be pronounced like a word or phrase—despite the existence of that im-

possible *Sesame Street* song, "Ab k'defkey jekyl m'nop kw'r stoov w'ksizz." There is nothing about the shape of an *A* that suggests its sound. Nor does the visual stimulus *B* sound "B-ish." Children learning the alphabet and learning to associate visually presented letters with their spoken names do so by **rote.** It is mechanical associative learning that requires time and repetition. If you think that learning the alphabet by rote is a simple child's task, now that it is behind you, try learning the Russian or Hebrew alphabet.

Now, if you had recognized THUNSTO-FAM as an acronym for the first two letters of each word in the phrase "THe UNited STates OF AMerica," you also would have reduced the number of chunks of information that had to be recalled. You could have considered the phrase to be a single chunk of information, and the rule that you must use the first two letters of each word of the phrase to be another chunk.

Reconsider the second challenge to memory on page 250. You were asked to remember nine chunks of visual information. Perhaps you could have used the acoustic codes "L" and "Square" for chunks three and five, but no obvious codes are available for the seven other chunks. Now look at Figure 7.3. If you had recognized that the elements in the challenge could be arranged as the familiar tic-tac-toe grid, remembering the nine elements might have required two chunks of information. The first would have been the mental image of the grid and the second would have been the rule for decoding: Each element corresponds to the shape of a section of the grid if read like words on a page (from upper left to lower right). The number sequence 1 through 9 would not in itself present a problem, because you learned this series by rote many years ago and have rehearsed it in countless calculations since.

Interference in Short-Term Memory. I mentioned that I often find myself running around looking for a pencil and a scrap of paper to write down a telephone number that has been given to me. If I keep on rehearsing the number while I'm looking, I'm okay. But I have also cursed myself repeatedly for failing to keep a pad and pencil by the telephone, and sometimes the

Rote • Mechanical associative learning that is based on repetition.

Displace • In memory theory, to cause chunks of information to be lost from short-term memory by adding new items.

FIGURE 7.3
A Familiar Grid The nine drawings in the second challenge to memory form this familiar tic-tac-toe grid when the numbers are placed inside them and they are arranged in numerical order, three shapes to a line. This method for recalling the shapes collapses nine chunks of information into two. One is the tic-tac-toe grid. The second is the rule for decoding the drawings from the grid.

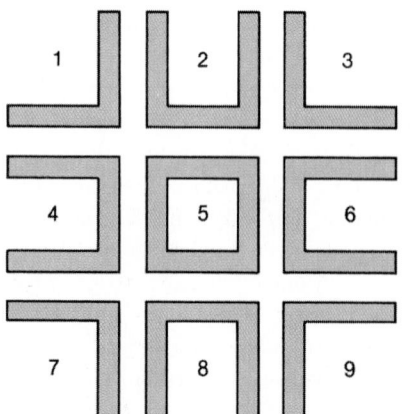

mental dressing-down interferes with my recollection of the number. (The moral of the story? Avoid self-reproach.) It has also happened that I have actually looked up a phone number for myself and been about to dial it when someone has asked me for the time or where I said we were going to dinner. Unless I say, "Now hold on a minute!" and manage to jot down the number on something, it's back to the phone book. Attending to distracting information, even briefly, prevents me from rehearsing the number, so it falls between the cracks of my short-term memory.

In an experiment with college students, Lloyd and Margaret Peterson (1959) demonstrated how prevention of rehearsal can wreak havoc with short-term memory. They asked students to remember three-letter combinations, such as HGB—normally, three easy chunks of information. They then had the students count backward from an arbitrary number, such as 181, by threes (that is, 181, 178, 175, 172, and so on). The students were told to stop counting and to report the letter sequence after the passage of the intervals of time shown in Figure 7.4. The percentage of letter combinations recalled correctly fell precipitously within seconds. After 18 seconds of interference, counting had dislodged the letter sequences in almost all of these bright young students' memories.

Psychologists say that the appearance of new information in short-term memory **displaces** the old information. Remember: Only a few bits of information at a time can be retained in short-term memory. Klatzky (1980) likens short-term memory to a shelf or workbench. Once it is full, some things fall off when new items are shoved on. Here, we have another possible explanation for the recency effect: The most recently learned bit of information is least likely to be displaced by additional information.

Displacement occurs at cocktail parties, and I'm not referring to the jostling of one's body by others in the crowd. The point is this: When you meet Jennifer or Jonathan at the party, there should be little trouble remembering the name. But then you may meet Tamara or Timothy and, still later, Stephanie or Steven. By that time you may have a hard time dredging up Jennifer

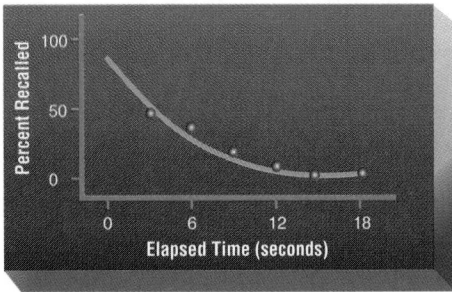

FIGURE 7.4
The Effect of Interference on Information in Short-Term Memory In this experiment, college students were asked to maintain a series of three letters in their memories while they counted backward by threes from an arbitrary number. After just 3 seconds, retention was cut by half. Ability to recall the words was almost completely lost by 15 seconds.

or Jonathan—unless, of course, you were very, very attracted to one of them. A passionate response would set that person apart and inspire a good deal of selective attention. Recall signal–detection theory from Chapter 4: If you were enamored enough, we may predict that the person's name (sensory signals) would be "detected" with a vengeance, and perhaps all the ensuing names would dissolve into background noise.

MINILECTURE: THE CAPACITY OF SHORT-TERM MEMORY

Displacement. Information can be lost to short-term memory by means of displacement. We may have little trouble remembering the names of the first one or two people we meet at a party. But as introductions continue, new names may displace the old, and we may forget the names of people we met only a few minutes earlier.

Long-term memory • The type or stage of memory capable of relatively permanent storage.

Repression • In Freud's psychodynamic theory, the ejection of anxiety-evoking ideas from conscious awareness.

Schema • A way of mentally representing the world, such as a belief or an expectation, that can influence perception of persons, objects, and situations.

Truth or Fiction Revisited. *It is true that it may be easier for you to recall the name of your first-grade teacher than of someone you just met at a party.* Your first-grade teacher's name is stored in long-term memory, whereas you may be juggling your new acquaintance's name with many others in short-term memory.

LONG-TERM MEMORY

Long-term memory is the third stage of processing of information. Think of your long-term memory as a vast storehouse of information containing names, dates, places, what Johnny did to you in second grade, and what Susan said about you when you were 12.

Some psychologists (Sigmund Freud was one) used to believe that nearly all of our perceptions and ideas were stored permanently. Of course, we might not be able to retrieve all of them, but such memories might be "lost" because of the unavailability of the proper cues, or they might be kept

beneath the surface of conscious awareness by the forces of **repression**. Adherents to this view often pointed to the work of neurosurgeon Wilder Penfield (1969). Many of Penfield's patients reported the appearance of images that had something of the feel of memories, when parts of their brains were electrically stimulated.

Today, most psychologists view this notion as being exaggerated. Memory researcher Elizabeth Loftus, for example, notes that the "memories" stimulated by Penfield's probes were impoverished in detail and not necessarily factual (Loftus & Loftus, 1980; Loftus, 1983).

Truth or Fiction Revisited. *It is not true that all of our experiences are permanently imprinted on the brain so that proper stimulation can cause us to remember them exactly.* Our memories are limited by such factors as the attention we pay to events (selective attention) and our inability to capture all of their details. Evidence is far from compelling that we store all of our experiences. To the contrary, we appear to be more likely to store incidents that have a greater impact on us—events more laden with personal meaning.

Now let us consider some important questions about long-term memory.

How Accurate Are Long-Term Memories?—Memory as Reconstructive. Elizabeth Loftus notes that memories are distorted by our biases and needs—by the ways in which we conceptualize our worlds. Cognitive psychologists speak of much of our knowledge of the world as being represented in terms of **schemas.**

To understand better what is meant by *schema,* consider the problems of travelers who met up with the legendary highwayman of ancient Greece, Procrustes. Procrustes had a quirk. He was not only interested in travelers' pocketbooks but also in their height. He had a concept—a schema—of just how tall people should be, and when people did not fit his schema, they were in for it. You see, Procrustes also had a very famous bed, a bed that comes down to us in history as a "Procrustean bed." He made his victims lie down in the bed, and when they were too short for it,

FIGURE 7.5
Memory as Reconstructive In their classic experiment, Carmichael, Hogan, and Walter (1932) presented participants with the figures in the left-hand box and made remarks of the sort suggested in the other boxes. For example, the experimenters might say, "This drawing looks like eyeglasses [or a dumbbell]." When participants later reconstructed the drawings, it was clear their drawings had been influenced by the experimenters' labels. That is, the experimenters had provided schemas according to which the subjects organized their experiences and reconstructed their memories.

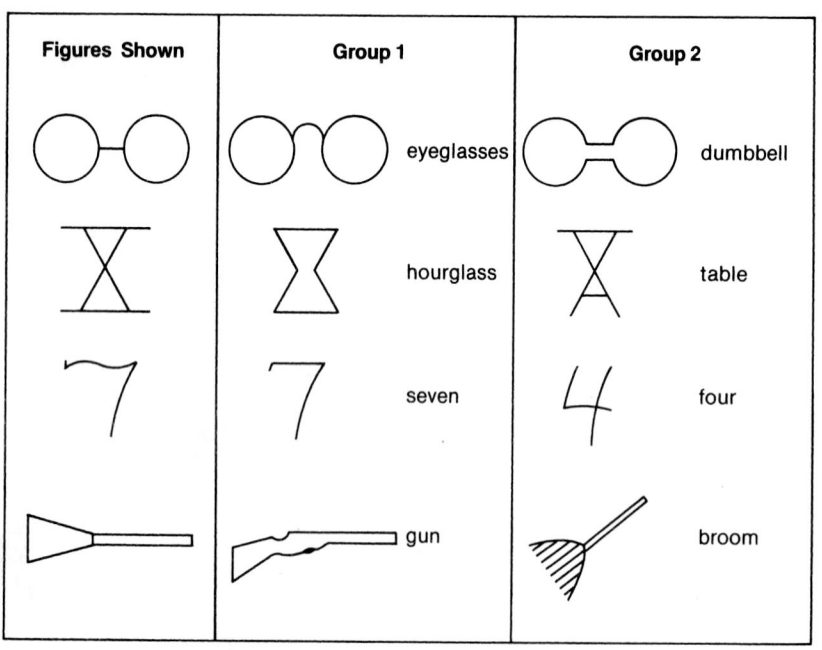

Figures Shown	Group 1		Group 2	
◯—◯	◯◯	eyeglasses	◯—◯	dumbbell
✕	✕	hourglass	✕	table
7	7	seven	4	four
⊢—	gun		broom	broom

he stretched them to make them fit. When they were too long for it, he is said to have practiced surgery on their legs. Many unfortunate passersby failed to survive.

Although the myth of Procrustes may sound absurd, it reflects a quirky truth about each of us. We all carry our cognitive Procrustean beds around with us—our unique ways of perceiving the world—and we try to make things and people fit.

Let me give you an example. Why don't you "retrieve" the fourth sheet of paper you prepared according to the instructions for the challenges to memory. The labels you wrote on the sheet will remind you of the figures. Please take a minute or two to draw them now. Then continue reading.

Now that you have made your drawings, turn to Figure 7.5 on page 262. Are your drawings closer in form to those in Group 1 or those in Group 2? I wouldn't be surprised if they were more like those in Group 1. After all, they were labeled like the drawings in Group 1. The labels serve as *schemas* for the drawings—ways of organizing your knowledge of them—and these schemas may have influenced your recollections.

Consider another example of the power of schemas in processing information. Loftus and Palmer (1974) showed people a film of a car crash and then asked them to fill out questionnaires that included a question about how fast the cars were going at the time. The language of the question varied subtly, however. Some people were asked to estimate how fast the cars were going when they "hit" one another. Others were asked to estimate the cars' speed when they "smashed" into one another. Those reconstructing the scene on the basis of the cue "hit" estimated a speed of 34 mph. People who watched the same film but reconstructed the scene on the basis of the cue "smashed" estimated a speed of 41 mph! In other words, the use of the word *hit* or *smashed* caused people to organize their knowledge about the crash in different ways. That is, the words served as diverse schemas that fostered the development of very different ways of processing information about the crash.

Participants in the same study were questioned again a week later: "Did you see any

How Fast Were These Cars Going When They Collided? Our schemas influence our processing of information. When shown pictures such as these, subjects who were asked how fast the cars were going when they *smashed* into one another offer higher estimates than subjects told they *hit* one another.

broken glass?" Since there was no broken glass shown in the film, positive replies were errors. Of those who had earlier been encouraged to process information about the accident in terms of one car "hitting" the other, 14% incorrectly answered yes. But 32% of the participants who had processed information about the crash in terms of one car "smashing" the other reported, incorrectly, that they had seen broken glass.

Findings such as these have important implications for eyewitness testimony.

Long-Term Memory and Eyewitness Testimony. Jean Piaget, the famed investigator of children's cognitive development, distinctly remembered an attempt to kidnap him from his baby carriage along the Champs Élysées. He recalled the excited throng, the abrasions on the face of the nurse who rescued him, the police officer's white baton, and the flight of the assailant. Although graphic, Piaget's memories were false. Years afterward, the nurse admitted that she had concocted the tale.

Lawyers, judges, and other legal professionals are vitally concerned about the accuracy of our memories as reflected in eyewitness testimony. For example, as noted

Eyewitness Testimony? How trustworthy is eyewitness testimony? Memories are reconstructive rather than photographic. The wording of questioners also influences the content of the memory. Attorneys are therefore sometimes instructed not to phrase questions that "lead" the witness.

MINILECTURE:
EYEWITNESS
TESTIMONY

by psychologist Elizabeth Loftus, misidentifications of suspects "create a double horror: The wrong person is devastated by this personal tragedy, and the real criminal is still out on the streets" (1993b, p. 550). Is there reason to believe that the statements of eyewitnesses would be any more factual than Piaget's?

There is cause for concern. The words chosen by an experimenter—and those chosen by a lawyer interrogating a witness—influence the reconstruction of memories (Loftus & Palmer, 1973). For example, an attorney for the plaintiff might ask the witness, "How fast was the defendant's car going when it *smashed into* the plaintiff's car?" In such a case, the car might be reported as going faster than if the question had been: "How fast was the defendant's car going when it *hit* the plaintiff's car?" Could the attorney for the defendant claim that use of the word *smashed* biased the witness? What of the jury who heard the word *smashed?* Would they not be biased toward assuming that the driver had been reckless?

Children tend to be more suggestible witnesses than adults, and preschoolers are more suggestible than older children (Ceci & Bruck, 1993). On the other hand, when questioned properly, even young children may be able to provide accurate and useful testimony (Ceci & Bruck, 1993).

There are cases in which the memories of eyewitnesses have been "refreshed" by hypnosis. Sad to say, hypnosis does more than amplify memories; it can also distort them (Loftus, 1994). One problem is that witnesses may accept and embellish suggestions made by the hypnotist. Another is that imagined events can seem as authentic as true events, but hypnotized people may report fantasized occurrences as compellingly as if they were real (Loftus, 1994).

There are also problems concerning the identification of criminals. For one thing, witnesses may pay more attention to the suspect's clothing than to more meaningful characteristics such as facial features, height, and weight. In one experiment, viewers of a videotaped crime incorrectly identified a man as the criminal because he wore the eyeglasses and T-shirt that had been worn by the perpetrator on the tape. The man who actually committed the crime was identified less often (Sanders, 1984).

Some other problems with eyewitness testimony:

- Identification of suspects is less accurate when suspects belong to ethnic or racial groups that differ from the witness's (Egeth, 1993).
- Identification of suspects is confused when interrogators make misleading suggestions (Lindsay & Johnson, 1989).
- Witnesses are perceived as more credible when they claim to be certain in their testimony (Wells, 1993), but there is little evidence that such claims are accurate (Bothwell and others, 1987; Yarmey, 1986).

As you can see, those in the legal profession are faced with a dilemma. It is recognized that our memories are distorted by our schemas—that is, the ways in which we organize experience. The ways in which we are questioned can color our recollections. And perhaps we do not pay as much attention as we should to fixed characteristics when we are trying to identify criminals. Yet research suggests that it may be possible to enhance the accuracy of eyewitness testimony. For example:

- Testimony is likely to be more accurate, and suspects are more likely to be convicted, when independent witnesses corroborate each other's testimony (Leippe, 1985; Lindsay and others, 1986).
- The accuracy of eyewitness testimony can be increased when the questioner carefully depicts the setting of the crime (Cutler and others, 1987) and asks witnesses to describe what happened rather than pump them full of suggestions (Sanders & Chiu, 1988).
- Witnesses who first view a "blank" police lineup (one that does not have a suspect) and make no identification are more likely to make accurate identifications in subsequent lineups that contain the culprit (Wells, 1993).
- Eyewitness identification is more accurate when police present suspects in sequence rather than showing suspects all at once in the same lineup (Wells, 1993).

In sum, eyewitness testimony has its problems. Yet there may be things that can be done to improve its accuracy (Wells, 1993; Wells & Luus, 1990). And what is the alternative? If we were to prevent witnesses from testifying, how many criminals would go free (Loftus, 1993b)?

How Much Information Can Be Stored in Long-Term Memory?

There is no evidence for any limit to the amount of information that can be stored in long-term memory. New information may replace older information in short-term memory, but there is no evidence that memories in long-term memory are lost by displacement. Long-term memories may last days, years, or for all practical purposes, a lifetime. From time to time, it may seem as if we have forgotten, or "lost," a long-term memory such as the names of elementary- or high-school classmates. Yet, it may be that we cannot find the proper cues to help us retrieve the information. If it is lost, it usually becomes lost only in the same way as when we misplace an object but know that it is still somewhere in the house or apartment. It is lost but not eradicated or destroyed.

Truth or Fiction Revisited. *It is true that there is no practical limit to the amount of information you can store in your memory.* At least no limit has been discovered to date.

Transferring Information from Short-Term to Long-Term Memory.

How is information transferred from short-term to long-term memory? By and large, the more often chunks of information are rehearsed, the more likely they are to be transferred to long-term memory (Rundus, 1971). We noted that repeating information over and over to prevent it from decaying or being displaced is termed *maintenance rehearsal*. Maintenance rehearsal does not attempt to give information meaning by linking it to past learning and is not considered an effective way to place information in permanent storage (Craik & Watkins, 1973).[1]

A more effective method is to make it more meaningful—or to purposefully

---

[1] Maintenance rehearsal, however, is responsible for rote learning.

relate new material to information that is already well known (Woloshyn and others, 1994). To better remember the components of levers, physics students might use seesaws, wheelbarrows, and oars as examples (Scruggs & Mastropieri, 1992). The nine chunks of information in our second challenge to memory were made easier to reconstruct once they were associated with the familiar tic-tac-toe grid in Figure 7.3. Relating new material to well-known material is known as **elaborative rehearsal** (Small, 1990). For example, have you seen this word before?

FUNTHOSTAM

Say it aloud. Do you know it? If you had used an acoustic code alone to memorize THUNSTOFAM, the list of letters you first saw on page 250, it might not have been easy to recognize FUNTHOSTAM as an incorrect spelling. Let us assume, however, that by now you have encoded THUNSTOFAM semantically as an acronym for "The United States of America." Then you would have been able to scan the spelling of the words in the phrase "The United States of America" to determine the correctness of FUNTHOSTAM. Of course, you would have found it to be incorrect.

As suggested earlier, pure repetition of a meaningless group of syllables, such as *thun-sto-fam,* would be relying on maintenance rehearsal for permanent storage. The process might be tedious (continued rehearsal) and unreliable. But usage of elaborative rehearsal—tying THUNSTOFAM to the name of a country—might make storage instantaneous and retrieval foolproof.

Truth or Fiction Revisited. *It is not true that learning must be meaningful if we are to remember it.* Nevertheless, elaborative rehearsal, which is based on the meanings of events or subject matter, is more efficient than maintenance rehearsal, which is based on rote repetition (Simpson and others, 1994).

You may recall that English teachers encouraged you to use new vocabulary words in sentences to help you remember them. Each new usage is an instance of elaborative rehearsal. Usage helps you build extended semantic codes that will help you retrieve

Elaborative rehearsal • A method for increasing retention of new information by relating it to information that is well known.

their meanings in the future. When I was in high school, foreign-language teachers told us that learning classical languages "exercises the mind" so that we would understand English better. Not exactly. The mind is not analogous to a muscle that responds to exercise. However, the meanings of many English words are based on foreign tongues. A person who recognizes that *retrieve* stems from roots meaning "again" *(re-)* and "find" *(trouver* in French) is less likely to forget that *retrieval* means "finding again" or "bringing back."

Think, too, of all the algebra and geometry problems we were asked to solve in high school. Each problem is an application of a procedure and, perhaps, of certain formulas and theorems. By repeatedly applying the procedures, formulas, and theorems in different contexts, we rehearse them elaboratively. As a consequence, we are more likely to remember them. Knowledge of the ways in which a formula or an equation is used helps us remember the formula. Also, by building theorem upon theorem in geometry, we relate new theorems to theorems that we already understand. As a result, we process information about them more deeply and remember them better.

Before proceeding to the next section, let me ask you to cover the preceding paragraph. Now, which of the following words is correctly spelled: *retrieval* or *retreival?* The spellings sound alike, so an acoustic code for reconstructing the correct spelling would fail. Yet a semantic code, such as the spelling rule "*i* before *e* except after *c,*" would allow you to reconstruct the correct spelling: retrieval.

Flashbulb Memories.

The attention which we lend to an experience is proportional to its vivid or interesting character; and it is a notorious fact that what interests us most vividly at the time is, other things equal, what we remember best. An impression may be so exciting emotionally as almost to leave a scar upon the cerebral tissues.

WILLIAM JAMES

Do you remember the first time you were in love? Can you remember how the streets and the trees looked somehow transformed? The vibrancy in your step? How generous you felt? How all of life's problems suddenly seemed to be solved?

Flashbulb Memories. Where were you and what were you doing when you learned that the Persian Gulf War had started in 1991, or that O. J. Simpson was involved in a chase on the Los Angeles freeways in 1994? Major happenings can illuminate everything about them, so that we clearly recall all the personal surrounding events. Many of us who are middle-aged or older will never forget where we were or what we were doing when we heard that President Kennedy had been shot.

We tend to remember events that occur under unusual, emotionally arousing circumstances more clearly. Those of us who are middle-aged and older tend to remember what we were doing when we heard that President John F. Kennedy had been shot in November 1963. Younger people tend to recall the events surrounding them on the day when the Persian Gulf War exploded in January 1991, or when they heard that O. J. Simpson was involved in a chase on the Los Angeles freeways. Similarly, we may remember in detail what we were doing when we learned of a relative's death. These are all examples of "flashbulb memories," because they preserve experiences in such detail (Brown & Kulik, 1977; Thompson & Cowan, 1986).

Why does the memory become etched when the "flashbulb" goes off? One factor is the distinctness of the memory. It is easier to discriminate stimuli that stand out. Such events are salient in themselves, and the feelings that are engendered by them are also rather special. It is thus relatively easy to pick them out from the storehouse of memories. Major events such as the assassi-nation of a president or the loss of a close relative also tend to have important effects on our lives, however. As a result, we are likely to dwell on them and form networks of associations; that is, we are likely to re-hearse them elaboratively. Our rehearsal may include great expectations about, or deep fears for, the future.

Organization in Long-Term Memory. The storehouse of long-term memory is usually well organized. Items are not just piled on the floor or thrown into closets. We tend to gather information about rats and cats into a certain section of the storehouse, perhaps the animal or mammal section. We put information about oaks, maples, and eucalyptus into the tree section.

Categorization is a basic cognitive function. Categorizing stimuli allows us to make predictions about specific instances and to store information efficiently (Corter & Gluck, 1992).

Preschoolers tend to organize their memories by grouping objects that share the same function (Lucariello & Nelson, 1985).

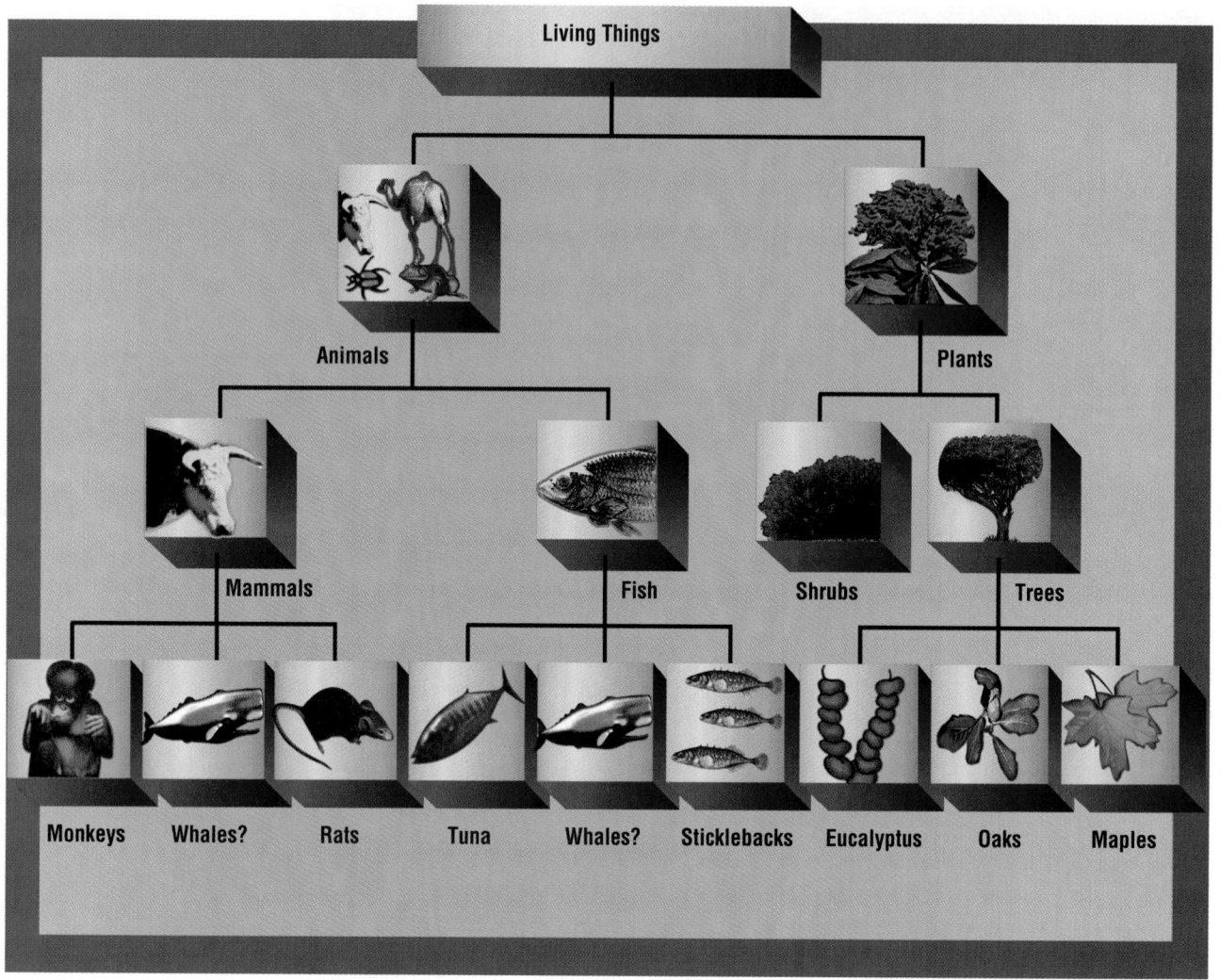

FIGURE 7.6
The Hierarchical Structure of Long-Term Memory Where are whales filed in the hierarchical cabinets of your memory? Your classification of whales may influence your answers to these questions: Do whales breathe underwater? Are they warm-blooded? Do they nurse their young?

At first, "toast" is grouped with "peanut butter sandwich" because both are eaten. Only during the early elementary school years are toast and peanut butter sandwich categorized as kinds of foods. Similarly, preschoolers and first graders may associate dogs and cats because they are often found together around the house (Björklund & de Marchena, 1984). Dogs and rabbits, however, are usually not placed in the same category until the concept "animal" is used to include them, which may not happen for a few more years.

As we develop, we tend to organize information according to a *hierarchical structure,* as shown in the graph in Figure 7.6. A hierarchy is an arrangement of items (or chunks of information) into groups or classes according to common or distinct features. As we work our way up the hierarchy shown in Figure 7.6, we find more encompassing, or **superordinate,** classes to which the items below belong. For example, all mammals are animals, but there are many types of animals to be found other than mammals.[2]

[2] A note to biological purists: Figure 7.6 is not intended to represent phyla, classes, orders, and so on accurately. Rather, it shows how an individual's classification scheme might be organized.

A Whale Nurses Her Young. Are whales categorized as mammals or fish in your memory? If the answer is fish, the content of this photograph may be of some surprise.

When items are correctly organized in long-term memory, you are more likely to recall—or know—accurate information about them (Hasselhorn, 1992; Schneider & Björklund, 1992). For instance, do you remember whether whales breathe underwater? If you did not know that whales are mammals (or, in Figure 7.6, **subordinate** to mammals), or if you knew nothing about mammals, a correct answer might depend on some remote instance of rote learning. That is, you might be depending on chancy episodic memory rather than on reliable semantic memory. For example, you might recall some details from a Public Broadcasting System documentary on whales. If you *did* know that whales are mammals, however, you would also know—or remember—that whales do not breathe underwater. How? You would reconstruct information about whales from knowledge about mammals, the group to which whales are subordinate. Similarly, you would know, or remember, that whales, because they are mammals, are warm-blooded, nurse their young, and are a good deal more intelligent than, say, tunas and sticklebacks, which are fish. Had you incorrectly classified whales as fish, you might have searched your memory and constructed the incorrect answer that they do breathe underwater.

Let us now consider some issues in the retrieval of information from long-term memory: the tip-of-the-tongue phenomenon, state-dependent memory, and context-dependent memory.

The Tip-of-the-Tongue Phenomenon. Have you ever been so close to re-trieving information that it seemed to be on "the tip of your tongue"? Still, you could not quite remember it? This is a frustrating experience, similar to reeling in a fish but having it drop off the line just before it breaks the surface of the water. Psychologists term this experience the **tip-of-the-tongue (TOT) phenomenon,** or the **feeling-of-knowing experience.**

In one TOT experiment, Brown and Mc-Neill (1966) defined some rather unusual words for students, such as *sampan,* which is a small riverboat used in China and Japan. Students were then asked to recall the words they had learned. Some of the students often had the right word "on the tips of their tongues" but reported words similar in meaning such as *junk, barge,* or *houseboat.* Still other students reported words that sounded similar such as *Saipan, Siam, sarong,* and *sanching.* Why?

To begin with, the words were unfamiliar, so elaborative rehearsal did not take place. The students, that is, did not have the opportunity to relate the words to other things that they knew. Brown and McNeill also suggested that our storage systems are indexed according to cues that include both the sounds and the meanings of words—according to both acoustic and semantic codes. By scanning words that are similar in sound and meaning to the word that is on the tip of the tongue, we sometimes find a useful cue and retrieve the word for which we are searching.

The feeling-of-knowing experience also seems to reflect incomplete or imperfect learning. In such cases, our answers may be "in the ballpark" if not on the mark.

MINILECTURE:
ORGANIZATION
AND LONG-
TERM MEMORY

Superordinate • Descriptive of a higher (inclusive) class or category in a hierarchy.

Subordinate • Descriptive of a lower (included) class or category in a hierarchy.

Tip-of-the-tongue phenomenon • The feeling that information is stored in memory although it cannot be readily retrieved. Also called the *feeling-of-knowing experience.*

Feeling-of-knowing experience • Same as *tip-of-the-tongue phenomenon.*

In some feeling-of-knowing experiments, people are often asked trivia questions. When they do not recall an answer, they are then asked to guess how likely it is that they will recognize the right answer if it is among a group of possibilities. People turn out to be very accurate in their estimations about whether or not they will recognize the answer. Similarly, Brown and McNeill found that the students in their TOT experiment proved to be very good at estimating the number of syllables in words they could not recall. The students often correctly guessed the initial sounds of the words and sometimes recognized words that rhymed with them.

Our sense that an answer is on the tips of our tongues thus often reflects incomplete knowledge. We may not know the exact answer, but we know something. (As a matter of fact, if we have good writing skills, we may present our incomplete knowledge so forcefully that we earn a good grade on an essay question on the topic!) At such times, the problem lies not in retrieval but in the original encoding and storage.

Context-Dependent Memory.   The context in which we acquire information can also play a role in retrieval. I remember walking down the halls of The Bronx apartment building where, as a child, I had lived many years earlier. I was suddenly assaulted by images of playing under the staircase, of falling against a radiator, of the shrill voice of a former neighbor calling for her child at dinnertime. Have you ever walked the halls of an old school and been assaulted by memories of faces and names that you would have guessed had been lost forever? Have you ever walked through your old neighborhood and recalled the faces of people or the aromas of cooking that were so real you salivated?

These are examples of **context-dependent memory.** Being in the proper context, that is, can dramatically enhance recall (Estes, 1972; Watkins and others, 1976). One fascinating experiment in context-dependent memory included a number of people who were "all wet." Members of a university swimming club were asked to learn lists of words either while they were submerged or literally high and dry (Godden & Baddeley, 1975). Students who learned the list underwa-

ter showed superior recall of the list when immersed. Those who had rehearsed the list ashore, similarly, showed better retrieval on terra firma.

Other studies have found that students do better on tests when they study in the room where the test is to be given (Smith and others, 1978). When police are interviewing witnesses to crimes, they have the witnesses verbally paint the scene as vividly as possible, or they visit the scene of the crime with the witnesses. People who mentally place themselves back in the context in which they encoded and stored information frequently retrieve it more accurately.

State-Dependent Memory.   **State-dependent memory** is an extension of context-dependent memory. It sometimes happens that we retrieve information better when we are in a physiological or emotional state that is similar to the one in which we encoded and stored the information. Drugs, for example, alter our physiological response patterns. They can influence the production and uptake of neurotransmitters involved in learning and memory and can modify the general state of alertness of the body. It also happens that material that is learned "under the influence" of a drug may be most readily retrieved when the person is again under the influence of that drug (Overton, 1985).

Our moods may also serve as cues that aid in the retrieval of memories. Feeling the rush of love may trigger images of other times when we had fallen in love. The grip of anger may prompt memories of frustration and rage. Gordon Bower (1981) ran experiments in which happy or sad moods were induced in people by hypnotic suggestion, and the subjects then learned lists of words. People who learned a list while in a happy mood showed better recall when a happy state was induced again. But people who had learned the list when a sad mood had been induced showed superior recall when they were saddened again. Bower suggests that in day-to-day life, a happy mood influences us to focus on positive events. As a result, we will have better recall of these happy events in the future. A sad mood, unfortunately, leads us to focus on and recall the negative. Happiness may feed on happiness, but sadness under extreme

Context-dependent memory • Information that is better retrieved in the context in which it was encoded and stored, or learned.

State-dependent memory • Information that is better retrieved in the physiological or emotional state in which it was encoded and stored, or learned.

circumstances can develop into a vicious cycle.

Reflections

Now that you have read the section on stages of memory, reflect on the following questions:

- Are you good or bad at remembering people's names? How about telephone numbers? What strategies do you use for storing and retrieving them?
- Do you know some people with excellent memories? Some with poor memories? How would you have explained why some people have good memories and others poor memories before you began to study psychology? How has your study of psychology affected the ways in which you would account for a good memory or a poor memory?
- Must you make a list to remember to buy what you need at a supermarket? If not, how do you remember what you need? (Or do you often fail to remember what you need?)
- Are there some things that you feel sure you will never forget? Why?
- How is it that these "Reflections" sections may help you remember the subject matter in this course?
- Have you ever had the experience of having something on "the tip of your tongue" but not being quite able to get at it? How does the text explain this experience?

The Levels-of-Processing Model of Memory

Not all psychologists view memory in terms of stages. Fergus Craik and Robert Lockhart (1972) suggest that we do not have a sensory memory, a short-term memory, and a long-term memory per se. Instead, our ability to remember things can also be viewed in terms of a single stage or dimension—the depth of our processing of information. Put it another way: According to Craik and Lockhart, we don't form enduring memories by getting information into the mental structure of long-term

memory. Rather, memories tend to endure when information is processed deeply—when it is attended to, encoded carefully, pondered, and rehearsed elaboratively or related to things we already know well.

Consider our by now familiar list of letters, THUNSTOFAM. In an experiment, we could ask one group of people to remember the list by repeating it aloud a few times, a letter at a time. Another group could be informed that it is an acronym for "The United States of America." If several months later each group were shown several similar lists of words and asked to select the correct list, which group do you think would be more likely to pick out THUNSTOFAM from the pack? It ought to be the group told of the acronym, because the information in that group would have been processed more deeply. It would have been semantically encoded and rehearsed elaboratively. The group engaging in more superficial information processing would be sticking to acoustic coding and maintenance rehearsal. In another example, consider why so many people have difficulty selecting the accurate drawing of the Lincoln penny. Is it perhaps because they have processed information about the appearance of a penny rather superficially? If they knew they were going to be quizzed about the features of a penny, however, wouldn't they process information about its appearance more deeply? That is, wouldn't they study the features and purposefully note whether the profile is facing toward the left or right, what the lettering says, and where the date goes?

Also weigh a fascinating experiment with three groups of college students, all of whom were asked to study a picture of a living room for 1 minute (Bransford and others, 1977). Their examination entailed different approaches, however. Two groups were informed that small x's were imbedded in the picture. The first of these groups was asked to find the x's by scanning the picture horizontally and vertically. The second group was informed that the x's could be found in the edges of the objects in the room and was asked to look for them there. The third group was asked, instead, to think about how it would use the objects pictured in the room. As a result of the divergent sets of instructions, the first two groups (the *x* hunters) processed information about the objects in the picture superficially. But the third group rehearsed the objects elaboratively—that is, the group members thought about the objects in terms of their meanings and uses. It should not be surprising that the third group remembered many times more objects than the first two groups.

Researchers more recently asked participants to indicate whether they recognized photos of faces that they had been shown under one of three conditions: being asked to recall the (1) gender or the (2) width of the nose of the person in the photo, or being asked to judge (3) whether the person is honest (Sporer, 1991). It is likely that asking people to judge other people's honesty stimulates deeper processing of the features of the faces (Bloom & Mudd, 1991). That is, they look at more facial features, study each in more detail, and attempt to relate what they see to their ideas about human nature.

Note that the levels-of-processing model finds uses for most of the concepts employed by those who think of memory in terms of stages. For example, adherents to this model also speak of the basic memory processes (encoding, storage, and retrieval) and of different kinds of rehearsal. The essential difference is that they view memory as consisting of a single dimension or entity that varies according to depth.

MINILECTURE:
TECHNIQUES
FOR
MEASURING
RETRIEVAL

Reflections

Now that you have read about the levels-of-processing model of memory, reflect on the following questions:

- You can remember the list of letters THUNSTOFAM by repeating it several times or by thinking of the phrase "The United States of America." Would the stage model of memory and the levels-of-processing model of memory agree or disagree on which method would lead to a longer lasting memory? Why?
- You probably do better in some subjects than others or at least find the information in some subjects easier to remember. Can you use the levels-of-processing model of memory to explain why the material in some subjects is easier to remember than the material in others?

We have been discussing remembering for quite some time. Since variety is supposed to be the spice of life, let's consider forgetting for a while.

Forgetting

What do DAL, RIK, BOF, and ZEX have in common? They are all **nonsense syllables.** Nonsense syllables are meaningless sets of two consonants with a vowel sandwiched in between. They were first used by German psychologist Hermann Ebbinghaus (1850–1909) and have since been used by many psychologists to study memory and forgetting.

Because nonsense syllables are intended to be meaningless, remembering them should depend on simple acoustic coding and maintenance rehearsal rather than on elaborative rehearsal, semantic coding, or other ways of making learning meaningful. Nonsense syllables provide a means of measuring simple memorization ability in studies of the three basic memory tasks of recognition, recall, and relearning. Studying these memory tasks has led to several conclusions about the nature of forgetting.

MEMORY TASKS USED IN MEASURING FORGETTING

Recognition. There are many ways of measuring **recognition.** In one study of high school graduates, Harry Bahrick and his colleagues (1975) interspersed photos of classmates with four times as many photos of strangers. Recent graduates correctly recognized persons who were former schoolmates 90% of the time, whereas those who had been out of school for 40 years recognized former classmates 75% of the time. A chance level of recognition would have been only 20% (one photo in five was of an actual classmate). Thus, even older graduates showed rather solid long-term recognition ability.

In many studies of recognition, psychologists ask participants to read a list of nonsense syllables. The participants then read a second list of nonsense syllables and indicate whether they recognize any of the syllables as having appeared on the first list. Forgetting is defined as failure to recognize a nonsense syllable that has been read before.

Recognition is the easiest type of memory task. This is why multiple-choice tests are easier than fill-in-the-blank or essay tests. We can recognize or identify photos of former classmates more easily than we can recall their names.

Recall. In his own studies of **recall,** another kind of memory task, Ebbinghaus would read lists of nonsense syllables aloud to the beat of a metronome and then see how many he could produce from memory. After reading through a list once, he usually would be able to recall seven nonsense syllables—the typical limit for short-term memory.

Psychologists also often use lists of pairs of nonsense syllables, called **paired associates,** to measure recall. A list of paired associates is shown in Figure 7.7. Study participants read through the lists pair by pair. Later, they are shown the first member of each pair and are asked to recall the second. Recall is more difficult than recognition. In a recognition task, one simply indicates whether an item has been seen before or which of a number of items is paired with a stimulus (as in a multiple-choice test). In a recall task, the person must retrieve a syllable with another syllable serving as a cue.

Retrieval is made easier if the two syllables can be meaningfully linked—encoded semantically—even if the "meaning" is stretched a bit. Consider the first pair of nonsense syllables in Figure 7.7. The image of a WOMan smoking a CEGarette may make CEG easier to retrieve when the person is presented with the cue WOM.

As we develop throughout childhood, our ability to recall information increases. This memory improvement is apparently linked to our growing ability to process (categorize) stimulus cues quickly (Howard & Polich, 1985). In one study, Kail and Nippold (1984) asked 8-, 12-, and 21-year-olds to name as many animals and pieces of furniture as they could during separate 7-minute intervals. The number of items recalled increased with age for both animals and furniture. For all age groups, items were retrieved according to classes. For example, in the animal category, a series of fish might be named, then a series of birds, and so on.

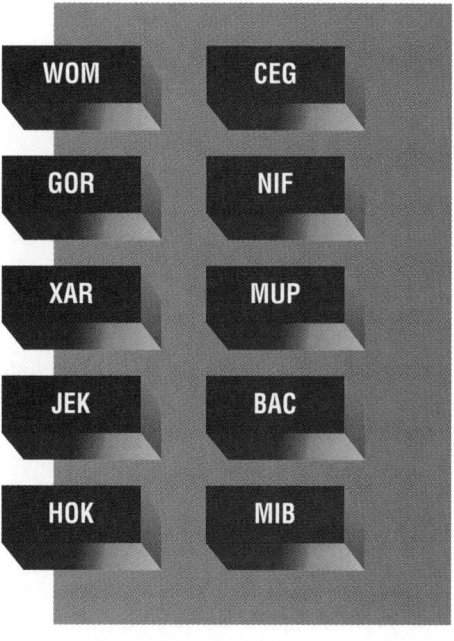

FIGURE 7.7
Paired Associates Psychologists often use paired associates, like those to the left, to measure recall. Retrieving CEG in response to the cue WOM is made easier by an image of a WOMan smoking a CEGarette.

It is easier to recall vocabulary words from foreign languages if you can construct a meaningful link between the foreign and English words (Atkinson, 1975). The *peso,* pronounced *pay-so,* is a unit of Mexican money. A link can be formed by finding a part of the foreign word, such as the *pe-* (pronounced *pay*) in *peso,* and constructing a phrase such as "You pay with money." When you read or hear the word *peso* in the future, you recognize the *pe-* and retrieve the link or phrase. From the phrase, you then reconstruct the translation, "a unit of money."

Some people who have been hypnotized show **posthypnotic amnesia.** They are unable, for example, to recall previously learned word lists (Kihlstrom, 1980). Spanos and his colleagues (1980, 1982) hypothesize that posthypnotic amnesia occurs when hypnotized subjects interpret the suggestion not to recall information as an "invitation" to refrain from attending to retrieval cues. A hypnotized person might be told that he or she will not be able to recall the colors of the spectrum upon awakening. This suggestion might be interpreted as an invitation *not* to focus on the acronym Roy G. Biv.

Relearning: Is Learning Easier the Second Time Around? **Relearning** is a third method of measuring retention. Do you remember having to learn all of the state capitals in grade school? What were

Nonsense syllables • Meaningless sets of two consonants, with a vowel sandwiched in between, that are used to study memory.

Recognition • In information processing, the easiest memory task, involving identification of objects or events encountered before.

Recall • Retrieval or reconstruction of learned material.

Paired associates • Nonsense syllables presented in pairs in experiments that measure recall.

Posthypnotic amnesia • Inability to recall material presented while hypnotized, following the suggestion of the hypnotist.

Relearning • A measure of retention. Material is usually relearned more quickly than it is learned initially.

the capitals of Wyoming and Delaware? Even when we cannot recall or recognize material that had once been learned, we can relearn it more rapidly the second time, such as Cheyenne for Wyoming and Dover for Delaware. Similarly, as we go through our 30s and 40s we may forget a good deal of our high school French or geometry. Yet, we could learn what took months or years much more rapidly the second time around.

To study the efficiency of relearning, Ebbinghaus (1885) devised the **method of savings.** First, he recorded the number of repetitions required to learn a list of nonsense syllables or words. Then, he recorded the number of repetitions required to relearn the list after a certain amount of time had elapsed. Next, he computed the difference between the number of repetitions required to arrive at the **savings.** If a list had to be repeated 20 times before it was learned, and 20 times again after a year had passed, there were no savings. Relearning, that is, was as tedious as the initial learning. However, if the list could be learned with only 10 repetitions after a year had elapsed, half the number of repetitions required for learning had been saved. (Ten is half of 20.)

Figure 7.8 is Ebbinghaus's classic curve of forgetting. As you can see, there was no loss of memory as measured by savings immediately after a list had been learned. However, recollection dropped precipitously during the first hour after learning a list. Losses of learning then became more gradual. Whereas retention dropped by half within the first hour, it took a month (31 days) for retention to be cut in half again. In other words, forgetting occurred most rapidly right after material was learned. We continue to forget material as time elapses but at a relatively slower rate.

Before leaving this section, I have one question for you: What are the capitals of Wyoming and Delaware?

INTERFERENCE THEORY

When we do not attend to, encode, and rehearse sensory input, we may forget it through decay of the trace of the image. Material in short-term memory, like material in sensory memory, can be lost through decay. It can also be lost through displacement, as may happen when we try to remember several new names at a party.

According to **interference theory,** we also forget material in short-term and long-term memory because newly learned material interferes with it. The two basic types of interference are retroactive interference (also called *retroactive inhibition*) and proactive interference (also called *proactive inhibition*).

Retroactive Interference. In **retroactive interference,** new learning interferes with the retrieval of old learning. A

FIGURE 7.8
Ebbinghaus's Classic Curve of Forgetting Recollection of lists of words dropped precipitously during the first hour after learning. Losses of learning then became more gradual. Whereas retention dropped by half within the first hour, it took a month (31 days) for retention to be cut in half again.

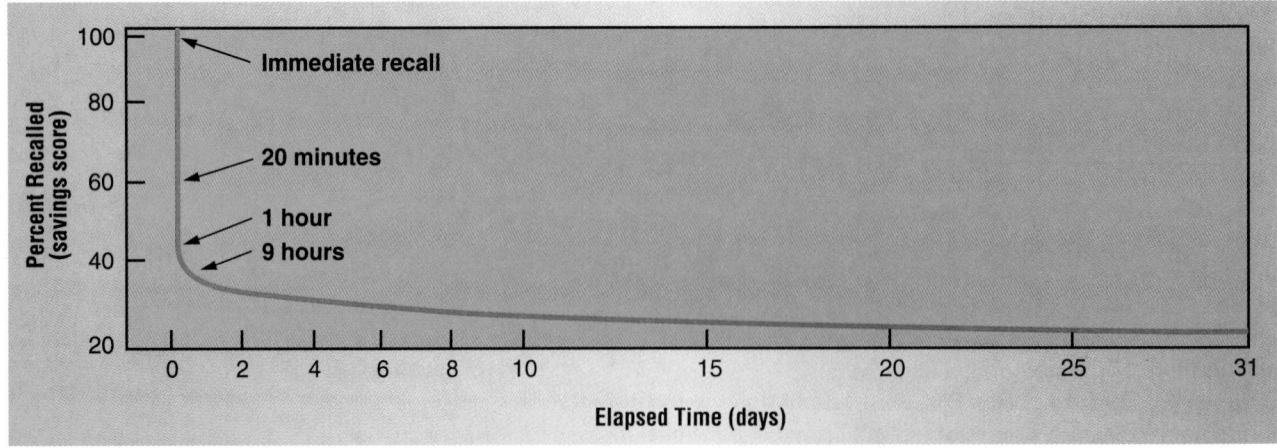

Interference. In retroactive interference, new learning interferes with the retrieval of old learning. In proactive interference, older learning interferes with the capacity to retrieve more recently learned material. High-school French vocabulary may "pop in," for example, when you are trying to retrieve Spanish words learned for a test in college.

medical student may memorize the names of the bones in the leg through rote repetition. Later, he or she may find that learning the names of the bones in the arm makes it more difficult to retrieve the names of the leg bones, especially if the names are similar in sound or in relative location on each limb.

Proactive Interference. In **proactive interference,** older learning interferes with the capacity to retrieve more recently learned material. High school Spanish may pop in when you are trying to retrieve college French or Italian words. All three are Romance languages, with similar roots and spellings. Old Japanese vocabulary words probably would not interfere with your ability to retrieve more-recently learned French or Italian, because many Japanese roots and sounds differ considerably from those of the Romance languages.

Consider motor skills. You may learn how to drive a standard shift on a car with three forward speeds and a clutch that must be let up slowly after shifting. Later, you learn to drive a car with five forward speeds and a clutch that must be released rapidly. For a

while, you make a number of errors on the five-speed car because of proactive interference. (Old learning interferes with new learning.) If you return to the three-speed car after driving the five-speed car has become natural, you may stall it a few times. This is because of retroactive interference (new learning interfering with the old).

REPRESSION

According to Sigmund Freud, we are motivated to forget painful memories and unacceptable ideas because they produce anxiety, guilt, and shame. (In terms of operant conditioning, anxiety, guilt, and shame serve as negative reinforcers. We learn to do that which is followed by their removal—in this case, to avoid thinking about certain events and ideas.) In Chapter 13, we shall see that psychoanalysts believe that repression is at the heart of disorders such as **dissociative amnesia.**

INFANTILE AMNESIA

When he interviewed people about their early experiences, Freud discovered that they could not recall events that happened

Method of savings • A measure of retention in which the difference between the number of repetitions originally required to learn a list and the number of repetitions required to relearn the list after a certain amount of time has elapsed is calculated.

Savings • The difference between the number of repetitions originally required to learn a list and the number of repetitions required to relearn the list after a certain amount of time has elapsed.

Interference theory • The view that we may forget stored material because other learning interferes with it.

Retroactive interference • The interference of new learning with the ability to retrieve material learned previously.

Proactive interference • The interference by old learning with the ability to retrieve material learned recently.

Dissociative amnesia • Amnesia thought to stem from psychological conflict or trauma. (See Chapter 13.)

prior to the age of 3 and that recall was very cloudy through the age of 5. This phenomenon is referred to as **infantile amnesia,** also called childhood amnesia. Many of us think that we have vivid recollections of key events of infancy. Yet research that attempts to verify such memories by interviewing independent older witnesses shows that they are usually inaccurate (e.g., Sheingold & Tenney, 1982).

Infantile amnesia has nothing to do with the fact that the events are of the distant past. Middle-aged and elderly people have vivid memories from the ages of 6 and 10, yet the events are many decades old. But 18-year-olds show steep declines in memory when they try to recall events earlier than the age of 6, even though these events are fewer than 18 years away (Wetzler & Sweeney, 1986).

Freud believed that young children have aggressive impulses and perverse lusts toward their parents, and he attributed infantile amnesia to their repression (Goleman, 1993). However, the events lost to infantile amnesia are not weighted in the direction of such "primitive" impulses. Many such incidents are pedestrian and emotionally bland. The effects of infantile amnesia are too broad for Freud's hypothesis to hold water.

Infantile amnesia probably reflects the interaction of physiological and cognitive factors. For example, a structure of the limbic system (the **hippocampus**) that is involved in the storage of memories does not become mature until we are about 2 years old. Also, myelination of brain pathways is incomplete for the first few years, contributing to the inefficiency of information processing and memory formation. There are also cognitive reasons for infantile amnesia. One is that very young children are not particularly interested in the past (Neisser, 1993). Another is that infants, in contrast to older children, tend not to weave specific events (episodes) together into meaningful stories of their own lives, or autobiographies (Hudson, 1993). Specific information (information about episodes) thus tends to be lost. Infants also do not make reliable use of language to symbolize or classify events. Their ability to *encode*

sensory input—that is, to apply the auditory and semantic codes that facilitate memory formation—is thus limited.

Truth or Fiction Revisited. *It is not true that we can remember important events that take place during the first 2 years of life.* (Really, Allyn, believe me.) Those early childhood memories that we are so certain we can see today are probably reconstructed and mostly inaccurate. Or else they may stem from a time when we were older than we think.

ANTEROGRADE AND RETROGRADE AMNESIA

In **anterograde amnesia,** there are memory lapses for the period following a trauma such as a blow to the head, an electric shock, or an operation. In some cases, it seems that the trauma interferes with all the processes of memory. The ability to pay attention, the encoding of sensory input, and rehearsal are all impaired. A number of investigators have linked certain kinds of brain damage—such as that to the hippocampus—to amnesia (Corkin and others, 1985; Squire and others, 1984).

Consider the classic case of a man with the initials H. M. Parts of the brain are sometimes lesioned to help people with epilepsy. In H. M.'s case, a section of the hippocampus was removed (Milner, 1966). Right after the operation, the man's mental functioning appeared to be normal. As time went on, however, it became quite clear that he had severe problems in the processing of information. For example, 2 years after the operation, H. M. believed that he was 27—his age at the time of the operation. When his family relocated to a new address, H. M. could not find his new home or remember the new address. He responded with appropriate grief to the death of his uncle, yet he then began to ask about his uncle and why he did not visit. Each time he was informed of his uncle's passing, he grieved as he had when he first heard of it. All in all, it seems that H. M.'s operation prevented him from transferring information from short-term memory to long-term memory.

In **retrograde amnesia,** the source of trauma prevents people from remembering

---

Infantile amnesia • Inability to recall events that occur prior to the age of 2 or 3. Also termed *childhood amnesia.*

Hippocampus • A structure in the limbic system that plays an important role in the formation of new memories.

Anterograde amnesia • Failure to remember events that occur after physical trauma because of the effects of the trauma.

Retrograde amnesia • Failure to remember events that occur prior to physical trauma because of the effects of the trauma.

Consolidation • The fixing of information in long-term memory.

Engram • (1) An assumed electrical circuit in the brain that corresponds to a memory trace. (2) An assumed chemical change in the brain that accompanies learning. (From the Greek *en-,* meaning "in," and *gramma,* meaning "something that is written or recorded.")

events that took place before the accident. A football player who is knocked unconscious or a person in an auto accident may be unable to recall events that occurred for several minutes prior to the trauma. The football player may not recall taking to the field. The person in the accident may not recall entering the car. It also sometimes happens that the individual cannot remember events that occurred for several years prior to the traumatic incident.

In one well-known case of retrograde amnesia, a man received a head injury in a motorcycle accident (Baddeley, 1982). When he regained consciousness, he had lost memory for all events after the age of 11. In fact, he appeared to believe that he was still 11 years old. During the next few months, he gradually recovered more knowledge of his past. He moved toward the present year by year, up until the critical motorcycle ride. But he never did recover the events just prior to the accident. The accident had apparently prevented the information that was rapidly unfolding before him from being transferred to long-term memory.

In terms of stages of memory, it may be that our perceptions and ideas need to **consolidate,** or rest undisturbed for a while, if they are to be transferred to long-term memory.

Reflections

Let's see if we can help you remember about forgetting by having you reflect on the following questions!

- Consider the memory tasks of recognition, recall, and relearning. What kinds of tasks do most of your tests rely on?
- Can you find an example of retroactive or proactive interference in your own life?
- What are your earliest memories? How do you know the proper dates of the experiences? How do you know how accurate your memories are? What types of experiences or processes are likely to distort these memories?

Let us now turn our attention to some of the biological events that appear to be involved in the formation of memories.

The Biology of Memory: From Engrams to Adrenaline

Psychologists generally assume that mental processes are accompanied by changes in the brain. In Chapters 2 and 3, we described some of the ways in which psychologists discover the changes that take place as we, say, solve math problems or listen to music. Psychologists similarly assume that changes in the brain accompany the encoding, storage, and retrieval of information—that is, memory.

Early in the century, many psychologists used the concept of the **engram** in their study of memory. Engrams were hypothesized electrical circuits in the brain that were assumed to correspond to memory traces—a neurological process that was believed to parallel a phenomenological experience. Biological psychologists such as Karl Lashley (1950) spent many fruitless years searching for such circuits or for the structures of the brain in which they might be housed.

During the 1950s and 1960s, research groups headed by James McConnell at the University of Michigan (McConnell and others, 1970) believed that they had found the elusive engram in ribonucleic acid (RNA). Whereas DNA "remembers" the genetic code from generation to generation, it was thought that the related organic compound, RNA, changed with experience so that personal events and knowledge could be stored and retrieved. RNA came to be dubbed "memory molecules." The McConnell group managed to condition flatworms to scrunch up when a light was shone by pairing the light with electric shock. Then they "taught" naive flatworms this response by feeding them RNA from chopped-up learners. When this research was young and filled with promise, many students joked that perhaps the fastest route to knowledge lay in doing to their professors what the worm researchers had done to their subjects. Unfortunately for this approach—but fortunately for professors—research with RNA could not be replicated

MINILECTURE: THE BIOLOGY OF MEMORY

by other investigators (Sommer, 1991). Psychologists thus turned elsewhere.

Much contemporary research on the biology of memory focuses on the roles of neurons, neurotransmitters, and hormones.

CHANGES AT THE NEURAL LEVEL

Rats that are reared in richly stimulating environments develop more dendrites and synapses in the cerebral cortex than rats reared in relatively impoverished environments (Rosenzweig and others, 1972). It also has been shown that the level of visual stimulation rats receive is associated with the number of synapses they develop in the visual cortex (Turner & Greenough, 1985). In sum, there is reason to believe that the storage of experience requires that the number of avenues of communication among brain cells be increased.

Thus, changes occur in the visual cortex as a result of visual experience. Changes are also likely to occur in the auditory cortex as a result of heard experiences. Information received through the other senses is just as likely to lead to corresponding changes in the cortical regions that represent them. The storage of experiences that are perceived by several senses is thus likely to involve numerous areas of the brain (Squire, 1986). The recollection of experiences, as in the production of visual images, also apparently involves neural activity in the appropriate regions of the brain (Kosslyn, 1994).

Research with sea snails such as *Aplysia* and *Hermissenda* has offered insight into the events that take place at existing synapses when learning occurs. *Aplysia,* for example, has only about 20,000 neurons compared with humans' *billions* (Kandel & Hawkins, 1992). As a result, researchers have actually been able to study how experience is reflected at the synapses of specific neurons. When sea snails are conditioned, more of the neurotransmitter serotonin is released at certain synapses. As a consequence, transmission at these synapses becomes more efficient as trials (learning) progress (Goelet and others, 1986; Kandel & Hawkins, 1992).

Many other naturally occurring chemical substances have been shown to play roles in memory. The hormone adrenaline, for example, generally stimulates bodily arousal and activity. It also strengthens memory when it is released into the bloodstream following instances of learning (Delanoy and others, 1982; Laroche & Bloch, 1982; McGaugh, 1983). The neurotransmitter acetylcholine (ACh) is also vital in memory formation, as is highlighted by the study of Alzheimer's disease (see Chapter 3).

Another hormone that can play a role in memory is antidiuretic hormone, also known as vasopressin. Vasopressin apparently stimulates social memory in male rats. Rats whose vasopressin activity has been blocked size up old acquaintances with full-body sniffs, a ritual normally reserved for strange rats (Angier, 1993). People given a synthetic form of vasopressin through nasal sprays have shown significant improvement in recall (McGaugh, 1983). Excess vasopressin, unfortunately, can have serious side effects such as constriction of the blood vessels.

CHANGES AT THE STRUCTURAL LEVEL

Consider the problems that beset H. M. following his epilepsy operation. Certain parts of the brain such as the hippocampus also appear to be involved in the formation of new memories—or the transfer of information from short-term memory to long-term memory. The hippocampus does not comprise the "storage bins" for memories themselves, because H. M.'s memories prior to the operation were not destroyed. Rather, the hippocampus is involved in relaying incoming sensory information to parts of the cortex. Therefore, it appears to be vital to the storage of new information even if old information can be retrieved without it (Murray & Mishkin, 1985; Squire, 1986).

Where are the storage bins? Figure 7.9 shows that the brain stores parts of memories in the appropriate areas of the sensory cortex (Moscovitch, 1994). Sights are stored in the visual cortex, sounds in the auditory cortex, and so on. The limbic system is largely responsible for integrating these shards of information when we recall an event. Research with animals and people with brain injuries suggests that an area in the frontal lobe (labeled "Place and Time")

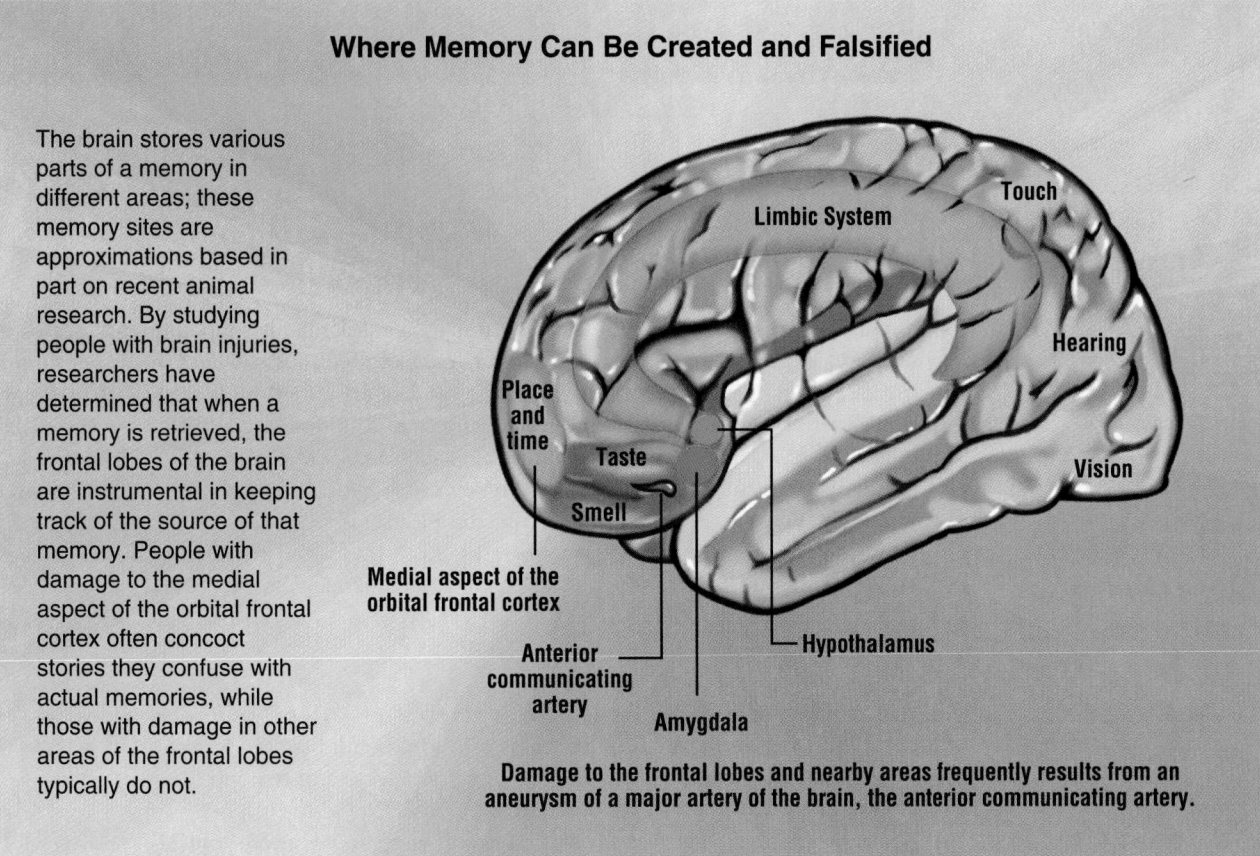

Where Memory Can Be Created and Falsified

The brain stores various parts of a memory in different areas; these memory sites are approximations based in part on recent animal research. By studying people with brain injuries, researchers have determined that when a memory is retrieved, the frontal lobes of the brain are instrumental in keeping track of the source of that memory. People with damage to the medial aspect of the orbital frontal cortex often concoct stories they confuse with actual memories, while those with damage in other areas of the frontal lobes typically do not.

Damage to the frontal lobes and nearby areas frequently results from an aneurysm of a major artery of the brain, the anterior communicating artery.

FIGURE 7.9
Where Memories Are Stored The brain apparently stores parts of memories in the appropriate areas of the sensory cortex. Memories of sights and sounds are kept in separate "bins" and pieced back together when we recall an event. An area in the frontal lobe (labeled "Place and Time") apparently stores much information as to the sources of memories.

stores information as to where and when an event occurred. People with damage to this part of the frontal lobe frequently attempt to fill in the memory gaps by making up stories as to when and where events have taken place.

The hippocampus, a part of the limbic system, is also involved in the where and when of things. We noted earlier that the hippocampus does not become mature until we are about 2 years old. Immaturity may be connected with infantile amnesia. Adults with hippocampal damage may be able to form new procedural memories, even though they cannot form new episodic ("where and when") memories. For example, they can acquire the skill of reading words backwards even though they

cannot recall individual practice sessions (Squire, 1986).

The thalamus, a structure near the center of the brain, appears to be involved in the formation of verbal memories. Part of the thalamus of an unfortunate Air Force cadet, known as N. A., was lesioned in a freak fencing accident. Following the episode, N. A. could no longer form verbal memories. However, his ability to form visual memories was unimpaired (Squire, 1986).

The encoding, storage, and retrieval of information thus involves biological activity on several levels. As we learn, new synapses are developed, and changes occur at existing synapses. Various parts and structures of the brain are also involved in the formation of different kinds of memories.

PSYCHOLOGY IN THE NEW MILLENNIUM

Getting Organized to the Max: Adventures in Living with an Electronic Memory

You say you have trouble remembering things like assignments, appointments, addresses, telephone numbers, ideas you wanted to include in a paper, and the like? Today's electronic organizers help people keep track of things, but they are rather crude devices. What might an electronic organizer be like in the new millennium? Consider a futuristic organizer that might also be connected with your household appliances and devices. . . .

Your alarm goes off in the morning and you instruct it firmly to shut off and try again in 7 minutes. You turn over and your Psytronics Electronic Organizer (E.O.) says, "Alan, it is now 6:45 on the morning of December 12, 2007. You asked me to get you up the first time today because you have a meeting with Sandra Hernandez at 8:30 A.M."

"No!" you say, banging the pillow.

"Do you want me to cancel?"

"No, no. Don't cancel. Keep bugging me."

"Alan, it is now 6:46 on the morning of December 12, 2007. You asked me to get you up the first time today because you have a meeting with Sandra Hernandez at 8:30 A.M."

"She's really very nice," you mutter. The organizer does not respond.

"What do I wear?" you say.

"Please note that you can arrange for apparel suggestions ahead of time. Is this a very formal business meeting, a slightly formal business meeting, a casual business meeting, a formal affair, a . . ."

"It's a slightly formal business meeting," you interject, annoyed with the organizer's mild upbraiding and not wanting to hear the entire menu.

"First choice would be the gray striped suit, the blue shirt with the white collar, the red and blue striped tie, black socks, and black wing tips. But I see that the red and blue striped tie is rumpled. [Another upbraiding? you wonder.] Do you wish alternatives?"

"No!"

"Alan, it is now 6:47 on the morning of December 12, 2007. You asked me to get you up the first time today because you have a meeting with Sandra Hernandez at 8:30 A.M. This is my third notice. You have two messages waiting. Neither one is from Sandra Hernandez."

"You can count."

"One message is marked urgent and is from your mother's E.O. Her message is as follows: 'Dear Alan: I hope that you will get out on time today and that your meeting will be very successful.'"

"Tell my mother's E.O. to butt out!"

"Do you wish me to notify your mother's E.O. that we no longer accept correspondence from that source."

"No, no. Forget it. I'm going to shower. Warm up the bathroom and start the coffee." (It took you months to get over using the word "please" with your E.O. But you still sometimes feel the urge to say "please". In the new millennium, psychologists are writing papers suggesting that electronic organizers be programmed not to follow instructions unless the user says "please," because the use of the polite term had all but dropped out of person-to-person language usage as a result of the introduction of the organizers.)

In the shower, you say, "Tell Sandra Hernandez's E.O. [electronic organizer] that I'm on schedule. Remind me of the four points I wanted to make at the meeting. Speak up because the water is running. What were the messages?"

A Woman Uses Her Electronic Organizer, Vintage 1990s. What forms will the electronic organizer take in the new millennium? How will it augment our own memories?

"The water usually does run in the shower." That's the private joke you programmed into the organizer. You smile, almost dutifully, but it's beginning to wear thin, even though the statement is made with a slightly novel inflection each time. After a pause, the organizer continues, "Do you want me to list the four points first or report the two messages first?"

A pretty crude organizer, you think; it used the word "first" two times when one would have done. Well, that's what happens when you lease something less than top of the line. Limited memory; limited *Grammarian*.

And so it goes. When you leave home, of course, you take the hand-held, battery-powered unit with you. It is connected to your larger home unit via wireless communication. You would not leave home without it. After all, you might forget something.

Now that you have read about the kind of electronic organizer that might come into usage in the new millennium, reflect on the following questions: Do you think the availability of such organizers would decrease your motivation to place information in your own long-term memory? From what you know of memory, would that "weaken" your memory or free you to focus on more important things?

Many people find using computers and today's electronic organizers to be complicated. Can you think of ways that psychologists could make such organizers user friendly, enough that it was easy—even fun—to learn how to use them?

Reflections

Now that you have read the section on the biology of memory, reflect on the following questions:

- Which biological theory of memory might have encouraged cannibalism? (Why is your psychology professor fortunate that research evidence has not confirmed this theory?)
- Assume that you could manufacture any chemical you wished and that it had no harmful side effects. What kinds of pills might you try taking during class or while reading textbooks to help you remember the subject matter?

Research into the biology of memory is in its infancy, but what an exciting area of research it is. What would it mean to you if you could read for an hour, pop a pill, and cause your new learnings to become consolidated in long-term memory? You would never have to reread the material; it would be at your fingertips for a lifetime. It would save a bit of study time, would it not?

A Final Challenge to Memory

Now that you've become an expert on memory, I'm going to give you a final challenge—an odd challenge but one that I bet you'll be able to meet quite well.

At the stroke of midnight on December 31, 2000, I challenge you to remember to say the following list of letters to yourself: T-H-U-N-S-T-O-F-A-M. As you join in the mass reveling of that special New Year's Eve—the one when we usher in the new millennium—repeat that list of letters silently to yourself. Oh, you may also kiss your partner, toot a horn, throw confetti into the air, and any number of other things. But also think T-H-U-N-S-T-O-F-A-M.

Why do I have such confidence in you? Why would I be willing to gamble that you'll be able to set aside other concerns for a few seconds on that New Year's Eve? There are two reasons. The first is that you'll surely be able to retrieve the letter list because of your enduring knowledge that it is an acronym for "The United States of America." The second is that this challenge is so unusual—so distinct from the other happenings in your life—that you may just store it deeply enough to jar your memory years into the future.

And if you don't meet this challenge, might you have the nagging thought that there was something you were going to do as the third millennium displaces the second? Might the challenge be—as some psychologists say—right on the tip of your tongue? And on that same New Year's Eve, my daughter Allyn—who will refuse to think T-H-U-N-S-T-O-F-A-M no matter what—will probably still be insisting that she can remember being born.

Summary

1. **What are the three kinds of memory suggested by Tulving?** These are episodic memory (memory for specific events that one has experienced), semantic memory (general knowledge), and procedural memory (skills).

2. **What are the three processes of memory?** These are encoding, storage, and retrieval. We commonly use visual, auditory, and semantic codes in the process of encoding.

3. **What are the three stages of memory proposed by the Atkinson-Shiffrin model?** These are sensory, short-term, and long-term memory.

4. **What are sensory registers?** These hold stimuli in sensory memory. Psychologists believe that information perceived through each sense has a register.

5. **What is the importance of Sperling's research?** Sperling demonstrated that visual stimuli are maintained in sensory memory for only a fraction of a second and that we can see more than we can report.

6. **What are icons and echoes?** Icons are the mental representations of visual stimuli, and echoes are the representations of auditory stimuli (sounds).

7. **What is the capacity of short-term memory?** We can hold seven chunks of information (plus or minus two) in short-term, or working, memory.

8. **How do psychologists explain the serial-position effect?** We tend to remember the initial items in a list because they are rehearsed most often (the primacy effect). We tend to remember the final items in a list because they are least likely to have been displaced by new information (the recency effect).

9. **How accurate are long-term memories?** Long-term memories are frequently biased because they are reconstructed according to our schemas—that is, our ways of organizing our experiences.

10. **How is information transferred from short-term to long-term memory?** There are two paths: maintenance rehearsal (rote repetition) and elaborative rehearsal (relating information to things known already).

11. **How is knowledge organized in long-term memory?** Knowledge tends to be organized according to a hierarchical structure with superordinate and subordinate concepts. We know things about members of a class when we have information about the class itself.

12. **What are context- and state-dependent memories?** Context dependence refers to the finding that we often retrieve information more efficiently when we are in the context in which we acquired it. State dependence refers to the finding that we often retrieve information better when we are in the same state of consciousness or mood as when we learned it.

13. **What is the levels-of-processing model?** This model views memory in terms of a single dimension—not three stages. It is hypothesized that we encode, store, and retrieve information more efficiently when we have processed it more deeply.

14. **What are nonsense syllables?** These are meaningless syllables first used by Ebbinghaus as a way of measuring the functions of memory.

15. **How do psychologists measure retention?** Retention is often tested through three types of memory tasks, in order of ascending difficulty: recognition, recall, and relearning.

16. **What is interference theory?** According to interference theory, people forget because learning can interfere with retrieval of other learnings. In retroactive interference, new learning interferes with old learning. In proactive interference, old learning interferes with new learning.

17. **What is repression?** This is Sigmund Freud's concept for motivated forgetting. Freud suggested that we are motivated to forget threatening or unacceptable material.

18. **What is infantile amnesia?** This term refers to inability to remember events from the first couple of years, apparently because of physiological and cognitive reasons.

19. **What are anterograde and retrograde amnesia?** In anterograde amnesia, a traumatic event such as hippocampal damage prevents formation of new memories. In retrograde amnesia, shock or other trauma prevents previously known information from being retrieved.

20. **What biological processes are associated with the processes of memory?** These processes entail development of synapses, changes at existing synapses, and changes in various sections of the brain—depending on the type of information that is being processed.

Psychology and Modern Life

Methods for Improving Memory

We beleaguered humans have come through an Ice Age, a Stone Age, an Iron Age, and, a bit more recently, an Industrial Revolution. Now we are trying to cope with the so-called Age of Information, in which there has been an exponential explosion of information—much of it scientific. Computers have been developed to process it. We, too, process information, and there is more of it to process than ever before. Fortunately, psychologists have helped devise a number of methods for promoting the retention of information. Let us consider some of them.

DRILL AND PRACTICE

Repetition (rote maintenance rehearsal) helps transfer information from short-term to long-term memory. Maintenance rehearsal may seem rather mechanical for a capable college student, but don't forget that this is how you learned the alphabet and how to count! We write spelling words over and over to remember them. Athletes and gymnasts repeat movements to facilitate their procedural memories. When you have formulas down pat, you can use your time pondering when to apply them, not trying to recall them. When the wide receiver has his moves down pat, he can focus on the defenders and not on his basic patterns.

Some students use flash cards to help them remember facts. For example, they might write "The originator of modern behaviorism is ____" on one side of the card and "John Broadus Watson" on the flip side.

In his book *Super Memory*, Douglas Herrmann (1991) recommends the following methods for helping to remember the name of someone you have just met:

1. Say the name out loud.

2. Ask your new acquaintance a question, using her or his name.

3. Use the person's name as many times as you can during your conversation. (Even seeking an opportunity to use the name will help you remember it.)

4. Write down the name, if possible, when the conversation has ended.

RELATE NEW INFORMATION TO WHAT IS ALREADY KNOWN

Relating new information to what is already known is a form of elaborative rehearsal that helps us to remember it (Willoughby and others, 1994). Herrmann (1991) also suggests that you can better remember the name of a new acquaintance by thinking of a rhyme for it. Now you have done some active thinking about the name, and you also have two tags for the person, not one. If you are trying to retrieve the spelling of the word *retrieve,* do so by retrieving the rule "*i* before *e* except after *c*." There are exceptions, of course: Remember that "weird" doesn't follow the rule because it's a "weird" word.

We normally expand our knowledge base by relating new items to things already known. Children learn that a cello is like a violin, only bigger. They learn that a bass fiddle is also like a violin, but bigger yet. We remember information about whales by relating whales to other mammals. Similarly, we will better recall information about porpoises and dolphins if we think of them as small whales (and not as friendly, intelligent fish).

The media are filled with stories about people who show psychological disorders of one kind or another. To help you remember the disorders discussed in Chapter 13, think of film or TV characters who were portrayed as having the disorders. Consider how the characters' behaviors were consistent (and inconsistent) with the descriptions in the text (and those offered by your professor). You will better remember the subject matter *and* become a good critic of media portrayals of psychological problems.

FORM UNUSUAL, EXAGGERATED ASSOCIATIONS

Psychologist Charles L. Brewer uses an interesting method to teach his psychology students the fundamentals of shaping:

In a recent class, Dr. Brewer first danced on his desk, then bleated like a sheep and finally got down on "all fours and oinked like a pig," he said. His antics were in response to a session he teaches on "successive approximation"—shaping behavior into a desired response.

To get students to "shape" him, he told them he would try to figure out what they wanted him to do. If he guessed wrong, they'd "boo and hiss," while if he did what they wanted, they'd applaud him—which is why he eventually acted like a pig. "I'll do anything to get them to learn," he said. (DeAngelis, 1994a, p. 40)

It is easier to recall stimuli that stand out, that separate themselves from the crowd. We pay more attention to them, and they tend to earn more of an emotional response. Sometimes, then, we better remember information when we create unusual, exaggerated associations.

Assume that you are trying to remember the geography of the cerebral cortex, as shown in Figure 3.10. Why not think of what you look like in right profile? (Use your left profile if it is better.) Then imagine a new imaging technique in which we can see through your skull, and we find four brightly colored lobes in the right hemisphere of your cerebral cortex. Not only that, but there are little people (homunculi) flapping about in the sensory and motor areas (see Figure 3.10 again). In fact, imagine that you're in a crowded line, and someone steps on your toe; thus, the homunculus in the sensory cortex has a throbbing toe. This is communicated to the association areas of the cortex, where you decide that you are rather annoyed. The language areas of the cortex think up some choice words that are relayed to the throat and mouth of the homunculus in the motor cortex, then sent into your throat and mouth. You also send some messages through the motor cortex that tighten your muscles, in readiness to attack.

Then you see that the perpetrator of the crime is a very attractive and apologetic stranger! What part of the occipital lobe is flashing the wonderful images?

The Method of Loci. Another example of forming unusual associations is the method of loci (pronounced LOW-sigh). With this method, you select a series of related images such as the parts of your body or the furniture in your home. Then you imagine an item from your shopping list, or another list you want to remember, as being attached to each image. Consider this meaty application: You might be better able to remember your shopping list if you imagine meatloaf in your navel or a strip of bacon draped over your nose.

By placing meatloaf or a favorite complete dinner in your navel, rather than a single item such as ground beef, you can combine several items into one chunk of information. At the supermarket, you recall the (familiar) ingredients for meatloaf and simply recognize whether or not you need each one.

USE MEDIATION

The method of mediation also relies on forming associations: You link two items with a third that ties them together.

What if you are having difficulty remembering that John's wife's name is Tillie? You can mediate between John and Tillie as follows. Reflect that the *john* is a slang term for bathroom. Bathrooms often have ceramic *tiles. Tiles,* of course, sounds like *Tillie.* So it goes: John → bathroom tiles → Tillie.

I used a combination of mediation and formation of unusual associations to help me remember foreign vocabulary words in high school. For example, the Spanish verb *trabajar* means "to work," in the sense of harassing, laboring, straining. Although -*jar* is pronounced "har," I nevertheless formed a mental image of a "trial by jars" when I laid eyes on the word. I saw myself running the gauntlet with strange enemies pouring jars down upon me until I was so laden that I could barely move. "Now," I thought, "that trial by jars was really *work*!" Trabajar → trial by jars → work. And how about *mujer* (pronounced moo-hair [almost]), meaning "woman"? Women have mo' hair than I do. Woman → mo' hair → mujer. This would no longer work, because now nearly all men also have more hair than I, but the association was so outlandish that it has stuck with me.

USE MNEMONIC DEVICES

Broadly speaking, the methods for jogging memory we have discussed all fall under the heading of *mnemonics,* or systems for remembering information. So-called

TABLE 7.1
Some Mnemonic Devices

DEVICE	INFORMATION ENCODED
	U.S. Presidents:
Washington And Jefferson Made Many A Joke.	Washington, Adams, Jefferson, Madison, Monroe, Adams, Jackson
Van Buren Had To Put The Frying Pan Back.	Van Buren, Harrison, Tyler, Polk, Taylor, Fillmore, Pierce, Buchanan
Lincoln Just Gasped, "Heaven Guard America."	Lincoln, Johnson, Grant, Hayes, Garfield, Arthur
Cleveland Had Coats Made Ready To Wear Home.	Cleveland, Harrison, Cleveland, McKinley, Roosevelt, Taft, Wilson, Harding
Coolidge Hurried Right To Every Kitchen Jar Nook.	Coolidge, Hoover, Roosevelt, Truman, Eisenhower, Kennedy, Johnson, Nixon
Ford Cut Right Brow.	Ford, Carter, Reagan, Bush
Poor Queen Victoria Eats Crow At Christmas.	The seven hills of Rome: Palatine, Quirinal, Viminal, Esquiline, Capitoline, Aventine, Caelian.
A True Conservative Can Not GOVern Virtuously; They Do Not Themselves Hate Avarice Altogether.	The Roman emperors: Augustus, Tiberius, Caligula, Claudius, Nero, Galba, Otho, Vitellius (the last three in the same year), Vespasian, Titus, Domitian, Nerva, Trajan, Hadrian, Antoninus Pius, Aurelius.
No Plan Like Yours To Study History Wisely.	The royal houses of England: Norman, Plantagenet, Lancaster, York, Tudor, Stuart, Hanover, Windsor.
X shall stand for playmates Ten. V for Five stalwart men. I for One, D for Five. M for a Thousand soldiers true. And L for Fifty, I'll tell you.	Translation of the Roman numerals, "D for Five" means D = 500.
Mary Eats Peanut Butter.	First four hydrocarbons of the Alkane class: Methane, Ethane, Propane, and Butane, in ascending order of the number of carbon atoms in their chains.
These Ten Valuable Amino Acids Have Long Preserved Life in Man.	Ten essential amino acids: Threonine, Tryptophan, Valine, Arginine, Histidine, Lysine, Phenylalanine, Leucine, Isoleucine, Methionine.
All Hairy Men Will Buy Razors.	Components of soil: Air, Humus, Mineral salts, Water, Bacteria, Rock particles.
Soak Her Toe.	Reminds one of *SohCahToa,* or: Sine = Opposite/Hypotenuse Cosine = Adjacent/Hypotenuse Tangent = Opposite/Adjacent.
Krakatoa Positively Casts Off Fumes; Generally Sulfurous Vapors.	Biological categories in descending order: Kingdom, Phylum, Class, Order, Family, Genus, Species, Variety.
On Old Olympia's Towering Tops, A Finn and A German Vault And Hop.	The 12 pairs of cranial nerves: Olfactory, Optic, Oculomotor, Trochlear, Trigeminal, Abducens, Facial, Auditory, Glossopharyngeal, Vagus, Accessory, Hypoglossal.
Never Lower Tillie's Pants; Mother Might Come Home.	The eight bones of the wrist: Navicular, Lunate, Triangular Pisiform, Multangular greater, Multangular lesser, Capitate, Hamate.
Camels Often Sit Down Carefully. Perhaps Their Joints Creak. Persistent Early Oiling Might Prevent Permanent Rheumatism.	The geological time periods: Cambrian, Ordovician, Silurian, Devonian, Carboniferous, Permian, Triassic, Jurassic, Cretaceous, Paleocene, Eocene, Oligocene, Miocene, Pliocene, Pleistocene, Recent.
Lazy French Tarts Sit Naked In Anticipation.	Nerves that pass through the superior orbital fissure of the skull: Lachrymal, Frontal, Trochlear, Superior, Nasal, Inferior, Abducent.

mnemonic devices usually combine chunks of information into a format such as an acronym, jingle, or phrase. For example, recalling the phrase "Every Good Boy Does Fine" has helped many people remember the musical keys E, G, B, D, F. In Chapter 3, we saw that the acronym *SAME* serves as a mnemonic device for distinguishing between afferent and efferent neurons. And in Chapter 4, we noted that most psychology students use the acronym *Roy G. Biv* to remember the colors of the rainbow, even though your "backward" author chose to use the "word" *vibgyor.*

Acronyms have found applications in many disciplines. Consider geography. The acronym *HOMES* stands for the Great Lakes: *H*uron, *O*ntario, *M*ichigan, *E*rie, and *S*uperior. In astronomy, the phrase "*Mer*cury's *v*ery *e*ager *m*other *j*ust *s*erved *us* *n*ine *p*otatoes" helps students recall the order of the planets Mercury, Venus, Earth, Mars, Jupiter, Saturn, Uranus, Neptune, and Pluto.

What about biology? You can remember that Dromedary camels have one hump while Bactrian camels have two by turning the letters *D* and *B* on their sides.

And how can you math students ever be expected to remember the reciprocal of pi (that is, 1 divided by 3.14)? Simple: Just remember the question "Can I remember the reciprocal?" and count the number of letters in each word. The reciprocal of pi, it turns out, is 0.318310. (Remember the last two digits as 10, not as one-zero.) A number of other phrases serve as mnemonic devices, as shown in Table 7.1.

Finally, how can you remember how to spell *mnemonics?* Easy—be willing to grant "a*MN*esty" to those who cannot.

Truth or Fiction Revisited. *It is true that you can use tricks to improve your memory.* The "tricks" all involve ways of forming associations.

Reflections

Now that you have read the section on methods of improving memory, reflect on the following questions:

- Which methods of encoding and storing information have you used to remember the following—that the number 1 has a "wun" sound; that the visual cortex is in the occipital lobe of the brain; that B. F. Skinner was a behaviorist; a shopping list?
- What strategies could you use to learn the names of your classmates? (How did you actually come to remember the names of those classmates who are most important to you?)
- Do you have use for any of the mnemonic devices shown in Table 7.1? Which ones? What mnemonic devices have you used to help you in this and other courses?

8

Thinking and Language

Truth or Fiction?

_____ It may be boring, but using the "tried and true" formula is the most efficient way to solve a problem.

_____ Only people are capable of solving problems by means of insight.

_____ The best way to solve a frustrating problem is to keep plugging away at it.

_____ Highly intelligent people are creative.

_____ We are more creative when we are paid to be creative.

_____ If A are B, and some B are C, then some A are C.

_____ If a couple has five sons, the sixth child is likely to be a daughter.

_____ An ice cream that is 97% fat free has less fat than an ice cream whose fat content makes up 10% of its calories.

_____ People change their opinions when they are shown to be wrong.

_____ The majority of people around the world speak at least two languages.

Outline

Truth or Fiction?
Concepts and Prototypes: Building Blocks of Thought
Problem Solving
   Approaches to Problem Solving: Getting from Here to There
   Factors That Affect Problem Solving
Creativity
   Creativity and Intelligence: Was Picasso Smart?
   Factors That Affect Creativity: Are Starving Artists More Creative?
Reasoning
   Types of Reasoning
Judgment and Decision Making
   Heuristics in Decision Making: If It Works, Must It Be Logical?
   The Framing Effect: Say That Again?
   Overconfidence: Is Your Hindsight 20–20?
Language
   Psychology in the New Millennium: Goals 2000: Helping Our Children Learn to Solve the Problems of the New Millennium
   Basic Concepts of Language
Language Development
   Development of Vocabulary
   Development of Syntax
   Toward More Complex Language
   Psychology in a World of Diversity: Black Dialect
   Theories of Language Development
Language and Thought
   The Linguistic-Relativity Hypothesis
Summary
Psychology and Modern Life
   Bilingualism and Bilingual Education

A t the age of 9, my daughter Jordan hit me with a problem about a bus driver that she had heard in school. Since I firmly believe in exposing students to the kinds of torture I have undergone, see what you can do with her problem:

You're driving a bus that's leaving from Pennsylvania. To start off with, there were 32 people on the bus. At the next bus stop, 11 people got off and 9 people got on. At the next bus stop, 2 people got off and 2 people got on. At the next bus stop, 12 people got on and 16 people got off. At the next bus stop, 5 people got on and 3 people got off. What color are the bus driver's eyes?

Now, I was not about to be fooled when I was listening to this problem. Although it seemed clear that I should be keeping track of how many people are on the bus, I had an inkling that a trick was involved. Therefore, I first instructed myself to remember that the bus was leaving from Pennsylvania. Being clever, I also kept track of the number of stops rather than the number of people getting on and off the bus. When I was finally hit with the question about the bus driver's eyes, I was at a loss. I protested that Jordan had said nothing about the bus driver's eyes, but she insisted that she had given me enough information to answer the question.

One of the requirements of problem solving is paying attention to relevant information. To do that, you need some familiarity with the type of problem it is. I immediately classified the bus driver problem as a trick question and paid attention to apparently superfluous information. But I wasn't good enough.

The vast human ability to solve problems has allowed people to build skyscrapers, create computers, and scan the interior of the body without surgery. Some people even manage to keep track of their children and balance their checkbooks. Problem solving is one aspect of thinking. **Thinking** is mental activity that is involved in understanding, processing, and communicating information. Thinking entails attending to information, mentally representing it, reasoning about it, and making judgments and decisions about it. The term *thinking* generally refers to conscious, planned attempts to make sense of things (Matlin, 1994). Cognitive psychologists usually do not characterize the less deliberate cognitive activities of daydreaming or the more automatic usages of language as thinking. Yet language is entwined with much of human thought. The uniquely human capacities to conceptualize mathematical theorems and philosophical treatises rely on language. Moreover, language allows us to communicate our thoughts and record them for posterity.

In this chapter we explore the broad topics of thinking and language. We begin with concepts, which provide building blocks of thought. We wend our way toward language, which lends human thought a unique richness and beauty.

Before we proceed, I have one question for you: What color were the bus driver's eyes?

Concepts and Prototypes: Building Blocks of Thought

I began the chapter with a problem posed by my daughter Jordan. Let me proceed with a riddle from my own childhood: "What's black and white and read all over?" Since this riddle was spoken, not written, and since it involved the colors black and white, you would probably assume that "read" was spelled "red." Thus, in seeking an answer, you might scan your memory for an object that was red although it also somehow managed to be black and white. The answer to the riddle, "newspaper," usually met with a good groan.

The word *newspaper* is a **concept.** *Red, black,* and *white* are also concepts—color concepts. Concepts are mental categories used to class together objects, relations, events, abstractions, or qualities that have common properties. Concepts are crucial to cognition. They represent aspects of the environment and of ourselves. In the cases of imagination and creativity, concepts can represent objects, events, activities, and ideas that never were. Much of thinking has to do with categorizing new objects and events and with manipulating the relationships among concepts.

We tend to organize concepts in hierarchies. The newspaper category includes objects such as your school paper and the *Los Angeles Times.* Newspapers, college textbooks, novels, and merchandise catalogs can be combined into higher-order categories such as *printed matter* or *printed devices that store information.* If you add CD-ROMs and floppy disks, you can create a still higher category, *objects that store information.* Now consider a question that requires categorical thinking: How are a newspaper and CD-ROM alike? Answers to such questions entail supplying the category that includes both objects. In this case, we can say that they both store information. That is, their functions are similar, even if their technology is very different. Here is another question: How are the brain and a CD-ROM alike? Yes, again, both can be said to store information. How are the brain and a CD-ROM different? To answer this question, we find a category in which only one of them belongs. For example, only the brain is a living thing. Functionally, moreover, the brain does much more than store information. The CD-ROM is an electronic device. People are not electronic devices. Could we, however, make the case that electricity is involved in human thinking? (Refer to the discussion of the neural impulse in Chapter 3.)

Prototypes are examples that best match the essential features of categories. In less technical terms, prototypes are good examples (Rosch, 1978). When new stimuli closely match people's prototypes of concepts, they are readily recognized as examples. Which animal seems more birdlike to you? A sparrow or an ostrich? Why? Which of the following better fits the prototype of a fish? A sea horse or a shark? Both self-love and maternal love may be forms of love, but more people readily agree that maternal love is a kind of love. Maternal love apparently better fits their prototype of love (Fehr & Russell, 1991).

Many lower animals can be said to possess instinctive or inborn prototypes of various concepts. Male robins attack round reddish objects that are similar in appearance to the breasts of other male robins—even when they have been reared in isolation and have thus never seen another male robin. People, however, generally acquire prototypes on the basis of experience. Many simple prototypes such as *dog* and *red* are taught by **exemplars.** We point to a dog and say "dog" or "This is a dog" to a child. Dogs are considered to be **positive instances** of the dog concept. **Negative instances**—that is, things that are not dogs—are then shown to the child while one says, "This is *not* a dog." Negative instances of one concept may be positive instances of another. So, in teaching a child, one may be more likely to say "This is not a dog—it's a cat" than simply, "This is not a dog."

Children may at first include horses and other four-legged animals within the dog schema or concept until the differences between dogs and horses are pointed out. (To them, the initial category could be more appropriately labeled "fuzzy-wuzzies.") In language development, the overinclusion of instances in a category (reference to horses as dogs) is labeled *overextension.* Children's prototypes become refined as the result of being shown positive and negative instances and being given verbal explanations.

Abstract concepts such as *bachelor* or *square root* are typically formed through verbal explanations that involve more basic concepts (Barsalou, 1992). If one points repeatedly to *bachelors* (positive instances) and *not bachelors* (negative instances), a child may eventually learn that bachelors are males or adult males. However, it is doubtful that this show-and-tell method would ever teach them that bachelors are adult human males

MINILECTURE: THE PROTOTYPE APPROACH

MINILECTURE: MENTAL IMAGES

Thinking • Mental activity that is involved in understanding, manipulating, and communicating about information. Thinking entails paying attention to information, mentally representing it, reasoning about it, and making decisions about it.

Concept • A mental category that is used to class together objects, relations, events, abstractions, or qualities that have common properties.

Prototype • A concept of a category of objects or events that serves as a good example of the category.

Exemplar • A specific example.

Positive instance • An example of a concept.

Negative instance • An idea, event, or object that is *not* an example of a concept. Concept formation is aided by presentation of positive and negative instances.

who are unmarried. The concept *bachelor* is best taught by explanation after the child understands the concepts of maleness and marriage.

Still more abstract concepts such as *justice, goodness, beauty,* and *love* may require complex explanations and many positive and negative instances as examples. These concepts are so abstract and instances so varied that no two people may agree on their definition. Or, if their definitions coincide, they may argue over positive versus negative instances (things that are beautiful and things that are ugly). What seems to be a beautiful work of art to me may impress you as meaningless jumbles of color. Thus the phrase, "Beauty is in the eye of the beholder."

Reflections

Now that you have read the opening sections of the chapter, reflect on the following questions:

- What strategy were you using to try to solve the bus driver problem? Were you misled or not? Why?
- When you were a child, some people were probably introduced to you as Aunt Bea or Uncle Harry. Do you remember when you first understood the concept of aunt or uncle? Can you think of ways of teaching these concepts to small children without using verbal explanation?

- Which concepts in this textbook have you found the most simple or most difficult to understand? Why?

Problem Solving

Now I have the pleasure of sharing something personal with you. One of the pleasures I derived from my own introductory psychology course lay in showing friends the textbook and getting them involved in the problems in the section on problem solving. First, of course, I struggled with the problems myself. Now it's your turn. Get some scrap paper, take a breath, and have a go at the following problems. The answers will be discussed in the following pages, but don't peek. *Try* the problems first.

1. Provide the next two letters in the series for each of the following:

   a. ABABABAB??
   b. ABDEBCEF??
   c. OTTFFSSE??

2. Draw straight lines through all the points in part A of Figure 8.1, using only *four* lines. Do not lift your pencil from the paper or retrace your steps. (The answer is given in Figure 8.5.)

3. Move three matches in part B of Figure 8.1 to make four squares of the same

FIGURE 8.1

Spotlight on Two Challenges to Problem-Solving Abilities Draw straight lines through all the points in Part A, using only four lines. Do not lift your pencil or retrace your steps. Move three matches in Part B to make four squares equal in size. Use all the matches.

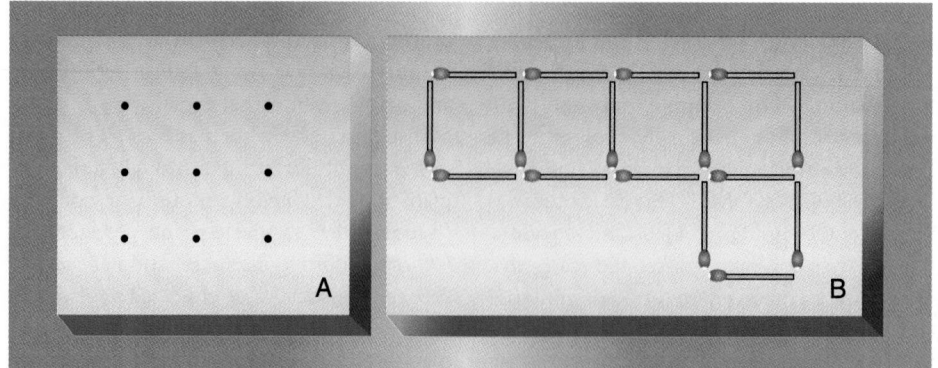

TABLE 8.1

Water-Jar Problems

| | THREE JARS ARE PRESENT WITH THE LISTED CAPACITY (IN OUNCES) | | | |
PROBLEM	JAR A	JAR B	JAR C	GOAL
1	21	127	3	100
2	14	163	25	99
3	18	43	10	5
4	9	42	6	21
5	20	59	4	31
6	23	49	3	20
7	10	36	7	3

For each problem, how can you use some combination of the three jars given, and a tap, to obtain precisely the amount of water shown?

Source: adapted from *Rigidity of Behavior* (p. 109), by Abraham S. Luchins and Edith H. Luchins, 1959, Eugene: University of Oregon Press.

size. You must use *all* the matches. (The answer is shown in Figure 8.5.)

4. You have three jars—A, B, and C—which hold the amounts of water, in ounces, shown in Table 8.1. For each of the seven problems in Table 8.1, use the jars in any way you wish to arrive at the indicated amount of water. Fill or empty any jar as often as you wish. How do you obtain the desired amount of water in each problem? (The solutions are discussed on pages 296, 298, and 300.)

APPROACHES TO PROBLEM SOLVING: GETTING FROM HERE TO THERE

What steps did you use to try to solve parts a and b of problem 1? Did you first make sure you understood the problem by rereading the instructions? Or did you dive right in as soon as you saw them on the page? Perhaps 1a and 1b came easily, but I'm sure that you studied 1c very carefully.

After you believed you understood what was required in each problem, you probably sought to discover the structure of the cycles in each series. Series 1a has repeated cycles of two letters: *AB, AB,* and so on. Series 1b may be seen as having four cycles of two consecutive letters: *AB, DE, BC,* and so on.

Again, did you solve 1a and 1b in a flash of insight, or did you try to find rules that govern the advance of each series? In series

1a, the rule is simply to repeat the cycle. Series 1b is more complicated, and different sets of rules can be used to describe it. One correct set of rules is that odd-numbered cycles (*1* and *3,* or *AB* and *BC*) simply repeat the last letter of the previous cycle (in this case *B*) and advance by one letter in the alphabet. The same rule applies to even-numbered cycles (*2* and *4,* or *DE* and *EF*).

If you found rules for problems 1a and 1b, you used them to produce the next letters in the series: *AB* in series 1a, and *CD* in series 1b. Perhaps you then evaluated the effectiveness of your rules by checking your answers against the solutions in the preceding paragraphs.

Question: What alternate sets of rules could you have found to describe these two series? Would you have generated the same answers from these rules?

In this section, we explore approaches to problem solving. We begin where you may have begun with the letters series: understanding the problem. Then we discuss various strategies for attacking the problem, including the use of algorithms, heuristic devices, or analogies.

Understanding the Problem. Let us begin our discussion of understanding problems by considering a bus driver problem that is very similar to the one my daughter Jordan gave me. This one is "official," however. That is, it appeared in the psychological literature:

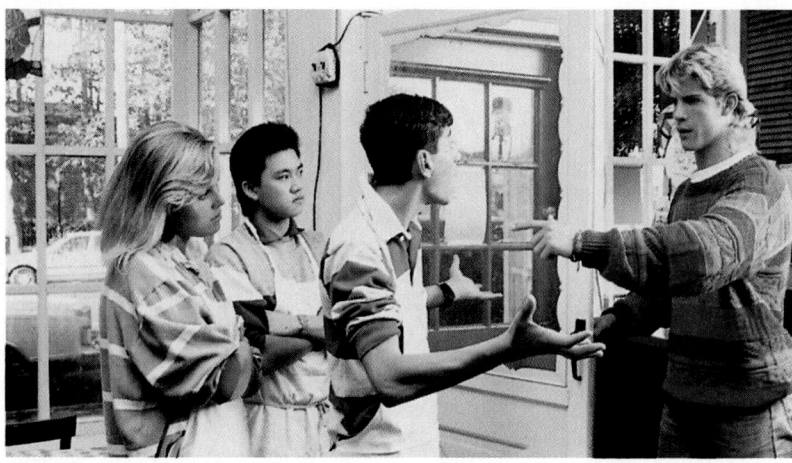

Heading for a Fight. Psychologists help people solve problems—for example, ways of averting aggression. In a particular form of therapy called problem-solving therapy, clients are encouraged to consider sample social provocations, generate multiple behavioral solutions (other than violent ones), try out the most promising, and evaluate their effectiveness.

Suppose you are a bus driver. On the first stop, you pick up 6 men and 2 women. At the second stop, 2 men leave and 1 woman boards the bus. At the third stop, 1 man leaves and 2 women enter the bus. At the fourth stop, 3 men get on and 3 women get off. At the fifth stop, 2 men get off, 3 men get on, 1 woman gets off and 2 women get on. What is the bus driver's name? (Halpern, 1989, p. 392).

Both versions of the bus driver problem demonstrate that a crucial factor in understanding a problem is focusing on the key information. If we assume that it is crucial to keep track of the numbers of people getting on and off the bus, we are focusing on information that turns out to be unessential. In fact, it distracts us from focusing on the crucial information.

When we are faced with a novel problem, how can we know which information is relevant and which is irrelevant? Background knowledge in the problem area helps. If you are given a chemistry problem, it helps if you have taken some courses in chemistry. If my daughter Jordan gives you a problem, it is helpful to expect the unexpected, or to head for the hills. (In case you still haven't noticed, by the way, the critical information you need to solve both bus

driver problems is indicated in the first sentence.)

Understanding a problem means constructing a coherent mental representation of the problem. I'll beat a horse to death by reminding you that psychologists cannot directly measure a person's mental representation of a problem or of anything else. However, psychologists make inferences about people's mental images from what people say and what they do—in this case, how they describe a problem and how they go about solving it.

The mental representation of the problem can include symbols or concepts, such as algebraic symbols or words. It can include lists, graphs, and visual images (Adeyemo, 1990). Successful understanding of a problem generally requires three features:

1. *The parts or elements of our mental representation of the problem relate to one another in a meaningful way.* If we are trying to solve a problem in geometry, our mental triangles should have angles that total 180 degrees and not 360 degrees.

2. *The elements of our mental representation of the problem correspond to the elements of the problem in the outer world.* If we are neutralizing an acid to wind up with a salt and water, our mental representation of water should be H_2O and not OH. The elements of our mental representations must include the key elements for solving the problem, such as the information in the first sentence of the bus driver problem. We prepare ourselves to solve a problem by familiarizing ourselves with its elements and defining our goals as clearly as possible. Part of understanding algebra and geometry problems is outlining all of the givens.

3. *We have a storehouse of background knowledge that we can apply to the problem.* We have taken the necessary coursework to solve problems in algebra and chemistry. The architect has a broad understanding of building materials and styles to apply to the problem of designing a particular structure for a particular site. A broad knowledge base may allow us to classify the problem or find analogies. When given a geometry problem involving a triangle, one may think, "Does this problem

seem to be similar to problems I've solved by using the quadratic equation?"

Algorithms. An **algorithm** is a specific procedure for solving a type of problem. An algorithm will invariably lead to the solution—if it is used properly, that is. Mathematical formulas—such as the Pythagorean Theorem—are examples of algorithms. They will yield correct answers to problems *as long as the right formula is used*. Finding the right formula to solve a problem may require scanning one's memory for all formulas that contain variables that represent one or more of the elements in the problem. The Pythagorean Theorem, for example, concerns triangles with right angles. Therefore, it is appropriate to consider using this formula for problems concerning right angles but not for others.

Consider anagram problems, in which we try to reorganize groups of letters into words. Some anagram problems require us to use every letter from the pool of letters; others allow us to use only some of the letter. How many words can you make from the pool of letters *DWARG?* If you were to use the algorithm termed the **systematic random search,** you would list every possible letter combination, using from one to all five letters. You could use a dictionary or a spell-checking computer software program to see whether each result is, in fact, a word. Such a method might be plodding, but it would work.

Systematic random searches are made practical in many cases by using a computer. If you were to use a computer to solve the DWARG anagram problem, you might instruct it to engage in a systematic random search as follows: First, instruct it to list every possible letter combination, using from one to five letters. Second, instruct it to run a spell-checking program on the potential solutions. Third, instruct it to print out only the combinations that are identified as words by the spell-checking program.

Did you develop an algorithm for solving the bus driver problem? Did it involve rereading the problem slowly, checking every word to determine whether it held a clue to the solution? Have you developed an algorithm for doing well in this course? Does it involve smiling at your professor now and then and keeping your fingers

crossed, or something a bit more . . . substantive?

Heuristics. **Heuristics** are rules of thumb that help us simplify and solve problems. Heuristics, in contrast to algorithms, do not guarantee a correct solution to a problem. They are shortcuts. When they work, they allow for more rapid solutions (Anderson, 1991). A heuristic device for solving the anagram problem would be to look for familiar letter combinations that are found in words and then to check the remaining letters for words that include these combinations. In *DWARG*, for example, we can find the familiar combinations *dr* and *gr*. We may then quickly find *draw, drag,* and *grad*. The drawback to this method, however, is that we might miss some words.

Truth or Fiction Revisited. *It is not true that using the "tried and true" formula is the most efficient way to solve a problem.* Using a tried and true formula—that is, an algorithm—may be less efficient than using a heuristic device.

One type of heuristic device is the **means-end analysis.** In using this heuristic device, we assess the difference between our current situation and our goals and then do what we can to reduce this discrepancy. Let's say that you are out in your car and lost. You know that your goal is west of your current location and on the other side of the railroad tracks. A heuristic device would be to drive toward the setting sun (west) and, at the same time, to remain alert for railroad tracks. If the road comes to an end and you must turn left or right, you can scan the distance in either direction for tracks. If you don't see any, turn right or left, but then, at the next major intersection, turn toward the setting sun again. Eventually you may get there. If not, you could use that most boring of algorithms: Ask people for directions until you find someone who knows the route.

When an inexperienced chess player is stuck for a move, she or he could engage in a systematic random search. That is, she could examine each piece remaining on the board and visualize every move the rules will allow each piece to make. Lengthy. She could make the process even lengthier by

Understanding • Constructing a coherent mental representation of a problem.

Algorithm • A systematic procedure for solving a problem that works invariably when it is correctly applied.

Systematic random search • An algorithm for solving problems in which each possible solution is tested according to a particular set of rules.

Heuristics • Rules of thumb that help us simplify and solve problems.

Means-end analysis • A heuristic device in which we try to solve a problem by evaluating the difference between the current situation and the goal.

imagining every possible countermove to each move, several moves hence. If there are many pieces on the board, it is not difficult to imagine the combinations quickly running into the billions. Chess players—even inexperienced chess players—tend to use heuristic devices or rules of thumb, however. The ultimate goal is to win the game. Chess players focus on subgoals, for example, such as trying to capture the center of the board, protecting the king, or trying out a Sicilian defense. They also use means-end analysis. They consider their subgoals and imagine ways of reducing the discrepancies between their current positions and their subgoals (for example, trying to castle to protect the king). Experienced players also search their memories for games that entailed similar or identical positions.

As we see in playing chess, one strategy of achieving a sizable goal is to break it up into more manageable subgoals. The goal of writing a term paper on psychological ways of managing stress can be broken down into subgoals such as making a list of the subtopics to be included (relaxation, exercise, and so forth), taking notes on recent research on each topic, creating a first draft in each area, and so on. This approach does not mean there is less work to do. However, it provides direction and helps outline a number of more readily attainable goals. It is thus easier to get going.

A few expert chess players are capable of reflecting on similar positions in classic games in historic chess matches. As we see in the following section, experts search for analogies that will help them achieve their goals.

Analogies. An *analogy* is a partial similarity among things that are different in other ways. During the cold war, some people in the United States believed in the so-called domino theory. Seeing nations as analogous to dominoes, they argued that if one nation were allowed to fall to communism, its neighbor would be likely to follow. In the late 1980s, a sort of reverse domino effect actually occurred as communism collapsed in Eastern Europe. When communism col-

lapsed in one nation, it became likely to collapse in neighboring nations as well.

The analogy heuristic applies the solution of an earlier problem to the solution of a new one. We use the analogy heuristic frequently, whenever we try to solve a new problem by referring to a previous problem (Halpern and others, 1990). Consider the water-jar problems in Table 8.1. Problem 2 is analogous to problem 1. Therefore, the approach to solving problem 1 works with problem 2. (Later we consider what happens when the analogy heuristic fails.)

Lawyers look for analogies (called *precedents*) when they prepare cases for argument. Precedents inform them as to what types of arguments have and have not worked in the past. Psychologists and physicians consider analogies (usually in the form of case studies) when they are attempting to understand a new case and create a treatment plan. Knowing what does *not* work can be as important as knowing what works.

The chess player might think, "Karpov was in a similar [analogous] position in 1977 and was checkmated in four moves when he moved his king." (Yes, she truly might summon up such a game.) People who are good at solving math problems tend to categorize the problem properly. That is, they recognize what *type* of problem it is—and thus summon up the right formulas. Solving a problem by analogy requires locating or retrieving relevant prior problems and adapting the solution of earlier problems to the current problem (Novick & Holyoak, 1991).

Let us see whether you can use the analogy heuristic to your advantage in the following number series problem: To solve problems 1a, 1b, and 1c on page 292 you had to figure out the rules that guide the order of the letters. Survey this series of numbers and find the rule that guides their order:

$$8, 5, 4, 9, 1, 7, 6, 3, 2, 0$$

Hint: The problem is somewhat analogous to problem 1c.[1]

---

[1] The analogous element is that there is a correspondence between these numbers and the first letter in the English word that spells them out (Matlin, 1994). What would you do to the words to arrive at this order?

FACTORS THAT AFFECT PROBLEM SOLVING

The way in which you approach a problem is central to how effective you are at solving it. Other factors also affect your effectiveness at problem solving. Three of them—your level of expertise, whether you fall prey to a mental set, and whether you develop insight into the problem—can be conceptualized as residing in you. A couple of problem characteristics also affect their solution: the extent to which the elements of the problem are fixed in function, and the way in which the problem is defined.

Expertise. To appreciate the role of expertise in problem solving, unscramble the following anagrams taken from Novick and Coté (1992). In each case, use all of the letters to form an actual English word:

DNSUO

RCWDO

IASYD

How long did it take you to unscramble each anagram? Would a person whose native language is English solve each problem (unscramble each anagram) more efficiently than a bilingual person who spoke another language in the home? Why or why not?

Experts solve problems more efficiently, more rapidly than novices do. (That is why they are called *experts*). Although it may be considered "smart" to be able to solve a particular kind of problem, experts do not necessarily exceed novices in general intelligence. Their areas of expertise may be quite limited. For example, the knowledge and skills required to determine whether a Northern Renaissance painting is a forgery are quite different from those that are used to find words that rhyme with elephant or to determine the area of a parallelogram. Generally speaking, experts at solving a certain kind of problem have a more extensive knowledge base in the area, have better memories for the elements in the problems, form mental images or representations that facilitate problem solving (Clement, 1991), relate the problem to other problems that are similar in structure, and have more efficient methods for problem solving (Hershey and others, 1990). These factors are interrelated. An art historian, for example, acquires a data base that permits her or him to understand the intricacies of paintings. As a result, her or his memory for paintings—and who painted them—expands vastly. People whose native language is English are likely to have a more extensive data base of English words, which should make them more efficient at unscrambling anagrams of English words. Their extensive English data base should also facilitate their learning and memory of new English words.

Novick and Coté (1992) found that the solutions to the three anagram problems seemed to "pop out" in under 2 seconds among "experts." The experts apparently had more efficient methods than the novices. Experts seemed to use parallel processing. That is, they dealt simultaneously with two or more elements of the problems—in this case, the anagrams. In the case of DNSUO, for example, they may have played with the order of the vowels (*UO* or *OU*) at the same time they tested which consonant (*D, N,* or *S*) was likely to precede them, arriving quickly at *sou* and *sound*. Novices were more likely to engage in serial processing—to handle one element of the problem at a time.

Mental Sets. Jordan hit me with another question: "A farmer had 17 sheep. All but 9 died. How many sheep did he have left?" Being a victim of a mental set, I assumed that this was a subtraction problem and gave the answer 8. She gleefully informed me that she hadn't said "9 died." She had said "*all but* 9 died." Therefore, the correct answer was 9. (Get it?) Put it another way: I had not *understood* the problem. My mental representation of the problem did not correspond to the actual elements of the problem. I resolved to actually pay attention when Jordan riddled me in the future.

Return to problem 1, part c, on page 292. To try to solve this problem, did you seek a pattern of letters that involved cycles and the alphabet? If so, it may be because parts a and b were solved by this approach.

The tendency to respond to a new problem with the same approach that helped solve earlier, similar-looking problems is termed a **mental set**. Mental sets usually

Jordan. The author's daughter, Jordan, posed the problem, "A farmer had 17 sheep. All but 9 died. How many sheep were left?" What is the answer?

Mental set • The tendency to respond to a new problem with an approach that was successfully used with similar problems.

MINILECTURE: BLOCKS TO PROBLEM SOLVING

make our work easier, but they can mislead us when the similarity between problems is illusory, as in part c of problem 1. Here is a clue: Part c is not an alphabet series. Each of the letters in the series *stands* for something. If you can discover what they stand for (that is, discover the rule), you will be able to generate the 9th and 10th letters. (The answer is in Figure 8.5 on p. 303.)

Have another look at water-jar problem 6. The formula $B-A-2C$ will solve this problem. Is that how you solved it? Note also that the problem could have been solved more efficiently by using the formula $A-C$. If the second formula did not occur to you, it may be because of the mental set you acquired from solving the first five problems.

Insight: Aha! To gain insight into the role of insight in problem solving, consider the following problem, which was posed by Janet Metcalfe:

> A stranger approached a museum curator and offered him an ancient bronze coin. The coin had an authentic appearance and was marked with the date 544 B.C. The curator

had happily made acquisitions from suspicious sources before, but this time he promptly called the police and had the stranger arrested. Why? (1986, p. 624)

I'm not going to give you the answer to this problem (drat?). Instead, I'll give you a guarantee. When you arrive at the solution, it will hit you all at once. You'll think "Aha!" or "Of course!" or something a bit less polite. It will seem as though there is a sudden reorganization of the pieces of information in the problem so that the solution leaps out at you—in a flash.

Problem solving by means of insight is very important in the history of psychology (Sternberg & Davidson, 1994). Consider a classic piece of research by a German psychologist who was stranded with some laboratory subjects on a Canary Island during World War I. Gestalt psychologist Wolfgang Köhler became convinced of the reality of insight when one of his chimpanzees, Sultan, "went bananas." Sultan had learned to use a stick to rake in bananas placed outside his cage. But now Herr Köhler (pronounced *hair curler*) gave Sultan a new problem. He placed the banana beyond the reach of the stick. However, he gave Sultan two bamboo poles that could be fitted together to make a single pole long enough to retrieve the delectable reward. The setup was similar to that shown in Figure 8.2.

As if to make this historic occasion more dramatic, Sultan at first tried to reach the banana with one pole. When he could not do so, he returned to fiddling with the sticks. Köhler left the laboratory after an hour or so of frustration (his own as well as Sultan's). An assistant was assigned the thankless task of observing Sultan. But soon afterward, Sultan happened to align the two sticks as he fiddled. Then, in what seemed to be a flash of inspiration, Sultan fitted them together and pulled in the elusive banana. Köhler was summoned to the laboratory. When he arrived the sticks fell apart, as if on cue. But Sultan regathered them, fit them firmly together, and actually tested the strength of the fit before retrieving another banana.

Köhler was impressed by Sultan's rapid "perception of relationships" and used the term **insight** to describe it. He noted that

Insight • In Gestalt psychology, a sudden perception of relationships among elements of the "perceptual field," permitting the solution of a problem.

Cognitive map • A mental representation or picture of the elements in a learning situation, such as a maze.

FIGURE 8.2

A Demonstration of Insight or Just Some Fiddling with Sticks? Gestalt psychologist Wolfgang Köhler ran experiments with chimpanzees to highlight the nature of problem solving by insight. This chimp must retrieve a stick outside the cage and attach it to a stick he already has before he can retrieve the distant circular object. While fiddling with two such sticks, Sultan, another chimp, seemed to suddenly recognize that the sticks could be attached. This is an example of problem solving by insight.

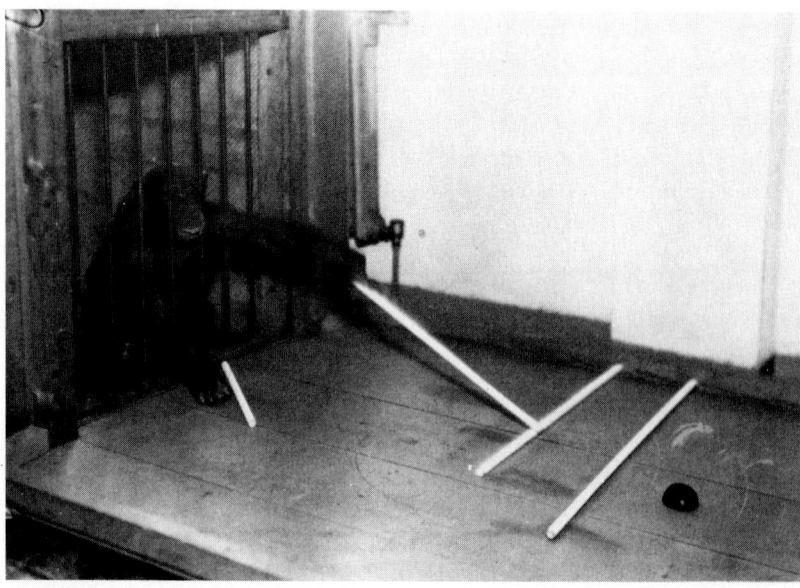

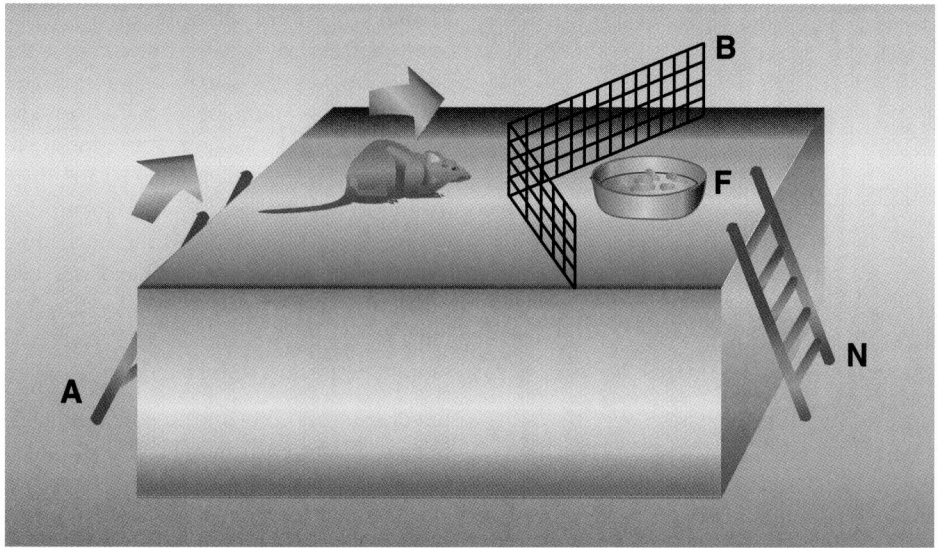

FIGURE 8.3
Bismarck Uses a Cognitive Map to Claim His Just Desserts Bismarck has learned to reach dinner by climbing ladder *A*. But now the food goal *(F)* is blocked by a wire mesh barrier *(B)*. Bismarck washes his face for a while, but then, in an apparent flash of insight, runs back down ladder *A* and up new ladder *N* to reach the goal.

such insights are not acquired gradually. Rather, they seem to occur "in a flash" when the elements of a problem have been arranged appropriately. Sultan also proved himself to be immediately capable of stringing several sticks together to retrieve various objects, not just bananas. It appeared that Sultan understood the principle of the relationship between joining sticks and reaching distant objects.

Soon after Köhler's findings were reported, psychologists in the United States demonstrated that even rats are capable of rudimentary forms of problem solving by insight. E. C. Tolman (1948), a University of California psychologist, showed that rats behaved as if they had acquired **cognitive maps** of mazes. Although they would learn many paths to a food goal, they would typically choose the shortest. If the shortest path was blocked, they would quickly switch to another.

Bismarck, one of University of Michigan psychologist N. R. F. Maier's laboratory rats, provided further evidence of insight in laboratory rats (Maier & Schneirla, 1935). Bismarck had been trained to climb a ladder to a tabletop where food was placed. On one occasion, Maier used a mesh barrier to prevent Bismarck from reaching his goal.

But, as shown in Figure 8.3, a second ladder to the table was provided. The second ladder was in clear view of the animal. At first, Bismarck sniffed and scratched and made every effort to find a path through the mesh barrier. Then Bismarck spent some time washing his face, an activity that apparently signals frustration in rats. Suddenly, Bismarck jumped into the air, turned, ran down the familiar ladder around to the new ladder, ran up the new ladder, and then claimed his just desserts. It seems that Bismarck suddenly perceived the relationships between the elements of his problem so that the solution occurred by insight. He seems to have had what Gestalt psychologists have termed an "Aha! experience."

Truth or Fiction Revisited. *It is not true that only people are capable of solving problems by means of insight.* Classic research evidence shows that lower animals, including apes and rats, are also capable of insight (a sudden reorganization of the perceptual field).

Let us return to the problems at the beginning of the section. How did you do with problem 1, part c, and problems 2 and 3? Students tend to fiddle around with them for a while, as Sultan fiddled with his

MINILECTURE:
COGNITIVE
MAPS

FIGURE 8.4
The Duncker Candle Problem
Can you use the objects shown on the table to attach the candle to the wall of the room so that it will burn properly?

Incubation • In problem solving, a hypothetical process that sometimes occurs when we stand back from a frustrating problem for a while and the solution "suddenly" appears.

Functional fixedness • The tendency to view an object in terms of its name or familiar usage.

Well-defined problem • A problem in which the original state, the goal, and the rules for reaching the goal are clearly spelled out.

Ill-defined problem • A problem in which the original state, the goal, or the rules are less than clear.

Creativity • The ability to generate novel solutions to problems.

sticks. The solutions, when they come, appear to arrive in a flash. Students set the stage for the flash of insight by studying the elements in the problems carefully, repeating the rules to themselves, and trying to imagine what a solution might look like. If you produced and then tried out solutions that did not meet the goals, you may have become frustrated and thought, "The heck with it! I'll come back to it later." Standing back from the problem may allow the **incubation** of insight. An incubator warms chicken eggs for a while so that they will hatch. Incubation in problem solving refers to standing back from the problem for a while as some mysterious process in us seems to continue to work on it. Later, the answer may occur to us in a flash of insight. When standing back from the problem is helpful, it may be because it provides us with some distance from unprofitable but persistent mental sets.

Truth or Fiction Revisited. *It is not true that the best way to solve a frustrating problem is to keep plugging away at it.* It may be better to distance oneself from the problem for a while and allow it to "incubate." Eventually you may solve the problem in what seems to be a flash of insight.

Have another look at the possible role of incubation in helping us overcome mental sets. Consider the seventh water-jar problem. What if we had tried all sorts of solutions involving the three water jars, and none had worked? What if we were then to stand back from this water-jar problem for a day or two? Is it not possible that with a little distance we might suddenly recall a 10, a

7, and a 3—three elements of the problem—and realize that we can arrive at the correct answer by using only two water jars? Our solution might seem too easy, and we might check Table 8.1 cautiously to make certain that the numbers are there as remembered. Perhaps our incubation period would have done nothing more than unbind us from the mental set that problem 7 *ought* to be solved by the formula $B - A - 2C$.

Functional Fixedness. **Functional fixedness** may also impair your problem-solving efforts. For example, first ask yourself what a pair of pliers is. Is it a tool for grasping, a paperweight, or a weapon? A pair of pliers could function as any of these, but your tendency to think of it as a grasping tool is fostered by your experience with it. You have probably only used a pair of pliers for grasping things. Functional fixedness is the tendency to think of an object in terms of its name or its familiar usage. Functional fixedness can be similar to a mental set in that it can make it difficult for you to use familiar objects to solve problems in novel ways.

Now that you know what functional fixedness is, let's see if you can overcome it by solving the Duncker candle problem. You enter a room that has the following objects on a table: a candle, a box of matches, and some thumbtacks (see Figure 8.4). Your task is to use the objects on the table to attach the candle to the wall of the room so that it will burn properly. (The answer is shown in Figure 8.5.)

You may know that soldiers in survival training in the desert are taught to view insects and snakes as sources of food rather than as pests or threats. But it would be understandable if you chose to show civilian functional fixedness for as long as possible if you were stuck in the desert.

The Definition of the Problem. Problems can be well-defined or ill-defined. In a **well-defined problem,** the original state, the goal, and the rules for reaching the goal are all clearly spelled out (Medin & Ross, 1992). The water-jar problems are well-defined in that we know the size of each jar (the original state), each goal state (exactly how much water is to be obtained), and the rules (how we may use the water jars to reach the goal). Well-defined problems also have specific ways in which we can determine whether we have reached a solution. For example, we know that we have solved the anagram problem, RCWDO, when we arrive at a correctly spelled English word—*crowd*.

In an **ill-defined problem,** the original state, the goal state, or the rules are less than clear. Consider the (unlikely) possibility that an architect is simply asked to design a house. You might think that an architect would savor such an ill-defined problem because of the freedom it grants. Yet, it is difficult for the architect to know when she or he has been successful. Of course, given the inadequate definition of the problem, the architect could always claim that under the circumstances, any design is a success. In the real world, an architect would likely be given a site for a house, a budget, a requested number of bedrooms, and information about the housing styles (for example, Georgian colonial or contemporary) that a client prefers.

There are various strategies for approaching ill-defined problems (Medin & Ross, 1992). One involves dividing the problem into subproblems. The architect might begin by thinking, Let me begin by designing an ideal master bedroom. Or one could implant structure on the problem where none existed. The architect might think, Let me assume that I must design a contemporary house for a bluff that sits high above a bay. Or one could just get started and stop when she or he has arrived at a solution. The architect could simply start sketching and see what happens.

Reflections

Now that you have read the section on problem solving, reflect on the following questions:

- How did you go about solving the problems presented at the beginning of the section? Which did you get right? Which did you get wrong? Why?
- Did you develop an algorithm for solving the bus driver problem? What is it? Did you attempt to use heuristic devices? What were they?

- How can you use subgoals to develop a strategy for doing well in this course? For doing well in an athletic event?
- Are you an expert at solving math problems? Social problems? Automobile problems? Musical problems? How did you get to be an expert?
- Can you think of an example in which a mental set or functional fixedness interfered with your ability to solve a problem?
- Can you think of an example in which you were struggling and then suddenly developed insight into a problem or an academic subject?

MINILECTURE: WELL-FORMED VS. ILL-FORMED PROBLEMS

Creativity

A creative person may be more capable of solving problems to which there are no preexisting solutions, no tried and tested formulas.

Creativity is an enigmatic concept. According to Sternberg (1985), we tend to perceive creative people as:

- Willing to take chances
- Unaccepting of limitations; trying to do the impossible

Creativity. This photograph shows Chinese American artist Hung Liu with her work "Burial at Little Golden Village." What traits are connected with creativity? What is the relationship between intelligence and creativity?

- Appreciating art and music
- Capable of using the materials around them to make unique things
- Questioning social norms and assumptions
- Willing to take an unpopular stand
- Inquisitive

A professor of mine once remarked that there is nothing new under the sun, only novel combinations of old elements. To him, the core of creativity was the ability to generate novel combinations of existing elements. Many psychologists concur. They view creativity as the ability to make unusual, sometimes remote, associations to the elements of a problem to generate new combinations that meet the goals (Boden, 1994). An essential aspect of a creative response is the leap from the elements of the problem to the novel solution (Amabile, 1990). A predictable solution is not particularly creative, even if it is difficult to arrive at.

According to Guilford (1967), creativity demands divergent thinking rather than convergent thinking. In **convergent thinking,** thought is limited to present facts as the problem-solver tries to narrow thinking to find the best solution. In **divergent thinking,** the problem-solver associates more fluently and freely to the various elements of the problem. The problem-solver allows "leads" to run a nearly limitless course to determine whether they will eventually combine as needed.

Successful problem solving may require both divergent and convergent thinking. At first, divergent thinking generates many possible solutions. Convergent thinking is then used to select the most probable solutions and reject the others.

CREATIVITY AND INTELLIGENCE: WAS PICASSO SMART?

It might seem that a creative person would be highly intelligent. However, the relationship between intelligence and creativity is moderate at best. Although creative people do tend to be intelligent, intelligence is no guarantee of creativity (Sternberg, 1990). For example, a Canadian study found that a group of highly intelligent ("gifted") boys and girls aged 9 to 11 was more creative than a group of less intelligent children. However, some of the gifted children were no more creative than their less intelligent peers (Kershner & Ledger, 1985). In this particular study, the girls were significantly more creative than the boys, especially on verbal tasks.

Moreover, tests that measure intelligence are not useful in measuring creativity. Intelligence test questions usually require convergent thinking to narrow in on the answer. On an intelligence test, an ingenious answer that differs from the designated answer is wrong. Tests of creativity are oriented toward determining how flexible and fluent thinking can be. Here, for example, is an item from a test used by Getzels and Jackson (1962) to measure associative ability, a factor in creativity: "Write as many meanings as you can for each of the following words: (a) duck; (b) sack; (c) pitch; (d) fair." Those who write several meanings for each word, rather than only one, are rated as being potentially more creative.

Another measure of creativity might ask people to produce as many words as possible that begin with T and end with N within a minute. Still another item might give people a minute to classify a list of names in as many ways as possible. In how many different ways can you classify the following group of names?

MARTHA   PAUL   JEFFRY
SALLY   PABLO   JOAN

Truth or Fiction Revisited. *It is not necessarily true that highly intelligent people are creative.* The statement is an overgeneralization. Although highly intelligent people are more likely to be creative than people with below-average intelligence, many intelligent people are relatively unimaginative.

FACTORS THAT AFFECT CREATIVITY: ARE STARVING ARTISTS MORE CREATIVE?

If there is only a modest connection between creativity and intelligence, what factors do contribute to creativity? Some factors reside within the person and some involve the social setting.

Convergent thinking • A thought process that attempts to narrow in on the single best solution to a problem.

Divergent thinking • A thought process that attempts to generate multiple solutions to problems.

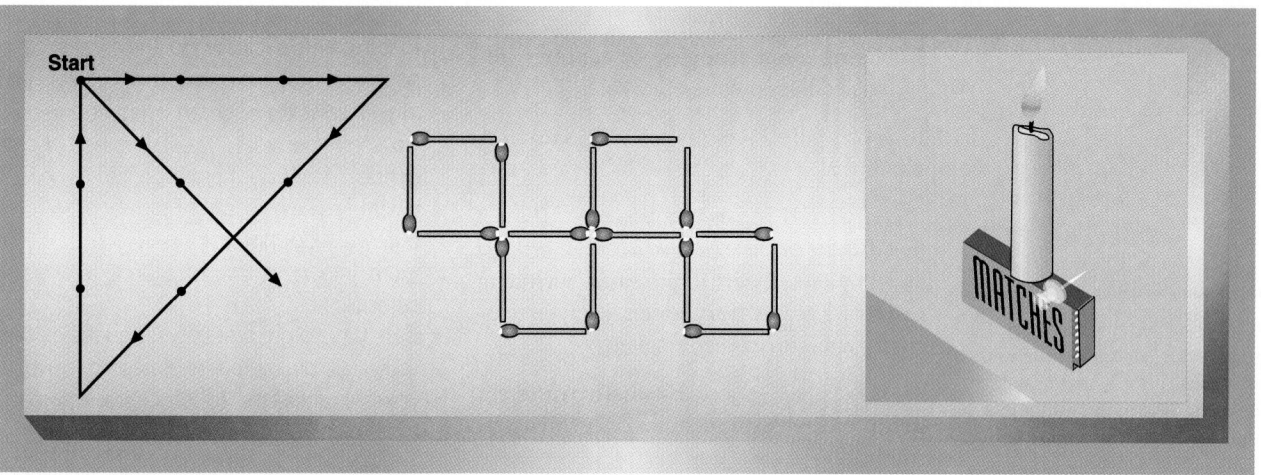

FIGURE 8.5
Answers to Problems on Pages 292 and 300 For problem 1C, note that each of the letters is the first letter of the numbers one through eight. Therefore, the two missing letters are *NT,* for *n*ine and *t*en. The solutions to problems 2 and 3 are shown in this illustration. Solving the Duncker candle problem requires using a thumbtack to pin the matchbox to the wall, then setting the candle on top of the box. Functional fixedness prevents many would-be problem-solvers from conceptualizing the matchbox as anything more than a device to hold the matches. Wrong answers include trying to affix the bottom of the candle to the wall with melted wax and trying to tack the candle to the wall.

Personal Factors. Guilford (1967) noted that creative people show flexibility, fluency (in generating words and ideas), and originality. Getzels and Jackson (1962) found that creative schoolchildren tend to express, rather than inhibit, their feelings and to be playful and independent. Creative people tend to be independent and nonconformist, but independence and nonconformity do not necessarily make a person creative. Negative stereotypes of creative artists have led to exaggerations of nonconformity.

Nevertheless, creative children are often at odds with their teachers because of their independence. Faced with the chore of managing upward of 30 pupils, teachers too often label quiet and submissive children as "good" children. These studies of creativity may also explain in part why there have been many more male than female artists throughout history, even though modern research does not find boys to be more creative than girls (e.g., Kershner & Ledger, 1985). Over the years, traits like independence and nonconformity are more likely to have been discouraged in females than in males, because they are inconsistent with the passive and compliant social roles tradi-tionally ascribed to females. Because of the women's movement, the number of women in the creative arts and sciences is growing rapidly today. In the past, the creativity of many girls may have been nipped in the bud.

Social Evaluation. Research evidence shows that concern about evaluation by other people reduces creativity. In one ex-periment, college students were asked to write poems under two very different sets of expectations (Amabile, 1990). Half the students were informed that the experi-menter intended to examine only their handwriting—not the aesthetic value of the poetry. The remaining students were informed that judges, who were poets, would supply them with written evalua-tions of their poetry's content and form. The students who expected to be evaluated according to the form and content of their work turned in significantly less creative poems.

Amabile (1990) found that the following four conditions reduce creativity:

1. Being watched while you are working
2. Being offered a reward for creativity

3. Competing for prizes

4. Having your choices or options restricted by someone else's rules

In short, when pressure prevails, creativity plummets.

Truth or Fiction Revisited. *It is not true that we are more creative when we are paid to be creative.* External pressures, including external rewards, very often dampen creativity rather than encourage it.

Brainstorming. **Brainstorming** is a group process that encourages creativity by stimulating a great number of ideas—even wild ideas—and suspending judgment until the process is completed. Note that brainstorming is not expected to work when other people evaluate one's ideas. A friendly atmosphere that supports wildly divergent ideas is assumed to be effective.

Matlin (1994) notes that psychologists have become somewhat skeptical of the brainstorming concept, however. For one thing, research evidence suggests that people who are working alone are often more creative than people who are working in groups. (Consider the cliché, "A camel is a horse made by a committee.") Moreover, the ideas produced by brainstorming are frequently poorer in quality than those produced by people working alone.

Reflections

Now that you have read the section on creativity, reflect on the following questions:

- Do you know people whom you consider to be creative? How do their traits compare with those discussed in this section?
- In your own experience, what are the connections between creativity and intelligence? Do you know people who are highly creative in art or some other area but who do not impress you as being more intelligent overall than the average person?
- Can you force creativity? You have certainly felt pressured at times to arrive at creative solutions to problems on tests. How did the pressure (for example, the amount of time left) affect you? Did it stimulate you to be more creative, or did it add to the difficulty? Why?
- Have you ever brainstormed as a group member attempting to come up with creative ideas—for example, on a class project? What was the experience like? Did the group process help or get in the way? How?

Reasoning

We are not done. I have more puzzles to solve, more weighty things to consider. Ponder this preposterous proposition:

If A are B, and some B are C,
then some A are C.

Is it true or false? What say you?

I confess that upon first seeing this proposition, I believed that it was true. It seemed that we were logically progressing to

---

Brainstorming • A group process that encourages creativity by stimulating a large number of ideas and suspending judgment until the process is completed.

Reasoning • The transforming of information to reach conclusions.

Deductive reasoning • A form of reasoning about arguments in which conclusions are deduced from premises. The conclusions are true if the premises are true.

Premise • A statement or assertion that serves as the basis for an argument.

Inductive reasoning • A form of reasoning in which we reason from individual cases or particular facts to a general conclusion.

─ Questionnaire ─

THE REMOTE ASSOCIATES TEST

One aspect of creativity is the ability to associate freely to all aspects of a problem. Creative people take far-flung ideas and piece them together in novel combinations. Following are items from the Remote Associates Test, which measures ability to find words that are distantly related to stimulus words. For each set of three words, try to think of a fourth word that is related to all three words. For example, the words *rough, resistance,* and *beer* suggest the word *draft* as in the phrases *rough draft, draft resistance,* and *draft beer.* The answers are given in Appendix B.

1.	charming	student	valiant	4.	dark	shot	sun	7.	attorney	self	spending
2.	food	catcher	hot	5.	Canadian	golf	sandwich	8.	arm	coal	peach
3.	hearted	feet	bitter	6.	tug	gravy	show	9.	type	ghost	story

higher-order categories at each step along the way (see Figure 8.6, Part A). For example, if apples (A) are fruit (B), and fruit (B) are food (C), then apples (A) are food (C). But so much for categorical thinking. So much for reasoning. I was bamboozled by the "some." My example with the apples omitted the word. Consider another example of this proposition, one that uses "some": If circles (A) are shapes (B), and *some* shapes (B) are squares (C), then some circles (A) are squares (C). Not so! By using the qualifying term "some," we can move both up to a higher-order category (from circles to shapes) and back down to a lower-order category (from shapes to squares) (see Figure 8.6, Part B).

Truth or Fiction Revisited. *It is not true that if A are B, and some B are C, then some A are C.* We can test the truthfulness of such abstract propositions by plugging in actual objects. Critical thinkers also pay special attention to statements that have qualifying words such as *some, sometimes, always,* or *never.*

TYPES OF REASONING

We have been toying with an example of reasoning. **Reasoning** is the transforming of information to reach conclusions. In this section we consider two kinds of reasoning: deductive reasoning and inductive reasoning.

Deductive reasoning is a form of reasoning in which the conclusion must be true if the premises are true. Consider this classic, three-sentence argument:

1. All persons are mortal.
2. Socrates is a person.
3. Therefore, Socrates is mortal.

Sentences 1 and 2 in this argument are called the **premises.** Premises provide the assumptions or basic information that allows people to draw conclusions. Sentence 3 is the conclusion. In this example, sentence 1 makes a statement about a category (persons). Sentence 2 assigns an individual (Socrates) to the category (persons). Sentence 3 concludes that what is true of the category (persons) is true for the member of the category (Socrates). The conclusion, sentence 3, is said to be *deduced* from the premises. The conclusion about Socrates is true if the premises are true.

In **inductive reasoning,** we reason from individual cases or particular facts to a general conclusion. Consider a transformation of the deductive reasoning example:

1. Socrates is a person.
2. Socrates is mortal.
3. Therefore, persons are mortal.

The conclusion happens to be correct, but it is illogical. The fact that one person is mortal does not guarantee that all people are mortal.

Inductive reasoning, then, does not permit us to draw absolute conclusions. Yet inductive reasoning is used all the time. We conclude that a certain type of food will or will not make us ill because of our experiences on earlier occasions. ("Buttered popcorn made me nauseous. This is buttered popcorn. Therefore, this will make me nauseous.") We assume that a cheerful smile and "Hello!" will work as an icebreaker with a new acquaintance because it has worked before. Although none of these conclusions is as logical as a deductive conclusion, inductive conclusions are correct often enough so that we can get on with our daily lives with some degree of confidence.

Inductive reasoning is also used in psychological research. We draw samples that we believe represent certain populations. We then conduct research with those samples. We assume that the conclusions we reach with the research samples will apply to the populations. However, we cannot be absolutely certain that our samples are representative. Even if they are, there may be a few cases in the population that are so unusual that we cannot generalize to them. Nevertheless, we are correct in our conclusions often enough that the research enterprise is largely successful.

Reflections

Now that you have read the section on reasoning, reflect on the following questions:

- Do you recognize the following kind of argument?
  1. John says that too much money is spent on education.

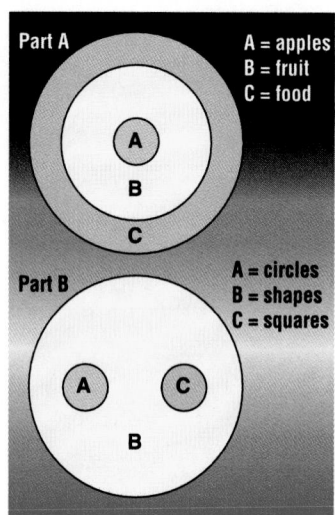

FIGURE 8.6
When Are A Also C?
In Part A of this figure, A (apples) are also C (food) because food represents a higher-order category that contains all apples. In Part B, however, C (squares) is not higher order than A (circles). Therefore, C does not contain A. B (shapes), however, is higher order than both A and C and contains both.

2. John is a (pick one: teacher, father, man, doctor, minister, congressional representative, talk show host).

3. Therefore, too much money is spent on education. What sort of appeal is used in this argument? Is the argument logical? Is the conclusion correct? Can you think of examples of similar kinds of arguments from your own experiences?

- Can you provide an example of deductive reasoning and an example of inductive reasoning that is connected with your own life?

Judgment and Decision Making

Representativeness heuristic • A decision-making heuristic in which people make judgments about samples according to the populations they appear to represent.

Availability heuristic • A decision-making heuristic in which our estimates of frequency or probability of events are based on how easy it is to find examples.

Anchoring and adjustment heuristic • A decision-making heuristic in which a presumption or first estimate serves as a cognitive anchor. As we receive additional information, we make adjustments, but tend to remain in the proximity of the anchor.

Decisions, decisions. Should you go for breakfast before classes begin or catch a few extra winks? Should you get married or remain single? (Should you get divorced or remain married?) Should you take a job or go on for advanced training when you complete your college program? If you opt for the job, cash will soon be jingling in your pockets. Yet, later you may wonder if you have the education to reach your potential. By furthering your education, you may have to delay independence and gratification, but you may find a more fulfilling position later on. Ah, decisions, decisions.

Other kinds of decisions are judgments about the nature of the world. We make judgments about which route to school or work will be the least crowded. We make judgments about where it is safe and convenient to live. We make judgments about political candidates and about which ice cream to buy.

You might like to think that people are so rational that they carefully weigh all the pluses and minuses when they make judgments or decisions. Or you might think that they insist upon finding and examining all the relevant information. Actually, people make most run-of-the-mill, daily decisions on the basis of limited information. They take shortcuts. They use heuristic devices—rules of thumb—in their judgments and decision making, just as they do in problem solving. Fortunately, the shortcuts tend not to land them in serious hot water—at least most of the time. In this section we con-

sider heuristic devices and two other factors in judgments and decision making: the framing effect and overconfidence.

HEURISTICS IN DECISION MAKING: IF IT WORKS, MUST IT BE LOGICAL?

Let us begin by asking you to imagine that you flip a coin six times. The coin has one head and one tail (take my word for it). In the following three possible outcomes, H stands for head and T stands for tail. Circle the sequence that is most likely:

H H H H H H

H H H T T T

T H H T H T

Did you select T H H T H T as the most likely sequence of events? Most people do (Matlin, 1994). Why? There are two reasons. First, people recognize that six heads in a row are unlikely. (The probability of achieving six heads is $\frac{1}{2} \times \frac{1}{2} \times \frac{1}{2} \times \frac{1}{2} \times \frac{1}{2} \times \frac{1}{2}$, or 1/64th.) Three heads and three tails are more likely than six heads (or six tails). Second, people recognize that the sequence of heads and tails ought to appear random. T H H T H T has a random look to it, whereas H H H T T T does not.

People can be said to select T H H T H T because of the **representativeness heuristic.** According to this decision-making heuristic, people make judgments about events (samples) according to the populations of events that they appear to represent. In this case, the sample of events is six coin tosses. The population is an infinite number of random coin tosses. But guess what, dear reader? *Each* of the sequences is equally likely (or unlikely). If the question had been whether six heads or three heads and three tails had been more likely, the correct answer would have been three and three. If the question had been whether heads and tails would be more likely to be consecutive or in random order, the correct answer would have been random order. But each of the three sequences shown is a specific sequence. What, in other words, is the probability of attaining the specific sequence T H H T H T? The probability that the first coin toss will result in a tail is

½. The probability that the second will result in a head is ½, and so on. Thus, the probability of attaining the exact sequence T H H T H T is identical to that of achieving any other specific sequence, that is: ½ × ½ × ½ × ½ × ½ × ½ = 1/64th. (Don't just sit there. Try this all out on a friend.)

Or consider this question: If a couple has five children, all of whom are boys, is their sixth child more likely to be a boy or a girl? Use of the representativeness heuristic would lead one to imagine that the couple is due for a girl. That is, five boys and one girl is closer than six boys to the assumed random distribution that accounts for roughly equal numbers of boys and girls in the world. But people with some knowledge of reproductive biology might predict that another boy is actually more likely, since five boys in a row may be too many to be a random biological event. On the other hand, if the couple's conception of a boy or girl were truly random, what would be the probability of conceiving another boy? Answer: ½.

Truth or Fiction Revisited. *It is not true that if a couple has five sons, the sixth child is likely to be a daughter.*

Another heuristic device used in decision making is the **availability heuristic.** According to this heuristic, our estimates of frequency or probability are based on how easy it is to find examples of relevant events. Let me ask you whether there are more art majors or sociology majors at your college. Unless you are familiar with the enrollment statistics, you will probably answer on the basis of the numbers of art majors and sociology majors that you personally know. Knowledge of these individuals is available to you.

Events that are more recent or more well-publicized tend to more available. Diseases such as emphysema and diabetes cause many times more death than accidents. Accidents are more likely to to reported in the media, however. Therefore, most people tend to exaggerate the number of deaths due to accidents but to underestimate the number of deaths due to emphysema and diabetes. Similarly, the media tend to focus on murder and other acts of violence, leading people to overestimate the incidence of aggression in our society (Silver and others, 1994). I am a metropolitan New Yorker. Many people from other parts of the United States judge the Big Apple by sensationalistic news reports of violence there. Thus, as I travel around the country, I constantly run into people who seem surprised that I feel that it is safe enough to live in the area.

The **anchoring and adjustment heuristic** suggests that there can be a good deal of inertia to our judgments. In forming opinions or making estimates, we have an initial view, or presumption. This is the anchor. As we receive additional information, we make adjustments. A bit begrudgingly. That is, if you grow up believing that one religion or one political party is the correct religion or political party, the belief serves as a cognitive anchor. When inconsistencies show up in your religion or political party, you may adjust your views of them, but perhaps not without some kicking and screaming.

Let us illustrate further by means of a math problem. Write each of the following multiplication problems on a separate piece of paper:

A. $8 \times 7 \times 6 \times 5 \times 4 \times 3 \times 2 \times 1$

B. $1 \times 2 \times 3 \times 4 \times 5 \times 6 \times 7 \times 8$

Show problem A to a few friends. Give them each 5 seconds to estimate the answer. Show problem B to other friends. Give them 5 seconds to estimate the answer as well.

The answers to the multiplication problems are the same since the order of the quantities being multiplied does not change the outcome. However, when Tversky and Kahneman (1982) showed these multiplication problems to high school students, the median estimate of students who were given version A was significantly higher than that of students who were given version B. Students who saw 8 in the first position offered an average estimate of 2,250. Students who saw 1 in the first position gave an average estimate of 512. That is, the estimate was larger when 8, not 1, served as the anchor. What, by the way, is the correct answer to the multiplication problems? Can you use the anchoring and adjustment heuristic to explain why both groups of students were so far off in their estimates?

THE FRAMING EFFECT: SAY THAT AGAIN?

If you were on a low-fat diet, would you be more likely to choose an ice cream that is 97% fat free or an ice cream whose fat content makes up 10% of its calorie content? On one shopping excursion, I was impressed with an ice cream package's claims that the product was 97% fat free. Yet when I read the package closely, I noticed that a 4-ounce serving had 160 calories, 27 of which were contributed by fat. Fat, then, accounted for 27/160ths, or 16.875%, of the ice cream's calorie content. But fat accounted for only 3% of the ice cream's *weight*. The packagers of the ice cream knew all about the *framing effect*. They understood that labeling the ice cream as "97% fat free" would make it sound more healthful than "Only 17% of calories from fat."

Truth or Fiction Revisited. *It is not true that an ice cream that is 97% fat free has less fat than an ice cream whose fat content makes up 10% of its calories.* The answer depends on how the measures are taken. A brand of ice cream I bought was 97% fat free in terms of the relative weights of the ingredients, but fat contributed 16.88% of the calories. In this case, if fat had contributed 10% of the calories, the ice cream would have been more than 98% fat free in terms of weight. We tend to be impressed with the "97% fat free" claim because of the framing effect.

The **framing effect** refers to the way in which wording, or the context in which information is presented, can influence decision making. Political groups are as aware as advertisers of the role of the framing effect. For example, proponents of legalized abortion refer to themselves as "pro-choice." Opponents of abortion refer to themselves as "pro-life." Thus each group frames itself in a way that is positive ("pro" something) and refers to a value (the values of freedom and of life) with which it would be difficult to argue.

Parents are also aware of the framing effect. My 3-year-old, Taylor, was invited to a play date at Abigail's house. I first asked Taylor, "Would you like to play with Abigail at her house?" The question met with a resounding no. I thought things over and reframed the question: "Would you like to play at Abigail's house and have a real fun time? She has lots of toys and games, and I'll pick you up real soon." This time Taylor's decision was yes.

Consider the following two possible survey questions to gain insight into the role of the framing effect—the effect of wording—in surveys:

1. Do you agree or disagree that women should have the same opportunities as men to seek fulfillment in the workplace?

2. Do you agree or disagree that women who have difficulty finding good day care for very young children should remain with the children in the home rather than work?

Try them out on your friends and see which earns greater agreement. Can you account for the difference?

The framing effect is also connected with the findings of Gestalt psychologists that the context in which information occurs affects its perception. In Part A of Figure 1.3 on page 14 we saw that circles of the same size might be perceived as smaller or larger because of their context. Similarly, the same symbol might be interpreted as either a B or the number 13, depending on its context (see Figure 1.3, Part B).

OVERCONFIDENCE: IS YOUR HINDSIGHT 20–20?

Whether our decisions are correct or incorrect, most of us tend to have overconfidence in them (Gigerenzer and others, 1991; Lundeberg and others, 1994). Overconfidence applies to judgments as wide-ranging as whether one will be infected by the virus that causes AIDS (Goldman & Harlow, 1993; van der Velde and others, 1994), predicting the outcome of elections (Hawkins & Hastie, 1990), asserting that one's answers to test items are correct (Lundeberg and others, 1994), and selecting stocks. Many people refuse to alter their judgments even in the face of statistical evidence that is running against them. (Have you ever known someone to maintain unrealistic confidence in a candidate who was far behind in the polls?)

Framing effect • The influence of wording, or the context in which information is presented, on decision making.

We also tend to view our situations with 20–20 hindsight. When we are proven wrong, we frequently find a way to show that we "knew it all along." We also at once become overconfident that we would have known the actual outcome if we had been privy to the information that became available after the event (Hawkins & Hastie, 1990). For example, if we had known that a key player would pull a hamstring muscle, we would have predicted a different outcome for the football game. If we had known that it would be blustery on Election Day, we would have predicted a smaller voter turnout and a different outcome of the election.

There are a number of reasons for overconfidence, even when our judgments are erroneous:

- We tend to be unaware of how flimsy our assumptions may be.

- We tend to focus on examples that confirm our judgments and to ignore events that do not.

- Our working memories have limited space, and we tend not to recall information that runs counter to our judgments.

- We work to bring about the events we believe in so that they sometimes come about as self-fulfilling prophecies.

- Even when people are told that they tend to be overconfident in their decisions, they usually fail to make use of this information (Gigerenzer and others, 1991). *You* are being informed, *right now,* that you may be overconfident about your decisions, even when they are based on faulty logic or inadequate information. Will *you* heed this advice, or will you continue to be overconfident and wing it day by day? (If you choose to continue to wing it, at least you'll be in good company.)

Truth or Fiction Revisited. *It is not necessarily true that people change their opinions when they are shown to be wrong.* In some cases they may, but the statement is too general to be true. Moreover, research evidence shows that people tend to only attend to information that confirms their judgments, whether or not they are correct. Also recall the anchoring and adjustment

heuristic. People's opinions, erroneous or correct, serve as their cognitive anchors. Thus, even when people do change their opinions, they change them, or adjust them, as little as possible. (To be human is to anchor and adjust?)

Reflections

Now that you have read the section on judgment and decision making, reflect on the following questions:

- Did you say that the "Truth or Fiction?" item "If a couple has five sons, the sixth child is likely to be a daughter" was truth or fiction? Why?

- Do you imagine that you could ever give up or seriously change your political or religious beliefs? Why or why not?

- Have you ever used the framing effect in trying to persuade someone to believe or do something? How?

- Do you tend to be confident in your decisions? Has your confidence—or overconfidence—ever gotten you into trouble? If so, how?

- Have you ever known people who have refused to change their minds even though they were shown to be wrong? How do you explain their reluctance to change?

Now that we have gained some insight into how people solve problems, reason, and make decisions, let us turn to the words and phrases they commonly use to think. Let us consider another aspect of cognitive science: the mechanics and development of language.

Language

When I was in high school, I was taught that people differ from other creatures that run, swim, or fly because only we use tools and language. Then I learned that lower animals also use tools. Otters use rocks to open clam shells. Chimpanzees toss rocks as weapons and use sticks to dig out grubs for food.

In recent years, our exclusive claim to language has also been questioned, because chimps and gorillas have been taught to use **symbols** to communicate. Some communicate by making signs with their hands. Others use plastic symbols or press keys on a computer keyboard. (See Figure 8.7.)

Language is the communication of thoughts and feelings by means of symbols that are arranged according to rules of grammar. Language makes it possible for one person to communicate knowledge to another and for one generation to communicate to another. Language creates a vehicle for recording experiences. Language allows us to don the eyes and ears of other people, to learn more than we could ever learn from direct experience. Language also provides many of the basic units of thought.

Language is one of our great strengths. Other species may be stronger, run faster, smell more keenly, even live longer, but only we have produced literature, music, mathematics, and science. Language ability has made all this possible.

Many species, including skylarks, have systems of communication. Birds warn other birds of predators. They communicate that they have taken possession of a certain tree or bush through particular chirps and shrieks. The "dances" of bees inform other bees of the location of a food source or a predator. Vervet monkeys make sounds that signal the distance and species of predators. But these are all inborn communication patterns. Swamp sparrows raised in isolation, for example, produce songs very similar to those produced by birds raised naturally in the wild (Brody, 1991). True language is distinguished from the communication systems of lower animals by properties such as semanticity, infinite

MINILECTURE:
BEE
LANGUAGE

Symbol • Something that stands for or represents another object, event, or idea.

Language • The communication of information by means of symbols arranged according to rules of grammar.

PSYCHOLOGY IN THE NEW MILLENNIUM

Goals 2000: Helping Our Children Learn to Solve the Problems of the New Millennium

Do you know where Slovenia is? In at least one way, Slovenia is more "on the map" than the United States.

That way has to do with how well children in the United States understand math. How do our kids fare? Not very well, according to comparisons of children in the United States with children from many other nations around the world. U.S. children chronically fall behind children in France, Germany, and Japan in most academic subjects. According to the 1994 *International Assessment of Educational Progress,* 13-year-olds in the United States rank 13th in science when compared with the children of 15 selected countries. Math? Children in the United States rank 14th out of the 15. They lag children in South Korea, Taiwan, Hungary, and Slovenia. Slovenia, then, could be said to have more prominence on the math map.

Does it matter that Asian and European children outperform children in the United States in math and science? Yes, according to Louis Gerstner, Jr. (1994), the chairperson of IBM. For one thing, U.S businesses are forced to pick up the slack. They have to spend about $60 billion a year teaching workers to perform tasks and to solve problems that they should have learned in school. Moreover, many businesses cannot upgrade their products or make their methods more efficient because they cannot teach their employees to do the necessary work. The bottom line is that it costs many businesses in the United States more money to produce less competitive products. The trend cannot last if the United States is to avert deterioration in its standard of living.

Of course, there is a still more important reason for upgrading the programs that teach children to reason and solve problems: The upgrading will enhance the quality of life of our children.

FIGURE 8.7
An Ape Uses Signs to Communicate Apes at Georgia State University's Language Research Center have been taught to express simple ideas by pressing keys on a computer-controlled keyboard.

Goals 2000. Recognizing educational deficiencies, President Clinton signed "Goals 2000" legislation in 1994 so that our children would have a more competitive future in the new millennium. The legislation addresses issues such as involving parents more in the educational process, using psychologists to train teachers, enhancing children's understanding of math and science, using psychologists to facilitate use of technologies, and employing psychologists to help assess educational progress (deGroot, 1994c).

Gerstner (1994) suggests a number of other measures:

• Increase the length of the school year. Children are out of school during the summer in the United States because of the historic need to work on the farm. However, farming in the United States now requires less than 2% of the labor force, and children are not needed at all to meet the nation's needs. Letting children's minds "lie fallow" during the summer means that in the fall they have to relearn much of what they have already covered rather than go on to new things. For disadvantaged children, having the summer off often means there is more time to simmer idly, or get in trouble, on the streets.

• Establish clear goals and the means for assessing them. Children learn more effectively when school systems and teachers establish concrete goals and systematically teach children to meet them. There should be more emphasis on what a 5th grader should understand about biology, what a 10th grader should understand in geometry.

• Provide rewards and incentives for students and teachers. Psychologists may debate why, but rewards work (most of the time). Students need to be rewarded for learning to solve problems and think critically. We cannot assume that children, especially young children, will want to learn for learning's sake. Some youngsters may need teacher approval and more tangible rewards. Teachers need to be rewarded for doing outstanding work. Strict seniority systems may protect teachers from arbitrary administrators, but they can also be punitive to teachers who would excel if they had incentives for doing so.

Semanticity • Meaning. The quality of language in which words are used as symbols for objects, events, or ideas.

Infinite creativity • The capacity to combine words into original sentences.

Syntax • The rules in a language for placing words in proper order to form meaningful sentences.

Displacement • The quality of language that permits one to communicate information about objects and events in another time and place.

Phonology • (foe-NOLL-oh-gee). The study of the basic sounds in a language.

Phoneme • (FOE-neem). A basic sound in a language.

Morpheme • (MORE-feem). The smallest unit of meaning in a language.

Inflections • Grammatical markers that change the forms of words to indicate grammatical relationships such as number and tense.

Semantics • The study of the meanings of a language—the relationships between language and objects and events.

Surface structure • The superficial grammatical construction of a sentence.

Deep structure • The underlying meaning of a sentence.

MINILECTURE: THE STRUCTURE OF LANGUAGE

MINILECTURE: THE BASICS OF LANGUAGE

creativity, and displacement (Ratner & Gleason, 1993).

Semanticity refers to the fact that the sounds (or signs) of a language have meaning. Words serve as symbols for actions, objects, relational concepts (*over, in, more,* and so on), and other ideas. The communications systems of the birds and the bees lack semanticity. Specific sounds and—in the case of bees—specific waggles do *not* serve as symbols.

Infinite creativity refers to the capacity to combine words into original sentences. An "original" sentence is *not* one that has never been spoken before. Rather, it is a sentence that is produced by the individual instead of imitated. To produce original sentences, children must have a basic understanding of **syntax,** or the structure of grammar. Two-year-old children string signs (words) together in novel combinations.

Displacement is the capacity to communicate information about events and objects in another time or place.[2] Language makes possible the efficient transmission of complex knowledge from one person to another and from one generation to another. Displacement permits parents to warn children of their own mistakes. Displacement allows children to tell their parents what they did in school.

BASIC CONCEPTS OF LANGUAGE

The basic concepts of language include *phonology* (sound[3]), *morphology* (units of meaning), *syntax* (word order), and *semantics* (the meanings of words and groups of words).

Phonology. **Phonology** is the study of the basic sounds in a language. There are 26 letters in the English alphabet but a greater number of **phonemes.** These include the *t* and *p* in *tip,* which a psycholinguist may designate as the /t/ and /p/ phonemes. The *o* in *go* and the *o* in *gone* are different phonemes. They are spelled with the same letter, but they sound different. English

speakers who learn French may be confused because /o/, as in the word *go,* has various spellings in French, including *o, au, eau,* even *eaux.*

Morphology. **Morphemes** are the smallest units of meaning in a language. A morpheme consists of one or more phonemes in a certain order. Some morphemes such as *dog* and *cat* function as words, but others must be used in combination. The words *dogs* and *cats* each consist of two morphemes. Adding /z/ to *dog* makes the word plural. Adding /s/ to *cat* serves the same function.

An *ed* morpheme at the end of a regular verb places it in the past tense, as with *add* and *added* and with *subtract* and *subtracted.* An *ly* morpheme at the end of an adjective often makes the word an adverb, as with *strong* and *strongly* and *weak* and *weakly.*

Morphemes such as *s* and *ed* tacked on to the ends of nouns and verbs are referred to as grammatical "markers," or **inflections.** Inflections change the forms of words to indicate grammatical relationships such as number (singular or plural) and tense (for example, present or past). Languages have grammatical rules for the formation of plurals, tenses, and other inflections.

Syntax.

since feeling is first
who pays any attention
to the syntax of things
will never wholly kiss you . . .

e. e. cummings

The lines from an e. e. cummings poem are intriguing because their syntax permits various interpretations. Syntax deals with the ways words are strung together, or ordered, into phrases and sentences (Lasnik, 1990). The rules for word order are the *grammar* of a language.

In English, statements usually follow the pattern *subject, verb,* and *object of the verb.* Note this example:

The young boy (subject) →
has brought (verb) → the book (object).

---

[2] The word *displacement* has a different meaning in Sigmund Freud's psychodynamic theory, as we shall see in Chapter 12.

[3] American Sign Language and Signed English, which are languages used by the deaf, are exceptions.

The sentence would be confusing if it were written "The young boy *has* the book *brought*." But this is how the words would be ordered in German. German syntax differs, and in German, a past participle *(brought)* is placed at the end of the sentence, whereas the helping verb *(has)* follows the subject. Although the syntax of German differs from that of English, children reared in German-speaking homes[4] acquire German syntax readily.

Semantics. **Semantics** is the study of meaning. It involves the relationship between language and the objects or events language depicts. Words that sound (and are spelled) alike can have different meanings, depending on their usage. Compare these sentences:

> A rock sank the boat.
>
> Don't rock the boat.

In the first sentence, *rock* is a noun and the subject of the verb *sank*. The sentence probably means that the hull of a boat was ripped open by an underwater rock, causing the boat to sink. In the second sentence, *rock* is a verb. The second sentence is usually used as a figure of speech in which a person is being warned not to change things—not to "make waves" or "upset the apple cart."

Compare these sentences:

> The chicken is ready for dinner.
>
> The lion is ready for dinner.
>
> The shark is ready for dinner.

The first sentence probably means that a chicken has been cooked and is ready to be eaten. The second sentence probably means that a lion is hungry or about to devour its prey. Our interpretation of the phrase "is ready for dinner" reflects our knowledge about chickens and lions. Whether we expect a shark to be eaten or to do some eating might reflect our seafood preferences or how recently we had seen the movie *Jaws*.

Let us differentiate between the *surface structure* and the *deep structure* of sentences (Lasnik, 1990). The **surface structure** in-volves the superficial grammatical construction of the sentence. The surface structure of the "ready for dinner" sentences is the same. The **deep structure** of a sentence refers to its underlying meaning. The "ready for dinner" sentences clearly differ in their deep structure. "Make me a peanut butter and jelly sandwich" has an ambiguous surface structure, allowing different interpretations of its deep meaning—and the typical child's response: "Poof! You're a peanut butter and jelly sandwich!"

What of the language of apes? Linguists Steven Pinker (1994a) and Herbert Terrace (1987) conclude that apes may not really use language because they may not produce it spontaneously, and they cannot master grammar. Michael Maratsos (1983) takes a different view. He argues that this strict standard is relatively new on the scene. "Apes can probably learn to use signs to communicate meanings," Maratsos writes. "As this used to be the old boundary for language, it seems unfair [now] to raise the ante and say that [using signs to communicate meaning] is not really language" (1983, p. 771).

MINILECTURE:
THE APE
LANGUAGE
DEBATE

Reflections

Now that you have read the section on language, reflect on the following questions:

- Can you imagine what life would be like without language? What do you believe you would have accomplished without language? What would be lacking? Why?
- Can you think of some English idioms or phrases that might be difficult for immigrants learning English to understand? Why?
- Have you ever known someone to claim that a pet could "speak" or understand English or another language? Did the pet really "speak"? Did the pet really "understand" language? What do you think?

Now that we have explored the properties and the basics of language, let us chronicle the "child's task" of acquiring language.

---

[4] No, homes do not really speak German or any other language. This is an example of idiomatic English. Idioms like these are readily acquired by children.

Language Development

Children appear to develop language in an invariant sequence of steps. We begin with the **prelinguistic** vocalizations of crying, cooing, and babbling.

Newborn children, as parents are well aware, have an unlearned but highly effective form of verbal expression: crying and more crying. Crying is accomplished by blowing air through the vocal tract. There are no distinct, well-formed sounds.

Crying is about the only sound that babies make during the first month. During the second month, they also begin **cooing.** Babies use their tongues when they coo. For this reason, coos are more articulated than cries. Coos are often vowel-like and may resemble extended "oohs" and "ahs." Cooing appears to be linked to feelings of pleasure or positive excitement. Babies do not coo when they are hungry, tired, or in pain.

Parents soon learn that different cries and coos can indicate different things: hunger, gas, or pleasure at being held or rocked.

Cries and coos are innate but can be modified by experience. When parents respond positively to cooing by talking to their babies, smiling at them, and imitating them, cooing increases. Early parent–child "conversations," in which parents respond to coos and then pause as the baby coos, may foster early infant awareness of turn-taking as a way of relating verbally to other people.

True language has *semanticity.* Sounds (or signs, in the case of sign language) are symbols. Cries and coos do not represent objects or events. Thus they are prelinguistic.

By about 8 months, cooing decreases markedly. By about the fifth or sixth month, children have begun to babble. **Babbling** is the first vocalizing that sounds like human speech. Children babble phonemes of several languages, including the throaty German *ch,* the clicks of certain African tribes, and rolling *r*'s. In babbling, babies frequently combine consonants and vowels, as in "ba," "ga," and, sometimes, the much valued "dada." "Dada" at first is purely coincidental (sorry, you Dads), despite the family's jubilation over its appearance.

Babbling, like crying and cooing, appears to be inborn. Children from cultures whose languages sound very different all seem to babble the same sounds, including many that they could not have heard (Gleason & Ratner, 1993). As time progresses, however, their babbling takes on more of the sounds of the languages spoken in their environments.

Children seem to single out the types of phonemes used in the home within a few months. By the age of 9 or 10 months, these phonemes are repeated regularly. Foreign phonemes begin to drop out. Thus, there is an overall reduction in the variety of phonemes that infants produce.

Babbling, like crying and cooing, is a prelinguistic event. Yet infants usually understand much of what others are saying well before they utter their first words. Comprehension precedes production, and infants demonstrate comprehension with their actions and gestures.

DEVELOPMENT OF VOCABULARY

Ah, that long-awaited first word! What a thrill! What a milestone! Sad to say, many parents miss it. They are not quite sure

Crying. Crying is a prelinguistic vocalization that most adults find aversive and strive to bring to an end.

when their infants utter their first word, often because the first word is not pronounced clearly or because pronunciation varies from usage to usage. *Ball* may be pronounced "ba," "bee," or even "pah." The majority of early words are nouns—names for things (Nelson and others, 1993).

Vocabulary acquisition is slow at first. It may take children 3 to 4 months to achieve a 10-word vocabulary after their first word is spoken (Nelson, 1973). By about 18 months, children are producing nearly two dozen words. Many words such as *no, cookie, mama, hi,* and *eat* are quite familiar. Others, like *allgone* and *bye-bye,* may not be found in the dictionary, but they function as words. Research evidence shows that reading to children increases their vocabulary, so parents do well to pull out the storybooks (Arnold and others, 1994; Robbins & Ehri, 1994).

Children try to talk about more objects than they have words for, and so they often extend the meaning of one word to refer to things and actions for which they do not have words. This phenomenon is termed **overextension.** At some point many children refer to horses as *doggies.* My daughter Allyn, at age 6, counted by tens as follows: sixty, seventy, eighty, ninety, *tenty.*

DEVELOPMENT OF SYNTAX

Although children first use one-word utterances, these utterances appear to express the meanings of sentences. Brief expressions that have the meanings of sentences are termed *telegraphic speech.* When we as adults write telegrams, we use principles of syntax to cut out all the "unnecessary" words. "Home Tuesday" might stand for "I expect to be home on Tuesday." Similarly, only the essential words are used in children's telegraphic speech—in particular, nouns, verbs, and some modifiers.

Single words that are used to express complex meanings are called **holophrases.** For example, *mama* may be used by the child to signify meanings as varied as "There goes Mama," "Come here, Mama," and "You are my Mama." Similarly, *poo-cat* can signify "There is a pussycat," "That stuffed animal looks just like my pussycat," or "I want you to give me my pussycat right now!" Most children readily teach

their parents what they intend by augmenting their holophrases with gestures, intonations, and reinforcers. That is, they act delighted when parents do as requested and howl when they do not.

Toward the end of the second year, children begin to speak in telegraphic two-word sentences. In the sentence "That ball," the words *is* and *a* are implied. Two-word utterances seem to appear at about the same time in the development of all languages (Slobin, 1973). Also, the sequence of emergence of the types of two-word utterances (for example, first, agent-action; then action-object, location, and possession) is the same in languages as diverse as English, Luo (an African tongue), German, Russian, and Turkish (Slobin, 1983).

Two-word utterances, although brief, show understanding of syntax. The child will say, "Sit chair" to tell a parent to sit in a chair, not "Chair sit." (Apes do not reliably make this distinction.) The child will say, "My shoe," not "Shoe my," to show possession. "Mommy go" means Mommy is leaving, whereas "Go Mommy" expresses the wish for Mommy to go away. For this reason, "Go Mommy" is not heard often.

TOWARD MORE COMPLEX LANGUAGE

Between the ages of 2 and 3, children's sentence structure usually expands to include the missing words in telegraphic speech. During the third year children usually add articles *(a, an, the),* conjunctions *(and, but, or),* possessive and demonstrative adjectives *(your, her, that),* pronouns *(she, him, one),* and prepositions *(in, on, over, around, under, and through).* Their grasp of syntax is shown in language oddities such as *your one* instead of, simply, *yours* and *his one* instead of *his.*

Usually between the ages of 2 and 3 children begin to combine phrases and clauses into complex sentences. An early example of a complex sentence is "You goed and Mommy goed, too." A more advanced example is "What will we do when we get there?"

One of the more intriguing language developments is **overregularization.** To understand children's use of overregularization, consider the formation of the past tense and of plurals in English. We add *d* or

Prelinguistic • Prior to the development of language.

Cooing • Prelinguistic, articulated, vowel-like sounds that appear to reflect feelings of positive excitement.

Babbling • The child's first vocalizations that have the sounds of speech.

Overextension • Overgeneralizing the use of words to objects and situations to which they do not apply—a normal characteristic of the speech of young children.

Holophrase • A single word used to express complex meanings.

Overregularization • The application of regular grammatical rules for forming inflections (e.g., past tense and plurals) to irregular verbs and nouns.

ed phonemes to regular verbs and *s* or *z* phonemes to regular nouns. Thus, *walk* becomes *walked* and *look* becomes *looked*. *Pussycat* becomes *pussycats* and *doggy* becomes *doggies*. There are also irregular verbs and nouns. For example, *see* becomes *saw, sit* becomes *sat,* and *go* becomes *went. Sheep* remains *sheep* (plural) and *child* becomes *children*.

At first, children learn a small number of these irregular verbs by imitating their parents. Two-year-olds tend to form them correctly—temporarily (Kuczaj, 1982)! Then they become aware of the syntactic rules for forming the past tense and plurals in English. As a result, they tend to make charming errors (Pinker, 1994a). Some 3- to 5-year-olds, for example, are more likely to say "I seed it" than "I saw it" and more likely to say "Mommy sitted down" than "Mommy sat down." They are likely to talk about the "gooses" and "sheeps" they "seed" on the farm and about all the "childs" they ran into at the playground. This tendency to regularize the irregular is what is meant by overregularization.

Some parents recognize that their children were at one point forming the past tense of irregular verbs correctly, and that they later began to make errors. The thing to remember is that overregularization *does represent an advance in the development of syntax.* Overregularization reflects knowledge of grammar—not faulty language development. In another year or two, *mouses* will be boringly transformed into *mice,* and Mommy will no longer have *sitted* down. Parents might as well enjoy overregularization while they can.

As language develops beyond the third year, children show increasing facility with the use of pronouns (such as *it* and *she*) and with prepositions (such as *in, before,* or *on*), which represent physical or temporal relationships among objects and events. Children's first questions are telegraphic and characterized by a rising pitch (which signifies a question mark in English) at the end. "More milky?" for example, can be translated into "May I have more milk?" or "Would you like more milk?" or "Is there more milk?"—depending on the context.

It is usually during the third year that the *wh* questions appear. Consistent with the child's general cognitive development, certain *wh* questions (*what, who,* and *where*) appear earlier than others (*why, when, which,* and *how*) (Bloom and others, 1982). *Why* is usually too philosophical for the 2-year-old, and *how* is too involved. Two-year-olds are also likely to be now-oriented, so *when,* too, is of less than immediate concern. By the fourth year, most children are spontaneously producing *why, when,* and *how* questions.

By the fourth year, children are asking questions, taking turns talking, and engaging in lengthy conversations. By the age of 6, their vocabularies have expanded to 10,000 words, give or take a few thousand. By 7 to 9, most children realize that words can have more than one meaning, and they are entertained by riddles and jokes that require semantic sophistication ("What's black and white and read all over?"). Between the elementary school and high school years, vocabulary continues to grow rapidly. There are also subtle advances in articulation and the capacity to use complex syntax.

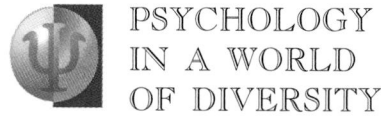

PSYCHOLOGY IN A WORLD OF DIVERSITY

BLACK DIALECT[5]

The Black dialect is spoken by segments of the African American community. To gain a taste of Black dialect, consider a study in which an audiotape of standard English was played to poor African American children who were asked to repeat what they had heard. The taped sentence was "I asked him if he did it, and he said he didn't do it." One 5-year-old girl recast the sentence in Black dialect as follows: "I asks him if he did it, and he says he didn't did it, but I knows he did" (Anastasiow & Hanes, 1976, p. 3).

As the example suggests, major differences between Black dialect and standard English lie in the use of verbs. Tenses are formed

---

[5] Also referred to as Black English Vernacular, or BEV (Pinker, 1994a, pp. 28–31).

How Do Students Respond When They Hear Black Dialect in the Classroom?
Black dialect is spoken by segments of the African American community. The major differences between Black dialect and standard English lie in the use of verbs. Many linguists note that the grammatical rules of Black dialect differ from those of standard English, but Black dialect has consistent rules.

differently in Black dialect. For example, "She-ah hit us" may be used in the place of the standard English "She will hit us." Consider the verb *to be*. In Black dialect, "He be gone" indicates the standard "He has been gone for a long while," and "He gone" signifies "He is gone right now" in standard English.

According to linguists, Black dialect is rooted in the remnants of West African languages used by slaves and the attempts of those slaves, who were denied formal education, to imitate the speech of the dominant White culture. Some observers believe that standard English verbs are used haphazardly in Black dialect, as if the bare bones of English are being adapted and downgraded. As a result, some school systems react to Black dialect with contempt (Lee, 1994). Yet, many linguists argue that Black dialect is a grammatical variant of standard English. The rules of Black dialect differ from those of standard English, but they are consistent rules and allow for the expression of complex thoughts (Pinker, 1994a). In other words, Black dialect is different but not inferior.

"To Be or Not to Be": Use of the Verb to Be in Black Dialect. Let us consider a couple of examples of rules in Black dialect—rules involving use of the verb *to be* and negation. In standard English, *be* is part of the infinitive form of the verb used in the formation of the future tense, as in "I'll be angry tomorrow." Thus, "I be angry" is incorrect. In Black dialect, *be* is used to denote a continuing state of being. "I am angry" would be perfectly good standard English *and* Black dialect. But the Black dialect sentence "I be angry" means in standard English, "I have been angry for a while" and is grammatical.

Black dialect also *omits* the verb *to be* in some cases (Lee, 1994), usually when standard English would use a contraction. For example, "She's the one I'm talking about" could be translated as "She the one I talking about." Omitting the verb in Black dialect is no more careless than contracting it in standard English. Contraction follows a rule of standard English; omission follows a rule of Black dialect. The Black dialect also frequently drops *ed* from the past tense and lacks the possessive *s* (Smitherman, 1994).

**"Not to Be or Not to Be Nothing":
Negation in Black Dialect.** Black dialect also differs in the use of the double negative. Consider the sentence, "I don't want no trouble," which is, of course, commendable. Middle-class White children would be corrected for this instance of double negation and encouraged to say either "I don't want any trouble" or "I want no trouble." Double negation is acceptable in Black dialect (Pinker, 1994a). However, many teachers who use standard English "jump on" African American children who speak this way (Lee, 1994).

Some African American children show biculturalism. They function competently within the dominant culture in the United States and within their own culture (LaFromboise and others, 1993). They take pride in their cultural identity and switch readily from standard English to Black dialect. They use standard English in a conference with their teacher or in a job interview but Black dialect as a sort of private code "in the neighborhood." Other children cannot switch back and forth (Lee, 1994). Then there are the children who refuse to adopt standard English because they do not want to be seen as trying to be better than African Americans who speak Black dialect. For them, speaking standard English is the equivalent of trying to be White. They would rather be "real" (Lee, 1994).

THEORIES OF LANGUAGE DEVELOPMENT

Since all normal humans talk but no house pets or house plants do, no matter how pampered, heredity must be involved in language. But since a child growing up in Japan speaks Japanese whereas the same child brought up in California would speak English, the environment is also crucial. Thus, there is no question about whether heredity or environment is involved in language, or even whether one or the other is "more important." Instead, . . . our best hope [might be] finding out *how* they interact. (Steven Pinker, 1990, p. 201)

Countless billions of children have acquired the languages spoken by their parents and passed them down, with minor changes, from generation to generation. Theories of language development are concerned with *how* they manage to do so. In language development, as in many other areas of psychology, we study the interactions between the influences of heredity (nature) and the environment (nurture). Let us see how these broad views are expressed in learning, nativist, and cognitive theories of language development.

Learning Views. Learning theorists claim that language develops according to laws of learning and is similar to other kinds of learned behavior (Gleason & Ratner, 1993). They usually refer to the concepts of imitation and reinforcement. From a social-cognitive perspective, parents serve as **models.** Children learn language, at least in part, by observation and imitation. It seems likely that many vocabulary words, especially nouns and verbs (including irregular verbs), are learned by imitation.

At first children accurately repeat the irregular verb forms they observe. This repetition can probably be explained in terms of modeling, but modeling does not explain all the events of learning. Children later begin to overregularize irregular verb forms *because of* knowledge of rules of syntax, not imitation. Nor does imitative learning explain how children spontaneously utter phrases and sentences they have *not* observed. Parents, for example, are unlikely to model utterances such as "bye-bye sock" and "allgone Daddy," but children do say them.

Sometimes children steadfastly avoid imitating language forms suggested by adults, even when the adults are insistent. Note the following exchange between 2-year-old Ben and a (very frustrated!) adult:

BEN: I like these candy. I like they.
ADULT: You like them?
BEN: Yes. I like they.
ADULT: Say *them.*
BEN: Them.
ADULT: Say "I like *them.*"
BEN: I like them.
ADULT: Good.
BEN: I'm good. These candy good too.

Models • In learning theory, persons who engage in behaviors that are imitated by others.

Psycholinguistic theory • The view that language learning involves an interaction between environmental influences and an inborn tendency to acquire language. The emphasis is on the inborn tendency.

Language acquisition device • In psycholinguistic theory, neural "prewiring" that facilitates the child's learning of grammar. Abbreviated *LAD.*

ADULT: Are they good?
BEN: Yes. I like they. You like they?
               (Kuczaj, 1982, p. 48)

In *Verbal Behavior,* B. F. Skinner outlined his view of the role of reinforcement in language development: "A child acquires verbal behavior when relatively unpatterned vocalizations, selectively reinforced, assume forms which produce appropriate consequences in a given verbal community" (Skinner, 1957, p. 31).

Skinner allows that prelinguistic vocalizations such as cooing and babbling are inborn. But parents reinforce children for babbling that approximates real words such as *da,* which in English resembles *dog* or *daddy.* Children, in fact, do increase their babbling when it results in adults smiling at them, stroking them, and talking back to them.

As the first year progresses, children babble the sounds of their native tongues with increasing frequency. "Foreign" sounds tend to drop out. The behaviorist explains this pattern of changing frequencies in terms of reinforcement (of the sounds of the adults' language) and extinction (of foreign sounds). An alternate (nonbehavioral) explanation is that children actively attend to the sounds in their linguistic environments and are intrinsically motivated to utter them.

From Skinner's (1957, 1983) perspective, children acquire an early vocabulary through shaping. That is, parents require that children's utterances come progressively closer to actual words before they are reinforced. Skinner views multiword utterances as complex stimulus-response chains that are also taught by shaping. As children's utterances increase in length, parents foster correct word order by uttering sentences to their children and reinforcing imitation. As with Ben, when children make grammatical errors, parents recast their utterances correctly. They then reinforce the children for repeating them.

But recall Ben's refusal to be shaped into correct syntax. If the reinforcement explanation were sufficient, parental reinforcement would facilitate children's learning of phonetics, syntax, and semantics. We do not have such evidence. For one thing, parents are more likely to reinforce their children

for the accuracy, or "truth value," of their utterances than for their grammatical correctness. Parents, in other words, generally accept the syntax of their children's vocal efforts. The child who points down and says, "The grass is purple" is not likely to be reinforced, despite correct syntax. But the enthusiastic child who shows her empty plate and blurts out "I eated it all up!" is likely to be reinforced, despite overregularization of *to eat.*

Selective reinforcement of children's pronunciation, in fact, may backfire. Children whose parents reward proper pronunciation but correct poor pronunciation develop vocabulary *more slowly* than children whose parents are more tolerant of pronunciation (Nelson, 1973).

Learning theory also cannot account for the invariant sequences of language development and for children's spurts in acquisition. Even the types of two-word utterances emerge in a consistent pattern in diverse cultures. Although timing differs from child to child, the types of questions used, passive versus active sentences, and so on, all emerge in the same order.

Nativist Views. The nativist view of language development holds that innate or inborn factors cause children to attend to and acquire language in certain ways (Maratsos, 1983). From this perspective, children bring an inborn tendency in the form of neurological "prewiring" to language learning (Pinker, 1994a).

According to **psycholinguistic theory,** language acquisition involves the interaction of environmental influences—such as exposure to parental speech and reinforcement—and an inborn tendency to acquire language, which Chomsky (1980, 1991) and some others refer to as a **language acquisition device** (LAD). Evidence for an LAD is found in the universality of human language abilities and in the invariant sequences of language development.

The inborn tendency suits the nervous system to learn grammar. On the surface, languages differ a great deal. However, the LAD serves children all over the world because languages share what Chomsky refers to as a "universal grammar"—an underlying deep structure or set of rules for turning ideas into sentences (Pinker, 1990,

1994a). Consider an analogy with computers: According to psycholinguistic theory, the universal grammar that resides in the LAD is the basic operating system of the computer, whereas the particular language that a child learns to use is the word-processing program.

Lenneberg (1967) proposes that there is a **sensitive period** for learning language that begins at about 18 to 24 months and lasts until puberty. This period reflects neural maturation. During the sensitive period, neural development (as in the differentiation of brain structures) provides a degree of plasticity that facilitates language learning.

Evidence for a sensitive period is found in recovery from brain injuries in some people. Injuries to the dominant hemisphere can impair or destroy the ability to speak (see Chapter 3). But prior to puberty, brain-injured children frequently recover a good deal of speaking ability.

Cognitive Views.   Cognitive views of language development focus on the relationships between cognitive development and language development. Cognitive theorists tend to hold a number of assumptions, including these:

1. Language development is made possible by cognitive analytical abilities (Bates and others, 1992; Maratsos, 1983).

2. Children are active agents in language learning. Children's motivation for learning syntax and vocabulary grows out of their "desire to express meanings that conceptual development makes available to them" (Maratsos, 1983).

Many cognitive theorists see language development as subordinate to cognitive development (Gleason & Ratner, 1993). Piaget (1976) argued that children must understand concepts before they can use words that describe the concepts. For example, children need to understand that objects (such as food) normally continue to exist whether or not you can still see them[6] before they begin to note their disappearance through phrases such as "All gone" (Gleason & Ratner, 1993). This view also holds that children learn words in order to describe classes or categories they have already created (Nelson, 1982). Children can learn the word *doggy* because they have already perceived the characteristics that distinguish dogs from other things.

Some cognitive theorists reverse the causal relationship and claim that children create cognitive classes in order to understand things that are labeled by words (Clark, 1993). When children hear the word *dog,* they strive to understand it by searching for characteristics that separate dogs from other things.

There may be something of value in each of these cognitive views (Greenberg & Kuczaj, 1982). In the early stages of language development, concepts often precede words so that many of the infant's words describe classes that have already developed. Later on, however, language is not the mere handmaiden of thought; language also influences thought.

Reflections

Now that you have read the section on language development, reflect on the following questions:

- Have you observed an infant learning language? How did she or he communicate desires and understanding of language before she or he could speak? What was her or his first word? (Are you sure?)
- Can you recall any of your own experiences in learning the language spoken in your home? Do you recall any "cute" errors you used to make in choice of words or in pronunciation?
- Did the adults in your life make an active effort to teach you to speak or develop more sophisticated language? What did they do? How well do you think it worked? What assumptions do you think they held about language development?

While we as adults continue to struggle with complex concepts to explain language development, 1- and 2-year-olds go right on learning language all around us. In many cases, as we see in the "Psychology and Modern Life" section, they learn more than one.

Sensitive period • In linguistic theory, the period from about 18 months to puberty when the brain is thought to be particularly capable of learning language because of plasticity.

Linguistic-relativity hypothesis • The view that language structures the way in which we view the world.

---

[6] This concept is referred to as *object permanence* by Piaget, as we see in Chapter 11.

Language and Thought

Theories of language development are of little importance to a 20-month-old who has just polished off her plate of chocolate chip cookies and exclaimed (or signed) "All gone!" In the previous section, we were concerned with how the child comes to say or sign "All gone" when she has finished her cookies. Now let us bring the chapter full circle by returning to matters of thinking: What does the child's use of "All gone" suggest about her thought processes? In other words, would the girl have *known* that there were no cookies left if she did not have a word to express this idea? (Modern theorists of language would answer yes [Larson, 1990; Miller, 1990; Pinker, 1990].) Do you always think in words? (Modern theorists of language would answer no [Larson, 1990; Miller, 1990; Pinker, 1990].) Can you think *without* using language? (Yes.) Would you be able to solve problems without using words or sentences? (That depends on the problem.)

Jean Piaget (1976) believed that language reflects knowledge of the world but that much knowledge can be acquired without language. For example, it is possible to have the concepts of roundness or redness even when we do not know or use the words *round* or *red*.

But is it possible for English speakers to have the thoughts experienced by people who speak other languages? This question brings us to consideration of the linguistic-relativity hypothesis.

THE LINGUISTIC-RELATIVITY HYPOTHESIS

Language may not be needed for all thought. According to the **linguistic-relativity hypothesis** proposed by Whorf (1956), however, language structures the ways in which we perceive the world. That is, the categories and relations we use to understand the world derive from our particular languages. Therefore, speakers of various languages conceptualize the world in different ways (Pinker, 1990).

According to the linguistic-relativity hypothesis, most English speakers' ability to think about snow may be rather limited

In an Igloo. The Inuit people of Alaska and the Canadian Northwestern Territories (shown here) have many more words for snow than most of us. They spend most of their lives in the snow, and the subtle gradations among various kinds of snow are meaningful to them.

when compared to that of the Inuit people. We have only a few words for snow, whereas the Inuit people have many words, related, for example, to whether the snow is hard-packed, falling, melting, or covered by ice. When we think about snow, we have fewer words to choose from and have to search for descriptive adjectives. The Inuit people, however, can readily find a single word that describes a complex weather condition. It might, then, be easier for them to think about this variety of snow in relation to other aspects of their world. Similarly, the Hanunoo people of the Philippines use 92 words for rice, depending on whether the rice is husked or unhusked and on how it is prepared. And we have one word for camel, whereas Arabs have more than 250.

In English, we have hundreds of words to describe different colors, but those who speak Shona use only three words for colors. People who speak Bassa use only two words for colors (Gleason, 1961), corresponding to light and dark. The Hopi Indians had two words for flying objects, one for birds and an all-inclusive word for anything else that may be found traveling through the air.

Does this mean that the Hopi were limited in their ability to think about bumblebees and airplanes? Are English speakers limited in their ability to think about skiing conditions? Are those who speak Shona and Bassa "color-blind" for practical purposes?

Probably not. People who use only a few words to distinguish colors seem to perceive the same color variations as people with dozens of words (Bornstein & Marks, 1982). For example, the Dani of New Guinea, like the Bassa, have just two words for colors: *mola,* which refers to warm colors, and *mili,* which refers to cool colors. Still, tasks in matching and memory show that the Dani can discriminate the many colors of the spectrum when they are motivated to do so. English-speaking skiers who are concerned about different skiing conditions have developed a comprehensive special vocabulary about snow, including the terms *powder, slush, ice, hard-packed,* and *corn snow,* that might enable them to communicate and think about snow with the facility of the Inuit people. When a need to expand a language's vocabulary arises, the speakers of that language apparently have little difficulty in meeting the need.

Modern cognitive scientists generally do not accept the linguistic-relativity hypothesis (Pinker, 1990). For one thing, adults use images and abstract logical propositions as units of thought, not only words (Larson, 1990; Miller, 1990). Infants, moreover, display considerable intelligence before they have learned to speak. Another criticism is that a language's vocabulary suggests the range of concepts that the speakers of the language have traditionally found important, not their cognitive limits. For example, a person magically lifted from the 19th century and placed inside an airplane would probably not think that she or he was flying inside a bird or a large insect, even if she or he had no word for airplane.

Reflections

Now that you have read the section on language and thought, reflect on the following questions:

- How sophisticated is your thinking about electronic data processing? For example, do you know what the terms *megabyte, random access memory, CD-ROM, local bus video,* and *PCMCIA card* mean? Does your knowledge of these terms affect your ability to think about computers? Why or why not?
- Does understanding of such words as *alliteration, trochaic foot,* and *pentameter* enhance your ability to appreciate poetry? Why or why not?

We noted that infants display considerable intelligence before they can speak. Yet knowledge of the meaning of words is one of the key measures of general intelligence. Chapter 9 explores the meaning and assessment of the enigmatic concept of intelligence. We see how intelligence is intertwined with other aspects of cognition, including memory, problem solving, reasoning, decision making, and language.

Before leaving this chapter, however, I have a final problem for you:

> You're driving a bus that's leaving from Pennsylvania. To start off with, there were 32 people on the bus. At the next bus stop, 11 people got off and 9 people got on. At the next bus stop, 2 people got off and 2 people got on. At the next bus stop, 12 people got on and 16 people got off. At the next bus stop, 5 people got on and 3 people got off.
>
> How many people are now on the bus?

Summary

1. **What is thinking?** Thinking is cognitive activity that is involved in understanding, processing, and communicating information. Thinking refers to conscious, planned attempts to make sense of the world.

2. **What are concepts?** Concepts are mental categories that group objects, events, or ideas with common properties. We tend to organize concepts in hierarchies.

3. **What are prototypes?** Prototypes are good examples of categories. When new instances closely match people's prototypes of concepts, they are readily recognized as examples.

4. **How do people approach problem solving?** People approach problem solving by first attempting to understand the problem. Then they use various strategies for attacking the problem, including algorithms, heuristic devices, and analogies.

5. **What are algorithms and heuristic devices?** Algorithms are specific procedures for solving problems (such as formulas) that will work invariably as long as they are applied correctly. Heuristics are rules of thumb that help us simplify and solve problems. Heuristics are less reliable than algorithms, but when they are effective, they allow us to solve problems more rapidly.

6. **What are some factors that affect problem solving?** Five key factors are one's level of expertise, whether one falls prey to a mental set, whether one develops insight into a problem, functional fixedness, and the definition of the problem.

7. **What is creativity?** Creativity is the ability to make unusual and sometimes remote associations to the elements of a problem to generate new combinations that meet goals.

8. **What factors appear to account for creativity?** There is only a moderate relationship between creativity and intelligence. Creative people show traits such as flexibility, fluency, and independence. The pressure of social evaluation appears to reduce creativity, and the effects of brainstorming in fostering creativity are debatable.

9. **What kinds of reasoning are there?** In deductive reasoning, one reaches conclusions about premises that are true so long as the premises are true. In inductive reasoning, we reason from individual cases or particular facts to a general conclusion that is not necessarily true.

10. **How do people make decisions?** People sometimes make decisions by carefully weighing the pluses and minuses. However, people making decisions frequently use rules of thumb or heuristics, which are shortcuts that are correct (or correct enough) most of the time. According to the representativeness heuristic, people make judgments about events according to the populations of events that they appear to represent. According to the availability heuristic, people's estimates of frequency or probability are based on how easy it is to find examples of relevant events. According to the anchoring and adjustment heuristic, we adjust our initial estimates as we receive additional information—but begrudgingly.

11. **What are some factors that affect decision making?** Our decisions are also influenced by the framing effect and overconfidence.

12. **What is language?** Language is the communication of thoughts and feelings through symbols that are arranged according to rules of grammar. Language has the properties of semanticity, infinite creativity, and displacement.

13. **What are the basic concepts of language?** The basic concepts of language include phonology, morphology, syntax, and semantics.

14. **What are prelinguistic vocalizations?** Crying, cooing, and babbling are prelinguistic.

15. **What is telegraphic speech?** Children's early utterances are telegraphic; that is, they eliminate unessential words. Two-word telegraphic utterances appear toward the end of the second year.

16. **How do psychologists explain language development?** Three kinds of theories are used: learning theories, nativist theories, and cognitive theories.

17. **What are some of the relationships between thought and language?** Thought is possible without language, but language facilitates thought. According to the linguistic-relativity hypothesis, language structures the ways in which we perceive the world. However, most modern cognitive scientists do not support the linguistic-relativity hypothesis.

Psychology and Modern Life

It may seem strange to people in the United States, but most people throughout the world speak two or more languages (Snow, 1993). Most countries have minority populations whose languages differ from the national tongue. Nearly all Europeans are taught English and the languages of neighboring nations. Consider the Netherlands. Dutch is the native tongue, but all children are also taught French, German, and English and expected to become fluent in each of them.

Truth or Fiction Revisited. *It is true that the majority of people around the world speak at least two languages.* Bilingualism is thus the normal state of affairs, not merely an issue for immigrants to the United States.

Bilingualism and Bilingual Education

For about 32 million people in the United States, English is a second language (Barringer, 1993b). Spanish, Russian, Chinese, or Arabic is spoken in the home and, per-

haps, the neighborhood. Table 8.2 provides a snapshot of the 25 languages most commonly spoken in the home in the United States in the 1990s. Much of the 38% jump in the numbers of speakers of foreign languages is due to waves of immigration from Latin America and Asia.

Early in the century, it was widely believed that children reared in bilingual homes were retarded in their cognitive and language development. The theory was that cognitive capacity was limited. Therefore, people who stored two linguistic systems were crowding their mental abilities (Lambert, 1990). However, the U.S. Bureau of the Census reports that more than 75% of Americans who first spoke another language in the home also speak English "well" or "very well" (Barringer, 1993b). Moreover, a careful analysis of older studies in bilingualism shows that the bilingual children observed often lived in families that were low in socioeconomic status and level of education. Yet these bilingual children were compared to middle-class monolingual children. Moreover, the achievement and intelligence tests were conducted in the

Bilingualism. Most people throughout the world speak two or more languages, and most countries have minority populations whose languages differ from the national tongue. It was once thought that children reared in bilingual homes were retarded in their cognitive and language development, but today most linguists consider it advantageous for children to be bilingual. Knowledge of more than one language certainly expands children's awareness of diverse cultures and broadens their perspectives.

monolingual child's language, which was the second language of the bilingual child (Reynolds, 1991). Lack of education and testing methods rather than bilingualism per se accounted for the apparent differences in achievement and intelligence.

Today, most linguists consider it advantageous for children to be bilingual. For one thing, knowledge of more than one language expands children's awareness of different cultures and broadens their perspectives (Diaz, 1985). For example, bilingual children are more likely to understand that the symbols used in language are arbitrary. Monolingual children are more likely to erroneously think that the word *dog* is somehow intertwined with the nature of the beast. Bilingual children therefore have somewhat more cognitive flexibility. Second, learning a second language does not crowd children's available "cognitive space." Instead, learning a second language has been shown to increase children's expertise in their first (native) language. Research evidence reveals that learning French enhances knowledge of the structure of English among Canadian children whose native language is English (Lambert and others, 1991). By contrast, the worst effect of bilingualism is apparently that children occasionally forget—for a moment—which language they are using (Taylor & Taylor, 1990).

Despite the advantages of bilingualism, many immigrants have not insisted on teaching their children the languages of the lands of origin. For example, in the effort to Americanize their children, many Mexican American immigrants have not taught their children Spanish in the home (Delgado-Gaitan, 1993). As a result, many first-generation Mexican Americans do not speak Spanish.

SECOND-LANGUAGE LEARNING AND AGE

We visited Israel, where the native language is Hebrew, when my daughter, Taylor, was 19 months old. Although we stayed for a month, my wife and I barely learned to understand a word of Hebrew. A few months after we returned to the United States, however, Taylor blurted out "Sleechah!" from her seat in our shopping cart when

we were trying to pass someone in an aisle of a supermarket. We realized that *sleechah* is the Hebrew for "Excuse me" and theorized that Taylor picked up the term in Israeli elevators when people were getting on and off. For a few months, when she wanted our attention, she would first try "Mommy" and "Daddy." If we were engrossed in something, however—or trying to get some sleep!—she would switch to *Eema* and *Abba,* which are the Hebrew for *mother* and *father.*

Whereas my wife and I had learned some Romance languages and German at an early age, Hebrew seemed impossible to us. There were no words in common with English, and the grammar was very different. Yet here was Taylor, who knew (or pretended to know) nothing about using a potty, soaking up Hebrew like a sponge.

Painstaking research as well as anecdotal evidence reveals that people who acquire second languages at earlier ages are more likely to become fluent and sound like native speakers (Snow, 1993; Taylor & Taylor, 1990). In one study, Tahka and associates (1981) found that children who arrived in England before the age of 7 learned to speak English with no trace of a foreign accent, whether their native tongue was Armenian, Cantonese, Hindi, or French. Those who learned English at age 14 and above had pronounced accents. Children even gain greater proficiency with American Sign Language (the language of the deaf) when they are taught it from birth (Newport & Supalla, 1993).

All in all, research evidence is consistent with Lenneberg's critical-period hypothesis. That is, young children acquire language more efficiently than older children and adults do—whether the language is their native language or another (Hurford, 1991).

BILINGUAL EDUCATION

Despite the positive aspects of bilingualism, many U.S. children who speak a different language in the home, especially older children, have problems learning English in school. Early in the century, the educational approach to teaching English to non-English-speaking children was simple: sink or swim. Children were taught in English

TABLE 8.2

Snapshot, U.S.A.: Bilingualism

LANGUAGE SPOKEN IN THE HOME	TOTAL NUMBER OF SPEAKERS, AGE 5 AND ABOVE 1990	1980	CHANGE (PERCENT)
TOTAL	**31,845,000**	**23,060,000**	**38%**
Spanish	17,339,000	11,549,000	50
French[1]	1,703,000	1,572,000	8
German	1,547,000	1,607,000	− 4
Italian	1,309,000	1,633,000	− 20
Chinese	1,249,000	632,000	98
Tagalog[2]	843,000	452,000	87
Polish	723,000	826,000	− 12
Korean	626,000	276,000	127
Vietnamese	507,000	203,000	150
Portuguese	430,000	361,000	19
Japanese	428,000	342,000	25
Greek	388,000	410,000	− 5
Arabic	355,000	227,000	57
Hindu, Urdu	331,000	130,000	155
Russian	242,000	175,000	39
Yiddish	213,000	320,000	− 34
Thai	206,000	89,000	132
Persian	202,000	109,000	85
French Creole[3]	188,000	25,000	654
Armenian	150,000	102,000	46
Navajo[4]	149,000	123,000	21
Hungarian	148,000	180,000	− 18
Hebrew	144,000	99,000	46
Dutch	143,000	146,000	− 3
Mon-Khmer[5]	127,000	16,000	676

Source: U.S. Bureau of the Census (1993).
[1] Spoken commonly in the home in New Hampshire, Maine, and Louisiana.
[2] Main language of the Philippines.
[3] Mainly spoken by Haitians.
[4] Native American language.
[5] Cambodian language.

from the outset. It was incumbent upon them to catch on as best they could. Most children swam. Some sank.

A more formal term for the sink-or-swim method is *total immersion*. Total immersion has a checkered history. There are, of course, many successes with total immersion, but there are also more failures than most educators are willing to tolerate. For this reason, bilingual education has been adopted in many school systems.

Bilingual-education legislation requires that non-English-speaking children be given the chance to study in their own lan-

guage to smooth the transition into U.S. life. The official purpose of federal bilingual programs is to help foreign-speaking children use their native tongue to learn English rapidly, then switch to a regular school program. Yet, the degree of emphasis on English differs markedly from program to program.

So-called transitional programs shoot their students into regular English-speaking classrooms as quickly as possible. Under a second technique, called the *maintenance method*, rapid mastery of English is still the goal. But students continue studying their own culture and language. A third approach, which has been tried in areas with large Hispanic populations, such as New York, Florida, Northern Virginia, and Southern California, is bilingual and bicultural: Programs encourage native-born U.S. children to achieve fluency in a foreign language even as immigrant children are learning English. In this method, all students study half a day in Spanish and half a day in English (Sleek, 1994).

Critics of the bilingual experiment contend that the movement is often more political than educational. For example, Spanish-surnamed children may be segregated in separate classes long after they can handle lessons in English. Such critics recognize the benefits of cultural pluralism but believe that the key to success in the United States is English.

It appears that bilingual education has been most successful if the following criteria are met:

- The bilingual program focuses specifically on teaching English and does not just start teaching other subjects in English, even at a low level.
- The child's parents understand and support the goals and methods of the program.

- Teachers, parents, and other members of the community have mutual respect for one another and for each others' languages (Lambert, 1992).

All in all, these principles of bilingual education can promote biculturalism as well as teach children English. They can help ensure that bilingual children will be proud of their ethnic heritages. Children can attain the language skills necessary to forge ahead in today's workplace and participate in political and social processes, while they retain a sense of ethnic identity and self-esteem.

Reflections

Now that you have read the section on bilingualism and bilingual education, reflect on the following questions:

- Did you grow up speaking a language other than English in the home? If so, what special opportunities and problems were connected with the experience? Are there some family members who never learned English very well? Why did they not learn more?
- Do you believe that children who do not speak English in the home should be taught in their native languages in U.S. schools? Why or why not?

9

Intelligence

Truth or Fiction?

_____ The terms *intelligence* and *IQ* can be used interchangeably.

_____ Two children can answer exactly the same items on an intelligence test correctly, yet one can be above average and the other below average in IQ.

_____ Non-Hispanic White Americans attain the highest scores on IQ tests.

_____ Early users of IQ tests administered them in English to immigrants who did not understand the language.

_____ Mental testing began in the 19th century.

_____ The use of culture-free intelligence tests eliminates socioeconomic and ethnic differences in IQ.

_____ Head Start programs have raised children's IQs.

Outline

Truth or Fiction?
Theories of Intelligence
  Factor Theories
  Gardner's Theory of Multiple Intelligences
  Sternberg's Triarchic Theory
Measurement of Intelligence
  Individual Intelligence Tests
    Psychology in the New Millennium:
    Artificial Intelligence
  Group Tests
    Psychology in a World of Diversity:
    Socioeconomic and Ethnic
    Differences in Intelligence
The Testing Controversy: Just What Do
  Intelligence Tests Measure?
  Is It Possible to Develop Culture-Free
  Intelligence Tests?
The Determinants of Intelligence:
  Where Does Intelligence Come
  From?
  Genetic Influences on Intelligence
  Environmental Influences on Intelligence
  On Ethnicity and Intelligence:
    A Concluding Note
  Psychology in the New Millennium:
    Will Music Provide Our Children
    with the Sweet Sounds of Success?
Summary
Psychology and Modern Life
  Mental Retardation and Giftedness

What form of life is so adaptive that it can survive in desert temperatures of 120 degrees Fahrenheit or Arctic climes of -40 degrees Fahrenheit? What form of life can run, walk, climb, swim, live underwater for months on end, and fly to the moon and back?

I won't keep you in suspense any longer. We are that form of life. Yet, our unclad bodies do not allow us to adapt to these extremes of temperature. Brute strength does not allow us to live underwater or travel to the moon. Rather, it is our **intelligence** that permits us to adapt to these conditions and to challenge our physical limitations. The human capacity to think about abstractions like space and time sets us apart from all other species (Campbell, 1994).

The term *intelligence* is familiar enough. At an early age, we gain impressions of how intelligent we are compared to others. We associate intelligence with academic success, advancement on the job, and appropriate social behavior. Psychologists use intelligence as a **trait** that may explain, at least in part, why people do (or fail to do) things that are adaptive and inventive.

Despite our familiarity with the concept of intelligence, intelligence cannot be seen, touched, or measured physically. However, as noted by Kimble (1994), the concept of intelligence is tied to predictors, such as scores on intelligence tests, and to behavior, such as school performance. Still, the concept of intelligence is subject to various interpretations. In this chapter, we discuss different ways of looking at intelligence. We see how intelligence is measured and discuss group differences in intelligence. Finally, we examine the determinants of intelligence: heredity and the environment.

Theories of Intelligence

Psychologists generally distinguish between **achievement** and intelligence. Achievement refers to knowledge and skills gained from experience. It involves specific content such as English, history, and math. The relationship between achievement and experience seems obvious: We are not surprised to find that a student who has taken Spanish, but not French, does better on a Spanish achievement test than on a French achievement test.

The meaning of *intelligence* is more difficult to pin down. Most psychologists agree that intelligence somehow provides the cognitive basis for academic achievement. Intelligence is usually perceived as underlying competence, or learning ability, whereas achievement involves acquired competencies or performance. Psychologists disagree, however, about the nature and origins of underlying competence, or learning ability.

FACTOR THEORIES

Many investigators have viewed intelligence as consisting of one or more mental abilities, or **factors**. Alfred Binet, the Frenchman who developed modern intelligence-testing methods about 100 years ago, believed that intelligence consisted of several related factors. Other investigators have argued that intelligence consists of from one to hundreds of factors.

In 1904, British psychologist Charles Spearman suggested that the behaviors we consider to be intelligent have a common underlying factor. He labeled this factor **g,** for "general intelligence." *G* represented broad reasoning and problem-solving abilities. Spearman supported this view by noting that people who excel in one area can usually excel in others. But he also noted that even the most capable people are relatively superior in some areas—whether in music or business or poetry. For this reason, he suggested that specific, or **s,** factors account for specific abilities.

To test his views, Spearman developed a statistical method called **factor analysis.** Factor analysis allows researchers to determine the relationships among large numbers of items such as those found on intelligence tests. Items that cluster together are labeled *factors.* In his research on relationships among tests of verbal, mathematical, and spatial reasoning, Spearman repeatedly found evidence supporting the existence of *s* factors. The evidence for *g* was more limited.

U.S. psychologist Louis Thurstone (1938) used factor analysis with various tests of specific abilities and also found only limited evidence for the existence of *g.* Thurstone concluded that Spearman had oversimplified the concept of intelligence. Thurstone's data suggested the presence of nine specific factors, which he labeled **primary mental abilities** (see Table 9.1). Thurstone suggested, for example, that we might have high word fluency, enabling us to rapidly

Going for a "Walk." Our human intelligence permits us to live underwater for months on end or to fly to the moon and back. Physically we are weaker than many other organisms. Our intelligence permits us to adapt successfully to the physical environment, however—to create new environments, even to go for leisurely "spacewalks." Who can say what wonders human intelligence will devise in the new millennium?

develop lists of words that rhyme, yet not enabling us to be efficient at solving math problems (Thurstone & Thurstone, 1963).

This view seems to make sense. Most of us know people who are good at math but poor in English, and vice versa. Nonetheless, some link seems to connect specific mental abilities. The data still show that the person with excellent reasoning ability is likely to have a larger-than-average vocabulary and better-than-average numerical ability. Few, if any, people exceed 99% of the population in one mental ability but are exceeded by 80 or 90% of the population in others.

Over the years, psychologist J. P. Guilford (1988) expanded the numbers of factors found in intellectual functioning to as many as 180. The problem with this expansionist

Intelligence • A complex and controversial concept. According to David Wechsler (1975), the "capacity . . . to understand the world [and] resourcefulness to cope with its challenges."

Trait • A distinguishing characteristic that is presumed to account for consistency in behavior.

Achievement • That which is attained by one's efforts and made possible by one's abilities.

Factor • A cluster of related items such as those found on an intelligence test.

g • Spearman's symbol for general intelligence, which he believed underlay more specific abilities.

s • Spearman's symbol for *specific* factors, or *s* factors, which he believed accounted for individual abilities.

Factor analysis • A statistical technique that allows researchers to determine the relationships among large numbers of items such as test items.

Primary mental abilities • According to Thurstone, the basic abilities that make up intelligence.

TABLE 9.1

Louis Thurstone's Primary Mental Abilities

ABILITY	DESCRIPTION
Visual and spatial abilities	Visualizing forms and spatial relationships
Perceptual speed	Grasping perceptual details rapidly, perceiving similarities and differences between stimuli
Numerical ability	Computing numbers
Verbal meaning	Knowing the meanings of words
Memory	Recalling information (words, sentences, etc.)
Word fluency	Thinking of words quickly (rhyming, doing crossword puzzles, etc.)
Deductive reasoning	Deriving examples from general rules
Inductive reasoning	Deriving general rules from examples

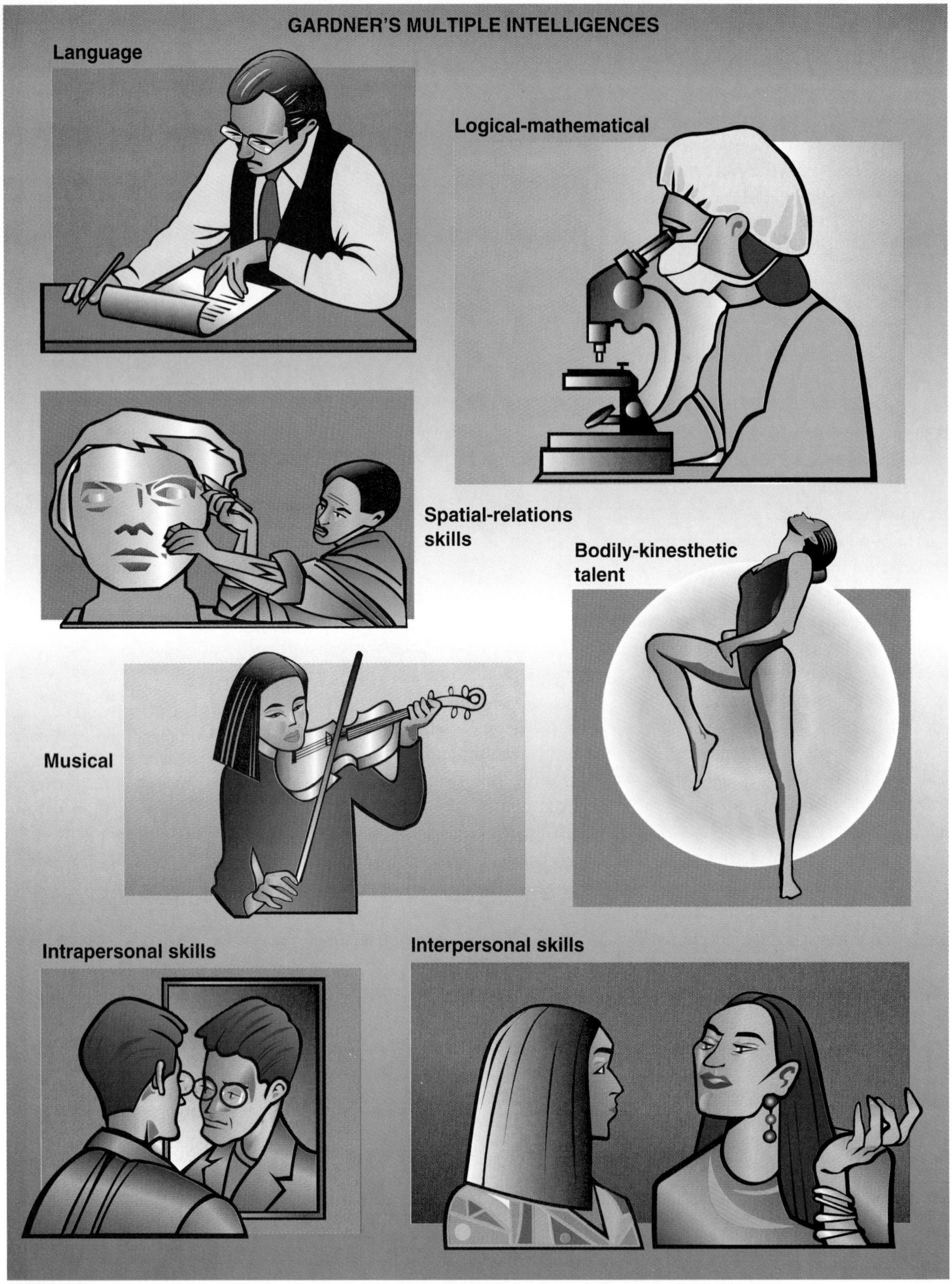

GARDNER'S MULTIPLE INTELLIGENCES

Language

Logical-mathematical

Spatial-relations skills

Bodily-kinesthetic talent

Musical

Intrapersonal skills

Interpersonal skills

FIGURE 9.1

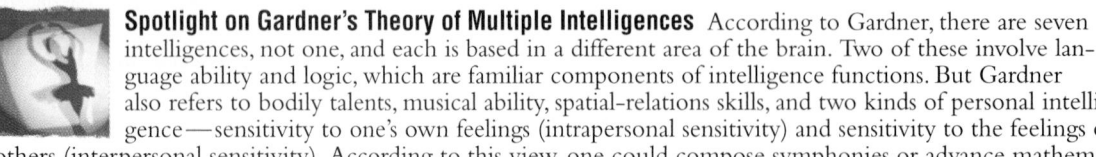

Spotlight on Gardner's Theory of Multiple Intelligences According to Gardner, there are seven intelligences, not one, and each is based in a different area of the brain. Two of these involve language ability and logic, which are familiar components of intelligence functions. But Gardner also refers to bodily talents, musical ability, spatial-relations skills, and two kinds of personal intelligence—sensitivity to one's own feelings (intrapersonal sensitivity) and sensitivity to the feelings of others (interpersonal sensitivity). According to this view, one could compose symphonies or advance mathematical theory while remaining average in, say, language skills.

approach seems to be that the greater the number of factors generated, the more overlap there is among them (Rebok, 1987).

GARDNER'S THEORY OF MULTIPLE INTELLIGENCES

Howard Gardner (1983; Gardner & Hatch, 1989) proposes the existence of seven kinds of intelligence. He refers to each as "an intelligence" because they can be so different from one another (see Figure 9.1). He also believes that each kind of intelligence has its neurological base in a different area of the brain. Two such "intelligences" involve language ability and logical-mathematical ability, which are familiar enough aspects of intelligence to other theorists. However, Gardner also refers to bodily-kinesthetic talents (of the sort shown by dancers, mimes, and athletes), musical talent, spatial-relations skills, and two kinds of personal intelligence: awareness of one's own inner feelings, and sensitivity to other people's feelings and the ability to respond to them appropriately. According to Gardner, one can compose symphonies or advance mathematical theory yet be average in, say, language and personal skills. (Are not some academic "geniuses" foolish in their personal lives?)

Critics of Gardner's view grant that people do function more intelligently in some aspects of life than in others. They also concur that many people have special talents, such as bodily-kinesthetic talents, whereas their overall intelligence appears to be quite average. However, they question whether such special talents are equivalent in meaning to what they see as a broader concept of intelligence (Scarr, 1985).

STERNBERG'S TRIARCHIC THEORY

Cognitive psychologist Robert Sternberg (1995) views intelligence in terms of information processing. He focuses on how information "flows" through us and is modified by us as we adapt to and act to change our environments.

Sternberg's analysis led him to construct a three-level, or **triarchic,** model of intelligence (see Figure 9.2). The levels are *contextual, experiential,* and *componental.* Individual differences are found at each level. The **contextual level** concerns the environmental setting. It is assumed that intelligent behavior permits people to adapt to the demands of their environments. For example, keeping a job by adapting one's behavior to the requirements of one's employer is adaptive. But if the employer is making unreasonable demands, reshaping the environment (by changing the employer's attitudes) or selecting an alternate environment (finding a more suitable job) is also adaptive.

On the **experiential level,** intelligent behavior is defined by the abilities to cope with novel situations and to process information automatically. The ability to quickly relate novel situations to familiar situations (to perceive the similarities and differences) fosters adaptation. Moreover, as a result of experience, we come to solve problems more rapidly. Intelligence and experience in reading permit the child to process familiar words more or less automatically and to decode new words efficiently. In sum, it is "intelligent" to profit from experience.

The **componental level** of intelligence consists of three processes: metacomponents, performance components, and knowledge-acquisition components. **Metacomponents** concern our awareness of our own intellectual processes. Metacomponents are involved in deciding what problem to solve, selecting appropriate strategies and formulas, monitoring the solution, and changing performance in the light of knowledge of results.

Performance components are the mental operations or skills used in solving problems or processing information. Performance components include encoding information, combining and comparing pieces of information, and generating a solution. Consider Sternberg's analogy problem:

Washington is to *one* as *Lincoln* is to
(a) 5, (b) 10, (c) 15, (d) 50?

To solve the analogy, we must first correctly *encode* the elements— *Washington, one,* and *Lincoln*—by identifying them and comparing them with other information. We must first encode *Washington* and *Lincoln* as the names of presidents[1] and then try to

Triarchic • (try-ARK-ick). Governed by three.

Contextual level • Those aspects of intelligent behavior that permit people to adapt to their environment.

Experiential level • Those aspects of intelligence that permit people to cope with novel situations and process information automatically.

Componential level • The level of intelligence that consists of metacomponents, performance components, and knowledge-acquisition components.

Metacomponents • Components of intelligence that are based on self-awareness of our intellectual processes.

Performance components • The mental operations used in processing information.

[1] There are other possibilities. Both are the names of memorials and cities, for example.

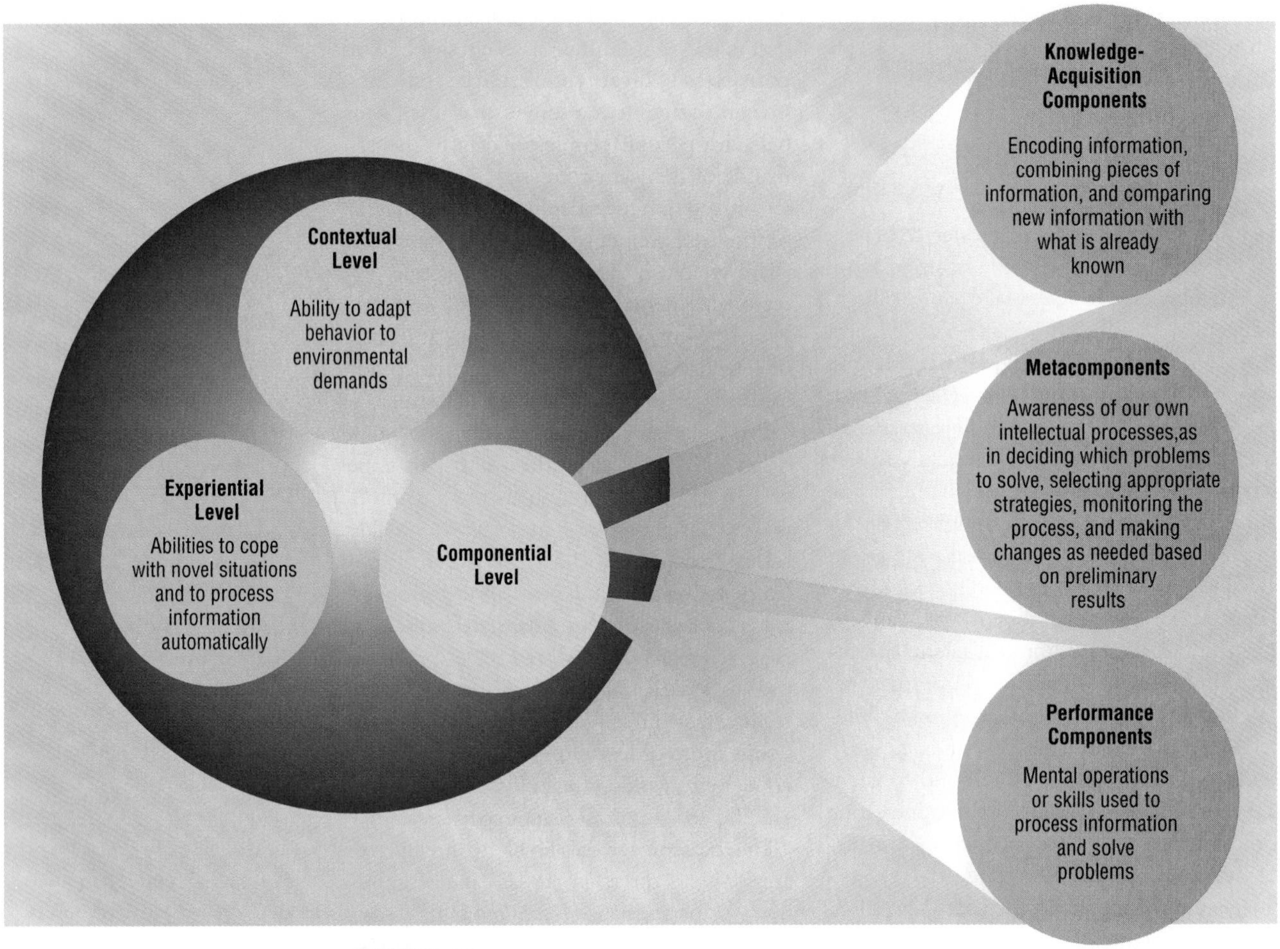

**Knowledge-
Acquisition
Components**

Encoding information,
combining pieces of
information, and comparing
new information with
what is already
known

**Contextual
Level**

Ability to adapt
behavior to
environmental
demands

Metacomponents

Awareness of our own
intellectual processes, as
in deciding which problems
to solve, selecting appropriate
strategies, monitoring the
process, and making
changes as needed based
on preliminary
results

**Experiential
Level**

Abilities to cope
with novel situations
and to process
information
automatically

**Componential
Level**

**Performance
Components**

Mental operations
or skills used to
process information
and solve
problems

FIGURE 9.2

Spotlight on Sternberg's Triarchic Model of Intelligence Robert Sternberg
views intelligence as consisting of contextual, experiential, and componential
levels. The componential level consists of metacomponents, performance
components, and knowledge-acquisition components.

combine *Washington* and *one* in a meaningful manner. Two possibilities quickly come
to mind. Washington was the first president,
and his picture is on the $1 bill. We can
then generate two possible solutions and try
them out. First, what number president was
Lincoln? Second, on what bill is Lincoln's
picture found? (Do you need to consult a
history book or peek into your wallet at
this point?)

Knowledge-acquisition components
are used in gaining new knowledge. These
include encoding information (for example,
Engelbert Humperdinck as the name of the
contemporary singer or as the name of the
19th-century composer of the opera *Hansel
and Gretel*), combining pieces of information, and comparing new information with
what is already known.

Sternberg's model is complex, but it does
a promising job of capturing what most investigators mean by intellectual functioning. David Wechsler, the originator of a
series of widely used intelligence tests, described intelligence in terms that are simpler but, I think, consistent with Sternberg's
view. Intelligence, wrote Wechsler, is the
"capacity of an individual to understand the
world [and the] resourcefulness to cope
with its challenges" (1975, p. 139). Intelligence, to Wechsler, involves accurate representation of the world (which Sternberg
describes as encoding, comparing new information to old information, and so on)
and effective problem solving (adapting to
one's environment, profiting from experience, selecting the appropriate formulas and
strategies, and so on).

Reflections

Now that you have read about theories of intelligence, reflect on the following questions:

- How would you have defined *intelligence* before you began reading this chapter? How do psychologists' definitions of intelligence agree with, or differ from, your own? How would you compare your definition with those you have read about?

- From your own experiences, what seem to be the relationships between general intelligence and special talents, such as musical or artistic ability? Do you know people who are "good at everything"? Do you know people who seem extremely talented in some areas but not in others? In what areas are they talented?

- What is the connection between intelligence and rapid processing of information? Do you know people who strike you as intelligent who process information somewhat slowly and deliberately?

Measurement of Intelligence

Although there are disagreements about the nature of intelligence, thousands of intelligence tests are administered by psychologists and educators every day. Let us explore some widely used intelligence tests.

INDIVIDUAL INTELLIGENCE TESTS

Many of the concepts of psychology have their origins in common sense (Kimble, 1994). The common sense notion that academic achievement depends on children's intelligence led the Frenchmen Alfred Binet and Theodore Simon to invent measures of intelligence early in this century.

The French public school system sought an instrument that could identify children who were unlikely to profit from the regular classroom so that they could receive special attention. The first version, the Binet–Simon scale, came into use in 1905. Since that time, it has undergone great revision and refinement. The current version is the Stanford–Binet Intelligence Scale (SBIS).

Despite his view that many factors are involved in intellectual functioning, Binet constructed his test to yield a single overall score so that it could be more easily used by the school system. He also assumed that intelligence increased with age. Therefore, older children should get more items right than younger children. Thus, Binet included a series of age-graded questions, as in Table 9.2, and he arranged them in order of difficulty.

The Binet–Simon scale yielded a score called a **mental age,** or MA. The MA shows the intellectual level at which a child is functioning. A child with an MA of 6 is functioning, intellectually, like the average child aged 6. In taking the test, children earned "months" of credit for each correct answer. Their MA was determined by adding the years and months of credit they attained.

Louis Terman adapted the Binet–Simon scale for use with children in the United States. The first version of the *Stanford–Binet Intelligence Scale (SBIS)*[2] was published in 1916. The SBIS included more items than the original test and was used with children aged 2 to 16. The SBIS also yielded an **intelligence quotient (IQ)** rather than an MA. American educators developed interest in learning the IQs of their pupils. The current version of the SBIS is used with children from the age of 2 upward and with adults.

Truth or Fiction Revisited. *It is not true that the terms* intelligence *and* IQ *can be used interchangeably. Intelligence* is a hypothetical concept on whose meanings psychologists do not agree. An *IQ* is a score on an intelligence test. What are some of the dangers in using the terms interchangeably?

The IQ reflects the relationship between a child's mental age and actual age, or chronological age (CA). Use of this ratio reflects the fact that the same MA score has different implications for children of different ages. That is, an MA of 8 is an above-average score for a 6-year-old, but an MA of 8 is below average for a 10-year-old. The

Knowledge-acquisition components • Components used in gaining knowledge, such as encoding and relating new knowledge to existing knowledge.

Mental age • The accumulated months of credit that a person earns on the Stanford-Binet Intelligence Scale. Abbreviated *MA*.

Intelligence quotient (IQ) • (1) Originally, a ratio obtained by dividing a child's score (or mental age) on an intelligence test by his or her chronological age. (2) Generally, a score on an intelligence test.

MINILECTURE: MEASURING INTELLIGENCE

---

[2] The test is so named because Terman carried out his work at Stanford University.

TABLE 9.2

Items Similar to Those on the Stanford–Binet Intelligence Scale

LEVEL (YEARS)	ITEM	LEVEL (YEARS)	ITEM
2 years	1. Children show knowledge of basic vocabulary words by identifying parts of a doll such as the mouth, ears, and hair. 2. Children show counting and spatial skills along with visual-motor coordination by building a tower of four blocks to match a model.	9 years	1. Children can point out verbal absurdities, as in this question: "In an old cemetery, scientists unearthed a skull which they think was that of George Washington when he was only 5 years of age. What is silly about that?" 2. Children show fluency with words, as shown by answering the questions: "Can you tell me a number that rhymes with snore?" "Can you tell me a color that rhymes with glue?"
4 years	1. Children show word fluency and categorical thinking by filling in the missing words when they are asked questions such as: "Father is a man; mother is a _____?" "Hamburgers are hot; ice cream is _____?" 2. Children show comprehension by answering correctly when they are asked questions such as: "Why do people have automobiles?" "Why do people have medicine?"	Adult	1. Adults show knowledge of the meanings of words and conceptual thinking by correctly explaining the differences between word pairs like "sickness and misery," "house and home," and "integrity and prestige." 2. Adults show spatial skills by correctly answering questions like: "If a car turned to the right to head north, in what direction was it heading before it turned?"

PSYCHOLOGY ψ IN THE NEW MILLENNIUM

Artificial Intelligence

Who can keep track of 10,000 topics like a computer?

PATRICK HAYES

Science has brought us a number of now-familiar artificial objects—artificial sweeteners, designer drugs, and artificial limbs, to name a few. But the new millennium promises to bring major developments in the realm of artificial intelligence, or *A.I.* As if there were not enough controversy about the nature and measurement of intelligence in people, A.I. is the replication of human intellectual functioning in computers.

The concept of A.I. has a lengthy history both in science fiction and in practice (Freedman, 1994; Gelernter, 1994). Think of HAL, the supercool computer that spoke softly but carried a big spaceship in the film *2001*. Not only was HAL capable of coordinating all the monitors and controls of a spaceship. HAL could also engage in such signature human activities as committing murder, lying with a straight . . . monitor, and striving to save his own . . . memory chips. The robot C3PO in *Star Wars* not only mimicked human intelligence. He also showed remarkably human anxieties and self-doubts. What of the *Terminator* films? The programming in the artificial combination of flesh and metal portrayed by Arnold Schwarzenegger presented him with options that enabled him to size up any situation and efficiently curse, kill, or utter notable Arnoldisms such as "I'll be back."

So much for Hollywood. The idea that human intelligence could be copied in computer form originated in the 1950s (Chartrand, 1993). It was predicted that machines with A.I. would one day be able to understand spoken language, decipher bad handwriting, search their memories for relevant information, reason, solve problems, make decisions, write books, and explain themselves out loud. At the time these predictions were visionary. Yet, that day—"one day"—is now. Within concrete limits, today's computers are very, very good at encoding information, storing it, retrieving it, and manipulating it to solve

TABLE 9.3

Subtests from the Wechsler Adult Intelligence Scale

VERBAL SUBTESTS	PERFORMANCE SUBTESTS
1. *Information:* "What is the capital of the United States?" "Who was Shakespeare?"	7. *Digit Symbol:* Learning and drawing meaningless figures that are associated with numbers.
2. *Comprehension:* "Why do we have ZIP Codes?" "What does 'A stitch in time saves 9' mean?"	8. *Picture Completion:* Pointing to the missing part of a picture.
3. *Arithmetic:* "If 3 candy bars cost 25 cents, how much will 18 candy bars cost?"	9. *Block Design:* Copying pictures of geometric designs using multicolored blocks.
4. *Similarities:* "How are good and bad alike?" "How are peanut butter and jelly alike?"	10. *Picture Arrangement:* Arranging cartoon pictures in sequence so that they tell a meaningful story.
5. *Digit Span:* Repeating a series of numbers forwards and backwards.	11. *Object Assembly:* Putting pieces of a puzzle together so that they form a meaningful object.
6. *Vocabulary:* "What does canal mean?"	

Items for verbal subtests 1, 2, 3, 4, and 6 are similar, but not identical, to actual test items on the WAIS.

German psychologist Wilhelm Stern in 1912 suggested use of the IQ to handle this problem.

$$IQ = \frac{\text{Mental Age (MA)}}{\text{Chronological Age (CA)}} \times 100$$

Stern computed IQ by the formula IQ = (Mental Age/Chronological Age) × 100, or

According to this formula, a child with an MA of 6 and a CA of 6 would have an IQ

problems and make decisions. In some ways, A.I. is even more than human. A.I. can crunch millions of numbers in a fraction of a second. A.I. can solve problems that would take people years to solve, if they could solve them at all without A.I. Given clear direction and the right formulas, computers can carry out many complex intellectual functions in a literal flash. "Who," asks Patrick Hayes (1993), a University of Illinois professor, "can keep track of 10,000 topics like a computer?"

In other ways, A.I. remains much less than human (Pinker, 1994b). Today's computers, even powerful mainframes, do not have the insights, intuitions, and creativity found in people (Gelernter, 1994). Their ability to produce original written material can be best described as lumbering. (So I still have a job.) The sparks of brilliance we find in computational ability turn to dense wood when we ask today's computers to exercise the human functions of writing prose or composing music. (I hope my computer's not reading this.)

Despite our increasing ability to pack huge amounts of memory into tiny chips of one kind or another, the possibility of a HAL—a computer that creates original thoughts and plays upon human psychologies—still seems like science fiction, at least by the year 2001.

The ultimate goal of A.I., notes Hayes, is the creation of a computer that has a human mind. Yet, some observers suggest that this goal is unnecessary. They believe that computer science will continue to evolve by improving on the things that computers already do better than people (Carter, 1993). Freedman (1994) describes projects involving antlike robots, hybrids of computer chips and neurons, even programs that mutate and mate—allowing the survival of the fittest programs. Steven Pinker likens these programs to "software animals that evolve in virtual worlds" (1994b, p. 13).

Whether or not scientists cease the effort to make computers think more like people, we will apparently continue to create computers that each have bits and pieces of humanlike intelligence (Gutknecht, 1992). But the whole that goes into that "piece of work" that defines the human being is likely to continue to elude us for the foreseeable future. That thought doesn't bother me a byte.

In the Eye of the Beholder—"HAL," That Is. HAL, the computer, spoke softly but carried a big spaceship in the classic science fiction film *2001* (shown in this photo). In the 1950s, it was predicted that machines with artificial intelligence would one day be able to understand spoken language, decipher bad handwriting, search their memories for relevant information, reason, solve problems, make decisions, write books, and explain themselves out loud. That day—"one day"—is now. What forms will artificial intelligence take in the new millennium?

of 100. Children who can handle intellectual problems as well as older children will have IQs above 100. For instance, an 8-year-old who does as well on the SBIS as the average 10-year-old will attain an IQ of 125. Children who do not answer as many items correctly as other children of their age will attain MAs lower than their CAs, and their IQ scores will be below 100.

Today, IQ scores on the SBIS are derived by seeing how children's and adults' performances deviate from those of other people of the same age. People who get more items correct than average attain IQ scores above 100, and people who answer fewer items correctly attain scores below 100.

Truth or Fiction Revisited. *It is true that two children can answer exactly the same items on an intelligence test correctly, yet* *one can be above average and the other below average in IQ.* This is because the ages of the children may differ. The more intelligent child would be the younger of the two.

David Wechsler developed a series of scales for use with children and adults. The Wechsler scales group test questions into a number of separate subtests (such as those shown in Table 9.3). Each subtest measures a different type of intellectual task. For this reason, the test shows how well a person does on one type of task (such as defining words) as compared with another (such as using blocks to construct geometric designs). In this way, the Wechsler scales highlight children's relative strengths and weaknesses, as well as measure overall intellectual functioning.

As you can see in Table 9.3, Wechsler described some of his scales as measuring

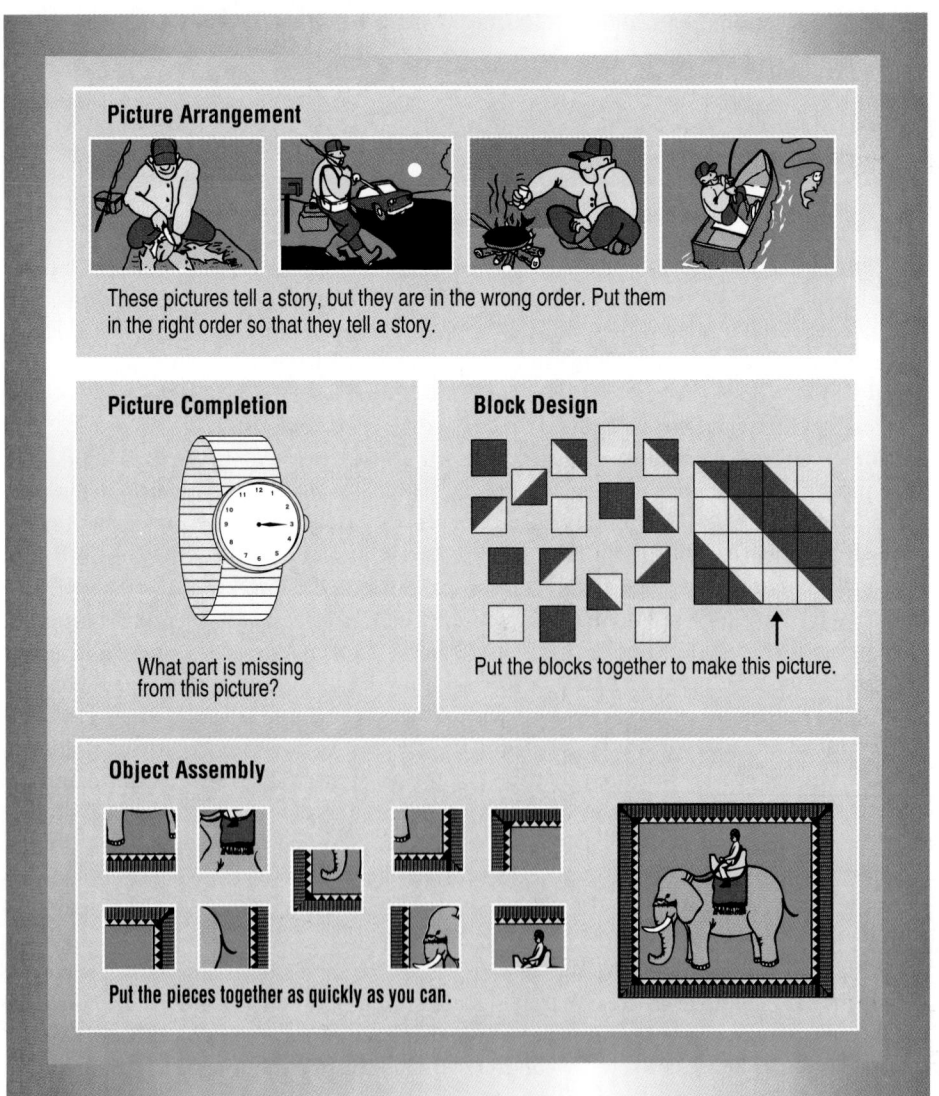

FIGURE 9.3
Performance Items of an Intelligence Test This figure shows a number of items that resemble those in the performance subtests of the Wechsler Adult Intelligence Scale.

verbal tasks and others as assessing *performance* tasks. In general, verbal subtests require knowledge of verbal concepts, whereas performance subtests require familiarity with spatial-relations concepts. (Figure 9.3 shows items similar to those found on the performance scales of the Wechsler tests.) But the two groupings are not that easily distinguished. For example, associating the name of the object being pieced together in subtest 11—a sign of word fluency and general knowledge as well as of spatial-relations ability—helps the person construct it rapidly. In any event, Wechsler's scales permit the computation of verbal and performance IQs.

Wechsler also introduced the concept of the deviation IQ. Instead of using mental and chronological ages to compute an IQ, he based IQ scores on how a person's answers compared with (or deviated from) those attained by people in the same age group. The average test result at any age level is defined as an IQ score of 100. Wechsler then distributed IQ scores so that the middle 50% of them would fall within the "broad average range" of 90 to 110.

As you can see in Figure 9.4, most IQ scores cluster around the average. Only 4% of the population have IQ scores of above 130 or below 70. Table 9.4 indicates the labels that Wechsler assigned to various IQ scores and the approximate percentages of the population who attain IQ scores at those levels.

GROUP TESTS

The SBIS and Wechsler scales are administered to one person at a time. This one-to-one ratio is considered optimal. It allows

Taking the Wechsler. The Wechsler intelligence scales consist of verbal and performance subtests such as the one shown above.

MINILECTURE: THE WECHSLER SCALES: THE WAIS

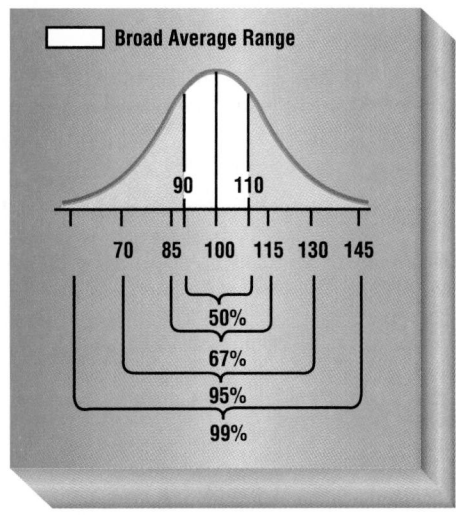

FIGURE 9.4
Approximate Distribution of IQ Scores Wechsler defined the deviation IQ so that 50% of scores would fall within the broad average range of 90–110. This bell-shaped curve is referred to as a *normal curve* by psychologists. It describes the distribution of many traits, including height.

TABLE 9.4
Variations in IQ Scores

RANGE OF SCORES	PERCENT OF POPULATION	BRIEF DESCRIPTION
130 and above	2	Very superior
120–129	7	Superior
110–119	16	Above average
100–109	25	High average
90–99	25	Low average
80–89	16	Slow learner
70–79	7	Borderline
Below 70	2	Intellectually deficient

the examiner to facilitate performance (within the limits of the standardized directions) and to observe the test taker closely. Examiners are thus alerted to factors that impair performance, such as language difficulties, illness, or a noisy or poorly lit room. But large institutions with few trained examiners, such as the public schools and armed forces, have also wished to estimate the intellectual functioning of their charges. They require tests that can be administered simultaneously to large groups of people.

Group tests for children, first developed during World War I, were administered to 4 million children by 1921, a couple of years after the war had ended (Cronbach, 1975). At first, these tests were heralded as remarkable instruments because they eased the huge responsibilities of school administrators. However, as the years passed they came under increasing attack, because many administrators relied on them completely to track children. The administrators did not seek other sources of information about the children's abilities and achievements (Reschly, 1981).

At their best, intelligence tests provide just one source of information as to the special abilities and talents of individual children. Children are not to be confused with numbers, especially those of IQ scores.

Reflections

Now that you have read about the measurement of intelligence, reflect on the following questions:

• Have you ever taken an intelligence test? Was it an individual test or a group test? What was the experience like? Were you informed as to how well you did on the test? Do you believe that the test assessed you fairly, or arrived at an accurate estimate of your intelligence?

• What types of items do you believe ought to be on intelligence tests? Do the tests discussed in this chapter appear to include the types of things that you consider important?

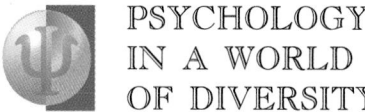

PSYCHOLOGY IN A WORLD OF DIVERSITY

SOCIOECONOMIC AND ETHNIC DIFFERENCES IN INTELLIGENCE

There is a body of research suggestive of differences in intelligence between socioeconomic and ethnic groups (Taylor & Richards, 1991). Lower-class U.S. children attain IQ scores some 10 to 15 points lower than those of middle- and upper-class children. African American children tend to attain IQ scores some 15–20 points lower than their White agemates (Helms, 1992; Storfer, 1990). Hispanic American and Native American children also score significantly below the norms of White children.

Several studies on IQ have confused the factors of social class and ethnicity because disproportionate numbers of African, Hispanic, and Native Americans are found among the lower socioeconomic classes (Patterson and others, 1990). When we limit our observations to particular ethnic groups, however, we still find an effect for social class. That is, middle-class Whites outscore lower-class Whites. Middle-class African, Hispanic, and Native Americans also all outscore lower-class members of their own ethnic groups.

Who's Smart? Asian children and Asian American children frequently outscore other American children on intelligence tests. Can we attribute the difference to genetic factors or to Asian parents' emphasis on acquiring the kinds of cognitive skills that enable children to fare well on such tests and in school? Sue and Okazaki (1990) suggest that Asian Americans place great value on education because they have been discriminated against in careers that do not require advanced education.

Research has also discovered differences between Asians and White people. Asian Americans, for example, frequently outscore White Americans on the math portion of the Scholastic Aptitude Test. Students in China (Taiwan) and Japan also outscore Americans on standardized achievement tests in math and science (Stevenson and others, 1986). British psychologist Richard Lynn (1982) has reported that Japanese (residing in Japan) attain higher IQ scores than White Britishers or U.S. citizens. The mean Japanese IQ was 111, which exceeds the top of the high-average range in the United States by a point. In the United States, moreover, people of Asian Indian, Korean, Japanese, Filipino, and Chinese extraction are more likely to graduate from high school and complete four years of college than White, African, and Hispanic Americans are (Sue & Okazaki, 1990). Asian Americans are vastly overrepresented in competitive colleges and universities. They make up only 2.4% of the U.S. population but account for 12% of the undergraduates at MIT, and 24% and 33%, respectively, at the University of California campuses at Berkeley and Irvine (*Chronicle of Higher Education*, 1992).

Truth or Fiction Revisited. *It is not true that non-Hispanic White Americans attain the highest scores on IQ tests.* Asian Americans tend to attain higher IQ scores. What hypotheses have been generated to account for this ethnic difference in IQ scores?

Lynn (1991) argues that the greater intellectual accomplishments of Asian students are in part genetically determined. According to Sue and Okazaki (1990), however, the higher scores of Asian students may reflect different values in the home, the school, or the culture at large rather than differences in underlying competence. They argue that Asian Americans have been discriminated against in careers that do not require advanced education, so they place relatively greater emphasis on the value of education. Steinberg and his colleagues (1992) claim that parental encouragement and supervision in combination with peer support for academic achievement partially explain the superior performances of White and Asian Americans as compared with African and Hispanic Americans.

Reflections

Now that you have read about socioeconomic and ethnic differences in intelligence, reflect on the following questions:

- It is a fact in the United States that lower-class children attain IQ scores some 10 to 15 points lower than those of middle- and upper-class children. As an intellectual exercise, first explain this finding from a genetic point of view. Then explain this finding from an environmental point of view. (Later in the chapter, we will explore both genetic and environmental contributions to intellectual functioning).
- Agree or disagree with the following statement and support your answer: "Studies on IQ have confused the factors of social class and ethnicity."
- What is your own ethnic background? Are there any stereotypes as to how people from your ethnic background perform on intelligence tests? If so, what is your reaction to these stereotypes? Why?

The Testing Controversy: Just What Do Intelligence Tests Measure?

I was almost one of the testing casualties. At 15, I earned an IQ test score of 82, three points above the track of the special education class. Based on this score, my counselor suggested that I take up bricklaying because I was "good with my hands." My low IQ, however, did not allow me to see that as desirable.

This testimony is offered by African American Robert L. Williams (1974, p. 32), who has since become a psychologist. It echoes the sentiments of many psychologists. A survey of psychologists and educational specialists by Mark Snyderman and Stanley Rothman (1987, 1990) found that most consider intelligence tests somewhat biased against African Americans and members of the lower classes. Elementary and secondary schools may also place too much emphasis on them in making educational placements.

During the 1920s, intelligence tests were misused to prevent the immigration of

MINILECTURE: GENDER COMPARISONS IN INTELLIGENCE

many Europeans and others into the United States (Kamin, 1982; Kleinmuntz, 1982). For example, test pioneer H. H. Goddard assessed 178 newly arrived immigrants at Ellis Island and claimed that "83% of the Jews, 80% of the Hungarians, 79% of the Italians, and 87% of the Russians were 'feeble-minded'" (Kleinmuntz, 1982, p. 333). Apparently it was of little concern to Goddard that these immigrants, by and large, did not understand English—the language in which the tests were administered.

Truth or Fiction Revisited. *It is true that early users of IQ tests administered them in English to immigrants who did not understand the language.*

Questions about the effects of social class on test performance, the role of tests in enhancing or inhibiting social mobility, and the like, have been asked at least since the use of mental testing in China 2,000 years ago (Matarazzo, 1990).

Truth or Fiction Revisited. *It is not true that mental testing began in the 19th century.* Records show that mental testing was used in China 2,000 years ago. Moreover, the ancient Chinese wondered about the relationship between socioeconomic status and test performance.

Twentieth-century misuse of intelligence tests has led psychologists such as Leon Kamin to complain, "Since its introduction to America the intelligence test has been used more or less consciously as an instrument of oppression against the underprivileged—the poor, the foreign born, and racial minorities" (Crawford, 1979, p. 664). Despite these historical notes and criticisms, group tests are administered to as many as 10 million children a year in the United States. But some states such as California and some cities have outlawed their use as the sole standard for placing children in special classrooms. Let us explore further some of the controversy concerning the use of both individual and group intelligence tests. Let us consider whether intelligence tests are still misused and misunderstood.

Intelligence tests measure traits that are required in modern, high-technology societies (Anastasi, 1983; Pearlman and others, 1980; Schmidt and others, 1981). The vo-

cabulary and arithmetic subtests on the Wechsler scales, for example, clearly reflect achievements in language skills and computational ability. It is generally assumed that the broad achievements measured by these tests reflect intelligence, but they might also reflect cultural familiarity with the concepts required to answer test questions correctly. In particular, the tests seem to reflect middle-class White culture in the United States (Garcia, 1981).

IS IT POSSIBLE TO DEVELOP CULTURE-FREE INTELLIGENCE TESTS?

If scoring well on intelligence tests requires a certain type of cultural experience, the tests are said to have a **cultural bias.** Children reared in African American neighborhoods could be at a disadvantage, not because of differences in intelligence but because of cultural differences (Helms, 1992) and economic deprivation. For this reason, psychologists such as Raymond B. Cattell (1949) and Florence Goodenough (1954) have tried to construct **culture-free** intelligence tests.

Cattell's Culture-Fair Intelligence Test evaluates reasoning ability through the child's ability to comprehend the rules that govern a progression of geometric designs, as shown in Figure 9.5. Goodenough's Draw-A-Person test is based on the premise that children from all cultural backgrounds have had the opportunity to observe people and note the relationships between the parts and the whole. Her instructions simply require children to draw a picture of a man or woman.

Culture-free tests have not lived up to their promise, however. Middle-class White children still outperform African American children, perhaps because they are more likely to be familiar with materials such as blocks and pencils and paper. They are more likely than disadvantaged children to have arranged blocks into various designs (practice relevant to the Cattell test) and more likely to have sketched animals, people, and inanimate objects (practice relevant to the Goodenough test). Too, culture-free tests do not predict academic success as well as other intelligence tests.

Cultural bias • A factor that provides an advantage for test takers from certain cultural or ethnic backgrounds.
Culture-free • Describing a test in which cultural biases are absent.
Determinants • Factors that set limits.

MINILECTURE: CULTURE-FAIR INTELLIGENCE TESTS

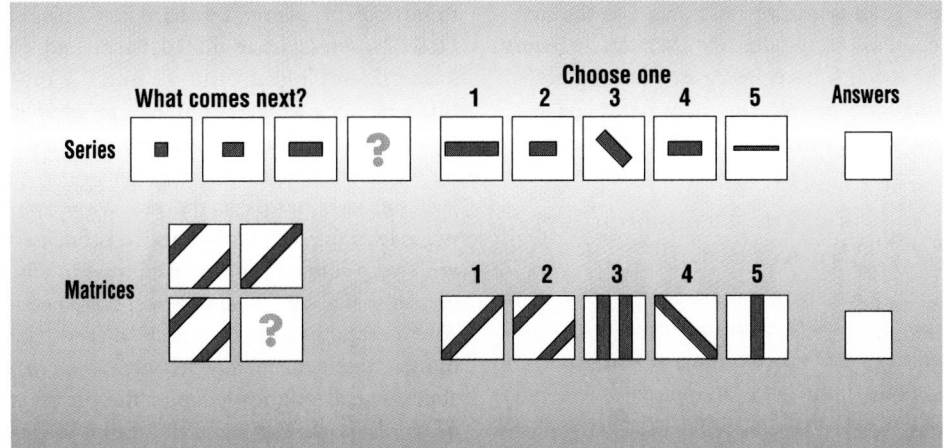

FIGURE 9.5
Sample Items from Raymond Cattell's Culture-Fair Intelligence Test Culture-fair tests attempt to exclude items that discriminate on the basis of cultural background rather than intelligence.

Truth or Fiction Revisited. *It is not true that the use of culture-free intelligence tests eliminates socioeconomic and ethnic differences in IQ.* Middle-class White children outperform African American children on "culture-free" tests.

Motivation to do well may also be a cultural factor. Because of socioeconomic and sociocultural differences, African American children often do not have the same motivation as White children to do well on tests (Tharp, 1991). Highly motivated children attain higher scores on intelligence tests than less-well-motivated children do (Collier, 1994). Perhaps there is no such thing as a culture-free intelligence test.

Reflections

Now that you have read about the testing controversy, reflect on the following questions:

• Agree or disagree with the following statement and support your answer: "It is not possible to construct a truly culture-free intelligence test."

• Consider your own ethnic group and the shared experiences of members of your ethnic group. Could you write an "intelligence test" that would provide members of your ethnic group an advantage? What types of items might you include? Would your test be a fair intelligence test, or would it be culturally biased?

The Determinants of Intelligence: Where Does Intelligence Come From?

Because the concept of intelligence is central to what it means to be human, psychologists have intensely debated the nature of intelligence. The measurement of social-class and ethnic differences in intelligence, and the history of measurement abuse, have added social and political dimensions to the debate.

One of the more heated areas of debate concerns the **determinants** of intelligence. That is, if different ethnic groups tend to score differently on intelligence tests, psychologists—like educators and other people involved in public life—want to know why. Yet this is one debate that is becoming supplied with important empirical findings. Here psychologists can point with pride to a rich mine of contemporary research into the roles of nature and nurture in the development of intelligence. Various ingenious approaches have been used to explore the elaborate interactions of genetic and environmental influences on intelligence.

GENETIC INFLUENCES ON INTELLIGENCE

Let us return to experiments with laboratory animals to point up some of the difficulties and shortcomings of research on genetic influences on *human* intelligence. Then we shall examine correlational research with humans.

Rats have been selectively bred for maze-learning ability (see Chapter 3). Maze-

bright parent rats tend to have maze-bright litters, whereas maze-dull parents tend to have maze-dull litters. But we must be cautious in generalizing from rats to people. The (spatial relations) superiority of the maze-bright rats did not generalize to all learning tasks, even for the rats. Moreover, maze-learning ability in rats is connected with very limited aspects of human intelligence: spatial ability and perceptual speed. The complex cognitive skills that define human intelligence rely heavily on verbal abilities such as knowledge of the meaning of words (vocabulary) and the ability to categorize objects and events, and on memory. However, the selective-breeding technique provides a model worth noting because it *cannot* be replicated with people for ethical, legal, and practical reasons. Research on genetic influences on human intelligence must thus employ different strategies, such as kinship studies, MZ–DZ twin studies, and adoptee studies.

For example, we can examine the IQ scores of closely and distantly related people who have been reared together or apart. If heredity is involved in human intelligence, closely related people ought to have more similar IQs than distantly related or unrelated people, even when they are reared separately.

Figure 9.6 is a composite of the results of more than 100 studies of IQ and heredity in human beings, as reported by Bouchard and associates (1990). The IQ scores of identical (MZ) twins are more alike than the scores for any other pairs, even when the twins have been reared apart. Correlations between the IQ scores of fraternal (DZ) twins, siblings, and parents and children are moderate. Correlations between children and their foster parents and between cousins are weak.

Large-scale twin studies are consistent with the data in Figure 9.6. For instance, a study of 500 pairs of MZ and DZ twins in Louisville, Kentucky (Wilson, 1983), found that the correlations in intelligence between MZ twins were about the same as those for MZ twins in Figure 9.6. The correlations in intelligence between DZ twin pairs were the same as those between other siblings. Research at the University of Minnesota with sets of twins who were reared together and others who were reunited in adulthood

FIGURE 9.6
Findings of Studies of the Relationship between IQ Scores and Heredity The data are a composite of hundreds of studies summarized in *Science* magazine (Bouchard and others, 1990). By and large, correlations are greater between pairs of people who are more closely related. Persons reared together have more similar IQ scores than persons who were reared apart. Such findings suggest that both genetic and environmental factors contribute to IQ scores.

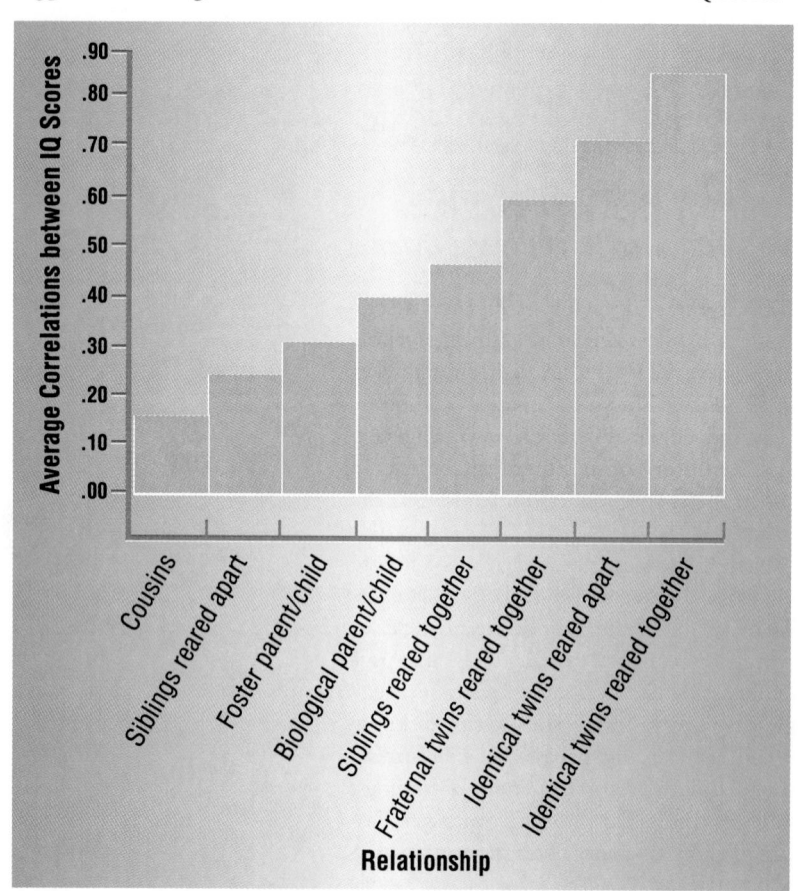

has obtained essentially similar results (Bouchard and others, 1990). In the MacArthur Longitudinal Twin Study, Robert Emde (1993) and his colleagues examined the intellectual abilities of 200 primarily White, healthy 14-month-old pairs of twins. They found that identical (MZ) twins were more similar than fraternal (DZ) twins in their spatial memory, their ability to categorize things, and their word comprehension. Emde and his colleagues concluded that genes tend to account for about 40% to 50% of the differences in cognitive skills in children (Adler, 1993a).

All in all, studies generally suggest that the **heritability** of intelligence is between 40% and 60% (Adler, 1993a; Bouchard and others, 1990; Plomin, 1989; Plomin & Rende, 1991). In other words, about half of the variations (the technical term is *variance*) in IQ scores among people can be accounted for by heredity. This is *not* the same as saying that you inherited about half of your intelligence. The implication of such a statement would be that you "got" the other half of your intelligence somewhere else. It means, rather, that about half of the difference between your IQ score and the IQ scores of other people can be explained in terms of genetic factors.

Even this view of the heritability of intelligence may be too broad to be highly accurate. Research also suggests that the heritability of verbal ability is greater than the heritability of factors such as spatial-relations ability and of memory (Thompson and others, 1991).

Note, too, that genetic pairs (such as MZ twins) reared together show higher correlations between IQ scores than similar genetic pairs (such as other MZ twins) who were reared apart. This finding holds for MZ twins, siblings, parents and children, and unrelated people. *For this reason, the same group of studies suggests that the environment plays a role in IQ scores.*

Another strategy for exploring genetic influences on intelligence is to compare the correlations between adopted children and their biological and adoptive parents (Coon and others, 1990). When children are separated from their biological parents at early ages, one can argue that strong relationships between their IQs and those of their natural parents reflect genetic influences. Strong re-lationships between their IQs and those of their adoptive parents might reflect environmental influences.

Several studies with 1- and 2-year-old children in Colorado (Baker and others, 1983), Texas (Horn, 1983), and Minnesota (Scarr & Weinberg, 1983) have found a stronger relationship between the IQ scores of adopted children and those of their biological parents than with the IQ scores of their adoptive parents. The Scarr and Weinberg report concerns African American children reared by White adoptive parents, and we shall return to its findings in the section on environmental influences on intelligence.

In sum, genetic factors account for about half of the variation in intelligence test scores among people. Environmental factors also affect scores on intelligence tests.

ENVIRONMENTAL INFLUENCES ON INTELLIGENCE

Studies on environmental influences also employ a variety of research strategies. One approach simply focuses on the situational factors that determine IQ scores. Remember that an IQ is a score on a test. Thus in some cases, the testing situation itself can explain part of the social-class difference in IQ. In one study, the experimenters (Zigler and others, 1982) simply made children as comfortable as possible during the test. Rather than being cold and impartial, the examiner was warm and friendly. Care was also taken to see that the children understood the directions. As one result, children's test anxiety was markedly reduced. As another, the children's IQ scores were 6 points higher than those for a control group treated in a more indifferent manner, and disadvantaged children made relatively greater gains from the procedure. *By doing nothing more than make testing conditions more optimal for all children, we may narrow the IQ gap between White and African American children.*

The home environment and styles of parenting also appear to have an effect on IQ (Coon and others, 1990; Olson and others, 1992; Steinberg and others, 1992b). Children of mothers who are emotionally responsive and verbally responsive, who

MINILECTURE: THE HERITABILITY OF INTELLIGENCE

Heritability • The degree to which the variations in a trait from one person to another can be attributed to, or explained by, genetic factors.

Head Start. Preschoolers placed in Head Start programs have made dramatic increases both in readiness for elementary school and in IQ scores.

provide appropriate play materials, who are involved with their children, and who provide varied daily experiences during the early years attain higher IQ scores later on (Bradley and others, 1989; Gottfried and others, 1994). The extent of home organization and safety has also been linked to higher IQs at later ages and to higher achievement test scores during the first grade (Bradley and others, 1989).

Dozens of other studies support the view that the child's early environment is linked to IQ scores and academic achievement. For example, McGowan and Johnson (1984) found that good parent–child relationships and maternal encouragement of independence were both positively linked to Mexican American children's IQ scores by the age of 3. A number of studies have also found that high levels of maternal restrictiveness and punishment at 24 months are linked to lower IQ scores later on (Bee and others, 1982; Yeates and others, 1983).

Government-funded efforts to provide preschoolers with enriched early environments have also led to intellectual gains. Head Start programs, for example, enhance the IQ scores, achievement test scores, and academic skills of poor children (Barnett & Escobar, 1990; Hauser-Cram and others,

1991; Zigler & Styfco, 1994) by exposing them to materials and activities that middle-class children take for granted. These include letters and words, numbers, books, exercises in drawing, pegs and pegboards, puzzles, toy animals, and dolls.

Truth or Fiction Revisited. *It is true that Head Start programs have raised children's IQs.* Critical thinkers, pay close attention to the definitions of terms. If you considered this statement to be false, refer to the definition of *IQ*.

There is now good research evidence that preschool intervention programs can have major long-term effects on children. During the elementary and high school years, graduates of preschool programs are less likely to be left back or placed in classes for slow learners. They are more likely to graduate from high school, go on to college, and earn higher incomes. Early childhood intervention also decreases the likelihood of juvenile delinquency, unemployment, and being on welfare (Schweinhart & Weikart, 1993; Zigler and others, 1992). In the mid-1990s, nearly three-quarters of a million children attended Head Start programs (Kassebaum, 1994).

As noted, the Minnesota adoption studies reported by Scarr and Weinberg suggest a

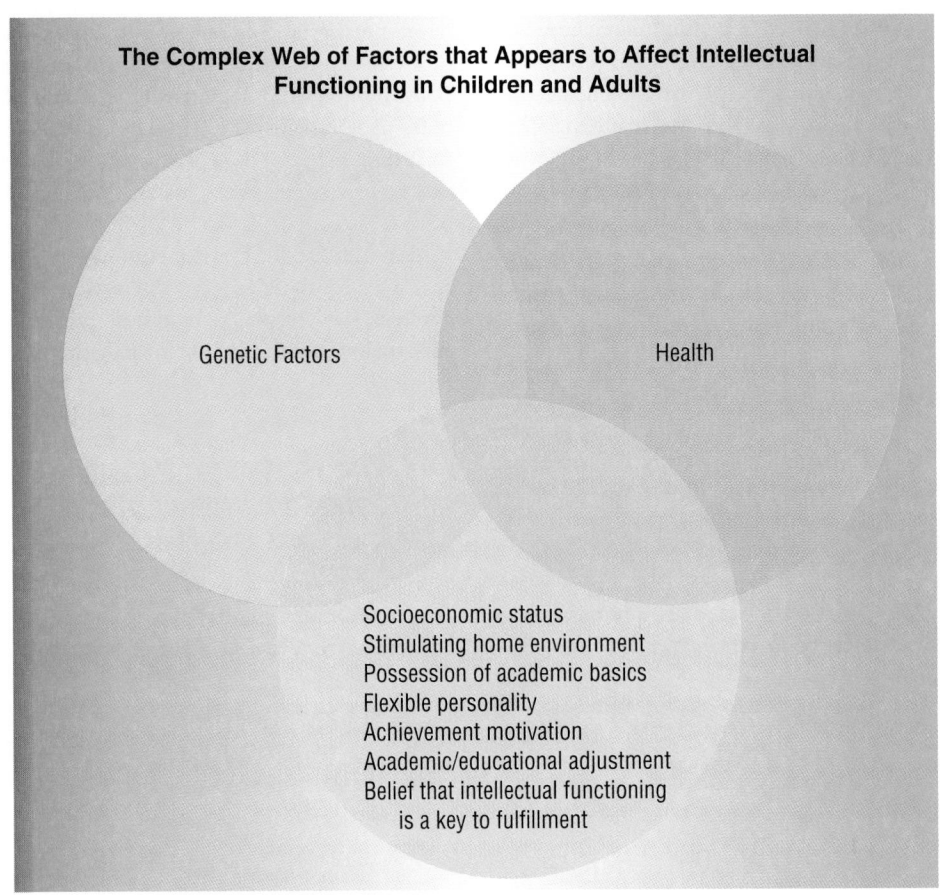

The Complex Web of Factors that Appears to Affect Intellectual Functioning in Children and Adults

Genetic Factors

Health

Socioeconomic status
Stimulating home environment
Possession of academic basics
Flexible personality
Achievement motivation
Academic/educational adjustment
Belief that intellectual functioning
is a key to fulfillment

FIGURE 9.7
The Complex Web of Factors That Appears to Affect Intellectual Functioning in Children and Adults Intellectual functioning appears to be influenced by the interaction of genetic factors, health, personality, and a host of sociocultural factors.

FIGURE 9.8 ▼
Beliefs of Psychologists and Educational Specialists Concerning Reasons for African American / White American Differences in IQ The largest group of psychologists and educational specialists views racial differences in IQ as reflecting the interaction of genetic and environmental factors. Source of data: Snyderman and Rothman (1987, 1990).

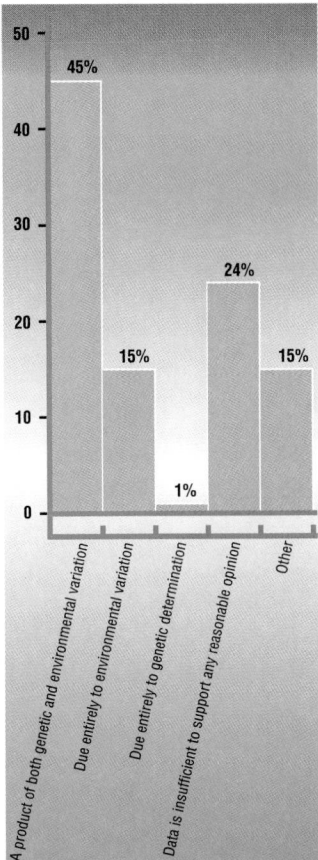

genetic influence on intelligence. But the same studies (Scarr & Weinberg, 1976, 1977) also suggest a role for environmental influences. African American children who were adopted during the first year by White parents above average in income and education showed IQ scores some 15 to 25 points higher than those attained by African American children reared by their natural parents (Scarr & Weinberg, 1976). Still, the adoptees' average IQ scores, about 106, remained somewhat below those of their adoptive parents' natural children— 117 (Scarr & Weinberg, 1977). Even so, the adoptive early environment closed a good deal of the IQ gap.

Environmental Influences on Adult Intellectual Functioning. Our focus has been on the intellectual development of children. However, psychologists are also concerned about intellectual functioning among adults. They have found that older people show some decline in general intellectual ability as measured by scores on intelligence tests. The drop-off is most acute

in processing speed (Schaie, 1994; Schaie & Willis, 1991). Speed is involved in timed items such as those found on the performance scales of the Wechsler Adult Intelligence Scale.

Certainly biological changes of aging are involved in the decline. For example, many older people show losses in sensory sharpness that affect their intellectual functioning. Moreover, people who retain good physical health tend to show higher levels of intellectual functioning in their later years (Schaie, 1994). It is unclear, however, whether good health is a causal factor in intelligence or whether a health-conscious lifestyle has cognitive as well as physical benefits (Gruber-Baldini, 1991).

The Seattle Longitudinal Study has been tracking intellectual changes among adults for more than 35 years as of this writing and has identified several environmental factors that affect intellectual functioning among older people (Schaie, 1993, 1994):

1. *Socioeconomic status.* People of high SES tend to maintain intellectual functioning more adequately than people low in

SES. High SES is also connected with above-average income and levels of education, a history of stimulating occupational pursuits, and the maintenance of intact families.

2. *Stimulating activities.* People who maintain their levels of intellectual functioning also tend to attend cultural events, travel, participate in professional organizations, and read extensively.

3. *Marriage to a spouse with a high level of intellectual functioning.* The spouse whose level of intellectual functioning is lower at the beginning of a marriage tends to narrow the gap as time elapses. Perhaps they are continually challenged.

4. *Flexible personality.*

We saw that Head Start programs have been effective in enhancing the intellectual development of children. It also turns out that training in reasoning and visual-spatial skills improves the cognitive functioning of older people (Schaie, 1994). The benefits of such training extend to performance on the practical tasks of daily living (Willis and others, 1992).

All in all, intellectual functioning at any age appears to reflect the interaction of a complex web of genetic, physical, personal, and sociocultural factors, as suggested by Figure 9.7.

ON ETHNICITY AND INTELLIGENCE: A CONCLUDING NOTE

Many psychologists believe that heredity and environment interact to influence intelligence. Forty-five percent of Snyderman

PSYCHOLOGY IN THE NEW MILLENNIUM

Will Music Provide Our Children with the Sweet Sounds of Success?

We can expect that technological innovations will overleap themselves in the new millennium. Parents will doubtlessly be concerned about what they can do to help their children grasp the new technologies. Whatever environmental factors are found to enhance children's intellectual functioning may well be music to parents' ears. But it may also turn out that music will be spatial reasoning to the children's ears.

Research in the 1990s suggests that listening to music and studying music may enhance one aspect of intellectual functioning—spatial reasoning. In October of 1993, the research team of Frances Rauscher, Gordon Shaw, and Katherine Ky—all of the University of California at Irvine—published an intriguing article in *Nature* on the effects of listening to Mozart. According to that study, listening to 10 minutes of Mozart's Piano Sonata K 448 on a number of occasions enhanced college students' scores on spatial reasoning tasks of the kind found on intelligence tests.

The research team of Rauscher, Shaw, Linda Levine, Ky, and Eric Wright reported the results of a follow-up study with preschoolers at the 1994 meeting of the American Psychological Association: "Music and spatial task performance: A causal relationship." They recruited 19 preschool children aged from 3 years to 4 years 9 months and gave them 8 months of music lessons, including singing and use of a keyboard. They then found that the children's scores on an object assembly task—like that of the object assembly subtest of the Wechsler Intelligence Scale for Children—significantly exceed those of 15 preschoolers who did not obtain the musical training.

How might listening to music or training in music affect spatial reasoning? Shaw, Wright, and a third researcher, Xiaodan Leng, theorize that musical activity and a number of other cognitive functions—such as spatial reasoning—share overlapping neural pathways (Martin, 1994). Musical training thus develops the neural firing patterns used in spatial reasoning, which may eventually help children solve geometry problems, design skyscrapers, navigate ships, even fit suitcases into the trunk of a car (Martin, 1994).

and Rothman's (1987, 1990) sample of 1,020 psychologists and educational specialists believe that African American-White differences in IQ are a "product of both genetic and environmental variation, compared to only 15% who feel the difference is entirely due to environmental variation [see Figure 9.8]. Twenty-four percent of experts do not believe there are sufficient data to support any reasonable opinion, [and 1%] indicate a belief in an entirely genetic determination" (1987, p. 141).

Diana Baumrind (1993) and Jacquelyne Jackson (1993) of the University of California Institute of Human Development argue that a strong belief in the predominance of genetic factors can undermine parental and educational efforts to enhance children's intellectual development. Jackson notes that such a view can be particularly harmful to African American children. Baumrind notes that parents are most effective when they believe their efforts will improve their children's functioning. Since parents cannot change their children's genetic codes, it is better for parents to assume that good parenting can make a difference.

Perhaps we need not be so concerned with whether we can sort out exactly "how much" of a person's IQ is due to heredity and how much is due to environmental influences. The largest number of psychologists and educators believe that IQ reflects the complex interaction of heredity, early childhood experiences, sociocultural factors and expectations, and even the atmosphere within which intelligence tests are conducted. Psychology has traditionally supported the dignity of the individual. It might be more appropriate for us to try to

Note the implications for Howard Gardner's theory of multiple intelligences. If the Rauscher team's research withstands the test of time and replication, it may be that musical talent and spatial skills represent one kind of intelligence and not two.

The researchers caution that their findings should be considered preliminary. It is not known, for example, whether the training effects endure or whether they will extend to older children, whose cerebral cortexes are more mature.

But perhaps the findings are enticing enough to encourage school administrators to maintain music programs, which are often among the first to go when school districts tighten the purse strings. Music, after all, may contribute to the sweet sounds of success.

The Sweet Sounds of Success? Research suggests that training in music advances children's spatial reasoning. Do musical activities and spatial reasoning share common neural pathways?

identify children *of all ethnic groups* whose environments place them at risk for failure and do what we can to enrich them.

Reflections

Now that you have read the section on the determinants of intelligence, reflect on the following questions:

• Does your own family seem to be generally similar in overall intellectual functioning? Are there one or more family members who appear to stand out from the others because of intelligence? If so, in what ways? Where do you seem to stand

in your family in terms of intellectual functioning?

• As you look back on your own childhood, can you point to any kinds of family or educational experiences that seem to have had an impact on your intellectual development? Would you say that your background, overall, was deprived or enriched? In what ways?

• When you look back on your own development, can you see ways in which genetic factors may have interacted with environmental factors to contribute to your intellectual functioning? Is it difficult, or impossible, to sort out genetic influences from environmental influences? If so, why?

Summary

1. **What is intelligence?** Achievement is what a person has learned. Intelligence is presumed to underlie achievement and has been defined by Wechsler as "capacity . . . to understand the world . . . and . . . resourcefulness to cope with its challenges."

2. **What are Spearman's and Thurstone's theories of intelligence?** Spearman and Thurstone believed that intelligence is composed of a number of factors. Spearman believed that a common factor, *g*, underlies all intelligent behavior but that people also have specific abilities, or *s* factors. Thurstone suggested that there are several primary mental abilities, including word fluency and numerical ability.

3. **What is Gardner's theory of intelligence?** Gardner believes that people have multiple intelligences, not one, and that each is based in a different area of the brain.

4. **What is the IQ?** Intelligence tests yield scores called intelligence quotients, or *IQs*. The Stanford–Binet Intelligence Scale, originated by Alfred Binet, derives IQ scores by dividing children's mental age scores by their chronological ages, then multiplying by 100. The Wechsler scales use deviation IQs, derived by comparing a person's performance with that of agemates.

5. **What kinds of items are found on intelligence tests?** The Wechsler scales are representative. They contain verbal and performance subtests that measure general information, comprehension, similarities (conceptual thinking), vocabulary, mathematics, block design (copying designs), and object assembly (piecing puzzles together).

6. **What is the controversy over culturally biased tests about?** It turns out that intelligence test scores reflect cultural factors as well as general learning ability. Cultural factors include familiarity with testing, socioeconomic status, familiarity with information concerning the mainstream culture, motivation, and academic adjustment.

7. **What are some socioeconomic and ethnic differences in IQ?** Lower-class U.S. children attain IQ scores some 10 to 15 points lower than those of middle- and upper-class children. African American children tend to attain IQ scores some 15–20 points lower than their White agemates. Asians and Asian Americans usually attain higher IQ scores than White Britishers or U.S. citizens.

8. **Where does intelligence come from?** The largest number of psychologists believe that intelligence reflects the interaction of genetic and environmental influences.

Psychology and Modern Life

Mental Retardation and Giftedness

The average IQ score in the United States is very close to 100. About 50% of U.S. children attain IQ scores in the broad average range from 90 to 110. Nearly 95% attain scores between 70 and 130. But what of the other 5%? Children who attain IQ scores below 70 are generally labeled as intellectually deficient or mentally retarded. Children who attain scores of 130 or above are usually labeled as gifted. Both of these labels create certain expectations. Both can place heavy burdens on children and their parents.

MENTAL RETARDATION

Mental retardation is typically assessed through a combination of children's IQ scores and behavioral observations. According to the American Association on Mental Retardation, mental retardation "refers to substantial limitations in present functioning [as] characterized by significantly sub-average intellectual functioning [including an IQ score of no more than 70 to 75], existing concurrently with related limitations in two or more of the following applicable adaptive skill areas: communication, self-care, home living, social skills, community use, self-direction, health and safety, functional academics, leisure and work" (Michaelson, 1993a). A number of scales have been developed to assess adaptive behavior. Items from the Vineland Adaptive Behavior Scales (Sparrow and others, 1984) are shown in Table 9.5.

Table 9.6 summarizes descriptions of a number of levels of retardation. Most of the children (about 80%) who are retarded are mildly retarded. Mildly retarded children, as the term implies, are most capable of adjusting to the demands of educational institutions and, eventually, to society at large. Mildly retarded children are also most likely to be mainstreamed in regular classrooms, as opposed to being placed in special-needs classes. Mainstreaming is intended to provide mildly retarded children with the best possible education and encourage socialization with children at all intellectual levels. Unfortunately, some mildly retarded children are overwhelmed by regular classrooms and are avoided by classmates.

Children with Down syndrome are most likely to fall within the moderately retarded range. As suggested in Table 9.6, moderately retarded children can learn to speak; to dress, feed, and clean themselves; and, eventually, to engage in useful work under supportive conditions, as in the sheltered workshop. However, they usually do not acquire skills in reading and arithmetic. Severely and profoundly retarded children may not acquire speech and self-help skills and remain highly dependent on others for survival throughout their lives.

TABLE 9.5
Items from the Vineland Adaptive Behavior Scales

Age Level	Item
2 years	Says at least 50 recognizable words Removes front-opening coat, sweater, or shirt without assistance
5 years	Tells popular story, fairy tale, lengthy joke, or plot of television program Ties shoelaces into a bow without assistance
8 years	Keeps secrets or confidences for more than one day
11 years	Uses the telephone for all kinds of calls, without assistance Watches television or listens to radio for information about a particular area of interest
16 years	Looks after own health Responds to hints or indirect cues in conversation

Source: adapted from *Vineland Adaptive Behavior Scales,* by S. S. Sparrow, D. A. Ballo, and D. V. Cicchetti, 1984, Circle Pines, MN: American Guidance Service.

Causes of Retardation. Some of the causes of retardation are biological. Retardation, for example, can stem from chromosomal abnormalities such as Down syndrome, genetic disorders such as phenylketonuria, and brain damage. Brain damage may have many origins, including accidents during childhood and problems during pregnancy. Prenatal maternal alcohol abuse, malnutrition, or diseases can all lead to retardation.

GIFTEDNESS

Giftedness involves more than excellence in the tasks provided by standard intelligence tests. Most educators include children who have outstanding abilities, are capable of high performance in a specific academic area such as language arts or mathematics, or who show creativity or leadership, distinction in the visual or performing arts, or bodily talents as in gymnastics and dancing.

Educators suggest that it is helpful to identify gifted children early and provide them with enriched experiences so they can develop their exceptional talents. I agree. But it is also essential to provide disadvantaged children with the richest possible educational experiences. Yet, if we enrich only the gifted and the disadvantaged, we risk creating a new class of relatively deprived students—the middle 95% of the school population. I would like to see us invest enough in education to enrich every child. (I'll climb down from my soapbox now.)

Reflections

Now that you have read about mental retardation and giftedness, reflect on the following questions:

- Do you know a person who is mentally retarded? What is known of the causes of the retardation? What social and other adjustment problems seem to be connected with the person's level of intellectual functioning? What kind of educational or training experiences is the person receiving? Do these experiences seem to be appropriate? Why or why not?
- Do you know a person who is intellectually gifted? Does this person also have special talents as in math, music, or art? Does the giftedness seem to be connected with social advantages or social problems? In what ways? What kinds of educational experiences is this person receiving? Do they seem to be appropriate? Why or why not?

TABLE 9.6

Levels of Retardation, Typical Ranges of IQ Scores, and Types of Adaptive Behaviors

APPROXIMATE IQ SCORE RANGE	PRESCHOOL AGE (0–5) MATURATION AND DEVELOPMENT	SCHOOL AGE (6–21) TRAINING AND EDUCATION	ADULT (21 AND OVER) SOCIAL AND VOCATIONAL ADEQUACY
Mild (50–70)	Often not noticed as retarded by casual observer but is slower to walk, feed self, and talk than most children.	Can acquire practical skills and useful reading and arithmetic to a 3rd to 6th grade level with special education. Can be guided toward social conformity.	Can usually achieve social and vocational skills adequate to self-maintenance; may need occasional guidance and support when under unusual social or economic stress.
Moderate (35–49)	Noticeable delays in motor development, especially in speech; responds to training in various self-help activities.	Can learn simple communication, elementary health and safety habits, and simple manual skills; does not progress in functional reading or arithmetic.	Can perform simple tasks under sheltered conditions; participates in simple recreation; travels alone in familiar places; usually incapable of self-maintenance.
Severe (20–34)	Marked delay in motor development; little or no communication skill; may respond to training in elementary self-help—e.g., self-feeding.	Usually walks, barring specific disability; has some understanding of speech and some response; can profit from systematic habit training.	Can conform to daily routines and repetitive activities; needs continuing direction and supervision in protective environment.
Profound (Below 20)	Gross retardation; minimal capacity for functioning in sensorimotor areas; needs nursing care.	Obvious delays in all areas of development; shows basic emotional responses; may respond to skillful training in use of legs, hands, and jaws; needs close supervision.	May walk, may need nursing care, may have primitive speech; will usually benefit from regular physical activity; incapable of self-maintenance.

10

Motivation and Emotion

Truth or Fiction?

_____ While Christmas Eve is a time of religious devotion in most Western nations, it has become a time of sexual devotion in Japan.

_____ Getting away from it all by going on a vacation from all sensory input for a few hours is relaxing.

_____ We appreciate things more when we have to work for them.

_____ Misery loves company.

_____ You may be able to fool a lie detector by squiggling your toes.

_____ Smiling can produce pleasant feelings.

_____ Because of better diets, young adults in the United States are trimmer in the 1990s than they were in the 1980s.

_____ Americans overeat by enough to feed the nation of Germany.

Outline

Truth or Fiction?
Coming to Terms with Motivation
Theories of Motivation: The Whys of Why
Instinct Theory: "Doing What Comes Naturally"?
Drive-Reductionism and Homeostasis: "Steady, Steady . . ."
Opponent-Process Theory: From Lambs to Lions
Humanistic Theory: "I've Got to Be Me"?
Cognitive Theory: "I Think, Therefore I Am Consistent"?
Sociocultural Theory
Evaluation: Which Whys Rise to the Occasion?
Hunger: Do You Go by "Tummy-Time"?
Sex: A Sociocultural Perspective
Organizing and Activating Effects of Sex Hormones
Psychology in the New Millennium: Sex Gets Interactive
Sexual Orientation
Psychology in a World of Diversity: Ethnicity and Sexual Orientation: A Matter of Belonging
Stimulus Motives
Sensory Stimulation and Activity
Exploration and Manipulation
Cognitive Consistency: Making Things Fit
Balance Theory
Cognitive-Dissonance Theory: "If I Did It, It Must Be Important"?
The Three A's of Motivation: Achievement, Affiliation, and Aggression
Achievement
Affiliation: "People Who Need People"
Aggression: Some Facts of Life and Death
Emotion: Adding Color to Life
Arousal, Emotions, and Lie Detection
How Many Emotions Are There? Where Do They Come From?
The Expression of Emotions
The Facial-Feedback Hypothesis
Theories of Emotion: *Is* Feeling First?
Summary
Psychology and Modern Life
Obesity: Coping with a Serious and Pervasive Problem

The Seekers were quite a group. Their brave leader, Marian Keech, dutifully recorded the messages that she believed were sent to her by the Guardians from outer space. One particular message was somewhat disturbing. It specified that the world would come to an end on December 21. A great flood was to engulf Lake City, the home of Ms. Keech and many of her faithful.

Another message brought good news, however. Ms. Keech received word that The Seekers would be spared the flood. Ms. Keech reported that she received messages through "automatic writing." The messengers would communicate through her. She would write down their words, supposedly without awareness. This bit of writing was perfectly clear: The Seekers would be saved by flying saucers at the stroke of midnight on the morning of the 21st.

In their classic observational study, Leon Festinger and his colleagues (1956) described how they managed to be present in Ms. Keech's household at the fateful hour. They pretended to belong to the faithful. Their actual purpose, however, was to observe the behavior of The Seekers during and following the prophecy's failure. The cognitive theory of motivation that Festinger was working on—**cognitive-dissonance theory**—suggested that there would be a discrepancy or conflict between two key cognitions: (1) Ms. Keech is a prophet, and (2) Ms. Keech is wrong.

How might such a conflict be resolved? One way would be for The Seekers to lose faith in Ms. Keech. But the researchers argued that according to cognitive-dissonance theory, The Seekers might be motivated to resolve the conflict by going out to spread the word and find additional converts. Otherwise the group would be painfully embarrassed.

Let us return to the momentous night. Many in the group had quit their jobs and gone on spending sprees before the end. Now they were all gathered together. They fidgeted as midnight approached, awaiting the flying saucers. Midnight came, but no saucers. Anxious glances were exchanged. Silence. Coughs. A few minutes passed by, tortuously slowly. Watches were checked, more glances exchanged. At 4:00 A.M. a bitter and frantic Ms. Keech complained that she sensed that members of the group were doubting her. At 4:45 A.M., however, she seemed suddenly relieved. Still another message was arriving, and Ms. Keech was spelling it out through automatic writing! The Seekers, it turned out, had managed to save the world through their faith. The universal powers that be had decided to let the world travel on in its sinful ways for a while longer. Why? Because of the faith of The Seekers, there was hope!

You guessed it. The faith of most of those present was renewed. They called wire services and newspapers to spread the word. All but three psychologists from the University of Minnesota. They went home, weary but enlightened, and wrote a book entitled *When Prophecy Fails,* which serves as one of the key documents of cognitive motivational theory.

Mr. Keech? He was a tolerant sort. He slept through it all.

The psychology of motivation is concerned with the *whys* of behavior. Why do we eat? Why do some of us strive to get ahead? Why do some of us ride motorcycles at breakneck speeds? Why do we try new things? Why were The Seekers in acute discomfort?

Coming to Terms with Motivation

Let us begin our journey into the *whys* of behavior with some definitions. **Motives** are hypothetical states within organisms that activate behavior and propel the organisms toward goals. Why do we say "hypothetical states"? We say so because motives are not seen and measured directly. Like many other psychological concepts, they are inferred from behavior (Kimble, 1994). Psychologists assume that behavior is largely caused by motives. *Needs, drives,* and *incentives* are closely related concepts.

Psychologists speak of physiological **needs** and psychological needs. We must meet physiological needs to survive. Examples include needs for oxygen, food, drink, pain avoidance, proper temperature, and elimination of waste products. Some physiological needs such as hunger and thirst are states of physical deprivation. When we have not eaten or drunk for a while, we develop needs for food and water. The body also has needs for oxygen, vitamins, minerals, and so on.

Examples of psychological needs are needs for achievement, power, self-esteem, social approval, and belonging. Psychological needs differ from physiological needs in two ways. First, psychological needs are not necessarily based on states of deprivation. A person with a need for achievement may have a history of success. Second, psychological needs may be acquired through experience, or learned. By contrast, physiological needs reside in the physical makeup of the organism. Because our biological makeups are similar, people share similar physiological needs. However, people are influenced by the sociocultural milieu, and needs may be expressed in divergent ways. All people need food, but some prefer a vegetarian diet whereas others prefer meat. Because learning enters into our psychological needs, people differ markedly in them (Capaldi, 1993).

Needs are said to give rise to **drives.** Depletion of food gives rise to the hunger drive, and depletion of liquids gives rise to the thirst drive. **Physiological drives** are the psychological counterparts of physio-

logical needs. When we have gone without food and water, our bodies may *need* these substances. However, our *experience* of the drives of hunger and thirst is psychological. Drives arouse us to action. Our drive levels tend to increase with the length of time we have been deprived. We are usually more highly aroused by the hunger drive when we have not eaten for several hours than when we have not eaten for, say, 5 minutes.

Psychological needs for approval, achievement, and belonging also give rise to drives. We can be driven to get ahead in the world of business just as surely as we can be driven to eat. The drives for achievement and power consume the daily lives of many people.

An **incentive** is an object, person, or situation perceived as being capable of satisfying a need or desirable for its own sake. Money, food, a sexually attractive person, social approval, and attention can all act as incentives that motivate behavior.

Reflections

Now that you have read the opening sections of the chapter, reflect on the following questions:

- Why do you think The Seekers were motivated to restore their faith in their leader?
- What are your most important biological needs? Psychological needs? How did you arrive at the list of your psychological needs?

In the following section, we explore theories of motivation. We ask the question: Just what is so motivating about motives? Researchers have spawned diverse views of the motives that propel us.

Theories of Motivation: The Whys of Why

Although psychologists agree that it is important to understand why people and lower animals do things, they do not agree about the whys of why—that is, the nature

Cognitive-dissonance theory • The view that we are motivated to make our cognitions or beliefs consistent.

Motive • A hypothetical state within an organism that propels the organism toward a goal. (From the Latin *movere,* meaning "to move.")

Need • A state of deprivation.

Drive • A condition of arousal in an organism that is associated with a need.

Physiological drives • Unlearned drives with a biological basis, such as hunger, thirst, and avoidance of pain.

Incentive • An object, person, or situation perceived as being capable of satisfying a need.

MINILECTURE: THEORIES OF MOTIVATION

Instinct • An inherited disposition to activate specific behavior patterns that are designed to reach certain goals.

Fixed-action pattern • An instinct; abbreviated *FAP*.

Ethologist • A scientist who studies the behavior patterns that characterize different species.

Releaser • In ethology, a stimulus that elicits an FAP.

Pheromones • Chemical secretions that are detected by other members of the same species and stimulate stereotypical behaviors.

Drive-reduction theory • The view that organisms learn to engage in behaviors that have the effect of reducing drives.

Primary drives • Unlearned, or physiological, drives.

Acquired drives • Drives that are acquired through experience, or learned.

Homeostasis • (HOME-me-oh-STAY-sis). The tendency of the body to maintain a steady state.

of motivation. Let us consider six theoretical perspectives on motivation: the instinct, drive-reductionist, opponent-process, humanistic, cognitive, and sociocultural theories.

INSTINCT THEORY: "DOING WHAT COMES NATURALLY"?

Animals are "prewired"—that is, born with preprogrammed tendencies—to respond to certain situations in certain ways. Birds reared in isolation from other birds build nests during the mating season even though they have never observed another bird building a nest (or, for that matter, seen a nest). Siamese fighting fish reared in isolation assume stereotypical threatening stances and attack other males when they are introduced into their tanks.

Behaviors such as these characterize particular species (species-specific) and do not rely on learning. They are called **instincts,** or **fixed-action patterns** (FAPs). Spiders spin webs. Bees "dance" to communicate the location of food to other bees. All this activity is inborn. It is genetically transmitted from generation to generation.

FAPs occur in response to stimuli that **ethologists** call **releasers.** Male members of many species are sexually aroused by

pheromones secreted by females. Pheromones release the FAP of sexual response.

The question arises as to whether people have instincts. Around the turn of the century, psychologists William James (1890) and William McDougall (1908) argued that people have instincts that foster self-survival and social behavior. James asserted that we have social instincts such as love, sympathy, and modesty. McDougall compiled 12 "basic" instincts, including hunger, sex, and self-assertion. Other psychologists have catalogued longer lists.

The psychoanalyst Sigmund Freud also used the term *instincts* to refer to physiological needs within people. Freud believed that the instincts of sex and aggression give rise to *psychic energy,* which is perceived as a feeling of tension. Tension motivates us to restore ourselves to a calmer, resting state. The behavior patterns we use to reduce tension are largely learned.

The psychodynamic views of Sigmund Freud also coincide reasonably well with those of a group of learning theorists who presented a drive-reduction theory of learning.

DRIVE-REDUCTIONISM AND HOMEOSTASIS: "STEADY, STEADY . . ."

According to **drive-reduction theory,** as framed by psychologist Clark Hull in the 1930s, **primary drives** such as hunger, thirst, and pain trigger arousal (tension) and activate behavior. We learn responses that reduce the drives. Through association, we also learn **acquired drives.** We may acquire a drive for money because money enables us to attain food, drink, and homes that protect us from predators and extremes of temperature. We might acquire drives for social approval and affiliation because other people, and their goodwill, help us to reduce primary drives, especially when we are infants. In all cases, tension reduction is the goal.

Primary drives like hunger are triggered when we are in a state of deprivation. Sensations of hunger motivate us to act to restore the bodily balance. The bodily tendency to maintain a steady state is called **homeostasis.** Homeostasis works much like a thermostat. When the room

A Fixed-Action Pattern. In the presence of other males, Siamese fighting fish assume instinctive threatening stances in which they circle one another while they extend their fins and gills. If neither male retreats, there will be conflict.

temperature drops below the set point, the heating system is triggered. The heat stays on until the set point is reached. Similarly, we eat until we are no longer hungry.

OPPONENT-PROCESS THEORY: FROM LAMBS TO LIONS

How does the fearful soldier come to experience feelings of confidence and bravery? How do motives to retreat turn into motives to attack? How do feelings of sexual infatuation turn to disgust? How do motives to cuddle and love turn into motives to run away? Why do many people experience rebound anxiety when they go off a tranquilizer? These are complex questions that require complex answers, but part of the explanation may be found in **opponent-process theory**. According to this view, originated by psychologist Richard Solomon, our emotions tend to trigger opposing emotions. Emotional reactions are followed by their opposites, rather than by neutral feelings, when the conditions that gave rise to the first emotion change (Kimble, 1994; Solomon, 1980).

Consider this example. The "green" soldier enters combat in awe of the enemy and full of fear. She or he survives. Opposing feelings (see Figure 10.8) of anger and anticipation are triggered. Repetitions of the experience strengthen the opposing emotion. With repeated exposures to combat, then, feelings of awe and fear may diminish so that the soldier eventually comes to view combat with feelings of bravery.

Kimble (1994) connects Solomon's opponent-process theory to other opponent processes that occur in people. For example, as noted in Chapter 4, we see afterimages following visual excitation—red where there was green, yellow where there was blue. Opponent processes may be ways in which the body attempts to maintain steady states.

HUMANISTIC THEORY: "I'VE GOT TO BE ME"?

Humanistic psychologists, particularly Abraham Maslow, note that the instinct and drive-reduction theories of motivation are basically defensive. These theories suggest that human behavior occurs in rather mechanical fashion and is aimed toward

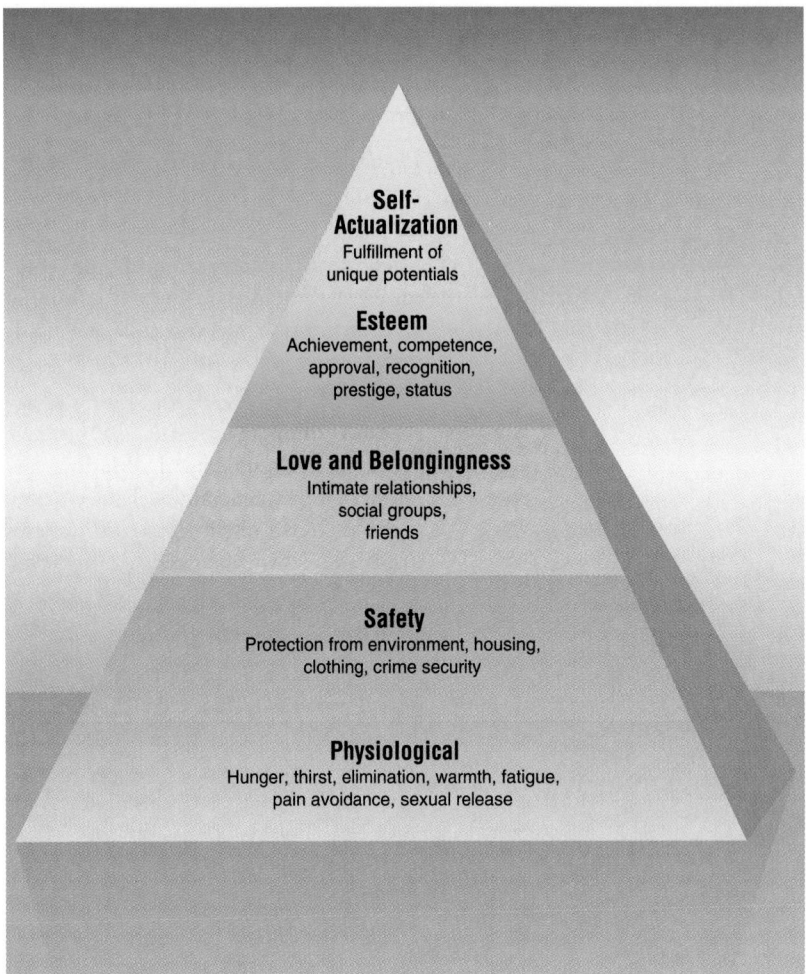

FIGURE 10.1
Maslow's Hierarchy of Needs Maslow believed that we progress toward higher psychological needs once basic survival needs have been met. Do you agree? Why or why not? Where do you fit in this pyramid?

survival and tension reduction. As a humanist, Maslow asserted that behavior is also motivated by the conscious desire for personal growth. Humanists note that people will tolerate pain, hunger, and many other sources of tension to achieve what they perceive as personal fulfillment.

Maslow believed that we are separated from lower animals by our capacity for **self-actualization,** or self-initiated striving to become whatever we believe we are capable of being. In fact, Maslow saw self-actualization to be as essential a human need as hunger.

Maslow (1970) organized human needs into a hierarchy, from physiological needs such as hunger and thirst, through self-actualization (see Figure 10.1.) He believed that in our lives, we naturally travel up through

Opponent-process theory • The view that our emotions trigger opposing emotions.

Self-actualization • According to Maslow and other humanistic psychologists, self-initiated striving to become what one is capable of being. The motive for reaching one's full potential, for expressing one's unique capabilities.

this hierarchy as long as we do not encounter insurmountable social or environmental hurdles. Maslow's hierarchy consists of the following:

1. *Physiological needs:* hunger, thirst, elimination, warmth, fatigue, pain avoidance, sexual release.
2. *Safety needs:* protection from the environment through housing and clothing; security from crime and financial hardship.
3. *Love and belongingness needs:* love and acceptance through intimate relationships, social groups, and friends. Maslow believed that in a generally well-fed society such as ours, much frustration stems from failure to meet needs at this level.
4. *Esteem needs:* achievement, competence, approval, recognition, prestige, status.
5. *Self-actualization:* fulfillment of our unique potentials. For many individuals, self-actualization involves needs for cognitive understanding (novelty, exploration, knowledge) and aesthetic needs (music, art, poetry, beauty, order).

COGNITIVE THEORY: "I THINK, THEREFORE I AM CONSISTENT"?

"I think, therefore I am," said the French philosopher René Descartes. If he had been a cognitive psychologist, he might have said, "I think, therefore I am *consistent*." Theorists such as Sandra Bem (1993) and Leon Festinger (1957) assert that people are motivated to achieve cognitive consistency. Bem argues that children try to follow the "gender schema" in their society—that is, expectations as to what behaviors are appropriate for males and females (see Chapter 12). Leon Festinger believed that people are motivated to hold harmonious beliefs and to justify their behavior. That is why we are more likely to appreciate things we must work for.

Cognitive theorists also note that people mentally represent their worlds (Rescorla, 1988). Jean Piaget and George Kelly (1955) hypothesized that people are born scientists who strive to understand the world so that they can predict and control events. Social-cognitive theorists (e.g., Bandura, 1989, 1991; Mischel, 1990, 1993; Rotter, 1972,

1990) assert that people are motivated by their expectations. On the basis of experience and reasoning, people expect that certain behaviors will lead to certain outcomes. They behave in ways that will enable them to achieve (or avert) these outcomes.

SOCIOCULTURAL THEORY

Sociocultural theory pervades other viewpoints. For example, primary drives may be inborn, but sociocultural experiences affect the *behavior* that satisfies them. Eating meat or fish, drinking coffee or tea, kissing lips or rubbing noses are all influenced by sociocultural factors. What stokes the sex drive is also determined by experiences within a sociocultural milieu. For example, women's breasts have become eroticized in Western culture and must usually be covered from public view. In some preliterate societies, however, the breasts are considered of interest to nursing children only, and women usually go bare-breasted. Among the Abkhasian people of Asia, men regard the female armpit as highly arousing. A woman's armpits are, therefore, a sight for her husband alone (Kammeyer and others, 1990).

Self-actualization also occurs within a given sociocultural milieu. Molière was lyrical in French; Toni Morrison is poetic in English. Many of the films created by John Huston reflected the European American sense of manifest destiny in pushing back the Western frontier. The films of Spike Lee reflect the African American experience and paint the United States from a very different vantage point.

The experiences of anthropologist Margaret Mead (1935) on the South Pacific island of New Guinea showed how the sociocultural milieu influences motives such as aggressiveness and nurturance. Among the Mundugumor, a tribe of headhunters and cannibals, women and men were both warlike and aggressive. The women considered motherhood to sidetrack them from more important activities, such as butchering inhabitants of neighboring villages. In contrast, women and men of the Arapesh tribe were both gentle and nurturant of children. Then there were the Tchambuli. In that tribe the women earned a living, while the men spent most of their time nurturing the children, primping, and gossiping.

EVALUATION: WHICH WHYS RISE TO THE OCCASION?

Instinct theory has been criticized for yielding circular explanations of behavior. If we say that mothers love and care for their children because of a maternal instinct, and then we take maternal care as evidence for such an instinct, we have come full circle. But we have explained nothing. We have only repeated ourselves. Instincts also occur within a given species. They give rise to stereotypical behaviors in all members of a class (such as adult females) within that species. There is so much variation in human behavior that it seems unlikely that much of it is instinctive. Consider William James's notion that sympathy is an instinct. Many people are cruel and cold-hearted; are we to assume that they possess less of this instinct? Such an assumption would be incompatible with the definition of an instinct.

Drive-reduction theory appears to apply in many situations involving physiological drives such as hunger and thirst. However, as well shall see in the "Psychology and Modern Life" section, we often eat when we are not hungry! Drive-reductionism also runs aground when we consider evidence that we often act to increase, rather than decrease, the tensions acting on us. Even when hungry, we may take the time to prepare a gourmet meal instead of a snack, although the snack would reduce the hunger drive as well. We drive fast cars, ride roller coasters, and sky dive for sport—all activities that heighten rather than decrease arousal. We often seek novel ways of doing things because of the stimulation they afford, shunning the tried and true. Yet, the tried and true would reduce tension more reliably. Some psychologists have theorized the existence of stimulus motives that surmount the limitations of drive-reduction theory.

Although opponent-process theory has received some empirical support, it fails to take into account many of the complexities of human behavior. The example with the soldier fails to consider cognitive issues such as belief in one's own abilities and the fatalistic belief of many soldiers that one dies when one's "time has come." In our discussion of theories of emotion, we will see that our emotional responses involve interactions among cognitive, physiological, and behavioral factors.

Critics of Maslow argue that there is too much individual variation for the hierarchy of motivation to apply to everyone. Some people whose physiological, safety, and love needs are met show little interest in achievement and recognition. Others seek distant, self-actualizing goals while exposing themselves to great danger. Some artists, musicians, and writers devote themselves fully to their art, even at the price of poverty.

Some psychologists criticize cognitive theory for its reliance on unobservable concepts such as expectations, rather than observable behavior. Other psychologists question whether the motives to understand and manipulate the environment are inborn. Could they be acquired as we learn that understanding allows us to satisfy physiological drives such as hunger and thirst?

The sociocultural perspective explains the *whys* of behavior at the boundaries of behavior, not at the core. It focuses on external influences that affect behavior. Many psychologists prefer to consider factors within the human being that motivate and shape behavior, such as the processes by which people understand and evaluate cultural influences.

MINILECTURE: THIRST

Reflections

Now that you have read the section on theories of motivation, reflect on the following questions:

- Do you believe that people have instincts? What kinds of instincts? What is your evidence for your belief?
- Have you ever felt powerful fear or infatuation and then had these feelings turn to anger or disgust? Can you put your finger on the factors that led to the change?
- What needs in Maslow's hierarchy are you attempting to meet by attending college?
- How have the ways in which you try to satisfy your needs been affected by sociocultural factors? Do people from other backgrounds try to satisfy the same

needs, or similar needs, in different ways? How so?

Perhaps no theory explains all of psychologists' observations or satisfies all objections. Yet, there is a wealth of research on motivation. Let us first consider the drives of hunger and sex. Hunger and sex are based on physiological needs. Because physiological drives are unlearned, they are also referred to as *primary drives*.

Hunger: Do You Go by "Tummy-Time"?

I go by tummy-time and I want my dinner.
SIR WINSTON CHURCHILL

MINILECTURE: HUNGER

We need food to survive, but food means more than survival to many of us. Food is a symbol of family togetherness and caring. We associate food with the nurturance of the parent–child relationship, with visits home during the holidays. Friends and relatives offer food when we enter their homes. Saying no may be interpreted as a personal rejection. Bacon and eggs, coffee with cream and sugar, meat and mashed pota-

toes—all seem to be part of sharing American values and agricultural abundance. What bodily mechanisms regulate the hunger drive? What psychological processes are at work?

In considering the bodily mechanisms that regulate hunger, let us begin with the mouth. This is an appropriate choice since we are discussing eating. Chewing and swallowing provide some sensations of **satiety.** If they did not, we might eat for a long time after we had taken in enough food. It takes the digestive tract time to metabolize food and provide signals of satiety to the brain by way of the bloodstream.

In classic "sham feeding" experiments with dogs, a tube was implanted in the animals' throats so that any food swallowed fell out of the body. Even though no food arrived at the stomach, the animals stopped feeding after a brief period (Janowitz & Grossman, 1949). However, they resumed feeding sooner than animals whose food did reach the stomach.

Let us proceed to the stomach, too, as we seek further regulatory factors in hunger. An empty stomach will lead to stomach contractions, which we call *hunger pangs.*

Hunger. How do *you* feel while you wait for someone to carve the meat? Hunger is a physiological drive that motivates us to eat. What makes us feel hungry? What makes us feel satiated? Why do many of us continue to eat when we have already supplied our bodies with the needed nutrients?

These pangs are not as influential as had once been thought. People and animals whose stomachs have been removed still regulate food intake to maintain normal weight. This finding led to the discovery of many other hunger regulatory mechanisms including blood sugar level, the hypothalamus, and even receptors in the liver.

When we are deprived of food, the level of sugar in the blood drops. The deficit is communicated to the hypothalamus (see Chapter 3). The drop in blood sugar apparently indicates that we have been burning energy and need to replenish it by eating.

Experiments with the Hypothalamus: The Search for "Start Eating" and "Stop Eating" Centers in the Brain. If you were just reviving from a surgical operation, fighting your way through the fog of the anesthesia, food would probably be the last thing on your mind. But when rats are operated on and a **lesion** in the **ventromedial nucleus** (VMN) of the hypothalamus is made, they will grope toward their food supplies as soon as their eyes open. Then they eat vast quantities of Purina Rat Chow or whatever else they can find.

The VMN might function like a stop-eating center in the rat's brain. If the VMN is electrically stimulated—that is, "switched on"—a rat will stop eating until the current is turned off. When the VMN is lesioned, the rat becomes **hyperphagic.** It will continue to eat until it has about doubled its normal weight (see Figure 10.2). Then it will level off its eating and maintain the higher weight. It is as if the set point of the stop-eating center has been raised to a higher level (Keesey, 1986).

VMN-lesioned rats are also more finicky about their food. They will eat more fats or sweet-tasting food, but they will actually eat less if their food is salty or bitter (Kimble, 1992).

The **lateral hypothalamus** might be a start-eating center in the rat's brain. If you electrically stimulate the lateral hypothalamus, the rat will start to eat. If you make a lesion in the lateral hypothalamus, the rat may stop eating altogether—that is, become **aphagic.** If you force-feed an aphagic rat for a while, however, it will begin to eat on its own and level off at a relatively low body

FIGURE 10.2
A Hyperphagic Rat This rodent winner of the basketball look-alike contest went on a food binge after it received a lesion in the ventromedial nucleus (VMN) of the hypothalamus. It is as if the lesion pushed the "set point" for body weight up several notches, and the rat's weight is now about five times normal. But now it eats only enough to maintain its pleasantly plump stature, so you need not be concerned that it will eventually burst. If the lesion had been made in the lateral hypothalmus, the animal might have become the "Twiggy" of the rat world.

weight. You have lowered the rat's set point. It is like turning the thermostat down from, say, 70 degrees Fahrenheit to 40 degrees Fahrenheit.

Other research suggests that receptors in the liver are also important in regulating hunger. These receptors appear to be sensitive to the blood-sugar level. In a state of food deprivation, blood sugar is low, and these receptors send rapid messages to the brain. After a meal, the blood-sugar level rises, and the receptors' rate of firing decreases (Novin and others, 1983).

Although many areas of the body work in concert to regulate the hunger drive, this is only part of the story. In human beings, the hunger drive is more complex. Psychological as well as physiological factors play an important role. How many times have you been made hungry by the sight or aroma of food? How many times have you eaten not because you were hungry but because you were at a relative's home or in a cafeteria? The chapter's "Psychology and Modern

Satiety • (SAY-she-uh-tee *or* sat-TIE-uh-tee). The state of being satisfied; fullness.

Lesion • An injury that results in impaired behavior or loss of a function.

Ventromedial nucleus • A central area on the underside of the hypothalamus that appears to function as a stop-eating center.

Hyperphagic • Characterized by excessive eating.

Lateral hypothalamus • An area at the side of the hypothalamus that appears to function as a start-eating center.

Aphagic • Characterized by undereating.

Life" section, on obesity, further explores psychological factors that affect our eating.

Reflections

Now that you have read the section on hunger, reflect on the following questions:

- What does food mean to you? Is food more than a way of satisfying the hunger drive? How so?
- How do you know when you are hungry? What bodily sensations do you experience?
- Do you eat when you are not hungry? For what reasons?

Sex: A Sociocultural Perspective

MINILECTURE:
THE SEXUAL
RESPONSE
CYCLE

Offshore from the misty coasts of Ireland lies the small island of Inis Beag. From the air it is a green jewel, warm and inviting. At ground level, things are somewhat different.

For example, the residents of Inis Beag do not believe that women experience orgasm. The woman who chances to find pleasure in sex is considered deviant. Premarital sex is all but unknown. Women engage in sexual relations to conceive children and to appease their husbands' carnal cravings. They need not worry about being called on for frequent performances, however, since the men of Inis Beag believe, erroneously, that sex saps their strength. Sex on Inis Beag is carried out in the dark—literally and figuratively—and with the nightclothes on. The man lies on top in the so-called missionary position. In accord with local concepts of masculinity, he ejaculates as fast as he can. Then he rolls over and falls asleep.

If Inis Beag does not sound like your cup of tea, you may find the atmosphere of Mangaia more congenial. Mangaia is a Polynesian pearl of an island, lifting languidly from the blue waters of the Pacific. It is on the other side of the world from Inis Beag—in more ways than one.

From an early age, Mangaian children are encouraged to get in touch with their sexuality through masturbation. Mangaian adolescents are expected to engage in sexual intercourse. They may be found on se-

cluded beaches or beneath the listing fronds of palms, diligently practicing techniques learned from village elders.

Mangaian women are expected to reach orgasm several times before their partners do. Young men want their partners to reach orgasm and compete to see who is more effective at bringing young women to multiple orgasms.

On the island of Inis Beag, a woman who has an orgasm is considered deviant. On Mangaia, multiple orgasms are the norm (Rathus and others, 1993). If we take a quick tour of the world of sexual diversity, we also find that:

- Nearly every society has an incest taboo, but some societies believe that a brother and sister who eat at the same table are engaging in a mildly sexual act. The practice is thus forbidden (Kammeyer and others, 1990).
- What is sexually arousing varies enormously among different cultures. Women's breasts and armpits stimulate a sexual response in some cultures, but not in others.
- Kissing is practiced nearly universally as a form of petting in the United States but is unknown among many cultures such as the Thonga of Africa and the Siriono of Bolivia. Upon first seeing European visitors kissing, a Thonga tribesman remarked, "Look at them—they eat each others' saliva and dirt."
- Sexual exclusiveness in marriage is valued highly in most parts of the United States, but among the Native American Aleut people of Alaska's Aleutian Islands, it is considered good manners for a man to offer his wife to a houseguest.
- The United States has its romantic Valentine's Day, but Japan has eroticized another day—Christmas Eve. (You read that right: Christmas Eve.) Christmas Eve may be a time of religious devotion in many Western nations, but it has become a time of sexual devotion in Japan. On Christmas Eve every single person must have a date that includes an overnight visit (Reid, 1990). During the weeks prior to Christmas, the media brim with reports on hotels for overnight stays, the correct attire, and breakfast ideas for the morning after. Where do Tokyo singles

like to go before their overnighter? Tokyo Disneyland.

Truth or Fiction Revisited. *It is true that Christmas Eve has become a time of sexual devotion in Japan, even while it is a time of religious devotion in most Western nations.* There is a good deal of social pressure on single people to have a date that includes an overnight stay.

The residents of Inis Beag and Mangaia have similar anatomic features but vastly different attitudes toward sex. Their sociocultural settings influence their patterns of sexual behavior and the pleasure they find—or do not find—in sex. Although sex is a natural function, perhaps no other natural function has been influenced so strongly by religious and moral beliefs, cultural tradition, folklore, and superstition (Rathus and others, 1993).

Now that we have considered sociocultural influences on sexual behavior, let us consider the roles of sex hormones. Then we turn our attention to sexual orientation.

ORGANIZING AND ACTIVATING EFFECTS OF SEX HORMONES

Sex hormones have many effects. They promote biological sexual differentiation, regulate the menstrual cycle, and affect sexual behavior.

Sex hormones have organizing and activating effects on behavior (Buchanan and others, 1992). They predispose lower animals toward masculine or feminine mating patterns—a directional or **organizing effect** (Crews, 1994). Hormones also affect the sex drive and promote sexual response—**activating effects.**

Sexual behavior among many lower animals is almost completely governed by hormones (Crews, 1994). The sex organs and brains of many species that are exposed to large doses of **testosterone** in utero (which occurs naturally when they share the uterus with many brothers or artificially as a result of hormone injections) become masculinized in structure (Crews, 1994). Such females are also predisposed toward masculine mating behaviors. If masculinized female rodents are given additional testosterone as adults, they attempt to mount other females about as often as males do (Goy &

McEwen, 1982). Prenatal testosterone organizes the brains of these females in the masculine direction, predisposing them toward masculine behaviors in adulthood. Testosterone in adulthood then apparently activates the masculine behavior patterns.

Testosterone is also important in human behavior. As testosterone levels rise among boys during puberty, so does their interest in sex and their number of orgasms (Angier, 1994b). Although males produce 10 to 20 times the amount of androgens produced by females, androgens affect the female as well as the male sex drive. However, even though puberty brings a rise in androgens in girls as well as boys, girls do not show as dramatic a rise in sexual interest and behavior (Angier, 1994b). Peer group influences and other psychosocial factors seem to be as important as hormones for girls (Angier, 1994b).

Female mice, rats, cats, and dogs are receptive to males only during **estrus,** when female sex hormones are plentiful. During estrus, female rats respond to males by hopping, wiggling their ears, and arching their backs with their tails to one side, thus making penetration possible. But, as noted by Kimble (1992),

> If we were to observe this same pair of rats one day [after estrus], when the female is into the first day of her new cycle, we would see a very different set of behaviors. While the male would still show signs of sexual interest, at least at first, his sniffing and attempted mounts would not be met with hopping, ear wiggling, and [back arching]. Indeed, the female is more likely to "chatter" her teeth at the male—an unmistakeable sign of rodent hostility. If the male is slow to grasp her meaning, she might turn her back to him and kick at his head, mule fashion. Clearly, it is over between them (pp. 310–311).

Women, by contrast, are sexually responsive during all phases of the menstrual cycle, even during menstruation, when hormone levels are low, and after **menopause.**

Men who are castrated or given drugs (antiandrogens) that decrease the amount of androgens in the bloodstream usually show gradual loss of sexual desire and of the

Organizing effects • The directional effects of sex hormones—for example, along stereotypically masculine or feminine lines.
Activating effects • The arousal-producing effects of sex hormones that increase the likelihood of dominant sexual responses.
Testosterone • A male hormone that promotes development of male sexual characteristics and that has activating effects on sexual arousal.
Estrus • The periodic sexual excitement of many female mammals, during which they can conceive and are receptive to the sexual advances of males.
Menopause • The cessation of menstruation.

capacities for erection and orgasm. Still, many castrated men remain sexually active for years. Perhaps for many people, fantasies, memories, and other cognitive stimuli are as important as hormones in sexual motivation. Women whose adrenal glands and ovaries have been removed (so that they no longer produce androgens) may gradually lose sexual interest and the capacity for sexual response. An active and enjoyable sexual history seems to ward off loss of sexual capacity, suggestive of the importance of cognitive and experiential factors in human sexual motivation. In human sexuality, biology is apparently not destiny.

SEXUAL ORIENTATION

Sexual orientation refers to the organization or directionality of one's erotic interests. **Heterosexual** people are sexually attracted to, and interested in forming romantic relationships with, people of the other gender. **Gay males** and **lesbians** are sexually attracted to, and interested in forming romantic relationships with, people of their own gender.[1] **Bisexuals** are

[1] In keeping with the suggestions of the American Psychological Association's (1991) Committee on Lesbian and Gay Concerns, I am using the terms *gay male* and *lesbian* instead of *homosexual* in our discussion of sexual orientation. As noted by the committee, there are several problems with the word *homosexual:* One, because it has been historically associated with concepts of deviance and mental illness, it may perpetuate negative stereotypes of gay men and lesbians. Two, the term is often used to refer to men only, thus rendering lesbians invisible. Third, the word is often ambiguous in meaning—that is, does it refer to sexual behavior or sexual orientation?

Sexual orientation • The direction of one's erotic interests (e.g., heterosexual, gay male, lesbian, or bisexual).

Heterosexual • A person whose sexual orientation is characterized by desire for sexual activity and the formation of romantic relationships with people of the other gender.

Gay male • A male whose sexual orientation is characterized by desire for sexual activity and the formation of romantic relationships with other males.

Lesbian • A female whose sexual orientation is characterized by desire for sexual activity and the formation of romantic relationships with other females.

Bisexual • A person whose sexual orientation is characterized by desire for sexual activity and the formation of romantic relationships with both women and men.

PSYCHOLOGY IN THE NEW MILLENNIUM

Sex Gets Interactive

There's nothing new about pulling down the curtains so that sexual activity remains a private matter. But a new wrinkle has been added by the black curtains at the computer expositions of the 1990s. The curtains shield high-tech peep shows that feature nude models on CD-ROMS produced by *Penthouse* and other purveyors of multimedia erotica. Sex has always followed hard on the heels of the technological innovations of the day. Four thousand years ago, the Sumerians celebrated the pleasures of sex in their early cuneiform writing on clay tablets (Tierney, 1994). Shortly after Gutenberg invented the printing press, a volume of erotic engravings appeared. (The year was 1524 A.D., and the work was soon suppressed by the pope.)

Today, we have multimedia interactivity. One could argue, of course, that sex has always been about as interactive a sphere of activity as one could have. But not until the 1990s did a *Penthouse* model saying "Let's get interactive" become available for your computer.

In one program produced by the CD-ROM company Interotica, entitled *Interactive Adventures,* a narrator introduces himself to a young woman in Los Angeles. The action soon comes to a halt with her face frozen on the monitor. The screen presents the computer operator with a menu of choices: retreating, asking the woman out to dinner, and inviting her to enjoy a sojourn in a hot tub. Retreating and the hot-tub proposition offer no rewards. (The hot-tub invitation is judged premature by this socially sophisticated program.) But the dinner invitation, followed up by additional "correct" choices, leads to a CD-ROM-mediated "sexual encounter."

Social critics point out that the advanced technology that makes such interactive adventures possible serves to maintain men's low-tech sexist illusions about women. As in pornographic books, films, and videocassettes, women are portrayed as objects whose function is to serve the cruder wishes of men. In such works, "love" is reduced to anonymous encounters in which women seek to fulfill men's sexual desires, not to develop relationships. Lisa Pilac, the editor of a magazine called *Future Sex,* suggests that "The link between sex and new technology is always going to be there, and I think women should get involved. We need to create our own erotic titles that appeal to women" (1994, p. H18).

sexually attracted to, and interested in forming romantic relationships with, both women and men.

The concept of *sexual orientation* is not to be confused with *sexual activity* (American Psychological Association, 1991). For example, engaging in sexual activity with members of one's own gender does not necessarily mean that one has a gay male or lesbian sexual orientation. Sociocultural factors inform us that male–male sexual behavior may reflect limited sexual opportunities or even ritualistic cultural practices, as in the case of the New Guinean Sambian people. American adolescent males may manually stimulate one another while fantasizing about girls. Men in prisons may similarly turn to each other as sexual outlets. Sambian male youths engage exclu-

sively in sexual practices with older males, since it is believed that they must drink "men's milk" to achieve the fierce manhood of the headhunter (Money, 1987). Their sexual activities are limited to female partners once they reach marrying age, however.

Research in the United States, Britain, France, and Denmark finds that about 3% of men surveyed identify themselves as gay (Hamer and others, 1993; Janus & Janus, 1993; Laumann and others, 1994). About 2% of the U.S. women surveyed consider themselves to have a lesbian sexual orientation (Janus & Janus, 1993; Laumann and others, 1994).

Origins of Sexual Orientation. Psychodynamic theory ties sexual orientation

Business people are already contemplating new ways of raking in the dollars from interactive erotica. Once fiber-optic cables have been installed in people's homes so that they are tuned in to the information superhighway, pay-per-view videophone sex is likely to replace telephone sex. Today, so-called "hot chats" are popular with computer on-line services. The services allow people with unusual sexual interests to conduct conversations with people who share their interests any place in the country by typing their comments onto their screens. It is easy to imagine video versions of the hot chat in the new millennium. If one wished to remain anonymous during an "interactive" session, one could perhaps don the computer-generated image of, say, Denzel Washington or Cindy Crawford.

Or consider what some futurists refer to as *cybersex* or *virtual sex* (Ravo & Nash, 1993). You don headphones, 3-D glasses, and a light bodysuit with miniature detectors that follow your movements and tiny stimulators for your skin. The detectors and stimulators are connected to computers that record your responses and create the impression of being touched by textures such as virtual satin, virtual wool, or virtual skin. The information superhighway allows you either to interact with another on-line person who is outfitted with similar gear or to be connected with a canned program.

What are some of the psychological implications of such new forms of interactive sex? If we could electronically dress up as movie stars, would our sense of self and our dignity as individuals suffer?

If we could at a moment's notice access a satisfying virtual sexual encounter with an appealing person (or program) who was only concerned about meeting our needs, would we become less sensitive to the needs of our real-life romantic partners? Would virtual sex provide additional outlets for people whose needs were not being fully met by others? Or would they become the preferred sexual outlets? If they did become preferred outlets, what would be the implications for the family? For children?

Would a virtual sex interaction be grounds for divorce?

It is comforting for an old fogy like me to note that family life remains a popular ideal despite provocative cuneiform writings on clay tablets, despite arousing engravings (and photographs) in printed media, despite adult films and videotapes, even despite telephone sex. On the other hand, we have not yet witnessed the most titillating interactions of the new millennium.

Sex On Line? What forms will "multimedia" and "interactivity" take in the new millennium? Today telephone sex is a hot industry. In the new millennium, will virtual sex become available on line?

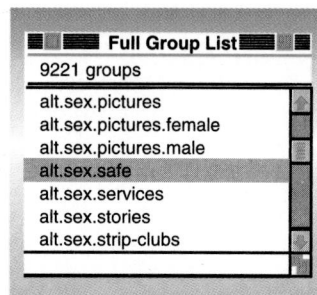

L'Abandon (Les Deux Amies.) This painting by Henri de Toulouse-Lautrec is of lesbian lovers.

Concordance • Agreement.

to identification with male or female figures. Identification, in turn, is related to resolution of the Oedipus and Electra complexes. In men, faulty resolution of the Oedipus complex would stem from a "classic pattern" of child rearing in which there is a "close binding" mother and a "detached hostile" father. Boys reared in such a home environment would identify with their mothers and not their fathers. Psychodynamic theory has been criticized, however, because many gay males have had excellent relationships with both parents. Also, the childhoods of many heterosexuals fit the "classic pattern." Because there is much variation among the families of gay men and lesbians, no single pattern applies to all cases (Isay, 1990).

From a learning-theory point of view, early reinforcement of sexual behavior (as by orgasm achieved through interaction with members of one's own gender) can influence one's sexual orientation. But many gay males and lesbians are aware of their sexual orientations before they have overt sexual contacts (Bell and others, 1981).

Biological theories focus on genetic and hormonal factors. There is ample evidence of familial patterns in sexual orientation (Pillard, 1990; Pillard & Weinrich, 1986). In one study, 22% of the brothers of 51 primarily gay men were either gay or bisexual

themselves. This is about four times the percentage found in the general population (Pillard & Weinrich, 1986). A study published in *Science* reported that genes connected with sexual orientation may be found on the X sex chromosome and transmitted from mother to child (Hamer and others, 1993). Moreover, according to research by Bailey and Pillard (1991), identical (MZ) twins have a higher **concordance** rate for a gay male sexual orientation than fraternal (DZ) twins: 52% for MZ twins versus 22% for DZ twins. Although genetic factors may partly determine sexual orientation, psychologist John Money, who has specialized in sexual behavior research, concludes that sexual orientation is "not under the direct governance of chromosomes and genes" (1987, p. 384).

Sex hormones predispose lower animals toward masculine or feminine mating patterns. Thus, it has been wondered whether gay males might be deficient in testosterone or whether lesbians might have lower-than-normal levels of estrogen and higher-than-normal levels of androgens in their bloodstreams. However, a gay male or lesbian sexual orientation has not been reliably linked to current (adult) levels of male or female sex hormones (Kimble, 1992).

But what of the effects of sex hormones on the developing fetus? We know that prenatal sex hormones can masculinize or feminize the brains of laboratory animals in the ways that they direct the development of brain structures.

Lee Ellis (1990; Ellis & Ames, 1987) theorizes that sexual orientation is hormonally determined prior to birth and is affected by genetic factors, drugs (such as androgens), and maternal stress. Why maternal stress? Stress causes the release of hormones such as adrenaline and cortisol, which can interact with testosterone and affect the prenatal development of the brain. Perhaps the brains of some gay males have been prenatally feminized, and the brains of some lesbians have been masculinized (Money, 1987). Even so, Money argues that prenatal hormonal influences would not induce a robotlike sexual orientation in humans and that socialization—or early learning experiences—would probably also play a role.

The determinants of sexual orientation are mysterious and complex. Research suggests that they may involve prenatal hormone levels—which can be affected by factors such as heredity, drugs, and maternal stress—and postnatal socialization. However, the precise interaction of these influences has eluded detection.

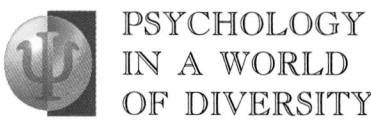

PSYCHOLOGY IN A WORLD OF DIVERSITY

ETHNICITY AND SEXUAL ORIENTATION: A MATTER OF BELONGING

Lesbians and gay men frequently suffer the slings and arrows of an outraged society. Because of societal prejudices, it is difficult for many young people to come to terms with an emerging lesbian or gay male sexual orientation (Rathus and others, 1993). You might assume that people who have been subjected to prejudice and discrimination—members of ethnic minority groups in the United States—would be more tolerant of a lesbian or gay male sexual orientation. However, according to psychologist Beverly Greene (1994) of St. John's University, such an assumption might not be warranted.

In an article that addresses the experiences of lesbians and gay men from ethnic minority groups, Greene (1994) notes that it is difficult to generalize about ethnic groups in the United States. For example, African Americans may find their cultural origins in the tribes of West Africa, but they have also been influenced by Christianity and the local subcultures of their North American towns and cities. Native Americans represent hundreds of tribal groups, languages, and cultures. By and large, however, a lesbian or gay male sexual orientation is rejected by ethnic minority groups in the United States. Lesbians and gay males are pressured to keep their sexual orientations a secret or to move to communities where they can live openly without sanction.

Within traditional Hispanic American culture, the family is the primary social unit. Men are expected to support and defend the family, and women are expected to be submissive, respectable, and deferential to men (Morales, 1992). Because women are expected to remain virgins until marriage, men sometimes engage in male–male sexual behavior without considering themselves gay (Greene, 1994). Hispanic American culture frequently denies the sexuality of women. Thus, women who label themselves lesbians are doubly condemned—because they are lesbians and because they are confronting others with their sexuality. Because lesbians are independent of men, most Hispanic American heterosexuals view Hispanic American lesbians as threats to the tradition of male dominance (Trujillo, 1991).

Asian American cultures emphasize respect for one's elders, obedience to parents, and sharp distinctions in masculine and feminine gender roles (Chan, 1992). The topic of sex is generally taboo within the family. Asian Americans, like Hispanic Americans, tend to assume that sex is unimportant to women. Women are also considered to be less important than men. Open admission of a lesbian or gay male sexual orientation is seen as a rejection of one's traditional cultural roles and a threat to the continuity of the family line (Chan, 1992; Garnets & Kimmel, 1991).

Because many African American men have had difficulty finding jobs, gender roles among African Americans have been more flexible than those found among White Americans and most other ethnic minority groups (Greene, 1994). Nevertheless, the African American community appears to strongly reject gay men and lesbians, pressuring them to remain secretive about their sexual orientations (Gomez & Smith, 1990; Poussaint, 1990). Greene (1994) hypothesizes a number of factors that influence African Americans to be hostile toward lesbians and gay men. One is strong allegiance to Christian beliefs and biblical scripture. Another is internalization of the dominant culture's stereotyping of African Americans as highly sexual beings. That is, many African Americans may feel a need to assert their sexual "normalcy" or even a sense of sexual superiority.

Prior to the European conquest, sex may not have been discussed openly by Native Americans, but sex was generally seen as a natural part of life. Individuals who incorporated both traditional feminine and masculine styles were generally accepted and even admired. The influence of the religions of colonists led to greater rejection of lesbians and gay men and to pressure to move off the reservation to the big city (Greene, 1994). Native American lesbians and gay men, like Asian American lesbians and gay men, thus often feel doubly removed from their families.

If any generalization is possible, it may be that lesbians and gay men find more of a sense of belonging in the gay community than in their ethnic communities.

Reflections

Now that you have read the section on sexual motivation, reflect on the following questions:

- What sociocultural factors have affected your sexual attitudes and behavior? Are your attitudes and behavior similar to or different from those of most of your classmates? Why or why not?
- What stimuli sexually arouse you? Why do you believe that they arouse you?
- What attitudes toward gay males and lesbians were expressed in your home, in your neighborhood? Have these attitudes affected your own beliefs? How? Has the information in this chapter changed your beliefs about gay males and lesbians? If so, how?

Stimulus Motives

One day when my daughter Taylor was 5 months old, I was batting her feet. (Why not?) She was sitting back in her mother's lap, and I repeatedly batted her feet up toward her middle with the palms of my hands. After a while, she began to laugh. When I stopped, she pushed a foot toward me, churned her arms back and forth, and blew bubbles as forcefully as she could. So I batted her feet again. She laughed and pushed them toward me again. This went on for a while, and it dawned on me that Taylor was doing what she could to make the stimulation last.

Physical needs give rise to drives like hunger and thirst. In such cases, organisms

are motivated to *reduce* the tension or stimulation that impinges on them. But in the case of **stimulus motives,** organisms seek to *increase* stimulation, like Taylor sought to have me bat her feet. Stimulus motives include sensory stimulation, activity, exploration, and manipulation of the environment.

Some stimulus motives provide a clear evolutionary advantage. People and lower animals who are motivated to learn about and manipulate the environment are more likely to survive. Learning about the environment increases awareness of resources and of potential dangers, and manipulation permits one to change the environment in beneficial ways. Learning and manipulation increase the chances of survival until sexual maturity and of transmitting whatever genetic codes may underlie these motives to future generations.

SENSORY STIMULATION AND ACTIVITY

When I was a teenager during the 1950s, I was unaware that some lucky students at McGill University in Montreal were being paid $20 a day (which, with inflation, would be well above $100 today) for doing absolutely nothing. Would you like such "work" for $100 a day? Don't answer too quickly. According to the results of classic research into **sensory deprivation,** you might not like it much at all.

Student volunteers were blindfolded in quiet cubicles (Bexton and others, 1954). Their arms were bandaged, and they could hear nothing but the dull, continuous hum of air conditioning. With nothing to do, many students slept for a while. After a few hours of sensory-deprived wakefulness, most felt bored and irritable. As time went on, many of them grew more uncomfortable, and some reported hallucinations, as of images of dots and geometric shapes.

Many students quit during the first day despite the financial incentive and the desire to contribute to science. Many of those who remained for a few days found it temporarily difficult to concentrate on simple problems afterward. For many, the experimental conditions did not provide a relaxing vacation. Instead, they instigated boredom and disorientation.

Stimulus motives • Motives to increase the stimulation impinging upon an organism.
Sensory deprivation • A research method for systematically decreasing the amount of stimulation that impinges upon sensory receptors.
Innate • Inborn, unlearned.

Truth or Fiction Revisited. *It is not true that getting away from it all by going on a vacation from all sensory input for a few hours is relaxing.* If carried out as it was at McGill University, such a "vacation" may be highly stressful.

Individual Differences in Desire for Stimulation. Some people seek higher levels of stimulation and activity than others. John is a couch potato, content to sit by the TV set all evening. Marsha doesn't feel right unless she's out on the tennis court or jogging. Cliff isn't content unless he has ridden his motorcycle over back trails at breakneck speeds, and Janet feels exuberant when she's catching the big wave or free-fall diving from an airplane. One's preference for tennis, motorcycling, or skydiving reflects one's geographical location, social class, and learning experiences. But it just may be that the levels of arousal at which we are comfortable would be too high or too low for other people. It also may be that these levels are determined to some degree by **innate** factors.

Questionnaire

THE SENSATION-SEEKING SCALE

Are you content to read or watch television all day? Or must you catch the big wave or bounce the bike across the dunes of the Mohave Desert? Psychologist Marvin Zuckerman (1980) has developed sensation-seeking scales that measure the level of stimulation or arousal a person will seek and predict how well he or she will fare in sensory-deprivation studies.

Zuckerman and his colleagues (1978) found four factors that are involved in sensation seeking: (1) seeking of thrill and adventure, (2) disinhibition (that is, tendency to express impulses), (3) seeking of experience, and (4) susceptibility to boredom. Other studies show that people high in sensation seeking are less tolerant of sensory deprivation. Sensation seekers are also more likely to use drugs and become involved in sexual experiences, to be drunk in public, and to volunteer for high-risk activities and unusual experiments (Kohn and others, 1979; Malatesta and others, 1981).

A shortened version of one of Zuckerman's scales follows. To gain insight into your own sensation-seeking tendencies, circle the choice, A or B, that best describes you. Then compare your answers to those in the answer key in Appendix B.

1. A. I would like a job that requires a lot of traveling.
   B. I would prefer a job in one location.

2. A. I am invigorated by a brisk, cold day.
   B. I can't wait to get indoors on a cold day.

3. A. I get bored seeing the same old faces.
   B. I like the comfortable familiarity of everyday friends.

4. A. I would prefer living in an ideal society in which everyone is safe, secure, and happy.
   B. I would have preferred living in the unsettled days of our history.

5. A. I sometimes like to do things that are a little frightening.
   B. A sensible person avoids activities that are dangerous.

6. A. I would not like to be hypnotized.
   B. I would like to have the experience of being hypnotized.

7. A. The most important goal in life is to live it to the fullest and experience as much as possible.
   B. The most important goal in life is to find peace and happiness.

8. A. I would like to try parachute jumping.
   B. I would never want to try jumping out of a plane, with or without a parachute.

9. A. I enter cold water gradually, giving myself time to get used to it.
   B. I like to dive or jump right into the ocean or a cold pool.

10. A. When I go on a vacation, I prefer the change of camping out.
    B. When I go on a vacation, I prefer the comfort of a good room and bed.

11. A. I prefer people who are emotionally expressive even if they are a bit unstable.
    B. I prefer people who are calm and even tempered.

12. A. A good painting should shock or jolt the senses.
    B. A good painting should give one a feeling of peace and security.

13. A. People who ride motorcycles must have some kind of unconscious need to hurt themselves.
    B. I would like to drive or ride a motorcycle.

Sensation Seeking? Is patriotism the sole motive of pilots of military aircraft such as the Lockheed A-117 Stealth fighter, or do fighter pilots also seek to raise their bodily arousal to more stimulating levels?

EXPLORATION AND MANIPULATION

Have you ever brought a dog or cat into a new home? At first, it may show general excitement. New kittens are also known to hide under a couch or bed for a few hours. But then they will begin to explore every corner of the new environment. When placed in novel environments, many animals appear to possess an innate motive to engage in exploratory behavior.

Once they are familiar with the environment, lower animals and people appear to be motivated to seek **novel stimulation.** For example, when they have not been deprived of food for a great deal of time, rats will often explore unfamiliar arms of mazes rather than head straight for the section of the maze in which they have learned to expect food. Animals that have just **copulated** and thereby reduced their sex drives will often show renewed interest in sexual behavior when presented with a novel sex partner. Monkeys will learn how to manipulate gadgets for the incentive of being able to observe novel stimulation through a window (see Figure 10.3). Children will spend hour after hour manipulating the controls of video games for the pleasure of zapping video monsters.

The question has arisen whether people and animals seek to explore and manipulate the environment *because* these activities help them reduce primary drives such as hunger and thirst or whether they engage in these activities for their own sake. Many psychologists do believe that such stimulating activities are reinforcing in and of themselves. Monkeys do seem to get a kick out of "monkeying around" with gadgets (see Figure 10.4). They learn how to manipulate hooks and eyes and other mechanical

FIGURE 10.3
The Allure of Novel Stimulation People and many lower animals are motivated to explore the environment and to seek novel stimulation. This monkey has learned to unlock a door for the privilege of viewing a model train.

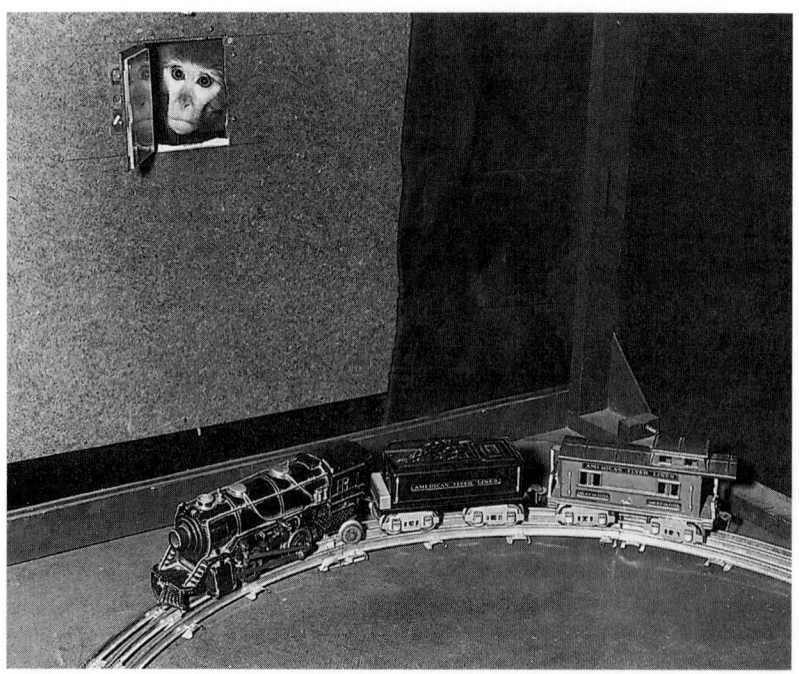

devices without any external incentives whatsoever (Harlow and others, 1950). Children engage in prolonged play with "busy boxes"—boxes filled with objects that honk, squeak, rattle, and buzz. They seem to find discovery of the cause-and-effect relationships in these gadgets pleasurable even though they are not rewarded with food, ice cream, or even hugs from parents.

Reflections

Now that you have read the section on stimulus motives, reflect on the following questions:

- Can you think of times when you were tired but "got a new wind" when you started to do something new or intriguing? Why do you think this happened?
- Do you find it relaxing to lie on the beach and "do nothing"? For how long? Or do you find it difficult to lie on the beach and do nothing? Why?

Cognitive Consistency: Making Things Fit

Cognitive theorists propose that organisms are motivated to create realistic mental maps of the world. Organisms therefore ad-

FIGURE 10.4
A Manipulation Drive? These young rhesus monkeys appear to monkey around with gadgets for the sheer pleasure of monkeying around. No external incentives or reinforcements are needed. Children similarly enjoy manipulating gadgets that honk, squeak, rattle, and buzz, even though the resultant honks and squeaks do not satisfy physiological drives such as hunger or thirst.

just their representations of the world, as needed, to reduce discrepancies and accommodate new information (Rescorla, 1988). In this section we consider two theories that address our efforts to create consistent mental maps: balance theory and cognitive-dissonance theory.

BALANCE THEORY

According to **balance theory,** originated by Fritz Heider (1958), we are motivated to maintain harmony among our beliefs and attitudes. For example, when people we like share our attitudes, there is balance and all is well (see Figure 10.5). It works the other way as well: If we support the president of the United States and she or he expresses an attitude, our own cognitions will remain in balance if we agree. For this reason, we

Novel stimulation • (1) An unusual source of arousal or excitement. (2) A hypothesized primary drive to experience new or different stimulation.

Copulate • To engage in sexual intercourse.

Balance theory • The view that people have a need to organize their perceptions, opinions, and beliefs in a harmonious manner.

FIGURE 10.5
Balance Theory According to Heider, we are motivated to maintain harmony among our attitudes. As in the triangle to the left, when people we like share our attitudes, there is a state of balance and all is well. However, as in the triangle in the center, when someone we care about disagrees with us, there is an uncomfortable state of imbalance that we may try to end by inducing the other person to change her or his attitude or by changing our feelings about the other person. The triangle on the right shows a state of nonbalance in which we dislike someone else, so that her or his attitudes are not of much interest to us one way or the other.

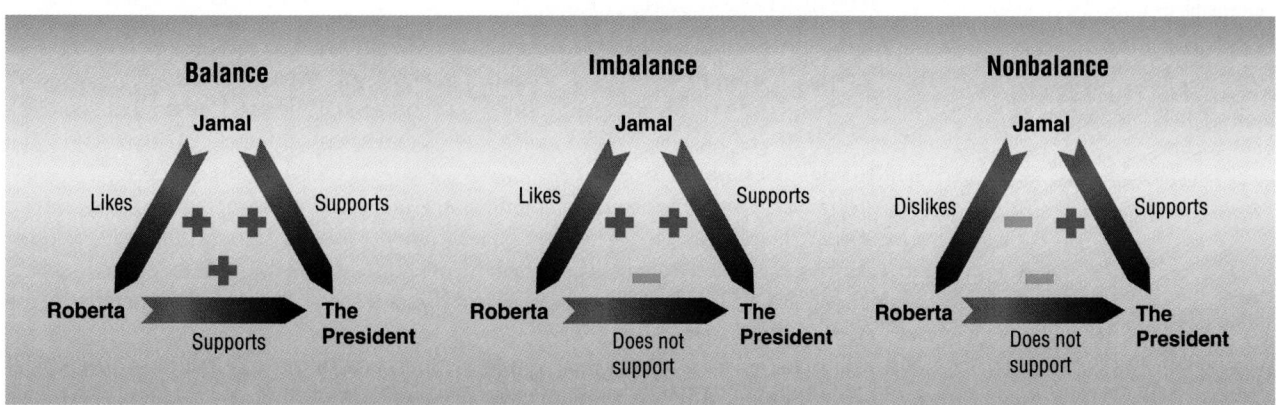

Are They "In Balance"?
According to balance theory, we are motivated to maintain harmony among our beliefs and attitudes. When people we care about share our attitudes, there is balance and all is well. But when someone we care about disagrees with us on important issues, a state of imbalance exists and the relationship could falter.

Nonbalance • In balance theory, a condition in which persons whom we dislike do not agree with us.

Imbalance • In balance theory, an uncomfortable condition in which persons whom we like disagree with us.

Attitude-discrepant behavior • Behavior that is inconsistent with an attitude and may have the effect of modifying an attitude.

Effort justification • In cognitive-dissonance theory, the tendency to seek justification (acceptable reasons) for strenuous efforts.

Thematic Apperception Test • A test devised by Henry Murray to measure needs through fantasy production.

MINILECTURE: ATTITUDE-DISCREPANT BEHAVIOR

are likely to develop favorable attitudes toward unfamiliar objects that the president seems to endorse. If we dislike other people, we might not care very much about their attitudes. They may disagree with us, but this state of **nonbalance** leaves us indifferent.

When someone we care about expresses a discrepant attitude, however, we *are* likely to be concerned (Orive, 1988). The relationship will survive if we like chocolate and our friend prefers vanilla, but what if the discrepancy concerns religion, politics, or child rearing? A state of **imbalance** now exists. What if the president, whom we like, reports favorably on an object we dislike? There is now an uncomfortable state of imbalance. What can we do to end such a state? We can try to induce others to change their attitudes. Or we can change our feelings about the other person.

COGNITIVE-DISSONANCE THEORY: "IF I DID IT, IT MUST BE IMPORTANT"?

Do I contradict myself?
Very well then I contradict myself,
(I am large, I contain multitudes.)
                    WALT WHITMAN, *SONG OF MYSELF*

Most of us are unlike Walt Whitman, according to cognitive-dissonance theory (Festinger, 1957; Festinger & Carlsmith, 1959). Whitman may not have minded contradicting himself, but most people do not like their attitudes (cognitions) to be inconsistent. Awareness that two cognitions are dissonant, or that our attitudes are incompatible with our behavior, is unpleasant and motivates us to reduce the discrepancy.

In the first and one of the best-known studies on cognitive dissonance, one group of participants received $1 for telling someone else that a boring task was interesting (Festinger & Carlsmith, 1959). A second group received $20 to describe the chore positively. Both groups were paid to engage in **attitude-discrepant behavior**—that is, behavior that ran counter to their cognitions. After "selling" the job to others, the participants were asked to rate their own liking for it. Ironically, the group paid *less* rated the task as more interesting. Why?

According to learning theory, the result would be confusing. After all, shouldn't we

learn to like that which is highly rewarding? But cognitive-dissonance theory would predict this "less-leads-to-more effect" for the following reason: The cognitions "I was paid very little" and "I told someone that this assignment was interesting" are dissonant. People tend to engage in **effort justification.** They tend to explain their behavior to themselves in such a way that unpleasant undertakings seem worth it. Study participants paid only $1 may have justified their lie by concluding that they may not have been lying in the first place. Similarly, we appreciate things more when they are more difficult to obtain.

Truth or Fiction Revisited. *It is true that we appreciate things more when we have to work for them.* This is an example of the principle of effort justification.

Consider another situation. Cognitive dissonance would be created if we were to believe that our preferred candidate was unlikely to win the American presidential election. One cognition would be that our candidate is better for the country or, at an extreme, would "save" the country from harmful forces. A second, and dissonant, cognition would be that our candidate does not have a chance to win. Research shows that in the presidential elections from 1952 to 1980, people by a four-to-one margin helped reduce such dissonance by expressing the belief that their candidate would win (Granberg & Brent, 1983). They often clung to these beliefs despite lopsided polls to the contrary.

Reflections

Now that you have read the section on cognitive consistency, reflect on the following questions:

- Have you ever changed your opinion of someone when you learned that she or he liked something that you disliked? What happened? Why did it happen?
- Were you ever subjected to difficult hazing upon joining a sorority, fraternity, or other kind of club? Did the experience affect your feelings about being a member of the group? How? Can you connect your experience to the concept of *effort justification?*

The Three A's of Motivation: Achievement, Affiliation, and Aggression

Let us consider some of the powerful motives that bind us together and tear us asunder: achievement, affiliation, and aggression. Harvard University psychologist Henry Murray (1938) hypothesized that each of these "A's" reflects a psychological need. Murray also referred to them as *social motives,* which he believed differed from primary motives such as hunger in that they were acquired through social learning. However, contemporary researchers do not rule out a role for hereditary predispositions toward these behavior patterns.

ACHIEVEMENT

We all know students who persist at academic tasks despite distractions. We all know adults who strive relentlessly to get ahead, to "make it," to earn vast sums of money, to invent, to accomplish the impossible. Such people are said to have strong achievement motivation.

Psychologist David McClelland (1958) helped pioneer the assessment of achievement motivation through fantasy. One method involves the **Thematic Apperception Test** (TAT), which was developed by Henry Murray. The TAT contains cards with pictures and drawings that are subject to various interpretations (see Chapter 12). Individuals are shown one or more TAT cards and asked to construct stories about the pictured theme: to indicate what led up to it, what the characters are thinking and feeling, and what is likely to happen.

One TAT card is similar to that in Figure 10.6. The meaning of the card is ambiguous—unclear. Is the boy dozing off, thinking about the violin, wishing he were out playing? Consider two stories that could be told about this card:

Story 1: "He's upset that he's got to practice the violin because he's behind in his assignments and

doesn't particularly like to work. He'd much rather be out playing with the other kids, and he'll probably sneak out to do just that."

Story 2: "He's thinking, 'Someday I'll be a great violinist. I'll play at Carnegie Hall, and everybody will be proud of me.' He practices constantly."

Formal standards enable psychologists to derive achievement motivation scores from stories such as these, but you need not be acquainted with them to see that the second story suggests more achievement motivation than the first. Classic studies find that people with high achievement motivation earn higher grades than people of comparable learning ability but lower achievement motivation. They are more likely to earn high salaries and be promoted than less motivated people with similar opportunities. They perform better at math problems and unscrambling anagrams such as decoding RSTA into *star, tars, arts,* or *rats.*

McClelland (1965) found that 83% of college graduates with high achievement motivation took positions characterized by risk, decision making, and the chance for great success, such as business management, sales, or businesses of their own making. Seventy percent of the graduates who chose nonentrepreneurial positions showed low

FIGURE 10.6
Tapping Fantasies in Personality Research This picture is similar to a Thematic Apperception Test card that is frequently used to measure the need for achievement. What is happening in this picture? What is the person thinking and feeling? What is going to happen? Your answers to these questions reflect your own needs as well as the content of the picture itself.

achievement motivation. People with high achievement motivation seem to prefer challenges and are willing to take moderate risks to achieve their goals.

What Flavor Is Your Achievement Motivation? Carol Dweck (1990) finds that achievement motivation can be driven by different forces. In the upcoming "Reflections" section, I ask you if you want to do well in this course. If you do, why is that so? Are you mainly motivated by performance goals? That is, is the course grade the key to you? If it is, it may be in part because your motives concern tangible rewards such as getting into graduate school, getting a good job, reaping approval from parents or your instructor, or averting criticism. Or are you motivated mainly by learning goals? Is your central motive the enhancing of your knowledge and skills—your abilities to understand and master the subject matter? Performance goals in life are usually met through extrinsic rewards—for example, a good income and prestige. Learning goals usually lead to intrinsic rewards, such as personal self-satisfaction. Many of us strive to meet both performance and learning goals in many subjects, and in other areas of life.

Development of Achievement Motivation. Parents with strong achievement motivation tend to encourage their children to think and act independently from an early age. In terms of schoolwork, parents help children develop learning goals by encouraging persistence, enjoyment, and independence in schoolwork (Ginsburg & Bronstein, 1993; Gottfried and others, 1994). They expose their children to new, stimulating experiences. Parents of children who develop performance goals are more likely to reward children with toys or money for getting good grades and to respond to poor grades with anger and the removal of privileges (Ginsburg & Bronstein, 1993; Gottfried and others, 1994). Parents of children with strong achievement motivation also show warmth and praise their children profusely for their accomplishments. Children of such parents frequently set high standards for themselves, associate their achievements with self-

worth, and come to attribute their achievements to their own efforts rather than to chance or to the intervention of others (Dweck, 1990; Ginsburg & Bronstein, 1993).

AFFILIATION: "PEOPLE WHO NEED PEOPLE"

The motive for **affiliation** prompts us to make friends, join groups, and to prefer to do things with others rather than go it alone. Affiliation motivation contributes to the social glue that creates families and civilizations. In this sense, it is certainly a positive trait. Yet, some people have such a strong need to affiliate that they find it painful to make their own decisions or to be in solitude. Research by Stanley Schachter suggests that a very high need to affiliate may indicate anxiety, such as when people "huddle together" in fear of some outside force.

In a classic experiment on the effects of anxiety on affiliation, Schachter (1959) manipulated study participants' anxiety levels by leading them to believe that they would receive either painful electric shocks (the high-anxiety condition) or mild electric shocks (the low-anxiety condition). Participants were then asked to wait while the shock apparatus was supposedly being set up. They could choose to wait alone or in a room with others. The majority (63%) of those who expected a painful shock chose to wait in a room with other people. Only one third (33%) of those who expected a mild shock chose to wait with others.

Truth or Fiction Revisited. *Schachter found that misery does love company—but only company of a special sort.* Highly anxious study participants were placed in two social conditions. In the first, they could choose either to wait alone or with others who would also receive painful shocks. Sixty percent of these people chose to affiliate—that is, to wait with others. In the second condition, highly anxious participants could choose to wait alone or with people they believed were not involved with the study. In this second condition, no one chose to affiliate.

Why did those in Schachter's study wish to affiliate only with people who shared

Affiliation • Association or connection with a group.

Theory of social comparison • The view that people look to others for cues about how to behave when they are in confusing or unfamiliar situations.

their misery? Schachter explained their choice through the **theory of social comparison.** This theory holds that in an ambiguous situation—that is, a situation in which we are not certain about what we should do or how we should feel—we will affiliate with people with whom we can compare feelings and behaviors. Schachter's anxious recruits could compare their reactions with those of other "victims," but not with people who had no reason to feel anxious. Anxious participants may also have resented uninvolved people for "getting away free."

AGGRESSION: SOME FACTS OF LIFE AND DEATH

Ponder some facts of life, and death:

- Following the demise of the cold war and the Soviet Union, you might have expected the world to become more peaceful. Yet civil wars and other conflicts rage on every continent.

- In the United States, violence replaced communicable diseases as the leading cause of death among young people during the past generation. Homicide has become the second-leading cause of death, following accidents, among 15- to 24-year-olds (Lore & Schultz, 1993).

- Aggression is not limited to foreign battlefields or dark streets and alleyways. Each year, more than a million U.S. children are brought to the attention of authorities as victims of child abuse.

- The video games *Mortal Kombat* and *Night Trap* are best-sellers with U.S. children. In *Mortal Kombat,* the player can decapitate the loser. In *Night Trap,* the player attempts to prevent a gang of vampires from capturing scantily clad sorority sisters. If the player fails, the vampires drain the women's blood from their necks.

Why do people treat each other like this? Let us consider some theories of aggression.

The Biological Perspective. Numerous biological structures and chemicals appear to be involved in aggression. One is the hypothalamus. In response to releasers, many lower animals show instinctive aggressive reactions. The hypothalamus appears to be involved in this inborn reaction pattern: Electrical stimulation of part of the hypothalamus triggers stereotypical aggressive behaviors in many lower animals. In people, however, whose brains are more complex, other brain structures apparently moderate possible instincts.

An offshoot of the biological perspective called *sociobiology* suggests that aggression is natural and even desirable for people. Sociobiology views much social behavior, including aggressive behavior, as genetically determined. Consider Darwin's theory of evolution. Darwin held that many more individuals are produced than can find food and survive into adulthood (Solomon and others, 1993). Therefore, a struggle for survival ensues. Those individuals who possess characteristics that provide them with an advantage in the struggle for existence are more likely to survive and contribute their genes to the next generation. In many species, such characteristics include aggressiveness. Because aggressive individuals are more likely to survive and reproduce, whatever genes are linked to aggressive behavior are more likely to be transmitted to subsequent generations.

The sociobiological view has been attacked on numerous grounds. One is that people's intelligence (their capacity to outwit other species), not their aggressiveness, appears to be the dominant factor in human survival. Another is that there is too much variation among and within societies to believe that people are dominated by, or at the mercy of, aggressive impulses. Finally, sociobiology seems to suggest that aggression is natural and desirable. Thus, efforts to control aggression can be seen as doomed to failure, even as morally questionable in that they interfere with the "natural order."

The Psychodynamic Perspective. Sigmund Freud believed that aggressive impulses were inevitable reactions to the frustrations of daily life. Children (and adults) normally desire to vent aggressive impulses on other people, including parents, because even the most attentive parents cannot gratify all of their demands immediately. Children, also fearing their parents' retribution and loss of love, come to repress most aggressive impulses. The Freudian perspective, in a sense, sees us as "steam engines." By holding in rather than venting "steam," we set the stage for future explosions. Pent-up aggressive impulses demand outlets. They may be expressed toward parents in roundabout ways such as destroying furniture, or they may be expressed toward strangers later in life.

According to psychodynamic theory, the best ways to prevent harmful aggression may be to encourage less harmful aggression. In the steam-engine analogy, verbal aggression (as through wit, sarcasm, or expression of negative feelings) may vent some of the aggressive steam in the unconscious. So might cheering on one's football team or attending prize fights. Psychoanalysts refer to the venting of aggressive impulses as **catharsis.** Catharsis is theorized to be a safety valve. But research findings on the usefulness of catharsis are mixed. Some studies suggest that catharsis leads to pleasant reductions in tension and a lowered likelihood of future aggression (e.g., Doob & Wood, 1972). Other studies, however, suggest that letting some steam escape actually encourages more aggression later on (e.g., Geen and others, 1975).

The Cognitive Perspective. Cognitive psychologists assert that our behavior is influenced by our values, by the ways in which we interpret our situations, and by choice. From the cognitive perspective, for example, people who believe that aggression is necessary and justified—as during wartime—are likely to act aggressively. People who believe that a particular war or act of aggression is unjust, or who universally oppose aggression, are less likely to behave aggressively (Feshbach, 1994).

One cognitive theory suggests that aggravating and painful events trigger unpleasant feelings (Rule and others, 1987). These feelings, in turn, prompt aggression. Aggression is *not* automatic, however. Cognitive factors intervene (Berkowitz, 1994). People *decide* whether they will strike out or not on the basis of factors such as their experiences with aggression and their interpretation of the other person's motives.

Researchers find that many aggressive people distort other people's motives. For example, they assume that other people mean them ill when they do not (Akhtar &

Bradley, 1991; Crick & Dodge, 1994; Dodge and others, 1990). Similarly, some date rapists tend to misread women's expressed wishes (e.g., Lipton and others, 1987; Malamuth and others, 1991).

Cognitively oriented psychotherapists note that we are more likely to respond aggressively to a provocation when we magnify the importance of the insult or otherwise stir up feelings of anger (e.g., Lochman, 1992; Lochman & Dodge, 1994).

Learning Perspectives. From the behavioral perspective, learning is acquired through principles of reinforcement. Organisms that are reinforced for aggressive behavior are more likely to behave aggressively in similar situations. Environmental consequences make it more likely that strong, agile organisms will be reinforced for aggressive behavior.

From the social-cognitive perspective, aggressive skills are acquired largely by observing others. Social-cognitive theorists, however, find roles for consciousness and choice. They believe that we are not likely to act aggressively unless we believe that aggression is appropriate under the circumstances.

The Sociocultural Perspective. The sociocultural perspective focuses on matters of ethnicity and gender in aggression. Note the following facts:

- African American men aged 15 to 34 are about 9 times as likely as non-Hispanic White Americans to be victims of homicide (Tomes, 1993).
- Hispanic American men are about 5 times as likely to be homicide victims (Tomes, 1993).
- Each year in the United States about 30 women per 1,000 are victims of violence at the hands of their male partners (Tomes, 1993).
- Perhaps half the women in the United States have been battered—that is, subjected to severe physical, sexual, or psychological abuse (Walker, 1993).

Sociocultural theorists note that U.S. culture—like the culture of the Mundugumor—has a way of breeding violence. For example, the countries of Thailand and

---

Catharsis • In psychodynamic theory, the purging of strong emotions or the relieving of tensions. (A Greek word meaning "purification.")

Emotion • A state of feeling that has cognitive, physiological, and behavioral components.

Sympathetic • Of the sympathetic division of the autonomic nervous system.

Parasympathetic • Of the parasympathetic division of the autonomic nervous system.

Jamaica discourage aggression in children and foster politeness and deference (Tharp, 1991). In the United States, by contrast, competitiveness, independence, and differentiation are widely encouraged. In Thailand and Jamaica, then, children are more likely to be "overcontrolled" and complain of sleeping problems, fears, and physical problems. In the United States, children are more likely to be "undercontrolled"—argumentative, disobedient, and belligerent (Tharp, 1991).

Reflections

Now that you have read the section on achievement, affiliation, and aggression, reflect on the following questions:

- Do you want to do well in this course? How hard will you strive to do well? How would you rate your own level of achievement motivation? When you consider your own life experiences, where does the achievement motivation (or lack of it) seem to come from?
- Do you feel a strong need to make friends, join groups, and do things with other people? Why or why not?
- Do you seem to be more in need of being around other people when you are upset about something? If so, why?
- What were your beliefs about why some people are more aggressive than others before you began this course? How has the information in this course, particularly in this chapter, affected your views? In what way?
- What do you think are the best ways to deal with aggressive criminals or aggressive nations? Why?

Emotion: Adding Color to Life

Emotions color our lives. We are green with envy, red with anger, blue with sorrow. The poets paint a thoughtful mood as a brown study. Positive emotions such as love and desire can fill our days with pleasure. Negative emotions such as fear, depression, and anger can fill us with dread and make each day a chore.

An emotion can at once be a response to a situation (in the way that fear is a response to a threat) and motivate behavior (in the way that anger can motivate us to act aggressively). An emotion can also be a goal in itself. We may behave in ways that will lead us to experience joy or feelings of love.

Emotions are states of feeling that have cognitive, physiological, and behavioral components (Carlson & Hatfield, 1992; Fischer and others, 1990; Haaland, 1992). Many strong emotions spark activity in the autonomic nervous system (LeDoux, 1986). Fear, which usually occurs in response to a threat, involves cognitions that one is in danger, predominantly **sympathetic** arousal (rapid heartbeat and breathing, sweating, muscle tension), and tendencies to avoid or escape from the situation (see Table 10.1). As a response to a social provocation, anger involves cognitions that a provocateur should be paid back, both sympathetic and **parasympathetic** arousal, and tendencies to attack. Depression usually involves cognitions of helplessness and hopelessness, predominantly parasympathetic arousal, and behavioral tendencies toward inactivity—or, sometimes—self-destruction. Joy, grief, jealousy, disgust, embarrassment, liking—all

TABLE 10.1

Components of Three Common Emotions

EMOTION	COMPONENTS		
	COGNITIVE	PHYSIOLOGICAL	BEHAVIORAL
Fear	Belief that one is in danger	Sympathetic arousal	Avoidance tendencies
Anger	Frustration or belief that one is being mistreated	Sympathetic and para-sympathetic arousal	Attack tendencies
Depression	Thoughts of helplessness, hopelessness, worthlessness	Parasympathetic arousal	Inactivity, possible self-destructive tendencies

have cognitive, physiological, and behavioral components. Generally speaking, the greater the autonomic arousal, the more intense the emotion (Chwalisz and others, 1988).

The connection between autonomic arousal and emotions has led to the development of many kinds of "lie detectors." Such instruments detect something, but do they detect specific emotional responses that signify lies?

AROUSAL, EMOTIONS, AND LIE DETECTION

One may smile, and smile, and be a villain.
SHAKESPEARE, HAMLET

Lying—for better and for worse—is an integral part of life (Saxe, 1991a). Political leaders lie to get elected. Some students lie about why they have not completed assignments (Greene & Saxe, 1990). ('Fess up!) The great majority of us lie to our lovers—most often about other relationships (Shusterman & Saxe, 1990). (Is it really true that you never held anyone's hand before?) People also lie about their qualifications to obtain jobs and, of course, to deny guilt for crimes. Although we are unlikely to subject our political leaders, students, and lovers to "lie detector" tests, such tests are frequently used in hiring and police investigative work.

Facial expressions often offer clues to deceit, but some people can lie with a straight face—or a smile. The use of devices to detect lies has a long, if not laudable, history:

> The Bedouins of Arabia . . . until quite recently required conflicting witnesses to lick a hot iron; the one whose tongue was burned was thought to be lying. The Chinese, it is said, had a similar method for detecting lying: Suspects were forced to chew rice powder and spit it out; if the powder was dry, the suspect was guilty. A variation of this test was used during the Inquisition. The suspect had to swallow a "trial slice" of bread and cheese; if it stuck to the suspect's palate or throat he or she was not telling the truth. (Kleinmuntz & Szucko, 1984, pp. 766–67)

These methods may sound primitive, even bizarre, but they are broadly consistent with modern psychological knowledge. Anxiety concerning being caught in a lie is linked to arousal of the sympathetic division of the autonomic nervous system. One sign of sympathetic arousal is lack of saliva, or dryness in the mouth. The emotions of fear and guilt are also linked to sympathetic arousal and, hence, dryness in the mouth.

Modern lie detectors, or polygraphs (see Figure 10.7), monitor indicators of sympathetic arousal while a witness or suspect is being examined: heart rate, blood pressure, respiration rate, and electrodermal response (sweating). But questions have been raised about the validity of the polygraph.

The American Polygraph Association (1992) claims that the polygraph is 85% to 95% accurate. Critics, however, find polygraphs less accurate and sensitive to more than lies (Bashore & Rapp, 1993; Furedy, 1990; Saxe, 1991b; Steinbrook, 1992). Studies have found that factors such as tensing muscles, drugs, and previous experience with polygraph tests all significantly reduce the accuracy rate (Steinbrook, 1992). In one experiment, people were able to reduce the accuracy rate to about 50% by biting their tongues (to produce pain) or pressing their toes against the floor (to tense muscles) while being interviewed (Honts and others, 1985).

FIGURE 10.7
What Do "Lie Detectors" Detect? The polygraph monitors heart rate, blood pressure, respiration rate, and sweat in the palms of the hands. Is the polygraph sensitive to lying only? Is it foolproof? Because of the controversy surrounding these questions, many courts no longer admit polygraph evidence.

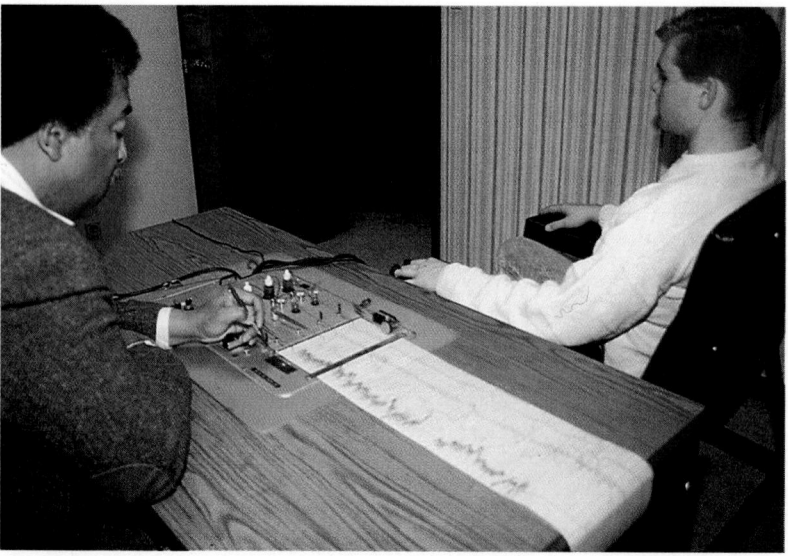

Truth or Fiction Revisited. *It is true that you may be able to fool a lie detector by squiggling your toes.* Squiggling creates patterns of autonomic arousal that may be misread by interpreters of polygraphs.

In a review of the literature, the government Office of Technology Assessment (OTA) found that there was little valid research into the use of the polygraph in preemployment screening, "dragnet" investigations (attempts to ferret out the guilty from many subjects), or determining who should be given access to classified information (U.S. Congress, 1983). OTA also looked into studies involving investigations of specific indictments. The studies' conclusions varied widely. In 28 studies judged to have adequate methodology, accurate detections of guilt ranged from 35% to 100%. Accurate judgments of innocence ranged from 12.5% to 94%.

In sum, no identifiable pattern of autonomic arousal has been connected with lying, and with lying alone (Bashore & Rapp, 1993; Saxe, 1991b; Steinbrook, 1992). Because of validity problems, results of polygraph examinations are no longer admitted as evidence in many courts. Polygraph interviews are still often conducted in criminal investigations and in job interviews, but these practices are also being questioned. Bashore and Rapp (1993) suggest that measures of electrical brain activity might be found to be more accurate than the polygraph.

HOW MANY EMOTIONS ARE THERE? WHERE DO THEY COME FROM?

The ancient Chinese believed that there were four basic or instinctive emotions—happiness, anger, sorrow, and fear. They arose, respectively, in the heart, liver, lungs, and kidneys (Carlson & Hatfield, 1992). (No, there is no evidence for this view.) Behaviorist John B. Watson (1924) believed that there were three basic or inborn emotions: fear, rage, and love. Others, such as Paul Ekman (1980, 1992) and Robert Plutchik (1984) have argued for somewhat larger numbers of basic emotions (see Figure 10.8). The question remains unresolved (Fischer and others, 1990).

In 1932, Katherine Bridges proposed that people are born with a single basic emotion—diffuse excitement—and that other

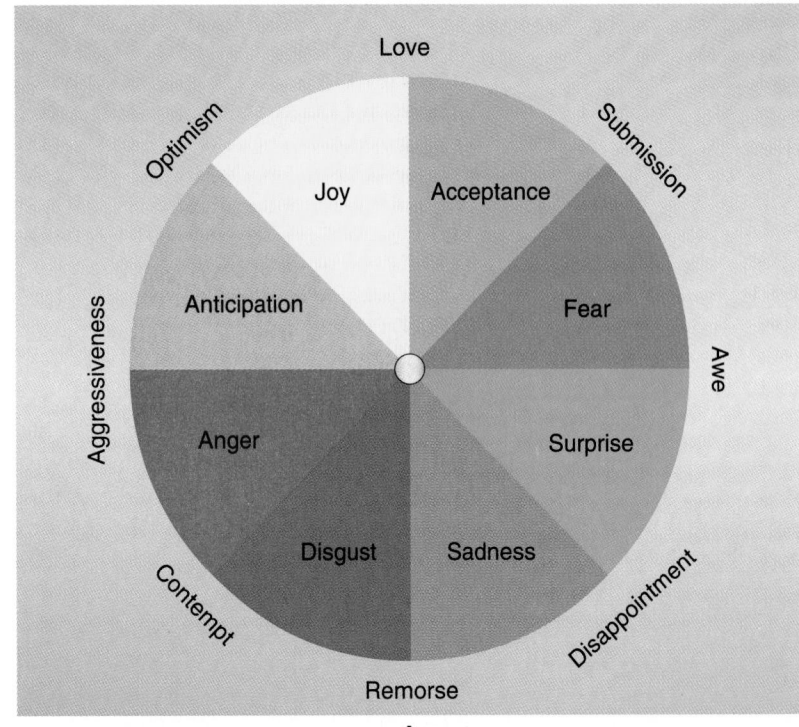

A

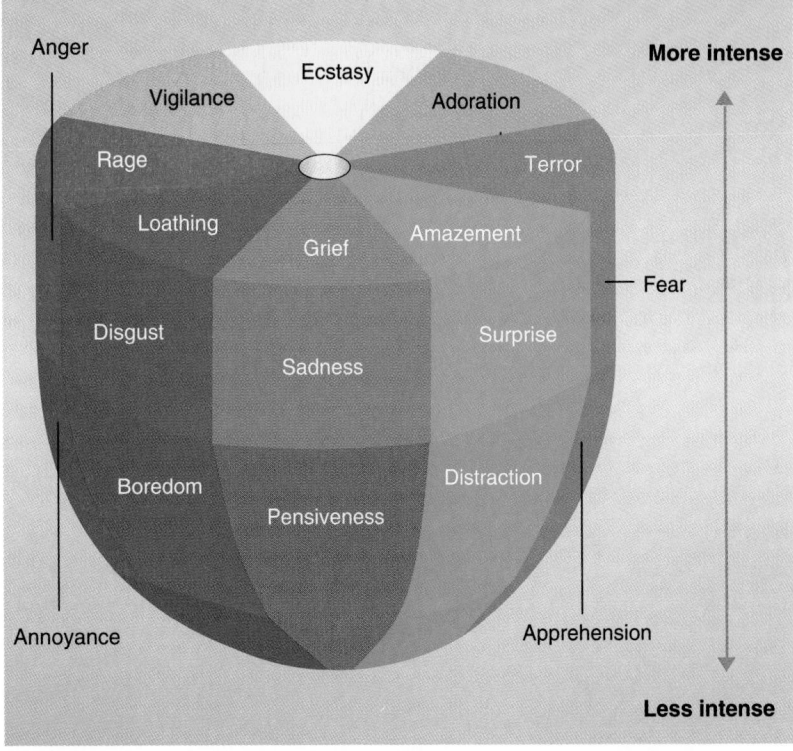

B

FIGURE 10.8
Plutchik's Theory of Emotions Part A shows Plutchik's "circle of emotions." Plutchik theorizes that there are eight basic, or primary, emotions. Secondary emotions such as love are derived from combinations of primary emotions—in this case, joy and acceptance. Part B shows Plutchik's "emotion solid." The vertical axis of this toplike figure represents degrees of emotional intensity. Intensity increases as we journey upward. Anger is more tense than the related emotion of annoyance, and rage is more intense still.

emotions become differentiated as children develop. Carroll Izard (1984, 1990, 1992) more recently argued that all emotions are present and differentiated at birth. However, they are not exhibited all at once. Instead, they emerge in response to the child's developing needs and maturational sequences. In keeping with Izard's view, researchers have found that infants appear to show a number of different emotions at ages earlier than those suggested by Bridges. In one study of the emotions shown by babies during their first 3 months, 99% of the mothers interviewed reported that their babies showed the emotion of interest. Ninety-five percent of mothers reported joy; 84%, anger; 74%, surprise; and 58%, fear (Johnson and others, 1982).

THE EXPRESSION OF EMOTIONS

There's no art
To find the mind's construction in the face.
SHAKESPEARE, *MACBETH*

Joy and sadness are found in diverse cultures around the world, but how can we tell when other people are happy or despondent? It turns out that the expression of many emotions may be universal (Rinn, 1991). Smiling is apparently a universal sign of friendliness and approval. Baring the teeth, as noted by Charles Darwin (1872) in the last century, may be a universal sign of anger. As the originator of the theory of

evolution, Darwin believed that the universal recognition of facial expressions would have survival value. For example, facial expressions could signal the approach of enemies (or friends) in the absence of language.

Most investigators (e.g., Brown, 1991; Buss, 1992; Ekman, 1992, 1994; Izard, 1992, 1994) concur that certain facial expressions suggest the same emotions in all people. Moreover, people in diverse cultures recognize the emotions manifested by the facial expressions. In classic research, Paul Ekman (1980) took photographs of people exhibiting the emotions of anger, disgust, fear, happiness, sadness, and surprise, similar to those shown in Figure 10.9. He then asked people around the world to indicate what emotions were being depicted. Those queried ranged from European college students to members of the Fore, a tribe that dwells in the New Guinea highlands. All groups, including the Fore, who had almost no contact with Western culture, agreed on the portrayed emotions. The Fore also displayed familiar facial expressions when asked how they would respond if they were the characters in stories that called for basic emotional responses. Ekman and his colleagues (1987) more recently obtained similar results in a study of 10 cultures in which participants were permitted to report that multiple emotions were shown by facial expressions. The participants generally agreed on which two emotions were being shown and which emotion was most intense.

FIGURE 10.9
Photographs Used in Research by Paul Ekman Ekman's research suggests that the expression of several basic emotions—such as happiness, anger, surprise, and fear—is universally recognized.

 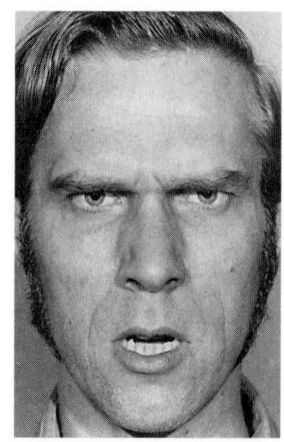 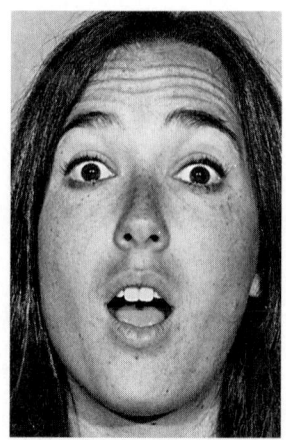 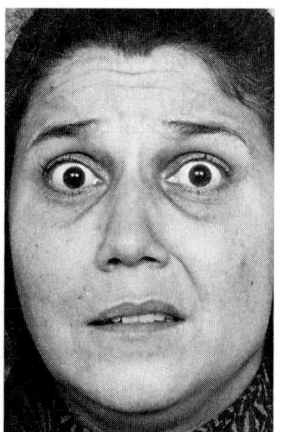

THE FACIAL-FEEDBACK HYPOTHESIS

We generally recognize that facial expressions reflect emotional states. In fact, various emotional states give rise to certain patterns of electrical activity in the facial muscles and in the brain (Cacioppo and others, 1988; Ekman and others, 1990).

The **facial-feedback hypothesis** argues, however, that the causal relationship between emotions and facial expressions can also work in the opposite direction. Consider Darwin's words:

> The free expression by outward signs of an emotion intensifies it. On the other hand, the repression, as far as possible, of all outward signs softens our emotions. (Darwin, 1872, p. 22)

Can smiling give rise to feelings of goodwill, for example, or frowning, to anger?

Psychological research has given rise to some interesting findings concerning the facial-feedback hypothesis. Inducing participants in experiments to smile, for example, leads them to report more positive feelings (Ekman, 1993b) and to rate cartoons as being more humorous (Laird, 1974). When induced to frown, they rate cartoons as being more aggressive (Laird, 1974). When participants pose expressions of pain, they rate electric shocks as being more painful (Colby and others, 1977; Lanzetta and others, 1976).

What are the possible links between facial feedback and emotion? One link is arousal. Intense contraction of facial muscles such as those used in signifying fear heightens arousal (Zuckerman and others, 1981). Self-perception of heightened arousal then leads to heightened emotional activity. Other links may involve changes in brain temperature and the release of neurotransmitters (Zajonc, 1985). Kinesthetic feedback of the contraction of facial muscles may also induce feeling states. Ekman (1993b) has found that the so-called Duchenne smile, which is characterized by "crow's feet wrinkles around the eyes and a subtle drop in the eye cover fold so that the skin above the eye moves down slightly toward the eyeball," can induce pleasant feelings.

Truth or Fiction Revisited. *It is true that smiling can produce pleasant feelings.* Research has shown that the Duchenne smile can indeed give rise to pleasant feelings.

You may have heard the British expression "keep a stiff upper lip" as a recommendation for handling stress. It might be that a "stiff" lip suppresses emotional response—as long as the lip is relaxed rather than quivering with fear or tension. But when a lip is stiffened through strong muscle tension, facial feedback may heighten emotional response. In the following section, we see that the facial-feedback hypothesis is related to the James–Lange theory of emotion.

THEORIES OF EMOTION: *IS* FEELING FIRST?

In Chapter 8, we asked you to consider the syntax of the following lines from an e. e. cummings poem:

since feeling is first
who pays any attention
to the syntax of things
will never wholly kiss you . . .

Now let us address the subject matter of the poem—no, not the kiss, but the question, *Does* feeling, in fact, come first?

Emotions have physiological, situational, and cognitive components, but psychologists have disagreed about how these components interact to produce feeling states and actions. Some psychologists argue that physiological arousal ("feeling" in the cummings poem) is a more basic component of emotional response than cognition and that the type of arousal we experience strongly influences our cognitive appraisal and our labeling of the emotion (e.g., Izard, 1984; Zajonc, 1984). For these psychologists, "feeling is first." Other psychologists argue that cognitive appraisal and physiological arousal are so strongly intertwined that one's cognitive processes may determine the emotional response (e.g., Lazarus, 1984, 1991a).

The "commonsense theory" of emotions is that something happens (situation) that is cognitively appraised (interpreted) by the person and the feeling state (a combination of arousal and thoughts) follows. For example, you meet someone new, appraise that person as being delightful, and feelings of

Facial-feedback hypothesis • The view that stereotypical facial expressions can contribute to stereotypical emotions.

MINILECTURE: THEORIES OF EMOTION

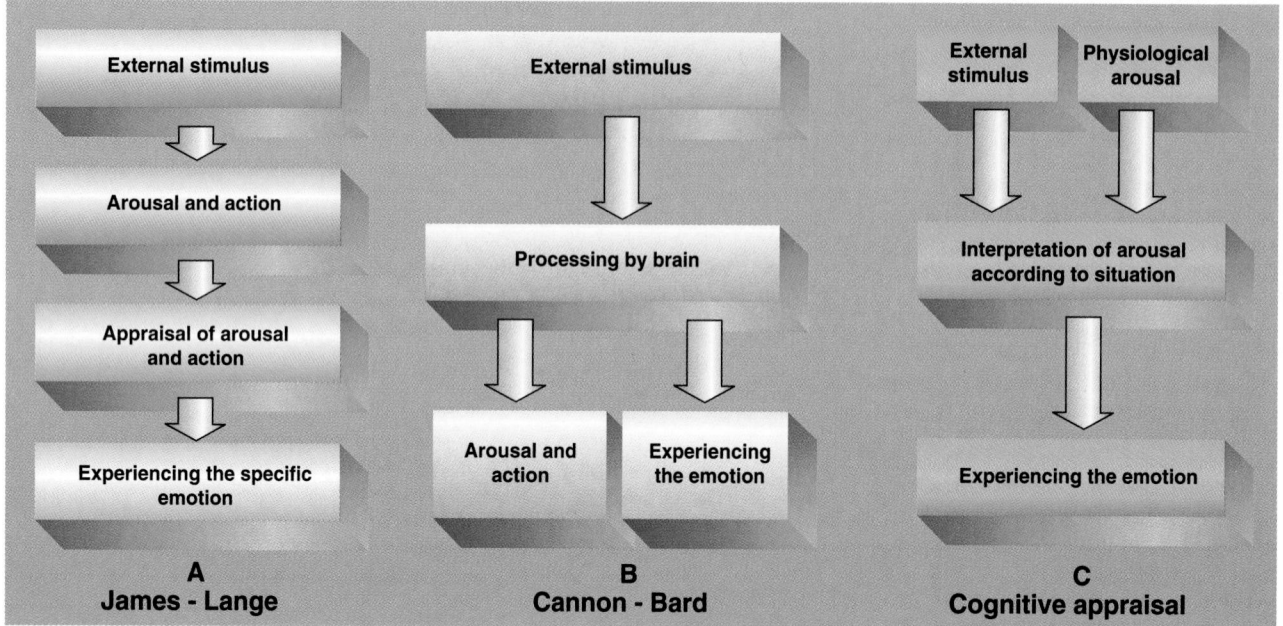

FIGURE 10.10

Spotlight on the Major Theories of Emotion Several theories of emotion have been advanced, each of which proposes a different role for the components of emotional response. According to the James–Lange theory (part A), events trigger specific arousal patterns and actions. Emotions result from our appraisal of our body responses. According to the Cannon–Bard theory (part B), events are first processed by the brain. Body patterns of arousal, action, and our emotional responses are then triggered simultaneously. According to the theory of cognitive appraisal (part C), events and arousal are appraised by the individual. The emotional response stems from the person's appraisal of the situation and his or her level of arousal.

attraction follow. Or you flunk a test, recognize that you're in trouble, and feel down in the dumps.

However, historic and contemporary theories of how the components of emotions interact are at variance with the common-sense view. Let us consider a number of more important theories and see if we can arrive at some useful conclusions.

The James–Lange Theory. At the turn of the century, William James suggested that our emotions follow, rather than cause, our behavioral responses to events. This view was also proposed by a contemporary of James's, the Danish physiologist Karl G. Lange. It is thus termed the James–Lange theory of emotion.

According to James and Lange (see Figure 10.10, part A), certain external stimuli instinctively trigger specific patterns of arousal and action such as fighting or fleeing. We then become angry *because* we act

aggressively. We then become afraid *because* we run away. Emotions are simply the cognitive representations (or by-products) of automatic physiological and behavioral responses.

Walter Cannon (1927) criticized the James–Lange assertion that each emotion has distinct physiological correlates. Cannon argued that the physiological arousal that accompanies emotion A is not as distinct from the arousal that accompanies emotion B as the theory asserts. We can also note that the James–Lange view ascribes a very meager function to human cognition; it denies the roles of cognitive appraisal, personal values, and personal choice.

On the other hand, the James–Lange theory is consistent with the facial-feedback hypothesis. That is, smiling apparently can induce pleasant feelings, "even though we don't know if the effect is strong enough to override sadness" (Ekman, 1993b). The theory also suggests that we may be able to change our feelings by changing our behavior. Changing one's behavior to change one's feelings is one aspect of behavior therapy, which is discussed in Chapter 14.

The Cannon–Bard Theory. Walter Cannon was not content to criticize the James–Lange theory. He (Cannon, 1927) and Philip Bard (1934) suggested that an event would trigger bodily responses (arousal and action) and the experience of an emotion simultaneously. As shown in Figure 10.10 (part B), when an event is perceived (processed by the brain), the brain stimulates autonomic and muscular activity (arousal and action) *and* cognitive activity (experience of the emotion). According to the Cannon–Bard theory, emotions *accompany* bodily responses. Emotions are not *produced by* bodily changes, as in the James–Lange theory.

The central criticism of the Cannon–Bard theory focuses on whether bodily responses (arousal and action) and emotions are actually stimulated simultaneously. For example, pain or the perception of danger may trigger arousal before we begin to feel distress or fear. Also, many of us have had the experience of having a "narrow escape" and then becoming aroused and shaky afterward, when we have finally had time to consider the damage that might have occurred.

What is needed is a theory that allows for an ongoing interaction of external events, physiological changes (such as autonomic arousal and muscular activity), and cognitive activities.

The Theory of Cognitive Appraisal. Recent theoretical approaches to emotion have stressed cognitive factors. Among those psychologists who argue that thinking comes first are Gordon Bower, Richard Lazarus, Stanley Schachter, and Robert Zajonc.

Stanley Schachter (1971) asserts that emotions have generally similar patterns of bodily arousal. The essential way in which they vary is along a weak–strong dimension that is determined by one's level of arousal. The label we give to an emotion largely depends on our cognitive appraisal of our situation. Cognitive appraisal is based on many factors, including our perception of external events and the ways in which other people seem to respond to those events (see Figure 10.10, part C). Given the presence of other people, we engage in social comparison to arrive at an appropriate response.

In a classic experiment, Schachter and Singer (1962) showed that arousal can be labeled quite differently, depending on a person's situation. The investigators told study participants that their purpose was to study the effects of a vitamin on vision. Half of the participants received an injection of adrenaline, a hormone that increases autonomic arousal (see Chapter 3). A control group received an injection of an inactive solution. Those given adrenaline then received one of three "cognitive manipulations," as shown in Table 10.2. Group 1 was told nothing about possible emotional effects of the "vitamin." Group 2 was deliberately misinformed; group members were led to expect itching, numbness, or other irrelevant symptoms. Group 3 was informed accurately about the increased arousal they would experience.

After receiving injections and cognitive manipulations, study participants were asked to wait, in pairs, while the experimental apparatus was being set up. Participants did not know that the person with whom they

TABLE 10.2

Injected Substances and Cognitive Manipulations in the Schachter–Singer Study

GROUP	SUBSTANCE	COGNITIVE MANIPULATION
1	Adrenaline	No information given about effects
2	Adrenaline	Misinformation given: itching, numbness, etc.
3	Adrenaline	Accurate information: physiological arousal
4	(Inactive)	None

Source: Schachter & Singer (1962).

were waiting was a confederate of the experimenter. The confederate's purpose was to model a response that the participant would believe resulted from the injection.

Some who took part in the experiment waited with a confederate who acted in a happy-go-lucky manner. He flew paper airplanes about the room and tossed paper balls into a wastebasket. Other participants-subjects waited with a confederate who acted angry, complaining about the experiment, tearing up a questionnaire, and departing the waiting room in a huff. As the confederates worked for their Oscars, the real participants were observed through a one-way mirror.

The people in groups 1 and 2 were likely to imitate the behavior of the confederate. Those exposed to the **euphoric** confederate acted jovial and content. Those exposed to the angry confederate imitated that person's complaining, aggressive ways. But those in groups 3 and 4 were less influenced by the confederate's behavior.

Schachter and Singer concluded that those in groups 1 and 2 were in an ambiguous situation. Members of these groups felt arousal from the adrenaline injection but had no basis for attributing it to any event or emotion. Social comparison with the confederate led them to attribute their arousal either to happiness or to anger, whichever was displayed by the confederate. Group 3 members expected arousal from the injection with no particular emotional consequences. These people did not imitate the confederate's display of happiness or anger because they were not in an ambiguous situation. Group 4 members had no physiological arousal for which they needed an attribution, except perhaps for some induced by observing the confederate. Group 4 members also failed to imitate the confederate.

Now, happiness and anger are quite different emotions. Happiness is a positive emotion, and anger, for most of us, is a negative emotion. Yet, Schachter and Singer suggest that any physiological differences between these two emotions are so slight that opposing cognitive appraisals of the same situation can lead one person to label arousal as happiness and another person to label arousal as anger. The Schachter–Singer

view could not be further removed from the James–Lange theory, which holds that each emotion has specific and readily recognized body sensations.

The truth, it happens, may lie somewhere in between.

In science, it must be possible to replicate experiments and attain identical or similar results. The Schachter and Singer study has been replicated with *different* results, however (Ekman, 1993a). For instance, a number of studies found that participants were less likely to imitate the behavior of the confederate and were likely to perceive unexplained arousal in negative terms such as nervousness, anger, even jealousy (Zimbardo and others, 1993).

Evaluation. What do we make of all this? Research by Paul Ekman and his colleagues (1983) suggests that the patterns of arousal that lead us to believe we are experiencing certain emotions are apparently more specific than suggested by Schachter and Singer—although less specific than suggested by James and Lange. It seems that there are some reasonably distinct patterns of arousal. Moreover, lack of control over our emotions and lack of understanding of what is happening to us appear to be disturbing experiences (Zimbardo and others, 1993). Thus our cognitive appraisals of our situations apparently do affect our emotional responses, even if not quite in the way envisioned by Schachter.

In sum, various components of an experience—cognitive, physiological, and behavioral—contribute to our emotional responses. People are thinking beings who gather information from all three sources in determining their behavioral responses and labeling their emotional responses. The fact that none of the theories we have discussed applies to all people in all situations is comforting. Our emotions are not quite as easily understood or manipulated as some theorists have suggested.

Reflections

Now that you have read the section on emotion, reflect on the following questions:

• Do you know people whom you consider to be highly emotional? What behavior

---

Euphoric • Characterized by feelings of well-being, elation.

patterns lead you to infer that they are emotional?

- Have you ever tried to discern whether someone was lying to you? What types of clues did you look for? Do you think that you were successful in determining the truth? Can you "keep a straight face"

when you lie? What does the expression *to keep a straight face* mean?

- Have you had any experiences that seem to support one of the theories of emotion presented in the chapter? What were they? Which theory do they seem to support?

Summary

1. **What are motives, needs, drives, and incentives?** A motive is a state within an organism that activates and directs behavior toward a goal. A physiological need is a state of deprivation. Needs give rise to drives, which are psychological in nature and arouse us to action. An incentive is perceived as being capable of satisfying a need.

2. **What are some psychological theories of motivation?** According to instinct theory, organisms are born with preprogrammed tendencies to behave in certain ways in certain situations. According to drive-reduction theory, we are motivated to engage in behavior that reduces drives. Humanistic psychologists argue that behavior can be growth-oriented; people are motivated to consciously strive for self-fulfillment. Maslow hypothesized that people have a hierarchy of needs, including an innate need for self-actualization. According to cognitive theory, people are motivated to understand and predict events and to make cognitions harmonious.

3. **What are physiological drives?** Physiological, or primary, drives are unlearned and generally function according to a homeostatic principle—the body's tendency to maintain a steady state.

4. **What factors give rise to the hunger drive?** Hunger is regulated by several internal mechanisms, including stomach contractions, blood-sugar level, receptors in the mouth and liver, and the responses of the hypothalamus. The ventromedial hypothalamus functions as a stop-eating center. Lesions in this area lead to hyperphagia in rats,

causing the animals to grow to several times their normal body weight, but their weight eventually levels off. The lateral hypothalamus has a start-eating center. External stimuli such as the aroma of food can also trigger hunger.

5. **What are the effects of sex hormones?** Sex hormones promote biological sexual differentiation, regulate the menstrual cycle, and have organizing (directional) and activating (motivational) effects on sexual behavior.

6. **What is sexual orientation?** One's sexual orientation is the direction of one's erotic interests. Gay males and lesbians are sexually aroused by, and interested in forming romantic relationships with, people of their own gender. Promising hypotheses concerning the origins of sexual orientation point to roles for genetic factors, prenatal hormonal influences, and socialization.

7. **What are stimulus motives?** Stimulus motives, like physiological motives, are innate, but they involve motives to increase rather than decrease stimulation. Sensory-deprivation studies show that lack of stimulation is aversive. People and many lower animals have needs for stimulation and activity, for exploration and manipulation. Sensation-seekers may seek thrills, act out on impulses, and be easily bored.

8. **Do people seek cognitive consistency?** According to balance theory, we are motivated to maintain harmony among our perceptions, beliefs, and attitudes. When people we care about express attitudes that differ from ours, we are in a state of imbalance and are motivated to try to restore the balance.

Cognitive-dissonance theory also hypothesizes that people dislike inconsistency between their attitudes and their behavior. Attitude-discrepant behavior apparently induces cognitive dissonance, which people can then reduce by changing their attitudes. People also engage in effort justification; that is, they tend to justify attitude-discrepant behavior to themselves by concluding that their attitudes may differ from what they thought they were.

9. **What is achievement motivation?** Achievement motivation is the need to accomplish things. People with high achievement motivation attain higher grades and earn more money than people of comparable ability with lower achievement motivation.

10. **What is the need for affiliation?** This is the need to be with other people. The need for affiliation prompts us to join groups and make friends. Anxiety tends to increase our need for affiliation, especially with people who share our predicaments.

11. **Why are people aggressive?** Diverse theories account for aggression in various ways. Sociobiological theory views aggression as instinctive and connected with evolution. Psychodynamic theory views aggression as stemming from inevitable frustrations. Learning theories view aggression as stemming from experience and reinforcement. Cognitive perspectives predict that people are aggressive when they see aggression as being appropriate for them.

12. **What is an emotion?** An emotion is a state of feeling with cognitive, physiological, and behavioral components. Emotions motivate behavior and also serve as goals.

13. **Are emotions expressed in the same way in different cultures?** They are according to Ekman, whose research shows that there are several basic emotions whose expression is recognized around the world.

14. **What is the facial-feedback hypothesis?** This is the view that exhibiting intense facial expressions can heighten emotional response. Evidence for the hypothesis is mixed.

15. **What is the James–Lange theory of the activation of emotions?** According to James–Lange theory, emotions have specific patterns of arousal and action that are triggered by certain external events. The emotion follows the behavioral response.

16. **What is the Cannon–Bard theory of the activation of emotions?** The Cannon–Bard theory proposes that processing of events by the brain gives rise simultaneously to feelings and bodily responses. According to this view, feelings accompany bodily responses.

17. **What is the cognitive-appraisal theory of the activation of emotions?** According to Schachter and Singer's theory of cognitive appraisal, emotions have largely similar patterns of arousal. The emotion a person will experience in response to an external stimulus reflects that person's appraisal of the stimulus—that is, the meaning of the stimulus to him or her.

18. **Does research support any of these theories?** Research seems to suggest that although patterns of arousal are more specific than suggested by the theory of cognitive appraisal, cognitive appraisal does play an important role in determining our responses to events.

Psychology and Modern Life

Obesity: Coping with a Serious and Pervasive Problem

There is no sincerer lover than the lover of food.
GEORGE BERNARD SHAW

The two biggest sellers in any bookstore are the cookbooks and the diet books. The cookbooks tell you how to prepare the food and the diet books tell you how not to eat any of it.
ANDY ROONEY

Obesity is one of the banes of modern life. For example, even though young Americans in the 1990s are eating a lower-fat diet than they were in the 1980s, they weigh 10 pounds more on the average than they did in the 1980s ("Despite Better Diets," 1994; see Table 10.3).

Truth or Fiction Revisited. *It is not true that young adults in the United States are trimmer in the 1990s than they were in the 1980s.* Although young Americans now eat less fat and their cholesterol levels are 9 points lower on the average, they actually weigh in, on average, at 10 pounds more. Eating more and exercising less are two of the reasons ("Despite Better Diets," 1994).

Here are some other facts about weight:

• One out of four American adults is obese—that is, weighs more than 20% above his or her recommended weight (Kuczmarski, 1992).

• Americans consume 815 billion calories of food each day, which is 200 billion calories more than they need to maintain their weight (Jenkins, 1988). The excess calories could feed a nation of 80 million people (Jenkins, 1988).

Truth or Fiction Revisited. *It is true that Americans overeat by enough to feed the nation of Germany.* They overeat by enough to feed another 80 million people!

• At any given time, 25% to 50% of the adult American population is on a diet (Bouchard, 1991).

• As compared with other women, overweight women are less likely to get married, have lower incomes, and complete fewer years of school (Gortmaker and others, 1993).

• Within a few years, the great majority of dieters regain most of the weight they have lost (Wilson, 1993).

This nation idealizes slender heroes and heroines. For those of us who "measure more than up" to TV and film idols, food may have replaced sex as the central source of guilt. Obese people encounter more than their fair share of illnesses, including heart disease, diabetes, gout, respiratory problems, even certain kinds of cancer (Leary, 1991; Manson and others, 1990). Obesity is also connected with psychological, social, and economic problems (Fitzgibbon and others, 1993; Stunkard & Sørensen, 1993). If obesity is connected with health problems and unhappiness with the image reflected in the mirror, why do so many people overeat? Psychological research has made major contributions to our knowledge concerning why so many people are obese and what can be done about it.

Heredity. Obesity runs in families. It used to be the conventional wisdom that obese parents encouraged their children to be overweight by having fattening foods in

TABLE 10.3

Snapshot, U.S.A.: Average Weight in Pounds of Americans Aged 25–30 in the 1980s versus the 1990s

	1985–1986	1992–1993	GAIN IN POUNDS
African American men	174.2	185.8	11.6
White men	171.1	181.9	10.8
African American women	158.5	166.2	7.7
White women	140.6	150.8	10.2

Based on a survey of 5,115 Americans.
Source of data: Cora E. Lewis, University of Alabama at Birmingham. Cited in "Despite Better Diets, Adults in Their 20s Are Weighing More," *The New York Times,* March 18, p. A17.

the house and setting poor examples. However, a study of Scandinavian adoptees by Stunkard and his colleagues (1990) found that children bear a closer resemblance in weight to their biological parents than to their adoptive parents. Heredity, then, plays a role.

Fat Cells. The efforts of obese people to maintain a slender profile might be sabotaged by microscopic units of life within their own bodies: fat cells. No, fat cells are not overweight cells. They are adipose tissue, or cells that store fat. Hunger might be related to the amount of fat stored in these cells. As time passes after a meal, the blood-sugar level drops. Fat is then drawn from these cells to provide further nourishment. At some point, referred to as the *set point,* the hypothalamus is signaled of the fat deficiency in these cells, triggering the hunger drive.

People with more adipose tissue than others feel food-deprived earlier, even though they may be equal in weight. This might be because more signals are being sent to the brain. Obese people, and *formerly* obese people, tend to have more adipose tissue than people of normal weight. Thus, many people who have lost weight complain that they are always hungry when they try to maintain normal weight levels.

Fatty tissue also metabolizes food more slowly than muscle. For this reason, a person with a high fat-to-muscle ratio will metabolize food more slowly than a person of the same weight with a lower fat-to-muscle ratio. In other words, two people identical in weight will metabolize food at different rates, according to their bodies' distribution of muscle and fat. Obese people are therefore doubly handicapped in their efforts to lose weight—not only by their extra weight but also by the fact that much of their body is composed of adipose tissue.

In a sense, the normal distribution of fat cells could be considered "sexist." The average man is 40% muscle and 15% fat, whereas the average woman is 23% muscle and 25% fat. Therefore, if a man and woman with typical distributions of muscle and fat are of the same weight, the woman—who has more fat cells—will have to eat less to maintain that weight.

Dieting and Metabolism. People on diets and those who have lost substantial amounts of weight burn fewer calories. That is, their metabolic rates slow down (Shah & Jeffery, 1991).

Fat cells might play a role in triggering internal sensations of hunger, but they cannot compel us to eat. Below we shall review evidence that obese people are actually less sensitive than normal-weight people to internal sensations of hunger.

Other factors, such as stress and our emotional states, also play a role in obesity (Greeno & Wing, 1994). Dieting efforts may be impeded by negative emotions like depression and anxiety (Cools and others, 1992).

Methods of Weight Control. Before discussing methods of losing weight, let us note that not everyone who is a few pounds overweight should be trying to slim down (Brownell, 1993; Brownell & Rodin, 1994). As noted by social critics, women are under extreme pressure to conform to an unnaturally slender female ideal (Bordo, 1993; Wolf, 1991). Moreover, many attempts to lose weight are ineffective. On the other hand, for many obese people, and especially for severely obese people, shedding excess pounds lowers the risks of diseases such as diabetes and heart disease (Brody, 1992d).

Research on motivation and on cognitive and behavioral methods of therapy has enhanced our knowledge of healthful ways of losing weight. Sound weight-control programs do not involve fad diets such as fasting, eliminating carbohydrates, or eating excessive amounts of grapefruit or rice. Instead, they involve major changes in lifestyle that include improving nutritional knowledge, decreasing calorie intake, exercising, and modifying behavior (Brownell & Rodin, 1994; Brownell & Wadden 1992).

Nutritional knowledge helps ensure that we will not deprive ourselves of essential food elements and suggests strategies for losing weight without making us feel overly deprived. For example, eating foods that are low in saturated fats and cholesterol is not only good for the heart. Because dietary fat is converted to bodily fat more efficiently than carbohydrates are, a low-fat diet also leads to weight loss (Brownell & Wadden, 1992; Wood and others, 1991). Nutritional

A Sampler of Dietary Methods. At any given time, 25% to 50% of the adult American population is on a diet. Dieting, as a matter of fact, has become the "normal" pattern of eating for women in the United States. Dozens of diets vie for attention on the bookshelves on any given day. How can we know which contain truth and which contain fiction? How can we separate the wheat from the chaff?

knowledge also leads to suggestions for taking in fewer calories, which is a common avenue to reduction. Taking in fewer calories doesn't only mean eating smaller portions. It means switching to some lower-calorie foods—relying more on fresh, unsweetened fruits and vegetables (eating apples rather than apple pie), lean meats, fish and poultry, and skim milk and cheese. It means cutting down on—or eliminating—butter, margarine, oils, and sugar.

The same foods that help us control our weight also tend to be high in vitamins and fiber and low in fats. Such foods may thus also lower our risk of developing heart disease, cancer, and a number of other illnesses.

Dieting plus exercise is more effective than dieting alone for shedding pounds (Epstein and others, 1984; Wood and others, 1991) and keeping them off (Perri and others, 1988). Remember that when we restrict calories, our metabolic rates compensate by slowing down (Brownell & Wadden, 1992). Dieters may reach plateaus from which they cannot shed additional pounds unless they starve themselves. Exercise burns calories and builds muscle tissue. Muscle metabolizes more calories than bodily fat (Brownell & Wadden, 1992). A long-term exercise program may also lower the set point for body weight (Keesey, 1986).

Cognitive and behavioral methods have also provided many strategies for losing weight. Here are a number of suggestions for losing weight based on cognitive-behavioral principles:

Establish calorie-intake goals and heighten awareness of whether you are meeting them. Get a book that shows how many calories are found in various foods, and keep a diary of your calorie intake.

Use low-calorie substitutes for high-calorie foods. Fill your stomach with celery rather than cheesecake and enchiladas. Eat preplanned low-calorie snacks instead of binge eating a jar of peanuts or a container of ice cream.

Take a 5-minute break between helpings. Ask yourself whether you're still hungry. If not, stop eating.

Avoid sources of external stimulation (temptations) to which you have succumbed in the past. Shop at the mall that has the Alfalfa Sprout, not the Gushy Gloppy Shoppe. Plan your meal before entering a restaurant. (Avoid ogling that tempting, full-color menu.) Attend to your own plate, not to the sumptuous dish at the next table. (Your salad probably looks greener to them, anyhow.) Shop from a list. Walk briskly through the supermarket, preferably after dinner when you're no longer hungry. Don't be sidetracked by pretty packages (fattening things may come in them). Keep out of the kitchen. Study, watch TV, or write letters elsewhere. Keep fattening foods out of the house. Prepare only enough food to remain within your calorie goals.

Exercise to burn more calories and maintain your predieting metabolic rate. Reach for your mate, not your plate (to coin a phrase). Jog rather than eat an unplanned snack. Build exercise routines by a few minutes each week.

Reward yourself for meeting calorie goals—but not with food. Imagine how great you'll look in that new swimsuit next summer. Do not go to see that great new film unless you have met your weekly calorie goal. Each time you meet your weekly calorie goal, put cash in the bank toward a vacation or new camera.

Use imagery to help yourself lose weight. Tempted by a fattening dish? Imagine that it's rotten, that you would be nauseated by it and have a sick taste in your mouth for the rest of the day. Tempted to binge? Strip before the mirror and handle a fatty area of your body. Ask yourself if you *really* want to make it larger or if you would prefer to exercise self-control.

Mentally walk through solutions to problem situations. Consider how you will politely refuse when cake is handed out at the office party. Rehearse your next visit to "the relatives"—the ones who tell you how painfully thin you look and try to stuff you like a pig. Imagine how you'll politely (but firmly) refuse seconds, and thirds, despite all their protestations.

Above all, if you slip from your plan for a day, don't blow things out of proportion. Dieters are often tempted to binge, especially when they rigidly see themselves either as perfect successes or complete failures (Polivy & Herman, 1985) or when they experience powerful emotions—either positive or negative (Cools and others, 1992). Consider the weekly or monthly trend, not just the day. Credit yourself for the long-term trend. If you do binge, resume dieting the next day.

Losing weight—and keeping it off—is not easy, but it can be done. Making a personal commitment to losing weight and formulating a workable plan for doing so are two of the keys.

Reflections

Now that you have read the section on obesity, reflect on the following questions:

- How do you feel about your own weight and body shape? Why?
- How many dieters do you know? How successful are they? What methods, if any, seem to work for them?
- Agree or disagree with the following statement and support your answer: "People who are overweight simply eat too much."

NOTES

11

Developmental Psychology

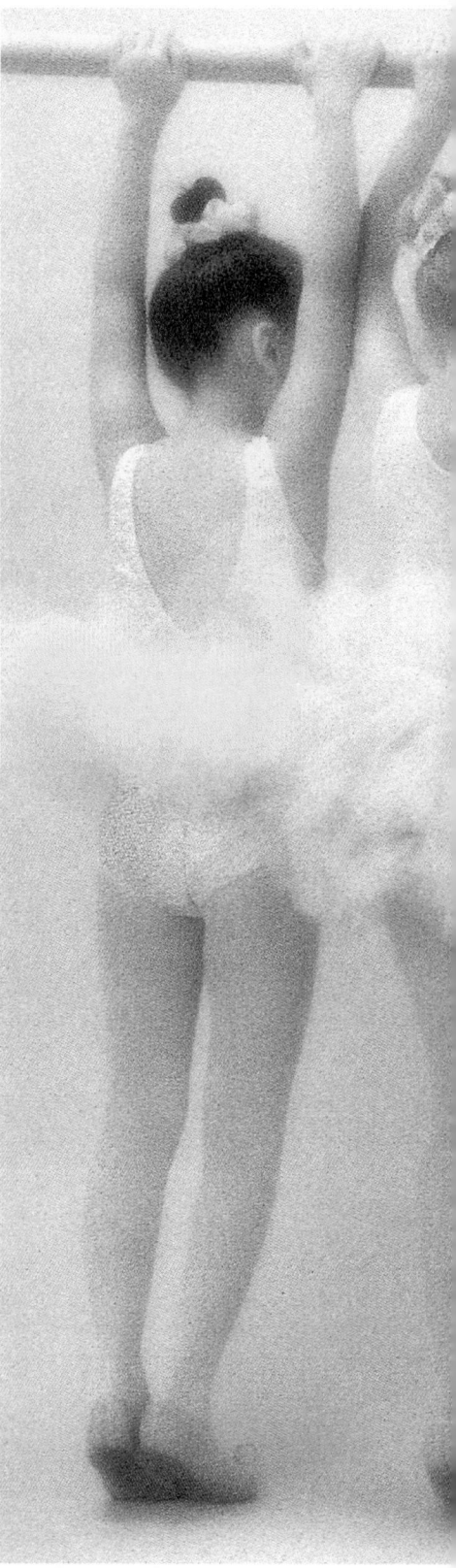

Truth or Fiction?

_____ Fertilization takes place in the uterus.

_____ Your heart started beating when you were only one-fifth of an inch long and weighed a fraction of an ounce.

_____ The way to a baby's heart is through its stomach—that is, babies become emotionally attached to those who feed them.

_____ The highest level of moral reasoning involves relying on our own views of what is right and wrong.

_____ Girls are capable of becoming pregnant when they have their first menstrual periods.

_____ Menopause signals the end of a woman's sexual interests.

_____ Mothers suffer from the "empty-nest syndrome" when the youngest child leaves home.

_____ Most older people are dissatisfied with their lives.

_____ Children placed in day care are more aggressive than children cared for in the home.

_____ Child abusers have frequently been abused as children themselves.

Outline

Truth or Fiction?

Controversies in Developmental Psychology

  Does Development Reflect Nature or Nurture?

  Is Development Continuous or Discontinuous?

  Psychology in the New Millennium: How Many of You Are There? How Many Will There Be?

Prenatal Development

Physical Development

  Reflexes

  Perceptual Development

Social Development

  Attachment

  Dimensions of Child Rearing

Cognitive Development

  Jean Piaget's Cognitive-Developmental Theory

  Information-Processing Approaches to Cognitive Development

  Lawrence Kohlberg's Theory of Moral Development

  Psychology in a World of Diversity: Are the Stages of Moral Development Universal? Evidence for Gender and Ethnocentric Biases

Adolescence

  Physical Development

  Social and Personality Development

  Psychology in a World of Diversity: Gender and Ethnic Factors in Adolescent Identity Formation

Adult Development

  Young Adulthood

  Middle Adulthood

  Late Adulthood

Summary

Psychology and Modern Life

  Day Care

  Child Abuse

There is no cure for birth or death save to enjoy the interval.

GEORGE SANTAYANA

When I approach a child, he inspires in me two sentiments: tenderness for what he is, and respect for what he may become.

LOUIS PASTEUR

On a summerlike day in October, Megan and her husband Michael rush out to their jobs as usual. While Megan, a buyer for a New York department store, is arranging for dresses from the Chicago manufacturer to arrive in time for the spring line, a very different drama is unfolding in her body. Hormones are causing a follicle (egg container) in one of her ovaries to rupture and release an egg cell, or ovum. Megan, like other women, possessed from birth all the egg cells she would ever have. How this ovum was selected to ripen and be released this month is unknown. But in any case, Megan will be capable of becoming pregnant for only a couple of days following ovulation.

When it is released, the ovum begins a slow journey down a 4-inch-long fallopian tube to the uterus. It is within this tube that one of Michael's sperm cells will unite with the egg.

Truth or Fiction Revisited. *It is not true that fertilization takes place in the uterus.* Fertilization normally occurs in a fallopian tube.

Like many other couples, Megan and Michael engaged in sexual intercourse the night before. But unlike most other couples, their timing and methodology were preplanned. Megan used a kit bought in a drugstore to predict when she would ovulate. She chemically analyzed her urine for the presence of luteinizing hormone, which surges 1 to 2 days prior to ovulation. The results suggested that Megan would be most likely to conceive today.

When Megan and Michael made love, he ejaculated hundreds of millions of sperm, with about equal numbers of Y and X sex chromosomes. By the time of conception, only a few thousand had survived the journey to the fallopian tubes. Several bombarded the ovum, attempting to penetrate. Only one succeeded. It carried a Y sex chromosome, so the couple conceived a boy. The fertilized ovum, or **zygote,** is 1/175th of an inch across—a tiny stage for the drama yet to unfold.

Developmental psychologists would be pleased to study the development of Michael and Megan's new son from conception throughout his lifetime. There are several reasons for this. One approach to the explanation of adult behavior lies in the discovery of early influences and developmental sequences. An answer to the question of why we behave in certain ways lies in outlining the development of behavior patterns over the years. There also is interest in the effects of genetics, of early interactions with parents and **siblings,** and of the school and the community on traits such as aggressiveness and intelligence.

Developmental psychologists also seek insight into the causes of developmental abnormalities. This avenue of research can contribute to children's health and psychological well-being. For instance, should pregnant women abstain from smoking and drinking? Is it safe for the **embryo** for pregnant women to take aspirin for a headache or tetracycline to ward off a bacterial invasion? Need we be concerned about placing our children in day care? What factors contribute to child abuse? Developmental psychologists are also concerned about issues in adult development. For example, what conflicts and disillusionments can we expect as we journey through our 30s, 40s, and 50s? The information acquired by developmental psychologists can help us make decisions about how we rear our children and lead our own lives.

Of course, there is another very good reason for studying development. Thousands of psychologists enjoy it.

Controversies in Developmental Psychology

Throughout this textbook, we have seen that psychologists see things in very different ways. Diverse views give rise to controversies in developmental psychology as well.

DOES DEVELOPMENT REFLECT NATURE OR NURTURE?

There is continuing interest in sorting out what human behavior is the result of nature and of nurture. What aspects of behavior originate in a person's genes—that is, nature—and are biologically "programmed" to unfold in the child as long as minimal nutrition and social experience are provided? What aspects of behavior can be largely traced to environmental influences such as nutrition and learning—that is, nurture?

Psychologists seek to understand the influences of nature in our genetic heritage, in the functioning of the nervous system, and in the process of **maturation.** Psychologists look for the influences of nurture in our nutrition, cultural and family backgrounds, and opportunities to learn about the world, including early cognitive stimulation and formal education. American psychologist Arnold Gesell (1880–1961) leaned heavily toward natural explanations of development, arguing that all areas of development are self-regulated by the unfolding of natural plans and processes. John Watson and other behaviorists leaned heavily toward environmental explanations. (Watson, of course, was focusing primarily on adaptive behavior patterns, whereas Gesell was focusing on many aspects of

development, including physical and motor growth and development.) Today, nearly all researchers would agree, broadly speaking, that nature and nurture interact as children develop.

IS DEVELOPMENT CONTINUOUS OR DISCONTINUOUS?

Do developmental changes occur gradually (continuously) or in major qualitative leaps (discontinuously) that dramatically alter our bodies and behavior?

Watson and other behaviorists have viewed human development as being a continuous process in which the effects of learning mount gradually, with no major sudden qualitative changes. Maturational theorists, in contrast, believe that there are a number of rapid qualitative changes that usher in new **stages** of development. Maturational theorists point out that the environment, even when enriched, profits us little until we are ready, or mature enough, to develop in a certain direction. For example, newborn babies will not imitate their parents' speech, even when parents speak clearly and deliberately. Nor does aided

Zygote • A fertilized ovum.
Siblings • Brothers and sisters.
Embryo • (EM-bree-oh). The baby from the third through the eighth weeks following conception, during which time the major organ systems undergo rapid differentiation.
Maturation • (mat-your-RAY-shun). The orderly unfolding of traits, as regulated by the genetic code.
Stage • A distinct period of life that is qualitatively different from other stages.

Which Aspects of Development Are Continuous, and Which Are Discontinuous? The adolescent growth spurt is an example of discontinuity in development. Psychologists debate whether or not other aspects of development—such as cognitive development—are most accurately described as continuous or discontinuous.

practice in "walking" during the first few months after birth significantly accelerate the emergence of independent walking.

Stage theorists such as Sigmund Freud (see Chapter 12) and Jean Piaget saw development as being discontinuous. Both theorists saw biological changes as providing the potential for psychological changes. Freud focused on the ways in which physical sexual developments might provide the basis for personality development. Piaget centered on the ways in which maturation of the nervous system permitted cognitive advances. Stage theorists see the sequences of development as being invariant, although they allow for individual differences in timing.

Certain aspects of physical development do appear to occur in stages. For example, from the age of 2 to the onset of **puberty**, children gradually grow larger. Then the adolescent growth spurt occurs, ushered in by hormones and characterized by rapid biological changes in structure and function (as in the development of the sex organs) as well as in size. So it would appear that a new stage of life has begun. Psychologists disagree more strongly on whether aspects

PSYCHOLOGY IN THE NEW MILLENNIUM

How Many of You Are There? How Many Will There Be?

Puberty • (PEW-burr-tee or POO-burr-tee). The period of early adolescence during which hormones spur rapid physical development.

Fetus • (FEE-tuss). The baby from the third month following conception through childbirth, during which time there is maturation of organ systems and dramatic gains in length and weight.

How valuable would your individual existence be if another one of you could be developed on demand? What if a dozen or more of you could be brought to life?

Some fear that our increasing control of genetics will make possible scenarios like that portrayed by Aldous Huxley in his still-powerful 1932 novel *Brave New World*. Through a method called "Bokanovsky's Process," egg cells from parents who were ideally suited to certain types of labor were made to "bud." From these buds, up to 96 people with identical genetic makeups were developed—filling the labor niches required by society.

In the novel, the director of a "hatchery" leads a group of students on a tour. One student is foolish enough to question the advantage of Bokanovsky's Process:

"My good boy!" The Director wheeled sharply round on him. "Can't you see? Can't you see?" He raised a hand; his expression was solemn. "Bokanovsky's Process is one of the major instruments of social stability!"

Major instruments of social stability (wrote the student).

Standard men and women; in uniform batches. The whole of a small factory staffed with the products of a single Bokanovskied egg.

"Ninety-six identical twins working 96 identical machines!" The voice was almost tremulous with enthusiasm. "You really know where you are. For the first time in history." He quoted the planetary motto. "Community, Identity, Stability." Grand words. "If we could Bokanovskify indefinitely the whole problem would be solved."

Bokanovsky's Process was science fiction when Huxley wrote *Brave New World*. Today, however, reproductive technologies have made the creation of genetically identical people possible. Techniques very similar to that described by Huxley have been developed for making identical cattle. With cattle, the cells that make up the developing embryo are divided one or more times, and each new cluster of cells develops into an animal (Kolata, 1993c). In what the Vatican refers to as "A Perverse Choice" (1993), researchers are also using cloning to create multiple human embryos from one.

In one approach, an ovum (egg cell) is first fertilized with sperm in the laboratory *(in vitro)*. The fertilized ovum begins to divide. If the dividing mass of cells is separated into clusters at this early stage, each cluster may develop into a separate organism. The embryos of development such as cognitive development, attachment, and gender-typing occur in stages.

Let us now turn to the developments that occur between conception and birth. Although they are literally "out of sight," our most dramatic biological changes occur within this short span of 9 months.

Prenatal Development

During the months following conception, the single cell formed by the union of sperm and egg will multiply—becoming two, then four, then eight, and so on. By the time a **fetus** is ready to be born, it will contain trillions of cells. Prenatal development is divided into three periods: the germinal stage (approximately the first 2 weeks), the embryonic stage (which lasts from 2 weeks to about 2 months after conception), and the fetal stage.

The Germinal Stage. The zygote divides repeatedly as it proceeds on its 3- to 4-day journey to the uterus. The ball-like mass of multiplying cells wanders about the

MINILECTURE:
PRENATAL
DEVELOPMENT

could be implanted in one or more women to develop to maturity. Or else some embryos can be frozen to be implanted if the natural parents (or adoptive parents) desire a genetically identical child.

In another approach, the material containing genetic information is surgically extracted from an egg donated by another woman. The nutrients that will nourish the development of the egg are retained. The fertilized nucleus of the first egg is then transplanted into the donor's egg, and cell division begins. The egg with the transplanted genetic information is then implanted in a woman's uterus, where it develops into a person with the genetic characteristics determined by the nucleus.

These technologies are reasonably familiar even today, but they raise many ethical concerns. One involves human dignity, a core concern for psychologists. One reason we consider people to be dignified and valuable is because of their uniqueness. Imagine a world, however, in which every child and adult had one or more frozen identical twins in embryo form. If a child died by accident, would the parents develop a frozen embryo to replace the lost child? *Would* that replace the lost child? Would some frozen embryos be developed to term to provide donor organs for people who were ill? Would society desire that a dozen twins be developed to maturity when a Toni Morrison, a Mozart, a Mary Cassatt, or an Einstein was discovered?

Would society, on the other hand, attempt to lower the incidence of certain genetic disorders or antisocial behavior by preventing the twins of less fortunate individuals from being developed to maturity?

Or imagine this scenario: Parents "invest" frozen embryos that are the twins of their children in embryo banks. As their children develop, "bankers" take photographs and administer psychological tests. Could it happen that the twins of the brightest, most attractive children would be sold to the highest bidder? What would happen in societies that valued brawny soldiers? Dull workers of the sort envisioned by Huxley? Boys? Girls?

Some ethicists argue that parents' embryos are their own and that it is not society's place to prevent parents from cloning them (Kolata, 1993d). Others argue that such cloning would lead us into a "tunnel of madness" ("A Perverse Choice," 1993). As we head toward the new millennium, many of our technologies are developing at paces that threaten our ability to cope with them in a productive, ethical manner. As citizens, it is our duty to keep abreast of technical innovations and to ensure that their applications are beneficial. Unfortunately, people of goodwill often have very different views of what is beneficial.

An Exercise Class for Pregnant Women. Years ago, the rule of thumb was that pregnant women were not to exert themselves. Today, it is recognized that exercise is healthful for pregnant women, because it promotes cardiovascular fitness and increases muscle strength. Fitness and strength are assets during childbirth—and at other times.

Germinal stage • The first stage of prenatal development during which the dividing mass of cells has not become implanted in the uterine wall.

Period of the ovum • Another term for the *germinal stage.*

Cephalocaudal • (SEFF-uh-lo-CAW-d'l). Proceeding from top to bottom.

Proximodistal • (PROX-ee-mo-DISS-t'l). Proceeding from near to far.

Androgens • (AND-row-jennz). Male sex hormones.

Amniotic sac • (am-knee-OTT-tick). A sac within the uterus that contains the embryo or fetus.

Placenta • (pluh-SENT-uh). A membrane that permits the exchange of nutrients and waste products between the mother and her developing child but does not allow the maternal and fetal bloodstreams to mix.

uterus for another 3 to 4 days before beginning to become implanted in the uterine wall. Implantation takes another week or so. The period from conception to implantation is called the **germinal stage,** or the **period of the ovum.**

A few days into the germinal stage, cells are separating into groups according to what they will become. Inner layers of cells are forming what will become the baby. The outer layer differentiates into membranes that will protect and nourish the embryo, including the umbilical cord; the placenta; the amniotic sac; and the chorion, which lines the placenta. Prior to implantation, the dividing ball of cells is nourished solely by the yolk of the original egg cell, and it does not gain in mass.

The Embryonic Stage. The embryonic stage lasts from implantation until about the eighth week of development. During this stage, the major body organ systems differentiate. Development follows two general trends—**cephalocaudal** and **proximodistal.** As you can see from the relatively large heads of embryos and fetuses during prenatal development (see Figure 11.1), the growth of the head precedes the growth of the lower parts of the body. If you also think of the body as containing a

central axis that coincides with the spinal cord, the growth of the organ systems close to this axis (that is, *proximal*) takes precedence over the growth of the extremities (*distal* areas). Relatively early maturation of the brain and the major organ systems allows them to participate in the nourishment and further development of the embryo.

During the third week after conception, the head and the blood vessels begin to form. During the fourth week, a primitive heart begins to beat and pump blood—in an organism that is one-fifth of an inch long. The heart will continue to beat without rest every minute of every day for perhaps 80 or 90 years.

Truth or Fiction Revisited. *It is true that your heart started beating when you were only one-fifth of an inch long and weighed a fraction of an ounce.* This occurred about 3 to 4 weeks following conception.

Arm buds and leg buds begin to appear toward the end of the first month. Eyes, ears, nose, and mouth begin to take shape. By this time, the nervous system, including the brain, has also begun to develop.

The upper arms and legs develop first, followed by the forearms and lower legs. Next come hands and feet, followed at 6 to 8 weeks by webbed fingers and toes. By the end of the second month, the limbs are elongating and separated. The webbing is gone. The head has become rounded and the facial features distinct—all in an embryo about 1 inch long and weighing 1/30th of an ounce. During the second month, the nervous system begins to transmit messages. By the end of the embryonic period, teeth buds have formed. The embryo's kidneys are filtering acid from the blood, and its liver is producing red blood cells.

By 5 to 6 weeks, the embryo is only a quarter to a half an inch long, yet nondescript sex organs have formed. By about the seventh week, the genetic code (XY or XX) begins to assert itself, causing sex organs to differentiate. If a Y sex chromosome is present, testes form and begin to produce **androgens,** which further masculinize the sex organs. In the absence of male sex hormones, the embryo develops female sex organs.

The embryo and fetus develop suspended within a protective **amniotic sac** in the mother's uterus. The sac is surrounded by a clear membrane and contains amniotic fluid. The fluid serves as a sort of natural air bag, allowing the child to move or even jerk around without injury. It also helps maintain an even temperature.

The **placenta** permits the embryo (and later on, the fetus) to exchange nutrients

FIGURE 11.1
Embryos and Fetuses at Various Intervals of Prenatal Development

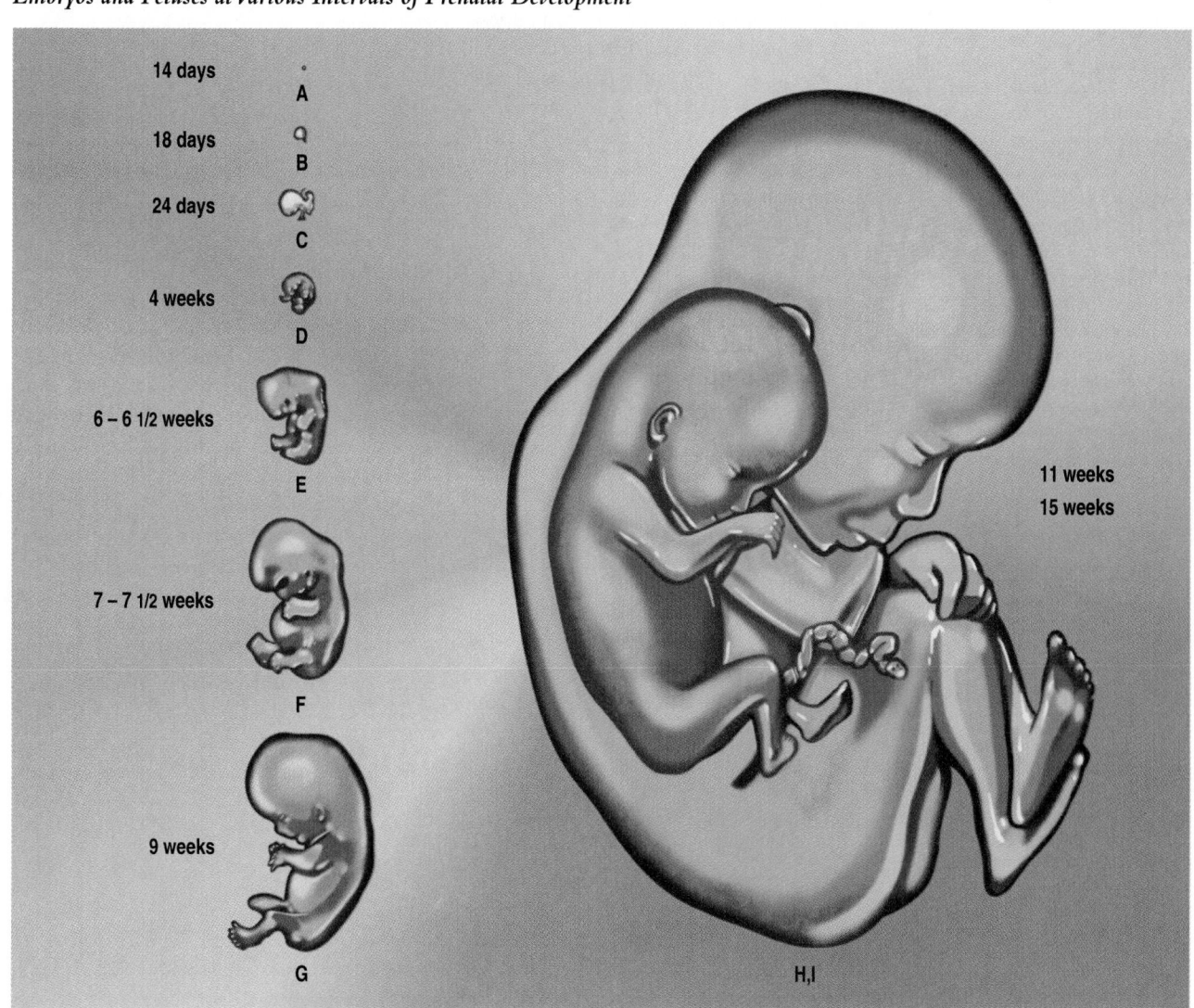

14 days — A
18 days — B
24 days — C
4 weeks — D
6 – 6 1/2 weeks — E
7 – 7 1/2 weeks — F
9 weeks — G
11 weeks / 15 weeks — H,I

and wastes with the mother. The placenta is unique in origin: It grows from material supplied by both mother and embryo. The fetus is connected to the placenta by the **umbilical cord.** The mother is connected to the placenta by the system of blood vessels in the uterine wall.

The circulatory systems of mother and baby do not mix. A membrane in the placenta permits only certain substances to pass through. Oxygen and nutrients are passed from the mother to the embryo. Carbon dioxide and other wastes are passed from the child to the mother, where they are removed by the mother's lungs and kidneys. Unfortunately, a number of other substances can pass through the placenta. They include some microscopic disease organisms—such as those that cause syphilis and German measles—and some chemical agents, including Accutane (a prescription drug for acne), aspirin, narcotics, alcohol, and tranquilizers. Because these and other agents may be harmful to the embryo and fetus, pregnant women are advised to consult their physicians about the advisability of using any chemical agents, even those that are available without prescription.

The Fetal Stage. The fetal stage lasts from the beginning of the third month until birth. The fetus begins to turn and respond to external stimulation at about the ninth or tenth week. By the end of the third month, all the major organ systems have been formed. The fingers and toes appear to be fully formed. The eyes can be clearly distinguished, and the gender of the fetus can be determined visually.

The fourth through sixth months are characterized by maturation of fetal organ systems and dramatic gains in size. The brain continues to mature, contributing to the fetus's ability to regulate its own basic body functions. During these months, the fetus advances from 1 *ounce* to 2 *pounds* in weight and grows three to four times in length, from about 4 to 14 inches. Soft, downy hair grows above the eyes and on the scalp. The skin turns ruddy because of blood vessels that show through the surface. (During the final 3 months, fatty layers will give the red a pinkish hue.)

In the middle of the fourth month, the mother usually detects the first fetal move-

ments. By the end of the sixth month, the fetus moves its limbs so vigorously that the mother may complain of being kicked. The fetus opens and shuts its eyes, sucks its thumb, alternates between periods of wakefulness and sleep, and perceives light. It also turns somersaults which can be clearly perceived by the mother. The umbilical cord is composed so that it will not break or become dangerously wrapped around the fetus, no matter how many acrobatic feats the fetus performs.

During the last 3 months, the organ systems of the fetus continue to mature. The heart and lungs become increasingly capable of sustaining independent life. The fetus gains about 5½ pounds and doubles in length. Newborn boys average about 7½ pounds and newborn girls about 7 pounds.

Physical Development

Physical development includes gains in height and weight; maturation of the nervous system; and development of bones, muscles, and the sex organs.

The most dramatic gains in height and weight occur during prenatal development. Within 9 months, a child develops from a nearly microscopic cell to a **neonate** about 20 inches in length. Weight increases by the billions. During infancy, dramatic gains continue. Babies usually double their birth weight in about 5 months and triple it by the first birthday. Their height increases by about 10 inches in the first year. Children grow another 4 to 6 inches during the second year and gain some 4 to 7 pounds.

Following the gains of infancy, children gain about 2 to 3 inches a year until they reach the adolescent growth spurt. Weight gains also remain fairly even at about 4 to 6 pounds per year.

In one of the more fascinating aspects of the development of the nervous system, newborn babies show a number of automatic behavior patterns that are essential to survival—reflexes.

REFLEXES

Soon after you were born, a doctor or a nurse probably pressed her fingers against the palms of your hands. Although you

---

Umbilical cord • (um-BILL-lick-al). A tube between the mother and her developing child through which nutrients and waste products are conducted.

Neonate • A newly born child.

Reflex • A simple unlearned response to a stimulus.

Rooting • The turning of an infant's head toward a touch, such as by the mother's nipple.

Sphincter • (SFINK-ter). A ringlike muscle that circles a body opening such as the anus. An infant will exhibit the sphincter reflex (have a bowel movement) in response to intestinal pressure.

would have had no "idea" as to what to do, most likely you grasped the fingers firmly—so firmly that you could actually have been lifted from your cradle by holding on! Grasping at birth is inborn, just one of the neonate's many **reflexes.** Reflexes are simple, unlearned, stereotypical responses that are elicited by specific stimuli. They do not involve higher brain functions. They occur automatically, without thinking.

Many reflexes such as the breathing reflex have survival value. The breathing rate is regulated by body levels of oxygen and carbon dioxide. We take in oxygen and give off carbon dioxide. Newborns normally take their first breath before the umbilical cord is cut. The breathing reflex continues to work for a lifetime, though we can take conscious control of breathing when we choose to do so.

Newborn children do not "know" that it is necessary to eat to survive, so it is fortunate that they have **rooting** and sucking reflexes. Neonates will turn their heads (root) toward stimuli that prod or stroke the cheek, chin, or corners of the mouth. They will suck objects that touch their lips. Neonates reflexively withdraw from painful stimuli (the withdrawal reflex), and they draw up their legs and arch their backs in response to sudden noises, bumps, or loss of support while being held (the startle, or Moro, reflex). They reflexively grasp objects that press against the palms of their hands (the grasp, or palmar, reflex). They spread their toes when the soles of their feet are stimulated (the Babinski reflex). Babies also show sneezing, coughing, yawning, blinking, and other reflexes. It is guaranteed that you will learn about the **sphincter** reflex if you put on your best clothes and hold an undiapered neonate on your lap for a while. Pediatricians assess the adequacy of babies' neural functioning largely by testing their reflexes.

As children develop, their muscles and neural functions mature, and they learn to coordinate sensory and motor activity. Many reflexes drop out of their storehouse of responses. Many processes, such as the elimination of wastes, come under voluntary control. Some highlights of children's motor development are chronicled in Figure 11.2.

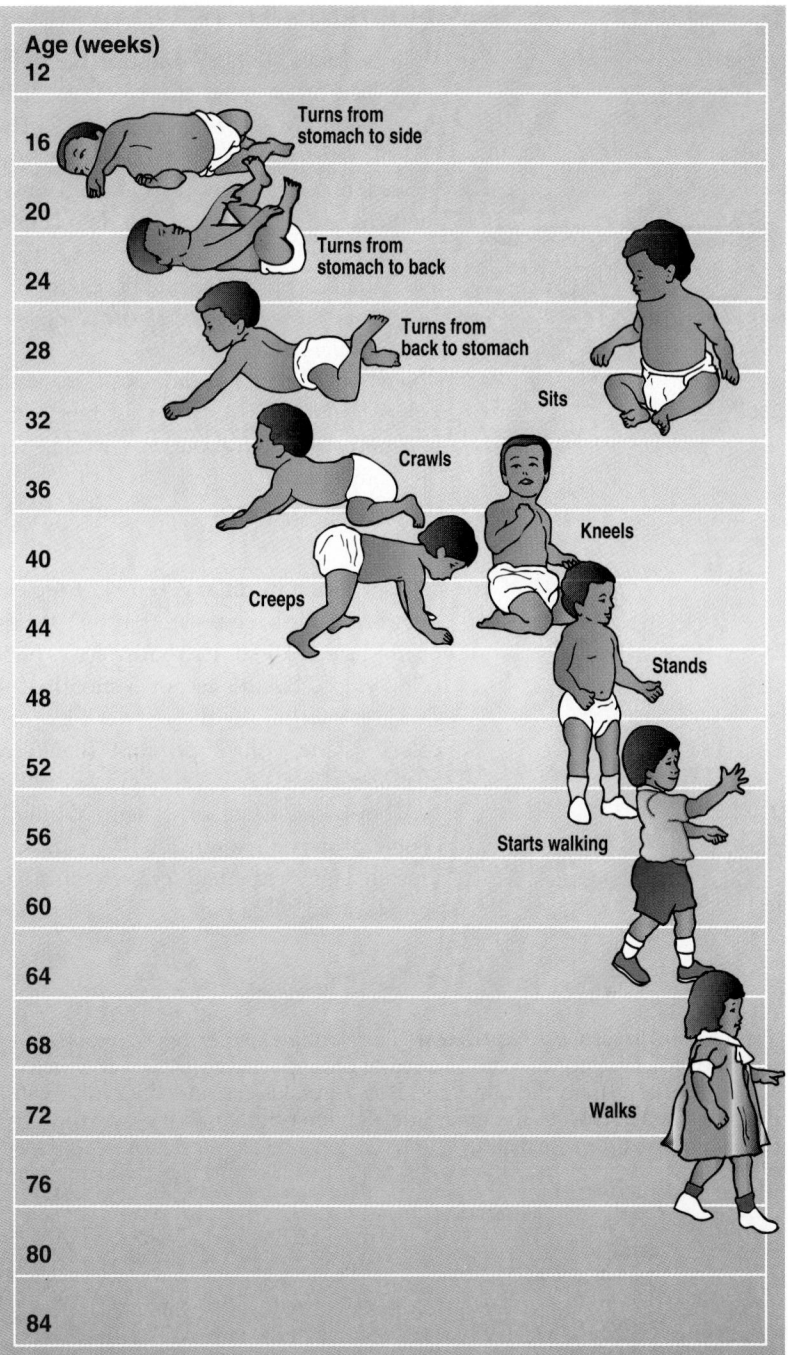

FIGURE 11.2

Spotlight on Motor Development in Infancy At birth, infants appear to be bundles of aimless "nervous energy." They have reflexive responses, but they also engage in random movements. Random movement is replaced by purposeful activity as they mature. Motor development proceeds in an orderly sequence. Practice prompts sensorimotor coordination, but maturation is essential. During the first six months, cells in the motor and sensorimotor areas of the brain mature to allow activities such as crawling and, later, walking. The times in the figure are approximate: An infant who is a bit behind may develop with no problems at all, and a precocious infant will not necessarily become a rocket scientist (or gymnast).

PERCEPTUAL DEVELOPMENT

William James (1890) wrote that the newborn baby must sense the world as "one great booming, buzzing confusion." The neonate emerges from being literally suspended in a temperature-controlled environment to being—again, in James's words—"assailed by eyes, ears, nose, skin, and entrails at once." Despite his eloquence, James may have exaggerated the disorganization of the neonate's world.

Newborn children spend about 16 hours a day sleeping and do not have much opportunity to learn about the world. Yet, they are capable of perceiving the world reasonably well soon after birth (Pick, 1991).

Vision. The **pupillary reflex** is present at birth. At birth, cones are less well-developed than rods, so newborns have poor color vision. By the age of 3 months, infants can discriminate most, if not all, of the colors of the visible spectrum (Banks & Shannon, 1993; Teller & Lindsey, 1993). Newborns can fixate on a light. Within a couple of days, they can follow, or track, a moving light with their eyes (Kellman & von Hofsten, 1992).

FIGURE 11.3
The Classic Visual Cliff Experiment This young explorer has the good sense not to crawl out onto an apparently unsupported surface, even when Mother beckons from the other side. Rats, pups, kittens, and chicks also will not try to walk across to the other side. (So don't bother asking why the chicken crossed the visual cliff.)

Neonates do not show **visual accommodation.** They see as though looking through a fixed-focus camera. They are thus nearsighted and see objects 7 to 9 inches away most clearly. By about the age of 4 months, however, infants seem able to focus about as well as adults can. Visual acuity makes dramatic gains during the first 2 months (Hainline & Abramov, 1992) and approaches adult levels by 1 year of age (Haith, 1990).

Response to Complex Visual Stimulation and the Human Face. The visual preferences of infants are measured by the amount of time, termed **fixation time,** that they spend looking at one stimulus instead of another. In classic research by Robert Fantz (1961), 2-month-old infants preferred visual stimuli that resembled the human face to newsprint, a bull's-eye, and featureless disks colored red, white, and yellow. Subsequent research suggests that the complexity of facelike patterns may be more important than their content at this age. For example, babies have been shown facelike patterns that differ either according to the number of elements or the degree to which they are organized to match the human face. Five- to 10-week-old babies fixate longer on patterns that have high numbers of elements. The organization of the elements—that is, the degree to which they resemble the face—is less important. By 15 to 20 weeks, the organization of the pattern also matters. Babies then dwell longer on facelike patterns (e.g., Haaf and others, 1983).

Infants thus seem to have an inborn preference for complex visual stimulation. However, preference for faces as opposed to other equally complex stimuli may not emerge until infants have had experience with people. Nurture as well as nature appears to influence infants' preferences.

Depth Perception. Classic research shows that infants tend to respond to cues for depth by the time they are able to crawl (at about 6 to 8 months). Most also have the good sense to avoid crawling off ledges and table tops into open space (Campos and others, 1978). Note the setup (Figure 11.3) in the classic "visual cliff" experiment run by Walk and Gibson (1961). An

8-month-old infant crawls freely above the portion of the glass with a checkerboard pattern immediately beneath but hesitates to crawl over the portion of the glass beneath which the checkerboard has been dropped a few feet. Since the glass alone would support the infant, this is a "visual cliff," not an actual cliff.

Psychologists can assess infants' "emotional" responses to the visual cliff long before they can crawl. For example, Joseph Campos and his colleagues (1970) found that 1-month-old infants showed no emotional response, as measured by changes in heart rate, when placed face down on the visual cliff. At about 2 months of age, the infants showed decreases in heart rate when so placed, which psychologists interpret as interest. The heart rates of 9-month-olds accelerated when the infants were placed on the cliff, which is interpreted as a fear response. Moreover, 8 of 10 crawling infants studied by Walk and Gibson refused to venture onto the visually unsupported glass surface, even when their mothers beckoned.

Hearing. Months before they are born, fetuses respond to sounds. Their middle and inner ears normally mature before birth (Aslin and others, 1983). Normal neonates thus hear well unless their middle ears are clogged with amniotic fluid. In such cases, hearing improves rapidly. Most neonates reflexively turn their heads toward unusual sounds and suspend other activities. This finding, along with findings about visual tracking, suggests that infants are preprogrammed to survey their environments. Neonates are more responsive to high-pitched than low-pitched sounds. On the other hand, speaking or singing softly in a low-pitched tone soothes infants (Papousek and others, 1991). This is well known to parents who use lullabies to get infants to sleep (Trehub and others, 1993).

Three-day-old babies prefer their mothers' voices to those of other women, but they do not show similar preferences for the voices of their fathers (DeCasper & Prescott, 1984; Freeman and others, 1993). By birth, of course, babies have had many months of "experience" in the uterus. For at least 2 or 3 months, babies have been capable of sensing sounds. Because they are predominantly exposed to sounds produced by their mothers, learning may contribute to neonatal preferences.

Smell: The Nose Knows Early. Neonates can discriminate distinct odors such as those of onions and licorice. Newborns breathe more rapidly and are more active when presented with powerful odors—and they turn away from unpleasant odors (Rieser and others, 1976). They can become used to even powerful odors, as can adults. The nasal preferences of babies are similar to those of adults. Newborn infants spit, stick out their tongues, and literally wrinkle their noses at the odor of rotten eggs. But they smile and show licking motions in response to chocolate, strawberry, vanilla, and honey.

The sense of smell, like the sense of hearing, may provide a vehicle for mother–infant recognition. Within the first week, nursing infants prefer to turn to look at their mothers' nursing pads (which can be discriminated only by the sense of smell) rather than those of strange women (Macfarlane, 1975). By 15 days, nursing infants prefer their mothers' underarm odors to those of other women (Porter and others, 1992). Bottle-fed babies do not show this preference.

Taste. Shortly after birth, infants show the ability to discriminate taste. They suck liquid solutions of sugar and milk but grimace and refuse to suck salty or bitter solutions. Sweet solutions tend to calm newborns (Blass & Smith, 1992). The tongue pressure of 1-day-old infants sucking on a nipple correlates with the amount of sugar in their liquid diet.

Touch. Newborn babies are sensitive to touch. Many reflexes (rooting and sucking are two) are activated by pressure against the skin. Newborns are relatively insensitive to pain, however, which may be adaptive considering the squeezing of the birth process. Sensitivity increases dramatically within a few days.

The sense of touch is an extremely important avenue of learning and communication for babies. Not only do the skin senses provide information, but sensations of skin against skin also appear to provide

Pupillary reflex • (PEW-pill-air-ee). The automatic adjustment of the irises to permit more or less light to enter the eye.
Visual accommodation • Automatic adjustment of the thickness of the lens in order to focus on objects.
Fixation time • The amount of time spent looking at a visual stimulus.

Allyn. At the age of 2, the author's daughter Allyn nearly succeeded in preventing the publication of an earlier edition of this book by pulling him away from the computer when he was at work. Because of their mutual attachment, separation was painful.

Attachment • The enduring affectional tie that binds one person to another.

Secure attachment • A type of attachment characterized by positive feelings toward attachment figures and feelings of security.

Insecure attachment • A negative type of attachment, in which children show indifference or ambivalence toward attachment figures.

feelings of comfort and security that may contribute to the formation of affectionate bonds between infants and caregivers, as we shall see in the section on attachment.

Reflections

Now that you have read the opening sections of this chapter, reflect on the following questions:

• Which aspects of your own development seem to be most influenced by nature or nurture? Why?

• Which aspects of your own development seem to have been most discontinuous? Why?

• How can you make use of knowledge of prenatal development in your own life?

• What are your beliefs concerning why newborn babies have reflexes and why they drop out as the weeks and months proceed? Is it possible to scientifically test your beliefs? Why or why not?

• Agree or disagree with the following statement and support your answer: "The newborn baby must sense the world as 'one great booming, buzzing confusion.'"

Social Development

At just 2 years, my daughter Allyn almost succeeded at preventing publication of an earlier edition of this book. When I locked myself into my study, she positioned herself outside the door and called, "Daddy, oh Daddy." Next came, "Pencer, oh Pencer." At other times, she would bang on the door or cry outside. When I would give in (several times a day) and open the door, she would run in and say, "I want you to pick up me" and hold out her arms or climb into my lap. Then she would say, "I want to play." I would beg, "I'm in the middle of something. Just give me a second to finish it." Then, when I would look back at my monitor, she would try to turn my face to hers or turn the computer off. Or, if I were trying to jot down some notes from a journal, she would try to yank them from my hands and toss them across the room. (I have sometimes wanted to do that to the journals, too.) Although we were separate human beings, it was as though she were very much *attached* to me.

I am a psychologist. Solutions thus came easily. For example, I could write outside the home. But this solution had the drawback of distancing me from my family. Another solution was to let my daughter cry and ignore her. If I refused to reinforce crying, crying would become extinguished. There were only two problems with this solution. First, I was incapable of ignoring her crying. Second, I didn't *want* to extinguish her efforts to get to me. Feelings of attachment, you see, are a two-way street.

Attachment is one of the issues involved in the social development of the child. In this section we discuss attachment and dimensions of child rearing.

ATTACHMENT

Mary Ainsworth (1989), one of the preeminent researchers in attachment, defines **attachment** as an emotional tie that is formed between one animal or person and another specific individual. Attachment keeps organisms together and tends to endure. Attachment is essential to the very survival of the infant (Bowlby, 1988).

The behaviors that define attachment include (1) attempts to maintain contact or nearness and (2) shows of anxiety when separated. Babies and children try to maintain contact with caregivers to whom they are attached. They engage in eye contact, pull and tug at them, ask to be picked up, and may even jump in front of them in such a way that they will be "run over" if they are not picked up!

Attachment is one measure of the care that infants receive. The mothers of **securely attached** children are more likely to be affectionate and reliable caregivers (Cox and others, 1992; Isabella, 1993). Securely attached children are happier, more sociable with unfamiliar adults, more cooperative with parents, and get along better with peers than do **insecurely attached** children (Belsky and others, 1991; Thompson, 1991a). Securely attached preschoolers have longer attention spans, are less impulsive, and better at solving problems (Frankel & Bates, 1990; Lederberg & Mobley, 1990). At ages 5 and 6, securely attached children are liked better by their peers and teachers, are more competent, and have fewer behavior problems than insecurely attached peers

(Lyons-Ruth and others, 1993; Youngblade & Belsky, 1992).

Stages of Attachment. The study of attachment is greatly indebted to the individual and collaborative efforts of Mary D. Salter Ainsworth and John Bowlby (1991)—whose "partnership [has] endured for 40 years across time and distance" (p. 333). In a review of their research, they refer to critical cross-cultural studies such as one conducted by Ainsworth in Uganda, which led to a theory of the stages of attachment.

Ainsworth tracked the attachment behaviors of Ugandan infants. She noted their efforts to maintain contact with the mother, their protests when separated, and their use of the mother as a base for exploring the environment. At first, the Ugandan infants showed **indiscriminate attachment.** That is, they preferred being held or being with someone to being alone, but they showed no preferences. Specific attachment to the mother began to develop at about 4 months of age and grew intense by about 7 months of age. Fear of strangers, if it developed at all, followed by 1 or 2 months.

From studies such as these, Mary Ainsworth identified three stages of attachment:

1. The **initial-preattachment phase,** which lasts from birth to about 3 months and is characterized by indiscriminate attachment

2. The **attachment-in-the-making phase,** which occurs at about 3 or 4 months and is characterized by preference for familiar figures

3. The **clear-cut-attachment phase,** which occurs at about 6 or 7 months and is characterized by intensified dependence on the primary caregiver—usually the mother

Bowlby noted that children's attachment behaviors are also characterized by fear of strangers ("stranger anxiety"). But not all children show fear of strangers.

Theoretical Views of Attachment. Attachment, like so many other behavior patterns, seems to develop as a result of the interaction of nature and nurture.

A BEHAVIORAL VIEW OF ATTACHMENT: MOTHER AS A REINFORCER. Early in the century, behaviorists argued that attachment behaviors are learned through conditioning. Caregivers feed their infants and tend to their other physiological needs. Thus, infants associate their caregivers with gratification and learn to approach them to meet their needs. From this perspective, a caregiver becomes a conditioned reinforcer. The feelings of gratification that are associated with meeting basic needs generalize into feelings of security when the caregiver is present.

HARLOW'S VIEW OF ATTACHMENT: MOTHER AS A SOURCE OF CONTACT COMFORT. Classic research by psychologist Harry F. Harlow cast doubt on the behaviorist view that attachment is learned mechanically. Harlow had noted that infant rhesus monkeys reared without mothers or companions became attached to pieces of cloth in their cages. They maintained contact with them and showed distress when separated from them. Harlow conducted a series of experiments to find out why (Harlow, 1959).

In one study, Harlow placed rhesus monkey infants in cages with two surrogate mothers, as shown in Figure 11.4. One "mother" was made from wire mesh from which a baby bottle was extended. The other surrogate mother was made of soft, cuddly terry cloth. Infant monkeys spent most of their time clinging to the cloth mother, even though "she" did not gratify the need for food. Harlow concluded that monkeys—and perhaps humans—have a primary (unlearned) need for **contact comfort** that is as basic as the need for food. Gratification of the need for contact comfort, rather than food, might be why infant monkeys (and humans) cling to their mothers.

Truth or Fiction Revisited. *It is not true that the way to a baby's heart is through its stomach. That is, babies do not necessarily become emotionally attached to those who feed them.* Contact comfort may be a stronger wellspring of attachment. Let's put it another way: The path to a monkey's heart may be through its skin, not its stomach.

Harlow and Zimmerman (1959) found that a surrogate mother made of terry cloth

Attachment. Feelings of attachment bind most parents tightly to their children. According to Ainsworth, attachment is an emotional bond between one animal or person and another specific individual. Secure attachment paves the way for healthy social development.

Indiscriminate attachment • Showing attachment behaviors toward any person.

Initial-preattachment phase • The first phase in forming bonds of attachment, characterized by indiscriminate attachment.

Attachment-in-the-making phase • The second phase in forming bonds of attachment, characterized by preference for familiar figures.

Clear-cut-attachment phase • The third phase in forming bonds of attachment, characterized by intensified dependence on the primary caregiver.

Contact comfort • A hypothesized primary drive to seek physical comfort through contact with another.

FIGURE 11.4
Attachment in Infant Monkeys
Although this rhesus monkey infant is fed by the wire "mother," it spends most of its time clinging to the soft, cuddly terry-cloth "mother." It knows where to get a meal, but contact comfort is apparently a more central determinant of attachment in infant monkeys (and infant humans?) than is the feeding process, as indicated by the accompanying graph.

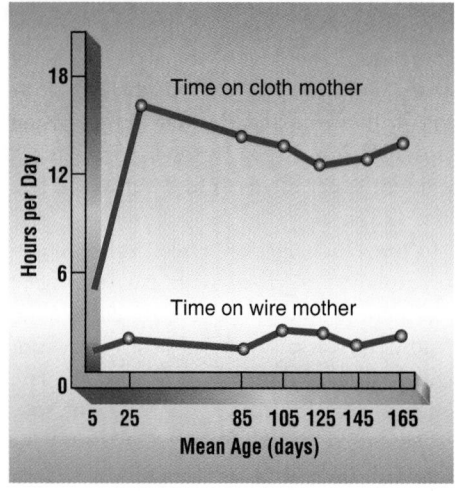

Critical period • A period of time when a fixed-action pattern can be elicited by a releasing stimulus.

Imprinting • A process occurring during a critical period in the development of an organism, in which that organism responds to a stimulus in a manner that will afterward be difficult to modify.

could also serve as a comforting base from which a rhesus infant could explore the environment. Toys such as stuffed bears (see Figure 11.5) and oversized wooden insects were placed in cages with rhesus infants and their surrogate mothers. When the infants were alone or had wire surrogate mothers for companions, they cowered in fear as long as the "bear monster" or "insect monster" was present. But when the terry-cloth mothers were present, the infants clung to them for a while, then explored the intruding "monster." With human infants, too, bonds of mother–infant attachment appear to provide a secure base from which infants feel encouraged to express their curiosity motives.

IMPRINTING: AN ETHOLOGICAL VIEW OF ATTACHMENT.   Ethologists note that for many animals, attachment is an inborn fixed-action pattern (FAP). The FAP of attachment, like other FAPs, is theorized to occur in the presence of a species-specific releasing stimulus and during a **critical period** of life.

Some animals become attached to the first moving object they encounter. The unwritten rule seems to be, "If it moves, it must be mother." It is as if the image of the moving object becomes "imprinted" on the young animal, and so the formation of an attachment in this manner is called **imprinting.**

Ethologist Konrad Lorenz (1981) became well known when pictures of his "family" of goslings were made public (see Figure 11.6). How did Lorenz acquire his following? He was present when the goslings hatched and during their critical periods, and he allowed them to follow him. The critical period for geese and some other animals is bounded, at the younger end, by the age at which they first engage in locomotion and, at the older end, by the age at which they develop fear of strangers. The goslings followed Lorenz persistently, ran to him when frightened, honked with distress at his departure, and tried to overcome barriers between them. If you substitute crying for honking, it all sounds rather human.

FIGURE 11.5
Security With its terry-cloth surrogate mother nearby, this infant rhesus monkey apparently feels secure enough to explore the "bear monster" placed in its cage. But infants with only wire surrogate mothers, or with no mothers, remain cowering in a corner when the bear or other "monsters" are introduced.

If imprinting occurs with children, it does not follow the mechanics that apply to waterfowl. Not all children develop fear of strangers. When they do, it occurs at about 6 to 8 months of age—*prior to* independent locomotion, or crawling, which usually occurs 1 or 2 months later. Yet, Ainsworth and Bowlby (1991) also hold an ethological view of human attachment, though the critical period with humans would be quite extended.

DIMENSIONS OF CHILD REARING

Investigators of parental approaches to child rearing have found it useful to classify them according to two broad dimensions: warmth–coldness and restrictiveness–permissiveness (Baumrind, 1991a, 1991b; MacDonald, 1992). These dimensions are independent. That is, warm parents can be restrictive or permissive. So can cold parents.

Warmth–Coldness. Whether parents respond to their children with warmth, love, and affection usually reflects their feelings toward their children, not a philosophy of child rearing. Warm parents are affectionate toward their children. They tend to hug and kiss them and to smile at them frequently. They behave in ways that communicate their happiness at having children and their enjoyment in being with them. Cold parents may not enjoy being with their children and may have few feelings of affection for them. They are likely to complain about their children's behavior, saying that they are naughty or have "minds of their own."

Research evidence clearly shows that warmth is superior to coldness in rearing children (Dix, 1991). Children of warm parents are more likely to be socially and emotionally well-adjusted and to internalize

FIGURE 11.6
Imprinting Quite a following? Konrad Lorenz may not look like Mommy to you, but these goslings became attached to him because he was the first moving object they perceived and followed. This type of attachment process is referred to as *imprinting*.

moral standards—that is, to develop a conscience (MacDonald, 1992; Miller and others, 1993).

Restrictiveness—Permissiveness.

Parents must generally decide how restrictive they will be toward many of their children's behavior patterns. Consider just a brief list: diet, noise (screaming, screeching, or demanding attention, especially when other children are sleeping or people are trying to converse), playing with dangerous objects or in dangerous places, damaging property, neatness, and aggression. Parents who are highly restrictive tend to impose many rules and to watch their children closely. Permissive parents impose few, if any, rules and supervise their children less closely. As a group, they are less concerned about cleanliness.

Parents may be permissive for different reasons. Some parents believe that children need the freedom to express their natural urges if they are to become self-directed and psychologically healthy. Others may be disinterested in their children and uninvolved.

The effects of restrictiveness on children depend on how "restrictiveness" is used. If it is used in the sense of consistent control and firm enforcement of rules, it can have positive results, especially when combined with support and affection (Putallaz & Hefflin, 1990). But when "restrictiveness" means physical punishment or intrusiveness, it is connected with disobedience and lower levels of academic performance (Olson and others, 1992; Westerman, 1990).

So-called **authoritative** (not authoritarian) parents combine warmth with positive forms of restrictiveness. Compared with other children, the children of authoritative parents have greater self-reliance, self-esteem, social competence, and achievement motivation (Baumrind, 1991b; Dumas & LaFreniere, 1993). It seems that demands for mature behavior combined with affection and support pay off.

Reflections

Now that you have read the section on social development, reflect on the following questions:

- How would you characterize your own attachment to the parent figures in your life? How did your feelings of attachment affect your behavior as a child?
- Would you characterize the parent figures in your life as having been warm or cold, restrictive or permissive? In what ways? How did the parenting style you experienced affect your feelings and behavior?

Cognitive Development

The developing thought processes of children—their cognitive development—is explored in this section. Cognitive functioning develops over a number of years, and children have ideas about the world that differ considerably from those of adults. Many of these ideas are charming but illogical. Swiss psychologist Jean Piaget (1896–1980) contributed significantly to our understanding of children's cognitive development.

JEAN PIAGET'S COGNITIVE-DEVELOPMENTAL THEORY

Piaget is more than a historical figure, large as he looms in the historical landscape of developmental psychology. His theory is still very much a contending presence in the free-for-all that defines current psychological theorizing.

HARRY BEILIN (1992)

In his early 20s, Jean Piaget obtained a job at the Binet Institute in Paris. His initial task was to develop a standardized version of the Binet intelligence test in French. In so doing, he questioned many children using potential test questions and became intrigued by their *incorrect* answers. Another investigator might have shrugged them off and forgotten them. Young Piaget realized that there were methods to his children's madness. The wrong answers reflected consistent, if illogical, cognitive processes.

Piaget hypothesized that children's cognitive processes develop in an orderly sequence of stages (1963). Although some children may be more advanced than others at particular ages, the developmental

---

Authoritative • The style of parenting characterized by warmth and restrictiveness.

Assimilation • (as-SIM-me-LAY-shun). According to Piaget, the inclusion of a new event into an existing scheme.

Scheme • According to Piaget, a hypothetical mental structure that permits the classification and organization of new information.

Accommodation • (ack-KOM-me-DAY-shun). According to Piaget, the modification of schemes so that information inconsistent with existing schemes can be integrated or understood.

TABLE 11.1

Piaget's Stages of Cognitive Development

STAGE	APPROXIMATE AGE	DESCRIPTION
Sensorimotor	Birth–2 years	Behavior suggests that child lacks language and does not use symbols or mental representations of objects in the environment. Simple responding to the environment (through reflexive schemes) draws to an end, and intentional behavior—such as making interesting sights last—begins. The child develops the object concept and acquires the basics of language.
Preoperational	2–7 years	The child begins to represent the world mentally, but thought is egocentric. The child does not focus on two aspects of a situation at once and therefore lacks conservation. The child shows animism, artificialism, and immanent justice.
Concrete operational	7–12 years	The child shows conservation concepts, can adopt the viewpoint of others, can classify objects in series (for example, from shortest to longest), and shows comprehension of basic relational concepts (such as one object being larger or heavier than another).
Formal operational	12 years and above	Mature, adult thought emerges. Thinking seems to be characterized by deductive logic, consideration of various possibilities before acting to solve a problem (mental trial and error), abstract thought (for example, philosophical weighing of moral principles), and the formation and testing of hypotheses.

sequence is invariant. Piaget identified four major stages of cognitive development (see Table 11.1): sensorimotor, preoperational, concrete operational, and formal operational.

Piaget regarded children as natural physicists who actively intend to learn about and manipulate their worlds. In the Piagetan view, children who squish their food and laugh enthusiastically, for example, are often acting as budding scientists. In addition to enjoying a response from parents, they are studying the texture and consistency of their food. (Parents, of course, often wish that their children would practice these experiments in the laboratory, not the house.)

Piaget's view differs markedly from the behaviorist view that people merely react to environmental stimuli rather than intending to interpret and act on the world. Piaget saw people as actors, not reactors. Piaget believed that people purposefully form cognitive representations of, and seek to manipulate, the world.

Piaget's Basic Concepts: Assimilation and Accommodation. Piaget described human thought, or intelligence, in terms of assimilation and accommodation. **Assimilation** is responding to a new stimulus through a reflex or existing habit. Infants, for example, usually try to place new objects in their mouths to suck, feel, or explore. Piaget would say that the child is assimilating a new toy to the sucking **scheme.** A scheme is a pattern of action or a mental structure that is involved in acquiring or organizing knowledge.

Accommodation is the creation of new ways of responding to objects or looking at the world. In accommodation, children transform existing schemes—action patterns or ways of organizing knowledge—to incorporate new events. Children (and adults) accommodate to objects and situations that cannot be integrated into existing schemes. The ability to accommodate to novel stimulation advances as a result of maturation and experience.

Most of the time, newborn children assimilate environmental stimulation according to reflexive schemes, although adjusting the mouth to contain the nipple is a primitive kind of accommodation. Reflexive behavior, to Piaget, is not characteristic of "true" intelligence. True intelligence

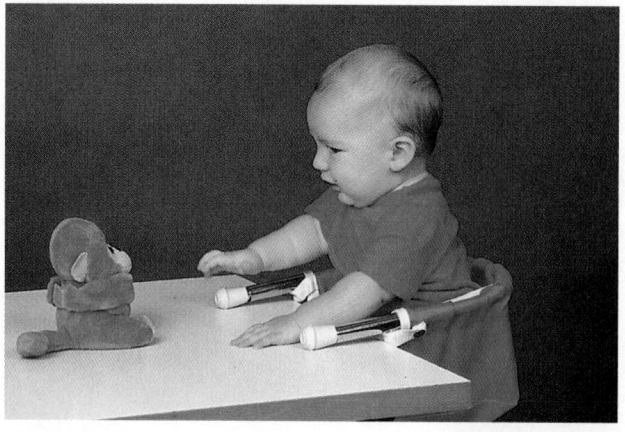
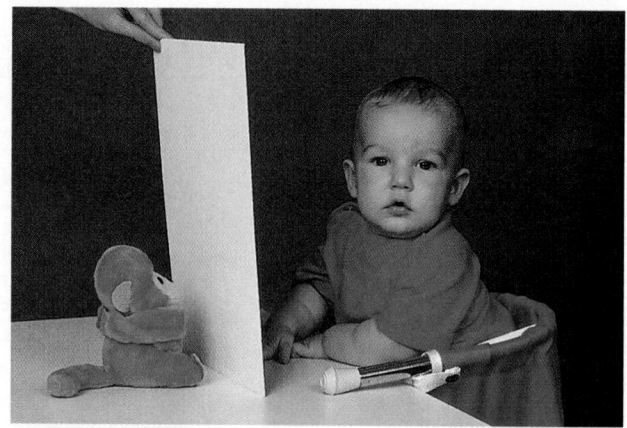

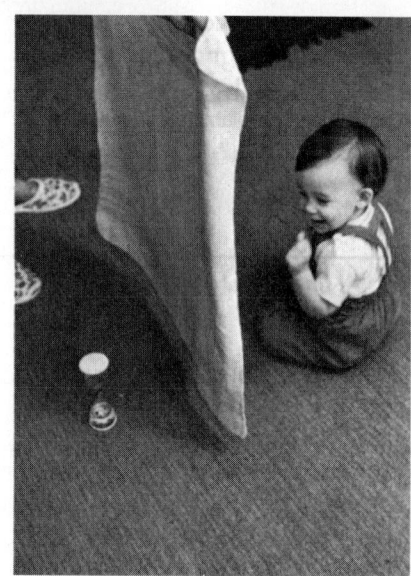

FIGURE 11.7

Object Permanence To the infant at the top, who is in the early part of the sensorimotor stage, out of sight is truly out of mind. Once a sheet of paper is placed between the infant and the toy monkey, the infant loses all interest in the toy. From evidence of this sort, Piaget concluded that the toy is not mentally represented. The bottom series of photos shows a child in a later part of the sensorimotor stage. This child does mentally represent objects and pushes through a towel to reach an object that has been screened from sight.

involves adapting to the world through a smooth, fluid balancing of the processes of assimilation and accommodation (Beilin, 1992). Let us now return to the stages of cognitive development.

The Sensorimotor Stage. The newborn infant is capable of assimilating novel stimulation only to existing reflexes (or ready-made schemes) such as the rooting and sucking reflexes. But by the time an infant reaches the age of 1 month, it will already show purposeful behavior by repeating behavior patterns that are pleasur-

able such as sucking its hand. During the first month or so, an infant apparently does not connect stimulation perceived through different senses. Crude turning toward sources of auditory and olfactory stimulation has a ready-made look about it that cannot be considered purposeful searching. But within the first few months, the infant begins to coordinate vision with grasping so that it simultaneously looks at what it is holding or touching.

A 3- or 4-month-old infant may be fascinated by its own hands and legs. It may become absorbed in watching itself open and close its fists. The infant becomes increasingly interested in acting on the environment to make interesting results (such as the sound of a rattle) last. Behavior becomes increasingly intentional and purposeful. Between 4 and 8 months of age, the infant explores cause-and-effect relationships such as the thump that can be made by tossing an object or the way kicking can cause a hanging toy to bounce.

Prior to the age of 6 months or so, out of sight is literally out of mind. Objects are not yet mentally represented. For this reason, as you can see in Figure 11.7, a child will make no effort to search for an object that has been removed or placed behind a screen. By the ages of 8 to 12 months, however, infants realize that objects removed from sight still exist and attempt to find them. In this way, they show what is known as **object permanence.**

During the second year of life, children begin to show interest in how things are constructed. It may be for this reason that they persistently touch and finger their parents' and their own faces. Toward the end of the second year, children begin to engage in mental trial and error before they try out overt behavior. For instance, when they look for an object you have removed, they will no longer begin their search in the last place it was seen. Rather, they may follow you, assuming that you are carrying the object even though it is not visible. It is as though they are anticipating failure in searching for the object in the place where it was most recently seen.

Because the first stage of development is dominated by learning to coordinate perception of the self and of the environment with motor (muscular) activity, Piaget termed it the **sensorimotor stage.** The sensorimotor stage comes to a close at about the age of 2, with the acquisition of the basics of language.

The Preoperational Stage.

When Tony gets little, I'll marry him, okay?
THE AUTHOR'S DAUGHTER TAYLOR,
AT AGE 2 YEARS 10 MONTHS.
(TONY WAS A WAITER AT A RESTAURANT.)

The **preoperational stage** is characterized by children's early use of words and symbols to represent objects and the relationships among them. But be warned—any resemblance between the logic of children between the ages of 2 to 7 and your own logic very often appears to be purely coincidental. Children may use the same words as adults do, but this does not mean their views of the world are similar to adults'. A major limit on preoperational children's thinking is that it tends to be one-dimensional—to focus on one aspect of a problem or situation at a time.

One consequence of one-dimensional thinking is **egocentrism.** Preoperational children cannot understand that other people do not see things as they do. When Allyn was 2½, I asked her to tell me about a trip to the store with her mother. "You tell me," she replied. Upon questioning, it seemed that she did not understand that I could not see the world through her eyes.

To egocentric preoperational children, all the world's a stage that has been erected to meet their needs and amuse them. When asked, "Why does the sun shine?" they may say, "To keep me warm." If asked, "Why is the sky blue?" they may respond, "'Cause blue's my favorite color." Preoperational children also show **animism.** They attribute life and consciousness to physical objects like the sun and the moon (Beilin, 1992). They also show **artificialism.** They believe that environmental events like rain and thunder are human inventions (Beilin, 1992). Asked why the sky is blue, 4-year-olds may answer, "'Cause Mommy painted it." Examples of egocentrism, animism, and artificialism are shown in Table 11.2.

To gain further insight into preoperational thinking, consider these problems:

1. Imagine that you pour water from a tall, thin glass into a low, wide glass. Now, does the low, wide glass contain more, less, or the same amount of water as was in the tall, thin glass? I won't keep you in suspense. If you said the same amount of water (with possible minor exceptions for spillage and evaporation), you were correct. Now that you're rolling, read on to the next problem.

2. If you flatten a ball of clay into a pancake, do you wind up with more, less, or the same amount of clay? If you said the same amount of clay, you are correct once more. To arrive at the correct answers to these questions, you must

MINILECTURE: OBJECT PERMANENCE

MINILECTURE: CONSERVATION

Object permanence • Recognition that objects removed from sight still exist, as demonstrated in young children by continued pursuit.

Sensorimotor stage • The first of Piaget's stages of cognitive development, characterized by coordination of sensory information and motor activity, early exploration of the environment, and lack of language.

Preoperational stage • The second of Piaget's stages, characterized by illogical use of words and symbols, spotty logic, and egocentrism.

Egocentric • (ee-go-SENT-trick). According to Piaget, assuming that others view the world as one does oneself.

Animism • The belief that inanimate objects move because of will or spirit.

Artificialism • The belief that natural objects have been created by human beings.

TABLE 11.2
Examples of Preoperational Thought

TYPE OF THOUGHT	SAMPLE QUESTIONS	TYPICAL ANSWERS
Egocentrism	Why does it get dark out?	So I can go to sleep.
	Why does the sun shine?	To keep me warm.
	Why is there snow?	For me to play in.
	Why is grass green?	Because that's my favorite color.
	What are TV sets for?	To watch my favorite shows and cartoons.
Animism (attributing life and consciousness to physical objects)	Why do trees have leaves?	To keep them warm.
	Why do stars twinkle?	Because they're happy and cheerful.
	Why does the sun move in the sky?	To follow children and hear what they say.
	Where do boats go at night?	They sleep like we do.
Artificialism (assuming that environmental events are human inventions)	What makes it rain?	Someone emptying a watering can.
	Why is the sky blue?	Somebody painted it.
	What is the wind?	A man blowing.
	What causes thunder?	A man grumbling.
	How does a baby get in Mommy's tummy?	Just make it first. (How?) You put some eyes on it, put the head on (etc.).

understand the law of **conservation.** This law holds that basic properties of substances such as mass, weight, and volume remain the same—or are *conserved*—when you change superficial properties such as their shape or arrangement.

Conservation requires the ability to think about, or **center** on, two aspects of a situation at once, such as height and width. Conserving the mass, weight, or volume of a substance requires recognition that a change in one dimension can compensate

FIGURE 11.8

Conservation The boy in these photographs agreed that the amount of water in two identical containers is equal. He then watched as water from one container was poured into a tall, thin container. In the left-hand photograph, he is examining one of the original containers and the new container. When asked whether he thinks that the amounts of water in the two containers are now the same, he says no. Apparently, he is impressed by the height of the new container, and, prior to the development of conservation, he focuses on only one dimension of the situation at a time—in this case, the height of the new container.

for a change in another. But the preoperational boy in Figure 11.8 focuses on just one dimension at a time. First, he is shown two tall, thin glasses of water and agrees that they have the same amount of water. Then, while he watches, water is poured from one tall glass into a squat glass. Now, he is asked which glass has more water. After mulling over the problem, he points to the tall glass. Why? When he looks at the glasses, he is "overwhelmed" by the fact that the thinner glass is taller. The preoperational child focuses on the most apparent dimension of the situation—in this case, the greater height of the thinner glass. He does not realize that the gain in width in the squat glass compensates for the loss in height. By the way, if you ask him whether any water has been added or taken away in the pouring process, he will readily reply no. But if you then repeat the question about which glass has *more* water, he will again point to the taller glass.

If all this sounds rather illogical, that is because it is illogical—or to be precise, preoperational.

After you have tried the experiment with the water, try the following. Make two rows with five pennies each. In the first row, place the pennies about half an inch apart. In the second row, place the pennies 2 to 3 inches apart. Ask a 4- to 5-year-old child which row has more pennies. What do you think the child will say? Why?

Piaget (1962) found that the moral judgment of preoperational children is also one-dimensional. Five-year-olds are slaves to rules and authority. When you ask them why something should be done in a certain way, they may insist "Because that's the way to do it!" or "Because my Mommy says so!" Right is right and wrong is wrong. Why? "Because!"—that's why.

According to most older children and adults, an act is a crime only when there is criminal intent. Accidents may be hurtful, but the perpetrators are usually seen as blameless. But in the court of the one-dimensional, preoperational child, there is **objective responsibility.** People are sentenced (and harshly!) on the basis of the amount of damage they have done, not their motive or intentions.

To demonstrate objective responsibility, Piaget would tell children stories and ask them which character was naughtier and why. John, for instance, accidentally breaks 15 cups when he opens a door. Henry breaks one cup when he sneaks into a kitchen cabinet to find forbidden jam. The preoperational child usually judges John to be naughtier. Why? He broke more cups.

The Concrete-Operational Stage. By about the age of 7, the typical child is entering the stage of **concrete operations.** In this stage, which lasts until about the age of 12, children show the beginnings of the capacity for adult logic. However, their logical thought, or operations, generally involves tangible objects rather than abstract ideas. Concrete operational children are capable of **decentration;** they can center simultaneously on two dimensions of a problem. This attainment has implications for moral judgments, conservation, and other intellectual undertakings.

Children now become **subjective** in their moral judgments. They center on the motives of wrongdoers as well as the amount of damage done when assigning guilt. Concrete-operational children judge Henry more harshly than John, since John's misdeed was an accident.

Concrete-operational children understand the laws of conservation. The boy in Figure 11.8, now a few years older, would say that the squat glass still has the same amount of water. If asked why, he might reply, "Because you can pour it back into the other one." An answer to this effect also suggests awareness of the concept of **reversibility**—recognition that many processes can be reversed or undone so that things can be restored to their previous condition. Centering simultaneously on the height and the width of the glasses, the boy recognizes that the loss in height compensates for the gain in width.

Concrete-operational children can conserve number as well as weight and mass. They recognize that there is the same number of pennies in each of the rows described earlier, even though one row may be spread out to look longer than the other.

Children in this stage are less egocentric. They are able to take on the roles of others and to view the world, and themselves, from other peoples' perspectives. They recognize that people see things in different

Conservation • According to Piaget, recognition that basic properties of substances such as weight and mass remain the same when superficial features change.

Center • According to Piaget, to focus one's attention.

Objective responsibility • According to Piaget, the assignment of blame according to the amount of damage done rather than the motives of the actor.

Concrete-operational stage • Piaget's third stage, characterized by logical thought concerning tangible objects, conservation, and subjective morality.

Decentration • (DEE-sent-TRAY-shun). Simultaneous focusing on more than one dimension of a problem, so that flexible, reversible thought becomes possible.

Subjective moral judgment • According to Piaget, moral judgments that are based on the motives of the perpetrator.

Reversibility • According to Piaget, recognition that processes can be undone, that things can be made as they were.

ways because of different situations and different sets of values.

During the concrete-operational stage, children's own sets of values begin to emerge and acquire stability. Children come to understand that feelings of love between them and their parents can endure even when someone feels angry or disappointed at the moment.

The Formal-Operational Stage.

The stage of **formal operations** is the final stage in Piaget's theory. It begins at about the time of puberty and is the stage of cognitive maturity. Not all children enter this stage at puberty, and some people never reach it.

Formal-operational children (and adults) think abstractly. They become capable of solving geometric problems about circles and squares without reference to what the circles and squares may represent in the real world. Children derive rules for behavior from general principles and can focus, or center, on many aspects of a situation at once in arriving at judgments and solving problems.

In a sense, it is during the stage of formal operations that people tend to emerge as theoretical scientists—even though they may see themselves as having little or no interest in science. They become capable of dealing with hypothetical situations. They realize that situations can have different outcomes, and they think ahead, experimenting with different possibilities. Children—adolescents by now—also conduct experiments to determine whether their hypotheses are correct. These experiments are not conducted in the laboratory. Rather, adolescents may try out different tones of voice, ways of carrying themselves, and ways of treating others to see what works best for them.

Children in this stage can reason deductively, or draw conclusions about specific objects or people once they have been classified accurately. Adolescents can be somewhat proud of their new logical abilities. A new sort of egocentrism can develop in which adolescents emotionally press for acceptance of their logic without recognition of the exceptions or practical problems that are often considered by adults. Consider this example: "It is wrong to hurt people.

MINILECTURE:
FORMAL
OPERATIONS

Industry A occasionally hurts people (perhaps through pollution or economic pressures). Therefore, Industry A must be severely punished or dismantled." This thinking is logical. By impatiently pressing for immediate major changes or severe penalties, however, one may not fully consider various practical problems such as thousands of resultant layoffs.

Evaluation of Piaget's Cognitive-Developmental Theory.

A number of questions, such as the following, have been raised concerning the accuracy of Piaget's views:

1. *Was Piaget's timing accurate?* Some critics argue that Piaget's methodology led him to underestimate the abilities of children. U.S. researchers have used different methods and have found, for example, that preschoolers are less egocentric and that children are capable of conservation at earlier ages than Piaget's research suggested. On the other hand, Piaget himself admitted that the ages at which his subjects showed certain developments were a function of the methods he used (Beilin, 1992). Piaget himself, therefore, was not locked into particular age norms.

2. *Is cognitive development discontinuous?* The most damaging criticism leveled at Piaget is that cognitive skills such as egocentrism and conservation appear to develop more continuously than Piaget thought—rather than in stages. Flavell and his colleagues (1993) argue that cognitive development does not appear to be very stagelike. Although cognitive developments appear to build on other cognitive developments, the process may be more gradual than discontinuous.

3. *Are developmental sequences invariant?* Here, Piaget's views have fared better. It seems that the sequences of development are indeed invariant, as Piaget believed. I also think it is fair to say that the sequences of development might be more essential to Piaget's theory than their timing.

In sum, Piaget's theoretical edifice has been rocked, but it has not been dashed to rubble. Research continues to wear away at his timing and at his belief that the stages of cognitive development are discontinuous, but his views on the sequences of development remain relatively inviolate.

Many psychologists regard Piaget as a towering figure in the study of cognitive development, but his approach is not the only one. There are many others, including information-processing approaches.

INFORMATION-PROCESSING APPROACHES TO COGNITIVE DEVELOPMENT

Whereas Piaget viewed children as budding scientists, psychologists who study **information processing** view children (and adults) as akin to computer systems. Children, like computers, attain information ("input") from the environment, store it, retrieve and manipulate it, then respond to it overtly ("output") (Harnishfeger & Bjorklund, 1990). One goal of the information-processing approach is to learn how children store, retrieve, and manipulate information—how their "mental programs" develop. Information-processing theorists also study the development of children's strategies for processing information.

Case (1992) and Pascual-Leone (1980) focus on children's capacity for memory and their use of cognitive strategies, such as the ways in which they focus their attention. They assume that neurological developments permit the expansion of working memory. They note that certain Piagetan tasks require several cognitive strategies instead of one and that young children may fail at them because they cannot simultaneously hold many pieces of information in their working memories. Put it this way: Preschoolers can solve problems with one or two steps, but older children can retain information from early steps as they carry out later steps.

Reconsider Piaget's story of the cups, the one in which John breaks 15 cups accidentally while Henry breaks one while trying to steal jam. Some aspects of development that Piaget believed to reflect qualitative changes in thought may actually reflect growing capacity for storage and retrieval of information (Gelman & Baillargeon, 1983).

Most 5-year-olds say that John is naughtier because he broke more cups. Eight-year-olds usually condemn Henry because he was doing something wrong at the time. Piaget explained this age difference in terms of 5-year-olds' tendencies to focus on the amount of damage done, rather than the intentions of the wrongdoer. However, many 5-year-olds say that John is naughtier simply because they can remember that he broke more cups but not all the details of the stories. When the stories are repeated carefully, even 5-year-olds often consider the motives of the cup-breaker.

Development of Selective Attention. A basic strategy for solving problems is simply to attend to their elements. The ability to focus one's attention and screen out distractions advances steadily through middle childhood. Younger children tend to focus their attention on one element of a problem at a time—a major reason that they lack conservation. Older children, in contrast, attend to multiple aspects of the problem at once, which permits them to conserve number, volume, and so on.

A classic experiment by Eleanor Maccoby and John Hagen (1965) illustrates how selective attention develops during middle childhood. The researchers showed 6- to 12-year-olds pictures of elephants, buckets, scooters, and other things and told them to remember only the colors of the pictures' *backgrounds*. They were told that the subjects themselves were immaterial. Recall of background colors improved regularly with age. The 12-year-olds recalled about twice as many colors as the 6-year-olds. Then the researchers turned the tables on the children by asking them to recall the *subjects* of the pictures. Ironically, the 12-year-olds recalled *fewer* subjects correctly than the 6-year-olds, apparently because of their greater ability to focus their attention as originally directed.

Automaticity. Another contributor to children's abilities to solve problems is increasing automaticity in applying cognitive strategies (Case, 1992). If you ask young children how many objects there are in three sets of two, they may have to count them one by one to arrive at a total of six. But older children, with larger working memories, familiarity with multiplication tables, and more perceptual experience, are

Formal-operational stage • Piaget's fourth stage, characterized by abstract logical thought; deduction from principles.

Information processing • An approach to cognitive development that deals with children's advances in the input, storage, retrieval, manipulation, and output of information.

likely to arrive at a total of six automatically when three groups of two are perceived. Automaticity in adding, multiplying, and so on allows older children to solve math problems that have several steps. Younger children, meanwhile, become lost in individual steps.[1]

Metamemory. **Metamemory** refers to children's awareness of the functioning of their memory processes. Older children show greater insight into how their memories work (Hashimoto, 1991; Kail, 1990). They are more capable of using strategies to remember things. For example, 2- and 3-year-olds do not use rehearsal (repetition) when asked to remember a list of items. Four- and 5-year-olds will usually repeat the list aloud if someone else suggests that they do, and they use rehearsal spontaneously by 6 or 7 (Flavell and others, 1993).

If you were trying to remember a new phone number, you would know to rehearse it several times or to write it down before doing a series of math problems. Ten-year-olds are also aware that new mental activities (the math problems) can interfere with old ones (rehearsing the telephone number) and usually suggest jotting down the number before trying the problems. Few 5-year-olds see the advantage of jotting the number down before doing the math problems, however.

Let us now turn our attention to Lawrence Kohlberg's theory of moral development and see how children process information that leads to judgments of right and wrong.

LAWRENCE KOHLBERG'S THEORY OF MORAL DEVELOPMENT

Psychologist Lawrence Kohlberg (1981) originated a cognitive-developmental theory of children's moral reasoning. Before we describe Kohlberg's views, read the following tale he used in his research and answer the questions that follow.

In Europe a woman was near death from a special kind of cancer. There was one drug that the doctors thought might save her. It was a form of radium that a druggist in the same town had recently discovered. The drug was expensive to make, but the druggist was charging ten times what the drug cost him to make. He paid $200 for the radium and charged $2,000 for a small dose of the drug. The sick woman's husband, Heinz, went to everyone he knew to borrow the money, but he could only get together about $1,000, which was half of what it cost. He told the druggist that his wife was dying and asked him to sell it cheaper or let him pay later. But the druggist said: "No, I discovered the drug and I'm going to make money from it." So Heinz got desperate and broke into the man's store to steal the drug for his wife. (Kohlberg, 1969)

What do you think? Should Heinz have tried to steal the drug? Was he right or wrong? As you can see from Table 11.3, the issue is more complicated than a simple yes or no. Heinz is caught up in a moral dilemma in which a legal or social rule (in this case, laws against stealing) is pitted against a strong human need (Heinz's desire to save his wife). According to Kohlberg's theory, children and adults arrive at yes or no answers for different reasons. These reasons can be classified according to the level of moral development they reflect.

As a stage theorist, Kohlberg argues that the stages of moral reasoning follow an invariant sequence. Children progress at different rates, and not all children (or adults) reach the highest stage. But children must go through stage 1 before they enter stage 2, and so on. According to Kohlberg, there are three levels of moral development and two stages within each level.

The Preconventional Level. The **preconventional level** applies to most children through about the age of 9. Children at this level base moral judgments on the consequences of behavior. For instance, stage 1 is oriented toward obedience and punishment. Good behavior is obedient and allows one to avoid punishment.

MINILECTURE: KOHLBERG'S THEORY OF MORAL DEVELOPMENT

---

[1] In Chapter 9, we saw that automaticity in processing information is an element in Robert Sternberg's (1995) theory of intelligence.

TABLE 11.3

Kohlberg's Levels and Stages of Moral Development

STAGE OF DEVELOPMENT	EXAMPLES OF MORAL REASONING THAT SUPPORT HEINZ'S STEALING THE DRUG	EXAMPLES OF MORAL REASONING THAT OPPOSE HEINZ'S STEALING THE DRUG
LEVEL I: PRECONVENTIONAL		
STAGE 1: Judgments guided by obedience and the prospect of punishment (The consequences of the behavior.)	It isn't wrong to take the drug. After all, Heinz tried to pay the druggist for it, and it's only worth $200, not $2,000.	It's wrong to take the drug because taking things without paying is against the law; Heinz will get caught and go to jail.
STAGE 2: Naively egoistic, instrumental orientation (Things are right when they satisfy people's needs.)	Heinz ought to take the drug because his wife really needs it. He can always pay the druggist back.	Heinz shouldn't take the drug. If he gets caught and winds up in jail, it won't do his wife any good.
LEVEL II: CONVENTIONAL		
STAGE 3: Good-boy orientation (That which helps others and is socially approved is right.)	Stealing is a crime, so it's bad, but Heinz should take the drug to save his wife or else people would blame him for letting her die.	Stealing is a crime. Heinz shouldn't just take the drug because his family will be dishonored and they will blame him.
STAGE 4: Law-and-order orientation (Doing one's duty and showing respect for authority are right.)	Heinz must take the drug to do his duty to save his wife. Eventually, he has to pay the druggist for it, however.	If everybody took the law into his or her own hands, civilization would fall apart, so Heinz shouldn't steal the drug.
LEVEL III: POSTCONVENTIONAL		
STAGE 5: Contractual, legalistic orientation (It is moral to weigh pressing human needs against society's need to maintain the social order.)	This thing is complicated because society has a right to maintain law and order, but Heinz has to take the drug to save his wife.	I can see why Heinz feels he has to take the drug, but laws exist for the benefit of society as a whole and can't simply be cast aside.
STAGE 6: Universal ethical principles orientation (People must act in accord with universal ethical principles and their own conscience, even if they must break the law in doing so.)	This is a case in which the law comes into conflict with the sanctity of human life. Heinz must take the drug because his wife's life is more important than the law.	If Heinz, in his own conscience, believes that stealing the drug is worse than letting his wife die, he should not take it. People have to make sacrifices to do what they believe is right.

Metamemory • Knowledge of the functions and processes in one's own memory, as shown by use of cognitive strategies to retain information.

Preconventional level • According to Kohlberg, a period during which moral judgments are based largely on expectation of rewards or punishments.

Conventional level • According to Kohlberg, a period during which moral judgments largely reflect social conventions. A "law and order" approach to morality.

In stage 2, good behavior allows people to satisfy their needs and those of others. (Heinz's wife needs the drug; therefore, stealing the drug—the only way of attaining it—is not wrong.)

The Conventional Level. In the **conventional level** of moral reasoning, right and wrong are judged by conformity to conventional (family, church, societal) standards of right and wrong. According to the stage 3 "good-boy orientation," it is

moral to meet the needs and expectations of others. Moral behavior is what is "normal"—what the majority does. (Heinz should steal the drug because that is what a "good husband" would do. It is "natural" or "normal" to try to help one's wife. *Or,* Heinz should *not* steal the drug because "good people do not steal.")

In stage 4, moral judgments are based on rules that maintain the social order. Showing respect for authority and doing one's duty are valued highly. (Heinz must steal the drug; it would be his responsibility if he let his wife die. He would pay the druggist when he could.) Many people do not mature beyond the conventional level.

Stage 3 moral judgments are found most frequently among 13-year-olds, and stage 4 judgments most often among 16-year-olds (Kohlberg, 1963).

The Postconventional Level. In the **postconventional level,** moral reasoning is based on the person's own moral standards. In each instance, moral judgments are derived from personal values, not from conventional standards or authority figures. In stage 5's contractual, legalistic orientation, it is recognized that laws stem from agreed-upon procedures and that many laws have great value and should not be violated. But under exceptional circumstances, laws cannot bind the individual. (Although it is illegal for Heinz to steal the drug, in this case it is the right thing to do.)

Stage 6 thinking relies on supposed universal ethical principles such as those of human life, individual dignity, justice, and **reciprocity.** Behavior that is consistent with these principles is moral. If a law is unjust or contradicts the rights of the individual, it is wrong to obey it.

Postconventional people look to their consciences as the highest moral authority. This point has created confusion. To some it suggests that it is right to break the law when it is convenient. But this interpretation is incorrect. Kohlberg means that postconventional people must do what they believe is right even if it counters social rules or laws or requires personal sacrifice.

Not all people reach the postconventional level of moral reasoning. Postconventional moral judgments were absent among the 7- to 10-year-olds in Kohlberg's (1963) sample of American children. Postconventional judgments are found more frequently during the early and middle teens. By age 16, stage 5 reasoning is shown by about 20% and stage 6 reasoning by about 5% of adolescents. However, stage 3 and 4 judgments are made more frequently at all ages, 7 through 16, studied by Kohlberg and other investigators (Colby and others, 1983; Rest, 1983).

Evaluation of Kohlberg's Theory. Research suggests that moral reasoning

does follow a developmental sequence (Snarey and others, 1985), even though most children do not reach postconventional thought. Postconventional thought, when found, first occurs during adolescence. It also seems that formal operational thinking is a precedent for postconventional reasoning, which requires the capacities to understand abstract moral principles and to empathize with the attitudes and emotional responses of other people (Flavell and others, 1993).

Consistent with Kohlberg's theory, children do not appear to skip stages as they progress (Flavell and others, 1993). When children are exposed to adult models who enact a lower stage of moral reasoning, they can be induced to follow along (Bandura & McDonald, 1963). Children exposed to examples of moral reasoning above and below their own stage generally prefer the higher stage, however (Rest, 1983). Thus the thrust of moral development is from lower to higher, even if children can be sidetracked by social influences.

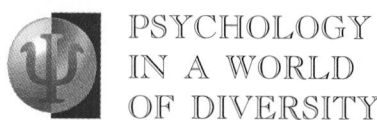

PSYCHOLOGY IN A WORLD OF DIVERSITY

ARE THE STAGES OF MORAL DEVELOPMENT UNIVERSAL? EVIDENCE FOR GENDER AND ETHNOCENTRIC BIASES

One of the more controversial notions in the history of child development is that males show higher levels of moral development than females. From his psychoanalytic perspective, Freud assumed that males would have stronger "superegos" than females because of the wrenching Oedipus complex and the male's consequent identification with authority figures and social codes. But Freud's views on the Oedipus complex were speculative, and his views on women reflected the ignorance and prejudice of his times.

In more recent years, however, some researchers have reported gender differences in moral development in the United States in terms of responses to Heinz's dilemma. Some studies have found that boys reason at higher levels of moral development than

---

Postconventional level • According to Kohlberg, a period during which moral judgments are derived from moral principles and people look to themselves to set moral standards.

Reciprocity • Mutual action.

Adolescence • The period of life bounded by puberty and the assumption of adult responsibilities.

girls. Carol Gilligan (1982; Gilligan and others, 1989) argues that this gender difference reflects different patterns of socialization for boys and girls.

Gilligan makes her point through two examples of responses to Heinz's dilemma. Eleven-year-old Jake views the dilemma as a math problem. He sets up an equation showing that life has greater value than property. Heinz is thus obligated to steal the drug. Eleven-year-old Amy vacillates. She notes that stealing the drug and letting Heinz's wife die would both be wrong. Amy searches for alternatives, such as getting a loan, stating that it would profit Heinz's wife little if he went to jail and were no longer around to help her.

According to Gilligan, Amy is showing a pattern of reasoning that is as sophisticated as Jake's. Still, Amy would be rated as showing a lower level of moral development. Gilligan asserts that Amy, like other girls, has been socialized into focusing on the needs of others and foregoing simplistic judgments of right and wrong. As a consequence, Amy is more likely to appear to show stage 3 reasoning, which focuses in part on empathy for others. Jake, by contrast, has been socialized into making judgments based purely on logic. To him, clear-cut conclusions are to be derived from a set of premises. Amy was aware of the logical considerations that struck Jake, of course. However, she processed them as one source of information—not as the sole acceptable source. It is ironic that Amy's empathy, a trait that has "defined the 'goodness' of women," marks Amy "as deficient in moral development" (Gilligan, 1982, p. 18). Prior to his death in 1987, Kohlberg had begun efforts to correct the sexism in his scoring system.

Kohlberg's critics have suggested that postconventional reasoning, especially stage 6 reasoning, may reflect Kohlberg's personal ideals and not a natural, universal stage of development. Stage 6 reasoning is based on supposedly omnipresent ethical principles. The principles of justice, equality, integrity, and reverence for life may have a high appeal to you, but you were reared in a culture that idealizes them. They are not universal, however—witness the brutality of Adolph Hitler, Joseph Stalin, and Saddam Hussein. These principles are more reflec-

tive of Western ideals than of cognitive development. In his later years, Kohlberg virtually dropped stage 6 reasoning from his theory, in recognition of these problems.

Truth or Fiction Revisited. *It is true within our culture that the highest level of moral reasoning involves relying on our own views of what is right and wrong. However, postconventional thought is not found in all cultures, and there is more support for stage 5 reasoning than for stage 6 reasoning.*

Reflections

Now that you have read the section on cognitive development, reflect on the following questions:

- Think of children you know or have known. (You were a child yourself once!) How does their behavior and some of the things they say seem reminiscent of the stages described by Piaget?
- Can you provide some examples of assimilation and accommodation in your own learning about the various areas of psychology?
- What cognitive strategies are you using to learn the material in this chapter? Are they planned or automatic?
- Agree or disagree with the following statement and support your answer: "Postconventional moral judgments represent the highest level of moral reasoning."
- How would you characterize your own level of cognitive development, both in terms of Piaget's and Kohlberg's theories of development? Support your characterizations.

Adolescence

Adolescence is a time of transition from childhood to adulthood. In our society, adolescents often feel that they are "neither fish nor fowl," as the saying goes—neither children nor adults. Although adolescents may be old enough to reproduce and are as large as their parents, they are often treated quite differently. They may not be eligible for driver's licenses until they are 16 or 17.

Adolescents. In our culture, adolescents are "neither fish nor fowl." Although they may be old enough to reproduce and may be as large as their parents, adolescents are often treated like children.

Secondary sex characteristics • Characteristics that differentiate the sexes, such as distribution of body hair and depth of voice, but that are not directly involved in reproduction.

Menarche • (men-ARK-key or may-NARSH). The beginning of menstruation.

They cannot attend R-rated films unless accompanied by an adult. They are prevented from working long hours. They are required to remain in school usually through age 16. They may not marry until they reach the "age of consent." Let us consider the physical, social, and personal changes of adolescence.

PHYSICAL DEVELOPMENT

Adolescence is heralded by puberty. Puberty begins with the appearance of **secondary sex characteristics** such as body hair, deepening of the voice in males, and rounding of the breasts and hips in females. In boys, pituitary hormones stoke the testes to increase the output of testosterone, causing the penis and testes to grow and bodily hair to appear. By the early teens, erections become common, and boys may ejaculate. Ejaculatory ability usually precedes the presence of mature sperm by at least a year. Ejaculation is thus not evidence of reproductive capacity.

In girls, pituitary secretions cause the ovaries to begin to secrete estrogen, which stimulates growth of breast tissue and fatty and supportive tissue in the hips and buttocks. Thus the pelvis widens, rounding the hips. Small amounts of androgens produced by the adrenal glands, along with estrogen, spur growth of pubic and underarm hair. Estrogen and androgens together stimulate the growth of female sex organs. Estrogen production becomes cyclical in puberty and regulates the menstrual cycle. First menstruation, or **menarche,** usually occurs between the ages of 11 and 14. Girls cannot become pregnant until they begin to ovulate, however, which may occur as much as two years later.

Truth or Fiction Revisited. *It is not usually true that girls are capable of becoming pregnant when they have their first menstrual periods.* Menarche can precede ovulation by a year or more.

Puberty ends when the long bones make no further gains in length so that full height is attained. But adolescence ends with psychosocial markers such as assumption of adult responsibilities. Adolescence is a psychological concept with biological aspects, but puberty is a biological concept.

The stable growth patterns in height and weight that characterize early and middle childhood come to an abrupt end with the adolescent growth spurt, which lasts for 2 to 3 years. Adolescents add some 8 to 12 inches in height. Most boys wind up taller and heavier than most girls.

In boys, the muscle mass increases notably in weight, and there are gains in shoulder width and chest circumference. Adolescents may eat enormous quantities of food to fuel their growth spurts. Adults fighting the battle of the bulge stare at them in wonder as they wolf down french fries and shakes at the fast-food counter and later go out for pizza.

SOCIAL AND PERSONALITY DEVELOPMENT

In the last century, psychologist G. Stanley Hall described adolescence as a time of *Sturm und Drang*—storm and stress. Certainly, many American teenagers abuse drugs, have unplanned pregnancies, contract sexually transmitted diseases, become involved in violence, and encounter psychological and social problems that are connected with academic failure and suicide attempts (Garland & Zigler, 1993; Gentry & Eron, 1993; Kazdin, 1993). Nearly 1 in 10 adolescent girls becomes pregnant each year. Nearly 10% of teenaged boys and 20% of teenaged girls attempt suicide. Alcohol-related incidents are the overall leading cause of death among adolescents.

Hall attributed the conflicts and distress of adolescence to biological changes. Research evidence suggests that the hormonal changes of adolescence may have some effect on the activity levels, mood swings, and aggressive tendencies of many adolescents (Buchanan and others, 1992). Overall, however, it would appear that cultural influences and social expectations may have a greater impact on adolescents than hormones do (Buchanan and others, 1992).

Yet the picture of adolescence as a state of constant rebellion against parents and society is overblown. Yes, adolescence is a time of redefinition of parent–child relationships. However, many of these changes are positive and not negative (Collins, 1990; Steinberg, 1991). Moreover, there are many individual differences.

Adolescents do strive to become more independent from their parents. This striving is manifested by some bickering, especially in early adolescence (Smetana and others, 1991). Conflicts typically center around the details of everyday family life—issues such as homework, chores, money, appearance, curfews, and dating (Galambos & Almeida, 1992; Smetana and others, 1991). Arguments are common when adolescents maintain that personal choices, such as those that concern clothes and friends, should be made by them and not their parents (Smetana and others, 1991).

The striving for independence is also characterized by withdrawal from family life, at least relative to the prior involvement. In one study, children ranging in age from 9 to 15 carried electronic pagers for a week so that they could report what they were doing and whom they were with when signaled (Larson & Richards, 1991). The amount of time spent with the family decreased dramatically as age increased. The 15-year-olds spent only half as much time with their families as the 9-year-olds. Yet, this change does not mean that most adolescents spend their time on the streets. For 15-year-old boys in the study, time with the family tended to be replaced by time spent alone. For older girls, this time was divided between friends and solitude.

Adolescents, like younger children, interact with their mothers more so than with their fathers. When parent–adolescent conflict arises, then, it is more likely to be with the mother. But most adolescents also see their mothers as more supportive than their fathers, as knowing them better, and as being more likely to tolerate their opinions (Collins & Russell, 1991; Noller & Callan, 1990). Teenagers are also more likely to seek and follow advice from their mothers than their fathers (Greene & Grimsley, 1991).

Some distancing from parents is adaptive for adolescents (Galambos, 1992). After all, they do have to form relationships outside the family. But greater independence does not necessarily mean that adolescents become emotionally detached from their parents or fall completely under the influence of their peers. Most adolescents continue to feel love, respect, and loyalty toward their parents (Montemayor & Flannery, 1991). Adolescents who feel close to their parents actually show greater self-reliance and independence than those who are distant from their parents. Adolescents who retain close ties with parents also fare better in school and have fewer adjustment problems (Davey, 1993; Papini & Roggman, 1992; Steinberg, 1991).

Despite parent–adolescent conflict over issues of control, many studies confirm that parents and adolescents share quite similar social, political, religious, and economic views (Paikoff & Collins, 1991). In sum, there are frequent parent–adolescent differences on issues of personal control. However, there is apparently no "generation gap" on broader matters.

Ego Identity versus Role Diffusion.

According to psychoanalyst Erik Erikson, the major challenge of adolescence is the creation of an adult identity. This is accomplished primarily through choosing and developing a commitment to an occupation or a role in life. But identity extends to sexual, political, and religious beliefs and commitments.

Erikson (1963) theorizes that adolescents experience a life crisis of *ego identity versus role diffusion.* If this crisis is resolved properly, adolescents develop a firm sense of who they are and what they stand for. This sense of **ego identity** can carry them through difficult times and color their achievements with meaning. If they do not resolve this life crisis properly, they may experience **role diffusion.** They then spread themselves thin, running down one blind alley after another and placing themselves at the mercy of leaders who promise to give them the sense of identity they cannot mold for themselves.

PSYCHOLOGY IN A WORLD OF DIVERSITY

GENDER AND ETHNIC FACTORS IN ADOLESCENT IDENTITY FORMATION

Erik Erikson's views of the development of identity were intended to apply primarily to males (Archer, 1992; Patterson and others, 1992). In Erikson's theory, the stage of identity development includes embracing a

philosophy of life and commitment to a career. It is in the next stage that people develop the capacity to form intimate relationships. Erikson believed that the development of interpersonal relationships was more important to women's identity than occupational and ideological issues. Revealing his theoretical indebtedness to Sigmund Freud, Erikson believed that women's identities are intimately connected with women's roles as wives and mothers, whereas men's identities do not depend on their roles as husbands and fathers. Erikson argued, therefore, that women tend to resolve concerns about identity and intimacy simultaneously and resolve identity concerns later than men (Patterson and others, 1992).

Yet contemporary research shows that women in the United States approach identity formation in a manner that is much more similar to, than different from, men (Archer, 1992). The realities of contemporary life in the United States call for full participation of women in the workplace. It is not surprising, then, that female adolescents' concern about their occupational plans is about equal to that of males. Female adolescents, however, also voice concern about the interrelatedness of family concerns and occupational concerns in their daily lives (Archer, 1992). This is not surprising when we consider that despite their investment in the workplace, U.S. women still often have the primary responsibility for rearing the children and maintaining the home (Archer, 1991).

Identity formation is more complicated for adolescents from ethnic minority groups (Cross, 1991; Spencer & Markstrom-Adams, 1990). Unlike adolescents who are a part of the dominant culture, minority adolescents may be faced with two sets of cultural values: those of their ethnic group and those of the dominant culture (Markstrom-Adams, 1992; Phinney & Rosenthal, 1992). When these values are in conflict, the minority adolescent needs to reconcile the differences and, frequently, decide where she or he stands. Maha Alkhateeb, an Arab American Muslim adolescent, explains why she skipped the prom: "At the time of the prom, I was sad, but just about everyone I

Ego identity • Erikson's term for a firm sense of who one is and what one stands for.

Role diffusion • Erikson's term for lack of clarity in one's life roles—a function of failure to develop ego identity.

Intimacy versus isolation • Erikson's life crisis of young adulthood, which is characterized by the task of developing abiding intimate relationships.

Trying 20s • Sheehy's term for the third decade of life, when people are frequently occupied with advancement in the career world.

knew had sex that night, which I think was immoral. Now, I like saying that I didn't go. I didn't go there just because it was a cool thing to do" ("Muslim Women," 1993, p. B9).

There may also be a scarcity of realistic role models for minority youth. Many African American role models are in show business or athletics, and the reality is that there are very few "jobs" in these arenas. When minority youth identify too strongly with the dominant culture, they risk being rejected by their friends and families.

Biracial adolescents or adolescents whose parents are of different religions wrestle not only with these issues, but with issues as to what constitutes their own dominant cultural heritage (Gibbs, 1992; Johnson, 1992; Miller, 1992). Parents from different ethnic groups may spend their lives together, but their values may not dwell so contentedly side by side within the minds of their children.

Establishing Intimate Relationships. According to Erik Erikson, establishing intimate relationships is a central task of young adulthood.

Reflections

Now that you have read the section on adolescence, reflect on the following questions:

- Consider some of the stereotypes of the adolescent, as captured in the phrase "storm and stress." Do these stereotypes describe your own experiences as an adolescent? How or how not?

- Consider your own sociocultural background and your experiences as an adolescent. How did your gender or ethnic group influence the formation of your own identity? Did the process of building your identity require you to resolve any conflicts related to your gender or ethnicity?

Adult Development

Development continues throughout a lifetime. Many theorists, including Erik Erikson and Daniel Levinson, believe that adult concerns and involvements are patterned so that we can speak of stages of adult development. Let us consider the adult years according to three broad categories: young adulthood, middle adulthood, and late adulthood.

YOUNG ADULTHOOD

Young, or early, adulthood covers the two decades from ages 20 to 40. According to Erik Erikson (1963), young adulthood is the stage of **intimacy versus isolation.** Erikson saw the establishment of intimate relationships as central to young adulthood. Young adults who have evolved a firm sense of identity during adolescence are now ready to "fuse" their identities with those of other people through marriage and abiding friendships.

Erikson warns that we may not be able to commit ourselves to others until we have achieved ego identity, or established stable life roles. Achieving ego identity is the central task of adolescence. Lack of personal stability is connected with the high divorce rate in teenage marriages.

Erikson argues that people who do not reach out to develop intimate relationships risk retreating into isolation and loneliness.

Adults in their 20s tend to be fueled by ambition as they strive to establish their pathways in life. Journalist Gail Sheehy (1976) labeled the 20s the **Trying 20s**—a period during which people basically strive to advance themselves in the career world.

In one phase of her work, reported in her book *Passages,* Sheehy (1976) interviewed

Dream • In this usage, Levinson's term for the overriding drive of youth to become someone important, to leave one's mark on history.

Age-30 transition • Levinson's term for the ages from 28 to 33, which are characterized by reassessment of the goals and values of the 20s.

Catch 30s • Sheehy's term for the fourth decade of life, when many people undergo major reassessments of their accomplishments and goals.

Generativity versus stagnation • Erikson's term for the crisis of middle adulthood, characterized by the task of being productive and contributing to younger generations.

Midlife transition • Levinson's term for the ages from 40 to 45, which are characterized by a shift in psychological perspective from viewing ourselves in terms of years lived to viewing ourselves in terms of the years we have left.

Midlife crisis • A crisis experienced by many people during the midlife transition when they realize that life may be more than halfway over, and they reassess their achievements in terms of their dreams.

MINILECTURE:
PSYCHOSOCIAL
DEVELOPMENT
IN ADULTHOOD

115 people drawn largely from the middle and upper classes, including many managers, executives, and other professionals. In another phase, she examined 60,000 questionnaires filled out by readers of *Redbook* and *Esquire* magazines, reported in her 1981 book *Pathfinders.* The young adults in her samples were concerned about establishing their pathways in life, finding their places in the world. They were generally responsible for their own support, made their own choices, and were largely free from parental influences.

During our 20s, many of us feel "buoyed by powerful illusions and belief in the power of the will [so that] we commonly insist . . . that what we have chosen to do is the one true course in life" (Sheehy, 1976, p. 33). This "one true course" usually turns out to have many swerves and bends. As we develop, what seemed to be important one year can lose some of its allure the next. That which we hardly noticed can gain prominence.

Gender Differences in Developmental Patterns of Young Adulthood. Most Western men consider separation and individuation to be key goals of personality development during young adulthood (Guisinger & Blatt, 1994). For women, however, the establishment and maintenance of social relationships are also of primary importance (Gilligan and others, 1990, 1991; Jordan and others, 1991). Women are relatively more likely to be guided by changing patterns of attachment and caring. In becoming adults, men are likely to undergo a transition from restriction to control. Women, as pointed out by Gilligan (1982), are relatively more likely to undergo a transition from being cared for to caring for others, however.

According to Daniel Levinson's in-depth study of 40 men, published in 1978 as *The Seasons of a Man's Life,* men enter the adult world in their early 20s. Upon entry, they are faced with the tasks of exploring adult roles (in terms of careers, intimate relationships, and so on) and of establishing stability in the chosen roles. At this time, men also often adopt a **dream**—the drive to "become" someone, to leave their mark on history—which serves as a tentative blueprint for their lives.

Although there are very important differences in the development of women and men, a study by Ravenna Helson and Geraldine Moane (1987) of the University of California found that between the ages of 21 and 27, college women do develop in terms of individuation and autonomy. That is, they, like men, tend to assert increasing control over their own lives. College women, of course, are relatively liberated and career-oriented in comparison with their less-well-educated peers.

The Age-30 Transition. Levinson labeled the ages of 28 to 33 the **age-30 transition.** For many, this is a period of reassessment of the choices made during their early 20s. A number of researchers have noted that women frequently encounter a crisis that begins between the ages of 27 and 30 (Reinke and others, 1985). During the early 30s, many of the women studied by Helson and Moane (1987) felt exploited by others, alone, weak, limited, and as if they would "never get myself together." Concerns about nearing the end of the fertile years, opportunities closing down, and heightened responsibilities at home and work all make their contributions.

For men and women, the late 20s and early 30s are commonly characterized by self-questioning: "Where is my life going?" "Why am I doing this?" Sheehy (1976) labeled the 30s the **Catch 30s** because of such reassessment. During our 30s, we often find that the lifestyles we adopted during our 20s do not fit as comfortably as we had anticipated.

One response to the disillusionments of the 30s, according to Sheehy,

> is the tearing up of the life we have spent most of our 20s putting together. It may mean striking out on a secondary road toward a new vision or converting a dream of "running for president" into a more realistic goal. The single person feels a push to find a partner. The woman who was previously content at home with children chafes to venture into the world. The childless couple reconsiders children. And almost everybody who is married . . . feels a discontent. (1976, p. 34)

Settling Down. According to Levinson, the ages of about 33 to 40 are characterized by settling down. Men during this period still strive to forge ahead in their careers, their interpersonal relationships, and their communities. During the latter half of their 30s, men are also concerned about "becoming one's own man." That is, they desire independence and autonomy in their careers and adult relationships. Promotions and pay increases are important as signs of success.

Sheehy found that young adults who had successfully ridden out the storm of reassessments of the Catch 30s begin the process of "rooting" at this time. They feel a need to put down roots, to make a financial and emotional investment in their homes. Their concerns become more focused on promotion or tenure, career advancement, and long-term mortgages.

Settling Down. According to some chroniclers of adult development, the 30s are often characterized by settling down, or planting roots, as in taking on the responsibilities of a home.

MIDDLE ADULTHOOD

Middle adulthood spans the years from 40 to 60 or 65.

Generativity versus Stagnation. Erikson (1963) labels the life crisis of the middle years that of **generativity versus stagnation.** In other words, are we still striving to produce or to rear our children well, or are we marking time, treading water? Generativity by and large requires doing things that we believe are worthwhile. In so doing, we enhance and maintain our self-esteem. Generativity also involves the Eriksonian ideal of helping shape the new generation. This shaping may involve rearing our own children or generally working to make the world a better place. Many of us find great satisfaction in these tasks.

Levinson's Seasons. According to Levinson, there is a **midlife transition** at about age 40 to 45 that is characterized by a dramatic shift in psychological perspective. Previously, we had thought of our ages largely in terms of the number of years that have elapsed since birth. Once the midlife transition takes place, however, there is a tendency to think of our ages in terms of the number of years we have left.

Men in their 30s still think of themselves as part of the Pepsi Generation, older brothers to "kids" in their 20s. At about age

40 to 45, however, some marker event—illness, a change on the job, the death of a friend or of a parent, or being beaten at tennis by one's child—leads men to realize that they are a full generation older than 20-year-olds.

During this transition, it strikes men that life may be more than halfway over. There may be more to look back on than forward to. It dawns on men that they'll never be president or chairperson of the board. They'll never play shortstop for the Dodgers. They mourn their own youth and begin to adjust to the specter of old age and the finality of death.

The Midlife Crisis. The midlife transition may trigger a crisis referred to as the **midlife crisis.** The middle-level, middle-aged businessperson looking ahead to another 10 to 20 years of grinding out accounts in a Wall Street cubbyhole may encounter severe depression. The woman with two teenagers, an empty house from 8:00 to 4:00, and a 40th birthday on the way might feel that she is coming apart at the seams. Both feel entrapment and loss of purpose. Some people are propelled into extramarital affairs at this time by the desire to prove to themselves that they remain attractive.

Is Middle Age the End of Young Adulthood? How do the middle-aged differ from young adults? To what extent are the biological changes of aging inevitable? How much control can we exert over our own aging?

Until midlife, the men studied by the Levinson group were largely under the influence of their dream—the overriding drive of youth to "become," to be the great scientist or novelist, to leave one's mark on history. At midlife, they found they must come to terms with the discrepancies between their dream and their actual achievements. Middle-aged people who free themselves from their dream find it easier to enjoy the passing pleasures of the day.

Levinson's study was carried out with men. Women, as suggested by Sheehy and other writers (e.g., Reinke and others, 1985) may undergo a midlife transition a number of years earlier. Sheehy (1976) writes that women enter midlife about 5 years earlier than men, at about age 35 instead of 40. Once they turn 35, women are usually advised to have their fetuses routinely tested for Down syndrome and other chromosomal disorders. At age 35, women also enter higher risk categories for side effects from birth control pills.

The study of college women by Helson and Moane (1987) suggests that many women in their early 40s may already be emerging from some of the fears and uncertainties that are first confronting men. For example, they found that women at age 43 are more likely than women in their early 30s to feel confident; to exert an influence on their communities; to feel secure and committed; to feel productive, effective, and powerful; and to extend their interests beyond their own families.

Menopause. **Menopause,** or the cessation of menstruation, usually occurs during the late 40s or early 50s, although there are wide variations. Menopause is the final stage of a broader female experience, the climacteric, which is caused by a falling off in the secretion of the hormones estrogen and progesterone. The climacteric begins with irregular periods and ends with menopause.[2] With menopause, ovulation also draws to an end. There is some atrophy of breast tissue and a decrease in the elasticity of the skin. There can also be a loss of bone density that leads to osteoporosis in late adulthood (Brody, 1993b).

During the climacteric, many women encounter symptoms such as hot flashes (uncomfortable sensations characterized by heat and perspiration) and loss of sleep (Azar, 1994a). However, women are more likely to suffer from depression prior to menopause, when they may buckle from the combined demands of the workplace, child rearing, and home-making (Brody, 1993b). In most cases, mood changes are relatively mild. According to psychologist Karen Matthews, who has been following a sample of 451 women through menopause, some women do encounter problems. "But studies show that they are in the minority," Matthews (1994, p. 25) points out. "The vast majority have no problem at all getting through the menopausal transition."

Menopause does not signal the end of a woman's sexual interests (Brody, 1993b). Many women find the separation of sex from reproduction to be sexually liberating. Some of the physical problems that may stem from falloff in hormone production may be alleviated by hormone-replacement therapy (Belchetz, 1994). A more important issue may be the meaning of menopause to the individual. Women who equate menopause with loss of femininity are likely to encounter more distress than those who do not (Rathus and others, 1993).

Truth or Fiction Revisited. *It is not true that menopause signals the end of a woman's sexual interests.* Many women find the separation of sex from reproduction to be sexually liberating.

Manopause (Manopause?). Have you heard this joke?

An older man hears a frog talking while he is walking down the street. "Pick me up and kiss me," the frog says, "I'm really a beautiful young woman who was cursed. If you kiss me, I'll turn back into her and be your love slave forever." The man thinks for a minute. Then he picks up the frog and puts it in his pocket. "Hey" calls the frog from his pocket. "Aren't you going to kiss me? Don't

---

[2] There are many other reasons for irregular periods, and women who encounter them are advised to discuss them with their doctors.

you want me to turn back into a ravishing woman who will be your slave?" The man pauses, then says, "To be honest with you, at this age I think I'd rather have a talking frog in my pocket."

The joke is supposed to represent male menopause. It suggests that once male menopause occurs, a novel event, such as a talking frog, may hold more allure than sex.

Men cannot really experience menopause, of course. After all, they have never menstruated. Yet now and then we hear the term *male menopause,* or "manopause." Middle-aged or older men may be loosely alluded to as menopausal. This epithet is doubly offensive: It reinforces the negative, harmful stereotypes of aging people, especially aging women, as crotchety and irritable. Nor is the label particularly consistent with the biology or psychology of aging.

For women, menopause is a time of relatively acute age-related declines in sex hormones and fertility. In men, however, the decline in the production of male sex hormones and fertility is more gradual. Moreover, some viable sperm are produced even in late adulthood. It is therefore not surprising to find a man in his 70s or older fathering a child. On the other hand, many men in their 50s and 60s experience intermittent problems in achieving and maintaining erections (Sheehy, 1993), which may or may not be connected with hormone production.

Men can remain sexually active and father children at advanced ages. For both genders, attitudes toward the biological changes of aging—along with one's general satisfaction with life—apparently affect sexual behavior as profoundly as the biological changes themselves.

The Empty-Nest Syndrome. In earlier decades, psychologists placed great emphasis on a concept referred to as the **empty-nest syndrome** that applied to women in particular. It was assumed that women experienced a profound sense of loss when the youngest child went off to college, got married, or moved into an apartment. Research findings paint more of a mixed and optimistic picture, however. Certainly there can be problems, and these

apply to both parents. Perhaps the largest of these is letting go of one's children after so many years of mutual interdependence (Bell, 1983). The stresses of letting go can be compounded when the children are also ambivalent about becoming independent.

Many mothers report increased marital satisfaction and personal changes such as greater mellowness, self-confidence, and stability after the children have left home, however (Reinke and others, 1985). Middle-aged women show increased dominance and assertiveness, an orientation toward achievement, and greater influence in the worlds of politics and work (Serlin, 1980; Sheehy, 1976). It is as if they are cut free from traditional shackles by the knowledge that their child-bearing years are behind them.

Truth or Fiction Revisited. *It is not true that mothers in general suffer from the "empty-nest syndrome" when the youngest child leaves home.* Most mothers (and fathers) do not suffer when the youngest child leaves home.

Role reversals are not uncommon in family life once the children have left home (Wink & Helson, 1993). Given traditional sociocultural expectations of men and women, men are frequently more competent than their wives in the world outside the family during the early stages of marriage, and their wives are more emotionally dependent. But in the postparental period, these differences decrease or actually become reversed both because of the women's enhanced status in the world of work and because of the influence of the mother role.

LATE ADULTHOOD
You know you're getting old when you stoop to tie your shoes and wonder what else you can do while you're down there.
GEORGE BURNS

Late adulthood begins at age 65. One reason that developmental psychologists have become concerned about the later years is that with improved health care and knowledge of the importance of diet and exercise, more Americans than ever before are 65 or older. By the year 2000, nearly 35 million Americans, more than 13% of the population, will be 65 or older (Farley, 1993b). In

Menopause • (MEN-no-paws). The cessation of menstruation.
Empty-nest syndrome • A sense of depression and loss of purpose felt by some parents when the youngest child leaves home.

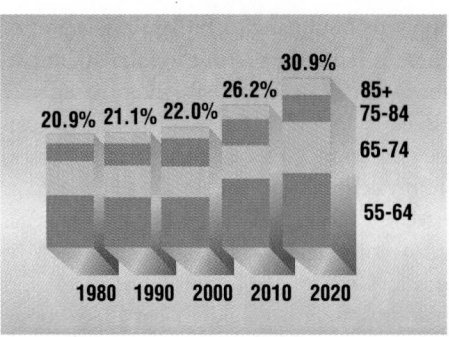

FIGURE 11.9
The Aging of America Because of factors such as improved health care, diet, and exercise, Americans are living longer. By the year 2020, for example, about 31% of us will be at least 55 years old, as compared with about 21% today.

Reaction time • The amount of time required to respond to a stimulus.

Longevity • A long span of life.

Ego integrity versus despair • Erikson's term for the crisis of late adulthood, characterized by the task of maintaining one's sense of identity despite physical deterioration.

1900, only 1 American in 30 was over 65, as compared with 1 in 9 in 1970. By 2020, perhaps 1 American in 5 will be 65 or older (Figure 11.9). Another reason for the increased interest in aging is the recognition that, in a sense, *all* development involves aging. A third reason for studying the later years is to learn how we can further promote the health and psychological well-being of older people.

Physical Development. Various changes—some of them problematic—do occur during the later years. Changes in calcium metabolism lead to increased brittleness in the bones and heightened risk of breaks from accidents like falls. The skin becomes less elastic and subject to wrinkles and folds.

The senses become less acute. Older people see and hear less acutely (Belsky, 1984b). Because of a decline in the sense of smell, they may use more spice to flavor their food. Older people require more time (called **reaction time**) to respond to stimuli. Older drivers need more time to respond to traffic lights, other vehicles, and changing road conditions.

As we grow older, our immune systems also function less effectively, leaving us more vulnerable to disease.

Cognitive Development. Older people usually show some decline in reaction time, intellectual functioning, and memory. However, we understand very little about

why this occurs. Losses of sensory acuity and of motivation to do well may contribute to lower scores. Psychologist B. F. Skinner (1983) argued that much of the falloff is due to an "aging environment" rather than an aging person. That is, in many instances the behavior of older people goes unreinforced. Note that nursing home residents who are rewarded for remembering recent events show improved scores on tests of memory (Langer and others, 1979; Wolinsky, 1982).

In some cases, supposedly irreversible cognitive changes reflect psychological problems such as depression (Albert, 1981). Such changes are neither primarily cognitive nor irreversible. If the depression is treated effectively, intellectual performance may also improve.

Theories of Aging. Although it may be hard to believe that it will happen to us, everyone who has so far walked the Earth has aged—which may not be a bad fate, considering the alternative. Why do we age? Various factors, some of which are theoretical, apparently contribute to aging.

Heredity plays a role. **Longevity** runs in families. People whose parents and grandparents lived into their 80s and 90s have a better chance of reaching these years themselves.

Environmental factors also influence aging. People who exercise regularly seem to live longer. Disease, stress, obesity, and cigarette smoking can contribute to an early death. Fortunately, we can exert control over some of these factors.

Older people show better health and psychological well-being when they do exert control over their own lives (Rodin, 1986; Wolinsky, 1982). About 29% of older people will spend at least some time in a nursing home (Kemper & Murtaugh, 1991), however, where many of them surrender much of their independence. Even in the nursing home, older people fare better when they are kept well-informed and allowed to make decisions on matters that affect them.

Disturbances in the abilities of cells to regenerate and repair themselves accompany aging. It is unclear whether these disturbances are genetically preprogrammed or are caused by external factors (such as ultraviolet light) or by an accumulation of random internal changes. More research is needed into the basic processes of aging, including the relationships between biological processes, lifestyle, and psychological problems such as confusional states and Alzheimer's disease (Lonergan & Krevans, 1991).

Ego Integrity versus Despair. According to Erikson, late adulthood is the stage of **ego integrity versus despair.** The basic challenge is to maintain the belief that life is meaningful and worthwhile in the face of the inevitability of death. Ego integrity derives from wisdom, as well as from the acceptance of one's life span as occurring at a certain point in the sweep of history and as being limited. We spend most of our lives accumulating things and relationships. Erikson also argues that adjustment in the later years requires the wisdom to be able to let go.

Erikson was optimistic. He believed that we can maintain a sense of trust through life and avoid feelings of despair.

Stereotypes of Older People. Aging is not without its problems. One key problem experienced by older people, however, concerns the stereotypes that younger people tend to have of them. One such stereotype is that older people tend to be crotchety, irritable, and difficult to satisfy. However, a study of people retired for 18 to 120 months found that 75% rated retirement as mostly good (Hendrick and others, 1982a). More than 90% were generally satisfied with life. More than 75% reported their health as good or excellent.

Truth or Fiction Revisited. *It is not true that most older people are dissatisfied with their lives.*

As at any age, adjustment among older people is related to financial security and physical health. The sicker we are, the less likely we are to be well-adjusted. There is also a link between financial status and physical health. Older people who are poor are more likely to report ill health than the financially secure (Birren, 1983). This finding would seem to call for better health care for the aged, and it does. But it may also be that people who have been healthier

over the years are better able to provide for their own financial security.

There are some stereotypes concerning living arrangements for older people. One has them living with children; another, in institutions. Still another has them buying recreational vehicles and taking off for condominiums or retirement communities in the Sunbelt. First, let us put to rest the stereotype that older people are generally dependent on others. According to the U.S. Bureau of the Census, nearly 70% of heads of households aged at least 65 own their own homes.

Despite the stereotype of taking off for the Sunbelt, the majority of older people remain in their hometowns and cities. Moving is stressful at any age. Most older people apparently prefer to remain in familiar locales.

Here, too, there are some stereotypes. Older people are often seen as living in poverty or at the mercy of their children and external forces such as government support. Unfortunately, some of these stereotypes are based on reality. People who no longer work are usually dependent on savings and fixed incomes such as pensions and Social Security payments. The flip side of the coin is that nationwide, only about 13% of those aged 65 and above live below the poverty level. But the financial status of older African Americans is worse. Two out of three live below the poverty level.

On Death and Dying.
Of all the wonders that I yet have heard,
It seems to me most strange that men should fear;
Seeing that death, a necessary end,
Will come when it will come.
SHAKESPEARE, *JULIUS CAESAR*

Death is the last great taboo. Psychiatrist Elisabeth Kübler-Ross commented on our denial of death in her landmark book *On Death and Dying:*

> We use euphemisms, we make the dead look as if they were asleep, we ship the children off to protect them from the anxiety and turmoil around the house if the [person] is fortunate enough to die at home, [and] we don't allow children to visit their dying parents in the hospitals. (1969, p. 8)

From her work with terminally ill patients, Kübler-Ross found some common responses to news of impending death. She identified five stages of dying through which many patients pass, and she suggested that older people who suspect that death is approaching may undergo similar stages:

1. *Denial.* In the denial stage, people feel "It can't be me. The diagnosis must be wrong."

2. *Anger.* Denial usually gives way to anger and resentment toward the young and healthy and, sometimes, toward the medical establishment—"It's unfair. Why me?"

3. *Bargaining.* Next, people may try to bargain with God to postpone death, promising, for example, to do good deeds if they are given another 6 months, another year.

4. *Depression.* With depression come feelings of loss and hopelessness—grief at the specter of leaving loved ones and life itself.

5. *Final acceptance.* Ultimately, an inner peace may come, a quiet acceptance of the inevitable. Such "peace" does not resemble contentment; it is nearly devoid of feeling.

Psychologist Edwin Shneidman (1984), who has specialized in the concerns of suicidal and dying individuals, acknowledges the presence of feelings such as those described by Kübler-Ross, but he does not perceive them to be linked in sequence. Instead, Shneidman suggests that dying people show a variety of emotional and cognitive responses that tend to be fleeting or relatively stable, to ebb and flow, and to reflect pain and bewilderment. He also points out that the kinds of responses shown by individuals reflect their personality traits and their philosophies of life.

"Lying Down to Pleasant Dreams . . . " The American poet William Cullen Bryant is best known for his poem "Thanatopsis," which he composed at the age of 18. "Thanatopsis" expresses Erik Erikson's goal of ego integrity—optimism that we can maintain a sense of trust through life. By meeting squarely the challenges of our adult lives, perhaps we can take our leave with dignity. When our time comes to "join the innumerable caravan"—the billions who have died before us—perhaps we can depart life with integrity.

Live, wrote the poet, so that

. . . when thy summons comes to join
The innumerable caravan which moves
To that mysterious realm, where each shall take
His chamber in the silent halls of death,
Thou go not, like the quarry-slave at night,
Scourged to his dungeon, but, sustained and
*   soothed*
By an unfaltering trust, approach thy grave
Like one that wraps the drapery of his couch
About him, and lies down to pleasant dreams.

Bryant, of course, wrote "Thanatopsis" at age 18, not at 85, the age at which he died. At that advanced age, his feelings—and his verse—might have differed. But literature and poetry, unlike science, need not reflect reality. They can serve to inspire and warm us.

Reflections

Now that you have read the section on adult development, reflect on the following questions:

- Consider the middle-aged and older people in your own life. Are their behavior and personalities in any way consistent with the descriptions in this section? How or how not?

- How do you feel about the use of the term *manopause* to describe men who have reached middle age or the later years? Do you believe that the term is of any value or just serves to perpetuate stereotypes? Explain.

- Erik Erikson wrote that one aspect of wisdom is the ability to visualize one's role in the march of history and to accept one's own death. Do you believe that acceptance of death is a sign of wisdom? (Or that wisdom means being able to accept one's own death?) Why or why not?

Summary

1. **Does development reflect nature or nurture?** Development appears to reflect an interaction between nature (genetic factors) and nurture (environmental influences). Nature provides a reaction range for the development of traits, and nurture modifies the expression of traits. Maturational theorists focus on the influences of nature, whereas learning theorists focus on environmental influences.

2. **Is development continuous or discontinuous?** Stage theorists such as Freud and Piaget view development as being discontinuous. According to them, we undergo distinct periods of development that differ in quality and follow an orderly sequence. Learning theorists, in contrast, tend to view psychological development as a continuous process.

3. **What are the stages of prenatal development?** These are the germinal, embryonic, and fetal stages. During the germinal stage, the zygote divides as it travels through the fallopian tube and becomes implanted in the uterine wall. The major organ systems are formed during the embryonic stage, and the fetal stage is highlighted by maturation and gains in size.

4. **What are the highlights of physical development?** Physical development occurs most rapidly prenatally and then during the first 2 years after birth. There is also an adolescent growth spurt during which we make dramatic gains in height and weight.

5. **What are reflexes?** Reflexes are unlearned, stereotypical responses to stimuli that in many cases are essential to infant survival. Examples include breathing, sucking, and swallowing.

6. **How do babies perceive the environment?** Newborn babies can see quite well and show greater interest in complex visual stimuli than in simple stimuli. Infants are capable of depth perception by the time they can crawl. Newborns can normally hear and show preferences for their mothers' voices. Newborns can discriminate different odors and tastes and show preferences for pleasant odors and sweet foods.

7. **What are the stages of attachment?** According to Ainsworth, there are three stages of attachment: the initial-preattachment phase, which is characterized by indiscriminate attachment; the attachment-in-the-making phase, which is characterized by preference for familiar figures; and the clear-cut-attachment phase, which is characterized by intensified dependence on the primary caregiver.

8. **What are some of the theories of attachment?** Behaviorists have argued that children become attached to their mothers through conditioning, because their mothers feed them and attend to other needs. Harlow's studies with rhesus monkeys suggest that an innate motive, contact comfort, may be more important than conditioning in the development of attachment. The ethological view of attachment suggests that there are critical developmental periods during which animals such as geese and ducks will become imprinted on, or attached to, an object that they follow.

9. **What are the dimensions of child rearing?** Two broad, independent dimensions of child rearing have been found: warmth–coldness and restrictiveness–permissiveness.

10. **How did Jean Piaget view children?** Piaget saw children as budding scientists who actively strive to make sense of the perceptual world. He defined intelligence as involving processes of assimilation (responding to events according to existing schemes) and accommodation (changing schemes to permit effective responses to new events).

11. **What are the stages of cognitive development according to Piaget?** Piaget's view of cognitive development includes four stages: sensorimotor (prior to use of symbols and language);

preoperational (characterized by egocentric thought, animism, artificialism, and inability to center on more than one aspect of a situation); concrete operational (characterized by conservation, less egocentrism, reversibility, and subjective moral judgments); and formal operational (characterized by abstract logic).

12. **How do information-processing theorists view cognitive development?** Information-processing theorists view cognitive development in terms of expansion of working memory, growing automaticity in problem solving, development of more sophisticated "mental programs," and increasing self-knowledge of the functioning of one's own cognitive processes.

13. **How did Kohlberg view moral development?** Kohlberg focused on the processes of moral reasoning. He hypothesized that these processes develop through three "levels," with two stages within each level.

14. **What is adolescence?** Adolescence is a period of life that begins at puberty (a biological marker) and ends with assumption of adult responsibilities (a psychosocial marker). Changes that lead to reproductive capacity and secondary sex characteristics are stimulated by testosterone in the male and by estrogen and androgens in the female. Adolescents frequently yearn for independence from their parents.

15. **What are some of the major events of young adulthood?** Young adulthood is generally characterized by striving to advance in the business world and the development of intimate ties.

16. **What are some of the major events of middle adulthood?** Middle adulthood is a time of crisis and further reassessment for many, a time when we must come to terms with the discrepancies between our achievements and the dreams of youth. Some middle-aged adults become depressed when the youngest child leaves home (the so-called "empty-nest syndrome"), but many report increased satisfaction, stability, and self-confidence.

17. **What are some of the changes that occur during late adulthood?** Older people show less sensory acuity, and reaction time increases. Presumed cognitive deficits sometimes reflect declining motivation or psychological problems such as depression.

18. **What factors are involved in longevity?** Heredity plays a role in longevity. We do not know exactly why people age, but lifestyle factors such as exercise, diet, and the maintenance of responsibility can apparently delay aging.

19. **Are there "stages of dying"?** Kübler-Ross identifies five stages of dying among the terminally ill: denial, anger, bargaining, depression, and final acceptance. Other investigators find that psychological reactions to approaching death are more varied than Kübler-Ross suggests, however.

Psychology and Modern Life

One of the facts of modern life is that most American mothers are in the workforce. In the 1990s, only about 7% of U.S. families fit the once traditional model of the bread-winner husband and the full-time home-maker wife (Silverstein, 1991). Today about two mothers in three work outside the home. This figure includes more than half of mothers of children who are younger than 1 year of age (U.S. Bureau of the Census, 1993). When both parents spend the day on the job, the children must be cared for by others. As a consequence, millions of American preschoolers are placed in day care, although some older "latchkey" children come home from school and care for themselves until their parents arrive. Parents, of course, are very concerned about what happens to children in day care. Our first topic thus concerns the effects of day care. We also offer pointers on selecting a day-care center.

Another fact of modern life is that more than 2 million children in the United States are reported to be neglected or abused by parents each year (Colon & Colon, 1989). Many more cases of abuse and neglect may go unreported (Emery, 1989; Giovannoni, 1989). Our second topic in this section is thus child abuse—why parents abuse their children and what can be done about it.

Day Care

What are the effects of day care on parent–child bonds of attachment? On children's social development?

Studies of the effects of day care on parent–child attachment are somewhat mixed. On the one hand, children in full-time day care show less distress when their mothers leave them and are less likely to seek their mothers out when they return. Some psychologists suggest that this apparent distancing from the mother is a sign of potential insecure attachment (Belsky, 1990). Others suggest, however, that the children are adapting to repeated separations from, and reunions with, their mothers (Field, 1991; Lamb and others, 1992; Thompson 1991b). Yet, children in full-time day care whose mothers are anxious and dissatisfied with their marriages are more likely to be insecurely attached to their

mothers than children whose mothers are better adjusted (Belsky & Rovine, 1988). Overall, however, most children who are in full-time day care and those who are cared for by their mothers throughout the day are securely attached (Clarke-Stewart, 1989).

Day care seems to have positive and negative influences on children's social development. First, the positive: Infants with day-care experience are more peer oriented and play at higher developmental levels. Children in day care are also more likely to share their toys. They are more independent, self-confident, and outgoing. They are also more helpful and cooperative with peers and adults (Clarke-Stewart, 1991; Field, 1991).

Now, the negative: Some studies have found that children who were in day care are less compliant and more aggressive toward peers and adults than are other children (Vandell & Corasaniti, 1990). The negative characteristics found among children placed in day care suggest a common theme: Day care promotes interest in peers and the development of social skills, but children tend not to receive the individual attention or resources they want. Placed in a competitive situation, many become more aggressive to attempt to meet their needs. On the other hand, Clarke-Stewart (1990) interprets the greater noncompliance and aggressiveness of children placed in day care as signs of greater independence rather than social maladjustment.

Truth or Fiction Revisited. *It is true that children placed in day care are more aggressive than children cared for in the home.* Perhaps they are so because they have become more independent.

There are thus some research findings that suggest that children placed in full-time day care may be less secure and more aggressive and noncompliant than children reared in the home. However, some psychologists attribute these research findings to children's adaptation to day care and to the series of separations from, and reunions with, parents that day care involves.

SELECTING A DAY-CARE CENTER

Because it is economically, vocationally, and socially unrealistic for most parents to spend

Day Care. Because most parents in the United States are in the work force, day care is a major influence on the lives of millions of children. Parents are understandably concerned that their children will be provided with positive and stimulating experiences.

the day at home, most parents strive to secure day care that will foster the social and emotional development of their children.

Selecting a day-care center can be an overwhelming task. Standards for day-care centers vary from locale to locale, so licensing is no guarantee of adequate care. To help make a successful choice, parents can weigh factors such as the following:

1. Is the center licensed? By what agency? What standards must be met to acquire a license?

2. What is the ratio of children to caregivers? Everything else being equal, caregivers can do a better job when there are fewer children in their charge.

3. What are the qualifications of the center's caregivers? How well aware are they of children's needs and patterns of development? Day-care workers are typically poorly paid, and financial frustrations lead many of the best to seek work in other fields. Children apparently fare better when their caregivers have specific training in child development. If the administrators of a day-care center are reluctant to discuss the training and experience of their caregivers, consider another center.

4. How safe is the environment? Do toys and swings seem to be in good condition? Are dangerous objects out of reach? Would strangers have a difficult time breaking in? Ask something like, "Have children been injured in this center?" Administrators should report previous injuries without hesitation.

5. What is served at mealtime? Is it nutritious and appetizing? Will *your child* eat it?

6. Which caregivers will be responsible for *your* child? What are their backgrounds? How do they seem to relate to children? To your child?

7. What toys, games, books, and other educational materials are provided?

8. What facilities are provided to promote the motor development of your child? How well supervised are children when they use things like swings and tricycles?

9. Are the hours offered by the center convenient for your schedule?

10. Is the location of the center convenient?

As you can see, the considerations can be overwhelming. Perhaps no day-care center within reach will score perfectly on every factor. Some factors are more important than others, however. Perhaps this list of considerations will help you focus your primary concerns.

Child Abuse

Children are much more likely than adults to be victimized. For example, the rates of assault and robbery against teenagers are two to three times greater than for adults (Finkelhor & Dziuba-Leatherman, 1994). Children are five times more likely to be raped than adults (Kilpatrick, 1992).

Why do adults, and particularly parents, victimize their children? The small stature and relative weakness of children provide one answer (Finkelhor & Dziuba-Leatherman, 1994). That is, if one is seeking a victim, it is certainly safer to select a victim who cannot retaliate. But many other factors also contribute to child abuse by parents: situational stress, history of child abuse in at least one of the parent's families of origin, acceptance of violence as a way of coping with stress, failure to become attached to the children, substance abuse, and rigid attitudes about child rearing (Belsky, 1993; Kaplan, 1991). Unemployment is a particularly predisposing source of stress. Child abuse increases during periods of rising unemployment (Trickett and others, 1991).

Stress is also created by the crying infants themselves (Green and others, 1987). Infants who are already in pain of some kind and relatively difficult to soothe are ironically more likely to be abused (Frodi, 1985). Cognitive biases appear to be at work in many abusive parents: Abusive mothers are more likely than nonabusive mothers to assume that their children's stress-producing behavior is intentional, even when it is not (Bauer & Twentyman, 1985).

Sad to say, abused children show an alarming incidence of personal and social problems and psychological disorders (Malinosky-Rummell & Hansen, 1993). Maltreatment can disturb basic patterns of attachment. Abused children are less likely than nonabused agemates to venture out to explore the world (Aber & Allen, 1987). Abused children are more likely to show emotional problems such as anxiety and depression (Malinosky-Rummell & Hansen, 1993; Stone, 1993) and to have lower self-esteem than children who are not abused (Cicchetti & Olson, 1990). Physically abused children are also more likely to be violent than nonabused children are (Dodge and others, 1990; Rothbart & Ahadi, 1994). When they become adults, they are more likely to be violent toward their dates and their spouses (Malinosky-Rummell & Hansen, 1993).

Child abuse runs in families to some degree (Simons and others, 1991). However, *the majority of children who are abused do* not *abuse their own children as adults* (Kaufman & Zigler, 1989). Why does abuse run in families? There are several hypotheses (Belsky, 1993). One is that parents serve as role models. If children observe their parents using violence as a means of coping with stress and anger, they are less likely to learn to diffuse anger through techniques such as humor, verbal expression, reasoning, or even "counting to 10." Another possibility is more cognitively oriented—that children adopt parents' strict philosophies of physical discipline. Exposure to violence in their own homes leads some children to view abuse as normal. Certainly, people can find justifications for violence—if they are seeking them. One is the age-old adage "Spare the rod, spoil the child." A third hypothesis is based on findings that abused children develop problems in empathy, in regulating their emotions, and with aggressive behavior themselves. That is, abuse and neglect foster hostile personalities in children who, when they have their own children, are liable to continue the pattern of abuse and neglect.

Truth or Fiction Revisited. *It is true that child abusers have frequently been abused as children.* However, the majority of them do not abuse their own children.

WHAT TO DO

Dealing with child abuse is frustrating in itself. Social agencies and courts can find it difficult to distinguish between "normal" hitting or spanking and abuse. Because of the American belief that parents have the right to rear their children as they wish, police and courts usually try to avoid involvement in "domestic quarrels" and "family disputes."

However, the alarming incidence of child abuse has spawned new efforts at detection and prevention. Many states require helping professionals such as psychologists and physicians to report any suspicion of child abuse. Many states require *anyone* who suspects child abuse to report it to authorities.

Many locales also have child abuse hotlines. Their phone numbers are available from the telephone information service. Private citizens who suspect child abuse may call for advice. Parents who are having difficulty controlling aggressive impulses toward their children are encouraged to use the hotlines. Some hotlines are serviced by groups such as Parents Anonymous, which involve parents who have had similar difficulties and which may help callers diffuse feelings of anger in less harmful ways.

12

Personality: Theories and Measurement

Truth or Fiction?

_____ According to Sigmund Freud, the human mind is like a vast submerged iceberg, only the tip of which rises above the surface into conscious awareness.

_____ According to Freud, biting one's fingernails or smoking cigarettes as an adult is a sign of conflict during very early childhood.

_____ Obese people are jolly.

_____ We are more likely to persist at difficult tasks when we believe we shall succeed.

_____ Psychologists can invariably determine whether a person has told the truth on a personality test.

_____ There is a psychological test made up of inkblots, one of which looks like a bat.

_____ Men behave more aggressively than women do.

_____ Children's preferences for gender-typed toys and activities remain flexible until the resolution of the Oedipus or Electra complexes at the ages of 5 or 6.

Outline

Truth or Fiction?
"Why Are They Sad and Glad and Bad?" Introduction to Personality
The Psychodynamic Perspective
Sigmund Freud's Theory of Psychosexual Development
Other Psychodynamic Theorists
Evaluation of the Psychodynamic Perspective
Psychology in a World of Diversity: Individuality versus Relatedness: The Rust Pile for Iron John?
The Trait Perspective
From Hippocrates to the Present Day
Hans Eysenck
The Big Five Factor Structure
Evaluation of the Trait Perspective
The Learning Perspective
Behaviorism
Social-Cognitive Theory
Evaluation of the Learning Perspective
The Humanistic–Existential Perspective
Abraham Maslow and the Challenge of Self-Actualization
Carl Rogers' Self Theory
Evaluation of the Humanistic–Existential Perspective
Psychology in the New Millennium: The Sociocultural Perspective: The Individual in the New Multicultural United States
Measurement of Personality
Objective Tests
Projective Tests
Summary
Psychology and Modern Life
Gender Differences: Vive la Différence or Vive la Similarité?
On Becoming a Woman or a Man: The Development of Gender Differences

An unlearned carpenter of my acquaintance once said in my hearing: "There is very little difference between one [person] and another; but what little there is, is very important." This distinction seems to me to go to the heart of the matter.

WILLIAM JAMES

I was reading Dr. Seuss's *One Fish, Two Fish, Red Fish, Blue Fish* to my daughter, Taylor, when she was 2 years old. The sneaky author set up a trap for fathers. A part of the book reads that "Some [fish] are sad. And some are glad. And some are very, very bad. Why are they sad and glad and bad? I do not know. Go ask your dad."

Thanks, Dr. Seuss.

For many months I had just recited this section and then moved on. On one particular day, however, Taylor's cognitive development had apparently flowered, and she would not let me get away with glossing over this. Why, indeed, she wanted to know, were some fish sad, whereas others were glad and bad? I paused and then, being a typical American dad, I gave the answer I'm sure has been given by thousands of other fathers:

"Uh, some fish are sad and others are glad or bad because of, uh, the interaction of nature and nurture—I mean, you know, heredity and environmental factors."

To which Taylor laughed and replied "Not!"

"Why Are They Sad and Glad and Bad?" Introduction to Personality

I'm still not certain whether Taylor thought my words came out silly or that my psychological theorizing was simplistic or off base. But this question applied to people—that is, why people are sad or glad or bad—is the kind of question that is of interest to psychologists who investigate matters of **personality.**

Now, people do not necessarily agree on what the word *personality* means. Many lay people equate personality with liveliness, as in, "She's got a lot of personality." Others characterize a person's personality as consisting of the most striking or dominant traits, as in a "shy personality" or a "happy-go-lucky personality." Psychologists who investigate personality tend to define it as the reasonably stable patterns of emotions, motives, and behavior that distinguish people from one another (Prigatano, 1992).

Psychologists also seek to explain how personality develops—that is, why some (people) are sad or glad or bad—and to predict how people with certain features of personality will respond to life's demands. In this chapter, we explore five perspectives on personality: the psychodynamic, trait, learning, humanistic–existential, and sociocultural perspectives. Then we discuss methods of measuring whether people are sad, glad, bad, and lots of other things—personality tests.

The Psychodynamic Perspective

There are several **psychodynamic theories** of personality, but they have a number of things in common. Each teaches that personality is characterized by a dynamic struggle. Drives such as sex, aggression, and

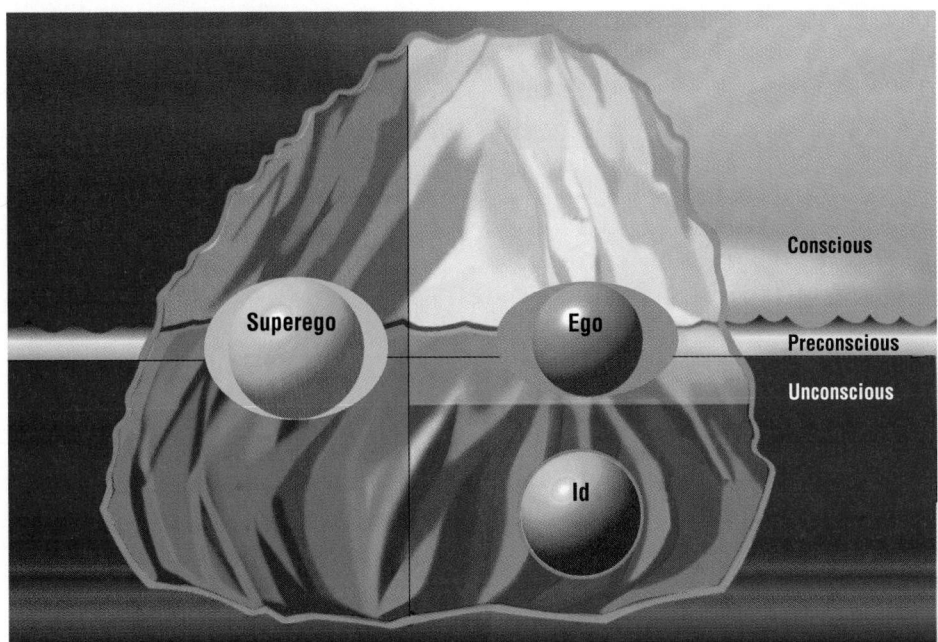

FIGURE 12.1

Spotlight on the Human Iceberg (According to Freud) According to psychodynamic theory, only the tip of human personality rises above the surface of the mind into conscious awareness. Material in the preconscious can become conscious if we direct our attention to it, but unconscious material tends to remain shrouded in mystery.

the need for superiority come into conflict with laws, social rules, and moral codes. The laws and social rules become internalized. We make them parts of ourselves. After doing so, the dynamic struggle becomes a clashing of opposing *inner* forces. At any moment, our behavior, thoughts, and emotions represent the outcome of these inner contests.

Each psychodynamic theory owes its origin to the thinking of Sigmund Freud.

SIGMUND FREUD'S THEORY OF PSYCHOSEXUAL DEVELOPMENT

He was born with a shock of dark hair—in Jewish tradition, the sign of a prophet. In 1856, in a Czechoslovakian village, an old woman told his mother that she had given birth to a great man. The child was reared with great expectations. His sister, in fact, was prohibited from playing the piano when Freud was reading or reflecting in his room.[1] In manhood, Sigmund Freud himself would be cynical about the prophecy. Old women, after all, would earn greater

favors by forecasting good tidings than doom. But the forecast about Freud was not pure fantasy. Few have influenced our thinking about human nature so deeply.

Freud was trained as a physician. Early in his practice, he was astounded to find that some people apparently experienced loss of feeling in a hand or paralysis of the legs in the absence of any medical disorder. These odd symptoms often disappeared once people had recalled and discussed stressful events and feelings of guilt or anxiety that seemed to be related to the symptoms. For a long time, these events and feelings had been hidden beneath the surface of awareness. Even so, they had the capacity to influence people's behavior.

From this sort of clinical evidence, Freud concluded that the human mind is like an iceberg (Loftus & Klinger, 1992). Only the tip of an iceberg rises above the surface of the water, while the great mass of it darkens the deep (see Figure 12.1). Freud came to believe that people, similarly, are only aware of a small number of the ideas and impulses that dwell within their minds. Freud argued that the greater mass of the mind—our

Personality • The distinct patterns of behavior, thoughts, and feelings that characterize a person's adaptation to life.

Psychodynamic theory • Sigmund Freud's perspective, which emphasizes the importance of unconscious motives and conflicts as forces that determine behavior.

---

[1] My wife believes that Freud's sister was running into typical 19th-century sexism. She might have been prevented from playing the piano if playing interfered with the activities of any man, not just the "local family genius."

Conscious • Self-aware.

Preconscious • Capable of being brought into awareness by the focusing of attention.

Unconscious • In psychodynamic theory, not available to awareness by simple focusing of attention.

Repression • A defense mechanism that protects the person from anxiety by ejecting anxiety-evoking ideas and impulses from awareness.

Psychoanalysis • In this usage, Freud's method of exploring human personality.

Self-insight • Accurate awareness of one's motives and feelings.

Resistance • A blocking of thoughts whose awareness could cause anxiety.

Psychic structure • In psychodynamic theory, a hypothesized mental structure that helps explain different aspects of behavior.

Id • The psychic structure, present at birth, that represents physiological drives and is fully unconscious.

Pleasure principle • The governing principle of the id—the seeking of immediate gratification of instinctive needs.

Ego • The second psychic structure to develop, characterized by self-awareness, planning, and delay of gratification.

Reality principle • Consideration of what is practical and possible in gratifying needs; the governing principle of the ego.

deepest images, thoughts, fears, and urges—remain beneath the surface of conscious awareness, where little light illumines them.

Truth or Fiction Revisited. *According to Sigmund Freud, it is true that the human mind is like a vast submerged iceberg, only the tip of which rises above the surface into conscious awareness.* We will see that most personality theorists credit conscious thought with more importance than Freud did.

Freud labeled the region that pokes through into the light of awareness the **conscious** part of the mind. He called the regions that lay below the surface the *preconscious* and the *unconscious.* The **preconscious** mind contains elements of experience that are presently out of awareness but that can be made conscious simply by focusing on them. The **unconscious** mind is shrouded in mystery. It contains biological instincts such as sex and aggression. Some unconscious urges cannot be experienced consciously because mental images and words could not portray them in all their color and fury. Other unconscious urges may be kept below the surface by repression.

Repression is the automatic ejection of anxiety-evoking ideas from awareness. Research evidence suggests that many people repress ugly childhood experiences (Myers & Brewin, 1994). Perhaps "something shocking happens, and the mind pushes it into some inaccessible corner of the unconscious" (Loftus, 1993a). Repression may also protect us from perceiving morally unacceptable impulses.

In the unconscious mind, primitive drives seek expression. Internalized values try to keep them in check. The resultant conflict can precipitate outbursts and psychological problems.

We cannot view the unconscious mind directly. Freud explored the unconscious through a method of mental detective work called **psychoanalysis.** In this method, people are prodded to talk about anything that pops into their minds while they remain comfortable and relaxed. People may gain **self-insight** by pursuing some of the thoughts that pop into awareness. But they are also motivated to evade threatening subjects. The same repression that ejects unacceptable thoughts from awareness prompts

resistance, or the desire to avoid thinking about or discussing them. Repression and resistance can make psychoanalysis a tedious process that lasts for years, even decades.

The Structure of Personality. When is a structure not a structure? When it is a mental or **psychic structure.** Sigmund Freud labeled the clashing forces of personality *psychic structures.* They cannot be seen or measured directly, but their presence is suggested by behavior, expressed thoughts, and emotions. Freud hypothesized the existence of three psychic structures: the id, ego, and superego.

The **id** is present at birth. It represents physiological drives and is fully unconscious. Freud described the id as "a chaos, a cauldron of seething excitations" (1964, p. 73). The conscious mind might find it inconsistent to love and hate a person at the same time, but Freud believed that conflicting emotions could dwell side by side in the id. In the id, we can feel hatred for our mothers for failing to immediately gratify all of our needs even as we sense love for them.

The id follows what Freud termed the **pleasure principle.** It demands instant gratification of instincts without consideration of law, social custom, or the needs of others.

The **ego** begins to develop during the first year of life, largely because a child's demands for gratification cannot all be met immediately. The ego "stands for reason and good sense" (Freud, 1964, p. 76), for rational ways of coping with frustration. The ego curbs the appetites of the id and makes plans that are compatible with social convention. Thus, a person can find gratification yet avoid social disapproval. The id lets you know that you are hungry. The ego formulates the idea of microwaving some enchiladas.

The ego is guided by the **reality principle.** It takes into account what is practical along with what is urged. The ego also provides the conscious sense of self.

Although most of the ego is conscious, some of its business is carried out unconsciously. For instance, the ego also acts as a censor that screens the impulses of the id. When the ego senses that improper impulses are rising into awareness, it may use

TABLE 12.1

Some Defense Mechanisms of the Ego, According
to Psychodynamic Theory

DEFENSE MECHANISM	DEFINITION	EXAMPLES
Repression	The ejection of anxiety-evoking ideas from awareness.	A student forgets that a difficult term paper is due. A patient in therapy forgets an appointment when anxiety-evoking material is to be discussed.
Regression	The return, under stress, to a form of behavior characteristic of an earlier stage of development.	An adolescent cries when forbidden to use the family car. An adult becomes highly dependent on his parents following the breakup of his marriage.
Rationalization	The use of self-deceiving justifications for unacceptable behavior.	A student blames her cheating on her teacher's leaving the room during a test. A man explains his cheating on his income tax by saying "Everyone does it."
Displacement	The transfer of ideas and impulses from threatening or unsuitable objects to less threatening objects.	A worker picks a fight with her spouse after being criticized sharply by her supervisor.
Projection	The thrusting of one's own unacceptable impulses onto others so that others are assumed to harbor them.	A hostile person perceives the world as being a dangerous place. A sexually frustrated person interprets innocent gestures of others as sexual advances.
Reaction formation	Assumption of behavior in opposition to one's genuine impulses in order to keep impulses repressed.	A person who is angry with a relative behaves in a "sickly sweet" manner toward that relative. A sadistic individual becomes a physician.
Denial	Refusal to accept the true nature of a threat.	Belief that one will not contract cancer or heart disease although one smokes heavily. "It can't happen to me."
Sublimation	The channeling of primitive impulses into positive, constructive efforts.	A person paints nudes for the sake of "beauty" and "art." A hostile person becomes a tennis star.

Defense mechanism • In psychodynamic theory, an unconscious function of the ego that protects it from anxiety-evoking material by preventing accurate recognition of this material.

Superego • The third psychic structure, which functions as a moral guardian and sets forth high standards for behavior.

Identification • In psychodynamic theory, the unconscious assumption of the behavior of another person.

Moral principle • The governing principle of the superego, which sets moral standards and enforces adherence to them.

psychological defenses to deter them from surfacing. Repression is one such psychological defense, or **defense mechanism.** Various defense mechanisms are described in Table 12.1.

The **superego** develops throughout early childhood, usually incorporating the moral standards and values of parents and important members of the community through **identification.** The superego functions according to the **moral principle.** The superego holds forth shining examples of an ideal self and also acts like the conscience, an internal moral guardian. Throughout life, the superego monitors the intentions of the ego and hands out judgments of right

and wrong. It floods the ego with feelings of guilt and shame when the verdict is negative.

The ego hasn't an easy time of it. It stands between id and superego, braving the arrows of each. It strives to satisfy the demands of the id and the moral sense of the superego. The id may urge, "You are sexually aroused!" But the superego may warn, "You're not married." The poor ego is caught in the middle.

From the Freudian perspective, a healthy personality has found ways to gratify most of the id's demands without seriously offending the superego. Most of the id's remaining demands are contained or

Eros • In psychodynamic theory, the basic instinct to preserve and perpetuate life.

Libido • (1) In psychodynamic theory, the energy of Eros; the sexual instinct. (2) Generally, sexual interest or drive.

Erogenous zone • An area of the body that is sensitive to sexual sensations.

Psychosexual development • In psychodynamic theory, the process by which libidinal energy is expressed through different erogenous zones during different stages of development.

Oral stage • The first stage of psychosexual development, during which gratification is hypothesized to be attained primarily through oral activities.

Weaning • Accustoming a child not to suck the mother's breast or a baby bottle.

Fixation • In psychodynamic theory, arrested development. Attachment to objects of an earlier stage.

repressed. If the ego is not a good problem-solver, or if the superego is too stern, the ego will have a hard time of it.

Stages of Psychosexual Development. Freud stirred controversy within the medical establishment of his day by arguing that sexual impulses are pivotal factors in personality development, even among children. Freud saw children's basic ways of relating to the world, such as sucking their mothers' breasts and moving their bowels, as entailing sexual feelings.

Freud believed that a major instinct, which he termed **Eros,** is aimed at preserving and perpetuating life. Eros is fueled by psychological, or psychic, energy that Freud labeled **libido.** Libidinal energy involves sexual impulses, so Freud considered it to be *psychosexual*. Libidinal energy would be expressed through sexual feelings in different parts of the body, or **erogenous zones,** as the child developed. To Freud, human development involves the transfer of libidinal energy from one zone to another. He hypothesized five periods of **psychosexual development:** oral, anal, phallic, latency, and genital.

During the first year of life, a child experiences much of its world through the mouth. If it fits, into the mouth it goes.

This is the **oral stage.** Freud argued that oral activities such as sucking and biting bring the child sexual gratification as well as nourishment.

Freud believed that children would encounter conflicts during each stage of psychosexual development. During the oral stage, conflict would center around the nature and extent of oral gratification. Early **weaning** could lead to frustration. Excessive gratification, on the other hand, could lead an infant to expect that it would routinely be handed everything in life. Insufficient or excessive gratification in any stage could lead to **fixation** in that stage and to the development of traits characteristic of that stage. Oral traits include dependency, gullibility, and optimism or pessimism.

Freud theorized that adults with an **oral fixation** could experience exaggerated desires for "oral activities," such as smoking, overeating, alcohol abuse, and nail biting. Like the infant whose very survival depends on the mercy of an adult, adults with oral fixations may be disposed toward clinging, dependent interpersonal relationships.

Truth or Fiction Revisited. *According to Freud, it is true that biting one's fingernails or smoking cigarettes as an adult is a sign of conflict during very early childhood.* Freud believed that adult problems tend to have their origins in childhood conflicts that are long lost to conscious awareness.

Note that according to psychodynamic theory, people are largely at the mercy of events that occurred long before they can weigh alternatives and make decisions about how to behave. Freud's own "oral fixation," cigar smoking, seems to have advanced the cancer of the mouth and jaw that killed him in 1939.

During the **anal stage,** sexual gratification is attained through contraction and relaxation of the muscles that control elimination of waste products. Elimination, which was controlled reflexively during most of the first year of life, comes under voluntary muscular control, even if such control is not reliable at first. The anal stage is said to begin in the second year of life.

During the anal stage, children learn to delay the gratification of eliminating as soon as they feel the urge. The general issue of self-control may become a source of conflict between parent and child. **Anal**

The Oral Stage? According to Sigmund Freud, the first year is the oral stage of development. If it fits, into the mouth it goes. What, according to Freud, are the effects of insufficient or excessive gratification during the oral stage? Is there evidence for his views?

fixations may stem from this conflict and lead to two sets of anal traits. So-called **anal-retentive** traits involve excessive use of self-control. They include perfectionism, a strong need for order, and exaggerated neatness and cleanliness. **Anal-expulsive** traits, on the other hand, "let it all hang out." They include carelessness, messiness, even **sadism.**

Children enter the **phallic stage** during the third year of life. During this stage, the major erogenous zone is the phallic region (the **clitoris** in girls). Parent–child conflict is likely to develop over masturbation, which parents may treat with punishment and threats. During the phallic stage, children may develop strong sexual attachments to the parent of the other gender and begin to view the parent of the same gender as a rival for the other parent's affections. Boys may want to marry Mommy, and girls may want to marry Daddy.

Feelings of lust and jealousy are difficult for children to handle. Home life would be tense indeed if they were aware of them. Thus, these feelings remain unconscious, but their influence is felt through fantasies about marriage and hostility toward the parent of the same gender. Freud labeled this conflict in boys the **Oedipus complex,** after the legendary Greek king who unwittingly killed his father and married his mother. Similar feelings in girls give rise to the **Electra complex.** According to Greek legend, Electra was the daughter of the king Agamemnon. She longed for him after his death and sought revenge against his slayers—her mother and her mother's lover.

The Oedipus and Electra complexes become resolved by about the ages of 5 or 6. Children then repress their hostilities toward, and identify with, the parent of the same gender. Identification leads to playing the social and gender roles of the parent of the same gender and internalizing that parent's values. Sexual feelings toward the parent of the other gender are repressed for a number of years. When the feelings emerge during adolescence, they are **displaced,** or transferred, to socially appropriate members of the other gender.

By the age of 5 or 6, Freud believed that children would have been in conflict with their parents over sexual feelings for several years. The pressures of the Oedipus and Electra complexes would motivate them to repress all sexual urges. In so doing, they would enter **latency,** a period of life during which sexual feelings remain unconscious. They would use this period to focus on schoolwork and to consolidate earlier learning, most notably of appropriate gender-role behaviors. During the latency phase, it would not be uncommon for children to prefer playmates of their own gender.

Freud wrote that we enter the final stage of psychosexual development, or **genital stage,** at puberty. Adolescent males again experience sexual urges toward their mothers and adolescent females toward their fathers. However, the **incest taboo** encourages repression of these impulses and their displacement onto other adults or adolescents of the other gender. Boys still might seek girls "just like the girl that married dear old Dad." Girls still might be attracted to men who resemble their fathers.

People in the genital stage prefer, by definition, to find sexual gratification through intercourse with a member of the other gender. In Freud's view, oral or anal stimulation, masturbation, and homosexual activity would all represent **pregenital** fixations and immature forms of sexual conduct. They would not be consistent with the life instinct Eros.

OTHER PSYCHODYNAMIC THEORISTS

Several personality theorists are intellectual heirs of Sigmund Freud. Their theories, like Freud's, include roles for unconscious motivation, for motivational conflict, and for defensive responses to anxiety that involve repression and cognitive distortion of reality. In other respects, theories differ considerably.

Carl Jung.

The brain is viewed as an appendage of the genital glands.

CARL JUNG (on Freud's psychodynamic theory)

Carl Jung (1875–1961) was a Swiss psychiatrist who had been a member of Freud's inner circle. He fell into disfavor with Freud when he developed his own psychodynamic theory—**analytical psychology.** As suggested by the above quotation, Jung downplayed the importance of the sexual

Oral fixation • Attachment to objects and behaviors characteristic of the oral stage.

Anal stage • The second stage of psychosexual development, when gratification is attained through anal activities.

Anal fixation • Attachment to objects and behaviors characteristic of the anal stage.

Anal-retentive • Descriptive of behaviors and traits that have to do with "holding in," or self-control.

Anal-expulsive • Descriptive of behaviors and traits that have to do with unregulated self-expression such as messiness.

Sadism • Attaining gratification from inflicting pain on, or humiliating, others.

Phallic stage • The third stage of psychosexual development, characterized by a shift of libido to the phallic region.

Clitoris • An external female sex organ that is highly sensitive to sexual stimulation.

Oedipus complex • A conflict of the phallic stage in which the boy wishes to possess his mother sexually and perceives his father as a rival in love.

Electra complex • A conflict of the phallic stage in which the girl longs for her father and resents her mother.

Displaced • Transferred.

Latency • A phase of psychosexual development characterized by repression of sexual impulses.

Genital stage • The mature stage of psychosexual development, characterized by preferred expression of libido through intercourse with an adult of the other gender.

Incest taboo • The cultural prohibition against marrying or having sexual relations with a close blood relative.

Pregenital • Characteristic of stages less mature than the genital stage.

Analytical psychology • Jung's psychodynamic theory, which emphasizes the collective unconscious and archetypes.

instinct. He saw it as but one of several important instincts.

Jung, like Freud, was intrigued by unconscious processes. He believed that we not only have a *personal* unconscious that contains repressed memories and impulses but also an inherited **collective unconscious.** The collective unconscious contains primitive images, or **archetypes,** that reflect the history of our species. Examples of archetypes are the All-Powerful God, the young hero, the fertile and nurturing mother, the wise old man, the hostile brother, even fairy godmothers, wicked witches, and themes of rebirth or resurrection. Archetypes themselves remain unconscious, but Jung declared that they influence our thoughts and emotions and render us responsive to cultural themes in stories and films.

Despite his interest in the collective unconscious, Jung granted more importance to conscious motives than Freud did. Jung believed that one of the archetypes is a **Self,** a unifying force of personality that gives direction and purpose to human behavior. According to Jung, the Self aims to provide the personality with wholeness or fullness.

Alfred Adler. Alfred Adler (1870–1937), another follower of Freud, also believed that Freud had placed too much emphasis on sexual impulses. Adler believed that people are basically motivated by an **inferiority complex.** In some people, feelings of inferiority may be based on physical problems and the need to compensate for them. Adler believed, however, that all of us encounter some feelings of inferiority because of our small size as children, and these feelings give rise to a **drive for superiority.** For instance, the English poet Lord Byron, who had a crippled leg, became a champion swimmer. Adler as a child was crippled by rickets and suffered from pneumonia, and it may be that his theory developed in part from his own childhood striving to overcome repeated bouts of illness.

Adler, like Jung, believed that self-awareness plays a major role in the formation of personality. Adler spoke of a **creative self,** a self-aware aspect of personality that strives to overcome obstacles and develop the individual's potential. Because each person's

potential is unique, Adler's views have been termed **individual psychology.**

Adler introduced the term *sibling rivalry* to describe the jealousies that are found among brothers and sisters.

Karen Horney. Karen Horney (1885–1952) agreed with Freud that childhood experiences played a major role in the development of adult personality. But like many other neoanalysts, she believed that sexual and aggressive impulses take a backseat in importance to social relationships. Moreover, she disagreed with Freud that anatomical differences between the genders lead girls to feel inferior to boys.

Horney, like Freud, saw parent–child relationships to be of paramount importance. Small children are completely dependent. When their parents treat them with indifference or harshness, they develop feelings of insecurity and what Horney terms **basic anxiety.** Children also resent neglectful parents, and Horney theorized that a **basic hostility** would accompany basic anxiety. Horney agreed with Freud that children would repress rather than express feelings of hostility toward their parents because of fear of reprisal and, just as important, fear of driving them away. But in contrast to Freud, she also believed that genuine and consistent love could mitigate the effects of even the most traumatic childhoods.

Erik Erikson. Erik Erikson (1902–1994) also believed that Freud had placed undue emphasis on sexual instincts. He asserted that social relationships are more crucial determinants of personality. To Erikson, the general climate of the mother–infant relationship is more important than the details of the feeding process or the sexual feelings that might be stirred by contact with the mother. Erikson also argued that, to a large degree, we are the conscious architects of our own personalities. His view grants more powers to the ego than Freud had allowed. Within Erikson's theory, it is possible for us to make real choices. Within Freud's theory, we may think that we are making choices, but we may only be rationalizing the compromises forced upon us by intrapsychic warfare.

Erikson, like Freud, is known for devising a comprehensive developmental theory of

Collective unconscious • Jung's hypothesized store of vague racial memories.

Archetypes • Basic, primitive images or concepts hypothesized by Jung to reside in the collective unconscious.

Self • In analytical psychology, a conscious, unifying force to personality that provides people with direction and purpose.

Inferiority complex • Feelings of inferiority hypothesized by Adler to serve as a central motivating force.

Drive for superiority • Adler's term for the desire to compensate for feelings of inferiority.

Creative self • According to Adler, the self-aware aspect of personality that strives to achieve its full potential.

Individual psychology • Adler's psychodynamic theory, which emphasizes feelings of inferiority and the creative self.

Basic anxiety • Horney's term for lasting feelings of insecurity that stem from harsh or indifferent parental treatment.

Basic hostility • Horney's term for lasting feelings of anger that accompany basic anxiety but are directed toward nonfamily members in adulthood.

Psychosocial development • Erikson's theory of personality and development, which emphasizes social relationships and eight stages of growth.

Ego identity • A firm sense of who one is and what one stands for.

TABLE 12.2
Erik Erikson's Stages of Psychosocial Development

TIME PERIOD	LIFE CRISIS	THE DEVELOPMENTAL TASK
Infancy (0–1)	Trust versus mistrust	Coming to trust the mother and the environment—to associate surroundings with feelings of inner goodness
Early childhood (2–3)	Autonomy versus shame and doubt	Developing the wish to make choices and self-control to exercise choice
Preschool years (4–5)	Initiative versus guilt	Adding planning and "attacking" to choice, becoming active and on the move
Grammar school years (6–12)	Industry versus inferiority	Becoming eagerly absorbed in skills, tasks, and productivity; mastering the fundamentals of technology
Adolescence	Identity versus role diffusion	Connecting skills and social roles to formation of career objectives
Young adulthood	Intimacy versus isolation	Committing the self to another; engaging in sexual love
Middle adulthood	Generativity versus stagnation	Needing to be needed; guiding and encouraging the younger generation; being creative
Late adulthood	Integrity versus despair	Accepting the timing and placing of one's own life cycle; achieving wisdom and dignity

Source: Erikson, 1963, pp. 247–269.

personality. But whereas Freud proposed stages of psycho*sexual* development, Erikson proposed stages of psycho*social* development. Rather than label a stage after an erogenous zone, Erikson labeled stages after the traits that might be developed during that stage (see Table 12.2). Each stage is named according to the possible outcomes. For example, the first stage of **psychosocial development** is named the stage of trust versus mistrust because of the two possible major outcomes. (1) A warm, loving relationship with the mother (and others) during infancy might lead to a sense of basic trust in people and the world. (2) A cold, nongratifying relationship might generate a pervasive sense of mistrust. Erikson believed that most of us would wind up with some blend of trust and mistrust—hopefully more trust than mistrust. A basic sense of mistrust could mar the formation of relationships for a lifetime unless we come to recognize and challenge it. For Erikson, the goal of adolescence is the attainment of **ego identity,** not genital sexuality.

Erikson extended Freud's five developmental stages to eight. Freud's developmental theory ends with adolescence. Erikson's includes the changing concerns of adulthood.

EVALUATION OF THE PSYCHODYNAMIC PERSPECTIVE

Psychodynamic theories have had tremendous appeal. They are "rich" theories. They involve many concepts and explain many varieties of human behavior and traits.

Although concepts such as "intrapsychic conflict" and "psychic energy" strike many psychologists as unscientific today, Freud fought for the idea that human personality and behavior are subject to scientific analysis. Freud's theorizing took place at a time when many people still viewed grave psychological problems as signs of possession by the Devil or evil spirits, as they had during the Middle Ages. Freud argued that psychological disorders stem from problems within the individual—not evil spirits. Freud's thinking contributed to the development of compassion for, and methods of helping, people with psychological disorders.

Psychodynamic theory has also focused the attention of scientists and helping professionals on the far-reaching effects of childhood events. The developmental theories of Freud and Erikson suggest ways in which early childhood traumas can affect us for a lifetime. Horney believed that Freud was too pessimistic about the ability of children to recover from trauma and that Freud underestimated the saving powers of love. Yet, Freud and other psychodynamic theorists are to be credited for suggesting that personality and behavior *develop* and that it is important for us as parents to be aware of the emotional needs of our children.

Freud has helped us recognize that sexual and aggressive urges are commonplace and that there is a difference between acknowledging these urges and acting on them. As W. Bertram Wolfe put it, "Freud found sex an outcast in the outhouse, and left it in the living room an honored guest."

Freud also noted that people have defensive ways of looking at the world. His list of defense mechanisms have become part of everyday parlance. Whether or not we attribute these cognitive distortions to unconscious ego functioning, our thinking may be distorted by our efforts to avert anxiety and guilt. If these concepts no longer strike us as being innovative, it is largely because of the influence of Sigmund Freud. Psychodynamic theorists also innovated many methods of psychotherapy, which we describe in Chapter 14.

Despite their richness, psychodynamic theories, particularly the original psychodynamic views of Sigmund Freud, have met with criticism. Some followers of Freud, such as Horney and Erikson, have argued that Freud placed too much emphasis on human sexuality and neglected the importance of social relationships. Other followers have argued that Freud placed too much emphasis on unconscious motives. They assert that people consciously seek self-enhancement and intellectual pleasures. They do not merely try to gratify the dark demands of the id.

A number of critics note that "psychic structures" such as the id, ego, and superego have no substance. They are little more than useful fictions—poetic ways to express inner conflict. It is debatable whether Freud ever attributed substance to the psychic structures. He, too, may have seen them more as poetic fictions than as

"things." If so, his critics have the right to use other descriptive terms and write better "poems."

Some critics have argued that Freud's hypothetical mental processes fail as scientific concepts because they can neither be observed nor can they predict observable behavior with precision (Robinson, 1993). Scientific propositions must be capable of being proved false. But Freud's statements about mental structures are unscientific because no conceivable type of evidence can disprove them. Any behavior can be explained in terms of these hypothesized (but unobservable) "structures."

Nor have the stages of psychosexual development escaped criticism. Children begin to masturbate as early as the first year, not in the phallic stage. As parents know from discovering their children play "doctor," the latency stage is not as sexually latent as Freud believed. Much of Freud's thinking concerning the Oedipus and Electra complexes remains speculation. The evidence for some of Erikson's developmental views seems somewhat sturdier. For example, adolescents who fail to develop ego identity seem to encounter problems developing intimate relationships later on.

Freud's method of gathering evidence from the clinical session is also suspect (Robinson, 1993). Therapists may subtly influence clients to produce what they expect to find. Therapists may also fail to separate reported facts from their own interpretations. Also, Freud and many other psychodynamic theorists restricted their evidence gathering to case studies with individuals who sought therapy for adjustment problems. Their clients were also mostly White and drawn from the middle and upper classes. Persons seeking therapy are likely to have more problems than the general population.

Reflections

Now that you have read about psychodynamic theories of personality, reflect on the following questions:

• Do you believe that you are aware of all of your feelings? Why or why not? What would Freud have said about your answer?

- Agree or disagree with the following statement and support your answer: "People are basically antisocial. Their primitive impulses must be suppressed and repressed if they are to function productively within social settings."
- If you were fixated in a stage of psychosocial development, which stage would it be? Why?

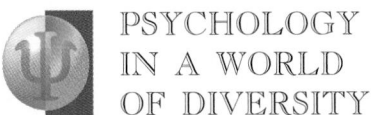 PSYCHOLOGY IN A WORLD OF DIVERSITY

INDIVIDUALITY VERSUS RELATEDNESS: THE RUST PILE FOR IRON JOHN?

Most Western theories of personality and human development have been accused of having a "phallocentric" and individualist bias (Jordan and others, 1991). This criticism applies to the views of Freud, Erikson, Piaget, and Kohlberg, among others. Each view uses the yardsticks of male development as the norms. Each view neglects important aspects of personality development, such as the relatedness of the individual to other people (Guisinger & Blatt, 1994). In Western culture, the male view is that the self is supreme and distinct from other people. Moreover, separation and individuation are presented as the highest goal of personality development. Yet social critics (e.g., Gilligan and others, 1991; Jordan and others, 1991) consider a crucial aspect of a woman's sense of self to be her relatedness—her establishment and maintenance of social relationships.

Guisinger and Blatt (1994) suggest that the male tendency toward individualism might arise from the different developmental tasks faced by boys and girls. For example, when a boy recognizes that he and his mother are not of the same gender, he must set himself apart from her. This process of differentiation may lead boys to greater concern about being separate and distinct from other people. For girls, of course, differentiation from the mother is unnecessary.

Gender stereotypes and cultural expectations also enter the picture early. True, in our society the great majority of women

are in the workforce. Yet girls are still taught from an early age that they will have the primary responsibilities for homemaking and child rearing. We live in an age in which women and men share child-rearing chores more than they did in the past. However, developmental research still shows that women are more likely than men to supply the emotional glue that holds the family together.

Guisinger and Blatt (1994) suggest women's and men's personality development may frustrate both genders. Women's relational development is both an undervalued strength and a source of vulnerability for women. Women are often at risk of losing themselves in their relationships and experience an inadequately developed sense of self. Although men today may be more involved as fathers than they were in past generations, young daughters may still learn to invest themselves in attempting to engage their relatively distant fathers. Later, they attempt to engage other men in relationships and may chronically feel that men care less about them than they care about the men.

Men tend to underemphasize interpersonal relatedness. Although their needs to be strong individuals may prevent them

Is This "Iron John"? Do Western theories of personality present the masculine gender-role stereotype—as characterized by separation and individuation—as the highest goal of personality development? Women more so than men emphasize interpersonal relatedness as a key goal of personality development. Although their needs to be strong individuals may prevent men from getting in touch with their feelings, they may suffer from feelings of alienation and grief over lack of relatedness to other people.

Trait • A relatively stable aspect of personality that is inferred from behavior and assumed to give rise to consistent behavior.

Lexical hypothesis • The view that fundamental human differences in personality traits may be studied by surveying which traits are described by many of the world's languages in single words. People, that is, from various cultures will need concise ways of describing common personality traits.

Factor analysis • A statistical technique that identifies variables or traits that tend to belong together or, as items on a personality test, to be answered in the same direction. For example, test items assessing organization, thoroughness, and reliability would tend to be answered in the same direction to form a factor that can be labeled *conscientiousness*.

from admitting to, or getting in touch with, their feelings, they may suffer from feelings of alienation and grief over their loss of relatedness to others, including other men (Bly, 1990; Keen, 1991). Consider the title of Robert Bly's popular book, *Iron John.* It is well known that Iron Johns are less likely than women to reveal intimate information about themselves (Dindia & Allen, 1992). As one result, they are less likely than women to have intimate friends, even though they may be part of a large sporting crowd. Iron Johns may do many things "with the guys" but feel that they have no one to talk to. Moreover, just as women are likely to struggle to engage distant men, men are likely to have chronic problems in their relationships with women.

The Trait Perspective

In most of us by the age of thirty, the character has set like plaster, and will never soften again.
WILLIAM JAMES

FIGURE 12.2
Three Personality Profiles According to Cattell's Personality Factors How do the traits of writers, airline pilots, and creative artists compare? Where would you place yourself within these personality dimensions?

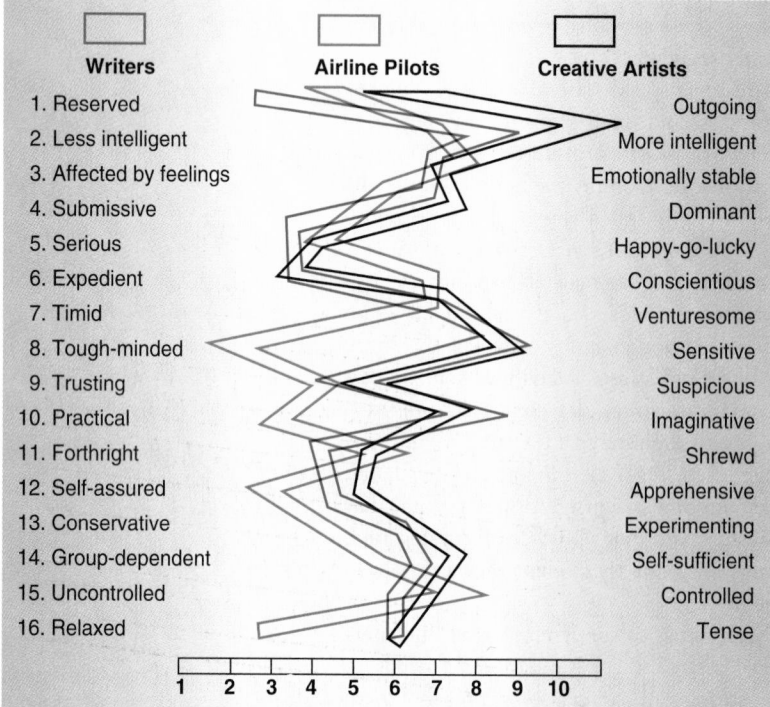

The notion of **traits** is very familiar. If I asked you to describe yourself, you would probably do so in terms of traits such as bright, sophisticated, and witty. (That is you, is it not?) We also describe other people in terms of traits.

Traits are reasonably stable elements of personality that are inferred from behavior. If you describe a friend as "shy," it may be because you have observed social anxiety or withdrawal in the friend's encounters. Traits are assumed to account for consistent behavior in diverse situations. You probably expect your "shy" friend to be retiring in most social confrontations—"all across the board," as the saying goes. The concept of traits also finds a place in other approaches to personality. Recall that throughout Freud's stages of psychosexual development, he linked development of certain traits to children's experiences.

FROM HIPPOCRATES TO THE PRESENT DAY

The history of the trait approach is very old. It dates at least to Hippocrates (ca. 460–377 B.C.), the physician of the Golden Age of Greece (Maher & Maher, 1994). The assumption has generally been that traits are embedded in people's bodies, but the biological rationales have varied. Hippocrates believed that traits are embedded in people's bodily fluids, or humors, and give rise to certain types of personalities. In his view, these types, and mixtures of these types, depend on the balance of four "basic fluids," or humors, in the body. Yellow bile was associated with a choleric (quick-tempered) disposition; blood, a sanguine (warm, cheerful) one; phlegm, a phlegmatic (sluggish, calm, cool) disposition; and black bile, a melancholic (gloomy, pensive) temperament. Disease was believed to reflect an imbalance in humors. Methods such as bloodletting and vomiting were recommended to restore the balance and one's health (Maher & Maher, 1994). Although Hippocrates' theoretical edifice lies in ruins, the terms *choleric, sanguine,* and so on remain in use.

Early in the 20th century, William Sheldon suggested that personality traits are linked to body types (Maher & Maher, 1994). His types were derived from distinctions between layers of embryonic tissue. Sheldon's theory has not drawn much interest in recent years, in part because it perpetuated stereotypes such as the notion that obese people are jolly.

Truth or Fiction Revisited. *It is not true that obese people are jolly.* For the statement to be true, it would have to apply universally. Moreover, this view serves to perpetuate a stereotype.

More enduring trait theories, like that of Gordon Allport, have assumed that traits are heritable and embedded in the nervous system. They have relied on the mathematical technique of factor analysis in the attempt to determine basic human traits.

Sir Francis Galton was among the first scientists to recognize the **lexical hypothesis,** which holds that many of the world's languages will use single words to describe fundamental human differences in personality (Goldberg, 1993). More than 50 years ago, Gordon Allport and a colleague (Allport & Oddbert, 1936) catalogued some 18,000 human traits from a search through word lists of the sort found in dictionaries. Some were physical traits such as short, black, and brunette. Others were behavioral traits such as shy and emotional. Still others were moral traits such as honest. This exhaustive list has served as the basis for personality research by many other psychologists, including Raymond Cattell.

Psychologists such as Raymond Cattell (1965) have used **factor analysis** to reduce this universe of traits to smaller lists of traits that show common features. Cattell also distinguished between surface traits and source traits. **Surface traits** describe characteristic ways of behaving—for example, cleanliness, stubbornness, thrift, and orderliness. We may observe that these traits form meaningful patterns that are suggestive of underlying traits. (Cleanliness, stubbornness, and so on, were all referred to as *anal retentive* traits by Freud.)

Cattell refined the Allport catalogue by removing unusual terms and grouping the remaining traits under **source traits**—the underlying traits from which surface traits are derived. Cattell argued that psychological measurement of a person's source traits would enable us to predict his or her behavior in various situations.

Cattell's research led him to suggest the existence of 16 source traits, and these traits can be measured by means of his Sixteen Personality Factors Scale. The "16 PF" is frequently used in psychological research that explores differences between groups of people and individuals. Figure 12.2. shows the differences, according to the 16 PF, between airline pilots, creative artists, and writers. Notice that the pilots are more stable, conscientious, tough-minded, practical, controlled, and relaxed than the other two groups. The artists and writers are more intelligent, sensitive, and imaginative.

HANS EYSENCK

British psychologist Hans J. Eysenck (1960; Eysenck & Eysenck, 1985) has focused much of his research on the relationships between two important traits: **introversion–extroversion** and emotional stability–instability (the last also known as **neuroticism**). Carl Jung was first to distinguish between introverts and extroverts. Eysenck added the dimension of emotional stability–instability to introversion–extroversion. He has catalogued

Surface traits • Cattell's term for characteristic, observable ways of behaving.
Source traits • Cattell's term for underlying traits from which surface traits are derived.
Introversion • A source trait characterized by intense imagination and the tendency to inhibit impulses.
Extroversion • A source trait characterized by tendencies to be socially outgoing and to express feelings and impulses freely.
Neuroticism • Eysenck's term for emotional instability.

Creative Artists. Artist Faith Ringgold (right) works on a quilt with a colleague. What traits are shown by creative artists? What are their strengths, their weaknesses? How do their personalities compare, say, to those of airline pilots? How do psychologists measure traits?

MINILECTURE:
TRAIT
THEORIES

various personality traits according to where they are "situated" along these dimensions or factors (see Figure 12.3). For instance, an anxious person would be high both in introversion and in neuroticism—that is, preoccupied with his or her own thoughts and emotionally unstable.

Eysenck notes that his scheme is reminiscent of that suggested by Hippocrates.

According to Eysenck's dimensions, the choleric type would be extroverted and unstable; the sanguine type, extroverted and stable; the phlegmatic type, introverted and stable; and the melancholic type, introverted and unstable.

THE BIG FIVE FACTOR STRUCTURE

Empirical studies (Digman, 1990; Trull, 1992) suggest that there may be five basic personality factors (Goldberg, 1993; Kim-

ble, 1994). These factors include the two found by Eysenck—introversion–extroversion and emotional stability–instability—and three suggested by Raymond Cattell: conscientiousness, agreeableness, and openness to new experience (akin to Cattell's experimenting–conservative dimension) (see Table 12.3). Although many personality theorists, especially Louis Thurstone, Raymond Cattell, and Donald Fiske, can be said to have had a part in the development of the Big Five, Tupes and Christal (1992) are usually given major credit because of their key studies for the U.S. Air Force (Goldberg, 1993; McCrae, 1992). In recent years, the Big Five have found practical applications in areas such as personnel selection and classification (Goldberg, 1993) and psychological disorders (Clark and others, 1994; Widiger & Costa, 1994).

There continues to be disagreement on the number of basic personality factors.

FIGURE 12.3
Eysenck's Personality Dimensions and Hippocrates' Personality Types Various personality traits shown in the outer ring fall within the two major dimensions of personality suggested by Hans Eysenck. The inner circle shows how Hippocrates' personality types—choleric, sanguine, phlegmatic, and melancholic—fit within Eysenck's dimensions.

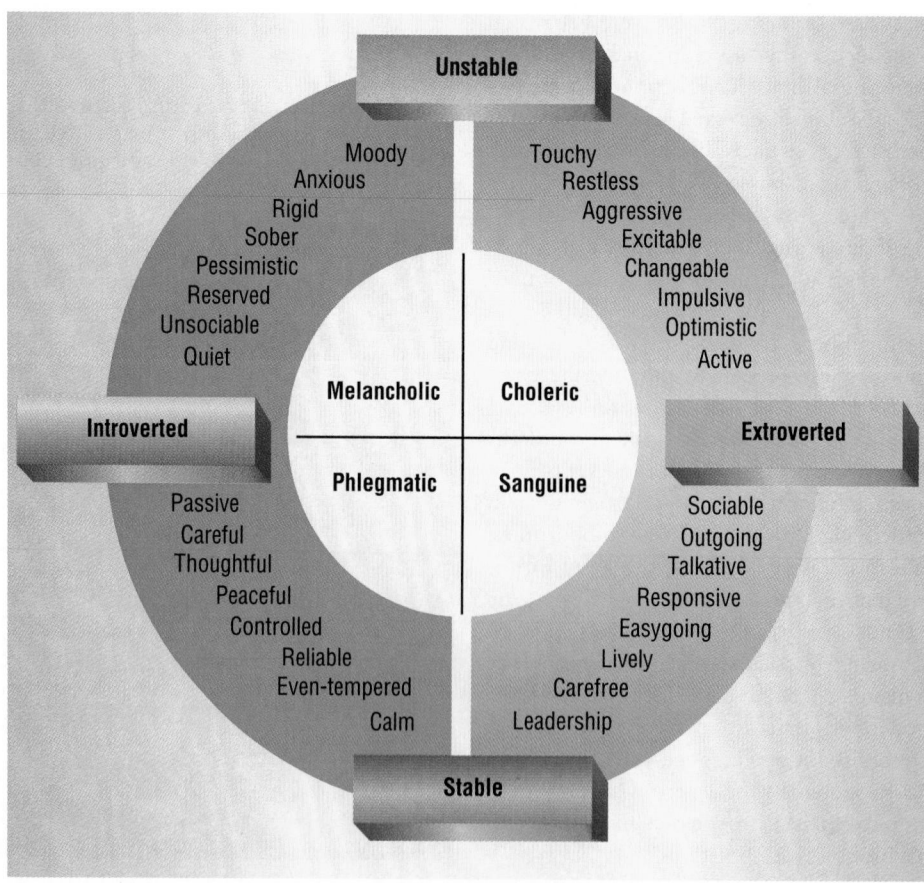

TABLE 12.3
The Big Five Personality Factors

FACTOR	NAME	TRAITS CONTRASTED OR INCLUDED
I	Extroversion	Contrasts talkativeness, assertiveness, and activity with silence, passivity, and reserve
II	Agreeableness	Contrasts kindness, trust, and warmth with hostility, selfishness, and distrust
III	Conscientiousness	Contrasts organization, thoroughness, and reliability with carelessness, negligence, and unreliability
IV	Emotional stability	Includes traits such as nervousness, moodiness, temperamentality, and sensitivity to negative stimuli
V	Openness to experience (versus closed-mindedness)	Contrasts imagination, curiosity, and creativity with shallowness and imperceptiveness

Sources: Clark and others, 1994; Goldberg, 1993.

Zuckerman (1992), for example, questions the ways in which researchers determine which personality factors are basic and which are not. Hans Eysenck is less charitable. He argues that the Big Five factor theory is unscientific, even "a grotesque product of the imagination" (Eysenck, 1993, p. 1299).

EVALUATION OF THE TRAIT PERSPECTIVE

Trait theories, like psychodynamic theories, have their strengths and weaknesses.

Trait theorists have focused much attention on the development of useful tests such as Cattell's Sixteen Personality Factors Scale to measure traits. Others are discussed in the section on measurement of personality.

Trait theorists have also spawned theories concerning the fit between personality and jobs. The qualities that suit us for various kinds of work can be expressed in terms of our abilities, our personality traits, and our interests. By using interviews and tests to learn about our abilities and our traits, testing and counseling centers can make valuable suggestions about the likelihood for our success and fulfillment in various kinds of jobs.

Freud developed his theories about "oral," "anal," and other traits on the basis of clinical case studies. However, trait theorists have administered broad personality tests to thousands of people and have used sophisticated statistical techniques to identify the basic traits, or factors, that tend to describe us.

One weakness of trait theory is that it is descriptive, not explanatory. Trait theory focuses on describing traits rather than tracing their origins or investigating how they may be modified. Moreover, the "explanations" that are provided by trait theory are often criticized as being **circular explanations.** That is, they restate what is observed and do not explain what is observed. Saying that John failed to ask Marsha on a date *because* of shyness is an example of a circular explanation: We have merely restated John's (shy) behavior as a trait (shyness).

The trait concept requires that traits show stability. Although many personality traits seem to do so, behavior may vary more from situation to situation than trait theory would allow (Mischel, 1993). People who are high in **self-consciousness** try to show consistent behavior from situation to situation (Carver & Scheier, 1981; Duval and others, 1992; Underwood & Moore, 1981). However, other people show more variability in behavior. Even identical twins show increasingly greater differences in traits as they grow up and grow apart (McCartney and others, 1990).

Circular explanation • An explanation that merely restates its own concepts instead of offering additional information.
Self-consciousness • The tendency to take critical note of one's own behavior.

Reflections

Now that you have learned about trait theory, reflect on the following questions:

- To what traits do you refer when you are describing yourself? What is your evidence for referring to these traits?
- Where would you place athletes and artists in terms of the dimensions of introversion–extroversion and neuroticism? Where would you place yourself?

The Learning Perspective

The learning perspective has also contributed to the understanding of personality. We shall focus on two learning approaches: behaviorism and social-cognitive theory.

BEHAVIORISM

You have freedom when you're easy in your harness.

ROBERT FROST

At Johns Hopkins University in 1924, psychologist John B. Watson announced the battle cry of the behaviorist movement:

> Give me a dozen healthy infants, well-formed, and my own specified world to bring them up in and I'll guarantee to take any one at random and train him to become any type of specialist I might suggest—doctor, lawyer, merchant-chief and, yes, even beggar-man and thief, regardless of his talents, penchants, tendencies, abilities, vocations, and the race of his ancestors. (p. 82)

Watson thus proclaimed that situational variables or environmental influences—not internal, person variables—are the important shapers of human preferences and behaviors. As a counterbalance to the psychoanalysts and structuralists of his day, Watson argued that unseen, undetectable mental structures must be rejected in favor of that which can be seen and measured. In the 1930s, Watson's hue and cry was taken up by B. F. Skinner, who agreed that we should avoid trying to see within the "black box" of the organism and emphasized the effect that reinforcements have on behavior.

The views of John B. Watson and B. F. Skinner largely discard the notions of personal freedom, choice, and self-direction. Most of us assume that our wants originate within us. But Skinner suggested that environmental influences such as parental approval and social custom shape us into *wanting* certain things and *not wanting* others (Delprato & Midgley, 1992).

In his novel *Walden Two*, Skinner (1948) described a Utopian society in which people are happy and content, because they are allowed to do as they please. However, they have been trained or conditioned from early childhood to engage in **prosocial** behavior and to express prosocial attitudes. Because of their reinforcement histories, they *want* to behave in a decent, kind, and unselfish way (Dinsmoor, 1992). They see themselves as being free because society makes no effort to force them to behave as they do as adults.

Skinner elaborated on his beliefs about people and society in *Beyond Freedom and Dignity* (1972). According to Skinner, adaptation to the environment requires acceptance of behavior patterns that ensure survival. If the group is to survive, it must construct rules and laws that foster social harmony. People are then rewarded for following these rules and punished for disobeying them. None of us is really free, even though we think of ourselves as coming together freely to establish the rules and as choosing to follow them.

Some object to behaviorist notions because they sidestep the roles of human consciousness and choice. Others argue that people are not so blindly ruled by pleasure and pain. People have rebelled against the so-called necessity of survival by choosing pain and hardship over pleasure, or death over life. Many people have sacrificed their own lives to save those of others.

The behaviorist defense might be that the apparent choice of pain or death is forced on the altruist as inevitably as conformity to social custom is forced on others. The altruist is also shaped by external influences, even if those influences differ from those that affect many other people.

SOCIAL-COGNITIVE THEORY

Social-cognitive theory[2] is a contemporary view of learning that is being developed by Albert Bandura (1986, 1989, 1991) and other psychologists (e.g., Cantor, 1990; Dweck, 1990; Higgins, 1990; Mischel, 1990). Social-cognitive theory focuses on the importance of learning by observation and on the cognitive processes that underlie

Prosocial • Behavior that is characterized by helping others and making a contribution to society.

Social-cognitive theory • A cognitively oriented learning theory in which observational learning and person variables such as values and expectancies play major roles in individual differences.

Person variables • Factors within the person, such as expectancies and competencies, that influence behavior.

Expectancies • Personal predictions about the outcomes of potential behaviors.

Subjective value • The desirability of an object or event.

Model • In social-cognitive theory, an organism that exhibits behaviors that others will imitate or acquire through observational learning.

Competencies • Knowledge and skills.

Encode • Interpret; transform.

[2] Formerly termed *social-learning theory.*

individual differences. Social-cognitive theorists see people as influencing the environment just as the environment influences them. Social-cognitive theorists agree with behaviorists and other empirical psychologists that discussions of human nature should be tied to observable experiences and behaviors. They assert, however, that variables within people—**person variables**—must also be considered if we are to understand them.

One goal of all psychological theories is the prediction of behavior. Social-cognitive theorist Julian B. Rotter (1972) argues that we cannot predict behavior from situational variables alone. Whether a person will behave in a certain way also depends on the person's **expectancies** about that behavior's outcomes and the perceived or **subjective values** of those outcomes.

To social-cognitive theorists, people are self-aware and engage in purposeful learning. People are not simply at the mercy of the environment. Instead, they seek to learn about their environment. They alter and construct the environment to make reinforcers available.

Social-cognitive theorists also note the importance of rules and symbolic processes in learning. Children, for example, learn more effectively how to behave in specific situations when parents explain the rules involved. In inductive methods of discipline, parents use the situation to teach children about general rules and social codes that should govern their behavior. Inductive methods are more effective at fostering desirable behavior than punishment alone.

Observational Learning. Observational learning (also termed **modeling** or *cognitive learning*) refers to acquiring knowledge by observing others. For operant conditioning to occur, an organism (1) must engage in a response, and (2) that response must be reinforced. But observational learning occurs even when the learner does not perform the observed behavior. Therefore, direct reinforcement is not required either. Observing others extends to reading about them or perceiving what they do and what happens to them in media such as radio, television, and film.

Our expectations stem from our observations of what happens to ourselves and other people. For example, teachers are more likely to call on males and are more accepting of "calling out" in class from males than females (Sadker & Sadker, 1994). As a result, many males expect to be rewarded for calling out. Females, however, may learn that they will be reprimanded for behaving in what traditionalists might term an "unladylike" manner.

Social-cognitive theorists view behavior as stemming from the interaction between person variables and situational variables. Person variables include competencies, encoding strategies, expectancies, subjective values, and self-regulatory systems and plans (Mischel, 1993, pp. 403–411; see Figure 12.4).

Competencies: What Can You Do? **Competencies** include knowledge of rules that guide conduct, concepts about ourselves and other people, and skills (Cantor, 1990). Our ability to use information to make plans depends on our competencies.

Competencies include knowledge of the physical world, of cultural codes of conduct, and of the behavior expected in certain situations. They include academic skills such as reading and writing, athletic skills such as swimming and tossing a football, social skills such as knowing how to ask someone out on a date, job skills, and many others.

Individual differences in competencies reflect genetic variation, nourishment, differences in learning opportunities, and other environmental factors. Generally speaking, people do not perform well at given tasks unless they have the competencies needed to do so.

Encoding Strategies: How Do You See It? Different people **encode** (symbolize or represent) the same stimuli in different ways, and their encoding strategies are an important factor in their overt behavior. One person might encode a tennis game as a chance to bat the ball back and forth and have some fun; another might encode the same game as a demand to perfect his or her serve. One person might encode a date that doesn't work out as a sign of her

How Do Competencies Contribute to Performance? There are great individual differences in our competencies, based on genetic variation, nourishment, differences in learning opportunities, and other environmental factors. What factors contribute to this girl's performance on the balance beam?

or his social incompetence; another might encode the dating experience as reflecting the fact that people are not always "made for each other."

Some people make themselves miserable by encoding events in self-defeating ways (see Chapter 13). A linebacker may encode an average day on the field as a failure because he didn't get any sacks. A college student may encode one refusal to accept a date as a disaster that reflects on his or her worth as a human being. Cognitive and behavior therapists foster adjustment by challenging individuals to view life in more productive ways.

Expectancies: What Will Happen?

There are various kinds of expectancies in social-cognitive theory. Some expectancies are predictions about what will follow

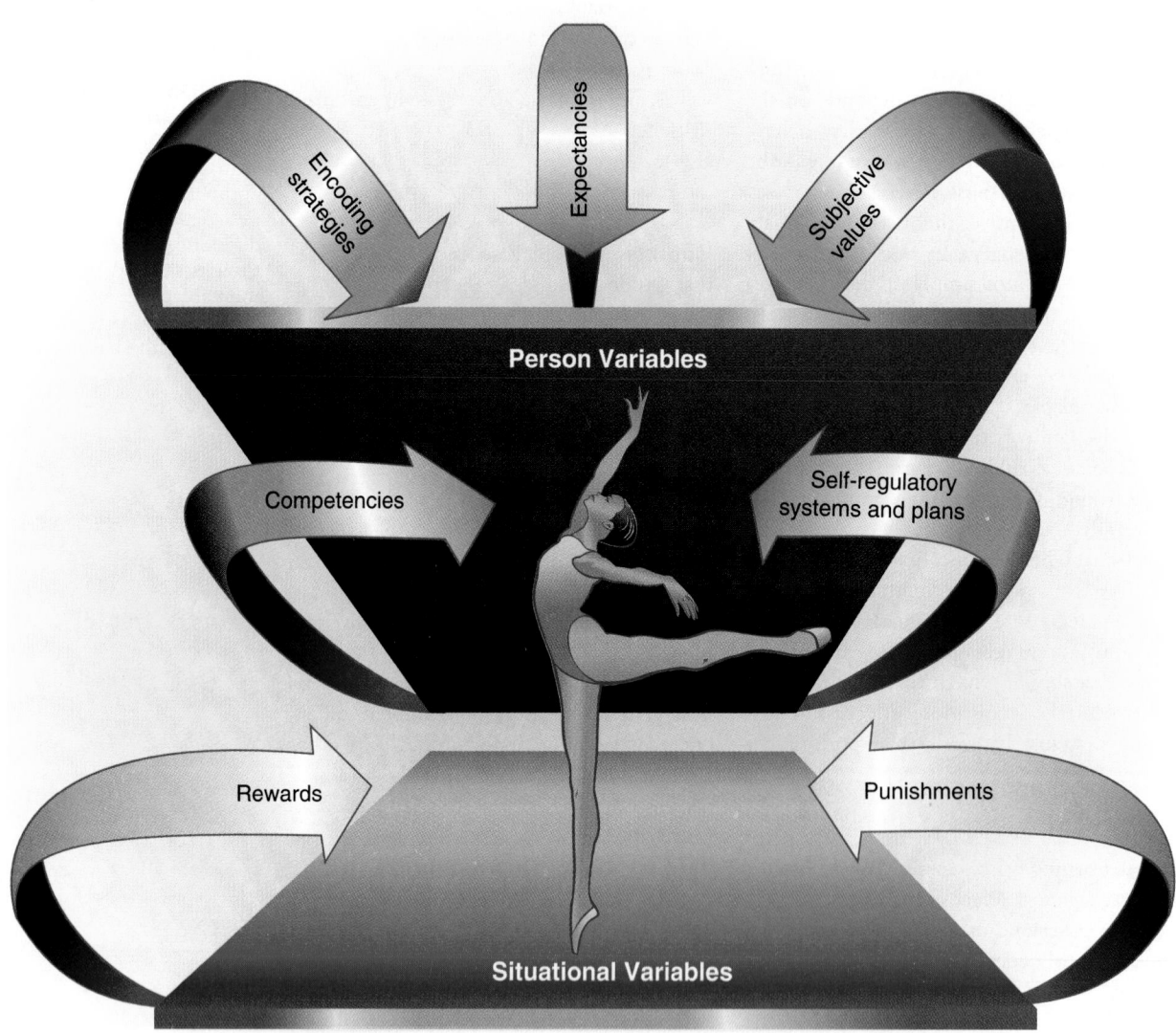

FIGURE 12.4

Spotlight on Social-Cognitive Theory According to social–cognitive theory, person variables and situational variables interact to influence behavior.

various stimuli or signs **(stimulus-outcome relations)**. For example, some people predict other people's behavior on the basis of signs such as "tight lips" or "shifty eyes" (Ross & Nisbett, 1991). Other expectancies involve what will happen if we engage in certain behaviors **(behavior-outcome relations)**. Still other expectancies are **self-efficacy expectations**. These are our beliefs that we can accomplish things such as speak before a group, or do a backflip into a swimming pool, or solve math problems (Pajares & Miller, 1994).

The human ability to manipulate symbols allows us to foresee the potential outcomes of what we do. Expectancies are based on our observations of others and on our own experiences.

Competencies influence expectancies, and expectancies, in turn, influence motivation to perform. People with positive self-efficacy expectations are more likely to try difficult tasks than people who do not believe that they can master them. As noted by Bandura and his colleagues Linda Reese and Nancy Adams:

> In their daily lives people must make decisions about whether to attempt risky courses of action or how long to continue, in the face of difficulties, those they have undertaken. [Social-cognitive theory suggests that] people tend to avoid situations they believe exceed their coping capabilities, but they undertake and perform assuredly activities they judge themselves capable of managing. . . .
>
> Self-judged efficacy also determines how much of an effort people will make and how long they will keep at a task despite obstacles or adverse experiences. . . . Those who have a strong sense of efficacy exert greater effort to master the challenges. . . . (1982, p. 5)

Truth or Fiction Revisited. *It is true that we are more likely to persist at difficult tasks when we believe we shall succeed.* Positive self-efficacy expectations apparently motivate us to persevere. Bandura (1986) suggests that one way in which psychotherapy helps people is by changing their self-efficacy expectations from "I can't" to "I can." As a result, people are motivated to try out new patterns of behavior.

Subjective Values: What Is It Worth? Because of our different learning histories, we each may place a different value on the same outcome. What is frightening to one person may entice another. What is somewhat desirable to one may be irresistible to another. From the social-cognitive perspective, in contrast to behaviorist perspective, we are not controlled by stimuli. Instead, stimuli have meanings for us, and these meanings are one factor in influencing behavior.

The subjective value of a particular stimulus or reward is related to our experience with it or similar rewards. Experience may be direct or observational. Because of experience, our feelings about the outcome may be positive or negative. If you became nauseated the last time you drank a glass of iced tea, its subjective value as an incentive may diminish, even on a hot day.

Self-Regulatory Systems and Plans: How Can You Achieve It? Social-cognitive theory recognizes that one of the features of being human is our tendency to regulate our own behavior, even in the absence of observers and external constraints. We set goals and standards for ourselves, construct plans for achieving them, and congratulate or criticize ourselves, depending on whether or not we reach them (Bandura, 1991).

Self-regulation amplifies our opportunities for influencing our environment. We can select the situations to which we expose ourselves and the arenas in which we shall contend. Based on our expectancies, we may choose to enter the academic or athletic worlds. We may choose marriage or the single life. And, when we cannot readily select our environment, we can to some degree select our responses within an environment—even an aversive one. For example, if we are undergoing an uncomfortable medical procedure, we may try to focus on something else—the cracks in the tiles on the ceiling or an inner fantasy—to reduce the stress.

Stimulus-outcome relations • Predictions as to what events will follow certain stimuli or signs.

Behavior-outcome relations • Predictions as to the outcomes (reinforcement contingencies) of one's behavior.

Self-efficacy expectations • Beliefs to the effect that one can handle a task.

EVALUATION OF THE LEARNING PERSPECTIVE

Learning theorists have made monumental contributions to the scientific understanding of behavior, but they have also left some psychologists dissatisfied.

Psychodynamic theorists and trait theorists propose the existence of psychological structures that cannot be seen and measured directly. Learning theorists—particularly behaviorists—have dramatized the importance of referring to publicly observable variables, or behaviors, if psychology is to be accepted as a science.

Similarly, psychodynamic theorists and trait theorists focus on internal variables such as intrapsychic conflict and traits to explain and predict behavior. Learning theorists have emphasized the importance of environmental conditions, or situational variables, as determinants of behavior.

Learning theorists have elaborated on the conditions that foster learning—even automatic kinds of learning. They have shown that involuntary responses—including fear responses—may be conditioned, that we can learn to do things because of reinforcements, and that many broad behavior patterns are acquired by observing others.

Learning theorists have devised methods for helping individuals solve adjustment problems that probably would not have been derived from any other theoretical perspective. These include the behavioral, extinction-based, fear-reduction methods of flooding and systematic desensitization and the operant-conditioning method of biofeedback training.

On the other hand, behaviorism is limited in its ability to explain personality. Behaviorism does not describe, explain, or even suggest the richness of inner human experience. We experience thoughts and feelings and peruse our complex inner maps of the world, and behaviorism does not deal with these phenomena. To be fair, however, the "limitations" of behaviorism are self-imposed. Personality theorists have traditionally dealt with thoughts, feelings, and behavior, whereas behaviorism, in its insistence on studying only that which is observable and measurable, deals with behavior alone.

Critics of social-cognitive theory cannot accuse its supporters of denying the importance of cognitive activity and feelings. But they often contend that social-cognitive theory has not derived satisfying statements about the development of traits or accounted for self-awareness. Also, social-cognitive theory—like its intellectual forebear, behaviorism—may not have paid sufficient attention to genetic variation in explaining individual differences in behavior.

Social-cognitive theorists seem to be working on these theoretical flaws. Social-cognitive theorists, unlike behaviorists, view people as active, not as reacting mechanically to environmental pressures. In the area of psychological disorders, social-cognitive theorists grant that inherited or biological factors may interact with situational factors to give rise to abnormal behavior.

Reflections

Now that you have learned about the learning perspective on personality, reflect on the following questions:

- Given cultural and social conditioning, is true freedom possible? To behaviorists, our telling ourselves that we have free will is determined by the environment. Is free will merely an illusion? What is the evidence for your belief?
- Which theorists believe that people are "ruled" by pleasure and pain? Do you share this belief? Why or why not?
- Social-cognitive theorists suggest that our self-efficacy expectations are connected with how hard we work at things. Do examples from your own life support this view?

Now let us consider theories that begin with the assumption of consciousness and dwell on the importance of our cognitive functioning.

The Humanistic— Existential Perspective

You are unique, and if that is not fulfilled, then something has been lost.

MARTHA GRAHAM

High tech, artificial intelligence, space exploration—these are a few of the artifacts of modern life. Genocide and world war are others. Amid upheaval, humanists and existentialists dwell on the meaning of life. Their self-awareness of their being in the world is the hub of the humanistic–existential search for meaning. Because of their focus on conscious, subjective experience, humanistic–existential theories have also been referred to as **phenomenological.**

The term **humanism** has a lengthy history and diverse meanings. It became a third force in American psychology in the 1950s and 1960s, in part in response to the predominant psychodynamic and behavioral models. Humanism also represented a reaction to the "rat race" spawned by industrialization and automation. Humanists opposed the posting of people on the gray, anonymous treadmills of industry. "Alienation" from inner sources of meaning distressed them. Against this backdrop emerged the humanistic views of Abraham Maslow and Carl Rogers.

Existentialism in part reflects the horrors of mass destruction of human life through war and genocide. The term *existentialism* implies that our existence, or being, in the world is more central to human nature than theories or abstractions about human nature.

The European existentialist philosophers Jean-Paul Sartre and Martin Heidegger saw human life as trivial in the grand scheme of things, leading to feelings of alienation. But the Swiss psychiatrists Ludwig Binswanger and Medard Boss argued that seeing human existence as meaningless could give rise to withdrawal and apathy—even suicide. Psychological salvation therefore requires implanting personal meaning on things and making personal choices. Yes, there is pain in life, and yes, life sooner or later comes to an end, but people can see the world for what it is and they can make real, **authentic** choices.

Freud argued that defense mechanisms prevent us from seeing the world as it is. Therefore, the concept of free choice is meaningless. Behaviorists view freedom as an illusion determined by social forces. Social-cognitive theorists also speak of external or situational forces that influence us.

To existentialists, we are really and painfully free to do as we choose with our lives.

Humanists and existentialists share a search for meaning in life and a belief that freedom and personal responsibility are the essence of being human. Let us now consider the views of Abraham Maslow and Carl Rogers.

ABRAHAM MASLOW AND THE CHALLENGE OF SELF-ACTUALIZATION

Humanists see Freud as preoccupied with the "basement" of the human condition. Freud wrote that people are basically motivated to gratify defensive, biological drives. Humanistic psychologist Abraham Maslow argued that people also have growth-oriented needs for **self-actualization**—to become all that they can be. Because people are unique, they must follow unique paths to self-actualization. Self-actualization requires taking risks. People who adhere to the "tried and true" may find their lives degenerating into monotony and predictability. (Maslow's theoretical *hierarchy of needs* is discussed in Chapter 10.)

CARL ROGERS' SELF THEORY

Carl Rogers (1902–1987) was a minister before he became a psychologist. Like Maslow, he wrote that people shape themselves through free choice and action.

Rogers defined the *self* as an "organized, consistent, conceptual **gestalt** composed of perceptions of the characteristics of the 'I' or 'me' and the perceptions of the relationships of the 'I' or 'me' to others and to various aspects of life, together with the values attached to these perceptions" (1959, p. 200). Your self is your center of experience. It is your ongoing sense of who and what you are, your sense of how and why you react to the environment and how you choose to act on the environment. Your choices are made on the basis of your values, and your values are also parts of your self.

To Rogers, the sense of self is inborn, or innate. The self provides the experience of being human in the world. It is the guiding principle behind personality structure and behavior.

Phenomenological • Having to do with conscious, subjective experience.

Humanism • The view that people are capable of free choice, self-fulfillment, and ethical behavior.

Existentialism • The view that people are completely free and responsible for their own behavior.

Authentic • Genuine; consistent with one's values and beliefs.

Self-actualization • In humanistic theory, the innate tendency to strive to realize one's potential.

Gestalt • In this usage, a quality of wholeness.

Unique. According to humanistic psychologists like Carl Rogers, each of us views the world and ourselves from a unique frame of reference. What is important to one individual may hold little meaning for another.

The Self-Concept and Frames of Reference. Our self-concepts comprise our impressions of ourselves and our evaluations of our adequacy. It may be helpful to think of us as rating ourselves according to various scales or dimensions such as good–bad, intelligent–unintelligent, strong–weak, and tall–short.

Rogers believed that we all have unique ways of looking at ourselves and the world, or unique **frames of reference.** It may be that we each use a different set of dimensions in defining ourselves and that we judge ourselves according to different sets of values. To one person, achievement–failure may be the most important dimension. To another person, the most important dimension may be decency–indecency. A third person may not even think in terms of decency.

Self-Esteem and Positive Regard. Rogers assumed that we all develop a need for self-regard, or **self-esteem,** as we develop and become aware of ourselves. At first, self-esteem reflects the esteem in which others hold us. Parents help children develop self-esteem when they show them **unconditional positive regard**—that is, when they accept them as having intrinsic merit regardless of their behavior at the moment. But when parents show children **conditional positive regard**—accept them only when they behave in a desired manner—children may learn to disown the thoughts, feelings, and behaviors that parents have rejected. Conditional positive regard may lead children to develop **conditions of worth,** or to think that they are worthwhile only if they behave in certain ways.

Because each of us is thought to have a unique potential, children who develop conditions of worth must be somewhat disappointed in themselves. We cannot fully live up to the wishes of others and remain true to ourselves. This does not mean that the expression of the self inevitably leads to conflict. Rogers was optimistic about human nature. He believed that we hurt others or act in antisocial ways only when we are frustrated in our efforts to develop our potential. But when parents and others are loving and tolerant of our differentness, we, too, are loving—even if some of our preferences, abilities, and values differ from those of our parents.

However, children in some families learn that it is bad to have ideas of their own, especially about sexual, political, or religious matters. When they perceive their parents' disapproval, they may come to see themselves as rebels and label their feelings as being selfish, wrong, or evil. If they wish to retain a consistent self-concept and self-esteem, they may have to deny many of their genuine feelings, or disown parts of themselves. In this way, the self-concept becomes distorted. According to Rogers, anxiety often stems from partial perception of feelings and ideas that are inconsistent with the distorted self-concept. Since anxiety is unpleasant, such individuals may deny that these feelings and ideas exist.

Psychological Congruence and the Self-Ideal. When we accept our feelings as our own, we experience psychological integrity or wholeness. There is a "fit" between our self-concept and our behavior, thoughts, and emotions, which Rogers called **congruence.**

According to Rogers, the path to self-actualization requires getting in touch with our genuine feelings, accepting them as ours, and acting on them. This is the goal of Rogers's method of psychotherapy, person-centered therapy, which we discuss in Chapter 14. Here, it is sufficient to say that person-centered therapists provide an atmosphere in which clients can cope with the anxieties of focusing on disowned parts of the self.

Rogers also believed that we have mental images of what we are capable of becoming, or **self-ideals.** We are motivated to reduce the discrepancy between our self-concepts and our self-ideals. As we undertake the process of actualizing ourselves, our self-ideals may gradually grow more complex. Our goals may become higher or change in quality. The self-ideal is something like a carrot dangling from a stick strapped to a burro's head. The burro strives to reach the carrot, as though it were a step or two away, without recognizing that its own progress also causes the carrot to advance. Rogers believed that the process of striving to meet meaningful goals, the good struggle, yields happiness.

EVALUATION OF THE HUMANISTIC–EXISTENTIAL PERSPECTIVE

Humanistic–existential theories usually have tremendous appeal for college students because of their focus on the importance of personal experience. We tend to treasure our conscious experiences (our "selves") and those of the people we care about. For lower organisms, to be alive is to move, to process food, to exchange oxygen and carbon dioxide, and to reproduce one's kind. But for human beings, an essential aspect of life is conscious experience—the sense of one's self as progressing through space and time. Humanistic–existential theorists grant consciousness the cardinal role it occupies in our daily lives.

Psychodynamic theories see us largely as victims of our childhoods, whereas learning theories, to some degree, see us as "victims of circumstances"—or, at least, as victims of situational variables. But humanistic–existential theorists envision us as being free to make choices. Psychodynamic theorists and learning theorists wonder whether our sense of freedom is merely an illusion. Humanistic–existential theorists begin with an assumption of personal freedom.

Humanistic–existential theorists have made important innovations and contributions to the practice of psychotherapy, such as person-centered therapy, the type of therapy originated by Carl Rogers (see Chapter 14).

Ironically, the primary strength of the humanistic–existential approaches—their focus on conscious experience—is also their primary weakness. Conscious experience is private and subjective. Therefore, the validity of formulating theories in terms of

consciousness has been questioned. On the other hand, some psychologists (e.g., Bevan & Kessel, 1994) believe that the science of psychology can afford to loosen its methods somewhat if loosening will help it to better address the richness of human experience.

The concept of self-actualization—so important to Maslow and Rogers—cannot be proved or disproved. Like an id or a trait, a self-actualizing force cannot be observed or measured directly. It must be inferred from its supposed effects.

Self-actualization, like trait theory, yields circular explanations for behavior. When we see someone engaged in what seems to be positive striving, we gain little insight by attributing this behavior to a self-actualizing force. We have done nothing to account for the origins of the self-actualizing force. And when we observe someone who is not engaged in growth-oriented striving, it seems arbitrary to "explain" this outcome by suggesting that the self-actualizing tendency has been blocked or frustrated. It could also be that self-actualization is an acquired need, rather than an innate need, and that it is found in some, but not all, of us.

Humanistic–existential theories, like learning theories, have little to say about the development of traits and personality types. Humanistic–existential theorists assume that we are all unique, but they do not predict the sorts of traits, abilities, and interests we shall develop.

Reflections

Now that you have read about the humanistic–existential perspective, reflect on the following questions:

- Humanistic–existentialist theorists argue that life's difficulties are more bearable when our lives have meaning. Do you consider your life meaningful? If so, in what way? Do your beliefs help sustain you when times are difficult?
- Maslow believed that self-actualization requires taking risks. Are you a self-actualizer? Why do you think that you are—or are not?
- What factors in your own life seem to have contributed to your self-esteem? Do your experiences seem to support Rogers's views on the origins of self-esteem?

Frame of reference • One's unique patterning of perceptions and attitudes according to which one evaluates events.

Self-esteem • One's evaluation and valuing of oneself.

Unconditional positive regard • A persistent expression of esteem for the value of a person, but not necessarily an unqualified acceptance of all of the person's behaviors.

Conditional positive regard • Judgment of another person's value on the basis of the acceptability of that person's behaviors.

Conditions of worth • Standards by which the value of a person is judged.

Congruence • According to Rogers, a fit between one's self-concept and one's behaviors, thoughts, and feelings.

Self-ideal • A mental image of what we believe we ought to be.

The Sociocultural Perspective: The Individual in the New Multicultural United States

Thirteen-year-old Hannah brought her lunch tray to the table in the cafeteria. Her mother Julie eyed in horror the french fries, the plate of mashed potatoes in gravy, the bag of potato chips, and the large paper cup brimming with soda. "You cannot eat that!" she said. "It's garbage!"

"Oh come on, Mom! Chill, okay?" Hannah rejoined, before taking her tray to sit with friends rather than with us.

I spend my Saturdays with my children at the Manhattan School of Music. Not only do they study voice, piano, and violin, they—and I—have widened our cultural perspective by relating to families and students from all parts of the world.

Julie and Hannah are Korean Americans. Flustered, Julie shook her head and said, "I've now been in the United States longer than I was in Korea, and I still can't get used to the way children act here." A Polish American parent, Barbara, at the table chimed in, "I never would have spoken to my parents the way Thomas speaks to me. I would have been . . . whipped or beaten."

"I try to tell Hannah she is part of the family," Julie continued. "She should think of other people. When she talks that way, it is embarrassing."

"Over here children are not part of the family," said Ken, an African American parent. "They are either part of their own crowd or they are 'individuals.'"

"Being an individual does not mean that you must be mean to your mother," Julie said. "What do you think, Spencer? You're the psychologist."

I think I made some unhelpful comments about the ketchup on the french fries having vitamin C and some slightly helpful comments about what is typical for teenagers in the United States. But I'm not sure, because I was thinking deeply about Hannah at the time. Not about her lunch, but about the formation of her personality and the influences on her behavior.

It was occurring to me that personality in our new multicultural United States could not be understood without reference to the sociocultural perspective. Moreover, as we head toward the new millennium, trends in immigration are making the population an even richer mix. Multiple traditions will characterize our nation as it evolves into a "social mosaic" (Portes & Stepick, 1993).

Back to Hannah. Perhaps there were some unconscious psychodynamic influences operating on Hannah. Her traits included exceptional intelligence and musical aptitude, which were at least partly determined by her heredity. Clearly, she was consciously striving to become a great violinist. But one could not make inroads into Hannah's personality structure without also considering the **sociocultural perspective**—the sociocultural influences acting on her.

Here was a youngster strongly affected by her school peers—she was completely at home in her blue jeans and with her luncheon choices. She was also a daughter in an Asian American immigrant group that views education as a key to success in our culture (Gibson & Ogbu, 1991; Ogbu, 1993). Belonging to this ethnic group had certainly contributed to her personal ambition. But being a Korean American had not prevented her from becoming an outspoken American teenager. (Would she have been outspoken if she had been reared in Korea, I wondered, but this question can never be answered with certainty.) Predictably, her outspoken behavior had struck her mother as brazen and inappropriate (Lopez & Hernandez, 1986). Julie was deeply offended by behavior that rolls off my back with my own children. Julie reeled off the things that were "wrong" with Hannah from her Korean

Sociocultural perspective • The view that focuses on the roles of ethnicity, gender, culture, and socioeconomic status in personality formation, behavior, and mental processes.

Individualist • A person who defines herself or himself in terms of personal traits and gives priority to her or his own goals.

Three Generations of the Wong Family. Chinese American artist Hung Liu's triptych traces the history of the Wong family, as they emigrated from China, and then over the course of two generations in the United States. Contemporary descendants of the Wongs are influenced by acculturation and intermarriage with Americans from other backgrounds.

American perspective. I listed some things that were very right with Hannah and encouraged Julie to worry less.

Let us consider ways in which sociocultural factors can affect one's sense of self.

Individualism versus Collectivism. In a sense, Julie's complaint was that Hannah saw herself too much as an individual and an artist rather than as a family member and a Korean girl. Cross-cultural research reveals that people in the United States and many northern European nations tend to be individualistic. **Individualists** tend to define themselves in terms of their personal identities and to give priority to their personal goals. When asked to complete the statement "I am," they are likely to respond in terms of their

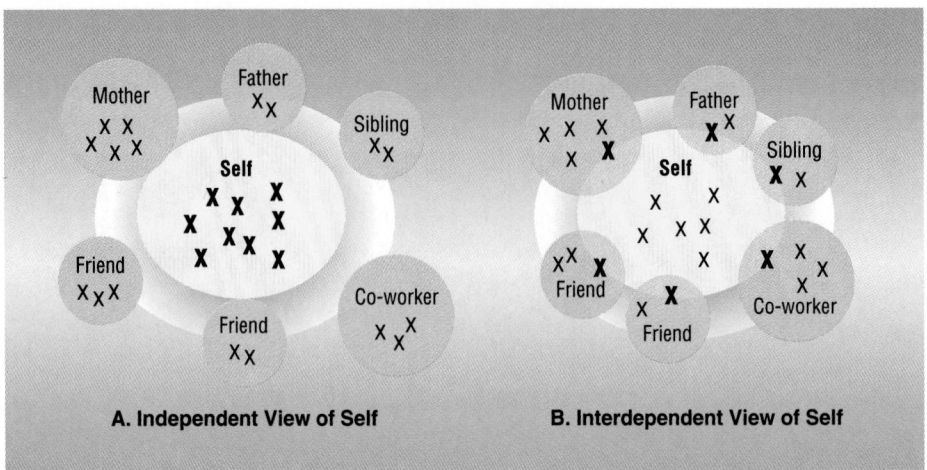

FIGURE 12.5
The Self in Relation to Others from the Individualist and Collectivist Perspectives To an individualist, the self is separate from other people (Part A). To a collectivist, the self is complete only in terms of relationships to other people (Part B). (Based on Markus & Kitayama, 1991.)

Collectivist • A person who defines herself or himself in terms of relationships to other people and groups and gives priority to group goals.

Acculturation • The process of adaptation in which immigrants and native groups identify with a new, dominant culture by learning about that culture and making behavioral and attitudinal changes.

personality traits ("I am outgoing," "I am artistic") or their occupations ("I am a nurse," "I am a systems analyst") (Triandis, 1990). In contrast, many people from cultures in Africa, Asia, and Central and South America tend to be collectivistic. **Collectivists** tend to define themselves in terms of the groups to which they belong and to give priority to the goals of their group. They feel complete only in terms of their social relationships with others (Markus & Kitayama, 1991; see Figure 12.5). When asked to complete the statement "I am," they are more likely to respond in terms of their families, gender, or nation ("I am a father," "I am a Buddhist," "I am a Japanese") (Draguns, 1988; Triandis, 1990, 1994).

The seeds of individualism and collectivism are found in the cultures in which the person grows up. The capitalist system fosters individualism to some degree. It assumes that individuals are entitled to amass personal fortunes and that the process of doing so creates jobs and wealth for large numbers of people. The individualist perspective is found in the self-reliant heroes and antiheroes in the Western media—from Homer's Odysseus to Clint Eastwood's gritty cowboys and Walt Disney's Princess Jasmine (in the film *Aladdin*). The traditional writings of the East have exalted people who resisted personal temptations to do their duty and promote the welfare of the group.

There are, of course, conflicting ideals within a given culture, individual differences and even gender differences. In the United States, for example, children are taught to share with other children as well as to be "Number 1." Children are encouraged to give to charity as well as to be independent and successful.

Note, too, that neither individualism nor collectivism in their extreme form is desirable. Extreme greed or selfishness tears the social fabric. Extreme collectivism discourages inventiveness and creativity and denies the dignity of the individual.

Sociocultural Factors and the Self. Sociocultural factors also affect the self-concept and self-esteem of the individual. Carl Rogers noted that our self-concepts tend to reflect the ways in which other people see us. Thus, members of the dominant culture in the United States are likely to have a positive sense of self. They share in the expectations of personal achievement and respect that are typically accorded those who ascend to power. Similarly, members of ethnic groups who have been subjected to discrimination and poverty may have poorer self-concepts and lower self-esteem than members of the dominant culture (Greene, 1993, 1994; Lewis-Fernández & Kleinman, 1994).

There are some ironies, however. Many in the United States, particularly women, are unhappy with their appearance. This is because the cultural ideal is found in female models who average 9% taller and 16% slimmer than the average U.S. woman (Williams, 1992).

Despite the persistence of racial prejudices, an American Association of University Women (1992) survey found that African American girls are likely to be happier with their appearances than White girls are. Sixty-five percent of African American elementary schoolgirls said they were happy with the way they were, as compared with 55% of White girls. By high school age, 58% of African American girls remained happy with the way they were, as compared with a surprisingly low 22% of White girls. Why the great discrepancy? It appears that the parents of African American girls teach them that there is nothing wrong with them if they do not match the ideals of the dominant culture; the world treats them negatively because of prejudice, not because of who they really are or what they do (Williams, 1992). The White girls are more likely to look inward and blame themselves for not attaining the unreachable ideal.

Acculturation and Self-Esteem. Should Hindu women who immigrate to the United States surrender the sari in favor of California Casuals? Should Russian immigrants teach their children Russian in the home? Should African American children be acquainted with the music and art of African peoples? Should women from traditional Islamic societies lift the veil and enter the workplace alongside American Murphy Browns? How does **acculturation** affect the psychological well-being of immigrants and their families?

Self-esteem is connected with patterns of acculturation among immigrants to the United States. There are various patterns of acculturation. Some immigrants are completely assimilated by the dominant culture. They lose the language and customs of their country of origin and become like the dominant culture in the new host country. Others maintain separation. They retain the language and customs of their country of origin and never become comfortable with the language and customs of the new host country. Still others become bicultural. They become fluent in the languages of their country of origin and their new country and integrate the customs and values of both cultures.

Research evidence suggests that people who identify with the bicultural pattern have the highest self-esteem (Phinney and others, 1992). For example, Mexican Americans who are more proficient in English are less likely to be anxious and depressed than less proficient Mexican Americans (Salgado de Snyder and others, 1990). The ability to adapt to the ways of the new society, combined with a supportive cultural tradition and a sense of ethnic identity, apparently helps people to adjust.

The Sociocultural Perspective in the New Millennium. The sociocultural perspective provides valuable insights into the roles of ethnicity, gender, culture, and socioeconomic status in personality formation. When we ignore sociocultural factors, we deal only with the core of the human being—the potentials that permit adaptation to external forces. Sociocultural factors are external forces that are internalized and affect all of us. They run through us deeply, touching many aspects of our cognitions, motives, emotions, and behavior. Without reference to sociocultural factors, we may be able to understand generalities about behavior and cognitive processes. However, we will not be able to understand how individuals think, behave, and feel about themselves within a given cultural setting. The sociocultural perspective enhances our sensitivity to cultural differences and expectations and allows us to appreciate much of the richness of human behavior and mental processes.

Reflections

Now that you have read about the sociocultural perspective, reflect on the following questions:

- When you were a child, were you given conflicting messages about the importance of competing successfully and of sharing? Do you think the experiences in your own home were more oriented toward encouraging individualism or collectivism? How so?

- How have sociocultural factors affected your own self-concept?

- For how many generations have the families of your parents been in the United States? What acculturation problems did your forebears experience? If you do not have specific information about their experiences, what do you imagine they might have been like? Why?

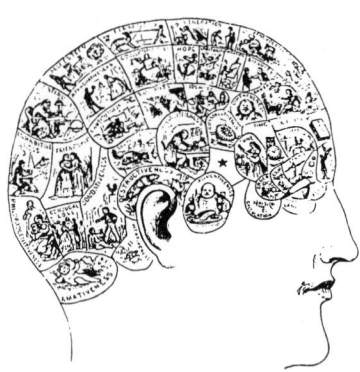

FIGURE 12.6
A Phrenologist's Map of the "Mental Functions."

Phrenology • The analysis of personality by measuring the shape and protuberances of the skull.

Behavior-rating scale • A systematic means for recording the frequency with which target behaviors occur.

Aptitude • A natural ability or talent.

Objective tests • Tests whose items must be answered in a specified, limited manner. Tests whose items have concrete answers that are considered correct.

Standardized test • A test that is given to a large number of respondents so that data concerning the typical responses can be accumulated and analyzed.

Forced-choice format • A method of presenting test questions that requires a respondent to select one of a number of possible answers.

Validity scales • Groups of test items that indicate whether a person's responses accurately reflect that individual's traits.

Clinical scales • Groups of test items that measure the presence of various abnormal behavior patterns.

Response set • A tendency to answer test items according to a bias—for instance, to make oneself seem perfect or bizarre.

Measurement of Personality

If you had asked a phrenologist about your personality in the last century, she or he might have measured the bumps on your head. **Phrenology** was based on the erroneous belief that traits, abilities, and mental functions dwell in specific places in the head and could be measured from the outside (see Figure 12.6).

Although psychologists tend to date the beginning of psychological assessment as the end of the 19th century—with the works of Francis Galton, James McKeen Cattell, Alfred Binet, and others—there is evidence that many people were selected for government service on the basis of assessment of individual differences in mental and physical abilities 2,500 years ago during the Golden Age of Greece (Matarazzo, 1990). In China some 2,000 years ago, objective tests were also used to select applicants for civil service (Bowman, 1989). These tests measured aptitudes such as verbal and mathematical abilities as well as knowledge of law and geography. All these measures took a sample of behavior to predict future behavior. Contemporary measures of personality similarly sample behavior, usually in the form of a self-report, to predict future behavior. Standardized interviews are often used. Many psychologists even have computers conduct some routine interviews (Bloom, 1992). Some measures of personality are **behavior-rating scales,** which assess overt behavior in settings such as the classroom or mental hospital. With behavior-rating scales, trained observers usually check off each occurrence of a specific behavior within a certain time frame—say, a 15-minute period. Standardized objective and projective tests are used more frequently, and they will be discussed in this section.

Measures of personality are used to make important decisions such as whether a person is suited for a certain type of work, for a particular class in school, or for a drug to reduce agitation (Saccuzzo, 1994). As part of their admissions process, graduate schools often ask professors to rate prospective students on scales that assess traits such as intelligence, emotional stability, and cooperation. Students may take tests of **aptitudes** and interests to gather insight into whether they are suited for certain occupations. It is assumed that students who share the aptitudes and interests of people who are well-adjusted in certain positions are also likely to be well-adjusted in those positions.

OBJECTIVE TESTS

Objective tests present respondents with a **standardized** group of test items in the form of a questionnaire. Respondents are limited to a specific range of answers. One test might ask respondents to indicate whether items are true or false for them. Another might ask respondents to select the preferred activity from groups of three.

Some tests have a **forced-choice format,** in which respondents are asked to indicate which of two statements is more true for them or which of several activities they prefer. The respondents are not given the option of answering "none of the above." Forced-choice formats are frequently used in interest inventories, which help predict whether one would be well-adjusted in a certain occupation. The following item is similar to those found in occupational interest inventories:

> I would rather
> a. be a forest ranger.
> b. work in a busy office.
> c. play a musical instrument.

Research evidence suggests that test results are comparable whether such tests are administered by paper and pencil or by computer (Mead & Drasgow, 1993).

The Minnesota Multiphasic Personality Inventory (MMPI) contains hundreds of items presented in a true–false format. The MMPI was intended to be used by clinical and counseling psychologists to help diagnose psychological disorders (see Chapter 13). Accurate measurement of people's problems should point to appropriate treatment. The MMPI has become the most widely used psychological test in the clinical setting (Helmes & Reddon, 1993; Lubin and others, 1985). It is also the most widely used instrument for personality measurement in psychological research.

TABLE 12.4
Commonly Used Validity and Clinical Scales of the MMPI

SCALE	ABBREVIATION	POSSIBLE INTERPRETATIONS
	VALIDITY SCALES	
Question	?	Corresponds to number of items left unanswered
Lie	L	Lies or is highly conventional
Frequency	F	Exaggerates complaints or answers items haphazardly
Correction	K	Denies problems
	CLINICAL SCALES	
Hypochondriasis	Hs	Has bodily concerns and complaints
Depression	D	Is depressed, guilty; has feelings of guilt and helplessness
Hysteria	Hy	Reacts to stress by developing physical symptoms, lacks insight
Psychopathic deviate	Pd	Is immoral, in conflict with the law; has stormy relationships
Masculinity/femininity	Mf	High scores suggest interests and behavior patterns considered stereotypical of the other gender
Paranoia	Pa	Is suspicious and resentful, highly cynical about human nature
Psychasthenia	Pt	Is anxious, worried, high-strung
Schizophrenia	Sc	Is confused, disorganized, disoriented; has bizarre ideas
Hypomania	Ma	Is energetic, restless, active, easily bored
Social introversion	Si	Is introverted, timid, shy; lacks self-confidence

Psychologists can score tests by hand, send them to computerized scoring services, or have them scored by on-site computers. Computers generate reports by interpreting the test record according to certain rules or by comparing it with records in memory. Computer-based interpretations are controversial (Spielberger & Piotrowski, 1990). Although they are efficient, questions have been raised as to their validity (Butcher, 1987).

The MMPI is usually scored for the 4 **validity scales** and 10 **clinical scales** described in Table 12.4. The validity scales suggest whether answers are likely to represent the person's thoughts, emotions, and behaviors, although they cannot guarantee that deception will be disclosed.

Truth or Fiction Revisited. *Psychologists cannot invariably determine whether a person has told the truth on a personality test.* However, validity scales allow psychologists to make educated guesses.

The validity scales in Table 12.4 assess different **response sets,** or biases, in answering the questions. People with high L scores, for example, may be attempting to present themselves as excessively moral and well-behaved individuals. People with high F scores may be trying to seem bizarre or are answering haphazardly. However, there are questions concerning the accuracy of the validity scales (Helmes & Reddon, 1993). For example, F-scale scores are elevated among people with schizophrenia, who may be answering bizarrely because of their psychological disorders rather than because of misrepresentation. Many personality measures have some kind of validity scale. The clinical scales of the MMPI assess the problems shown in Table 12.4, as well as stereotypical masculine or feminine interests and introversion.

The MMPI scales were constructed empirically on the basis of actual clinical data rather than on the basis of psychological theory. A test-item bank of several hundred items was derived from questions often asked in clinical interviews. Here are some of the items that were used:

Is this Test Taker Telling the Truth? How can psychologists determine whether or not people are answering test items honestly? What are the validity scales of the MMPI?

My father was a good man.   T   F
I am very seldom troubled by
     headaches.   T   F
My hands and feet are usually
     warm enough.   T   F
I have never done anything
     dangerous for the thrill of it. T   F
I work under a great deal of
     tension.   T   F

The items were administered to people with previously identified symptoms such as depressive or schizophrenic symptoms. Items that successfully set apart people with these symptoms were included on scales named accordingly. Figure 12.7 shows the

personality profile of a 27-year-old barber who consulted a psychologist because of depression and difficulty in making decisions. The barber scored abnormally high on the Hs, D, Pt, Sc, and Si scales, suggestive of concern with body functions (Hs), depression (D), persistent feelings of anxiety and tension (Pt), insomnia and fatigue, and some difficulties relating to other people (Sc, Si). Note that the high Sc score does not in itself indicate that the barber should be diagnosed with schizophrenia.

In addition to the standard validity and clinical scales, investigators of personality have derived many experimental scales such as those that measure neuroticism, religious orthodoxy, assertiveness, substance abuse,

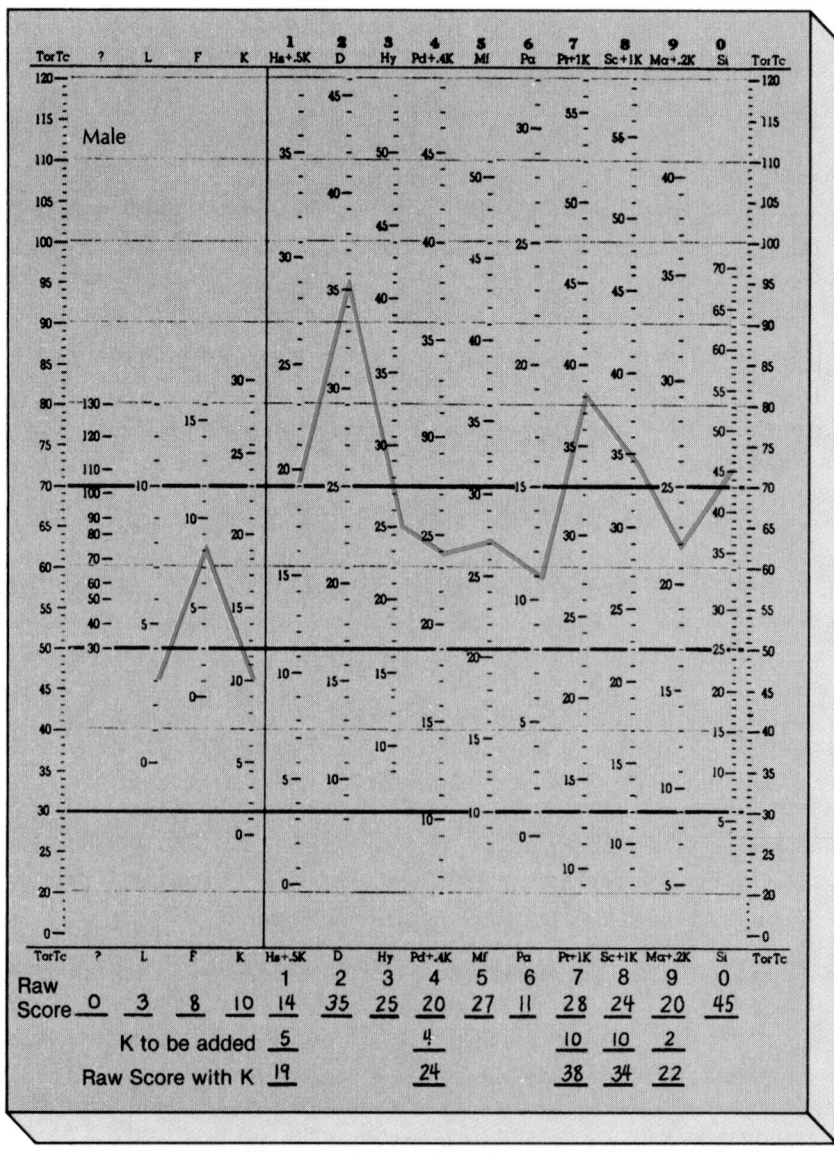

FIGURE 12.7
An MMPI Personality Profile
This profile was attained by a depressed barber. On this form, scores at the standard level of 50 are average for males, and scores above the standard score of 70 are considered abnormally high. The raw score is the number of items answered in a certain direction on a given MMPI scale. K is the correction scale. A certain percentage of the K-scale score is added onto several clinical scales to correct for denial of problems.

even well-being. The MMPI remains a rich mine for unearthing elements of personality.

PROJECTIVE TESTS

You may have heard that there is a personality test that asks people what a drawing or inkblot looks like and that people commonly answer "a bat." There are a number of such tests, the best known of which is the Rorschach inkblot test, named after its originator, Swiss psychiatrist Hermann Rorschach (1884–1922).

The Rorschach Inkblot Test. The Rorschach test is a **projective test.** In projective techniques, there are no clear, specified answers. People are presented with **ambiguous** stimuli such as inkblots or vague drawings and may be asked to report what these stimuli look like to them or to tell stories about them. Because there is no one proper response, it is assumed that people *project* their own personalities into their responses. The meanings they attribute to these stimuli are assumed to reflect their personalities as well as the drawings or blots themselves.

Actually, the facts of the matter are slightly different. There may be no single "correct" response to the Rorschach inkblot shown in Figure 12.8, but some responses would clearly not be in keeping with the features of the blot. Figure 12.8 could be a bat or a flying insect, the pointed face of an animal, the face of a jack-o'-lantern, or many other things. But responses like "an ice cream cone," "diseased lungs," or "a metal leaf in flames" are not suggested by the blot and may suggest personality problems.

Truth or Fiction Revisited. *It is true that there is a psychological test made up of inkblots, one of which looks like a bat.* This is the Rorschach inkblot test. The Rorschach inkblot test contains 10 cards. Five are in black and white and shades of gray. Five use a variety of colors. Subjects are given the cards, one by one, and are asked what they look like or what they could be. The subjects can give no, one, or several responses to each card. They can hold the card upside down or sideways.

Responses are scored according to location, determinants, content, and form level.

The location is the section of the blot chosen — the whole card or a major or minor detail. Determinants include features of the blot such as shading, texture, or color that influence the response. The content is the *what* of the response — for instance, a bat, a jack-o'-lantern, or a human torso. Form level indicates whether the response is consistent with the shape of the blot and also indicates the complexity of the response. A response that reflects the shape of the blot is a sign of adequate **reality testing.** A response that richly integrates several features of the blot is a sign of high intellectual functioning. The Rorschach test is thought to provide insight into a person's intelligence, interests, cultural background, degree of introversion or extroversion, level of anxiety, reality testing, and a host of other variables.

The Thematic Apperception Test. The Thematic Apperception Test (TAT) was developed in the 1930s by psychologist Henry Murray at Harvard University. It consists of drawings like that shown in Figure 10.6 (see p. 375) that are open to a variety of interpretations. Individuals are given the cards one at a time and are asked to make up stories about them.

The TAT has been widely used in research into motivation as well as in clinical practice. The notion is that we are likely to be preoccupied with our own needs to some degree and that our needs will be projected into our responses to ambiguous situations. The TAT is also widely used to assess attitudes toward other people, especially parents, lovers, and spouses.

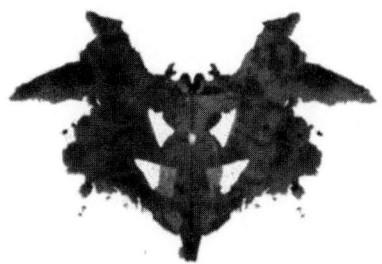

FIGURE 12.8
A Rorschach Inkblot What does this look like? What could it be?

Projective test • A psychological test that presents ambiguous stimuli onto which the test taker projects his or her own personality in making a response.

Ambiguous • Having two or more possible meanings.

Reality testing • The capacity to perceive one's environment and oneself according to accurate sensory impressions.

Reflections

Now that you have read about psychological measurement of personality, reflect on the following questions:

- Did you ever take any psychological tests? For what purposes? What were your feelings about the tests at the time? Did they seem valid to you? Why or why not?
- Do you believe that psychological tests should be used as the sole means for making decisions about people's personalities or assessing psychological problems? Why or why not?

Summary

1. **How do psychologists define "personality"?** Personality comprises the reasonably stable patterns of behavior, including thoughts and emotions, that distinguish one person from another. These behavior patterns characterize a person's ways of adapting to the demands of his or her life.

2. **What is the role of conflict in Sigmund Freud's psychodynamic theory?** Psychodynamic theory, originated by Sigmund Freud, assumes that we are driven largely by unconscious motives. Conflict is inevitable as basic instincts of hunger, sex, and aggression come up against social pressures to follow laws, rules, and moral codes. At first this conflict is external, but as we develop, it becomes intrapsychic.

3. **What are the psychic structures in psychodynamic theory?** The unconscious id is the psychic structure present at birth. The id represents psychological drives and operates according to the pleasure principle, seeking instant gratification. The ego is the sense of self or "I." The ego develops through experience and operates according to the reality principle. It takes into account what is practical and possible in gratifying the impulses of the id. Defense mechanisms protect the ego from anxiety by repressing unacceptable ideas or distorting reality. The superego is the moral sense, a partly conscious psychic structure that develops largely through identification with others.

4. **What are Freud's stages of psychosexual development?** People undergo psychosexual development as psychosexual energy, or libido, is transferred from one erogenous zone to another during childhood. There are five stages of development: oral, anal, phallic, latency, and genital.

5. **What is Carl Jung's theory?** Jung's psychodynamic theory, called analytical psychology, features a collective unconscious and numerous archetypes, both of which reflect the history of our species.

6. **What is Alfred Adler's theory?** Adler's psychodynamic theory, called individual psychology, features the inferiority complex and the compensating drive for superiority.

7. **What is Karen Horney's theory?** Horney's psychodynamic theory focuses on parent–child relationships and the possible development of feelings of basic anxiety and basic hostility. Later in life, repressed hostility can lead us to relate to others in a neurotic manner.

8. **What is Erik Erikson's theory?** Erikson's psychodynamic theory of psychosocial development highlights the importance of early social relationships rather than the gratification of childhood sexual impulses. Erikson extended Freud's five developmental stages to eight, including stages for periods of adulthood.

9. **What are traits?** Traits are personality elements that are inferred from behavior and that account for behavioral consistency. Trait theory adopts a descriptive approach to personality.

10. **What are Gordon Allport's views?** Allport saw traits as embedded in the nervous system and as steering behavior.

11. **What are Raymond Cattell's views?** Cattell distinguished between surface traits (characteristic ways of behaving that seem to be linked in an orderly manner) and source traits (underlying traits from which surface traits are derived). Cattell constructed a test that measures 16 source traits.

12. **What are Hans Eysenck's views?** Eysenck theorized that there are two broad, independent personality dimensions (introversion–extroversion and emotional stability–instability) and described our personalities according to combinations of these dimensions.

13. **What is the Big Five factor structure?** Mathematical analyses that seek common factors in multiple personality traits often tend to arrive at a list of five factors: extroversion, agreeableness,

conscientiousness, emotional stability, and openness to experience.

14. **How do behaviorists view personality?** Behaviorists place emphasis on the situational determinants of behavior. John B. Watson, the father of modern behaviorism, rejected notions of mind and personality altogether. Watson and B. F. Skinner discarded notions of personal freedom and argued that environmental contingencies can shape people into wanting to do the things that the physical environment and society require of them.

15. **How do social-cognitive theorists view personality?** Social-cognitive theory, in contrast to behaviorism, has a cognitive orientation and focuses on learning by observation. To predict behavior, social-cognitive theorists consider situational variables (rewards and punishments) and person variables (competencies, encoding strategies, expectancies, subjective values, and self-regulatory systems and plans).

16. **What is Carl Rogers' self theory?** Self theory begins with the assumption of the existence of the self. According to Rogers, the self is an organized and consistent way in which a person perceives his or her "I" to relate to others and the world. The self is innate and will attempt to become actualized (develop its unique potential) when the person receives unconditional positive regard. We all have need of self-esteem. Conditions of worth may lead to a distorted self-concept, disowning parts of the self, and anxiety.

17. **What is the sociocultural perspective?** This is the view that focuses on the roles of ethnicity, gender, culture, and socioeconomic status in personal-ity formation, behavior, and mental processes. Sociocultural theorists are interested in issues such as individualism versus collectivism and the effects of sociocultural factors on the sense of self.

18. **What are objective tests?** Objective tests present test takers with a standardized set of test items that they must respond to in specific, limited ways (as in multiple-choice tests or true–false tests). A forced-choice format requires respondents to indicate which of two or more statements is true for them or which of several activities they prefer.

19. **What is the Minnesota Multiphasic Personality Inventory (MMPI)?** The MMPI is the most widely used psychological test in the clinical setting. The MMPI is an objective personality test that uses a true–false format to assess abnormal behavior. It contains validity scales as well as clinical scales.

20. **What are projective tests?** Projective tests present ambiguous stimuli and permit the test taker a broad range of responses.

21. **What is the Rorschach inkblot test?** The foremost projective technique is the Rorschach, in which test takers are asked to report what inkblots look like or could be. Rorschach responses are scored according to location, determinants, content, and form level.

22. **What is the Thematic Apperception Test?** The TAT consists of ambiguous drawings that test takers are asked to interpret. The TAT is widely used in research on social motives as well as in clinical practice.

Psychology and Modern Life

MINILECTURE:
GENDER
COMPARISONS
IN
INTELLIGENCE

A Female Architectural Engineer. Women remain underrepresented in many kinds of careers. Although women have made marked recent gains in medicine and law, their numbers remain relatively low in careers in math and engineering. Why? What can we do about it?

Modern life has challenged our concepts of what it means to be a woman and what it means to be a man. The anatomical differences between women and men are obvious and are connected with the biological role of each gender in the process of reproduction. Biologists, therefore, have a relatively easy time of it describing and interpreting the gender differences they study.

The task of psychology is more complex and wrapped up with sociocultural and political issues. Differences in personality between women and men are not so obvious as biological differences.

Put it another way: To fulfill certain biological roles, women and men have to be biologically different. Throughout history, it has also been assumed that women and men must be psychologically different to fulfill different roles in the family and society at large.

Psychological research has led us to question whether women and men are actually different in personality, however. If they are different in personality, just *how* different are they? And, of course, if they are different, psychologists are vitally concerned with just how that difference came about. In the case of anatomy, it is clear that gender differences are predominantly genetic. In the case of personality, psychological and sociocultural influences also come into play.

Gender Differences: Vive la Différence or Vive la Similarité?

In this chapter, we noted that the typical male view is that separation and individuation are the supreme goals of personality development (Guisinger & Blatt, 1994). Yet a key, crucial aspect of a woman's sense of self often concerns her ability to establish and maintain relationships (Gilligan and others, 1991; Jordan and others, 1991). It was also noted that women's relational development provides a source of vulnerability for women—the risk that they may lose themselves in their relationships. Men, on the other hand, may experience a chronic sense of alienation.

What other psychological differences are found between women and men? Key studies on the question span three decades.

DIFFERENCES IN COGNITIVE ABILITIES

It was once believed that males were more intelligent than females because of their greater knowledge of world affairs and their skill in science and industry. We now recognize that greater male knowledge and skill reflected not differences in intelligence but the systematic exclusion of females from world affairs, science, and industry. Studies in the assessment of intelligence do not show overall differences in cognitive abilities between males and females. However, a classic review of the research literature by Eleanor Maccoby and Carol Nagy Jacklin (1974) found persistent suggestions that girls are somewhat superior to boys in verbal ability. Males, on the other hand, seem to be somewhat superior in visual–spatial abilities. Differences in mathematical ability are more complex.

Girls seem to acquire language somewhat faster than boys. Girls make more prelinguistic vocalizations and utter their first word a half month earlier. They acquire additional words more rapidly, and their pronunciation is clearer (Hyde & Linn, 1988; Nelson, 1973). High school girls excel in spelling, punctuation, reading comprehension, solving verbal analogies (such as Washington:one::Lincoln:?), and solving anagrams (scrambled words). Also, far more

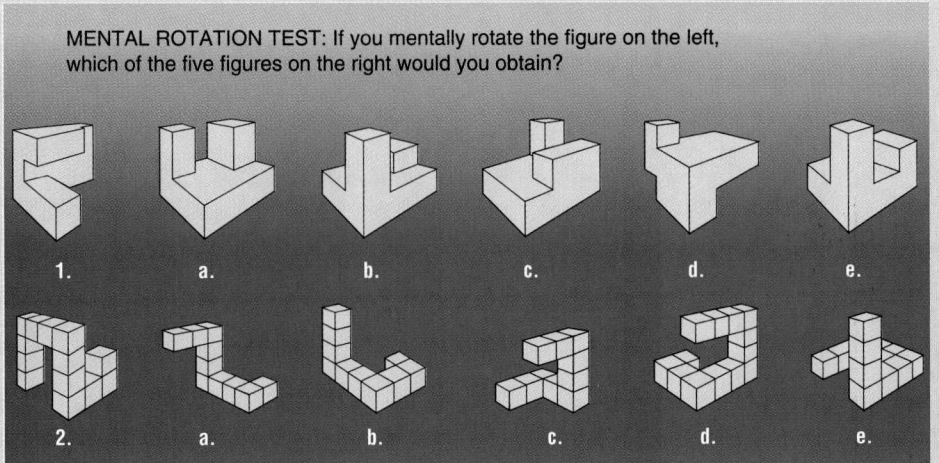

MENTAL ROTATION TEST: If you mentally rotate the figure on the left, which of the five figures on the right would you obtain?

FIGURE 12.9
Rotating Figures in Space Males as a group outperform females on spatial-relations tasks, such as rotating figures in space and picturing the results. However, females do as well as males when they receive some training in the task.

boys in the United States than girls have reading problems, ranging from reading below grade level to severe disabilities. On the other hand, at least males headed toward college seem to catch up in verbal skills.

Males apparently excel in visual-spatial abilities. Beginning in adolescence, boys usually outperform girls on tests of spatial ability (Maccoby & Jacklin, 1974; Halpern, 1986). These tests assess skills such as mentally rotating figures in space (see Figure 12.9) and finding figures embedded within larger designs (see Figure 12.10).

Concerning math, differences at all ages are small and narrowing (Hyde and others, 1990). Females excel in computational ability in elementary school, however, and males excel in mathematical problem solving in high school and in college (Hyde and others, 1990). Differences in problem solving are reflected on the mathematics test of the Scholastic Aptitude Test (SAT). The mean score is 500, and about two thirds of the test takers receive scores between 400 and 600. Boys outperform girls on SAT math items (Byrnes & Takahira, 1993). Twice as many boys as girls attain scores over 500 (Benbow & Stanley, 1980). According to Byrnes and Takahira (1993), boys' superiority in math does not reflect gender per se. Instead, boys do as well as they do because of prior knowledge of math and their strategies for approaching math problems.

In any event, psychologists note that three factors should caution us not to attach too much importance to apparent gender differences in cognition:

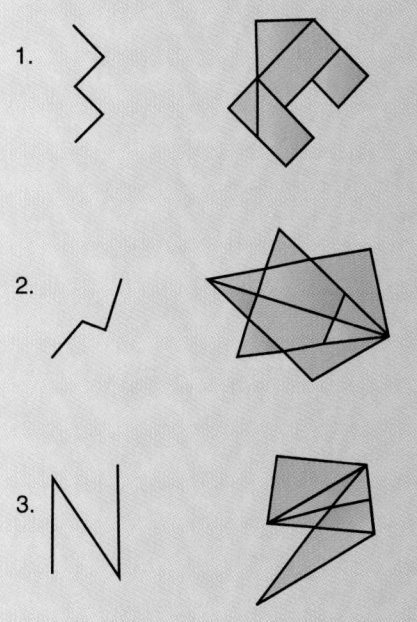

EMBEDDED-FIGURES TEST: Study the figure on the left. Then cover it up and try to find where it is hidden in the figure on the right. The left-hand figure may need to be shifted in order to locate it in the right-hand figure.

FIGURE 12.10
Items from an Embedded-Figures Test.

1. In most cases, they are small. In the case of verbal abilities and mathematics, differences are getting smaller (Hyde and others, 1990; Maccoby, 1990).

2. These gender differences are *group* differences. Variation in these skills is larger *within* the groups than between males and females (Maccoby, 1990). Millions of females outdistance the "average" male in math and spatial abilities. Men have produced their Shakespeares. Women have produced their Madame Curies.

3. The small differences that appear to exist may largely reflect sociocultural expectations and environmental influences (Tobias, 1982). Spatial and math abilities are stereotyped as masculine in our culture. Female introductory psychology students given just 3 hours of training in various visual-spatial skills, such as rotating geometric figures, showed no performance deficit in these skills when compared with men (Stericker & LeVesconte, 1982).

DIFFERENCES IN AGGRESSION

In most cultures, it is the males who march off to war and who battle for glory and shaving-cream commercial contracts. Most psychological studies of aggression have found that male children and adults behave more aggressively than females (Eagly, 1987; Maccoby, 1990; Maccoby & Jacklin, 1980).

Truth or Fiction Revisited. *It is true that men behave more aggressively than women do*—at least in most cultures. The issue is whether this gender difference is inborn or reflects sociocultural conditioning.

In a classic review of 72 studies concerning gender differences in aggression, Ann Frodi and her colleagues (1977) found that females are more likely to act aggressively under some circumstances than others:

1. Females are more likely to feel anxious or guilty about behaving aggressively. These feelings tend to inhibit aggression.

2. Females behave as aggressively as males when they have the means to do so and believe that their behavior is justified.

3. Females are more likely to empathize with the victim—to put themselves in the victim's place.

4. Gender differences in aggression decrease when the victim is anonymous. Anonymity may prevent females from empathizing with their victims.

OTHER DIFFERENCES IN PERSONALITY

Despite the stereotype of women as gossips and chatterboxes, research in communication styles suggests that males in many situations spend more time talking than women. Males are also more likely to introduce new topics and to interrupt (Hall, 1984). Females, on the other hand, seem more willing to reveal their feelings and personal experiences (Dindia & Allen, 1992). Females are less likely than males to curse—with the exception of women who are bucking gender-role stereotypes.

Women interact at closer distances to one another than men do. Women seek more space between themselves and strangers of the other gender than males do (Rüstemli, 1986). Men are made more uncomfortable by strangers who sit across from them, whereas women feel more "invaded" by strangers who sit next to them. In libraries, men tend to pile books protectively in front of them. Women strategically place books and coats to discourage others from taking adjacent seats.

In the realm of sexual behavior, men are more likely than women to masturbate. Men also hold more permissive attitudes toward casual sex than women do (Oliver & Hyde, 1993).

On Becoming a Woman or a Man: The Development of Gender Differences

There are thus a number of gender differences in personality. They include minor differences in cognitive functioning and differences in aggressiveness and communication styles. In this section, we consider the biological and psychological factors that appear to contribute to the development of gender differences.

BIOLOGICAL INFLUENCES

Biological views on gender differences tend to focus on two issues: brain organization and sex hormones.

Brain Organization. A number of studies suggest that we can speak of "left brain" versus "right brain" functions. Language skills seem to depend more on left-brain functioning, whereas right-brain functioning may be more involved in spatial relations and in aesthetic and emotional responses. The brain hemispheres may be even more specialized in males than in females (Bryden, 1982).

Evidence for this view derives from adults who receive brain injuries. Men with damage to the left hemisphere are more likely to show verbal deficits than women with similar damage (McGlone, 1980). Men with damage to the right hemisphere are more likely to show spatial-relations deficits than similarly injured women.

Gender differences in brain organization might, in part, explain why women exceed men in verbal skills that require some spatial organization, such as reading, spelling, and crisp articulation of speech. Men might be superior at more specialized spatial-relations tasks, however, such as interpreting road maps and visualizing objects in space.

Sex Hormones. Sex hormones are responsible for prenatal differentiation of sex organs. Prenatal sex hormones may also "masculinize" or "feminize" the brain by creating predispositions that are consistent with some gender-role stereotypes (Crews, 1994). Yet Money (1977, 1987) argues that social learning plays a stronger role in the development of gender identity, personality traits, and preferences. Money claims that social learning is powerful enough to counteract many prenatal predispositions.

Some evidence for the possible role of hormonal influences derives from animal studies (Crews, 1994). Male rats are generally superior to females in maze-learning ability, for example, a task that requires spatial skills. Female rats that are exposed to androgens in the uterus or soon after birth learn maze routes as rapidly as males, however. Female rodents that are exposed to androgens in the uterus, like males, also roam larger distances and mark larger territories than most females do (Vandenbergh, 1993).

Males are more aggressive than females, and aggression in lower animals has been connected with the male sex hormone testosterone. As Benderly puts it, this finding has led to one scientific version of the view that "boys have no choice but to be boys" (1993, p. 10). However, cognitive psychologists argue that boys (and girls) can choose whether or not to act aggressively, regardless of the levels of hormones in their bloodstreams.

Let us now consider psychological views of the development of gender differences.

PSYCHODYNAMIC THEORY

Sigmund Freud explained the acquisition of gender roles in terms of identification. Freud believed that gender identity remains flexible until the resolution of the Oedipus and Electra complexes at about the age of 5 or 6. Appropriate gender-typing requires that boys identify with their fathers and surrender the wish to possess their mothers. Girls have to surrender the wish to have a penis and identify with their mothers.

Boys and girls develop stereotypical preferences for toys and activities much earlier than might be predicted by psychodynamic theory, however. Even within their first year, boys are more explorative and independent. Girls are relatively more quiet, dependent, and restrained (Etaugh & Rathus, 1995). By 18 to 36 months, girls are more likely to play with soft toys and dolls and to dance. Boys of this age are more likely to play with blocks and toy cars, trucks, and airplanes.

Truth or Fiction Revisited. *It is not true that children's preferences for gender-typed toys and activities remain flexible until the resolution of the Oedipus or Electra complexes at the ages of 5 or 6.* Children's preferences for gender-typed toys and activities become rather fixed by the age of 3.

Let us consider the ways in which cognitive theories account for gender-typing.

Acquiring Gender Roles. What psychological factors contribute to the acquisition of gender roles? Psychodynamic theory focuses on the concept of identification. Social-cognitive theory focuses on the roles of imitation of the behavior patterns of adults of the same gender and reinforcement by parents and peers.

SOCIAL-COGNITIVE THEORY

Social-cognitive theorists explain the acquisition of gender roles and gender differences in terms of observational learning, identification,[3] and socialization.

Children learn much of what is considered masculine or feminine by observational learning, as suggested by an experiment conducted by David Perry and Kay Bussey (1979). In this study, children learned how behaviors are gender-typed by observing the *relative frequencies* with which men and women performed them. However, the adult role models expressed arbitrary preferences for one item from each of 16 pairs of items—pairs such as oranges

versus apples and toy cows versus toy horses—as 8- and 9-year-old boys and girls observed. The children were then asked to show their own preferences. Boys selected an average of 14 of 16 items that agreed with the "preferences" of the men. Girls selected an average of only 3 of 16 items that agreed with the choices of the men.

Social-cognitive theorists view identification as a broad, continuous learning process in which children are influenced by rewards and punishments to imitate adults of the same gender—particularly the parent of the same gender. In identification, as opposed to imitation, children do not simply imitate a certain behavior pattern. They also try to become broadly like the model.

[3] But the social-cognitive concept of identification differs from the psychodynamic concept, as noted in this section.

Socialization also plays a role. Parents and other adults—even other children—inform children about how they are expected to behave. They reward children for behavior they consider gender-appropriate. They punish (or fail to reinforce) children for behavior they consider inappropriate. Girls, for example, are given dolls while they still sleep in cribs. They are encouraged to rehearse caretaking behaviors in preparation for traditional feminine adult roles.

The Development of Gender Differences in Aggressive Behavior.

Concerning the greater aggressiveness of boys, Maccoby and Jacklin note that:

> Aggression in general is less acceptable for girls, and is more actively discouraged in them, by either direct punishment, withdrawal of affection, or simply cognitive training that "that isn't the way girls act." Girls then build up greater anxieties about aggression, and greater inhibitions against displaying it. (1974, p. 234)

Girls frequently learn to respond to social provocations by feeling anxious about the possibility of acting aggressively, whereas boys are generally encouraged to retaliate (Frodi and others, 1977).

From the social-cognitive perspective, males and females both tend to view aggression as a way in which people control other people. Men are more aggressive than women, however, because men tend to think of aggression as a more or less legitimate weapon in the male struggle for status and power (Campbell, 1993). Women, by contrast, usually think of aggression as the result of a failure of self-control.

Classic experiments highlight the importance of social learning in female aggressiveness. For example, studies by Bandura and his colleagues (1963b) found that boys are more likely than girls to imitate aggressive models they see in films. Other research suggests that this gender difference may be attributed to the sociocultural milieu in which aggression occurs. In one study, for example, college women competed with men to see who could respond more quickly to a stimulus (Richardson and others, 1979). There were four blocks of trials, with six trials in each block. They

could not see their opponents. The loser of each trial received an electric shock whose intensity was set by the opponent on the same sort of fearsome-looking console used in the Milgram experiments on obedience to authority (see Figure 2.1, p. 43). Women competed under one of three experimental conditions: public, private, or with a supportive other. In the public condition, another woman observed the study participant silently. In the private condition, there was no observer. In the supportive-other condition, another woman urged the participant to retaliate strongly when her opponent selected high shock levels. As shown in Figure 12.11, women in the private and supportive-other conditions selected increasingly higher levels of shock in retaliation. Presumably, the women assumed that an observer, though silent, would frown on aggressive behavior. This assumption is likely to reflect the women's own early socialization experiences. Women who were unobserved or urged on by a supportive other apparently felt free to violate the gender norm of nonaggressiveness when their situations called for aggressive responses.

Social-cognitive theory has helped outline the ways in which rewards, punishments, and modeling foster "gender-appropriate" behavior. Gender-schema theory suggests that we tend to assume gender-appropriate behavior patterns as a result of blending our self-concepts with sociocultural expectations.

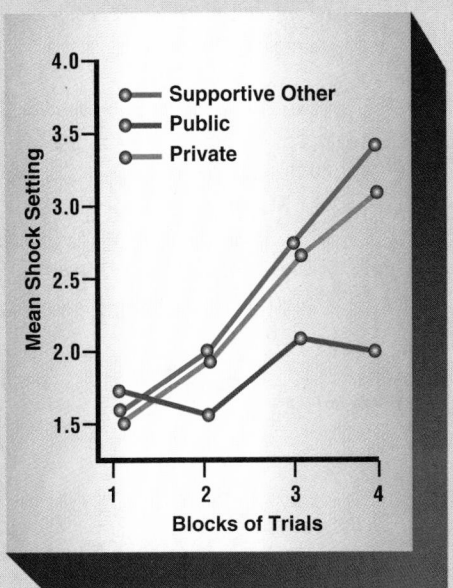

FIGURE 12.11
Mean Shock Settings Selected by Women in Retaliation Against Male Opponents
Women in the Richardson study chose higher shock levels for their opponents when they were alone or when another person (a "supportive other") urged them on.

GENDER-SCHEMA THEORY: BLENDING THE SELF-CONCEPT WITH SOCIOCULTURAL EXPECTATIONS

You have heard the expression, "looking at the world through rose-colored glasses." According to Sandra Bem (1993), the originator of gender-schema theory, people look at the social world through "the lenses of gender." Bem argues that our culture polarizes females and males by organizing social life around mutually exclusive gender roles or scripts. Children, and later adults, come to internalize, or accept, the polarizing scripts without realizing it. Unless parents or unusual events encourage them to challenge the validity of gender polarization, children attempt to construct identities that are consistent with the "proper" script. Most children perceive gender polarization as normal. They reject behavior—in others and in themselves—that deviates from it. Children's self-esteem soon becomes wrapped up in the ways in which they measure up to the gender schema.

Within gender-schema theory, gender identity is sufficient to prompt "gender-appropriate" behavior. Once children understand the labels *boy* and *girl,* they have a basis for blending their self-concepts with the gender schema of their culture. No external reinforcement is required. Children who have developed a sense of being male or being female, which usually occurs by the age of 3, actively seek information about the gender schema. As in social-cognitive theory, children seek to learn what is considered appropriate for them by observation.

There is evidence that the polarized female–male scripts serve as cognitive anchors within our culture. In one study, for example, Carol Martin and Charles Halverson (1983) showed 5- and 6-year-old boys and girls pictures of actors engaged in "gender-consistent" or "gender-inconsis-

tent" activities. The gender-consistent pictures showed boys in activities such as playing with trains or sawing wood and girls in activities such as cooking and cleaning. Gender-inconsistent pictures showed actors of the other gender engaged in these gender-typed activities. Each child was shown a randomized collection of pictures that included only one picture of each activity. One week later, the children were asked who had engaged in a pictured activity, a male or a female. Boys and girls both answered wrong significantly more often when the picture they had seen showed gender-*inconsistent* activity. Their processing of information had been distorted to conform to the gender schema.

In sum, brain organization and sex hormones may contribute to gender-typed behavior and play a role in verbal ability, math skills, and aggression. Yet the effects of social learning may counteract biological influences. Social-cognitive theory outlines the environmental factors that influence children to assume "gender-appropriate" behavior. Gender-schema theory focuses on how children blend their self-identities with the gender schema of their culture.

Reflections

Now that you have read about gender differences and gender-typing, reflect on the following questions:

- Would you say that your own patterns of cognitive skills and personality traits are more consistent with stereotypical female or male patterns? Have your patterns of cognition and personality affected your self-concept? If so, in what way?

- What view of gender-typing seems best to describe your own experiences with gender-typing? Can you recall any experiences that seem to have contributed to your gender-typing?

NOTES

13

Psychological Disorders

Truth or Fiction?

_____ A man shot the president of the United States in front of millions of television witnesses, yet was found not guilty by a court of law.

_____ In the Middle Ages, innocent people were drowned to prove that they were not possessed by the Devil.

_____ Some people have more than one identity, and the identities may have different allergies and eyeglass prescriptions.

_____ It is abnormal to feel depressed.

_____ You can never be too rich or too thin.

_____ Some college women control their weight by going on cycles of binge eating and self-induced vomiting.

_____ People who truly love each other enjoy the sexual aspects of their relationship.

_____ People who threaten suicide are only seeking attention.

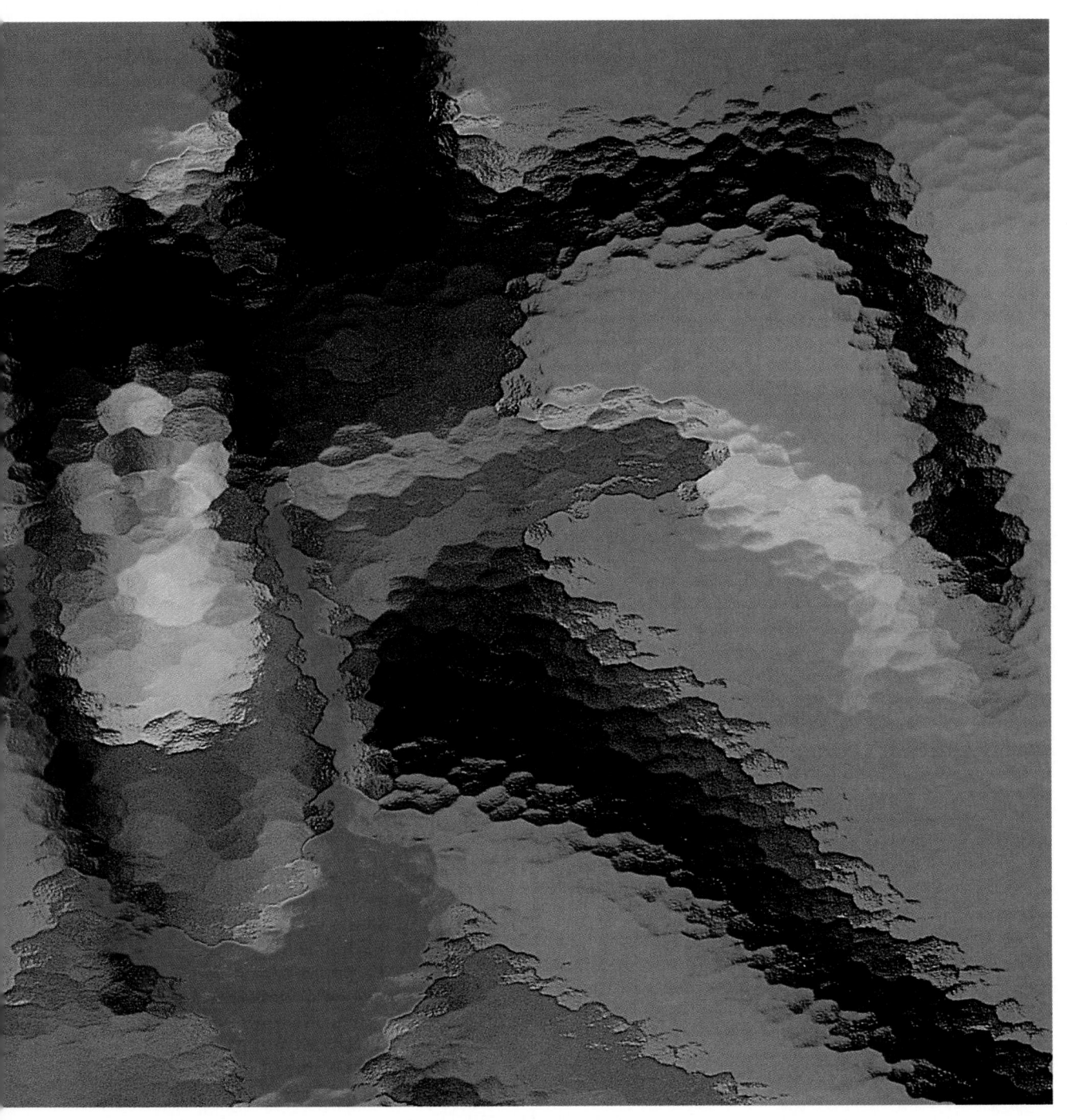

Outline

Truth or Fiction?
What Are Psychological Disorders?
Classifying Psychological Disorders
  Psychology in the New Millennium:
    Will Your Problems Be Diagnosed
    by a Computer?
Anxiety Disorders
  Types of Anxiety Disorders
  Theoretical Views
Dissociative Disorders
  Types of Dissociative Disorders
  Theoretical Views
Somatoform Disorders
  Types of Somatoform Disorders
  Theoretical Views
Mood Disorders
  Types of Mood Disorders
  Theoretical Views
Schizophrenia
  Types of Schizophrenia
  Theoretical Views
Personality Disorders
  Types of Personality Disorders
  Theoretical Views
Eating Disorders
  Types of Eating Disorders
  Psychology in a World of Diversity:
    Eating Disorders: Why the Gender
    Gap?
  Theoretical Views
Sexual Dysfunctions
  Types of Sexual Dysfunctions
  Theoretical Views
Summary
Psychology and Modern Life
  Suicide

The Ohio State campus lived in terror one long fall. Four college women were abducted, were forced to cash checks or obtain money with their instant-cash cards, then were raped. A mysterious phone call led to the arrest of a 23-year-old drifter, William, who had been dismissed from the Navy.

William was not the boy next door.

Psychologists and psychiatrists who interviewed William concluded that 10 personalities—8 male and 2 female—resided within him (Scott, 1994). His personality had been "fractured" by an abusive childhood. The personalities showed distinct facial expressions, vocal patterns, and memories. They even performed differently on personality and intelligence tests.

Arthur, the most rational personality, spoke with a British accent. Danny and Christopher were quiet adolescents. Christene was a 3-year-old girl. It was Tommy, a 16-year-old, who had enlisted in the Navy. Allen was 18 and smoked. Adelena, a 19-year-old lesbian personality, had committed the rapes. Who had made the mysterious phone call? Probably David, aged 9, an anxious child personality.

The defense claimed that William's behavior was caused by a psychological disorder: **dissociative identity disorder** (also referred to as **multiple personality disorder**). Several distinct identities or personalities dwelled within him. Some were aware of the others. Some believed that they were the sole occupants. Billy, the core identity, had learned to sleep as a child to avoid the abuse of his father. A psychiatrist asserted that Billy had also been "asleep," in a "psychological coma," during the abductions. Billy should therefore be found innocent by reason of **insanity.**

Billy was found not guilty by reason of insanity. He was committed to a psychiatric institution and released 6 years later.

In 1982, John Hinckley was also found not guilty of the assassination attempt on President Reagan's life by reason of insanity. Expert witnesses testified that he should be diagnosed with **schizophrenia.** Hinckley, too, was committed to a psychiatric institution.

Truth or Fiction Revisited. *It is true that a man shot the president of the United States in front of millions of television witnesses and was found not guilty by a court of law.* He was found not guilty by reason of insanity.

Dissociative identity disorder and schizophrenia are two **psychological disorders.** If William and John had lived in Salem, Massachusetts, in 1692, just 200 years after Columbus set foot in the New World, they might have been hanged as witches. At that time, most people assumed that psychological disorders were caused by possession by the Devil. Nineteen people lost their lives that year in that colonial town for allegedly practicing the arts of Satan.

Throughout human history, most people have attributed unusual behavior and psychological disorders to demons. The ancient Greeks by and large believed that the gods punished humans by causing confusion and madness. An exception was Hippocrates, the Greek physician of the Golden Age of art and literature (4th century B.C.). Hippocrates made the radical suggestion that psychological disorders are caused by an abnormality of the brain. The notion that biology could affect thoughts, feelings, and behavior was to lie dormant for about 2,000 years.

During the Middle Ages in Europe, as well as during the early days of European colonization of the rocky coast of Massachusetts, it was generally believed that psychological disorders were signs of possession by agents of the Devil. Possession could stem from retribution, or God's having the Devil possess your soul as punishment for sins. Agitation and confusion were ascribed to retribution. Possession was also believed to result from deals with the Devil, in which people traded their souls for earthly gains. Such traders were called witches. Witches were held responsible for unfortunate events ranging from a neighbor's infertility to a poor crop. At least 200,000 accused witches were killed during the next 2 centuries. Europe was no place to practice strange ways. The goings-on at Salem were trivial by comparison.

Ingenious "diagnostic" tests were used to ferret out possession. The water-float test was based on the principle that pure metals sink to the bottom during smelting, whereas impurities float to the surface. Suspects were thus kept in deep water. Those who sank to the bottom and drowned were judged to be pure. Suspects who managed to keep their heads above water were assumed to be "impure" and in league with the Devil. Then they were in real trouble. This ordeal is the origin of the phrase, "Damned if you do and damned if you don't."

Truth or Fiction Revisited. *It is true that innocent people were drowned in the Middle Ages to prove that they were not possessed by the Devil. The method was based on a water-float test designed to determine whether metals are pure.*

Few people in the United States today would argue that unusual or unacceptable behavior is caused by demons. Still, the language continues to harbor phrases suggestive of demonology. How many times have you heard the expressions "Something got the best of me" or "The Devil made me do it"?

In this chapter, we first define what is meant by a psychological disorder. We then discuss various psychological disorders, including anxiety disorders, dissociative disorders, somatoform disorders, mood disorders,

Exorcism. This medieval woodcut represents the practice of exorcism, in which a demon is expelled from a person who has been "possessed."

schizophrenia, personality disorders, eating disorders, and sexual dysfunctions.

What Are Psychological Disorders?

Psychology is the study of behavior and mental processes. Psychological disorders are patterns of behavior or mental processes that are connected with notable distress or disability. However, they are not predictable responses to specific events.

For example, some psychological disorders are characterized by anxiety or depression, but many of us are anxious or depressed now and then without being considered disordered. It is appropriate to be anxious before a big date or on the eve of a midterm exam. It is appropriate to be depressed if a friend is upset with you or if you have failed at a test or job.

Dissociative identity disorder • A disorder in which a person appears to have two or more distinct identities or personalities that may alternately emerge. (A term first used in DSM-IV.)

Multiple personality disorder • The previous DSM term for *dissociative identity disorder.*

Insanity • A legal term descriptive of a person judged to be incapable of recognizing right from wrong or of conforming his or her behavior to the law.

Schizophrenia • (skit-so-FREE-knee-uh). A psychotic disorder characterized by loss of control of thought processes and inappropriate emotional responses.

Psychological disorders • Patterns of behavior or mental processes that are connected with emotional distress or significant impairment in functioning.

When, then, are feelings like anxiety and depression deemed to be abnormal or signs of a psychological disorder? For one thing, anxiety and depression may suggest a disorder when they are not appropriate to our situations. It is inappropriate to be depressed when things are going well or to be distraught when entering an elevator or looking out of a fourth-story window. The magnitude of the problem may also suggest that a disorder is present. Though some anxiety is to be expected before a job interview, feeling that your heart is pounding so intensely that it might leap out of your chest—and then avoiding the interview—are not. Nor is it usual to sweat so profusely that your clothing literally becomes soaked.

Behavior or mental processes are suggestive of psychological disorders when they meet some combination of the following criteria:

1. *They are unusual.* Although people with psychological disorders are in a minority, uncommon behavior or mental processes are not in themselves abnor-

mal. Only one person holds the record for running or swimming the fastest mile. That person is different from you and me but is not abnormal. Only a few people qualify as geniuses in mathematics, but mathematical genius is not a sign of a psychological disorder.

Rarity or statistical deviance may not be sufficient for behavior or mental processes to be labeled abnormal, but it helps. Most people do not see or hear things that are not there, and "seeing things" and "hearing things" are considered abnormal. We must also consider the situation. Although many of us feel "panicked" when we recall that a term paper or report is due, most of us do not have panic attacks "out of the blue." Unpredictable panic attacks are thus suggestive of psychological disorder.

2. *They suggest faulty perception or interpretation of reality.* It is considered normal to talk to God through prayer, but people who claim that God talks back to them may be committed to a psychiatric

Hallucinations. Hallucinations are among the more flagrant features of schizophrenia. They are perceptions that occur in the absence of external stimulation that cannot be distinguished from real perceptions, as in "hearing voices" or "seeing things." Are the cats in this Sandy Skoglund photograph real or hallucinatory?

institution. Our society considers it normal to be inspired by religious beliefs, but abnormal to believe that God is literally speaking to you. "Hearing voices" and "seeing things" are considered **hallucinations.** Similarly, **ideas of persecution** such as believing that the Mafia or the FBI is "out to get you," are considered signs of disorder. (Unless they *are* out to get you, of course.)

3. *They suggest severe personal distress.* Anxiety, depression, exaggerated fears, and other psychological states cause personal distress, and severe personal distress may be considered abnormal. Anxiety and depression may also be appropriate responses to one's situation, however, as in the case of a real threat or loss. In such cases, they are not abnormal unless they persevere long after the source of distress has been removed or after most people would have adjusted.

4. *They are self-defeating.* Behavior or mental processes that cause misery rather than happiness and fulfillment may be suggestive of psychological disorders. Chronic drinking that impairs work and family life and cigarette smoking that impairs health may thus be deemed abnormal.

5. *They are dangerous.* Behavior or mental processes that are hazardous to the self or others may be considered suggestive of psychological disorders. People who threaten or attempt suicide may be considered abnormal, as may people who threaten or attack others. Yet criminal behavior or aggressive behavior in athletic contests does not necessarily imply a psychological disorder.

6. *Behavior is socially unacceptable.* We must consider the cultural context of a behavior pattern in judging whether or not the behavior is normal. In the United States, it is deemed normal for males to be aggressive in sports and in combat. In other situations warmth and tenderness are valued. (Yet, as noted in Chapter 12, "Iron John" may not readily adapt to "peacetime.") Many in the United States admire women who are self-assertive, yet Hispanic American, Asian American,

and "traditional" non-Hispanic White American groups may find outspoken women to be brazen and insolent.

Classifying Psychological Disorders

Toss some people, apes, seaweed, fish, and sponges into a room—preferably a well-ventilated room. Stir slightly. What do you have? It depends on how you classify this hodgepodge.

Classify them as plants versus animals and you lump the people, chimpanzees, fish, and, yes, sponges together. Classify them as stuff that carries on its business on land or underwater, and we throw in our lots with just the chimps. How about those that swim and those that don't? Then the chimps, the fish, and some of us are pigeonholed together.

Classification is at the heart of science (Barlow, 1991). Without labeling and ordering psychological disorders, investigators would not be able to communicate with each other, and progress would be at a standstill. The most widely used classification scheme for psychological disorders[1] is the *Diagnostic and Statistical Manual* (DSM) of the American Psychiatric Association (Maser and others, 1991). The DSM was developed to provide a uniform way of classifying psychological disorders (Widiger and others, 1991), and it has undergone several revisions.

The current edition of the DSM—DSM-IV—employs a multiaxial, or multidimensional, system of assessment. It provides a broad range of information about an individual's functioning, not just a diagnosis. The axes are shown in Table 13.1.

Separating the diagnostic categories into two axes provides diagnostic flexibility. People may receive Axis I or Axis II diagnoses or a combination of the two.

Axis III, general medical conditions, lists physical disorders or problems that may affect people's functioning or response to

Hallucination • (hal-LOOSE-sin-nay-shun). A perception in the absence of sensory stimulation that is confused with reality.

Ideas of persecution • Erroneous beliefs that one is being victimized or persecuted.

---

[1] The American Psychiatric Association refers to psychological disorders as *mental disorders.*

TABLE 13.1

The Multiaxial Classification System of DSM-IV

AXIS	TYPE OF INFORMATION	BRIEF DESCRIPTION
Axis I	Clinical Syndromes (a wide range of diagnostic classes, such as substance-related disorders, anxiety disorders, mood disorders, schizophrenia, somatoform disorders, and dissociative disorders)	Patterns of abnormal behavior that impair functioning and are stressful to the individual
Axis II	Personality Disorders	Deeply ingrained, maladaptive ways of perceiving others and behaviors that are stressful to the individual or those who relate to the individual
Axis III	General Medical Conditions	Chronic and acute illnesses, injuries, allergies, and so on, that affect functioning and treatment, such as cardiovascular disorders, athletic injuries, and allergies to medication
Axis IV	Psychosocial and Environmental Problems	Stressors that occurred during the past year that may have contributed to the development of a new mental disorder or the recurrence of a prior disorder or that may have exacerbated an existing disorder
Axis V	Global Assessment of Functioning	Overall judgment of current functioning and the highest level of functioning in the past year according to psychological, social, and occupational criteria

psychotherapy or drug treatment. Axis IV, psychosocial and environmental problems, includes difficulties that may affect the diagnosis, treatment, or outcome of a psychological disorder (see Table 13.2). Axis V, the global assessment of functioning, allows the clinician to rate the client's current level of functioning and highest level of functioning prior to the onset of the psychological disorder. The purpose is to help set goals as to what kinds of psychological functioning are to be restored.

The DSM-IV groups disorders on the basis of observable features or symptoms, which is logical enough. However, early editions of the DSM grouped many disorders on the basis of assumptions about their causes (Millon, 1991). Because Freud's psychodynamic theory was widely accepted at the time, one major diagnostic category contained the so-called neuroses.[2] From the psychodynamic perspective, all neuroses—no matter how differently people with various neuroses might behave—stemmed

from unconscious neurotic conflict. Each neurosis was thought to reflect a way of coping with unconscious fear that primitive impulses might break loose. As a result, sleepwalking was included as a neurosis (psychoanalysts assumed that sleepwalking contained impulses by permitting their partial expression during the night). Now that the focus is on the observable, sleepwalking is classified as a sleep disorder, not as a kind of neurosis. I mention all this because the words *neurosis* and *neurotic* are still heard today. Without some explanation, it might seem strange that they have been largely abandoned by professionals.

We must also consider the reliability and validity of the DSM categories. The reliability of a diagnosis such as dissociative identity disorder is its consistency, usually measured as the extent of agreement among professionals who make diagnoses. For example, the agreement rates among pairs of professionals for diagnoses of schizophrenia and mood disorders are about

---

[2] The neuroses included what are today referred to as anxiety disorders, dissociative disorders, somatoform disorders, mild depression, and some other disorders, such as sleepwalking.

TABLE 13.2
Psychosocial and Environmental Problems

PROBLEM CATEGORIES	EXAMPLES
Problems with primary support groups	Death of family members; health problems of family members; marital disruption in the form of separation, divorce, or estrangement; physical or sexual abuse in the family; birth of a sibling
Problems related to the social environment	Death or loss of a friend; living alone or in social isolation; problems adjusting to a new culture (acculturation problems); discrimination; problems adjusting to the transitions of the life cycle, such as retirement
Educational problems	Academic problems; illiteracy; problems with classmates or teachers; impoverished or inadequate school environment
Occupational problems	Work-related problems, including problems with supervisors and co-workers, heavy workload, unemployment, adjusting to a new job, job dissatisfaction, sexual harassment, discrimination
Housing problems	Homelessness or inadequate housing; problems with landlords or neighbors; an unsafe neighborhood
Economic problems	Financial hardships or poverty; inadequate public support
Problems with access to health care	Lack of health insurance; inadequate health care services; problems with transportation to health care facilities
Problems related to the legal or criminal justice systems	Victimization by crime; involvement in a law suit or trial; arrest, imprisonment
Other psychosocial or environmental problems	Natural or technological disaster; war; lack of social services

Source: Adapted from DSM-IV (American Psychiatric Association, 1994).

81% and 83%, respectively (Spitzer and others, 1979). These are reasonably respectable numbers. One reason that the DSM is reliable is that the diagnostic categories have been narrowed in recent years, meaning that fewer people are likely to show the lists of behaviors required for various diagnoses. There is a downside to this reliability: Some observers wonder whether the descriptions of some diagnostic categories are so narrow that many people who actually have the disorders, such as many people with schizophrenia, fail to be properly diagnosed (Andreasen, 1990).

The validity of a diagnosis is the degree to which it reflects an *actual* disorder. For example, there is question as to whether the kinds of depression listed in the DSM are really all that distinct (Keller and others, 1990) and whether "substance abuse" is really all that different from "substance dependence" (Helzer & Schuckit, 1990).

Some professionals, like psychiatrist Thomas Szasz, believe that the categories described in the DSM are really "problems in living" rather than "disorders." They are not disorders, at least, in the sense that high blood pressure, cancer, and the flu are disorders. Szasz argues that labeling people with problems in living as being "sick" degrades them and encourages them to evade their personal and social responsibilities. Since sick people are encouraged to obey doctors' orders, Szasz (1984) also contends that labeling people as "sick" accords too much power to health professionals. Instead, troubled people need to be encouraged to take greater responsibility for solving their own problems.

In sum, questions remain about classification. These include questions about the reliability and validity of the diagnostic categories in the DSM and broader philosophical questions. Yet, in considering abnormal behavior, I shall refer to the DSM. This is a convenience, however, and not an endorsement.

Reflections

Now that you have read the opening sections of the chapter on psychological disorders, reflect on the following questions:

- Do any family members or friends have psychological disorders? How do you know? Do the behaviors or mental processes of the people affected appear to correspond to the six criteria discussed in the chapter? How are the disorders being treated? How have you, the rest of the family, or friends reacted to them?
- Do you believe that people who try to commit suicide have psychological disorders? Why or why not? (We will talk about suicide in this chapter's "Psychology and

Modern Life" section. Think about your initial impressions now.)
- Had you heard of the term *neurotic* before reading this chapter? What had you imagined it to mean? What does it mean?
- Can you think of a way in which classification plays a key role in a science other than psychology? How about biology or chemistry?

Let us now consider the more prominent psychological disorders.

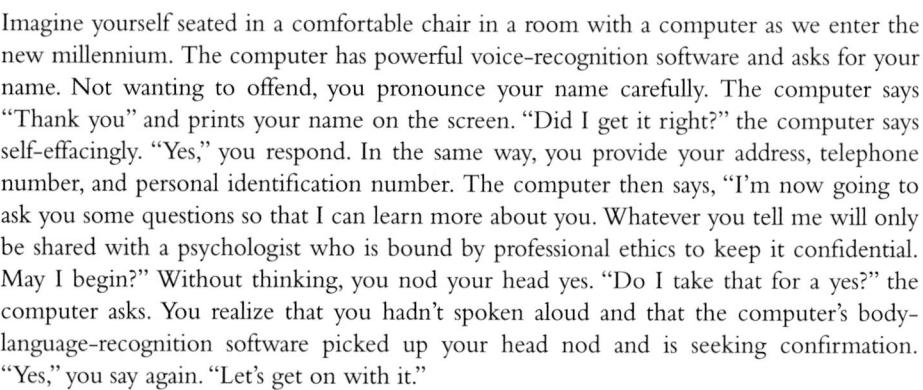

PSYCHOLOGY IN THE NEW MILLENNIUM

Will Your Problems Be Diagnosed by a Computer?

Will Your Problems be Diagnosed by a Computer in the New Millennium? Research shows that many people are willing to disclose more personal matters to a computer than to another human being. Use of the computer for diagnostic purposes also frees clinicians to spend more time directly working with people.

Imagine yourself seated in a comfortable chair in a room with a computer as we enter the new millennium. The computer has powerful voice-recognition software and asks for your name. Not wanting to offend, you pronounce your name carefully. The computer says "Thank you" and prints your name on the screen. "Did I get it right?" the computer says self-effacingly. "Yes," you respond. In the same way, you provide your address, telephone number, and personal identification number. The computer then says, "I'm now going to ask you some questions so that I can learn more about you. Whatever you tell me will only be shared with a psychologist who is bound by professional ethics to keep it confidential. May I begin?" Without thinking, you nod your head yes. "Do I take that for a yes?" the computer asks. You realize that you hadn't spoken aloud and that the computer's body-language-recognition software picked up your head nod and is seeking confirmation. "Yes," you say again. "Let's get on with it."

This scenario presupposes that you have been having some personal problems and have finally decided to go for help. The helping professional asked if you would have a dialogue with her computer as a way of learning more about your problems. Living in a world of computers, you assumed that the interaction would be worthwhile. So here you are.

Sound far-fetched? Actually, primitive computers have been interviewing people for more than 20 years. One current system is named CASPER, which stands for Computerized Assessment System for Psychotherapy Evaluation and Research. A CASPER interview lasts about 30 minutes. It covers a wide range of topics, such as demographic information, family relations, social activities, sexual behavior, life satisfaction, and problems connected with physical and psychological disorders. Questions and response options, such as the following, are shown on the screen:

> "About how many days in the past month did you have difficulty falling asleep, staying asleep, or waking too early (include sleep disturbed by bad dreams)?" "During the past month, how have you been getting along with your spouse/partner? (1) Very satisfactory; (2) Mostly satisfactory; (3) Sometimes satisfactory, sometimes unsatisfactory; (4) Mostly unsatisfactory; (5) Very unsatisfactory." (Farrell and others, 1987, p. 692)

The person presses a numeric keypad to respond. CASPER is a branching program that produces additional questions to follow up on problems suggested by people's responses. If

Anxiety Disorders

Anxiety is characterized by subjective and physical features (Beck and others, 1988). Subjective features include fear of the worst happening, fear of losing control, nervousness, and inability to relax. Physical features reflect arousal of the sympathetic branch of the autonomic nervous system. They entail trembling, sweating, a pounding or racing heart, elevated blood pressure (a flushed face), and faintness. Anxiety is an appropriate response to a threat. Anxiety can be abnormal, however, when its extent is out of proportion to the threat or when it "comes out of the blue"—that is, when events do not seem to warrant it.

TYPES OF ANXIETY DISORDERS

The anxiety disorders include phobic, panic, generalized anxiety, obsessive–compulsive, post-traumatic stress, and acute stress disorders.

the person reports difficulty sleeping, CASPER delves into whether sleep has become a key problem—"something causing you great personal distress or interfering with your daily functioning" (Farrell and others, 1987, p. 693). If the person responds yes, the computer will investigate still more deeply. People may also add or drop complaints; that is, people can change their minds.

Research has shown that people are generally capable of completing CASPER interviews with little difficulty, and most respond favorably to the interview (Bloom, 1992; Farrell and others, 1987). People also appear to report a greater number of problems to CASPER than to a live clinician. Perhaps the computer helps identify problems that the person would be unwilling to report to another person. Or perhaps the computer seems more willing to take the time needed to record all complaints.

Computer diagnostic programs apparently offer some advantages over traditional human interviewers (Farrell and others, 1987):

1. Computers can be programmed to ask specific sets of questions in definite order, whereas people sometimes omit important questions or allow the interview to veer off course into less critical issues.

2. As with CASPER, people may be less disconcerted about reporting personal matters to a computer because computers do not respond emotionally or judgmentally.

3. Use of the computer for purposes of diagnosis also frees clinicians to spend their time more productively in direct clinical services.

As such programs become capable of handling vastly increased amounts of information, they are also likely to become more accurate at diagnosis and more capable of identifying unusual problems. They may also readily connect the person's complaints to similar cases in the literature, indicating what course of treatment has been most effective. On the other hand, it may be that computerized psychological testing will not be for everyone. Research shows that younger, better-educated people who are experienced with computers react more favorably to computerized assessment (Spinhoven and others, 1993).

Yet a review of the research literature suggests that some computer programs are as capable as trained clinicians of obtaining pertinent information from a client and arriving at an accurate diagnosis (Bloom, 1992). Is the scenario sketched at the outset of this feature a foregone conclusion?

Specific phobia • Persistent fear of a specific object or situation.

Social phobia • An irrational, excessive fear of public scrutiny.

Claustrophobia • (claws-troe-FOE-bee-uh). Fear of tight, small places.

Acrophobia • (ack-row-FOE-bee-uh). Fear of high places.

Agoraphobia • (ag-or-uh-FOE-bee-uh). Fear of open, crowded places.

Panic disorder • The recurrent experiencing of attacks of extreme anxiety in the absence of external stimuli that usually elicit anxiety.

Generalized anxiety disorder • Feelings of dread and foreboding and sympathetic arousal of at least 6 months' duration.

Obsession • A recurring thought or image that seems beyond control.

Compulsion • An apparently irresistible urge to repeat an act or engage in ritualistic behavior such as hand washing.

Panic Disorder. This man was overcome by feelings of panic as he was walking to his car. The physical aspects of panic attacks tend to be stronger than those of other kinds of anxiety, including shortness of breath, dizziness, and pounding of the heart. Many people with panic disorder fear that they will have heart attacks.

Phobias. There are several types of phobias, including specific phobias, social phobia, and agoraphobia. **Specific phobias** are excessive, irrational fears of specific objects or situations. **Social phobias** are persistent fears of scrutiny by others or of doing something that will be humiliating or embarrassing. Stage fright and speech anxiety are common social phobias.

Some people with social phobia cannot sign their names in public, as in the case of Brett:

Brett had a signature phobia. She was literally terrified of signing her name in public. She had structured her life to avoid situations requiring a signature. She paid cash rather than by credit card. She filed documents by mail rather than in person. She even registered her car in her husband's name so that he would be responsible for signing the motor vehicle forms. Like many people with phobias, Brett was clever at restructuring her life so that she could avoid exposing herself to these fearful situations. She had even kept her phobia from her husband for 15 years.

Brett's phobia was maintained by an underlying fear of social embarrassment. She feared ridicule for an illegible or sloppy signature, or that authority figures like bank officers or motor vehicle officials would think that her signature was phony or a forgery. Brett knew that she could prove her identity by other means than her signature and also recognized that no one really cared whether or not her signature was legible. Brett had created a vicious cycle of anxiety: She felt she must prevent her hands from shaking so that she could write legibly. But her anxiety was so strong that she began to shake whenever her signature was required. The more she tried to fend off the anxiety, the stronger it became. Her anxiety confirmed her belief that her signature would be ridiculed. (Adapted from Nevid and others, 1994)

One specific phobia is fear of elevators. Some people will not enter elevators despite the hardships they incur (such as walking six flights of steps) as a result. Yes, the cable *could* break. The ventilation *could* fail. One *could* be stuck waiting in midair for repairs. These problems are uncommon, however, and it does not make sense for most of us to repeatedly walk flights of stairs to elude them. Similarly, some people with specific phobias for hypodermic needles will not have injections, even to treat profound illness. Injections can be painful, but most people with phobias for needles would gladly suffer an even more painful pinch if it would help them fight illness. Other specific phobias include **claustrophobia** (fear of tight or enclosed places), **acrophobia** (fear of heights), and fear of mice, snakes, and other creepy-crawlies.

Phobias can seriously disrupt one's life. A person may know that a phobia is irrational yet still experience acute anxiety and avoid the phobic article or circumstance.

Fears of animals and imaginary creatures are common among children. **Agoraphobia** is among the most widespread phobias among adults. Agoraphobia is derived from the Greek meaning "fear of the marketplace," or of being out in open, busy areas. Persons with agoraphobia fear being in places from which it might be difficult to escape or in which help might be unavailable if they become disquieted. In practice, people who receive this label are often loath to venture out of their homes, especially when they are alone. They find it difficult to hold jobs or to sustain an ordinary social life.

Panic Disorder.

My heart would start pounding so hard I was sure I was having a heart attack. I used to go to the emergency room. Sometimes I felt dizzy, like I was going to pass out. I was sure I was about to die.

KIM WEINER

Panic disorder is an abrupt attack of acute anxiety that is not triggered by a specific object or situation. People with panic disorder experience strong physical sensations such as shortness of breath, heavy sweating, quaking, and pounding of the heart (Goleman, 1992). As was the case with Kim Weiner (1992), they are particularly aware of cardiac sensations (Ehlers & Breuer, 1992), and it is not unusual for them to think they are having a heart attack. People may also experience choking sensations; nausea; numbness or tingling; flushes or chills; chest pain; and fear of dying, going crazy, or losing control. Panic attacks may last from a minute or two to an hour or more. Afterwards, people usually feel spent.

Perhaps half of us panic now and then (Wilson and others, 1991). The diagnosis of panic disorder is reserved for people who undergo series of attacks or live in dread of attacks. Fewer than 10% of us meet this standard (Wilson and others, 1992).

Because panic attacks seem to descend from nowhere, some people who have had them generally remain in the home for fear of having an attack in public. In such cases, they are diagnosed as having panic disorder with agoraphobia.

Generalized Anxiety Disorder. The central feature of **generalized anxiety disorder** is persistent anxiety. As with panic disorder, the anxiety cannot be attributed to a phobic object, situation, or activity. Rather, it seems to be free floating. Features may include motor tension (shakiness, inability to relax, furrowed brow, fidgeting); autonomic overarousal (sweating, dry mouth, racing heart, lightheadedness, frequent urinating, diarrhea); feelings of dread and foreboding; and excessive vigilance, as shown by distractibility, insomnia, and irritability.

Obsessive–Compulsive Disorder.
Obsessions are recurrent, anxiety-provoking thoughts or images that seem irrational and beyond control (Foa, 1990). They are so compelling and recurrent that they disrupt daily life. They may include doubts about whether one has locked the doors and shut the windows, or images such as one mother's repeated fantasy that her children had been run over by traffic on the way home from school. A woman became obsessed with the idea that she had contaminated her hands with Sani-Flush and that the chemicals were spreading to everything she touched. A 16-year-old boy found "numbers in my head" whenever he was about to study or take a test.

Compulsions are thoughts or behaviors that tend to reduce the anxiety connected with obsessions (Foa, 1990). They are

Obsessive–Compulsive Disorder? This photograph, *Red Library #2,* by Laurie Simmons, is suggestive of certain features of obsessive–compulsive disorder. The "woman" in this compulsively neat room is apparently transfixed by the absence of perfection. It seems that one picture is missing. People with obsessive–compulsive disorder engage in repetitious behaviors as a way of managing troubling thoughts.

seemingly irresistible urges to engage in acts, often repeatedly, such as elaborate washing after using the bathroom. The impulse is recurrent and forceful, interfering with daily life. The woman who felt contaminated by Sani-Flush spent 3 to 4 hours daily at the sink and complained, "My hands look like lobster claws."

A Traumatic Experience from the Vietnam War. Physical threats and other traumatic experiences can lead to post-traumatic stress disorder (PTSD). PTSD is characterized by intrusive memories of the experience, recurrent dreams about it, and the sudden feeling that it is, in fact, recurring (as in "flashbacks").

Post-traumatic stress disorder • A disorder that follows a distressing event outside the range of normal human experience and that is characterized by features such as intense fear, avoidance of stimuli associated with the event, and reliving of the event. Abbreviated *PTSD.*

Acute stress disorder • A disorder, like PTSD, that is characterized by feelings of anxiety and helplessness and caused by a traumatic event. Unlike PTSD, acute stress disorder occurs within a month of the event and lasts from 2 days to 4 weeks. (A category first included in DSM-IV.)

Concordance • (con-CORD-ants). Agreement.

Post-Traumatic Stress Disorder.

Fire, stabbings, shootings, suicides, medical emergencies, accidents, bombs, and hazardous material explosions—these are just some of the traumatic experiences firefighters confront on a fairly regular basis. Because of such experiences, one study found that the prevalence of **post-traumatic stress disorder** (PTSD) among firefighters was 16.5%. This rate was 1% higher than the rate among Vietnam veterans and compared to a rate of 1% to 3% among the general population (DeAngelis, 1995).

PTSD is known by intense and persistent feelings of anxiety and helplessness that are caused by a traumatic experience such as a physical threat or assault of oneself or one's family, destruction of one's community, or witnessing a death. PTSD may occur many months after the event. PTSD has troubled many combat veterans and people who have seen their homes and communities inundated by floods, swept away by tornadoes, or subjected to toxic hazards (Baum & Fleming, 1993). A study of victims of Hurricane Andrew, which assailed South Florida, found that one man in four and about one woman in three (36%) had

developed PTSD (Ironson, 1993). A national study of more than 4,000 women found that PTSD had occurred among about one woman in four who had been victimized by crime (Resnick and others, 1993; see Figure 13.1).

The event that precipitates PTSD is incessantly reexperienced as intrusive memories, recurrent dreams, and flashbacks—the sudden feeling that the event is recurring. When combat veterans with PTSD imagine the events of the battlefield, they show a great deal of muscle tension and other physiological signs of anxiety (Orr and others, 1993; Pitman and others, 1990).

People with PTSD typically attempt to avoid thoughts and activities connected to the traumatic event. They may also display sleep problems, irritable outbursts, difficulty concentrating, extreme vigilance, and an intensified "startle" response.

Acute Stress Disorder. **Acute stress disorder,** like PTSD, is characterized by feelings of anxiety and helplessness that are caused by a traumatic event. However, whereas PTSD can occur 6 months or more after the traumatic event and tends to persist, acute stress disorder occurs within a month of the event and lasts from 2 days to 4 weeks. Women who have been raped, for example, experience immediate high levels of distress that tend to peak in severity about 3 weeks after the assault (Davidson & Foa, 1991; Rothbaum and others, 1992).

THEORETICAL VIEWS

According to the psychodynamic perspective, phobias symbolize conflicts of childhood origin. Psychodynamic theory explains generalized anxiety as persistent difficulty in maintaining repression of primitive impulses. Psychoanalysts view obsessions as the leakage of unconscious impulses and compulsions as acts that allow people to keep such impulses partly repressed.

Some learning theorists consider phobias to be conditioned fears that were acquired in early childhood. Therefore, their origins are beyond memory. Avoidance of feared stimuli is reinforced by reduction of anxiety. In the case of women who have been raped, evidence suggests that exposure to the situation (for example, the neighborhood, one's workplace) in which the attack occurred, in the absence of further attack, can extinguish some of the post-traumatic distress (Wirtz & Harrell, 1987).

Social-cognitive theorists note a role for observational learning in fear acquisition (Bandura and others, 1969). If parents squirm, grimace, and shudder at mice, blood, or dirt on the kitchen floor, children might encode these stimuli as being awful and imitate their behavior. Learning theorists suggest that generalized anxiety is often nothing more than fear that has been associated with situations so broad that they are not readily identified, such as social relationships or personal achievement. Cognitive theorists suggest that anxiety can be maintained by thinking that one is in a terrible situation and is helpless to change it. Mineka (1991) argues that people with anxiety disorders are cognitively biased toward paying more attention to threatening objects or situations. Psychoanalysts and learning theorists broadly agree that compulsive behavior reduces anxiety.

Cognitive theorists note that our appraisals of the magnitude of the threats in events help determine whether events are traumatic and lead to PTSD (Creamer and others, 1992). People with panic attacks tend to misinterpret bodily cues and to view them as threats (Meichenbaum, 1993). Obsessions and compulsions may serve to divert people's attention from more intimidating issues such as "What am I to do with my life?" When anxieties are acquired at a young age, we may later interpret them as enduring traits and label ourselves as "people who fear _____" (you fill it in). We then live up to the labels. We also entertain thoughts that heighten and perpetuate anxiety such as "I've got to get out of here," or "My heart is going to leap out of my chest." Such ideas intensify physical signs of anxiety, disrupt planning, magnify the aversiveness of stimuli, motivate avoidance, and decrease self-efficacy expectations about ability to manage the situation. Belief that we shall not be able to handle a threat heightens anxiety, whereas belief that we are in control lessens anxiety (Bandura and others, 1985).

Biological factors play a role in anxiety disorders. Genetic factors are implicated in

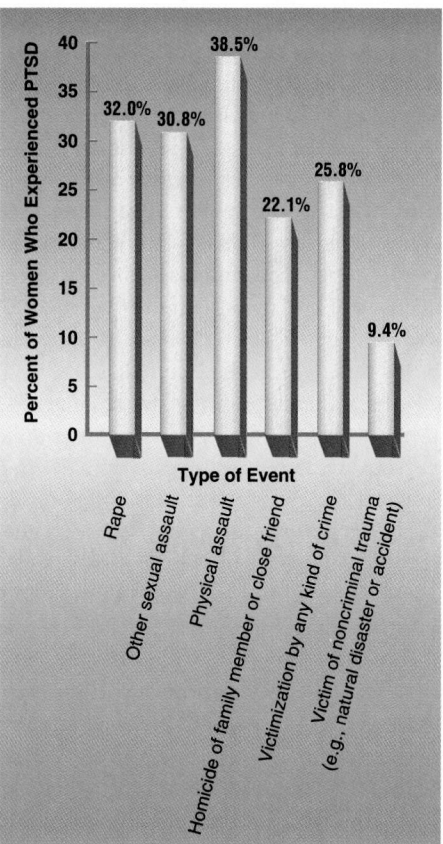

FIGURE 13.1
Incidence of Post-Traumatic Stress Disorder among Female Victims of Crime and among Nonvictims According to Resnick and her colleagues (1993), about one woman in four (25.8%) who was victimized by crime could be diagnosed with PTSD at some point following the crime. By contrast, fewer than one woman in 10 (9.4%) who was not victimized by crime experienced PTSD.

most psychological disorders, including anxiety disorders (Carey & DiLalla, 1994). For one thing, anxiety disorders tend to run in families (Michels & Marzuk, 1993b; Turner and others, 1987). Twin studies also find the **concordance** rate for anxiety disorders to be higher among pairs of identical than fraternal twins (Torgersen, 1983). Adoptee studies similarly show that the biological parent places the child at risk for anxiety and related traits (Pedersen and others, 1988).

Susan Mineka (1991) suggests that people (and nonhuman primates) are genetically predisposed to fear stimuli that may have once posed a threat to their ancestors. Evolutionary forces would have favored the survival of individuals who were predisposed toward acquiring fears of large animals, spiders, snakes, heights, entrapment, sharp objects, and strangers. In laboratory experiments, people view photographs of various objects and then receive electric shock (Hugdahl & Ohman, 1977; Ohman and others, 1976). Participants more readily acquire fear reactions to some stimuli (for example, spiders and snakes) than others (for example, flowers and houses), as measured by sweat in the palm of the hand. These experiments, however, do not show that the participants are genetically predisposed to develop fear responses to stimuli such as snakes and spiders. The participants were reared in a society in which many people react negatively to these creepy-crawlies. Thus their learning experiences, and not genetic factors, may have predisposed them to fear these stimuli.

Perhaps a predisposition toward anxiety—in the form of a highly reactive autonomic nervous system—can be inherited. What might make a nervous system "highly reactive"? In the case of panic disorder, faulty regulation of serotonin and norepinephrine may be involved (Clum and others, 1993). In other anxiety disorders, one possibility is that receptor sites in the brain are not sensitive enough to **gamma-aminobutyric acid (GABA),** an inhibitory neurotransmitter that may help quell anxiety reactions. The **benzodiazepines,** a class of drugs that reduce anxiety, are thought to work by increasing the sensitivity of receptor sites to GABA. However, it is unlikely that excesses or deficiencies in the levels of a single neurotransmitter can explain any psychological disorder (Michels & Marzuk, 1993a).

Many cases of anxiety disorders may reflect the interaction of biological and psychological factors. In panic disorder, biological imbalances may initially trigger attacks. However, subsequent fear of attacks—and of the bodily cues that signal the onset of attacks—may heighten people's discomfort and give them the idea there is nothing they can do about them (McNally, 1990; Meichenbaum, 1993). Feelings of helplessness increase fear. People with panic disorder can thus be helped by psychological methods that provide ways of reducing physical discomfort—including regular breathing—and that show them that there are, after all, things they can do to cope with attacks (Clum and others, 1993; Klosko and others, 1990). The origins of many psychological disorders are apparently quite complex. They would appear to involve the interaction of biological, psychological, and perhaps other factors.

Gamma-aminobutyric acid (GABA) • (a-me-no-byoo-TIE-rick). An inhibitory neurotransmitter that is implicated in anxiety reactions.

Benzodiazepines • (ben-zoe-die-AZZ-uh-peans). A class of drugs that reduce anxiety; minor tranquilizers.

Dissociative disorders • (diss-SO-she-uh-tivv). Disorders in which there are sudden, temporary changes in consciousness or self-identity.

Dissociative amnesia • (am-KNEE-she-uh). A dissociative disorder marked by loss of memory or self-identity; skills and general knowledge are usually retained. Previously termed *psychogenic amnesia.*

Malingering • Pretending to be ill to escape duty or work.

Dissociative fugue • (FYOOG). A dissociative disorder in which one experiences amnesia and then flees to a new location. Previously termed *psychogenic fugue.*

Reflections

Now that you have read the section on anxiety disorders, reflect on the following questions:

• Have you ever felt anxious? Did your anxiety strike you as being normal under the circumstances? Why or why not?

• Do you know anyone with a phobia? What kind of phobia? Does the phobia seriously interfere with his or her life? How so?

• Do you ever find yourself "in a panic"? Under what circumstances? What is the difference between "being in a panic" and having a panic disorder?

• Do you know any people who are obsessive–compulsive? What behavior leads you to apply this label?

• Do you tend to pay a great deal of attention to potential threats or to put them out of your mind? How does your response to threats affect your feelings about them?

Dissociative Disorders

In the **dissociative disorders,** there is a separation of mental processes such as thoughts, emotions, identity, memory, or consciousness—the processes that make the person feel whole (Spiegel & Cardeña, 1991).

TYPES OF DISSOCIATIVE DISORDERS

The DSM lists several dissociative disorders, including dissociative amnesia, dissociative fugue, dissociative identity disorder, and depersonalization.

Dissociative Amnesia. In **dissociative amnesia,** there is sudden inability to recall important personal information. Memory loss cannot be attributed to organic problems such as a blow to the head or alcoholic intoxication. It is thus a psychological dissociative disorder, and not an organic disorder. In the most common example, the person cannot recall events for a number of hours after a stressful incident, as in warfare or in the case of the uninjured survivor of an accident. In generalized amnesia, people forget their entire lives.

Amnesia may last for hours or years. Termination of amnesia is also sudden.

People sometimes claim that they cannot recall engaging in socially unacceptable behavior, promising to do something, and so on. Claiming to have a psychological problem such as amnesia in order to escape responsibility is known as **malingering.** Current research methods do not guarantee that we can distinguish malingerers from people with dissociative disorders.

Dissociative Fugue. In **dissociative fugue,** the person shows loss of memory for the past and travels abruptly from his or her home or place of work. Either the person does not think about the past, or the person reports a past filled with invented memories. Following recovery, the events that occurred during the fugue are not recalled.

Dissociative Identity Disorder. Dissociative identity disorder (formerly termed *multiple personality disorder*) is the name given to William's disorder, as described at the beginning of the chapter. In this disorder, two or more identities or personalities, each with distinct traits and memories, "occupy" the same person, with or without awareness of the others. Different identities might even have different eyeglass prescriptions (Braun, 1988).

Braun reports cases in which assorted identities showed different allergic responses. In one person, an identity named

Timmy was not sensitive to orange juice. But when other identities who alternated control over him drank orange juice, they would break out with hives. Hives would also erupt after Timmy drank orange juice if another identity emerged while the juice was being digested. If Timmy reappeared when the allergic reaction was present, the itching of the hives would cease and the blisters would start to subside. In other cases reported by Braun, different identities in one person might show various responses to the same medicine. Or one identity might exhibit color blindness while others had intact color vision.

Truth or Fiction Revisited. *It is true that some people have more than one identity, and the identities may have different allergies and eyeglass prescriptions.* However, many individuals may feign dissociative identity disorder in an effort to evade responsibility for unacceptable behavior.

A few celebrated cases have been portrayed in the popular media. In one that became the subject of the film *The Three Faces of Eve,* a timid housewife named Eve White harbored two other identities: Eve Black, a sexually aggressive, antisocial personality; and Jane, an emerging identity who was able to accept the existence of her primitive impulses, yet show socially appropriate behavior. Finally, the three faces merged into one—Jane. Ironically, Jane (Chris Sizemore, in real life) reportedly split into 22 identities later on. Another well-publicized case is

Dissociative Identity Disorder. In the film *The Three Faces of Eve,* Joanne Woodward played three personalities in the same woman: the shy, inhibited Eve White (lying on couch); the flirtatious and promiscuous Eve Black (in dark dress); and a third personality (Jane) who could accept her sexual and aggressive impulses and still maintain her sense of identity.

Feelings of Depersonalization. Episodes of depersonalization are typified by a sense of detachment from oneself. It may seem that one is outside one's own body or walking in a dream.

that of Sybil, a woman with 16 identities who was played by Sally Field in a film.

Depersonalization Disorder.

Depersonalization disorder is characterized by persistent or recurrent feelings that one is detached from one's own body, as if one is observing one's thought processes from the outside. One may also feel as though he or she is functioning on automatic pilot or as if in a dream.

The case of Richie illustrates a transient (passing) episode of depersonalization:

> "We went to Orlando with the children after school let out. I had also been driving myself hard, and it was time to let go. We spent three days 'doing' Disneyworld, and it got to the point where we were all wearing shirts with mice and ducks on them and singing Disney songs like 'Yo ho, yo ho, a pirate's life for me.' On the third day I began to feel unreal and ill at ease while we were watching these middle-American Ivory-soap teenagers singing and dancing in front of Cinderella's Castle. The day was finally cooling down, but I broke into a sweat. I became shaky and dizzy and sat down on the cement next to the 4-year-old's stroller without giving

[my wife] an explanation. There were strollers and kids and [adults'] legs all around me, and for some strange reason I became fixated on the pieces of popcorn strewn on the ground. All of a sudden it was like the people around me were all silly mechanical creatures, like the dolls in the 'It's a Small World' [exhibit] or the animals on the 'Jungle Cruise.' Things sort of seemed to slow down, the way they do when you've smoked marijuana, and there was this invisible wall of cotton between me and everyone else.

> "Then the concert was over and my wife was like 'What's the matter?' and did I want to stay for the Electrical Parade and the fireworks or was I sick? Now I was beginning to wonder if I was going crazy and I said I was sick, that my wife would have to take me by the hand and drive us back to the [motel]. Somehow we got back to the monorail and turned in the strollers. I waited in the herd [of people] at the station like a dead person, my eyes glazed over, looking out over kids with Mickey Mouse ears and Mickey Mouse balloons. The mechanical voice on the monorail almost did me in and I got really shaky.

> "I refused to go back to the Magic Kingdom. I went with the family to Sea World, and on another day I dropped [my wife] and the kids off at the Magic Kingdom and picked them up that night. My wife thought I was goldbricking or something, and we had a helluva fight about it, but we had a life to get back to and my sanity had to come first." (Nevid and others, 1994)

THEORETICAL VIEWS

According to psychodynamic theory, people with dissociative disorders use massive repression to avert recognition of improper impulses (Vaillant, 1994). In dissociative amnesia and fugue, the person forgets a profoundly disturbing event or impulse. In dissociative identity disorder, the person expresses unacceptable impulses through alternate identities. In depersonalization, the person stands outside—removed from the turmoil within.

According to learning theorists, people with dissociative disorders have learned *not to think* about disturbing acts or impulses to avoid feelings of guilt and shame. Technically speaking, *not thinking about these matters* is reinforced[3] by *removal* of the aversive stimuli of guilt and shame.

Social-cognitive theory suggests that many people come to role-play dissociative identity disorder through observational learning. This is not quite the same thing as faking, because people can "forget to tell themselves" that they have assumed a role. Reinforcers are made available by role-playing individuals with dissociative identity disorder: Drawing attention to oneself and escaping responsibility for unacceptable behavior are two (Spanos and others, 1985; Thigpen & Cleckley, 1984).

Perhaps all of us are capable of dividing our awareness so that we become unaware, at least temporarily, of events that we usually focus more attention on. The dissociative disorders raise fascinating questions about the nature of human self-identity and memory (Kihlstrom and others, 1994). Perhaps it is no marvel that attention can be divided. Perhaps the marvel is that human consciousness normally integrates experience into a meaningful whole.

Reflections

Now that you have read the section on dissociative disorders, reflect on the following questions:

• Have you ever known people to claim that they had "amnesia" for some episode or event? Now that you have read this section, do you think that the term was used correctly? Why or why not?

• Have you ever felt removed from the world—as though the things around you could not be really happening? Now that you have read this section, do these feelings seem connected with depersonalization? Why or why not?

• Have you seen a film or a TV show in which a character was supposed to have dissociative identity disorder (perhaps it was called "multiple personality")? What kind of behavior did the character display? Does the behavior seem consistent with the description of the disorder in the text? In the film or TV show, what were the supposed origins of the disorder?

Somatoform Disorders

In **somatoform disorders,** people show or complain of physical problems such as paralysis, pain, or the persistent belief that they have a serious disease, yet no evidence of a physical abnormality can be found.

TYPES OF SOMATOFORM DISORDERS

In this section, we discuss two somatoform disorders: conversion disorder and hypochondriasis.

Conversion Disorder. **Conversion disorder** is characterized by a major change in, or loss of, physical functioning, although there are no medical findings to explain the loss of functioning. The behaviors are not intentionally produced. That is, the person is not faking.

If you lost the ability to see at night, or if your legs became paralyzed, you would understandably show concern. But some people with conversion disorder show indifference to their symptoms, a remarkable feature referred to as **la belle indifférence.** Conversion disorder is so named because it appears to "convert" a source of stress into a physical difficulty.

During World War II, a number of bomber pilots developed night blindness. They could not carry out their nighttime missions, although no damage to the optic nerves was found. In rare cases, women with large families have been reported to become paralyzed in the legs, again with no medical findings.

Depersonalization disorder • A dissociative disorder in which one experiences persistent or recurrent feelings that one is not real or is detached from one's own experiences or body.

Somatoform disorders • (so-MAT-oh-form). Disorders in which people complain of physical (somatic) problems even though no physical abnormality can be found.

Conversion disorder • A disorder in which anxiety or unconscious conflicts are "converted" into physical symptoms that often have the effect of helping the person cope with anxiety or conflict.

La belle indifférence • (lah bell an-DEEF-fay-rants). A French term descriptive of the lack of concern sometimes shown by people with conversion disorders.

---

[3] This is an example of negative reinforcement, because the frequency of behavior—in this case, the frequency of diverting one's attention from a certain topic—is increased by *removal* of a stimulus—in this case, by removal of feelings of, say, guilt or shame.

Hypochondriasis • (high-poe-con-DRY-uh-sis). Persistent belief that one has a medical disorder despite lack of medical findings.

Major depression • A severe depressive disorder in which the person may show loss of appetite, psychomotor behaviors, and impaired reality testing.

Psychomotor retardation • Slowness in motor activity and (apparently) in thought.

Bipolar disorder • A disorder in which the mood alternates between two extreme poles (elation and depression). Also referred to as *manic-depression*.

Manic • Elated, showing excessive excitement.

Rapid flight of ideas • Rapid speech and topic changes, characteristic of manic behavior.

Hypochondriasis. Persons with **hypochondriasis** insist that they are suffering from profound physical illness, even though no medical evidence can be found. They become preoccupied with minor physical sensations and maintain their belief despite medical reassurance. They may run from doctor to doctor, seeking the one who will find the causes of the sensations. Fear may disrupt work or home life.

THEORETICAL VIEWS

Consistent with psychodynamic theory, early versions of the DSM labeled what are now referred to as somatoform disorders as "hysterical neuroses." "Hysterical" derives from the word *hystera,* the Greek term for the uterus or womb. Like many other Greeks, Hippocrates believed that hysteria was a sort of female trouble that was caused by a wandering uterus. It was erroneously thought that the uterus could roam the body—that it was not anchored in place! As the uterus meandered, it could cause pains and odd sensations almost anywhere. The Greeks also believed that pregnancy anchored the uterus and ended hysterical complaints. What did Greek physicians thus prescribe to bring monthly aches and pains to an end? Good guess.

Even in the earlier years of the 20th century, it was suggested that strange sensations and medically unfounded complaints were largely the province of women. Moreover, considering the problem to be a neurosis suggested that it stemmed from unconscious childhood conflicts. The psychodynamic view of conversion disorders is that the symptoms protect the individual from feelings of guilt or shame or from another source of stress. Conversion disorders, like dissociative disorders, often seem to serve a purpose. The "blindness" of the pilots may have afforded them respite from stressful missions or may have allowed them to evade the guilt from bombing civilian populations.

Reflections

Now that you have read the section on somatoform disorders, reflect on the following questions:

- What kinds of problems do you think are involved in trying to determine whether someone has a medical problem or a conversion disorder?
- Have you heard the term *hypochondriac* used sarcastically or as an insult? How so?

Mood Disorders

Mood disorders are characterized by disturbance in expressed emotions. The disruption generally involves depression or elation. Most instances of depression are normal, or "run-of-the-mill." If you have failed an important test, if a business investment has been lost, or if your closest friend becomes ill, it is understandable and fitting for you to be depressed about it. It would be odd, in fact, if you were *not* affected by adversity.

Truth or Fiction Revisited. *It is not abnormal to feel depressed.* It is normal—indeed, it is psychologically appropriate—for one to feel depressed when one's situation is depressing. As with anxiety disorders, feelings of depression are considered abnormal when they are magnified beyond one's circumstances or when there is no apparent reason for them.

TYPES OF MOOD DISORDERS

In this section, we discuss two mood disorders: major depression and bipolar disorder.

Major Depression. Depression is the "common cold" of psychological problems, perhaps affecting upward of 10% of us at any given time (Alloy and others, 1990). People with run-of-the-mill depression may feel sad, blue, or "down in the dumps." They may complain of lack of energy, loss of self-esteem, difficulty concentrating, loss of interest in other people and usually enjoyable activities, pessimism, crying, and thoughts of suicide.

These feelings tend to be more intense among people with **major depression.** People with major depression may also show poor appetite and serious weight loss, agitation or **psychomotor retardation,** inability to concentrate and make decisions, complaints of "not caring" anymore, and suicide attempts.

Persons with major depression may also show faulty perception of reality—so-called psychotic behaviors. Psychotic behaviors include delusions of unworthiness, guilt for imagined wrongdoings, even ideas that one is rotting from disease. There may also be hallucinations such as of the Devil administering just punishment or of strange bodily sensations.

Bipolar Disorder.   In **bipolar disorder,** formerly known as manic-depression, there are mood swings from elation to depression. These cycles seem to be unrelated to external events. In the elated, or **manic** phase, people may show excessive excitement or silliness, carrying jokes too far. They may show poor judgment, sometimes destroying property, and be argumentative. Roommates may avoid them, finding them abrasive. Manic people often speak rapidly ("pressured speech") and jump from topic to topic, showing **rapid flight of ideas.** It is hard to get a word in edgewise. They may make extremely large contributions to charity or give away expensive possessions. They may not be able to sit still or to sleep restfully.

Depression is the other side of the coin. People with bipolar depression often sleep more than usual and are lethargic. People with major (or unipolar) depression are more likely to have insomnia and agitation. People with bipolar depression also exhibit social withdrawal and irritability.

Some people with bipolar disorder attempt suicide on the way down from the elated phase. They will do almost anything to escape the depths of depression that lie ahead.

THEORETICAL VIEWS

Depression is an appropriate reaction to losses and unpleasant events. Problems such as marital discord, physical discomfort, incompetence, and failure or pressure at work all contribute to feelings of depression. We tend to be more depressed by things we bring upon ourselves, such as academic problems, financial problems, unwanted pregnancy, conflict with the law, arguments, and fights (Hammen & Mayol, 1982; Simons and others, 1993). Employed mothers are frequently depressed by the difficulty of finding adequate child care (Ross, 1993). Many people recover from depression less readily than others, however. People who remain depressed have lower self-esteem (Andrews & Brown, 1993), are less likely to be able to solve social problems (Marx and others, 1992; Nezu & Ronan, 1985), and have less social support (Asarnow and others, 1987; Pagel & Becker, 1987).

Women are more likely than men to be diagnosed with depression (Nolen-Hoeksema & Girgus, 1994; Russo, 1990b). Belle (1990) points out that women—especially single mothers—have lower socioeconomic status than men in our society and that depression and other psychological disorders have traditionally been more common among poor people. Capable, hard-working women are likely to become depressed when they see how society limits their opportunities (Rothbart & Ahadi, 1994).

Psychodynamic Views.   Psychoanalysts suggest various explanations for depression. In one, people at risk for depression are overly concerned about hurting others' feelings or losing their approval. As a result, they hold in rather than express feelings of anger. Anger becomes turned inward and is experienced as misery and self-hatred. From the psychodynamic perspective, bipolar disorder may be seen as alternating dominance of the personality by the superego and the ego. In the depressive phase of the disorder, the superego dominates, flooding the individual with exaggerated ideas of wrongdoing and associated feelings of guilt and worthlessness. After a while, the ego defends itself by rebounding and asserting supremacy, accounting for the elation and self-confidence that in part characterize the manic phase. Later, in response to the excessive display of ego, feelings of guilt return, again plunging the person into depression.

Learning Views.   Many people with depressive disorders have an external locus of control. That is, they do not believe that they can control events to achieve desired outcomes (Weisz and others, 1993). Some people with depressive disorders lack skills, such as social skills, that might lead to rewards (Gotlib, 1984).

Research has also found links between depression and **learned helplessness.** In one study, Seligman (1975) taught dogs that they were helpless to escape an electric shock by preventing them from leaving a cage in which they received repeated shock. Later, a barrier to a safe compartment was removed, allowing the animals a way out. When they were shocked again, however, the dogs made no effort to escape. They had apparently learned that they were helpless. Seligman's dogs were also, in a sense, reinforced for doing nothing. That is, the shock *eventually* stopped when the dogs were showing helpless behavior—inactivity and withdrawal. "Reinforcement" might have increased the likelihood of repeating their "successful behavior"—that is, doing nothing—in a similar situation. This helpless behavior resembles that of people who are depressed.

Cognitive Factors. The concept of learned helplessness bridges learning and cognitive approaches in that it is an attitude,

Why Did He Miss That Tackle? This football player is compounding his feelings of depression by attributing his shortcomings on the field to factors that he cannot change. For example, he tells himself that he missed the tackle because of stupidity and lack of athletic ability. He ignores the facts that his coaching was poor and that his teammates failed to come to his support.

a general expectation. Other cognitive factors also contribute to depression. For example, perfectionists set themselves up for depression through irrational self-demands. They are likely to fall short of their (unrealistic) expectations and, as a result, to feel depressed (Hewitt & Flett, 1993; Persons and others, 1993).

People with depression pay more attention to negative information (Mineka, 1991). They tend to be self-critical (Zuroff & Mongrain, 1987) and pessimistic (Alloy & Ahrens, 1987; Pyszczynski and others, 1987). People, moreover, who respond to feelings of depression by focusing on their symptoms and the possible causes and effects of their symptoms tend to prolong depressive episodes (Nolen-Hoeksema, 1991). Susan Nolen-Hoeksema and her colleagues (1993) found that women are more likely than men to focus on their symptoms and thereby prolong feelings of depression. Men seem somewhat more likely to try to fight off negative feelings by distracting themselves (Parrot & Sabini, 1990). She points out that men are more likely to distract themselves by turning to alcohol, however, thus exposing themselves and their families to additional problems (Nolen-Hoeksema, 1991).

Seligman and his colleagues note that when things go wrong, we may think of the causes of failure as *internal* or *external, stable* or *unstable, global* or *specific.* Let us explain these various **attributional styles** through the example of having a date that does not work out. An internal attribution involves self-blame, as in "I really loused it up," whereas an external attribution places the blame elsewhere (as in "Some couples just don't take to each other," or, "She was the wrong sign for me"). A stable attribution ("It's my personality") suggests a problem that cannot be changed, whereas an unstable attribution ("It was the head cold") suggests a temporary condition. A global attribution of failure ("I have no idea what to do when I'm with people") suggests that the problem is quite large. A specific attribution ("I have problems making small talk at the very outset of a relationship") chops the problem down to a manageable size.

Research shows that people who are depressed are more likely than other people to attribute the causes of their failures to internal, stable, and global factors—factors they are relatively helpless to change (Gotlib and others, 1993; Metalsky and others, 1993; Seligman and others, 1984). Such attributions can give rise to feelings of hopelessness.

Biological Factors. Researchers are also searching for biological factors in mood disorders. Depression, for example, is often associated with the trait of **neuroticism,** which is heritable (Clark and others, 1994). Anxiety is also connected with neuroticism, and mood and anxiety disorders are frequently found in the same person (Clark and others, 1994).

Mood swings also tend to run in families (Wachtel, 1994), and there is a higher concordance rate for bipolar disorder among identical than fraternal twins (Goodwin & Jamison, 1990; D. N. Klein and others, 1985). It has been estimated that about 80% of the risk of bipolar disorder involves genetic factors (McGuffin & Katz, 1986).

Other researchers focus on the actions of the neurotransmitters serotonin and noradrenaline (Cooper and others, 1991; Michels & Marzuk, 1993b). Deficiencies in serotonin may create a general disposition toward mood disorders. Serotonin deficiency *combined with* noradrenaline deficiency may be linked with depression. People with severe depression often respond to antidepressant drugs that heighten the action of noradrenaline and serotonin. Also, the metal lithium, which is the major chemical treatment for bipolar disorder, apparently flattens out manic-depressive cycles by moderating levels of noradrenaline.

Many cases of depression may reflect the interaction of biological factors (such as neurotransmitters) and psychological factors (such as learned helplessness). For example, Seligman (1975) and Weiss (1982) found that dogs that learn that they are helpless to escape electric shocks also have less noradrenaline available to the brain. Helplessness is thus linked to low noradrenaline levels. The relationship might be a vicious cycle: A depressing situation may decrease the action of noradrenaline, and this chemical change may aggravate depression.

Relationships between mood disorders and biological factors are complex and under intense study. Even if people are biologically predisposed toward depression, self-efficacy expectations and attitudes—particularly attitudes about whether one can change things for the better—may also play a role.

Reflections

Now that you have read the section on mood disorders, reflect on the following questions:

- Do you think that you would find it easy or difficult to admit to having feelings of depression? Why?
- How would you distinguish between "normal" depression or "normal" enthusiasm and a mood disorder?
- Do you ever feel depressed? What kinds of experiences lead you to feel depressed? When you fall short of your goals, do you tend to be merciless in your self-criticism or to blame other people or "circumstances"? Do your views of your shortcomings tend to worsen or to ease your feelings of depression?
- Did you ever feel that there was nothing you could do to improve your situation or to solve a personal problem? How did the feeling that you could do nothing affect your mood?

Schizophrenia

Joyce was 19. Her husband Ron brought her into the emergency room because she had slit her wrists. When she was interviewed, her attention wandered. She seemed distracted by things in the air, or something she might be hearing. It was as if she had an invisible earphone.

She explained that she had cut her wrists because the "hellsmen" had told her to. Then she seemed frightened. Later she said that the hellsmen had warned her not to reveal their existence. She had been afraid that they would punish her for talking about them.

Ron told the emergency room staff that Joyce had been married to him for about a year. At first they had

Learned helplessness • A model for the acquisition of depressive behavior, based on findings that organisms in aversive situations learn to show inactivity when their operants go unreinforced.

Attributional style • (at-rib-BYOO-shun-al). One's tendency to attribute one's behavior to internal or external factors, stable or unstable factors, and so on.

Neuroticism • A personality trait characterized largely by persistent anxiety.

MINILECTURE:
DEFINING
SCHIZO-
PHRENIA

Delusions • False, persistent beliefs that are unsubstantiated by sensory or objective evidence.

Stupor • (STEW-pour). A condition in which the senses and thought are dulled.

Paranoid schizophrenia • A type of schizophrenia characterized primarily by delusions—commonly of persecution—and by vivid hallucinations.

Disorganized schizophrenia • A type of schizophrenia characterized by disorganized delusions and vivid hallucinations.

Catatonic schizophrenia • A type of schizophrenia characterized by striking impairment in motor activity.

been together in a small apartment in town. But Joyce did not want to be near other people and had convinced him to rent a bungalow in the country. There she would make fantastic drawings of goblins and monsters during the days. Now and then she would become agitated and act as if invisible things were giving her instructions.

"I'm bad," Joyce would mutter. "I'm bad." She would begin to jumble her words. Ron would then try to convince her to go to the hospital, but she would refuse. Then the wrist cutting would begin. Ron thought he had made the cottage safe by removing knives and blades. But Joyce would always find something.

Then Joyce would be brought to the hospital, have stitches put in, be kept under observation for a while, and medicated. She would explain that she cut herself because the hellsmen had told her that she was bad and must die. After a few days she would deny hearing the hellsmen, and she would insist on leaving the hospital.

Ron would take her home. The pattern continued.

When the emergency room staff examined Joyce's wrists and heard that she believed she had been following the orders of "hellsmen," they suspected that she could be diagnosed with schizophrenia. Schizophrenia touches every aspect of people's lives. Schizophrenia is characterized by disturbances in (1) thought and language, (2) perception and attention, (3) motor activity, and (4) mood, and by (5) withdrawal and absorption in daydreams or fantasy.

Schizophrenia has been referred to as the worst disorder affecting human beings (Carpenter & Buchanan, 1994). It afflicts nearly 1% of the population worldwide. Its onset is relatively early in life, and its adverse effects tend to endure. It has been estimated that one third to one half of the homeless people in the United States have schizophrenia (Bachrach, 1992).

Schizophrenia is known primarily by disturbances in thought, which are inferred from verbal and other behavior. Persons with schizophrenia may show loosening of

associations. Unless we are daydreaming or allowing our thoughts to wander, our thinking is normally tightly knit. We start at a certain point, and the things that come to mind (the associations) tend to be logically and coherently connected. But people with schizophrenia often think in an illogical, disorganized manner. Their speech may be jumbled. They may combine parts of words into new words or make rhymes in a meaningless fashion. People with schizophrenia may also jump from topic to topic, conveying little useful information. They usually have no insight that their thoughts and behavior are abnormal.

Many people with schizophrenia have **delusions**—for example, delusions of grandeur, persecution, or reference. In the case of delusions of grandeur, a person may believe, for example, that he is Jesus or a person on a special mission, or he may have grand, illogical plans for saving the world. Delusions tend to be unshakable, despite disconfirming evidence. Persons with delusions of persecution may believe that they are sought by the Mafia, CIA, FBI, or some other group or agency. A woman with delusions of reference expressed the belief that national news broadcasts contained coded information about her. A man with such delusions complained that neighbors had "bugged" his walls with "radios." Other people with schizophrenia may have delusions to the effect that they have committed unpardonable sins, that they are rotting away from a hideous disease, or that they or the world do not really exist.

The perceptions of people with schizophrenia often include hallucinations—imagery in the absence of external stimulation that the person cannot distinguish from reality. In Shakespeare's play, after the killing of King Duncan, feelings of guilt apparently cause Macbeth to hallucinate a knife:

Is this a dagger which I see before
  me,
The handle toward my hand? Come,
  let me clutch thee:
I have thee not, and yet I see thee
  still.
Art thou not, fatal vision, sensible
To feeling as to sight? or art thou but
A dagger of the mind, a false creation,
Proceeding from the heat-oppressed
  brain?

Macbeth is a fictional character, of course. Joyce, however, a true case study, apparently believed that she heard "hellsmen." Other hallucinators may see colors or even obscene words spelled out in midair. Auditory hallucinations are most common.

Motor activity may become wild and excited or may slow to a **stupor.** There may be strange gestures and peculiar facial expressions. Emotional response may be flat or blunted, or inappropriate—as in giggling at bad news. Research evidence suggests that many people with schizophrenia experience emotional responses but that their expression is inhibited (Kring and others, 1993). People with schizophrenia tend to withdraw from social contacts and become wrapped up in their own thoughts and fantasies.

TYPES OF SCHIZOPHRENIA

There are three major types of schizophrenia: paranoid, disorganized, and catatonic.

Paranoid Type. People with **paranoid schizophrenia** have systematized delusions and, frequently, related auditory hallucinations. They usually show delusions of grandeur and persecution, but they may also show delusions of jealousy, in which they believe that a spouse or lover has been unfaithful. They may show agitation, confusion, and fear, and may experience vivid hallucinations that are consistent with their delusions. The person with paranoid schizophrenia often constructs a complex or systematized delusion involving themes of wrongdoing or persecution.

The disorganized and catatonic subtypes are relatively rare (Andreasen, 1990).

Disorganized Type. People with **disorganized schizophrenia** show incoherence, loosening of associations, disorganized behavior, disorganized delusions, fragmentary delusions or hallucinations, and flat or highly inappropriate emotional responses. Extreme social impairment is common among people with disorganized schizophrenia. They may also show silliness and giddiness of mood, giggling, and nonsensical speech. They may neglect their appearance and hygiene and lose control of their bladder and their bowels. Emilio showed some of these behaviors:

A 40-year-old man who looks more like 30 is brought to the hospital by his mother, who reports that she is afraid of him. It is his twelfth hospitalization. He is dressed in a tattered overcoat, baseball cap, and bedroom slippers, and sports several medals around his neck. His affect ranges from anger (hurling obscenities at his mother) to giggling. He speaks with a childlike quality and walks with exaggerated hip movements and seems to measure each step very carefully. Since stopping his medication about a month ago, . . . he has been hearing voices and looking and acting more bizarrely. He tells the interviewer he has been "eating wires" and lighting fires. His speech is generally incoherent and frequently falls into rhyme. (Adapted from Spitzer and others, 1989, pp. 137–138)

Catatonic Type. People with **catatonic schizophrenia** show striking impairment in motor activity. Impairment is characterized by slowing of activity into a stupor that may change suddenly into an agitated phase. Catatonic individuals may hold unusual, even difficult postures for hours, even as their limbs grow swollen or

Paranoid Schizophrenia. People with paranoid schizophrenia hold systematized delusions, often involving ideas that they are being persecuted or are on a special mission. Although they cannot be argued out of their delusions, their cognitive functioning is relatively intact compared to that of people with disorganized or catatonic schizophrenia.

Catatonic Schizophrenia. People with catatonic schizophrenia show striking motor impairment and may hold unusual positions for hours at a time.

Waxy flexibility • A feature of catatonic schizophrenia in which persons maintain postures into which they are placed.

Mutism • (MU-tizm). Refusal to talk.

stiff. A striking feature is **waxy flexibility,** in which they maintain positions into which they have been manipulated by others. Catatonic individuals may also show **mutism,** but afterward they usually report that they heard what others were saying at the time.

People who show grossly psychotic characteristics such as hallucinations, delusions, incoherence, or disorganized behavior, but do not fit the definitions of these three types of schizophrenia, are considered to be of an undifferentiated type.

THEORETICAL VIEWS

Psychologists have investigated various factors that may contribute to schizophrenia.

Psychodynamic Views. According to the psychodynamic perspective, schizophrenia is the overwhelming of the ego by sexual or aggressive impulses from the id. The impulses threaten the ego and cause intense intrapsychic conflict. Under this threat, the person regresses to an early phase of the oral stage in which the infant has not yet learned that it and the world are separate.

Fantasies become confused with reality, giving birth to hallucinations and delusions. Primitive impulses may carry more weight than social norms.

Critics point out that schizophrenic behavior is not the same as infantile behavior. Moreover, psychoanalysts have not been able to predict schizophrenia on the basis of theoretically predisposing childhoods.

Learning Views. Learning theorists explain schizophrenia through conditioning and observational learning. From this perspective, people show schizophrenic behavior when it is more likely than normal behavior to be reinforced. This may occur when the person is reared in a socially unrewarding or punitive situation. Inner fantasies then become more reinforcing than social realities.

People in the psychiatric hospital may learn what is "expected" of them by observing others. Hospital staff may reinforce schizophrenic behavior by paying more attention to people who behave bizarrely. This view is consistent with folklore that the child who disrupts the class earns more attention from the teacher than the "good" child.

Critics note that many of us are reared in socially punitive settings but are apparently immune to extinction of socially appropriate behavior. Others develop schizophrenic behavior without the opportunity to observe other people with schizophrenia.

Sociocultural Views. Many investigators have considered whether and how social and cultural factors such as poverty, discrimination, and overcrowding contribute to schizophrenia—especially among people who are genetically vulnerable to schizophrenia. Some sociocultural theorists suggest that adequate "treatment" of schizophrenia requires changing society to eradicate social ills, rather than changing the person whose behavior is deviant. Such theorists point out that schizophrenia is most common among the lowest socioeconomic classes (e.g., Kety, 1980). A classic study in New Haven, Connecticut, showed that the rate of schizophrenia was twice as high in the lowest socioeconomic class as in the next class in the socioeconomic ladder (Hollingshead & Redlich, 1958).

Critics of this view suggest that low socioeconomic status may be a *consequence* and not an *antecedent* of schizophrenia. People with schizophrenia may drift downward in social status because they lack the social skills and cognitive abilities to function at higher levels. Thus, they may wind up in more impoverished areas in disproportionately high numbers.

Evidence for the hypothesis that people with schizophrenia drift downward in socioeconomic status is mixed (Nevid and others, 1994). Many people with schizophrenia do drift downward occupationally in comparison with their fathers' occupations. Many are also reared in families in which the fathers come from the lowest socioeconomic class, however. Because the stresses of poverty may play a role in the development of schizophrenia, many researchers are interested in the possible interactions of psychosocial stressors and biological factors (Carpenter & Buchanan, 1994).

Biological Risk Factors. Research has suggested that there are three biological risk factors for schizophrenia: heredity, complications during pregnancy and birth, and birth during the winter (Carpenter & Buchanan, 1994).

Schizophrenia, like many other psychological disorders, runs in families (Grove and others, 1991). People with schizophrenia constitute about 1% of the population. However, children with one parent diagnosed as schizophrenic have about a 10% chance of being diagnosed as schizophrenic themselves. Children with two such parents have about a 35–40% chance of doing so (Gottesman, 1991; Straube & Oades, 1992). Twin studies also find about a 40–50% concordance rate for the diagnosis among pairs of identical (MZ) twins, whose genetic codes are the same, as compared with about a 10% rate among pairs of fraternal (DZ) twins (Gottesman, 1991; Straube & Oades, 1992). Sharing genes with people who have schizophrenia apparently places one at risk.

However, these kinship studies did not generally control for environmental influences. Adoptee studies do, and they find that the biological parent typically places the child at greater risk than the adoptive

parent—even though the child has been reared by the adoptive parent (Gottesman, 1991; Carpenter & Buchanan, 1994).

Whereas evidence for a genetic role in schizophrenia seems strong, heredity cannot be the sole factor. If it were, we might expect a 100% concordance rate for schizophrenia between pairs of identical twins, as opposed to the 40–50% rate found in research (Carpenter & Buchanan, 1994). It also turns out that many people with schizophrenia have undergone complications during pregnancy and birth. For example, the mothers of many people who are diagnosed with schizophrenia had influenza during the sixth or seventh month of pregnancy (C. E. Barr and others, 1990; Sham and others, 1992; Torrey and others, 1992). Maternal starvation has also been implicated (Susser & Lin, 1992). Individuals diagnosed with schizophrenia are also somewhat more likely to be born during the winter than would be predicted by chance (Carpenter & Buchanan, 1994). Considered together, these three biological risk factors suggest that schizophrenia involves atypical development of the central nervous system (Bracha and others, 1992; Carpenter & Buchanan, 1994). As we see next, problems in the nervous system may involve neurotransmitters as well as the development of brain structures.

The Dopamine Theory of Schizophrenia. Over the years, much research has also been conducted into the chemistry of schizophrenia. Numerous chemical substances have been thought to play a role. Much current focus is on the neurotransmitter dopamine (Carpenter & Buchanan, 1994). According to the dopamine theory of schizophrenia, people with schizophrenia use more dopamine than other people, although they do not necessarily produce more of it. Why? They may have more dopamine receptors in the brain than other people, or their dopamine receptors may be hyperactive (Davis and others, 1991). Postmortem studies of the brains of people with schizophrenia have yielded evidence consistent with both possibilities.

Many researchers agree that dopamine plays a role in schizophrenia but argue that other neurotransmitters are also involved (Maas and others, 1993; van Kammen and

MINILECTURE:
CAUSES OF
SCHIZO-
PHRENIA

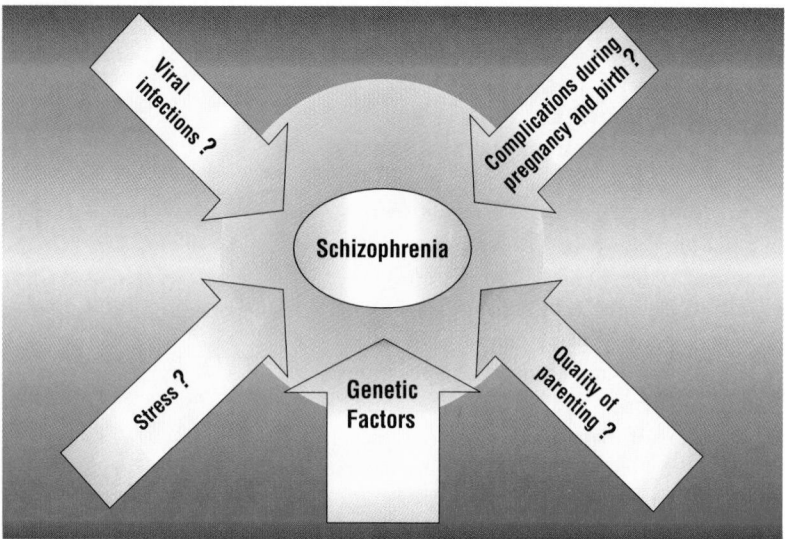

FIGURE 13.2

Spotlight on a Multifactorial Model of Schizophrenia According to the multifactorial model of schizophrenia, people with a genetic vulnerability to the disorder experience increased risk for the schizophrenia when they encounter problems such as viral infections, birth complications, stress, and poor parenting. People without a genetic vulnerability would not be at risk of developing schizophrenia, despite such problems.

Personality disorders • Enduring patterns of maladaptive behavior that are sources of distress to the individual or others.

Paranoid personality disorder • A disorder characterized by persistent suspiciousness, but not involving the disorganization of paranoid schizophrenia.

Schizotypal personality disorder • A disorder characterized by oddities of thought and behavior, but not involving bizarre psychotic behaviors.

Schizoid personality disorder • A disorder characterized by social withdrawal.

others, 1990). Supportive evidence is found in the fact that drugs that act on dopamine alone are not always effective in the treatment of schizophrenia (Carpenter & Buchanan, 1994).

Because so many psychological and biological factors have been implicated in schizophrenia, most investigators today favor a *multifactorial* model of schizophrenia. According to this model, genetic factors create a predisposition toward schizophrenia (see Figure 13.2). A genetic vulnerability to the disorder then interacts with other factors such as viral infections, complications during pregnancy and birth, stress, and the quality of parenting to produce the disorder (Michels & Marzuk, 1993a; Gottesman, 1991).

Reflections

Now that you have read the section on schizophrenia, reflect on the following questions:

• Have you ever heard the expression "split personality"? Does the expression seem to apply more to dissociative identity disorder or schizophrenia? Why?

• Had you heard of hallucinations or delusions before reading this section? Did your impressions of the meanings of these words match the descriptions in the text? What were the differences?

• Can you imagine what it might be like to have schizophrenia? Can you imagine why it might be frightening not to be able to distinguish between reality and hallucinations?

Personality Disorders

Personality disorders, like personality traits, are characterized by enduring patterns of behavior. Personality disorders, however, are inflexible and maladaptive. They impair personal or social functioning and are a source of distress to the individual or to other people (Widiger & Costa, 1994).

TYPES OF PERSONALITY DISORDERS

There are a number of personality disorders, including the paranoid, schizotypal, schizoid, antisocial, and avoidant personality disorders. The defining trait of the **paranoid personality disorder** is the tendency to interpret other people's behavior as threatening or demeaning. Persons with the disorder do not show grossly disorganized thinking. However, they are mistrustful of others, and their social relationships suffer for it. They may be suspicious of coworkers and supervisors, but they can generally hold onto jobs.

Schizotypal personality disorder is characterized by peculiarities in thought, perception, and behavior such as excessive fantasy and suspiciousness, feelings of being unreal, or odd usage of words. The bizarre behaviors that characterize schizophrenia are absent, so this disorder is schizo*typal,* not schizophrenic. Because of their oddities, persons with the disorder are often maladjusted on the job.

The **schizoid personality** is defined by indifference to relationships and flat emotional response. People with schizoid personality are "loners." They do not develop warm, tender feelings for others. They have

TABLE 13.3

Characteristics of People Diagnosed
with Antisocial Personality Disorder

Persistent violation of the rights of others	Persistent lying
Irresponsibility	Sexual promiscuity
Lack of loyalty or of formation of enduring relationships	Substance abuse
Failure to maintain good job performance over the years	Impulsivity
Failure to develop or adhere to a life plan	Glibness; superficial charm
History of truancy	Exaggerated sense of self-worth
History of delinquency	Inability to tolerate boredom
History of running away	At least 18 years of age

Sources: Hare and others, 1991; Harris and others, 1994; White and others, 1994.

Antisocial personality disorder • The diagnosis given a person who is in frequent conflict with society, yet who is undeterred by punishment and experiences little or no guilt and anxiety.

Avoidant personality disorder • A personality disorder in which the person is generally unwilling to enter relationships without assurance of acceptance because of fears of rejection and criticism.

few friends and rarely get married. Some people with schizoid personality do very well on the job, as long as continuous social interaction is not required. Hallucinations and delusions are absent.

Persons with **antisocial personality disorder** persistently violate the rights of others and are in conflict with the law (see Table 13.3). They often show a superficial charm and are at least average in intelligence. Striking features are their lack of guilt or anxiety about their misdeeds and their failures to learn from punishment and form meaningful bonds with other people (Widiger, 1990). Though they are often heavily punished by parents and rejected by peers for their misconduct, they carry on their impulsive, careless styles of life (Patterson, 1993; White and others, 1994). Many people with antisocial personality disorder are also alcoholic (Sher & Trull, 1994). Whereas women are more likely than men to have anxiety and depressive disorders, men are more likely to have antisocial personality disorder (Russo, 1990b).

People with **avoidant personality disorder** are generally unwilling to enter relationships without assurance of acceptance because of fear of rejection and criticism. As a result, they may have few close relationships outside their immediate families. Unlike people with schizoid personality, however, people with avoidant personality have interest in, and feelings of warmth toward, other people.

THEORETICAL VIEWS

Many of the theoretical accounts of personality disorders derive from the psychodynamic model. Traditional Freudian theory focuses on Oedipal problems as the foundation for many psychological disorders, including personality disorders. Faulty resolution of the Oedipus complex might lead to antisocial personality disorder since the moral conscience, or superego, is believed to depend on proper resolution of the Oedipus complex. Research concurs with psychodynamic theory that lack of guilt, as found among people with antisocial personality disorder, is more likely to develop

People with Antisocial Personalities. Some people with antisocial personalities fit the stereotype of the amoral, violent career criminal. Gary Gilmore (left) was executed after being convicted of two murders. As a child, Gilmore showed conduct problems at home and in school. He began a violent career in adolescence. He never held a steady job or maintained a committed relationship. Though he was intentionally cruel, he never showed guilt or remorse for his misdeeds. As the fictional corporate raider Gordon Gekko in the film *Wall Street,* Michael Douglas (right) lied and cheated to gain insider information that enabled him to make millions and break up companies for a profit. Motivated by the dollar sign, Gekko had no feelings for the thousands of workers he dispossessed.

among children who receive parental rejection and punishment rather than warmth and affection (Baumeister and others, 1994; Zahn-Waxler & Kochanska, 1990). Psychodynamic theory proposed that men were more likely to experience feelings of guilt than women because men were subjected to the throes of the Oedipus complex. However, empirical research shows that women are more likely than men to feel guilty about moral transgressions (Baumeister and others, 1994; Tangney, 1990). Men, by contrast, are more likely to fear being caught.

Learning theorists suggest that childhood experiences can contribute to maladaptive ways of relating to others (personality disorders) in adulthood. Cognitive psychologists find that antisocial adolescents encode social information in ways that bolster their misdeeds. For example, they tend to interpret other people's behavior as threatening, even when it is not (Crick & Dodge, 1994; Dodge and others, 1990; Lochman, 1992). Cognitive therapists have encouraged some antisocial adolescents to view social provocations as problems to be solved rather than as threats to their "manhood," with some favorable initial results (Lochman, 1992).

From a trait-theory perspective, Widiger and Costa (1994) note that many personality disorders seem to be extreme variations of normal personality traits. Referring to the Big Five model of personality, they note that people with schizoid personalities tend to be highly introverted. People with avoidant personalities tend to be both introverted and emotionally unstable (neurotic).

Genetic factors may be involved in some personality disorders (Nigg & Goldsmith, 1994). For example, antisocial personality disorder tends to run in families. Adoptee studies reveal higher incidences of antisocial behavior among the biological than the adoptive relatives of persons with the disorder (Cloninger & Gottesman, 1987). There is also evidence that genetic influences are moderate at best. The family environment also contributes to antisocial behavior (Carey, 1992).

If there are genetic factors in antisocial personality disorder, they may influence the individual's characteristic level of arousal of the nervous system. Consider that antisocial

personality disorder is characterized by deficiency in self-control (Sher & Trull, 1994). People with the disorder are unlikely to show guilt for their misdeeds or to be deterred by punishment. Low levels of guilt and anxiety may reflect lower-than-normal levels of arousal, which, in turn, may have a partial genetic basis (Lykken, 1982). Experiments show that people with antisocial personality disorder do not learn as rapidly as others equal in intelligence when the payoff is avoidance of impending electric shock. But when their levels of arousal are increased by injections of adrenaline, they learn to avoid punishment as rapidly as others (Schachter & Latané, 1964; Chesno & Kilmann, 1975). Patrick and his colleagues (1993) found that people with antisocial personality disorder did not show a startle response to unpleasant slides that included mutilated people and snakes. This finding provides additional evidence that antisocial personality disorder is connected with a deficit in the biological systems that regulate fear.

A lower-than-normal level of arousal would not ensure the development of an antisocial personality. Perhaps a person must also be reared under conditions that do not foster the self-concept of a law-abiding citizen. Punishment for deviant behavior would then be unlikely to induce feelings of guilt and shame. The individual might well be "undeterred" by punishment.

Reflections

Now that you have read the section on personality disorders, reflect on the following questions:

- Agree or disagree with the following statement and support your answer: "Criminals have antisocial personality disorder."
- Do you know some people whom you consider to have "bad personalities"? How does the term "bad personality" differ from the diagnosis of personality disorder?

Eating Disorders

Most of us deprive ourselves or consume vast quantities of food now and then. The **eating disorders** listed in the DSM are

Eating disorders • Psychological disorders that are characterized by distortion of the body image and gross disturbances in eating patterns.

Anorexia nervosa • A life-threatening eating disorder characterized by refusal to maintain a healthful body weight, intense fear of being overweight, a distorted body image, and, in females, lack of menstruation (amenorrhea.)

characterized by persistent, gross disturbances in eating patterns, however.

TYPES OF EATING DISORDERS

The eating disorders include anorexia nervosa and bulimia nervosa.

Anorexia Nervosa. There is a saying that you can never be too rich or too thin. Excess money may be pleasant enough, but as in the case of Karen, one can certainly be too thin.

> Karen was the 22-year-old daughter of a renowned English professor. She had begun her college career full of promise at the age of 17. But two years ago, after "social problems" occurred, she had returned to live at home and taken progressively lighter course loads at a local college. Karen had never been overweight, but about a year ago her mother noticed that she seemed to be gradually "turning into a skeleton."
>
> Karen spent hours every day shopping at the supermarket, butcher, and bakeries; and in conjuring up gourmet treats for her parents and younger siblings. Arguments over her lifestyle and eating habits had divided the family into two camps. The camp led by her father called for patience. That headed by her mother demanded confrontation. Her mother feared that Karen's father would "protect her right into her grave" and wanted Karen placed in residential treatment "for her own good." The parents finally compromised on an outpatient evaluation.
>
> At an even 5 feet, Karen looked like a prepubescent 11-year-old. Her nose and cheekbones protruded crisply, like those of an elegant young fashion model. Her lips were full, but the redness of the lipstick was unnatural, as if too much paint had been dabbed on a corpse for the funeral. Karen weighed only 78 pounds, but she had dressed in a stylish silk blouse, scarf, and baggy pants so that not one inch of her body was revealed. More striking than her mouth was the redness of her rouged cheeks. It was unclear whether she had used too much makeup or whether minimal makeup had caused the stark contrast between the parts of her face that were covered and those that were not.
>
> Karen vehemently denied that she had a problem. Her figure was "just about where I want it to be" and she engaged in aerobic exercise daily. A deal was struck in which outpatient treatment would be tried as long as Karen lost no more weight and showed steady gains back to at least 90 pounds. Treatment included a day hospital with group therapy and two meals a day. But word came back that Karen was artfully toying with her food—cutting it up, sort of licking it, and moving it about her plate—rather than eating it. After three weeks Karen had lost another pound. At that point her parents were able to persuade her to enter a residential treatment program where her eating behavior could be more carefully monitored. (Nevid and others, 1994, p. 519)

Karen was diagnosed with **anorexia nervosa,** a life-threatening disorder characterized by refusal to maintain a healthful body weight, intense fear of being overweight, a distorted body image, and, in females, lack of menstruation (amenorrhea.) People with anorexia usually weigh less than 85% of their expected body weight.

By and large, eating disorders afflict women during adolescence and young adulthood (Levine, 1987). Nearly 1 in 200 school-aged girls has trouble gaining or maintaining weight. The incidences of anorexia nervosa and bulimia nervosa have increased markedly in recent years (Strober, 1986). Women with anorexia greatly outnumber men with the disorder, as noted in the following "Psychology in a World of Diversity" feature.

Women with anorexia may drop 25% or more of their body weight in a year. Severe weight loss triggers amenorrhea. Their general health declines.

Truth or Fiction Revisited. *The statement that "You can never be too rich or too thin" is false.* I won't pass judgment on whether or not you can be too rich. You can clearly be too thin, however. About 4% of women with anorexia die from related problems such as weakness or imbalances in body chemistry (Herzog and others, 1988).

In the typical pattern, girls notice some weight gain after menarche and decide that it must come off. However, dieting—and, often, exercise—continue at a fever pitch. They persist after girls reach average body weights, even after family members and others have told them that they are losing too much. Girls with anorexia almost always adamantly deny that they are wasting away. They may point to their fierce exercise regimens as proof. Their body images are distorted (Williamson and others, 1993). Penner and his colleagues (1991) studied women who averaged 31% below their ideal body weights, according to Metropolitan Life Insurance Company charts. The women, ironically, overestimated the size of parts of their bodies by 31%! Whereas others perceive women with anorexia as "skin and bones," the women frequently sit before the mirror and see themselves as heavy.

Many people with anorexia become obsessed with food. They are constantly around it. They may engross themselves in cookbooks, take on the family shopping chores, and prepare elaborate dinners for others.

Bulimia nervosa • An eating disorder characterized by recurrent cycles of binge eating followed by dramatic measures to purge the food.

PSYCHOLOGY IN A WORLD OF DIVERSITY

EATING DISORDERS: WHY THE GENDER GAP?

The typical person with anorexia or bulimia is a young White female of higher socioeconomic status, although anorexia is also becoming more prevalent among other ethnic groups and older age groups (Mitchell & Eckert, 1987). Women with eating disorders vastly outnumber men with them.

Theorists account for the gender gap in different ways. Because anorexia is connected with amenorrhea, some psychodynamic theorists suggest that anorexia represents an effort by the girl to remain prepubescent. Anorexia allows the girl to avoid growing up, separating from the

family, and assuming adult responsibilities. Because of the loss of fatty deposits, her breasts and hips flatten. In their fantasies, perhaps, women with anorexia remain children, sexually undifferentiated.

Cognitive-behavioral approaches suggest that weight loss acquires its powerful reinforcement value because of a combination of feelings of personal perfectibility and the cultural idealization of the slender female (Vitousek & Manke, 1994). Brenner (1992) notes that female models, who tend to represent the female ideal, are 9% taller and 16% slimmer than the average woman. Sixteen percent! For most women, that is at least 16 pounds!

Consider the sociocultural aspects of eating disorders: As the cultural ideal grows slimmer, women with average or heavier-than-average figures come under more pressure to control their weight (Bordo, 1993; Wolf, 1991). Agras and Kirkley (1986) documented the interest in losing weight by counting the numbers of diet articles printed in three women's magazines since the year 1900: *Ladies' Home Journal, Good Housekeeping,* and *Harper's Bazaar.* Diet articles were absent until the 1930s. During the 1930s and 1940s, only about one article appeared in every 10 issues. During the 1950s and 1960s, the number of diet articles jumped to about one in every other issue. During the 1980s, however, the number mushroomed to about 1.3 articles per issue. This means that in recent years, there has been an average of *more than one* diet article per issue!

Bulimia Nervosa. The case of Nicole provides a vivid account of a young woman diagnosed with **bulimia nervosa:**

Nicole awakens in her cold dark room and already wishes it was time to go back to bed. She dreads the thought of going through this day, which will be like so many others in her recent past. She asks herself the question every morning, "Will I be able to make it through the day without being totally obsessed by thoughts of food, or will I blow it again and spend the day [binge eating]?" She tells herself that today she will begin a new life, today she will start to live like a normal human being. However, she is not at all convinced that the choice is hers. (Boskind-White & White, 1983, p. 29)

It turns out that this day Nicole begins by eating eggs and toast. Then she binges on cookies; doughnuts; bagels smothered with butter, cream cheese, and jelly; granola; candy bars; and bowls of cereal and milk—all within 45 minutes. When she cannot take in any more food, she turns her attention to purging what she has eaten. She goes to the bathroom, ties back her hair, turns on the shower to mask any noise she will make, drinks a glass of water, and makes herself vomit. Afterward she vows, "Starting tomorrow, I'm going to change." But she knows that tomorrow it will probably be the same story.

Truth or Fiction Revisited. *It is true that some college women control their weight by going on cycles of binge eating followed by self-induced vomiting.* Many other women do so as well. People who behave in this way are diagnosed with bulimia nervosa. Bulimia nervosa is defined as recurrent cycles of binge eating followed by dramatic measures to purge the food. Binge eating frequently follows food deprivation, as through severe dieting (Polivy and others, 1994). A binge involves eating much larger-than-normal quantities of food and a sense of loss of control over eating (Wilson & Walsh, 1991). Purging includes self-induced vomiting, fasting or strict dieting, use of laxatives, and vigorous exercise. As with anorexia, there is overconcern about body shape and weight (Gleaves and others, 1993). Like anorexia, bulimia afflicts many more women than men.

On a Binge. Bulimia nervosa is defined as recurrent cycles of binge eating and the taking of dramatic measures, such as self-induced vomiting, to purge the food. Many more women than men are afflicted with the eating disorders of anorexia nervosa and bulimia nervosa.

THEORETICAL VIEWS

Numerous explanations of anorexia nervosa and bulimia nervosa have been advanced. Some psychoanalysts suggest that anorexia represents an unconscious effort by the girl to cope with sexual fears, particularly the prospect of pregnancy. Others suggest that adolescents may use refusal to eat as a weapon against their parents. One study compared mothers of adolescents with eating disorders with mothers of adolescents without such problems. Mothers of adolescents with eating disorders were relatively more likely to be unhappy with their families' functioning, to have problems with eating and dieting themselves, to think that their daughters should lose weight, and to consider their daughters unattractive (Pike & Rodin, 1991). The researchers speculate that some adolescents develop eating disorders as ways of coping with feelings of loneliness and alienation they experience in the home. Could binge eating, as suggested by Humphrey (1986), symbolize the effort to gain parental nurturance and comfort? Could purging be a symbolic ridding oneself of negative feelings toward the family?

Other psychologists view anorexia as an excessive fear of gaining weight that derives from cultural idealization of the slender female. This ideal may contribute to distortion of the body image.

Reflections

Now that you have read the section on eating disorders, reflect on the following questions:

- Are you happy with your body shape? Do you feel pressure to be thinner than you are? Why or why not?
- Consider your sociocultural background. Are women from this background traditionally expected to be well-rounded in

shape or slender? What attitudes are connected with weight and body shape within your traditions?

Sexual Dysfunctions

Sexual dysfunctions involve persistent difficulty in becoming sexually aroused or reaching orgasm. Millions of Americans are troubled by sexual dysfunctions (Spector & Carey, 1990). Many readers—or their partners—will be troubled by a sexual dysfunction at one time or another.

TYPES OF SEXUAL DYSFUNCTIONS

The sexual dysfunctions include hypoactive sexual desire disorder, female sexual arousal disorder, male erectile disorder, orgasmic disorder, premature ejaculation, dyspareunia, and vaginismus.

In **hypoactive sexual desire disorder,** a person lacks interest in sexual activity and frequently reports an absence of sexual fantasies. The diagnosis exists because of the assumption that sexual fantasies and interests are normal responses that may be blocked by anxiety or other factors.

In women, sexual arousal is characterized by lubrication of the vaginal walls that facilitates entry by the penis. Sexual arousal in men is characterized by erection. Almost all women now and then have difficulty becoming or remaining lubricated. Almost all men have occasional difficulty attaining or maintaining an erection through intercourse. These events are considered dysfunctions (**female sexual arousal disorder** and **male erectile disorder**) when they are persistent or recurrent.

In **orgasmic disorder,** the man or woman, although sexually excited, is persistently delayed in reaching orgasm or does not reach orgasm at all. Orgasmic disorder is more common among women than men. In **premature ejaculation,** the male persistently ejaculates with minimal sexual stimulation, too soon to permit his partner or himself to enjoy sexual relations fully. Other dysfunctions include **dyspareunia** and **vaginismus.**

The Importance of Communication. Sexual relationships are usually no better than other aspects of relationships. Communication problems are linked to sexual as well as general marital dissatisfaction. Sex therapists help couples open lines of communication.

THEORETICAL VIEWS

Some sexual dysfunctions reflect biological problems. Lack of desire, for example, can reflect diabetes and diseases of the heart and lungs. Fatigue can dampen sexual desire and inhibit orgasm. Depressants such as alcohol, narcotics, and tranquilizers can also impair sexual response. Physical factors can interact with psychological factors. For instance, dyspareunia can heighten anxiety, and extremes of anxiety can dampen sexual arousal.

Physically or psychologically painful sexual experiences, such as rape, can block future sexual response (Koss, 1993). A sexual relationship is usually no better than other aspects of a relationship or marriage. Couples who have problems communicating are at a disadvantage in expressing their sexual desires.

Cognitive psychologists point out that irrational beliefs and attitudes can contribute to sexual dysfunctions (Ellis, 1987). If we believe that we need a lover's approval at all times, we may catastrophize the importance of one disappointing sexual episode. If we demand that each sexual encounter be perfect, we set ourselves up for inevitable failure.

In most cases of sexual dysfunction, the physical and psychological factors we have outlined lead to yet another psychological factor—**performance anxiety,** or fear of whether we shall be able to perform sexually. People with performance anxiety may focus on recollections of past failures and expectations of another disaster rather than enjoy erotic sensations and fantasies (Barlow, 1986). Performance anxiety can make it difficult for a man to attain erection, yet spur him to ejaculate prematurely. Performance anxiety can also prevent a woman from becoming adequately lubricated or can contribute to vaginismus.

Truth or Fiction Revisited. *It is not necessarily true that people who truly love each* other enjoy the sexual aspects of their relationships. The statement is too broad to be true. Sexual dysfunctions can occur even when the relationship is loving. Fortunately there are treatments for sexual dysfunctions—referred to as sex therapy—and a good overall relationship between sex partners facilitates therapy.

Sex therapy is largely indebted to the pioneering work of Masters and Johnson (1970), although other therapists have also innovated many important techniques. Sex therapy generally focuses on (1) reducing performance anxiety, (2) changing self-defeating expectations, and (3) fostering sexual skills or competencies. Readers who are interested in learning more about sex therapy are advised to consult a human sexuality textbook, contact their state's psychological association, or ask their professors or college counseling centers for referral.

Reflections

Now that you have read the section on sexual dysfunctions, reflect on the following questions:

- Consider your sociocultural background once more. Are women from this background traditionally expected to derive as much pleasure or satisfaction from sex as men are? Why or why not?
- Do sexual dysfunctions seem to be things that can or can't happen to you? Why?
- How is it that a negative sexual experience could lead to a sexual dysfunction? Can you offer an example?

Although the causes of many psychological disorders remain in dispute, a number of therapy methods have been devised to deal with them. Those methods are the focus of Chapter 14.

Sexual dysfunctions • Persistent problems in becoming sexually aroused or reaching orgasm.

Hypoactive sexual desire disorder • A sexual dysfunction characterized by lack of interest in sexual activity.

Female sexual arousal disorder • A sexual dysfunction characterized by difficulty in becoming sexually aroused, as defined by vaginal lubrication, or in sustaining arousal long enough to engage in satisfying sexual relations.

Male erectile disorder • A sexual dysfunction characterized by difficulty in becoming sexually aroused, as defined by achieving erection, or in sustaining arousal long enough to engage in satisfying sexual relations.

Orgasmic disorder • A sexual dysfunction in which one has difficulty reaching orgasm, although one is sexually aroused.

Premature ejaculation • Ejaculation that occurs prior to the couple's desires.

Dyspareunia • Painful sex.

Vaginismus • Involuntary contraction of the muscles surrounding the vagina, which makes entry difficult or impossible.

Performance anxiety • Fear about whether one will be able to perform adequately.

Summary

1. **What are psychological disorders?** Psychological disorders are characterized by unusual behavior, socially unacceptable behavior, faulty perception of reality, personal distress, dangerous behavior, or self-defeating behavior.

2. **How are psychological disorders classified?** The most commonly used system for classifying psychological disorders is the Diagnostic and Statistical Manual (DSM-IV) of the American Psychiatric Association. The DSM-IV is a "multiaxial" system with five axes. The axes assess clinical syndromes, personality disorders, general medical conditions, psychosocial and environmental problems, and global assessment of functioning.

3. **What are anxiety disorders?** Anxiety disorders are characterized by motor tension, feelings of dread, and overarousal of the sympathetic branch of the autonomic nervous system. Anxiety disorders include irrational, excessive fears, or phobias; panic disorder, which is characterized by sudden attacks in which people typically fear that they may be losing control or going crazy; generalized anxiety; obsessive–compulsive disorders, in which people are troubled by intrusive thoughts or impulses to repeat some activity; and post-traumatic stress disorder (PTSD), in which a stressful event is followed by persistent fears and intrusive thoughts about the event.

4. **How do psychologists explain anxiety disorders?** Psychoanalysts tend to view anxiety disorders as representing problems in maintaining repression of primitive impulses. Many learning theorists view phobias as conditioned fears. Cognitive theorists focus on ways in which people interpret threats. People may also be genetically predisposed to acquire certain kinds of fears. Anxiety disorders tend to run in families, and some psychologists suggest that biochemical factors that create a predisposition toward anxiety disorders may be inherited.

5. **What are dissociative disorders?** Dissociative disorders are characterized by sudden temporary changes in consciousness or self-identity. They include dissociative amnesia, or "motivated forgetting" of personal information; dissociative fugue, which involves forgetting plus fleeing and adopting a new identity; dissociative identity disorder (multiple personality), in which a person behaves as if more than one personality occupies the body; and depersonalization, which is characterized by feelings that one is not real or that one is standing outside oneself.

6. **What are somatoform disorders?** People with somatoform disorders show or complain of physical problems, although no medical evidence can be found. The somatoform disorders include conversion disorder and hypochondria.

7. **What are mood disorders?** Mood disorders are characterized by disturbances in expressed emotions. Major depression is characterized by persistent feelings of sadness, loss of interest, feelings of worthlessness or guilt, inability to concentrate, and physical features that may include disturbances in the regulation of eating and sleeping. Feelings of unworthiness and guilt may be so excessive that they are considered delusional. In bipolar disorder, there are mood swings between elation and depression.

8. **How do psychologists explain mood disorders?** Research emphasizes possible roles for learned helplessness, attributional styles, and neurotransmitters in depression. People who are depressed are more likely than other people to make internal, stable, and global attributions for failures. It might be that a deficiency in the neurotransmitter serotonin creates a predisposition toward mood disorders. A concurrent deficiency of noradrenaline might contribute to depression, whereas a concurrent excess of noradrenaline might contribute to manic behavior.

9. **What is schizophrenia?** Schizophrenia is characterized by disturbances in (1) thought and language, such as loosening of associations and delusions; (2) perception and attention, as found in hallucinations; (3) motor activity, as shown by a stupor or by excited behavior; and (4) mood, as in flat or inappropriate emotional responses. It is also characterized by withdrawal and absorption in daydreams or fantasy.

10. **How do psychologists explain schizophrenia?** There is a tendency for schizophrenia to run in families, suggestive of genetic factors. According to the dopamine theory, people with schizophrenia may utilize more dopamine than people without the disorder do because of a greater-than-normal number of dopamine receptors in the brain. People with schizophrenia may also have relatively greater sensitivity to dopamine. Multifactorial approaches view schizophrenia in terms of the interaction of psychological and biological factors.

11. **What are personality disorders?** Personality disorders are inflexible, maladaptive behavior patterns that impair personal or social functioning and are a source of distress to the individual or others. The defining trait of paranoid personality disorder is suspiciousness. Persons with schizotypal personality disorders show oddities of thought, perception, and behavior. Social withdrawal is the major characteristic of schizoid personality disorder. Persons with antisocial personality disorders persistently violate the rights of others and encounter conflict with the law. They show little or no guilt or shame over their misdeeds and are largely undeterred by punishment.

12. **How do psychologists explain antisocial personality disorder?** Research suggests that antisocial personality disorder may develop from some combination of inconsistent discipline, an antisocial father, cynical processing of social information, and lower-than-normal levels of arousal, which would help explain why persons with the disorder are undeterred by punishment.

13. **What are the eating disorders?** The eating disorders include anorexia nervosa and bulimia nervosa. Anorexia is characterized by refusal to eat and extreme thinness. Bulimia is characterized by cycles of binge eating and purging. Women are more likely than men to have these disorders.

14. **How do psychologists explain eating disorders?** Although there are psychodynamic explanations of the eating disorders, most psychologists look to cultural idealization of the very slender female as a major contributor.

15. **What are sexual dysfunctions?** Sexual dysfunctions are problems in becoming sexually aroused or reaching orgasm. Dysfunctions include lack of sexual desire, female sexual arousal disorder, male erectile disorder, orgasmic disorder, premature ejaculation, dyspareunia, and vaginismus.

16. **What are the causes of sexual dysfunctions?** Sexual dysfunctions now and then reflect physical factors, such as disease, but most reflect psychosocial factors such as psychosexual trauma, troubled relationships, and irrational beliefs. Any of these may lead to performance anxiety, which compounds sexual problems.

Psychology
and
Modern
Life

College students have so much to live for, so many possibilities. Possibilities of learning, of love, of appreciation of the arts, of a meaningful career, of parenthood, of travel—of distant experiences shrouded in mystery and allure. Yet about 10,000 college students attempt suicide each year. Although college students would seem to have "everything to live for," suicide is more common among college students than among nonstudents.

In this "Psychology and Modern Life" feature, we consider the distressing problem of suicide. We will see that it affects people of all age groups, of all socioeconomic backgrounds. Psychologists have learned much about why people commit suicide and have also devised ways of helping people who are considering suicide. Unfortunately, psychologists cannot always be there.

Suicide

We have seen that college students are at greater risk of committing suicide than are nonstudents. Consider some other facts about suicide:

- Three times as many women as men attempt suicide, but about four times as many men succeed (see Figure 13.3; Rich and others, 1988; CDC, 1985a).

- Men prefer to use guns or hang themselves, but women prefer to use sleeping pills. Males, that is, tend to use quicker and more lethal means. A study of 204 San Diego County suicides found that males were more likely to use guns (60% of the males versus 28% of the females) (Rich and others, 1988). Females more often used drugs or poisons (44% of the females versus 11% of the males).

- Although African Americans are more likely than White Americans to live in poverty and suffer from discrimination, the suicide rate is about twice as high among White Americans (Figure 13.3).

- One in four Native American teenagers has attempted suicide—a rate that is four times higher than that of other U.S. teenagers (Resnick and others, 1992). Among Zuni adolescents of New Mexico, the rate of completed suicides is more than twice the national rate (Howard-Pitney and others, 1992).

- Teenage suicides loom large in the media spotlight, but older people are actually much more likely to commit suicide (Richman, 1993; Figure 13.4). The suicide rate among older people is nearly twice the national rate.

All in all, about 30,000 people each year take their lives in the United States (Michels & Marzuk, 1993a). Most suicides are linked to feelings of depression and hopelessness (Beck and others, 1990; Lewinsohn and others, 1994a, 1994b). Suicidal people find life more dull, empty, and boring than do nonsuicidal people. They feel more anxious, excitable, submissive, angry, guilt-ridden, helpless, and inadequate. Among Native American Zuni adolescents in New Mexico, drug abuse, problems in school, and problems in communicating with other people are also connected with suicide (Howard-Pitney and others, 1992). UCLA suicide scholar Edwin Shneidman (1985, 1987) notes that suicide attempters

FIGURE 13.3
Suicide Rates According to Gender and Ethnicity Men are more likely than women to commit suicide. Women, however, make more suicide attempts. How can we account for this discrepancy? White people are also more likely to commit suicide than African Americans.

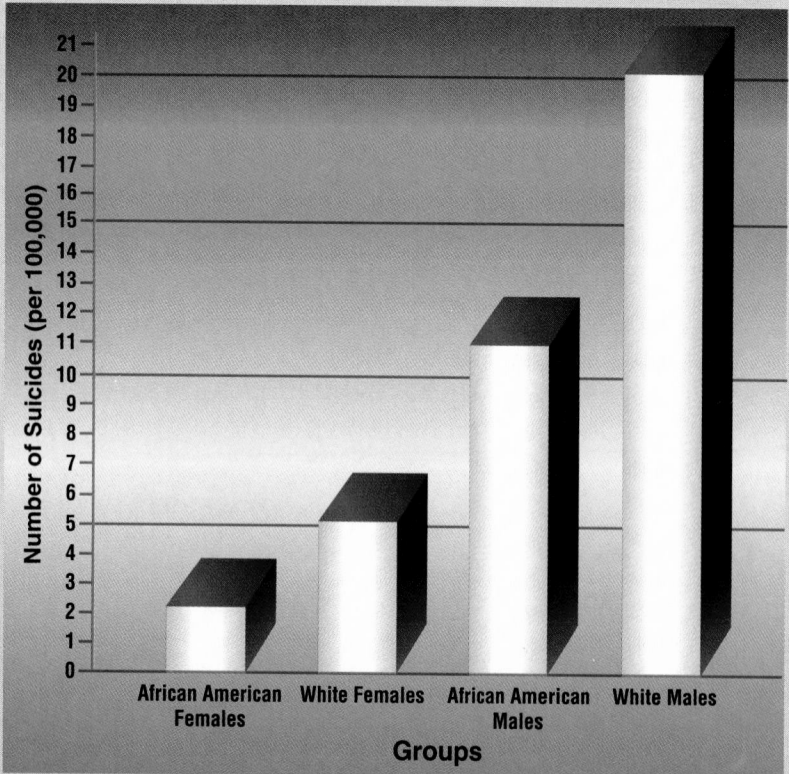

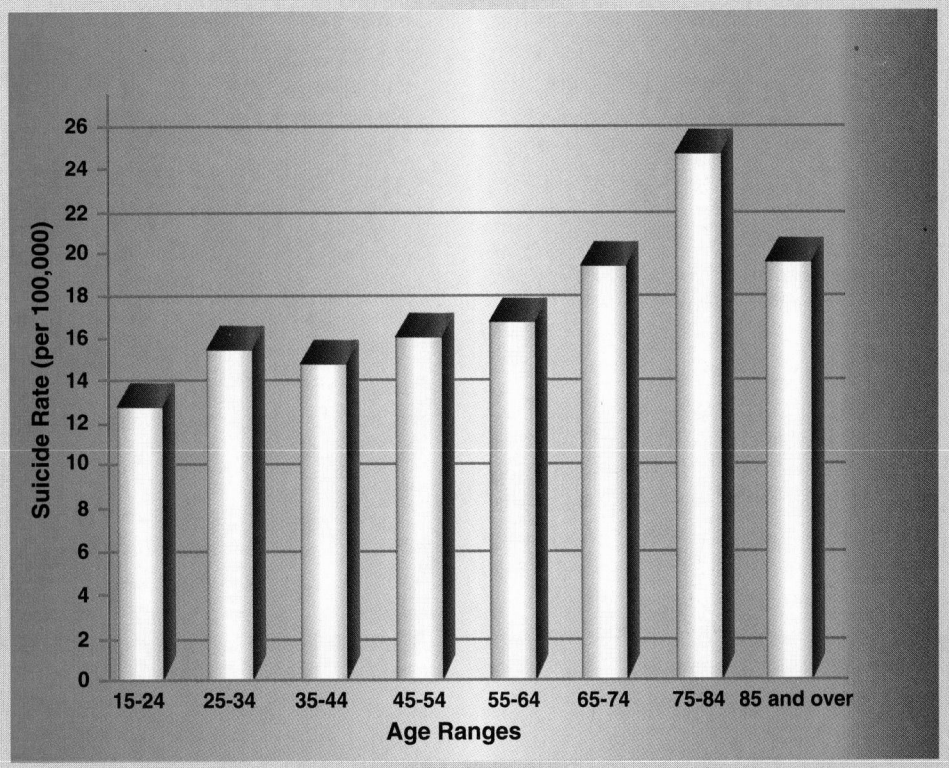

FIGURE 13.4
Suicide Rates According to Age
Older people (aged 65 and above) are more likely to commit suicide than the young and the middle-aged, yet suicide is the second leading cause of death among college students.

are usually trying to end extreme psychological anguish.

Suicide attempts are more frequent following stressful events, especially events that entail loss of social support—as in the loss of a spouse, friend, or relative. People under stress who consider suicide have been found to be less capable of solving problems—particularly interpersonal problems—than nonsuicidal people (Rotheram-Borus and others, 1990; Sadowski & Kelley, 1993; Schotte and others, 1990). Suicidal people are thus less likely to find productive ways of changing the stressful situation.

Suicide, like so many other psychological problems, tends to run in families. Nearly one in four people who attempts suicide reports that a family member has committed suicide (Sorensen & Rutter, 1991). Psychological disorders among family members may also make a contribution (Sorensen & Rutter, 1991; Wilson, 1991). The causal connections are unclear, however. Do suicide attempters inherit disorders that can lead to suicide? Does the family environment subject several family members to feelings of hopelessness? Does the suicide of a family member give one the idea of committing suicide or create the impression that

one is somehow fated to commit suicide? Perhaps these possibilities and others—such as poor problem-solving ability—form a complex web of contributory factors.

Myths about Suicide. Some believe that people who threaten suicide are only seeking attention. The serious just "do it." Actually, most people who commit suicide give clear clues concerning their intentions (Nevid and others, 1994).

Truth or Fiction Revisited. *It is not true that people who threaten suicide are only seeking attention.* The statement is too general to be accurate. Although there are some pretenders, many people who threaten suicide attempt to take their lives. Some believe that those who fail at suicide attempts are only seeking attention. But many people who commit suicide have made prior attempts (Lewinsohn and others, 1994). Contrary to myth, discussion of suicide with a person who is depressed does not prompt suicide. Extracting a promise that the person will not commit suicide before calling or visiting a helping professional seems to prevent some suicides.

Some believe that only "insane" people (meaning people who are out of touch with reality) would take their own lives. However, suicidal thinking is not necessarily a sign of psychosis, neurosis, or personality disorder. Instead, the contemplation of suicide can reflect a narrowing of the range of options that people think are available to them (Rotheram-Borus and others, 1990; Schotte and others, 1990).

SUICIDE PREVENTION

Imagine that you are having a heart-to-heart talk on campus with one of your best friends, Jamie. Things haven't been going well, you know. Jamie's grandmother died a month ago, and they were very close. Jamie's coursework has been suffering, and things have also been going downhill with the person Jamie has been seeing regularly. But you are not prepared when Jamie looks you straight in the eye and says, "I've been thinking about this for days, and I've decided that the only way out is to kill myself."

If someone tells you that he or she is considering suicide, you may feel frightened and flustered or feel that an enormous burden has been placed on you. It has. In such a case, your objective should be to encourage the person to consult a health-care provider, or to consult one yourself, as soon as possible. But if the person refuses to talk to anyone else and you feel that you can't break free for a consultation, there are a number of things you can do:

1. Draw the person out. Edwin Shneidman, cofounder of the Los Angeles Suicide Prevention Center, suggests asking questions such as "What's going on?" "Where do you hurt?" "What would you like to see happen?" (1985, p. 11) Questions such as these may encourage people to express frustrated psychological needs and provide some relief. They also give you time to assess the danger and think.

2. Be empathetic. Show that you understand how upset the person is. Do *not* say, "Don't be silly."

3. Suggest that measures other than suicide might be found to solve the problem,

even if they are not evident at the time. Shneidman (1985) suggests that suicidal people can typically see only two solutions to their problems—either death or a magical resolution of their problems. Therapists thus attempt to "widen the mental blinders" of suicidal people.

4. Ask how the person intends to commit suicide. People with concrete plans and a weapon are at greater risk. Ask if you might hold on to the weapon for a while. Sometimes the person says yes.

5. Suggest that the person go *with you* to obtain professional help *now*. The emergency room of a general hospital, the campus counseling center or infirmary, or the campus or local police will do. Some campuses have hot lines you can call. Some cities have suicide prevention centers with hot lines that people can use anonymously.

6. Extract a promise that the person will not commit suicide before seeing you again. Arrange a concrete time and place to meet. Get professional help as soon as you are apart.

7. Do *not* tell people threatening suicide that they're silly or crazy. Do *not* insist on contact with specific people like parents or a spouse. Conflict with these people may have led to the suicidal thinking.

Above all, remember that your primary objective is to consult a helping professional. Don't go it alone for one moment more than you have to.

Reflections

Now that you have read the section on suicide, reflect on the following questions:

- Is any of the information on suicide, or on people who attempt suicide, a surprise to you? If so, in what way?

- Agree or disagree with the following statement and support your answer: "It is abnormal to consider committing suicide."

- Has anyone ever talked to you about thoughts of suicide? How did you feel? What did you say? Would any of the suggestions made in this section have been of use to you?

A Suicide-Prevention Hot Line. At suicide-prevention centers, trained staff stand by hotlines around the clock. If someone you know is threatening suicide, consult a professional as soon as possible.

NOTES

14

Methods of
Therapy

Truth or Fiction?

_____ People in Merry Old England used to visit the local insane asylum for a fun night out on the town.

_____ Well-adjusted women wish to remain in the home and rear children.

_____ To be of help, psychotherapy must continue for months, perhaps years.

_____ Some psychotherapists interpret clients' dreams.

_____ Other psychotherapists encourage their clients to take the lead in the therapy session.

_____ Still other psychotherapists tell their clients precisely what to do.

_____ Lying around in your reclining chair and fantasizing can be an effective way of confronting your fears.

_____ Smoking cigarettes can be an effective treatment for helping people to . . . stop smoking cigarettes.

_____ You might be able to gain control over bad habits merely by keeping a record of where and when you practice them.

_____ The originator of a surgical technique intended to reduce violence learned that it was not always successful . . . when one of his patients shot him.

_____ Psychotherapy is ineffective unless the therapist and the client match in ethnic background.

Outline

Truth or Fiction?
What Is Therapy? In Search of That "Sweet Oblivious Antidote"
History of Therapies
Psychodynamic Therapies
Traditional Psychoanalysis: "Where Id Was, There Shall Ego Be"
Psychology in a World of Diversity: Women and Psychotherapy
Modern Psychodynamic Approaches
Humanistic–Existential Therapies
Person-Centered Therapy: Removing Roadblocks to Self-Actualization
Transactional Analysis: I'm OK — You're OK — We're All OK
Gestalt Therapy: Getting It Together
Cognitive Therapies
Rational-Emotive Therapy: Overcoming "Musts" and "Shoulds"
Cognitive Therapy: Correcting Cognitive Errors
Cognitive Restructuring: "No, No, Look at It This Way"
Behavior Therapy: Adjustment Is What You Do
Fear-Reduction Methods
Aversive Conditioning
Operant Conditioning Procedures
Self-Control Methods
Group Therapies
Encounter Groups
Couple Therapy
Family Therapy
Does Psychotherapy Work?
Problems in Conducting Research on Psychotherapy
Analyses of Therapy Effectiveness
Biological Therapies
Drug Therapy
Psychology in the New Millennium: Beyond Wellness: Are Biological Treatments for Personality Improvement in the Offing?
Electroconvulsive Therapy
Psychosurgery
Does Biological Therapy Work?
Summary
Psychology and Modern Life
Psychotherapy in the New Multicultural United States
Psychology in a World of Diversity: Ethnic Matching of Clients and Therapists

J asmine, a 19-year-old college sophomore, has been crying almost without let-up for several days. She feels that her life is falling apart. Her college aspirations lie in shambles. She has brought shame upon her family. Thoughts of suicide have crossed her mind. She can barely drag herself out of bed in the morning. She is avoiding friends. She can pinpoint some sources of stress in life: a couple of less-than-shining grades, an argument with a boyfriend, friction with roommates. Still, her misery seemed to descend on her from nowhere.

Jasmine is depressed—so depressed that family and friends have finally prevailed upon her to seek professional help. Had she broken her leg, her treatment from a qualified professional would have followed a fairly standard course. Yet treatment of psychological problems and disorders like depression may be approached from very different perspectives. Depending on whom Jasmine sees, she may be

- Lying on a couch talking about anything that pops into awareness and exploring the hidden meanings of a recurrent dream.

- Sitting face to face with a gentle, accepting therapist who places the major burden for what happens in therapy on Jasmine's shoulders.

- Listening to a frank, straightforward therapist assert that her problems stem from self-defeating attitudes and perfectionistic beliefs.

- Taking pills.

- Participating in some combination of the above.

These methods, though different, all represent methods of therapy. To make sense of what is happening to Jasmine, we first define *psychotherapy*. We consider the history of therapy and examine several of the major current psychotherapies including psychodynamic, humanistic–existential, cognitive, behavior, and group therapies. After exploring these approaches to psychotherapy, we shall turn our attention to biological therapies including drug therapy, electroconvulsive shock therapy, and psychosurgery. The chapter's "Psychology and Modern Life" section addresses therapy in the new multicultural United States. We shall see that people from different ethnic backgrounds have different attitudes toward psychotherapy and profit from culturally sensitive approaches to therapy.

What Is Therapy? In Search of That "Sweet Oblivious Antidote"[1]

The form of therapy practiced by a psychologist or another helping professional is related to her or his assumptions about personality and psychological disorders. Treatment is not, or ought not to be, a matter of chance.

Although there are many different kinds of psychotherapy, they have a number of things in common. **Psychotherapy** is a systematic interaction between a therapist and a client that brings psychological principles to bear on influencing the client's thoughts, feelings, or behavior in order to help the client overcome psychological disorders, adjust to problems in living, or develop as an individual.

---

[1] The phrase is from Shakespeare's *Macbeth,* as seen in the following pages.

Quite a mouthful? True. But note the essentials:

1. *Systematic Interaction.* Psychotherapy is a systematic interaction between a client and a therapist. The client's needs and goals and the therapist's theoretical point of view interact to determine how the therapist and client relate to one another.

2. *Psychological Principles.* Psychotherapy brings psychological principles to bear on the client's problems or goals. Psychotherapy is based on psychological theory and research in areas such as personality, learning, motivation, and emotion. Psychotherapy is not based on, say, religious or biological principles, although there is no reason why psychotherapy cannot be compatible with both.

3. *Thoughts, Feelings, and Behavior.* Psychotherapy influences clients' thoughts, feelings, and behavior. Psychotherapy can be aimed at any or all of these aspects of human psychology.

4. *Psychological Disorders, Adjustment Problems, and Personal Growth.* Psychotherapy is used with at least three types of clients. First, there are people who have

psychological disorders. Other people seek help in adjusting to problems such as social shyness, weight problems, loss of a spouse, or career confusion. Still other people use psychotherapy because they want to learn more about themselves and reach their full potential as individuals, creative artists, parents, and members of social groups. Table 14.1 lists reasons that a sample of Connecticut residents consulted psychologists, psychiatrists, marriage and family counselors, clergy, and other helping professionals.

HISTORY OF THERAPIES

Ancient and medieval "treatments" of psychological disorders often reflected the demonological model. As such, they tended to involve cruel practices such as exorcism and death by hanging or burning, as was practiced some 300 years ago. In Europe and the United States, some people who could not meet the demands of everyday life were also thrown into prisons (Grob, 1994). Others begged in city streets, stole produce and food animals from farms, or entered marginal societal niches occupied by prostitutes and petty thieves. A few might have found their ways to monasteries or other retreats

MINILECTURE: APPROACHES TO PSYCHOTHERAPY

MINILECTURE: THE HISTORY OF THERAPY

Psychotherapy • A systematic interaction between a therapist and a client that brings psychological principles to bear on influencing the client's thoughts, feelings, or behavior to help that client overcome abnormal behavior or adjust to problems in living.

TABLE 14.1

Reasons Connecticut Residents Consulted Psychologists and Other Helping Professionals

REASON	PERCENT
Mild depression	37
Marital problems	35
Problems in child rearing	20
Problems with social relationships	11
Problems with relationships at work	11
Suicidal thoughts	11
Dependence on alcohol or other drugs	7
Severe depression	7
Desire to quit smoking	6
Being obsessed about something	6
Sexual dysfunctions	6
Eating disorders/weight loss	4
Abuse by one's spouse or partner	4
Hallucinations/hearing voices	4

Note: The sum is greater than 100% because participants could list more than one reason for consulting the professional.
Source: Adapted from "The Public's Knowledge about Psychologists and Other Mental Health Professionals" (Table 2, p. 841), by B. I. Murstein & P. A. Fontaine, 1993, *American Psychologist, 48,* pp. 839–845.

St. Mary's of Bethlehem. This famous London institution is the source of the term *bedlam*.

Asylum • (uh-SIGH-lum). An institution for the care of the mentally ill.

lation until the daily stresses created by noise, overcrowding, and unsanitary conditions undoubtedly heightened the problems they were meant to ameliorate. Inmates were frequently chained and beaten. Some were chained for decades.

The word *bedlam* is derived from the name of the London asylum St. Mary's of Bethlehem, which opened its gates in 1547. Here, unfortunate people were chained between the inner and outer walls, whipped, and allowed to lie in their own waste. And here, the ladies and gentlemen of the British upper class might go for a stroll on a lazy afternoon to take in the sights. The admission for such amusement? One penny.

Truth or Fiction Revisited. *It is true that people in Merry Old England used to visit the local insane asylum for a fun night out on the town.* St. Mary's of Bethlehem was the best known asylum.

Humanitarian reform movements began in the 18th century. In Paris, Philippe Pinel unchained the patients at the asylum known as La Bicêtre. The populace was amazed that most patients, rather than running amok, profited from kindness and greater freedom. Many could eventually function in society once more. Reform movements were later led by the Quaker

that offered a kind word and some support. Generally speaking, they died early.

Asylums. **Asylums** often had their origins in European monasteries. They were the first institutions meant primarily for persons with psychological disorders. Their function was human warehousing, not treatment. Asylums mushroomed in popu-

The Unchaining of the Patients at La Bicêtre. Frenchman Philippe Pinel sparked the humanitarian reform movement symbolized by unchaining the patients at this Parisian asylum.

TABLE 14.2

Functions of a Community Mental Health Center

Outpatient treatment
Short-term hospitalization
Partial hospitalization (e.g., patient sleeps in the hospital and works outside during the day)
Crisis intervention
Community consultation and education about abnormal behavior

The Community Mental-Health Centers Act provided funds for community agencies that attempt to intervene in psychological disorders as early as possible and to maintain people in the community.

William Tuke in England and by Dorothea Dix in America.

Mental Hospitals. Mental hospitals gradually replaced asylums in the United States. In the mid-1950s, more than a million people resided in state, county, Veterans Administration, or private facilities. Treatment, not warehousing, is the function of the mental hospital. Still, because of high patient populations and understaffing, many people have received little attention. Even today, with somewhat improved conditions, one psychiatrist may be responsible for the welfare of several hundred people on a weekend.

The Community Mental Health Movement. Since the 1960s, efforts have been made to maintain as many mental patients as possible in the community. The Community Mental-Health Centers Act of 1963 provided funds for creating hundreds of community mental health centers, in which people would be charged according to their ability to pay, in order to accomplish this goal. These centers attempt to maintain new patients as outpatients, to serve patients from mental hospitals who have been released into the community, and to provide other services listed in Table 14.2. Today, the majority of the people with chronic psychological disorders live in the community, not the hospital.

Critics note that many people who had resided in hospitals for decades were suddenly discharged to "home" communities that seemed foreign and frightening. Many discharged people do not receive adequate follow-up care in the community. Many join the ranks of the nation's homeless (Carling, 1990; Levine & Rog, 1990). Some people try to return to the protected world

of the hospital and become trapped in a "revolving door" between the hospital and the community.

Reflections

Now that you have read the opening sections of this chapter, reflect on the following questions:

- Have people you know said they have gone for "therapy"? What kind of therapy? What are your attitudes toward people who seek professional help for psychological or adjustment problems? Why?

- Had you heard of insane asylums or mental hospitals? What pictures were conjured up in your mind? How did your impressions match the information in this chapter?

- Is there a community mental health center or home for homeless people in your neighborhood? How would your family or your neighbors feel about having these agencies in your neighborhood? Why?

Let us consider the different kinds of therapies available today.

Psychodynamic Therapies

Psychodynamic therapies are based on the thinking of Sigmund Freud, the founder of psychodynamic theory. Broadly speaking, they are based on the view that our problems largely reflect early childhood experiences and internal conflicts. According to Freud, this internal conflict involves the shifting of psychic, or libidinal, energy

Psychoanalysis • Freud's method of psychotherapy.

Abreaction • (AB-ree-ACK-shun). In psychoanalysis, expression of previously repressed feelings and impulses to allow the psychic energy associated with them to spill forth.

Catharsis • (cuh-THAR-sis). Another term for *abreaction*.

Free association • In psychoanalysis, the uncensored uttering of all thoughts that come to mind.

Resistance • The tendency to block the free expression of impulses and primitive ideas—a reflection of the defense mechanism of repression.

Interpretation • An explanation of a client's utterance according to psychoanalytic theory.

Wish fulfillment • A primitive method used by the id to attempt to gratify basic instincts.

Phallic symbol • A sign that represents the penis.

Manifest content • In psychodynamic theory, the reported content of dreams.

Latent content • In psychodynamic theory, the symbolized or underlying content of dreams.

among the three psychic structures—the id, ego, and superego. The sway of psychic energy determines our behavior. When primitive urges threaten to break through from the id or when the superego floods us with excessive guilt, it prompts the establishment of defenses and creates distress. Freud's psychodynamic therapy method—psychoanalysis—aims to modify the flow of energy among these structures, largely to bulwark the ego against the torrents of energy loosed by the id and the superego. With impulses and feelings of guilt and shame placed under greater control, clients are emotionally freed to develop more adaptive behavior patterns.

Not all psychodynamically oriented therapists view internal conflict in terms of unconscious forces. In this section, we first outline Freud's psychoanalytic methods for shoring up the ego—"traditional" psychoanalysis. We then examine more modern psychoanalytic approaches, whose concepts of conflict and methods differ from those of Freud.

TRADITIONAL PSYCHOANALYSIS: "WHERE ID WAS, THERE SHALL EGO BE"

Canst thou not minister to a mind diseas'd,
Pluck out from the memory a rooted sorrow,
Raze out the written troubles of the brain,
And with some sweet oblivious antidote
Cleanse the stuff'd bosom of that perilous stuff
Which weighs upon the heart?

SHAKESPEARE, *MACBETH*

In this passage, Macbeth asks a physician to minister to Lady Macbeth after she has gone mad. In the play, her madness is in part caused by current events—namely, her guilt for participating in murders designed to seat her husband on the throne of Scotland. There are also hints of more deeply rooted and mysterious problems, however, such as conflicts about infertility.

If Lady Macbeth's physician had been a traditional psychoanalyst, he might have asked her to lie down on a couch in a slightly darkened room. He would have sat just behind her and encouraged her to talk about anything that came to mind, no matter how trivial, no matter how personal. To avoid interfering with her self-exploration, he might have said little or nothing for ses-

sion after session. That would have been par for the course. A traditional **psychoanalysis,** you see, can extend for months, or years.

Psychoanalysis is the clinical method devised by Freud for plucking "from the memory a rooted sorrow," for razing "out the written troubles of the brain." Psychoanalysis is the method used by Freud and his followers to "cleanse . . . that perilous stuff which weighs upon the heart"—to provide insight into the conflicts presumed to lie at the roots of a person's problems. Insight involves a number of things: knowledge of the experiences that lead to conflicts and maladaptive behavior; identification and labeling of feelings and conflicts that lie below conscious awareness; and objective evaluation of one's beliefs and ideas, feelings, and behavior.

Psychoanalysis also seeks to allow the client to express emotions and impulses that are theorized to have been dammed up by the forces of repression. Freud was fond of saying, "Where id was, there shall ego be." In part, he meant that psychoanalysis could shed light on the inner workings of the mind. Freud did not believe that we ought to, or need to, become conscious of all of our conflicts and primitive impulses, however. Instead, he sought to replace impulsive and defensive behavior with coping behavior. He believed that impulsive behavior reflects the urges of the id. Defensive behavior such as timidly avoiding confrontations represents the ego's compromising efforts to protect the client from these impulses and the possibility of retaliation. Coping behavior would allow the client to partially express these impulses, but in socially acceptable ways. In so doing, the client would find gratification but avoid social and self-condemnation.

In this way, a man with a phobia for knives might discover he had been repressing the urge to harm someone who had taken advantage of him. He might also find ways to confront his antagonist verbally. A woman with a conversion disorder—for example, paralysis of the legs—could see that her disability allows her to avoid unwanted pregnancy without guilt. She might also realize her resentment at being pressed into a stereotypical feminine gender role and decide to expand her options.

Freud also believed that psychoanalysis allows the client to spill forth the psychic energy that was repressed by conflicts and guilt. He called this spilling forth **abreaction,** or **catharsis.** Abreaction would provide feelings of relief by alleviating some of the forces assaulting the ego.

Free Association.

Early in his career as a therapist, Freud found that hypnosis allowed his clients to focus on repressed conflicts and talk about them. The relaxed "trance state" provided by hypnosis seemed to allow clients to break through to topics of which they were otherwise unaware. Freud also found that many clients denied the accuracy of this material once they were out of the trance, however. Other clients found these revelations to be premature and painful. Freud thus turned to **free association,** a more gradual method of breaking down the walls of defense that block insight into unconscious processes.

In free association, the client is made comfortable, as by lying on a couch, and is asked to talk about any topic that comes to mind. No thought is to be censored—that is the cardinal rule. Psychoanalysts ask their clients to wander "freely" from topic to topic, but they do not believe that the process *within* the client is fully free. Repressed impulses press for release. A client may begin to free associate with meaningless topics, but pertinent repressed material may eventually surface.

The ego persists in trying to repress unacceptable impulses and threatening conflicts. As a result, clients might show **resistance** to recalling and discussing threatening ideas. Clients might claim "My mind is blank" when they are about to entertain such thoughts. They might accuse the analyst of being demanding or inconsiderate. They might "forget" their appointment when threatening material is due to be uncovered.

The therapist observes the dynamic struggle between the compulsion to utter and resistance. Through discreet remarks, the analyst subtly tips the balance in favor of uttering. A gradual process of self-discovery and self-insight ensues. Now and then, the analyst offers an **interpretation** of an utterance, showing how it suggests resistance or deep-seated feelings and conflicts.

A View of Freud's Consulting Room at Berggasse 19 in Vienna. Freud would sit in the chair by the head of the couch while a client free associated. The cardinal rule of free association is that no thought is to be censored.

Dream Analysis.

Sometimes a cigar is just a cigar.
SIGMUND FREUD, ON DREAM ANALYSIS

Freud often had clients jot down their dreams upon waking so that they could be discussed in therapy. Freud considered dreams the "royal road to the unconscious." He believed that dreams were determined by unconscious processes as well as by the events of the day. Unconscious impulses tend to be expressed in dreams as a form of **wish fulfillment.**

But unacceptable sexual and aggressive impulses are likely to be displaced onto objects and situations that reflect the client's era and culture. These objects become symbols of the unconscious wishes. For example, long, narrow dream objects might be **phallic symbols,** but whether the symbol takes the form of a spear, rifle, or spacecraft partially reflects one's cultural background.

In psychodynamic theory, the perceived content of the dream is called its shown or **manifest content.** Its presumed hidden or symbolic content is referred to as its **latent content.** A man might dream that he is flying. Flying is the manifest content of the dream. Freud usually interpreted flying as being symbolic of erection, so issues concerning sexual potency might make up the latent content of such a dream.

Truth or Fiction Revisited. *It is true that some psychotherapists interpret clients' dreams.* Psychoanalysis is a case in point. Despite his interest in possible dream symbols, even Freud allowed that "Sometimes a cigar is just a cigar."

Paul Robinson (1993), an intellectual historian and supporter of psychoanalysis, notes that psychoanalysis saw its heyday in the 1950s. Since then, its influence and adherents have declined. One reason, suggested by Robinson, is that intellectuals and the public fell too quickly and too deeply in love with psychoanalysis. Thus there is a rebound. Other forces that contributed to the decline of psychoanalysis include the rise of the women's movement, which as noted in the following feature on "Women and Psychotherapy," has found psychoanalysis to be degrading to women.

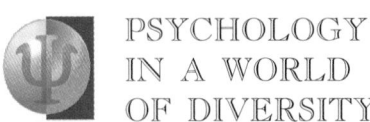

PSYCHOLOGY IN A WORLD OF DIVERSITY

WOMEN AND PSYCHOTHERAPY

Why discuss women and psychotherapy? Don't psychotherapy and the theories on which therapy is based apply to both genders? They do. But the most prominent form of therapy in the 20th century, psychoanalysis, set forth a view of women that has reinforced male dominance and the view that a woman's place is in the home (Robinson, 1993).

Traditional psychoanalysis professes that it is normal for little girls to experience penis envy. However, proper resolution of the Oedipus complex results in women's (unconsciously) replacing the desire for a penis of their own with the desire to bear children. Well-adjusted women, according to the theory, accept the authority of their husbands and wish to remain in the home and rear children. This degrading view of women has been attacked as groundless not only by critics of psychoanalysis, but also by modern-day ego analysts such as Karen Horney (Robinson, 1993).

Truth or Fiction Revisited. *It is not true that well-adjusted women wish to remain in the home and rear children.* This traditional psychodynamic view has not found empiri-

cal support and has been fiercely attacked by critics.

Social critics have attacked traditional psychodynamic theory as one more cultural ideology that subjugates women (Lerman & Porter, 1990; Greene, 1993; Robinson, 1993). For example, women who act assertively have often been perceived by traditional psychoanalysts as suffering from unresolved penis envy, whereas assertive men were viewed as appropriately masculinized. A more enlightened approach to therapy emerged as a response not only to psychoanalysis but also to male dominance of the mental health professions.

Psychoanalysts have a tendency to interpret clients' expressions of anger and indignation as *transference*—that is, as signs of maladjustment and reactions to historic events and figures in their lives. However, women have had ample cause to be angry toward, and suspicious of, male therapists. Anger is, after all, an appropriate response to prejudice and discrimination. Only 40 to 50 years ago most therapists considered women who chose to work to be maladjusted.

Most contemporary therapists are guided by the goal of raising awareness of the harmful effects of discrimination against, and harassment of, women on the job, of placement of men in positions of dominance over women, and of treatment of women as sex objects.

The Case of Women and Depression. Sociocultural theorists note that social inequality, rather than individual psychopathology, creates and maintains many of the problems presented in psychotherapy. This is particularly so when clients are members of oppressed groups, such as women (Brown, 1992). For example, women are more likely than men to be depressed (Coryell and others, 1992; Weissman and others, 1991). A major survey of five U.S. communities showed that major depression affected 7% of the women surveyed during their lifetimes, as compared to 2.6% of the men (Weissman and others, 1991).

Some therapists, like many uneducated lay people, assume that biological gender differences largely explain why women are more likely to get depressed. How often do we hear degrading remarks such as "It must be that time of the month" when women express feelings of anger or irritation? Hormonal changes during the menstrual cycle and childbirth may contribute to depression in women (McGrath and others, 1990). However, a panel convened by the American Psychological Association attributed most of the difference to the greater stresses placed on women (McGrath and others, 1990). Women are more likely to encounter socioeconomic and sociocultural stressors such as physical and sexual abuse, poverty, single parenthood, and sexism. Women are also more likely than men to support others who are undergoing stress. In supporting others, they heap additional caregiving burdens on themselves (Shumaker & Hill, 1991). One panel member, Bonnie Strickland, expressed surprise that still more women are not clinically depressed, given that they are treated as second-class citizens.

A part of "therapy" for women, then, is to modify the overwhelming demands that are made of women in contemporary society (Comas-Diaz, 1994). The pain may lie in the individual, but the cause often lies in society.

MODERN PSYCHODYNAMIC APPROACHES

Some psychoanalysts adhere faithfully to Freud's protracted techniques. They continue to practice traditional psychoanalysis. In recent years, however, briefer, less intense forms of psychodynamic therapy have been devised (Koss and others, 1986; Strupp, 1992). These methods are "psychoanalytically oriented." They make treatment available to clients who do not have the time or money for protracted therapy (Strupp, 1992). Also, frankly, many of these therapists believe that protracted therapy is not needed or justifiable in terms of the ratio of cost to benefits.

Truth or Fiction Revisited. *It is not true that psychotherapy must continue for months, perhaps years, to be of help. There are many effective brief forms of psychotherapy.*

Although some modern psychodynamic therapies continue to focus on revealing unconscious material and on breaking through psychological defenses or resis-

tance, there are a number of differences from traditional psychoanalysis. One is that client and therapist usually sit face to face, as opposed to the client's reclining on a couch. The therapist is usually more directive than the traditional psychoanalyst. Modern therapists often suggest productive behavior instead of focusing solely on self-insight. Finally, there is usually more focus on the ego as the "executive" of personality. Accordingly, there is less emphasis on the role of the id. For this reason, many modern psychodynamic therapists are considered **ego analysts.**

Many of Freud's followers, the "second generation" of psychoanalysts—from Jung and Adler to Horney and Erikson—believed that Freud had placed too much emphasis on sexual and aggressive impulses and underestimated the importance of the ego. Freud, for example, aimed to establish conditions under which clients could spill forth psychic energy and eventually shore up the position of the ego. Erikson, in contrast, spoke to clients directly about their values and concerns and encouraged them to consciously fashion desired traits and behavior patterns. Freud saw clients as perpetual victims of the past and doubted their ability to overcome childhood trauma. Karen Horney, on the other hand, deemed clients capable of overcoming early abuse and deprivation through self-understanding and adult relationships (Quinn, 1987). Even Freud's daughter, the psychoanalyst Anna Freud (1895–1982), was more concerned with the ego than with unconscious forces and conflicts.

Today, there are many psychodynamic therapies. Many approaches show the influence of Sigmund Freud. As a group they continue to use terms such as *conflict* and *ego.* They differ in the prominence they ascribe to unconscious forces and in their perception of the role of the ego.

Ego analyst • A psychodynamically oriented therapist who focuses on the conscious, coping behavior of the ego instead of the hypothesized, unconscious functioning of the id.

Reflections

Now that you have read the section on psychoanalysis, reflect on the following questions:

- Did you have a picture of psychoanalysis in your mind before reading this section? What was it like? Did it differ from the information presented in this chapter?

- Does it make you or other people you know feel good to talk with someone about your problems? Are there some thoughts or experiences you are unwilling to talk about or share with others? How do you think a psychoanalyst would respond if you brought them up? Why?

person-centered therapy, believed that childhood experiences gave rise to the conditions of worth that troubled his clients here and now. Rogers and Fritz Perls, the originator of Gestalt therapy, recognized that early incorporation of other people's values often leads clients to "disown" parts of their own personalities.

Humanistic – Existential Therapies

Whereas psychodynamic therapies focus on internal conflicts and unconscious processes, humanistic–existential therapies focus on the quality of clients' subjective, conscious experience. Whereas psychodynamic therapies tend to focus on the past, and particularly on early childhood experiences, humanistic–existential therapies usually focus on what clients are experiencing today —in "the here and now."

These differences are frequently ones of *emphasis,* however. The past has a way of influencing current thoughts, feelings, and behavior. Carl Rogers, the originator of

PERSON-CENTERED THERAPY: REMOVING ROADBLOCKS TO SELF-ACTUALIZATION

Person-centered therapy was originated by Carl Rogers (1951). Rogers believed that we are free to make choices and control our destinies, despite the burdens of the past.

Rogers also believed that we have natural tendencies toward health, growth, and fulfillment. Given this view, Rogers wrote that psychological problems arise from roadblocks placed in the path of our own self-actualization. Because others show us selective approval when we are young, we learn to disown the disapproved parts of

Person-Centered Therapy. By showing the qualities of unconditional positive regard, empathic understanding, genuineness, and congruence, person-centered therapists create an atmosphere in which clients can explore their feelings.

ourselves. We don masks and façades to earn social approval. We may learn to be seen but not heard—not even heard, or examined fully, by ourselves. As a result, we might experience stress and discomfort and the feeling that we—or the world—are not real.

Person-centered therapy aims to provide insight into the parts of us that we have disowned so that we can feel whole. It stresses the importance of a warm, therapeutic atmosphere that encourages client self-exploration and self-expression. Therapist acceptance of the client is thought to foster client self-acceptance and self-esteem. Self-acceptance frees the client to make choices that develop his or her unique potential.

Person-centered therapy is nondirective. The client takes the lead, listing and exploring problems. The therapist reflects or paraphrases expressed feelings and ideas, helping the client get in touch with deeper feelings and follow the strongest leads in the quest for self-insight.

Truth or Fiction Revisited. *It is true that some psychotherapists encourage their clients to take the lead in the therapy session.* Person-centered therapists provide an example.

Person-centered therapy is practiced widely in college and university counseling centers, not just to help students experiencing, say, anxieties or depression but also to help them make decisions. Many college students have not yet made career choices or wonder whether they should become involved with particular people or in sexual activity. Person-centered therapists provide an encouraging atmosphere in which clients can verbally explore choices and make decisions. Person-centered therapists do not tell clients what to do. Instead, they help clients arrive at their own decisions.

The effective person-centered therapist also shows four qualities: unconditional positive regard, empathic understanding, genuineness, and congruence. **Unconditional positive regard** is respect for clients as important human beings with unique values and goals. Clients are provided with a sense of security that encourages them to follow their own feelings. Psychoanalysts might hesitate to encourage clients to freely express their impulses be-

cause of the fear that primitive forces might be unleashed. Person-centered therapists believe that people are basically *pro*social, however. If people follow their own feelings, rather than act defensively, they should not be abusive or *anti*social.

Empathic understanding is shown by accurately reflecting the client's experiences and feelings. Therapists try to view the world through their clients' **frames of reference** by setting aside their own values and listening closely.

Whereas psychoanalysts are trained to be opaque, person-centered therapists are trained to show **genuineness.** Person-centered therapists are open about their feelings. It would be harmful to clients if their therapists could not truly accept and like them, even though their values might differ from those of the therapists. Rogers admitted that he sometimes had negative feelings about clients, usually boredom. He usually expressed these feelings rather than hold them in (Bennett, 1985). Person-centered therapists must also be able to tolerate differentness, because they believe that every client is different in important ways.

Person-centered therapists also try to show **congruence,** or a fit between their thoughts, feelings, and behavior. Person-centered therapists serve as models of integrity to their clients.

TRANSACTIONAL ANALYSIS: I'M OK—YOU'RE OK— WE'RE ALL OK

Transactional analysis (TA) is also rooted in the psychodynamic tradition. According to Thomas Harris, author of *I'm OK— You're OK* (1967), many of us suffer from inferiority complexes of the sort described by the psychoanalyst Alfred Adler. Even though we have become adults, we might continue to see ourselves as dependent children. We might think other people are OK but not see ourselves as being OK.

Within TA, *I'm not OK—You're OK* is one of four basic "life positions," or ways of perceiving relationships with others. A major goal of TA is to help people adopt the life position *I'm OK—You're OK,* in which they accept others and themselves. Unfortunately, people tend to adopt "games," or

Person-centered therapy • Carl Rogers's method of psychotherapy, which emphasizes the creation of a warm, therapeutic atmosphere that frees clients to engage in self-exploration and self-expression.

Unconditional positive regard • Acceptance of the value of another person, although not necessarily acceptance of everything the person does.

Empathic understanding • (em-PATH-ick). Ability to perceive a client's feelings from the client's frame of reference. A quality of the good person-centered therapist.

Frame of reference • One's unique patterning of perceptions and attitudes, according to which one evaluates events.

Genuineness • Recognition and open expression of the therapist's own feelings.

Congruence • (con-GREW-ants). A fit between one's self-concept and behaviors, thoughts, and emotions.

Transactional analysis • A form of psychotherapy that deals with how people interact and how their interactions reinforce attitudes, expectations, and "life positions." Abbreviated *TA.*

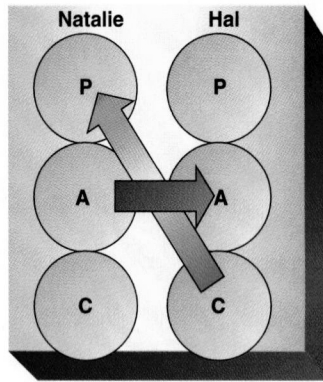

FIGURE 14.1
A Crossed Transaction Trans-actions are social exchanges. "Crossed" transactions hamper communication. In this crossed transaction, Natalie asks Hal, "Did you have a good time tonight?" Hal replies, "Why do you wanna know?" Thus communication is broken off.

styles of relating to others, that are designed to confirm one of the unhealthy life positions: I'm OK—You're not OK, I'm not OK—You're OK, or I'm not OK—You're not OK.

Psychiatrist Eric Berne (1976), the originator of TA, described our personalities as containing three "ego states": **Parent, Child,** and **Adult.** The "parent" is a moralistic ego state. The "child" is an irresponsible and emotional ego state. The "adult" is a rational ego state. It is easy to confuse the child ego state with the id, the adult ego state with the ego, and the parent ego state with the superego. But note that these are three hypothesized *ego states,* or ways of coping. The id is unconscious and so is some of the functioning of the superego. In TA, however, we can be fully conscious of the child and parent ego states.

Many interpersonal troubles occur because people tend to relate to each other as parents, children, or adults. A social exchange between two people is called a **transaction.** A transaction is said to fit, or be **complementary,** when a social exchange follows the same lines. In one type of complementary transaction, people relate as adults. A transaction can also be complementary, even if it is upsetting, when two people relate as parent and child (Parent: "You shouldn't have done that"; Child: "I'm sorry, I promise it won't happen again"). Communication breaks down when the social exchange between the parties does not follow complementary lines (as in Figure 14.1).

NATALIE (adult to adult):	Did you have a good time tonight?	
HAL (child to parent):	Why do you wanna know?	

Or:

BILL (adult to adult):	Nan, did you see the checkbook?	
NAN (parent to child):	A place for everything and everything in its place!	

TA is often carried out with couples who complain of communication problems. It encourages people to relate to each other as adults.

GESTALT THERAPY: GETTING IT TOGETHER

Gestalt therapy was originated by Fritz Perls (1893–1970). Gestalt therapy, like person-centered therapy, aims to help individuals integrate conflicting parts of the personality. Perls used the term *Gestalt* to signify his interest in providing the conflicting parts of the personality an integrated form or shape. He aimed to have his clients become aware of inner conflict, accept the reality of conflict rather than deny it or keep it repressed, and make productive choices despite misgivings and fear.

Although Perls's ideas about conflicting personality elements owe much to psychodynamic theory, his form of therapy, unlike psychoanalysis, focuses on the here and now. In Gestalt therapy, clients undergo exercises to heighten awareness of current feelings and behavior rather than explore the past. Perls also believed, along with Carl Rogers, that people are free to make choices and to direct their personal growth. Unlike person-centered therapy, however, Gestalt therapy is highly directive. The therapist leads the client through planned experiences.

One Gestalt technique that increases awareness of internal conflict is the **dialogue.** Clients undertake verbal confrontations between opposing wishes and ideas. An example of these clashing personality elements is "top dog" and "underdog." One's top dog might conservatively suggest, "Don't take chances. Stick with what you have or you might lose it all." One's frustrated underdog might then rise up and assert, "You never try anything. How will you ever get out of this rut if you don't take on new challenges?" Heightened awareness of the elements of conflict can clear the path toward resolution, perhaps through compromise.

Body language also provides insight into conflicting feelings. Clients might be instructed to attend to the ways in which they furrow their eyebrows and tense their facial muscles when they express ideas that they think they support. In this way, they often find that their body language asserts feelings that they have been denying.

To increase clients' understanding of opposing points of view, Gestalt therapists might encourage them to argue in favor of ideas opposed to their own. They might also have clients role-play people who are important to them to become more in touch with their points of view.

Whereas psychodynamic theory views dreams as the "royal road to the unconscious," Perls saw the stuff of dreams as disowned parts of the personality. Perls would often ask clients to role-play the elements in their dreams to get in touch with these parts. In *Gestalt Therapy Verbatim,* Perls—known to clients and friends alike as Fritz—describes a session in which a client, Jim, is reporting a dream:

JIM: I just have the typical recurring dream which I think a lot of people might have if they have a background problem, and it isn't of anything I think I can act out. It's the distant wheel—I'm not sure what type it is—it's coming towards me and ever-increasing in size. And then finally, it's just above me and it's no height that I can determine, it's so high. And that's—

FRITZ: If you were this wheel, . . . what would you do with Jim?

JIM: I am just about to roll over Jim. (Perls, 1971, p. 127)

Perls encourages Jim to undertake a dialogue with the wheel. Jim comes to see that the wheel represents fears about taking decisive action. Through this insight, the "wheel" becomes more manageable in size, and Jim is able to use some of the "energy" that he might otherwise have spent in worrying to begin taking charge of his life.

Reflections

Now that you have read the section on humanistic—existential therapies, reflect on the following questions:

- How would you feel if you went for help and your therapist followed your lead rather than offered concrete advice? Why?
- Have you experienced unconditional positive regard or conditional positive regard in your home life? How do you think your experiences have shaped your self-esteem?
- Do you believe that you are "OK"? Why or why not?

- Do you feel that parts of your personality pull you in different directions? If so, how?

Let us now turn our attention to another group of therapies that are concerned with subjective experience and the here and now—cognitive therapies. But whereas humanistic—existential therapists tend to focus on clients' personalities, cognitive therapists tend to focus on mental processes such as thoughts, strategies for interpreting experience, plans, problem-solving techniques, and attitudes—especially self-defeating attitudes.

Cognitive Therapies

There is nothing either good or bad, but thinking makes it so.

SHAKESPEARE, *HAMLET*

In this line from *Hamlet,* Shakespeare did not mean to suggest that injuries and misfortunes are painless or easy to manage. Rather, he meant that our cognitive appraisals of unfortunate circumstances can heighten our discomfort and impair our coping ability. In so doing, Shakespeare was providing a kind of motto for cognitive therapists.

Although there are many cognitively oriented therapists and more than one type of **cognitive therapy,** cognitive therapists would generally agree with Carl Rogers that people are free to make choices and develop in accord with their concepts of what they are capable of being. Cognitive therapists would also agree with Fritz Perls that it is appropriate for clients to focus on the here and now. Cognitive therapists, like Perls, are also reasonably directive in their approaches.

Cognitive therapists focus on the beliefs, attitudes, and automatic types of thinking that create and compound their clients' problems (Beck, 1993; Ellis, 1993). Cognitive therapists, like psychodynamic and humanistic—existential therapists, are interested in fostering client self-insight, but they aim to heighten clients' insight into *current cognitions* as well as those of the past (Jones & Pulos, 1993). Cognitive therapists also aim to directly *change* maladaptive cognitions to reduce negative feelings, to provide more accurate perceptions of the self

Parent • In TA, a moralistic ego state.

Child • In TA, an irresponsible, emotional ego state.

Adult • In TA, a rational, adaptive ego state.

Transaction • In TA, an exchange between two people.

Complementary • In TA, descriptive of a transaction in which the ego states of two people interact harmoniously.

Gestalt therapy • Fritz Perls's form of psychotherapy, which attempts to integrate conflicting parts of the personality through directive methods designed to help clients perceive their whole selves.

Dialogue • A Gestalt therapy technique in which clients verbalize confrontations between conflicting parts of their personality.

Cognitive therapy • A form of therapy that focuses on how clients' cognitions (expectations, attitudes, beliefs, etc.) lead to distress and may be modified to relieve distress and promote adaptive behavior.

and others, and to orient the client toward solving problems (Jones & Pulos, 1993).

Let us look at the approaches and methods of some major cognitive therapists.

RATIONAL-EMOTIVE THERAPY: OVERCOMING "MUSTS" AND "SHOULDS"

Albert Ellis (1977, 1993), the founder of **rational-emotive therapy,** points out that our beliefs about events, as well as the events themselves, shape our responses to them. Moreover, many of us harbor a number of irrational beliefs that can give rise to problems or magnify their impact. Two of the most important ones are the belief that you must have the love and approval of people who are important to you and the belief that you must prove yourself to be thoroughly competent, adequate, and achieving. (Others are elaborated in Chapter 15.)

Ellis's methods are active and directive. He does not sit back like the traditional psychoanalyst and occasionally offer an interpretation. Instead, he urges clients to seek out their irrational beliefs, which can be hard to pinpoint. He then shows clients how their beliefs lead to misery and challenges them to change their beliefs. According to Ellis, we need less misery and less blaming but more action.

COGNITIVE THERAPY: CORRECTING COGNITIVE ERRORS

Psychiatrist Aaron Beck (1991, 1993) also focuses on clients' cognitive distortions. He questions patients in a manner that encourages them to see the irrationality of their own ways of thinking—how, for example, their minimizing of their accomplishments and their pessimistic assumptions that the worst will happen heightens feelings of depression. Beck, like Ellis, notes that our cognitive distortions can be fleeting and automatic, difficult to detect. His therapy methods help clients pin them down and challenge them.

Beck notes in particular the pervasive influence of four basic types of cognitive errors that contribute to clients' miseries:

Rational-emotive therapy • Albert Ellis's form of cognitive psychotherapy which focuses on how irrational expectations create anxiety and disappointment and which encourages clients to challenge and correct these expectations.

1. Clients may *selectively perceive* the world as a harmful place and ignore evidence to the contrary.

2. Clients may *overgeneralize* on the basis of a few examples. For example, they may perceive themselves as worthless because they were laid off at work or as grossly unattractive because they were refused a request for a date.

3. Clients may *magnify,* or blow out of proportion, the importance of negative events. As noted in the discussion of Ellis's views, clients may catastrophize flunking a test by assuming they will flunk out of college or catastrophize losing a job by believing that they will never work again and that serious harm will befall their families.

4. Clients may engage in *absolutist thinking,* or looking at the world in black and white rather than in shades of gray. In doing so, a rejection on a date takes on the meaning of a lifetime of loneliness; a discomforting illness takes on life-threatening proportions.

The concept of pinpointing and modifying errors may become more clear from reading an excerpt from a case in which a 53-year-old engineer obtained cognitive therapy for severe depression. The engineer had left his job and become inactive. As reported by Beck and his colleagues, the first treatment goal was to foster physical activity—even things like raking leaves and preparing dinner—because activity is incompatible with depression. Then:

> [The engineer's] cognitive distortions were identified by comparing his assessment of each activity with that of his wife. Alternative ways of interpreting his experiences were then considered.
>
> In comparing his wife's résumé of his past experiences, he became aware that he had (a) undervalued his past by failing to mention many previous accomplishments, (2) regarded himself as far more responsible for his "failures" than she did, and (3) concluded that he was worthless since he had not succeeded in attaining certain goals in the past. When the two

accounts were contrasted, he could discern many of his cognitive distortions. In subsequent sessions, his wife continued to serve as an "objectifier."

In midtherapy, [he] compiled a list of new attitudes that he had acquired since initiating therapy. These included:

1. "I am starting at a lower level of functioning at my job, but it will improve if I persist."
2. "I know that once I get going in the morning, everything will run all right for the rest of the day."
3. "I can't achieve everything at once."
4. "I have my periods of ups and downs, but in the long run I feel better."
5. "My expectations from my job and life should be scaled down to a realistic level."
6. "Giving in to avoidance [e.g., staying away from work and social interactions] never helps and only leads to further avoidance."

He was instructed to reread this list daily for several weeks even though he already knew the content. (Rush and others, 1975)

Rereading the list of productive attitudes is a variation of the cognitive technique of having clients rehearse or repeat rational ideas so that they come to replace cognitive distortions and irrational beliefs. The engineer gradually became less depressed in therapy and returned to work and an active social life. Along the way, he learned to combat inappropriate self-blame for problems, perfectionistic expectations, magnifications of failures, and overgeneralizations from failures.

Becoming aware of cognitive errors and modifying catastrophizing thoughts help provide us with coping ability under stress. Internal, stable, and global attributions of failure lead to depression and feelings of helplessness. Cognitive therapists also alert clients to cognitive errors such as these so that the clients can change their attitudes and pave the way for effective behavior.

Is He "Just Exploding" or Has He Decided to Erupt? Many people claim that they just explode when they are provoked and are unaware of the thoughts that mediate provocations and their reactions. Cognitive therapists have devised a number of methods to help them get in touch with, and restructure, their fleeting, enraging thoughts.

COGNITIVE RESTRUCTURING: "NO, NO, LOOK AT IT THIS WAY"

What would you do if someone purposefully bumped into your cart at the supermarket and then said, "What the hell's the matter with you? Why don't you look where you're going?"? I would not be surprised if some male readers interpreted (or cognitively structured) this provocation as threats to their "manhood" and took an aggressive stance. A few might even "explode" and hit the provocateur without any discussion. Yet other readers might structure or interpret this event as a challenge to solve a social problem and generate nonviolent solutions.

In cognitive restructuring, clients are shown how their interpretations of events can lead to maladaptive responses. They are then helped to restructure or rethink their situations so that they can generate more-adaptive responses (Dodge and others, 1990). Consider aggressive people who see themselves as "exploding" at any provocation. Exploding, to them, is an automatic response to an insult. Aggressive behavior is not automatic in people, however, even when they are sorely provoked. People usually *decide* to act aggressively (Berkowitz, 1994). Cognitive restructuring can help people interpret provocations as social problems demanding a solution rather than as threats to their honor.

Lochman (1992) recently recruited fourth- to sixth-grade boys who were labeled as aggressive and disruptive by teachers into an anger-coping program that included cognitive restructuring of social provocations. The boys were taught to use calming thoughts to curb impulsive behavior (for example, to tell themselves "Stop!" and "Think!" when they were provoked), to restructure social provocations as problems demanding solutions rather than as threats, and to generate and practice nonviolent responses. Three years after treatment, the boys who received anger-coping training could not be distinguished from boys considered to be nonaggressive.

Participants in such programs not only cognitively restructure social provocations. They also use problem solving and practice social skills (Lochman and others, 1993). Rehearsing social skills is usually considered a behavior-therapy technique, but cognitive and behavioral methods are frequently used in tandem. Many theorists, in fact, consider cognitive therapy to be a collection of techniques that belong within the province of behavior therapy, which is discussed in the following section. Some members of this group prefer the name "cognitive *behavior* therapy." Others argue that the term *behavior therapy* is broad enough to include cognitive techniques. Many cognitive therapists and behavior therapists differ in focus, however. Behavior therapists deal with client cognitions to change *overt* behavior. Cognitive therapists also see the value of tying treatment outcomes to observable behavior, but they tend to assert that cognitive change is itself a key goal.

Reflections

Now that you have read the section on cognitive therapy, reflect on the following questions:

- Do you believe that you must have the love and approval of people who are important to you? (How do you think you

can know if you do?) If so, does this belief ever give rise to feelings of frustration, anxiety, or depression in you?

- Do you believe that you must prove yourself to be thoroughly competent, adequate, and achieving? (How do you think you can know if you do?) If so, does this belief ever give rise to feelings of frustration, anxiety, or depression in you?

- Do you ever engage in any of Beck's cognitive errors? For example, do you magnify the importance of negative events? (Here we go again: How do you think you can know if you do?) If so, does this belief ever give rise to feelings of frustration, anxiety, or depression in you?

Behavior Therapy: Adjustment Is What You Do

Behavior therapy—also called *behavior modification*—is the direct promotion of desired behavioral change by means of systematic application of principles of learning. Many behavior therapists incorporate cognitive processes in their theoretical outlook and cognitive procedures in their methodology (Meichenbaum, 1993). For example, techniques such as systematic desensitization, covert sensitization, and covert reinforcement ask clients to focus on visual imagery. Behavioral methods for treating bulimia nervosa focus on clients' irrational attitudes toward their weight and body shape as well as foster healthful eating habits (Wilson & Fairburn, 1993).

Behavior therapists rely heavily on principles of conditioning and observational learning. They help clients discontinue self-defeating behavior patterns such as overeating, smoking, and phobic avoidance of harmless stimuli. They also help clients acquire adaptive behavior patterns such as the social skills required to start social relationships and to say no to insistent salespeople.

Behavior therapists may help clients gain "insight" into maladaptive behavior in the sense of fostering awareness of the circumstances in which it occurs. They do not foster insight in the psychoanalytic sense of unearthing the childhood origins of

Behavior therapy • Systematic application of the principles of learning to the direct modification of a client's problem behaviors.

Systematic desensitization • Wolpe's method for reducing fears by associating a hierarchy of images of fear-evoking stimuli with deep muscle relaxation.

Hierarchy • An arrangement of stimuli according to the amount of fear they evoke.

problems and the symbolic meanings of maladaptive behavior. Behavior therapists, like other therapists, may also build warm, therapeutic relationships with clients, but they see the efficacy of behavior therapy as deriving from specific, learning-based procedures (Wolpe, 1990). Behavior therapists insist that their methods be established by experimentation (Wolpe, 1990) and that therapeutic outcomes be assessed in terms of observable, measurable behavior.

Let us consider some behavior-therapy techniques.

FEAR-REDUCTION METHODS

Behavior therapists use many methods for reducing fears, including flooding (see Chapter 6), systematic desensitization, and modeling.

Systematic Desensitization.

Adam has a phobia for receiving injections. His behavior therapist treats him as he reclines in a comfortable padded chair. In a state of deep muscle relaxation, Adam observes slides projected on a screen. A slide of a nurse holding a needle has just been shown three times, 30 seconds at a time. Each time Adam has shown no anxiety. So now a slightly more discomforting slide is shown: one of the nurse aiming the needle toward someone's bare arm. After 15 seconds, our armchair adventurer notices twinges of discomfort and raises a finger as a signal (speaking might disturb his relaxation). The projector operator turns off the light, and Adam spends 2 minutes imagining his "safe scene"—lying on a beach beneath the tropical sun. Then the slide is shown again. This time Adam views it for 30 seconds before feeling anxiety.

Adam is undergoing **systematic desensitization,** a method for reducing phobic responses originated by psychiatrist Joseph Wolpe (1990). Systematic desensitization is a gradual process. Clients learn to handle increasingly disturbing stimuli while anxiety to each one is being counterconditioned. About 10 to 20 stimuli are arranged in a sequence, or **hierarchy,** according to their

Overcoming Fear of Flying. This woman has undergone group systematic desensitization in order to overcome her fear of flying. For several sessions, she engaged in tasks such as viewing pictures of airplanes and imagining herself in one. Now in the final stages of her program, she actually flies in an airplane with the support of group members and her therapist.

capacity to elicit anxiety. In imagination or by being shown photos, the client travels gradually up through this hierarchy, approaching the target behavior. In Adam's case, the target behavior was the ability to receive an injection without undue anxiety.

Wolpe developed systematic desensitization on the assumption that maladaptive anxiety responses, like other behaviors, are learned or conditioned. He reasoned that they can be unlearned by counterconditioning or by extinction. In counterconditioning, a response that is incompatible with anxiety is made to appear under conditions that usually elicit anxiety. Muscle relaxation is incompatible with anxiety. For this reason, Adam's therapist is teaching Adam to experience relaxation in the presence of (usually) anxiety-evoking slides of needles. (Muscle relaxation is usually achieved by means of *progressive relaxation,* which we describe in Chapter 15 as a method for lowering the arousal that attends anxiety reactions.)

Remaining in the presence of phobic imagery, rather than running from it, is also likely to enhance our self-efficacy expectations (Galassi, 1988). Self-efficacy expectations are negatively correlated with levels of adrenaline in the bloodstream (Bandura and

MINILECTURE: TREATING MALADAPTIVE VOMITING

FIGURE 14.2
Modeling Modeling is a behavior-therapy technique that is based on principles of observational learning. In these photos, people with a fear of snakes observe, then imitate, models who are unafraid. Parents often try to convince children that something tastes good by eating it before them and saying "Mmm!"

others, 1985). Raising clients' self-efficacy expectations may thus help lower their adrenaline levels, counteract feelings of nervousness, and lessen the physical signs of anxiety.

Truth or Fiction Revisited. *It is true that lying around in your reclining chair and fantasizing can be an effective way of confronting your fears.* This description is consistent with the method of systematic desensitization.

Modeling. **Modeling** relies on observational learning. In this method, clients observe, then imitate, people who approach and cope with the objects or situations the clients fear. Bandura and his colleagues (1969) found that modeling worked as well

as systematic desensitization—and more rapidly—in reducing fear of snakes (see Figure 14.2). Modeling, like systematic desensitization, is likely to increase self-efficacy expectations in coping with feared stimuli.

AVERSIVE CONDITIONING

Aversive conditioning is one of the more controversial procedures in behavior therapy. In aversive conditioning, painful or aversive stimuli are paired with unwanted impulses, such as desire for a cigarette or desire to engage in antisocial behavior, to make the goal less appealing. For example, to help people control alcohol intake, tastes of different alcoholic beverages can be paired with drug-induced nausea and vomiting or with electric shock.

Aversive conditioning has been used with problems as divergent as cigarette smoking (Lichtenstein & Glasgow, 1992), sexual abuse (Rice and others, 1991), and retarded children's self-injurious behavior. **Rapid smoking** is an aversive-conditioning method designed to help smokers quit. In this method, the would-be quitter inhales every 6 seconds. In another aversive-conditioning method for quitting smoking, the hose of an everyday hair dryer is hooked up to a chamber with several lit cigarettes. Smoke is blown into the quitter's face as he or she also smokes a cigarette. In a third, branching pipes are used so that the smoker draws in smoke from two or more cigarettes simultaneously. In all of these methods, overexposure renders once-desirable cigarette smoke aversive. The quitter becomes motivated to avoid, rather than seek, cigarettes and stops smoking on a preplanned date. Many reports have shown a quit rate of 60% or higher at 6-month follow-ups. Yet interest in these methods for quitting smoking has waned because of side effects such as raising the blood pressure and decreasing the blood's capacity to carry oxygen.

Truth or Fiction Revisited. *It is true that smoking cigarettes can be an effective treatment for helping people to stop smoking cigarettes.* The trick is to inhale enough smoke so that it is aversive rather than enjoyable.

In one study of aversive conditioning in the treatment of alcoholism, 63% of the 685 people treated remained abstinent for 1 year afterward, and about a third remained abstinent for at least 3 years (Wiens & Menustik, 1983). It may seem ironic that punitive aversive stimulation is sometimes used to stop children from punishing themselves, but people sometimes hurt themselves to obtain sympathy and attention from others. If self-injury leads to more pain than anticipated and no sympathy, it might be discontinued.

OPERANT CONDITIONING PROCEDURES

We usually prefer to relate to people who smile at us rather than ignore us and to take courses in which we do well rather than fail. We tend to repeat behavior that is rein-

Aversive Conditioning. In aversive conditioning, unwanted behaviors take on a noxious quality as a result of pairing them repeatedly with aversive stimuli. Overexposure is making cigarette smoke aversive to the smoker in this photograph.

forced. Behavior that is not reinforced tends to become extinguished. Behavior therapists have used these principles of operant conditioning with people with psychotic disorders as well as clients with milder problems.

The staff at one mental hospital was at a loss about how to encourage withdrawn people with schizophrenia to eat regularly. Ayllon and Haughton (1962) observed that staff members were exacerbating the problem by coaxing them into the dining room, even feeding them. Increased staff attention apparently reinforced their lack of cooperation. Some rules were changed. People who did not arrive at the dining hall within 30 minutes after serving were locked out. Staff could not interact with them at mealtime. With uncooperative behavior no longer reinforced, the people diagnosed with schizophrenia quickly changed their eating habits.

The Token Economy. Many psychiatric wards and hospitals now use **token economies** in which tokens such as poker chips must be used by residents to purchase TV viewing time, extra visits to the canteen, or private rooms. The tokens are reinforcements for productive activities such as making beds, brushing teeth, and socializing. Whereas token economies have not eliminated all features of schizophrenia, they have enhanced activity levels and cooperation among people diagnosed with the disorder. Tokens have also been used successfully in programs designed to modify the behavior of children with conduct disorders. For example, Schneider and Byrne (1987) gave children tokens for helpful

Modeling • A behavior-therapy technique in which a client observes and imitates a person who approaches and copes with feared objects or situations.

Aversive conditioning • A behavior-therapy technique in which undesired responses are inhibited by pairing repugnant or offensive stimuli with them.

Rapid smoking • An aversive-conditioning method for quitting smoking in which the would-be quitter inhales every 6 seconds, thus rendering once-desirable cigarette smoke aversive.

Token economy • A controlled environment in which people are reinforced for desired behaviors with tokens (such as poker chips) that may be exchanged for privileges.

behaviors such as volunteering and removed tokens for behaviors such as arguing and inattention.

Successive Approximations. The operant conditioning method of **successive approximations** is often used to help clients build good habits. Let us use a (not uncommon!) example: You wish to study 3 hours an evening but can only maintain concentration for half an hour. Rather than attempting to increase study time all at once, you could do so gradually by, say, 5 minutes an evening. After every hour or so of studying, you could reinforce yourself with 5 minutes of people-watching in a busy section of the library.

Social-Skills Training. In social-skills training, behavior therapists decrease social anxiety and build social skills through operant-conditioning procedures that employ **self-monitoring,** coaching, modeling, role playing, **behavior rehearsal,** and **feedback.** Social-skills training has been used to help formerly hospitalized mental patients maintain jobs and apartments in the community.

Social-skills training is effective in groups. Group members can role-play important people—such as parents, spouses, or potential dates—in the lives of other members. The trainee then can engage in behavior rehearsal with the role player.

Assertiveness Training. Are you a person who can't say no? Do people walk all over you? Brush off those footprints and get some assertiveness training! Assertiveness training is a kind of social-skills training that helps clients demand their rights and express their genuine feelings. Assertiveness training helps clients decrease social anxieties, but it has been used to optimize the functioning of individuals without problems.

Assertive behavior can be contrasted with both *nonassertive* (submissive) behavior and *aggressive* behavior. Assertive people express their genuine feelings, stick up for their legitimate rights, and refuse unreasonable requests. But they do not insult, threaten, or belittle. Assertive people also do not shy away from meeting people and building relationships, and they express positive feelings such as liking and love. The nearby

Rathus Assertiveness Schedule will afford you insight into how assertive you are.

Biofeedback Training. Through **biofeedback training** (BFT), therapists help clients become more aware of, and gain control over, various bodily functions. Therapists attach clients to devices that measure bodily changes such as heart rate. "Bleeps" or other electronic signals are used to indicate (and thereby reinforce) bodily changes in the desired direction. (Knowledge of results is a powerful reinforcer.) The electromyograph (EMG), for example, monitors muscle tension. It has been used to augment control over muscle tension in the forehead and elsewhere, thereby alleviating anxiety and stress.

BFT also helps clients voluntarily regulate functions such as heart rate and blood pressure that were once thought to be beyond conscious control. Hypertensive clients use a blood-pressure cuff and electronic signals to gain control over their blood pressure. The electroencephalograph (EEG) monitors brain waves and can be used to teach people how to produce alpha waves, which are associated with relaxation. Some people have overcome insomnia by learning to produce brain waves associated with sleep.

SELF-CONTROL METHODS

Do mysterious forces sometimes seem to be at work? Forces that delight in wreaking havoc on New Year's resolutions and other efforts to take charge of bad habits? Just when you go on a diet, that juicy pizza stares at you from the TV set. Just when you resolve to balance your budget, that sweater goes on sale. Behavior therapists have developed a number of self-control techniques to help people cope with such temptations.

Functional Analysis of Behavior. Behavior therapists usually begin with a **functional analysis** of the problem behavior. In this way, they help determine the stimuli that trigger problem behavior and the reinforcers that maintain it. You can use a diary to jot down each instance of a problem behavior. Note the time of day, location, your activity (including your thoughts and feelings), and reactions (yours and others'). Functional analysis serves a number of

---

Successive approximations • In operant conditioning, a series of behaviors that gradually become more similar to a target behavior.

Self-monitoring • Keeping a record of one's own behavior to identify problems and record successes.

Behavior rehearsal • Practice.

Feedback • In assertiveness training, information about the effectiveness of a response.

Biofeedback training • The systematic feeding back to an organism of information about a bodily function so that the organism can gain control of that function. Abbreviated *BFT*.

Functional analysis • A systematic study of behavior in which one identifies the stimuli that trigger problem behavior and the reinforcers that maintain it.

Questionnaire

THE RATHUS ASSERTIVENESS SCHEDULE

How assertive are you? Do you stick up for your rights, or do you allow others to walk all over you? Do you say what you feel or what you think other people want you to say? Do you initiate relationships with attractive people, or do you shy away from them?

One way to gain insight into how assertive you are is to take the following self-report test of assertive behavior. Once you have finished, turn to Appendix B to find out how to calculate and interpret your score.

DIRECTIONS: Indicate how well each item describes you by using this code:

3 = very much like me   − 1 = slightly unlike me
2 = rather like me   − 2 = rather unlike me
1 = slightly like me   − 3 = very much unlike me

_____ 1. Most people seem to be more aggressive and assertive than I am.*

_____ 2. I have hesitated to make or accept dates because of "shyness."*

_____ 3. When the food served at a restaurant is not done to my satisfaction, I complain about it to the waiter or waitress.

_____ 4. I am careful to avoid hurting other people's feelings, even when I feel that I have been injured.*

_____ 5. If a salesperson has gone to considerable trouble to show me merchandise that is not quite suitable, I have a difficult time saying "No."*

_____ 6. When I am asked to do something, I insist upon knowing why.

_____ 7. There are times when I look for a good, vigorous argument.

_____ 8. I strive to get ahead as well as most people in my position.

_____ 9. To be honest, people often take advantage of me.*

_____ 10. I enjoy starting conversations with new acquaintances and strangers.

_____ 11. I often don't know what to say to people I find attractive.*

_____ 12. I will hesitate to make phone calls to business establishments and institutions.*

_____ 13. I would rather apply for a job or for admission to a college by writing letters than by going through with personal interviews.*

_____ 14. I find it embarrassing to return merchandise.*

_____ 15. If a close and respected relative were annoying me, I would smother my feelings rather than express my annoyance.*

_____ 16. I have avoided asking questions for fear of sounding stupid.*

_____ 17. During an argument, I am sometimes afraid that I will get so upset that I will shake all over.*

_____ 18. If a famed and respected lecturer makes a comment which I think is incorrect, I will have the audience hear my point of view as well.

_____ 19. I avoid arguing over prices with clerks and salespeople.*

_____ 20. When I have done something important or worthwhile, I manage to let others know about it.

_____ 21. I am open and frank about my feelings.

_____ 22. If someone has been spreading false and bad stories about me, I see him or her as soon as possible and "have a talk" about it.

_____ 23. I often have a hard time saying "No."*

_____ 24. I tend to bottle up my emotions rather than make a scene.*

_____ 25. I complain about poor service in a restaurant and elsewhere.

_____ 26. When I am given a compliment, I sometimes just don't know what to say.*

_____ 27. If a couple near me in a theater or at a lecture were conversing rather loudly, I would ask them to be quiet or to take their conversation elsewhere.

_____ 28. Anyone attempting to push ahead of me in a line is in for a good battle.

_____ 29. I am quick to express an opinion.

_____ 30. There are times when I just can't say anything.*

Reprinted from Rathus, 1973a, pp. 398-406.

Functional Analysis. Behavior therapists often help people modify problem behavior through functional analysis. This method helps people determine the stimuli that trigger the problem behavior and the reinforcers that maintain it. You can use a diary to jot down each instance of a problem behavior. Note the time of day, location, your activity (including your thoughts and feelings), and reactions (yours and others'). Functional analysis makes you more aware of the environmental context of your behavior and can boost your motivation to change.

purposes. It makes you more aware of the environmental context of your behavior and can boost your motivation to change.

Truth or Fiction Revisited. *It is true that you might be able to gain control over bad habits merely by keeping a record of where and when you practice them.* The record may help motivate you, make you more aware of the problems, and suggest strategies for behavior change.

Brian used functional analysis to master his nail biting. Table 14.3 shows a few items from his notebook. He discovered that boredom and humdrum activities seemed to serve as triggers for nail biting. He began to watch out for feelings of boredom as signs to practice self-control. He also made some changes in his life so that he would feel bored less often.

There are numerous self-control strategies aimed at (1) the stimuli that trigger behavior, (2) the behaviors themselves, and (3) reinforcers.

Strategies Aimed at Stimuli That Trigger Behavior

Restriction of the stimulus field. Gradually exclude the problem behavior from more environments. For example, at first make smoking off limits in the car, then in the office. Or practice the habit only outside the environment in which it normally occurs.

Avoidance of powerful stimuli that trigger habits. Avoid obvious sources of temptation. People who go window-shopping often wind up buying more than windows. If eating at The Pizza Glutton tempts you to forget your diet, eat at home or at The Celery Stalk instead.

Stimulus control. Place yourself in an environment in which desirable behavior is likely to occur. Maybe it's difficult to lift your mood directly at times, but you can place yourself in the audience of that uplifting concert or film. It might be difficult to force yourself to study, but how about

TABLE 14.3
Excerpts from Brian's Diary of Nail Biting for April 14

INCIDENT	TIME	LOCATION	ACTIVITY (THOUGHTS, FEELINGS)	REACTIONS
1	7:45 A.M.	Freeway	Driving to work, bored, not thinking	Finger bleeds, pain
2	10:30 A.M.	Office	Writing report	Self-disgust
3	2:25 P.M.	Conference	Listening to dull financial report	Embarrassment
4	6:40 P.M.	Living room	Watching evening news	Self-disgust

A functional analysis of problem behavior like nail biting increases awareness of the environmental context in which it occurs, spurs motivation to change, and, in highly motivated people, might lead to significant behavioral change.

rewarding yourself for spending time in the library?

Strategies Aimed at Behavior.

Response prevention. Make unwanted behavior difficult or impossible. Impulse buying is curbed when you shred your credit cards, leave your checkbook home, and carry only a couple of dollars. You can't reach for the strawberry cream cheese pie in your refrigerator if you have left it at the supermarket (that is, have not bought it).

Competing responses. Engage in behaviors that are incompatible with the bad habits. It is difficult to drink a glass of water and a fattening milk shake simultaneously. Grasping something firmly is a useful competing response for nail biting or scratching.

Chain breaking. Interfere with unwanted habitual behavior by complicating the process of engaging in it. Break the chain of reaching for a readily available cigarette and placing it in your mouth by wrapping the pack in aluminum foil and placing it on the top shelf in the closet. Rewrap the pack after taking one. Put your cigarette in the ashtray between puffs, or put your fork down between mouthfuls of dessert. Ask yourself if you really want more.

Successive approximations. Gradually approach targets through a series of relatively painless steps. Increase studying by only 5 minutes a day. Decrease smoking by pausing for a minute when the cigarette is smoked halfway, or by putting it out a minute before you would wind up eating the filter. Decrease your daily intake of food by 50 to 100 calories every couple of days, or cut out one type of fattening food every few days.

Strategies Aimed at Reinforcements.

Reinforcement of desired behavior. Why give yourself something for nothing? Make pleasant activities such as going to films, walking on the beach, or reading a new novel contingent upon meeting reasonable, daily behavioral goals. Put one dollar away toward that camera or vacation trip each day you remain within your calorie limit.

Response cost. Heighten awareness of the long-term reasons for dieting or cutting down on smoking by punishing yourself for not meeting a daily goal or for practicing a bad habit. Make out a check to your most hated cause and mail it at once if you bite your nails or inhale that cheesecake.

"Grandma's method." Remember Grandma's method for inducing children to eat their vegetables? Simple: no veggies, no dessert. In this method, desired behaviors such as studying and brushing teeth can be increased by insisting that they be done before you carry out a favored or frequently occurring activity. For example, don't watch television unless you have studied first. Don't leave the apartment until you've brushed your teeth. You can also place reminders of new attitudes you're trying to acquire on little cards and read them regularly. For example, in quitting smoking, you might write "Every day it becomes a little easier" on one card and "Your lungs will turn pink again" on another. Place these cards and others in your wallet, and read them like clockwork before you leave the house.

Covert sensitization. Create imaginary horror stories about problem behavior. Psychologists have successfully reduced overeating and smoking by having clients imagine that they become acutely nauseated at the thought of fattening foods or that a cigarette is made from vomit. Some horror stories are not so "imaginary." Deliberately focusing on heart strain and diseased lungs every time you overeat or smoke, rather than ignoring these long-term consequences, might also promote self-control.

Covert reinforcement. Create rewarding imagery for desired behavior. When you have achieved a behavioral goal, fantasize about how wonderful you are. Imagine friends and family patting you on the back.

Truth or Fiction Revisited. *It is true that some psychotherapists tell their clients precisely what to do.* That is, they outline behavioral prescriptions for their clients. Behavior therapists, Gestalt therapists, and some cognitive therapists provide examples.

Reflections

Now that you have read the section on behavior therapy, reflect on the following questions:

- Does behavior therapy strike you as "behavioral"? Do some methods seem more behavioral than others? Explain.
- Can you relate the methods discussed in this section to principles of conditioning and observational learning? As an example, how about the methods of fear reduction?
- Consider some of your own life concerns. Do you think they can be dealt with by means of behavior therapy? Why or why not?

Group Therapies

When a psychotherapist has several clients with similar problems—whether anxiety, depression, adjustment to divorce, or lack of social skills—it often makes sense to treat these clients in groups of 6 to 12 rather than conduct individual therapy sessions. The methods and characteristics of the group will reflect the needs of the members and the theoretical orientation of the leader. For example, in group psychoanalysis, clients might interpret one another's dreams. In a person-centered group, they might provide an accepting atmosphere for self-exploration. Members of behavior-therapy groups might obtain joint desensitization to anxiety-evoking stimuli or practice social skills together.

There are several advantages to group therapy:

1. Group therapy is economical. It allows the therapist to work with several clients at once. Since good therapists are usually busy, the group format allows them to see people who might otherwise have to wait.

2. As compared with one-to-one therapy, group therapy provides a greater fund of information and life experience for clients to draw upon. When a group member explains how something worked out (or didn't work out) for him or her, it might have more impact than a theoretical discussion or a secondhand story from a therapist.

Group Therapy. Group therapy has a number of advantages over individual therapy for many clients. It's economical, provides a fund of information and experience for clients to draw upon, elicits group support and reassurance, and provides the opportunity to relate to other people. On the other hand, some clients do require individual attention.

3. Appropriate behavior receives group support. Clients usually appreciate approval from their therapists, but an outpouring of peer approval is quite powerful.

4. When we run into troubles, it is easy to imagine that we are different from other people or inferior. Group members frequently learn that other people have had similar problems and self-doubts. Affiliating with people who have similar problems is reassuring.

5. Group members who show improvement provide hope for other members.

6. Many individuals seek therapy because of problems relating to other people. People who seek therapy for other reasons are also frequently socially inhibited. Members of groups have the opportunity to practice social skills in a relatively nonthreatening atmosphere. In a group consisting of men and women of different ages, group members can role-play one another's employers, employees, spouses, parents, children, and friends. A 20-year-old can practice refusing unreasonable requests from a 47-year-old as a way of learning how to refuse such requests from a parent. Members can role-play asking one another out on dates, saying no (or yes) to sexual requests, and so on.

On the other hand, group therapy is not for everyone. Some clients will fare better with individual treatment. Many clients prefer not to disclose their problems to a group. They may be inhibited in front of others, or they may want individual attention. Because many clients who are willing to enter groups also share these concerns, it is the responsibility of the therapist to insist that group disclosures be kept confidential, to establish a supportive atmosphere, and to ensure that group members receive the attention they need.

Many types of therapy can be conducted either individually or in groups. Encounter groups, couple therapy, and family therapy are conducted in group format only.

ENCOUNTER GROUPS

Encounter groups are not appropriate for treating serious psychological problems. Rather, they are intended to promote personal growth by heightening awareness of one's own needs and feelings and those of others. This goal is sought through intense confrontations, or encounters, between strangers. Like ships in the night, group members come together out of the darkness, touch one another briefly, then sink back into the shadows of one another's lives. But something is thought to be gained from the passing.

Encounter groups stress interactions between group members in the here and now. Discussion of the past may be outlawed. Interpretation is out. Expression of genuine feelings toward others is encouraged. When group members think that a person's social mask is phony, they might descend en masse to rip it off.

Professionals recognize that encounter groups can be damaging when they urge overly rapid disclosure of intimate matters or when several members attack one member in unison. Responsible leaders do not tolerate these abuses and try to keep their groups moving in growth-enhancing directions.

COUPLE THERAPY

Couple therapy helps unmarried and married couples enhance their relationships by improving communication skills and helping them manage conflict (Markman and others, 1993). There are often power imbalances in relationships, and couple therapy helps individuals find "full membership" in the couple. Correcting power imbalances increases marital happiness and can decrease the incidence of domestic violence. Ironically, the partner with *less* power in the relationship is usually the violent partner. Violence would sometimes appear to be a way of compensating for inability to share power in other areas of the relationship (Babcock and others, 1993).

The main approach to couple therapy today appears to be cognitive-behavioral (Jacobson & Addis, 1993; Markman and others, 1993). It focuses on teaching couples specific communications skills (such as how to listen to one another and how to express feelings), ways of handling feelings like depression and anger, and ways of solving problems.

Encounter group • A type of group that aims to foster self-awareness by focusing on how group members relate to each other in a setting that encourages open expression of feelings.

FAMILY THERAPY

In **family therapy,** one or more families constitute the group. Family therapy may be undertaken from various theoretical viewpoints. One is the "systems approach," in which the family system of interaction is studied and modified to enhance the growth of family members and of the family unit as a whole (Annunziata & Jacobson-Kram, 1995; Mikesell and others, 1995).

It is often found that family members with low self-esteem cannot tolerate different attitudes and behaviors from other family members. Faulty family communications also create problems. It is also not uncommon for the family to present an "identified patient"—that is, the family member who has *the* problem and is *causing* all the trouble. Yet family therapists usually assume that the identified patient is a scapegoat for other problems within and among family members. It is a sort of myth: Change the bad apple—or identified patient—and the barrel—or family—will be functional once more.

The family therapist—who is often a specialist in this field—attempts to teach the family to communicate more effectively and to encourage growth and the eventual autonomy, or independence, of each family member. In doing so, the family therapist will also show the family how the identified patient has been used as a focus for the problems of other members of the group.

There are many other types of groups: marathon groups, sensitivity-training groups, and psychodrama, to name just a few.

Reflections

Now that you have read the section on group therapies, reflect on the following questions:

- If you went for therapy, do you think that you would prefer being treated on a one-to-one basis or in a group? Why?
- Could a couple or a family you know of profit from couple therapy or family therapy? If so, in what way? Can you foresee problems in encouraging a couple or family to go for therapy? What might they be?

Now that we have explored some of the types of psychotherapy in use today, let us

Family therapy • A form of therapy in which the family unit is treated as the client.

consider a question that may have occurred to you: Does psychotherapy work?

Does Psychotherapy Work?

Many of us know people who swear by their therapists, but the evidence is often shaky—for example, "I was a wreck before, but now . . . ," or "I feel so much better now." Anecdotes like these are encouraging, but we do not know what would have happened to these people had they not sought help. Many people feel better about their problems as time goes on, with or without therapy. Sometimes, happily, problems seem to go away by themselves. Sometimes, people find solutions on their own. Then, too, we hear some stories about how therapy was to no avail and about people hopping fruitlessly from therapist to therapist.

PROBLEMS IN CONDUCTING RESEARCH ON PSYCHOTHERAPY

Before we report on research into the effectiveness of therapy, let us review some of the problems of this kind of research (Figure 14.3 summarizes these problems).

Problems in Running Experiments on Psychotherapy. The ideal method for evaluating a treatment—such as a method of therapy—is the experiment. However, "Experiments [on therapeutic methods] are not easy to arrange and control, outcomes are difficult to measure—often even to define—and results are often disappointing" (Smith & Sechrest, 1991, p. 233).

Consider psychoanalysis. In well-run experiments, individuals are randomly assigned to experimental and control groups. Thus, a sound experiment on psychoanalysis might require randomly assigning people seeking therapy to psychoanalysis and to a control group or other kinds of therapy for comparison (Lurbosky and others, 1993). A person may have to remain in traditional psychoanalysis for years to attain results, however. Could we create control "treatments" comparable in duration? Moreover,

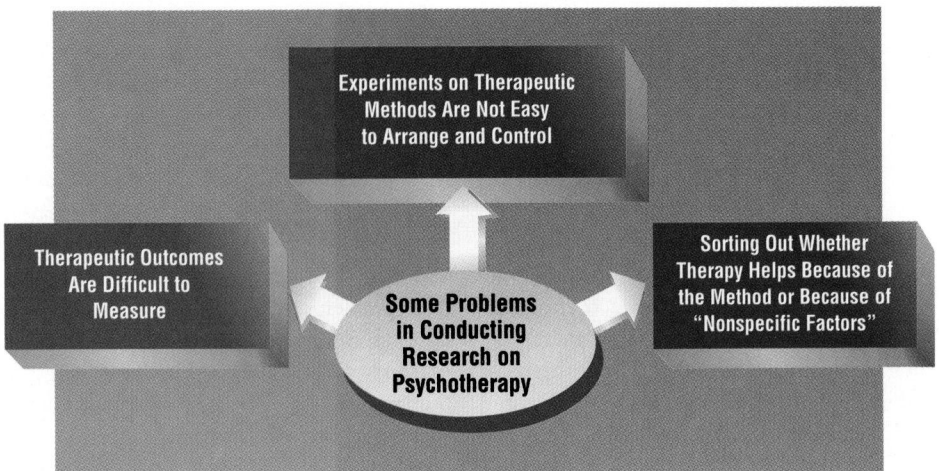

FIGURE 14.3

Spotlight on Problems in Conducting Research on Psychotherapy Numerous problems make it difficult to conduct research on psychotherapy. For example, experiments on therapy methods are difficult to arrange and control. It is hard to measure the outcomes of therapy, many of which are subjective. It may also be difficult to sort out the effects of the therapy method from those of nonspecific factors, such as instilling a sense of hope.

some people seek psychoanalysis per se rather than psychotherapy in general. Would it be ethical to assign them at random to other treatments or to a no-treatment control group? Clearly not.

In an ideal experiment, participants and researchers are blind as to the treatment the participants obtain. In the Lang (1975) experiment on the effects of alcohol discussed in Chapter 2, participants were blind as to whether they had ingested alcohol. In this way, the researchers could control for participants' expectations about alcohol's effects. In an ideal experiment on therapy, individuals would be similarly blind as to the type of therapy they are obtaining—or as to whether they are obtaining a placebo (Carroll and others, 1994). It is difficult to mask the type of therapy clients are obtaining, however (Margraf and others, 1991). Even if we could conceal it from clients, could we hide it from therapists?

Problems in Measuring the Outcomes of Therapy. Consider problems we run into when measuring the outcomes of therapy (Azar, 1994b). Behavior therapists define their goals in behavioral terms—such as a formerly phobic individual being able to obtain an injection or

look out of a 20th-story window. Therefore, behavior therapists do not encounter too many problems in this area. But what of the person-centered therapist who fosters insight and self-actualization? Or of the cognitive therapist who alters the ways in which clients perceive the world or who replaces irrational beliefs with rational ones? We cannot directly measure an insight, self-actualization, or a rational belief. We must assess what clients say and do and make inferences about such variables.

There are also problems with the amount of change. A therapy method may produce statistically significant changes that are not necessarily meaningful (Christiensen, 1994). The issue is not simply whether psychologists can use sophisticated mathematic means to show that clients change. The question is whether such change makes profound differences in clients' lives.

Are Clinical Judgments Valid? Because of problems such as these, many clinicians believe that important clinical questions cannot be answered through research (Newman & Howard, 1991). For them, clinical judgment is the basis for evaluating the effectiveness of therapy. Unfortunately, therapists have a stake in believing that their clients profit from treatment. Therapists are not unbiased judges, even when they try to be.

Does Therapy Help Because of the Method or Because of "Nonspecific Factors"? It is a staggering task to sort out the benefits of therapy per se from other aspects of the therapy situation. These aspects are termed *nonspecific factors* and refer to features that are found in most therapies, such as the instillation of hope and the relationship with a therapist (Crits-Christoph & Mintz, 1991). Common threads among therapists include the showing of warmth and empathy and the encouragement of exploration (Burns & Nolen-Hoeksema, 1992; Lambert and others, 1986; Rounsaville and others, 1987). The benefits of therapy could thus stem largely from such nonspecific factors. If so, the method itself might have little more value than a "sugar pill" has in combating physical ailments.

What Is the Experimental Treatment in Psychotherapy Outcome Studies? We may also inquire, what exactly is the experimental "treatment" being evaluated? Various therapists may say that they are practicing psychoanalysis, but they differ as individuals and in their training. It is therefore difficult to specify just what is happening in the therapeutic session (Luborsky and others, 1993).

ANALYSES OF THERAPY EFFECTIVENESS

Despite these evaluation problems, research into the effectiveness of therapy has been highly encouraging (Barlow, 1994; Lipsey & Wilson, 1993). Since the late 1970s, this research has relied heavily on a technique termed **meta-analysis** by researcher Gene Glass. Meta-analysis combines and averages the results of individual studies. Generally speaking, the included studies address similar issues in a similar way. Moreover, the analysts judge them to have been conducted in a valid manner.

In their classic early use of meta-analysis, Mary Lee Smith and Gene Glass (1977) analyzed the results of dozens of outcome studies on types of therapies. They concluded that people who obtained psy-

chodynamic therapy showed greater well-being, on the average, than 70% to 75% of those who did not obtain treatment. Similarly, nearly 75% of the clients obtaining person-centered therapy were better off than people without treatment. Psychodynamic and person-centered therapies appear to be most effective with well-educated, verbal, strongly motivated clients who report problems with anxiety, depression (of light to moderate proportions), and interpersonal relationships. Neither form of therapy appears to be effective with people with psychotic disorders such as major depression, bipolar disorder, and schizophrenia. Smith and Glass (1977) found that people who obtained TA were better off than about 72% of those without treatment. People who obtained Gestalt therapy showed greater well-being than about 60% of those without treatment. The effectiveness of psychoanalysis, person-centered therapy, and TA was thus reasonably comparable. Gestalt therapy fell behind.

Smith and Glass (1977) did not include cognitive therapies in their meta-analysis because many cognitive approaches were relatively new at the time of their study. Because behavior therapists also incorporate many cognitive techniques, it can be difficult to sort out which aspects—cognitive or otherwise—of behavioral treatments are most effective. However, many meta-analyses of cognitive-behavioral therapy have been conducted since the early work of Smith and Glass. Their results are strongly encouraging (Lipsey & Wilson, 1993).

A number of studies of cognitive therapy per se have also been conducted. For example, they show that rational-emotive therapy helps people with emotional problems such as anxiety and depression (Engels and others, 1993; Haaga & Davison, 1993). Modifying self-defeating beliefs of the sort outlined by Beck also frequently alleviates anxiety and depression (Robins & Hayes, 1993; Whisman and others, 1991). Cognitive therapy may be helpful with people with severe depression who are usually considered responsive only to biological therapies (Hollon and others, 1991, 1993; Simons and others, 1986). Cognitive therapy has also helped people with personality disorders (Beck & Freeman, 1990). It has even helped outpatients with schizophrenia

Meta-analysis • A method for combining and averaging the results of individual research studies.

(who are also using drug therapy) to modify delusional beliefs (Chadwick & Lowe, 1990).

Behavior therapy has provided people with strategies for alleviating anxiety, depression, social-skills deficits, and problems in self-control. These strategies have proved effective for most clients in terms of quantifiable behavioral change (Lazarus, 1990). Behavior therapists have also been innovative with a number of problems such as anxiety and sexual disorders for which there had not previously been effective treatments. Overall, Smith and Glass (1977) found behavior-therapy techniques to be somewhat more effective than psychodynamic or humanistic–existential methods. About 80% of people who obtained behavior-therapy treatments such as systematic desensitization and strategies for self-control showed greater well-being than people who did not. The 80% figure compares favorably with percentages in the low to middle 70s for people who obtained psychodynamic and humanistic–existential therapies.

Many studies that directly compare treatment techniques find behavior-therapy, psychodynamic, and humanistic–existential approaches to be about equal in overall effectiveness (Berman and others, 1985; Smith and others, 1980). Psychodynamic and humanistic–existential approaches seem to foster greater self-understanding. Behavior therapy (including cognitive-behavioral therapy) shows superior results in treatment of specific problems such as headaches (Blanchard, 1992b) and anxiety disorders (Borkovec & Costello, 1993). Behavior therapy has also been effective in helping coordinate the care of institutionalized people, including people with schizophrenia and those with mental retardation (Spreat & Behar, 1994). However, there is little evidence that behavior therapy alone is effective in treating the quirks of thought found in people with severe psychotic disorders (Wolpe, 1990).

Thus, it is not enough to ask which type of therapy is most effective. We must ask which type of therapy is most effective for a particular problem (Beutler, 1991; Shoham-Salomon, 1991; Snow, 1991). What are its advantages? What are its limitations? Clients may successfully use systematic desensitization to overcome stage fright, as measured by ability to speak to a group of people. If clients also want to know why they have stage fright, however, behavior therapy alone will not provide the answer.

Reflections

Now that you have read the section on whether psychotherapy works, reflect on the following questions:

- Agree or disagree with the following statement and support your answer: "Psychotherapy is just common sense."
- Justin swears he feels much better because of psychoanalysis. Deborah swears by her experience with Gestalt therapy. Are these endorsements acceptable as scientific evidence? Why or why not?
- Agree or disagree with the following statement and support your answer: "It has never been shown that psychotherapy does any good."
- Agree or disagree with the following statement and support your answer: "The effects of traditional psychoanalysis cannot be determined by the experimental method."
- Do you believe that you might profit from psychotherapy? Why or why not?

Biological Therapies

In the 1950s, Fats Domino popularized the song "My Blue Heaven." Fats was singing about the sky and happiness. Today, "blue heavens" is one of the street names for the 10-milligram dose of the antianxiety drug Valium. Clinicians prescribe Valium and other drugs for people with various psychological disorders. In this section, we discuss drug therapy, electroconvulsive therapy, and psychosurgery, three biological, or medical, approaches to treating people with psychological disorders.

MINILECTURE: BIOLOGICAL THERAPIES

DRUG THERAPY

In this section, we discuss antianxiety drugs, antipsychotic drugs, antidepressants, and lithium.

Antianxiety Drugs. Most antianxiety drugs (also called *minor tranquilizers*) belong to the chemical class *benzodiazepines.* Valium (diazepam) is a benzodiazepine. Other benzodiazepines include chlordiazepoxide (for example, Librium), oxazepam (Serax), and alprazolam (Xanax). Antianxiety drugs are usually prescribed for outpatients who complain of generalized anxiety or panic attacks, although many people also use them as sleeping pills. Valium and other antianxiety drugs depress the activity of the central nervous system (CNS). The CNS, in turn, decreases sympathetic activity, reducing the heart rate, respiration rate, and feelings of nervousness and tension.

Most people use antianxiety drugs for brief periods of time (Shader & Greenblatt, 1993). Some people come to tolerate small dosages of these drugs very quickly, how-

ever (Gillin, 1991). When tolerance occurs, dosages must be increased for the drug to remain effective. Some people become embroiled in tugs-of-war with their clinicians when the clinicians become concerned about how much they are taking. Clinicians may ask people to cut down "for their own good." People sometimes resent clinicians for getting them started with the drug and then playing moralists.

Sedation (feelings of being tired or drowsy) is the most common side effect of antianxiety drugs (Shader & Greenblatt, 1993). Problems that may be associated with withdrawal from them include **rebound anxiety.** That is, some people who have been using these drugs regularly report that their anxiety returns in exacerbated form once they discontinue them. Antianx-

---

PSYCHOLOGY IN THE NEW MILLENNIUM

Rebound anxiety • Strong anxiety that can attend the suspension of usage of a tranquilizer.
Antidepressant • Acting to relieve depression.

Beyond Wellness: Are Biological Treatments for Personality Improvement in the Offing?

Biological therapies for psychological disorders may date to prehistoric times. They hark back at least to ancient times, when the Greeks and Romans used mineral water (containing lithium) to treat people with bipolar disorder. Only in the 20th century, however, have we gained insights into how biological approaches to therapy affect the biochemical processes of the human body. This knowledge raises the possibility that biological treatments may soon be used to take us a step beyond freedom from disorder. They may be used to improve people's personalities.

One current drug that some have seen as personality-enhancing is the antidepressant drug Prozac (Newman, 1994). In *Listening to Prozac,* psychiatrist Peter D. Kramer (1993) writes that Prozac not only lifted depression in a number of his patients, but also caused a transformation in personality. Kramer claimed that Prozac could give introverted people the social skills of the salesperson. Prozac could free the inhibited person to be impetuous. Kramer argues that Prozac not only leads to predictable improvements such as reduced sluggishness (that is, reversal of the depressive symptom of psychomotor retardation) and enhanced ability to concentrate. He believes that Prozac also improves memory functioning, enhances social poise, increases resilience to setbacks, allows people to slough off insults, and heightens mental agility and thoughtfulness.

Kramer's critics, such as Daniel X. Freedman (1993), former editor of the journal *Archives of General Psychiatry,* argue that Prozac's effects are much more limited. Freedman allows that Kramer's *Listening to Prozac* demonstrates how drugs and psychotherapy can together provide helpful treatment for depression and other psychological problems. Yet Freedman argues that the number of users of Prozac "who experience startling personality changes is rather small. Indeed, it will be news to the millions of [people] who take it for depression [and other psychological problems] that this drug can cause dramatic changes in temperament" (p. 6).

iety drugs can induce physical dependence, as evidenced by withdrawal symptoms such as tremulousness, sweating, insomnia, and rapid heartbeat.

Antipsychotic Drugs. People diagnosed with schizophrenia are likely to take antipsychotic drugs (also called *major tranquilizers*). In most cases, antipsychotic drugs reduce agitation, delusions, and hallucinations (Gilman and others, 1990; Michels & Marzuk, 1993). Many antipsychotic drugs, including phenothiazines (for example, Thorazine) and clozapine (Clozaril) are thought to act by blocking dopamine receptors in the brain (Carpenter & Buchanan, 1994; Michels & Marzuk, 1993). Research along these lines supports the dopamine theory of schizophrenia.

Antidepressants. People with major depression often take so-called **antidepressant** drugs. Antidepressants are also sometimes helpful with people with eating disorders (Craighead & Agras, 1991) and panic disorder (Clum and others, 1993). Problems in the regulation of noradrenaline and serotonin may be involved in these other disorders as well as depression. Antidepressants are believed to work by increasing the amount of one or both of these neurotransmitters available in the brain, which can affect both depression and eating disorders. However, cognitive-behavior therapy addresses irrational attitudes concerning weight and body shape, fosters normal eating habits, and helps people resist the urges to binge and purge. Cognitive-behavior therapy is therefore apparently more

Regardless of the effects—or limitations—of Prozac, many biological therapies, including drugs with psychological effects, are in the research pipeline (Newman, 1994). One or more of them may foster remarkable changes in personality. If that is so, what questions are raised for society to ponder?

The value of psychological and biological approaches to alleviating psychological disorders would appear to be unquestioned. But who will decide what is an ideal personality? Who will decide on the directions into which we take the normal into the supernormal?

If drugs that can eliminate shyness are available, will outgoing mothers use them on timid children? Will people who are naturally reserved, and who might prefer to remain diffident, feel pressured to use drugs that abolish reservations so that they can compete in a millennium of "drug-engineered personalities" (Freedman, 1993, p. 6)? In ousting shyness, do we also eradicate introversion and introspection? Do we risk having a society of smiling, outgoing risk-takers?

If chemicals are available to make us well-adjusted, do we risk forgoing the fruits of people with "tortured" personalities such as Vincent van Gogh, Sylvia Plath, and Edgar Allan Poe? Would the person with antisocial personality disorder obtain a chemical conscience? Would Shakespeare's *Hamlet,* which is about the internal conflicts of literature's "melancholy Dane," be reinterpreted as a reminder of the perils of remaining pill-free?

If the powers that be in the new millennium—or the style—were to dictate that gender differences created the dangers of prejudice and discrimination, would all gender differences in cognition and personality be chemically or surgically erased? On the other hand, if political powers—or, again, the style—were to revert to a fierce traditionalism, would all men be chemically hyped into macho males and all women chemically laced into super-nurturant, ultra-feminine modes?

If the new millennium brings ways of transforming personality in specified directions, we will face many ethical and practical issues concerning what it means to be human. Will psychologists argue that "perfecting" the individual actually destroys the dignity of the individual? If so, why?

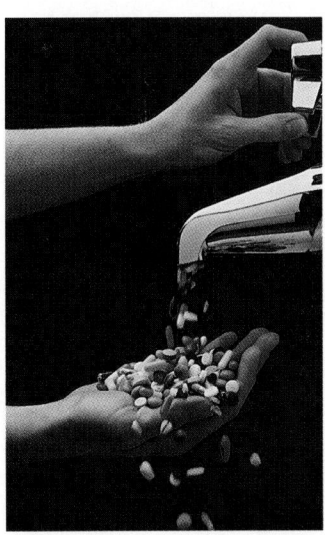

What Is in the Research Pipeline? There are many biological therapies for psychological disorders. However, researchers are developing a number of treatments that may improve people's personalities in the new millennium. If we were to use chemicals to make us well-adjusted, would we forgo the fruits of "tortured" artists such as Vincent van Gogh? What do you think?

Monoamine oxidase inhibitors • (MON–oh–ah–mean OX–see–dase). Antidepressant drugs that work by blocking the action of an enzyme that breaks down noradrenaline and serotonin. Abbreviated *MAO inhibitors.*

Tricyclic antidepressants • (try–SIGH–click). Antidepressant drugs that work by preventing the re-uptake of noradrenaline and serotonin by transmitting neurons.

Serotonin-uptake inhibitors • Antidepressant drugs that work by blocking the re-uptake of serotonin by presynaptic neurons.

Sedative • Relieving nervousness or agitation.

Electroconvulsive therapy • Treatment of disorders like major depression by passing an electric current (that causes a convulsion) through the head. Abbreviated *ECT.*

Psychosurgery • Surgery intended to promote psychological changes or to relieve disordered behavior.

Prefrontal lobotomy • The severing or destruction of a section of the frontal lobe of the brain.

effective than antidepressants with people with bulimia (Wilson & Fairburn, 1993).

There are various kinds of antidepressant drugs. Each type increases the brain concentrations of noradrenaline or serotonin (Potter and others, 1991). **Monoamine oxidase (MAO) inhibitors** block the activity of an enzyme that breaks down noradrenaline and serotonin. Nardil and Parnate are examples of MAO inhibitors. **Tricyclic antidepressants** such as Tofranil and Elavil prevent re-uptake of noradrenaline and serotonin by the axon terminals of the transmitting neurons. **Serotonin-uptake inhibitors,** such as fluoxetine hydrochloride (Prozac) and sertraline (Zoloft), also block the re-uptake of serotonin by presynaptic neurons. As a result, the neurotransmitters remain in the synaptic cleft for a greater amount of time, enhancing the probability that they will influence receiving neurons.

Antidepressants tend to alleviate the physical aspects of depression. For example, they tend to increase a person's activity level and to reduce eating and sleeping disturbances (Lyons and others, 1985). Severely depressed people often have insomnia, and it is not unusual for antidepressant drugs, which have a strong **sedative** effect, to be given at bedtime. Typically, antidepressant drugs must build up to a therapeutic level, which may take several weeks. Because overdoses of antidepressants can be lethal, some people enter the hospital during the build-up period to prevent suicide attempts.

Lithium. It could be said that the ancient Greeks and Romans were among the first to use the metal lithium as a psychoactive drug. They would prescribe mineral water for people with bipolar disorder. They had no inkling as to why this treatment sometimes helped, but it might have been because mineral water contains lithium. A salt of the metal lithium (lithium carbonate), in tablet form, flattens out cycles of manic behavior and depression for most people. It apparently moderates the level of noradrenaline available to the brain.

Because lithium is more toxic than most drugs, the dose must be carefully monitored during early phases of therapy by repeated analysis of blood samples. It might be necessary for persons with bipolar disorder to

use lithium indefinitely, just as a medical patient with diabetes must continue insulin to control the illness. Lithium also has been shown to have the side effects of impairing memory and depressing motor speed (Shaw and others, 1987). Memory impairment is reported as the primary reason that people discontinue lithium (Jamison & Akiskal, 1983).

ELECTROCONVULSIVE THERAPY

Electroconvulsive therapy (ECT) was introduced by Italian psychiatrist Ugo Cerletti in 1939 for use with people with psychological disorders. Cerletti had noted that some slaughterhouses used electric shock to render animals unconscious. The shocks also produced convulsions. Cerletti erroneously believed, as did other European researchers of the period, that convulsions were incompatible with schizophrenia and other major psychological disorders.

ECT was originally used for a variety of psychological disorders. Because of the advent of antipsychotic drugs, however, the American Psychiatric Association (1990) now recommends ECT mainly for people with major depression who are not responsive to antidepressants. ECT is still sometimes obtained by people with intense manic episodes, schizophrenia, and other disorders, however (Sakheim, 1990).

People typically obtain one ECT treatment three times a week for up to 10 sessions. Electrodes are attached to the temples, or on one side of the head only (in "unilateral ECT"), and an electrical current strong enough to produce a convulsion is induced. The shock causes unconsciousness, so people do not recall it. Still, people take a sedative so they sleep during treatment. In the past, people who obtained ECT flailed about wildly during the convulsions, sometimes breaking bones. Today, they take muscle-relaxing drugs, and convulsions are barely perceptible to onlookers.

ECT is controversial for many reasons. First, many professionals are distressed by the thought of passing electric shock through the head and producing convulsions, even if they are suppressed by drugs. Second are the side effects. ECT disrupts recall of recent events. Although memory

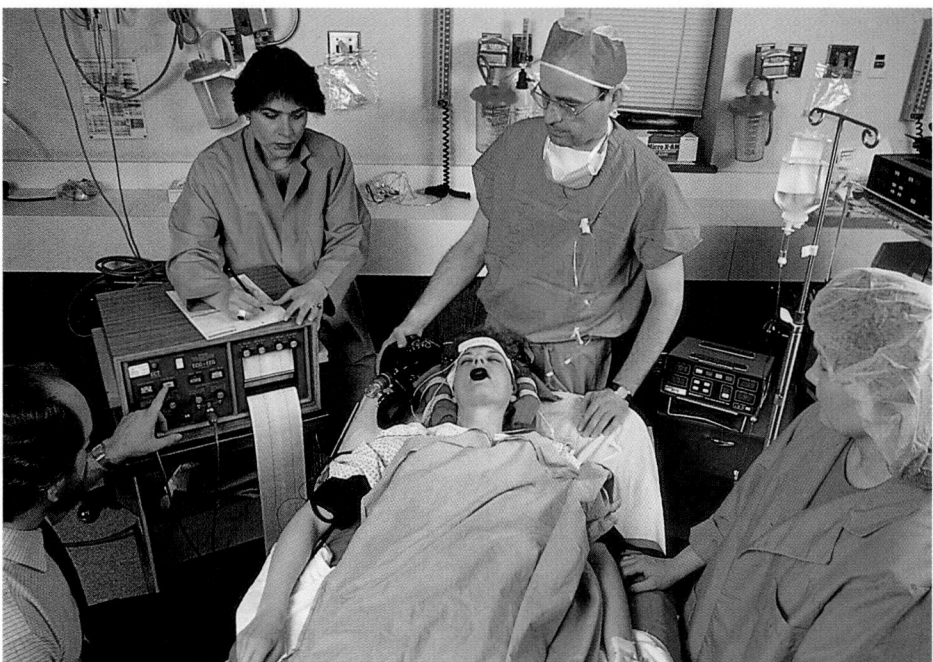

Electroconvulsive Therapy. In ECT, electrodes are placed on each side of the patient's head and a current is passed in between. A seizure is induced in this way. ECT is used mainly in cases of major depression when antidepressant drugs fail. ECT is quite controversial: Many believe that it is barbaric, and there are side effects.

functioning usually seems near normal for most people a few months after treatment, some appear to have permanent memory impairment (Coleman, 1990). Third, nobody knows *why* ECT works. For reasons such as these, ECT was outlawed in Berkeley, California, by voter referendum in 1982. This decision was later overturned in the courts, but it remains of interest because it marked the first time that a specific treatment found its way to the ballot box.

PSYCHOSURGERY

Psychosurgery is more controversial than ECT. The best-known modern technique, the **prefrontal lobotomy,** has been used with people with severe disorders. In this method, a picklike instrument is used to crudely sever the nerve pathways that link the prefrontal lobes of the brain to the thalamus. The prefrontal lobotomy was pioneered by the Portuguese neurologist Antonio Egas Moniz and was brought to the United States in the 1930s. As pointed out by Valenstein (1986), the theoretical rationale for the operation was vague and misguided. Moreover, Moniz's reports of success were exaggerated. Nevertheless, the prefrontal lobotomy was performed on more than a thousand people by 1950 in an effort to reduce violence and agitation. Anecdotal evidence of the method's unreliable outcomes is found in an ironic footnote to history: One of Dr. Moniz's "failures" shot him, leaving a bullet lodged in his spine and paralyzing his legs.

Truth or Fiction Revisited. *It is true that the originator of a surgical technique intended to reduce violence learned that it was not always successful . . . when one of his patients shot him.* The technique in question is the prefrontal lobotomy.

The prefrontal lobotomy also has a host of side effects including hyperactivity and distractibility, impaired learning ability, overeating, apathy and withdrawal, epileptic-type seizures, reduced creativity, and, now and then, death. Because of these side effects, and because of the advent of antipsychotic drugs, the prefrontal lobotomy has been largely discontinued in the United States.

DOES BIOLOGICAL THERAPY WORK?

There is little question that drug therapy has helped many people with severe psychological disorders. For example, antipsychotic drugs largely account for the lessened need for restraint and supervision (padded cells, straitjackets, hospitalization, and so on) used with people diagnosed with schizophrenia. Antipsychotic drugs have allowed hundreds of thousands of former hospital residents to lead largely normal lives in the community, hold jobs, and maintain family lives. Most problems related to these drugs concern their side effects.

On the other hand, most comparisons of psychotherapy (in the form of cognitive therapy) and drug therapy for depression suggest that cognitive therapy is at least comparable in effectiveness to the tricyclic antidepressants (Hollon and others, 1991, 1993; Imber and others, 1990; Robinson and others, 1990; Wexler & Cicchetti, 1992). Cognitive therapy may also provide coping skills that reduce the risk of recurrence of depression once treatment ends (Hollon and others, 1993). Moreover, most research suggests that a combination of antidepressant medication and psychotherapy is no more effective than either form of treatment alone (Burns & Nolen-Hoeksema, 1992; Robinson and others, 1990; Wexler & Cicchetti, 1992). Perhaps antidepressant medication is most appropriate for people who fail to respond to psychotherapy.

Many psychologists and psychiatrists are comfortable with the short-term use of antianxiety drugs in helping clients manage periods of unusual anxiety or tension. Supporters of the use of antianxiety drugs admit that they do not cure anxiety disorders, however (Shader & Greenblatt, 1993). Many people use antianxiety drugs routinely to dull the arousal that stems from anxiety-producing lifestyles or interpersonal problems. Rather than make the often painful decisions required to confront their problems and change their lives, they prefer to pop a pill. Unfortunately, some clinicians also find it easier to prescribe antianxiety drugs than to help people examine their lives and change anxiety-evoking conditions. The clinician's lot is not eased by the fact that many people want pills, not conversation.

In spite of the controversies that surround ECT, there is evidence that it brings many immobilized people out of their depression when antidepressant drugs fail (Janicak and others, 1985; NIMH, 1985). Moreover, depressed people who use ECT have a lower mortality rate following treatment than those who do not (Martin and others, 1985). This finding is in part attributable to a lower suicide rate. There are also suggestions that memory impairment is minimized by using the lowest dose of electricity required to produce seizures (Sakheim and others, 1985).

In sum, drug therapy and perhaps ECT seem to be desirable for some disorders that do not respond to psychotherapy alone. Yet common sense and research evidence suggest that psychotherapy is preferable for problems such as anxiety, mild depression, and interpersonal conflict. No chemical can show a person how to change an idea or solve an interpersonal problem. In some cases, chemicals only dull the pain of failure and postpone the day when people must seize control of their lives.

Reflections

Now that you have read the section on biological therapies, reflect on the following questions:

- Agree or disagree with the following statement and support your answer: "Drugs cause more problems than they solve when they are used to treat people with psychological disorders."
- Agree or disagree with the following statement and support your answer: "Biological treatments only provide a sort of Band-Aid therapy for psychological disorders. They don't get at the heart of the problems."

Summary

1. **What is psychotherapy?** Psychotherapy is a systematic interaction between a therapist and client that brings psychological principles to bear in helping the client overcome psychological disorders or adjust to problems in living.

2. **What are the goals of traditional psychoanalysis?** The goals are to provide self-insight, allow the spilling forth (catharsis) of psychic energy, and replace defensive behavior with coping behavior.

3. **What are the methods of traditional psychoanalysis?** Methods include free association and dream analysis.

4. **How do modern psychodynamic approaches differ from traditional psychoanalysis?** Modern approaches are briefer and more directive, and the therapist and client usually sit face to face.

5. **What are the goals and traits of the person-centered therapist?** The person-centered therapist uses nondirective methods to help clients overcome obstacles to self-actualization. Therapists show unconditional positive regard, empathic understanding, genuineness, and congruence.

6. **What are the goals and methods of transactional analysis (TA)?** TA helps people adopt healthy life positions ("I'm OK — You're OK"); fosters complementary transactions, or exchanges; encourages people to interact as adults rather than as children or parents; and alerts people to the "games" they play to retain self-defeating life positions.

7. **What are the goals and methods of cognitive therapies?** Cognitive therapies aim to provide clients with insight into irrational beliefs and cognitive distortions and to replace these cognitive errors with rational beliefs and accurate perceptions. Ellis notes that clients often show one or more of his 10 irrational beliefs, including excessive needs for approval and perfectionism. Beck notes that clients may become depressed because of their minimizing of accomplishments, catastrophizing of failures, and general pessimism. Cognitive restructuring helps clients interpret events in ways that foster adaptive behavior.

8. **What are some behavior therapy fear-reduction methods?** These include flooding, systematic desensitization, and modeling. Systematic desensitization counterconditions fears by gradually exposing clients to a hierarchy of fear-evoking stimuli while they remain deeply relaxed.

9. **What is aversive conditioning?** This is a behavior-therapy method for discouraging undesirable behavior by repeatedly pairing the goals (for example, alcohol, cigarette smoke, deviant sex objects) with aversive stimuli so that the goals become aversive rather than tempting.

10. **What are operant-conditioning procedures in behavior therapy?** These are behavior-therapy methods that foster adaptive behavior through principles of reinforcement. Examples include the token economy, successive approximations, social-skills training, and biofeedback training.

11. **What are behavioral self-control methods?** These are behavior-therapy methods for adopting desirable behavior patterns and breaking bad habits. They focus on modifying the antecedents (stimuli that act as triggers) and consequences (reinforcers) of behavior and on modifying the behavior itself.

12. **What are the advantages of group therapy?** Group therapy is more

economical than individual therapy. Moreover, group members profit from each other's social support and funds of experiences.

13. **Does psychotherapy work?** Apparently it does. Complex statistical analyses show that people who obtain most forms of psychotherapy fare better than people who do not. Psychodynamic and person-centered approaches are particularly helpful with highly verbal and motivated individuals. Cognitive and behavior therapies are probably most effective. Behavior therapy also helps in the treatment of people with mental retardation and severe psychological disorders.

14. **What are the uses of drug therapy?** Antipsychotic drugs help many people with schizophrenia by blocking the action of dopamine receptors. Antidepressants often help people with severe depression, apparently by raising the levels of noradrenaline and serotonin available to the brain. Lithium often helps persons with bipolar disorder, apparently by moderating levels of noradrenaline. The use of antianxiety drugs for daily tensions and anxieties is not recommended, because people rapidly build tolerance, drugs do not solve personal or social problems, and people attribute resultant calmness to the drugs and not to their self-efficacy.

15. **What is electroconvulsive therapy (ECT)?** ECT passes an electrical current through the temples, inducing a seizure and frequently relieving severe depression. ECT is controversial because of side effects such as loss of memory and because nobody knows why it works.

16. **What is psychosurgery?** Psychosurgery is an extremely controversial method for alleviating severe agitation by severing nerve pathways in the brain. The best-known psychosurgery technique, the prefrontal lobotomy, has been largely discontinued because of side effects.

Psychology and Modern Life

Psychotherapy in the New Multicultural United States

The United States, they are a-changing. Most of the "prescriptions" for psychotherapy discussed in this chapter were originated by, and intended for use with, European Americans. Yet the United States has many millions of African Americans, Asian Americans, Hispanic Americans, and Native Americans who seek or would profit from the benefits of psychotherapy.

But wait, you might interject. Aren't people people? Sure they are. And what people have in common is that their attitudes toward psychotherapy, and their abilities to profit from psychotherapy, are influenced by their ethnic backgrounds. For example, people from ethnic minority groups are less likely than European Americans to voluntarily seek therapy (Cheung & Snowden, 1990; Ho, 1985; Yamamoto, 1986). They are also more likely to quit therapy after a visit or two (Tharp, 1991). There are many reasons for their lower participation rate, such as:

- Lack of recognition that therapy is indicated

- Ignorance of the availability of professional services

- Distrust of professionals, particularly White professionals and (in the case of many women) male professionals (Greene, 1992)

- Language barriers (American Psychological Association, 1993; Martinez, 1986)

- Reluctance to open up about personal matters to strangers—especially strangers who are not members of one's ethnic group (LaFramboise, 1994)

- Cultural inclinations toward other approaches to problem solving, such as religious approaches (LaFramboise, 1994)

- Negative experiences with professionals

It might seem that it would be wisest for ethnic minorities to work only with therapists who share their ethnic backgrounds, and, perhaps, for women to work with female therapists. There are two problems with this approach, however. First, there are not enough minority therapists to go around (Allison and others, 1994; LaFramboise, 1994). In a recent year, for example,

only 8 of the 68 psychologists employed by the U.S. Indian Health Service, which provides services to people living on reservations, were Native Americans (DeAngelis, 1993). Second, such limitations would unfairly stereotype European American therapists as insensitive, particularly males. They would similarly unfairly characterize therapists from ethnic minority groups as sensitive. Neither stereotype is necessarily true. One cannot make assumptions about the cultural sensitivity of the therapist on the basis of ethnicity alone (Bernal & Castro, 1994; Greene, 1991). (This issue is discussed further in the following feature, "Ethnic Matching of Clients and Therapists.")

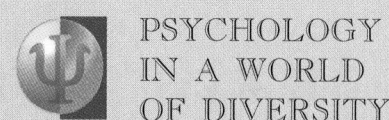

PSYCHOLOGY IN A WORLD OF DIVERSITY

ETHNIC MATCHING OF CLIENTS AND THERAPISTS

Most U.S. psychotherapists are non-Hispanic White Americans whose primary language is English (Allison and others, 1994; Bernal & Castro, 1994). Are such therapists as effective in treating people from ethnic minority groups as therapists drawn from the clients' own ethnic groups?

According to the "cultural-responsiveness hypothesis," people in therapy respond better when the therapist shares their ethnic background, including their language (Sue and others, 1991). Yet the evidence is mixed on whether ethnic matching actually enhances the benefits of therapy (Sue, 1988). A large-scale Los Angeles study found partial support for the cultural-responsiveness hypothesis (Sue and others, 1991). Matching of therapists and clients was connected with lower rates of dropping out of therapy for all ethnic groups. However, ethnic matching was not linked to treatment outcome, except in the case of Mexican Americans. The benefits of ethnic matching were greatest for Mexican Americans and Asian Americans whose primary language was not English.

Although matching therapists to clients on the basis of ethnicity has some benefits, ethnicity is not the sole determinant of therapeutic effectiveness. Therapist sensitivity and ability to establish rapport are also

Can White Therapists Conduct Effective Psychotherapy with Members of Minority Groups? Why are members of minority groups less likely than the White majority to seek therapy for their problems? What kinds of issues arise when majority therapists engage in therapy with members of minority groups?

crucial factors in therapeutic effectiveness, whether one is treating people of one's own ethnicity or from a different background (Sue, 1988).

Truth or Fiction Revisited. *It is not necessarily true that psychotherapy is ineffective unless the therapist and the client match in ethnic background.* Therapists who differ from clients in ethnic background can be effective if they are sensitive to ethnic differences and develop rapport.

Generally speaking, clinicians need to avoid stereotypes and be sensitive to the cultural heritages, languages, and values of the people they see in psychotherapy (American Psychological Association, 1993; Comas-Diaz, 1994; Lee & Richardson, 1991). Majority clinicians need to avoid stereotypes and be sensitive to the languages, behavior patterns, and values of minority group members in making diagnoses and doing therapy (American Psychological Association, 1993; Bernal & Castro, 1994; Comas-Diaz, 1994; Greene, 1992).

The need to avoid stereotyping is a generalization. Let us consider some of the particular issues involved in conducting

psychotherapy with African Americans, Asian Americans, Hispanic Americans, and Native Americans.

AFRICAN AMERICANS AND PSYCHOTHERAPY

In addition to the particular psychological problems that are presented by African American clients, therapists often need to help them develop ways of coping with prejudice and discrimination. Some African Americans also show low self-esteem because of the internalization of negative stereotypes that are maintained by the dominant culture (Greene, 1992; Pinderhughes, 1989).

African Americans are frequently reluctant to seek psychological help, both because of cultural assumptions that people should manage their own problems and because of mistrust of the therapy process. African Americans tend to assume that people are supposed to be resilient to stress and manage their problems by themselves. Signs of emotional weakness such as tension, anxiety, and depression are stigmatized and may lead to the individual's being perceived—by herself or himself as well as others—as having a "nervous breakdown" (Boyd-Franklin, 1989; Childs, 1990; Greene, 1993). The cultural expectation that people should get over such feelings by themselves often discourages them from seeking psychological intervention until the problem becomes more serious.

Many African American clients are then suspicious of their therapists—especially when therapists are non-Hispanic White Americans. They may withhold personal information because of the history of racial discrimination in such areas as employment, housing, education, and access to health care (Boyd-Franklin, 1989; Greene, 1990, 1993). When African Americans are suspicious, it is often because of awareness of the potential for maltreatment and exploitation. African American clients frequently minimize their vulnerability to exploitation by being less self-disclosing, especially when the relationship with the therapist is just under way (Boyd-Franklin, 1989; Greene, 1986).

Therapists need to be familiar with African American culture and alert to their own attitudes and feelings about African Americans (Greene, 1992; Pinderhughes, 1989). Therapists—regardless of their ethnicity—are exposed to the same stereotypes of African Americans as other people are and need to examine whether they believe them. Therapists need to confront their own prejudices and strive to replace stereotypes with knowledge of their African American clients as individuals (Mays, 1985).

Then there is the issue of cultural literacy. Therapists need to be aware of the cultural characteristics of African American families (American Psychological Association, 1993). There are typically strong kinship bonds among family members that often include people who are not biologically related. A close friend of a parent, for example, may enact some parenting role and be addressed as "Aunt." African American families usually have a strong spiritual and religious orientation. Households tend to be multigenerational. Because African American women have a long history of working outside the home, gender roles may be relatively flexible, and child rearing may be shared by various family members (Boyd-Franklin, 1989; Collins, 1990; Ferguson-Peters, 1985; Greene, 1990; McAdoo & McAdoo, 1985). Grandmothers, for example, often function as parents and are experienced psychologically as parents. They may even be referred to by the children as "mother."

ASIAN AMERICANS AND PSYCHOTHERAPY

Asian Americans tend to stigmatize people with psychological disorders, so that troubled people may deny such problems exist and refuse to seek help for them (Sue, 1991). Asian Americans, especially recent immigrants, may also not understand or believe in Western approaches to psychotherapy. For example, Western psychotherapy typically encourages people to express their feelings openly, a mode of behavior that may conflict with traditional Asian public restraint. Western insight-oriented therapies also tend to be unstructured, open-ended, and ambiguous. Many Asians prefer to receive advice that is structured and concrete. Western therapists usually try to help clients clarify their feelings and arrive at their own decisions. Asians often prefer therapists to function as authority figures who provide direct advice (Isomura and others, 1987).

Asian Americans also tend to view psychological health differently. They tend to believe that psychological health requires diverting one's thoughts from painful experiences or "morbid" concerns. Many Western therapy approaches aim to help clients get in touch with negative thoughts and feelings, however (Sue, 1991).

Because of the tendency to turn away from painful thoughts, many Asians experience and express psychological complaints as physical symptoms (Zane & Sue, 1991). Rather than thinking of themselves as being anxious, they may focus on physical features of anxiety such as a pounding heart and heavy sweating. Rather than thinking of themselves as depressed, they may center on their fatigue and low levels of energy.

To help Asian Americans, therapists—whether Asian American or of another ethnic group—must be sensitive to the cultural beliefs and values of Asians and use knowledge of these beliefs and values in therapy (American Psychological Association, 1993). Therapy must be consistent with clients' cultural expectations. Consider the therapeutic relationship between therapists and Japanese clients. Traditional Japanese culture endorses restraint in self-disclosure. Therapists who work with Japanese clients must thus be patient and not anticipate early self-disclosures (Henkin, 1985).

There can also be other conflicts between the goals of Western therapy and the values of a certain culture. Psychology emphasizes the dignity and importance of the individual, for example, and many Japanese are reared with cultural beliefs that the individual is subordinate to the group (Henkin, 1985).

HISPANIC AMERICANS AND PSYCHOTHERAPY

Hispanic American subcultures differ a great deal from one another. One cannot assume that cultural values that are found among Cuban Americans will also be found among Mexican Americans, Puerto Ricans, and Hispanic Americans from South America (Greene, 1994). Yet some values and beliefs do appear to be shared by the many Hispanic American subgroups, including adherence to a definite patriarchal (male dominated) family structure and strong kinship ties. Many Hispanic Americans also share the following values:

> One's identity is in part determined by one's role in the family. The male, or macho, is the head of the family, the provider, the protector of the family honor, and the final decision maker. The woman's role *(marianismo)* is to care for the family and the children. Obviously, these roles are changing, with women entering the work force and achieving greater educational opportunities. Cultural values of *respeto* (respect), *confianza* (trust), *dignidad* (dignity), and *personalismo* (personalism) are highly esteemed and are important factors in working with many [Hispanic Americans]. (De la Cancela & Guzman, 1991, p. 60)

Therapists need to be aware of potential conflicts between the traditional Hispanic American value of interdependency on the family and the typical non-Hispanic White American belief in independence and self-reliance (De la Cancela & Guzman, 1991). Psychotherapy is apparently more effective when therapists respect cultural differences in values rather than attempt to remold people from ethnic minority groups according to the values of the dominant culture (De la Cancela & Guzman, 1991).

Other problems that may sap the effectiveness of therapy arise from the cultural gulf that may exist between the middle-class, non-Hispanic White American therapist and the often poor Hispanic American client (Malgady and others, 1990). Measures such as the following may help bridge the gaps between psychotherapists and Hispanic American clients:

1. Interacting with clients in the language requested by clients or, if this is not possible, referring clients to professionals who can do so (American Psychological Association, 1993). Enlisting bilingual/bicultural staff and establishing a therapeutic atmosphere that accepts Hispanic American cultural values (Malgady and others, 1990).

2. Using methods that are consistent with Hispanic American clients' values. One might also tailor the treatment approach to the client's level of acculturation, as suggested by number of generations in the United States, number of years in the United States, fluency in English, level of education, relationships with people from the dominant culture, and similar factors (American Psychological Association, 1993). More acculturated clients may be assumed to share more of the values of the dominant culture (Ruiz, 1981).

3. Innovating therapy methods that incorporate clients' cultural values. Malgady and his colleagues (1990), for example, have integrated cultural values into psychotherapy through the use of *cuento therapy* with Puerto Ricans. *Cuento therapy* is a form of storytelling that adapts Hispanic folktales, or *cuentos,* in such a way that the characters serve as models for adaptive behavior. The child characters in the stories embody culturally desirable and effective values and behavior patterns.

NATIVE AMERICANS AND PSYCHOTHERAPY

Many psychological disorders among Native Americans involve the disruption in traditional culture caused by European appropriation of their lands and European attempts to cut them off from their tribal language and cultural traditions (LaFramboise, 1994). Native Americans have also been denied full access to the dominant Western culture (LaFramboise, 1994). Loss of cultural identity and social disorganization have set the stage for problems such as alcoholism, substance abuse, and depression. These problems dispose Native American adults to a high incidence of child abuse and neglect which, in turn, contribute to feelings of depression among adolescents. Adolescents may then try to escape their feelings through alcohol and other drugs (Berlin, 1987).

Many Native American cultures classify their problems according to those that are believed to arise from outside influences ("White man's sicknesses"), such as alcoholism and drug addiction, and those that arise from lack of harmony with traditional tribal life and thought ("Indian sicknesses") (Trimble, 1991). "White man's medicine" may be sought to cope with "White man's sicknesses." Traditional healers, shamans, and medicine men and women may be asked to treat "Indian sicknesses."

Theresa LaFramboise (1994) argues that if psychologists are to help Native Americans cope with psychological disorders, they must do so in a way that is sensitive to their culture, customs, and values. Efforts at preventing such disorders should focus on strengthening Native American cultural identity, pride, and cohesion, and helping Native Americans regain a sense of mastery over their world. When cultural and language differences create so great a gulf between Native Americans and the dominant culture, perhaps only trained Native Americans will be able to provide effective counseling.

Therapists can also use indigenous ceremonies that reflect clients' cultural or religious traditions (Timpson and others, 1988). Purification and cleansing rites are therapeutic for many Native Americans in the United States and elsewhere, as among the Brazilian *umbanda,* the African–Cuban *santeria,* and the Haitian *vodou* (Lefley, 1990). Such rites are commonly sought by Native Americans who believe that their problems are caused by failure to placate malevolent spirits or to perform required rituals (Lefley, 1990).

Reflections

Now that you have read the section on multicultural issues in psychotherapy, reflect on the following questions:

- Consider your sociocultural background. Do people from your background generally feel comfortable with the thought of going for psychotherapy? Why or why not?
- Do you think that the goals of psychoanalysis and other forms of psychotherapy are consistent with the values and customs of people from your particular background? Why or why not?
- Would you feel comfortable seeing a psychotherapist who was from another ethnic background? Why or why not? A psychotherapist of the other gender? Why or why not?

15

Health Psychology

Truth or Fiction?

_____ Since variety's the spice of life, the more change the merrier.

_____ A sense of humor can moderate the impact of stress.

_____ Single men live longer than married men.

_____ At any given moment, countless microscopic warriors within our bodies are carrying out search-and-destroy missions against foreign agents.

_____ Poor people in the United States eat less than more affluent people.

_____ Stress can influence the course of cancer.

_____ People are more likely to comply with doctor's orders when they are issued by an authoritarian physician.

_____ Harvard University alumni who exercise regularly live 2 years longer, on the average, than their sedentary counterparts.

Outline

Truth or Fiction?
Health Psychology
Stress: Presses, Pushes, and Pulls
  Sources of Stress: Don't Hassle Me?
  Psychological Moderators of Stress
  The General Adaptation Syndrome
  Effects of Stress on the Immune System
A Multifactorial Approach to Health
    and Illness
  Human Diversity and Health: Nations
    within the Nation
    Psychology in a World of Diversity:
    Health and Socioeconomic Status:
    The Rich Get Richer and the Poor
    Get . . . Sicker
  Headaches
  Coronary Heart Disease
  Asthma
  Cancer
    Psychology in the New Millennium:
    Health Psychology in the 21st
    Century: The Shape of Things to
    Come
Compliance with Medical Advice
  Encouraging Compliance by Enhancing
    Physician–Patient Interactions
Summary
Psychology and Modern Life
  Ways of Coping with Stress

Sirens. Ambulances. Stretchers. The emergency room at Dallas's public Parkland Memorial Hospital is a busy place. Sirens wail endlessly as ambulances pull up to the doors and discharge people in need of prompt attention. Because of the volume of patients, beds line the halls, and people who do not require immediate care cram the waiting room. Many hours may pass before they are seen. It is not unusual for people who are not considered in danger to wait for 10 to 12 hours.

All this may sound rather foreboding, but good things are happening at Parkland as well. One of them is the attention that physicians attempt to pay to people's psychological needs as well as to their physical needs. Influenced both by his own clinical experience and Native American wisdom about the healing process, for example, Dr. Ron Anderson teaches his medical students that caring about patients is not just an outdated ideal that typifies backwoods practices. Rather, it is a powerful weapon against disease.

TV journalist Bill Moyers describes Anderson on rounds with students:

> I listen as he stops at the bedside of an elderly woman suffering from chronic asthma. He asks the usual questions: "How did you sleep last night?" "Is the breathing getting any easier?" His next questions surprise the medical students: "Is your son still looking for work?" "Is he still drinking?" "Tell us what happened right before the asthma attack." He explains to his puzzled students. "We know that anxiety aggravates many illnesses, especially chronic conditions like asthma. So we have to find out what may be causing her episodes of stress and help her find some way of coping with it. Otherwise she will land in here again, and next time we might not be able to save her. We cannot just prescribe medication and walk away. That is medical neglect. We have to take the time to get to know her, how she lives, her values, what her social supports are. If we don't know that her son is her sole support and that he's out of work, we will be much less effective in dealing with her asthma." (Moyers, 1993, p. 2)

Health Psychology

Note some key concepts from the slice of hospital life reported by Moyers: "Anxiety aggravates many illnesses." "We have to find out what may be causing . . . stress and . . . find some way of coping with it." "We cannot just prescribe medication and walk away." "We have to take the time to get to know [patients], how [they] live, [their] values, what [their] social supports are."

Anderson and Moyers have collaborated to create a fine introduction to the field of health psychology. **Health psychology** studies the relationships between psychological factors and the prevention and treatment of physical illness (Taylor, 1990). The case of the woman with asthma is a useful springboard for discussion because, in recent years, health psychologists have been exploring the ways in which

- psychological factors such as stress, behavior patterns, and attitudes can lead to or exacerbate physical illness;

Daily Hassles. Daily hassles are notable daily conditions and experiences that are threatening or harmful to a person's well-being. The hassles shown in these photographs center around commuting. What are the daily hassles in your life?

- people can cope with stress;
- stress and **pathogens** can interact to influence the immune system (Kiecolt-Glaser & Glaser, 1992);
- people decide whether or not to seek health care;
- health-care providers can encourage people to comply with professional advice;
- psychological forms of intervention such as health education (for example, concerning nutrition, smoking, and exercise) and behavior modification can contribute to physical health (Blanchard, 1992a; Castelli, 1994; Dubbert, 1992; Lehrer and others, 1992).

Because of the links between psychological factors and physical health, an estimated 3,500 psychologists are now found on the faculties of medical schools (Matarazzo, 1993). Psychologists are found in medical schools' departments of family practice, neurology, pediatrics, psychiatry, and rehabilitation medicine, among others (Michaelson, 1993b; Wiggins, 1994). In this chapter, we consider a number of issues in health psychology: sources of stress, factors that moderate the impact of stress, the body's response to stress, ways in which stress is related to physical illnesses, and the psychology of being sick, including the improvement of physician–patient relationships. In the "Psychology and Modern Life" section, we explore ways of coping with stress.

Stress: Presses, Pushes, and Pulls

Americans will put up with anything provided it doesn't block traffic.

DAN RATHER

In physics, stress is defined as a pressure or force exerted on a body. Tons of rock pressing on the earth, one car smashing into another, a rubber band stretching—all are types of physical stress. Psychological forces, or stresses, also "press," "push," or "pull." We may feel "crushed" by the "weight" of a big decision, "smashed" by adversity, or "stretched" to the point of "snapping."

In psychology, **stress** is the demand made on an organism to adapt, to cope, or to adjust. Some stress is healthful and necessary to keep us alert and occupied. Stress researcher Hans Selye (1980) referred to such healthful stress as **eustress.** But intense or

Health psychology • The field of psychology that studies the relationships between psychological factors (e.g., attitudes, beliefs, situational influences, and behavior patterns) and the prevention and treatment of physical illness.

Pathogen • A microscopic organism (e.g., bacterium or virus) that can cause disease.

Stress • The demand that is made on an organism to adapt.

Eustress • (YOU-stress). Stress that is healthful.

MINILECTURE: STRESS AND STRESSORS

Life Changes. Life changes differ from daily hassles in that they tend to be more episodic. Life changes can also be positive as well as negative. What is the relationship between life changes and illness? Is the relationship causal?

Daily hassles • Notable daily conditions and experiences that are threatening or harmful to a person's well-being.

Uplifts • Notable pleasant daily conditions and experiences.

prolonged stress can overtax our adjustive capacity, dampen our moods, impair our ability to experience pleasure, and harm the body (Berenbaum & Connelly, 1993; Cohen and others, 1993; Repetti, 1993).

SOURCES OF STRESS: DON'T HASSLE ME?

Let us consider various sources of stress, including daily hassles, life changes, conflict, irrational beliefs, and Type A behavior.

Daily Hassles. It is the last straw that will break the camel's back—so goes the

saying. Similarly, stresses can pile atop one another until we can no longer cope. Some of these stresses are **daily hassles,** or notable daily conditions and experiences that are threatening or harmful to a person's well-being. Others are life changes. Lazarus and his colleagues (1985) analyzed a scale that measures daily hassles and their opposites—**uplifts**—and found that hassles could be grouped as follows:

1. *Household hassles:* preparing meals, shopping, and home maintenance
2. *Health hassles:* physical illness, concern about medical treatment, and the side effects of medication
3. *Time-pressure hassles:* having too many things to do, too many responsibilities, and not enough time
4. *Inner-concern hassles:* being lonely and fearful of confrontation
5. *Environmental hassles:* crime, neighborhood deterioration, and traffic noise
6. *Financial-responsibility hassles:* concern about owing money such as mortgage payments and loan installments
7. *Work hassles:* job dissatisfaction, not liking one's work duties, and problems with coworkers
8. *Future-security hassles:* concerns about job security, taxes, property investments, stock market swings, and retirement

These hassles are linked to psychological variables such as nervousness, worrying, inability to get going, feelings of sadness, and feelings of aloneness. For example, 83% of people in the United States will be victimized by a violent crime at some time, and victimization is connected with problems such as anxiety, physical complaints, hostility, and depression (Norris & Kaniasty, 1994).

Life Changes: "Going Through Changes." According to Holmes and Rahe (1967), too much of a good thing can make you ill. You might think that marrying Mr. or Ms. Right, finding a prestigious job, and moving to a better neighborhood all in the same year would propel you into a state of bliss. It might. But all these events, one on top of the other, may also lead to headaches, high blood pressure, and other ailments. As pleasant as they may be, they all entail major life changes, and life changes are another source of stress.

Life changes differ from daily hassles in two important ways: (1) Many life changes are positive and desirable, whereas all hassles, by definition, are negative. (2) Hassles tend to occur on a daily basis, whereas life changes are more isolated.

Richard Lazarus and his colleagues (e.g., Kanner and others, 1981) constructed a list of 117 daily hassles. They asked study participants to indicate which of these hassles they had encountered and how intense they were. Holmes and Rahe (1967) constructed a scale to measure the impact of life changes by assigning marriage an arbitrary weight of 50 "life-change units." Then they asked participants to assign units to other life changes, using marriage as the baseline. Most events were rated as less stressful than marriage. A few were more stressful, such as the death of a spouse (100 units) and divorce (73 units). Changes in work hours and residence (20 units each) were included, regardless of whether they were negative or positive. Positive life changes such as an outstanding personal achievement (28 units) and going on vacation (13 units) also made the list.

Hassles, Life Changes, and Illness.

Hassles and life changes—especially negative life changes—affect us psychologically. They can cause us to worry and dampen our moods. But stressors such as hassles and life changes also predict physical illnesses such as heart disease and cancer, even athletic injuries (Kanner and others, 1981; Smith and others, 1990; Stewart and others, 1994). Holmes and Rahe found that people who "earned" 300 or more life-change units within a year according to their scale were at greater risk for illness. Eight of 10 developed medical problems as compared with only 1 of 3 people whose life-change-unit totals for the year were below 150.

Truth or Fiction Revisited. *Although variety may be the very spice of life, psychologists have not found that "the more change the merrier."* Changes, even changes for the better, are sources of stress in that they require adjustment. Since stress is connected with physical illness, it may even be that too

much of a good thing—too many positive life changes—can make one ill.

Questions about the Links between Hassles, Life Changes, and Illness.

Although the links between daily hassles, life changes, and illness seem to have been supported by a good deal of research, critical thinking reveals a number of limitations:

1. *Correlational Evidence.* The links that have been uncovered between hassles, life changes, and illness are correlational rather than experimental. It may seem logical that the hassles and life changes caused the disorders, but these variables were not manipulated experimentally. Rival explanations of the data are therefore possible (Figure 15.1). One is that people who are predisposed toward

FIGURE 15.1

Spotlight on the Relationships among Daily Hassles, Life Changes, and Physical Illness There are positive correlations between daily hassles and life events, on the one hand, and illness on the other. It may seem logical that hassles and life changes cause illness, but research into the issue is correlational and not experimental. The results are therefore subject to rival interpretations. One is that people who are predisposed toward medical or psychological problems encounter or generate more hassles and amass more life-change units.

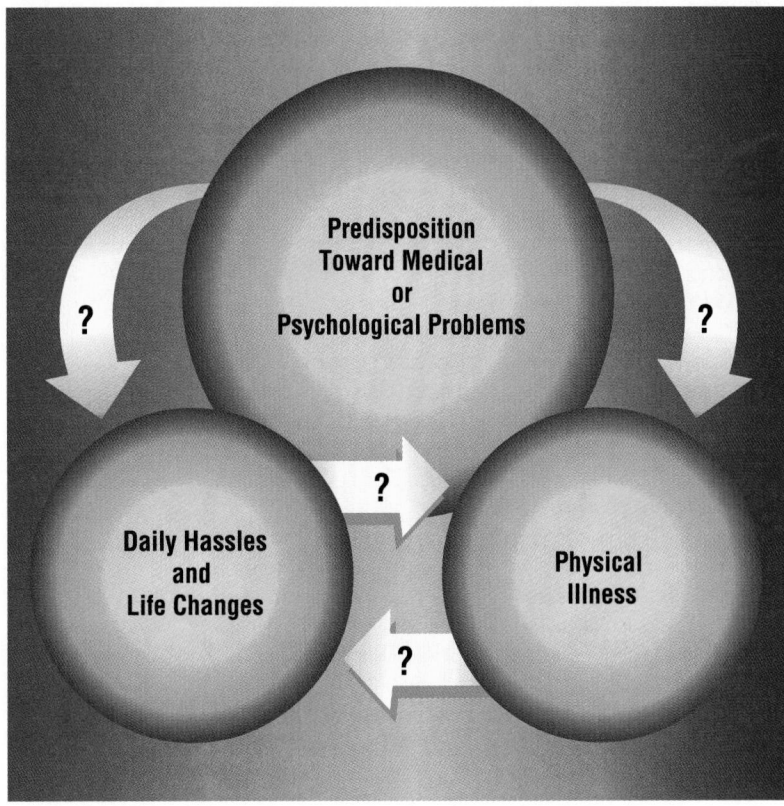

Questionnaire

SOCIAL READJUSTMENT RATING SCALE

Life changes can be a source of stress. How much stress have you experienced in the past year as a result of life changes? To compare your stress to that encountered by other college students, complete this questionnaire.

DIRECTIONS: Indicate how many times (frequency) you have experienced the following events during the past 12 months. Then multiply the frequency (do not enter a number larger than five) by the number of life-change units (value) associated with each event. Write the product in the column to the right (total). Then add up the points and check the key in Appendix B.

EVENT	VALUE	FREQUENCY	TOTAL
1. Death of a spouse, lover, or child	94	_____	_____
2. Death of a parent or sibling	88	_____	_____
3. Beginning formal higher education	84	_____	_____
4. Death of a close friend	83	_____	_____
5. Miscarriage or stillbirth of pregnancy of self, spouse, or lover	83	_____	_____
6. Jail sentence	82	_____	_____
7. Divorce or marital separation	82	_____	_____
8. Unwanted pregnancy of self, spouse, or lover	80	_____	_____
9. Abortion of unwanted pregnancy of self, spouse, or lover	80	_____	_____
10. Detention in jail or other institution	79	_____	_____
11. Change in dating activity	79	_____	_____
12. Death of a close relative	79	_____	_____
13. Change in marital situation other than divorce or separation	78	_____	_____
14. Separation from significant other whom you like very much	77	_____	_____
15. Change in health status or behavior of spouse or lover	77	_____	_____
16. Academic failure	77	_____	_____
17. Major violation of the law and subsequent arrest	76	_____	_____
18. Marrying or living with lover against parents' wishes	75	_____	_____
19. Change in love relationship or important friendship	74	_____	_____
20. Change in health status or behavior of a parent or sibling	73	_____	_____
21. Change in feelings of loneliness, insecurity, anxiety, boredom	73	_____	_____
22. Change in marital status of parents	73	_____	_____
23. Acquiring a visible deformity	72	_____	_____
24. Change in ability to communicate with a significant other whom you like very much	71	_____	_____
25. Hospitalization of a parent or sibling	70	_____	_____
26. Reconciliation of marital or love relationship	68	_____	_____
27. Release from jail or other institution	68	_____	_____
28. Graduation from college	68	_____	_____
29. Major personal injury or illness	68	_____	_____
30. Wanted pregnancy of self, spouse, or lover	67	_____	_____
31. Change in number or type of arguments with spouse or lover	67	_____	_____
32. Marrying or living with lover with parents' approval	66	_____	_____
33. Gaining a new family member through birth or adoption	65	_____	_____
34. Preparing for an important exam or writing a major paper	65	_____	_____
35. Major financial difficulties	65	_____	_____
36. Change in the health status or behavior of a close relative or close friend	65	_____	_____
37. Change in academic status	64	_____	_____
38. Change in amount and nature of interpersonal conflicts	63	_____	_____
39. Change in relationship with members of your immediate family	62	_____	_____
40. Change in own personality	62	_____	_____
41. Hospitalization of yourself or a close relative	61	_____	_____
42. Change in course of study, major field, vocational goals, or work status	60	_____	_____
43. Change in own financial status	59	_____	_____
44. Change in status of divorced or widowed parent	59	_____	_____
45. Change in number or type of arguments between parents	59	_____	_____
46. Change in acceptance by peers, identification with peers, or social pressure by peers	58	_____	_____

EVENT	VALUE	FREQUENCY	TOTAL
47. Change in general outlook on life	57	_____	_____
48. Beginning or ceasing service in the armed forces	57	_____	_____
49. Change in attitudes toward friends	56	_____	_____
50. Change in living arrangements, conditions, or environment	55	_____	_____
51. Change in frequency or nature of sexual experiences	55	_____	_____
52. Change in parents' financial status	55	_____	_____
53. Change in amount or nature of pressure from parents	55	_____	_____
54. Change in degree of interest in college or attitudes toward education	55	_____	_____
55. Change in the number of personal or social relationships you've formed or dissolved	55	_____	_____
56. Change in relationship with siblings	54	_____	_____
57. Change in mobility or reliability of transportation	54	_____	_____
58. Academic success	54	_____	_____
59. Change to a new college or university	54	_____	_____
60. Change in feelings of self-reliance, independence, or amount of self-discipline	53	_____	_____
61. Change in number or type of arguments with roommate	52	_____	_____
62. Spouse or lover beginning or ceasing work outside the home	52	_____	_____
63. Change in frequency of use of amounts of drugs other than alcohol, tobacco, or marijuana	51	_____	_____
64. Change in sexual morality, beliefs, or attitudes	50	_____	_____
65. Change in responsibility at work	50	_____	_____
66. Change in amount or nature of social activities	50	_____	_____
67. Change in dependencies on parents	50	_____	_____
68. Change from academic work to practical fieldwork experience or internship	50	_____	_____
69. Change in amount of material possessions and concomitant responsibilities	50	_____	_____
70. Change in routine at college or work	49	_____	_____
71. Change in amount of leisure time	49	_____	_____
72. Change in amount of in-law trouble	49	_____	_____
73. Outstanding personal achievement	49	_____	_____
74. Change in family structure other than parental divorce or separation	48	_____	_____
75. Change in attitude toward drugs	48	_____	_____
76. Change in amount and nature of competition with same gender	48	_____	_____
77. Improvement of own health	47	_____	_____
78. Change in responsibilities at home	47	_____	_____
79. Change in study habits	46	_____	_____
80. Change in number or type of arguments or close conflicts with close relatives	46	_____	_____
81. Change in sleeping habits	46	_____	_____
82. Change in frequency of use or amounts of alcohol	45	_____	_____
83. Change in social status	45	_____	_____
84. Change in frequency of use or amounts of tobacco	45	_____	_____
85. Change in awareness of activities in external world	45	_____	_____
86. Change in religious affiliation	44	_____	_____
87. Change in type of gratifying activities	43	_____	_____
88. Change in amount or nature of physical activities	43	_____	_____
89. Change in address or residence	43	_____	_____
90. Change in amount or nature of recreational activities	43	_____	_____
91. Change in frequency of use or amounts of marijuana	43	_____	_____
92. Change in social demands or responsibilities due to your age	43	_____	_____
93. Court appearance for legal violation	40	_____	_____
94. Change in weight or eating habits	39	_____	_____
95. Change in religious activities	37	_____	_____
96. Change in political views or affiliations	34	_____	_____
97. Change in driving pattern or conditions	33	_____	_____
98. Minor violation of the law	31	_____	_____
99. Vacation or travel	30	_____	_____
100. Change in number of family get-togethers	30	_____	_____

Source: *Self-Assessment and Behavior Change Manual* (pp. 43–47), by Peggy Blake, Robert Fry, & Michael Pesjack, 1984, New York: Random House. Reprinted by permission of Random House, Inc.

medical or psychological problems encounter more hassles and amass more life-change units. For example, medical disorders may contribute to sexual problems, arguments with spouses or in-laws, changes in living conditions and personal habits, and changes in sleeping habits before they are diagnosed. People may also generate the life events that then lead to physical and psychological disorders (Simons and others, 1993).

2. *Positive versus Negative Life Changes.* Other aspects of the research into the relationship between life changes and illness have also been challenged. For instance, positive life changes be less disturbing than hassles and negative life changes, even when their number of life-change units is high (Lefcourt and others, 1981).

3. *Personality Differences.* People with different kinds of personalities respond to life stresses in different ways (Vaillant, 1994). For example, people who are easygoing or psychologically hardy are less likely to become ill under the impact of stress.

4. *Cognitive Appraisal.* The stress of an event reflects the meaning the event has to the individual (Lazarus, 1991b; Whitehead, 1994). Pregnancy, for example, can be a positive or negative life change, depending on whether one wants and is prepared to have a child. We cognitively appraise hassles, traumatic experiences, and life changes (Creamer and others, 1992; Kiecolt-Glaser, 1993; Lazarus, 1991a). In responding to them, we take into account their perceived danger, our values and goals, our beliefs in our coping ability, our social support, and so on. The same event is less taxing to people who have greater coping ability and support.

Despite these methodological flaws, hassles and life changes still require adjustments. It seems wise to be aware of the hassles and life changes in our lifestyles.

Conflict.

I am
At war 'twixt will and will not.
SHAKESPEARE, *MEASURE FOR MEASURE*

Have you ever felt "damned if you did and damned if you didn't"? Regretted that you

couldn't do two things, or be in two places, at the same time? This is **conflict**—being torn in two or more directions by opposing motives. Conflict is frustrating and stressful. Psychologists often break conflicts down into four types: approach–approach, avoidance–avoidance, approach–avoidance, and multiple approach–avoidance.

An **approach–approach conflict** (Figure 15.2, Part A) is the least stressful form of conflict. Here, each of two goals is positive and within reach. You may not be able to decide between pizza or tacos, Tom or Dick, or a trip to Nassau or Hawaii. Conflicts are usually resolved by making decisions. People in conflict may **vacillate** until they make a decision.

An **avoidance–avoidance conflict** (Figure 15.2, Part B) is more stressful, because you are motivated to avoid each of two negative goals. However, avoiding one requires approaching the other. You may be fearful of visiting the dentist but also fear that your teeth will decay if you do not. You may not want to contribute to the Association for the Advancement of Lost Causes, but you fear that your friends will consider you cheap or uncommitted if you do not. Each goal is negative in an avoidance–avoidance conflict. When an avoidance–avoidance conflict is highly stressful, and no resolution is in sight, some people withdraw from the conflict by focusing their attention on other matters or by suspending behavior altogether. Highly conflicted people have refused to get out of bed in the morning and start the day.

The same goal can produce both approach and avoidance motives, as in the **approach–avoidance conflict** (Figure 15.2, Part C). People and things have their pluses and minuses, their good points and their bad points. Cream cheese pie may be delicious, but oh the calories! Goals producing mixed motives may seem more attractive from a distance but more repulsive up close. Many couples repeatedly break up, then reunite. When they are apart and lonely, they may recall each other fondly and swear that they could make it work "the next time." But after they again spend time together, they may find themselves facing the same old aggravations and think, "How could I have ever believed this so-and-so would change?"

Conflict • Being torn in different directions by opposing motives. Feelings produced by being in conflict.

Approach–approach conflict • A type of conflict in which the goals that produce opposing motives are positive and within reach.

Vacillate • Move back and forth.

Avoidance–avoidance conflict • A type of conflict in which the goals are negative, but avoidance of one requires approaching the other.

Approach–avoidance conflict • A type of conflict in which the same goal produces approach and avoidance motives.

Multiple approach–avoidance conflict • A type of conflict in which each of a number of goals produces approach and avoidance motives.

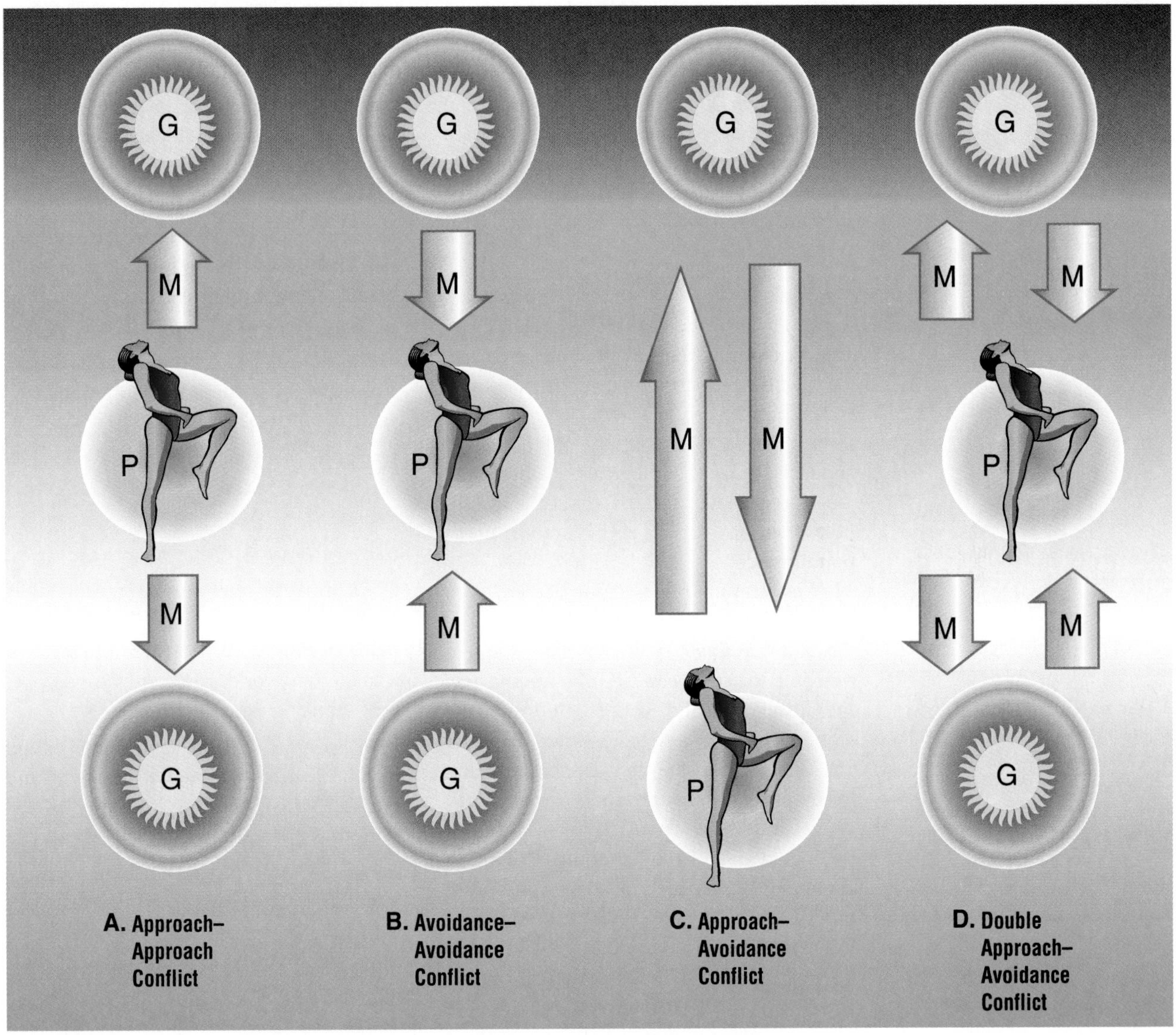

**A. Approach–
Approach
Conflict**

**B. Avoidance–
Avoidance
Conflict**

**C. Approach–
Avoidance
Conflict**

**D. Double
Approach–
Avoidance
Conflict**

FIGURE 15.2

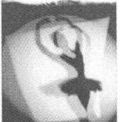 **Spotlight on Models for Conflict** Part A shows an approach–approach conflict, in which a person (P) has motives (M) to reach two goals (G) that are desirable, but approach of one requires exclusion of the other. Part B shows an avoidance–avoidance conflict in which both goals are negative, but avoiding one requires approaching the other. Part C shows an approach–avoidance conflict, in which the same goal has desirable and undesirable properties. Part D shows a double approach–avoidance conflict, which is the simplest kind of *multiple* approach–avoidance conflict. In a multiple approach–avoidance conflict, two or more goals have mixed properties.

The most complex form of conflict is the **multiple approach–avoidance conflict,** in which each of several alternative courses of action has its promising and distressing aspects. An example with two goals is shown in Figure 15.2, Part D. This sort of conflict might arise on the eve of an examination, when you are faced with the choice of studying or, say, going to a film. Each alternative has its positive and negative aspects: "Studying's a bore, but I won't have to worry about flunking. I'd love to see the movie, but I'd just be worrying about how I'll do tomorrow."

All forms of conflict entail motives that aim in opposite directions. When one motive is much stronger than the other—such as when you feel "starved" and are only slightly concerned about your weight—it will probably not be too stressful to act in accord with the powerful motive and, in this case, to eat. When each conflicting motive is powerful, however, you may encounter high levels of stress and confusion about the proper course of action. At such times, you are faced with the need to make a decision. Yet decision making can also be stressful, especially when there is no clear correct choice.

Irrational Beliefs: Ten Doorways to Distress. Psychologist Albert Ellis (1977, 1993) notes that our beliefs about events, as well as the events themselves, can be stressors. Consider a case in which one is fired from a job and is anxious and depressed about it. It may seem logical that losing the job is responsible for the misery, but Ellis points out how beliefs about the loss compound misery.

Let us examine this situation according to Ellis's A → B → C approach: Losing the job is an *activating event* (A). The eventual outcome, or *consequence* (C), is misery. Between the activating event (A) and the consequence (C), however, lie *beliefs* (B), such as: "This job was the most important thing in my life," "What a no-good failure I am," "My family will starve," "I'll never find a job as good," "There's nothing I can do about it." Beliefs such as these compound misery, foster helplessness, and divert us from planning and deciding what to do next. The belief "There's nothing I can do about it" fosters helplessness. The belief "What a no-good failure I am" internalizes the blame and may be an exaggeration. The belief "My family will starve" may also be an exaggeration.

We can diagram the situation like this:

Activating events → Beliefs → Consequences

Anxieties about the future and depression over a loss are normal and to be expected. However, the beliefs of the person who lost the job tend to **catastrophize** the extent of the loss and to contribute to anxiety and depression. By heightening emotional reaction to the loss and fostering feelings of helplessness, these beliefs also impair coping ability. They lower people's self-efficacy expectations.

Ellis proposes that many of us harbor irrational beliefs. We carry them with us. They

are our personal doorways to distress. They can give rise to problems in themselves. When problems assault us from other sources, these beliefs can magnify their effect. How many of these beliefs do you harbor? Are you sure?

Irrational Belief 1: You must have sincere love and approval almost all the time from the people who are important to you.

Irrational Belief 2: You must prove yourself to be thoroughly competent, adequate, and achieving at something important.

Irrational Belief 3: Things must go the way you want them to go. Life is awful when you don't get your first choice in everything.

Irrational Belief 4: Other people must treat everyone fairly and justly. When people act unfairly or unethically, they are rotten.

Irrational Belief 5: When there is danger or fear in your world, you must be preoccupied with and upset by it.

Irrational Belief 6: People and things should turn out better than they do. It's awful and horrible when you don't find quick solutions to life's hassles.

Irrational Belief 7: Your emotional misery stems from external pressures that you have little or no ability to control. Unless these external pressures change, you must remain miserable.

Irrational Belief 8: It is easier to evade life's responsibilities and problems than to face them and undertake more rewarding forms of self-discipline.

Irrational Belief 9: Your past influenced you immensely and must therefore continue to determine your feelings and behavior today.

Irrational Belief 10: You can achieve happiness by inertia and inaction, or by just enjoying yourself from day to day.

Ellis finds it understandable that we would want the approval of others but irrational to believe that we cannot survive without it. It would be nice to be competent in everything we do, but it's unreasonable to expect it. Sure, it would be nice to serve and volley like a tennis pro, but most of us haven't the

Catastrophize • (kuh-TASS-trow-fize). To interpret negative events as being disastrous; to "blow out of proportion."

Type A behavior • Behavior characterized by a sense of time urgency, competitiveness, and hostility.

Type A Behavior. The Type A behavior pattern is characterized by a sense of time urgency, competitiveness, and hostility.

time or natural ability to perfect the game. Demanding self-perfection prevents us from going out on the courts on weekends and batting the ball back and forth for fun. Belief 5 is a prescription for perpetual emotional upheaval. Beliefs 7 and 9 lead to feelings of helplessness and demoralization. Sure, Ellis might say, childhood experiences can explain the origins of irrational beliefs, but it is our own cognitive appraisal—here and now—that causes us misery. Research supports the connections between irrational beliefs (for example, excessive dependence on social approval and perfectionism) and feelings of anxiety and depression (Hewitt & Flett, 1993; Persons and others, 1993). Later in the chapter, we shall see how combating irrational beliefs may alleviate stress.

Type A Behavior. Some people create stress for themselves through the **Type A behavior** pattern. Type A people are highly driven, competitive, impatient, and aggressive (Thoresen & Powell, 1992). They feel rushed and under pressure and keep one eye glued firmly on the clock. They are not only prompt but often early for appointments. They eat, walk, and talk rapidly and become restless when others work slowly. They attempt to dominate group discussions. Type A people find it difficult to surrender control or to share power. They are often reluctant to delegate authority in the workplace and thus increase their own workloads. Type A people "accentuate the negative." They are merciless in their self-criticism when they fail at a task (Moser & Dyck, 1989). They even seek out negative information about themselves in order to better themselves (Cooney & Zeichner, 1985).

Type A people find it difficult just to go out on the tennis court and bat the ball back and forth. They watch their form, perfect their strokes, and demand regular self-improvement. The irrational belief that they must be perfectly competent and achieving in everything they undertake seems to be their motto.

Type B people, in contrast, relax more readily and focus more on the quality of life. They are less ambitious and less impatient, and they pace themselves. Type A people earn higher grades and more money than Type B's of equal intelligence. Type A people also seek greater challenges than Type B's (Ortega & Pipal, 1984).

Are you Type A? The nearby questionnaire should afford you some self-insight into the matter.

—— Questionnaire ——

ARE YOU TYPE A OR TYPE B?

Complete the questionnaire by placing a check mark under the Yes if the behavior pattern described is typical of you and under the No if it is not. Try to work rapidly and leave no item blank. Then read the nearby section on Type A behavior and turn to the scoring key in Appendix B.

DO YOU:

		YES	NO
1.	Strongly accent key words in your everyday speech?	___	___
2.	Eat and walk quickly?	___	___
3.	Believe that children should be taught to be competitive?	___	___
4.	Feel restless when watching a slow worker?	___	___
5.	Hurry other people to get on with what they're trying to say?	___	___
6.	Find it highly aggravating to be stuck in traffic or waiting for a seat at a restaurant?	___	___
7.	Continue to think about your own problems and business even when listening to someone else?	___	___
8.	Try to eat and shave, or drive and jot down notes at the same time?	___	___
9.	Catch up on your work on vacations?	___	___
10.	Bring conversations around to topics of concern to you?	___	___
11.	Feel guilty when you spend time just relaxing?	___	___
12.	Find that you're so wrapped up in your work that you no longer notice office decorations or the scenery when you commute?	___	___
13.	Find yourself concerned with getting more *things* rather than developing your creativity and social concerns?	___	___
14.	Try to schedule more and more activities into less time?	___	___
15.	Always appear for appointments on time?	___	___
16.	Clench or pound your fists or use other gestures to emphasize your views?	___	___
17.	Credit your accomplishments to your ability to work rapidly?	___	___
18.	Feel that things must be done *now* and quickly?	___	___
19.	Constantly try to find more efficient ways to get things done?	___	___
20.	Insist on winning at games rather than just having fun?	___	___
21.	Interrupt others often?	___	___
22.	Feel irritated when others are late?	___	___
23.	Leave the table immediately after eating?	___	___
24.	Feel rushed?	___	___
25.	Feel dissatisfied with your current level of performance?	___	___

PSYCHOLOGICAL MODERATORS OF STRESS

There is no one-to-one relationship between the amount of stress we undergo and physical illness or psychological distress. Physical factors account for some of the variability in our responses: Some people inherit predispositions toward specific disorders. Psychological factors also play a role, however (Holahan & Moos, 1990). They can influence, or *moderate,* the effects of sources of stress. In this section, we discuss a number of psychological moderators of stress: self-efficacy expectations, psychological hardiness, a sense of humor, predictability, and social support.

Self-Efficacy Expectations: "The Little Engine That Could." Our **self-efficacy expectations** affect our abilities to withstand stress (Bandura, 1982, 1991). For example, when we are faced with fear-inducing objects, high self-efficacy expectations are accompanied by relatively *lower* levels of adrenaline and noradrenaline in the bloodstream (Bandura and others, 1985). Adrenaline is secreted when we are under stress. It arouses the body by means such as accelerating the heart rate and releasing glucose from the liver. As a result, we may have "butterflies in the stomach" and feelings of nervousness. Excessive arousal can impair our ability to manage stress by boosting our motivation beyond optimal levels and by distracting us from the tasks at hand. People with higher self-efficacy expectations thus have biological as well as psychological reasons for remaining calmer.

People who are self-confident are less prone to become depressed in response to negative life events (Holahan & Moos, 1991). Moreover, people with positive self-efficacy expectations respond more positively to treatment for depression (Hoberman and others, 1988). People with higher self-efficacy expectations are more likely to lose weight or quit smoking and are less likely to relapse afterward (DiClemente and others, 1991).

Psychological Hardiness. **Psychological hardiness** also helps people resist stress. The research on psychological hardiness is largely indebted to the pioneering work of Suzanne Kobasa (1979) and her colleagues. They studied business executives who resisted illness despite heavy loads of stress. In one phase of her research, hardy and nonhardy executives completed a battery of psychological tests. Kobasa found that the hardy executives differed from the nonhardy in three important ways (Kobasa and others, 1982, pp. 169–170):

1. Hardy individuals were high in *commitment*. That is, they showed a tendency to involve themselves in, rather than experience alienation from, whatever they were doing or encountering.
2. Hardy individuals were high in *challenge*. They believed that change rather than stability is normal in life. They appraised change as an interesting incentive to personal growth, not as a threat to security.
3. Hardy individuals were also high in perceived *control* over their lives. They felt and behaved as though they were influential rather than helpless in facing the various rewards and punishments of life. Psychologically hardy people tend to have what Julian B. Rotter (1990) terms an internal **locus of control.**

According to Kobasa, hardy people are more resistant to stress because they see themselves as *choosing* to face it. They also interpret, or encode, the stress impacting

upon them as making life more interesting, not as compounding pressure. Their activation of control allows them to regulate to some degree the amount of stress they will encounter at any given time (Maddi & Kobasa, 1984). Other researchers have found that even the *illusion* of being in control of one's situation tends to enhance one's mood in the face of stress (Alloy & Clements, 1992).

Kobasa and Pucetti (1983) suggest that psychological hardiness helps individuals by buffering stressful life events. Buffering stress gives people the opportunity to draw on social supports (Ganellen & Blaney, 1984) and to use coping mechanisms such as controlling what they will be doing from day to day. Type A individuals who show psychological hardiness are more resistant to illness, including coronary heart disease, than Type A individuals who do not (Friedman & Booth-Kewley, 1987; Krantz and others, 1988).

A sense of control is essential to psychological hardiness. You may wish to complete the nearby questionnaire to see whether you believe that you are in charge of your own life.

Self-Efficacy Expectations and Performance. Outstanding athletes like Oksana Baiul tend to have high self-efficacy expectations. That is, they believe in themselves. High self-efficacy expectations—beliefs that we can cope—moderate the impact of stress upon us.

Self-efficacy expectations • Our beliefs that we can bring about desired changes through our own efforts.

Psychological hardiness • A cluster of traits that buffer stress and are characterized by commitment, challenge, and control.

Locus of control • The place (locus) to which an individual attributes control over the receiving of reinforcers—either inside or outside the self.

Sense of Humor: Does "A Merry Heart Doeth Good Like a Medicine"? The idea that humor lightens the burdens of the day and helps us cope with stress has been with us for millennia (Lefcourt & Martin, 1986). Consider the biblical maxim "A merry heart doeth good like a medicine" (Proverbs 17:22).

In *Anatomy of an Illness*, Norman Cousins (1979) reported his bout with a painful collagen illness that is similar to arthritis. He found that ten minutes of belly laughter of the sort he experienced while watching Marx Brothers movies relieved much of his pain. Laughter allowed him to sleep. It may also have reduced his inflammation, which is consistent with some findings that emotional responses such as happiness and anger may have beneficial effects on the immune system (Kemeny, 1993). The benefits of humor may also reflect the cognitive shifts they entail and the emotional changes that accompany them.

Research has also shown that humor can moderate the effects of stress. In one study, students completed a negative-life-events checklist and a measure of mood disturbance (Martin & Lefcourt, 1983). The mood-disturbance measure also yielded a stress score. Students self-rated their sense of humor. Behavioral assessments were made of their ability to produce humor under stress. Overall, there was a significant relationship between negative life events and stress scores: High accumulations of negative life events predicted higher levels of stress. However, students who had a greater sense of humor and who produced humor in difficult situations were less affected by negative life events than other students.

Truth or Fiction Revisited. *It is true that a sense of humor can moderate the*

Questionnaire

LOCUS OF CONTROL SCALE

Psychologically hardy people tend to have an internal locus of control. They believe that they are in control of their own lives. Persons with an external locus of control, in contrast, tend to see their fates as being out of their hands.

Are you more of an "internal" or more of an "external"? To learn more about your perception of your locus of control, respond to this questionnaire, which was developed by Nowicki and Strickland (1973).

Place a check mark in either the Yes or the No column for each question, and, when you are finished, turn to the answer key in Appendix B.

	YES	NO
1. Do you believe that most problems will solve themselves if you just don't fool with them?	____	____
2. Do you believe that you can stop yourself from catching a cold?	____	____
3. Are some people just born lucky?	____	____
4. Most of the time, do you feel that getting good grades meant a great deal to you?	____	____
5. Are you often blamed for things that just aren't your fault?	____	____
6. Do you believe that if somebody studies hard enough he or she can pass any subject?	____	____
7. Do you feel that most of the time it doesn't pay to try hard because things never turn out right anyway?	____	____
8. Do you feel that if things start out well in the morning, it's going to be a good day no matter what you do?	____	____
9. Do you feel that most of the time parents listen to what their children have to say?	____	____
10. Do you believe that wishing can make good things happen?	____	____
11. When you get punished, does it usually seem it's for no good reason at all?	____	____
12. Most of the time, do you find it hard to change a friend's opinion?	____	____
13. Do you think cheering more than luck helps a team win?	____	____
14. Did you feel that it was nearly impossible to change your parents' minds about anything?	____	____
15. Do you believe that parents should allow children to make most of their own decisions?	____	____
16. Do you feel that when you do something wrong there's very little you can do to make it right?	____	____
17. Do you believe that most people are just born good at sports?	____	____
18. Are most other people your age stronger than you are?	____	____

impact of stress. In an experiment run by Martin and Lefcourt, humor played its conjectured stress-buffering role.

Predictability. Ability to predict a stressor apparently moderates its impact. Predictability allows us to brace ourselves for the inevitable and, in many cases, to plan ways of coping with it. Experiments show that crowding is less aversive when we are forewarned about how crowding might make us feel (Baum and others, 1981; Paulus & Matthews, 1980).

There is also a relationship between the desire to assume control over one's situation and the usefulness of information about impending stressors (Lazarus & Folkman, 1984). Predictability is of greater benefit to **"internals"**—that is, to people who wish to exercise control over their situations—than to **"externals"** (Affleck and others, 1987; Martelli and others, 1987). People who want information about medical procedures and what they will experience cope better with pain when they obtain that information (Ludwick-Rosenthal & Neufeld, 1993).

Animal research tends to support the view that there are advantages to predictability, especially when predictability allows one to control a stressor (Weinberg & Levine, 1980). Signaling laboratory rats that a stressor is approaching apparently buffers its impact.

In one study, Weiss (1972) placed three sets of rats matched according to age and weight into individual soundproof cages, as shown in Figure 15.3. The rat on the left received electric shock following a signal. It could then terminate the shock by turning the wheel. The rat in the center was shocked in tandem with the rat to the left, but it received no warning signal and could

Internals • People who perceive the ability to attain reinforcements as being largely within themselves.
Externals • People who perceive the ability to attain reinforcements as being largely outside themselves.

	YES	NO
19. Do you feel that one of the best ways to handle most problems is just not to think about them?	____	____
20. Do you feel that you have a lot of choice in deciding who your friends are?	____	____
21. If you find a four-leaf clover, do you believe that it might bring you good luck?	____	____
22. Did you often feel that whether or not you did your homework had much to do with what kind of grades you got?	____	____
23. Do you feel that when a person your age is angry with you, there's little you can do to stop him or her?	____	____
24. Have you ever had a good-luck charm?	____	____
25. Do you believe that whether or not people like you depends on how you act?	____	____
26. Did your parents usually help you if you asked them to?	____	____
27. Have you ever felt that when people were angry with you, it was usually for no reason at all?	____	____
28. Most of the time, do you feel that you can change what might happen tomorrow by what you did today?	____	____
29. Do you believe that when bad things are going to happen they are just going to happen no matter what you try to do to stop them?	____	____
30. Do you think that people can get their own way if they just keep trying?	____	____
31. Most of the time do you find it useless to try to get your own way at home?	____	____
32. Do you feel that when good things happen, they happen because of hard work?	____	____
33. Do you feel that when somebody your age wants to be your enemy there's little you can do to change matters?	____	____
34. Do you feel that it's easy to get friends to do what you want them to do?	____	____
35. Do you usually feel that you have little to say about what you get to eat at home?	____	____
36. Do you feel that when someone doesn't like you, there's little you can do about it?	____	____
37. Did you usually feel it was almost useless to try in school, because most other children were just plain smarter than you were?	____	____
38. Are you the kind of person who believes that planning ahead makes things turn out better?	____	____
39. Most of the time, do you feel that you have little to say about what your family decides to do?	____	____
40. Do you think it's better to be smart than to be lucky?	____	____

do nothing to terminate the shock. The rat to the right received no signal and no electric shock. However, it was placed in the identical apparatus, including having electrodes attached to its tail, to control for any effects of this unnatural environment.

As shown in Figure 15.4, shock led to ulceration in the rats—the definition of stressful experience in this study. The rats to the right, which received no signal and no shock, showed hardly any ulceration. Rats that received shock without warning showed the greatest amount of ulceration. Rats given warning signals and allowed to terminate the shock also developed ulcers, but to a significantly lesser degree.

The Weiss study suggests that inescapable stressors may be less harmful when they are predictable and when we act purposefully upon their arrival. The predictability of a stressor is to some degree a situational variable. But if we learn what we can about the sources of stress in our lives—concurrent and impending—and commit ourselves to regulating them as best we can, we may, like Weiss's warned rats, be able to brace ourselves and plan effective responses. We may not avert stress completely, but we may buffer its impact.

Social Support. Social support, like psychological hardiness, seems to buffer the effects of stress (Burman & Margolin, 1992; Coyne & Downey, 1991; Holahan & Moos, 1990). Introverts, people who lack social skills, and people who live by themselves seem more prone to developing infectious diseases under stress (Cohen & Williamson, 1991).

Social supports include:

1. *Emotional concern* (listening to people's problems and expressing feelings of sympathy, caring, understanding, and reassurance).

2. *Instrumental aid* (the material supports and services that facilitate adaptive behavior). For example, after a disaster, the

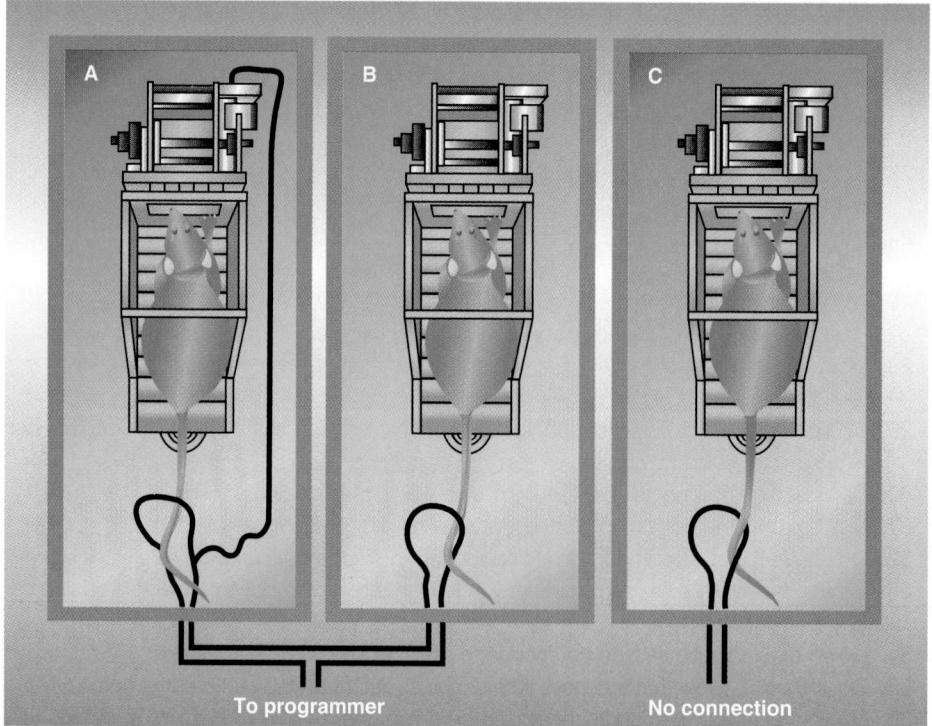

FIGURE 15.3
The Experimental Setup in the Weiss Study on Ulcer Formation in Rats The rat to the left is signaled prior to receiving electric shock and can terminate the shock by turning the wheel. The rat in the center receives a shock of the same intensity and duration but is not warned of its onset and cannot terminate it. The rat to the right receives no signal and no shock.

government may arrange for low-interest loans so that survivors can rebuild. Relief organizations may provide foodstuffs, medicines, and temporary living quarters.

3. *Information* (guidance and advice that enhance people's ability to cope).

4. *Appraisal* (feedback from others as to how one is doing). This kind of support involves helping people interpret, or "make sense of," what has happened to them.

5. *Socializing* (simple conversation, recreation, even going shopping with another person). Beneficial effects are derived from socializing itself, even in ways that are not oriented toward solving problems.

Research supports the value of social support. Older people who have social support recover more rapidly from physical disabilities (Wilcox and others, 1994). People who have buddies who help them start exercising or quit drinking or smoking are more likely to succeed (Gruder and others, 1993). Social support appears to protect us, and to help us recover, from feelings of depression (Lewinsohn and others, 1994b; McLeod and others, 1992). A study of men who were infected with the AIDS virus (the human immunodeficiency virus [HIV]) showed that men with more satisfying social support were less depressed and found HIV-related symptoms less stressful than men with less satisfying social support (Hays and others, 1992). Stress is less likely to induce high blood pressure in women who have social support than in women who do not (Linden and others, 1993).

People who receive social support may even live longer, as was found in studies of Alameda County, California (Berkman & Breslow, 1983) and Tecumseh, Michigan (House and others, 1982). In the Tecumseh study, adults were followed during a 12-year period. The mortality rate was significantly lower for men who were married, who regularly attended meetings of voluntary associations, and who frequently engaged in social leisure activities.

Truth or Fiction Revisited. *It is not true that single men live longer than married men.* Actually, married men live longer than single men.

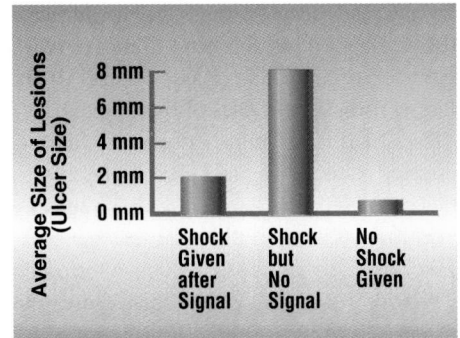

FIGURE 15.4
Effects of Predictability and Ability to Control a Stressor on Ulcer Formation in Rats
Rats that received no signals or shocks formed hardly any ulcers, as shown in Part C. Rats that received shocks but could not predict or terminate them showed the most ulcer formation. Part A shows that rats that were warned of impending shocks and could terminate them showed more ulcer formation than rats that were not shocked but not nearly as much ulceration as rats that could not predict the onset of shocks.

THE GENERAL ADAPTATION SYNDROME

How is it that too much of a good thing—or that stress—can make us ill? Hans Selye suggested that the body under stress is like a clock with an alarm system that does not shut off until its energy is dangerously depleted.

Selye (1976) observed that the body's response to different stressors shows some similarities or generalities, whether the stressor is a bacterial invasion, perceived danger, or a major life change. He labeled this response the **general adaptation syndrome** (GAS). The GAS consists of three stages: an alarm reaction, a resistance stage, and an exhaustion stage.

The Alarm Reaction. The **alarm reaction** is triggered by perception of a stressor. This reaction mobilizes or arouses the body in preparation for defense. Early in the century, physiologist Walter Cannon termed this alarm system the **fight-or-flight reaction.** The alarm reaction involves a number of bodily changes that are initiated by the brain and further regulated

General adaptation syndrome • Selye's term for a hypothesized three-stage response to stress. Abbreviated *GAS.*

Alarm reaction • The first stage of the GAS, which is triggered by the impact of a stressor and characterized by sympathetic activity.

Fight-or-flight reaction • An innate adaptive response to the perception of danger.

MINILECTURE: SELYE'S GENERAL ADAPTATION SYNDROME

by the endocrine system and the sympathetic division of the autonomic nervous system (ANS) (Gallucci and others, 1993). Let us consider the roles of these systems.

Stress has a domino effect on the endocrine system (Figure 15.5). The hypothalamus secretes corticotrophin-releasing hormone (CRH). CRH causes the pituitary gland to secrete adrenocorticotrophic hormone (ACTH). ACTH then causes the adrenal cortex to secrete cortisol and other corticosteroids (steroidal hormones produced by the adrenal cortex). Corticosteroids help protect the body by combating allergic reactions (such as difficulty breathing) and by producing inflammation. Inflammation increases circulation to parts of the body that are injured. It ferries in hordes of white blood cells to fend off invading pathogens.

Two other hormones that play a major role in the alarm reaction are secreted by the adrenal medulla. The sympathetic division of the ANS activates the adrenal medulla, causing a mixture of adrenaline

and noradrenaline to be released. The mixture arouses the body to cope with threats and stress by accelerating the heart rate and causing muscle tissue and the liver to release glucose (sugar). Energy is thus provided for the fight-or-flight reaction, which was inherited from a time when many stressors were life threatening. This reaction activates the body so that it is prepared to fight or flee from a predator. Many of the bodily changes that occur in the fight-or-flight reaction are outlined in Table 15.1. Historically, the reaction was triggered by a predator at the edge of a thicket or by a sudden rustling in the undergrowth. Today, it is also aroused when you chafe at the bit in stop-and-go traffic or learn that your mortgage payments are going to be increased. Once the threat is removed, the body returns to a lower state of arousal.

The Resistance Stage. If the alarm reaction mobilizes the body and the stressor is not removed, we enter the adaptation stage, or **resistance stage,** of the GAS. The

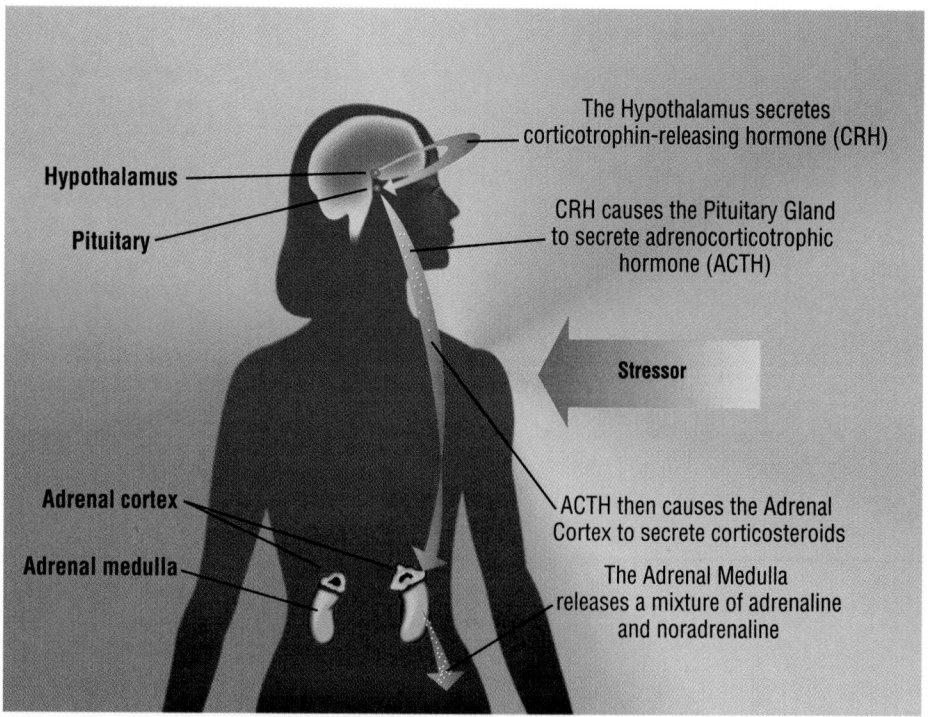

FIGURE 15.5
Stress and the Endocrine System Stress has a domino effect on the endocrine system, leading to the release of corticosteroids and a mixture of adrenaline and noradrenaline. Corticosteroids combat allergic reactions (such as difficulty breathing) and cause inflammation. Adrenaline and noradrenaline arouse the body to cope by accelerating the heart rate and providing energy for the fight-or-flight reaction.

Are Their Alarm Systems Going Off as They Take Out a Loan? The alarm reaction of the general adaptation syndrome can be triggered by daily hassles and life changes—such as taking out a large loan—as well as by physical threats. When the stressor persists, diseases of adaptation may eventually develop.

Resistance stage • The second stage of the GAS, characterized by prolonged sympathetic activity in an effort to restore lost energy and repair damage. Also called the *adaptation stage*.

Exhaustion stage • The third stage of the GAS, characterized by weakened resistance and possible deterioration.

levels of endocrine and sympathetic activity are not as high as in the alarm reaction. Still, they are greater than normal. In this stage, the body attempts to restore lost energy and repair bodily damage.

The Exhaustion Stage. If the stressor is still not adequately dealt with, we may enter the final or **exhaustion stage** of the GAS. Our individual capacities for resisting stress vary, but all of us eventually become exhausted when stress persists indefinitely. Our muscles become fatigued. We deplete our bodies of resources required for combating stress. With exhaustion, the parasympathetic division of the ANS may predominate. As a result, our heartbeats and respiration rates slow down. Many aspects of sympathetic activity are reversed. It might sound as if we would profit from the respite, but remember that we are still under stress—and possibly an external threat. Continued stress in the exhaustion stage may lead to what Selye terms "diseases of adaptation"—from allergies and hives to ulcers and coronary heart disease—and, ultimately, to death.

Let us now consider the effects of stress on the body's immune system. Our discussion will pave the way for understanding the links between various psychological factors and physical illnesses.

TABLE 15.1

Components of the Alarm Reaction

Corticosteroids are secreted	Muscles tense
Adrenaline is secreted	Blood shifts from internal organs to the skeletal musculature
Noradrenaline is secreted	Digestion is inhibited
Respiration rate increases	Sugar is released from the liver
Heart rate increases	Blood coagulability increases
Blood pressure increases	

The alarm reaction is triggered by various types of stressors. It is defined by release of corticosteroids and adrenaline and by activity of the sympathetic branch of the autonomic nervous system. It prepares the body to fight or flee from a source of danger.

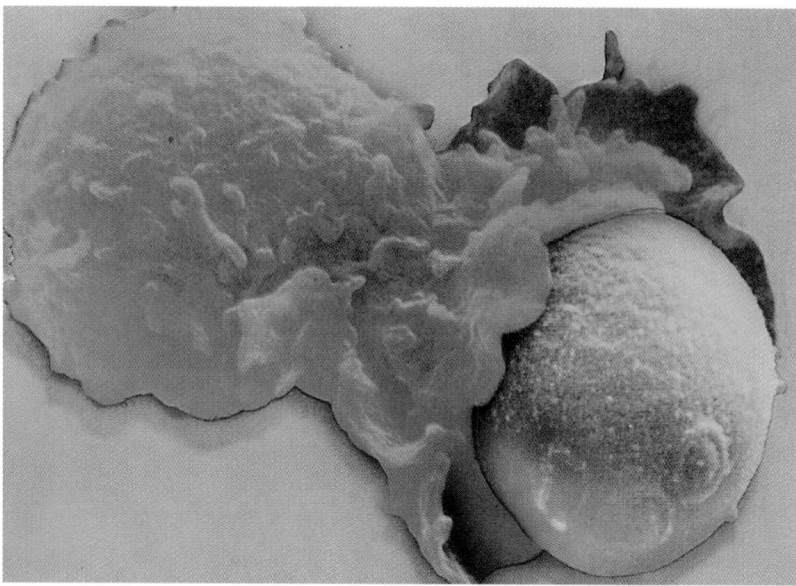

FIGURE 15.6
Microscopic Warfare The immune system helps us to combat disease. It produces white blood cells (leukocytes), such as the one shown here, that routinely engulf and kill pathogens such as bacteria and viruses. Leukocytes recognize pathogens by the shapes of their surfaces. The surface shapes are termed *antigens* (short for "antibody generators") because the body reacts to their presence by developing specialized proteins (the *antibodies*) that attach to the pathogens, inactivating them and marking them for destruction.

Immune system • (im-YOON). The system of the body that recognizes and destroys foreign agents (antigens) that invade the body.

Leukocytes • (LOO-coe-sites). White blood cells. (Derived from the Greek words *leukos,* meaning "white," and *kytos,* literally meaning "a hollow" but used to refer to cells.)

Antigen • (ANT-tee-jenn *or* ANT-eye-jenn). A substance that stimulates the body to mount an immune-system response to it. (The contraction for *anti*body *gen*erator.)

EFFECTS OF STRESS ON THE IMMUNE SYSTEM

Research shows that chronic stress suppresses the **immune system** (Coe, 1993; O'Leary, 1990). Research also demonstrates how psychological factors such as control and social support moderate the effects of stress on the immune system. Let us first review the nature and functions of the immune system. Then we shall consider the effects of stress on the immune system in more detail.

Nature and Functions of the Immune System. Given the complexities of our bodies and the fast pace of scientific change, it is common for us to think of ourselves as being dependent on trained professionals to cope with illness. Yet, we actually do most of this coping by ourselves, by means of our immune systems.

The immune system has several functions that help us combat disease. One way we combat physical disorders is by producing white blood cells that routinely engulf and kill pathogens such as bacteria, fungi, and viruses; worn-out body cells; even cells that have changed into cancerous cells. White blood cells are technically termed **leukocytes** (Figure 15.6). Leukocytes carry on microscopic warfare. They engage in search-and-destroy missions. They "recognize" and then eradicate foreign agents and unhealthy cells.

Leukocytes recognize foreign agents by the shapes of their surfaces. The surface shapes are termed **antigens.** The body reacts to antigens by developing specialized proteins, or **antibodies,** that attach to the foreign agents, inactivating them and marking them for destruction. The immune system "remembers" how to battle antigens by maintaining antibodies to them in the bloodstream, often for years.[1]

Inflammation is another function of the immune system. When injury occurs, blood vessels in the area first contract (to stem bleeding) but then dilate. Dilation increases the flow of blood to the damaged area, causing the redness and warmth that characterize inflammation. The increased blood supply also floods the region with white blood cells to combat invading microscopic life forms such as bacteria that might otherwise use the local damage as a port of entry into the body.

Truth or Fiction Revisited. *It is true that countless microscopic warriors within our bodies are carrying out search-and-destroy missions against foreign agents at any given moment.* The warriors are the white blood cells of the immune system.

Stress and the Immune System. Psychologists, biologists, and medical researchers have combined their efforts in a field of study that addresses the relationships between psychological factors, the nervous system, the endocrine system, the immune system, and disease: **psychoneuroimmunology** (Ader, 1993; Kiecolt-Glaser & Glaser, 1992). One of the major concerns of psychoneuroimmunology is the effect of stress on the immune system.

[1] Vaccination is the introduction of a weakened form of an antigen (usually a bacteria or a virus) into the body to stimulate the production of antibodies. Antibodies can confer immunity for many years, in some cases for a lifetime. Smallpox has been eradicated by means of vaccination, and scientists are searching for a vaccine against the AIDS virus.

One of the reasons that stress eventually exhausts us is that it stimulates us to produce steroids. Steroids suppress the functioning of the immune system. Suppression has negligible effects when steroids are secreted intermittently. However, persistent secretion of steroids decreases inflammation and interferes with the formation of antibodies. As a consequence, susceptibility to various illnesses, including the common cold (Cohen and others, 1993), increases.

An experiment with laboratory rats and electric shock mirrored the method of Weiss (1972), described earlier. In the later study, however, the dependent variable was activity of the immune system, not ulcer formation (Laudenslager and others, 1983). The rats were exposed to inevitable electric shocks, but, as in the Weiss study, one group of rats could terminate the shock. Rats that could not exert control over the stressor showed immune-system deficits. Rats that could terminate the shock showed no deficiency.

One study with people focused on dental students (Jemmott and others, 1983). Students showed lower immune-system functioning, as measured by lower levels of antibodies in the saliva, during stressful school periods than immediately following vacations. Moreover, students with many friends showed less suppression of the immune system than students with few friends. Social support apparently buffered school stresses.

Other studies have found that the stress of examinations depresses immune-system response to the Epstein-Barr virus, which causes fatigue and other problems (Glaser and others, 1991, 1993). Moreover, students who are lonely show greater suppression of the immune system than students who have more social support. In a study of older people, it was found that a combination of relaxation training, which decreases sympathetic activity, and training in coping skills *improves* the functioning of the immune system (Glaser and others, 1991).

Reflections

Now that you have read the section on stress, reflect on the following questions:

• What kinds of life changes and daily hassles are you experiencing these days? Do you find these events stressful? How do you know?

• Hassles and life changes can predict physical illness. Does this mean that we should try to avoid making changes in our lives? Why or why not?

• What kinds of conflict, if any, are you in? What are you doing to attempt to resolve these conflicts?

• Are you a Type A person? Why do you think that you are or are not?

• Agree or disagree with the following statement and support your answer: "It is better not to know about bad things that are going to happen."

• Why do you think that married men live longer than single men do? (See Figure 15.7.) Is it because marriage is a more healthful state than singleness, or do these findings reflect a selection factor? That is, do the same factors that lead men to get married and to stay married also lead to better health? If so, what might these factors be?

Antibodies • Substances formed by white blood cells that recognize and destroy antigens.

Inflammation • (IN-flam-MAY-shun). Increased blood flow to an injured area of the body, resulting in redness, warmth, and an increased supply of white blood cells.

Psychoneuroimmunology • (sigh-coe-new-row-im-you-NOLL-oh-gee). The field that studies the relationships between psychological factors (e.g., attitudes and overt behavior patterns) and the functioning of the immune system.

FIGURE 15.7
Why Do Married Men Live Longer than Single Men? Does marriage lead to longevity, or does another factor contribute both to longevity and a tendency to get married? What might that other factor (or factors) be?

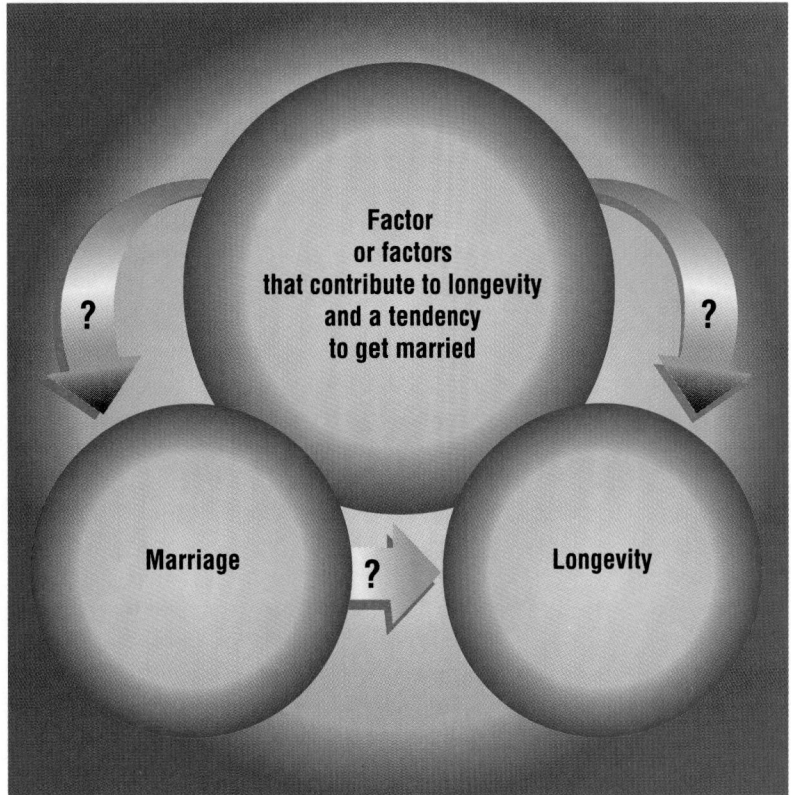

• Do you tend to get ill—for example, to "catch what's going around"—at a certain time of the year? If so, what time of year? Why do you think that you are more vulnerable to illness at this time of year?

Now that we have considered the nature of stress and the body's response to stress, let us more broadly consider the factors involved in physical illness.

A Multifactorial Approach to Health and Illness

The only way to keep your health is to eat what you don't want, drink what you don't like, and do what you'd rather not.

MARK TWAIN

Why do people get sick? Why do some of us develop cancer? Why do others have heart attacks? Why do still others seem to be immune to these illnesses? Why do some of us seem to come down with everything that is going around, while others ride out the roughest winters with nary a sniffle? There is no single, simple answer to these questions. The likelihood of contracting an illness—whether a case of the flu or a kind of cancer—can reflect the interaction of many factors (Coie and others, 1993; Stokols, 1992). Biological factors such as family history of disease, pathogens, inoculations, injuries, age, and gender may strike us as the most obvious causes of disease. However, as shown in Table 15.2, psychological, social, technological, and natural environmental factors also play key roles in health and illness. For example, the Los Angeles earthquake of 1994 not only killed more than 40 people and cost billions of dollars. It also caused life changes to pile atop one another by disrupting community life. Services that had been taken for granted, such as electricity and water, were lost. Businesses and homes were destroyed, so that people had to rebuild or relocate. Such disasters reveal the thinness of the veneer of technology on which civilization depends. It is understandable that many survivors report stress-related problems such as anxiety and depression for months after the fact.

Many diseases are influenced by psychological factors, such as our attitudes and patterns of behavior (Ader, 1993; Angell, 1993; Farley, 1993a). Psychological states such as anxiety and depression can also impair the functioning of the immune system, rendering us more vulnerable to physical disorders (Esterling and others, 1993; Herbert & Cohen, 1993; Kemeny and others, 1994; Weisse, 1992).

In this section, we first focus on some of the sociocultural factors that are connected with health and illness, as reflected in human diversity. Then we discuss a number of health problems including headaches, heart disease, asthma, and cancer. In each case we consider the interplay of biological, psychological, social, technological, and environmental factors in the origins of the problem. Although these are medical problems, we also explore ways in which psychologists have contributed to their treatment.

HUMAN DIVERSITY AND HEALTH: NATIONS WITHIN THE NATION

In 1990, a cigarette company began to market a new brand, Uptown, which was specifically designed to appeal to African Americans. There was such a clamor from civil rights groups and the media, however, that the ad campaign was canceled, and manufacture of the brand was discontinued ("Decline in Smoking," 1993). The cigarette brand Virginia Slims is designed and marketed to appeal to women (McCarthy, 1990). Virginia Slims is very much alive and economically successful, sad to say. In fact, whereas most population groups are now smoking less than they did a generation ago, young career women are smoking more. We thus find a greater incidence of lung cancer and other smoking-related illnesses within this group than we have in past years.

Health psychologists have noted that in the realms of health-related behaviors and the incidence of various physical disorders, we are many nations and not just one. Many factors influence whether people make an effort to prevent illness or succumb to illness. As noted in Table 15.2, they include ethnicity, gender, level of education, and socioeconomic status.

TABLE 15.2

Factors in Health and Illness: Biological, Psychological, Social, Technological, and Natural Environmental

BIOLOGICAL	PSYCHOLOGICAL		SOCIAL: SOCIO-ECONOMIC AND SOCIOCULTURAL	TECHNOLOGICAL	NATURAL ENVIRONMENTAL
	PERSONALITY	BEHAVIORAL			
Family history of illness	Self-efficacy expectations	Diet (intake of calories, fats, fiber, vitamins, etc.)	Socioeconomic status	Adequacy of available health care	Natural disasters (earthquakes, floods, hurricanes, drought, extremes of temperature, tornados)
Exposure to infectious pathogens (e.g., bacteria and viruses)	Psychological hardiness	Consumption of alcohol	Availability and use of social support vs. peer rejection or isolation	Vehicular safety	Radon
Functioning of the immune system	Psychological conflict (approach–approach, avoidance–avoidance, approach–avoidance)	Cigarette smoking	Family circumstances; social class, family size, conflict, disorganization	Architectural features (e.g., injury-resistant design, nontoxic construction materials, aesthetic design, air quality, noise insulation)	
Inoculations	Optimism	Level of physical activity	Social climate in the workplace, sexual harassment	Aesthetics of residential, workplace, communal architecture, and landscape architecture	
Medication history	Attributional style (how one explains one's failures to oneself)	Sleep patterns	Prejudice and discrimination	Water quality	
Congenital disabilities, perinatal complications	Health locus of control (belief that one is in charge of one's own health)	Safety practices (e.g., driving with seat belts; careful driving; practice of sexual abstinence, monogamy, or "safe sex"; attaining of comprehensive prenatal care)	Major life changes of a social nature such as death of a spouse or divorce	Solid waste treatment and sanitation	
Physiological conditions (e.g., hypertension, serum cholesterol level)	Introversion/extroversion	Regular medical and dental checkups	Health-related cultural and religious beliefs and practices	Pollution	
Reactivity of the cardiovascular system (e.g., "hot reactor")	Coronary-prone (Type A) personality	Compliance with medical and dental advice	Major economic life changes such as taking out a large mortgage or losing one's job	Radiation	
Pain and discomfort	Tendencies to express feelings of anger and frustration	Interpersonal/social skills	Health promotion programs in the workplace or the community	Global warming	
Age	Depression/anxiety		Health-related legislation	Ozone depletion	
Gender	Hostility/suspiciousness		Availability of health insurance		
			Availability of transportation to health-care facilities		

This table incorporates elements from Coie and others (1993) and from Stokols (1992).

For example, African Americans between the ages of 25 and 64 have a much higher mortality rate than White Americans in the same age group. Moreover, this gap has been widening over the past few decades (Pappas and others, 1993). The death rate does not appear to be due to ethnicity per se, but rather to factors such as income (Angell, 1993) and level of education (Guralnik and others, 1993). (African Americans tend to be poorer and less well educated than White Americans.) African Americans have less access to health care than White Americans do. African Americans are also more likely to live in unhealthful neighborhoods, eat high-fat diets, and smoke (Pappas and others, 1993).

Disproportionate numbers of deaths from AIDS also occur within ethnic minorities in the United States, predominantly among African Americans and Hispanic Americans (St. Lawrence, 1993). Only 12% of the U.S. population is African American (*The Outlook*, 1993), but African Americans account

MINILECTURE: PERSONALITY AND HEALTH

for more than 30% of those with AIDS (CDC, 1993). Only 9% of the population is Hispanic American (*The Outlook,* 1993), but Hispanic Americans account for more than 16% of people with AIDS (CDC, 1993). Yet minority adolescents still perceive AIDS to be a disease of White gay males. Thus, they perceive themselves to be at little risk for contracting AIDS (St. Lawrence, 1993).

The incidence of sickle-cell anemia is highest among African and Hispanic Americans. The incidence of Tay-Sachs disease is greatest among Jews of East European origin. The connection between these disorders and the ethnic groups they assault is genetic.

African Americans are five to seven times more likely than European Americans to suffer from hypertension (Leary, 1991). However, African Americans are also more likely to suffer from hypertension than Black Africans are. Many health professionals thus infer that environmental factors that are found among many African Americans—such as stress, diet, and smoking—contribute to high blood pressure in people who are genetically vulnerable to it (Betancourt & López, 1993; Leary, 1991).

Anorexia and bulimia nervosa are uncommon among poor people, but obesity is most prevalent among them (see Chapter 10). The incidence of obesity is also greater among cultural groups in which many people associate obesity with happiness and health—as among some Haitian (Laguerre, 1981) and Puerto Rican groups (Harwood, 1981). Poor urban neighborhoods foster obesity because junk food is heavily promoted and many residents eat as a way of coping with stress (Freeman, 1991).

Truth or Fiction Revisited. *It is not true that poor people in the United States eat less than more affluent people.* Obesity is actually most prevalent among the lowest socioeconomic groups. Why? (This is not to deny the sad fact that some poor people in the United States go hungry.)

African Americans are more likely than White Americans to have heart attacks and to die from them (Becker and others, 1993). Early diagnosis and treatment might help decrease the racial gap (Ayanian, 1993). African Americans with heart disease are less likely than White Americans to

obtain procedures such as bypass surgery, even in Veterans Administration hospitals, where diagnosis and treatment are free (Whittle and others, 1993).

African Americans are also more likely than White Americans to contract most forms of cancer. Possibly because of genetic factors, the incidence of lung cancer is significantly higher among African Americans than White Americans (Blakeslee, 1994; "Smoke Rises," 1993). Once they contract cancer, African Americans are more likely than White Americans to die from it (Andersen, 1992; Bal, 1992). The discouraging results for African Americans are connected with their lower socioeconomic status (Baquet and others, 1991). Consider research on women with breast cancer. Cancer is more curable when it is detected early. Yet women who do not carry health insurance coverage, or who have Medicaid (public health insurance for people of low socioeconomic status), are less likely than women who have private health insurance to detect cancer early and are more likely to die from it (Ayanian and others, 1993).

Also consider some cross-cultural differences in health. Death rates from cancer are higher in nations such as the Netherlands, Denmark, England, Canada, and—yes—the United States, where the population has a high daily fat intake (Cohen, 1987). Death rates from cancer are much lower in nations such as in Thailand, the Philippines, and Japan, where the daily fat intake is markedly lower. Don't assume that the difference is racial just because Thailand, the Philippines, and Japan are Asian nations! The diets of Japanese Americans are similar in fat content to those of other Americans—and so are their death rates from cancer.

Because of dietary differences, Japanese American men living in California and Hawaii are two to three times more likely to become obese than Japanese men who live in Japan (Curb & Marcus, 1991).

Then consider a few gender differences. Men are more likely than women to have coronary heart disease. Women are apparently "protected" by high levels of estrogen until menopause (Brody, 1993b). After menopause, women are dramatically more likely to incur heart disease.

At all ages, men are more likely than women to drink alcohol heavily. Heavy drinking is found less often among older people than among young and middle-age adults.

The gender of the physician can also make a difference. According to a study of more than 90,000 women, women whose internists or family practitioners are women are more likely to have screenings for cancer (mammograms and Pap smears) than women whose internists or family practitioners are men (Lurie and others, 1993). It is unclear from this study, however, whether female physicians are more likely than their male counterparts to encourage women to seek preventive care, or whether women who choose female physicians are also more likely to seek preventive care. Other research shows that female physicians are more likely than male physicians to conduct breast examinations properly (Hall and others, 1990).

There are also health-care "overusers" and "underusers" among diverse cultural groups and within each gender. By and large, however, women are more likely than men to regard unusual or painful sensations as symptoms and seek health care. Men are more likely to ignore these sensations until they are forced to attend to them. Irish Americans are likely to stoically deny pain. Jewish Americans tend to practice prevention and seek medical care in a timely manner. Hispanic Americans visit physicians less often than African Americans and non-Hispanic White Americans do because of lack of health insurance, difficulty speaking English, misgivings about medical technology, and—for illegal aliens—fear of deportation (Perez-Stable, 1991; Thompson, 1991).

Let us now focus on the relationships between biological, psychological, and other factors and illnesses such as headaches, heart disease, and cancer.

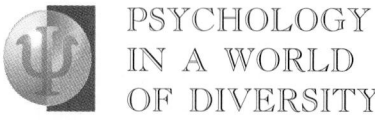

PSYCHOLOGY IN A WORLD OF DIVERSITY

HEALTH AND SOCIOECONOMIC STATUS: THE RICH GET RICHER AND THE POOR GET . . . SICKER

Socioeconomic status (SES) and health have been intimately connected throughout history (Abraham, 1993; Rogers & Ginzberg, 1993). Generally speaking, people

higher in SES enjoy better health and lead longer lives (Adler and others, 1994). The question is *why*.

Nancy Adler and her colleagues (1994) suggest possible explanations for the link between health and SES. One possibility is that the connection between health and SES is not causal, but that SES and health may both reflect genetic factors. For example, a genetically based solid constitution might lead both to good health and social standing. Second, poor health might lead to socioeconomic "drift" (that is, loss of social standing). Third, SES might affect biological functions that, in turn, influence one's health.

How might SES influence health? SES is defined in part in terms of level of education. That is, people who attain low levels of education are also likely to be low in SES. Less well-educated people are more likely to smoke (Winkleby and others, 1991), and smoking is connected with many physical illnesses. People lower in SES are also less likely to exercise and more likely to be obese—both of which are, again, linked to poor health outcomes (Ford and others, 1991).

Moreover, psychological stress places people at greater risk of physical illness. By altering hormonal responses and suppressing the immune response, people under stress are more likely to develop illnesses ranging from gastrointestinal disorders to heart attacks, and to succumb to infectious agents (Cohen and others, 1993). People who are lower in SES are more likely to suffer stress for two reasons. First, poor people are more likely to encounter stressors, such as daily financial hassles, crowding, and pollution. Second, poor people are less likely to have the resources to cope with stressful experiences (Adler and others, 1994).

Let us also not forget that poorer people also have less access to health care (Abraham, 1993; Rogers & Ginzberg, 1993). The problem is compounded by the fact that people of low SES are less likely to be educated concerning the values of regular health checkups and of early medical intervention when symptoms arise.

Socioeconomic status • One's social and financial level, as indicated by measures such as income, level of education, and occupational status. Abbreviated *SES*.

HEADACHES

Headaches are among the most common stress-related physical ailments. Nearly 20%

of people in the United States suffer from severe headaches.

Muscle-Tension Headache. The single most frequent kind of headache is the muscle-tension headache. We are likely to contract muscles in the shoulders, neck, forehead, and scalp during the first two stages of the GAS. Persistent stress can lead to persistent contraction of these muscles, giving rise to muscle-tension headaches. Such headaches usually come on gradually. They are most often characterized by dull, steady pain on both sides of the head and feelings of tightness or pressure.

Migraine Headache. Most other headaches, including the severe **migraine headache,** are vascular in nature—that is, stemming from changes in the blood supply to the head (Welch, 1993). There is often a warning aura that may be characterized by visual problems and perception of unusual odors. The attacks themselves are often attended by intensified sensitivity to light, loss of appetite, nausea, vomiting, sensory and motor disturbances such as loss of balance, and changes in mood. The so-called common migraine headache is identified by sudden onset and throbbing on one side of the head. The so-called classic migraine is known by sensory and motor disturbances that precede the pain.

The origins of migraine headaches are not clearly understood. It is believed, however, that they can be induced by barometric pressure; pollen; specific drugs; the chemical monosodium glutamate (MSG), which is often used to enhance the flavor of food; chocolates; aged cheeses; beer, champagne, and red wines; and the hormonal changes connected with menstruation (Brody, 1992a). Type A behavior may also be an important contributor to migraine headaches. In one study, 53% of 30 people who have migraines showed the Type A behavior pattern, as compared with 23% of 30 people who have muscle-tension headaches (Rappaport and others, 1988).

Regardless of the original source of the headache, we can unwittingly propel ourselves into a vicious cycle. Headache pain is a stressor that can lead us to increase, rather than relax, muscle tension in the neck, shoulders, scalp, and face.

Treatment. Aspirin and ibuprofen frequently decrease pain, including headache pain. They inhibit the production of the prostaglandins that help initiate transmission of pain messages to the brain. Drugs that affect the blood flow in the brain help many people with migraine (Welch, 1993). Behavioral methods can also help. Progressive relaxation focuses on decreasing muscle tension and has been shown to be highly effective in relieving muscle-tension headaches (Blanchard, 1992b; Blanchard and others, 1990a, 1991). Biofeedback training that alters the flow of blood to the head has helped many people with migraine headaches (Blanchard and others, 1990b; Gauthier and others, 1994). People who are sensitive to MSG or red wine can ask that MSG be left out of their dishes and can switch to a white wine.

Why, under stress, do some of us develop ulcers, others develop coronary heart disease, and still others suffer no physical problems? In the following sections, we see that there may be an interaction between stress and predisposing biological and psychological differences between individuals.

CORONARY HEART DISEASE

Coronary heart disease (CHD) causes nearly half the deaths in the United States (USDHHS, 1991). Consider the risk factors for CHD:

1. *Family History.* People with a family history of CHD are more likely to develop CHD themselves (Marenberg and others, 1994).

2. *Physiological Conditions.* Obesity, high **serum cholesterol** levels (Keil and others, 1993; Manson and others, 1990; Rossouw and others, 1990; Stampfer and others, 1991), and **hypertension** are examples.

   About one American in five has hypertension, or abnormally high blood pressure (Leary, 1991). When high blood pressure has no identifiable causes, it is referred to as *essential hypertension*. There appears to be a genetic component to essential hypertension (Caulfield and others, 1994). However, our blood pressure also rises in situations in which we are on constant guard against threats,

---

Migraine headaches • (MY-grain). Throbbing headaches that are connected with changes in the supply of blood to the head.

Serum cholesterol • (SEE-rum coe-LESS-ter-all). Cholesterol found in the blood.

Hypertension • (HIGH-purr-TEN-shun). High blood pressure.

whether in combat, in the workplace, or in the home. When we are under stress, we may believe that we can feel our blood pressure "pounding through the roof," but this notion is usually inaccurate. Most people cannot recognize symptoms of hypertension. It is thus important to have our blood pressure checked regularly.

3. *Patterns of Consumption.* Patterns include heavy drinking, smoking, overeating, and eating food high in cholesterol, like saturated fats (Castelli, 1994; Jeffery, 1991; Keil, 1993). Smoking raises the blood level of cholesterol and weakens the walls of blood vessels (Bartecchi and others, 1994).

4. *Type A Behavior.* Evidence is mixed as to whether the Type A behavior pattern— or one or more of its components, such as hostility—places people at risk for CHD. However, most studies suggest that there is at least a modest relationship between Type A behavior and CHD (Thoresen & Powell, 1992). It also seems that alleviating Type A behavior patterns may reduce the risk of *recurrent* heart attacks (Friedman & Ulmer, 1984).

5. *Hostility and Holding in Feelings of Anger* (Kneip and others, 1993; Suarez and others, 1993).

6. *Job Strain.* Overtime work, assembly-line labor, and exposure to conflicting demands all make their contributions (Jenkins, 1988). High-strain work, which makes high demands on workers but affords them little personal control, places workers at the highest risk (Karasek and others, 1982; Krantz and others, 1988). As shown in Figure 15.8, the work of waiters and waitresses may best fit this description.

7. *Chronic Fatigue and Chronic Emotional Strain.*

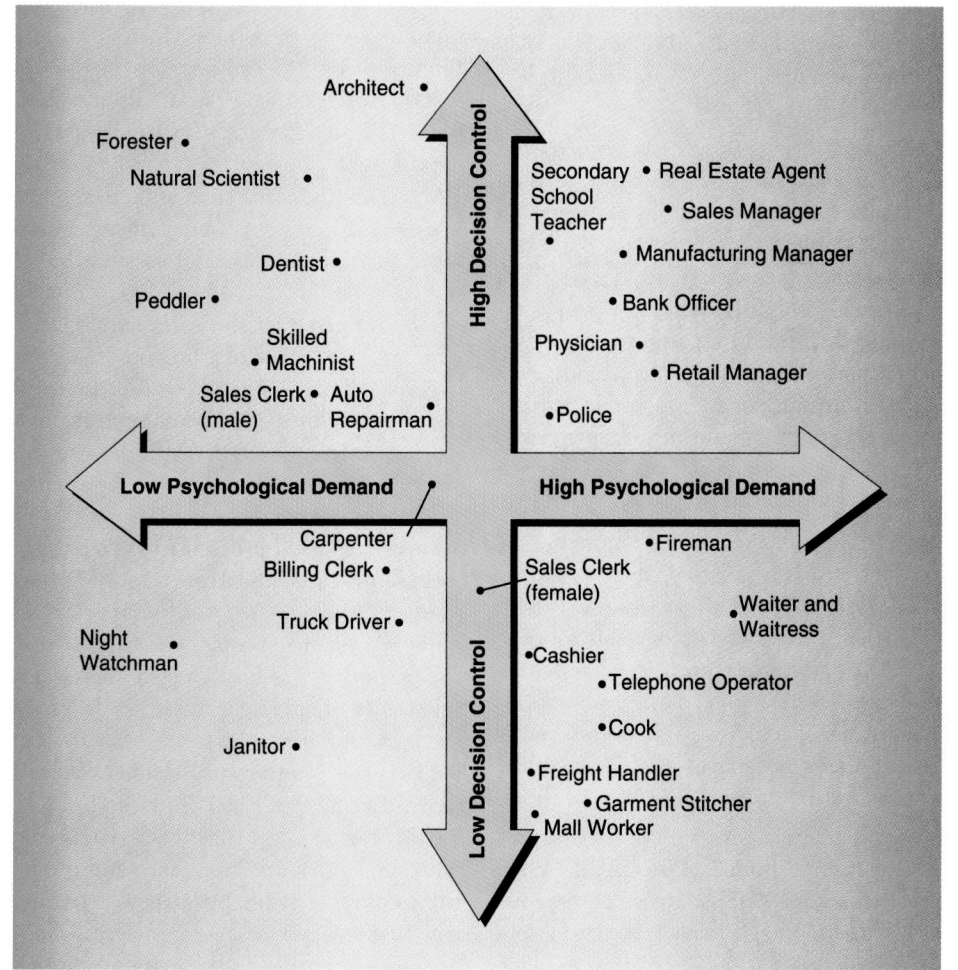

FIGURE 15.8
The Job-Strain Model This model highlights the psychological demands made by various occupations and the amount of personal (decision) control they allow. Occupations characterized by both high demand and low decision control place workers at greatest risk for heart disease.

8. *A Physically Inactive Lifestyle* (Dubbert, 1992; Lakka and others, 1994).

Behavior Modification for Reducing Risk Factors for Coronary Heart Disease. Once CHD has been diagnosed, there are a number of medical treatments, including surgery and medication. However, persons who have not had CHD (as well as those who have) can profit from behavior modification that is intended to reduce the risk factors. These methods include the following:

1. *Stopping Smoking.* (See methods in Chapter 5.)

2. *Weight Control.* (See methods in Chapter 10.)

3. *Reducing Hypertension.* Relaxation training (Agras and others, 1983), meditation (Benson and others, 1973), aerobic exercise (Brownell & Wadden, 1992; Danforth and others, 1990), maintenance of normal weight, and cutting down on dietary salt (Langford and others, 1985) all show promise in the treatment of hypertension.

4. *Lowering Low-Density Lipoprotein (Harmful) Serum Cholesterol.* The major method involves cutting down on foods high in cholesterol and saturated fats, but exercise and medication may also help (Castelli, 1994). Interestingly, people assume that foods that are low in fat will not taste as good as high-fat foods, even when their flavor is comparable. Participants in one laboratory experiment rated food labeled "high-fat" as tasting better than food labeled "low-fat" (Wardle & Solomons, 1994). However, they were tasting the same exact food!

5. *Modifying Type A Behavior.* The advice offered in the "Psychology and Modern Life" section can modify Type A behavior and decrease the risk of heart attacks, even for people who have previously had them (Friedman & Ulmer, 1984; Roskies and others, 1986).

6. *Exercise.* Sustained physical activity protects people from CHD (Castelli, 1994; Curfman, 1993b). However, studies in the United States (Mittelman and others, 1993) and Germany (Willich and others, 1993) show that strenuous physical exertion by people who are not used to exercise can trigger heart attacks. Sedentary people are therefore advised to begin exercise programs under their physicians' guidance.

We conclude this section with good news for readers of this book: *Better educated* people are more likely to modify health-impairing behavior and reap the benefits of change (Angell, 1993; Guralnik and others, 1993; Johnston and others, 1992; Pappas and others, 1993).

ASTHMA

Asthma is a respiratory disorder characterized by episodic constriction of the main tubes of the windpipe (the bronchi), over-secretion of mucus, and inflammation of air passageways (Israel and others, 1990). People with asthma may wheeze and intermittently find it difficult to breathe. Asthma affects about 9% of African American children and 6% of White children in the United States (DeAngelis, 1994b). Nearly 5,000 Americans die from asthma each year. African Americans and older people are the most vulnerable (Altman, 1993).

Although the causes of asthma are unknown, the lungs of people with asthma are more irritable than those of people who do not have the disease (Altman, 1993). Attacks can be triggered by allergic reactions; cold, dry air; stress; emotional responses such as anger; laughing too hard; and exercise (McFadden & Gilbert, 1994). Although the link to stress is less than fully clear, the stress of worrying about an attack can apparently help bring one on.

There are medical treatments for asthma, including bronchodilators and inhaled steroids (Altman, 1993). A number of reports suggest that people with asthma may also improve their breathing by muscle relaxation training, biofeedback that helps relax facial muscles, and family therapy that reduces the interpersonal stresses that affect asthmatic children (Lehrer and others, 1992). Asthma has also been connected with respiratory infections and with maternal smoking during pregnancy (Martinez and others, 1992). Such evidence again suggests an interaction between the psychological and the physiological.

CANCER

Cancer is characterized by the development of abnormal, or mutant, cells that reproduce rapidly and rob the body of nutrients. Cancerous cells may take root anywhere: in the blood (leukemia), bones, digestive tract, lungs, and genital organs. If not controlled early, the cancerous cells may metastasize (establish colonies elsewhere in the body). We apparently develop cancer cells frequently. However, the immune system normally surveys the body and destroys cancer cells. Evidence suggests that people whose immune systems are compromised by physical or psychological factors are more likely to develop tumors (Antoni, 1987; Greenberg, 1987).

Risk Factors. As with many other disorders, people can inherit dispositions toward cancer (Eysenck, 1991). Carcinogenic genes may remove the usual brakes on cell division, allowing cells to propagate wildly. Or they may allow mutations to accumulate unchecked in other genes (Kolata, 1993b). However, many behavior patterns markedly heighten the risk for cancer, such as smoking (Bartecchi and others, 1994), drinking alcohol (especially in women), ingesting animal fats (Willett and others, 1990), and sunbathing (which because of ultraviolet light causes skin cancer). Prolonged psychological conditions such as depression or stress may also heighten the risk (Antoni, 1987).

Stress and Cancer. Researchers have begun to uncover links between stress and cancer. For example, a study of children with cancer by Jacob and Charles (1980) revealed that a significant percentage had encountered severe life changes within a year of the diagnosis, often involving the death of a loved one or the loss of a close relationship.

Numerous studies also connect stressful life events to the onset of cancer among adults. However, this research has been criticized because it tends to be retrospective (Krantz and others, 1985). That is, people with cancer are interviewed about events preceding their diagnoses and about their psychological well-being prior to the onset of the disease. Self-reports are confounded by problems in memory and other

inaccuracies. Moreover, the causal relationships in such research are clouded. For example, development of the illness might have precipitated stressful events. Stress, in other words, might have been the result of the illness rather than the cause.

Experimental research that could not be conducted with humans has been conducted with rats and other animals. In one type of study, animals are injected with cancerous cells or with viruses that cause cancer and then exposed to various conditions. In this way, it can be determined which conditions influence the likelihood that the animals' immune systems will be able to fend off the disease. Such experiments with rodents suggest that once cancer has affected the individual, stress can influence its course. In one study, for example, rats were implanted with small numbers of cancer cells so that their own immune systems would have a chance to successfully combat them (Visintainer and others, 1982). Some of the rats were then exposed to inescapable shocks. Others were exposed to escapable shocks or to no shock. The rats exposed to the most stressful condition—the inescapable shock—were half as likely as the other rats to reject the cancer and two times as likely to die from it.

In a study of this kind with mice, Riley (1981) studied the effects of a cancer-causing virus that can be passed from mothers to offspring by means of nursing. This virus typically produces breast cancer in 80% of female offspring by the time they have reached 400 days of age. Riley placed one group of female offspring at risk for cancer in a stressful environment of loud noises and noxious odors. Another group was placed in a less stressful environment. At the age of 400 days, 92% of the mice that developed under stressful conditions developed breast cancer, compared with 7% of those in the control group. Moreover, the high-stress mice showed increases in levels of steroids, which depress the functioning of the body's immune system and lower blood levels of disease-fighting antibodies. However, the bottom line in this experiment is of major interest: By the time another 200 days had elapsed, the mice in the low-stress condition had nearly caught up to those in the high-stress condition in the incidence of cancer. Stress appears to have hastened along the inevitable for many of these mice. However, low stress levels did not prevent the ultimate outcome.

Truth or Fiction Revisited. *It is true that stress can influence the course of cancer.* Whether stress ever affects the ultimate outcome remains an open question.

Psychological Factors in the Treatment of Cancer. Not only must people with cancer cope with the biological aspects of their illnesses. They are also often faced with a host of psychological problems. These include feelings of anxiety and depression about treatment methods and the eventual outcome, changes in body image after the removal of a breast or testicle, feelings of vulnerability, and family problems. For example, some families criticize members with cancer for feeling sorry for themselves or for not fighting hard enough (Andersen and others, 1994; Rosenthal, 1993b). Psychological stress due to cancer can impair the immune system, setting the stage for additional health problems, such as respiratory tract infections (Andersen and others, 1994).

It is understandable that people with cancer will be sad about it, but severe depres-sion is often treatable in people with cancer (Holland, 1993). In earlier years, a person who survived cancer who complained that his treatment left him unable to function sexually might be told that he was lucky to be alive by his physician (Holland, 1993). Today people are more likely to be treated with sensitivity.

Many people with cancer are more concerned about their pain, or the pain they fear they will experience in the late stages of the illness, than they are about death. People may refuse narcotics like morphine for fear that they will no longer be effective later on, when they "really need it." Or they may fear that they will become addicted. Accurate information is often helpful because specialists today say that addiction is not a problem for people with cancer (Brody, 1994). Psychological methods such as relaxation, meditation, biofeedback training, and exercise can also be of help (Lang & Patt, 1994).

There are also psychological interventions for the nausea that often accompanies chemotherapy. People in chemotherapy who also obtain relaxation training and guided imagery techniques have significantly less nausea and vomiting than people in chemotherapy who do not use these methods. Moreover, their blood pressure and pulse rates are lower, and their moods are less negative than those of people in chemotherapy who do not obtain the psychological help (Burish and others, 1987). Studies with preteenagers and teenagers find that playing video games also lessens the discomfort of chemotherapy (Kolko & Rickard-Figueroa, 1985; Redd and others, 1987). The children focus on battling computer-generated monsters rather than the effects of the chemicals being injected.

Yes, cancer is a medical disorder. However, health psychologists have improved the treatment of people with cancer. For example, a crisis like cancer can induce perceptions that life has spun out of control and become unpredictable. Control and predictability are factors in psychological hardiness, so perceptions of lack of control and unpredictability can lead to psychological vulnerability and heighten stress. Health psychology therefore stresses the value of encouraging people with cancer to remain in charge of their lives (Jacox and others,

How Have Health Psychologists Helped This Youngster with Cancer?
Cancer is a medical disorder, but psychologists have contributed to the treatment of people with cancer. For example, psychologists help people with cancer remain in charge of their lives, combat feelings of hopelessness and helplessness, cope with stress, and manage the side effects of chemotherapy.

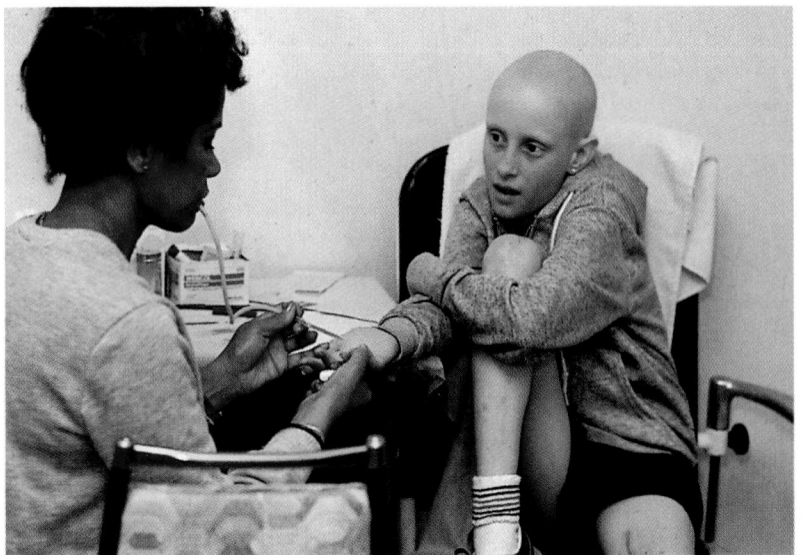

1994). Yes, cancer does require medical treatment and, in too many cases, there are few options. However, people with cancer can still choose their attitudes. A 10-year follow-up of women with breast cancer found a significantly higher survival rate for women who met their diagnosis with anger and a "fighting spirit" rather than stoic acceptance (Pettingale and others, 1985). Emotional states like hostility, anxiety, even horror are all associated with increased rates of survival in people with breast cancer. Desire to fight the illness is apparently a vital treatment component.

Health psychologists have also found that the feelings of hopelessness and helplessness that often accompany the diagnosis of cancer may hinder recovery (Levy and others, 1985). Such feelings can depress the responsiveness of the person's immune system (Brody, 1994). Hospitalization itself is stressful because it removes people from their normal sources of social support and reduces their sense of control. If handled insensitively, hospitalization may further depress people's own ability to fight illness.

Psychologists are teaching coping skills to people with cancer to relieve psychological as well as physical distress. In one study, cognitive-behavioral coping methods were found superior to supportive group therapy and a no-treatment control condition in reducing emotional distress and helping people with cancer meet the demands of daily life (Telch & Telch, 1986). Treatment included relaxation training, stress management techniques, assertive communication training, cognitive restructuring, problem-solving techniques, management of emotions, and pleasant activities. Coping skills are beneficial in themselves and help people with cancer regain a sense of control and mastery.

Yet another psychological application is helping people in chemotherapy keep up their strength by eating. The problem is that chemotherapy often causes nausea. Nausea then becomes associated with foods eaten earlier in the day, causing enduring taste aversions in about 45% of people in chemotherapy (Carey & Burish, 1988). So people with cancer, who are often already losing weight because of their illness, may find that taste aversions exacerbate the problems caused by lack of appetite. To combat such taste aversions, Bernstein (1985) recommends eating atypical foods prior to chemotherapy. If taste aversions develop, they are associated with the unusual food, and people's appetites for dietary staples may remain unaffected. Relaxation training also appears to increase food intake in people with cancer in chemotherapy (Carey & Burish, 1987).

In sum, cancer is frightening and, in many cases, there may be little that we can do about its eventual outcome. However, we are not helpless in the face of cancer. We can take measures like the following:

1. We can limit our exposure to the behavioral risk factors for cancer.

2. We can modify our diets by reducing intake of fats and increasing our intake of fruits and vegetables (Mevkens, 1990; Willett and others, 1990). Crucifers such as broccoli, cauliflower, and cabbage appear to be of particular value (Angier, 1994a). (Yes, Grandma was right.)

3. We can have regular medical checkups to detect cancer early. Unfortunately, people may not go for regular checkups or diagnostic procedures, such as mammograms to detect breast cancer, unless they believe that they are susceptible to the disease, believe in the benefits of mammography, and are not put off by barriers such as inconvenience or cost (Aiken and others, 1994).

4. We can regulate the amount of stress that affects us.

5. If we are struck by cancer, we can battle it energetically rather than assume the roles of passive victims.

Health psychologists are also investigating the role of chronic stress in inflammatory diseases such as arthritis, premenstrual distress, digestive diseases such as colitis, and metabolic diseases such as diabetes and hypoglycemia. The relationships among behavior patterns, attitudes, and illness are complex and under intense study. With some stress-related illnesses, it may be that stress determines whether the person will contract the disease at all. In others, it may be that an optimal environment merely delays the inevitable or that a stressful environment merely hastens the onset of the inevitable. Then, too, in different illnesses stress may have different effects on the person's ability to recover. In the "Psychology and Modern Life" section, we focus on a number of behavior patterns that help provide relief from stress and have other important health benefits as well.

Reflections

Now that you have read the section on a multifactorial approach to physical illness, reflect on the following questions:

* Agree or disagree with the following statement and support your answer: "Good

PSYCHOLOGY IN THE NEW MILLENNIUM

Health Psychology in the 21st Century: The Shape of Things to Come

The title of this feature is adapted from the title of an address by Margaret A. Chesney (1993), who served as president of the APA Division of Health Psychology. In her address, Chesney discusses several implications she finds in the current AIDS epidemic for health psychology in the 21st century.

During the 1980s, she notes, coronary-prone behavior received the lion's share of attention from researchers in health psychology. Although some observers wondered whether this focus was the most desirable for the advancement of health psychology, it now seems that it was valuable indeed. For example, the focus on coronary-prone behavior led to vastly increased understanding of the roles of stressors, cognitive appraisal, and personality factors (especially hostility) in CHD.

AIDS has clearly become the focus of research in health psychology in the 1990s, and some researchers are again wondering whether excessive attention is being paid to the topic. Chesney argues that the focus is well deserved because AIDS is having such a devastating effect on the lives of so many people. Moreover, the experience of the AIDS epidemic is pointing health psychology toward five trends that are likely to achieve yet greater prominence in the 21st century (Chesney, 1993):

* *Early identification of people at risk for disease.* The experience of the AIDS epidemic is showing that health psychology needs to foster the early identification of people who are at risk for health problems. Risk for many disorders, such as cancer, is defined largely in terms of family history (Arbeit, 1990) and patterns of consumption such as eating, smoking, and drinking alcohol. In the case of AIDS, however, risk is defined more in terms of people's behavior and mental processes—factors that place people at risk of being infected with the AIDS virus (HIV). Sociocultural considerations are also connected with risk. In the United States, for example, non-Hispanic White men are most likely to be infected with HIV through male–male sexual practices. African American men are equally likely to be infected through male–male sexual practices and injecting ("shooting up") drugs (CDC, 1993). Globally speaking, however, male–female sexual behavior is the most common method of transmitting HIV.

* *Rising expectation for programs that are successful at encouraging people to change high-risk behavior.* Health psychology needs to learn more about the planning and execution of programs that foster healthful behavioral changes. For example, most people in the United States have become generally aware of the threat and modes of transmission of HIV. Yet knowledge of danger alone apparently does not produce sufficient behavioral changes concerning sexual practices and injecting drugs (Chesney & Coates, 1990; Rotheram-Borus and others, 1991). (Nor does knowledge of danger alone stop people from smoking or drinking to excess.)

health is basically a matter of heredity or good luck. People cannot really do much to enhance their health or stave off illness."
• Consider your sociocultural background: What health problems are more common, or less common, among people of your

background than among the U.S. population at large? Why do you think these problems are more common or less common among people of your background?
• Agree or disagree with the following statement and support your answer: "Some people can 'refuse' to become ill."

• *Growing numbers of people who are coping with chronic diseases.* Health psychologists are developing more effective methods of helping people cope with chronic diseases. Today more than 31 million Americans are 65 or older. That number will increase to about 60 million by the year 2020. Almost 4 out of 5 people aged 65 or above have at least one chronic condition such as heart disease, hypertension, arthritis, and declining cognitive functioning (Chesney, 1993). In addition to younger people who are at risk for serious illnesses, such as AIDS, the increasing numbers of older people will profit from enhanced coping strategies being devised and tested today (e.g., Antoni, 1992; Ironson and others, 1992).

• *A shift toward inclusion of community and public health perspectives.* Psychology advances the dignity of the individual, and health psychology has traditionally focused on the health of the individual. However, the advent of the AIDS epidemic has spurred health psychologists to also consider community and public health perspectives. Health psychologists, for example, are now working with community psychologists to explore more effective ways of changing norms and values in the community at large. Health psychologists are studying barriers to behavioral change among community groups that are likely to engage in high-risk behavior.

• *The need to address health problems on a global scale.* There is increasing awareness that health psychology must address health problems on a global scale. AIDS is the first deadly epidemic that has had a truly global impact (Mann, 1992). Efforts at prevention and treatment have therefore spilled across national borders. Since chronic illnesses such as cancer and heart disease also know no boundaries, it would appear that the international perspective is here to stay.

Fostering Healthful Behavioral Changes. Health psychology needs to learn more about the planning and execution of programs that foster healthful behavioral changes. In this photo, a teacher begins to make children aware of the dangers of AIDS in a primary school.

Despite healthful behavior patterns, all of us become sick from time to time. In the following section, we explore what psychologists have learned about why people comply—or do not comply—with medical advice.

Compliance with Medical Advice

Individual differences truly hit home when it comes to our behavior concerning the prevention or treatment of illness. Some of us refuse to go to the doctor unless we are completely incapable of functioning. Others rush off to the doctor at the drop of a hat. Some of us deny symptoms such as pain. Others exaggerate pain. Some of us make good use of visits to the doctor. Others do not. Some of us comply with medical advice. Others ignore it.

Once we have seen the doctor, how many of us comply with her or his advice? According to the National Council on Patient Information and Education, one person in five does not fill prescriptions. One in seven discontinues medication too soon. One in three fails to get refills as prescribed. All in all, 30% to 50% of prescriptions are taken erroneously (Brody, 1992c). Only a minority of people follow advice that involves lifestyle changes, such as changing eating, drinking, smoking, or exercise habits (Brody, 1992c; Dunbar-Jacob, 1993).

Why don't people take medical advice? Consider some of the reasons:

The health problem may cause fewer symptoms or difficulties in lifestyle than the recommended diagnosis or treatment, at least in the short run (Brody, 1992c). Magnetic resonance imaging (MRI) is a valuable diagnostic tool for many neurological (brain) conditions. Although it is painless, MRI can require that people lie motionless for 2 hours or more in a tube, whose wall is only inches from their faces (Shuchman, 1993). Being closed in this way causes some people to panic. People often discontinue medications when they encounter side effects, especially unexpected side effects. Accurate information about potential emotional responses or side effects appears

to encourage compliance (Keown and others, 1984; McCrank, 1993).

The symptoms of the disease may disappear before the treatment has run its course, leading people to stop treatment. Other people may try to take charge of their treatment by increasing the dosage of drugs or other treatments when symptoms are more severe. It helps if physicians carefully explain the courses of the illnesses and how the prescribed treatments do their work.

People tend to deny health problems unless they are forced to face them. For example, as compared with college students who obtain normal serum cholesterol test results, students who obtain borderline-high test results rate cholesterol as a less serious health threat. They also rate the test as less accurate and see high cholesterol levels as more common (Croyle and others, 1993).

Many people resist being dependent on drugs (Conrad, 1992). In some cases, they discontinue treatment as a way of denying their health problem.

The costs of the treatment or the prescribed changes in lifestyle are impossible or impractical from the person's point of view. The effective health-care professional is aware of and deals with the realities of individuals' lives as well as textbook information (Moyers, 1993).

People may resist instructions from physicians whom they perceive as being authoritarian and condescending (Brody, 1992c; Gastorf & Galanos, 1983). People are more likely to adhere to advice from physicians who are perceived as being competent, friendly, warm, and concerned (Brody, 1992c; DiNicola & DiMatteo, 1984).

Truth or Fiction Revisited. *It is not true that people are more likely to comply with doctor's orders when they are issued by an authoritarian physician.* People are more likely to comply when physicians are competent, friendly, warm, and concerned—not authoritarian.

People are more likely to comply with medical advice when they believe that it will work (Bandura, 1990). Women, for example, are more likely to engage in breast self-examination when they believe that they will really be able to detect abnormal growths (Alagna & Reddy, 1984). People with diabetes are more likely to use insulin when they believe that their regimens will help control their blood-sugar levels (Brownlee-Duffeck and others, 1987).

People are less likely to comply when they fear the outcome of compliance. For example, Kathryn Kash (1993) of the Sloan-Kettering Cancer Center surveyed 217 women at high risk for breast cancer because close relatives (mothers, sisters) had been stricken with the illness. Only 40% of the women performed breast self-examinations for cancer on a monthly basis. The tendency to seek early detection through self-examination and medical examination, including mammography, was connected with the women's levels of fear. Women with greater fear of learning they had breast cancer were less likely to seek early detection.

People are more likely to adhere to treatment when their physicians make specific follow-up appointments rather than say something like "Come back to see me in a couple of months" (DiMatteo and others, 1993).

Some people do not comply with medical instructions and procedures because of lack of social support. One study found that men with supportive spouses are more likely to change their nutritional and activity patterns to avert heart disease (Doherty and others, 1983). People can increase the likelihood of their own compliance by asking clinicians for a referral to a support group that deals with their problem (Brody, 1992c).

Sociocultural factors are also involved in compliance. It has been shown, for example, that Hispanic Americans are more likely to comply with medical instructions when they are issued by personnel who have an understanding of Hispanic-American culture. A study in Zimbabwe, Africa, points out that some people do not comply with medical regimens because of belief in traditional rather than scientific methods of healing (Zyazema, 1984).

There was a time when medical training was almost completely technical, but research findings like these have prompted medical schools to train students how to relate to patients as people (Moyers, 1993).

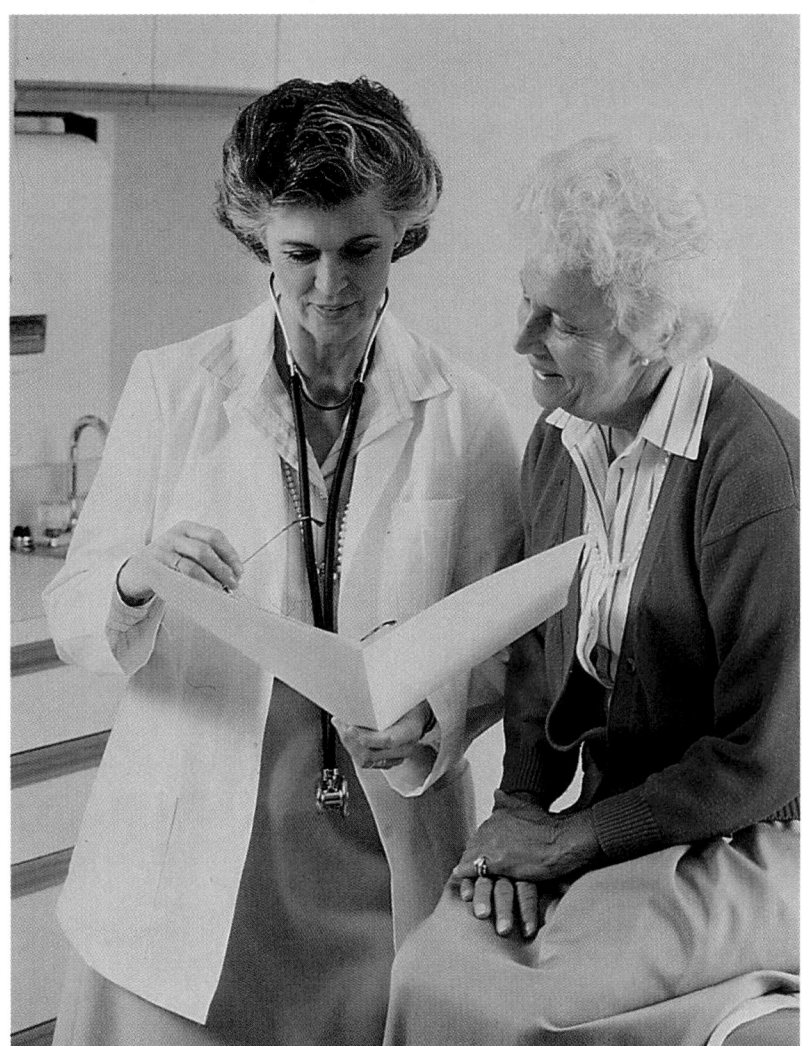

A Physician-Patient Interaction. People are more satisfied with medical visits, and more likely to comply with medical advice, when the doctor is caring and friendly. People also need to understand why treatments have been prescribed. People are more likely to follow regimens when they believe that they will be effective.

ENCOURAGING COMPLIANCE BY ENHANCING PHYSICIAN–PATIENT INTERACTIONS

Because of the anxiety the symptoms of illnesses provoke, most people try not to think about the symptoms when they first appear (Moyers, 1993). By the time people visit the physician, they may be quite anxious about them. Anxiety during the physician–patient interview sometimes causes people to forget to mention some symptoms and to forget to ask questions that had been on their minds. Health psychologists have found that giving people a few minutes before their visits to mull over their questions leads them to ask more and heightens their satisfaction with the interview (DiMatteo and others, 1993). Nurses and physicians can ask people to jot down their questions in the waiting room and offer them pads of paper to do so.

Another issue is the physician's so-called bedside manner. For example, in an experiment to determine which aspects of a physician's nonverbal behavior contributed to visitors' satisfaction, Harrigan and Rosenthal (1983) manipulated behaviors such as leaning forward versus sitting back. It was found that people evaluated physicians most positively when they leaned forward rather than sat back, nodded their heads in response to verbalizations, and kept their arms open rather than folded. People are also more satisfied when their doctors encourage them to ask questions. Such satisfaction is not a frivolous goal. It has a direct bearing on wellness (Dunbar-Jacob,

1993). People who find their doctors to be warm and interested, and who gather the information they need to know about their illnesses and treatments, are more likely to comply with medical advice.

It thus seems that there are a number of things that the medical profession (and we!) can do to enhance the physician–patient relationship and improve the prospects of profiting from medical advice.

Reflections

Now that you have read the section on compliance with medical advice, reflect on the following questions:

- Consider your sociocultural background: Do people of your background tend to be overutilizers or underutilizers of health care? Why?
- When you are ill, do you take medicine or follow other health regimens as prescribed? Why or why not? If you are dissatisfied with your health-related behavior, what can you do about it?

Summary

1. **What is health psychology?** Health psychology studies the relationships between psychological factors and the prevention and treatment of physical illness.

2. **What is stress?** Stress is the demand made on an organism to adjust. Whereas some stress is desirable to keep us alert and occupied, too much stress can tax our adjustive capacities and contribute to physical illness.

3. **What are some sources of stress?** Sources of stress include daily hassles, life changes, conflict, irrational beliefs, and Type A behavior. Type A behavior is characterized by aggressiveness, time urgency, and competitiveness.

4. **What psychological factors moderate the impact of stress?** These include positive self-efficacy expectations, psychological hardiness, a sense of humor, predictability of stressors, and social support. Self-efficacy expectations encourage us to persist in difficult tasks and to endure discomfort.

Psychological hardiness is characterized by commitment, challenge, and control.

5. **What is the general adaptation syndrome (GAS)?** The GAS is a body response triggered by perception of a stressor and consists of three stages: the alarm, resistance, and exhaustion stages.

6. **What is the role of the endocrine system in the body's response to stress?** The hypothalamus and pituitary glands secrete hormones that stimulate the adrenal cortex to release corticosteroids. Corticosteroids help resist stress by fighting inflammation and allergic reactions. Adrenaline and noradrenaline are secreted by the adrenal medulla, and adrenaline arouses the body by activating the sympathetic nervous system.

7. **What is the role of the autonomic nervous system (ANS) in the body's response to stress?** The sympathetic division of the ANS is highly

active during the alarm and resistance stages of the GAS. This activity is characterized by rapid heartbeat and respiration rate, release of stores of sugar, muscle tension, and other responses that spend the body's stores of energy. The parasympathetic division of the ANS predominates during the exhaustion stage of the GAS. Its activity is characterized by responses such as digestive processes that help restore the body's reserves of energy.

8. **What are the functions of the immune system?** One function of the immune system is to engulf and kill pathogens, worn-out body cells, and cancerous cells. Another is to "remember" pathogens to facilitate future combat against them. A third function is to facilitate inflammation, which increases the numbers of white blood cells brought to a damaged area.

9. **What are the effects of stress on the immune system?** By stimulating the release of corticosteroids, stress depresses the functioning of the immune system. (For example, steroids counter inflammation.)

10. **What kinds of headaches are there, and how are they related to stress?** The most common kinds are muscle-tension headaches and migraine headaches. Stress causes and compounds headache pain by stimulating muscle tension.

11. **What are the risk factors for coronary heart disease?** They include family history; physiological conditions such as hypertension and high levels of serum cholesterol; behavior patterns such as heavy drinking, smoking, eating fatty foods, and Type A behavior; work overload; chronic tension and fatigue; and physical inactivity.

12. **What are the risk factors for cancer?** Risk factors for cancer include family history, smoking, drinking alcohol, eating animal fats, sunbathing, and stress.

13. **What behavioral measures contribute to the prevention and treatment of cancer?** The following measures do: controlling our exposure to behavioral risk factors for cancer, going for regular medical checkups, regulating the amount of stress impacting upon us, and vigorously fighting cancer if we have it.

14. **What factors influence compliance with medical instructions and procedures?** Factors that influence compliance include the physician's bedside manner (we are more likely to comply with advice from competent, friendly, concerned physicians), belief that the advice will be effective, ability to cope with side effects, sociocultural factors, and social support.

Psychology and Modern Life

What do these things have in common: (1) telling yourself that you can live with another person's disappointment, (2) taking a deep breath and telling yourself to relax, (3) taking the scenic route to work, and (4) jogging for half an hour? These are all methods psychologists suggest for helping us cope with the stresses of modern life.

Ways of Coping with Stress

Stress takes many forms and can harm our psychological well-being and physical health. Let us highlight a number of ways of coping with stress: controlling irrational thoughts, lowering arousal, modifying the Type A behavior pattern, and—a method you might find somewhat surprising—exercising.

CONTROLLING IRRATIONAL THOUGHTS

Consider the following experiences to see whether you encounter pressures from your own thoughts:

1. You have difficulty with the first item on a test and become absolutely convinced that you will flunk.

2. You want to express your genuine feelings but think that you might make another person angry or upset.

3. You haven't been able to get to sleep for 15 minutes and assume that you will lie awake the whole night and feel "wrecked" in the morning.

4. You're not sure what decision to make, so you try to put your conflicts out of your mind by going out, playing cards, or watching TV.

5. You decide not to play tennis or go jogging because your form isn't perfect and you're in less than perfect condition.

If you have had these or similar experiences, it may be because you harbor a number of the irrational beliefs identified by Albert Ellis (see page 572). These beliefs may make you overly concerned about the approval of others (experience 2 in the preceding list) or perfectionistic (experience 5). They may lead you to think that you can solve problems by pretending that they do not exist (experience 4) or that a minor setback will invariably lead to greater problems (experiences 1 and 3).

How, then, do we change irrational or catastrophizing thoughts? The answer is deceivingly simple: We change these thoughts by changing them. However, change may require work. Moreover, before we can change our thoughts, we must become aware of them.

Three Steps for Controlling Catastrophizing Thoughts. Meichenbaum and Jaremko (1983) suggest a three-step procedure for controlling the irrational and catastrophizing thoughts that often accompany feelings of anxiety, conflict, or tension:

1. Develop awareness of these thoughts through careful self-examination. Study the examples at the beginning of this section or in Table 15.3 to see if they apply to you. (Also carefully read Ellis's irrational beliefs on page 572, and ask yourself whether any of them govern your behavior.) When you encounter anxiety or frustration, pay careful attention to your thoughts. Are they helping to point toward a solution, or are they compounding your problems?

2. Prepare thoughts that are incompatible with the irrational and catastrophizing thoughts and practice saying them firmly to yourself. (If nobody is nearby, why not say them firmly aloud?)

3. Reward yourself with a mental pat on the back for effective changes in beliefs and thought patterns.

LOWERING AROUSAL

Stress tends to trigger intense activity of the sympathetic branch of the autonomic nervous system—or, briefly, arousal. Arousal is a sign that something may be wrong, a message to survey the situation and take appropriate action. But once you are aware that a stressor is acting upon you and have developed a plan to cope with it, it is no longer helpful to have blood pounding so fiercely through your arteries. Psychologists and other scientists have developed many methods for teaching people to lower excessive arousal. They include meditation, biofeedback (both discussed in Chapter 5), and progressive relaxation.

Meditation seems to focus on the cognitive components of a stress reaction. Biofeedback can be directed at various physiological functions such as heart rate

TABLE 15.3
Controlling Irrational Beliefs and Thoughts

IRRATIONAL THOUGHTS	INCOMPATIBLE (COPING) THOUGHTS
"Oh my God, I'm going to lose all control!"	"This is painful and upsetting, but I don't have to go to pieces."
"This will never end."	"This will come to an end even if it's hard to see right now."
"It'll be awful if Mom gives me that look."	"It's more pleasant when Mom's happy with me, but I can live with it if she isn't."
"How can I go out there? I'll look like a fool."	"So you're not perfect; that doesn't mean that you're going to look stupid. And so what if someone thinks you look stupid? You can live with that, too. Just stop worrying and have some fun."
"My heart's going to leap out of my chest! How much can I stand?"	"Easy—hearts don't leap out of chests. Stop and think! Distract yourself. Breathe slowly, in and out."
"What can I do? There's nothing I can do!"	"Easy—stop and think. Just because you can't think of a solution right now doesn't mean there's nothing you can do. Take it a minute at a time. Breathe easy."

Do irrational beliefs and catastrophizing thoughts compound the stress you experience? Cognitive psychologists suggest that you can cope with stress by becoming aware of self-defeating beliefs and thoughts and replacing them with rational, calming beliefs and thoughts.

and muscle tension. Progressive relaxation focuses on reducing muscle tension. All three methods lower arousal, enhance self-efficacy expectations, and promote an internal locus of control.

Progressive Relaxation.

In the 1930s, Edmund Jacobson, the originator of progressive relaxation, noted that people tense their muscles when they are under stress. They thus compound their discomfort. Jacobson developed the method of progressive relaxation to teach people how to relax these tensions. In this method, people purposefully tense a muscle group before relaxing it. This sequence allows them to (1) develop awareness of their muscle tensions and (2) differentiate between feelings of tension and relaxation. The method is "progressive" because people move on, or progress, from one muscle group to another.

Progressive relaxation lowers the arousal of the alarm reaction. It has been found to be useful for stress-related illnesses ranging from headaches (Blanchard and others, 1990a) to hypertension (Agras and others, 1983). You can experience muscle relaxation in the arms by doing the following:

Settle down in a reclining chair, dim the lights, and loosen tight clothing. Use the instructions that follow. They can be memo-rized (slight variations from the text will do no harm), recorded and played back, or read aloud by a friend. For instructions concerning relaxation of the entire body, consult a behavior therapist or other helping professional familiar with the technique.

Settle back as comfortably as you can. Let yourself relax to the best of your ability. . . . Now, as you relax like that, clench your right fist, just clench your fist tighter and tighter, and study the tension as you do so. Keep it clenched and feel the tension in your right fist, hand, forearm . . . and now relax. Let the fingers of your right hand become loose, and observe the contrast in your feelings. . . . Now, let yourself go and try to become more relaxed all over. . . . Once more, clench your right fist really tight . . . hold it, and notice the tension again. . . . Now let go, relax; your fingers straighten out, and you notice the difference once more. . . . Now repeat that with your left fist. Clench your left fist while the rest of your body relaxes; clench that fist tighter and feel the tension . . . and now relax. Again enjoy the contrast. . . . Repeat that once more, clench the left fist, tight

Coping with the Type A Sense of Time Urgency. The San Francisco Recurrent Coronary Prevention Project has helped many Type A heart-attack victims modify their behavior in an effort to avert future attacks. Type A individuals modify their behavior to alleviate their sense of time urgency, their hostility, and "self-destructive tendencies" such as smoking, gorging on high-fat foods, and drinking heavily.

and tense. . . . Now do the opposite of tension—relax and feel the difference. Continue relaxing like that for a while. . . . Clench both fists tighter and together, both fists tense, forearms tense, study the sensations . . . and relax; straighten out your fingers and feel that relaxation. Continue relaxing your hands and forearms more and more. . . . Now bend your elbows and tense your biceps, tense them harder and study the tension feelings . . . all right, straighten out your arms, let them relax and feel that difference again. Let the relaxation develop. . . . Once more, tense your biceps; hold the tension and observe it carefully. . . . Straighten the arms and relax; relax to the best of your ability. . . . Each time, pay close attention to your feelings when you tense up and when you relax. Now straighten your arms, straighten them so that you feel most tension in the triceps muscles along the back of your arms; stretch your arms and feel that tension. . . . And now relax. Get your arms back into a comfortable position. Let the relaxation proceed on its own. The arms should feel comfortably heavy as you allow them to relax. . . . Straighten the arms once more so that you feel the tension in the triceps muscles;

straighten them. Feel that tension . . . and relax. Now let's concentrate on pure relaxation in the arms without any tension. Get your arms comfortable and let them relax further and further. Continue relaxing your arms even further. Even when your arms seem fully relaxed, try to go that extra bit further; try to achieve deeper and deeper levels of relaxation. (Wolpe & Lazarus, 1966, p. 177)

Controlling catastrophizing thoughts along with lowering the arousal of your alarm reaction reduces the effect of the stressor. These methods give you the chance to develop a plan for effective action. When effective action is not possible, controlling your thoughts and your level of arousal can enhance your capacity to tolerate discomfort.

MODIFYING THE TYPE A BEHAVIOR PATTERN

Type A behavior is identified by a sense of time urgency, hostility, and hard-driving, self-destructive behavior patterns. Meyer Friedman (one of the originators of the Type A concept) and Diane Ulmer reported in 1984 on some of the results of the San Francisco Recurrent Coronary Prevention Project (RCPP). The RCPP was designed to help Type A people who had had heart attacks modify their behavior to avert future attacks. After 3 years, participants placed in a treatment group in which they learned to reduce Type A behavior patterns had only one-third as many recurrent heart attacks as participants placed in a control group.

The three broad RCPP guidelines were alleviating participants' sense of time urgency, their hostility, and their self-destructive tendencies. They were also counseled to give up smoking, eat a low-fat diet, and establish a peaceful environment. The buffering effects of a sense of humor were noted, too.

Alleviating Your Sense of Time Urgency. Stop driving yourself—get out and walk. Too often, we jump out of bed to the sound of an abrasive alarm, hop into a shower, fight commuter crowds, and arrive at class or work with no time to spare. Then we become involved in our hectic day. For Type A people, the day begins urgently and never lets up.

The first step in coping with a sense of time urgency is confronting and replacing the beliefs that support it. Friedman and Ulmer (1984) note that Type A individuals tend to harbor the following beliefs:

1. "My sense of time urgency has helped me gain social and economic success" (p. 179). *The idea that impatience and irritation contribute to success, according to Friedman and Ulmer, is absurd.*

2. "I can't do anything about it" (p. 182). The belief that we cannot change ourselves is self-defeating and irrational, as noted by Albert Ellis. *Even in late adulthood, note Friedman and Ulmer, old habits can be discarded and new habits can be acquired.*

Friedman and Ulmer (1984) also use many exercises to help combat the sense of time urgency. Note this sampling:

1. Engage in more social activities with family and friends.

2. Spend a few minutes each day recalling events from the distant past. Check old photos of family and friends.

3. Read books—literature, drama, politics, biographies, science, nature, science fiction (not books on business or on climbing the corporate ladder!).

4. Visit museums and art galleries for their aesthetic value—not for speculation on the price of paintings.

5. Go to the movies, ballet, and theater.

6. Write letters to family and friends.

7. Take a course in art or begin violin or piano lessons.

8. Remind yourself daily that life is by nature unfinished, and you do not need (and should not want) to have all your projects finished on a given date.

9. Ask a family member what he or she did that day and actually *listen* to the answer.

Psychologist Richard Suinn (1982) adds the following suggestions for alleviating the sense of time urgency:

10. Get a nice-sounding alarm clock!

11. Move about slowly when you awake. Stretch.

12. Drive more slowly. This saves energy, lives, and traffic citations. It's also less stressful than racing the clock.

13. Don't wolf lunch. Get out; make it an occasion.

14. Don't tumble words out. Speak more slowly. Interrupt less frequently.

15. Get up earlier to sit and relax, watch the morning news with a cup of tea, or meditate. This may mean going to bed earlier.

16. Leave home earlier and take a more scenic route to work or school. Avoid rush-hour jams.

17. Don't carpool with last-minute rushers. Drive with a group that leaves earlier or use public transportation.

18. Have a snack or relax at school or work before the "day" begins.

19. Don't do two things at once. Avoid scheduling too many classes or appointments back to back.

20. Use breaks to read, exercise, or meditate. Limit intake of stimulants like caffeine. Try decaffeinated coffee.

21. Space chores. Why have the car and typewriter repaired, work, shop, and drive a friend to the airport all in one day?

22. If rushed, allow unessential work to go until the next day.

23. Set aside some time for yourself: for music, a hot bath, exercise, relaxation. (If your life will not permit this, get a new life.)

Alleviating Your Hostility. Friedman and Ulmer (1984) note that hostility, like time urgency, is supported by a number of irrational beliefs. It is up to us to begin again by recognizing our irrational beliefs and replacing them with new beliefs. Irrational beliefs that support hostility include the following:

1. "I need a certain amount of hostility to get ahead in the world" (p. 222). *Becoming readily irritated, aggravated, and angered does not contribute to getting ahead.*

2. "I can't do anything about my hostility" (p. 222). Is any comment necessary?

3. "Other people tend to be ignorant and inept" (p. 223). Surely some of them are, but the world is what it is. Albert Ellis

points out that we just expose ourselves to aggravation by demanding that other people be what they are not.

4. "I don't believe I can ever feel at ease with doubt and uncertainty" (p. 225). There are ambiguities in life; certain things remain unpredictable. Becoming irritated and aggravated doesn't make things less uncertain.

5. "Giving and receiving love is a sign of weakness" (p. 228). This belief is rugged individualism carried to the extreme. It can isolate us from social support.

Friedman and Ulmer (1984) also offer a number of suggestions in addition to replacing irrational beliefs:

1. Tell your spouse and children that you love them.

2. Make some new friends.

3. Let friends know that you stand ready to help them.

4. Get a pet. (Take care of it!)

5. Don't talk to another person about subjects on which you know that the two of you hold divergent and set opinions.

6. When other people do things that fall short of your expectations, consider the situational factors such as level of education or cultural background that might govern their behavior. Don't assume that they intend to distress you.

7. Look for the beauty and joy in things.

8. Stop cursing so much.

9. Express appreciation for the help and encouragement of others.

10. Play to lose, at least some of the time. (Ouch?)

11. Say "Good morning" in a cheerful manner.

12. Look at your face in the mirror at various times during the day. Search for signs of aggravation and anger and ask yourself if you need to look like that.

Modifying Your Self-Destructive Behavior Patterns. Friedman and Ulmer (1984) assert that Type A individuals harbor (frequently unconscious) wishes to destroy themselves. We cannot accept this view without evidence. However, many of us do overeat, gorge on high-fat foods, drink heavily, fail to exercise, and work 16-hour workdays even though we know that such behavior can be harmful.

We can monitor our behavior throughout the day and determine whether it is health-enhancing or health-impairing. If we are doing things that are health-impairing, are we going to continue them or modify them? If we're not going to modify them, why not? Are we going to tell ourselves we cannot change? Do we think so little of ourselves that we do not think it is worth it to change our behavior?

Honest self-reflection is in order.

EXERCISING: RUN FOR YOUR LIFE?

I like long walks, especially when they are taken by people who annoy me.
FRED ALLEN

Exercise, particularly aerobic exercise, can enhance our psychological well-being and help us cope with stress as well as foster physical health. *Aerobic exercise* refers to exercise that requires a sustained increase in the consumption of oxygen. Aerobic exercise promotes cardiovascular fitness. Aerobic exercises include, but are not limited to, running and jogging, running in place, walking (at more than a leisurely pace), aerobic dancing, jumping rope, swimming, bicycle riding, basketball, racquetball, and cross-country skiing.

Anaerobic exercises, in contrast, involve short bursts of muscle activity. Examples of anaerobic exercises are weight training, calisthenics (which usually allow rest periods between exercises), and sports such as baseball, in which there are infrequent bursts of strenuous activity. Anaerobic exercises can strengthen muscles and improve flexibility.

Physiological Benefits of Exercise. The major physiological effect of exercise is the promotion of fitness. Fitness includes muscle strength; muscle endurance; suppleness or flexibility; cardiorespiratory, or aerobic, fitness; and changes in body composition so that the ratio of muscle to fat is increased, usually as a result of both building muscle and reducing fat (Curfman, 1993a). Cardiovascular fitness, or "condition," means that the body can use greater amounts of oxygen during vigorous activity and pump more blood with each heartbeat.

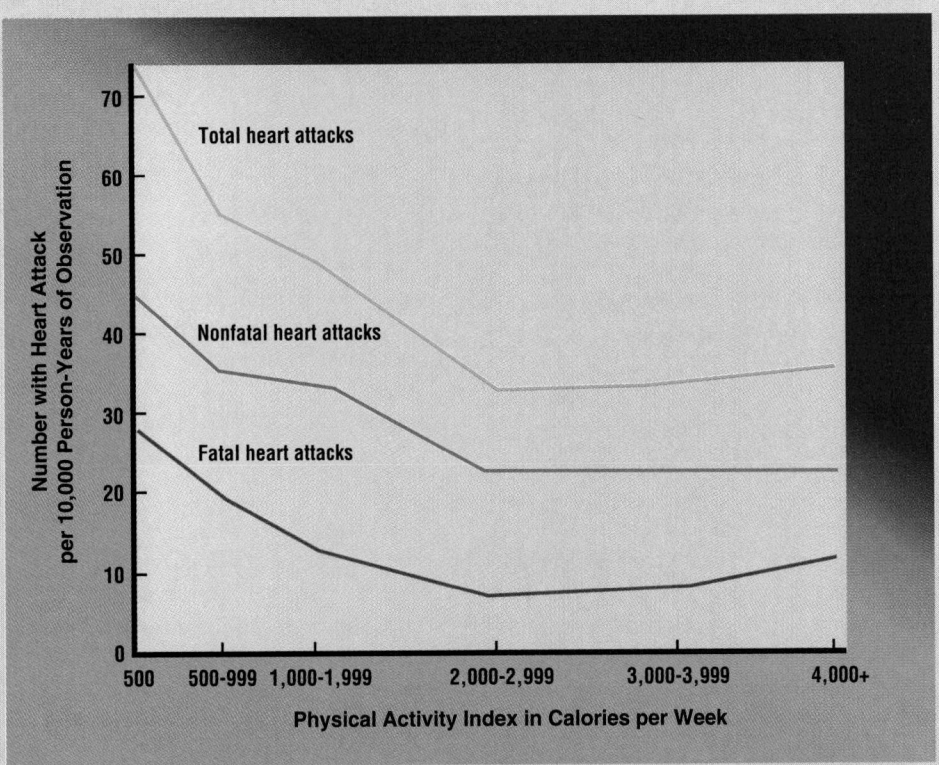

Total heart attacks

Nonfatal heart attacks

Fatal heart attacks

Number with Heart Attack per 10,000 Person-Years of Observation

Physical Activity Index in Calories per Week

FIGURE 15.9
Incidence of Heart Attacks and Level of Physical Activity Paffenbarger and his colleagues have correlated the incidence of heart attacks with level of physical activity among 17,000 Harvard alumni. The incidence of heart attacks declines as the activity level rises to burning about 2,000 calories a week by means of physical activity. Above 2,000 calories a week, however, the incidence of heart attacks begins to climb gradually again, although not steeply.

Because conditioned athletes' hearts pump more blood with each beat, they usually have a slower pulse rate—that is, fewer heartbeats per minute. However, during aerobic exercise, they may double or triple their resting heart rates for minutes at a time.

Research suggests that sustained physical activity not only fosters fitness but also reduces the incidence of heart attacks and the mortality rate (Castelli, 1994; Curfman, 1993a). In one research program, Paffenbarger and his colleagues (1986, 1993) have been tracking some 17,000 Harvard University alumni by means of university records and questionnaires. They have correlated the group's incidence of heart attacks with their levels of physical activity. As shown in Figure 15.9, the incidence of heart attacks among the alumni declines as the physical activity level rises to burning about 2,000 calories a week—the exercise equivalent of jogging about 20 miles a week. Above 2,000 calories, the incidence of heart attacks begins to climb again, but not steeply. Inactive alumni run the highest risks of heart attacks. Alumni who burn at least 2,000 calories a week through exercise live 2 years longer, on the average, than their less active counterparts.

Truth or Fiction Revisited. *It is true that Harvard University alumni who exercise regularly live 2 years longer, on the average, than their sedentary counterparts.*

Of course, there is an important limitation to Paffenbarger's research: It is correlational, not experimental. It is possible that persons in better health choose to engage in, and enjoy, higher levels of physical activity. If such is the case, then their lower incidence of heart attacks and their lower mortality rates would be attributable to their initial superior health, not to physical activity.

Aerobic exercise raises blood levels of high-density lipoproteins (HDL, or "good cholesterol") (Castelli, 1994; Curfman, 1993b; Wood and others, 1991). HDL lowers the amount of low-density lipoproteins (LDL, or "bad cholesterol") in the blood. This is another way in which exercise may lower the risk of heart attacks.

Aerobic exercise also appears to strengthen the functioning of the immune system (Antoni and others, 1990, 1991). Participants in one experiment rode exercise bicycles for three 45-minute sessions a week over a 10-week period. After 10 weeks of training, they significantly raised their volume of oxygen consumption (a measure of fitness) along with the functioning of their immune systems (Laperriere and others, 1990, 1991).

Psychological Benefits of Exercise. Psychologists have been keenly interested in the effects of exercise on psychological variables. Articles have appeared on exercise as "therapy"—for example, "running therapy" (Greist, 1984).

Consider the case of depression. Depression is characterized by inactivity and feelings of helplessness. Exercise is, in a sense, the opposite of inactivity. Success at exercise might also help alleviate feelings of helplessness. In a notable experiment, McCann and Holmes (1984) assigned mildly depressed college women at random to aerobic exercise, a progressive-relaxation placebo, and a no-treatment control group. The relaxation group showed some improvement, but aerobic exercise made dramatic inroads on students' depression. Other experiments also suggest that exercise—aerobic and nonaerobic—alleviates feelings of depression, at least among mildly and moderately depressed individuals (Buffone, 1984; Greist, 1984; Norvell & Belles, 1993).

Exercise has also been shown to decrease anxiety and hostility (Norvell & Belles, 1993) and to boost self-esteem (Sonstroem, 1984).

Getting Started. So, how about you? Are you considering climbing aboard the exercise bandwagon? If so, consider the following suggestions:

1. Unless you have engaged in sustained and vigorous exercise recently, seek the advice of a medical expert. If you smoke, have a family history of heart disease, are overweight, or are over 40, get a stress test.
2. Consider joining a beginner's aerobics class. Group leaders are not usually experts in physiology, but at least they "know the steps." You'll also be among other beginners and derive the benefits of social support.
3. Get the proper equipment to facilitate performance and help avert injury.
4. Read up on the activity you are considering. Books, magazines, and newspaper articles will give you ideas as to how to get started and how fast to progress.
5. Try to select activities that you can sustain for a lifetime. Don't worry about building yourself up rapidly. Enjoy yourself. Your strength and endurance will progress on their own. If you do not enjoy what you're doing, you're not likely to stick to it.
6. Keep a diary or log and note your progress. If running, note the paths or streets you follow, the distance you run, the weather conditions, and any remarkable details that come to mind. Check your notes now and then to remind yourself of enjoyable paths and experiences.
7. If you feel severe pain, don't try to exercise "through" it. Soreness is to be expected for beginners (and old-timers now and then). In that sense, soreness, at least when intermittent, is normal. But sharp pain is abnormal and a sign that something is wrong.
8. Have fun!

Reflections

Now that you have read the section on coping with stress, reflect on the following questions:

- How do you cope with life changes and daily hassles? Are you satisfied with your ways of coping? If not, can you apply some of the suggestions in this section to your own life? If not, why not?
- Do you have any methods of relaxing? What are they? How do they compare to the methods described in this chapter?
- Are you a Type A person? Why do you think that you are or are not? If you are, do you believe that you should do something about it? Do any of the suggestions in this section apply to you? If not, why not?
- Agree or disagree with the following statement and support your answer: "I am in charge of my own life. I can regulate the amount of stress I experience."

Modern life has its stresses, and none of us is completely immune to them. However, psychological knowledge can help us recognize the sources of stress in our life and cope with them.

NOTES

16

Social Psychology

Truth or Fiction?

_____ Airing a TV commercial repeatedly hurts sales.

_____ First impressions have powerful effects on our social relationships.

_____ We take others to task for their misdeeds but tend to see ourselves as victims of circumstances when our conduct falls short of our ideals.

_____ Beauty is in the eye of the beholder.

_____ People are perceived as being more attractive when they are smiling.

_____ Love makes the world go round—romantic love is found in every culture in the world, that is.

_____ Group decisions tend to represent conservative compromises of the opinions of the group members.

_____ Nearly 40 people stood by and did nothing while a woman was being stabbed to death.

Outline

Truth or Fiction?

Attitudes

The A–B Problem: Do We Do as We
Think?

Origins of Attitudes

Changing Attitudes through Persuasion

Prejudice

Social Perception

Primacy and Recency Effects: The
Importance of First Impressions

Attribution Theory: You're Free but I'm
Caught in the Middle?

Body Language

Psychology in the New Millennium:
Can Psychologists Usher in an Age
of Peace?

**Interpersonal Attraction: Liking and
Loving**

Physical Attractiveness: How Important Is
Looking Good?

Similarity: Do "Opposites Attract" or Do
"Birds of a Feather Flock Together"?

Reciprocity: If You Like Me, You Must
Have Excellent Judgment

Love: Doing What Comes . . .
Culturally?

Social Influence

Obedience to Authority: Does Might
Make Right?

Conformity: Do Many Make Right?

Psychology in a World of Diversity:
Muslim Women Face Pressure to
Conform in the United States

Group Behavior

Social Facilitation: Monkey See, Monkey
Do Faster?

Group Decision Making

Polarization and the Risky Shift

Groupthink

Mob Behavior and Deindividuation

Altruism and the Bystander Effect: Some
Watch While Others Die

Summary

Psychology and Modern Life

Gender Polarization: Gender Stereotypes
and Their Costs

Psychology in a World of Diversity:
Machismo/Marianismo
Stereotypes and Hispanic
Culture

Candy and Stretch. A new technique for controlling weight gains? No, these are the names of a couple who have just met at a camera club that doubles as a meeting place for singles.

Candy and Stretch stand above the crowd—literally. Candy, an attractive woman in her early 30s, is almost 6 feet tall. Stretch is more plain-looking, but wholesome, in his late 30s, and 6 feet 5 inches.

Stretch has been in the group for some time. Candy is a new member. Let's listen in on them as they make conversation during a coffee break.[1] As you will see, there are some differences between what they say and what they are thinking:

	THEY SAY	THEY THINK
STRETCH:	Well you're certainly a welcome addition to our group.	(Can't I ever say something clever?)
CANDY:	Thank you. It certainly is friendly and interesting.	(He's cute.)
STRETCH:	My friends call me Stretch. It's left over from my basketball days. Silly, but I'm used to it.	(It's safer than saying my name is David Stein.)
CANDY:	My name is Candy.	(At least my nickname is. He doesn't have to hear Hortense O'Brien.)
STRETCH:	What kind of camera is that?	(Why couldn't a girl named Candy be Jewish? It's only a nickname, isn't it?)
CANDY:	Just this old German one of my uncle's. I borrowed it from the office.	(He could be Irish. And that camera looks expensive.)
STRETCH:	May I? (He takes her camera, brushing her hand and then tingling with the touch.) Fine lens. You work for your uncle?	(Now I've done it. Brought up work.)
CANDY:	Ever since college. It's more than being just a secretary. I get into sales, too.	(So okay, what if I only went for a year. If he asks what I sell, I'll tell him anything except underwear.)
STRETCH:	Sales? That's funny. I'm in sales, too, but mainly as an executive. I run our department. I started using cameras on trips. Last time I was in the Bahamas. I took—	(Is there a nice way to say used cars? I'd better change the subject.) (Great legs! And the way her hips move—)

[1] Source of dialogue: *Pairing*, by G. R. Bach and R. M. Deutsch, 1970, New York: Peter H. Wyden.

	THEY SAY	**THEY THINK**
CANDY:	Oh! Do you go to the Bahamas, too? I love those islands.	(So I went just once, and it was for the brassiere manufacturers' convention. At least we're off the subject of jobs.)
STRETCH:		(She's probably been around. Well, at least we're off the subject of jobs.)
	I did a little underwater work there last summer. Fantastic colors. So rich in life.	(And lonelier than hell.)
CANDY:		(Look at that build. He must swim like a fish. I should learn.)
	I wish I'd had time when I was there. I love the water.	(Well, I do. At the beach, anyway, where I can wade in and not go too deep.)

So begins a relationship. Candy and Stretch have a drink and talk, sharing their likes and dislikes. Amazingly, they seem to agree on everything—from cars to clothing to politics. The attraction is very strong, and neither is willing to risk turning the other off by disagreeing.

Soon they feel that they have fallen in love. They still agree on everything they discuss, but they scrupulously avoid one topic: religion. Their religious differences became apparent when they exchanged last names. But that doesn't mean they have to talk about it.

They also put off introducing each other to their parents. The O'Briens and the Steins are narrow-minded about religion. If the truth be known, so are Candy and Stretch.

What happens in this tangled web of deception? After some deliberation, and not without misgivings, they decide to get married. Do they live happily ever after? We can't say. "Ever after" isn't here yet.

We do not have all the answers, but we have some questions. Candy and Stretch's relationship began with a powerful attraction. What is *attraction?* How do we determine who is attractive? Candy and Stretch fell in love. What is *love?* They pretended to share each other's *attitudes?* What are attitudes? Also, why were they so reluctant to disagree?

Candy and Stretch were both a bit prejudiced about religion. What is *prejudice?* Why didn't they introduce each other to their parents? Did they fear that their parents would want them to *conform* to their own standards? Would their parents try to *persuade* them to limit dating to people of their own religions? Would they *obey?*

Attraction, attitudes, prejudice, conformity, persuasion, obedience—these topics are the province of the branch of psychology called **social psychology.** Social psychologists study the nature and causes of our behavior and mental processes in social situations. The social psychological topics we discuss in this chapter include attitudes, social perception, attraction, social influence, and group behavior.

Social psychology • The field of psychology that studies the nature and causes of individual thoughts, feelings, and overt behavior in social situations.

Attitudes

How do you feel about abortion, Japanese cars, and the Republican party? The only connection I draw among these items is that people have *attitudes* toward them. They each tend to elicit cognitive evaluations (such as approval or disapproval), feelings (liking, disliking, or something stronger), and behavioral tendencies (as of approach or avoidance). Although I asked you how you "feel," attitudes are not just feelings or emotions (Pratkanis and others, 1989). Most psychologists agree that thinking—judgment—is primary. Feelings and behavior follow (Breckler & Wiggins, 1989; Eagly & Chaiken, 1993; Petty & Cacioppo, 1986).

Attitudes are behavioral and cognitive tendencies that are expressed by evaluating particular people, places, or things with some degree of favor or disfavor (Eagly & Chaiken, 1993). Attitudes are learned and affect behavior (Shavitt, 1990; Snyder & DeBono, 1989). Attitudes can foster love or hate. They can give rise to helping behavior or to mass destruction. They can lead to social conflict or to conflict resolution. Attitudes can change, but they tend to remain stable unless shoved. Most people do not change their religion or political affiliation without serious reflection or coercion.

THE A–B PROBLEM: DO WE DO AS WE THINK?

Our definition of attitude implies that our behavior is consistent with our cognitions—our beliefs and our feelings. When we are free to do as we wish, it often is. But, as indicated by the term **A–B problem,** the links between attitudes (A) and behaviors (B) tend to be weak to moderate (Eagly & Chaiken, 1993). For example, research reveals that attitudes toward health-related behaviors such as use of alcohol and cigarettes, and drunken driving, are not strong or consistent predictors of these behaviors (Stacy and others, 1994).

A number of factors influence the likelihood that we can predict behavior from attitudes:

1. *Specificity.* We can better predict specific behavior from specific attitudes than from global attitudes. We can better predict church attendance by knowing people's attitudes toward church attendance than by knowing whether they are Christian. A study of female juvenile delinquents found that prostitutes made weaker judgments against prostitution than other delinquents did (Bartek and others, 1993).

2. *Strength of attitudes.* Strong attitudes are more likely to determine behavior than weak attitudes (Fazio, 1990). A person who believes that the nation's destiny depends on Republicans taking control of Congress is more likely to vote than a person who leans toward Republicanism but does not believe that the outcome of elections makes much difference.

3. *Vested interest.* People are more likely to act on their attitudes when they have a vested interest in the outcome (Johnson & Eagly, 1989). People are more likely to vote for (or against) unionization of their workplace, for example, when they believe that their job security depends on the outcome.

4. *Accessibility.* People are more likely to express their attitudes when they are accessible—that is, when they are brought to mind (Fazio, 1990; Krosnick, 1989). This is why politicians attempt to "get out the vote" by means of media blitzes just prior to an election. It does politicians little good to have supporters who forget them on election day. Attitudes that have strong emotional impact are more accessible (Wu & Shaffer, 1987), which is one reason that politicians strive to get their supporters "worked up" over the issues.

Candy and Stretch avoided discussing matters on which they differed. One motive might have been to avoid heightening the *accessibility* of their clashing attitudes. By keeping them under the table, Candy and Stretch might be less likely to act on them and go their separate ways.

ORIGINS OF ATTITUDES

You were not born a Republican or a Democrat. You were not born a Catholic or a Jew—although your parents may have practiced one of these religions when you came along. Political, religious, and other attitudes are learned.

Conditioning. Conditioning may play a role in the acquisition of attitudes. Laboratory experiments have shown that attitudes toward national groups can be influenced by associating them with positive words (such as *gift* or *happy*) or negative words (such as *ugly* and *failure*) (Lohr & Staats, 1973). President George Bush's references to Iraq's Saddam Hussein as "another Hitler" prior to the Persian Gulf War encouraged people to associate their hatred for Hitler with Hussein. Parents often reward children for saying and doing things that are consistent with their own attitudes. Patriotism is encouraged by approving of

---

Attitude • An enduring mental representation of a person, place, or thing that evokes an emotional response and affected behavior.

A–B problem • The issue of how well we can predict behavior on the basis of attitudes.

Stereotype • A fixed, conventional idea about a group.

Elaboration likelihood model • The view that persuasive messages are evaluated (elaborated) on the basis of central and peripheral cues.

children when they sing the national anthem or wave the flag.

Observational Learning. Attitudes formed through direct experience may be stronger and easier to recall, but we also acquire attitudes by observing others. The approval or disapproval of peers molds adolescents to prefer short or long hair, blue jeans, or preppy sweaters. Television shows us that body odor, bad breath, and the frizzies are dreaded diseases—and, perhaps, that people who use harsh toilet paper are somehow un-American.

Cognitive Appraisal. Yet, all is not so mechanical. Now and then we also evaluate information and attitudes on the basis of evidence. We may revise **stereotypes** on the basis of new information (Weber & Crocker, 1983). We are especially likely to scrutinize our attitudes when we know that we shall have to justify them to people who may dissent (Tetlock, 1983).

Still, initial attitudes tend to serve as cognitive anchors. They help mold the ways in which we perceive the world and interpret events. Attitudes we encounter later are thus often judged in terms of how much they deviate from the initial set. Accepting larger deviations demands greater adjustments in information processing (Quattrone, 1982). For this reason, perhaps, great deviations are apt to be resisted. Yet once people begin to think deeply about issues, changes in attitudes are likely to persist (Verplanken, 1991).

CHANGING ATTITUDES THROUGH PERSUASION

Let advertisers spend the same amount of money improving their product that they do on advertising and they wouldn't have to advertise it.

WILL ROGERS

Rogers's social comment sounds on the mark, but he was probably wrong. It does little good to have a wonderful product if its existence remains a secret.

Petty and Cacioppo (1986) have devised the **elaboration likelihood model** for understanding the processes by which people examine the information in persuasive messages. According to this view, there are at least two routes to persuading others to change attitudes—that is, two ways of responding to, or elaborating, persuasive messages. The first, or central route, involves thoughtful consideration of arguments and evidence (Eagly & Chaiken, 1993). The second, or peripheral route, involves associating objects with positive or negative cues. When politicians avow that, "This bill is supported by Jesse Jackson (or Jesse Helms)," they are seeking predictable, knee-jerk reactions, not careful consideration of a bill's merits. Other cues are rewards (such as a smile or a hug), punishments (such as parental disapproval), and factors such as the trustworthiness and attractiveness of the communicator.

Advertisements, which are a form of persuasive communication, also rely on central and peripheral routes. Some ads focus on the quality of the product (central route). Others attempt to associate the product with appealing images (peripheral route). Ads for Total cereal, which highlight its nutritional benefits, provide information about the quality of the product. So, too, do the "Pepsi Challenge" taste-test ads, which claim that Pepsi tastes better than Coca-Cola. Marlboro cigarette ads that focus on the masculine, rugged image of the "Marlboro man"[2] offer no information about the product itself. Nor do Virginia Slims cigarette ads, which show attractive women smoking.

In this section, we shall examine one central factor in persuasion—the nature of the message itself—and three peripheral factors: (1) the messenger, (2) the context of the message, and (3) the audience. We shall also examine a method of persuasion used frequently by persons seeking charitable contributions: the foot-in-the-door technique.

The Persuasive Message: Say What? Say How? Say How Often? How do we respond when TV commercials are repeated until we have memorized

MINILECTURE: FACTORS IN PERSUASIVE COMMUNICATION

---

[2] The rugged actor in the original TV commercials died from lung cancer. Cigarettes were apparently more rugged than he.

Would You Buy These Products?
Advertisers use a combination of central and peripheral cues to hawk their wares. What factors contribute to the persuasiveness of messages? To the persuasiveness of communicators? Why is Michael Jordan considered an MVE ("Most Valuable Endorser")?

every dimple on the actors' faces? Research suggests that familiarity breeds content, not contempt.

You might not be crazy about *zebulons* and *afworbu's* at first, but Zajonc (1968) found that people began to react favorably toward these bogus Turkish words[3] on the basis of repeated exposure. Political candidates who become well known to the public through regular TV commercials attain more votes (Grush, 1980). People respond more favorably to abstract art (Heingartner & Hall, 1974), classical music (Smith & Dorfman, 1975), and photographs of African Americans (Hamm and others, 1975) and college students (Moreland & Zajonc, 1982) on the basis of repetition. Love for classical art and music may begin through exposure in the nursery, not the college appreciation course.

Truth or Fiction Revisited. *It is not true that airing a TV commercial repeatedly hurts sales.* Repeated exposure frequently leads to liking and acceptance.

The more complex the stimuli, the more likely it is that frequent exposure will have favorable effects (Saegert & Jellison, 1970; Smith & Dorfman, 1975). The 100th playing of a Bach fugue may be less tiresome than the 100th performance of a pop tune.

In two-sided arguments, the communicator recounts the arguments of the opposition in order to refute them. Such arguments can be especially effective when the audience is at first uncertain about its position (Sorrentino and others, 1988). Theologians and politicians sometimes expose their followers to the arguments of the opposition. By refuting them one by one, they impart to their followers a kind of psychological immunity to them. Two-sided product claims, in which advertisers admitted their product's weak points in addition to highlighting its strengths, are the most believable (Bridgwater, 1982).

It would be nice to think that people are too sophisticated to be persuaded by a **fear appeal.** However, grisly films of operations on cancerous lungs are more effective than matter-of-fact presentations for changing attitudes toward smoking (Leventhal and others, 1967). Films of bloodied gums and decayed teeth are also more effective than logical discussions for boosting toothbrushing (Dembroski and others, 1978). Sun tanning has been shown to increase the likelihood of skin cancer. Interestingly, however, warnings against sun tanning were shown to be more effective among a group of Wake Forest University students when they were based on risks to students' *appearance* (premature aging, wrinkling, and scarring of the skin) rather than on the risk to their health (Jones & Leary, 1994). That is, students who read essays about the sun's cosmetic effects were more likely to say they would protect themselves from the sun than were students who read essays about the sun and cancer. Generally speaking, fear appeals are most effective when they are strong, when the audience believes the dire outcomes, and when the audience believes that it can change (Eagly & Chaiken, 1993; Robberson & Rogers, 1988).

Audiences also tend to believe arguments that appear to run counter to the vested interests of the communicator (Eagly & Chaiken, 1993). People may pay more attention to a whaling-fleet owner's claim than to a conservationist's that whales are becoming extinct. If the president of Chrysler or General Motors said that Toyotas and Hondas were superior, you can bet that we would prick up our ears.

The Persuasive Communicator: Whom Do You Trust? Would you buy a used car from a person convicted of larceny? Would you attend weight-control classes run by a 350-pound leader? Would you leaf through fashion magazines featuring homely models? Probably not. Research shows that persuasive communicators show expertise (Hennigan and others, 1982), trustworthiness, attractiveness, or similarity to their audiences (Mackie and others, 1990; Wilder, 1990). Because of the adoration of their fans, sports superstars such as Michael Jordan have also solidified their places as endorsers of products (Goldman, 1993). Fans may consider Jordan to be an MVP, or Most Valuable Player. To Madison Avenue, however, Jordan is an MVE, or Most Valuable Endorser (Goldman, 1993).

Fear appeal • A type of persuasive communication that influences behavior on the basis of arousing fear instead of rational analysis of the issues.

---

[3] *Zebulun,* it happens, is the name of Jacob's 10th son, as reported in *Genesis.* Driving through the Carolinas one summer, your author noted a town named Zebulon. (I'm a repository of useless information.)

TV news anchors enjoy high prestige. One study (Mullen and others, 1987) found that before the 1984 presidential election, Peter Jennings of ABC News had shown significantly more favorable facial expressions when reporting on Ronald Reagan than on Walter Mondale. Tom Brokaw of NBC and Dan Rather of CBS had not shown favoritism. The researchers also found that viewers of ABC News voted for Reagan in greater proportions than viewers of NBC or CBS News. It is tempting to conclude that viewers were subtly persuaded by Jennings to vote for Reagan—and maybe this happened in a number of cases. But Sweeney and Gruber (1984) have shown that viewers do not simply absorb, spongelike, whatever the tube feeds them. Instead, they show **selective avoidance** and **selective exposure.** They tend to switch channels when they are faced with news coverage that counters their own attitudes. They also seek communicators whose outlooks coincide with their own. Thus, it may simply be that Reaganites favored Jennings over Brokaw and Rather.

The Context of the Message: "Get 'Em in a Good Mood."

You are too shrewd to let someone persuade you by buttering you up, but perhaps someone you know would be influenced by a sip of wine, a bite of cheese, and a sincere compliment. Atmospheric elements like good food and pleasant music boost acceptance of persuasive messages. When we are in a good mood, we are apparently less likely to carefully evaluate the situation (Mackie & Worth, 1989; Petty and others, 1991; Schwarz and others, 1991).

It is also counterproductive to call your dates fools when they differ with you—even though their ideas are bound to be foolish if they do not concur with yours. Agreement and praise are more effective at encouraging others to embrace your views. Appear sincere or else your compliments will look manipulative. (It seems unsporting to divulge this information.)

The Persuaded Audience: Are You a Person Who Can't Say No?

Why do some people have sales resistance? Why do others enrich the lives of every door-to-door salesperson? It may be that people with high self-esteem and low social anxiety are more likely to resist social pressure (Santee & Maslach, 1982). Baumeister and Covington (1985) challenge the view that persons with low self-esteem are more open to persuasion, however. Persons with high self-esteem may also be persuaded, but they may be less willing to confess that others have influenced them. Knowledge of the areas that a communicator is addressing also tends to lessen persuadability (Wood, 1982).

A classic study by Schwartz and Gottman (1976) reveals the cognitive nature of the social anxiety that can make it hard for some of us to refuse requests. Schwartz and Gottman found that people who comply with unreasonable requests are more apt to report thinking, "I was worried about what the other person would think of me if I refused," "It is better to help others than to be self-centered," or "The other person might be hurt or insulted if I refused." People who did not comply reported thoughts such as, "It doesn't matter what the other person thinks of me," "I am perfectly free to say no," or "This request is an unreasonable one" (p. 916).

The Foot-in-the-Door Technique.

You might suppose that contributing money to door-to-door solicitors for charity will get you off the hook. That is, they'll take the cash and leave you alone for a while. Actually, the opposite is true. The next time they mount a campaign, they may call on generous you to go door to door! Organizations compile lists of persons they can rely on. Giving an inch apparently encourages others to go for a yard. They have gotten their "foot in the door."

Consider a classic experiment on the **foot-in-the-door technique** by Freedman and Fraser (1966). Groups of women received phone calls from a consumer group requesting that they let a six-person crew drop by their homes to catalog their household products. The job could take hours. Only 22% of one group acceded to this irksome entreaty. But 53% of another group of women assented to a visit from this wrecking crew. Why was the second group more compliant? The pliant group had been phoned a few days earlier and had

Selective avoidance • Diverting one's attention from information that is inconsistent with one's attitudes.

Selective exposure • Deliberately seeking and attending to information that is consistent with one's attitudes.

Foot-in-the-door technique • A method for inducing compliance in which a small request is followed by a larger request.

Prejudice • The belief that a person or group, on the basis of assumed racial, ethnic, sexual, or other features, will possess negative characteristics or perform inadequately.

Discrimination • The denial of privileges to a person or group because of prejudice.

agreed to answer a few questions about the soap products they used. They had been primed for the second request. The caller had gotten a "foot in the door."

Research suggests that people who accede to small requests become more amenable to larger ones because they come to see themselves as the kind of people who help in this way (Eisenberg and others, 1987). Regardless of how the foot-in-the-door technique works, if you want to say no, it may be easier to do so (and stick to your guns) the first time a request is made. Later may be too late.

In the following section, we discuss a particularly troubling kind of attitude: prejudice.

PREJUDICE

I imagine one of the reasons people cling to their hates so stubbornly is because they sense, once hate is gone, they will be forced to deal with pain.

JAMES BALDWIN

Indifference, to me, is the epitome of evil.

ELIE WIESEL

I am free of all prejudices. I hate everyone equally.

W. C. FIELDS

People have condemned billions of other people. Without ever meeting them. Without ever learning their names.

Prejudice is an attitude toward a group that leads people to evaluate members of that group negatively. On a cognitive level, prejudice is linked to expectations that the target group will behave poorly, say, in the workplace or by engaging in criminal behavior. On an affective level, prejudice is associated with negative feelings such as dislike or hatred. Behaviorally, prejudice is connected with avoidance, aggression, and discrimination.

Discrimination. One form of negative behavior that results from prejudice is called **discrimination.** Many groups have suffered discrimination in the United States— women, gay males and lesbians, older people, and ethnic groups such as African Americans, Asian Americans, Hispanic Americans, Irish Americans, Jewish Americans, and Native Americans (Takaki, 1993). Discrimination takes many forms, including

Stereotyping. How well is this child performing on her test? An experiment by Darley and Gross showed that our expectations concerning a child's performance on a test are linked to our awareness of that child's socioeconomic background.

denial of access to jobs, housing, and the voting booth—even avoidance of eye contact (Neuberg, 1989). Many people have forgotten that African American men gained the right to vote decades before women did.

Stereotypes. Are Jewish Americans shrewd and ambitious? Are African Americans superstitious and musical? Are gay men and lesbians unfit for military service? Such ideas are stereotypes—prejudices about groups that lead people to interpret their observations in a biased fashion (Herek, 1993). Table 16.1 shows common stereotypes about various sociocultural groups.

Sources of Prejudice. The sources of prejudice are many and varied. Let us consider some contributors:

1. *Assumptions of dissimilarity.* We are apt to like people who share our attitudes. In forming impressions of others, we are influenced by attitudinal similarity and dissimilarity (Duckitt, 1992). People of different religions and races often have different backgrounds, however, giving rise to dissimilar attitudes. Even when people of different races share important values, they may assume they do not.

2. *Social conflict.* There is a lengthy history of social and economic conflict between

MINILECTURE:
STEREOTYPE
AND
PREJUDICE

people of different races and religions. For example, Southern White people and African Americans have competed for jobs, giving rise to negative attitudes, even lynchings (Hepworth & West, 1988).

3. *Social learning.* Children acquire some attitudes from others, especially parents. Children tend to imitate their parents, and parents reinforce their children for doing so (Duckitt, 1992). In this way, prejudices can be transmitted from generation to generation.

4. *Information processing.* One cognitive view is that prejudices act as cognitive filters through which we perceive the social world. Prejudice is a way of processing social information. It is easier to attend to, and remember, instances of behavior that are consistent with our prejudices than it is to reconstruct our mental categories (Bodenhausen, 1988; Devine, 1989; Dovidio and others, 1986; Fiske, 1993). If you believe that Jewish Americans are stingy, it is easier to recall a Jewish American's negotiation of a price than a Jewish American's charitable donation. If you believe that Californians are "airheads," it may be easier to recall TV images of surfing than of scientific conferences at Caltech and Berkeley.

5. *Social categorization.* A second cognitive perspective focuses on people's tendencies to divide the social world into "us" and "them." People usually view those who belong to their own groups—the "in-group"—more favorably than those who do not—the "out-group" (Duckitt, 1992; Linville and others, 1989; Schaller & Maas, 1989). Moreover, there is a tendency for us to assume that out-group members are more alike, or homogeneous, in their attitudes and behavior than members of our own groups (Judd & Park, 1988; Wilder, 1986). Our isolation from out-group members makes it easier to maintain our stereotypes.

6. *Victimization by prejudice.* Ironically, people who have been victims of prejudice sometimes attempt to gain a sense of pride by asserting their superiority over other socioeconomic or ethnic groups (Van Brunt, 1994).

Intergroup Contact. Intergroup contact can reduce feelings of prejudice when people work together toward common goals.

Reflections

Now that you have read the section on attitudes, reflect on the following questions:

- Agree or disagree with the following statement and support your answer: "People vote their consciences."

- What are your political attitudes? Liberal? Conservative? Middle of the road? (Something else?) How did you develop these attitudes? (Are you sure?) Do your political attitudes represent the attitudes of many people from your sociocultural background? Why or why not?

- Are you entertained by any radio or TV commercials? Which ones? Why? Did these commercials ever convince you to buy a product? Which product? Was the commercial accurate?

- Do you ever get involved in arguments in which you try to change other people's attitudes? Can you provide an example? Do you tend to win or lose such arguments? Why?

TABLE 16.1
Some Stereotypes of Sociocultural Groups within the United States

African Americans	**Irish Americans**	**Jewish Americans**
Physically powerful and well-coordinated	Sexually repressed	Cheap, shrewd in business
Unclean	Heavy drinkers	Clannish
Unintelligent and superstitious	Overly religious	Control banks, Wall Street, and the media
Musically talented	Political and nationalistic	Wealthy and showy
Excellent as lovers	Outgoing, witty, and literary	Big-nosed
Lazy	Hot-tempered ("fighting Irish")	Pushy
Emotional and aggressive	**Italian Americans**	Smothering mother
Flashy (gaudy clothes and big cars)	Overly interested in food	**Polish Americans**
Chinese Americans	Ignorant, suspicious of education	Unintelligent and uneducated
Deceitful	Clannish	Overly religious
Inscrutable	Great singers	Dirty
Wise	Great shoemakers and barbers	Racist, bigoted
Cruel	Hot-tempered and violent	Boorish, uncultured
Polite, quiet, and deferential	Connected to the Mafia	**White Anglo-Saxon Protestants ("WASPs")**
Possessing strong family ties	Talk with their hands	Hard-working, ambitious, thrifty
Law-abiding	Cowardly in battle	Honorable
Hispanic Americans	**Japanese Americans**	Wealthy, powerful
Macho	Ambitious, hard-working, and competitive	Insensitive, emotionally cold
Unwilling to learn English	Intelligent, well-educated	Polite, well-mannered, genteel
Disinterested in education	Obedient, servile women	Snobbish
Not concerned about being on welfare	Sneaky	Guilt-ridden do-gooders
Warm, expressive	Poor lovers	
Lazy	Possessing strong family ties	
Hot-tempered and violent	Great imitators, not originators	
	Law-abiding	

Stereotypes are fixed, conventional ideas about groups of people and can give rise to prejudice and discrimination. Do you believe the stereotypes listed in this table? What is the evidence for your beliefs?
Sources of stereotypes: *Sociology in a changing world,* 3d ed., by W. Kornblum, 1994, Fort Worth: Harcourt Brace College Publishers; *A different mirror: A history of multicultural America,* by R. Takaki, 1993, Boston: Little, Brown & Company.

Social perception • A subfield of social psychology that studies the ways in which we form and modify impressions of others.

- What stereotypes, if any, do you hold of other ethnic groups, such as those included in Table 16.1? How did these stereotypes develop? Has taking this course affected your tendency to hold such stereotypes? If so, in what way?

Let us now turn our attention to some of the factors involved in the formation of our impressions of other people.

Social Perception

In this section, we shall explore some factors that contribute to **social perception:** primacy and recency effects, attribution theory, and body language. Then, we shall survey the determinants of interpersonal attraction.

PRIMACY AND RECENCY EFFECTS: THE IMPORTANCE OF FIRST IMPRESSIONS

Why do you wear your best outfit to a job interview? Why do defense attorneys dress their clients neatly and cut their hair before they are seen by the jury? Because first impressions are important and reasonably accurate (Burnstein & Schul, 1982; Wyer, 1988).

When I was a teenager, a young man was accepted or rejected by his date's parents the first time they were introduced. If he was considerate and made small talk, her parents would allow the couple to stay out past curfew, even to watch submarine races at the beach during the early morning hours. If he was boorish or uncommunicative, he was a cad forever. Her parents would object to him, no matter how hard he worked to gain their favor later on.

First Impressions. Why is it important to make a good first impression? What are some ways of doing so?

MINILECTURE: ATTRIBUTION

Primacy effect • The tendency to evaluate others in terms of first impressions.

Recency effect • The tendency to evaluate others in terms of the most recent impression.

Attribution • A belief concerning why people behave in a certain way.

Attribution process • The process by which people draw inferences about the motives and traits of others.

Dispositional attribution • An assumption that a person's behavior is determined by internal causes such as personal attitudes or goals.

First impressions often make or break us. This is the **primacy effect.** We infer traits from behavior. If we act considerately at first, we are labeled considerate. The trait of consideration is used to explain and predict our future behavior. If, after being labeled considerate, one keeps a date out past curfew, this lapse is likely to be seen as an exception to a rule—excused by circumstances or external causes. If one is first seen as inconsiderate, however, several months of considerate behavior may be perceived as a cynical effort to "make up for it."

Participants in a classic experiment on the primacy effect read different stories about "Jim" (Luchins, 1957). The stories consisted of one or two paragraphs. One-paragraph stories portrayed Jim as friendly or unfriendly. These paragraphs were also used in the two-paragraph stories but were read in opposite order. Of those reading only the "friendly" paragraph, 95% rated Jim as friendly. Of those who read just the "unfriendly" paragraph, 3% rated him as friendly. Seventy-eight percent of those who read two-paragraph stories in the "friendly–unfriendly" order labeled Jim as friendly. When they read the paragraphs in the reverse order, only 18% rated Jim as friendly.

Truth or Fiction Revisited. *It is true that first impressions have powerful effects on our social relationships.* People apparently interpret future events in the light of first impressions. If you have made a poor first impression with someone, should you attempt to change her or his impression or just give up on the relationship?

How can we encourage people to pay more attention to more recent impressions? Luchins accomplished this by allowing time to elapse between presenting the paragraphs. In this way, fading memories allowed more recent information to take precedence. This is the **recency effect.** Luchins found a second way to counter first impressions: He simply asked people in the study to avoid snap judgments and to weigh all the evidence.

ATTRIBUTION THEORY: YOU'RE FREE BUT I'M CAUGHT IN THE MIDDLE?

At the age of 3, one of my daughters believed that a friend's son was a boy because he *wanted* to be a boy. Since she was 3 at the time, this error in my daughter's **attribution** for the boy's gender is understandable. Adults tend to make somewhat similar attribution errors, however. No, adults do not believe that people's preferences have much to do with their gender. However, adults do tend to exaggerate the role of choice in other aspects of their behavior.

An assumption about why people do things is called an attribution for behavior (Jones, 1990). Our inference of the motives and traits of others through the observation of their behavior is called the **attribution process.** We now focus on attribution theory, or the processes by which people draw conclusions about the factors that influence one another's behavior.

Attribution theory is very important, because our attributions lead us to perceive others either as purposeful actors or as victims of circumstances.

Dispositional and Situational Attributions. Social psychologists describe two types of attributions—dispositional attributions and situational attributions. **Dispositional attributions** ascribe a person's behavior to internal factors, such as personality traits and free will. **Situational attributions** attribute a person's actions to external factors such as social influence or socialization.

The Fundamental Attribution Error.

People tend to attribute too much of other people's behavior to internal factors such as free will (Kimble, 1994). This bias in the attribution process is the **fundamental attribution error.** When we observe the behavior of others, we apparently focus too much on their actions and too little on the circumstances that surround their actions. We tend to be more aware of the networks of forces acting on ourselves.

One reason for the fundamental attribution error is that we tend to infer traits from behavior. When we overhear a woman screaming at her husband in a supermarket, we tend to assume that she is impulsive and boisterous. We are usually not aware of the many things that her husband might have done to infuriate her. The fundamental attribution error is linked to another bias in the attribution process: the actor–observer effect.

The Actor–Observer Effect.

When we see ourselves and others engaging in behavior that we do not like, we tend to see the others as willful actors but to perceive ourselves as victims of circumstances (Fiske & Taylor, 1984). The tendency to attribute the behavior of others to dispositional factors and our own behavior to situational influences is termed the **actor–observer effect** (Jellison & Green, 1981.)

Consider an example. When parents and children argue about the children's choice of friends or dates, the parents infer traits from behavior and tend to perceive their children as stubborn, difficult, and independent. The children also infer traits from behavior. They may thus perceive their parents as bossy and controlling. Parents and children alike attribute the others' behavior to internal causes. They both make dispositional attributions about other people's behavior, that is.

How do the parents and children perceive themselves? The parents probably see themselves as being forced into combat by

The Actor–Observer Effect. Who is at fault here? When parents and teenagers argue about the teenagers' choice of friends or dates, the parents tend to perceive the teenagers as stubborn and independent. But the children may perceive their parents as bossy and controlling. Parents and children alike make dispositional attributions for each others' behavior. But the parents and teenagers both tend to see their own behavior as being motivated by situational factors. Teenagers often see themselves as being caught between peer pressures and parental restrictiveness. Parents, on the other hand, tend to see themselves as being forced to act out of love of, and fear for what might happen to, their impetuous children.

their children's foolishness. If they become insistent, it is in response to their children's stubbornness. The children probably see themselves as responding to peer pressures and, perhaps, to sexual urges that may have come from within but do not seem "of their own making." The parents and the children both tend to see their own behavior as being motivated by external factors. That is, they make situational attributions for their own behavior.

Truth or Fiction Revisited. *It is true that we take others to task for their misdeeds but tend to see ourselves as victims of circumstances when our conduct falls short of our ideals.* This bias in the attribution process is referred to as the actor–observer effect. What factors seem to account for the actor–observer effect?

The actor–observer effect extends to our perceptions of the in-group (an extension of ourselves) and the out-group. Consider conflicts between nations. Both sides may engage in brutal acts of violence. Each side usually considers the other to be calculating, inflexible, and—not infrequently—sinister. Each side also typically views its own people as victims of circumstances and

Situational attribution • An assumption that a person's behavior is determined by external circumstances such as the social pressure found in a situation.

Fundamental attribution error • The tendency to assume that others act predominantly on the basis of their dispositions, even when there is evidence suggesting the importance of their situations.

Actor–observer effect • The tendency to attribute our own behavior to situational factors but to attribute the behavior of others to dispositional factors.

TABLE 16.2

Factors Leading to Internal or External Attributions of Behavior

	INTERNAL ATTRIBUTION	**EXTERNAL ATTRIBUTION**
Consensus	Low: Few people behave this way.	High: Most people behave this way.
Consistency	High: The person behaves this way frequently.	Low: The person does not behave this way frequently.
Distinctiveness	Low: The person behaves this way in many situations.	High: The person behaves this way in few situations.

We are more likely to attribute behavior to internal, dispositional factors when it is low in consensus, high in consistency, and low in distinctiveness. In the example given in the textbook, we will be most likely to attribute a complaint about one's food to external factors if other people also complain (high consensus) and if the complainer usually does not complain about food (high distinctiveness).

Self-serving bias • The tendency to view one's successes as stemming from internal factors and one's failures as stemming from external factors.

Consensus • General agreement.

its own violent actions as being vindicated or dictated by the situation. After all, we may look at the other side as being in the wrong, but can we expect the out-group to agree with us?[4]

The Self-Serving Bias. There is also a **self-serving bias** in the attribution process. We are likely to ascribe our successes to internal, dispositional factors but our failures to external, situational influences (Baumgardner and others, 1986; Van der Plight & Eiser, 1983). When we have done well on a test or impressed a date, we are likely to credit these outcomes to our intelligence and charm. But when we fail, we are likely to ascribe them to bad luck, an unfairly demanding test, or our date's bad mood.

It seems that we extend the self-serving bias to others in our perceptions of why we win or lose when we gamble. When we win bets on football games, we tend to attribute our success to the greater ability of the winning team—a dispositional factor (Gilovich, 1983). But when we lose our bets, we tend to ascribe the game's outcome to a fluke, such as an error by a referee.

An ironic twist to the self-serving bias is that we tend to see ourselves as less self-centered than others (Rempel and others, 1985).

There are exceptions to the self-serving bias. We are more likely to own up to our responsibility for our failures when we think that other people will not accept situational attributions (Reiss and others, 1981). Depressed people are also more likely than nondepressed people to ascribe their failures to internal factors, even when dispositional attributions are not justified.

Another interesting attribution bias is a gender difference in attributions for friendly behavior. Men are more likely than women to interpret a woman's friendliness toward men as flirting (Abbey, 1987). Perhaps gender roles apparently still lead men to expect that "decent" women are passive.

Factors Contributing to the Attribution Process: Consensus, Consistency, and Distinctiveness. According to Kelley and Michela (1980), our attribution of behavior to internal or external causes can be influenced by three factors: consensus, consistency, and distinctiveness. When few people act in a certain way—that is, when **consensus** is low—we are likely to attribute behavior to dispositional (internal) factors. Consistency refers to the degree to which the same person acts in the same way on other occasions. Highly consistent behavior can often be attributed to dispositional factors. Distinctiveness is the extent to which the person responds differently in different situations. If the person acts similarly in different situations, distinctiveness is low. We are thus likely to attribute his or her behavior to dispositional factors.

Let us apply the criteria of consensus, consistency, and distinctiveness to a

---

[4] I am not suggesting that all nations are equally blameless (or blameworthy) for their brutality toward other nations. I am merely pointing out that there is a tendency for the people of a nation to perceive themselves as being driven to unwanted behavior. Yet, they are also likely to perceive other nations' negative behavior as willful and directed by national dispositions.

customer in a restaurant. She takes one bite of her blueberry cheesecake and calls for the waiter. She argues that her food is inedible and demands that it be replaced. The question is whether she complained as a result of internal causes (for example, because she is difficult to please) or external causes (that is, because the food really is bad). Under the following circumstances, we are likely to attribute her behavior to internal, dispositional causes: (1) No one else at the table is complaining, so consensus is low. (2) She has returned food on other occasions, so consistency is high. (3) She complains in other restaurants also, so distinctiveness is low (see Table 16.2).

Under the following circumstances, however, we are likely to attribute her behavior to external, situational causes: (1) Everyone else at the table is also complaining, so consensus is high. (2) She has not returned food on other occasions, so consistency is low. (3) She usually does not complain at restaurants, so distinctiveness is high. Given these conditions, we are likely to believe that the blueberry cheesecake really is awful, and our friend is justifiably responding to the circumstances.

BODY LANGUAGE

Body language is important in social perception. Nonverbal behavior can express internal states, such as feelings. It can regulate social interactions (Patterson, 1991). People even use body language to deceive other people as to how they feel (DePaulo, 1992).

At an early age, we learn that the ways people carry themselves provide cues to how they feel and are likely to behave (Saarni, 1990). You may have noticed that when people are "uptight," they may also be rigid and straight-backed. People who are relaxed are more likely, literally, to "hang loose." Factors such as eye contact, posture, and distance between people provide broadly recognized cues to their moods and feelings toward their companions. When people face us and lean toward us, we may assume that they like us or are interested in what we are saying. If we are privy to a conversation between a couple and observe that the woman is leaning toward the man, but that the man is sitting back and toying with his hair, we are likely

to infer that he is not having any of what she is selling (DePaulo and others, 1978).

Touching also communicates. Women are more likely than men to touch other people when they are interacting with them (Stier & Hall, 1984). In one touching experiment, Kleinke (1977) showed that appeals for help can be more effective when the distressed person engages in physical contact with people being asked for aid. A woman obtained more dimes for phone calls when she touched the person she was asking for money on the arm. In another experiment, waitresses obtained higher tips when they touched patrons on the hand or the shoulder while making change (Crusco & Wetzel, 1984).

In these experiments, touching was noncontroversial. It was usually gentle, brief, and occurred in familiar settings. However, when touching suggests greater intimacy than is desired, it can be seen as negative. A study in a nursing home found that responses to being touched depended on factors such as the status of the staff member, the type of touch, and the part of the body that was touched (Hollinger & Buschmann, 1993). Touching was considered positive when it was appropriate to the situation and did not appear to be condescending. Touching was seen as negative when it was controlling, unnecessary, or overly intimate.

Body language can also be used to establish and maintain territorial control (Brown & Altman, 1981), as anyone who has had to step aside because a football player was walking down the hall can testify. Werner and her colleagues (1981) found that players in a game arcade used touching as a way of signaling others to keep their distance. Solo players engaged in more touching than did groups, perhaps because they were surrounded by strangers.

Gazing and Staring: The Eyes Have It. We usually feel that we can learn much from eye contact. When others "look us squarely in the eye," we may assume that they are being assertive or open with us. Avoidance of eye contact may suggest deception or depression. Gazing is interpreted as a sign of liking or friendliness (Kleinke, 1986). In one penetrating study, as a matter of fact, men and women were asked to gaze into each other's eyes for two

Can Psychologists Usher in an Age of Peace?

One of the most pressing human issues concerns conflict and warfare. It would be nice to think that technological advances would somehow minimize human brutality. However, the fact is that technological innovations have been repeatedly used by warlords and governments as more efficient ways of maiming and killing.

Fortunately, psychologists have not given in to the view that we are helpless to blunt human tendencies to harm other people. In fact, groups of psychologists who have been planning for the future have given "zealous nationalism and what motivates some groups to start war [while other] groups are able to live in peace" a prominent place on their agenda (Meade, 1994, p. 15).

Many matters discussed in this book relate to war and peace. Chapter 10 explores the origins of aggression and measures that psychologists are developing to deal with it on an individual level (see, e.g., Crick & Dodge, 1994; Lochman & Dodge, 1994). Chapter 2 and this chapter discuss the human tendency to obey authority figures, even when authority figures demand that people act brutally. Although we have outlined the forces that act on individuals in the presence of authority figures, can we hope that readers of this book will act to prevent authority figures from committing crimes against humanity in the new millennium? (That answer now lies in your hands, not mine.)

This chapter also deals with stereotyping and prejudice (Herek, 1993)—the creation of attitudes that lead to discrimination and, too often, to violence. Here, too, we consider the tendency to label some people as members of the in-group and others as members of the out-group, and to deal harshly with those who are classified in the out-group (Duckitt, 1992; McCauley, 1989). Will readers of this book recognize and speak out against stereotyping and prejudice in the new millennium?

Here let us also consider how psychologists might refer to theory and research concerning attributional processes to heighten the chances of peace.

Can Psychologists Use Attribution Theory to Mediate International Conflicts?
Biases in the attribution process interfere with people's ability to understand other nations' motives for their behavior. As a result, people may blame others when blame is undue, and conflict may result. At times, biases in the attribution process even cloud nations' perceptions of themselves.

Psychologists conduct individual and group therapy. Can they also mediate international conflicts? Theory and research concerning the attribution process provide psychologists with the following ideas for doing so:

• *Helping Nations Avoid Jumping to the Conclusion That Other Nations Are Always to Blame for Their Behavior.* People, and nations, tend to attribute too much of other people's and nations' behavior to dispositional factors. That is, they make the fundamental attribution error. The fact is that people and nations are influenced by situational variables as well as by dispositional variables. A handful of these include financial hardship, shortsighted leaders, conflict among ethnic groups, unwise alliances, the promise of reward, and the threat of punishment.

When one nation is offended by another nation's behavior, leaders might try to empathize and imagine the internal and external pressures that are impacting on the other nation and its leaders. Empathy might foster understanding and the discovery of ways to encourage more suitable behavior.

- *Helping Nations Avoid Jumping to the Conclusion That They Are Never to Blame for Their Own Behavior.* Psychologists have also learned that people—and, presumably, nations—tend to be highly aware of the situational forces that are acting upon them and influencing their own behavior. Nations may tend to focus on situational factors to the point that they ignore the roles of dispositional factors—for example, the role that is played by their leader's own decisions. A nation may see itself as leaning toward war because of a shortage of natural resources and pressure from an ally; however, its leaders make decisions on the basis of these and other factors. Recognition of the importance of the decision making can help place the onus for poor decisions where it belongs—on specific leaders rather than nations.

    Do you ever say to yourself, "How can I be expected to relax and be a nice guy when I'm going to this pressure cooker of a college?" or "How can I let an insult go unpunished?"? Situational and dispositional variables interact to influence nations' behavior as well as our own. When nations focus on the situational variables, they may lose sight of their own causal role in aggressive behavior.

- *Helping a Nation Recognize That Other Nations May Tend to Blame It for Things That Are Not Its Fault.* Partly because of its wealth, partly because of its history, and partly because it is a big target, the United States is frequently blamed for world problems that are not of its making. Other people, not only we, are subject to biases in the attribution process. For example, they may attribute too much of our nation's behavior to dispositional factors. Similarly, our parents, employers, professors, lovers, and friends may think that we are being stubborn, mean, or even stupid when we do not accede to their requests. When in conflict, it is useful for us, and for our nation, to explain the forces that we perceive to be acting upon us. We thus give other people, or other nations, the information that will permit them to empathize with us. It is useless to say things such as "You would never understand" and then cut off communication.

- *Helping a Nation Recognize That Other Nations Often See Themselves as Forced into Their Behavior.* We tend to see ourselves as victims of circumstances, as compelled by our situations. Consider the U.S. involvement in Vietnam in the 1960s and 1970s. The United States perceived itself as coming to the aid of South Vietnamese friends who valued democracy and sought protection from invaders from the North. But many North Vietnamese perceived themselves as attempting to unify their country and resist the influence of a superpower from the other side of the world.

    It is helpful to try to perceive events from the perspective of one's adversary. It helps to realize that other people can feel forced into their behavior, just as we can. Then we can begin to focus on the forces that compel us all—not just on our own sense of injury.

Can psychologists help make the new millennium an age of peace? Can psychologists succeed where national leaders, philosophers, kings and queens, and great historic figures have failed? Perhaps they can. Perhaps not. But there are two compelling reasons why psychologists will try to help. One is that psychology brings a unique perspective to world problems. Another is that even if psychologists fail, the greater crime would be not to try to help.

Can Psychologists Help Make the New Millennium an Age of Peace? Will the horrors of war, as depicted here, be behind us? How can psychologists apply knowledge of the social psychological topic of attribution theory to foster interpersonal and international understanding?

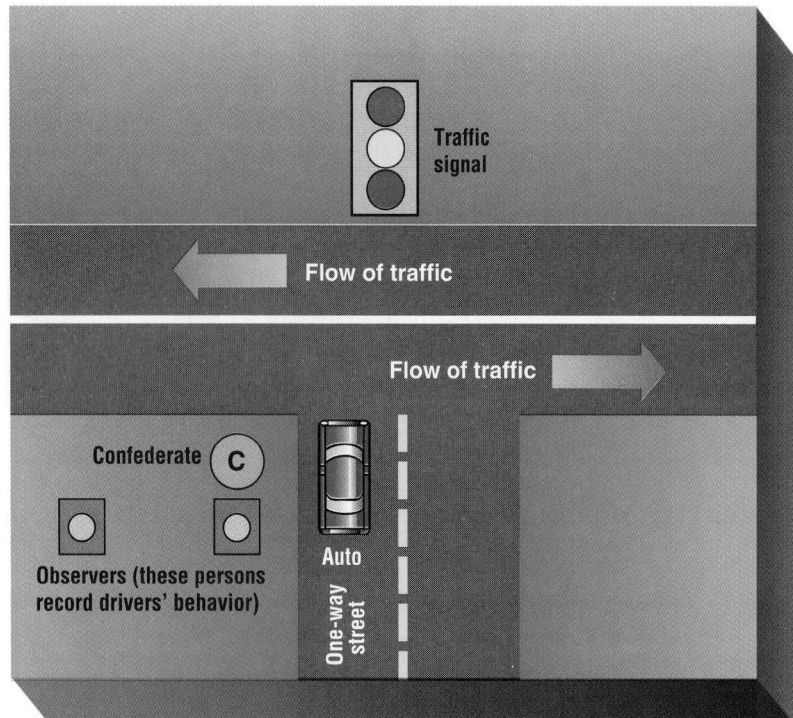

FIGURE 16.1
Diagram of an Experiment in Hard Staring and Avoidance In the Greenbaum and Rosenfeld study, the confederate of the experimenter stared at some drivers and not at others. Recipients of the stares drove across the intersection more rapidly once the light turned green. Why?

Attraction • In social psychology, an attitude of liking or disliking (negative attraction).

minutes (Kellerman and others, 1989). Afterward, they reported passionate feelings toward one another. (Watch out!)

Gazes differ, of course, from persistent hard stares. Hard stares are interpreted as provocations or signs of anger. Adolescent males sometimes engage in staring contests as an assertion of dominance. The male who looks away first loses. In a classic series of field experiments, Phoebe Ellsworth and her colleagues (1972) subjected drivers stopped at red lights to hard stares from riders of motor scooters (see Figure 16.1). People who were stared at crossed the intersection more rapidly than people who were not when the light changed. People who are stared at show higher levels of physiological arousal than people who are not (Strom & Buck, 1979).

Reflections

Now that you have read the section on social perception, reflect on the following questions:

- Think of an instance in which you tried to make a good first impression on someone. How did you do it? Why was it important to try to make a good first impression?
- Give an example of an instance in which you, or someone you know, tried to excuse your behavior by making a situational attribution. Do you make the fundamental attribution error of attributing too much of other people's behavior to choice? Give an example.
- How do you feel when strangers touch you? Why? How do you feel when a physician or nurse touches you during an examination? Why?
- Did you ever leave a situation in which you were stared at in order to lower feelings of arousal and avert the threat of danger?

Interpersonal Attraction: Liking and Loving

Whether we are discussing the science of physics, a pair of magnetic toy dogs, or a couple in a singles bar, attraction is a force that draws bodies together. In psychology, **attraction** is also thought of as a force that draws bodies, or people, together—an attitude of liking. Magnetic "kissing" dogs are usually constructed so that the heads attract one another, but (unlike their flesh-and-blood counterparts) a head and tail repel one another. Attraction can lead to feelings of liking and loving. We shall see that when there is a matching of the heads—that is, a meeting of the minds—people experience *positive attraction* to one another. As with the toy dogs, when we believe that another person's opinions are, well, asinine, we experience *negative attraction* and are repelled.

PHYSICAL ATTRACTIVENESS: HOW IMPORTANT IS LOOKING GOOD?

Are we all so intelligent and sophisticated that we rank physical appearance low on the roster of qualities we seek in a date—below sensitivity and warmth, for example? No. Physical appearance has been found to

"Looking Good." Tia Carrere, Andy Garcia, Naomi Campbell, and Kevin Costner are among those who set the standards for beauty in the new multicultural United States. How important is physical attractiveness? What are our stereotypes of attractive people? Do we see them as being more successful? As making better spouses and parents?

be a key factor in attraction and consideration of partners for dates and marriage (Green and others, 1984). Physical attractiveness also influences prospective employers during job interviews (Mack & Rainey, 1990).

Is Beauty in the Eye of the Beholder? What determines physical allure? Are our standards subjective—that is, "in the eye of the beholder"? Or is there agreement on what is appealing?

Some aspects of beauty appear to be cross-cultural. For example, a study of people in England and Japan found that both British and Japanese men considered women with large eyes, high cheekbones, and narrow jaws to be most attractive (Perrett and others, 1994). In his research, Perrett created computer composites of the faces of 60 women and, as shown in Part A of Figure 16.2, of the 15 women who were rated the most attractive. He then used computer enhancement to exaggerate the differences between the composite of the 60 and the composite of the 15 most attractive, arriving at the image shown in Part B of Figure 16.2. Part B, which shows higher cheekbones and a narrower jaw than Part A, was rated as the most attractive image. Similar results were found for the image of a Japanese woman. Works of art suggest that the ancient Greeks and Egyptians favored similar facial features (Etcoff, 1994).

Psychologist Judith Langlois (1994) has found that the tendency to prefer attractive faces, as determined by amount of time spent looking at various faces, is found in infants by the age of 2 months. She concludes that infants' preferences are likely to be inborn.

In our society, tallness is an asset for men, but tall women are viewed less positively (Sheppard & Strathman, 1989). College women prefer their dates to be about 6 inches taller than they are. College men tend to fancy women who are about $4\frac{1}{2}$ inches shorter (Gillis & Avis, 1980).

FIGURE 16.2

What Features Contribute to Facial Attractiveness? In both England and Japan, features such as large eyes, high cheekbones, and narrow jaws contribute to perceptions of the attractiveness of women. Part A shows a composite of the faces of 15 women rated as the most attractive of a group of 60. Part B is a composite in which the features of these 15 women are exaggerated—that is, developed further in the direction that separates them from the average of the entire 60.

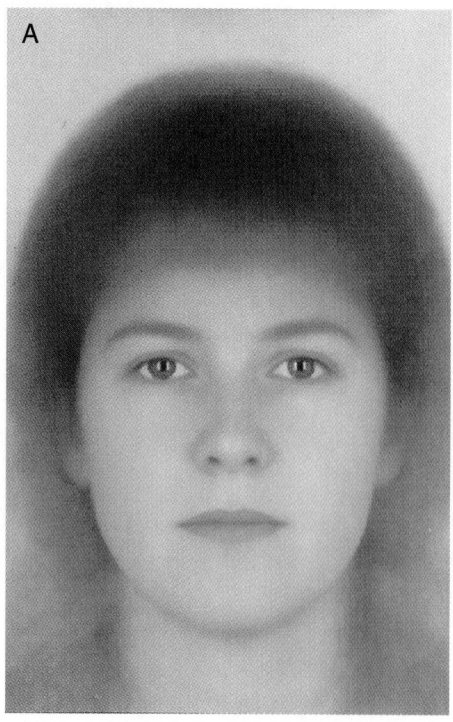
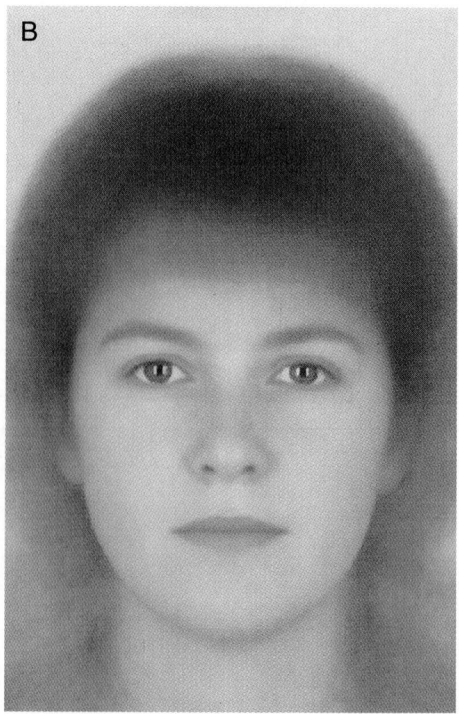

Stretch and Candy were tall. Since we tend to connect tallness with social dominance, many women of Candy's height may be concerned that their stature will compromise their femininity. Some women fear that shorter men are disinclined to ask them out. A few walk with a hunch, trying to downplay their height. A neighbor of the author describes herself as 5 feet 13 inches tall.

Although preferences for facial features may transcend time and culture, preferences for body weight and shape may be more culturally determined (Etcoff, 1994). For example, plumpness has been valued in many cultures. Grandmothers who worry that their granddaughters are starving themselves often come from cultures in which stoutness is acceptable or desirable.[5] In current Western society, both genders find slenderness engaging (Franzoi & Herzog, 1987). Women generally favor men with a V-taper (Horvath, 1981).

Truth or Fiction Revisited. *It is not true that beauty is in the eye of the beholder,* despite the familiarity of the adage. It appears that some aspects of physical appeal may be innate or inborn. There are also cultural standards for beauty that influence people who are reared in that culture.

Although both genders perceive overweight people as unappealing, there are fascinating gender differences in perceptions of desirable body shapes. College men generally find their current physique similar to the ideal male build and to the one that women find most appealing (Fallon & Rozin, 1985). College women, in contrast, generally see themselves as markedly heavier than the figure that is most appealing to men and heavier still than the ideal (see Figure 16.3). Both mothers and fathers of college students see themselves as heavier than their ideal weights (Rozin & Fallon, 1988). Both genders err in their estimates of the other's likes, however. Men of both generations actually prefer women to be heavier than women presume. Women of both generations fancy men who are slimmer than the men imagine.

A flat-chested look was a hallmark of the enchanting profile of the 1920s flapper era,

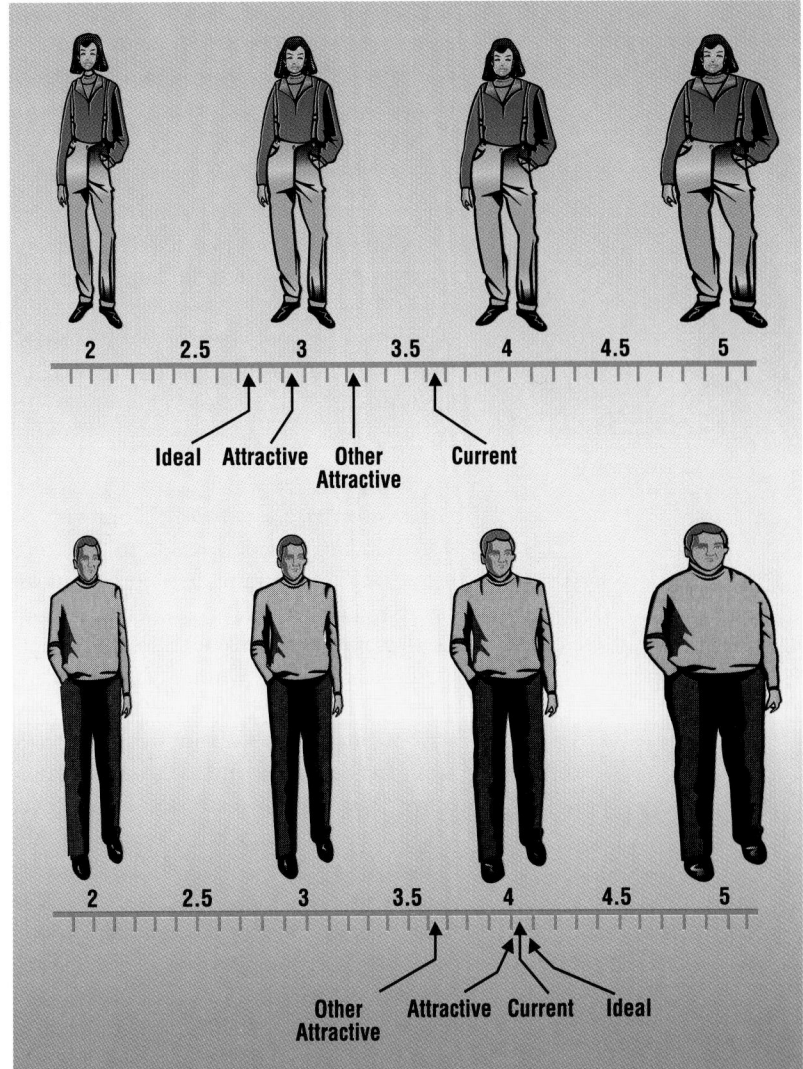

FIGURE 16.3
Can You Ever Be Too Thin? Research suggests that most college women believe they are heavier than they ought to be. However, men actually prefer women to be a bit heavier than women assume the men would like them to be.

but U.S. women today are likely to think of their bust size as too small (even though they consider themselves to be generally too heavy!). Despite the medical risks, about 120,000 U.S. women a year had breast-implant surgery for cosmetic reasons through 1991. The numbers included such public figures (pardon the pun) as Cher and Mariel Hemingway (Williams, 1992). Ironically, we tend to perceive large-busted women as less intelligent, competent, moral, and modest than women with smaller

---

[5] The other side of the coin, as noted in Chapter 13's discussion of anorexia nervosa, is that some granddaughters *are* literally starving themselves today.

breasts (Kleinke & Staneski, 1980). Unless there is known to be a silicone implant, this is clearly a case in which people overattribute a physical feature to dispositional factors!

"Pretty Is as Pretty Does"? Men and women are both perceived as more attractive when they are smiling (Reis and others, 1990). There is thus ample reason to, as the song goes, "put on a happy face" when you are meeting people or looking for a date.

Truth or Fiction Revisited. *It is true that people are perceived as being more attractive when they are smiling.* Does this research finding provide a reason to "put on a happy face" early in the development of social relationships?

Other aspects of behavior also affect interpersonal attraction. Women shown videotapes of prospective dates prefer men who act outgoing and self-expressive (Riggio & Wolf, 1984). College men who show dominance (operationally defined as control over a social interaction with a professor) in a videotape are rated as more attractive by women (Sadalla and others, 1987). College men respond negatively to women who show self-assertion and social dominance, however (Riggio & Wolf, 1984; Sadalla and others, 1987). Despite the liberating forces of recent years, the cultural stereotype of the ideal woman still finds a place for demureness. I am *not* suggesting that self-assertive, expressive women take a back seat to make themselves appealing to traditional men; assertive women might find nothing but conflict with such men anyhow.

"Your Daddy's Rich and Your Ma Is Good Lookin'": Gender Differences in the Importance of Physical Attractiveness.
Your Daddy's rich
And your Ma is good lookin',
So hush, little baby,
Don't you cry.

"SUMMERTIME," FROM THE OPERA
PORGY AND BESS

College men and women report that the importance of physical attractiveness depends on the type of relationship (Nevid, 1984). In relationships that are predomi-

nantly sexual, the physical attractiveness of one's partner is the primary consideration. Psychological traits such as honesty, fidelity, warmth, and sensitivity become relatively more important in long-term, meaningful relationships.

Men are relatively more swayed than women by their partners' physical characteristics, however. Women place relatively greater emphasis on personal qualities such as warmth, assertiveness, need for achievement, and wit.

These findings are replicated in studies on mate selection. Women tend to place greater emphasis than men on traits such as professional status, consideration, dependability, kindness, and fondness for children. Men place relatively greater emphasis on physical allure, cooking ability (can't they turn on the microwave oven themselves?), even thrift (Buss, 1994; Feingold, 1992a).

On the surface, gender differences in the traits that affect perceptions of attractiveness seem unbearably sexist—and perhaps they are. Some sociobiologists believe that evolutionary forces favor the survival of men and women with these preferences because they provide reproductive advantages (Fisher, 1992). As reviewed in Rathus and his colleagues (1993), physical features such as cleanliness, good complexion, clear eyes, good teeth and good hair, firm muscle tone, and a steady gait are universally appealing to both genders. Perhaps such traits have value as markers of better reproductive potential in prospective mates. According to the "parental investment model," a woman's appeal is strongly connected with her age and health, both of which are markers of reproductive capacity. The value of men as reproducers, however, could be more intertwined with factors that contribute to a stable environment for child rearing—such as social standing and reliability (Feingold, 1992a). For such reasons, sociobiologists speculate that these qualities may have grown relatively more alluring to women over the millennia (e.g., Buss, 1994; Fisher, 1992).

Sociobiological theory is largely speculative, however, and not fully consistent with all the evidence (Kakutani, 1992). Women, as men, are attracted to physically appealing people. Too, women tend to marry men similar to them in physical attractiveness and socioeconomic standing. Aging men are more likely than younger men to die from natural causes. The wealth they accrue may not always be transmitted to their spouses and children, either. Many women may be more able to find reproductive success by mating with a fit, younger male than with an older, higher-status male. Even sociobiologists allow that despite any innate predispositions, many men are sexually interested in older women. Human behavior is certainly flexible.

Stereotypes of Attractive People: Do Good Things Come in Pretty Packages? By and large, we rate what is beautiful as good. We expect physically attractive people to be poised, sociable, popular, intelligent, mentally healthy, fulfilled, persuasive, and successful in their jobs and marriages (Eagly and others, 1991; Feingold, 1992b). Unattractive people are more likely to be judged as outside of the mainstream—for example, politically radical or psychologically disordered (Brigham, 1980; O'Grady, 1982; Unger and others, 1982). Unattractive college students are also more apt to rate themselves as susceptible to personal problems.

These stereotypes seem to have some basis in reality. For one thing, attractive people do seem less likely to develop psychological disorders. The disorders of unattractive people are also more severe (e.g., Archer & Cash, 1985; Farina and others, 1986; Burns & Farina, 1987). For another, attractiveness correlates positively with popularity, social skills, and sexual experience (Feingold, 1992b). The correlations between physical attractiveness and most measures of mental ability and personality are trivial, however (Feingold, 1992b).

One way to interpret the data on the correlates of beauty is to assume that they are all innate. In other words, we can believe that beauty and social competence go genetically hand in hand. We can believe that biology is destiny and throw up our hands in despair. Another (more adaptive!) interpretation is that we can do things to make ourselves more attractive and also more successful and fulfilled. Smiling, for example, is linked to attractiveness. So is having a decent physique or figure (which we can work on) and attending to grooming and dress. So don't give up the ship.

The Matching Hypothesis. Do opposites attract, or do we tend to pair off with people who look and think as we do? As suggested by these photographs, similarity often runs at least skin-deep.

Attractive people are also more likely to be judged innocent of crimes in mock jury experiments and observational studies (Michelini & Snodgrass, 1980). When found guilty, they are given less severe sentences (Stewart, 1980). Perhaps we assume that attractive people have less need to resort to deviant behavior to achieve their goals. Even when they have erred, perhaps they will have more opportunity for personal growth and be more likely to change their evil ways.

Attractive children learn early of the expectations of others. Even during the first year, adults tend to rate attractive babies as good, smart, likeable, even well-behaved (Stephan & Langlois, 1984). Parents, teachers, and other children expect attractive children to get good grades and be popular, well-behaved, and talented.

The Matching Hypothesis: Who Is "Right" for You? Have you ever refrained from asking out an extremely attractive person for fear of rejection? Do you feel more comfortable when you approach someone who is a bit less attractive?

If so, you're not alone. Although we may rate highly attractive people as being most desirable, we will not necessarily be left to blend in with the wallpaper. According to the **matching hypothesis,** we tend to ask out people who are similar to ourselves in physical attractiveness rather than the local Denzel Washington or Cindy Crawford look-alike. The central motive for asking out "matches" seems to be fear of rejection by more attractive people (Bernstein and others, 1983).

The matching hypothesis does not apply to physical appeal only. We are also more likely to get married to people who are similar to us in their personality traits (Buss, 1994; Lesnik-Oberstein & Cohen, 1984), attitudes, and even their weight (Schafer & Keith, 1990).

SIMILARITY: DO "OPPOSITES ATTRACT" OR DO "BIRDS OF A FEATHER FLOCK TOGETHER"?

This is the land of free speech. So do we respect the right of others to reveal their ignorance by disagreeing with us? Perhaps. But it has been observed since ancient times that we tend to like people who agree with us. Similarity in attitudes and tastes is a key contributor to initial attraction, friendships, and love relationships (Cappella & Palmer, 1990; Griffin & Sparks, 1990).

Psychological research supports the lure of similarity in attitudes (Griffin & Sparks, 1990; Park & Flink, 1989). Not all attitudes

are equal, however. Attitudes toward religion and children are more important in mate selection than characteristics like kindness and professional status (e.g., Buss & Barnes, 1986; Howard and others, 1987).

We also tend to *assume* that alluring people share our attitudes (Dawes, 1989; Marks and others, 1981). Is this wish fulfillment? When physical attraction is strong, as with Candy and Stretch, perhaps we want to think that the kinks in the relationship will be small or that we can iron them out. Similarly, we tend to assume that the presidential candidates we support share our political views (Brent & Granberg, 1982). We may even forget public statements that conflict with our views (Johnson & Judd, 1983). Then, once they are in office, we may be disillusioned when they swerve from our expectations.

Similarity in tastes and distastes is also important to relationships. Friends tend to be similar in academic skills (Tesser and others, 1984), substance use and abuse, and sexual attitudes (Eisenman, 1985; Rodgers and others, 1984). May and Hamilton (1980) found that college women rated photos of male strangers as more attractive when they were listening to music that they like (in most cases, rock) as compared with music that they don't like (in this experiment, avant-garde classical). If a couple's taste in music differs, one member may grow more appealing at the same time the second is losing appeal in the other's eyes—all because of what is on the stereo. Does this mean that you should find out what music your date likes and play it when you're together? Certainly not if you're planning a long-term relationship! Do you want to have music you hate blaring from the stereo for the next 50 years?

RECIPROCITY: IF YOU LIKE ME, YOU MUST HAVE EXCELLENT JUDGMENT

Has anyone told you how good-looking, brilliant, and mature you are? That your taste is refined? That all in all, you are really something special? If so, have you been impressed by his or her fine judgment?

Reciprocity is also a powerful determinant of attraction (Condon & Crano, 1988). We tend to return feelings of admiration.

Matching hypothesis • The view that people tend to choose persons similar to themselves in attractiveness and attitudes in the formation of interpersonal relationships.

Reciprocity • In interpersonal attraction, the tendency to return feelings and attitudes that are expressed about us.

Romantic love • An intense, positive emotion that involves sexual attraction, feelings of caring, and the belief that one is in love.

Triangular model of love • Sternberg's view that love involves combinations of three components: intimacy, passion, and decision/commitment.

We tend to be more open, warm, and helpful when we are interacting with strangers who seem to like us (Clark and others, 1989; Curtis & Miller, 1986). Men tend to be attracted to women who engage them in conversation, maintain eye contact, and lean toward them while speaking, even when their attitudes are dissimilar (Gold and others, 1984).

We have seen how our feelings of attraction are influenced by physical attractiveness, attitudinal similarity, and so on. Let us now see what we mean when we say that feelings of attraction have blossomed into love.

LOVE: DOING WHAT COMES . . . CULTURALLY?

Love—the ideal for which we make great sacrifice. Love—the sentiment that launched a thousand ships in the Greek epic *The Iliad*. Through the millennia, poets have sought to capture love in words. Dante Alighieri, the poet who shed some light on the Dark Ages, wrote of "the love that moves the sun and the other stars." Poet Robert Burns wrote that his love was like "a red, red rose." Love is beautiful and elusive. Passion and **romantic love** are also earthy and lusty, surging with sexual desire.

We use the label "love" to describe everything from affection to sex ("making love"). During adolescence, lust is often tagged as love. We use "love" to describe lust, because sexual desire in the absence of a committed relationship may be viewed as primitive—especially by parents who fear that adolescents may become pregnant if they give in to it. "Being in love" puts the cultural stamp of approval on sexual feelings. "Love" can be discussed even at the dinner table.

The Love Triangle. No, this love triangle does not refer to two men wooing the same woman. It refers to Robert Sternberg's **triangular model of love.** Sternberg (1986, 1988) believes that love can include combinations of three components: intimacy, passion, and decision/commitment (see Figure 16.4).

Intimacy refers to a couple's closeness, to their mutual concern and sharing of feelings and resources. Passion means romance and sexual feelings. Decision/commitment

Romantic Love. There are many kinds of love. Romantic love is an intense, positive emotion that involves sexual attraction, feelings of caring, a cultural setting that idealizes love, and the *belief* that one is "in love."

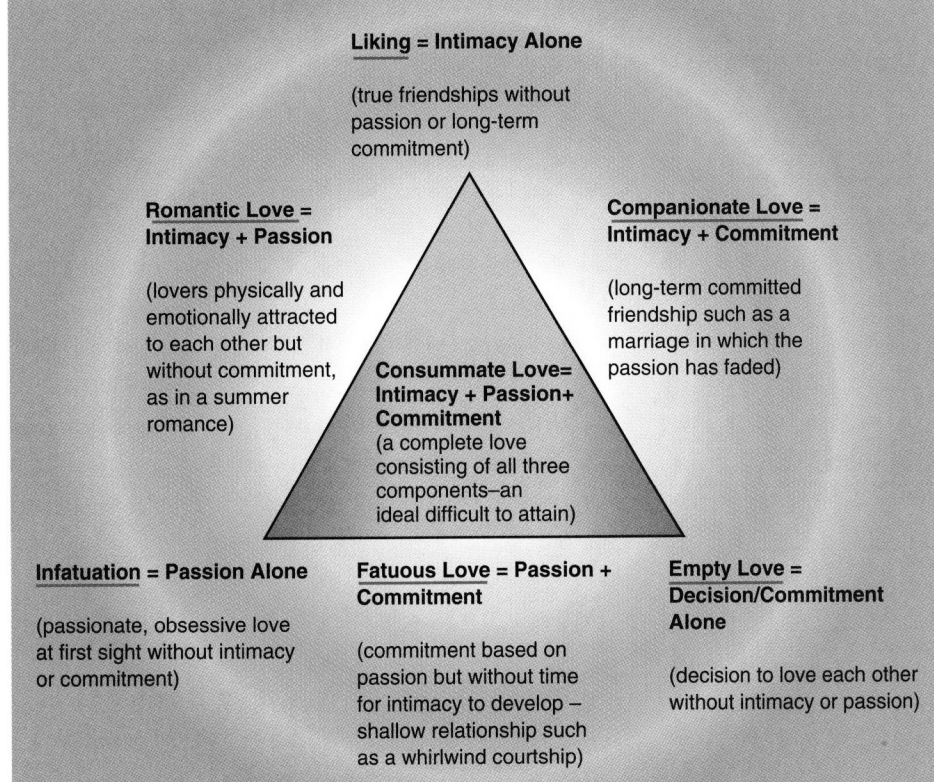

Liking = Intimacy Alone

(true friendships without passion or long-term commitment)

Romantic Love = Intimacy + Passion

(lovers physically and emotionally attracted to each other but without commitment, as in a summer romance)

Companionate Love = Intimacy + Commitment

(long-term committed friendship such as a marriage in which the passion has faded)

Consummate Love= Intimacy + Passion+ Commitment
(a complete love consisting of all three components–an ideal difficult to attain)

Infatuation = Passion Alone

(passionate, obsessive love at first sight without intimacy or commitment)

Fatuous Love = Passion + Commitment

(commitment based on passion but without time for intimacy to develop – shallow relationship such as a whirlwind courtship)

Empty Love = Decision/Commitment Alone

(decision to love each other without intimacy or passion)

FIGURE 16.4
The Triangular Model of Love
According to this model, love has three components: intimacy, passion, and decision/commitment. The ideal of consummate love consists of romantic love plus commitment.

refers to deciding that one is in love and, in the long term, the commitment to enhance and maintain the relationship. Passion is most crucial in short-term relationships. Intimacy and commitment are relatively more important in enduring relationships. The ideal form of love, which combines all three, is **consummate love.** Consummate love, within this model, is romantic love plus commitment.

Romantic Love in Contemporary Western Culture: A Sociocultural Approach. Romantic love is characterized by passion and intimacy. Passion involves feelings of fascination, as shown by preoccupation with the loved one; sexual craving; and the desire for exclusiveness (a special relationship with the loved one). Intimacy involves caring—championing the interests of the loved one; sacrificing one's own interests, if necessary. College undergraduates see helping one's lover as being more central to the concept of love than seeking to meet one's own needs with one's lover (Steck and others, 1982). ("Ask not what your lover can do for you; ask what you can do for your lover.") People who are dating, or who expect to be dating one another, are cognitively biased toward evaluating one another positively (Fiske, 1993). They tend to pay attention to information that confirms their romantic interests. In less technical terms, romantic lovers often idealize one another. They magnify each other's positive features and overlook their flaws.

To experience romantic love, in contrast to attachment or sexual arousal, one must

---

— Questionnaire —

THE LOVE SCALE

Are you in love?

The following love scale was developed at Northeastern University in Boston. To compare your own score with those of Northeastern University students, simply think of your dating partner or partners and fill out the scale with each of them in mind. Then compare your scores to those in Appendix B.

DIRECTIONS: Circle the number that best shows how true or false the items are for you.

1. I look forward to being with _____ a great deal.

   definitely false   1 2 3 4 5 6 7   definitely true

2. I find _____ to be sexually exciting.

   definitely false   1 2 3 4 5 6 7   definitely true

3. _____ has fewer faults than most people.

   definitely false   1 2 3 4 5 6 7   definitely true

4. I would do anything I could for _____.

   definitely false   1 2 3 4 5 6 7   definitely true

5. _____ is very attractive to me.

   definitely false   1 2 3 4 5 6 7   definitely true

6. I like to share my feelings with _____.

   definitely false   1 2 3 4 5 6 7   definitely true

7. Doing things is more fun when _____ and I do them together.

   definitely false   1 2 3 4 5 6 7   definitely true

8. I like to have _____ all to myself.

   definitely false   1 2 3 4 5 6 7   definitely true

9. I would feel horrible if anything bad happened to _____.

   definitely false   1 2 3 4 5 6 7   definitely true

10. I think about _____ very often.

    definitely false   1 2 3 4 5 6 7   definitely true

11. It is very important that _____ cares for me.

    definitely false   1 2 3 4 5 6 7   definitely true

12. I am most content when I am with _____.

    definitely false   1 2 3 4 5 6 7   definitely true

13. It is difficult for me to stay away from _____ for very long.

    definitely false   1 2 3 4 5 6 7   definitely true

14. I care about _____ a great deal.

    definitely false   1 2 3 4 5 6 7   definitely true

    Total Score for Love Scale: ___

be exposed to a culture that idealizes the concept. In Western culture, romantic love blossoms within the fairy tales about Sleeping Beauty, Cinderella, Snow White, and all their princes charming. It matures with romantic novels, television tales and films, and the personal tales of friends and relatives about dates and romances.

Truth or Fiction Revisited. *Romantic love is not found in every culture in the world. Romantic love is found only in cultures that idealize the concept.*

Reflections

Now that you have read the section on interpersonal attraction, reflect on the following questions:

- Agree or disagree with the following statement and support your answer: "Beauty is in the eye of the beholder."
- What do the men you know look for in a date? What do the women look for? Are the desired traits similar or dissimilar? In what ways?
- What do the men you know look for in a mate? What do the women look for in a mate? Are the desired traits similar or dissimilar to those sought in a date? In what ways?
- Agree or disagree with the following statement and support your answer: "Opposites attract."
- Are you in love? Have you been in love? How do you know when you are in love? How does being in love differ from being infatuated or sexually aroused?

Social Influence

Most of us would be reluctant to wear blue jeans to a funeral, to walk naked on city streets, or, for that matter, to wear clothes at a nudist colony. Other people and groups can exert enormous pressure on us to behave according to their norms. **Social influence** is the area of social psychology that studies the ways in which people alter the thoughts, feelings, and behavior of others. We already learned how attitudes can be changed through persuasion. In this section, we shall describe a couple of classic experiments to show various ways in which people influence others to engage in destructive obedience and to conform to social norms.

OBEDIENCE TO AUTHORITY: DOES MIGHT MAKE RIGHT?

Throughout history soldiers have followed orders—even when it comes to slaughtering innocent civilians. The Turkish slaughter of Armenians, the Nazi slaughter of Jews, the Serbian slaughter of Bosnian Muslims, the slaughter in Rwanda—these are historic and not so historic examples of the tragedies that can arise from following orders. We may say that we are horrified by such crimes, and that we can't imagine why people engage in them. But how many of us would resist orders issued by authority figures?

The Milgram Studies. Stanley Milgram also wondered how many of us would resist authority figures who made immoral requests. To find out, he ran a series of experiments that we reviewed in Chapter 2. People responded to newspaper ads to participate in research on "the effects of punishment on learning." The experiment required a "teacher" and a "learner." The newspaper-ad recruit was appointed the teacher—supposedly by chance.

Figures 2.1 and 2.2 show the bogus shock apparatus that was employed in the studies and the layout of the laboratory. "Teachers" were given the task of administering shock to learners when they made errors. The shock was to increase with each consecutive error. Despite the professed purpose of the research, Milgram's sole aim was to determine how many people would deliver high levels of apparently painful electric shock to "learners."

In various phases of Milgram's research, nearly half or the majority of participants complied throughout the series, believing that they were delivering 450-volt, XXX-rated shocks. These findings held for men from the New Haven community, for Yale students, and for women as well as men.

Many people thus obey the commands of others, even when pressed to perform immoral tasks. But *why?* Why did Germans "just follow orders" and commit atrocities?

MINILECTURE: CONFORMITY, COMPLIANCE, AND OBEDIENCE

Consummate love • The ideal form of love within Sternberg's model, which combines passion, intimacy, and commitment.

Social influence • The area of social psychology that studies the ways in which people influence the thoughts, feelings, and behavior of others.

Why did "teachers" obey the experimenter? We do not have all the answers, but we can offer a number of hypotheses:

1. *Socialization.* Despite the expressed American ideal of independence, we are socialized to obey authority figures such as parents and teachers from early childhood. Obedience to immoral demands may be the ugly sibling of socially desirable respect for authority figures (Blass, 1991).

2. *Lack of social comparison.* In Milgram's experimental settings, experimenters showed command of the situation. "Teachers" were on the experimenter's ground and very much on their own. Being on their own, they did not have the opportunity to compare their ideas and feelings with those of people in the same situation. They were thus less likely to have a clear impression of what to do.

3. *Perception of legitimate authority.* One phase of Milgram's research took place within the hallowed halls of Yale University. Those participating in the study there might have been overpowered by the reputation and authority of the setting. An experimenter at Yale might have appeared to be very much the legitimate authority figure—as might a government official or a high-ranking officer in the military. Yet, further research showed that the university setting contributed to compliance but was not fully responsible for it. The percentage of individuals complying with the experimenter's demands dropped from 65% to 48% when Milgram (1974) replicated the study in a dingy storefront in a nearby town. At first glance, this finding might seem encouraging. But the main point of the Milgram studies is that most of us remain willing to engage in morally reprehensible acts at the behest of a legitimate-looking authority figure. Hitler and his henchmen were very much the legitimate authority figures in Nazi Germany. "Science" and Yale University legitimized the authority of the experimenters in the Milgram studies. The problem of acquiescence to authority figures remains.

4. *The foot-in-the-door technique.* The foot-in-the-door technique might also have contributed to the obedience of the teachers (Gilbert, 1981). Once they had begun to deliver shocks to learners, they might have found it progressively more difficult to extricate themselves. Soldiers, similarly, are first taught to obey unquestioningly in innocuous matters such as dress and drill. By the time they are ordered to risk their lives, they have been saluting smartly and following commands for quite some time.

5. *Inaccessibility of values.* People are more likely to act in accord with their attitudes when their attitudes are readily available, or accessible. Most people believe that it is wrong to harm innocent people. But as the teachers in the Milgram experiments became more and more aroused, their attitudes might have become less accessible. As a consequence, it might have become progressively more difficult for them to behave according to them.

6. *Buffers.* Several buffers decreased the effect of the learners' pain on the teachers. Learners (confederates of the experimenter), for example, were in another room. When they were in the same room with teachers—that is, when teachers had full view of their victims—the compliance rate dropped from 65% to 40% (Miller, 1986). Moreover, when the teacher held the learner's hand on the shock plate, the compliance rate dropped to 30%. In modern warfare, opposing soldiers may be separated by great distances. They may be little more than a blip on a radar screen. It is one thing to press a button to launch a missile or to aim a piece of artillery at a distant troop carrier or a distant ridge. It is another to hold a weapon to the victim's throat.

There are thus numerous theoretical explanations for obedience. Regardless of the exact nature of the forces that acted on the participants in the Milgram studies, Milgram's research has alerted us to a real and present danger—the tendency of many, if not most, people to obey an authority figure even when the figure's demands contradict the person's moral values. It has happened before. Unless we remain alert, it will happen again.

Conformity. In the military, individuals are taught to conform until the group functions in machine-like fashion. What pressures toward conformity do you experience? From whom? Do you accede to them? Are you aware of doing so?

Conform • To change one's attitudes or overt behavior to adhere to social norms.

Social norms • Explicit and implicit rules that reflect social expectations and influence the ways people behave in social situations.

In the section on conformity, we describe another classic study. Imagine how you would behave if you were involved in it.

CONFORMITY: DO MANY MAKE RIGHT?

We are said to **conform** when we change our behavior to adhere to social norms. **Social norms** are widely accepted expectations concerning social behavior. Explicit social norms require us to whisper in libraries and to slow down when driving past a school. One unspoken or implicit social norm is to face front in elevators. Another implicit norm is to be fashionably late for social gatherings.

The tendency to conform to social norms is often a good thing. Many norms have evolved because they favor comfort and survival. Group pressure can also promote maladaptive behavior, as when people engage in risky behavior because "everyone is doing it."

Let us look at a classic experiment on conformity run by Solomon Asch in the early 1950s. We shall then examine factors that promote conformity.

Seven Line Judges Can't Be Wrong: The Asch Study. Do you believe what you see with your own eyes? Seeing is believing, is it not? Not if you were a participant in the Asch (1952) study.

You would enter a laboratory room with seven other participants in an experiment on visual discrimination. There was a man at the front of a room with some cards with lines drawn on them.

The eight of you would be seated in a series. You would be given the seventh seat, a minor fact at the time. The man would explain the task. There was a single line on the card on the left. Three lines were drawn on the card at the right (Figure 16.5). One line was the same length as the line on the other card. You and the other participants need only call out, one at a time, which of the three lines—1, 2, or 3—was the same length. Simple.

You would try it out. Those to your right spoke out in order: "3," "3," "3," "3," "3," "3." Now it was your turn. Line 3 was clearly the same length as the line on the first card, so you said "3." The fellow after you then chimed in: "3." That's all there was to it. Two other cards were then set up

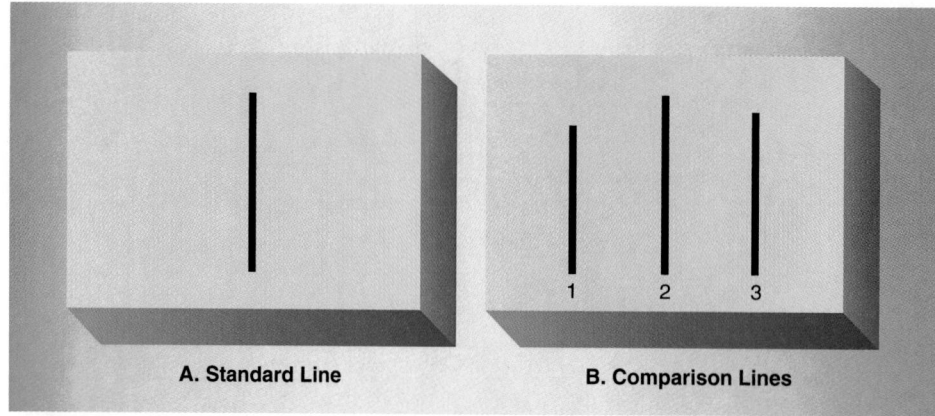

A. Standard Line   B. Comparison Lines

FIGURE 16.5
Cards Used in the Asch Study on Conformity Which line on card B—1, 2, or 3—is the same length as the line on card A? Line 2, right? But would you say "2" if you were a member of a group and six people answering ahead of you all said "3"? Are you sure?

in the front of the room. This time line 2 was clearly the same length as the line on the first card. The answers: "2," "2," "2," "2," "2," "2." Your turn again: "2," you said, and perhaps your mind began to wander. Your stomach was gurgling a bit. That night you would not even mind dorm food particularly. The fellow after you said, "2."

Another pair of cards was held up. Line 3 was clearly the correct answer. The six people on your right spoke in turn: "1," "1 . . ." Wait a second! ". . . 1," "1—" You forgot about dinner and studied the lines briefly. No, 1 was too short, by a good half an inch. But ". . . 1," "1," and suddenly it was your turn. Your hands had quickly become sweaty and there was a lump in your throat. You wanted to say 3, but was it right? There was really no time, and you had already paused noticeably: "1," you said, "1," the last fellow confirmed matter-of-factly.

Now your attention was riveted on the chore. Much of the time you agreed with the other seven line judges, but sometimes you did not. And for some reason beyond your understanding, they were in perfect agreement, even when they were wrong—assuming that you could trust your eyes. The experiment was becoming an uncomfortable experience, and you began to doubt your judgment.

The discomfort in the Asch study was caused by the pressure to conform. Actually, the other seven recruits were confederates of the experimenter. They prearranged

a number of incorrect responses. The sole purpose of the study was to see whether you would conform to the erroneous group judgments.

How many people in Asch's study caved in? How many went along with the crowd rather than assert what they thought to be the right answer? Seventy-five percent. *Three of four agreed with the majority wrong answer at least once.*

Factors Influencing Conformity. Several personal and situational factors prompt conformity to social norms. Personal factors include the desires to be liked by other members of the group and to be right (Insko, 1985), low self-esteem, high self-consciousness, social shyness (Santee & Maslach, 1982), and lack of familiarity with the job. Situational factors include group size and social support.

There has been a great deal of controversy about whether women conform to social norms more than men do. Old-fashioned stereotypes portray men as rugged individualists and women as civilizing influences, so it is not surprising that women have been generally perceived as more conformist. Yet, many psychologists argue that there are no major gender differences in conformity. Eagly (1987) suggests that people perceive women as being easier to "push around" because women usually have lower social status than men—in society at large and in the workforce.

Situational factors include the number of people who hold the majority opinion and the presence of at least one other person who shares the discrepant opinion. Likelihood of conformity, even to incorrect group judgments, increases rapidly as a group grows to five members, then rises more slowly to about eight members (Tanford & Penrod, 1984). At about that point, the maximum chance of conformity is reached.

Finding just one other person who supports your minority opinion is apparently enough to encourage you to stick to your guns (Morris and others, 1977).

PSYCHOLOGY IN A WORLD OF DIVERSITY

MUSLIM WOMEN FACE PRESSURE TO CONFORM IN THE UNITED STATES

Asking me why I don't feel comfortable praying in front of other people here in the United States is like asking me why I don't wear shorts in Cairo.
                    MAYADA EL-ZOGHBI, A 24-YEAR-OLD EGYPTIAN WOMAN WHO GREW UP IN EGYPT AND MINNESOTA[6]

"People look at me and they're like, 'She wants to work here?'" complained 19-year-old Maha Alkhateeb. After a frustrating job search at the mall, she pulled off her hejab, the black scarf with which many Muslim women cover their hair, and allowed her long, dark hair to cascade out.

Wanda Khan, 37, suffered a similar setback in Charlotte, North Carolina. She was denied a teaching job because of her hejab. "I know that I am more than qualified," she said, "but a school official told me that there is a school policy against wearing hats. I told him it was a religious thing, and that I couldn't remove it, and that I would take it up with the school board."

Muslim women find that they are usually treated as an oddity in the United States. Maha's mother, Sharifa, explained that most people in the United States think of Muslim women as wearing huge sheets, with three children trailing behind them, and with "her trailing behind her husband who just finished beating her."

Support Groups. Because of the need to support one another and address practical problems, Muslim women across the nation are organizing neighborhood groups and national associations. Sharifa Alkhateeb is president of the North American Council for Muslim Women. Some groups focus on studying the Koran, which is the Islamic bible. Others debate the merits of wearing veils. (There is nothing in the Islamic religion that requires the hejab per se, but wearing one is a traditional way for Muslim women to meet Islamic mandates for modesty.) Many groups explore ways of getting other people in the United States to accept them in malls, PTAs, and investment banks. They frequently convene to discuss ways of tackling school boards that do not excuse their children for Muslim holidays and businesses that deny jobs to Muslims.

"Muslim women here are starting to mobilize because they feel demonized," noted Yvonne Haddad, a professor at the University of Massachusetts. The act of organizing brings Muslim women out from behind their husbands and fathers, who have traditionally been first to try to decode the cultural values and language of a new host nation. "When it looks like things are falling apart, the women step up," Professor Haddad said. "They used to defer to men, but when they see things aren't getting done, they organize themselves."

Muslim women in the United States are also likely to step out because of freedoms and mobility they lacked in their countries of origin. For some, the issue seems to be how to continue to embrace Islam and at the same time adopt appealing values of the dominant U.S. culture concerning women's independence, self-assertiveness, and advancement in the workplace.

Balancing the Sacred and the Secular. Ferial Masry, 44, is a Saudi Arabian immigrant who runs a photography shop in Southern California. Ferial, like many other Arabian Americans, attempts to balance the sacred and the secular in her personal life. She studies Islamic history and takes Arabic

---

[6] Citations in this feature are drawn from "Muslim Women Bridging Culture Gap," 1993, *The New York Times,* November 8, p. B9.

folk dancing but also lets her children watch the cable channel Nick at Nite.

"Here in America, you are constantly forced to question the things we took for granted back home," Ferial explains. "Here, you need to really understand your values and get the children to feel close to their culture while still letting them assimilate."

Skipping the Prom. Maha Alkhateeb is one of a number of young Muslim American women who find that Islamic religious obligations muddle an already flustering adolescence. Stringent Islamic practices, such as praying five times a day and fasting from dawn to sunset during Ramadan, can be burdensome for Muslims living in the United States. The United States is a generally secular society. Many Americans consider such overt and frequent religious displays to be oddities. Fasting during the month of Ramadan made Maha's gym class arduous, her clothing drew scorn from classmates, and her values led her to skip the prom. She explains about the prom: "At the time of the prom, I was sad, but just about everyone I knew had sex that night, which I think was immoral. Now, I like saying that I didn't go. I didn't go there just because it was a cool thing to do."

Mayada el-Zoghbi, a 24-year-old Egyptian who grew up spending time in Minnesota and Egypt, is now a graduate student at Columbia University. In keeping with Islamic tradition, Mayada fasts during Ramadan and abstains from alcohol. On the other hand, she prays "occasionally," not the traditional five times per day. Moreover, she goes out dancing and on dates—practices that are frowned upon by traditional Muslims. Dorm life, she notes, makes it difficult to pray as often as her family would expect her to pray. "Asking me why I don't feel comfortable praying in front of other people here in the United States is like asking me why I don't wear shorts in Cairo," she explains. "I just can't."

Reflections

Now that you have read the section on social influence, reflect on the following questions:

- Why do you think that the majority of participants in the Milgram studies obeyed orders? How would you describe the pressures acting on them?
- It has been shown that people who value being right more than being liked by others are less likely to conform to group pressure (Insko and others, 1985). Which is more important to you?
- Can you think of some instances in which you have conformed to social pressure? (Would you wear blue jeans if everyone else wore slacks or skirts?) Have the pressures placed on you by your own sociocultural group ever come into conflict with the values and customs of the United States at large? If so, how?

Group Behavior

To be human is to belong to groups. Groups help us satisfy the needs for affection, attention, and belonging (Robbins, 1989). They empower us to do things we could not manage by ourselves.

In this section, we look at a number of aspects of group behavior: social facilitation, group decision making, mob behavior, and the bystander effect.

SOCIAL FACILITATION: MONKEY SEE, MONKEY DO FASTER?

One effect of groups on individual behavior is **social facilitation,** or the effects on performance that result from the presence of others. Bicycle riders and runners tend to move more rapidly when they are members of a group. This effect is not limited to people. Dogs and cats eat more rapidly around others. Even roaches—yes, roaches—run more rapidly when other roaches are present (Zajonc, 1980).

According to Robert Zajonc (1980), the presence of others influences us by increasing our levels of arousal, or motivation. When our levels of arousal are highly increased, our performance of simple, dominant responses is facilitated. Our performance of complex, recently acquired responses may be impaired, however. For this reason, a well-rehearsed speech may be

Social Facilitation. Runners tend to move more rapidly when they are members of a group. Does the presence of others raise our levels of arousal or give rise to evaluation apprehension?

delivered more masterfully before a larger audience. An offhand speech or a question-and-answer session may be hampered by a large audience.

Social facilitation may be influenced by **evaluation apprehension** as well as level of arousal (Bray & Sugarman, 1980; Sanna & Shotland, 1990). Our performance before a group is affected not only by the presence of others, but also by concern that they are evaluating us. When giving a speech, we may "lose our thread" if we are distracted by the audience and focus too much on its apparent reaction to us (Seta, 1982). If we believe that we have begun to flounder, evaluation apprehension may skyrocket. As a result, our performance may falter further.

The presence of others can also impair performance—not when we are acting *before* a group, but when we are anonymous members *of* a group (Harkins, 1987; Shepperd, 1993). Workers, for example, may "goof off" or engage in "social loafing" on humdrum jobs when they believe they will not be found out and held accountable. There is then no evaluation apprehension. There may also be **diffusion of responsibility** in groups. Each person may feel less obligation to help because others are pres-

ent. Group members may also reduce their efforts if an apparently capable member makes no contribution but "rides free" on the efforts of others.

GROUP DECISION MAKING

In 1986 and 1987, President Ronald Reagan's popularity took a drubbing when it was alleged that he had authorized the sale of American weapons to Iran to try to gain the release of American hostages being held by pro-Iranian groups in Lebanon. This occurred at a time when the American public was very hostile toward Iran. Reagan had also sworn he would never negotiate with terrorists and had branded Iran a "terrorist nation." The decision to trade weapons for hostages apparently resulted from heated discussions in the White House during which the secretaries of state and defense took one position and the national security adviser took another position.

How do group decisions get made? Social psychologists have found a number of "rules," or **social decision schemes,** that govern much of group decision making (Davis and others, 1984; Kerr & MacCoun, 1985; Stasser and others, 1989). Note some examples:

Social facilitation • The process by which a person's performance is increased when other members of a group engage in similar behavior.

Evaluation apprehension • Concern that others are evaluating our behavior.

Diffusion of responsibility • The spreading or sharing of responsibility for a decision or behavior within a group.

Social decision schemes • Rules for predicting the final outcome of group decision making on the basis of the members' initial positions.

1. *The majority-wins scheme.* In this commonly used scheme, the group arrives at the decision that was initially supported by the majority. This scheme appears to guide decision making most often when there is no objectively correct decision. An example would be a decision about which car models to build when their popularity has not been tested in the court of public opinion.

2. *The truth-wins scheme.* In this scheme, as more information is provided and opinions are discussed, the group comes to recognize that one approach is objectively correct. For example, a group deciding whether to use SAT scores in admitting students to college would profit from information about whether these scores actually predict college success.

3. *The two-thirds majority scheme.* This scheme is frequently adopted by juries, who tend to convict defendants when two-thirds of the jury initially favors conviction.

4. *The first-shift rule.* In this scheme, the group tends to adopt the decision that reflects the first shift in opinion expressed by any group member. If a car-manufacturing group is equally divided on whether to produce a convertible, it may opt to do so after one group member initially opposed to the idea changes her mind. If a jury is deadlocked, the members may eventually follow the lead of the first juror to switch his position.

Now let us consider whether group members are likely to make compromise decisions or to take relatively extreme viewpoints as a result of diverse initial positions.

POLARIZATION AND THE RISKY SHIFT

We might think that a group decision would be more conservative than an individual decision. After all, shouldn't there be an effort to compromise, to "split the differences"? We might also expect that a few mature individuals would be able to balance the opinions of daredevils. Groups do not generally seem to work in these ways, however.

Consider the **polarization** effect. As an individual, you might recommend that your company risk $500,000 to develop or market a new product. Other company executives, polled individually, might risk similar amounts. If you were gathered for a group decision, however, you would probably recommend either an amount well above this figure or nothing at all (Burnstein, 1983). This group effect is called *polarization,* or the taking of an extreme position. If you had to gamble on which way the decision would go, however, you would do better to place your money on movement toward the higher sum—that is, to bet on a **risky shift.** Why?

One possibility is that a group member may reveal information the others had not been aware of. This information may clearly point in one direction or the other. With doubts removed, the group becomes polarized. It moves decisively in the appropriate direction. It may also be that social facilitation occurs in the group setting and that increased motivation prompts more extreme decisions.

Why, however, do groups tend to take greater, not smaller, risks than those that would be ventured by their members as individuals? One answer is diffusion of responsibility (Burnstein, 1983; Myers, 1983). If the venture flops, it will not be you alone to blame. Remember the self-serving bias: You can always say (and tell yourself) that the failure was, after all, a group decision. You thus protect your self-esteem (Larrick, 1993). If the venture pays off handsomely, on the other hand, you can attribute the outcome to your cool analysis and trumpet abroad your influential role in the group decision-making process.

Truth or Fiction Revisited. *It is not true that group decisions tend to represent conservative compromises of the opinions of the group members.* Group decisions tend to be riskier than the average decision that would be made by each group member acting as an individual—probably because of diffusion of responsibility.

GROUPTHINK

Groupthink is a problem that sometimes arises in group decision making (Janis, 1982). Group problem solving may

Polarization • In social psychology, taking an extreme position or attitude on an issue.

Risky shift • The tendency to make riskier decisions as a member of a group than as an individual acting independently.

Groupthink • A process in which group members are influenced by cohesiveness and a dynamic leader to ignore external realities as they make decisions.

degenerate into groupthink when a group senses an external threat. Groupthink is usually unrealistic and fueled by a dynamic group leader. The perception of external threat heightens group cohesiveness and serves as a source of stress. When under stress, group members tend not to consider all their options carefully (Keinan, 1987). Flawed decisions are therefore common.

Groupthink has been connected with fiascos such as President Kennedy's decision to support the Bay of Pigs invasion of Cuba, the Watergate affair, and NASA's decision to launch the *Challenger* space shuttle despite engineers' warnings that cold weather might endanger the launching (Aldag & Fuller, 1993). The Iran-Contra affair of the 1980s, which made Colonel Oliver North a household phrase, offers another example. Janis notes five characteristics of groupthink that play roles in such flawed group decisions:

1. *Feelings of invulnerability.* Each decision-making group might have believed that it was beyond the reach of critics or the law—in some cases, because the groups consisted of powerful individuals close to the president of the United States.

2. *Group belief in its rightness.* These groups apparently believed in the rightness of what they were doing. In some cases, the groups were carrying out the president's wishes. In the case of the *Challenger* launch, NASA had a track record of nearly unblemished success.

3. *The discrediting of information opposed to the group's decision.* At the time that Oliver North's group decided to divert funds from (secret) sales of arms to Iran to the Contras, it was illegal for the U.S. government to do so. The group apparently discredited the law by (1) deciding that it was inconsistent with the best interests of the United States and (2) enlisting private citizens to divert profits from sales to the Contras so that the U.S. government was not directly involved.

4. *Pressures on group members to conform.* Groupthink pressures group members to conform (McCauley, 1989).

5. *Stereotyping of members of the out-group.* Oliver North's group reportedly stereotyped persons who would oppose them as communist "sympathizers"; "knee-

An Angry Mob Is Contained by Police. Mob actions such as race riots and lynchings sometimes seem to operate on a psychology of their own. Do mobs elicit the beast in us? How is it that mild-mannered people commit mayhem as members of a mob?

jerk liberals"; and, in the case of the Congress that had made helping the Contras illegal, "slow-acting," "vacillating" (i.e., voting to aid the Contras in one bill and prohibiting aid to the Contras in another), and "irresolute."

The negative outcomes of groupthink can be averted when group leaders encourage group members to remain skeptical about options and to feel free to ask probing questions and disagree with other members.

MOB BEHAVIOR AND DEINDIVIDUATION

Gustave Le Bon (1960), the French social thinker, branded mobs and crowds irrational, like a "beast with many heads." Mob actions such as race riots and lynchings sometimes seem to operate on a psychology of their own. Do mobs elicit the beast in us? How is it that mild-mannered people commit mayhem as members of a mob? In seeking an answer, let us examine a lynching and the baiting type of crowd that often seems to attend threatened suicides.

The Lynching of Arthur Stevens. In their classic volume *Social Learning and Imitation,* Neal Miller and John Dollard

(1941) vividly described a southern lynching. Arthur Stevens, an African American, was accused of murdering his lover, a White woman, when she wanted to break up with him. Stevens was arrested and confessed to the crime. The sheriff feared violence and moved Stevens to a town 200 miles distant during the night. But his location was uncovered. The next day, a mob of a hundred persons stormed the jail and returned Stevens to the scene of the crime.

Outrage spread from person to person like a plague bacillus. Laborers, professionals, women, adolescents, and law-enforcement officers alike were infected. Stevens was tortured and murdered. His corpse was dragged through the streets. The mob then went on a rampage in town, chasing and assaulting other African Americans. The riot ended only when troops were sent in to restore law and order.

Deindividuation. When we act as individuals, fear of consequences and self-evaluation tend to prevent antisocial behavior. But as members of a mob, we may experience **deindividuation,** a state of reduced self-awareness and lowered concern for social evaluation (Mann and others, 1982). Many factors lead to deindividuation, including anonymity, diffusion of responsibility, arousal due to noise and crowding, and a focus on emerging group norms rather than one's own values (Diener, 1980). Under these circumstances, crowd members behave more aggressively than they would as individuals.

Police know that mob actions are best averted early by dispersing the small groups that may gather into a crowd. On an individual level, perhaps we can resist deindividuation by instructing ourselves to stop and think whenever we begin to feel highly aroused as group members. If we dissociate ourselves from such groups when they are forming, we shall be more likely to remain critical and avoid behavior that we shall later regret.

The Baiting Crowd in Cases of Threatened Suicide. As individuals, we often feel compassion when we observe people who are so distressed that they are considering suicide. Why is it, then, that when people who are considering suicide

threaten to jump from a ledge, the crowd often baits them, urging them on?

Such baiting occurred in 10 of 21 cases of threatened suicide studied by Mann (1981). Analysis of newspaper reports suggested a number of factors that might have prompted deindividuation among crowd members. They all contributed to anonymity: The crowds were large. It was dark (past 6 P.M.). The victim and the crowd were distant from one another (with the victim, for example, on a high floor). Baiting was also linked to high temperatures (the summer season) and lengthy episodes. Crowd members were thus likely to be tired and under stress.

ALTRUISM AND THE BYSTANDER EFFECT: SOME WATCH WHILE OTHERS DIE

The nation was shocked by the murder of 28-year-old Kitty Genovese in New York City. Murder was not unheard of in the Big Apple, but Kitty had screamed for help as her killer stalked her for more than half an hour and stabbed her in three separate attacks (Rosenthal, 1994). Thirty-eight neighbors heard the commotion. Twice their voices and their bedroom lights interrupted the assault. Each time the attacker returned. Still, nobody came to her aid. No one even called the police. Why? Some witnesses said matter-of-factly that they did not want to get involved. One said that he was tired. Still others said "I don't know." As a nation, are we a callous bunch who would rather watch than help when others are in trouble?

Truth or Fiction Revisited. *It is true that nearly 40 people stood by and did nothing while a woman was being stabbed to death. Their failure to come to her aid has been termed the* bystander effect. What factors determine whether we help others who are in trouble?

The Helper: Who Helps? Some theorists (e.g., Guisinger & Blatt, 1994; Rushton, 1989) suggest that **altruism** is a natural aspect of human nature. Self-sacrifice sometimes helps close relatives or others who are similar to us to survive. Ironically, self-sacrifice is selfish from a genetic or sociobiological point of view. It helps us perpetuate a

---

Deindividuation • The process by which group members may discontinue self-evaluation and adopt group norms and attitudes.

Altruism • Unselfish concern for the welfare of others.

MINILECTURE: KITTY GENOVESE

genetic code similar to our own. This view suggests that we are more likely to be altruistic with our relatives rather than strangers, however. The Kitty Genoveses of the world remain out of luck unless they are surrounded by kinfolk or friends.

Most psychologists focus on the roles of a helper's mood and personality traits. By and large, we are more likely to help others when we are in a good mood (Berkowitz, 1987; Manucia and others, 1984). Perhaps good moods impart a sense of personal power (Cunningham and others, 1990). We may help others when we are miserable ourselves, however, if our own problems work to increase our empathy or sensitivity to the plights of others (Thompson and others, 1980). People with a high need for approval may help others to earn social approval (Satow, 1975). People who are empathic, who can take the perspective of others, are also likely to help (Batson and others, 1989a).

There are many reasons why bystanders are reluctant to aid people in distress. First, bystanders may not fully understand what they are seeing and fail to recognize that an emergency exists. The more ambiguous the situation, that is, the less likely bystanders are to help (Shotland & Heinold, 1985). Perhaps some who heard Kitty Genovese's calls for help were not certain as to what was happening. (But remember that others admitted they did not want to get involved.) Second, bystanders who are not certain that they possess the competencies to take charge of the situation may stay on the sidelines for fear of making a social blunder and being subject to ridicule (Pantin & Carver, 1982). Or they may fear getting hurt themselves. (Perhaps some who heard Kitty Genovese thought, "If I try to intervene I may get killed or make an idiot of myself.") Bystanders who believe that others get what they deserve may rationalize not helping by thinking that a person would not be in trouble unless this outcome was just (Lerner and others, 1975). (Perhaps some who heard Kitty Genovese thought, "She probably wouldn't be under attack if she hadn't done something bad to the guy.")

A sense of personal responsibility increases the likelihood of helping. Such responsibility may stem from having made a verbal commitment to help (e.g., Moriarty, 1975) or from having been designated by others as being responsible for carrying out a helping chore (Maruyama and others, 1982). This, of course, is the central question: How can people be made to feel responsible for one another?

The Victim: Who Is Helped? Although gender roles have been changing, it is traditional for men to help women in our society. Women were more likely than men to receive help, especially from men, when they dropped coins in Atlanta (a southern city) than in Seattle or Columbus (northern cities) (Latané & Dabbs, 1975). The researchers suggest that traditional gender roles persevere more strongly in the South.

Women are also more likely than men to be helped when their cars have broken

Whom Do You Help? Psychologists have dressed the same person in different ways in experiments to determine how appearance influences our decisions to help others.

down on the highway or they are hitchhiking (Pomazal & Clore, 1973). There may be sexual overtones to some of this "altruism." Attractive and unaccompanied women are most likely to be helped by men (Benson and others, 1976; Snyder and others, 1974).

As in the research on interpersonal attraction, similarity also seems to promote helping behavior. Poorly dressed people are more likely to succeed in requests for a dime with poorly dressed strangers. Well-dressed people are more likely to get money from well-dressed strangers (Hensley, 1981).

Situational Determinants of Helping: "Am I the Only One Here?"

It may seem logical that a group of people would be more likely to have come to the aid of Kitty Genovese than a lone person. After all, a group could more effectively have overpowered her attacker. Research by Darley and Latané (1968) suggests that a lone person may have been more likely to try to help her, however.

In their classic experiment, male participants were performing meaningless tasks in cubicles when they heard a (convincing) recording of a person apparently having an epileptic seizure. When the men thought that four other persons were immediately available to help, only 31% made an effort to help the victim. When they thought that no one else was available, however, 85% of them tried to offer aid. As in other areas of group behavior, it seems that diffusion of responsibility inhibits helping behavior in groups or crowds. When we are in a group, we are often willing to let George (or Georgette) do it. When George isn't around, we are more willing to help others ourselves. (Perhaps some who heard Kitty Genovese thought, "Why should I get involved? Other people can hear her too.")

In most studies on the bystander effect, the bystanders are strangers (Latané & Nida, 1981). Research shows that bystanders who are acquainted with victims are more likely to respond to the social norm of helping others in need (Rutkowski and others,

1983). Aren't we also more likely to give to charity when asked directly by a coworker or supervisor in the socially exposed situation of the office as compared with a letter received in the privacy of our own homes?

We are more likely to help when we understand what is happening (for instance, if we clearly see that the woman whose car has broken down is alone), when the environment is familiar (when we are in our hometown rather than a strange city), and when we have the competencies. Registered nurses, for example, are more likely than people with no medical training to come to the aid of accident victims (Cramer and others, 1988).

Reflections

Now that you have read the section on group behavior, reflect on the following questions:

- Families, classes, religious groups, political parties, nations, circles of friends, bowling teams, sailing clubs, conversation groups, therapy groups—to how many groups do you belong? How does belonging to groups influence your behavior?

- Do you work harder or less hard than you would as an individual when you are given a group assignment? Why?

- Have you ever been a member of a committee or other group decision-making body? Did the group make the decisions democratically, or did a powerful leader emerge? Were the decisions made more or less conservative than the decisions you would probably have made on your own? Why?

- Have you ever done something as a member of a mob that you would not have done if you had been acting on your own? What? How did being a member of the mob influence you?

- Altruism and the bystander effect highlight the fact that we are members of a vast, interdependent social fabric. The next time you see a stranger who is in need of help, what will you do? Are you sure?

Summary

1. **What do social psychologists do?** Social psychologists study the factors that influence our thoughts, feelings, and behaviors in social situations.

2. **What are attitudes?** Attitudes are enduring mental representations of people, places, and things that elicit emotional reactions and influence behavior.

3. **What is the elaboration likelihood model for understanding persuasive messages?** According to this model, persuasion occurs through central and peripheral routes. Change occurs through the central route by means of consideration of arguments and evidence. Peripheral routes involve associating the objects of attitudes with positive or negative cues, such as attractive or unattractive communicators.

4. **What factors affect the persuasiveness of messages?** Repeated messages generally "sell" better than messages delivered once. People tend to show greater response to fear appeals than to purely factual presentations. This is especially so when the appeals offer concrete advice for avoiding negative outcomes. Persuasive communicators tend to show expertise, trustworthiness, attractiveness, or similarity to the audience.

5. **What is the foot-in-the-door technique?** In this technique, people are asked to accede to large requests after they have acceded to smaller requests.

6. **What is prejudice?** Prejudice is an attitude toward a group that includes negative evaluations, negative affect, and avoidance behavior or discrimination. Sources of prejudice include attitudinal dissimilarity (or the assumption that members of out-groups hold different attitudes), social conflict, social learning, authoritarianism, and the tendency to divide the social world into two categories: "us" and "them."

7. **What is the importance of first impressions?** First impressions can last (the primacy effect) because we tend to label or describe people in terms of the initial behavior we see.

8. **What is the attribution process?** Our inference of the motives and traits of others through the observation of their behavior is called the attribution process. In dispositional attributions, we attribute people's behavior to internal factors such as their personality traits and decisions. In situational attributions, we attribute people's behavior to their circumstances or external forces.

9. **What are some biases in the attribution process?** According to the actor–observer effect, we tend to attribute the behavior of others to internal, dispositional factors, whereas we tend to attribute our own behavior to external, situational factors. The so-called fundamental attribution error is the tendency to attribute too much of other people's behavior to dispositional factors.

10. **What can we infer from body language?** People who feel positively toward one another position themselves close together and touch. Gazing into another's eyes can be a sign of love, but a hard stare is an aversive challenge.

11. **What is interpersonal attraction?** In social psychology, attraction is an attitude of liking (positive attraction) or disliking (negative attraction).

12. **What factors contribute to attraction?** In our culture, slenderness is found to be attractive in both men and women, and tallness is valued in men. We are more attracted to good-looking people. We tend to assume that attractive people are more likely to be talented and less likely to engage in criminal behavior. Attitudinal similarity and reciprocity also enhance feelings of attraction.

13. **What is the matching hypothesis?** According to the matching hypothesis, we tend to seek dates and mates at our own level of attractiveness, largely because of fear of rejection.

14. **Will people obey authority figures who command them to engage in improper behavior?** Many or most people in the Milgram studies on obedience complied with the demands of authority figures even when these demands seemed immoral. Factors contributing to obedience include socialization, lack of social comparison, perception of legitimate authority figures, the foot-in-the-door technique, inaccessibility of values, and buffers between perpetrator and victim.

15. **What factors contribute to conformity?** Personal factors such as low self-esteem, high self-consciousness, and shyness contribute to conformity. Group size is also a factor.

16. **What is social facilitation?** Social facilitation refers to the effects on performance that result from the presence of others. The presence of others may facilitate performance for reasons such as increased arousal and evaluation apprehension. However, when we are anonymous group members, task performance may fall off. This phenomenon is termed social loafing.

17. **How do group decisions differ from individual decisions?** Group decisions tend to be more polarized and risky than individual decisions, largely because groups diffuse responsibility. Group decisions may be highly productive when group members are knowledgeable, there is an explicit procedure for arriving at decisions, and there is a process of give and take.

18. **How do groups make decisions?** Social psychologists have identified several decision-making schemes including the majority-wins scheme, the truth-wins scheme, the two-thirds majority scheme, and the first-shift rule.

19. **What is groupthink?** Groupthink is an unrealistic kind of decision making that is fueled by the perception of external threats to the group or to those the group wishes to protect. Groupthink is facilitated by feelings of invulnerability, group belief in its rightness, the discrediting of information opposed to the group's decision, pressures on group members to conform, and stereotyping of members of the outgroup.

20. **How do social psychologists explain mob behavior?** Highly emotional crowds may induce attitude-discrepant behavior through the process of deindividuation, which is a state of reduced self-awareness and lowered concern for social evaluation.

21. **What is the bystander effect?** According to the bystander effect, we are unlikely to aid others in distress when we are members of crowds. Crowds tend to diffuse responsibility.

Psychology and Modern Life

I have yet to hear a man ask for advice on how to combine marriage and a career.

GLORIA STEINEM

"Why Can't a Woman Be More Like a Man?" You may recognize this song title from the musical *My Fair Lady*. In the song, Henry Higgins laments that women are emotional and fickle, whereas men are logical and dependable.

In this chapter we explored the nature of stereotypes—fixed, conventional ideas about a group of people—and how they give rise to prejudice and discrimination. The excitable woman is a stereotype. The logical man is also a stereotype. Higgins's stereotypes reflect the gender polarization found in Western culture.

Stereotypes shape our expectations: We assume that all group members share the stereotypes we attribute to the group. Cultural expectations of men and women involve complex clusters of stereotypes, called *gender roles,* that define the ways in which men and women are expected to behave. In this section, we discuss the nature of gender polarization in Western culture and explore its costs.

Gender Polarization: Gender Stereotypes and Their Costs

Sandra Lipsitz Bem (1993) writes that three beliefs about women and men have prevailed throughout the history of Western culture and polarized our views of women and men:

1. that women and men have basically different psychological and sexual natures,

2. that men are the superior, dominant gender, and

3. that gender differences and male superiority are "natural."

What does "natural" mean? Throughout most of history, people viewed naturalness in terms of religion, or God's scheme of things (Bem, 1993). For the past century or

so, naturalness has been seen in biological, evolutionary terms—at least by most scientists.

What are perceived as the "natural" gender roles? In what Bem (1993) refers to as our "gender-polarizing society," people tend to see the feminine gender role as warm, emotional, dependent, gentle, helpful, mild, patient, submissive, and interested in the arts. The typical masculine gender role is perceived as independent, competitive, tough, protective, logical, and competent at business, math, and science. Women are typically expected to care for the kids and cook the meals.

U.S. gender polarization is connected with the traditional distribution of men into breadwinning roles and women into homemaking roles (Eagly & Steffen, 1984; Hoffman & Hurst, 1990). When the wife works, she is less likely to be perceived as stereotypically feminine—unless she works because of financial necessity and not because of choice. Despite the persistence of the stereotype that men put bread on the table, 6 of every 10 new U.S. jobs in the 1990s are being filled by women (National Institute of Occupational Safety and Health, 1990).

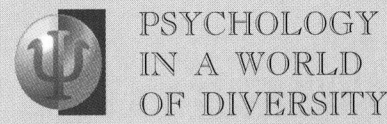

PSYCHOLOGY IN A WORLD OF DIVERSITY

MACHISMO/MARIANISMO STEREOTYPES AND HISPANIC CULTURE[7]

People who are unfamiliar with the diversity that exists among the peoples of Latin America tend to perceive all Hispanic Americans as part of a single culture. Although most of them do share some common cultural traditions, most notably the Spanish language and devotion to Christianity, each Latin American nation has its own cultural tradition, as well as distinct subcultures. The differences between the

---

[7] This guest feature was written by Rafael Art. Javier, PhD. Dr. Javier is associate clinical professor of psychology and director of the Center for Psychological Services and Clinical Studies at St. John's University in Jamaica, New York. Dr. Javier was born in the Dominican Republic and educated in philosophy in the Dominican Republic, Puerto Rico, and Venezuela, and in psychology and psychoanalysis at New York University. Dr. Javier is a practicing psychoanalyst and maintains a research interest in psycholinguistic research and psychotherapy with ethnic minorities.

peoples of Latin America can be seen in their dress styles, their use of language, and their music and literary traditions. Argentineans, for example, are more European in their dress and music. In the Dominican Republic and Puerto Rico, the influence of African and Native Carib Indian cultures blossoms forth in colorful dress and percussion instruments in music.

Machismo.

Machismo is a cultural stereotype that defines masculinity in terms of an idealized view of manliness. To be macho is to be strong, virile, and dominant. Each Hispanic culture puts its own particular cultural stamp on the meaning of machismo, however. In the Spanish-speaking cultures of the Caribbean and Central America, the macho code encourages men to restrain their feelings and maintain an emotional distance. In my travels in Argentina and some other Latin American countries, however, I have observed that men who are sensitive and emotionally expressive are not perceived as compromising their macho code. More research is needed into differences in cultural conceptions of machismo and other gender roles among various Hispanic groups.

Marianismo.

In counterpoint to the macho ideal among Hispanic peoples is the cultural idealization of femininity embodied in the concept of marianismo. The marianismo stereotype, which derives its name from the Virgin Mary, refers to the ideal of the virtuous woman as one who "suffers in silence," submerging her needs and desires to those of her husband and children. With the marianismo stereotype, the image of a woman's role as a martyr is raised to the level of a cultural ideal. According to this cultural stereotype, a woman is expected to demonstrate her love for her husband by waiting patiently at home and having dinner prepared for him at any time of day or night he happens to come home, to have his slippers ready for him, and so on. The feminine ideal is one of suffering in silence and being the provider of joy, even in the face of pain. Strongly influenced by the patriarchal Spanish tradition, the marianismo stereotype has historically been used to maintain women in a subordinate position in relation to men.

Acculturation: When Traditional Stereotypes Meet the Financial Realities of Life in the United States.

Acculturation—the merging of cultures that occurs when immigrant groups become assimilated into the mainstream culture—has challenged this traditional machismo/marianismo division of marital roles among Hispanic couples in the United States. I have seen in my own work treating Hispanic American couples in therapy that marriages are under increasing strain from the conflict between traditional and modern expectations about marital roles. Hispanic American women have been entering the workforce in increasing numbers, usually in domestic or child-care positions. Yet, they are still expected to assume responsibility for tending their own children, keeping the house, and serving their husbands' needs when they return home. In many cases, a reversal of traditional roles occurs in which the wife works and supports the family, while the husband remains at home because he is unable to find or maintain employment.

It is often the Hispanic American husband who has the greater difficulty accepting a more flexible distribution of roles within the marriage and giving up a rigid set of expectations tied to traditional machismo/marianismo gender expectations. Although some couples manage to reshape their expectations and marital roles in the face of changing conditions, many relationships buckle under the strain and end in divorce. While I do not expect either the machismo or marianismo stereotype to disappear entirely, I would not be surprised to find a greater flexibility in gender role expectations as a product of continued acculturation.

COSTS OF GENDER POLARIZATION

Gender polarization exacts costs in terms of education, activities, careers, psychological well-being, and interpersonal relationships.

Costs in Terms of Education.

Polarization has historically worked to the disadvantage of women. In past centuries, girls were considered to be unsuited to education. Even the great Swiss-French philosopher Jean-Jacques Rousseau, who was in the forefront of an open approach to education, believed that girls were basically irrational and naturally disposed to child rearing and homemaking tasks—certainly not to commerce, science, and industry.

In the United States today, boys and girls are looked upon as being about equal in overall learning ability. Girls are expected to excel in language arts, and boys, in math and science, however. Such expectations dissuade girls from taking advanced courses in the "male domain." Boys take more math courses in high school than girls do (AAUW, 1992), and math courses open doorways to occupations in the natural sciences, engineering, and economics, among many other fields. There are several reasons why American boys are more likely than American girls to feel at home with math (AAUW, 1992):

1. Fathers are more likely than mothers to help children with math homework.

2. Advanced math courses are more likely to be taught by men.

3. Teachers often show higher expectations for boys in math courses.

4. Teachers of math courses spend more time instructing and interacting with boys than girls.

Given these experiences, we should not be surprised that by junior high, boys view themselves as more competent in math than girls do, even when they receive identical grades (AAUW, 1992). Boys are more likely to have positive feelings about math. Girls are more liable to have math anxiety. It becomes increasingly hard to convince high school and college women to take math courses, even when they have superior ability. Even girls who excel in math and science are less likely than boys to choose careers in math and science (AAUW, 1992).

Reviews of the research (AAUW, 1992; Sadker & Sadker, 1994)) reveal that:

• Teachers pay more attention to boys than to girls.

• Girls continue to lag behind boys on achievement test scores in math and science.

• Girls are reporting an increased incidence of sexual harassment by boys.

• A number of standardized tests are biased against girls, which hurts their chances of being accepted into college and receiving scholarships.

• Textbooks still tend to ignore or stereotype women.

• Girls receive virtually no information about pressing concerns such as sexual discrimination, sexual abuse and harassment, and depression.

If women are to find their places in professions related to math, science, and engineering, we may need to provide more female role models in these professions. As we enter the new millennium, such models will help shatter the stereotype that these occupations are meant for men. We also need to encourage girls to take more courses in math and science. Experimental programs such as Operation Smart (for *Science, Math, and Relevant Technology*), run by Girls Inc., show that with a little encouragement, many female middle-schoolers overcome any anxieties they may have about math and science (Marriott, 1991).

Costs in Terms of Careers. Women are less likely than men to enter careers in math, science, and engineering. Although women are awarded more than half of the bachelor's degrees in the United States, they receive fewer than one third of the degrees in science and engineering. Moreover, women account for only 15% of the nation's scientists and engineers (Hafner, 1993). Why? It is partly because math, science, and engineering are perceived as being inconsistent with the feminine gender role. Many little girls are dissuaded from thinking about professions such as engineering and architecture because they are given dolls, not firetrucks and blocks, to play with (Marriott, 1991). Many boys are likewise deterred from entering child-care and nursing professions because others look askance at them when they reach for dolls.

Then there are the inequities in the workplace which are based on gender polarization. For example, women earn less than men for comparable work. Women are less likely than men to be promoted into responsible managerial positions (Kilborn, 1995; Rosenberg and others, 1993). Once in managerial positions, women often feel pressured to be "tougher" than men in order to seem as tough. They also feel pressured to pay more attention to their appearance than men do, because coworkers pay more attention to what they wear, how they crop their hair, and so forth. If they don't look crisp and tailored every day, others will think they are unable to exert the force to remain in command. If they dress up too much, however, they may be denounced as fashion plates rather than serious workers! Female managers who choose to be deliberate in decision making—and, consequently, to take some time—may stand accused of being "wishy-washy." What happens when female managers change their minds? They run the risk of being labeled fickle and indecisive, rather than flexible and willing to consider new information.

Women in the workplace are also often expected to engage in traditionally feminine tasks, such as making the coffee or cleaning up after the conference lunch, along with the jobs they were hired to do. Finally, women usually have the dual responsibility of being the major caretaker for the children in the home.

Costs in Psychological Well-Being and Interpersonal Relationships.

Polarization also interferes with our psychological well-being and our interpersonal relationships. Women who assume the traditional feminine gender role appear to have lower self-esteem than women who also show masculine traits (Flaherty & Dusek, 1980; Spence and others, 1975). They are also likely to believe that women are to be seen and not heard. They are

therefore unlikely to assert themselves by making their needs and wants known. As a consequence, they are likely to encounter frustration.

Men who accept the traditional masculine gender role are less likely to feel comfortable performing the activities involved in caring for children, such as bathing them, dressing them, and feeding them (Bem, 1993). Such men are less likely to ask for help—including medical help—when they need it (Rosenstock & Kirscht, 1979). They are also less likely to be sympathetic and tender or express feelings of love in their marital relationships (Coleman & Ganong, 1985).

Reflections

Now that you have read the section on gender polarization, reflect on the following questions:

- Do you think that there are some kinds of work that are women's work and others that are men's work? If so, what? Would you permit individual women and men to differ with you and to undertake work that you believe is meant for the other gender?
- Have you ever received special treatment from a teacher or from a school on the basis of your gender? What was it? How did you feel about it? How do you feel about it now?
- Gender polarization has compromised the quality of life for hundreds of millions of women and men. Have you been guilty of gender polarization? What will you do to eliminate the bane of gender polarization in the new millennium?

NOTES

17

Applied Psychology

Truth or Fiction?

_____ Efficient, skillful employees are evaluated more highly than hard-working employees who must struggle to get the job done.

_____ Psychologists help design computer keyboards and aircraft controls.

_____ TV commercials must be likable if they are to influence us to buy the advertised products.

_____ You can improve your athletic performance by imagining yourself making the right moves.

_____ Teachers who know more about a subject do a better job of teaching it.

_____ Most Americans believe that some women like to be talked into sex.

_____ Any healthy woman can successfully resist a rapist if she really wants to.

_____ Only gay males and substance abusers are at serious risk for contracting AIDS.

Outline

Truth or Fiction?
Industrial/Organizational Psychology
  Currents in Industrial/Organizational
    Psychology
  Recruitment and Placement
    Psychology in a World of Diversity:
      "But You're Not in Hong Kong":
      Asian Americans Fight a
      Stereotype through Assertiveness
      Training
  Training and Instruction
  Appraisal of Workers' Performance
    Psychology in a World of Diversity:
      Women Scientists Lagging in
      Industry Jobs
  Organizational Theory
    Psychology in the New Millennium:
      U.S. Corporations in the 21st
      Century: Will Psychology Prevent
      the Behemoths from Falling?
Human Factors
  Criteria for Evaluating Person–Machine
    Systems and Work Environments
  Criteria for Evaluating the Coding in
    Displays
Consumer Psychology
  Task Analysis of Consumer Behavior
  Marketing Research
Environmental Psychology
  Environmental Activism
  Noise: Of Muzak, Rock 'n' Roll, and
    Low-Flying Aircraft
  Temperature: Getting Hot under the
    Collar
  Of Aromas and Air Pollution: Facilitating,
    Fussing, and Fuming
  Crowding and Personal Space: "Don't
    Burst My Bubble, Please"
Community Psychology
  Levels of Prevention
    Psychology in a World of Diversity:
      "At the Heart of What
      Psychology Should Be Doing in
      the Community"
Forensic Psychology
  The Insanity Plea
Sports Psychology
  Task Analysis of Athletic Performances
  How Sports Psychologists Help Athletes
    Handle "Choking"
  Positive Visualization
  Peak Performance
Educational Psychology
  Teaching Practices
  Classroom Management
  Planning and Teaching
  Teaching Exceptional Students
  Tests and Grades
Summary
Psychology and Modern Life
  Primary Prevention of Rape
  Primary Prevention of AIDS

olumnist Russell Baker once wrote, "The goal of all inanimate objects is to resist man and ultimately to defeat him." He must know my stove personally. Each morning it tries to do me in. It has four burners, two in back and two in front, but the burner controls are lined up in a neat row. Unless I strain my eyes looking for the tiny "F" or "B" that shows which one governs which burner, I wind up minutes later with a pot of cold water and a red-eyed burner glaring wrathfully at me. Then I hop into my shower—the one with the single knob that is turned clockwise for hot (or is it cold?) and counterclockwise for cold (or is it hot?). Each morning I risk burning or freezing as I relearn which is which.

Next, I encounter my car, whose "smart sticks" are much smarter than I. I usually turn on the lights when it begins to rain and the windshield wipers to welcome the twilight. I know that if I turn one of them clockwise (or is it counterclockwise?), I get intermittent wiping, and if I turn it counterclockwise (or is it clockwise?), I get rapid wiping, but I'm not sure which. To gas up, I have to release the gas tank cover. Unfortunately, the control is out of sight on the floor to the side of the driver's seat, next to two others that feel just like it. So I'm as likely to pop open the hood or the trunk as the door to the gas tank. (The attendant always smiles.)

If I were not a psychologist, I would think that I'm just inept. But as a professional, I recognize all these problems as shortcomings in human-factors engineering. The field called human factors, or human factors in engineering, ensures that equipment and facilities are compatible with human behavior patterns and mental processes. That is, they are reasonably easy to work, or work in, and safe. But the machines surrounding me were either designed by sadists or left to chance.

Many industrial/organizational psychologists further specialize in human factors. Human-factors design is one example of **applied psychology.** There are many kinds of applied psychologists, but they all use psychological knowledge and methods to solve problems in the world outside the laboratory. They apply knowledge from psychology's basic areas—for example, biology and behavior, sensation and perception, learning, memory, motivation, and personality—to meet people's needs. Clinical psychologists are the largest subgroup of applied psychologists. Clinical psychologists apply psychological knowledge from areas such as biology, learning, motivation, and personality to the evaluation and treatment of psychological disorders. Counseling psychologists apply psychological knowledge to help people with academic, vocational, and adjustment problems. Health psychologists apply psychological knowledge to the prevention and treatment of illness (see Chapter 15). In this chapter, we explore a number of other areas of applied psychology including industrial/organizational psychology and the related fields of human factors and consumer psychology, environmental psychology, community psychology, forensic psychology, sports psychology, and educational psychology.

Industrial/Organizational Psychology

It has been said that the business of the United States is business. From broad questions concerning the economy to the details of our own workplaces, earning a living—and the way we feel about earning a living—are vital concerns.

Psychologists are involved in many issues that concern the workplace. **Industrial/organizational (I/O) psychologists** are employed by corporations and other groups to help in matters such as the following:

- Devising psychological tests for recruitment of people for industrial positions
- Interviewing individuals who are being recruited for industrial positions
- Measuring performance on the job
- Motivating workers to increase productivity
- Enhancing job satisfaction
- Helping organizations function more efficiently
- Identifying and modifying stressors in the workplace
- Making person–machine systems user friendly and efficient
- Studying and modifying the behavior of consumers

CURRENTS IN INDUSTRIAL/ ORGANIZATIONAL PSYCHOLOGY

I/O psychology is born of several movements and contains many currents (Landy, 1992). First is the testing movement, which focuses on the measurement of individual differences in personality and aptitudes. The assumption is that there are relationships among a person's intelligence, personality traits (for example, sociable or shy, domineering or self-abasing), and aptitudes (for example, mechanical or musical) on the one hand and the requirements of jobs on the other. People whose personal attributes fit the requirements of their jobs are better adjusted and more productive in their work.

Second is the human-relations (or human-potential) movement, as set forth by Carl Rogers and Abraham Maslow. Rogers argued that we possess unique talents and abilities. Ideally, the environment ought to encourage each of us to develop them (see Chapter 12).

Third is the industrial-engineering movement. This movement has sparked interest in efficient, user-friendly person–machine systems and has prompted psychologists to become involved in human factors.

Many I/O psychologists also apply the behavioral and cognitive perspectives. Behavioral principles have been used in industry, for example, to train workers in step-by-step fashion, to modify problem work behaviors, and to make sure that workers are rewarded for targeted behaviors. When required work behaviors are made explicit and the reinforcers (for example, raises, bonuses, promotions, and time off) for completing tasks are spelled out, morale rises and complaints about favoritism decrease. Companies as diverse as Chase Manhattan, Procter & Gamble, Ford, Standard Oil of Ohio, Emery Air Freight, General Electric, B. F. Goodrich, and Connecticut General Life Insurance have used behavior modification in some form.

The influences of cognitive psychology are being felt in issues ranging from biases in the appraisal of worker performance to the ways in which workers' information-processing capacities impact on the design of work environments (Landy, 1992). For example, supervisors tend to rate employees according to how much they like them. They also evaluate "hard workers" more positively than other workers, even if they accomplish less (Tsui & O'Reilly, 1989).

We shall consider some of the functions and findings of I/O psychologists in the areas of job recruitment, training, and evaluation.

RECRUITMENT AND PLACEMENT

People sometimes get hired for reasons that are irrelevant to potential to perform in the job. Now and then, people are hired because they are physically attractive (Mack & Rainey, 1990). On other occasions, nepotism reigns. Relatives or friends of friends get chosen. By and large, however, businesses seek employees who can do the job and are likely to be reasonably satisfied with it. Employees who are satisfied with their jobs have lower absenteeism and turnover (quit) rates. I/O psychologists facilitate recruitment procedures by analyzing jobs, specifying the skills and personal attributes that are needed in a position, and constructing tests and interview procedures to determine whether job candidates have these skills and attributes. These procedures

Applied psychology • The application of fundamental psychological methods and knowledge to the investigation and solution of human problems.

Industrial psychology • The field of psychology that studies the relationships between people and work.

Organizational psychology • The field of psychology that studies the structure and functions of organizations.

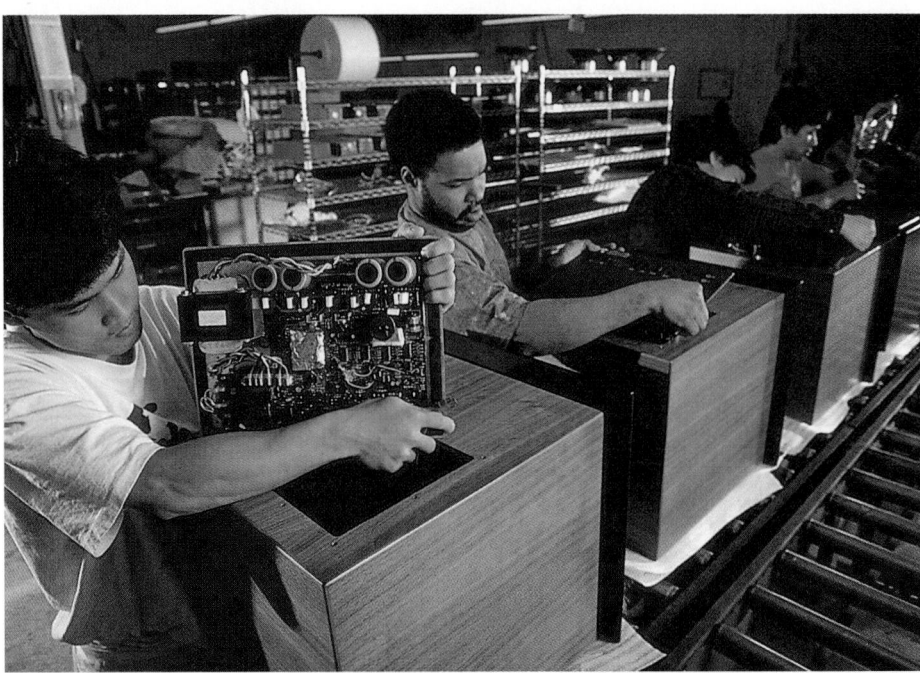

The Assembly Line. Although the assembly line is an integral part of contemporary industrial life, many workers sing the "assembly-line blues." Assembly-line workers may repeat one task hundreds of times a day and never see the finished product. Experimental work-redesign programs are helping many such workers—and their companies.

can enhance job satisfaction and productivity (Hunter & Schmidt, 1983; Katzell & Thompson, 1990).

Personnel Tests. Personnel tests most likely to be used by organizations include tests of (1) intellectual abilities, (2) spatial and mechanical abilities, (3) perceptual accuracy, (4) motor abilities, and (5) personality and interests. Test performances are correlated with specific job requirements. For this reason, many employers are more concerned about candidates' verbal and numerical abilities than their overall level of intellectual functioning, as might be measured by the Wechsler scales.

Tests of mechanical comprehension are appropriate for many factory workers, construction workers, and of course, mechanics. They include items such as indicating which of two pairs of shears would cut metal better. Spatial-relations ability is needed in any job that requires the ability to visualize objects in three dimensions. Examples include drafting, clothing design, and architecture. Tests of perceptual accuracy are useful for clerical positions, such as

bank tellers and secretaries. Some items on these tests require that respondents compare columns of letters, words, or numbers and indicate which do or do not match. Tests of motor abilities are useful for jobs that require strength, coordination, rapid reaction time, or dexterity. Moving furniture, driving certain kinds of equipment, and sewing all require some motor skills.

The relationships between personality and performance in a job are somewhat less clear. It seems logical that one might wish to hire a candidate for a sales position who has a strong need to persuade others. Many businesses have used personality tests to measure candidates' general "stability," however. Such use has sometimes been criticized as an invasion of privacy.

Interest Inventories. Psychologists have devised a number of interest inventories, such as the Strong/Campbell Interest Inventory and others, that predict adjustment in various occupations. Interest in an occupation does not guarantee ability to excel in that occupation, however. Fortunately, there are many types of jobs in a broad occupational area. Consider medicine. There are medical technicians (X-ray technicians, blood analysts, and so on), nurses, physical therapists, physicians, and many other specific occupations. Assessment of interests and aptitudes can help one zero in on a potentially fulfilling career.

PSYCHOLOGY IN A WORLD OF DIVERSITY

"BUT YOU'RE NOT IN HONG KONG": ASIAN AMERICANS FIGHT A STEREOTYPE THROUGH ASSERTIVENESS TRAINING

In his novel *Rising Sun,* Michael Crichton (1992) writes that Japanese corporate culture encourages consensus building. Individualism and face-to-face confrontation are common American approaches to arriving at corporate decisions. In the United States, many groups of Asian Americans, including Japanese Americans and Chinese Americans, also tend to be stereotyped as passive, soft-spoken, and unassertive—and consequently as poor managers and poor decision makers (Louie, 1993). A young Chinese American executive at a California high-tech firm complains that his efforts to build consensus are often criticized with statements such as, "Why can't you come out and make a decision?" (Louie, 1993).

In many Asian cultures, direct eye contact, expansive movements, and impassioned speech during a discussion are considered threatening (Crichton, 1992; Louie, 1993). Asians and many Asian Americans are thus socialized into less confrontational patterns of body language. Either way, many Asian Americans are stereotyped. Politeness is often misinterpreted as wimpiness. Yet because forceful behaviors run counter to the stereotype, many Asian Americans who are being dynamic and decisive in typical American fashion are branded as aggressive—just as dynamic, decisive women are often besmirched as masculine or bitchy.

Enter Assertiveness Training? Assertiveness training, which was popular during the Me Decade of the 1970s, is making something of a comeback among Asian Americans (Louie, 1993). Participants in assertiveness training workshops are taught both nonverbal and verbal assertive behaviors. Nonverbal assertiveness includes direct eye contact, sitting upright, and leaning toward the person one is addressing. Verbal exercises focus on expressing one's feelings, using the word "I" rather than being self-deprecating, making reasonable requests, saying no, and emphatic repetition of one's positions.

Training also focuses on the clashes between Asian and American cultures. Participants talk through their feelings about the place of Asian values such as desire for harmony, respect for authority, loyalty toward one's group or corporation, perseverance without complaint, and control of emotions in the American workplace.

A participant in one such workshop complained that none of this would be necessary if she had remained in Hong Kong. "But you're not in Hong Kong," replied the workshop leader (Louie, 1993), "so what are you going to do about that?"

Asian Americans Buck Stereotypes in the U.S. Business World. Many groups of Asian Americans, including Japanese Americans and Chinese Americans, tend to be stereotyped as passive, soft-spoken, and unassertive—and consequently as poor managers and decision makers in the business world. One of the causes of the stereotyping is that in many Asian cultures, direct eye contact, expansive movements, and impassioned speech—all of which are common enough in the United States—are considered to be threatening. Therefore, some Asian Americans are turning to assertiveness training to modify stereotypical behavior. Participants in assertiveness training are taught nonverbal and verbal assertive skills such as direct eye contact, leaning toward the person one is addressing, making reasonable requests, and emphatically repeating their positions.

TRAINING AND INSTRUCTION

I/O psychologists are versed in principles of learning, and worker training and instruction is the most commonly reported way of enhancing productivity (Katzell & Thompson, 1990). Training provides workers with appropriate skills. Equipping them to solve job problems also reduces the stress they will encounter and enhances their feelings of self-worth. More than 90% of American corporations train their workers (Goldstein & Buxton, 1982).

Training programs usually follow when managers identify a need for improved performance in a given job. A formal needs assessment has three components: (1) organizational analysis, (2) task analysis, and (3) person or worker analysis.

Organizational analysis is appraisal of the goals and resources of the corporation or other institution. Consider IBM. The goals of IBM include such varied items as selling computers, identifying future markets, and pure scientific development (advancement of the sciences for their own sake, although commercial opportunities are certainly acted upon). The resources of IBM include factory workers, managers, sales personnel, doctoral-level scientists, and so on.

Task analysis involves appraisal of the duties (breaking them down into subparts) of a person in a given job title. For example, a police officer is expected to carry out duties ranging from operating vehicles under varied weather conditions and transporting prisoners to chasing animals, counseling juveniles, giving street direc-

tions, controlling crowds, and using weapons. Person analysis deals with the question of who should be trained. Trainees can include persons already in a job and new recruits.

Learning objectives are usually established on the basis of the needs analysis. Learning objectives are designed to give employees the skills, the knowledge, and, sometimes, the attitudes they will need to perform well on the job. Why attitudes? A factory worker might resist wearing protective devices, even when taught how to do so, if he has the attitude that safety devices are for sissies. I have observed barehanded gardeners injuring themselves on thorns and barehanded construction clean-up workers injuring themselves on glass shards, nails, and so on all because of the self-defeating attitude that "real men" don't use protective gloves.

Once objectives are established, psychologists help devise ways to gain and maintain the workers' attention, to present materials in step-by-step fashion, to promote retention, and to evaluate the effectiveness of the training program.

APPRAISAL OF WORKERS' PERFORMANCE

Workers fare better and productivity is enhanced when workers receive individualized guidance and reinforcers are based on accurate appraisal of their performance. Criticism of workers' performance is necessary if workers are to improve, and it is important that criticisms be delivered constructively (Weisinger, 1990; see Table 17.1). Destructive criticism saps workers'

Organizational analysis • Evaluation of the goals and resources of an organization.

Task analysis • The breaking down of a job or behavior pattern into its component parts.

Halo effect • The tendency for one's general impression of a person to influence one's perception of aspects of, or performances by, that person.

TABLE 17.1

Criticism: The Good and the Bad

CONSTRUCTIVE	DESTRUCTIVE
Specific: The manager says exactly what the person is doing wrong, such as, "This is what I didn't like, and why."	**Vague:** Offers no specifics but makes blanket condemnation, such as, "That was a lousy job."
Supportive: Gives the sense that the criticism is meant to help the person do better.	**Blames the person:** Attributes the problem to personality or some other unchangeable trait.
Problem solving: Suggests a solution or offers to help find a way to improve things.	**Threatening:** Makes the person feel attacked, such as, "Next time, you're through."
Timely: Gives the message soon after the problem occurs.	**Pessimistic:** Offers no hope for change or suggestions for doing better.

Source: Goleman (1990).

motivation and belief in their own ability to perform adequately. Constructive criticism helps workers feel that they are being shown how to perform better (Baron, 1990).

Biases in the Appraisal Process. In an ideal world, appraisal of workers' performances would be based solely on how well they do their jobs. Managers do give the largest salary increments to workers whose objective performances are rated most positively (Alexander & Barrett, 1982), but research into appraisal of performance shows that biases are also at work. One bias is a tendency for supervisors to focus on the *worker* rather than the worker's performance. Raters may form general impressions of workers and then evaluate them on the basis of these impressions rather than on how well they carry out their tasks (Isen & Baron, 1990). A supervisor is more likely to positively appraise the performance of a subordinate who is also a friend (Fiske, 1993). Managers should therefore be evaluated by subordinates as well as by their superiors (Higan and others, 1994).

The tendency to rate workers according to general impressions (for example, of liking or disliking) is an example of the **halo effect.** The halo effect can be overcome by instructing raters to focus on how well workers perform specific tasks.

Behavioral I/O psychologists suggest that the criteria for appraisal be objective. They should be publicly observable behaviors that are outlined to workers and supervisors beforehand (Hedge & Kavanaugh, 1988). Workers are ideally rated according to whether they complete their tasks. Workers are not penalized for intangibles such as "poor attitude." Task analysis allows managers to create objective standards.

Another bias in appraisal is the tendency to evaluate workers according to how much effort they put into their work (Dugan, 1989; Knowlton & Mitchell, 1980).

Truth or Fiction Revisited. *It is not true that efficient, skillful employees are evaluated more highly than hard-working employees who must struggle to get the job done.* Supervisors often focus on employees' efforts, sometime more so than on their performance. Hard work is not necessarily good work, however. (Should students who work harder than you do be given higher grades on tests, even when you get the answers right and they make errors?)

We tend to overestimate the role of dispositional (internal) factors in our attributions for other people's behavior (see Chapter 16). This attribution error extends into the workplace (Mohrman and others, 1989). For example, U.S. workers have been criticized in recent years for flagging productivity. That is, as productivity in Japan and some other nations began to surpass our own, there was a tendency to assume that U.S. workers were lazy. More perceptive critics of the workplace have noted that situational factors such as the greater use of robots in foreign countries have contributed to the (apparent) lagging of U.S. workers.

 PSYCHOLOGY IN A WORLD OF DIVERSITY

WOMEN SCIENTISTS LAGGING IN INDUSTRY JOBS[1]

Women working as scientists and engineers are making little progress in breaking into industry, and a Federal research council says companies are largely to blame.

The National Research Council, an arm of the National Academy of Sciences, convened a conference a year ago to determine why women make up 45 percent of the work force but only 12 percent of the scientists and engineers working in industry. A report issued by a research council committee said that women must contend with sexist attitudes and unequal pay and that companies are doing little to help them juggle a career and family.

"I thought surely things were getting better, but when I saw the statistics I was amazed," said Dr. Betsy Ancker-Johnson, a retired vice president at GM and an

[1] Reprinted with permission from "Women Scientists Lagging in Industry Jobs," 1994, *The New York Times,* January 18, p. C5.

engineer who helped prepare the report. "The message is for companies to take advantage of the talent that's available," she said. "But also for women: don't forget you're going to work your tail off."

Women tend to choose careers in life sciences, behavioral sciences, and social sciences, fields in which industry plays a fairly small part, the report acknowledged. In 1989, 75 percent of science degrees awarded to women were in those fields, as against 46 percent for men.

But the research council said other factors were at work, including these:

- The median salary of female scientists with bachelor's degrees and up to two years of experience was 73 percent that of their male colleagues in 1990, $21,000 vs. $29,500. Those with doctorates made 88 percent of the median male salary, $35,500 vs. $40,400. Salary discrepancies also existed among women of different races.

- Female scientists are twice as likely as men to leave industry for academic or government work. They also quit twice as often as their female counterparts in government. The ratio remains the same regardless of whether the women are married or have children.

- Companies make it difficult for women to learn about job openings because scientific jobs are often filled through "good old boy" networks.

- Women are subjected to paternalism by a vanguard of older male scientists. One woman reported that a male oceanography professor had told her, "Women can only count plankton," not do in-depth research.

- Corporations do little to accommodate female scientists with children. The council recommended that companies offer quality day care and flexible work schedules so women could return to the laboratory quickly and not lose their edge by taking a long maternity leave.

"You can drop in and out of other careers, but if you're trying to be on the leading edge of science you just can't do that," Dr. Ancker-Johnson said. "An employee that is confident that the child is getting good care will be more productive."

The report advised companies to emulate programs started by six concerns: the Xerox Corporation, Alcoa, the Aerospace Corporation, AT&T Bell Laboratories, Scios Nova, and Barrios Technology. Among other things, they established scholarships and mentorships to recruit women, publicized job openings, equalized salaries, developed maternal leave policies, and held frequent meetings to gather feedback from female scientists.

At the biotechnology firm Scios Nova, the report noted, an African American woman who is a vice president is among the five highest-paid employees, and women earn the highest bonuses in its incentive program.

ORGANIZATIONAL THEORY

Organizations are composed of individuals, but they can have natures of their own. Organizations have formal characteristics such as chains of command, channels of communication, and policies concerning hiring, compensation, and retirement. They also have informal characteristics such as "personalities," which may be impersonal and cold, warm and family-like, authoritarian, or permissive (Schein, 1990).

The traits of individuals involve relatively stable ways of responding to the demands of life. The characteristics of organizations also form traits. They are consistent ways in which organizations respond to economic, political, and other challenges to organizational life. As with individuals, we speak of corporations as adapting or failing to adapt to environments, such as economic environments. We speak of them as growing and thriving or as being sick and dying or disintegrating.

Organizational adaptations may be required if businesses are to remain competitive. Many corporations heighten their competitiveness by stripping away layers of middle management and cutting costs, for example. We speak of them as becoming "leaner and meaner." Many formerly staid corporations have changed their personalities and acquired "lean and hungry" looks.

As with other areas of psychology, there are different theoretical approaches to structuring organizations. Three broad

Corporate Identity. Corporations, like people, can be thought of as having personalities or identities. The Transamerica "pyramid" in San Francisco was designed to help lend the corporation a jaunty, upward-looking appearance. The pyramid also dominates the San Francisco skyline, which may be suggestive of permanence and strength.

approaches are in sway today: *classic organization theories, contingency theories,* and *human-relations theories.* **Classic organization theories** propose that there is one best way to structure an organization—from the skeleton outward. Organization is based on the required levels of authority and supervision, that is. Classic organization theories frequently rely on a **bureaucracy,** which ideally frees workers from the injustices of favoritism and nepotism and enables them to make long-range plans. Other elements of classic organization theories include the division of labor and the delegation of authority.

Contingency theories hold that there are many valid ways to structure organizations and that organizational approaches are *contingent on* factors such as organizational goals, workers' characteristics, and the political or economic environment. A classic bureaucracy might make sense when timeliness and accuracy in production are central corporate objectives. When scientific innovation is the major goal, however, a less centralized, authoritarian organization might be more facilitative.

Human-relations theories begin structuring with the individual, the worker. They argue that the behavior of the organization cannot be predicted or controlled without considering the characteristics and needs of the worker. From this perspective, efficient organizational structure will reflect the cognitive processes of individuals as these processes are applied to problem solving, decision making, and the quests for self-expression and self-fulfillment. Let us consider three human-relations approaches: McGregor's Theory Y, Argyris's developmental theory, and Ouchi's Theory Z.

Human - Relations Approaches.

Douglas McGregor's (1960) **Theory Y** is based on the assumption that workers are motivated to assume responsibility and that worker apathy and misbehavior stem from shortcomings of the organization. Theory Y holds that management's central task is to structure the organization so that organizational goals will be congruent with workers' goals. Workers cannot be expected to be productive if their personal goals are at odds with those of the organization.

Classic organization theories • Theories that hold that organizations should be structured from the skeleton (governing body) outward.

Bureaucracy • An administrative system characterized by departments and subdivisions whose members frequently are given long tenure and inflexible work tasks.

Contingency theories • Theories that hold that organizational structure should depend on factors such as goals, workers' characteristics, and the overall economic or political environment.

Human-relations theories • Theories that hold that efficient organizations are structured according to the characteristics and needs of the individual worker.

Theory Y • McGregor's view that organizational goals should be congruent with workers' goals.

PSYCHOLOGY IN THE NEW MILLENNIUM

U.S. Corporations in the 21st Century: Will Psychology Prevent the Behemoths from Falling?

The bronze statue called the Colossus of Rhodes dominated the Mediterranean Sea in ancient times. In more recent years, U.S. corporations like IBM and GM dominated the financial world. The Colossus was struck down by an earthquake 60 years after it was erected. IBM, GM, and other U.S. corporate giants have been struck by financial earthquakes during their century of origin. Whereas all traces of the Colossus have disappeared, IBM, GM, and other corporations have suffered the fate of being downsized. That is, they have lost market share and thousands of employees have been let go.

What brought these colossi to their knees? Was it competition at home and abroad? Was it bad products? Bad planning? Bad management? Bad luck?

Bad planning and bad management are certainly two of the reasons. Many corporations have failed because of bad management, changes in market forces, and the changing nature of the workforce (Hogan and others, 1994). Psychologists can help by improving methods of selecting, training, and evaluating managers for sensitive positions (Hogan and others, 1994). As we reach the new millennium, only 15% of new workers will be White males, as compared with more than 40% during the 1980s. As the workforce becomes more diverse—including more minority and female employees—we should be increasing the numbers of minority group members and women in management (Hogan and others, 1994).

The chairperson of IBM notes that many companies, including IBM, have made the mistake of being complacent (Gerstner, 1994). They were content to continue to use outdated practices. They resisted change. Then market forces swept them away. How could this happen?

According to industrial/organizational psychologist Harry Levinson (1994), the reasons for the shortsightedness were basically psychological. The companies had faults that we find in individual people. For example, they were vain or conceited. Top-level managers bonded closely like family members. It thus became difficult for them to evaluate each other objectively. Many managers also failed to try to solve highly complex problems because it was easier to pretend that things were simple.

Levinson notes that each corporation also made the error of becoming "one big family." That is, too many people were promoted from within and they became too attached to one another.

Levinson suggests a number of psychologically based changes U.S. corporations can make to remain competitive in the new millennium:

- Corporate boards and top managers must become aware of the psychological problems that make their corporations inefficient and maladaptive.

- New managers should be brought in from outside the corporation so that their perspectives are not colored by the corporation's own views or by attachment to individuals within the corporation.

- Room should be made for "creatively abrasive" people in organizations. As noted by Thomas J. Watson, Jr., the founder of IBM, "I never hesitated to promote someone I didn't like. . . . I look for those sharp, scratchy, almost unpleasant guys who see and tell you about things as they really are. If you can get enough of them around you, and have patience enough to hear them out, there's no limit to where you can go" (Watson & Petre, 1990, p. 290).

So, where will U.S. organizations be in the new millennium? Will they again fall prey to keeping it "all in the family"? Or will they listen to industrial/organizational psychologists and look for some "sharp, scratchy" managers from the outside?

Will Psychology Prevent the Behemoths from Falling in the New Millennium? In recent decades, many once-great U.S. corporations have fallen—that is, lost market share and downsized. Industrial/organizational psychologists are finding ways to help by ending complacency and by improving methods of selecting, training, and evaluating managers for sensitive positions.

Chris Argyris (1972) notes a number of developmental principles and suggests that organizations are structured efficiently when they allow their workers to develop. Argyris notes that individuals develop

- from passive to active organisms,
- from dependent to independent organisms,
- from organisms capable of dealing with concrete issues to organisms capable of dealing with abstract issues, and
- from organisms with few abilities to organisms with many abilities.

Ouchi's (1981) **Theory Z** combines some of the positive features of the Japanese workplace with some of the realities of the U.S. workplace to foster company loyalty and heighten productivity. Perhaps the most salient feature of many Japanese workplaces is their paternalism. That is, they offer security through lifetime employment, involvement of workers' families in company activities, and the subsidizing of housing and education for workers' families. Many U.S. firms, in contrast, lay off workers with every economic downturn. Ouchi's theory compromises by suggesting that U.S. firms offer long-term employment when possible. Restructuring to avoid layoffs would enhance workers' loyalty.

There is traditionally a high division of labor and specialization in the U.S. workplace, leading to feelings of being pigeonholed and lack of a sense of control over the whole product. Japanese career paths tend to be relatively nonspecialized, allowing for sideways movement and variety. Again, a compromise of a moderately specialized career path is suggested. In the traditional U.S. workplace, decision making and responsibility are in the hands of relatively few supervisors. In Japan, decision making tends to be consensual—and responsibility collective. In Japan, moreover, managers often eat with laborers and share their bathrooms. The importing of the quality circle and the creation of other methods for enhancing employees' sense of participation in the decision-making process are also consistent with the compromises of Theory Z. Although the Japanese are highly competitive in the world marketplace, managers within given firms

tend to reach decisions by means of consensus, in contrast to the typical U.S. winner-take-all approach. Therefore, another Theory-Z Japanese import is a consensus management system in which managers tend to feel that "nobody has lost."

Psychologists are highly concerned with the dignity of the individual. They thus tend to gravitate toward organizational structures that allow for workers' self-development and self-satisfaction. In many cases, this leaning also heightens productivity.

Human Factors

I was griping about the ways in which displays are *coded*. The controls of my stove, shower, and car hassle me because they are arbitrary, inconvenient, and, to some degree, dangerous. To use the vernacular, they are "user *un*friendly." Psychologists in **human factors** apply knowledge of biology, sensation and perception, learning, memory, and motivation in enhancing the efficiency and safety of person–machine systems and work environments.

CRITERIA FOR EVALUATING PERSON–MACHINE SYSTEMS AND WORK ENVIRONMENTS

Psychologists have been involved in human factors since the 19th century. In 1898, APA president Hugo Munsterberg studied industrial safety. In evaluating the efficiency and safety of stoves and other kinds of equipment, human-factors psychologists use performance criteria, physiological criteria, subjective criteria, and accident-and-injury criteria.

Performance standards involve the quality of the performance made possible by the design. For example, how rapidly can the task (such as finding the proper water temperature in the shower!) be carried out? Can it be performed without making errors? (Am I likely to turn on the correct burner of the stove?)

Physiological standards involve the physical changes caused by operating the equipment. For example, are switches difficult to throw? Does working in a certain factory raise the blood pressure or damage the

Theory Z • Ouchi's view that adapts positive features of the Japanese workplace to the U.S. workplace.

Human factors • The field that studies the efficiency and safety of person–machine systems and work environments.

An Intimidating Display. Display panels of modern instruments can be overwhelming unless their coding is helpful. I/O psychologists attribute the following characteristics to good coding: detectability, discriminability, compatibility, meaningfulness, standardization, and multidimensionality.

lungs? Does the screen of the computer monitor cause eye strain? Does the keyboard contribute to carpal-tunnel syndrome?

Subjective criteria include psychological factors such as boredom and job satisfaction. For many people, assembly-line work is boring and nonsatisfying. There can be high absenteeism and turnover in such humdrum positions. Keyboards are more enjoyable to work when they make responsive clacks. Quiet keyboards are frustrating. Computer programmers also attempt to choose pleasing color combinations for the screen.

Designs also foster or prevent accidents and injuries. Are we at risk of burning our hands (or our houses down!) when we cannot readily find the control that governs the burner? Fortunately, I have not yet been injured in the shower, but making the water hotter when I think I am cooling it down could have dangerous consequences. How many times do we injure ourselves by using dangerous tools? Part of the problem may lie in failure to follow rules of safety. Tools are often not as safe in design as they could be, however.

CRITERIA FOR EVALUATING THE CODING IN DISPLAYS

I don't want you to think that I'm obsessed with my stove, so I'll talk about word processing for a minute. My current "enhanced" computer keyboard has nicely marked keys that say "Insert" and "Delete." With my previous (unenhanced) keyboard, I had to press a function key simultaneously with keys for regular letters. It wasn't too difficult, however, because the "D" key was used for deleting and the "S" key, which is next to it, was used for inserting. Think of the designer's quandary: Should the "S" or "I" key be used to insert material? The "I" key begins with the proper letter, but the "S" key sat next to the "D" key and in the section of the keyboard that housed all the codes. It worked out fine.

The "Men" and "Women" restroom signs are adequate for people who read English, and "Caballeros" and "Damas" are helpful for speakers of Spanish. But the universal nonverbal code is a stick figure of a man or woman. Here the code (the figure) is inherently related to the function of the design. That is, one door is meant for men to walk through, the other for women. Consider, however, an arbitrary but popular code: Decaffeinated coffee is often served from pots that are color-coded orange. If you think about it logically, perhaps decaffeinated coffee should be color-coded green or blue. Orange is a warm color (see Chapter 4), and oranges and reds are more likely than greens and blues to be used to signal danger or increases in intensity. Since caffeine is the "dangerous" substance, shouldn't caffeinated coffee be coded orange or red? Nevertheless, practice seems to defeat logic.

Good codes have the following characteristics:

- *Detectability.* Good codes are readily detected or sensed. I have difficulty detecting the gas tank cover release lever because it is out of sight (down along the side of my seat).

- *Discriminability.* Good codes can be discriminated from other symbols of the kind. My gas tank cover release switch is next to the hood and trunk releases, and the three are similar in design—not easy to tell apart.

- *Compatibility.* Good codes are consistent with our expectations. The stick figure of a man is compatible with our expectation that the room being coded is the "men's room." For reasons noted, the color orange is incompatible with *decaffeinated* coffee.

- *Meaningfulness.* When possible, good codes symbolize the information in question. The stick figure of the man symbolizes men. The "do not enter" symbol is a meaningful barrier. The meaning of orange as the symbol for decaffeinated coffee runs contrary to the color's "meaning," however.

- *Standardization.* When possible, the same code should be used universally. Consistency in usage could be the saving grace of using the color orange to signify decaffeinated coffee. Using green to mean go and red to mean stop is universal in traffic lights.

- *Multidimensionality.* Codes are made easier to recognize when they employ two or more dimensions. Traffic stop signs, for example, employ an octagonal shape and are red in color. A green stop sign would confuse drivers and create hazardous crossings. Red traffic lights are always on top: Top to bottom, they are arranged red, amber, green. You may not ever think about this array, but if you drove up to an intersection with a different grouping, it wouldn't feel right, and there might be accidents.

Psychologists who engage in human-factors design, like other psychologists, are empirically oriented. In addition to deriving design concepts from psychological theory, they try them out before implementing them. Consider, for example, the four designs in Figure 17.1. Which telegraphs itself as the best symbol for an elevator? As you can see from the numbers beneath the designs, the third was identified as the symbol for an elevator by 87% of the participants in one study (Mackett-Stout & Dewar, 1981). *None* correctly identified the symbol on the left. From this type of research, the more effective designs would be selected. If no code were correctly identified by the great majority of those queried, perhaps designers would return to the drawing board.

Figure 17.2 provides some other examples of good symbols. Part A of Figure 17.3 shows my problem with the electric stove: The burners are grouped in a square, but the controls form a line. In his book *The Psychology of Everyday Things,* psychologist Donald Norman (1988) agrees with me that if the controls were in a square pattern

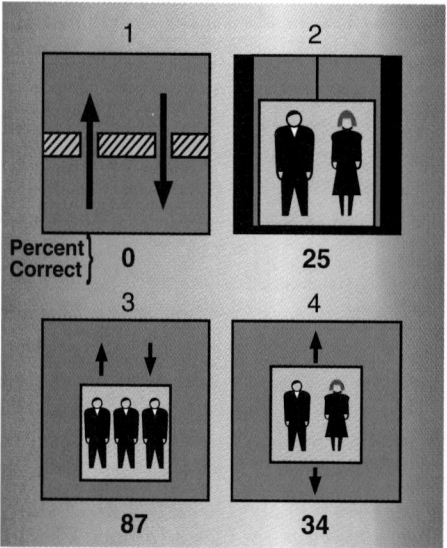

FIGURE 17.1
Elevator Symbols Psychologists in human factors evaluate symbols' effectiveness at communicating ideas. Which of these symbols best signifies an elevator to you?

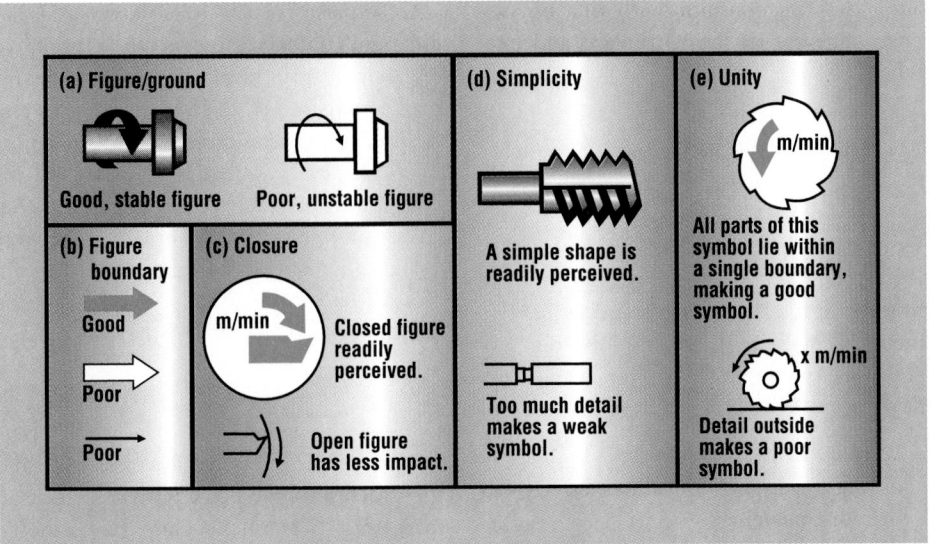

FIGURE 17.2
Visual-Code Symbols Psychologists in human factors apply knowledge of sensation and perception in the design of effective visual-code symbols.

that corresponded to the arrangement of the burners (see Part B of Figure 17.3), I wouldn't be heating the air and pouring ice-cold water over my poor wife's tea bags. Finally, note how the shape-coded cockpit

control knobs in Figure 17.4 discourage a pilot from accidentally activating the wrong mechanism.

Truth or Fiction Revisited. *It is true that psychologists help design computer keyboards and aircraft controls.* Design of such person–machine systems is an example of the field of human-factors engineering. Human-factors engineering can make our devices and machines safer and more user friendly. In a following section, we shall explore some of the ways in which environmental psychologists are learning more

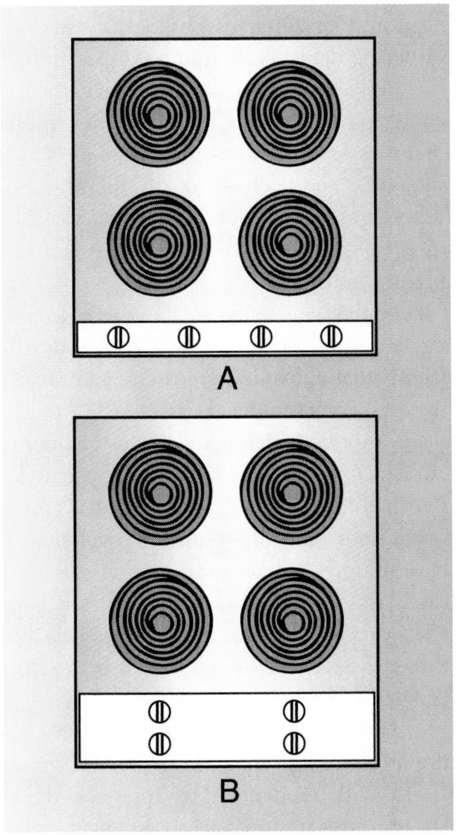

◀ **FIGURE 17.3**
Two Stove-Top Configurations Well-designed regulation systems are readily interpreted by users (are "user friendly"). Which control regulates which burner? Is it easier to determine which regulates which in stove-top A or stove-top B?

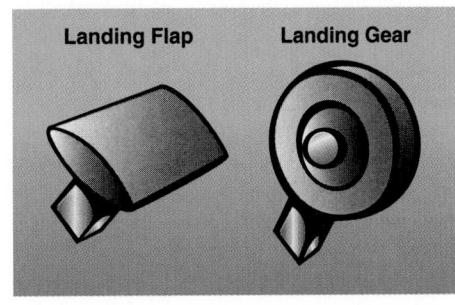

FIGURE 17.4
Shape-Coded Control Knobs How does the shape of each airplane control knob help signal its function?

about our relationships with our physical environment—in the workplace and elsewhere.

Consumer Psychology

Consumer psychology applies psychological methods to the investigation and modification of consumer behavior and mental processes. We encounter topics of concern to consumer psychologists every day. Here is just a brief list:

- Why are consumers loyal to a brand? For example, why do consumers buy Miller beer or Budweiser?

- What characteristics do consumers attribute to various brands? For example, what are consumers' impressions of American cars versus Japanese cars?

- How can consumer attitudes toward products be modified? How can brand images be enhanced? For example, how can consumers be persuaded that the reliability of American cars and electronic devices is improving? Why did Pepsico hire Ray Charles to endorse Diet Pepsi?

- What is the best way to market a new product? Should there be a national advertising blitz, or should the product first be tested in a local market?

TASK ANALYSIS
OF CONSUMER BEHAVIOR

Consumer psychologists have undertaken task analyses of consumer behavior and found that it often involves a number of steps: deciding to make a purchase, selecting the brand, shopping, buying the product, and evaluating how well it meets one's needs (Robertson and others, 1984). Consumer psychologists study ways of intervening at each stage to enhance the probability that consumers will decide to make a purchase and choose a certain brand. Advertising is used not only to help consumers tell brands apart but also to encourage them to buy. Packaging similarly helps consumers distinguish between brands. If the packages are "pretty" enough, consumers may assume that "good things" come in them. First impressions count in the supermarket as well as in interpersonal relationships.

An experiment by Julie Baker and her colleagues (1992) provides an example of research into consumer behavior. The researchers recruited 147 undergraduates and exposed them to a combination of atmospheric factors (music and lighting) and social factors (such as the friendliness of employees) in a store. These factors were found to enhance the students' pleasure and arousal, and consequently to increase the likelihood that they would make purchases.

MARKETING RESEARCH

Consumer psychologists, like other psychologists, are empirically oriented, and their methods have had a powerful effect on marketing personnel. They have shown marketing managers how to test hypotheses concerning the effectiveness of advertising, marketing, and so on through marketing research. In this method, a consumer population is targeted—for example, yuppies, baby boomers, or teenagers. Representative samples are then drawn from the target population. Their responses to product names, ads, packages, and the products themselves are measured. So-called taste tests of soft drinks apply methods used by psychologists who study sensation and perception. Consumer psychologists find ways of having drinkers indicate their preferences for the flavors of various beverages. Participants may simply report that they prefer brand A over the notorious brand X. Or they may rate each drink on, for example, scales from 1 to 10 according to variables such as sweetness, stimulation, general liking, and so on.

In applying principles of social psychology, consumer psychologists also study the factors that enhance advertisements' persuasiveness. For example, does sex sell? Are cars made more appealing to viewers when an attractive woman drives them or yearns for the male driver? And what about all those sexy jeans ads? Consumer psychologists have found that although some ads may catch the eye, such as the photo on page 671, you may remember the models but forget the product when the ad is too sexy (Edgley, 1989; Severn, 1990).

Social psychologists have found that an attitude of liking—toward people—is associated with tendencies to approach them. Do attitudes toward advertisements transfer

Consumer psychology • The field of psychology that studies the nature, causes, and modification of consumer behavior and mental processes.

An Enticing Advertisement. Ads such as this certainly gain readers' attention. The question is whether readers remember the product and when to use it or whether the ad actually distracts readers from this information.

into approach or avoidance tendencies toward the products, however? Not necessarily. Consumer psychologists have found that it doesn't matter whether a commercial is likable or irritating. What is important is that the viewer can remember the product and when to use it (Baron & Byrne, 1991).

Truth or Fiction Revisited. *It is not true that TV commercials must be likable if they are to influence us to buy the advertised products.* It is sufficient that commercials prompt the viewer to remember the product and when to use it.

Reflections

Now that you have read the sections on industrial/organizational psychology, human factors, and consumer psychology, reflect on the following questions:

- Agree or disagree with the following statement and support your answer: "Corporations and individual workers are natural adversaries. What is better for one is worse for the other."
- What is the halo effect? Can you offer examples of how the halo effect applies to your relationships with friends and family members?

- Consider a place in which you or a family member has worked. What was the organizational structure like? What was the effect of the structure on workers?
- Let's consider some human factors together. Flip through the pages of the book now in your hands. Is it easy to find the features of the book (for example, key terms, "Psychology in a World of Diversity" features, where one topic leaves off and another begins)? What "codes" were used to signal these features? Have you found the book to be user friendly? If so, in what ways?
- The text claims that ads need not be likable to be effective. Can you think of an ad or an ad campaign that you dislike but which encouraged you to check out a product?

Environmental Psychology

What do you picture when you hear the phrase "the environment"? Is it vast tracts of wilderness? Is it deep, rolling oceans? Or do you picture shore birds draped in oil as a

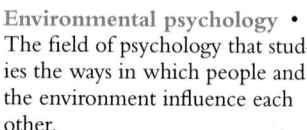

Environmental psychology •
The field of psychology that studies the ways in which people and the environment influence each other.

What Is Our Impact on Planet Earth? As these photographs of the Exxon Valdez oil spill (top) and the setting afire of the oil wells of Kuwait (bottom) suggest, people's impact on planet Earth has been less than benevolent. Environmental psychologists study the ways in which people and the physical environment influence each other. One concern of environmental psychologists is finding ways to persuade people to change their environmental behavior.

result of an oil spill? Do you think of billowing summer storm clouds and refreshing rain, or do you conjure up visions of fire-blackened clouds and acid rain? All this—the beauty and the horror—is the province of environmental psychology.

Environmental psychologists study the ways in which people and the physical en-

vironment influence each other. As people, we have needs that must be met if we are to remain physically and psychologically healthy. Environmental conditions such as temperature and population density affect our capacities to meet these needs. People also affect the environment. We have pushed back forests and driven many species to extinction. In recent years, our impact has mushroomed. So have the controversies over the greenhouse effect, the diminution of the ozone layer, and acid rain. Many of us have an aesthetic interest in the environment and appreciate the remaining bastions of wilderness. Protecting the environment also ultimately means protecting ourselves, however—for it is in the environment that we flourish or fade away.

In this section, we touch on environmental activism. We then consider some findings of environmental psychologists concerning the effects of atmospheric conditions, noise, heat, and crowding.

ENVIRONMENTAL ACTIVISM

Since people cause much environmental damage, environmental psychologists try to find ways to persuade people to change their environmental behavior (Stokols, 1992). Most people consider themselves pro-environment. Many think of themselves as "environmentalists." People may not put their behaviors where their mouths are, however (Hamilton, 1985). Many people are unaware of the individual impact they have on the environment—for example, how much electricity, natural gas, and water they consume (Kushler, 1989). Research has shown that when people obtain accurate information as to the resources they use—and squander—they are more likely to modify their behavior. When homeowners begin to read their meters and check for drafts, they become more likely to weatherize their homes (Aronson, 1990).

Research into cognitive-dissonance theory has shown that we may change our attitudes when we are compelled to change our behavior. People who must conform to antidiscrimination laws may become less prejudiced. People may similarly grumble when "bottle bills" are passed—laws that require them to pay high deposits on bottled beverages and return the used bottles to regain their money. As time passes, however, their behavior tends to conform and their attitudes tend to grow positive (Kahle & Beatty, 1987). Similar patterns are found when communities legislate the recycling of aluminum cans, newspapers, and bottles.

NOISE: OF MUZAK, ROCK 'N' ROLL, AND LOW-FLYING AIRCRAFT

Environmental psychologists apply knowledge of sensation and perception to design environments that induce positive emotional responses and contribute to human performance. They may thus suggest soundproofing certain environments or using pleasant background sounds such as music or recordings of water in natural environments (rain, the beach, brooks, and so on). Noise can be aversive, however—especially loud noise. How do you react when chalk is scraped on the blackboard or when an airplane screeches low overhead?

Office Design. Environmental psychologists study the ways in which aspects of the physical environment influence behavior, including work behavior. Thus they consider issues such as colors for office walls, what kinds of music facilitate work, and so on.

At the Disco. Couples may enjoy high noise levels (up to 140 dB) at the discotheque. Less desirable noises of only 80 dB, however, can decrease feelings of attraction, put a damper on helping behavior, and contribute to aggressive behavior.

The decibel (dB) is used to express the loudness of noise. The hearing threshold is defined as zero dB. Your school library is probably about 30 to 40 dB. A freeway is about 70 dB. One hundred forty dB is painfully loud, and 150 dB can rupture your eardrums. After 8 hours of exposure to 110 to 120 dB, your hearing may be damaged (rock groups play at this level). High noise levels are stressful and can lead to illnesses such as hypertension, neurological and intestinal disorders, and ulcers (Cohen and others, 1986, Topf, 1989).

High noise levels also impair daily functioning. They foster forgetfulness, perceptual errors, even dropping things (Smith & Stansfield, 1986). Children who are exposed to greater traffic noise on the lower floors of apartment complexes or to loud noise from low-flying airplanes at their schools may encounter stress, hearing loss, and impairments in learning and memory. Time to adjust and subsequent noise abatement do not seem to reverse their cognitive and perceptual deficits (Cohen and others, 1986).

Couples may enjoy high noise levels at the disco, but grating noises of 80 dB seem to decrease feelings of attraction. They cause couples to stand farther apart. Loud noise also dampens helping behavior. People are less likely to help pick up a dropped

package when the background noise of a construction crew is at 92 dB than when it's at 72 dB (Page, 1977). They're even less willing to make change for a quarter.

If you and your date have had a fight and are then exposed to a sudden tire blowout, look out. Angered people are more likely to behave aggressively when exposed to a sudden noise of 95 dB than one of 55 dB (Donnerstein & Wilson, 1976).

TEMPERATURE: GETTING HOT UNDER THE COLLAR

Environmental psychologists also study the ways in which temperature can facilitate or impair behavior and mental processes. When a car's engine is too hot, there may be great demands on the circulatory system. The water may overheat and the radiator may pop its cap. Extremes of heat can also make excessive demands on our bodies' circulatory systems, leading to dehydration, heat exhaustion, heat stroke, even a heart attack.

When it is too cold, the body responds by attempting to generate and retain heat. The metabolism increases. We shiver. Blood vessels in the skin constrict, decreasing flow of blood to the periphery of the body, where its warmth can be transmitted more easily to the outside.

Despite their obvious differences, both hot and cold temperatures are aversive events with some similar consequences, the first of which is increased arousal. A number of studies suggest that moderate shifts in temperature are mildly arousing. They may thus facilitate learning and performance, increase feelings of attraction, and have other positive effects. Extreme temperatures cause performance and activity levels to deteriorate, however.

Environmental psychologists, applying knowledge concerning the psychology of motivation, point out that small changes in arousal tend to get our attention, motivate us to perform, and facilitate the performance of tasks. Great increments in arousal, as can result from major deviations from ideal temperatures, are aversive and hinder the performance of complex tasks. We try to cope with uncomfortable temperatures through clothing, air conditioning, or traveling to more amenable climes. Extreme temperatures can sap our ability to cope, however.

Heat apparently makes some people hot under the collar. That is, high temperatures are connected with aggression. The frequency of car honking at traffic lights in Phoenix increases with the temperature (Kenrick & MacFarlane, 1986). In Houston, murders and rapes are most likely to occur when the temperature is in the 90s Fahrenheit (Anderson & DeNeve, 1992). In Raleigh, North Carolina, the incidence of rape and aggravated assault escalates with the average monthly temperature (Cohn, 1990; Simpson & Perry, 1990).

Some psychologists (e.g., Anderson & DeNeve, 1992) suggest that the probability of aggressive behavior continues to increase as the temperature soars. Other psychologists (e.g., Bell, 1992) argue that once temperatures become extremely aversive, people tend to avoid aggressive behavior so that they will not be doubly struck by hot temper and hot temperature. The evidence does not absolutely support either view. Thus, the issue remains, well, heated.

OF AROMAS AND AIR POLLUTION: FACILITATING, FUSSING, AND FUMING

Environmental psychologists also investigate the effects of odors ranging from perfumes to auto fumes, industrial smog, cigarette smoke, fireplaces, even burning leaves. For example, the lead in auto fumes may impair children's intellectual functioning in the same way that eating lead-based paint does.

Carbon monoxide, a colorless, odorless gas found in cigarette smoke and auto fumes, decreases the capacity of the blood to carry oxygen. Carbon monoxide impairs learning ability and perception of the passage of time. It may also contribute to highway accidents. Residents of Los Angeles, New York, and various other major cities are accustomed to warnings to remain indoors or to be inactive in order to reduce air consumption when atmospheric inversions allow smog to accumulate. In December 1952, atmospheric conditions in London caused high amounts of smog to collect, leading to an estimated 4,000 excess deaths (Schenker, 1993). High levels of air pollution have also been connected with the

mortality rate in U.S. cities (Dockery and others, 1993).

People tend to become psychologically accustomed to air pollution. For example, newcomers to polluted regions such as Southern California are more concerned about the air quality than long-term residents (Evans and others, 1982). Acceptance of pollution backfires when long-term illnesses result.

Unpleasant-smelling pollutants, like other forms of aversive stimulation, decrease feelings of attraction and heighten aggression (Baron & Byrne, 1991).

CROWDING AND PERSONAL SPACE: "DON'T BURST MY BUBBLE, PLEASE"

Psychologists distinguish between "density" and "crowding." *Density* refers to the number of people in an area. *Crowding* suggests an aversive high-density social situation.

All instances of density are not equal. Whether we feel crowded depends on who is thrown in with us and our interpretation of the situation. Environmental psychologists apply principles of information processing and social psychology to explain why.

A fascinating experiment illustrates the importance of cognitive factors—in this case, attributions for arousal—in transforming high density into crowding. Worchel and Brown (1984) showed small groups of people films when the people were spaced comfortably apart or uncomfortably close. There were four different films. Three were arousing (either humorous, sexual, or violent), and one was unarousing.

As shown in Figure 17.5, viewers who sat more closely together generally felt more crowded than those seated farther apart. Note that those who were seated at appropriate distances from one another uniformly rated the seating arrangements as uncrowded. Among those who were seated inappropriately close, viewers of the unarousing film felt most crowded. Viewers of the arousing films felt less crowded. Why? The researchers suggest that viewers who were packed in could attribute their arousal to the content of the films. Viewers of the unarousing film could not. Thus, they were likely to attribute their arousal to the seating arrangements.

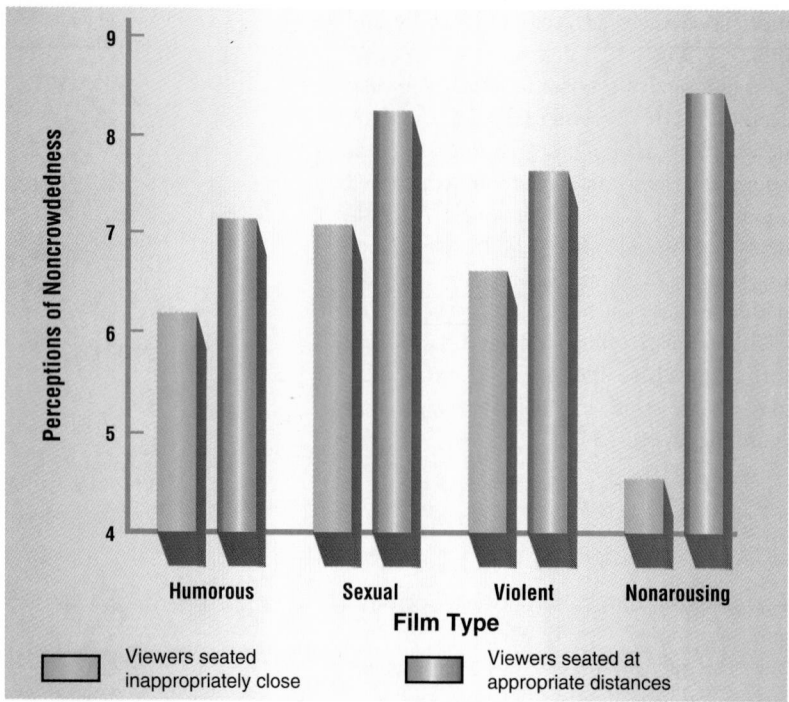

FIGURE 17.5
Type of Film and Appraisal of High-Density Seating In a study by Worchel and Brown (1984), viewers seated inappropriately close or at appropriate distances watched four kinds of films. Of the individuals seated too closely, those who could attribute their arousal to the film were less likely to experience crowding than those who could not.

Psychological Moderators of the Impact of High Density. A sense of control enhances psychological hardiness (see Chapter 15). Examples from everyday life suggest that a sense of control—of choice—over the situation also helps us cope with the stress of being packed in. When we are at a concert, a disco, or a sports event, we may encounter higher density than we do in those frustrating ticket lines. But we may be having a wonderful time. Why? We have *chosen* to be at the concert and are focusing on our good time (unless a tall or noisy person sits in front of us). We feel in control.

We tend to moderate the effects of high density in subway cars and other mass-transportation vehicles by ignoring fellow passengers and daydreaming, by reading newspapers and books, and by finding humor in the situation. Some of us catch a snooze and wake up in time for our stops.

Some Effects of City Life. Big city dwellers are more likely to experience stim-ulus overload and fear crime than suburbanites and rural folk. Overwhelming crowd stimulation, bright lights, shop windows, and so on cause them to narrow their perceptions to a particular face, destination, or job. The pace of life literally picks up—pedestrians walk faster in bigger cities (Sadalla and others, 1990).

City dwellers are less willing to shake hands with, make eye contact with, or help strangers (Milgram, 1977; Newman & McCauley, 1977). People who move to the city from more rural areas adjust by becoming more deliberate in their daily activities. They plan ahead to take safety precautions, and they increase their alertness to potential dangers.

Farming, anyone?

Personal Space. One adverse effect of crowding is the invasion of **personal space.** Personal space is an invisible boundary, sort of a bubble, that surrounds you. You are likely to become anxious and, perhaps, angry when others invade your space. This may happen when someone sits down across from or next to you in an otherwise empty cafeteria or stands too close in an elevator. Personal space appears to serve protective and communicative functions.

People sit and stand closer to people of the same race, similar age, or similar socio-economic status. Dating couples come closer together as the attraction between them increases.

North Americans and northern Europeans apparently distance themselves from others more so than southern Europeans, Asians, and Middle Easterners do (Baron & Byrne, 1991). A study by Pagan and Aiello (1982) suggests the contribution of cultural experiences. Puerto Ricans tend to interact more closely than Americans of northern European extraction. Pagan and Aiello found that Puerto Ricans reared in New York City required more personal space when interacting with others of the same gender than did Puerto Ricans reared in Puerto Rico.

People in some cultures apparently learn to cope with high density and also share their ways of coping with others (Gillis and others, 1986). Asians in crowded cities such as Tokyo and Hong Kong interact more harmoniously than North Americans and

Britishers, who dwell in less dense cities. The Japanese are used to being packed sardinelike into subway cars by white-gloved pushers employed by the transit system. Imagine the rebellion that would occur at such treatment in American subways! It has been suggested that Asians are accustomed to adapting to the environment, whereas Westerners are more prone to try to change the environment.

Southern Europeans apparently occupy a middle ground between Asians, on the one hand, and northern Europeans on the other. They are more outgoing and comfortable with interpersonal propinquity than northern Europeans but not as tolerant of crowding as Asians.

Reflections

Now that you have read the section on environmental psychology, reflect on the following questions:

- As you read this book, crises loom concerning the disposal of toxic wastes, industrial and vehicular emissions and safety, population growth, devastation of the rain forest, pollution, and a host of other environmental issues (Geller, 1990; Stokols, 1992). You dwell on planet Earth. This is your home. What can you do to become informed? What can you do to encourage people to modify their environmental behavior?
- How do loud noises and extremes of temperature affect your behavior? Can you think of some examples?
- Agree or disagree with the following statement and support your answer: "Crowding people together is aversive."

Community Psychology

Clinical psychologists treat psychological disorders. **Community psychologists** use knowledge of biology, learning, motivation, and personality to prevent them. Community mental health centers (CMHCs) deal with psychological problems in the community rather than in the hospital. Hospitalization has not been shown to be of help

with many people who have psychological disorders. Moreover, removal of the individual from the community can sever ties to social realities and obligations. As a result, disorders are sometimes intensified rather than alleviated. Some functions of the CMHC were designed to maintain people with disorders in the community. Partial hospitalization allows them to sleep in a community hospital and work outside during the day. Through community consultation and education, disorders may be averted or identified during their formative stages.

LEVELS OF PREVENTION

Prevention takes place at three levels: primary, secondary, and tertiary. **Primary prevention** aims to deter problems before they start. There is not much community psychologists can do about genetic predispositions toward psychological disorders. However, genetic predispositions tend to interact with psychological and social factors to spawn disorders. These factors include unemployment, lack of education, drug abuse, teenage pregnancy, marital conflict, and substandard housing. By consulting with community leaders, agencies and institutions, and lawmakers, community psychologists try to change stressful conditions that contribute to psychological disorders (Edgerton, 1994). Community psychologists apply knowledge of developmental psychology, psychological disorders, and social psychology when they consult with groups such as Big Brothers and Boys' Clubs to help avert delinquency among high-risk youth. Yoshikawa (1994) has shown, for example, that a combination of comprehensive family support and early childhood education can reduce the prevalence of chronic juvenile delinquency. Many community psychologists follow a so-called systems approach: They study the ways in which the criminal-justice, educational, welfare, and health-care systems can work together to foster psychological well-being among groups at risk.

The aim of **secondary prevention** is to catch psychological problems in their formative stages and to stay their advancement. Groups such as Parents Anonymous and suicide prevention centers provide ways for

Personal space • An invisible boundary that surrounds a person and serves protective functions.

Community psychology • A field of psychology, related to clinical psychology, that focuses on the prevention of psychological problems and the maintenance of distressed persons in the community.

Primary prevention • In community psychology, the deterrence of psychological problems.

Secondary prevention • In community psychology, the early detection and treatment of psychological problems.

distressed people to express their concerns before child abuse gets out of hand or they kill themselves. Community psychologists also work with teachers and others to sensitize them to early signs of psychological disorders or abuse.

Tertiary prevention deals with psychological disorders that have ripened. There is much overlap between psychological treatment, as in psychotherapy and behavior therapy, and tertiary prevention. In tertiary prevention, however, there is a community emphasis. The focus is on rallying community forces to shore up the ties of people with disorders to family and vocational life. Halfway houses, partial hospitalization, and consultation with employers and family groups are as likely to be used as the methods of therapy outlined in Chapter 14.

Tertiary prevention • In community psychology, the treatment of ripened psychological problems.

Forensic psychology • The field that applies psychological knowledge within the criminal-justice system.

PSYCHOLOGY IN A WORLD OF DIVERSITY

"AT THE HEART OF WHAT PSYCHOLOGY SHOULD BE DOING IN THE COMMUNITY"[2]

The community can teach more than a textbook (deGroot, 1994a).

Eleven-year-old Shalise had grown accustomed to the sounds of a man and woman arguing in the apartment above hers. Now she is getting used to the sounds of silence. Two months ago, the woman upstairs shot her husband, and their child went to live with his grandmother.

Like most children in her neighborhood, Shalise is used to the shootings, arrests, and drug dealing that go on around her. But Shalise is lucky in one way: She is one of 55 Bladensburg Elementary School students in the Home School Empowerment program, a joint project of the county school system and the University of Maryland.

Community psychologist Ray Lorion, PhD, director of the clinical community psychology program at the University of Maryland, has a team of graduate students who work with the school system to provide social and academic support.

For 4 hours a week, Shalise meets with Lorion's students for tutoring in math, manners, and self-esteem.

"Shalise really is a bright girl, but she feels like no one listens to her," said Pam Flores, a student in the clinical community psychology program at the university. "That's part of my job, to listen to her and to make her feel better about herself. She always says 'I can't do this; I can't do that.' I've taught her to say, 'I can't do this . . . yet.'"

Established in 1991, the program has made great strides in improving the children's self-esteem and confidence, as well as reading and math skills. The program also provides intense, hands-on training in clinical and community psychology for University of Maryland students. The graduate students have been able to conduct studies of drug use among elementary school students and develop special programs for high-risk children.

"I think this gets at the heart of what psychology should be doing in the community," Flores said.

Reflections

Now that you have read the section on community psychology, reflect on the following questions:

- You have heard the expression "An ounce of prevention is worth a pound of cure." How might dealing with problems such as unemployment, lack of education, drug abuse, teenage pregnancy, marital conflict, and substandard housing help prevent psychological disorders?
- Can you think of some agencies in your home or college community where community psychology students could get valuable hands-on experience in attempting to prevent psychological disorders, spouse abuse, and so on?

In recent years, community psychologists and other psychologists have also been concerned about the primary prevention of rape and AIDS. Prevention of these

[2] This feature is adapted from "Tutors Help Students Boost Self-Esteem," by Gabrielle deGroot, 1994b, *APA Monitor,* 25(5), p. 45.

problems is the focus of the chapter's "Psychology and Modern Life" section.

Forensic Psychology

Forensic psychologists apply psychological knowledge to the functioning of the criminal-justice system. Some apply knowledge concerning social psychology and information processing in the investigation of the legal process. Because the testimony of eyewitnesses has an impact on juries (Wolf & Bugaj, 1990), they study the use of eyewitness testimony, which has many shortcomings (see Chapter 7). They also investigate ways in which the behavior of judges, attorneys, and defendants influences jury decisions (Davis, 1989).

Many forensic psychologists are employed by law-enforcement agencies. They apply knowledge of personality, personality assessment, and the psychology of learning to facilitate the recruitment and training of police officers. There is a high burnout rate among police officers, and some psychologists apply therapy methods to help police find ways of coping with stress. They apply knowledge of psychological disorders and social psychology to help train police to handle special problems—for example, assessing the dangerousness of persons they suspect of crimes or are trying to apprehend, and handling suicide threats, hostage crises, and family disputes.

THE INSANITY PLEA

Some forensic psychologists apply psychological knowledge in the evaluation of persons who commit crimes. They testify about defendants' competence to stand trial or participate in their own defense, as well as about whether defendants should be found not guilty by reason of insanity. In Chapter 13, I mentioned a couple of cases in which individuals were found not guilty of crimes by reason of insanity. One involved William, who was diagnosed with dissociative identity disorder (multiple personality). The other person, John Hinckley, was found not guilty of an assassination attempt on President Reagan. Hinckley was

diagnosed with schizophrenia. In both cases, the defendants were committed to psychiatric institutions rather than given prison sentences. William was discharged a number of years ago, but Hinckley remains hospitalized.

In pleading insanity, lawyers use the so-called M'Naghten rule, named after Daniel M'Naghten, who tried to assassinate the British prime minister, Sir Robert Peel, in 1843. M'Naghten had delusions that Peel was persecuting him, and he killed Peel's secretary in the attempt. The court found M'Naghten not guilty by reason of insanity, referring to what has become the M'Naghten rule. The rule is that the accused did not understand what she or he was doing at the time of the act, did not realize it was wrong, or was succumbing to an irresistible impulse. Some of the implications of the M'Naghten rule are highlighted by the Lorena Bobbitt case.

The Lorena Bobbitt Case: Irresistible Impulse or Planned Revenge? In June 1993, following years of physical and sexual abuse, Lorena Bobbitt severed her husband's penis with a knife. The penis was surgically reattached. In November 1993, the husband—John Wayne Bobbitt, a former marine—was tried and found not guilty of marital rape. (Some observers speculated that the jury may have believed that he was guilty but had already paid for his crimes at the hands of his wife.) In January 1994, Lorena Bobbitt was tried and found not guilty of the malicious wounding of her husband by reason of insanity. The jury maintained that she had been acting out an irresistible impulse.

The Lorena Bobbitt case epitomizes some of the problems with the M'Naghten rule for determining guilt or innocence for criminal behavior. How can we determine with certainty whether other people know right from wrong or are acting out an irresistible impulse at any given moment (Scott, 1994)? We can only interview people and observe them—often, hours or weeks after a crime is committed—and draw our own conclusions. In the typical insanity defense, defense attorneys employ expert witnesses—usually psychologists and psychiatrists. On the basis of interviews

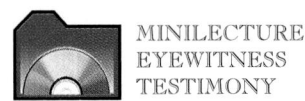

MINILECTURE:
EYEWITNESS
TESTIMONY

or previous knowledge of the defendant, the witnesses usually testify that the accused was insane at the time of the act. The prosecution typically presents opposing experts who testify that the accused was sane at the time of the act. Such back-and-forth testimony characterized the Lorena Bobbitt trial.

A parade of witnesses corroborated Lorena Bobbitt's testimony of marital abuse. They recounted seeing her with bruises all over her body. Lorena testified that she could not recall maiming her husband. The court appointed two forensic psychologists and a psychiatrist. They testified that Lorena Bobbitt was a battered woman with post-traumatic stress disorder and severe depression at the time of the mutilation. The judge's charge to jurors required that for them to find that Lorena Bobbitt had experienced an irresistible impulse at the time of the crime, they would have to believe that Lorena Bobbitt's mind was so impaired by psychological disorder that she had not been able to resist the impulse to maim her husband.

Commenting on the verdict, Stanford law professor Lawrence Friedman said, "Fifty years ago, Lorena Bobbitt would have been convicted without a shadow of a doubt. [The jury] would not have listened to any argument that the deed was justified by a history of abuse. [The jury] would have focused on the act itself, which horrifies all males" (Sachs, 1994, p. 99). Other attorneys expressed the view that a finding of temporary insanity allows a jury to acquit a guilty defendant who has won its sympathy (Sachs, 1994).

Many people, including some government officials, would ban the insanity plea (DeAngelis, 1994d). Such banning "is an attempt to deal with a perception that the world is getting more violent," notes psychologist–lawyer Donald Bersoff (1994, p. 28). "That's combined with the perception that people are literally getting away with murder because of the insanity defense."

Practically speaking, there may not be all that much cause for concern, however. Although the public estimates that the insanity defense is used in about 37% of felony cases, it is actually raised in only 1% (Silver and others, 1994).

Sports psychology • The field of psychology that studies the nature, causes, and modification of the behavior and mental processes of people involved in sports.

Reflections

Now that you have read the section on forensic psychology, reflect on the following questions:

- Can you draw on your knowledge of aggression, psychological disorders, and social psychology to think of ways in which police might handle hostage crises? Can you think of any such crises that ended in disaster and how disaster might have been averted?
- The jury in the Lorena Bobbitt case maintained that she had experienced an irresistible impulse. Put on your critical thinking cap. Consider definitions. What is an *irresistible impulse?* Is a craving for a chocolate candy bar an irresistible impulse? Is a craving for a cigarette an irresistible impulse to a habitual smoker? Is a craving for a drink an irresistible impulse to an alcoholic? Can sexual feelings become so overpowering that they are irresistible? How can we know whether an impulse is irresistible or merely tantalizing?

Sports Psychology

Among the welter of a spirited tennis crowd, I overheard a conversation between two women:

"Do you think there's anything I could do to play like Steffi Graf?"
"The first thing you've got to do is get Steffi Graf's genes."
A pause. Then: "But she's wearing a skirt."

Clothes may make the man, or woman, but probably not the athlete. Why does Steffi Graf outplay most other women on the tennis circuit? There is a combination of reasons, including motivation, dedication, long hours of training, superb coaching—as well as her ability to cope with stardom and the crowds. And, yes, "genes"—not jeans. Heredity plays a role in terms of her physical strength, her coordination, her reaction time, and her eyesight.

TASK ANALYSIS OF ATHLETIC PERFORMANCES

Sports psychologists apply psychological methods and knowledge to the study and modification of the behavior and mental processes of people involved in sports. Sports psychologists do task analyses of athletic performances just as I/O psychologists do task analyses of work performances. They break athletic performances down into their components to discover ways of enhancing the performance of each. In doing so, they apply knowledge about biology (the facts concerning human limits and health hazards), motivation, learning (for example, the roles of cognitive understanding, repetition, and reinforcement), self-efficacy expectations ("I can do it"), and coping with stress. They apply this knowledge and knowledge about group processes to help coaches. Many amateur and professional teams have psychologists as well as coaches.

Note some of the issues sports psychologists deal with:

• How can athletes focus their attention on their own performance and not on the crowd or on competing athletes?

• How can athletes use cognitive strategies such as mental practice and positive visualization to enhance performance?

• What is the role of emotions in performance? For example, did tennis pro John McEnroe's on-court cursing and arguing spark his achievement motivation and concentration, or did they distract him and cost him matches?

• What are the relationships between sports and psychological well-being?

• How can knowledge of group behavior be applied to enhance team cohesiveness?

• How can psychologists help athletes handle "choking"?

Let us consider this last issue further—the problem of "choking."

HOW SPORTS PSYCHOLOGISTS HELP ATHLETES HANDLE "CHOKING"

Buffalo Bills placekicker Scott Norwood had toiled for many years preparing for the 1991 Super Bowl. For several hours a day, he perfected his form on the field. He kicked field goals from various distances and in all extremes of weather. Then, when

Scott Norwood at the Super Bowl. Buffalo Bills placekicker Scott Norwood trained for years, under extremes of weather. Then, in the waning seconds of the January 1991 Super Bowl—when a relatively short kick would have given the Bills a victory over the Giants—he choked. Instead of splitting the uprights, the ball spun off to the side. One of the functions of sports psychologists is to help athletes handle choking through techniques like relaxation and positive visualization.

his opportunity to win the game with a short field goal arose, he "choked." He shanked the ball in the final seconds of the game, handing the victory to Buffalo's downstate rivals—the New York Giants.

A critical outing also had a devastating effect one fall on Penn State placekicker Herb Menhardt. Penn State was facing its second loss in three games. With a fourth down on the Iowa 37-yard line and 50 seconds to play, the coach took a chance on the untested Menhardt, a first-year student. As 75,000 anxious Penn State fans looked on at Beaver Stadium, Menhardt hooked the 54-yard kick wide to the left, leaving Iowa with a 7–6 victory. As a result, Matt Bahr got the starting placekicking job, which eventually landed him in the pros.

Menhardt quit the team and didn't return until his junior year. "I had to live with that kick for years," Menhardt noted. "Matt won the starting job, and I had to accept being a failure. I had nightmares about it, and all my so-called friends mocked me. I decided to give up on football. I knew I could kick, but I had to live with that one kick."

Choking during an athletic contest, as when taking a test, is especially cruel. The athlete, like the student, may have sweated long hours preparing for a crucial performance. Then it's over in a matter of seconds or minutes. Yet, it may devastate one's self-esteem and taint one's life.

Fortunately, Menhardt had an opportunity to work with sports psychologists Charles Stebbins and Kevin Hickey. They taught him a variety of coping skills. Some were largely perceptual and physical—such as helping him develop his peripheral vision, sense of balance, and response time. They taught him relaxation skills. Menhardt learned to breathe deeply and regularly under stress. He was shown how to relax muscle groups as he told himself to relax.

POSITIVE VISUALIZATION

Like many other performers, Menhardt was also shown how to use the technique of positive visualization. He envisioned himself going through the motions in a critical game situation. He pictured blocking the crowd out of his mind and focusing on the ball. He moved fluidly toward the ball as if in a trance—as if he and the performance were one—and booted the ball flawlessly through the posts.

Truth or Fiction Revisited. *It is true that you can improve your athletic performance by imagining yourself making the right moves.* This is an example of the technique of positive visualization. Positive visualization helps you rehearse the desired behavior and enhances self-efficacy expectations.

After his new combination of athletic, behavioral, and cognitive training, Menhardt returned to the team and made a last-second 54-yard goal against North Carolina State. He gave Penn State the winning margin: 9–6. That season, he went on to convert 14 field goals in 20 attempts and all of his 28 kicks after touchdowns.

PEAK PERFORMANCE

Menhardt was now engaging in what sports psychologists refer to as "peak performances." Peak performances are characterized by

- intense concentration
- ability to screen out the crowd and, when appropriate, the competitors (successful field-goal kickers and quarterbacks do not usually "hear footsteps" or focus on the opposition's defenders rushing in)

- a sense of power and control over the situation
- lack of pain and fatigue
- the sense that time has slowed down, as if the performance is being carried out in slow motion (Browne & Mahoney, 1984). Great hitters in baseball have fine eyesight and timing. They report that they can "see" the ball exceptionally clearly. When they are at their peak, even fastballs seem to linger in the air as they come across the plate.

It also seems that peak performances can elude athletes who pursue them intentionally, or who "try too hard." A useful prescription includes training adequately—that is, enhancing endurance and fine-tuning skills—learning how to regulate one's breathing and relax muscle groups that are unessential to performance, and spending some practice time picturing oneself performing flawlessly under adverse conditions.

Reflections

Now that you have read the section on sports psychology, reflect on the following questions:

- Have you or someone you know ever "choked" during an athletic performance? What caused you or the other person to choke? Now that you look back on it with this psychology course "under your belt," can you think of any ways in which you could have handled the situation?
- Can you think of ways in which you can use positive visualization in an athletic contest? Or of ways to use positive visualization to improve your performance in class and on tests?

We could say that sports psychology is about educating athletes to enhance their performance. Let us now turn our attention to educational psychology, which is concerned with the enhancement of learning in general.

Educational Psychology

Discussion of educational psychology brings our book full circle. After all, educating students in psychology is what it is all about.

Educational psychologists apply knowledge from many areas of psychology to the processes of teaching and learning (Woolfolk, 1995). They apply knowledge of developmental psychology to determine when children are ready to undertake certain kinds of learning and whether teaching practices can be modified to meet the needs of older people. They apply knowledge of learning and memory to present instructional materials in ways that will foster comprehension and retention. They apply knowledge of motivation to find ways to encourage students to become involved with, and attend to, subject matter. They apply knowledge of test construction and statistics to develop tests that assess aptitudes and achievement. They apply knowledge of social psychology to enhance teacher–student and student–student relationships.

Let us survey some of the concerns of educational psychologists.

TEACHING PRACTICES

Psychologist Joseph Palladino (1994) helps his students learn about neuropsychology by having them pretend that they are neurons. He helps them understand the nature of different psychological disorders by acting them out in class.

Educational psychologists help instructors find ways of teaching effectively. A first step is the analysis of the outcomes of learning—that is, whether students are expected to show changes in their attitudes, motor skills, verbal information, intellectual skills (for example, knowing how to add and subtract), or cognitive strategies for processing information (for example, paying attention and rehearsing information). A number of psychologists, like Jerome Bruner, argue in favor of **discovery learning.** That is, they claim that children should be placed in resource-rich environments and be allowed to work on their own to discover basic principles. Others, like David Ausubel, value **expository teaching.** They prefer to set forth facts and ideas in an orderly manner.

Research has shown that teachers who are too busy or unwilling to answer student questions discourage learning and inhibit students from participating in class discussions (Newman, 1990). Teachers who encourage students to ask questions and who provide clear answers encourage students to take an active role in learning (Karabenick & Sharma, 1994). Psychologists also help teachers develop ways of teaching problem solving and critical thinking. Let us consider some of the activities of educational psychologists, beginning with their contributions to classroom management.

CLASSROOM MANAGEMENT

Educational psychologists study ways of motivating and managing students in the classroom. Teachers can develop ways of motivating students if they ask themselves how they can help foster positive attitudes toward learning activities and how the activities can help meet students' needs (Wlodkowski, 1982). How can teachers marshall students' needs for achievement and mastery? There is also a link between teacher expectations and how well students do. Therefore, teachers should not assume that a student will perform badly because of her or his sociocultural background or "attitude." Teacher expectations have ways of becoming **self-fulfilling prophecies.**

Teachers can help motivate students in the following ways (DeAngelis, 1994; Woolfolk, 1995):

1. By making the classroom and the lesson interesting and inviting
2. By ensuring that students can fulfill their needs for affiliation and belonging
3. By making the classroom a safe and pleasant place
4. By recognizing that students' backgrounds can give rise to diverse patterns of needs
5. By helping students take appropriate responsibility for their successes and failures
6. By encouraging students to perceive the links between their own efforts and their achievements
7. By helping students set attainable short-term goals

Classrooms are special environments crowded with people, learning resources, tasks, and time pressures (Doyle, 1986).

Educational psychology • The field of psychology that studies the nature, causes, and enhancement of teaching and learning.
Discovery learning • Bruner's view that children should work on their own to discover basic principles.
Expository teaching • Ausubel's method of presenting material in an organized form, moving from broad to specific concepts.
Self-fulfilling prophecy • An expectation that is confirmed because of the behavior of those who hold the expectation.

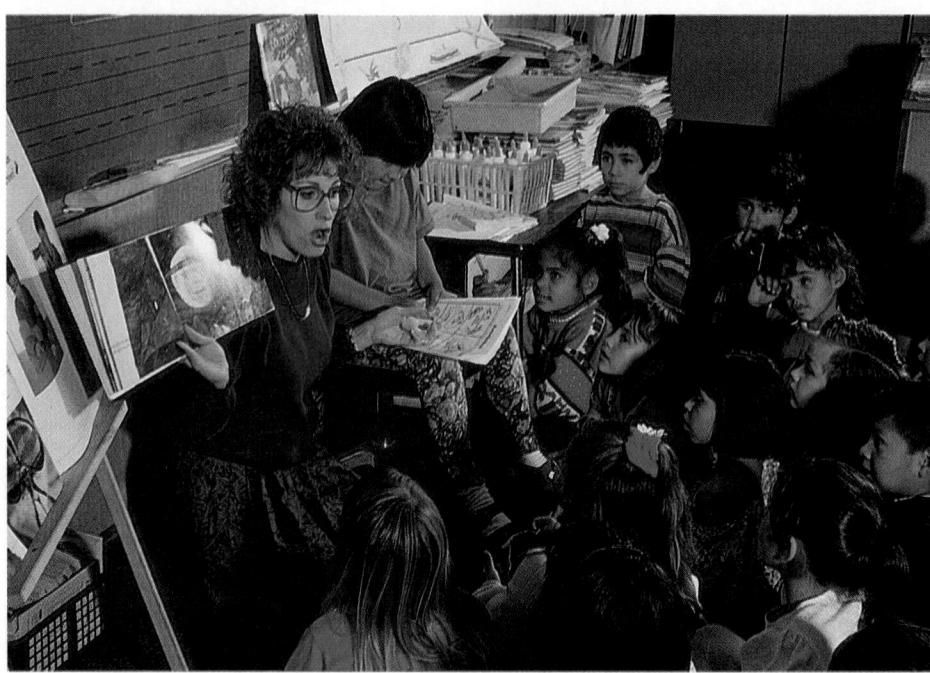

A Class Act. Educational psychologists help instructors find ways of teaching effectively. For example, they connect various teaching methods to the outcomes of learning (e.g., whether students are expected to show changes in their attitudes, motor skills, verbal information, intellectual skills, or cognitive strategies for processing information).

Everything seems to happen at once. Some events—such as the burning out of a light bulb or a child's becoming ill—can make them unpredictable places. Despite the unpredictables, classrooms become more manageable when concrete procedures and rules are spelled out to students. For example, elementary school students need rules concerning being polite and helpful, taking care of the school, avoiding aggressive behavior, keeping the bathroom neat, and behaving in the cafeteria. Young students need concrete examples. Saying "Be good" is not sufficient. Children need multiple examples of "good" behavior spelled out. Class procedures involve ways in which students are expected to enter and leave the room, whether they must raise their hands to participate in class discussion, and how they will find out about and hand in assignments. Teachers who state rules clearly and insist that they be followed during the early weeks of school usually encounter fewer behavior problems as the year progresses. Educational psychologists also devise ways for dealing with defiant and violent students. Many teachers are instructed in the methods of behavior modification described in Chapter 6.

PLANNING AND TEACHING

Educational psychologists find it valuable for teachers to set **instructional objectives.** Communication of objectives helps students focus on the essential aspects of the material. Objectives can be general (the student should be able to reason in solving simple math problems) and specific (the student should be able to add single digits when written in the form, $3 + 5 = x$). A classification system, or **taxonomy**, of instructional objectives divides them into three domains: cognitive, affective (emotional), and psychomotor (concerning the development of physical abilities and skills). Examples of objectives in the cognitive domain include acquisition of knowledge, comprehension of subject matter, and ability to apply concepts to solve problems.

Educational psychologists conduct research into which teaching formats best enable teachers to meet instructional objectives. For example, in the **recitation** approach, teachers pose questions that students answer. Other basic teaching formats include the lecture approach, group discussion, seatwork and homework, and individualized instruction. In the latter format, students are taught on a one-to-one basis. They are then given time to read about or apply the subject matter on their own. It is interesting to note that individualized instruction, which is usually prized because of the presumably ideal teacher-to-student ratio, has *not* been shown to be superior for elementary and secondary students. Perhaps it leaves immature students too much time on their own. However, individualized instruction seems to benefit college students (Bangert and others, 1983), who are presumably better capable of managing their time.

There are some interesting findings concerning teacher characteristics and student learning. For example, it has *not* been shown that teachers who know more about a subject do a better job of teaching it, particularly at the elementary level. Students learn more when their teachers manage the classroom well and present material in a clear, organized fashion (Cantrell and others, 1977; Hines and others, 1985).

Truth or Fiction Revisited. *It is not true teachers who know more about a subject do a better job of teaching it—at least in the lower grades.* The statement is too general to be true and discounts other key teaching factors, such as communication skills and organization. Such factors seem to be just as important, if not more important, than knowledge of content areas with young children. The situation may differ in college, where students are better able to organize subject matter for themselves.

TEACHING EXCEPTIONAL STUDENTS

Exceptional students have special needs. They may have physical and health problems, communication problems, behavior disorders, specific learning disabilities, or mental retardation or—at the other intellectual extreme—giftedness. Educational psychologists study ways of maximizing instructional effectiveness with exceptional students and of integrating them into regular classrooms when possible so they will not suffer from losses in self-esteem.

The practice of placing exceptional students in educational environments that are as normal as possible is referred to as **mainstreaming.** Since the passage of the Education for All Handicapped Children Act in 1975, exceptional children have been afforded the **least-restrictive placement**—that is, put in settings that are as normal and as much in the mainstream of education as possible. On the other hand, educational psychologists have also labored to develop instructional methods that will benefit exceptional children who receive supplementary instruction or who must be placed in special classes.

TESTS AND GRADES

Educational psychologists also develop methods for assessing students and assigning grades. Assessment includes standardized tests that measure intelligence (for example, the Wechsler and Stanford–Binet scales), aptitudes (for example, the SATs and GREs), achievement in specific subjects (for example, the California Achievement Tests and the advanced tests of the GREs), and problems that affect learning (for example, perceptual and motor problems, as measured by the Bender Gestalt Test). Schools use such tests to assess learning ability and to see how well children are reading or computing math problems as compared with agemates. Colleges and graduate programs use tests to make admissions decisions.

Such tests can be **norm-referenced** or **criterion-referenced.** Students' performances on norm-referenced tests are compared with the average performance of others. In other words, how well one does on the Wechsler scales or on the GREs depends on how well one performs relative to other people who take the tests. On the Wechsler scales for children, test takers' performances are compared with a nationwide sample that represents their agemates. Norms for the GRE are based on numbers of items answered correctly by young adults interested in pursuing graduate education—a rather select group.

In criterion-referenced testing, test takers' scores are compared with a fixed performance standard. In other words, criterion-referenced testing might be used to determine whether one can use long division, type 60 words a minute, or speak Spanish fluently. A good score on the norm-referenced GRE advanced test in Spanish means that you answered more questions correctly than the average test

---

Instructional objective • A clear statement of what is to be learned.

Taxonomy • Classification system.

Recitation • A teaching format in which teachers pose questions that are answered by students.

Exceptional students • The term applied to students whose educational needs are special because of physical and health problems, communication problems, behavior disorders, specific learning disabilities, mental retardation, or intellectual giftedness.

Mainstreaming • The practice of placing exceptional students in educational environments that are as normal as possible.

Least-restrictive placement • Placement of exceptional students in settings that are as normal and as much in the mainstream of education as possible, in accord with the Education for All Handicapped Children Act.

Norm-referenced testing • A testing approach in which scores are derived by comparing the number of items answered correctly with the average performance of others.

Criterion-referenced testing • A testing approach in which scores are based on whether one can perform up to a set standard.

taker, not that you can understand or speak Spanish. A road test for a driver's license is a criterion-referenced test; either you can drive successfully according to the set standard or you can't.

Educational psychologists are also interested in classroom evaluation and testing. They study the reliability and validity of various kinds of tests such as multiple-choice tests versus essay tests. They have found, for example, that long tests are more reliable than brief tests. They have learned that the grading of multiple-choice tests is more objective, or fair, than the grading of essay tests. The grading of essays (and course grades themselves), like the appraisal of workers, can also be influenced by the halo effect—that is, the teacher's general impression of the student. However, the consistency of essay test grades can be enhanced by writing a model answer and then assigning points to its various parts (Gronlund, 1985). Covering students' names while grading also increases fairness. (But penmanship can also affect grades!)

Educational psychologists also investigate the effects of grading. Grades provide students with more than just feedback about how much they have achieved. They also affect students' self-esteem and motivation. For that reason, some teachers try to encourage students they perceive as underachievers by grading them on their (presumed) abilities and not on their actual achievements. In elementary schools, teachers are frequently allowed to give children two grades for the same subject matter area: One reflects achievement and the other is based on "judgment calls" and intangibles such as effort.

Reflections

Now that you have read the section on educational psychology, reflect on the following questions:

• Which of your teachers have been most effective over the years? Can you explain their effectiveness in terms of psychological concepts discussed in this textbook?

• Which of your teachers have been most effective and least effective in controlling the behavior of students in the classroom? How do you account for the differences?

• How do you respond to tests and grades? Can you think of alternatives to them? How else could we motivate students and assess learning?

• What grade will you earn for this course? Will it be determined by norm-referenced testing or criterion-referenced testing? Will your grade reflect the amount of work you have put into the course? Will it influence your attitude toward psychology? What do you think?

• Of the human being, Shakespeare wrote, "What a piece of work is man!" What has this course taught you about our favorite "piece of work"?

Summary

1. **What is applied psychology?** Applied psychology refers to a number of fields of psychology such as industrial/organizational or environmental psychology that apply fundamental psychological methods and knowledge to the investigation and solution of human problems.

2. **What is industrial/organizational (I/O) psychology?** I/O psychologists apply psychological expertise to assist in worker recruitment, training, and appraisal; enhance job satisfaction; and structure organizations to function efficiently.

3. **How do I/O psychologists facilitate recruitment?** I/O psychologists facilitate recruitment procedures by analyzing jobs to specify the skills and personal attributes that are required. They also construct personnel tests and interview procedures to assess the presence of these skills and attributes.

4. **How do I/O psychologists facilitate training?** Training programs usually follow when managers identify a need for improved performance in a given job. Steps in devising training programs include assessing needs, establishing learning objectives, devising methods for gaining and maintaining attention, presenting material, and evaluating program effectiveness.

5. **What have I/O psychologists learned about employee appraisal?** Appraisal of a worker's performance is a cognitive process that is subject to distortions. For example, workers may be judged on the basis of general impressions instead of work performance.

6. **What are the various approaches to organizational theory?** There are three basic approaches to organizational theory: the classic approach, which tends to rely on a bureaucracy, division of labor, and delegation of authority; contingency approaches, which tie organizational structures to organizational objectives and environmental demands; and human-relations approaches, which place the worker first.

7. **What are the major human-relations approaches?** Three important human-relations theories are McGregor's Theory Y, which is based on the assumption that workers are motivated to take responsibility for their work behavior; Argyris's view that organizations are structured efficiently when they allow their workers to develop; and Ouchi's Theory Z, which combines some of the positive features of the Japanese workplace with some of the realities of the American workplace.

8. **What is human-factors psychology?** This is the field that ensures that equipment and facilities are compatible with human behavior patterns and mental processes—that is, they are reasonably easy to work, or work in, and safe.

9. **What criteria do human-factors psychologists use in evaluating person–machine systems and for work environments?** They use performance criteria, physiological criteria, subjective criteria, and accident-and-injury criteria.

10. **What criteria do human-factors psychologists use for evaluating the coding in displays?** They consider the displays' detectability, discriminability, compatibility, meaningfulness, standardization, and multidimensionality.

11. **What is consumer psychology?** Consumer psychology applies psychological methods to the investigation and modification of consumer behavior and mental processes.

12. **What kinds of questions are considered by consumer psychologists?** They consider issues such as why consumers are loyal to one brand over another, the qualities or characteristics that consumers associate with various brands, and how consumer attitudes toward products can be modified.

13. **What is environmental psychology?** Environmental psychologists study the ways in which people and

the physical environment influence each other. They investigate the ways in which factors such as noise, temperature, pollution, and population density affect human behavior and mental processes.

14. **What is community psychology?** Community psychology is related to clinical psychology but focuses on the prevention of psychological problems and the maintenance of distressed individuals in the community.

15. **What kinds of prevention are there?** Primary prevention is the modification of the community environment to preclude the emergence of problems. Secondary prevention is the early detection and treatment of problems. Tertiary prevention is the treatment of developed problems.

16. **What is forensic psychology?** Forensic psychology is the application of psychological knowledge to the functioning of the criminal-justice system.

17. **What kinds of issues are dealt with by forensic psychologists?** Forensic psychologists study ways in which witnesses, judges, defendants, and attorneys affect the legal process. Forensic psychologists participate in the recruitment, training, and counseling of police personnel. They also testify as to the competence of defendants to participate in their own defense.

18. **What is sports psychology?** Sports psychology is the application of psychological methods and knowledge to the study and modification of the behavior and mental processes of people involved in sports.

19. **What kinds of issues do sports psychologists deal with?** In addition to task analysis of athletic performances, sports psychologists are concerned with issues such as how athletes can use cognitive strategies like mental practice and positive visualization to enhance performance, how sports contribute to mental health, how team cohesiveness can be enhanced, how coaching methods can be improved, how athletes can handle "choking," and how athletes can attain peak performance.

20. **What is educational psychology?** Educational psychologists apply their knowledge from many areas of psychology to the processes of teaching and learning.

21. **How do educational psychologists contribute to teaching practices?** They analyze the outcomes of learning and the effects of different kinds of teaching such as discovery learning and expository teaching.

22. **How do educational psychologists contribute to classroom management?** They study ways of motivating and managing students in the classroom setting. They relate instructional methods to students' needs and point out the value of concrete school rules and procedures.

23. **How do educational psychologists contribute to planning and teaching?** They explain how to use instructional objectives according to a taxonomy. They conduct research into which teaching formats best enable teachers to meet their objectives.

24. **What are exceptional students?** Exceptional students are students whose needs are special because of physical and health problems, communication problems, behavior disorders, specific learning disabilities, or mental retardation or—at the other intellectual extreme—giftedness.

Psychology and Modern Life

Prevention is a buzzword in community psychology and in modern life. The old saying "An ounce of prevention is worth a pound of cure" contains much wisdom. The saying is especially pertinent to the cases of rape and AIDS. The aftermath of rape can include physical harm, anxiety, depression, sexual dysfunctions, sexually transmitted diseases, and pregnancy (Kimerling & Calhoun, 1994; Koss, 1993). AIDS, of course, is lethal.

In this section, we discuss the problems of rape and AIDS. We explore why, for some males, sexual behavior is adversarial rather than loving and cooperative. We see that prevention includes changing sociocultural attitudes as well as taking personal actions. We explore why some people continue to jeopardize their physical health—in fact, their lives—by acting as if AIDS did not exist. In both cases, we outline prescriptions for prevention.

Primary Prevention of Rape

From 14% to 25% of women in the United States have been raped (Koss, 1993). Parents regularly encourage their daughters to be wary of strangers and strange places—

Kristine, Amy, and Karen. These college women are among the many thousands who claim to have been raped by dates. The great majority of rapes are committed by dates or acquaintances, not by strangers. People differ in their perceptions of where encouragement leaves off and rape begins. For this reason, many colleges require students to attend seminars on date rape. Male students are taught that "No" means *stop—now.*

places where they are prey to men. Certainly the threat of rape from strangers is real enough. Yet only one rape in five is carried out by a complete stranger (Gibbs, 1991). The great majority are committed by acquaintances.

Date rape is a pressing concern on college campuses, where thousands of women have been victimized and there is much controversy as to what exactly constitutes rape. Nine percent of one sample of 6,159 college women reported that they had given in to sexual intercourse as a result of threats or physical force (Koss and others, 1987). Consider the case of Ann:

> I first met him at a party. He was really good looking and he had a great smile. I wanted to meet him but I wasn't sure how. I didn't want to appear too forward. Then he came over and introduced himself. We talked and found we had a lot in common. I really liked him. When he asked me over to his place for a drink, I thought it would be OK. He was such a good listener, and I wanted him to ask me out again.
>
> When we got to his room, the only place to sit was on the bed. I didn't want him to get the wrong idea, but what else could I do? We talked for awhile and then he made his move. I was so startled. He started by kissing. I really liked him so the kissing was nice. But then he pushed me down on the bed. I tried to get up and I told him to stop. He was so much bigger and stronger. I got scared and I started to cry. I froze and he raped me.
>
> It took only a couple of minutes and it was terrible, he was so rough. When it was over he kept asking me what was wrong, like he didn't know. He had just forced himself on me and he thought that was OK. He drove me home and said he wanted to see me again. I'm so afraid to see him. I never thought it would happen to me. (Trenton State College, 1991)

If we add to these statistics on rape instances in which women are subjected to forced kissing and petting, the numbers grow more alarming. At a major university,

40% of 201 male students surveyed admitted to using force to unfasten a woman's clothing, and 13% reported that they had forced a woman to engage in sexual intercourse (Rapaport & Burkhart, 1984). Forty-four percent of the college women in the Koss study (Koss and others, 1987) reported that they had "given in to sex play" because of a "man's continual arguments and pressure."

WHY DO MEN RAPE WOMEN?

Boys . . . have sex earlier now, with more impunity, with a more casual commitment, in a cultural environment saturated with soft porn and cinematic violence.
ANNA QUINDLEN (1993)

Why do men coerce women into sexual activity? Sex is not the only reason. Many social scientists argue that rape is often a man's way of expressing social dominance over, or anger toward, women (Ellis, 1991; Malamuth and others, 1991). In fact, many rapists have long records as violent offenders (Fairstein, 1993; Vachss, 1993). With some rapists, violence also appears to enhance sexual arousal. Thus they are motivated to combine sex with aggression (Barbaree & Marshall, 1991).

Many social critics contend that American culture socializes men—including the nice young man next door—into becoming rapists (Malamuth and others, 1991; Prentky & Knight, 1991; Stermac and others, 1990). Males are often reinforced for aggressive and competitive behavior (Nelson, 1994). The date rapist could be said to be asserting culturally expected dominance over women. Sexually coercive college men are more likely than noncoercive college men to believe that aggression is legitimate behavior (Rapaport & Burkhart, 1984).

College men frequently perceive dates' protests as part of an adversarial sex game. One male undergraduate said "Hell, no" when asked whether a date had consented to sex. He added, ". . . but she didn't say no, so she must have wanted it, too. . . . It's the way it works" (Celis, 1991). Consider the comments of Jim, the man who victimized Ann:

> I first met her at a party. She looked really hot, wearing a sexy dress that showed off her great body. We started

talking right away. I knew that she liked me by the way she kept smiling and touching my arm while she was speaking. She seemed pretty relaxed so I asked her back to my place for a drink. . . . When she said yes, I knew that I was going to be lucky!

> When we got to my place, we sat on the bed kissing. At first, everything was great. Then, when I started to lay her down on the bed, she started twisting and saying she didn't want to. Most women don't like to appear too easy, so I knew that she was just going through the motions. When she stopped struggling, I knew that she would have to throw in some tears before we did it.

> She was still very upset afterwards, and I just don't understand it! If she didn't want to have sex, why did she come back to the room with me? You could tell by the way she dressed and acted that she was no virgin, so why she had to put up such a big struggle I don't know. (Trenton State College, 1991)

RAPE MYTHS: DO YOU HARBOR BELIEFS THAT ENCOURAGE RAPE?

The U.S. sociocultural milieu harbors a number of myths about rape—myths that tend to blame the victim, not the aggressor. For example, a majority of Americans aged 50 and above believe that the woman is partly responsible for being raped if she dresses provocatively (Gibbs, 1991). A majority of Americans believe that some women like to be talked into sex.

Truth or Fiction Revisited. *It is true that most Americans believe that some women like to be talked into sex.* A majority of Americans—including a majority of American *women*—believe that some women do like to be talked into having sex. Does this belief encourage men to be persistent with their dates?

Other myths include the notions that "Only bad girls get raped," "Any healthy woman can resist a rapist if she wants to," and "Women only cry rape when they've been jilted or have something to cover up" (Burt, 1980, p. 217). These myths deny the impact of the assault and transfer blame

--- Questionnaire ---

CULTURAL MYTHS THAT CREATE A CLIMATE THAT SUPPORTS RAPE

The following statements are based on a questionnaire by Martha Burt (1980). Read each statement and indicate whether you believe it to be true or false by circling the T or the F. Then turn to the key in Appendix B to learn of the implications of your answers.

T F 1. A woman who goes to the home or apartment of a man on their first date implies that she is willing to have sex.

T F 2. Any female can get raped.

T F 3. One reason that women falsely report a rape is that they frequently have a need to call attention to themselves.

T F 4. Any healthy woman can successfully resist a rapist if she really wants to.

T F 5. When women go around braless or wearing short skirts and tight tops, they are just asking for trouble.

T F 6. In the majority of rapes, the victim is promiscuous or has a bad reputation.

T F 7. If a girl engages in necking or petting and she lets things get out of hand, it is her own fault if her partner forces sex on her.

T F 8. Women who get raped while hitchhiking get what they deserve.

T F 9. A woman who is stuck-up and thinks she is too good to talk to guys on the street deserves to be taught a lesson.

T F 10. Many women have an unconscious wish to be raped and may then unconsciously set up a situation in which they are likely to be attacked.

T F 11. If a woman gets drunk at a party and has intercourse with a man she's just met there, she should be considered "fair game" to other males at the party who want to have sex with her too, whether she wants to or not.

T F 12. Many women who report a rape are lying because they are angry and want to get back at the man they accuse.

T F 13. Many, if not most, rapes are merely invented by women who discovered they were pregnant and wanted to protect their reputation.

---

onto the victim. They contribute to a social climate that is too often lenient toward rapists and unsympathetic toward victims.

Truth or Fiction Revisited. *It is not true that any healthy woman can successfully resist a rapist if she really wants to.* Feminists argue that myths such as this foster a social climate that encourages rape.

You may complete the nearby questionnaire on cultural myths and rape if you want to learn whether you harbor some of the more common myths.

WHAT TO DO

Don't accept rides from strange men—and remember that all men are strange.
ROBIN MORGAN

Testosterone does not have to be toxic.
ANNA QUINDLEN

From the sociocultural perspective, primary prevention of rape involves publicly examining and challenging the widely held cultural attitudes and ideals that contribute to rape. The traditions of male dominance and rewards for male aggressiveness take a daily toll on the lives of women. We can encourage our colleges and universities to require students to attend lectures and seminars on rape. Many colleges now require students to attend orientation sessions on rape. The point here is for men to learn that "No" means "No," despite the widespread belief that some women like to be talked into sex. We can encourage community and national leaders to pay more attention to the problem.

On a personal level, there are things that women can do now to protect themselves. *The New Our Bodies, Ourselves,* written by the Boston Women's Health Book Collective (1992), lists numerous suggestions that may be of help in preventing rape by strangers:

• Establish signals and arrangements with other women in an apartment building or neighborhood.

• List only first initials in the telephone directory or on the mailbox.

• Use deadbolt locks.

Rape-Crisis Counseling. Rape-crisis centers help victims cope with the aftermath of rape. They offer concrete advice concerning medical and legal issues and also lend emotional support. The psychological effects of rape can endure, coloring interpersonal relationships for years to come.

- Keep windows locked and obtain iron grids for first-floor windows.
- Keep entrances and doorways brightly lit.
- Have keys ready for the front door or the car.
- Do not walk alone in the dark.
- Avoid deserted areas.
- Never allow a strange man into your apartment or home without checking his credentials.

- Drive with the car windows up and the doors locked.
- Check the rear seat of the car before entering.
- Avoid living in an unsafe building.
- Do not pick up hitchhikers (including women).
- Do not talk to strange men in the street.
- Shout "Fire!" not "Rape!" People crowd around fires but avoid scenes of violence.

The following tactics may help prevent date rape (Hanson & Gidycz, 1993; Rathus & Fichner-Rathus, 1994):

- Avoid getting into secluded situations until you know your date very well. (As noted in the nearby questionnaire, some men interpret a date's willingness to accompany them to their room as an agreement to engage in sexual activity.) But be aware that victims of date rapes have sometimes gotten to know their assailants.
- Be wary when a date attempts to control you in any way, such as frightening you by driving rapidly or taking you some place you would rather not go.
- Be very assertive and clear concerning your sexual intentions. A Lehigh University dean encourages women to be forceful and clear in their communications, spoken and nonverbal (Volchko, 1991). Some rapists, particularly date rapists, tend to misinterpret women's wishes. If their dates begin to implore them to stop during kissing or petting, they construe pleading as "female game playing." So if kissing or petting is leading where you don't want it to go, speak up.
- When dating a person for the first time, try to date in a group.
- Talk to your date about his attitudes toward women. If you get the feeling that he believes that men are in a war with women, or that women try to "play games" with men, you may be better off dating someone else.
- You can explore attitudes by discussing items from the nearby questionnaire with a man you are considering dating. You can say something like, "You know, my friend's date said that . . . What do you think about it?" It's a good way to find

out if he has attitudes that can lead to trouble.

Primary Prevention of AIDS

It really is demeaning for someone in my situation to have the 1990s' version of leprosy, to have to walk around on eggshells when we know that I am absolutely no danger to anyone. . . . You can kiss me, you can hug me, you can shake my hand, you can drink out of the same glass. I can sneeze on you, I can cough on you — you're not going to get it from me.

ARTHUR ASHE (1992), FORMER TENNIS
PLAYER AND WIMBLEDON CHAMPION, WHO
DIED OF AIDS IN 1993

The "1990s' version of leprosy" is acquired immunodeficiency syndrome (AIDS). AIDS is a fatal condition in which one's immune system is so weakened that it falls prey to "opportunistic" diseases. (Opportunistic diseases are those that would not stand much of a chance of developing in people whose immune systems were intact.) AIDS is caused by the human immunodeficiency virus (HIV). Although it takes an average (median) of 10 years for people who are infected with HIV to develop AIDS, researchers believe that perhaps 99% of those who are infected will eventually develop AIDS (Kolata, 1991b).

HIV is transmitted by heterosexual vaginal intercourse, anal intercourse, sharing contaminated hypodermic needles (as when a group of people "shoots up" a drug), transfusions of contaminated blood, and childbirth (Glasner & Kaslow, 1990). There is no evidence that public toilets, holding or hugging an infected person, or living or attending school with one transmit the virus.

HIV has an affinity for, and kills, white blood cells called CD4 lymphocytes[3] (or, more simply, CD4 cells) that are found in the immune system. CD4 cells recognize viruses and other germs and "instruct" other white blood cells — called B lymphocytes — to make antibodies. When CD4 cells are depleted, the body is left vulnerable to opportunistic diseases.

HIV has infected fewer Americans than most other sexually transmitted diseases. A survey of some 16,000 students at 19 universities found HIV antibodies present in only 30. That amounts to 2 of every 1,000 blood samples tested, or 0.2% (Gayle and others, 1990). However, because AIDS is fatal, this finding is cause for concern.

AIDS is characterized by fatigue, fever, unexplained weight loss, swollen lymph nodes, diarrhea, and, in many cases, impairment in learning and memory (Grant & Heaton, 1990). Opportunistic infections such as the following take hold: Kaposi's sarcoma, a cancer of the blood cells that is seen in many gay males who contract AIDS; PCP (pneumocystis carinii pneumonia), a kind of pneumonia that is characterized by coughing and shortness of breath; and, in women, invasive cancer of the cervix.

Men who engage in sexual activity with other men have been most prone to infection by HIV (CDC, 1993). Nearly 75% of cases diagnosed in the early 1980s were among gay males, but the percentage of gays among new cases has declined. People who inject ("shoot up") illicit drugs have also been widely affected. Although people who inject drugs accounted for only about 15% of cases in the early 1980s, they now account for about 25% of cases overall. Other people who have been at particular risk include sex partners of people who inject drugs, babies born to women who inject drugs or whose sex partners inject drugs, prostitutes, men who visit prostitutes, sex partners of men who visit infected prostitutes, and people receiving blood transfusions — for example, surgery patients and hemophiliacs. This last avenue of infection has become rare because the medical community routinely screens blood supplies (Busch and others, 1991).

People tend to underestimate their risk of being infected with HIV (van der Velde and others, 1994). This finding holds true for impoverished inner city residents (Hobfoll and others, 1993) as well as college students (Goldman & Harlow, 1993). Because AIDS has often been characterized as

---

[3] Also called T_4 *cells* or *helper T cells.*

transmitted by anal intercourse (a practice that is not uncommon among gay males) and the sharing of contaminated needles, many heterosexual, non-drug-abusing Americans have dismissed the threat of AIDS to them (Kolata, 1993a). Yet heterosexual intercourse accounts for a majority of cases worldwide (Goodgame, 1990; Kolata, 1993a). Although gay males and drug abusers have been hit hardest by the epidemic, HIV infection cuts across all boundaries of gender, sexual orientation, ethnicity, and socioeconomic status.

Truth or Fiction Revisited. *It is not true that only gay males and substance abusers are at serious risk for contracting AIDS.* We all need to be aware of the risk factors and take appropriate precautions.

Infection by HIV is generally diagnosed by blood tests that show antibodies to the virus. Because it can take months after infection for antibodies to develop, repeated tests may be in order.

Unfortunately, we do not have a safe, effective vaccine for HIV. Nor is there a cure for AIDS. A number of antiviral drugs and behavioral interventions are under investigation, singly and in combination. Drug therapy has not cured anyone of AIDS to date (Eckholm, 1994). The only known way to effectively cope with AIDS is by *prevention* (Chesney, 1993; Kelly and others, 1993).

WHAT TO DO
You're not just sleeping with one person, you're sleeping with everyone they ever slept with.
DR. THERESA CRENSHAW, PRESIDENT,
AMERICAN ASSOCIATION OF SEX EDUCATORS,
COUNSELORS AND THERAPISTS

Most college students appear to be reasonably well-informed about HIV transmission and AIDS (Wulfert & Wan, 1993). However, knowledge of AIDS and methods of HIV transmission are apparently insufficient in themselves to induce self-protective behavior (Bandura, 1990). Many college students assume that a partner would not be infected with HIV. They simply hope for the best—even in the age of AIDS (Wulfert & Wan, 1993).

What can we do to prevent the transmission of HIV? A number of things.

1. *Refuse to deny the prevalence and harmful nature of AIDS.* Many people try to put AIDS and other sexually transmitted diseases (STDs) out of their minds and wing it when it comes to sex. The first and most important aspect of primary prevention is psychological: keeping AIDS in mind—refusing to play the dangerous game (at least for the moment) that it does not exist or is unlikely to strike you. Other measures involve modifying our behavior.

2. *Remain abstinent.* One way to curb the sexual transmission of HIV is sexual abstinence. Most people who remain abstinent do so while they are looking for Mr. or Ms. Right, of course. They thus eventually face the risk of engaging in sexual intercourse. Moreover, students want to know just what "abstinence" means. Does it mean avoiding sexual intercourse (yes) or any form of sexual activity with another person (not necessarily)? Kissing, hugging, and petting to orgasm (without coming into contact with semen or

vaginal secretions) are generally considered safe.

3. *Engage in a monogamous relationship with someone who is not infected.* Sexual activity within a monogamous relationship with an uninfected person is safe. The questions here are how certain one can be that one's partner is indeed uninfected and monogamous.

For those who are unwilling to abstain from sexual relationships or to limit themselves to a monogamous relationship, some things can be done that make sex safer—if not perfectly safe:

4. *Be selective.* Engage in sexual activity only with people well known to you who are not at high risk for being infected with HIV.

5. *Inspect one's partner's genitals.* People who have been infected by HIV often have other sexually transmitted diseases. Examining one's partner's genitals for blisters, discharges, chancres, rashes, warts, lice, and unpleasant odors during foreplay may yield signs of such diseases.

6. *Wash one's own genitals before and after contact.* Washing beforehand helps protect one's partner. Washing promptly afterward with soap and water helps remove germs.

7. *Use spermicides.* Many spermicides kill HIV as well as sperm. Check with a pharmacist.

8. *Use condoms.* Latex condoms (but not condoms made from animal membrane) protect the man from vaginal

(or other) body fluids and protect the woman from having infected semen enter the vagina.

9. *Contribute to research on AIDS.* If you can afford it, make a contribution to the American Foundation for AIDS Research (AMFAR) or to the Pediatric AIDS Foundation. Both organizations are based in Los Angeles.

10. *When in doubt, stop.* If one is not sure that sex is safe, one can stop and mull things over or seek expert advice.

If you think about it, this last point is rather good general advice. When in doubt, why not stop and think, regardless of whether the doubt is about one's sex partner, one's college major, or a financial investment? In sex and in most other areas of life, hesitating when in doubt pays off in many, many ways.

Reflections

Now that you have read the sections on the primary prevention of rape and AIDS, reflect on the following questions:

• Agree or disagree with the following statement and support your answer: "A woman who is raped is partly to blame if she agrees to go to the man's room or home."

• Agree or disagree with the following statement and support your answer: "One's behavior, and not one's group membership, places one at risk of HIV infection."

• Agree or disagree with the following statement and support your answer: "Safe sex is the answer to the AIDS epidemic."

APPENDIX A

Statistics

Imagine that some visitors from outer space arrive outside Madison Square Garden in New York City. Their goal this dark and numbing winter evening is to learn all they can about the inhabitants of planet Earth. They are drawn inside the Garden by lights, shouts, and warmth. The spotlighting inside rivets their attention to a wood-floored arena where the New York Apples are hosting the California Quakes in a briskly contested basketball game.

Our visitors use their sophisticated instruments to take some measurements of the players. Some surprising statistics are sent back to the planet of their origin: It appears that (1) 100% of Earthlings are male, and (2) the height of Earthlings ranges from 6 feet 1 inch to 7 feet 2 inches.

Statistics is the name given the science concerned with obtaining and organizing numerical measurements or information. Our imagined visitors have sent home some statistics about the sex and size of human beings that are at once accurate and misleading. Although they accurately measured the basketball players, their small **sample** of Earth's **population** was quite distorted. Fortunately for us Earthlings, about half of us are female. And the **range** of heights observed by the aliens, of 6 feet 1 to 7 feet 2, is both restricted and too high. People vary in height by more than 1 foot and 1 inch. And our **average** height is not between 6 feet 1 inch and 7 feet 2 inches but a number of inches below.

Psychologists, like our imagined visitors, are vitally concerned with measuring human as well as animal characteristics and traits—not just physical characteristics like sex and height but also psychological traits like intelligence, aggressiveness, anxiety, or self-assertiveness. By observing the central tendencies (averages) and variations in measurements from person to person, psychologists can state that some person is average or above average in intelligence or that another person is less assertive than, say, 60% of the population.

But psychologists, unlike our aliens, are careful in their attempts to select a sample that accurately represents the entire population. Professional basketball players do not represent the human species. They are taller, stronger, and more agile than the rest of us, and they make more shaving-cream commercials.

In this appendix, we shall survey some of the statistical methods used by psychologists to draw conclusions about the measurements they take in research activities. First, we shall discuss *descriptive statistics* and learn what types of statements we can make about the height of basketball players and some other human traits. Then, we shall discuss the *normal curve* and learn why basketball players are abnormal—at least in terms of height. We shall explore *correlation coefficients* and provide you with some less-than-shocking news: More intelligent people attain higher grades than less intelligent people. Finally, we shall have a brief look at inferential *statistics* and see why we can be bold enough to say that the difference in height between basketball players and other people is not just a chance accident, or fluke. Basketball players are in fact statistically significantly taller than the general population.

DESCRIPTIVE STATISTICS

Being told that someone is a "10" is not very descriptive unless you know something about how possible scores are distributed and how frequently one finds a 10. Fortunately—for 10s, if not for the rest of us—one is usually informed that someone is a 10 on a scale of 1 to 10 and that 10 is the positive end of the scale. If this is not sufficient, one will also be told that 10s are few and far between—rather unusual statistical events.

This business of a scale from 1 to 10 is not very scientific, to be sure, but it does suggest something about **descriptive statistics.** We can use descriptive statistics to clarify our understanding of a distribution of scores such as heights, test grades, IQs, or increases or decreases in measures of sexual arousal following the drinking of alcohol.

Statistics • Numerical facts assembled in such a manner that they provide significant information about measures or scores. (From the Latin word *status,* meaning "standing" or "position.")

Sample • Part of a population.

Population • A complete group from which a sample is selected.

Range • A measure of variability; the distance between extreme measures or scores.

Average • Central tendency of a group of measures, expressed as mean, median, and mode.

Descriptive statistics • The branch of statistics that is concerned with providing information about a distribution of scores.

Frequency distribution • An ordered set of data that indicates how frequently scores appear.

Histogram • A graphic representation of a frequency distribution that uses rectangular solids. (From the Greek *bistoria,* meaning "narrative," and *gramma,* meaning "writing" or "drawing.")

Polygon • A closed figure. (From the Greek *polys,* meaning "many," and *gōnia,* meaning "angle.")

MINILECTURE: CENTRAL TENDENCY

For example, descriptive statistics can help us to determine measures of central tendency, or averages, and to determine how much variability there is in the scores. Being a 10 loses some of its charm if the average score is an 11. Being a 10 is more remarkable in a distribution whose scores range from 1 to 10 than in one that ranges from 9 to 10.

Let us now examine some of the concerns of descriptive statistics: the frequency distribution, measures of central tendency (types of averages), and measures of variability.

The Frequency Distribution. A **frequency distribution** takes scores or items of raw data, puts them into order as from lowest to highest, and groups them according to class intervals. Table A.1 shows the rosters for a recent California Quakes–New York Apples basketball game. The members of each team are listed according to the numbers on their uniforms. Table A.2 shows a frequency distribution of the heights of the players of both teams combined, with a class interval of 1 inch.

It would also be possible to use 3-inch class intervals, as in Table A.3. In determining how large a class interval should be, a researcher attempts to collapse that data into a small enough number of classes to ensure that they will appear meaningful at a glance. But the researcher also attempts to maintain a large enough number of cate-

gories to ensure that important differences are not obscured.

Table A.3 obscures the fact that no players are 6 feet 4 inches tall. If the researcher believes that this information is extremely important, a class interval of 1 inch may be maintained.

Figure A.1 shows two methods for representing the information in Table A.3 with graphs. Both in frequency **histograms** and frequency **polygons,** the class intervals are typically drawn along the horizontal line, or X-axis, and the number of scores (persons, cases, or events) in each class is drawn along the vertical line, or Y-axis. In a histogram, the number of scores in each class interval is represented by a rectangular solid so that the graph resembles a series of steps. In a polygon, the number of scores in each class interval is plotted as a point, and the points are then connected to form a many-sided geometric figure. Note that class intervals were added at both ends of the horizontal axis of the frequency polygon so that the lines could be brought down to the axis to close the geometric figure.

Measures of Central Tendency.
Never try to walk across a river just because it has an average depth of four feet.
MARTIN FRIEDMAN

There are three types of measures of central tendency, or averages: *mean, median,* and *mode.* Each tells us something about the way

TABLE A.1
Rosters of Quakes versus Apples at New York

CALIFORNIA			NEW YORK		
2	Callahan	6′-7″	3	Roosevelt	6′-1″
5	Daly	6′-11″	12	Chaffee	6′-5″
6	Chico	6′-2″	13	Baldwin	6′-9″
12	Capistrano	6′-3″	25	Delmar	6′-6″
21	Brentwood	6′-5″	27	Merrick	6′-8″
25	Van Nuys	6′-3″	28	Hewlett	6′-6″
31	Clemente	6′-9″	33	Hollis	6′-9″
32	Whittier	6′-8″	42	Bedford	6′-5″
41	Fernando	7′-2″	43	Coram	6′-2″
43	Watts	6′-9″	45	Hampton	6′-10″
53	Huntington	6′-6″	53	Ardsley	6′-10″

A glance at the rosters for a recent California Quakes-New York Apples basketball game shows you that the heights of the team members, combined, ranged from 6 feet 1 inch to 7 feet 2 inches. Are the heights of the team members representative of those of the general male population?

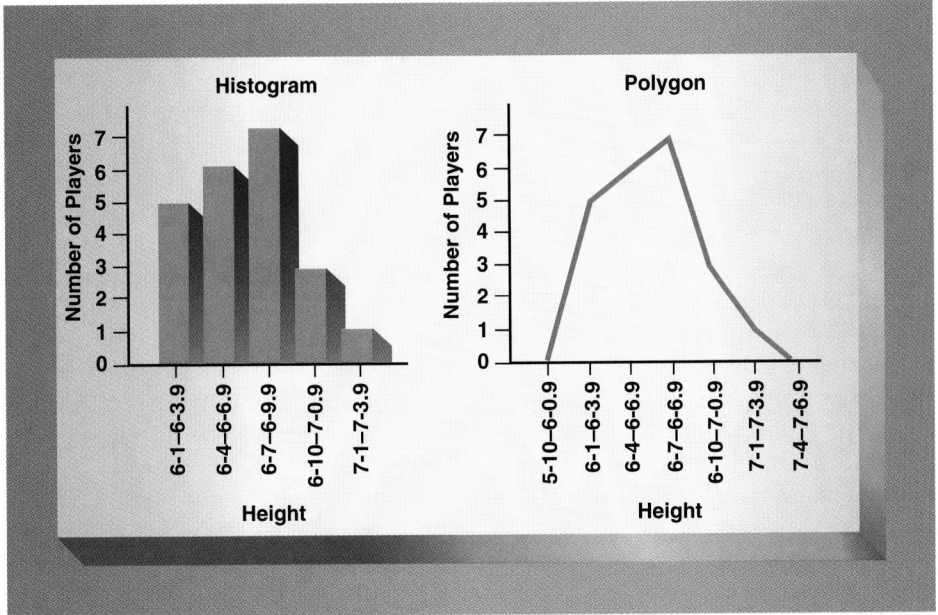

FIGURE A.1
Two Graphical Representations of the Data in Table A.3.

Mean • A type of average calculated by dividing the sum of scores by the number of scores. (From the Latin *medius*, meaning "middle.")

Median • The score beneath which 50% of the class fall. (From the Latin *medius*, meaning "middle.")

Mode • The most frequently occurring number or score in a distribution. (From the Latin *modus*, meaning "measure.")

in which the scores in a distribution may be summarized by a typical or representative number.

The **mean** is what most people think of as "the average." The mean is obtained by adding up all the scores in a distribution and then dividing this sum by the number of scores. In the case of our basketball players, it would be advisable first to convert all heights into one unit, such as inches (6′1″ becomes 73″, and so on). If we add all the heights in inches, then divide by the number of players, or 22, we obtain a mean height of 78.73″, or 6′6.73″.

The **median** is the score of the middle case in a frequency distribution. It is the score beneath which 50% of the cases fall. In a distribution with an even number of cases, such as the distribution of the heights of the 22 basketball players in Table A.2, the median is determined by finding the mean of the two middle cases. Listing these 22 cases in ascending order, we find that the 11th case is 6′6″ and the 12th case is 6′7″. Thus the median is (6′6″ + 6′7″)/2, or 6′6½″.

In the case of the heights of the basketball players, the mean and the median are similar, and either serves as a useful indicator of the central tendency of the data. But sup-

pose we are attempting to determine the average savings of 30 families living on a suburban block. Let us assume that 29 of the 30 families have savings between $8,000 and $12,000, adding up to $294,000. But the 30th family has savings of $1,400,000! The mean savings for a family on this block would thus be $56,467. A mean can be greatly distorted by one or two extreme scores, and for such distributions the median is a better indicator of the central tendency. The median savings on our hypothetical block would lie between $8,000 and $12,000 and so would be more representative of the central tendency of savings. Studies of the incomes of American families usually report median rather than mean incomes just to avoid the distortions that would result from treating incomes of the small numbers of multimillionaires in the same way as other incomes.

The **mode** is simply the most frequently occurring score in a distribution. The mode of the data in Table A.1 is 6′9″ because this height occurs most often. The median class interval for the data in Table A.3 is 6′6½″ to 6′9½″. In these cases, the mode is somewhat higher than the mean or median height.

TABLE A.2

Frequency Distribution of Heights of Basketball Players, with a One-inch Class Interval

CLASS INTERVAL	NUMBER OF PLAYERS IN CLASS
6-1 to 6-1.9	1
6-2 to 6-2.9	2
6-3 to 6-3.9	2
6-4 to 6-4.9	0
6-5 to 6-5.9	3
6-6 to 6-6.9	3
6-7 to 6-7.9	1
6-8 to 6-8.9	2
6-9 to 6-9.9	4
6-10 to 6-10.9	2
6-11 to 6-11.9	1
7-0 to 7-0.9	0
7-1 to 7-1.9	0
7-2 to 7-2.9	1

TABLE A.3

Frequency
Distribution of Heights
of Basketball Players,
with a Three-inch
Class Interval

CLASS INTERVAL	NUMBER OF PLAYERS IN CLASS
6-1 to 6-3.9	5
6-4 to 6-6.9	6
6-7 to 6-9.9	7
6-10 to 7-0.9	3
7-1 to 7-3.9	1

MINILECTURE:
VARIABILITY

Bimodal • Having two modes.
Range • The difference between the highest and the lowest scores in a distribution.
Standard deviation • A measure of the variability of a distribution, attained by the formula

$$\sqrt{\frac{\text{Sum of } d^2}{N}}$$

In some cases, the mode is a more appropriate description of a distribution than the mean or median. Figure A.2 shows a **bimodal** distribution, or a distribution with two modes. In this hypothetical distribution of the test scores, the mode at the left indicates the most common class interval for students who did not study, and the mode at the right indicates the most frequent class interval for students who did. The mean and median test scores would probably lie within the 55–59 class interval, yet use of that interval as a measure of central tendency would not provide very meaningful information about the distribution of scores. It might suggest that the test was too hard, not that a number of students chose not to study. One would be better able to visualize the distribution of scores if it is reported as a bimodal distribution. Even in similar cases in which the modes are not exactly equal, it might be more appropriate to describe a distribution as being bimodal or even multimodal.

Measures of Variability. Measures of variability of a distribution inform us about the spread of scores, or about the typical distances of scores from the average score. Measures of variability include the *range* of scores and the *standard deviation*.

The **range** of scores in a distribution is defined as the difference between the highest score and the lowest score, and it is ob-

tained by subtracting the lowest score from the highest score. The range of heights in Table A.2 is 7'2" minus 6'1", or 1'1". It is important to know the range of temperatures if we move to a new climate so that we may anticipate the weather and dress appropriately. A teacher must have some understanding of the range of abilities or skills in a class to teach effectively.

The range is an imperfect measure of variability because of the manner in which it is influenced by extreme scores. In our earlier discussion of the savings of 30 families on a suburban block, the range of savings is $1,400,000 to $8,000, or $1,392,000. This tells us little about the typical variability of savings accounts, which lie within a restricted range of $8,000 to $12,000. The **standard deviation** is a statistic that indicates how scores are distributed about a mean of a distribution.

The standard deviation considers every score in a distribution, not just the extreme scores. Thus, the standard deviation for the distribution on the right in Figure A.3 would be smaller than that of the distribution on the left. Note that each distribution has the same number of scores, the same mean, and the same range of scores. But the standard deviation for the distribution on the right is smaller than that of the distribution on the left, because the scores tend to cluster more closely about the mean.

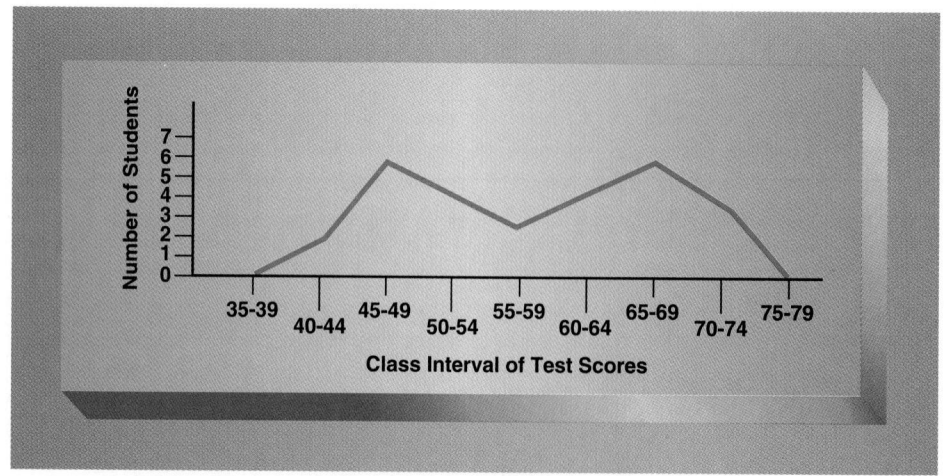

FIGURE A.2
A Bimodal Distribution This hypothetical distribution represents students' scores on a test. The mode at the left represents the central tendency of students who did not study, and the mode at the right represents the mode of students who did study.

The standard deviation (S.D.) is calculated by the formula

$$S.D. = \sqrt{\frac{\text{Sum of } d^2}{N}}$$

where *d* equals the deviation of each score from the mean of the distribution, and *N* equals the number of scores in the distribution.

Let us find the mean and standard deviation of the IQ scores listed in column 1 of Table A.4. To obtain the mean, we add all the scores, attain 1,500, and then divide by the number of scores (15) to obtain a mean of 100. We obtain the deviation score *(d)* for each IQ score by subtracting the score from 100. The *d* for an IQ of 85 equals 100 minus 85, or 15, and so on. Then we square each *d* and add these squares. The S.D. equals the square root of the sum of squares (1,426) divided by the number of scores (15), or 9.75.

As an additional exercise, we can show that the S.D. of the test scores on the left (in Figure A.3) is greater than that for the scores on the right by assigning the grades points according to a 4.0 system. Let A = 4, B = 3, C = 2, D = 1, and F = 0. The S.D. for each distribution of test scores is computed in Table A.5. The greater S.D.

for the distribution on the left indicates that the scores in that distribution are more variable, or tend to be farther from the mean.

THE NORMAL CURVE

Many human traits and characteristics such as height and intelligence seem to be distributed in a pattern known as a normal distribution. In a **normal distribution,** the mean, median, and mode all fall at the same data point or score. Scores cluster most heavily about the mean, fall off rapidly in either direction at first (as shown in Figure A.4), and then taper off more gradually.

The curve in Figure A.4 is bell shaped. This type of distribution is also called a **normal curve.** It is hypothesized to reflect the distribution of variables in which different scores are determined by chance variation. Height is thought to be largely determined by chance combinations of genetic material. A distribution of the heights of a random sample of the population approximates normal distributions for men and women, with the mean of the distribution for men a few inches higher than the mean for women.

Test developers traditionally assumed that intelligence was also randomly or normally

TABLE A.4
Hypothetical Scores Attained from an IQ Testing

IQ SCORE	*d* (DEVIATION SCORE)	d^2 (DEVIATION SCORE SQUARED)
85	15	225
87	13	169
89	11	121
90	10	100
93	7	49
97	3	9
97	3	9
100	0	0
101	− 1	1
104	− 4	16
105	− 5	25
110	− 10	100
112	− 12	144
113	− 13	169
117	− 17	289

Sum of IQ scores = 1,500
Sum of d^2 scores = 1,426

$$\text{Mean} = \frac{\text{Sum of scores}}{\text{Number of scores}}$$
$$= \frac{1,500}{15} = 100$$

Standard Deviation (S.D.)
$$= \sqrt{\frac{\text{Sum of } d^2}{\text{Number of Scores}}}$$
$$= \sqrt{\frac{1,426}{15}} = \sqrt{95.07} = 9.75$$

Normal distribution • A symmetrical distribution in which approximately 68% of cases lie within a standard deviation of the mean.

Normal curve • Graphic presentation of a normal distribution, showing a bell shape.

FIGURE A.3
Hypothetical Distributions of Student Test Scores Each distribution has the same number of scores, the same mean, and even the same range, but the standard deviation is greater for the distribution on the left because the scores tend to be farther from the mean.

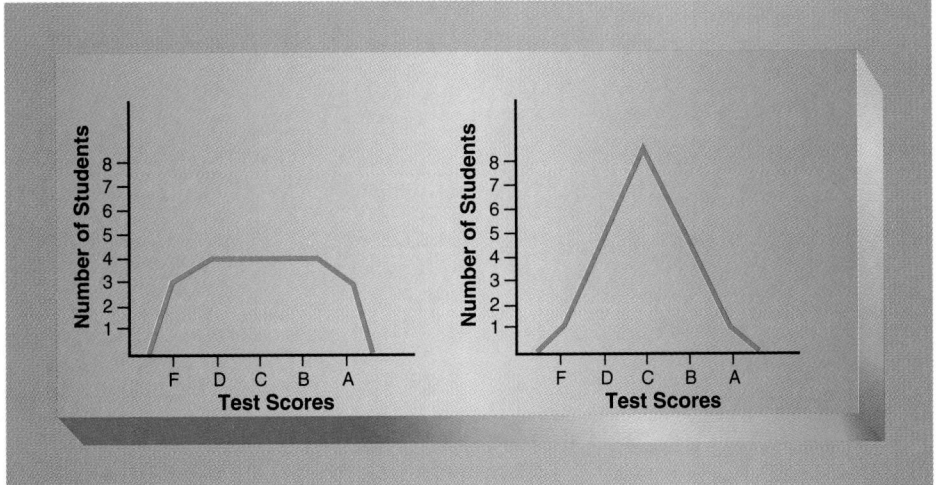

TABLE A.5

Computation of
Standard Deviations
for Test-score
Distributions in
Figure A.3

DISTRIBUTION AT LEFT:			DISTRIBUTION AT RIGHT:		
GRADE	d	d^2	GRADE	d	d^2
A (4)	2	4	A (4)	2	4
A (4)	2	4	B (3)	1	1
A (4)	2	4	B (3)	1	1
B (3)	1	1	B (3)	1	1
B (3)	1	1	B (3)	1	1
B (3)	1	1	C (2)	0	0
B (3)	1	1	C (2)	0	0
C (2)	0	0	C (2)	0	0
C (2)	0	0	C (2)	0	0
C (2)	0	0	C (2)	0	0
C (2)	0	0	C (2)	0	0
D (1)	−1	1	C (2)	0	0
D (1)	−1	1	C (2)	0	0
D (1)	−1	1	D (1)	−1	1
D (1)	−1	1	D (1)	−1	1
F (0)	−2	4	D (1)	−1	1
F (0)	−2	4	D (1)	−1	1
F (0)	−2	4	F (0)	−2	4
Sum of grades = 36			Sum of grades = 36		
Mean grade = 36/18 = 2			Mean grade = 36/18 = 2		
Sum of d^2 = 32			Sum of d^2 = 16		
S.D. = $\sqrt{32/18}$ = 1.33			S.D. = $\sqrt{16/18}$ = 0.94		

Correlation coefficient • A number between −1.00 and +1.00 that indicates the degree of relationship between two variables.

distributed among the population. For that reason, they constructed intelligence tests so that scores would be distributed as close to "normal" as possible. In actuality, IQ scores are also influenced by environmental factors and chromosomal abnormalities, so the resultant curves are not perfectly normal. Most IQ tests have means defined as scores of 100 points, and the Wechsler scales are constructed to have standard deviations of 15 points, as shown in Figure A.4. This means that 50% of the Wechsler scores fall between 90 and 100 (the "broad average" range), about 68% (or two of three) fall between 85 and 115, and more than 95% fall between 70 and 130—that is, within two S.D.s of the mean.

The Scholastic Assessment Test (SATs) were constructed so that the mean scores would be 500 points, and an S.D. would be 100 points. Thus, a score of 600 would equal or excel that of some 84 to 85% of the test takers. Because of the complex interaction of variables determining SAT scores, the distribution of SAT scores is not exactly normal either. The normal curve is an idealized curve.

THE CORRELATION COEFFICIENT

What is the relationship between intelligence and educational achievement? Between cigarette smoking and lung cancer in human beings? Between introversion and frequency of dating among college students? We cannot run experiments to determine whether the relationships between these variables are causal, because we cannot manipulate the independent variable. For example, we cannot randomly assign a group of people to cigarette smoking and another group to nonsmoking. People must be permitted to make their own choices, and so it is possible that the same factors that lead people to choose to smoke may also lead to lung cancer. However, the **correlation coefficient** may be used to show that there is a relationship between smoking and cancer.

The correlation coefficient is a statistic that describes the relationship between two variables. It varies from +1.00 to −1.00; therefore, a correlation coefficient of +1.00 is called a perfect positive correlation, a

FIGURE A.4

A Bell-Shaped or Normal Curve In a normal curve, approximately 68 percent of the cases lie within a standard deviation (S.D.) from the mean, and the mean, median, and mode all lie at the same score. IQ tests and Scholastic Assessment Tests have been constructed so that distributions of scores approximate the normal curve.

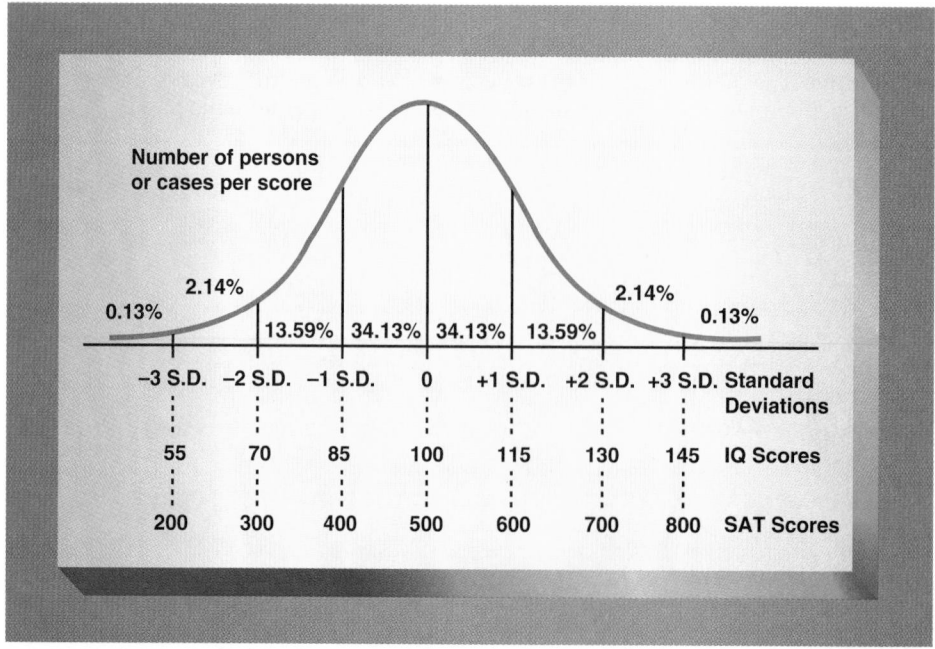

coefficient of −1.00 is a perfect negative correlation, and a coefficient of 0.00 shows no correlation between variables. The meanings of various correlation coefficients are discussed further in Chapter 2.

INFERENTIAL STATISTICS

In a study reported in Chapter 9, children enrolled in a Head Start program earned a mean IQ score of 99, whereas children similar in background who were not enrolled in Head Start earned a mean IQ score of 93. Is this difference of six points in IQ significant, or does it represent chance fluctuation of scores? In a study reported in Chapter 2, people who believed they had drunk alcohol chose higher levels of electric shock to be applied to persons who had provoked them than did people who believed they had not drunk alcohol. Did the difference in level of shock chosen reflect an actual difference between the two groups, or could it have been a chance fluctuation? Inferential statistics help us make decisions about whether differences found between such groups reflect real differences or just fluctuations.

Figure A.5 shows the distribution of heights of 1,000 men and 1,000 women selected at random. The mean height for men is greater than the mean height for women.

Can we draw the conclusion, or **infer,** that this difference in heights represents the general population of men and women? Or must we avoid such an inference and summarize our results by stating only that the sample of 1,000 men in the study had a higher mean height than that of the sample of 1,000 women in the study?

If we could not draw inferences about populations from studies of samples, our research findings would be very limited indeed—limited only to the specific individuals studied. However, the branch of statistics known as **inferential statistics** uses mathematical techniques in such a way that we can draw conclusions about populations from which samples have been drawn.

Statistically Significant Differences. In determining whether differences in measures taken of research samples may be applied to the populations from which they were drawn, psychologists use mathematical techniques that indicate whether differences are statistically significant. Was the difference in IQ scores for children attending and those not attending Head Start significant? Did it represent only the children participating in the study, or can it be applied to all children represented by the sample? Is the difference between the height of men and the height of

Infer • To draw a conclusion, to conclude. (From the Latin *in,* meaning "in," and *ferre,* meaning "to bear.")

Inferential statistics • The branch of statistics concerned with the confidence with which conclusions drawn about samples may be extended to the populations from which they were drawn.

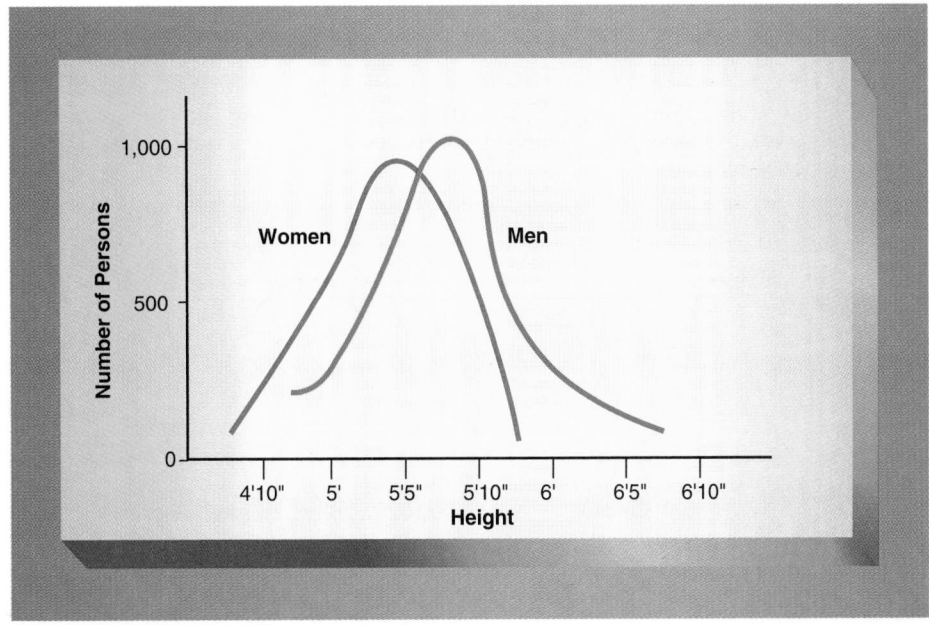

FIGURE A.5
Distribution of Heights for Random Samples of Men and Women Inferential statistics permit us to apply our findings to the populations sampled.

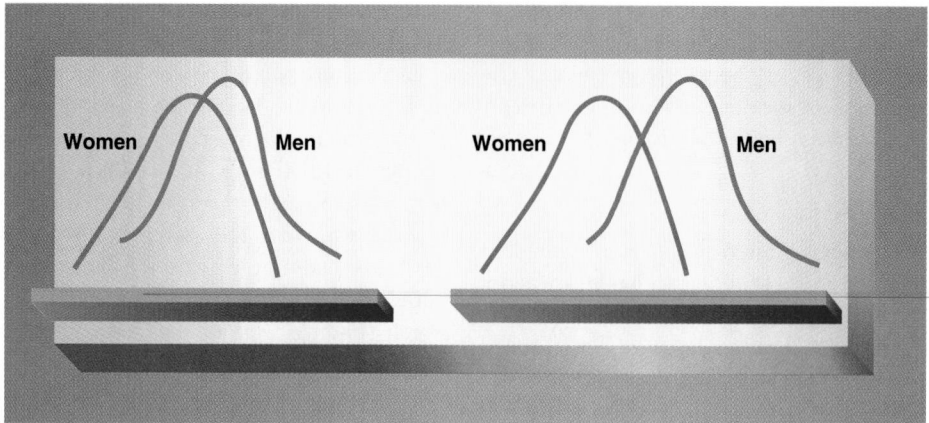

FIGURE A.6
Psychologists use group means and standard deviations to determine whether the difference between group means is statistically significant. The difference between the means of the groups on the right is greater and thus more likely to be statistically significant.

women in Figure A.5 statistically significant? Can we apply our findings to all men and women?

Psychologists use formulas involving the means and standard deviations of sample groups to determine whether group differences are statistically significant. As you can see in Figure A.6, the farther apart the group means are, the more likely it is that the difference between them is statistically significant. This makes a good deal of common sense. After all, if you were told that your neighbor's car had gotten one-tenth of a mile more per gallon of gasoline than your car had last year, you might assume

that this was a chance difference. But if the difference was farther apart, say 14 miles per gallon, you might readily believe that this difference reflected an actual difference in driving habits or efficiency of the automobiles.

As you can see in Figure A.7, the smaller the standard deviations (a measure of variability) of the two groups, the more likely it is that the difference of the means is statistically significant. As an extreme example, if all women sampled were exactly 5'5" tall, and all men sampled were exactly 5'10", we would be highly likely to assume that the difference of 5 inches in group means is

FIGURE A.7
The variability of the groups on the left is smaller than the variability of the groups on the right. Thus, it is more likely that the difference between the means of the groups on the left is statistically significant.

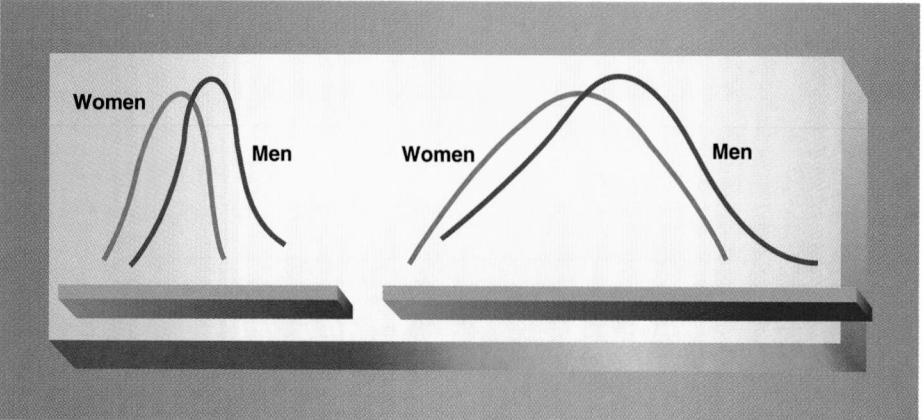

statistically significant. But if the heights of women varied from 2' to 14', and the heights of men varied from 2'1" to 14'3", we might be more likely to assume that the 5-inch difference in group means could be attributed to chance fluctuation.

Samples and Populations. Inferential statistics are mathematical tools that psychologists apply to samples of scores to determine whether they can generalize their findings to populations of scores. Thus, they must be quite certain that the samples involved actually represent the populations from which they were drawn.

As you learned in Chapter 2, psychologists often use the techniques of random sampling and stratified sampling of populations to draw representative samples. If the samples studied do not accurately represent their intended populations, it matters very little how sophisticated the statistical techniques of the psychologist may be. We could use a variety of statistical techniques on the heights of the New York Apples and California Quakes, but none would tell us much about the height of the general population.

APPENDIX B

Answer Keys for Questionnaires

SCORING KEY FOR "WHY DO YOU DRINK?" (CHAPTER 5, P. 189)

Why do you drink? Score your questionnaire by seeing how many items you answered for each of the reasons for drinking listed at left. Consider the key to be *suggestive* only. For example, if you answered several items in the manner indicated on the *addiction* factor, it may be wise to seriously examine what your drinking means to you. But do not interpret a few test-item scores as binding evidence of addiction.

Addiction	Social Reward
1. T	**3**. T
6. F	**8**. T
32. T	**23**. T
38. T	
40. T	Celebration
	10. T
Anxiety/	**24**. T
Tension	**25**. T
Reduction	
7. T	Religion
9. T	**11**. T
12. T	
15. T	Social Power
18. T	**2**. T
26. T	**13**. T
31. T	**19**. T
33. T	**30**. T
Pleasure/Taste	Scapegoating
2. T	(Using alcohol
5. T	as an excuse for
16. T	failure or social
27. T	misconduct)
28. T	**14**. T
35. T	**15**. T
37. T	**20**. T
	21. T
Transforming	**39**. T
Agent	
2. T	Habit
4. T	**17**. T
19. T	**29**. T
22. T	
28. T	
30. T	
34. T	
36. T	

SCORING KEY FOR "THE REMOTE ASSOCIATES TEST" (CHAPTER 8, P. 304)

1. Prince	4. Glasses	7. Defense
2. Dog	5. Club	8. Pit
3. Cold	6. Boat	9. Writer

SCORING KEY FOR "THE SENSATION-SEEKING SCALE" (CHAPTER 10, P. 371)

Because this is a shortened version of a questionnaire, no norms are available. However, answers in agreement with the following key point in the direction of sensation seeking:

1. A	5. A	9. B	13. B
2. A	6. B	10. A	
3. A	7. A	11. A	
4. B	8. A	12. A	

SCORING KEY FOR "THE RATHUS ASSERTIVENESS SCHEDULE" (CHAPTER 14, P. 541)

Tabulate your score as follows: For those items followed by an asterisk (★), change the signs (plus to minus; minus to plus). For example, if the response to an asterisked item was 2, place a minus sign (−) before the 2. If the response to an asterisked item was −3, change the minus sign to a plus sign (+) by adding a vertical stroke. Then add up the scores of the 30 items.

Scores on the assertiveness schedule can vary from +90 to −90. Table B.1 will show you how your score compares with those of 764 college women and 637 men from 35 campuses across the United States. For example, if you are a woman and your score is 26, it exceeds that of 80% of the women in the sample. A score of 15 for a male exceeds that of 55–60% of the men in the sample.

ANSWER KEY FOR THE "SOCIAL READJUSTMENT RATING SCALE" (CHAPTER 15, PP. 568–569)

Add all the scores in the "Total" column to arrive at your final score.

FINAL SCORE _____

Interpretation. Your final score is indicative of the amount of stress you have experienced during the past 12 months (see Table B.2).

Research has shown that the probability of encountering physical illness within the *following* year is related to the amount of stress experienced during the *past* year. That is, college students who experienced minor stress have a 28% chance of becoming ill; mild stress, a 45% chance; moderate stress, a 70% chance; and major stress, an 82% chance. Moreover, the seriousness of the illness also increases with the amount of stress.

It should be recognized that these percentages reflect previous research with college students. Do not assume if you have encountered a great deal of stress that you are "doomed" to illness. Also keep in mind that a number of psychological factors moderate the impact of stress, as discussed in Chapter 15. For example, psychologically hardy college students could theoretically

TABLE B.1

WOMEN'S SCORES	PER- CENTILE	MEN'S SCORES
55	99	65
48	97	54
45	95	48
37	90	40
31	85	33
26	80	30
23	75	26
19	70	24
17	65	19
14	60	17
11	55	15
8	50	11
6	45	8
2	40	6
− 1	35	3
− 4	30	1
− 8	25	− 3
− 13	20	− 7
− 17	15	− 11
− 24	10	− 15
− 34	5	− 24
− 39	3	− 30
− 48	1	− 41

withstand the same amount of stress that could enhance the risk of illness for non-hardy individuals.

ANSWER KEY FOR "ARE YOU TYPE A OR TYPE B?" (CHAPTER 15, P. 574)

As described in Chapter 15, type A's are ambitious, hard driving, and chronically discontent with their current achievements. Type B's, in contrast, are more relaxed and more involved with the quality of life.

TABLE B.2

FINAL SCORE	AMOUNT OF STRESS
From 0 to 1,500	Minor stress
1,501–3,500	Mild stress
3,501–5,500	Moderate stress
5,501 and above	Major stress

The questionnaire was developed from descriptions of type A people by Friedman and Ulmer (1984), Matthews and her colleagues (1982), and Musante and others (1983). Yesses suggest the type A behavior pattern, which is marked by a sense of time urgency and constant struggle. In appraising your type, you need not be overly concerned with the precise number of "yes" answers; we have no normative data for you. But as Friedman and Rosenman (1974, p. 85) note, you should have little trouble spotting yourself as "hard core" or "moderately afflicted"—that is, if you are honest with yourself.

ANSWER KEY FOR THE "LOCUS OF CONTROL SCALE" (CHAPTER 15, PP. 576–577)

Place a check mark in the blank space in the scoring key (Table B.3) each time your answer agrees with the answer in the key. The number of check marks is your total score.

Interpreting Your Score.

Low Scorers (0–8). About one respondent in three earns a score of from 0 to 8. Such respondents tend to have an internal locus of control. They see themselves as being responsible for the reinforcements they attain (and fail to attain) in life.

Average Scorers (9–16). Most respondents earn from 9 to 16 points. Average scorers may see themselves as partially in control of their lives. Perhaps they see themselves as being in control at work but not in their social lives—or vice versa.

High Scorers (17–40). About 15% of respondents attain scores of 17 or above. High scorers tend to see life largely as a game of chance and success as a matter of luck or the generosity of others.

NORMS FOR "THE LOVE SCALE" (CHAPTER 16, P. 634)

The Love Scale was validated with a sample of 220 undergraduates, aged 19–24 (mean age = 21), from Northeastern University. Students were asked to indicate whether

TABLE B.3

Scoring Key

1. Yes ___	21. Yes ___
2. No ___	22. No ___
3. Yes ___	23. Yes ___
4. No ___	24. Yes ___
5. Yes ___	25. No ___
6. No ___	26. No ___
7. Yes ___	27. Yes ___
8. Yes ___	28. No ___
9. No ___	29. Yes ___
10. Yes ___	30. No ___
11. Yes ___	31. Yes ___
12. Yes ___	32. No ___
13. No ___	33. Yes ___
14. Yes ___	34. No ___
15. No ___	35. Yes ___
16. Yes ___	36. Yes ___
17. Yes ___	37. Yes ___
18. Yes ___	38. No ___
19. Yes ___	39. Yes ___
20. No ___	40. No ___

TOTAL SCORE _____

TABLE B.4

Love-Scale Scores of Northeastern University Students

CONDITION	N*	MEAN SCORES
Absolutely in love	56	89
Probably in love	45	80
Not sure	36	77
Probably not in love	40	68
Definitely not in love	43	59

*N = Number of students

they were "absolutely in love," "probably in love," "not sure," "probably not in love," or "definitely not in love" with a person they were dating. Then they answered the items on the Love Scale with the same person in mind.

Table B.4 shows the mean score for each category. Mean scores for men and women in each of the five categories did not differ, so they were lumped together. If your Love-Scale score for your date is 84, it may be that your feelings lie somewhere in between those of Northeastern University students who claimed that they were "probably in love" and "absolutely in love."

Be warned: A number of students broke into arguments after taking the Love Scale—their "love" for one another differed by a few points! Please do not take the scale so seriously. Such scales are fun, but they will not hold up in court as grounds for divorce. Rely on your feelings, not on your scores.

ANSWER KEY FOR "CULTURAL MYTHS THAT CREATE A CLIMATE THAT SUPPORTS RAPE" (CHAPTER 17, P. 691)

Actually, each item, with the exception of number 2, represents a cultural myth that tends to support rape. Item number 2, sad to say, is absolutely true. Agreement with any of these items shows an endorsement of such a myth.

PHOTO CREDITS

A13

LITERARY CREDITS

GLOSSARY

A

A–B problem The issue of how well we can predict behavior on the basis of attitudes.

Abreaction In psychodynamic theory, the expression of previously repressed feelings and impulses to allow the psychic energy associated with them to spill forth.

Absolute refractory period A phase following a neuron's firing during which an action potential cannot be triggered.

Absolute threshold The minimal amount of energy that can produce a sensation.

Abstinence syndrome A characteristic cluster of symptoms that results from sudden decrease in the level of usage of a drug on which one is physiologically dependent.

Accommodation According to Piaget, the modification of existing concepts or schemas so that new information can be integrated or understood.

Acculturation The process of adaptation in which immigrants and native groups identify with a new, dominant culture by learning about that culture and making behavioral and attitudinal changes.

Acetylcholine A neurotransmitter that controls muscle contractions. Abbreviated *ACh*.

Achievement Accomplishment; that which is attained by one's efforts and presumed to be made possible by one's abilities.

Acoustic code Mental representation of information as a sequence of sounds.

Acquired drives Drives that are acquired through experience, or learned.

Acquired immunodeficiency syndrome A fatal, sexually transmitted disease caused by the human immunodeficiency virus (HIV) that destroys cells of the immune system, leaving the body vulnerable to opportunistic diseases. Abbreviated *AIDS*.

Acquisition trial In conditioning, a presentation of stimuli such that a new response is learned and strengthened.

Acronym A word that is composed of the first letters of the elements of a phrase.

Acrophobia Fear of high places.

Action potential The electrical impulse that provides the basis for the conduction of a neural impulse along an axon of a neuron.

Activating effects The arousal-producing effects of sex hormones that increase the likelihood of dominant sexual responses.

Activation-synthesis model The view that dreams reflect activation by the reticular activating system and synthesis of activated cognitions by the cerebral cortex.

Active coping A response to stress that manipulates the environment or changes the response patterns of the individual to permanently remove the stressor or to render it harmless.

Actor–observer effect In attribution theory, the tendency to attribute our own behavior to situational factors but to attribute the behavior of others to dispositional factors.

Acupuncture The practice, originated in ancient China, of piercing parts of the body with needles to deaden pain and treat illness.

Adaptation stage See *resistance stage*.

ADH Abbreviation of antidiuretic hormone.

Adipose tissue Tissue that contains fat.

Adjustment The process of responding to stress.

Adolescence The stage of development between childhood and adulthood that is bounded by the advent of puberty and the capacity to assume adult responsibilities.

Adrenal cortex The outer part of the adrenal gland, which produces steroids.

Adrenaline A hormone produced by the adrenal medulla that stimulates the sympathetic division of the autonomic nervous system. Also called *epinephrine*.

Adrenal medulla The inner part of the adrenal gland, which produces adrenaline.

Adrenocorticotrophic hormone A pituitary hormone that regulates the adrenal cortex. Abbreviated *ACTH*.

Adult In transactional analysis, a rational, adaptive ego state.

Aerobic exercise Exercise that requires sustained increase in oxygen consumption.

Affective disorders Disorders characterized primarily by prolonged disturbances of mood or emotional response. (Now referred to as *mood disorders*.)

Afferent neuron A neuron that transmits messages from sensory receptors to the spinal cord and brain. Also called *sensory neuron*.

Affiliation The social motive to be with others and to cooperate.

Afterimage The lingering impression made by a stimulus that has been removed.

Age regression In hypnosis, taking on the role of childhood, frequently accompanied by vivid recollections of the early years.

Agoraphobia Fear of open, crowded places.

AIDS Acronym for *Acquired Immunodeficiency Syndrome*. A disorder of the immune system caused by human immunodeficiency virus (HIV) and characterized by suppression of the immune response, leaving the body prey to opportunistic diseases.

Alarm reaction The first stage of the general adaptation syndrome, which is triggered by the impact of a stressor and characterized by heightened sympathetic activity.

Alcoholism Drinking that persistently impairs personal, social, or physical well-being.

Algorithm A specific procedure such as a formula for solving a problem that will work invariably if it is applied correctly.

All-or-none principle The principle that a neuron fires an impulse of the same strength whenever its action potential has been triggered.

Alpha waves Rapid, low-amplitude brain waves that have been linked to feelings of relaxation.

Altered states of consciousness States other than the normal waking state, including sleep, meditation, the hypnotic trance, and the distorted perceptions that can be caused by use of certain drugs.

Alternate-form reliability The consistency of a test as determined by correlating scores attained on one form of the test with scores attained on another form. The Scholastic Assessment Tests and Graduate Record Exams, for example, have many forms.

Altruism Selflessness; unselfish concern for the welfare of others.

Alzheimer's disease A progressive disease that is associated with degeneration of hippocampal cells that produce acetylcholine. It is symptomized by the inability to form new memories and the loss of other cognitive functions.

Ambiguous Having two or more possible meanings.

Amenorrhea Absence of menstruation.

American Sign Language The communication of meaning through the use of symbols that are formed by moving the hands and arms and associated gestures. Abbreviated *ASL*.

Amino acid Protein involved in metabolism.

Amniocentesis A method for tapping amniotic fluid and examining fetal chromosomes that have been sloughed off, making it possible to determine the presence of genetic abnormalities and the sex of the fetus.

Amniotic fluid Fluid within the amniotic sac, formed largely from the fetus's urine, that protects the fetus from jarring or injury.

Amniotic sac A sac within the uterus that contains the embryo or fetus.

Amotivational syndrome Loss of ambition or motivation to achieve.

Amphetamines Stimulants such as Dexedrine and Benzedrine that are derived from *alpha-methyl-beta-phenyl-ethyl-amine*. Abuse can trigger symptoms that mimic schizophrenia.

Amplitude Height. The extreme range of a variable quantity.

Amygdala A part of the limbic system that apparently facilitates stereotypical aggressive responses.

Anabolic steroids Steroids, the chief of which is testosterone, that promote the growth of muscle tissue by creating protein and other substances. Anabolic steroids also foster feelings of invincibility. See also *corticosteroids*.

Anaerobic exercise Exercise that does not require sustained increase in oxygen consumption, such as weight lifting.

Anal expulsive A Freudian personality type characterized by unregulated self-expression such as messiness.

Anal fixation In psychodynamic theory, attachment to objects and behaviors characteristic of the anal stage.

Analgesia (1) A conscious state in which pain is reduced or terminated. (2) A method for inducing such a state.

Analogous hues Colors that lie next to one another on the color wheel, forming families of harmonious colors such as yellow and orange, and green and blue.

Anal retentive A Freudian personality type characterized by self-control such as excessive neatness and punctuality.

Anal stage   In psychodynamic theory, the second stage of psychosexual development, in which gratification is obtained through anal activities like eliminating wastes.

Analyst   A person who practices psychoanalysis, Freud's method of psychotherapy.

Analytical psychology   Jung's psychodynamic theory which emphasizes archetypes, a collective unconscious, and a unifying force of personality called the Self.

Anchoring and adjustment heuristic   A decision-making heuristic in which a presumption or first estimate serves as a cognitive anchor. As we receive additional information, we make adjustments, but tend to remain in the proximity of the anchor.

Androgen   Male sex hormone.

Anger   (1) A negative emotion frequently characterized by a provocation, cognitions that one has been taken advantage of and should seek revenge, and aggressive behavioral tendencies. (2) The second stage in Kübler-Ross's theory of dying.

Angiotensin   A kidney hormone that signals the hypothalamus of depletion of body fluids.

Animism   The belief, characteristic of preoperational thought, that inanimate objects move because of will or spirit.

Anorexia nervosa   An eating disorder characterized by maintenance of an abnormally low body weight, intense fear of weight gain, a distorted body image, and, in females, amenorrhea.

Anosmia   Lack of sensitivity to a specific odor.

ANS   Abbreviation for *autonomic nervous system.*

Antecedent   An event or thing that occurs before another. (An *antecedent* of behavior is not necessarily a *cause* of behavior.)

Anterograde amnesia   Failure to remember events that occur after physical trauma because of the effects of the trauma.

Antibodies   Substances formed by white blood cells that recognize and destroy antigens.

Antidepressant drug   A drug that acts to relieve depression.

Antidiuretic hormone   A pituitary hormone that conserves body fluids by increasing the reabsorption of urine. Abbreviated *ADH.*

Antigen   A substance that stimulates the body to mount an immune-system response to it. (The contraction for *anti*body *gen*erator.)

Antisocial personality disorder   The diagnosis given a person who is in frequent conflict with society yet is undeterred by punishment and experiences little or no guilt and anxiety. Also referred to as *psychopathy* or *sociopathy.*

Anvil   A bone of the middle ear.

Anxiety   A psychological state characterized by tension and apprehension, foreboding and dread.

Aphagic   Characterized by undereating.

Aphasia   Impaired ability to comprehend or express oneself through speech.

Apnea   A life-threatening sleep disorder that is characterized by temporary discontinuation of breathing during sleep.

Applied psychology   The application of fundamental psychological methods and knowledge to the investigation and solution of human problems.

Applied research   Research conducted in an effort to find solutions to particular problems.

Approach–approach conflict   Conflict involving two positive but mutually exclusive goals.

Approach–avoidance conflict   Conflict involving a goal with positive and negative features.

Aptitude   A natural ability or talent.

Archetypes   In Jung's personality theory, primitive images or concepts that reside in the collective unconscious.

Arousal   (1) A general level of activity or preparedness for activity in an organism. (2) A general level of motivation in an organism.

Arteriosclerosis   A disease characterized by thickening and hardening of the arteries.

Artificialism   The belief, characteristic of preoperational thought, that natural objects have been created by human beings.

Assertiveness training   A form of social-skills training—including techniques such as coaching, modeling, feedback, and behavior rehearsal—that teaches clients to express their feelings and seek fair treatment

Assimilation   According to Piaget, the inclusion of a new event into an existing concept or schema.

Association areas   Parts of the cerebral cortex involved in learning, thought, memory, and language.

Asthma   Recurrent attacks of difficult breathing and wheezing.

Astigmatism   A visual disorder in which vertical and horizontal contours cannot be focused on simultaneously.

Astrology   A pseudoscience that is based on the notion that the positions of the sun, the moon, and the stars affect human affairs and that one can foretell the future by studying the positions of these bodies.

Asylum   (1) An early institution for the care of the mentally ill. (2) A safe place, or refuge.

Attachment   The enduring affectional tie that binds one person to another.

Attachment-in-the-making phase   According to Ainsworth, the second phase in forming bonds of attachment, characterized by preference for familiar figures.

Attention-deficit/hyperactivity disorder   A disorder that begins in childhood and is characterized by a persistent pattern of lack of attention, with or without hyperactivity and impulsive behavior.

Attitude   An enduring mental representation of people, places, or things that evokes feelings and influences behavior.

Attitude-discrepant behavior   Behavior that is inconsistent with an attitude and may have the effect of modifying an attitude.

Attraction   A force that draws bodies or people together. In social psychology, an attitude of liking (positive attraction) or disliking (negative attraction).

Attribution   A belief about why people behave in a certain way.

Attributional style   One's tendency to attribute one's behavior to internal or external factors, stable or unstable factors, and so on.

Attribution process   The process by which people draw conclusions about the motives and traits of others.

Auditory   Having to do with hearing.

Auditory nerve   The axon bundle that transmits neural impulses from the organ of Corti to the brain.

Authoritarianism   Belief in the importance of unquestioning obedience to authority.

Autism   (1) Self-absorption. Absorption in daydreaming and fantasy. (2) A childhood disorder marked by problems such as failure to relate to others, lack of speech, and intolerance of change.

Autogenic training   A method for reducing tension involving repeated suggestions that the limbs are becoming warmer and heavier and that one's breathing is becoming more regular.

Autokinetic effect   The tendency to perceive a stationary point of light in a dark room as moving.

Autonomic nervous system   The division of the peripheral nervous system that regulates glands and involuntary activities like heartbeat, respiration, digestion, and dilation of the pupils. Abbreviated *ANS.* Also see *sympathetic* and *parasympathetic* branches of the *ANS.*

Autonomy   Self-direction. The social motive to be free, unrestrained, and independent.

Autonomy versus shame and doubt   Erikson's second stage of psychosocial development, during which the child develops (or does not develop) the wish to make choices and the capacity to exercise self-control.

Availability heuristic   A decision-making heuristic in which our estimates of frequency or probability of events are based on how easy it is to find examples.

Average   The central tendency of a group of measures, expressed as *mean, median,* or *mode.*

Aversive conditioning   A behavior-therapy technique in which a previously desirable or neutral stimulus is made obnoxious by being paired repeatedly with a repugnant or offensive stimulus.

Avoidance–avoidance conflict   Conflict involving two negative goals in which avoidance of one requires approaching the other.

Avoidance learning   An operant conditioning procedure in which an organism learns to exhibit an operant that permits it to avoid an aversive stimulus.

Axon   A long, thin part of a neuron that transmits impulses to other neurons from branching structures called *terminals.*

B

Babbling   The child's first verbalizations that have the sound of speech.

Babinski reflex   An infant's fanning of the toes in response to stimulation of the sole of the foot.

Backward conditioning   A classical-conditioning procedure in which the unconditioned stimulus is presented prior to the conditioned stimulus.

Balance theory   The view that people have a need to organize their perceptions, opinions, and beliefs in a harmonious manner.

Barbiturate   An addictive depressant used to relieve anxiety or induce sleep.

Bargaining   The third stage in Kübler-Ross's theory of dying, in which the terminally ill try to bargain with God to postpone death, usually by offering to do good deeds in exchange for time.

Barnum effect   The tendency to believe in the accuracy of a generalized personality report or prediction about oneself.

Basal ganglia   Ganglia located in the brain between the thalamus and the cerebrum that are involved in motor coordination.

Basic anxiety   Horney's term for enduring feelings of insecurity that stem from harsh or indifferent parental treatment.

Basic hostility   Horney's term for enduring feelings of anger that accompany basic anxiety but that are directed toward nonfamily members in adulthood.

Basilar membrane   A membrane to which the organ of Corti is attached. The basilar membrane lies coiled within the cochlea.

Behavior   The observable or measurable actions of people and lower animals.

Behavioral competencies   Skills.

Behavior genetics   The study of the genetic transmission of structures and traits that give rise to behavior.

Behaviorism   The school of psychology that defines psychology as the study of observable behavior and investigates the relationships between stimuli and responses.

Behaviorist   A psychologist who believes that psychology should address observable behavior and the relationships between stimuli and responses.

Behavior modification   Use of principles of learning to change behavior in desired directions.

Behavior-outcome relations   A kind of expectancy in social-cognitive theory: predictions as to the outcomes (reinforcement contingencies) of one's behavior.

Behavior rating scale   A systematic means of recording the frequency with which target behaviors occur. (An alternative to self-report methods of personality testing.)

Behavior rehearsal   Practice.

Behavior therapy   Use of the principles of learning in the direct modification of problem behavior.

Benzodiazepines   A class of drugs that reduce anxiety. Minor tranquilizers.

Bimodal   Having two modes.

Binocular cues   Stimuli that suggest depth by means of simultaneous perception by both eyes. Examples: retinal disparity and convergence.

Biofeedback training   The systematic feeding back to an organism information about a body function so that the organism can gain control of that function. Abbreviated *BFT*.

Biological psychologist   A psychologist who studies the relationships between biological processes and behavior.

Bipolar cells   Neurons that conduct neural impulses from rods and cones to ganglion cells.

Bipolar disorder   A disorder in which the mood inappropriately alternates between extremes of elation and depression. Formerly called *manic-depression*.

Blind   In experimental terminology, unaware of whether one has obtained a treatment.

Blind spot   The area of the retina where axons from ganglion cells meet to form the optic nerve. It is insensitive to light.

Blocking   In conditioning, the phenomenon whereby a new stimulus fails to gain the capacity to signal an unconditioned stimulus (US) when the new stimulus is paired repeatedly with a stimulus that already effectively foretells the US.

B lymphocytes   The white blood cells of the immune system that produce antibodies.

Bottom-up processing   The organization of the parts of a pattern to recognize, or form an image of, the pattern they compose.

Brainstorming   A group process that encourages creativity by stimulating a large number of ideas and suspending judgment until the process is completed.

Breathalyzer   A device that measures the quantity of alcohol in the body by analyzing the breath.

Brief reactive psychosis   A psychotic episode of less than 2 weeks in duration that follows a known stressful event.

Brightness constancy   The tendency to perceive an object as being just as bright even though lighting conditions change the intensity with which it impacts on the eye.

Broca's aphasia   A speech disorder caused by damage to Broca's area of the brain. It is characterized by slow, laborious speech and by difficulty articulating words and forming grammatical sentences.

Bulimia nervosa   An eating disorder characterized by recurrent episodes of binge eating followed by purging and by persistent overconcern with body shape and weight.

Bureaucracy   An administrative system characterized by departments and subdivisions whose members frequently are given long tenure and inflexible work tasks.

C

Cannon-Bard theory   The theory of emotion that holds that events are processed by the brain and that the brain induces patterns of activity and autonomic arousal *and* cognitive activity—that is, the experiencing of the appropriate emotion.

Carcinogen   An agent that gives rise to cancerous changes.

Cardinal trait   Allport's term for pervasive traits that steer practically all of a person's behavior.

Cardiovascular disorders   Diseases of the cardiovascular system, including heart disease, hypertension, and arteriosclerosis.

Case study   A carefully drawn biography that may be obtained through interviews, questionnaires, psychological tests, and, sometimes, historical records.

Catastrophize   To exaggerate or magnify the noxious properties of negative events; to "blow out of proportion."

Catatonic schizophrenia   A subtype of schizophrenia characterized by striking impairment in motor activity.

Catch 30s   Sheehy's term for the fourth decade of life, which is frequently characterized by major reassessment of one's accomplishments and goals.

Catecholamines   A number of chemical substances produced from an amino acid that are important as neurotransmitters (dopamine and norepinephrine) and as hormones (adrenaline and norepinephrine).

Catharsis   In psychodynamic theory, the purging of strong emotions or the relieving of tensions. Also called *abreaction*.

CD4 cells   The white blood cells of the immune system that recognize invading pathogens and are attacked by the human immunodeficiency virus (HIV). Also called *T helper cells* or T_4 *cells*.

Cellular-aging theory   The view that aging occurs because body cells lose the capacity to reproduce and maintain themselves.

Center   According to Piaget, to focus one's attention.

Central fissure   The valley in the cerebral cortex that separates the frontal and parietal lobes.

Central nervous system   The brain and spinal cord.

Central traits   Characteristics that are outstanding and noticeable but not necessarily all-pervasive.

Cephalocaudal   Proceeding from top to bottom.

Cerebellum   A part of the hindbrain involved in muscle coordination and balance.

Cerebral cortex   The wrinkled surface area of the cerebrum, often called "gray matter" because of the appearance afforded by the many cell bodies.

Cerebrum   The large mass of the forebrain, which consists of two hemispheres.

Chain breaking   A behavior-therapy self-control technique in which one disrupts problematic behavior by complicating its execution.

Chemotherapy   The use of drugs to treat medical problems or abnormal behavior.

Child   In transactional analysis, an irresponsible, emotional ego state.

Childhood amnesia   Inability to recall events that occurred before the age of 3. Also termed *infantile amnesia*.

Chorionic villus sampling   The detection of genetic abnormalities by sampling the membrane that envelops the amniotic sac and the fetus within. Abbreviated *CVS*.

Chromosomes   Genetic structures consisting of genes that are found in the nuclei of the body's cells.

Chronological age   A person's actual age—as contrasted with *mental age*.

Chunk   A stimulus or group of stimuli that are perceived or encoded as a discrete piece of information.

Circadian rhythm   (sir-KADE-ee-an). Referring to cycles that are connected with the 24-hour period of the earth's rotation. (A scientific term coined from the Latin roots *circa,* meaning "about," and *diem*, meaning "day.")

Circular explanation   An explanation that merely repeats its own concepts instead of offering additional information.

Cirrhosis of the liver   A disease caused by protein deficiency in which connective fibers replace active liver cells, impairing circulation of the blood. Alcohol does not contain protein; therefore, people who drink excessively may be prone to acquiring this disease.

Clairvoyance   The term means ability to perceive things in the absence of sensory stimulation. However, most psychologists do not believe that this ability exists. (A French word meaning "clear-sightedness.")

Classical conditioning   (1) According to cognitive theorists, the learning of relations among events so as to allow an organism to represent its environment. (2) According to behaviorists, a form of learning in which one stimulus comes to evoke the response usually evoked by a second stimulus by being paired repeatedly with the second stimulus. Also referred to as *respondent conditioning* or *Pavlovian conditioning*.

Classic organization theories   Theories that hold that organizations should be structured from the skeleton (governing body) outward.

Claustrophobia   Fear of tight, small places.

Clearcut-attachment phase   According to Ainsworth, the third phase in forming bonds of attachment, which is characterized by intensified dependence on the primary caregiver.

Client-centered therapy   See *person-centered therapy*.

Clinical scales   Groups of test items that measure the presence of various abnormal behavior patterns, as on the Minnesota Multiphasic Personality Inventory.

Closure   The tendency to perceive a broken figure as being complete or whole.

Cocaine   A powerful stimulant derived from coca leaves that is usually snorted, brewed, or injected.

Cochlea   The inner ear; the bony tube that contains the basilar membrane and the organ of Corti.

Cognitive   Having to do with mental processes such as sensation and perception, memory, intelligence, language, thought, and problem solving.

Cognitive-dissonance theory   The view that we are motivated to make our cognitions or beliefs consistent.

Cognitive map   A mental representation or picture of the elements in a learning situation, such as a maze.

Cognitive therapy   A form of psychotherapy that focuses on how people's cognitions (expectations, attitudes, beliefs, etc.) lead to distress and may be modified to relieve distress and promote adaptive behavior.

Collective unconscious   Jung's hypothesized store of vague racial memories and archetypes.

Collectivist   A person who defines herself or himself in terms of relationships to other people and groups and gives priority to group goals.

Color constancy   The tendency to perceive an object as being the same color even as lighting conditions change its appearance.

Common fate   The tendency to perceive elements that move together as belonging together.

Community psychology   A field of psychology, related to clinical psychology, that focuses on the prevention of psychological problems and the maintenance of distressed persons in the community.

Companionate love   A type of nonpassionate love characterized by intimacy, respect, trust, and commitment.

Competencies   Within social-learning theory, knowledge and skills.

Competing response   In behavior therapy, a response that is incompatible with an unwanted response.

Complementary   (1) In sensation and perception, descriptive of colors of the spectrum that, when combined, produce white or nearly white light. (2) In transactional analysis, descriptive of a transaction in which the ego states of two people interact harmoniously.

Componential level   According to Sternberg, the level of intelligence that consists of metacomponents, performance components, and knowledge-acquisition components.

Compulsion   An apparently irresistible urge to repeat an act or engage in ritualistic behavior, such as handwashing.

Computerized axial tomography   Formation of a computer-generated image of the anatomical details of the brain by passing a narrow X-ray beam through the head and measuring from different angles the amount of radiation that passes through. Abbreviated *CAT scan*.

Concept   A mental category that is used to class together objects, relations, events, abstractions, or qualities that have common properties.

Concordance   Agreement.

Concrete operational stage   Piaget's third stage of cognitive development, characterized by logical thought processes concerning tangible objects, conservation, reversibility, and subjective morality.

Conditional positive regard   In Rogers's self theory, judgment of another person's basic value as a human being on the basis of the acceptability of that person's behaviors.

Conditional reasoning   A form of reasoning about arguments that is used to reach conclusions about if–then relationships.

Conditioned reinforcer   Another term for *secondary reinforcer*.

Conditioned response   In classical conditioning, a learned response to a previously neutral stimulus. A response to a conditioned stimulus. Abbreviated *CR*.

Conditioned stimulus   A previously neutral stimulus that elicits a conditioned response because it has been paired repeatedly with a stimulus that had already elicited that response. Abbreviated *CS*.

Conditioning   A simple form of learning in which responses become associated with stimuli. See *classical conditioning* and *operant conditioning*.

Conditions of worth   Standards by which the value of a person, or the self, is judged.

Conductive sensory deafness   The forms of deafness in which there is loss of conduction of sound through the middle ear.

Cone   A cone-shaped photoreceptor in the eye that transmits sensations of color.

Confederate   In experimental terminology, a person who pretends to be a participant in a study but who is in league with the experimenter.

Confidential   Secret, not to be disclosed.

Conflict   (1) Being torn in different directions by opposing motives. (2) Feelings produced by being in conflict.

Conform   To change one's attitudes or overt behavior to adhere to social norms.

Conformity   Behavior that is in accordance with group norms and expectations.

Congruence   In Rogers's self theory, a fit between one's self-concept and one's behaviors, thoughts, and feelings. A quality shown by the person-centered therapist.

Conscious   Aware, in the normal waking state.

Consciousness   A complex and controversial concept in psychology. Consciousness has several meanings in addition to the normal waking state; see *sensory awareness, direct inner awareness,* and *self*.

Consensus   General agreement.

Conservation   According to Piaget, recognition that certain properties of substances remain constant even though their appearance may change. For example, the weight and mass of a ball of clay remain constant (are conserved) even if the ball is flattened into a pancake.

Consolidation   The fixing of information in long-term memory.

Consonant In harmony.

Construe Interpret.

Consultation The provision of professional advice or services.

Consumer psychology The field of psychology that studies the nature, causes, and modification of consumer behavior and mental processes.

Consummate love In Sternberg's triangular model, the kind of love characterized by passion, intimacy, and commitment.

Contact comfort (1) The pleasure attained from physical contact with another. (2) A hypothesized primary drive to seek physical comfort through physical contact with another.

Context-dependent memory Information that is better retrieved in the context in which it was encoded and stored, or learned.

Contextual level According to Sternberg, those aspects of intelligent behavior that permit people to adapt to their environment.

Contiguous Next to one another.

Contingency theory (1) In conditioning, the view that learning occurs when stimuli provide information about the likelihood of the occurrence of other stimuli. (2) In industrial/organizational psychology, a theory that holds that organizational structure should depend on factors such as goals, workers' characteristics, and the overall economic or political environment.

Continuity As a rule of perceptual organization, the tendency to perceive a series of stimuli as having unity.

Continuous reinforcement A schedule of reinforcement in which every correct response is reinforced. See *partial reinforcement*.

Control group A group of participants in an experiment who do not receive the experimental treatment but for whom all other conditions are comparable with those of individuals in the experimental group.

Conventional level According to Kohlberg, a period of moral development during which moral judgments largely reflect social conventions. A "law and order" approach to morality.

Convergence A binocular cue for depth based on the inward movement of the eyes as they attempt to focus on an object that is drawing nearer.

Convergent thinking A thought process that attempts to narrow in on the single best solution to a problem.

Conversion disorder A disorder in which anxiety or unconscious conflicts are "converted" into physical symptoms that often have the effect of helping the person cope with the anxiety or conflicts.

Cooing Prelinguistic, articulated, vowel-like sounds that appear to reflect feelings of positive excitement.

Cornea Transparent tissue that forms the outer surface of the eyeball.

Corpus callosum A thick bundle of fibers that connects the two hemispheres of the cerebrum.

Correlational research A method of scientific investigation that studies the relationships between variables. Correlational research can imply but cannot show cause and effect, because no experimental treatment is introduced.

Correlation coefficient A number ranging from +1.00 to −1.00 that expresses the strength and direction (positive or negative) of the relationship between two variables.

Corticosteroids Steroids produced by the adrenal cortex that regulate carbohydrate metabolism and increase resistance to stress by fighting inflammation and allergic reactions. Also called *cortical steroids*.

Cortisol A hormone (steroid) produced by the adrenal cortex that helps the body cope with stress by counteracting inflammation and allergic reactions.

Counterconditioning A behavior-therapy technique that involves the repeated pairing of a stimulus that elicits a problematic response (such as fear) with a stimulus that elicits an antagonistic response (such as relaxation instructions) so that the first stimulus loses the capacity to evoke the problematic response. See also *systematic desensitization* and *aversive conditioning*.

Countertransference In psychoanalysis, the generalization to the client of feelings toward another person in the analyst's life.

Covert reinforcement A behavior-therapy self-control technique in which one creates pleasant imagery to reward desired behavior.

Covert sensitization A behavior-therapy self-control technique in which one creates aversive imagery and associates it with undesired behavior.

CR Conditioned response.

Creative self According to Adler, the self-aware aspect of personality that strives to achieve its full potential.

Creativity The ability to generate novel solutions to problems. A trait characterized by originality, ingenuity, and flexibility.

Cretinism A condition caused by thyroid deficiency in childhood and characterized by mental retardation and stunted growth.

Criteria Plural of *criterion*.

Criterion A standard; a means for making a judgment.

Criterion-referenced testing A testing approach in which scores are based on whether or not one can perform up to a set standard.

Critical period A period in an organism's development during which it is capable of certain types of learning.

CS Conditioned stimulus.

Cultural bias A factor hypothesized to be present in intelligence tests that provides an advantage for test takers from certain cultural or ethnic backgrounds but that does not reflect actual intelligence.

Culture-fair Describing a test in which there are no cultural biases. On such a test, test takers from different cultural backgrounds would have an equal opportunity to earn scores that reflect their true abilities.

Cumulative incidence The occurrence of an event or act by a given time or age.

Cumulative recorder An instrument used in operant conditioning laboratory procedures to automatically record the frequency of targeted responses.

D

Daily hassles Notable daily conditions and experiences that are threatening or harmful to a person's well-being.

Dark adaptation The process of adjusting to conditions of lower lighting by increasing the sensitivity of rods and cones.

Debrief To receive information about a procedure that has been completed.

Decibel A unit expressing the loudness of a sound. Abbreviated *dB*.

Deductive reasoning A form of reasoning about arguments in which conclusions are deduced from premises. The conclusions are true if the premises are true.

Deep structure The underlying meaning of a sentence as determined by interpretation of the meanings of the words.

Defense mechanisms In psychodynamic theory, unconscious functions of the ego that protect it from anxiety-evoking material by preventing accurate recognition of this material.

Defensive coping A response to stress that reduces the stressor's immediate effect but frequently at some cost to the individual. Defensive coping may involve self-deception and does not change the environment or the person's response patterns to permanently remove or modify the effects of the stressor. Contrast with *active coping*.

Deindividuation The process by which group members may discontinue self-evaluation and adopt group norms and attitudes.

Delayed conditioning A classical-conditioning procedure in which the CS is presented several seconds before the US and remains in place until the response occurs.

Delirium tremens A condition characterized by sweating, restlessness, disorientation, and hallucinations that occurs in some chronic users of alcohol when there is a sudden decrease in the level of drinking. Abbreviated *DTs*.

Delta-9-tetrahydrocannabinol The major active ingredient in marijuana. Abbreviated *THC*.

Delta waves Strong, slow brain waves usually emitted during stage 4 sleep.

Delusions False, persistent beliefs that are unsubstantiated by sensory or objective evidence.

Delusions of grandeur Erroneous beliefs that one is a grand person, like Jesus or a secret agent on a special mission.

Delusions of persecution Erroneous beliefs that one is being threatened or persecuted.

Dendrites Rootlike structures attached to the soma of a neuron that receive impulses from other neurons.

Denial   (1) A defense mechanism in which threatening events are misperceived to be harmless. (2) The first stage in Kübler-Ross's theory of dying.

Dependent variable   A measure of an assumed effect of an independent variable. An outcome measure in a scientific study.

Depersonalization disorder   A dissociative disorder characterized by persistent or recurrent feelings that one is not real or is detached from one's own experiences or body.

Depolarization   The reduction of the resting potential of a cell membrane from about 70 millivolts toward zero.

Depressant   A drug that lowers the nervous system's rate of activity.

Depression   (1) A negative emotion frequently characterized by sadness, feelings of helplessness, and a sense of loss. (2) The fourth stage in Kübler-Ross's theory of dying.

Descriptive statistics   The branch of statistics that is concerned with providing descriptive information about a distribution of scores.

Desensitization   The type of sensory adaptation in which we become less sensitive to constant stimuli. Also called *negative adaptation*.

Determinant   A factor that defines or sets limits.

Deviation IQ   A score on an intelligence test that is derived by determining how far an individual's score deviates from the norm. On the Wechsler scales, the mean IQ score is defined as 100, and approximately two of three scores fall between 85 and 115.

Diabetes   A disorder caused by inadequate secretion or utilization of insulin and characterized by excess sugar in the blood.

Diagnosis   A decision or opinion about the nature of a diseased condition.

Dialogue   A Gestalt therapy technique in which people verbalize confrontations between conflicting parts of their personality.

Dichromat   A person who is sensitive to the intensity of light and to red and green or blue and yellow and who thus is partially color-blind.

Difference threshold   The minimal difference in intensity that is required between two sources of energy so that they will be perceived as being different.

Differentiation   The modification of tissues and organs in structure, function, or both during the course of development.

Diffusion of responsibility   The spreading or sharing of responsibility for a decision or behavior among the members of a group.

Direct coping   See *active coping*.

Direct inner awareness   One of the definitions of consciousness: knowledge of one's own thoughts, feelings, and memories, without use of sensory organs.

Discovery learning   Bruner's view that children should work on their own to discover basic principles.

Discrimination   (1) In conditioning, the tendency for an organism to distinguish between a conditioned stimulus and similar stimuli that do not forecast an unconditioned stimulus. (2) In social psychology, the denial of privileges to a person or a group on the basis of prejudice.

Discrimination training   Teaching an organism to show a conditioned response to only one of a series of similar stimuli by pairing that stimulus with the unconditioned stimulus and presenting similar stimuli in the absence of the unconditioned stimulus.

Discriminative stimulus   In operant conditioning, a stimulus that indicates that reinforcement is available.

Disinhibit   In social-cognitive theory, to trigger a response that is usually inhibited, generally as a consequence of observing a model engage in the behavior without negative consequences.

Disorganized schizophrenia   A subtype of schizophrenia characterized by disorganized delusions and vivid hallucinations. Formerly *hebephrenic schizophrenia*.

Disorientation   Gross confusion. Loss of awareness of time, place, and the identity of people.

Displacement   (1) In information processing, the causing of chunks of information to be lost from short-term memory by adding too many new items. (2) In psychodynamic theory, a defense mechanism that involves the transference of feelings or impulses from threatening or unacceptable objects onto unthreatening or acceptable objects. (3) As a property of language, the ability to communicate information about events in other times and places.

Dispositional attribution   An assumption that a person's behavior is determined by internal causes such as personal attitudes or goals. Contrast with *situational attribution*.

Dissociative amnesia   A dissociative disorder marked by loss of episodic memory or self-identity. Skills and general knowledge are usually retained. Formerly termed *psychogenic amnesia*.

Dissociative disorder   A disorder in which there is a sudden, temporary change in consciousness or self-identity, such as dissociative amnesia, dissociative fugue, dissociative identity disorder, or depersonalization disorder.

Dissociative fugue   A dissociative disorder in which one experiences amnesia, then flees to a new location. Formerly termed *psychogenic fugue*.

Dissociative identity disorder   A dissociative disorder in which a person has two or more distinct identities or personalities. Formerly termed *multiple personality disorder*.

Dissonant   Incompatible, discordant.

Divergent thinking   A thought process that attempts to generate multiple solutions to problems. Free and fluent associations to the elements of a problem.

Dizygotic twins   Twins who develop from separate zygotes. Fraternal twins. Abbreviated *DZ twins*. Contrast with *monozygotic twins*.

DNA   Deoxyribonucleic acid. The substance that carries the genetic code and makes up genes and chromosomes.

Dominant trait   In genetics, a trait that is expressed. See *recessive trait*.

Dopamine   A neurotransmitter that is involved in Parkinson's disease and theorized to play a role in schizophrenia.

Double approach–avoidance conflict   Conflict involving two goals, each of which has positive and negative aspects.

Double-blind study   A study in which neither the participants nor the persons measuring results know who has obtained the treatment.

Down syndrome   A chromosomal abnormality caused by an extra chromosome in the 21st pair ("trisomy 21") and characterized by slanted eyelids and mental retardation.

Dream   A form of cognitive activity—usually a sequence of images or thoughts—that occurs during sleep. Dreams may be vague and loosely plotted or vivid and intricate.

Drive   A condition of arousal within an organism that is associated with a need.

Drive for superiority   Adler's term for the desire to compensate for feelings of inferiority.

Drive-reduction theory   The view that organisms are motivated to learn to engage in behaviors that have the effect of reducing drives.

DSM   The *Diagnostic and Statistical Manual of the Mental Disorders*, a publication of the American Psychiatric Association. A frequently used compendium of psychological disorders.

Duct   Passageway.

Duplicity theory   A combination of the place and frequency theories of pitch discrimination.

Dyslexia   A severe reading disorder characterized by problems such as letter reversals, reading as if one were seeing words reflected in a mirror, slow reading, and reduced comprehension.

Dyspareunia   Persistent or recurrent pain during or after sexual intercourse.

E

Eardrum   A thin membrane that vibrates in response to sound waves, transmitting them from the outer ear to the middle and inner ears.

Eating disorders   Psychological disorders that are characterized by distortion of the body image and gross disturbances in eating patterns. See *anorexia nervosa* and *bulimia nervosa*.

Echo   A mental representation of an auditory stimulus that is held briefly in sensory memory.

Echoic memory   The sensory register that briefly holds mental representations of auditory stimuli.

Eclectic   Selecting from various systems or theories.

ECT   Acronym for *electroconvulsive therapy*.

Educational psychology   The field of psychology that studies the nature, causes, and enhancement of teaching and learning.

Efferent neuron   A neuron that transmits messages from the brain or spinal cord to muscles or glands. Also called *motor neuron*.

Effort justification   In cognitive-dissonance theory, the tendency to seek justification (acceptable reasons) for strenuous efforts.

Ego   In psychodynamic theory, the second psychic structure to develop. The ego is governed by the reality principle and its functioning is characterized by self-awareness, planning, and capacity to tolerate frustration and delay gratification.

Ego analyst   A psychodynamically oriented therapist who focuses on the conscious, coping behavior of the ego instead of the hypothesized unconscious functioning of the id.

Egocentric   According to Piaget, assuming that others view the world as oneself does. Unable or unwilling to view the world as through the eyes of others.

Ego identity   Erikson's term for the sense of who one is and what one stands for.

Ego identity versus role diffusion   Erikson's fifth stage of psychosocial development, which challenges the adolescent to connect skills and social roles to career objectives.

Ego integrity   Erikson's term for a firm sense of identity during the later years, characterized by the wisdom to accept the fact that life is limited and the ability to let go.

Ego integrity versus despair   Erikson's eighth stage of psychosocial development, which challenges persons to accept the limits of their own life cycles during the later years.

Eidetic imagery   The maintenance of detailed visual memories over several minutes.

Elaboration likelihood model   The view that persuasive messages are evaluated (elaborated) on the basis of central and peripheral cues.

Elaborative rehearsal   A method for increasing retention of new information by relating it to information that is well known.

Electra complex   In psychodynamic theory, a conflict of the phallic stage in which the girl longs for her father and resents her mother.

Electroconvulsive therapy   Treatment of disorders like major depression by passing an electric current through the head, causing a convulsion. Abbreviated *ECT*.

Electroencephalograph   An instrument that measures electrical activity of the brain (brain waves). Abbreviated *EEG*.

Electromyograph   An instrument that measures muscle tension. Abbreviated *EMG*.

Elicit   To bring forth, evoke.

Embryo   The developing organism from the third through the eighth weeks following conception, during which time the major organ systems undergo rapid differentiation.

Embryonic period   The period of prenatal development between the period of the ovum and fetal development, approximately from the third through the eighth weeks following conception.

Embryo transfer   Transfer of an embryo from the fallopian tube of its mother into the uterus of another woman, where it becomes implanted and develops.

Emetic   Causing vomiting.

Emotion   A state of feeling that has cognitive, physiological, and behavioral components.

Emotional appeal   A type of persuasive communication that influences behavior on the basis of feelings that are aroused instead of rational analysis of the issues.

Empathic understanding   Ability to perceive a client's feelings from the client's frame of reference. A quality of a good person-centered therapist.

Empathy   Ability to understand and share another person's feelings.

Empirical   Experimental. Emphasizing or based on observation and measurement, in contrast to theory and deduction.

Empty-nest syndrome   A sense of depression and loss of purpose that is experienced by some parents when the youngest child leaves home.

Encoding   Modifying information so that it can be placed in memory. The first stage of information processing.

Encounter group   A structured group process that aims to foster self-awareness by focusing on how group members relate to each other in a setting that encourages frank expression of feelings.

Endocrine system   The body's system of ductless glands that secrete hormones and release them directly into the bloodstream.

Endorphins   Neurotransmitters that are composed of amino acids and are functionally similar to morphine.

Engram   (1) An assumed electrical circuit in the brain that corresponds to a memory trace. (2) An assumed chemical change in the brain that accompanies learning.

Enkephalins   Types of endorphins that are weaker and shorter-acting than beta-endorphin.

Enuresis   Lack of bladder control at an age by which control is normally attained.

Environmental psychology   The field of psychology that studies the ways in which people and the physical environment influence one another.

Epilepsy   Temporary disturbances of brain functions that involve sudden neural discharges.

Epinephrine   A hormone produced by the adrenal medulla that stimulates the sympathetic division of the ANS. Also called *adrenaline*.

Episodic memory   Memories of specific events experienced by a person.

Equilibrium   Another term for the *vestibular sense*.

Erogenous zone   An area of the body that is sensitive to sexual sensations.

Eros   In psychodynamic theory, the basic life instinct, which aims toward the preservation and perpetuation of life.

Estrogen   A generic term for several female sex hormones that promote growth of female sexual characteristics and regulate the menstrual cycle.

Estrus   The periodic sexual excitement of many female mammals, during which they are capable of conceiving and are receptive to sexual advances by males.

Ethical   Moral; referring to one's system of deriving standards for determining what is moral.

Ethologist   A scientist who studies behavior patterns that are characteristic of various species.

Euphoria   Feelings of extreme well-being, elation.

Eustress   Stress that is healthful.

Evaluation apprehension   Concern that others are evaluating our behavior.

Exceptional students   The term applied to students whose educational needs are special because of physical and health problems, communication problems, behavior disorders, specific learning disabilities, mental retardation, or intellectual giftedness.

Excitatory synapse   A synapse that influences receiving neurons in the direction of firing by increasing depolarization of their cell membranes.

Excitement phase   The first phase of the sexual response cycle, characterized by erection in the man and by vaginal lubrication and clitoral swelling in the woman.

Exhaustion stage   The third stage of the general adaptation syndrome, characterized by parasympathetic activity, weakened resistance, and possible deterioration.

Existentialism   The view that people are completely free and responsible for their own behavior.

Expectancies   A person variable in social-learning theory. Personal predictions about the outcomes of potential behaviors—"if–then" statements.

Experiential level   According to Sternberg, those aspects of intelligence that permit people to cope with novel situations and process information automatically.

Experiment   A scientific method that seeks to discover cause-and-effect relationships by introducing independent variables and observing their effects on dependent variables.

Experimental group   A group of participants who obtain a treatment in an experiment.

Expository teaching   Ausubel's method of presenting material in an organized form, moving from broad to specific concepts.

Expressive vocabulary   The sum total of the words that one can use in the production of language.

External eater   A person who eats predominantly in response to external stimuli, such as the time of day, the smell of food, or the presence of people who are eating. See *internal eater*.

"Externals"   People who have an external locus of control—who perceive the ability to attain reinforcements as largely outside themselves.

Extinction   An experimental procedure in which stimuli lose their ability to evoke learned responses because the events that had followed the stimuli no longer occur. (The learned responses are said to be *extinguished*.)

Extinction trial   In conditioning, a performance of a learned response in the absence of its predicted consequences so that the learned response becomes inhibited.

Extrasensory perception   Perception of external objects and events in the absence of sensation. Abbreviated *ESP*. A controversial area of investigation. (*Not* to be confused with hallucinations, which typify certain psychological disorders and are defined as confusion of fantasies with reality.)

Extroversion   A source trait in which one's attention is directed to persons and things outside the self, often associated with a sociable, outgoing approach to others and the free expression of feelings and impulses. Opposite of *introversion*.

F

Facial-feedback hypothesis   The view that stereotypical facial expressions can contribute to the experiencing of stereotypical emotions.

Factor   A cluster of related items such as those found on an intelligence test.

Factor analysis   A statistical technique that allows researchers to determine the relationships among a large number of items such as test items.

Fallopian tube   A tube that conducts ova from an ovary to the uterus.

Family therapy   A form of therapy in which the family unit is treated as the client.

Farsighted   Capable of seeing distant objects with greater acuity than nearby objects.

Fat cells   Cells that store fats. Also called *adipose tissue.*

Fear   A negative emotion characterized by perception of a threat, sympathetic nervous system activity, and avoidance tendencies.

Feature detectors   Neurons in the visual cortex that fire in response to specific features of visual information, such as lines or edges presented at particular angles.

Feedback   Information about one's own behavior.

Feeling-of-knowing experience   See *tip-of-the-tongue phenomenon.*

Female sexual arousal disorder   A sexual dysfunction characterized by difficulty in becoming sexually aroused, as defined by vaginal lubrication, or sustaining arousal long enough to engage in satisfying sexual relations.

Feminists   People (of both genders) who seek social change and legislation to reverse discrimination against women and to otherwise advance the concerns of women.

Fetus   The developing organism from the third month following conception through childbirth, during which time there are maturation of organ systems and dramatic gains in length and weight.

Fight-or-flight reaction   Cannon's term for a hypothesized innate adaptive response to the perception of danger.

File-drawer problem   In research, the tendency to file away (and forget) negative results, such that positive results tend to achieve greater visibility or impact than they may deserve.

Final acceptance   The fifth stage in Kübler-Ross's theory of dying, which is characterized by lack of feeling.

Fissure   Valley—referring to the valleys in the wrinkled surface of the cerebral cortex.

Fixation   In psychodynamic theory, arrested development. Attachment to objects of an earlier stage.

Fixation time   The amount of time spent looking at a visual stimulus. A measure of interest in infants.

Fixed-action pattern   An instinct; abbreviated *FAP.*

Fixed-interval schedule   A partial reinforcement schedule in which a fixed amount of time must elapse between the previous and subsequent times that reinforcement is made available.

Fixed-ratio schedule   A partial reinforcement schedule in which reinforcement is made available after a fixed number of correct responses.

Flashbacks   Distorted perceptions or hallucinations that occur days or weeks after usage of a hallucinogenic drug (usually LSD) but that mimic the effects of the drug.

Flashbulb memories   Memories that are preserved in great detail because they reflect intense emotional experiences.

Flat affect   Monotonous, dull emotional response.

Flooding   A behavioral fear-reduction technique that is based on principles of classical conditioning. Fear-evoking stimuli (CSs) are presented continuously in the absence of actual harm so that fear responses (CRs) are extinguished.

Foot-in-the-door technique   A method of persuasion in which compliance with a large request is encouraged by first asking the recipient of the request to comply with a smaller request.

Forced-choice format   A method of presenting test questions that requires a respondent to select one of a number of possible answers.

Forensic psychology   The field that applies psychological knowledge within the criminal-justice system.

Formal-operational stage   Piaget's fourth stage of cognitive development, characterized by abstract logical and theoretical thought and deduction from principles.

Fovea   A rodless area near the center of the retina where vision is most acute.

Frame of reference   In self theory, one's unique patterning of perceptions and attitudes, according to which one evaluates events.

Framing effect   The influence of wording, or the context in which information is presented, on decision making.

Free association   In psychoanalysis, the uncensored uttering of all thoughts that come to mind.

Free-floating anxiety   Chronic, persistent anxiety. Anxiety that is not tied to particular events.

Frequency distribution   An ordered set of data that indicates how frequently scores appear.

Frequency theory   The theory that the pitch of a sound is reflected in the frequency of the neural impulses that are generated in response.

Frontal lobe   The lobe of the cerebral cortex that is involved with movement and that lies to the front of the central fissure.

Frustration   (1) The thwarting of a motive. (2) The emotion produced by the thwarting of a motive.

Functional analysis   A systematic study of behavior in which one identifies the stimuli that trigger it (antecedents) and the reinforcers that maintain it (consequences).

Functional fixedness   The tendency to view an object in terms of its name or familiar usage; an impediment to creative problem solving.

Functionalism   The school of psychology, founded by William James, that emphasizes the uses or functions of the mind.

Fundamental attribution error   A bias in social perception characterized by the tendency to assume that others act predominantly on the basis of their dispositions, even when there is evidence suggesting the importance of their situations.

G

g   Spearman's symbol for general intelligence, a general factor that he hypothesized underlay more specific abilities.

Galvanic skin response   A sign of sympathetic arousal detected by the amount of sweat in the hand. The greater the amount of sweat, the more electricity is conducted across the skin, suggesting greater sympathetic arousal. Abbreviated *GSR.*

Ganglia   Plural of *ganglion.* A group of neural cell bodies found elsewhere in the body other than the brain or spinal cord.

Ganglion   See *ganglia.*

Ganglion cells   Neurons whose axons form the optic fiber.

Ganzfeld procedure   In ESP research, a method for studying telepathy in which a "sender" tries to mentally transmit information to a "receiver" whose eyes and ears are covered. (*Ganzfeld* is German for "whole field.")

GAS   Abbreviation for general adaptation syndrome.

Gay male   A male who is sexually aroused by, and interested in forming romantic relationships with, other males.

Gender   The state of being female or male.

Gender constancy   The concept that one's gender remains the same, despite superficial changes in appearance or behavior.

Gender identity   One's sense of being female or male.

Gender polarization   The tendency in Western culture to view women and men as opposites in terms of personality and appropriate behavior patterns.

Gender role   A complex cluster of behaviors that characterizes traditional female or male behaviors.

Gender-schema theory   The view that gender identity plus knowledge of the distribution of behavior patterns into feminine and masculine roles motivates and guides the gender-typing of the child.

Gender stability   The concept that one's gender is a permanent feature.

Gender-typing   The process by which people acquire a sense of being female or male and acquire the traits considered typical of females or males.

Gene   The basic building block of heredity, which consists of deoxyribonucleic acid (DNA).

General adaptation syndrome Selye's term for a theoretical three-stage response to stress. Abbreviated *GAS*.

General anesthetics Methods that control pain by putting a person to sleep.

Generalization (1) The process of going from the particular to the general. (2) In conditioning, the tendency for a conditioned response to be evoked by stimuli that are similar to the stimulus to which the response was conditioned.

Generalized anxiety disorder Feelings of dread and foreboding and sympathetic arousal of at least 6 months' duration.

Generalized expectancies In social-learning theory, broad expectations that reflect extensive learning and that are relatively resistant to change.

Generativity versus stagnation Erikson's seventh stage of psychosocial development; the middle years during which persons find (or fail to find) fulfillment in expressing creativity and in guiding and encouraging the younger generation.

Genetic counseling Advice or counseling that concerns the probability that a couple's offspring will have genetic abnormalities.

Genetics The branch of biology that studies heredity.

Genital stage In psychodynamic theory, the fifth and mature stage of psychosexual development, characterized by preferred expression of libido through intercourse with an adult of the opposite gender.

Genuineness Recognition and open expression of one's feelings. A quality of the good person-centered therapist.

Germinal stage The first stage of prenatal development during which the dividing mass of cells has not become implanted in the uterine wall.

Gestalt psychology The school of psychology that emphasizes the tendency to organize perceptions into wholes, to integrate separate stimuli into meaningful patterns.

Gestalt therapy Fritz Perls's form of psychotherapy which attempts to integrate conflicting parts of the personality through directive methods designed to help clients perceive their whole selves.

Glass ceiling The unspoken limits that prevent many women from being promoted into the upper levels of management in organizations. The "ceiling" is the limit itself, and the concept of "glass" refers to women's ability to see through the limit they cannot penetrate.

Glaucoma An eye disease characterized by increased fluid pressure within the eye. A cause of blindness.

Glial cells Cells that nourish and insulate neurons, direct their growth, and remove waste products from the nervous system.

Grasp reflex An infant reflex in which an object placed on the palms or soles is grasped. Also called *palmar* or *plantar reflex*.

Gray matter In the spinal cord, the neurons and neural segments that are involved in spinal reflexes. They are gray in appearance. Also see *white matter*.

Groupthink A process in which group members, as they make decisions, are influenced by cohesiveness and a dynamic leader to ignore external realities.

Growth hormone A pituitary hormone that regulates growth.

Growth hormone releasing factor A hormone produced by the hypothalamus that causes the pituitary to secrete growth hormone.

GSR Abbreviation for *galvanic skin response*.

H

Habit A response to a stimulus that becomes automatic with repetition.

Habituate To become accustomed to a stimulus, as determined by no longer showing a response to the stimulus.

Hallucination A sensory experience in the absence of sensory stimulation that is confused with reality.

Hallucinogenic Giving rise to hallucinations.

Halo effect The tendency for one's general impression of a person to influence one's perception of aspects of, or performances by, that person.

Hammer A bone of the middle ear.

Hashish A psychedelic drug derived from the resin of *Cannabis sativa*. Often called "hash."

Hassle A source of annoyance or aggravation.

Health psychology The field of psychology that studies the relationships between psychological factors (e.g., attitudes, beliefs, situational influences, and overt behavior patterns) and the prevention and treatment of physical illness.

Hebephrenic schizophrenia See *disorganized schizophrenia*.

Hemoglobin The substance in the blood that carries oxygen.

Heredity The transmission of traits from one generation to another through genes.

Heroin A powerful opioid that provides a euphoric "rush" and feelings of well-being.

Hertz A unit expressing the frequency of sound waves. One Hertz, or *1 Hz*, equals one cycle per second.

Heterosexual A person who is sexually aroused by, and interested in forming romantic relationships with, people of the opposite gender.

Heuristic device A rule of thumb that helps us simplify and solve problems.

Higher-order conditioning (1) According to cognitive psychologists, the learning of relations among events, none of which evokes an unlearned response. (2) According to behaviorists, a classical-conditioning procedure in which a previously neutral stimulus comes to elicit the response brought forth by a *conditioned* stimulus by being paired repeatedly with that conditioned stimulus.

Hippocampus A part of the limbic system of the brain that plays an important role in the formation of new memories.

Histogram A graphic representation of a frequency distribution that uses rectangular solids.

HIV See *human immunodeficiency virus*.

Holocaust The name given the Nazi murder of millions of Jews during World War II.

Holophrase A single word used to express complex meanings.

Homeostasis The tendency of the body to maintain a steady state, such as body temperature or level of sugar in the blood.

Homosexuality See *sexual orientation, gay male, lesbian*.

Homunculus Latin for "little man." A homunculus within the brain was once thought to govern human behavior.

Hormone A substance secreted by an endocrine gland that promotes development of body structures or regulates bodily functions.

Horoscope A forecast based on astrological (pseudoscientific) principles. (From Greek roots referring to observation *[skopos]* of the hour *[hora]* during which one was born.)

Hot reactors People who respond to stress with accelerated heart rate and constriction of blood vessels in peripheral areas of the body.

Hue The color of light, as determined by its wavelength.

Human factors The field that studies the efficiency and safety of person–machine systems and work environments.

Human immunodeficiency virus The virus that gives rise to acquired immune deficiency syndrome (AIDS) by destroying cells of the immune system and leaving the body prey to opportunistic diseases. Abbreviated *HIV*. Sometimes referred to as "the AIDS virus."

Humanism The philosophy (and school of psychology) that asserts that people are conscious, self-aware, and capable of free choice, self-fulfillment, and ethical behavior.

Humanistic psychology The school of psychology that assumes the existence of the self and emphasizes the importance of consciousness, self-awareness, and the freedom to make choices.

Human-relations theories Theories that hold that efficient organizations are structured according to the characteristics and needs of the individual worker.

Hyperactivity A disorder found most frequently in young boys, characterized by restlessness and short attention span. It is thought to reflect immaturity of the nervous system.

Hyperglycemia A disorder caused by excess sugar in the blood that can lead to coma and death.

Hypermnesia Greatly enhanced memory.

Hyperphagic Characterized by excessive eating.

Hypertension High blood pressure.

Hyperthyroidism A condition caused by excess thyroxin and characterized by excitability, weight loss, and insomnia.

Hypnagogic state The drowsy interval between waking and sleeping, characterized by brief, hallucinatory, dreamlike experiences.

Hypnosis   A condition in which people appear to be highly suggestible and behave as though they are in a trance.

Hypoactive sexual desire disorder   Persistent or recurrent lack of sexual fantasies and of interest in sexual activity.

Hypochondriasis   Persistent belief that one has a medical disorder despite the lack of medical findings.

Hypoglycemia   A metabolic disorder that is characterized by shakiness, dizziness, and lack of energy. It is caused by a low level of sugar in the blood.

Hypothalamus   A bundle of nuclei below the thalamus involved in the regulation of body temperature, motivation, and emotion.

Hypothesis   An assumption about behavior that is tested through research.

Hypothesis testing   In concept formation, an active process in which we try to ferret out the meanings of concepts by testing our assumptions.

Hypothyroidism   A condition caused by a deficiency of thyroxin and characterized by sluggish behavior and a low metabolic rate.

Hysterical disorder, conversion type   Former term for *conversion disorder*.

I

Icon   A mental representation of a visual stimulus that is held briefly in sensory memory.

Iconic memory   The sensory register that briefly holds mental representations of visual stimuli.

Id   In psychodynamic theory, the psychic structure that is present at birth and that is governed by the pleasure principle. The id represents physiological drives and is fully unconscious.

Idealize   To think of as being perfect, without flaws.

Ideas of persecution   Erroneous beliefs (delusions) that one is being victimized or persecuted.

Identification   (1) In psychodynamic theory, unconscious incorporation of the personality of another person. (2) In social-learning theory, a broad, continuous process of imitation during which children strive to become like role models.

Identity crisis   According to Erikson, a period of inner conflict during which one examines his or her values and makes decisions about life roles.

Identity diffusion   See *role diffusion*.

Ill-defined problem   A problem in which the original state, the goal, or the rules are less than clear.

Illusions   Sensations that give rise to misperceptions.

Imbalance   In balance theory, an uncomfortable condition in which persons whom we like disagree with us.

Immune system   The system of the body that recognizes and destroys foreign agents (antigens) that invade the body.

Imprinting   A process that occurs during a critical period in an organism's development, in which that organism forms an attachment that will afterward be difficult to modify.

Incentive   An object, person, or situation perceived as being capable of satisfying a need.

Incest taboo   The cultural prohibition against marrying or having sexual relations with a close blood relative.

Incidence   The extent to which an event occurs.

Incubation   In problem solving, a hypothetical process that sometimes occurs when we stand back from a frustrating problem for a while and the solution suddenly appears.

Incus   A bone of the middle ear. Latin for "anvil."

Independent variable   A condition in a scientific study that is manipulated so that its effects may be observed.

Indiscriminate attachment   The showing of attachment behaviors toward any person.

Individualist   A person who defines herself or himself in terms of personal traits and gives priority to her or his own goals.

Individual psychology   Adler's psychodynamic theory which emphasizes feelings of inferiority and the creative self.

Individuation   The process by which one separates from others and gains control over one's own behavior.

Inductive reasoning   A form of reasoning in which we reason from individual cases or particular facts to a general conclusion.

Industrial psychology   The field of psychology that studies the relationships between people and work.

Industry versus inferiority   Erikson's fourth stage of psychosocial development in which the child is challenged to master the fundamentals of technology during the primary school years.

Infant   A very young organism, a baby.

Infantile autism   A developmental disorder of childhood, characterized by extreme aloneness, communication problems, preservation of sameness, and ritualistic behavior.

Infer   Draw a conclusion.

Inference   Conclusion.

Inferential statistics   The branch of statistics concerned with the confidence with which conclusions drawn about samples may be extended to the populations from which they were drawn.

Inferiority complex   Feelings of inferiority hypothesized by Adler to serve as a central source of motivation.

Inflammation   Increased blood flow to an injured area of the body, resulting in redness, warmth, and increased supply of white blood cells.

Inflections   Grammatical markers that change the forms of words to indicate grammatical relationships such as number and tense.

Information processing   The processes by which information is encoded, stored, and retrieved.

Informed consent   Agreement to participate in research after receiving information about the purposes of the study and the nature of the treatments.

Inhibited orgasm   Persistent or recurrent delay in, or absence of, orgasm in a sexually excited person who has been engaging in sexually stimulating activity.

Inhibited sexual desire   Lack of interest in sexual activity, usually accompanied by absence of sexual fantasies.

Inhibited sexual excitement   Persistent lack of sexual response during sexual activity.

Inhibitory synapse   A synapse that influences receiving neurons in the direction of not firing by encouraging changes in their membrane permeability in the direction of the resting potential.

Initial-preattachment phase   According to Ainsworth, the first phase in forming bonds of attachment, which is characterized by indiscriminate attachment.

Initiative versus guilt   Erikson's third stage of psychosocial development, during which the child is challenged to add planning and "attacking" to the exercise of choice.

Innate   Existing at birth. Unlearned, natural.

Innate fixed-action pattern   An instinct.

Inner ear   The cochlea.

Insanity   A legal term descriptive of a person judged to be incapable of recognizing right from wrong or of conforming his or her behavior to the law.

Insecure attachment   A negative type of attachment, in which children show indifference or ambivalence toward attachment figures.

Insight   (1) In Gestalt psychology, the sudden perception of relationships among elements of the perceptual field, allowing the sudden solution of a problem. (2) In psychotherapy, awareness of one's genuine motives and feelings.

Insomnia   A term for three types of sleeping problems: (1) difficulty falling asleep (sleep-onset insomnia); (2) difficulty remaining asleep; and (3) waking early.

Instinct   An inherited disposition to activate specific behavior patterns that are designed to reach certain goals.

Instinctive   Inborn, natural, unlearned.

Instructional objective   A clear statement of what is to be learned.

Instrumental conditioning   Another term for *operant conditioning*, reflecting the fact that in operant conditioning, the learned behavior is instrumental in achieving certain effects.

Instrumental learning   See *instrumental conditioning*.

Insulin   A pancreatic hormone that stimulates the metabolism of sugar.

Intellectualization A defense mechanism in which threatening events are viewed with emotional detachment.

Intelligence A complex and controversial concept: (1) Learning ability, as contrasted with achievement. (2) Defined by David Wechsler as the "capacity . . . to understand the world [and the] resourcefulness to cope with its challenges."

Intelligence quotient (1) Originally, a ratio obtained by dividing a child's mental age on an intelligence test by his or her chronological age. (2) Generally, a score on an intelligence test. Abbreviated *IQ*.

Interactionism An approach to understanding behavior that emphasizes specification of the relationships among the various determinants of behavior instead of seeking the first cause of behavior.

Interference theory The view that we may forget stored material because other learning interferes with it.

Internal eaters People who eat predominantly in response to internal stimuli, like hunger pangs. See *external eater*.

"Internals" People who have an internal locus of control—who perceive the ability to attain reinforcements as being largely within themselves.

Interneuron A neuron that transmits a neural impulse from a sensory neuron to a motor neuron.

Interpersonal attraction See *attraction*.

Interposition A monocular cue for depth based on the fact that closer objects obscure vision of objects behind them.

Interpretation In psychoanalysis, an analyst's explanation of a client's utterance according to psychodynamic theory.

Intimacy versus isolation Erikson's sixth stage of psychosocial development; the young adult years during which persons are challenged to commit themselves to intimate relationships with others.

Intonation The use of pitches of varying levels to help communicate meaning.

Intoxication Drunkenness.

Intrapsychic Referring to the psychodynamic movement of psychic energy among the psychic structures hypothesized by Sigmund Freud.

Introjection In psychodynamic theory, the bringing within oneself of the personality of another individual.

Introspection An objective approach to describing one's mental content.

Introversion A trait characterized by intense imagination and the tendency to inhibit impulses. Opposite of *extroversion*.

Intuitive The direct learning or knowing of something without conscious use of reason.

Involuntary Automatic, not consciously controlled—referring to functions like heartbeat and dilation of the pupils.

IQ Intelligence quotient. A score on an intelligence test.

Iris A muscular membrane whose dilation regulates the amount of light that enters the eye.

J

James–Lange theory The theory that certain external stimuli trigger stereotypical patterns of activity and autonomic arousal. Emotions are the cognitive representations of this behavior and arousal.

Just noticeable difference The minimal amount by which a source of energy must be increased or decreased so that a difference in intensity will be perceived. Abbreviated *jnd*.

K

Kinesthesis The sense that provides information about the position and motion of parts of the body.

Knobs Swellings at the ends of axon terminals. Also referred to as *bulbs* or *buttons*.

Knowledge-acquisition components According to Sternberg, components of intelligence that are used in gaining knowledge, such as encoding and relating new knowledge to existing knowledge.

Korsakoff's syndrome See Wernicke–Korsakoff syndrome.

L

La belle indifférence A French term descriptive of the lack of concern shown by some persons with conversion disorder.

LAD Acronym for *language acquisition device*.

Language The communication of information through symbols that are arranged according to rules of grammar.

Language acquisition device In psycholinguistic theory, neural "prewiring" that is theorized to facilitate the child's learning of grammar. Abbreviated *LAD*.

Larynx The structure in the throat that contains the vocal cords.

Latency stage In psychodynamic theory, the fourth stage of psychosexual development during which sexual impulses are repressed.

Latent content In psychodynamic theory, the symbolized or underlying content of dreams.

Latent learning Learning that is not exhibited at the time of learning but is shown when adequate reinforcement is introduced.

Lateral fissure The valley in the cerebral cortex that separates the temporal lobe from the frontal and parietal lobes.

Lateral hypothalamus An area at the side of the hypothalamus that appears to function as a start-eating center.

Law of effect Thorndike's principle that responses are "stamped in" by rewards and "stamped out" by punishments.

Learned helplessness A model for the acquisition of depressive behavior, based on findings that organisms in aversive situations learn to show inactivity when their operants are not reinforced.

Learning (1) According to cognitive theorists, the process by which organisms make relatively permanent changes in the way they represent the environment because of experience. These changes influence the organism's behavior. (2) According to behaviorists, a relatively permanent change in behavior that results from experience.

Least-restrictive placement Placement of exceptional students in settings that are as normal and as much in the mainstream of education as possible, in accord with the Education for All Handicapped Children Act.

Lens A transparent body between the iris and the vitreous humor of the eye that focuses an image onto the retina.

Lesbian A female who is sexually aroused by, and interested in forming romantic relationships with, other females.

Lesion An injury that results in impaired behavior or loss of a function.

Leukocytes The white blood cells of the immune system.

Libido (1) In psychodynamic theory, the energy of Eros, the sexual instinct. (2) Generally, sexual interest or drive.

Lie detector See *polygraph*.

Life-change units Numbers assigned to various life events that indicate the degree of stress they cause.

Light Electromagnetic energy of various wavelengths. The part of the spectrum of energy that stimulates the eye and produces visual sensations.

Limbic system A group of brain structures that form a fringe along the inner edge of the cerebrum. These structures are involved in memory and motivation.

Linguistic relativity hypothesis The view that language structures the way in which we perceive the world. As a consequence, our thoughts would be limited by the concepts available in our languages.

Linguists Scientists who study the structure, functions, and origins of language.

Locus of control The place (locus) to which an individual attributes control over the receiving of reinforcements—either inside or outside the self.

Long-term memory The type or stage of memory capable of relatively permanent storage.

Love A strong, positive emotion with many meanings. See, for example, *romantic love* and *attachment*.

Low-balling A sales method in which extremely attractive terms are offered to induce a person to make a commitment. Once the commitment is made, the terms are revised.

LSD Lysergic acid diethylamide. A hallucinogenic drug.

Lucid dream   A dream in which we seem to be awake and aware that we are dreaming.

Lysergic acid diethylamide   A hallucinogenic drug. Abbreviated *LSD*.

M

Magnetic resonance imaging   Formation of a computer-generated image of the anatomical details of the brain by measuring the signals that these structures emit when the head is placed in a strong magnetic field. Abbreviated *MRI*.

Mainstreaming   The practice of placing exceptional students in educational environments that are as normal as possible.

Maintenance rehearsal   Mental repetition of information in order to keep it in memory.

Major depression   A severe mood disorder in which the person may show loss of appetite, psychomotor symptoms, and impaired reality testing.

Major tranquilizer   A drug that decreases severe anxiety or agitation in psychotic patients or in violent individuals.

Male erectile disorder   A sexual dysfunction characterized by difficulty in becoming sexually aroused, as defined by achieving erection, or in sustaining arousal long enough to engage in satisfying sexual relations.

Malingering   Pretending to be ill to escape duty or work.

Malleus   A bone of the middle ear. Latin for "hammer."

Mania   A state characterized by elation and restlessness. (A Greek word meaning "madness.")

Manic-depression   Former term for *bipolar disorder*.

Manifest content   In the psychodynamic theory of dreams, the reported or perceived content of dreams.

Mantra   A word or sound that is repeated in transcendental meditation as a means of narrowing consciousness and inducing relaxation.

Marijuana   The dried vegetable matter of the *Cannabis sativa* plant. A mild hallucinogenic drug that is most frequently taken in by smoking.

Masochism   The attainment of gratification, frequently sexual, through the receiving of pain or humiliation.

Masturbation   Self-stimulation of the sexual organs.

Matching hypothesis   The view that people tend to choose persons similar to themselves in attractiveness and attitudes in the formation of interpersonal relationships.

Maturation   Changes that result from heredity and minimal nutrition but that do not appear to require learning or exercise. A gradual, orderly unfolding or developing of new structures or behaviors as a result of heredity.

Mean   A type of average calculated by dividing the sum of scores by the number of scores.

Means–end analysis   A heuristic device in which we try to solve a problem by evaluating the difference between the current situation and the goal.

Median   A type of average defined as the score beneath which 50% of the cases fall.

Mediation   In information processing, a method of improving memory by linking two items with a third that ties them together.

Medical model   The view that abnormal behavior is symptomatic of underlying illness.

Meditation   A systematic narrowing of attention that slows the metabolism and helps produce feelings of relaxation.

Medulla   An oblong-shaped area of the hindbrain involved in heartbeat and respiration.

Meiosis   A process of reduction division in which sperm and ova are formed, each of which contains 23 chromosomes.

Memory   The processes by which information is encoded, stored, and retrieved.

Memory trace   An assumed change in the nervous system that reflects the impression made by a stimulus. Memory traces are said to be "held" in sensory registers.

Menarche   The onset of menstruation.

Menopause   The cessation of menstruation.

Menstrual synchrony   The convergence of the menstrual cycles of women who spend time in close quarters.

Menstruation   The monthly shedding of the uterine lining by nonpregnant women.

Mental age   The accumulated months of credit that a test taker earns on the Stanford–Binet Intelligence Scale.

Mental set   (1) Readiness to respond to a situation in a set manner. (2) In problem-solving, a tendency to respond to a new problem with an approach that was successful with similar problems.

Mescaline   A hallucinogenic drug derived from the mescal (peyote) cactus. In religious ceremonies, Mexican Indians chew the buttonlike structures at the tops of the rounded stems of the plant.

Metabolism   In organisms, a continuous process that converts food into energy.

Metacognition   Awareness and control of one's cognitive abilities, as shown by the intentional use of cognitive strategies in solving problems.

Metacomponents   According to Sternberg, components of intelligence that are based on self-awareness of our intellectual processes.

Metamemory   Self-awareness of the ways in which memory functions, as shown by use of cognitive strategies to foster the effective encoding, storing, and retrieval of information.

Methadone   An artificial narcotic that is slower acting than, and does not provide the rush of, heroin. Methadone allows heroin addicts to abstain from heroin without experiencing an abstinence syndrome.

Methaqualone   An addictive depressant often referred to as "ludes."

Method of constant stimuli   A psychophysical method for determining thresholds in which the researcher presents stimuli of various magnitudes and asks the subject to report detection.

Method of loci   A method of retaining information in which chunks of new material are related to a series of well-established or well-known images.

Method of savings   A measure of retention in which the difference between the number of repetitions originally required to learn a list and the number of repetitions required to relearn the list after a certain amount of time has elapsed is calculated.

Microspectrophotometry   A method for analyzing the sensitivity of single cones to lights of different wavelengths.

Middle ear   The central part of the ear that contains three small bones, the "hammer," "anvil," and "stirrup."

Midlife crisis   According to theorists of adult development, a crisis experienced by many people at about age 40 when they realize that life may be halfway over and they feel trapped in meaningless life roles.

Migraine headache   A throbbing headache, usually occurring on one side of the head, that stems from change in the blood supply to the head. It is often accompanied by nausea and impaired vision.

Mind   That part of consciousness that is involved in perception and awareness.

Minor tranquilizer   A drug that relieves feelings of anxiety and tension.

Mitosis   The process of cell division by which the identical genetic code is carried into new cells in the body.

Mnemonics   A system for remembering in which items are related to easily recalled sets of symbols such as acronyms, phrases, or jingles.

Mode   A type of average defined as the most frequently occurring score in a distribution.

Model   In social-cognitive theory: (1) As a noun, an organism that engages in a response that is imitated by another organism. (2) As a verb, to engage in behavior patterns that are imitated by others.

Monoamine oxidase inhibitors   Antidepressant drugs that work by blocking the action of an enzyme that breaks down norepinephrine and serotonin. Abbreviated *MAO inhibitors*.

Monochromat   A person who is sensitive to the intensity of light only and thus colorblind.

Monocular cues   Stimuli that suggest depth and that can be perceived with only one eye, such as perspective and interposition.

Monozygotic twins   Twins who develop from the same zygote, thus carrying the same genetic instructions. Identical twins. Abbreviated *MZ twins*. See *dizygotic twins*.

Moral principle   In psychodynamic theory, the governing principle of the superego, which sets moral standards and enforces adherence to them.

Moro reflex   An infant reflex characterized by arching of the back and drawing up of the legs in response to a sudden, startling stimulus. Also called the *startle reflex*.

Morpheme   The smallest unit of meaning in a language.

Morphine A narcotic derived from opium that reduces pain and produces feelings of well-being.

Morphology The study of the units of meaning in a language.

Motion parallax A monocular cue for depth based on the perception that nearby objects appear to move more rapidly in relation to our own motion.

Motive A hypothetical state within an organism that propels the organism toward a goal.

Motor cortex The section of cerebral cortex that lies in the frontal lobe, just across the central fissure from the sensory cortex. Neural impulses in the motor cortex are linked to muscular responses.

Multiple approach–avoidance conflict A type of conflict in which a number of goals each produces approach and avoidance motives.

Multiple personality disorder The earlier term for *dissociative identity disorder:* A dissociative disorder in which a person has two or more distinct identities or personalities.

Mutation Sudden variations in the genetic code that usually occur as a result of environmental influences.

Mutism Refusal to talk.

Myelination The process by which the axons of neurons become coated with a fatty, insulating substance.

Myelin sheath A fatty substance that encases and insulates axons, permitting more rapid transmission of neural impulses.

N

n Ach The need for achievement; the need to master, to accomplish difficult things.

n Aff The need for affiliation; the need to be associated with groups.

Narcolepsy A sleep disorder characterized by uncontrollable seizures of sleep during the waking state.

Narcotics Drugs used to relieve pain and induce sleep. The term is usually reserved for opioids.

Native-language approach A method of teaching a second language in which children are at first taught in the language spoken in the home.

Naturalistic observation A method of scientific investigation in which organisms are observed carefully and unobtrusively in their natural environments.

Nature In behavior genetics, inherited influences on behavior, as contrasted with *nurture.*

Nearsightedness Inability to see distant objects with the acuity with which a person with normal vision can see distant objects.

Need A state of deprivation.

Need for achievement The need to master, to accomplish difficult things.

Need for affiliation The need for affiliation; the need to be associated with groups.

Negative correlation A relationship between two variables in which one variable increases as the other variable decreases.

Negative feedback Descriptive of a system in which information that a quantity (e.g., of a hormone) has reached a set point suspends action of the agency (e.g., a gland) that gives rise to that quantity.

Negative instance In concept formation, events that are *not* examples of a concept.

Negative reinforcer A reinforcer that increases the frequency of operant behavior when it is removed. Pain, anxiety, and disapproval usually, but not always, function as negative reinforcers. See *positive reinforcer.*

Neodissociation theory A theory that explains hypnotic events in terms of an ability to divide our awareness so that we can focus on hypnotic instructions and, at the same time, perceive outside sources of stimulation.

Neo-Freudians Theorists in the psychodynamic tradition who usually place less emphasis than Freud did on the importance of sexual impulses and unconscious determinants of behavior. Instead, they place more emphasis than Freud did on conscious motives and rational decision making.

Neonate A newborn child.

Nerve A bundle of axons from many neurons.

Neural impulse The electrochemical discharge of a neuron, or nerve cell.

Neuron A nerve cell.

Neuropeptide A short chain of amino acids (peptide) that functions as a neurotransmitter.

Neurosis One of a number of psychological disorders characterized chiefly by anxiety, feelings of dread and foreboding, and avoidance behavior. Neuroses are theorized to stem from unconscious conflict. (Contemporary systems of classifying psychological disorders focus more on observable behavior and therefore deemphasize this concept.)

Neuroticism A trait in which a person is given to emotional instability, anxiety, feelings of foreboding, inhibition of impulses, and avoidance behavior.

Neurotransmitter A chemical substance that is involved in the transmission of neural impulses from one neuron to another.

Nicotine A stimulant found in tobacco smoke.

Nightmare A frightening dream that usually occurs during rapid-eye-movement (REM) sleep.

Night terrors See *sleep terrors.*

Node of Ranvier A noninsulated segment of an otherwise myelinated axon.

Noise (1) In signal-detection theory, any unwanted signal that interferes with perception of the desired signal. (2) More generally, a combination of dissonant sounds.

Nonbalance In balance theory, a condition in which persons whom we dislike do not agree with us.

Nonconscious Descriptive of bodily processes, such as the growing of hair, of which we cannot become conscious. We may know that our hair is growing, but we cannot directly experience the biological process.

Non-rapid-eye-movement sleep Stages 1 through 4 of sleep, which are not characterized by rapid eye movements. Abbreviated *NREM sleep.*

Nonsense syllables Meaningless sets of two consonants, with a vowel sandwiched in between, that are used to study memory.

Norepinephrine A neurotransmitter whose action is similar to that of the hormone *epinephrine* and which may play a role in depression.

Normal curve A graphic presentation of a normal distribution, showing a bell shape.

Normal distribution A symmetrical distribution in which approximately two thirds of the cases lie within a standard deviation of the mean. A distribution that represents chance deviations of a variable.

Normative data Information concerning the behavior of a population.

Norm-referenced testing A testing approach in which scores are derived by comparing the number of items answered correctly with the average performance of others.

Novel stimulation (1) New or different stimulation. (2) A hypothesized primary drive to experience new or different stimulation.

Noxious Harmful, injurious.

Nuclear magnetic resonance See *magnetic resonance imaging.*

Nuclei Plural of *nucleus.* A group of neural cell bodies found in the brain or spinal cord.

Nurturance The quality of nourishing, rearing, and fostering the development of children, animals, or plants.

Nurture In behavior genetics, environmental influences on behavior, including factors such as nutrition, culture, socioeconomic status, and learning. Contrast with *nature.*

O

Objective Of known or perceived objects rather than existing only in the mind; real.

Objective morality According to Piaget, objective moral judgments assign guilt according to the amount of damage done rather than the motives of the actor.

Objective tests Tests whose items must be answered in a specified, limited manner. Tests that have concrete answers that are considered to be correct.

Object permanence Recognition that objects removed from sight still exist, as demonstrated in young children by continued pursuit.

Observational learning In social-learning theory, the acquisition of expectations and skills by observing the behavior of others. As opposed to operant conditioning, skill acquisition by means of observational learning occurs without the emission and reinforcement of a response.

Obsession A recurring thought or image that seems to be beyond control.

Occipital lobe The lobe of the cerebral cortex that is involved in vision. It lies below and behind the parietal lobe and behind the temporal lobe.

Odor   The characteristic of a substance that makes it perceptible to the sense of smell. An odor is a sample of the molecules of the substance being sensed.

Oedipus complex   In psychodynamic theory, a conflict of the phallic stage in which the boy wishes to possess his mother sexually and perceives his father as a rival in love.

Olfactory   Having to do with the sense of smell.

Olfactory membrane   A membrane high in each nostril that contains receptor neurons for the sense of smell.

Olfactory nerve   The nerve that transmits information about odors from olfactory receptors to the brain.

Opaque   (1) Not permitting the passage of light. (2) In psychoanalysis, descriptive of the analyst, who is expected to hide her or his own feelings from the client.

Operant behavior   Voluntary responses that are reinforced.

Operant conditioning   A simple form of learning in which an organism learns to engage in behavior because it is reinforced.

Operational definition   A definition of a variable in terms of the methods used to create or measure the variable.

Opioid   An addictive drug derived from the opium poppy, or similar in chemical structure, that provides a euphoric rush and depresses the nervous system.

Opponent-process theory   (1) In sensation and perception, the theory that color vision is made possible by three types of cones, some of which respond to red or green light, some to blue or yellow light, and some to the intensity of light only. (2) In motivation and emotion, the view that our emotions trigger opposing emotions.

Optic nerve   The nerve that transmits sensory information from the eye to the brain.

Optimal arousal   A level of arousal at which an organism has the greatest feelings of well-being or functions most efficiently.

Oral fixation   In psychodynamic theory, attachment to objects and behaviors characteristic of the oral stage.

Oral stage   The first stage in Freud's theory of psychosexual development, during which gratification is obtained primarily through oral activities like sucking and biting.

Organizational analysis   Evaluation of the goals and resources of an organization.

Organizational psychology   The field of psychology that studies the structure and functions of organizations.

Organizing effects   The directional effects of sex hormones—for example, along stereotypical masculine or feminine lines.

Organ of Corti   The receptor for hearing, which lies on the basilar membrane in the cochlea. Called the command post of hearing, it contains the receptor cells that transmit auditory information to the auditory nerve.

Orgasm   The height or climax of sexual excitement, involving involuntary muscle contractions, release of sexual tensions, and, usually, intense subjective feelings of pleasure.

Orienting reflex   An unlearned response in which an organism attends to a stimulus.

Osmoreceptors   Receptors in the hypothalamus that are sensitive to depletion of fluid in the body.

Osteoporosis   A condition caused by calcium deficiency and characterized by brittleness of the bones.

Outer ear   The funnel-shaped outer part of the ear that transmits sound waves to the eardrum.

Oval window   A membrane that transmits vibrations from the stirrup of the middle ear to the inner ear.

Ovaries   The female reproductive organs located in the abdominal cavity. The ovaries produce egg cells (ova) and the hormones estrogen and progesterone.

Overextension   Overgeneralizing the use of words into situations in which they do not apply (characteristic of the speech of young children).

Overregularization   The formation of plurals and past tenses of irregular nouns and verbs according to rules of grammar that apply to regular nouns and verbs (characteristic of the speech of young children).

Overtones   Tones higher in frequency than those played on an instrument. Overtones result from vibrations throughout the instrument.

Ovulation   The releasing of an egg cell (ovum) from an ovary.

Oxytocin   A pituitary hormone that stimulates labor (childbirth).

P

Paired associates   Nonsense syllables presented in pairs in experiments that measure recall. After viewing pairs, participants are shown one member of each pair and asked to recall the other.

Palmar reflex   See *grasp reflex*.

Pancreas   A gland behind the stomach whose secretions, including insulin, influence the level of sugar in the blood.

Panic disorder   The recurrent experiencing of attacks of extreme anxiety in the absence of external stimuli that usually elicit anxiety.

Paradoxical intention   Achieving one's goals by undertaking an apparently opposing course of action.

Paradoxical sleep   Another term for the period of sleep during which rapid eye movements occur. The term *paradoxical* reflects the fact that brain waves found during REM sleep suggest a level of arousal similar to that shown during the waking state.

Paranoia   A rare psychotic disorder in which a person shows a persistent delusional system but not the confusion of the paranoid schizophrenic.

Paranoid personality disorder   A disorder characterized by persistent suspiciousness but not the disorganization of paranoid schizophrenia.

Paranoid schizophrenia   A subtype of schizophrenia characterized primarily by delusions—commonly of persecution—and by vivid hallucinations.

Paraphilia   A disorder in which the person shows sexual arousal in response to unusual or bizarre objects or situations.

Parasympathetic nervous system   The branch of the autonomic nervous system that is most active during processes such as digestion and relaxation that restore the body's reserves of energy. See *sympathetic division*.

Parent   In transactional analysis, a moralistic ego state.

Parietal lobe   The lobe of the cerebral cortex that lies behind the central fissure and that is involved in body senses.

Partial reinforcement   One of several types of reinforcement schedules in which correct responses receive intermittent reinforcement, as opposed to *continuous reinforcement*.

Participant modeling   A behavior-therapy technique in which a client observes and imitates a person who approaches and copes with feared objects or situations.

Passionate love   See *romantic love*.

Pathogen   An organism such as a bacterium or virus that can cause disease.

Pathological gambler   A person who gambles habitually despite consistent losses. A compulsive gambler.

PCP   Phencyclidine; a hallucinogenic drug.

Peak experience   In humanistic theory, a brief moment of rapture that stems from the realization that one is on the path toward self-actualization.

Pelvic inflammatory disease   Inflammation of the woman's abdominal region that is caused by pathogens such as the gonorrhea bacterium and characterized by fever, local pain, and, frequently, fertility problems. Abbreviated *PID*.

Penis envy   In psychodynamic theory, jealousy of the male sexual organ attributed to girls in the phallic stage.

Pepsinogen   A substance that helps the body digest proteins.

Perceived self-efficacy   In social-learning theory, a person's belief that she or he can achieve goals through her or his own efforts.

Perception   The process by which sensations are organized into an inner representation of the world—a psychological process through which we interpret sensory information.

Perceptual organization   The tendency to integrate perceptual elements into meaningful patterns.

Performance anxiety   Fear concerning whether or not one will be able to perform adequately.

Performance components   According to Sternberg, the mental operations used in processing information.

Period of the ovum   The period following conception before the developing ovum (now fertilized) has become securely implanted in the uterine wall. Another term for the *germinal stage*.

Peripheral nervous system   The part of the nervous system consisting of the somatic nervous system and the autonomic nervous system.

Permeability   The degree to which a membrane allows a substance to pass through it.

Personality   The distinct patterns of behaviors, including thoughts and feelings, that characterize a person's adaptation to the demands of life.

Personality disorder   An enduring pattern of maladaptive behavior that is a source of distress to the individual or to others.

Personality structure   One's total pattern of traits.

Personal space   A psychological boundary that surrounds a person and permits that person to maintain a protective distance from others.

Person-centered therapy   Carl Rogers's method of psychotherapy, which emphasizes the creation of a warm, therapeutic atmosphere that frees clients to engage in self-expression and self-exploration.

Person variables   In social-learning theory, determinants of behavior that lie within the person, including competencies, encoding strategies, expectancies, subjective values, and self-regulatory systems and plans.

Perspective   A monocular cue for depth based on the convergence (coming together) of parallel lines as they recede into the distance.

pH   A chemical symbol expressing the acidity of a solution.

Phallic stage   In psychodynamic theory, the third stage of psychosexual development, characterized by shifting of libido to the phallic region and by the Oedipus and Electra complexes.

Phallic symbol   In psychodynamic theory, an object that represents the penis.

Phencyclidine   A hallucinogenic drug whose name is an acronym for its chemical structure. Abbreviated *PCP*.

Phenomenological   Having to do with subjective, conscious experience.

Phenothiazines   Drugs that act as major tranquilizers and that are effective in treating many cases of schizophrenic disorders.

Phenylketonuria   A genetic abnormality transmitted by a recessive gene, in which one is unable to metabolize phenylpyruvic acid, leading to mental retardation. Abbreviated *PKU*.

Pheromones   Chemical secretions detected by the sense of smell that stimulate stereotypical behaviors in other members of the same species.

Phi phenomenon   The perception of movement as a result of sequential presentation of visual stimuli, as with lights going on and off in a row on a theater marquee.

Phobic disorder   Excessive, irrational fear. Fear that is out of proportion to the actual danger and that interferes with one's life. Formerly called *phobic neurosis*.

Phoneme   A basic sound in a language.

Phonology   The study of the basic sounds in a language.

Photographic memory   See *iconic memory*.

Photoreceptors   Cells that respond to light. See *rod* and *cone*.

Phrenology   An unscientific method of analyzing personality by measurement of the shapes and protuberances of the skull.

Physiological   Having to do with the biological functions and vital processes of organisms.

Physiological dependence   Addiction to a drug, which occurs when regular usage renders the presence of the drug within the body the normal state.

Physiological drives   Unlearned drives with a biological basis, such as hunger, thirst, and avoidance of pain. Also called *primary drives*.

Physiological psychologists   Same as biological psychologists.

Pitch   The highness or lowness of a sound, as determined by the frequency of the sound waves.

Pituitary gland   The body's master gland, located in the brain, that secretes growth hormone, prolactin, antidiuretic hormone, and other hormones.

Placebo   A bogus treatment that controls for the effects of expectations. A so-called sugar pill.

Placenta   A membrane that permits the exchange of nutrients and waste products between the mother and the fetus but that does not allow the maternal and fetal bloodstreams to mix.

Place theory   The theory that the pitch of a sound is determined by the section of the basilar membrane that vibrates in response to it.

Plantar reflex   See *grasp reflex*.

Plateau phase   An advanced state of sexual arousal that precedes orgasm.

Pleasure principle   In psychodynamic theory, the principle that governs the id; the demanding of immediate gratification of instinctive needs.

Polarization   (1) In physiological psychology, the readying of a neuron for firing by creating an internal negative charge in relation to the body fluid outside the cell membrane. (2) In social psychology, the taking of an extreme position or attitude on an issue.

Polygenic   Determined by more than one gene.

Polygraph   An instrument that is theorized to be sensitive to whether or not an individual is telling lies by assessing four measures of arousal: heart rate, blood pressure, respiration rate, and galvanic skin response (GSR). Also called a *lie detector*.

Pons   A structure of the hindbrain involved in respiration.

Population   A complete group of organisms or events.

Positive correlation   A relationship between variables in which one variable increases as the other variable also increases.

Positive instance   In concept formation, an example of a concept.

Positive reinforcer   A reinforcer that increases the frequency of operant behavior when it is presented. Food and approval are usually, but not always, positive reinforcers. See *negative reinforcer*.

Positron-emission tomography   Formation of a computer-generated image of the neural activity of parts of the brain by tracing the amount of glucose used by the various parts. Abbreviated *PET scan*.

Postconventional level   According to Kohlberg, a period of moral development during which moral judgments are derived from moral principles and people look to themselves to set moral standards.

Posthypnotic amnesia   Inability to recall material presented while hypnotized, following the suggestion of the hypnotist.

Post-traumatic stress disorder   A disorder that follows a distressing event outside the range of normal human experience. It is characterized by symptoms such as intense fear, avoidance of stimuli associated with the event, and reliving of the event.

Pragmatics   The practical aspects of communication. Adaptation of language to fit the social context.

Precognition   The term means ability to foresee the future; however, most psychologists do not believe that this ability exists. (From the Latin *prae-*, meaning "before," and *cognitio*, meaning "knowledge.")

Preconscious   In psychodynamic theory, descriptive of material of which one is not currently aware but which can be brought into awareness by focusing one's attention. Also see *unconscious*.

Preconventional level   According to Kohlberg, a period of moral development during which moral judgments are based largely on expectation of rewards and punishments.

Prefrontal lobotomy   A form of psychosurgery in which a section of the frontal lobe of the brain is severed or destroyed.

Pregenital   In psychodynamic theory, characteristic of stages less mature than the genital stage.

Prejudice   The unfounded belief that a person or group—on the basis of assumed racial, ethnic, sexual, or other features—will possess negative characteristics or perform inadequately.

Prelinguistic   Prior to the development of language.

Premature ejaculation   Ejaculation that occurs before the couple are satisfied with the duration of coitus.

Premenstrual syndrome   A cluster of symptoms—which may include tension, irritability, depression, and fatigue—that some women experience before menstruating.

Premise   A statement or assertion that serves as the basis for an argument.

Prenatal   Prior to birth.

Preoperational stage   The second of Piaget's stages of cognitive development, characterized by illogical use of words and symbols, egocentrism, animism, artificialism, and objective moral judgments.

Presbyopia   Brittleness of the lens, a condition that impairs visual acuity for nearby objects.

Primacy effect   (1) In information processing, the tendency to recall the initial items in a series of items. (2) In social psychology, the tendency to evaluate others in terms of first impressions.

Primary colors   Colors that we cannot produce by mixing other hues; colors from which other colors are derived.

Primary drives   Unlearned drives; physiological drives.

Primary mental abilities   According to Thurstone, the basic abilities that compose human intelligence.

Primary narcissism   In psychodynamic theory, the type of autism that describes the newborn child who has not learned that he or she is separate from the rest of the world.

Primary prevention   In community psychology, the deterrence of psychological problems before they start.

Primary reinforcer   A stimulus that has reinforcement value without learning. Examples: food, water, warmth, and pain. See *secondary reinforcer.*

Primary sex characteristics   Physical traits that distinguish the sexes and that are directly involved in reproduction.

Primate   A member of an order of mammals including monkeys, apes, and human beings.

Prism   A transparent triangular solid that breaks down visible light into the colors of the spectrum.

Proactive interference   Interference from previously learned material in one's ability to retrieve or recall recently learned material. See *retroactive interference.*

Proband   The family member first studied or tested.

Procedural memory   Knowledge of ways of doing things; skill memory.

Productivity   A property of language; the ability to combine words into unlimited, novel sentences.

Progesterone   A sex hormone that promotes growth of the sexual organs and helps maintain pregnancy.

Prognosis   A prediction of the probable course of a disease.

Programmed learning   A method of learning, based on operant conditioning principles, in which complex tasks are broken down into simple steps. The proper performance of each step is reinforced. Incorrect responses go unreinforced but are not punished.

Progressive relaxation   Jacobson's method for reducing muscle tension, which involves alternate tensing and relaxing of muscle groups throughout the body.

Projection   In psychodynamic theory, a defense mechanism in which unacceptable ideas and impulses are cast out or attributed to others.

Projective test   A psychological test that presents questions for which there is no single correct response. A test that presents ambiguous stimuli into which the test taker projects his or her own personality in making a response.

Prolactin   A pituitary hormone that regulates production of milk and, in lower animals, maternal behavior.

Propinquity   Nearness.

Prosocial   Behavior that is characterized by helping others and making a contribution to society.

Prototype   A concept of a category of objects or events that serves as a good example of the category.

Proximity   Nearness. The perceptual tendency to group together objects that are near one another.

Proximodistal   Proceeding from near to far.

***Psi* communication**   (SIGH). The term means the transfer of information through an irregular or unusual process—not the usual senses. However, most psychologists do not believe that psi communication exists.

Psychedelic   Causing hallucinations or delusions or heightening perceptions.

Psychiatrist   A physician who specializes in the application of medical treatments to psychological disorders.

Psychic structure   In psychodynamic theory, a hypothesized mental structure that helps explain various aspects of behavior. See *id, ego,* and *superego.*

Psychoactive   Describing drugs that give rise to psychological effects.

Psychoanalysis   The school of psychology, founded by Sigmund Freud, that emphasizes the importance of unconscious motives and conflicts as determinants of human behavior. Also the name of Freud's methods of psychotherapy and clinical investigation.

Psychodynamic   Descriptive of Freud's view that various forces move within the personality, frequently clashing, and that the outcome of these clashes determines behavior.

Psychogenic amnesia   The earlier term for *dissociative amnesia:* A dissociative disorder marked by loss of episodic memory or self-identity. Skills and general knowledge are usually retained.

Psychogenic fugue   The earlier term for *dissociative fugue:* A dissociative disorder in which one experiences amnesia, then flees to a new location.

Psychokinesis   The term means ability to manipulate objects by thought processes. However, most psychologists do not believe that this ability exists.

Psycholinguist   A psychologist who studies how we perceive and acquire language.

Psycholinguistic theory   The view that language learning involves an interaction between environmental influences and an inborn tendency to acquire language. The emphasis is on the innate tendency.

Psychological androgyny   Possession of both instrumental and warmth–expressiveness traits.

Psychological dependence   Repeated use of a substance as a way of dealing with stress.

Psychological disorders   Patterns of behavior or mental processes that are connected with distress or disability and are not expectable responses to particular events.

Psychological hardiness   A cluster of traits that buffer stress and that are characterized by commitment, challenge, and control.

Psychology   The science that studies behavior and mental processes.

Psychomotor retardation   Slowness in motor activity and, apparently, in thought.

Psychoneuroimmunology   The field that studies the relationships between psychological factors (e.g., attitudes and overt behavior patterns) and the functioning of the immune system.

Psychopath   Another term for a person who shows an antisocial personality disorder.

Psychophysics   The study of the relationships between physical stimuli, such as light and sound, and their perception.

Psychophysiological   Having to do with physical illnesses that are believed to have psychological origins or to be stress-related. Also termed *psychosomatic.*

Psychosexual development   In psychodynamic theory, the process by which libidinal energy is expressed through different erogenous zones during different stages of development.

Psychosexual trauma   A distressing sexual experience that may have lingering psychological effects.

Psychosis   A major psychological disorder in which a person shows impaired reality testing and has difficulty meeting the demands of everyday life.

Psychosocial development   Erikson's theory of personality and development, which emphasizes the importance of social relationships and conscious choice throughout eight stages of development, including three stages of adult development.

Psychosomatic   Having to do with physical illnesses that are believed to have psychological origins or to be stress-related. Also termed *psychophysiological.*

Psychosurgery   Biological treatments in which specific areas or structures of the brain are destroyed to promote psychological changes or to relieve disordered behavior.

Psychotherapy   A systematic interaction between a therapist and a client that brings psychological principles to bear on influencing the client's thoughts, feelings, or behaviors to help that client overcome psychological disorders or adjust to problems in living.

Puberty   The period of early adolescence during which hormones spur rapid physical development.

Punishment   An unpleasant stimulus that suppresses the frequency of the behavior it follows.

Pupil   The apparently black opening in the center of the iris, through which light enters the eye.

Pupillary reflex   The automatic adjusting of the irises to permit more or less light to enter the eye.

Pure research   Research conducted without concern for immediate applications.

Q

Quality circle   A regularly scheduled meeting in which a group of workers discusses problems and suggests solutions in order to enhance the quality of products.

R

Rage response   Stereotypical aggressive behavior that can be brought forth in lower animals by electrical stimulation of the brain.

Random sample   A sample drawn in such a manner that every member of a population has an equal chance of being selected.

Random trial and error   In operant conditioning, refers to behavior that occurs prior to learning what behavior is reinforced. The implication is that in a novel situation, the organism happens upon the first correct (reinforced) response by chance.

Range   A measure of variability; the distance between extreme measures or scores in a distribution.

Rapid-eye-movement sleep   A stage of sleep characterized by rapid eye movements that have been linked to dreaming. Abbreviated *REM sleep*. See also *paradoxical sleep*.

Rapid flight of ideas   Rapid speech and topic changes, characteristic of manic behavior.

Rapid smoking   A type of aversive conditioning in which cigarettes are inhaled every few seconds, making the smoke aversive.

Rational-emotive therapy   Albert Ellis's form of cognitive psychotherapy, which focuses on how irrational expectations create negative feelings and maladaptive behavior and which encourages clients to challenge and correct these expectations.

Rationalization   In psychodynamic theory, a defense mechanism in which an individual engages in self-deception, finding justifications for unacceptable ideas, impulses, or behaviors.

Reaction formation   In psychodynamic theory, a defense mechanism in which unacceptable impulses and ideas are kept unconscious through the exaggerated expression of opposing ideas and impulses.

Reaction time   The amount of time required to respond to a stimulus.

Readiness   In developmental psychology, referring to a stage in the maturation of an organism when it is capable of engaging in a certain response.

Reality principle   In psychodynamic theory, the principle that guides ego functioning; consideration of what is practical and possible in gratifying needs.

Reality testing   The capacity to form an accurate mental representation of the world, including socially appropriate behavior, reasonably accurate knowledge of the motives of others, undistorted sensory impressions, and self-insight.

Reasoning   The transforming of information to reach conclusions.

Rebound anxiety   Strong anxiety that can attend the suspension of usage of a tranquilizer.

Recall   Retrieval or reconstruction of learned material.

Recency effect   (1) In information processing, the tendency to recall the last items in a series of items. (2) In social psychology, the tendency to evaluate others in terms of the most recent impression.

Receptive vocabulary   The extent of one's knowledge of the meanings of words that are communicated to one by others.

Receptor site   A location on a receiving neuron that is tailored to receive a neurotransmitter.

Recessive trait   In genetics, a trait that is not expressed when the gene or genes involved have been paired with *dominant* genes. However, recessive traits are transmitted to future generations and expressed if paired with other recessive genes. See *dominant trait*.

Reciprocity   (1) Mutual action. Treating others as one is treated. (2) In interpersonal attraction, the tendency to return feelings and attitudes that are expressed about us.

Recitation   A teaching format in which teachers pose questions that are answered by students.

Recognition   In information processing, a relatively easy memory task in which one identifies objects or events as having been encountered previously.

Reconstructive memories   Memories that are based on the piecing together of memory fragments with general knowledge and expectations rather than a precise picture of the past.

Reflex   A simple, unlearned response to a stimulus.

Refractory period   (1) In discussion of the nervous system, a period following firing during which a neuron's action potential cannot be triggered. (2) In human sexuality, a period following orgasm when a male is insensitive to further sexual stimulation.

Regression   In psychodynamic theory, return to a form of behavior characteristic of an earlier stage of development. As a defense mechanism, regression to less mature behavior is a means of coping with stress.

Reinforcement   A stimulus that follows a response and increases the frequency of that response. See *positive* and *negative*, *primary* and *secondary* reinforcers.

Relative refractory period   A phase following the absolute refractory period during which a neuron will fire in response to stronger-than-usual messages from other neurons.

Relaxation response   Benson's term for a cluster of responses brought about by meditation that lower the activity of the sympathetic division of the autonomic nervous system.

Relearning   A measure of retention. Material is usually relearned more quickly than it is learned initially.

Releaser   In ethology, a stimulus that elicits an instinctive response.

Reliability   In psychological measurement, consistency. Also see *validity*.

Replication   The repetition or duplication of scientific studies in order to double-check their results.

Representativeness heuristic   A decision-making heuristic in which people make judgments about events (samples) according to the populations they appear to represent.

Repression   In psychodynamic theory, the ejection of anxiety-provoking ideas, impulses, or images from awareness, without the awareness that one is doing so. A defense mechanism.

Resistance   During psychoanalysis, a blocking of thoughts, the awareness of which could cause anxiety. The client may miss sessions or verbally abuse the analyst as threatening material is about to be unearthed.

Resistance stage   The second stage of the general adaptation syndrome, characterized by prolonged sympathetic activity in an effort to restore lost energy and repair damage. Also called the *adaptation stage*.

Response   A movement or other observable reaction to a stimulus.

Response cost   A behavior-therapy self-control technique in which one uses self-punishment for practicing a bad habit or failing to meet a goal.

Response prevention   A behavior-therapy self-control technique in which one makes unwanted behaviors difficult or impossible.

Response set   A tendency to answer test items according to a bias—for example, with the intention of making oneself appear perfect or bizarre.

Resting potential   The electrical potential across the neural membrane when it is not responding to other neurons.

Restriction of the stimulus field   A behavior-therapy self-control technique in which a problem behavior is gradually restricted from more environments.

Reticular activating system   A part of the brain involved in attention, sleep, and arousal. Abbreviated *RAS*.

Retina   The area of the inner surface of the eye that contains rods and cones.

Retinal disparity   A binocular cue for depth based on the difference of the image cast by an object on the retinas of the eyes as the object moves closer or farther away.

Retrieval   The location of stored information and its return to consciousness. The third stage of information processing.

Retroactive interference   The interference by new learning in one's ability to retrieve material learned previously. See *proactive interference*.

Retrograde amnesia   Failure to remember events that occur prior to physical trauma because of the effects of the trauma.

Reversibility   According to Piaget, recognition that processes can be undone, leaving things as they were before. Reversibility is a factor in conservation of the properties of substances. See *conservation* and *concrete operational stage*.

Reward   A pleasant stimulus that increases the frequency of the behavior it follows.

Risky shift   The tendency to make riskier decisions as a member of a group than as an individual acting independently.

Rod   A rod-shaped photoreceptor in the eye that is sensitive to the intensity of light. Rods permit "black and white" vision.

Role diffusion According to Erikson, a state of confusion, insecurity, and susceptibility to the suggestions of others; the probable outcome if ego identity is not established during adolescence.

Role theory A theory that explains hypnotic events in terms of the person's ability to act *as though* he or she were hypnotized. Role theory differs from faking in that people cooperate and focus on hypnotic suggestions instead of cynically pretending to be hypnotized.

Romantic love An intense, positive emotion that involves arousal, a cultural setting that idealizes love, feelings of caring, and the belief that one is in love. Also called *passionate love*. Within Sternberg's triangular model, the kind of love that is characterized by passion and intimacy.

Rooting (1) A reflex in which an infant turns its head toward a touch, such as by the mother's nipple. (2) In adult development, the process of establishing a home, which frequently occurs in the second half of the 30s.

Rorschach Inkblot Test A projective personality test that presents test takers the task of interpreting inkblots.

Rote Mechanical associative learning that is based on repetition.

"Roy G. Biv" A mnemonic device for remembering the colors of the visible spectrum.

S

s Spearman's symbol for specific or "s" factors, which he believed account for individual abilities.

Saccadic eye movement The rapid jumps made by a reader's eyes as they fixate on different points in the text.

Sadism The attainment of gratification, frequently sexual, from inflicting pain on, or humiliating, others.

"SAME" The mnemonic device for remembering that *s*ensory neurons are called *a*fferent neurons and that *m*otor neurons are termed *e*fferent neurons.

Sample Part of a population.

Satiety The state of being satisfied; fullness.

Saturation The degree of purity of a color, as measured by its freedom from mixture with white or black.

Savings The difference between the number of repetitions originally required to learn a list and the number of repetitions required to relearn the list after a certain amount of time has elapsed.

Scapegoat A person or group upon whom the blame for the mistakes or crimes of others is cast.

Scatter diagram A graphic presentation formed by plotting the points defined by the intersections of two variables.

Schachter–Singer theory The theory of emotion that holds that emotions have generally similar patterns of bodily arousal, and that the label we give to an emotion depends on our level of arousal and our cognitive appraisal of our situation.

Schema A way of mentally representing the world, such as a belief or an expectation, that can influence perception of persons, objects, and situations.

Schizoid personality disorder A disorder characterized by social withdrawal.

Schizophrenia A psychotic disorder of at least 6 months' duration in which thought processes and reality testing are impaired and emotions are not appropriate to one's situation. Also see *schizophreniform disorder, brief reactive psychosis,* and *schizotypal personality disorder.*

Schizophreniform disorder A disorder whose symptoms resemble schizophrenia but that is relatively brief (2 weeks to less than 6 months in duration).

Schizotypal personality disorder A disorder characterized by oddities of thought and behavior but not involving bizarre psychotic symptoms. Formerly called *simple schizophrenia.*

Scientific method A method for obtaining scientific evidence in which a hypothesis is formed and tested.

Secondary colors Colors derived by mixing primary colors.

Secondary prevention In community psychology, the early detection and treatment of psychological problems.

Secondary reinforcer A stimulus that gains reinforcement value through association with other, established reinforcers. Money and social approval are secondary reinforcers. Also called *conditioned reinforcer.* See *primary reinforcer.*

Secondary sex characteristics Physical traits that differentiate the genders, such as the depth of the voice, but that are not directly involved in reproduction.

Secondary traits Allport's term for traits that appear in a limited number of situations and govern a limited number of responses.

Secure attachment A type of attachment characterized by positive feelings toward attachment figures and feelings of security.

Sedative A drug that soothes or quiets restlessness or agitation.

Selective attention The focus of consciousness on a particular stimulus.

Selective avoidance Diverting one's attention from information that is inconsistent with one's attitudes.

Selective exposure The deliberate seeking of, and attending to, information that is consistent with one's attitudes.

Self The totality of one's impressions, thoughts, and feelings. The center of consciousness that organizes sensory impressions and governs one's perceptions of the world.

Self-actualization According to Maslow and other humanistic psychologists, self-initiated striving to become what one is capable of being. The motive for reaching one's full potential, for expressing one's unique capabilities.

Self-efficacy expectations A kind of expectancy in social-cognitive theory: beliefs that one can bring about desired changes through one's own efforts.

Self-esteem One's evaluation of, and the placement of value on, oneself.

Self-fulfilling prophecy An expectation that is confirmed because of the behavior of those who hold the expectation.

Self-ideal A mental image of what we believe we ought to be.

Self-insight In psychodynamic theory, accurate awareness of one's own motives and feelings.

Self-monitoring A behavior-therapy technique in which one keeps a record of his or her behavior in order to identify problems and record successes.

Self-serving bias The tendency to view one's successes as stemming from internal factors and one's failures as stemming from external factors.

Self theory The name of Carl Rogers's theory of personality, which emphasizes the importance of self-awareness, choice, and self-actualization.

Semantic code Mental representation of information according to its meaning.

Semanticity Meaning. The property of language in which words are used as symbols for objects, events, or ideas.

Semantic memory General knowledge, as opposed to episodic memory.

Semantics The study of the relationships between language and objects or events. The study of the meaning of language.

Semicircular canals Structures of the inner ear that monitor body movement and position.

Sensation The stimulation of sensory receptors and the transmission of sensory information to the central nervous system.

Sensitive period In linguistic theory, the period from about 18 months to puberty when the brain is thought to be particularly capable of learning language because of plasticity.

Sensitization The type of sensory adaptation in which we become more sensitive to stimuli that are low in magnitude. Also called *positive adaptation.*

Sensorimotor stage The first of Piaget's stages of cognitive development, characterized by coordination of sensory information and motor activity, early exploration of the environment, and lack of language.

Sensorineural deafness The forms of deafness that result from damage to hair cells or the auditory nerve.

Sensory adaptation The processes by which organisms become more sensitive to stimuli that are low in magnitude and less sensitive to stimuli that are constant or ongoing in magnitude.

Sensory awareness One of the definitions of consciousness: knowledge of the environment through perception of sensory stimulation.

Sensory cortex The section of the cerebral cortex that lies in the parietal lobe, just behind the central fissure. Sensory stimulation is projected in this section of cortex.

Sensory deprivation (1) In general, insufficient sensory stimulation. (2) A research method for systematically decreasing the stimuli that impinge on sensory receptors.

Sensory memory The type or stage of memory first encountered by a stimulus. Sensory memory holds impressions briefly, but long enough so that series of perceptions are psychologically continuous.

Sensory register A system of memory that holds information briefly, but long enough so that it can be processed further. There may be a sensory register for every sense.

Septum A part of the limbic system that apparently restrains stereotypically aggressive responses.

Serial position effect The tendency to recall more accurately the first and last items in a series.

Serotonin A neurotransmitter, deficiencies of which have been linked to affective disorders, anxiety, and insomnia.

Serotonin re-uptake inhibitor An antidepressant medication that works by slowing the re-uptake of serotonin in the synaptic cleft.

Serum cholesterol A fatty substance (cholesterol) in the blood (serum) that has been linked to heart disease.

Set point A value that the body attempts to maintain. For example, the body tries to maintain a certain weight by adjusting the metabolism.

Sex chromosomes The 23rd pair of chromosomes, which determine whether a child will be male or female.

Sex flush A reddish hue on body surfaces that is caused by vasocongestion during sexual excitement.

Sexism The prejudgment that a person, on the basis of his or her gender, will possess negative traits or perform inadequately.

Sex norms Social rules or conventions that govern the ways in which males and females interact.

Sex role See *gender role.*

Sex therapy A number of cognitive and behavioral methods that seek to reverse sexual dysfunctions by reducing performance anxiety, reversing defeatist expectations, and fostering sexual competencies.

Sex-typing See *gender-typing.*

Sexual apathy Lack of interest in sexual activity.

Sexual dysfunctions Persistent or recurrent problems in achieving or maintaining sexual arousal or in reaching orgasm.

Sexual orientation The directionality of one's erotic and romantic interests—that is, toward people of the opposite gender, people of the same gender, or in the case of bisexuality, people of both genders. See *heterosexual, gay male, lesbian.*

Sexual response cycle A four-phase process that describes response to sexual stimulation in males and females.

Shadowing A monocular cue for depth based on the fact that opaque objects block light and produce shadows.

Sham False, pretended.

Shape constancy The tendency to perceive an object as being the same shape even though its retinal image changes in shape as the object rotates.

Shaping In operant conditioning, a procedure for teaching complex behaviors that at first reinforces approximations of these behaviors.

Short-term memory The type or stage of memory that can hold information for up to a minute or so after the trace of the stimulus decays. Also called *working memory.*

Siblings Brothers and sisters.

Signal-detection theory In psychophysics, the view that the perception of sensory stimuli is influenced by the interaction of physical, biological, and psychological factors.

Significant others Persons who have a major influence on one's psychosocial development, including parents, peers, lovers, and children.

Similarity As a rule of perceptual organization, the tendency to group together objects that are similar in appearance.

Simple phobia Persistent fear of a specific object or situation.

Simultaneous conditioning A classical conditioning procedure in which the CS and US are presented at the same time, and the CS remains in place until the response occurs.

Situational attribution An assumption that a person's behavior is determined by external circumstances, such as social pressure. Contrast with *dispositional attribution.*

Situational variables In social-learning theory, external determinants of behavior, such as rewards and punishments.

Size constancy The tendency to perceive an object as being the same size even as the size of its retinal image changes according to its distance.

Skewed distribution A slanted distribution, drawn out toward the low or high scores.

Sleep-onset insomnia Difficulty falling asleep.

Sleep spindles Short bursts of rapid brain waves that occur during stage 2 sleep.

Sleep terrors Frightening, dreamlike experiences that usually occur during deep stage 4 sleep.

Social-cognitive theory A cognitively oriented learning theory in which observational learning and person variables such as values and expectancies play major roles in individual differences. Also termed *cognitive social-learning theory* or *social-learning theory.*

Social-comparison theory The view that people look to others for cues about how to behave in confusing situations.

Social decision schemes Rules for predicting the final outcome of group decision making on the basis of the initial positions of the members.

Social facilitation The process by which a person's performance is increased when other members of a group engage in similar behavior.

Social influence The area of social psychology that studies the ways in which people influence the thoughts, feelings, and behavior of others.

Socialization Guidance of people—and children in particular—into socially desirable behavior by means of verbal messages, the systematic use of rewards and punishments, and other methods of teaching.

Social-learning theory See *social-cognitive theory.*

Social loafing The process by which a person's performance is decreased as a function of being a member of a group.

Social motives Learned or acquired motives such as the needs for achievement and affiliation.

Social norms Explicit and implicit rules that reflect social expectations and influence the ways people behave in social situations.

Social perception A subfield of social psychology that studies the ways in which we form and modify impressions of others.

Social phobias Irrational fears that involve themes of public scrutiny.

Social psychology The field of psychology that studies the nature and causes of people's thoughts, feelings, and behavior in social situations.

Sociobiology A biological theory of social behavior that assumes that the underlying purpose of behavior is to ensure the transmission of an organism's genes from generation to generation.

Sociocultural perspective The perspective in psychology that focuses on the roles of ethnicity, gender, culture, and socioeconomic status in personality formation, behavior, and mental processes.

Sociopath Another term for a person who shows an antisocial personality disorder.

Soma A cell body.

Somatic nervous system The division of the peripheral nervous system that connects the central nervous system (brain and spinal cord) with sensory receptors, muscles, and the surface of the body.

Somatoform disorders Disorders in which people complain of physical (somatic) problems although no physical abnormality can be found. See *conversion disorder* and *hypochondriasis.*

Source traits Cattell's term for underlying traits from which surface traits are derived.

Spectrograph An instrument that converts sounds to graphs or pictures according to their acoustic qualities.

Sphincter A ringlike muscle that circles a body opening such as the anus. An infant will exhibit the sphincter reflex (have a bowel movement) in response to intestinal pressure.

Spinal cord A column of nerves within the spine that transmits messages from the sensory receptors to the brain and from the brain to muscles and glands throughout the body.

Spinal reflex A simple, unlearned response to a stimulus that may involve only two neurons.

Split-brain operation An operation in which the corpus callosum is severed, usually in an effort to control epileptic seizures.

Split-half reliability A method for determining the internal consistency of a test (an index of reliability) by correlating scores attained on half the items with scores attained on the other half of the items.

Spontaneous recovery Generally, the recurrence of an extinguished response as a function of the passage of time. In classical conditioning, the eliciting of a conditioned response by a conditioned stimulus after some time has elapsed following the extinction of the conditioned response. In operant conditioning, the performance of an operant in the presence of discriminative stimuli after some time has elapsed following the extinction of the operant.

Sports psychology The field of psychology that studies the nature, causes, and modification of the behavior and mental processes of people involved in sports.

Stage In developmental psychology, a distinct period of life that is qualitatively different from other stages. Stages follow one another in an orderly sequence.

Standard deviation A measure of the variability of a distribution, obtained by taking the square root of the sum of difference scores squared divided by the number of scores.

Standardization The process of setting standards for a psychological test, accomplished by determining how a population performs on it. Standardization permits psychologists to interpret individual scores as deviations from a norm.

Standardized tests Tests for which norms are based on the performance of a range of individuals.

Stapes A bone of the middle ear. Latin for "stirrup."

Startle reflex See *moro reflex.*

State-dependent memory Information that is better retrieved in the physiological or emotional state in which it was encoded (stored) or learned.

Statistically significant difference As indicated by inferential statistics, a difference between two groups that is so large that it is not probable that it results from chance fluctuation.

Statistics Numerical facts assembled in such a manner that they provide useful information about measures or scores.

Stereotype A fixed, conventional idea about a group.

Steroids A family of hormones that includes testosterone, estrogen, progesterone, and corticosteroids.

Stimulant A drug that increases the activity of the nervous system.

Stimuli Plural of *stimulus.*

Stimulus (1) A feature in the environment that is detected by an organism or that leads to a change in behavior (a response). (2) A form of physical energy, such as light or sound, that impinges on the sensory receptors.

Stimulus control A behavior-therapy self-control technique in which one places oneself in an environment in which desired responses are likely to occur.

Stimulus discrimination The eliciting of a conditioned response by only one of a series of similar stimuli.

Stimulus generalization The eliciting of a conditioned response by stimuli that are similar to the conditioned stimulus.

Stimulus motives Motives to increase the stimulation impinging on an organism.

Stimulus-outcome relations A kind of expectancy in social-cognitive theory: predictions as to what events will follow certain stimuli or signs.

Stirrup A bone of the middle ear.

Storage The maintenance of information over time. The second stage of information processing.

Strabismus A visual disorder in which the eyes point in different directions and thus do not focus simultaneously on the same point.

Stratified sample A sample drawn in such a way that known subgroups within a population are represented in proportion to their numbers in the population.

Stress The demand made on an organism to adjust or adapt.

Stressor An event or stimulus that acts as a source of stress.

Stroboscopic motion A visual illusion in which the perception of motion is generated by presentation of a series of stationary images in rapid succession.

Structuralism The school of psychology, founded by Wilhelm Wundt, that argues that the mind consists of three basic elements—sensations, feelings, and images—that combine to form experience.

Structure-of-intellect model Guilford's three-dimensional model of intelligence, which focuses on the operations, contents, and products of intellectual functioning.

Stupor A condition in which the senses and thought processes are dulled.

Subject A participant in a scientific study. Many psychologists consider this term dehumanizing and no longer use it in reference to human participants.

Subjective Of the mind; personal; determined by thoughts and feelings rather than by external objects.

Subjective morality According to Piaget, subjective moral judgments assign guilt according to the motives of the actor. See *objective morality.*

Subjective value The desirability of an object or event.

Sublimation In psychodynamic theory, a defense mechanism in which primitive impulses—usually sexual or aggressive—are channeled into positive, constructive activities.

Subordinate Descriptive of a lower (included) class or category in a hierarchy; contained by another class; opposite of *superordinate.*

Substance abuse Persistent use of a substance despite the fact that it is disrupting one's life.

Substance dependence A term whose definition is in flux: Substance dependence is characterized by loss of control over use of a substance, but some professionals consider *physiological* dependence, as typified by tolerance, withdrawal, or both, is essential to the definition.

Successive approximations In operant conditioning, a series of behaviors that gradually become more similar to a target behavior.

Superego In psychodynamic theory, the psychic structure that is governed by the moral principle, sets forth high standards for behavior, and floods the ego with feelings of guilt and shame when it falls short.

Superordinate Descriptive of a higher (including) class or category in a hierarchy; containing another class; opposite of *subordinate.*

Suppression The deliberate, or conscious, placing of certain ideas, impulses, or images out of awareness. Contrast with *repression.*

Surface structure The superficial construction of a sentence as defined by the placement of words.

Surface traits Cattell's term for characteristic, observable ways of behaving. See *source traits.*

Survey A method of scientific investigation in which large samples of people answer questions.

Symbol Something that stands for or represents another thing.

Sympathetic nervous system The branch of the autonomic nervous system that is most active when the person is engaged in behavior or experiencing feeling states that spend the body's reserves of energy, such as fleeing or experiencing fear or anxiety.

Synapse A junction between neurons, consisting of a terminal knob of a transmitting neuron, the space between the neurons (synaptic cleft), and a dendrite or soma of a receiving neuron.

Synaptic cleft The space between neurons, across which messages are transmitted by means of neurotransmitters.

Syndrome A cluster of symptoms characteristic of a disorder.

Syntax The rules in a language for placing words in proper order to form meaningful sentences.

Systematic desensitization A behavior-therapy fear-reduction technique in which a hierarchy of fear-evoking stimuli are presented while the person remains in a state of deep muscle relaxation.

Systematic random search An algorithm for solving problems in which each possible solution is tested according to a particular set of rules.

T

TA Abbreviation for *transactional analysis.*

Tactile Of the sense of touch.

Target behavior Goal.

Task analysis The breaking down of a job or behavior pattern into its component parts.

Taste aversion A kind of classical conditioning in which a previously desirable or neutral food comes to be perceived as repugnant because it is associated with aversive stimulation.

Taste buds The sensory organs for taste. They contain taste cells and are located on the tongue.

Taste cells Receptor cells that are sensitive to taste.

TAT Thematic Apperception Test.

Taxonomy Classification system.

Telegraphic speech Speech in which only the essential words are used, as in a telegram.

Telepathy The term refers to the direct transference of thought from one person to another. However, most psychologists do not believe that telepathy exists.

Temporal lobe The lobe of the cerebral cortex that is involved in hearing. It lies below the lateral fissure, near the temples.

Terminal A small branching structure found at the tip of an axon.

Territory In sociobiology, the particular area acquired and defended by an animal, or pair of animals, for purposes of feeding and breeding.

Tertiary colors Colors derived by mixing primary and adjoining secondary colors.

Tertiary prevention In community psychology, the treatment of ripened psychological problems. See *primary* and *secondary prevention*.

Testes The male reproductive organs that produce sperm and the hormone testosterone.

Testosterone A male sex hormone (steroid) that is produced by the testes and promotes growth of male sexual characteristics and sperm.

Test–retest reliability A method for determining the reliability of a test by comparing (correlating) test takers' scores on separate occasions.

Texture gradient A monocular cue for depth based on the perception that nearby objects appear to have rougher or more detailed surfaces.

Thalamus An area near the center of the brain that is involved in the relay of sensory information to the cortex and in the functions of sleep and attention.

THC Delta-9-tetrahydrocannabinol. The major active ingredient in marijuana.

The Dream Levinson's term for the overriding drive of youth to become someone important, to leave one's mark on history.

T-helper lymphocytes The white blood cells of the immune system that recognize invading pathogens and are attacked by the human immunodeficiency virus (HIV). Also called *CD4 cells* and T_4 *cells*.

Thematic Apperception Test A projective test devised by Henry Murray to measure needs through the production of fantasy.

Theory A formulation of relationships underlying observed events. A theory involves assumptions and logically derived explanations and predictions.

Theory of social comparison The view that people look to others for cues about how to behave when they are in confusing or unfamiliar situations.

Theory Y McGregor's view that organizational goals should be congruent with workers' goals.

Theory Z Ouchi's view that adapts positive features of the Japanese workplace to the U.S. workplace.

Theta waves Slow brain waves produced during the hypnagogic state.

Thinking Mental activity that is involved in understanding, manipulating, and communicating about information. Thinking entails paying attention to information, mentally representing it, reasoning about it, and making decisions about it.

Threshold The point at which a stimulus is just strong enough to produce a response.

Thyroxin The thyroid hormone that increases the metabolic rate.

Timbre The quality or richness of a sound. The quality that distinguishes the sounds of one musical instrument from those of another.

Time out In operant conditioning, a method for decreasing the frequency of undesired behaviors by removing an organism from a situation in which reinforcement is available as a consequence of showing the undesired behavior.

Tip-of-the-tongue phenomenon The feeling that information is stored in memory although it cannot be readily retrieved. Also called the *feeling-of-knowing experience*.

TM Transcendental meditation.

Token economy A controlled environment in which people are reinforced for desired behaviors with tokens (such as poker chips) that may be exchanged for privileges.

Tolerance Habituation to a drug, with the result that increasingly higher doses of the drug are required to achieve similar effects.

Tolerance for frustration Ability to delay gratification, to maintain self-control when a motive is thwarted.

Top-down processing The use of contextual information or knowledge of a pattern to organize parts of the pattern.

Total immersion A method of teaching a second language in which all instruction is carried out in the second language.

Trace conditioning A classical-conditioning procedure in which the CS is presented and then removed before the US is presented.

Trait A distinguishing quality or characteristic of personality that is inferred from behavior and assumed to account for consistency in behavior.

Tranquilizers Drugs used to reduce anxiety and tension. See *minor* and *major tranquilizer*.

Transaction In transactional analysis, an exchange between two people.

Transactional analysis A form of psychotherapy that deals with how people interact and how their interactions reinforce attitudes, expectations, and "life positions." Abbreviated *TA*.

Transcendental meditation The simplified form of meditation brought to the United States by the Maharishi Mahesh Yogi in which one focuses on a repeated mantra. Abbreviated *TM*.

Transference In psychoanalysis, the generalization to the analyst of feelings toward another person in the client's life.

Trauma An injury or wound.

Treatment In experiments, a condition obtained by participants and whose effects are observed by the researchers.

Trial In conditioning, a presentation of the stimuli.

Triangular model Sternberg's model of love, which refers to combinations of passion, intimacy, and decision/commitment.

Triarchic Governed by three. (Referring to Sternberg's triarchic theory of intelligence.)

Trichromat A person with normal color vision.

Trichromatic theory The theory that color vision is made possible by three types of cones, some of which respond to red light, some to green, and some to blue.

Tricyclic antidepressants Antidepressant drugs that work by preventing the re-uptake of norepinephrine and serotonin by transmitting neurons.

Trust versus mistrust The first of Erikson's stages of psychosocial development, during which the child comes to (or not to) develop a basic sense of trust in others.

Trying 20s Sheehy's term for the third decade of life, which is frequently characterized by preoccupation with advancement in the career world.

Two-point threshold The least distance by which two rods touching the skin must be separated before an individual will report that there are two rods, not one, on 50% of occasions.

Type In personality theory, a group of traits that cluster in a meaningful way.

Type A behavior Behavior characterized by a sense of time urgency, competitiveness, and hostility.

U

Ulcer An open sore, as in the lining of the stomach.

Umbilical cord A tube between the mother and her fetus through which nutrients and waste products are conducted.

Unconditional positive regard In self theory, a consistent expression of esteem for the basic value of a person, but not necessarily an unqualified endorsement of all that person's behaviors. A quality shown by the person-centered therapist.

Unconditioned response An unlearned response. A response to an unconditioned stimulus. Abbreviated *UR*.

Unconditioned stimulus A stimulus that elicits a response from an organism without learning. Abbreviated *US*.

Unconscious In psychodynamic theory, descriptive of ideas and feelings that are not available to awareness, in many instances because of the *defense mechanism* of *repression*.

Unobtrusive Not interfering.

Uplifts Notable pleasant daily conditions and experiences.

UR Unconditioned response.

US Unconditioned stimulus.

Uterus The hollow organ within women in which the embryo and fetus develop.

V

Vaccination Purposeful infection with a small amount of an antigen, or weakened antigen, so that in the future the immune system will recognize and efficiently destroy the antigen.

Vaginismus Persistent or recurrent spasm of the muscles surrounding the outer part of the vaginal barrel, making entry difficult or impossible.

Validity The degree to which a test or instrument measures or predicts what it is supposed to measure or predict. Also see *reliability*.

Validity scale A group of test items that suggests whether or not the results of a test are valid—whether a person's test responses accurately reflect his or her traits.

Variable A condition that is measured or controlled in a scientific study. A variable can be altered in a measurable manner.

Variable-interval schedule A partial reinforcement schedule in which a variable amount of time must elapse between the previous and subsequent times that reinforcement is available.

Variable-ratio schedule A partial reinforcement schedule in which reinforcement is provided after a variable number of correct responses.

Vasopressin Another term for *antidiuretic hormone*.

Ventromedial nucleus A central area on the underside of the hypothalamus that appears to function as a stop-eating center. Abbreviated *VMN*.

Vestibular sense The sense that provides information about the position of the body relative to gravity. Also referred to as the sense of *equilibrium*.

Vicarious Taking the place of another person or thing. In vicarious learning, we learn from the experiences of others.

Visible light The band of electromagnetic energy that produces visual sensations.

Visual accommodation Automatic adjustment of the thickness of the lens in order to focus on objects.

Visual acuity Keenness or sharpness of vision.

Visual capture The tendency of vision to dominate the other senses.

Visual code Mental representation of information as a picture.

Volley principle A modification of the *frequency theory* of pitch perception. The hypothesis that groups of neurons may be able to achieve the effect of firing at very high frequencies by "taking turns" firing—that is, by firing in volleys.

Volt A unit of electrical potential.

W

Waxy flexibility A symptom of catatonic schizophrenia in which the person maintains a posture or position into which he or she is placed.

Weaning Accustoming the child not to suck the mother's breast or a baby bottle.

Weber's constant The fraction of the intensity by which a source of physical energy must be increased or decreased so that a difference in intensity will be perceived.

Well-defined problem A problem in which the original state, the goal, and the rules for reaching the goal are clearly spelled out.

Wernicke–Korsakoff syndrome An alcohol-related disorder that is characterized by loss of memory and that is thought to reflect nutritional deficiency.

Wernicke's aphasia An aphasia caused by damage to Wernicke's area of the brain. It is characterized by difficulty comprehending the meaning of spoken language and by the production of language that is grammatically correct but confused or meaningless in content.

White matter In the spinal cord, axon bundles that carry messages from and to the brain.

White noise Discordant sounds of many frequencies, which often produce a lulling effect.

Wish fulfillment In psychodynamic theory, a primitive method used by the id—such as in fantasy and dreams—to attempt to gratify basic impulses.

Working memory See *short-term memory*.

Y

Yerkes–Dodson law The principle that a high level of arousal increases performance on a relatively simple task, whereas a low level of arousal increases performance on a relatively complex task.

Z

Zygote A fertilized egg cell or ovum.

REFERENCES

AAUW. (1992). *How schools shortchange women: The A.A.U.W. report.* Washington, DC: American Association of University Women Educational Foundation.

Abbey, A. (1987). Misperceptions of friendly behavior as sexual interest: A survey of naturally occurring incidents. *Psychology of Women Quarterly, 11,* 173–194.

Aber, J. L., & Allen, J. P. (1987). Effects of maltreatment of young children on young children's socioemotional development: An attachment theory perspective. *Developmental Psychology, 23,* 406–414.

Abraham, L. K. (1993). *Mama might be better off dead: The failure of health care in urban America.* Chicago: University of Chicago Press.

Abramowitz, A. J., & O'Leary, S. G. (1991). Behavioral interventions for the classroom: Implications with students for ADHD. *School Psychology Review, 20,* 220–234.

Abravanel, E., & Gingold, H. (1985). Learning via observation during the second year of life. *Developmental Psychology, 21,* 614–623.

Adair, J. G., Dushenko, T. W., & Lindsay, R. C. L. (1985). Ethical regulations and their impact on research practice. *American Psychologist, 40,* 59–72.

Ader, D. N., & Johnson, S. B. (1994). Sample description, reporting, and analysis of sex in psychological research: A look at APA and APA division journals in 1990. *American Psychologist, 49,* 216–218.

Ader, R. (1993). Conditioned responses. In B. Moyers (Ed.), *Healing and the mind.* New York: Doubleday.

Adeyemo, S. A. (1990). Thinking imagery and problem-solving. *Psychological Studies, 35,* 179–190.

Adler, N. E., and others (1994). Socioeconomic status and health: The challenge of the gradient. *American Psychologist, 49,* 15–24.

Adler, T. (1990). Distraction, relaxation can help "shut off" pain. *APA Monitor, 21*(9), 11.

Adler, T. (1993a). Shy, bold temperament? It's mostly in the genes. *APA Monitor, 24*(1), 7, 8.

Adler, T. (1993b). Sleep loss impairs attention—and more. *APA Monitor, 24*(9), 22–23.

Affleck, G., Tennen, H., Pfeiffer, C., & Fifield, J. (1987). Appraisals of control and predictability in adapting to chronic disease. *Journal of Personality and Social Psychology, 53,* 273–279.

Agras, W. S., & Kirkley, B. G. (1986). Bulimia: Theories of etiology. In K. D. Brownell & J. P. Foreyt (Eds.), *Handbook of eating disorders.* New York: Basic Books.

Agras, W. S., Southam, M. A., & Taylor, C. B. (1983). Long-term persistence of relaxation-induced blood pressure lowering during the working day. *Journal of Consulting and Clinical Psychology, 51,* 792–794.

Aiken, L. S., West, S. G., Woodward, C. K., & Reno, R. R. (1994). Health beliefs and compliance with mammography-screening recommendations in asymptomatic women. *Health Psychology, 13,* 122–129.

Ainsworth, M. D. S. (1989). Attachments beyond infancy. *American Psychologist, 44,* 709–716.

Ainsworth, M. D. S., & Bowlby, J. (1991). An ethological approach to personality development. *American Psychologist, 46,* 333–341.

Akhtar, N., & Bradley, E. J. (1991). Social information processing deficits of aggressive children: Present findings and implications for social skills training. *Clinical Psychology Review, 11,* 621–644.

Albert, M. S. (1981). Geriatric neuropsychology. *Journal of Consulting and Clinical Psychology, 49,* 835–850.

Aldag, R. J., & Fuller, S. R. (1993). Beyond fiasco: A reappraisal of the groupthink phenomenon and a new model of group decision processes. *Psychological Bulletin, 113,* 533–552.

Alexander, R. A., & Barrett, G. U. (1982). Equitable salary increase judgments based upon merit and nonmerit considerations: A cross-national comparison. *International Review of Applied Psychology, 31,* 443–454.

Allen, L. (1993, August). Integrating a sociocultural perspective into the psychology curriculum. G. Stanley Hall lecture presented to the American Psychological Association, Toronto, Canada.

Allison, K. W., Crawford, I., Echemendia, R., Robinson, L. V., & Knepp, D. (1994). Human diversity and professional competence. *American Psychologist, 49,* 792-796.

Alloy, L. B., Abramson, L. Y., & Dykman, B. M. (1990). Depressive realism and nondepressive optimistic illusions: The role of the self. In R. E. Ingram (Ed.), *Contemporary psychological approaches to depression.* New York: Plenum.

Alloy, L. B., & Ahrens, A. H. (1987). Depression and pessimism for the future: Biased use of statistically relevant information in predictions for self versus others. *Journal of Personality and Social Psychology, 52,* 366–378.

Alloy, L. B., & Clements, C. M. (1992). Illusion of control: Invulnerability to negative affect and depressive symptoms after laboratory and natural stressors. *Journal of Abnormal Psychology, 101,* 234–245.

Allport, G. W., & Odbert, H. S. (1936). Trait names: A psycholexical study. *Psychological Monographs, 47,* 2–11.

Altman, L. K. (1991, June 18). W.H.O. says 40 million will be infected with AIDS virus by 2000. *The New York Times,* p. C3.

Altman, L. K. (1993, May 4). Rise in asthma deaths is tied to ignorance of many physicians. *The New York Times,* p. C3.

Amabile, T. M. (1990). Within you, without you: The social psychology of creativity, and beyond. In M. A. Runco & R. S. Albert (Eds.), *Theories of creativity.* Newbury Park, NY: Sage.

Amato, P. R. (1983). Helping behavior in urban and rural environments: Field studies based on taxonomic organization of helping episodes. *Journal of Personality and Social Psychology, 45,* 571–586.

American Psychiatric Association. (1990). *The practice of electroconvulsive therapy.* Washington, DC: American Psychiatric Press.

American Psychiatric Association (1994). *Diagnostic and statistical manual of the mental disorders* (4th ed.). Washington, DC: Author.

American Psychological Association, Committee on Gay and Lesbian Concerns. (1991). Avoiding heterosexual bias in language. *American Psychologist, 46,* 973–974.

American Psychological Association. (1992a). Big world, small screen: The role of television in American society. Washington, DC: Author.

American Psychological Association. (1992b). Ethical principles of psychologists and code of conduct. *American Psychologist, 47,* 1597–1611.

American Psychological Association. (1993). Guidelines for providers of psychological services to ethnic, linguistic, and culturally diverse populations. *American Psychologist, 48,* 45–48.

American Psychological Association. (1994). Publication manual of the American Psychological Association, 4th ed. Washington, DC: Author.

Anastasiow, N. J., & Hanes, M. L. (1976). *Language patterns of children in poverty.* Springfield, IL: Charles C. Thomas.

Andersen, B. L. (1992). Psychological interventions for cancer patients to enhance the quality of life. *Journal of Consulting and Clinical Psychology, 60,* 552–568.

Andersen, B. L., Kiecolt-Glaser, J. K., & Glaser, R. (1994). A biobehavioral model of cancer stress and disease course. *American Psychologist, 49,* 389–404.

Anderson, C. A., & DeNeve, K. M. (1992). Temperature, aggression, and the negative affect escape model. *Psychological Bulletin, 111,* 347–351.

Anderson, J. R. (1991). Is human cognition adaptive? *Behavioral and Brain Sciences, 14,* 471–517.

Andreasen, N. C. (1990, August/September). Schizophrenia. In American Psychiatric Association, *DSM-IV Update.* Washington, DC: American Psychiatric Association.

Andrews, B., & Brown, G. W. (1993). Self-esteem and vulnerability to depression. *Journal of Abnormal Psychology, 102,* 565–572.

Aneshensel, C. S., & Huba, G. J. (1983). Depression, alcohol use, and smoking over one year: A four-wave longitudinal causal model. *Journal of Abnormal Psychology, 92,* 134–150.

Angell, M. (1993). Privilege and health—What is the connection? *New England Journal of Medicine, 329,* 126–127.

Angier, N. (1993, August 13). Scientists detect a genetic key to Alzheimer's. *The New York Times,* pp. A1, A12.

Angier, N. (1994a). Benefits of broccoli confirmed as chemical blocks tumors. *The New York Times,* p. C11.

Angier, N. (1994b). Factor in female sexuality. *The New York Times,* p. C13.

Annunziata, J., & Jacobson-Kram, P. (1995). *Solving your problems together: Family therapy for the whole family.* Washington, DC: American Psychological Association.

Antoni, M. H. (1987). Neuroendocrine influences in psychoimmunology and neoplasia: A review. *Psychology and Health, 1,* 3–24.

Antoni, M. H. (1992, July). *Behavioral intervention effects on coping strategies, emotional expression and immune measures among individuals dealing with traumatic events: Implications for psycho-oncology?* Paper presented at the Second International Congress of Behavioral Medicine, Hamburg, Germany.

Antoni, M. H., and others (1990). Psychoneuroimmunology and HIV-1. *Journal of Consulting and Clinical Psychology, 58,* 38–49.

Antoni, M. H., and others (1991). Cognitive-behavioral stress management intervention buffers distress responses and immunologic changes following notification of HIV-1 seropositivity. *Journal of Consulting and Clinical Psychology, 59,* 906–915.

Archer, R. P., & Cash, T. F. (1985). Physical attractiveness and maladjustment among psychiatric patients. *Journal of Social and Clinical Psychology, 3,* 170–180.

Archer, S. L. (1991). Gender differences in identity development. In R. M. Lerner, A. C. Peterson, & J. Brooks-Gunn (Eds.), *Encyclopedia of Adolescence, I.* New York: Garland.

Archer, S. L. (1992). A feminist's approach to identity research. In G. R. Adams, T. P. Gullotta, & R. Montemayor (Eds.), *Adolescent identity formation.* Newbury Park, CA: Sage.

Argyris, C. (1972). *The applicability of organizational psychology.* Cambridge: Cambridge University Press.

Arnold, D. H., Lonigan, C. J., Whitehurst, G. J., & Epstein, J. N. (1994). Accelerating language development through picture book reading: Replication and extension to a videotape training format. *Journal of Educational Psychology, 86,* 235–243.

Aronson, E. (1990). Applying social psychology to desegregation and energy conservation. *Personality and Social Psychology Bulletin, 16,* 118–132.

Asarnow, J. R., Carlson, G. A., & Guthrie, D. (1987). Coping strategies, self-perceptions, hopelessness, and perceived family environments in depressed and suicidal children. *Journal of Consulting and Clinical Psychology, 55,* 361-366.

Asch, S. E. (1952). *Social psychology.* Englewood Cliffs, NJ: Prentice-Hall.

Ashe, A. (1992). Cited in A hug for Arthur Ashe (1992, April 14). *The New York Times,* p. A24.

Aslin, R. N., Pisoni, D. B., & Jusczyk, P. W. (1983). Auditory development and speech perception in infancy. In P. H. Mussen (Ed.), *Handbook of child psychology* (4th ed.). New York: Wiley.

Atkins, C. J., Kaplan, R. M., Timms, R. M., Reinsch, S., & Lofback, K. (1984). Behavioral exercise programs in the management of chronic obstructive pulmonary disease. *Journal of Consulting and Clinical Psychology, 52,* 591–603.

Atkinson, R. C. (1975). Mnemotechnics in second-language learning. *American Psychologist, 30,* 821–828.

Atkinson, R. C., & Shiffrin, R. M. (1968). Human memory: A proposed system and its control processes. In K. Spence (Ed.), *The psychology of learning and motivation* (Vol. 2). New York: Academic Press.

Ayanian, J. Z. (1993). Heart disease in black and white. *New England Journal of Medicine, 329,* 656–658.

Ayanian, J. Z., and others (1993). The relation between health insurance coverage and clinical outcome among women with breast cancer. *New England Journal of Medicine, 329,* 326–331.

Ayllon, T., & Haughton, E. (1962). Control of the behavior of schizophrenic patients by food. *Journal of the Experimental Analysis of Behavior, 5,* 343–352.

Azar, B. (1994a). Outcomes measurement is debated by profession. *APA Monitor, 25*(5), 29.

Azar, B. (1994b). Women are barraged by media on "the change." *APA Monitor, 25*(5), 24–25.

Azar, B. (1994c). Computers create global research lab. *APA Monitor, 25*(8), 1–16.

Azar, B. (1994d). Research made easier by computer networks. *APA Monitor, 25*(8), 16.

Babcock, J. C., Waltz, J., Jacobson, N. S., & Gottman, J. M. (1993). Power and violence: The relation between communication patterns, power discrepancies, and domestic violence. *Journal of Consulting and Clinical Psychology, 61,* 40–50.

Bachrach, L. L. (1992). What we know about homelessness among mentally ill persons: An analytical review and commentary. In H. R. Lamb, L. L. Bachrach, & F. I. Kass (Eds.), *Treating the homeless mentally ill.* Washington, DC: American Psychiatric Press.

Baddeley, A. (1994). Working memory: The interface between memory and cognition. In D. L. Schacter & E. Tulving (Eds.), *Memory systems 1994.* Cambridge, MA: The MIT Press, a Bradford Book.

Bahrick, H. P., Bahrick, P. O., & Wittlinger, R. P. (1975). Fifty years of memory for names and faces: A cross-sectional approach. *Journal of Experimental Psychology: General, 104,* 54–75.

Bailey, J. M., & Pillard, R. C. (1991). A genetic study of male sexual orientation. *Archives of General Psychiatry, 48,* 1089-1096.

Baker, L. A., DeFries, J. C., & Fulker, D. W. (1983). Longitudinal stability of cognitive ability in the Colorado adoption project. *Child Development, 54,* 290–297.

Bal, D. G. (1992). Cancer in African Americans. *Ca-A Cancer Journal for Clinicians, 42,* 5–6.

Bandura, A. (1973). *Aggression: A social learning analysis.* Englewood Cliffs, NJ: Prentice-Hall.

Bandura, A. (1986). *Social foundations of thought and action: A social-cognitive theory.* Englewood Cliffs, NJ: Prentice-Hall.

Bandura, A. (1989). Human agency in social cognitive theory. *American Psychologist, 44,* 1175–1184.

Bandura, A. (1990). Perceived self-efficacy in the exercise of control over AIDS infection. *Evaluation and Program Planning, 13,* 9–17.

Bandura, A. (1991). Human agency: The rhetoric and the reality. *The American Psychologist, 46,* 157–162.

Bandura, A., Blanchard, E. B., & Ritter, B. (1969). The relative efficacy of desensitization and modeling approaches for inducing behavioral, affective, and cognitive changes. *Journal of Personality and Social Psychology, 13,* 173–199.

Bandura, A., & McDonald, F. J. (1963). Influence of social reinforcement and the behavior of models in shaping children's moral judgments. *Journal of Abnormal and Social Psychology, 67,* 274–281.

Bandura, A., Reese, L., & Adams, N. E. (1982). Microanalysis of action and fear arousal as a function of differential levels of perceived self-efficacy. *Journal of Personality and Social Psychology, 43,* 5–21.

Bandura, A., & Rosenthal, T. L. (1966). Vicarious classical conditioning as a function of fear arousal. *Journal of Personality and Social Psychology, 3,* 54–62.

Bandura, A., Ross, D., & Ross, S. A. (1963a). A comparative test of the status envy, and the secondary reinforcement theories of identificatory learning. *Journal of Abnormal and Social Psychology, 67,* 527–534.

Bandura, A., Ross, S. A., & Ross, D. (1963b). Imitation of film-mediated aggressive models. *Journal of Abnormal and Social Psychology, 66,* 3–11.

Bandura, A., Taylor, C. B., Williams, S. L., Medford, I. N., & Barchas, J. D. (1985). Catecholamine secretion as a function of perceived coping self-efficacy. *Journal of Consulting and Clinical Psychology, 53,* 406–414.

Bangert, R., Kulik, J., & Kulik, C. (1983). Individualized systems of instruction in secondary schools. *Review of Educational Research, 53,* 143–158.

Banks, M. S., & Shannon, E. (1993). Spatial and chromatic visual efficiency in human neonates. In C. E. Granrud (Ed.), *Visual perception and cognition in infancy.* Hillsdale, NJ: Erlbaum.

Banyai, E. I., & Hilgard, E. R. (1976). A comparison of active-alert hypnotic induction with traditional relaxation induction. *Journal of Abnormal Psychology, 85,* 218–224.

Baquet, C. R., Horm, J. W., Gibbs, T., & Greenwald, P. (1991). Socioeconomic factors and cancer incidence among Blacks and Whites. *Journal of the National Cancer Institute, 83,* 551–557.

Barbaree, H. E., & Marshall, W. L. (1991). The role of male sexual arousal in rape: Six models. *Journal of Consulting and Clinical Psychology, 59,* 621–631.

Barbour, I. (1990). *Religion in an age of science: The Gifford lectures, 1989–1991* (Vol. 1). New York: HarperCollins.

Bard, P. (1934). The neurohumoral basis of emotional reactions. In C. A. Murchison (Ed.), *Handbook of general experimental psychology.* Worcester, MA: Clark University Press.

Barlow, D. H. (1986). Causes of sexual dysfunction: The role of anxiety and cognitive interference. *Journal of Consulting and Clinical Psychology, 54,* 140–148.

Barlow, D. H. (1991). Introduction to the special issue on diagnoses, definitions, and *DSM-IV:* The science of classification. *Journal of Abnormal Psychology, 100,* 243–244.

Barlow, D. H. (1994). Cited in Howard, K., Barlow, D., Christiensen, A., & Frank, E. *Evaluating outcomes of psychological interventions: Evaluating the effectiveness of psychotherapy.* Symposium conducted at the meeting of the American Psychological Association, Los Angeles.

Barnett, W. S., & Escobar, C. M. (1990). Economic costs and benefits of early intervention. In S. J. Meisels & J. P. Shonkoff (Eds.), *Handbook of early childhood intervention,* New York: Cambridge University Press.

Baron, R. A. (1990). Countering the effects of destructive criticism: The relative efficacy of four interventions. *Journal of Applied Psychology, 75,* 235–245.

Baron, R. A., & Byrne, D. (1991). *Social psychology: Understanding human interaction,* 6th ed. Boston: Allyn & Bacon.

Barr, C. E., Mednick, S. A., & Munk-Jorgensen, P. (1990). Exposure to influenza epidemics during gestation and adult schizophrenia: A 40-year study. *Archives of General Psychiatry, 47,* 869–874.

Barr, H. M., Streissguth, A. P., Darby, B. L., & Sampson, P. D. (1990). Prenatal exposure to alcohol, caffeine, tobacco, and spirin. *Developmental Psychology, 26,* 339–348.

Barringer, F. (1989, June 9). Divorce data stir doubt on trial marriage. *The New York Times,* pp. A1, A28.

Barringer, F. (1993a, April 15). Sex survey of American men finds 1% are gay. *The New York Times,* pp. A1, A18.

Barringer, F. (1993b, April 28). For 32 million Americans, English is a second language. *The New York Times,* p. A18.

Barsalou, L. W. (1992). *Cognitive psychology: An overview for cognitive scientists.* Hillsdale, NJ: Erlbaum.

Bartecchi., C. E., MacKenzie, T. D., & Schrier, R. W. (1994). The human cost of tobacco use. *New England Journal of Medicine, 330,* 907–912.

Bartek, S. E., Krebs, D. L., & Taylor, M. C. (1993). Coping, defending, and the relations between moral judgment and moral behavior in prostitutes and other female juvenile delinquents. *Journal of Abnormal Psychology, 102,* 66–73.

Bashore, T. R., & Rapp, P. E. (1993). Are there alternatives to traditional polygraph procedures? *Psychological Bulletin, 113,* 3–22.

Bates, E., Thal, D., & Janowsky, J. S. (1992). Early language development and its neural correlates. In I. Rapin & S. Segalowitz (Eds.), *Handbook of neuropsychology: Vol. 6. Child neurology.* Amsterdam: Elsevier.

Batson, C. D., and others (1989a). Negative state relief and the empathy–altruism hypothesis. *Journal of Personality and Social Psychology, 56,* 922–933.

Batson, C. D., and others (1989b). Religious prosocial motivation: Is it altruistic or egoistic? *Journal of Personality and Social Psychology, 57,* 873–884.

Bauer, W. D., & Twentyman, C. T. (1985). Abusing, neglectful, and comparison mothers' responses to child-related and non-child-related stressors. *Journal of Consulting and Clinical Psychology, 53,* 335–343.

Baum, A., Fisher, J. D., & Solomon, S. (1981). Type of information, familiarity, and the reduction of crowding stress. *Journal of Personality and Social Psychology,* 40, 11–23.

Baum, A., & Fleming, I. (1993). Implications of psychological research on stress and technological accidents. *American Psychologist, 48,* 665–672.

Baum, W., & Heath, J. I. (1992). Behavioral explanations and intentional explanations in psychology. *American Psychologist, 47,* 1312–1317.

Baumeister, R. F., & Covington, M. V. (1985). Self-esteem, persuasion, and retrospective distortion of initial attitudes. *Electronic Social Psychology, 1,* 1–22.

Baumeister, R. F., Stillwell, A. M., & Heatherton, T. F. (1994). Guilt: An interpersonal approach. *Psychological Bulletin, 115,* 243–267.

Baumgardner, A. H., Heppner, P. P., & Arkin, R. M. (1986). Role of causal attribution in personal problem solving. *Journal of Personality and Social Psychology, 50,* 636–643.

Baumrind, D. (1985). Research using intentional deception: Ethical issues revisited. *American Psychologist, 40,* 165–174.

Baumrind, D. (1986). Sex differences in moral reasoning: Response to Walker's (1984) conclusion that there are none. *Child Development, 57,* 511–521.

Baumrind, D. (1991a). The influence of parenting style on adolescent competence and substance abuse. *Journal of Early Adolescence, 11,* 56–95.

Baumrind, D. (1991b). Parenting styles and adolescent development. In J. Brooks-Gunn, R. Lerner, & A. C. Petersen (Eds.), *Encyclopedia of Adolescence, II.* New York: Garland.

Baumrind, D. (1993). The average expectable environment is not good enough: A response to Scarr. *Child Development, 64,* 1299–1317.

Beauchamp, G. K. (1981). Paper presented to the Conference on the Determination of Behavior by Chemical Stimuli. Hebrew University, Jerusalem.

Beauchamp, G. K. (1993). Cited in Blakeslee, S. (1993, September 7). Human nose may hold an additional organ for a real sixth sense. *The New York Times,* p. C3.

Beck, A. T. (1991). Cognitive therapy: A 30-year retrospective. *American Psychologist, 46,* 368–375.

Beck, A. T. (1993). Cognitive therapy: Past, present, and future. *Journal of Consulting and Clinical Psychology, 61,* 194–198.

Beck, A. T., Brown, G., Berchick, R. J., Stewart, B. L., & Steer, R. A. (1990). Relationship between hopelessness and ultimate suicide. *American Journal of Psychiatry, 147,* 190–195.

Beck, A. T., Epstein, N., Brown, G., & Steer, R. A. (1988). An inventory for measuring clinical anxiety: Psychometric properties. *Journal of Consulting and Clinical Psychology, 56,* 893–897.

Beck, A. T., & Freeman, A. (1990). *Cognitive therapy of personality disorders.* New York: Guilford.

Beck, A. T., & Haaga, D. A. F. (1992). The future of cognitive therapy. *Psychotherapy, 29,* 34–38.

Beck, J., Elsner, A., & Silverstein, C. (1977). Position uncertainty and the perception of apparent movement. *Perception and Psychophysics, 21,* 33–38.

Becker, K. L. (1990). *Principles and practice of endocrinology and metabolism.* Philadelphia: Lippincott.

Becker, L. B., and others. (1993). Racial differences in the incidence of cardiac arrest and subsequent survival. *New England Journal of Medicine, 329,* 600–606.

Bee, H. L., and others (1982). Prediction of IQ and language skill from perinatal status, child performance, family characteristics, and mother–infant interaction. *Child Development, 53,* 1134–1156.

Beilin, H. (1992). Piaget's enduring contribution to developmental psychology. *Developmental Psychology, 28,* 191–204.

Belchetz, P. E. (1994). Hormonal treatment of postmenopausal women. *New England Journal of Medicine, 330,* 1062–1071.

Bell, A. P., Weinberg, M. S., & Hammersmith, S. K. (1981). *Sexual preference: Its development in men and women.* Bloomington: University of Indiana Press.

Bell, P. A. (1992). In defense of the negative affect escape model of heat and aggression. *Psychological Bulletin, 111,* 342–346.

Belle, D. (1990). Poverty and women's mental health. *American Psychologist, 45,* 385–389.

Belsky, J. (1984). *The psychology of aging: Theory, research, and practice.* Monterey, CA: Brooks/Cole.

Belsky, J. (1990). Developmental risks associated with infant day care: Attachment insecurity, noncompliance and aggression? In I. S. Cherazi (Ed.), *Psychosocial issues in day care* (pp. 37–68). New York: American Psychiatric Press.

Belsky, J. (1993). Etiology of child maltreatment: A developmental–ecological analysis. *Psychological Bulletin, 114,* 413–434.

Belsky, J., Fish, M., & Isabella, R. (1991). Continuity and discontinuity in infant negative and positive emotionality: Family attachments and attachment consequences. *Developmental Psychology, 27,* 421–431.

Belsky, J., & Rovine, M. (1988). Nonmaternal care in the first year of life and infant–parent attachment security. *Child Development, 59,* 157–167.

Bem, D. J., & Honorton, C. (1994). Does Psi exist? Replicable evidence for an anomalous process of information transfer. *Psychological Bulletin, 115,* 4–18.

Bem, S. L. (1993). *The lenses of gender.* New Haven: Yale University Press.

Benbow, C. P., & Stanley, J. C. (1980). Sex differences in mathematical ability: Fact or artifact? *Science, 210,* 1029–1031.

Benderly, B. L. (1993, June 20). The perps are almost always male. *The New York Times Book Review,* p. 10.

Bennett, D. (1985). Rogers: More intuition in therapy. *APA Monitor, 16*(10), 3.

Benson, H. (1975). *The relaxation response.* New York: Morrow.

Benson, H., Manzetta, B. R., & Rosner, B. (1973). Decreased systolic blood pressure in hypertensive subjects who practiced meditation. *Journal of Clinical Investigation, 52,* 8.

Benson, P. L., Karabenick, S. A., & Lerner, R. M. (1976). Pretty pleases: The effects of physical attractiveness, race, and sex on receiving help. *Journal of Experimental Social Psychology, 12,* 409–415.

Berenbaum, H., & Connelly, J. (1993). The effect of stress on hedonic capacity. *Journal of Abnormal Psychology, 102,* 474–481.

Berkowitz, L. (1987). Mood, self-awareness, and willingness to help. *Journal of Personality and Social Psychology, 52,* 721–729.

Berkowitz, L. (1988). Frustrations, appraisals, and aversively stimulated aggression. *Aggressive Behavior, 14,* 3–11.

Berkowitz, L. (1994). Is something missing? Some observations prompted by the cognitive-neoassociationist view of anger and emotional aggression. In L. R. Huesmann (Ed.), *Aggressive behavior: current perspectives.* New York: Plenum.

Berlin, I. N. (1987). Effects of changing Native American cultures on child development. *Journal of Community Psychology, 15,* 299–306.

Berliner, D. (1993). Cited in Blakeslee, S. (1993, September 7). Human nose may hold an additional organ for real sixth sense. *The New York Times,* p. C3.

Berman, J. S., Miller, R. C., & Massman, P. J. (1985). Cognitive therapy versus systematic desensitization: Is one therapy superior? *Psychological Bulletin, 97,* 451–461.

Bernal, M. E., & Castro, F. G. (1994). Are clinical psychologists prepared for service and research with ethnic minorities? *American Psychologist, 49,* 797–805.

Berne, E. (1976). *Beyond games and scripts.* New York: Grove Press.

Bernstein, W. M., Stephenson, B. O., Snyder, M. L., & Wicklund, R. A. (1983). Causal ambiguity and heterosexual affiliation. *Journal of Experimental Social Psychology, 19,* 78–92.

Berntzen, D., & Götestam, K. G. (1987). Effects of on-demand versus fixed-interval schedules in the treatment of chronic pain with analgesic compounds. *Journal of Consulting and Clinical Psychology, 55,* 213–217.

Berquier, A., & Ashton, R. (1992). Characteristics of the frequent nightmare sufferer. *Journal of Abnormal Psychology, 101,* 246–250.

Bersoff, D. (1994). Cited in DeAngelis, T. (1994d). Experts see little impact from insanity plea ruling. *APA Monitor, 25*(6), 28.

Betancourt, H., & López, S. R. (1993). The study of culture, ethnicity, and race in American psychology. *American Psychologist, 48,* 629–637.

Beutler, L. E. (1991). Have all won and must all have prizes? *Journal of Consulting and Clinical Psychology, 59,* 226–232.

Beutler, L. E., & Kendall, P. C. (1991). Ethical dilemmas. *Journal of Consulting and Clinical Psychology, 59,* 245–255.

Bevan, W., & Kessel, F. (1994). Plain truths and home cooking: Thoughts on the making and remaking of psychology. *American Psychologist, 49,* 505–509.

Bexton, W. H., Heron, W., & Scott, T. H. (1954). Effects of decreased variation in the sensory environment. Canadian Journal of Psychology, *8,* 70–76.

Birch, H. G., & Rabinowitz, H. S. (1951). The negative effect of previous experience on productive thinking. *Journal of Experimental Psychology, 42,* 121-125.

Birren, J. E. (1983). Aging in America: Roles for psychology. *American Psychologist, 38,* 298–299.

Bishop, J. E. (1993, March 17). When smokers quit is a key to cancer risk. *The Wall Street Journal,* pp. B1, B7.

Bjorklund, D. F., & de Marchena, M. R. (1984). Developmental shifts in the basis of organization in memory: The role of associative versus categorical relatedness in children's free recall. *Child Development, 55,* 952–962.

Blakeslee, S. (1992a, January 7). Scientists unraveling chemistry of dreams. *The New York Times,* pp. C1, C10.

Blakeslee, S. (1992b, January 22). An epidemic of genital warts raises concern but not alarm. *The New York Times,* p. C12.

Blakeslee, S. (1992c, October 27). Nerve cell rhythm may be key to consciousness. *The New York Times,* pp. C1, C10.

Blakeslee, S. (1993, September 7). Human nose may hold an additional organ for a real sixth sense. *The New York Times,* p. C3.

Blakeslee, S. (1994, April 13). Black smokers' higher risk of cancer may be genetic. *The New York Times,* p. C14.

Blakeslee, S. (1995, March 21). How the brain might work: A new theory of consciousness. *The New York Times,* pp. C1, C10.

Blanchard, E. B. (1992a). Psychological treatment of benign headache disorders. *Journal of Consulting and Clinical Psychology, 60,* 537–551.
Blanchard, E. B. (1992b). Introduction to the special issue on behavioral medicine: An update for the 1990s. *Journal of Consulting and Clinical Psychology, 60,* 491–492.
Blanchard, E. B., and others (1990a). A controlled evaluation of thermal biofeedback and thermal feedback combined with cognitive therapy in the treatment of vascular headache. *Journal of Consulting and Clinical Psychology, 58,* 216–224.
Blanchard, E. B., and others (1990b). Placebo-controlled evaluation of abbreviated progressive muscle relaxation and of relaxation combined with cognitive therapy in the treatment of tension headache. *Journal of Consulting and Clinical Psychology, 58,* 210–215.
Blanchard, E. B., and others (1991). The role of regular home practice in the relaxation treatment of tension headache. *Journal of Consulting and Clinical Psychology, 59,* 467–470.
Blanck, P. D., Bellack, A. S., Rosnow, R. L., Rotheram-Borus, M. J., & Schooler, N. R. (1992). Scientific rewards and conflicts of ethical choices in human subjects research. *American Psychologist, 47,* 959–965.
Blass, E. M., & Smith, B. A. (1992). Differential effects of sucrose, fructose, glucose, and lactose on crying in 1- to 3-day-old human infants: Qualitative and quantitative considerations. *Developmental Psychology, 28,* 804–810.
Blass, T. (1991). Understanding behavior in the Milgram obedience experiment: The roles of personality, situations, and their interactions. *Journal of Personality and Social Psychology, 60,* 398–413.
Bloom, B. L. (1992). Computer assisted psychological intervention: A review and commentary. *Clinical Psychology Review, 12,* 169–197.
Bloom, J. D., & Williams, M. H. (1994). *Management and treatment of insanity acquittees: A model for the 1990s.* Washington, DC: American Psychiatric Press.
Bloom, L., Lahey, L., Hood, L., Lifter, K., & Fiess, K. (1980). Complex sentences: Acquisition of syntactic connectives and the semantic relations they encode. *Journal of Child Language, 7,* 235–261.
Bloom, L., Merkin, S., & Wootten, J. (1982). *Wh*-questions: Linguistic factors that contribute to the sequence of acquisition. *Child Development, 53,* 1084–1092.
Bloom, L., & Mudd, S. A. (1991). Depth of processing approach to face recognition: A test of two theories. *Journal of Experimental Psychology: Learning, Memory, and Cognition, 17,* 556–565.
Bly, R. (1990). *Iron John.* Reading, MA: Addison–Wesley.
Boden, M. A. (1994). What is creativity? In M. A. Boden (Ed.), *Dimensions of creativity.* Cambridge, MA: The MIT Press, a Bradford Book.
Bodenhausen, G. V. (1988). Stereotypic biases in social decision making and memory. *Journal of Personality and Social Psychology, 55,* 726–737.
Boneau, C. A. (1992). Observations on psychology's past and future. *American Psychologist, 47,* 1586–1596.
Bootzin, R. R., Epstein, D., & Wood, J. N. (1991). Stimulus control instructions. In P. Hauri (Ed.), *Case studies in insomnia.* New York: Plenum.
Bordo, S. (1993). *Unbearable weight: Feminism, Western culture, and the body.* Berkeley: University of California Press.
Borgida, E., & Campbell, B. (1982). Belief relevance and attitude-behavior consistency: The moderating role of personal experience. *Journal of Personality and Social Psychology, 42,* 239–247.
Borkovec, T. D., & Costello, E. (1993). Efficacy of applied relaxation and cognitive-behavioral therapy in the treatment of generalized anxiety disorder. *Journal of Consulting and Clinical Psychology, 61,* 611–619.
Borod, J. C. (1992). Interhemispheric and intrahemispheric control of emotion: A focus on unilateral brain damage. *Journal of Consulting and Clinical Psychology, 60,* 339–348.
Boskind-White, M., & White, W. C. (1983). *Bulimarexia: The binge/purge cycle.* New York: W. W. Norton.
Boston Women's Health Book Collective. (1992). *The new our bodies, ourselves.* New York: Simon & Schuster.
Bothwell, R. K., Deffenbacher, K. A., & Brigham, J. C. (1987). Correlation of eyewitness accuracy and confidence: Optimality hypothesis revisited. *Journal of Applied Psychology, 72,* 691–695.
Botvin, G. J., and others (1990). Preventing adolescent drug abuse through a multimodal cognitive-behavioral approach: Results of a 3-year study. *Journal of Consulting and Clinical Psychology, 58,* 437–446.
Bouchard, C. (1991). Is weight fluctuation a risk factor? *New England Journal of Medicine, 324,* 1887–1889.
Bouchard, T. J., Jr., Lykken, D. T., McGue, M., Segal, N. L., & Tellegen, A. (1990). Sources of human psychological differences: The Minnesota study of twins reared apart. *Science, 250,* 223–228.
Bower, G. H. (1981). Mood and memory. *American Psychologist, 36,* 129–148.
Bowlby, J. (1988). *A secure base.* New York: Basic Books.
Bowman, M. L. (1989). Testing individual differences in ancient China. *American Psychologist, 44,* 576–578.
Boyatzis, R. E. (1974). The effect of alcohol consumption on the aggressive behavior of men. *Quarterly Journal for the Study of Alcohol, 35,* 959–972.
Boyd-Franklin, N. (1989). *Black families in therapy: A multisystems approach.* New York: Guilford.
Bracha, H. S., Torrey, E. F., Gottesman, I. I., Bigelow, L. B., & Cunniff, C. (1992). Second-trimester markers of fetal size in schizophrenia: A study of monozygotic twins. *American Journal of Psychiatry, 149,* 1355–1361.
Bradley, R. H., and others (1989). Home environment and cognitive development in the first 3 years of life: A collaborative study involving six sites and three ethnic groups in North America. *Developmental Psychology, 25,* 217–235.
Bransford, J. D., Nitsch, K. E., & Franks, J. J. (1977). Schooling and the facilitation of knowing. In R. C. Anderson, R. J. Spiro, & W. E. Montague (Eds.), *Schooling and the acquisition of knowledge.* Hillsdale, NJ: Erlbaum.
Braun, B. G. (1988). *Treatment of multiple personality disorder.* Washington, DC: American Psychiatric Press.
Bray, N. W., Hersh, R. E., & Turner, L. A. (1985). Selective remembering during adolescence. *Developmental Psychology, 21,* 290–294.
Bray, R. M., & Sugarman, R. (1980). Social facilitation among interaction groups: Evidence for the evaluation-apprehension hypothesis. *Personality and Social Psychology Bulletin, 6,* 137–142.
Breckler, S. J., & Wiggins, E. C. (1989). Affect versus evaluation in the structure of attitudes. *Journal of Experimental Social Psychology, 25,* 253–271.
Brenner, J. (1992). Cited in Williams, L. (1992, February 6). Woman's image in a mirror: Who defines what she sees? *The New York Times,* pp. A1, B7.
Brent, E., & Granberg, D. (1982). Subjective agreement with the presidential candidates of 1976 and 1980. *Journal of Personality and Social Psychology, 42,* 393–403.
Brewin, C. R., Andrews, B., & Gotlib, I. H. (1993). Psychopathology and early experience: A reappraisal of retrospective reports. *Psychological Bulletin, 113,* 82–98.
Bridges, K. (1932). Emotional development in early infancy. *Child Development, 3,* 324–341.
Bridgwater, C. A. (1982). What candor can do. *Psychology Today, 16*(5), 16.
Brigham, J. C. (1980). Limiting conditions of the "physical attractiveness stereotype": Attributions about divorce. *Journal of Research in Personality, 14,* 365–375.
Brody, J. E. (1989, January 5). How women can begin to cope with premenstrual syndrome, a biological mystery. *The New York Times,* p. B12.
Brody, J. E. (1991, April 9). Not just music, bird song is a means of courtship and defense. *The New York Times,* pp. C1, C9.
Brody, J. E. (1992a, January 8). Migraines and the estrogen connection. *The New York Times,* p. C12.
Brody, J. E. (1992b, August 4). How the taste bud translates between tongue and brain. *The New York Times,* pp. C1, C8.
Brody, J. E. (1992c, September 16). Curable killer: Ignoring the doctor's orders. *The New York Times.*
Brody, J. E. (1992d, December 30). How weight loss changes risk. *The New York Times,* p. C6.
Brody, J. E. (1993, December 1). Liberated at last from the myths about menopause. *The New York Times,* p. C15.
Brody, J. E. (1994, March 16). Cancer pain is beatable, but too few know it. *The New York Times,* p. C12.
Bronstein, P., & Quina, K. (1988). (Eds.). *Teaching a psychology of people: Resources for gender and sociocultural awareness.* Washington, DC: American Psychological Association.
Broughton, R. S. (1991). *Parapsychology: The controversial science.* New York: Ballantine.
Brown, B. B., & Altman, J. (1981). *Territoriality and residential crime.* In P. A. Brantingham & P. L. Brantingham (Eds.), *Urban crime and environmental criminology.* Beverly Hills, CA: Sage.
Brown, D. E. (1991). *Human universals.* Philadelphia: Temple University Press.
Brown, L. S. (1992). A feminist critique of the personality disorders. In L. Brown & M. Balou (Eds.), *Personality and psychopathology: Feminist reappraisals.* New York: Guilford.
Brown, R., & Kulik, J. (1977). Flashbulb memories. *Cognition, 5,* 73–99.
Brown, R., & McNeill, D. (1966). The tip-of-the-tongue phenomenon. *Journal of Verbal Learning and Verbal Behavior, 5,* 325–337.
Brown, S. A. (1985). Expectancies versus background in the prediction of college drinking patterns. *Journal of Consulting and Clinical Psychology, 53,* 123–130.
Brown, S. A., Goldman, M. S., & Christiansen, B. A. (1985). Do alcohol expectancies mediate drinking patterns of adults? *Journal of Consulting and Clinical Psychology, 53,* 512–519.
Browne, A. (1993). Violence against women by male partners: Prevalence, outcomes, and policy implications. *American Psychologist, 48,* 1077–1087.
Browne, M. A., & Mahoney, M. J. (1984). Sport psychology. *Annual Review of Psychology, 35,* 605–625.
Brownell, K. D. (1993). Whether obesity should be treated. *Health Psychology, 12,* 339–341.
Brownell, K. D., & Rodin, J. (1994). The dieting maelstrom: Is it pos-sible and advisable to lose weight? *American Psychologist, 49,* 781–791.
Brownell, K. D., & Wadden, T. A. (1992). Obesity: Understanding a serious, prevalent, and refractory disorder. *Journal of Consulting and Clinical Psychology, 60,* 505–517.
Brownell, W. E. (1992). Cited in Browne, M. W. (1992, June 9). Ear's own sounds may underlie its precision. *The New York Times,* pp. C1, C8.
Brownlee-Duffeck, M., and others (1987). The role of health beliefs in the regimen adherence and metabolic control of adolescents and adults with diabetes mellitus. *Journal of Consulting and Clinical Psychology, 55,* 139–144.
Bruner, J. S. (1983). *Child's talk: Learning to use language.* New York: W. W. Norton.
Bryant, P. (1982). Piaget's questions. *British Journal of Psychology, 73,* 157–163.
Buchanan, C. M., Eccles, J. S., & Becker, J. B. (1992). Are adolescents the victims of raging hormones? Evidence for activational effects of hormones on moods and behavior at adolescence. *Psychological Bulletin, 111,* 62–107.
Budzynski, T. H., & Stoyva, J. M. (1984). Biofeedback methods in the treatment of anxiety and stress. In R. L. Woolfolk & P. M. Lehrer (Eds.), *Principles and practice of stress management.* New York: Guilford.
Buffone, G. W. (1984). Running and depression. In M. L. Sachs & G. W. Buffone (Eds.), *Running as therapy: An integrated approach.* Lincoln: University of Nebraska Press.
Bullock, M. (1985). Animism in childhood thinking: A new look at an old question. *Developmental Psychology, 21,* 217–225.
Bulman, R. J., & Wortman, C. B. (1977). Attribution of blame and coping in the "real world": Severe accident victims ract to their lot. *Journal of Personality and Social Psychology, 35,* 351–363.
Burish, T. G., Carey, M. P., Krozely, M. G., & Greco, F. A. (1987). Conditioned side effects induced by cancer chemotherapy: Prevention through behavioral treatment. *Journal of Consulting and Clinical Psychology, 55,* 42–48.
Burish, T. G., Snyder, S. L., & Jenkins, R. A. (1991). Preparing patients for cancer chemotherapy: Effect of coping preparation and relaxation interventions. *Journal of Consulting and Clinical Psychology, 59,* 518–525.
Burman, B., & Margolin, G. (1992). Analysis of the association between marital relationships and health problems: An interactional perspective. *Psychological Bulletin, 112,* 39–63.
Burns, D. D., & Nolen-Hoeksema, S. (1992). Therapeutic empathy and recovery from depression in cognitive-behavioral therapy: A structural equation model. *Journal of Consulting and Clinical Psychology, 60,* 441–449.
Burns, G. L., & Farina, A. (1987). Physical attractiveness and self-perception of mental disorder. *Journal of Abnormal Psychology, 96,* 161–163.
Burnstein, E. (1983). Persuasion as argument processing. In M. Brandstatter, J. H. Davis, & G. Stocker-Kreichgauer (Eds.), *Group decision processes.* London: Academic Press.
Burnstein, E., & Schul, Y. (1982). The informational basis of social judgments: Operations in forming an impression of another person. *Journal of Experimental Social Psychology, 18,* 217–234.
Burt, M. R. (1980). Cultural myths and supports for rape. *Journal of Personality and Social Psychology, 38,* 217–230.
Busch, M. P., and others (1991). Evaluation of screened blood donations for HIV-1 infection by culture and DNA amplification of pooled cells. *New England Journal of Medicine, 325,* 1–5.
Bushnell, E. W., Shaw, L., & Strauss, D. (1985). Relationship between visual and tactual exploration by 6-month-olds. *Developmental psychology,* 21, 591-600.
Buss, A. H. (1983). Social rewards and personality. *Journal of Personality and Social Psychology, 44,* 553–563.
Buss, A. H. (1986). *Social behavior and personality.* Hillsdale, NJ: Erlbaum.
Buss, D. M. (1992). Is there a universal human nature? *Contemporary Psychology, 37,* 1262–1263.
Buss, D. M. (1994). *The evolution of desire: Strategies of human mating.* New York: Basic Books.
Buss, D. M., Gomes, M., Higgins, D.S., & Lauterbach, K. (1987). Tactics of manipulation. *Journal of Personality and Social Psychology, 52,* 1219-1229.
Butcher, J. N. (1987). *Computerized psychological assessment: A practitioner's guide.* New York: Basic Books.
Byrnes, J., & Takahira, S. (1993). Explaining gender differences on SAT-math items. *Developmental Psychology, 29,* 805–810.

Cacioppo, J. T., Martzke, J. S, Petty, R. E., & Tassinary, L. G. (1988). Specific forms of facial EMG response index emotions during an interview. *Journal of Personality and Social Psychology, 54,* 552–604.
Campbell, A. (1993). *Men, women, and aggression.* New York: Basic Books.
Campbell, J. (1994). *Past, space, and self.* Cambridge, MA: The MIT Press, a Bradford Book.

Campos, J. J., Hiatt, S., Ramsey, D., Henderson, C., & Svejda, M. (1978). The emergence of fear on the visual cliff. In M. Lewis & L. Rosenblum (Eds.), *The origins of affect.* New York: Plenum.

Campos, J. J., Langer, A., & Krowitz, A. (1970). Cardiac responses on the visual cliff in prelocomotor infants. *Science, 170,* 196–197.

Cannon, W. B. (1927). The James–Lange theory of emotions: A critical examination and an alternative theory. *American Journal of Psychology, 39,* 106–124.

Cantor, N. (1990). From thought to behavior: "Having" and "doing" in the study of personality and behavior. *American Psychologist, 45,* 735–750.

Cantrell, R. P., Stenner, A. J., & Katzenmeyer, W. G. (1977). Teacher knowledge, attitudes, and classroom teaching correlates of student achievement. *Journal of Educational Psychology, 69,* 180–190.

Capaldi, E. D. (1993, August). The psychology of eating: Why we like the foods we like. G. Stanley Hall lecture presented to the American Psychological Association, Toronto, Canada.

Cappella, J. N., & Palmer, M. T. (1990). Attitude similarity, relational history, and attraction: The mediating effects of kinesic and vocal behaviors. *Communication Monographs, 5,* 161–183.

Carey, G. (1992). Twin imitation for antisocial behavior: Implications for genetic and family environment research. *Journal of Abnormal Psychology, 101,* 18–25.

Carey, G., & DiLalla, D. L. (1994). Personality and psychopathology: Genetic perspectives. *Journal of Abnormal Psychology, 103,* 32–43.

Carey, M. P., & Burish, T. G. (1987). Providing relaxation training to cancer chemotherapy patients: A comparison of three delivery techniques. *Journal of Consulting and Clinical Psychology, 55,* 732–737.

Carey, M. P., & Burish, T. G. (1988). Etiology and treatment of the psychological side effects associated with cancer chemotherapy: A critical review and discussion. *Psychological Bulletin, 104,* 307–325.

Carling, P. J. (1990). Major mental illness, housing, and supports: The promise of community integration. *American Psychologist, 45,* 969–975.

Carlson, J. G., & Hatfield, E. (1992). *Psychology of emotion.* Fort Worth, TX: Harcourt Brace Jovanovich.

Carmichael, L. L., Hogan, H. P., & Walter, A. A. (1932). An experimental study of the effect of language on the reproduction of visually perceived form. *Journal of Experimental Psychology, 15,* 73–86.

Carpenter, W. T., Jr., & Buchanan, R. W. (1994). Schizophrenia. *New England Journal of Medicine, 330,* 681–690.

Carroll, K. M., Rounsaville, B. J., & Nich, C. (1994). Blind man's bluff: Effectiveness and significance of psychotherapy and pharmacotherapy blinding procedures in a clinical trial. *Journal of Consulting and Clinical Psychology, 62,* 276–280.

Carver, C. S., & Gaines, J. G. (1987). Optimism, pessimism, and postpartum depression. *Cognitive Therapy and Research, 11,* 449–462.

Carver, C. S., & Scheier, M. F. (1981). *Attention and self-regulation: A control theory approach to human behavior.* New York: Springer–Verlag.

Case, R. (1992). *The mind's staircase: Exploring the conceptual underpinnings of children's thought and knowledge.* Hillsdale, NJ: Erlbaum.

Castelli, W. (1994). Cited in Brody, J. E. (1994, February 8). Scientist at work—William Castelli: Preaching the gospel of healthy hearts. *The New York Times,* pp. C1, C10.

Cattell, R. B. (1949). *The culture-free intelligence test.* Champaign, IL: Institute for Personality and Ability Testing.

Cattell, R. B. (1965). *The scientific analysis of personality.* Baltimore: Penguin.

Caulfield, M., and others (1994). Linkage of the angiotensinogen gene to essential hypertension. *New England Journal of Medicine, 330,* 1629–1633.

Ceci, S. J., & Bruck, M. (1993). Suggestibility of the child witness: A historical review and synthesis. *Psychological Bulletin, 113,* 403–439.

Celis, W. (1991, January 2). Students trying to draw line between sex and an assault. *The New York Times,* pp. A1, B8.

Celis, W. (1993, January 10). College curriculums shaken to the core. *Education Life [The New York Times],* Section 4A, pp. 16–18.

Center for Women in Government. (1992). Women in Public Service Survey. Rockefeller College of Public Affairs and Policy. Cited in Few women found in top public jobs. (1992, January 3). *The New York Times,* p. A12.

CDC (Centers for Disease Control). (1985). *Suicide surveillance: 1970–1980.* Washington, DC: U.S. Department of Health and Human Services.

CDC (Centers for Disease Control). (1991). Mortality attributable to HIV infection/AIDS—United States, 1981–1990. *Journal of the American Medical Association, 265,* 848.

CDC (Centers for Disease Control and Prevention). (1993, October). *HIV/AIDS surveillance: Third quarter edition. U.S. AIDS cases reported through September 1993.* Atlanta, GA: U.S. Department of Health and Human Services.

Cepeda-Benito, A. (1993). Meta-analytical review of the efficacy of nicotine chewing gum in smoking treatment programs. *Journal of Consulting and Clinical Psychology, 61,* 822–830.

Chadwick, P. D. J., & Lowe, C. F. (1990). Measurement and modification of delusional beliefs. *Journal of Consulting and Clinical Psychology, 58,* 225–232.

Chaiken, S., & Eagly, A. H. (1983). Communication modality as a determinant of persuasion: The role of communcator salience. *Journal of Personality and Social Psychology, 45,* 241–256.

Chan, C. (1992). Cultural considerations in counseling Asian American lesbians and gay men. In S. Dworkin & F. Gutierrez (Eds.), *Counseling gay men and lesbians: Journey to the end of the rainbow.* Alexandria, VA: American Association for Counseling and Development.

Chartrand, S. (1993, July 18). A split in thinking among keepers of artificial intelligence. *The New York Times,* p. E6.

Chassin, L., Mann, L. M., & Sher, K. J. (1988). Self-awareness theory, family history of alcoholism, and adolescent alcohol involvement. *Journal of Abnormal Psychology, 97,* 206–217.

Chesney, M. A. (1993). Health psychology in the 21st century: Acquired immunodeficiency syndrome as a harbinger of things to come. *Health Psychology 12,* 259–268.

Chesney, M. A., & Coates, T. J. (1990). Health promotion and disease prevention: AIDS puts the models to the test. In S. Petro and others (Eds.), *Ending the HIV epidemic* (pp. 48–62). Santa Cruz, CA: ETR Associates.

Chesno, F. A., & Kilmann, P. R. (1975). Effects of stimulation intensity on sociopathic avoidance learning. *Journal of Abnormal Psychology, 84,* 144–151.

Cheung, F. K., & Snowden, L. R. (1990). Community mental health and ethnic minority populations. *Community Mental Health Journal, 26,* 277–291.

Childs, E. K. (1990). Therapy, feminist ethics, and the community of color with particular emphasis on the treatment of Black women. In H. Lerman & N. Porter (Eds.), *Feminist ethics in psychotherapy* (pp. 195–203). New York: Springer.

Chitayat, D. (1993, February). Presentation to the Fifth International Interdisciplinary Congress on Women, University of Costa Rica, San Jose, Costa Rica.

Chomsky, N. (1980). Rules and representations. *Behavioral and Brain Sciences, 3,* 1–16.

Chomsky, N. (1991). Linguistics and cognitive science: Problems and mysteries. In A. Kasher (Ed.), *The Chomskyan turn.* Cambridge, MA: Blackwell.

Christiensen, A. (1994). Cited in Howard, K., Barlow, D., Christiensen, A., & Frank, E. *Evaluating outcomes of psychological interventions: Evaluating the effectiveness of psychotherapy.* Symposium conducted at the meeting of the American Psychological Association, Los Angeles.

Chronicle of Higher Education, March 18, 1992, pp. A35–A44.

Chwalisz, K., Diener, E., & Gallagher, D. (1988). Autonomic arousal feedback and emotional experience: Evidence from the spinal cord injured. *Journal of Personality and Social Psychology, 54,* 820–828.

Cialdini, R. B., & Fultz, J. (1990). Interpreting the negative mood-helping literature via "mega"-analysis: A contrary view. *Psychological Bulletin, 107,* 210–214.

Cicchetti, D., & Olson, K. (1990). The developmental psychopathology of child maltreatment. In M. Lewis & S. M. Miller (Eds.), *Handbook of developmental psychopathology* (pp. 261–279). New York: Plenum.

Clark, E. V. (1993). *The lexicon in acquisition.* New York: Cambridge University Press.

Clark, L. A., Watson, D., & Mineka, S. M. (1994). Temperament, personality, and the mood and anxiety disorders. *Journal of Abnormal Psychology, 103,* 103–116.

Clark, M. S., Mills, J. R., & Corcoran, D. M. (1989). Keeping track of needs and inputs of friends and strangers. *Personality and Social Psychology Bulletin, 15,* 533–542.

Clarke, A. C. (1993). The hammer of God. New York: Bantam.

Clarke-Stewart, K. A. (1989). Infant day care: Maligned or malignant? *American Psychologist, 44,* 266–273.

Clarke-Stewart, K. A. (1990). "The 'effects' of infant day care reconsidered": Risks for parents, children, and researchers. In N. Fox & G. G. Fein (Eds.), *Infant day care: The current debate* (pp. 61–86). Norwood, NJ: Ablex.

Clarke-Stewart, K. A. (1991). A home is not a school: The effects of child care on children's development. *Journal of Social Issues, 47,* 105–123.

Clement, J. (1991). Nonformal reasoning in experts and in science students: The use of analogies, extreme cases, and physical intuition. In J. Voss, D. Perkins, & J. Siegel (Eds.), *Informal reasoning and education.* Hillsdale, NJ: Erlbaum.

Clkurel, K., & Gruzelier, J. (1990). The effects of active alert hypnotic induction on lateral haptic processing. *British Journal of Experimental and Clinical Hypnosis, 11,* 17–25.

Cloninger, C. R., & Gottesman, I. I. (1987). Genetic and environmental factors in antisocial behavior disorders. In S. A. Mednick and others (Eds.), *The causes of crime: New biological approaches.* New York: Cambridge University Press.

Coe, C. (1993). Cited in Adler, T. (1993). Men and women affected by stress, but differently. *APA Monitor, 24*(7), 8–9.

Coe, W. C., & Yaskinski, E. (1985). Volitional experiences associated with breaching posthypnotic amnesia. *Journal of Personality and Social Psychology, 48,* 716–722.

Cohen, L. A. (1987, November). Diet and cancer. *Scientific American,* pp. 42–48, 53–54.

Cohen, S., Evans, G. W., Stokols, D., & Krantz, D. S. (1986). *Behavior, health, and environmental stress.* New York: Plenum.

Cohen, S., Tyrrell, D. A. J., & Smith, A. P. (1993). Negative life events, perceived stress, negative affect, and susceptibility to the common cold. *Journal of Personality and Social Psychology, 64,* 131–140.

Cohen, S., & Williamson, G. M. (1991). Stress and infectious disease in humans. *Psychological Bulletin, 109,* 5–24.

Cohn, E. G. (1990). Weather and violent crime. *Environment and Behavior, 22,* 280–294.

Coie, J. D., and others. (1993). The science of prevention: A conceptual framework and some directions for a national research program. *American Psychologist, 48,* 1013–1022.

Colby, A., Kohlberg, L., Gibbs, J., & Lieberman, M. (1983). A longitudinal study of moral judgment. *Monographs of the Society for Research in Child Development, 48*(Serial No. 200).

Colby, C. Z., Lanzetta, J. T., & Kleck, R. E. (1977). Effects of the expression of pain on autonomic and pain tolerance response to subject-controlled pain. *Psychophysiology, 14,* 537–540.

Coleman, L. (1990). Cited in Goleman, G. (1990, August 2). The quiet comeback of electroshock therapy. *The New York Times,* p. B5.

Coleman, M., & Ganong, L. H. (1985). Love and sex role stereotypes: Do macho men and feminine women make better lovers? *Journal of Personality and Social Psychology, 49,* 170–176.

Collier, G. (1994). *Social origins of mental ability.* New York: Wiley.

Collins, P. H. (1990). *Black feminist thought: Knowledge, consciousness, and the politics of empowerment.* Boston: Unwin Hyman.

Collins, W. A. (1990). Parent–child relationships in the transition to adolescence: Continuity and change in interaction, affect, and cognition. In. R. Montemayor, G. R. Adams, & T. P. Gullotta (Eds.), *From childhood to adolescence: A transitional period.* Newbury Park, CA: Sage.

Collins, W. A., & Russell, G. (1991). Mother–child and father–child relationships in middle childhood and adolescence: A developmental analysis. *Developmental Review, 11,* 99–136.

Colon, P. A., & Colon, A. R. (1989). The health of America's children. In F. J. Macehiarola & A. Gartner (Eds.), *Caring for America's Children, 37,* 45–47. New York: The Academy of Political Science.

Comas-Diaz, L. (1994, February). Race and gender in psychotherapy with women of color. *Winter roundtable on cross-cultural counseling and psychotherapy: Race and gender.* New York: Teachers College, Columbia University.

Condon, J. W., & Crano, W. D. (1988). Inferred evaluation and the relation between attitude similarity and interpersonal attraction. *Journal of Personality and Social Psychology, 54,* 789–797.

Conn, P. M., & Crowley, W. F., Jr. (1991). Gonadotropin-releasing hormone and its analogues. *New England Journal of Medicine, 324,* 93-103.

Conrad, P. (1992). Cited in Brody, J. E. (1992, September 16). Curable killer: Ignoring the doctor's orders. *The New York Times.*

Cools, J., Schotte, D. E., & McNally, R. J. (1992). Emotional arousal and overeating in restrained eaters. *Journal of Abnormal Psychology, 101,* 348–351.

Coon, H., Fulker, D. W., DeFries, J. C., & Plomin, R. (1990). Home environment and cognitive ability of 7-year-old children in the Colorado Adoption Project: Genetic and environmental etiologies. *Developmental Psychology, 26,* 459–468.

Cooney, J. L., & Zeichner, A. (1985). Selective attention to negative feedback in Type A and Type B individuals. *Journal of Abnormal Psychology, 94,* 110–112.

Cooper, H. M. (1979). Statistically combining independent studies: A meta-analysis of sex differences in conformity research. *Journal of Personality and Social Psychology, 37,* 131-146.

Cooper, J. R., Bloom, F. E., & Roth, R. H. (1991). *The biochemical basis of neuropharmacology.* New York: Oxford University Press.

Cooper, M. L., Peirce, R. S., & Huselid, R. F. (1994). Substance use and sexual risk taking among Black adolescents and White adolescents. *Health Psychology, 13,* 251–262.

Copeland, L. J., Jarrell, J. F., & McGregor, J. A. (Eds.). (1993). *Textbook of gynecology.* Philadelphia: W. B. Saunders.

Corkin, S., and others (1985). Analyses of global memory impairments of different etiologies. In D. S. Olton, E. Gamzu, & S. Corkin (Eds.), *Memory dysfunction.* New York: New York Academy of Sciences.

Corter, J. E., & Gluck, M. A. (1992). Explaining basic categories: Feature predictability and information. *Psychological Bulletin, 111,* 291–303.

Coryell, W., Endicott, J., & Keller, M. (1992). Major depression in a nonclinical sample: Demographic and clinical risk factors for first onset. *Archives of General Psychiatry,* 49, 117–125.

Costa, E. (1985). Benzodiazepine/GABA interactions: A model to investigate the neurobiology of anxiety. In A. H. Tuma & J. D. Maser (Eds.), *Anxiety and the anxiety disorders.* Hillsdale, NJ: Erlbaum.

Costa, P. T., Jr., & McCrae, R. R. (1984). Personality as a lifelong determinant of wellbeing. In C. Z. Malatesta & C. E. Izard (Eds.), *Emotion in adult development.* Beverly Hills, CA: Sage.

Cousins, N. (1979). *Anatomy of an illness as perceived by the patient: Reflections on healing and regeneration.* New York: W. W. Norton.

Cox, M. J., Owen, M. T., Henderson, V. K., & Margand, N. A. (1992). Prediction of infant–father and infant–mother attachment. *Developmental Psychology, 28,* 474–483.

Coyne, J. C., & Downey, G. (1991). Social factors and psychopathology: Stress, social support, and coping processes. *Annual Review of Psychology, 42,* 401–425.

Crabtree, A. (1994). *From Mesmer to Freud: Magnetic sleep and the roots of psychological healing.* New Haven, CT: Yale University Press.

Craighead, L. W., & Agras, W. S. (1991). Mechanisms of action in cognitive-behavioral and pharmacological interventions for obesity and bulimia nervosa. *Journal of Consulting and Clinical Psychology, 59,* 115–125.

Craik, F. I. M., & Lockhart, R. S. (1972). Levels of processing: A framework for memory research. *Journal of Verbal Learning and Verbal Behavior, 11,* 671–684.

Craik, F. I. M., & Watkins, M. J. (1973). The role of rehearsal in short-term memory. *Journal of Verbal Learning and Verbal Behavior, 12,* 599–607.

Cramer, R. E., McMaster, M. R., Bartell, P. A., & Dragna, M. (1988). Subject competence and minimization of the bystander effect. *Journal of Applied Social Psychology, 18,* 1133–1148.

Crawford, C. (1979). George Washington, Abraham Lincoln, and Arthur Jensen: Are they compatible? *American Psychologist, 34,* 664–672.

Crawford, H. J., & Barabasz, A. (1993). Phobias and fears: Facilitating their treatment with hypnosis. In J. Rhue, S. Lynn, & I. Kirsch (Eds.), *Clinical handbook of hypnosis.* Washington, DC: American Psychological Association.

Crawford, H. J., Brown, A. M., & Moon, C. E. (1993). Sustained attentional and disattentional abilities: Differences between low and highly hypnotizable persons. *Journal of Abnormal Psychology, 102,* 534–543.

Creamer, M., Burgess, P., & Pattison, P. (1992). Reaction to trauma: A cognitive processing model. *Journal of Abnormal Psychology, 101,* 452–459.

Crews, D. (1994). Animal sexuality. *Scientific American, 270*(1), 108–114.

Crichton, M. (1992). *Rising sun.* New York: Knopf.

Crick, F. & Koch, C. (1992). The problem of consciousness. *Scientific American, 267*(3), 152–159.

Crick, N. R., & Dodge, K. A. (1994). A review and reformulation of social information-processing mechanisms in children's social adjustment. *Psychological Bulletin, 115,* 74–101.

Crits-Christoph, P., & Mintz, J. (1991). Implications of therapist effects for the design and analysis of comparative studies of psychotherapies. *Journal of Consulting and Clinical Psychology, 59,* 20–26.

Cronbach, L. J. (1975). Five decades of public controversy over mental testing. *American Psychologist, 30,* 1–14.

Cross, W. (1991). *Shades of identity.* Philadelphia: Temple University Press.

Crowe, R. A. (1990). Astrology and the scientific method. *Psychological Reports, 67,* 163–191.

Croyle, R. T., Sun, Y., & Louie, D. H. (1993). Psychological minimization of cholesterol test results: Moderators of appraisal in college students and community residents. *Health Psychology, 12,* 503–507.

Crusco, A. H., & Wetzel, C. G. (1984). The Midas touch: The effects of interpersonal touch on restaurant tipping. *Personality and Social Psychology Bulletin, 10,* 512–517.

Crystal, A. J. (1988). The diagnosis of Alzheimer's disease and other dementing disorders. In M. K. Aronson (Ed.). *Understanding Alzheimer's Disease.* New York: Macmillan.

Cummings, E. M., Iannotti, R. J., & Zahn-Waxler, C. (1985). Influence of conflict between adults on the emotions and aggression of young children. *Developmental Psychology, 21,* 495–507.

Cummings, N. A. (1979). Turning bread into stones: Our modern antimiracle. *American Psychologist, 34,* 1119–1129.

Cunningham, M. R., Shaffer, D. R., Barbee, A. P., Wolff, P. L., & Kelley, D. J. (1990). Separate processes in the relation of elation and depression to helping: Social versus personal concerns. *Journal of Experimental Social Psychology, 26,* 13–33.

Curb, J. D., & Marcus, E. B. (1991). Body fat and obesity in Japanese Americans. *American Journal of Clinical Nutrition, 53,* 1552S–1555S.

Curfman, G. D. (1993a). The health benefits of exercise: A critical reappraisal. *New England Journal of Medicine, 328,* 574–576.

Curfman, G. D. (1993b). Is exercise beneficial—or hazardous—to your heart? *New England Journal of Medicine, 329,* 1730–1731.

Curry, S. J., Wagner, E. H., & Grothaus, L. C. (1991). Evaluation of intrinsic and extrinsic motivation interventions with a self-help smoking cessation program. *Journal of Consulting and Clinical Psychology, 59,* 318–324.

Curtis, R. C., & Miller, K. (1986). Believing another likes or dislikes you: Behavior making the beliefs come true. *Journal of Personality and Social Psychology, 51,* 284–290.

Cutler, B. L., Penrod, S. D., & Martens, T. K. (1987). Improving the reliability of eyewitness identification: Putting content into context. *Journal of Applied Psychology, 72,* 629–637.

Damasio, A. R., & Damasio, H. (1992). Brain and language. *Scientific American, 267*(3), 88–95.

Danforth, J. S., and others (1990). Exercise as a treatment for hypertension in low-socioeconomic-status Black children. *Journal of Consulting and Clinical Psychology, 58,* 237–239.

Darkes, J., & Goldman, M. S. (1993). Expectancy challenge and drinking reduction: Experimental evidence for a mediational process. *Journal of Consulting and Clinical Psychology, 61,* 344–353.

Darley, J. M., & Latané B. (1968). Bystander intervention in emergencies: Diffusion of responsibility. *Journal of Personality and Social Psychology, 8,* 377–383.

Darwin, C. A. (1872). *The expression of the emotions in man and animals.* London: J. Murray.

Davey, L. F. (1993, March). *Developmental implications of shared and divergent perceptions in the parent–adolescent relationship.* Paper presented at the biennial meeting of the Society for Research in Child Development, New Orleans.

Davidson, J. R., & Foa, E. G. (1991). Diagnostic issues in posttraumatic stress disorder: Considerations for the DSM-IV. *Journal of Abnormal Psychology, 100,* 346–355.

Davidson, T. M., & Bowers, K. S. (1991). Selective hypnotic amnesia: Is it a successful attempt to forget or an unsuccessful attempt to remember? *Journal of Abnormal Psychology, 100,* 133–143.

Davies, P. (1988). Alzheimer's disease and related disorders: An overview. In M. K. Aronson (Ed.), *Understanding Alzheimer's Disease.* New York: Scribner's.

Davis, J. H. (1989). Psychology and law: The last 15 years. *Journal of Applied Social Psychology, 19,* 119–230.

Davis, J. H., Tindale, R. S., Nagao, D. H., Hinsz, V. B., & Robertson, B. (1984). Order effects in multiple decisions by groups: A demonstration with mock juries and trial procedures. *Journal of Personality and Social Psychology, 47,* 1003–1012.

Davis, K. L., Kahn, R. S., Ko, G., & Davidson, M. (1991). Dopamine in schizophrenia: A review and reconceptualization. *American Journal of Psychiatry, 148,* 1474–1486.

Dawes, R. M. (1989). Statistical criteria for establishing a truly false consensus effect. *Journal of Experimental Social Psychology, 25,* 1–17.

Dean, G. (1987). Does astrology need to be true? Part II: The answer is no. *The Skeptical Inquirer, 11,* 257–273.

DeAngelis, T. (1993a). It's baaack: TV violence, concern for kid viewers. *APA Monitor, 24*(8), 16.

DeAngelis, T. (1993b). Law helps American Indians enter field. *APA Monitor, 24*(3), 26–27.

DeAngelis, T. (1994a). Educators reveal keys to success in classroom. *APA Monitor, 25*(1), 39–40.

DeAngelis, T. (1994b). Poor kids are focus of asthma studies. *APA Monitor, 25*(3), 26–27.

DeAngelis, T. (1994c). Psychologists' expertise is often essential in court. *APA Monitor, 25*(6), 1, 29.

DeAngelis, T. (1995). Firefighters' PTSD at dangerous levels. *APA Monitor, 26*(2), 36–37.

DeCasper, A. J., & Prescott, P. A. (1984). Human newborns' perception of male voices: Preference, discrimination, and reinforcing value. *Developmental Psychobiology, 17,* 481–491.

Decline in smoking levels off and officials urge a tax rise. (1993, April 2). *The New York Times,* p. A10.

DeFries, J. C., Plomin, R., & LaBuda, M. C. (1987). Genetic stability of cognitive development from childhood to adulthood. *Developmental Psychology, 23,* 4–12.

deGroot, G. (1994a). The community teaches more than any textbook. *APA Monitor, 25*(5), 44.

deGroot, G. (1994b). Psychologists are keys to school reforms. *APA Monitor, 25*(6), 38–39.

deGroot, G. (1994c). Tutors help students boost self-esteem. *APA Monitor, 25*(5), 45.

De La Cancela, V., & Guzman, L. P. (1991). Latino mental health service needs: Implications for training psychologists. In H. F. Myers and others (Eds.), *Ethnic minority perspectives on clinical training and services in psychology* (pp. 59–64). Washington, DC: American Psychological Association.

Delanoy, R. L., Merrin, J. S., & Gold, P. E. (1982). Moderation of long-term potentiation (LTP) by adrenergic agonists. *Neuroscience Abstracts, 8,* 316.

de Leon, M. J., George, A. E., & Ferris, S. H. (1986). Computed tomography and positron emission tomography correlates of cognitive decline in aging and senile dementia. In L. W. Poon (Ed.), *Handbook for clinical memory assessment of older adults.* Washington, DC: American Psychological Association.

Delgado, J. M. R. (1969). *Physical control of the mind.* New York: Harper & Row.

Delgado-Gaitan, C. (1993). Parenting in two generations of Mexican American families. *International Journal of Behavioral Development, 16,* 409–427.

Delprato, D. J., & Midgley, B. D. (1992). Some fundamentals of B. F. Skinner's behaviorism. *American Psychologist, 47,* 1507–1520.

Dembroski, T. M., Lasater, T. M., & Ramirez, A. (1978). Communicator similarity, fear-arousing communications, and compliance with health care recommendations. *Journal of Applied Social Psychology, 8,* 254–269.

Denmark, F. L. (1994). Engendering psychology. *American Psychologist, 49,* 329–334.

DePaulo, B. M. (1992). Nonverbal behavior and self-presentation. *Psychological Bulletin, 111,* 203–243.

DePaulo, B. M., Rosenthal, R., Eisenstat, R. A., Rogers, P. L., & Finkelstein, S. (1978). Decoding discrepant nonverbal cues. *Journal of Personality and Social Psychology, 38,* 313–323.

Depue, R. A., and others (1981). A behavioral paradigm for identifying persons at risk for bipolar depressive disorder. *Journal of Abnormal Psychology, 90,* 381–438.

Derryberry, D., & Tucker, D. M. (1992). Neural mechanisms of emotion. *Journal of Consulting and Clinical Psychology, 60,* 329–338.

Despite better diets, adults in their 20s are weighing more. (1994, March 18). *The New York Times,* p. A17.

DeValois, R. L., & Jacobs, G. H. (1984). Neural mechanisms of color vision. In I. Darian-Smith (Ed.), *Handbook of physiology* (Vol. 3). Bethesda, MD: American Physiological Society.

Devine, P. G. (1989). Stereotypes and prejudice: Their automatic and controlled components. *Journal of Personality and Social Psychology, 56,* 5–18.

Dewsbury, D. A. (1991). "Psychobiology." *American Psychologist, 46,* 198–205.

Diaz, R. M. (1985). Bilingual cognitive development: Addressing three gaps in current research. *Child Development, 56,* 1376–1388.

DiClemente, C. C., and others (1991). The process of smoking cessation. *Journal of Consulting and Clinical Psychology, 59,* 295–304.

Diener, E. (1980). Deindividuation: The absence of self-awareness and self-regulation in group members. In P. Paulus (Ed.), *The psychology of group influence.* Hillsdale, NJ: Erlbaum.

Digman, J. M. (1990). Personality structure: Emergence of the five-factor model. *Annual Review of Psychology, 41,* 417–440.

DiLalla, L. F., & Gottesman, I. I. (1991). Biological and genetic contributors to violence—Widom's untold tale. *Psychological Bulletin, 109,* 125–129.

Dill, C. A., Gilden, E. R., Hill, P. C., & Hanselka, L. L. (1982). Federal human subjects regulations: A methodological artifact. *Personality and Social Psychology Bulletin, 8,* 417–425.

DiMatteo, M. R., & DiNicola, D. D. (1982). *Achieving patient compliance: The psychology of the medical practitioner's role.* New York: Pergamon.

DiMatteo, M. R., and others (1993). Physicians' characteristics influence patients' adherence to medical treatment: Results from the Medical Outcomes Study. *Health Psychology, 12,* 93–102.

Dindia, K., & Allen, M. (1992). Sex differences in self-disclosure: A meta-analysis. *Psychological Bulletin, 112,* 106–124.

DiNicola, D. D., & DiMatteo, M. R. (1984). Practitioners, patients, and compliance with medical regimens: A social psychological perspective. In A. Baum, S. E. Taylor, & J. E. Singer (Eds.), *Handbook of psychology and health: Vol. 4. Social psychological aspects of health.* Hillsdale, NJ: Erlbaum.

Dinsmoor, J. A. (1992). Setting the record straight: The social views of B. F. Skinner. *American Psychologist, 47,* 1454–1463.

Dix, T. (1991). The affective organization of parenting: Adaptive and maladaptive processes. *Psychological Bulletin, 110,* 3–25.

Dockery, D. W., and others (1993). An association between air pollution and mortality in six U.S. cities. *New England Journal of Medicine, 329,* 1753–1759.

Dodge, K. A., Price, J. M., Bachorowski, J., & Newman, J. P. (1990). Hostile attributional biases in severely aggressive adolescents. *Journal of Abnormal Psychology, 99,* 385–392.

Doherty, W. J., Schrott, H. G., Metcalf, L., & Iasiello-Vailas, L. (1983). Effects of spouse support and health beliefs on medication adherence. *Journal of Family Practice, 17,* 837–841.

Dollard, J., Doob, L. W., Miller, N. E., Mowrer, O. H., & Sears, R. R. (1939). *Frustration and aggression.* New Haven, CT: Yale University Press.

Donnerstein, E. I., & Wilson, D. W. (1976). Effects of noise and perceived control on ongoing and subsequent aggressive behavior. *Journal of Personality and Social Psychology, 34,* 774–781.

Doob, A. N., & Wood, L. (1972). Catharsis and aggression: The effects of annoyance and retaliation on aggressive behavior. *Journal of Personality and Social Psychology, 22,* 236–245.

Dovidio, J. H., Evans, N., & Tyler, R. B. (1986). Racial stereotypes: The contents of their cognitive representations. *Journal of Experimental Social Psychology, 22,* 22–37.

Doyle, W. (1986). Classroom organization and management. In M. Wittrock (Ed.), *Handbook of research on teaching* (3rd ed). New York: Macmillan.

Draguns, J. G. (1988). Personality and culture: Are they relevant for the enhancement of quality of mental life? In P. R. Dasen, J. W. Berry, & N. Sartorius (Eds.), *Health and cross-cultural psychology: Toward applications.* Newbury Park, CA: Sage.

Dubbert, P. M. (1992). Exercise in behavioral medicine. *Journal of Consulting and Clinical Psychology, 60,* 613–618.

Duckitt, J. (1992). Psychology and prejudice: A historical analysis and integrative framework. *American Psychologist, 47,* 1182–1193.

Dugan, K. W. (1989). Ability and effort attributions: Do they affect how managers communicate performance feedback information? *Academy of Management Journal, 32,* 87–114.

Duke, M. P., & Nowicki, S. (1972). A new measure and social learning model for interpersonal distance. *Journal of Experimental Research in Personality, 6,* 119–132.

Dumas, J. E., & LaFreniere, P. J. (1993). Mother–child relationships as sources of support or stress: A comparison of competent, average, aggressive, and anxious dyads. *Child Development, 64.*

Dunbar-Jacob, J. (1993). Contributions to patient adherence: Is it time to share the blame? *Health Psychology, 12,* 91–92.

Duval, T. S., Duval, V. H., & Mulilis, J. (1992). Effects of self-focus, discrepancy between self and standard, and outcome expectancy favorability on the tendency to match self to standard or to withdraw. *Journal of Personality and Social Psychology, 62,* 340–348.

Dweck, C. S. (1990). Self-theories and goals: Their role in motivation, personality, and development. In R. A. Dienstbier (Ed.), *Nebraska Symposium on Motivation:* Vol. 38. (pp. 199–235). Lincoln: University of Nebraska Press.

Dywan, J., & Bowers, K. S. (1983). The use of hypnosis to enhance recall. *Science, 222,* 184–185.

Eagly, A. H. (1983). Gender and social influence: A social psychological analysis. *American Psychologist, 38,* 971–981.

Eagly, A. H. (1987). *Sex differences in social behavior: A social-role interpretation.* Hillsdale, NJ: Erlbaum.

Eagly, A. H., Ashmore, R. D., Makhijani, M. G., & Longo, L. C. (1991). What is beautiful is good, but . . .: A meta-analytic review of research on the physical attractiveness stereotype. *Psychological Bulletin, 110,* 109–128.

Eagly, A. H., & Chaiken, S. (1993). *The psychology of attitudes.* Fort Worth, TX: Harcourt Brace Jovanovich.

Eagly, A. H., & Steffen, V. J. (1984). Gender stereotypes stem from the distribution of men and women into social roles. *Journal of Personality and Social Psychology, 46,* 735–754.

Ebbeson, E. B., & Bowers, J. B. (1974). Proportion of risky to conservative arguments in a group discussion and choice shift. *Journal of Personality and Social Psychology, 29,* 316–327.

Ebbinghaus, H. (1913). *Memory: A contribution to experimental psychology.* (H. A. Roger & C. E. Bussenius, Trans.). New York: Columbia University Press. (Original work published 1885)

Eckholm, E. (1994, March 6). AIDS still immune to the onslaught of medical science. *The New York Times,* pp. E1, E4.

Edgerton, J. W. (1994). Working with key players for psychological and mental health services. *American Psychologist, 49,* 314–321.

Edgley, C. (1989). Commercial sex: Pornography, prostitution, and advertising. In K. McKinney & S. Sprecher (Eds.), *Human sexuality: The societal and interpersonal context.* Norwood, NJ: Ablex.

Edwards, D. J. A. (1972). Approaching the unfamiliar: A study of human interaction differences. *Journal of Behavioral Sciences, 1,* 249–250.

Edwards, D. L. (1991). A meta-analysis of the effects of meditation and hypnosis on measures of anxiety (Doctoral dissertation, Texas A&M University, 1990). *Dissertation Abstracts International, 52,* 1039B.

Egeth, H. E. (1993). What do we not know about eyewitness identification? *American Psychologist, 48,* 577–580.

Ehlers, A., & Breuer, P. (1992). Increased cardiac awareness in panic disorder. *Journal of Abnormal Psychology, 101,* 371–382.

Eidelson, R. J., & Epstein, N. (1982). Cognition and relationship maladjustment: Development of a measure of dysfunctional relationship beliefs. *Journal of Consulting and Clinical Psychology, 50,* 715–720.

Eisenberg, N., Cialdini, R. B., McCreath, H., & Shell, R. (1987). Consistency-based compliance: When and why do children become vulnerable? *Journal of Personality and Social Psychology, 52,* 1174–1181.

Eisenman, R. (1985). Marijuana use and attraction: Support for Byrne's similarity-attraction paradigm. *Perceptual and Motor Skills, 61,* 582.

Ekman, P. (1980). *The face of man.* New York: Garland.

Ekman, P. (1992). Are there basic emotions? *Psychological Review, 99,* 550–553.

Ekman, P. (1993a). Facial expression and emotion. *American Psychologist, 48,* 384–392.

Ekman, P. (1993b). Cited in D. Goleman (1993, October 26). One smile (only one) can lift a mood. *The New York Times,* p. C11.

Ekman, P. (1994). Strong evidence for universals in facial expression. *Psychological Bulletin, 115,* 268–287.

Ekman, P., Davidson, R. J., & Friesen, W. V. (1990). The Duchenne smile: Emotional expression and brain physiology II. *Journal of Personality and Social Psychology, 58,* 342–353.

Ekman, P., and others (1987). Universals and cultural differences in the judgments of facial expressions of emotion. *Journal of Personality and Social Psychology, 53,* 712–717.

Ekman, P., Levenson, R. W., & Friesen, W. V. (1983). Autonomic nervous system activity distinguishes among emotions. *Science, 221,* 1208–1210.

Ekman, P., & Oster, H. (1979). Facial expressions of emotion. Annual *Review of Psychology* (Vol. 30). Palo Alto, CA: Annual Reviews.

Elkins, R. L. (1980). Covert sensitization treatment of alcoholism. *Addictive Behaviors, 5,* 67–89.

Ellickson, P. L., Hays, R. D., & Bell, R. M. (1992). Stepping through the drug use sequence: Longitudinal scalogram analysis of initiation and regular use. *Journal of Abnormal Psychology, 101,* 441–451.

Ellis, A. (1977). The basic clinical theory of rational-emotive therapy. In A. Ellis & R. Grieger (Eds.), *Handbook of rational-emotive therapy.* New York: Springer.

Ellis, A. (1993). Reflections on rational-emotive therapy. *Journal of Consulting and Clinical Psychology, 61,* 199–201.

Ellis, L. (1990). Prenatal stress may effect sex-typical behaviors of a child. *Brown University Child Behavior and Development Letter, 6*(1), pp. 1-3.

Ellis, L. (1991). A synthesized (biosocial) theory of rape. *Journal of Consulting and Clinical Psychology, 59,* 631–642.

Ellis, L., & Ames, M. A. (1987). Neurohormonal functioning and sexual orientation: A theory of homosexuality–heterosexuality. *Psychological Bulletin, 101,* 233–258.

Ellsworth, P. C., Carlsmith, J. M., & Henson, A. (1972). The stare as a stimulus to flight in human subjects. *Journal of Personality and Social Psychology, 21,* 302–311.

Emde, R. (1993). Cited in Adler, T. (1993). Shy, bold temperament? It's mostly in the genes. *APA Monitor, 24*(1), 7, 8.

Emery, R. E. (1989). Family violence. *American Psychologist, 44,* 321–328.

Engels, G. I., Garnefski, N., & Diekstra, R. F. W. (1993). Efficacy of rational-emotive therapy: A quantitative analysis. *Journal of Consulting and Clinical Psychology, 61,* 1083–1090.

Engen, T. (1991). *Odor sensation and memory.* New York: Praeger.

Epstein, L. H., Wing, R. R., Koeske, R., & Valoski, A. (1984). Effects of diet plus exercise on weight change in parents and children. *Journal of Consulting and Clinical Psychology, 52,* 429–437.

Erikson, E. H. (1963). *Childhood and society.* New York: W. W. Norton.

Eron, L. D. (1982). Parent–child interaction, television violence, and aggression of children. *American Psychologist, 37,* 197–211.

Eron, L. D. (1993). Cited in DeAngelis, T. (1993b). It's baaack: TV violence, concern for kid viewers. *APA Monitor, 24*(8), 16.

Espenshade, T. (1993). Cited in Barringer, F. (1993, April 25). Polling on sexual issues has its drawbacks. *The New York Times,* p. A23.

Esterling, B. A., Antoni, M. H., Kumar, M., & Schneiderman, N. (1993). Defensivesness, trait anxiety, and Epstein–Barr viral capsid antigen antibody titers in healthy college students. *Health Psychology, 12,* 132–139.

Estes, W. K. (1972). An associative basis for coding and organization in memory. In A. W. Melton & E. Martin (Eds.), *Coding processes in human memory.* Washington, DC: Winston.

Etaugh, C., & Rathus, S. A. (1995). *The world of children.* Fort Worth: Harcourt Brace.

Etcoff, N. L. (1994). Cited in Brody, J. E. (1994, March 21). Notions of beauty transcend culture, new study suggests. *The New York Times,* p. A14.

Evans, D. A., and others (1989). Prevalence of Alzheimer's disease in a community population of older persons. *Journal of the American Medical Association, 262,* 2551–2556.

Evans, G. W., Jacobs, S. V., & Frager, N. B. (1982). Behavioral responses to air pollution. In A. Baum & J. E. Singer (Eds.), *Advances in environmental psychology* (Vol. 4). Hillsdale, NJ: Erlbaum.

Eysenck, H. J. (1991). *Smoking, personality, and stress: Psychosocial factors in the prevention of cancer and coronary heart disease.* New York: Springer–Verlag.

Eysenck, H. J. (1993). Comment on Goldberg. *American Psychologist, 48,* 1299–1300.

Eysenck, H. J., & Eysenck, M. W. (1985). *Personality and individual differences.* New York: Plenum.

Fabricius, W. V., & Wellman, H. M. (1983). Children's understanding of retrieval cue utilization. *Developmental Psychology, 19,* 15–21.

Fairstein, L. A. (1993). *Sexual violence: Our war against rape.* New York: William Morrow.

Fallon, A. E., & Rozin, P. (1985). Sex differences in perceptions of desirable body shape. *Journal of Abnormal Psychology, 94,* 102–105.

Fantz, R. L. (1961). The origin of form perception. *Scientific American, 204*(5), 66–72.

Farina, A., Burns, G. L., Austad, C., Bugglin, C. S., & Fischer, E. H. (1986). The role of physical attractiveness in the readjustment of discharged psychiatric patients. *Journal of Abnormal Psychology, 95,* 139–143.

Farley, F. (1993a). Cited in Michaelson, R. (1993). Farley calls for more money for health, behavior research. *APA Monitor, 24*(4), 7.

Farley, F. (1993b). Wisconsin on the Potomac. *APA Monitor, 24*(4), 3.

Farrell, A. D., Camplair, P. S., & McCullough, L. (1987). Identification of target complaints by computer interview: Evaluation of the Computerized Assessment System for Psychotherapy Evaluation and Research. *Journal of Consulting and Clinical Psychology, 55,* 691–700.

Farthing, G. W., Venturino, M., & Brown, S. W. (1984). Suggestion and distraction in the control of pain: Test of two hypotheses. *Journal of Abnormal Psychology, 93,* 266–276.

Fazio, R. H. (1990). Multiple processes by which attitudes guide behavior: The MODE model as an integrative framework. In M. P. Zanna (Ed.), *Advances in experimental social psychology.* San Diego, CA: Academic Press.

Fehr, B., & Russell, J. A. (1991). The concept of love viewed from a prototype perspective. *Journal of Personality and Social Psychology, 60,* 425–438.

Feingold, A. (1992a). Gender differences in mate selection preferences: A test of the parental investment model. *Psychological Bulletin, 112,* 125–139.

Feingold, A. (1992b). Good-looking people are not what we think. *Psychological Bulletin, 111,* 304–341.

Ferguson-Peters, M. (1985). Racial socialization of young Black children. In H. McAdoo & J. L. McAdoo (Eds.), *Black children* (pp. 159–173). Beverly Hills, CA: Sage.

Ferin, M., Jewelewicz, R., & Warren, M. (1993). *The menstrual cycle: Physiology, reproductive disorders, and infertility.* New York: Oxford University Press.

Feshbach, S. (1994). Nationalism, patriotism, and aggression: A clarification of functional differences. In L. R. Huesmann (Ed.), *Aggressive behavior: current perspectives.* New York: Plenum.

Festinger, L. (1957). *A theory of cognitive dissonance.* Evanston, IL: Row, Peterson.

Festinger, L., & Carlsmith, J. M. (1959). Cognitive consequences of forced compliance. *Journal of Abnormal and Social Psychology, 58,* 203–210.

Festinger, L., Riecken, H. W., Jr., & Schachter, S. (1956). *When prophecy fails.* Minneapolis: University of Minnesota Press.

Field, T. M. (1991). Young children's adaptations to repeated separations from their mothers. *Child Development, 62,* 539–547.

Findley, M. J., & Cooper, H. M. (1983). Locus of control and academic achievement: A literature review. *Journal of Personality and Social Psychology, 44,* 419–427.

Finkelhor, D., & Dziuba-Leatherman, J. (1994). Victimization of children. *American Psychologist, 49,* 173–183.

Fischbach, G. D. (1992). Mind and brain. *Scientific American, 267*(3), 48–57.

Fischer, K. W., Shaver, P. R., & Carochan, P. (1990). How emotions develop and how they organize development. *Cognition and Emotion, 4,* 81–127.

Fisher, C. B., & Fyrberg, D. (1994). Participant partners: College students weigh the costs and benefits of deceptive research. *American Psychologist, 49,* 417–427.

Fisher, H. E. (1992). *Anatomy of love: The natural history of monogamy, adultery and divorce.* New York: W. W. Norton.

Fiske, S. T. (1993). Controlling other people: The impact of power on stereotyping. *American Psychologist, 48,* 621–628.

Fiske, S. T., & Taylor, S. E. (1984). *Social cognition.* Reading, MA: Addison–Wesley.

Fitzgerald, L. F. (1993). Sexual harassment: Violence against women in the workplace. *American Psychologist, 48,* 1070–1076.

Fitzgibbon, M. L., Stolley, M. R., & Kirschenbaum, D. S. (1993). Obese people who seek treatment have different characteristics than those who do not seek treatment. *Health Psychology, 12,* 342–345.

Flaherty, J. F., & Dusek, J. B. (1980). An investigation of the relationship between psychological androgyny and components of self-concept. *Journal of Personality and Social Psychology, 38,* 984–992.

Flavell, J. H., Miller, P. H., & Miller, S. A. (1993). *Cognitive development* (3rd ed.). Englewood Cliffs, NJ: Prentice-Hall.

Flor, H., & Birbaumer, N. (1993). Comparison of the efficacy of electromyographic biofeedback, cognitive–behavioral therapy, and conservative medical intervention in the treatment of chronic musculoskeletal pain. *Journal of Consulting and Clinical Psychology, 61,* 653–658.

Flor, H., Fydrich, T., & Turk, D. C. (1992). Efficacy of multidisciplinary pain treatment centers: A meta-analytic review. *Pain, 49,* 221–230.

Foa, E. B. (1990, August/September). Obsessive–compulsive disorder. *DSM-IV Update.* Washington, DC: American Psychiatric Association.

Folkman, S., & Lazarus, R. S. (1985). If it changes it must be a process: Study of emotion and coping during three stages of a college examination. *Journal of Personality and Social Psychology, 48,* 150–170.

Ford, E. S., and others (1991). Physical activity behaviors in lower and higher socioeconomic status populations. *American Journal of Epidemiology, 133,* 1246–1256.

Foreyt, J. P. (1986). Treating the diseases of the 1980s: Eating disorders. *Contemporary Psychology, 31,* 658–660.

Fowler, R. D. (1992). Solid support needed for animal research. *APA Monitor, 23*(6), 2.

Francis, D. (1984). *Will you still need me, will you still feed me, when I'm 84?* Bloomington: Indiana University Press.

Frankel, K. A., & Bates, J. E. (1990). Mother–toddler problem solving: Antecedents in attachment, home behavior, and temperament. *Child Development, 61,* 810–819.

Franzoi, S. L., & Herzog, M. E. (1987). Judging physical attractiveness: What body aspects do we use? *Personality and Social Psychology Bulletin, 13,* 19–33.

Freed, C. R., and others (1992). Survival of implanted fetal dopamine cells and neurologic improvement 12 to 46 months after transplantation for Parkinson's disease. *New England Journal of Medicine, 327,* 1549–1555.

Freedman, D. (1994). *Brainmakers: How scientists are moving beyond computers to make a rival to the human brain.* New York: Simon & Schuster.

Freedman, D. X. (1993, August 8). On "Beyond wellness." *The New York Times Book Review,* p. 6.

Freedman, J. L., & Fraser, S. C. (1966). Compliance without pressure: The foot-in-the-door technique. *Journal of Personality and Social Psychology, 4,* 195–202.

Freedman, J. L., Wallington, S. A., & Bless, E. (1967). Compliance without pressure: The effect of guilt. *Journal of Personality and Social Psychology, 7,* 117–124.

Freeman, A. M. (1990, December 18). Deadly diet. *The Wall Street Journal,* pp. 1, B1.

Freeman, M. S., Spence, M. J., & Oliphant, C. M. (1993, June). *Newborns prefer their mothers' low-pass filtered voices over other female filtered voices.* Paper presented at the annual convention of the American Psychological Society, Chicago.

Freud, S. (1959). Analysis of a phobia in a 5-year-old boy. In *Collected papers* (Vol. 3). (A. & J. Strachey, Trans.). New York: Basic Books (Original work published 1909).

Freud, S. (1961). *Civilization and its discontents* (J. Strachey, Trans.). New York: W. W. Norton (Original work published 1930).

Freud, S. (1964a). New introductory lectures. In *Standard edition of the complete psychological works of Sigmund Freud* (Vol. 22). London: Hogarth (Original work published 1933).

Freud, S. (1964b). A religious experience. In *Standard edition of the complete psychological works of Sigmund Freud* (Vol. 21). London: Hogarth (Original work published 1927).

Friedman, H. S., & Booth-Kewley, S. (1987). Personality, type A behavior, and coronary heart disease: The role of emotional expression. *Journal of Personality and Social Psychology, 53,* 783–792.

Friedman, M., & Ulmer, D. (1984). *Treating type A behavior and your heart.* New York: Fawcett Crest.

Friman, P. C., Allen, K. D., Kerwin, M. L. E., & Larzelere, R. (1993). Changes in modern psychology: A citation analysis of the Kuhnian displacement thesis. *American Psychologist, 48,* 658–664.

Frodi, A. M. (1985). When empathy fails: Infant crying and child abuse. In B. M. Lester & C. F. Z. Boukydis (Eds.), *Infant crying.* New York: Plenum.

Frodi, A. M., Macauley, J., & Thome, P. R. (1977). Are women always less aggressive than men? A review of the experimental literature. *Psychological Bulletin, 84,* 634–660.

Furedy, J. J. (1990, July). *Experimental psychophysiology and pseudoscientific polygraphy: Conceptual concerns and practical problems.* Symposium at the 5th International Congress of Psychophysiology, Budapest, Hungary.

Furumoto, L. (1992). Joining separate spheres—Christine Ladd-Franklin, woman-scientist. *American Psychologist, 47,* 175–182.

Gable, D. (1993, July 26). Public wants TV crime reined in. *USA Today,* p. D3.

Galambos, N. L. (1992, October). Parent–adolescent relations. *Current Directions in Psychological Science,* 146–149.

Galambos, N. L., & Almeida, D. M. (1992). Does parent–adolescent conflict increase in early adolescence? *Journal of Marriage and the Family, 54,* 737–747.

Galassi, J. P. (1988). Four cognitive-behavioral approaches: Additional considerations. *The Counseling Psychologist, 16*(1), 102–105.

Gallucci, W. T., and others. (1993). Sex differences in sensitivity of the hypothalamic-pituitary-adrenal axis. *Health Psychology, 12,* 420–425.

Gallup, G. H., & Newport, F. (1991). Belief in paranormal phenomena among adult Americans. *Skeptical Inquirer, 15*(4), 137–146.

Ganellen, R. J., & Blaney, P. H. (1984). Hardiness and social support as moderators of the effects of life stress. *Journal of Personality and Social Psychology, 47,* 156–163.

Garcia, J. (1981). The logic and limits of mental aptitude testing. *American Psychologist, 36,* 1172–1180.

Garcia, J. (1993). Misrepresentation of my criticism of Skinner. *American Psychologist, 48,* 1158.

Garcia, J., Brett, L. P., & Rusiniak, K. W. (1989). Limits of Darwinian conditioning. In S. B. Klein & R. R. Mowrer (Eds.), *Contemporary learning theories: Instrumental conditioning theory and the impact of biological constraints on learning.* Hillsdale, NJ: Erlbaum.

Garcia, J., & Koelling, R. A. (1966). Relation of cue to consequences in avoidance learning. *Psychonomic Science 4,* 123–124.

Gardner, H. (1983). *Frames of mind: The theory of multiple intelligences.* New York: Basic Books.

Gardner, H., & Hatch, T. (1989). Multiple intelligences go to school: Educational implications of the theory of multiple intelligences. *Educational Researcher, 18*(8), 4–10.

Garland, A. F., & Zigler, E. (1993). Adolescent suicide prevention: Current research and social policy implications. *American Psychologist, 48,* 169–182.

Garnets, L., & Kimmel, D. (1991). In J. D. Goodchilds (Ed.). *Psychological perspectives on human diversity in America.* Washington, DC: American Psychological Association.

Gastorf, J. W., & Galanos, A. N. (1983). Patient compliance and physicians' attitude. *Family Practice Research Journal, 2,* 190–198.

Gauthier, J., Côte, G., & French, D. (1994). The role of home practice in the thermal biofeedback treatment of migraine headache. *Journal of Consulting and Clinical Psychology, 62,* 180–184.

Gayle, H. D., and others (1990). Prevalence of human immunodeficiency virus among university students. *New England Journal of Medicine, 323,* 1538–1541.

Gaziano, J. M., and others (1993). Moderate alcohol intake, increased levels of high-density lipoprotein and its subfractions, and decreased risk of myocardial infarction. *New England Journal of Medicine, 329,* 1829–1834.

Gazzaniga, M. S. (1992). *Nature's mind.* New York: Basic Books.

Gebhardt, D. L., & Crump, C. E. (1990). Employee fitness and wellness programs in the workplace. *American Psychologist, 45,* 262–272.

Geen, R. G., Stonner, D., & Shope, G. L. (1975). The facilitation of aggression by aggression: Evidence against the catharsis hypothesis. *Journal of Personality and Social Psychology, 31,* 721–726.

Geisinger, K. (1992). *Psychological testing of Hispanics.* Washington, DC: American Psychological Association.

Gelernter, D. (1994). *The muse in the machine: Computerizing the poetry of human thought.* New York: The Free Press.

Geller, E. S. (1990). Preventing injuries and deaths from vehicle crashes: Encouraging belts and discouraging booze. In J. Edwards and others (Eds.), *Social influence processes and prevention.* New York: Plenum.

Gelman, R., & Baillargeon, R. (1983). A review of some Piagetan concepts. In J. Flavell & E. Markman (Eds.), *Handbook of child psychology.* New York: Wiley.

Gentry, J., & Eron, L. D. (1993). American Psychological Association Commission on Violence and Youth. *American Psychologist, 48,* 89.

Gershon, E. S., & Rieder, R. O. (1992). Major disorders of mind and brain. *Scientific American, 267*(3), 126–133.

Gerstner, L. V., Jr. (1994, May 27). Our schools are failing. Do we care? *The New York Times,* p. A27.

Getzels, J. W., & Jackson, P. W. (1962). *Creativity and intelligence: Explorations with gifted students.* New York: Wiley.

Gfeller, J. D., Lynn, S. J., & Pribble, W. E. (1987). Enhancing hypnotic susceptibility: Interpersonal and rapport factors. *Journal of Personality and Social Psychology, 52,* 586–595.

Gibbs, J. T. (1992). Negotiating ethnic identity: Issues for Black–White biracial adolescents. In M. P. P. Root (Ed.), *Racially mixed people in America.* Newbury Park, CA: Sage.

Gibbs, N. (1991, June 3). When is it rape? *Time,* pp. 48–54.

Gibson, E. J., & Walk, R. D. (1960, April). The visual cliff. *Scientific American, 202,* 64–71.

Gibson, M., & Ogbu, J. (Eds.). (1991). *Minority status and schooling: A comparative study of immigrant and involuntary minorities.* New York: Garland.

Gigerenzer, G., Hoffrage, U., & Kleinbölting, H. (1991). Probabilistic mental models: A Brunswikian theory of confidence. *Psychological Review, 98,* 506–528.

Gilbert, S. (1993, April 25). Waiting game. *The New York Times Magazine,* pp. 70–72, 92.

Gilbert, S. J. (1981). Another look at the Milgram obedience studies: The role of the gradated series of shocks. *Personality and Social Psychology Bulletin, 7,* 690–695.

Gilligan, C. (1982). *In a different voice.* Cambridge, MA: Harvard University Press.

Gilligan, C., Lyons, P., & Hanmer, T. J. (Eds.). (1990). *Making connections.* Cambridge, MA: Harvard University Press.

Gilligan, C., Rogers, A. G., & Tolman, D. L. (Eds.). (1991). *Women, girls, and psychotherapy.* New York: Haworth.

Gilligan, C., Ward, J. V., & Taylor, J. M. (1989). *Mapping the moral domain: A contribution of women's thinking to psychological theory and education.* Cambridge, MA: Harvard University Press.

Gillin, J. C. (1991). The long and the short of sleeping pills. *New England Journal of Medicine, 324,* 1735–1736.

Gillin, J. C., & Byerley, W. F. (1990). The diagnosis and management of insomnia. *New England Journal of Medicine, 322,* 239–248.

Gillis, A. R., Richard, M. A., & Hagan, J. (1986). Ethnic susceptibility to crowding. *Environment and Behavior, 18,* 683–706.

Gillis, J. S., & Avis, W. E. (1980). The male-taller norm in mate selection. *Personality and Social Psychology Bulletin, 6,* 396–401.

Gilman, A. G., and others (1990). *Goodman and Gilman's the pharmacological basis of therapeutics* (8th ed.). New York: Pergamon.

Gilovich, T. (1983). Biased evaluation and persistence in gambling. *Journal of Personality and Social Psychology, 44,* 1110–1126.

Ginsburg, G., & Bronstein, P. (1993). Family factors related to children's intrinsic/extrinsic motivational orientation and academic performance. *Child Development, 64,* 1461–1474.

Giovannoni, J. (1989). Definitional issues in child maltreatment. In D. Cicchetti & V. Carlson (Eds.), *Child maltreatment: Theory and research on the causes and consequences of child abuse and neglect* (pp. 3–37). Cambridge: Cambridge University Press.

Glaser, R., and others (1991). Stress-related activation of Epstein–Barr virus. *Brain, Behavior, and Immunity, 5,* 219–232.

Glaser, R., and others (1993). Stress and the memory T-cell response to the Epstein-Barr virus. *Health Psychology, 12,* 435–442.

Glasgow, R. E., Klesges, R. C., Klesges, L. M., Vasey, M. W., & Gunnarson, D. F. (1985). Long-term effects of a controlled smoking program: A two and one-half year follow-up. *Behavior Therapy, 16,* 303–307.

Glasner, P. D., & Kaslow, R. A. (1990). The epidemiology of human immunodeficiency virus infection. *Journal of Consulting and Clinical Psychology, 58,* 13–21.

Gleason, J. B., & Ratner, N. B. (1993). Language development in children. In J. B. Gleason & N. B. Ratner (Eds.), *Psycholinguistics.* Fort Worth, TX: Harcourt Brace Jovanovich.

Gleaves, D. H., Williamson, D. A., & Barker, S. E. (1993). Confirmatory factor analysis of a multidimensional model of bulimia nervosa. *Journal of Abnormal Psychology, 102,* 173–176.

Glenn, S. S., Ellis, J., & Greenspoon, J. (1992). On the revolutionary nature of the operant as a unit of behavioral selection. *American Psychologist, 47,* 1326–1329.

Glover, J. A., Ronning, R. R., & Bruning, R. H. (1990). *Cognitive psychology for teachers.* New York: Macmillan.

Godden, D. R., & Baddeley, A. D. (1975). Context-dependent memory in two natural environments: On land and underwater. *British Journal of Psychology, 66,* 325–331.

Goelet, P., and others (1986). The long and the short of long-term memory—A molecular framework. *Nature, 322,* 419–422.

Gold, J. A., Ryckman, R. M., & Mosley, N. R. (1984). Romantic mood induction and attraction to a dissimilar other: Is love blind? *Personality and Social Psychology Bulletin, 10,* 358–368.

Gold, M. S. (1993). *Cocaine: Drugs of abuse: A comprehensive series for clinicians* (Vol. 3). New York: Plenum.

Goldberg, L. R. (1993). The structure of phenotypic personality traits. *American Psychologist, 48,* 26–34.

Goldberg, L. W. (1978). Differential attribution of trait-descriptive terms to oneself as compared to well-liked, neutral, and dis-liked others. *Journal of Personality and Social Psychology, 36,* 1012–1028.

Goldfarb, L. A., Dykens, E. M., & Gerrard, M. (1985). The Goldfarb Fear of Fat Scale. *Journal of Personality Assessment, 49,* 329–332.

Goldman, J. A., & Harlow, L. L. (1993). Self-perception variables that mediate AIDS-preventive behavior in college students. *Health Psychology, 12,* 489–498.

Goldman, K. (1993, June 1). Jordan & Co. play ball on Madison Avenue. *The Wall Street Journal,* p. B9.

Goldman-Rakic, P. S. (1992). Working memory and the mind. *Scientific American, 267*(3), 110–117.

Goldsmith, H. H. (1993). Cited in Adler, T. (1993). Shy, bold temperament? It's mostly in the genes. *APA Monitor, 24*(1), 7, 8.

Goldstein, I. L., & Buxton, V. M. (1982). Training and human performance. In M. D. Dunnette & E. A. Fleishman (Eds.), *Human Performance and Productivity, 1,* 135–177.

Goldstein, T. (1988, February 12). Women in the law aren't yet equal partners. *The New York Times,* p. B7.

Goleman, D. J. (1992, January 8). Heart seizure or panic attack? Disorder is a terrifying mimic. *The New York Times,* p. C12.

Goleman, D. J. (1993, April 6). Studying the secrets of childhood memory. *The New York Times,* pp. C1, C11.

Gomez, J., & Smith, B. (1990). Taking the home out of homophobia: Black lesbian health. In E. C. White (Ed.), *The Black women's health book: Speaking for ourselves.* Seattle: Seal Press.

Goodchilds, J. D. (1991). (Ed.). *Psychological perspectives on human diversity in America.* Washington, DC: American Psychological Association.

Goodgame, R. W. (1990). AIDS in Uganda—Clinical and social features. *New England Journal of Medicine, 323,* 383–389.

Goodman, L. A., Koss, M. P., Fitzgerald, L. F., Russo, N. F., & Keita, G. W. (1993). Male violence against women: Current research and future directions. *American Psychologist, 48,* 1054–1058.

Goodwin, D. W. (1985). Alcoholism and genetics. *Archives of General Psychiatry, 42,* 171–174.

Goodwin, F. K., & Jamison, K. R. (1990). *Manic-depressive illness.* New York: Oxford University Press.

Gortmaker, S. L., and others. (1993). Social and economic consequences of over-weight in adolescence and young adulthood. *New England Journal of Medicine, 329,* 1008–1012.

Gotlib, I. H., Lewinsohn, P. M., Seeley, J. R., Rohde, P., & Redner, J. E. (1993). Negative cognitions and attributional style in depressed adolescents: An examination of stability and specificity. *Journal of Abnormal Psychology, 102,* 607–615.

Gottesman, I. I. (1991). *Schizophrenia genesis: The origins of madness.* New York: Freeman.

Gottfried, A. E., Fleming, J. S., & Gottfried, A. W. (1994). Role of parental motivational practices in children's academic intrinsic motivation and achievement. *Journal of Educational Psychology, 86,* 104–113.

Graesser, A. C., & Nakamura, G. V. (1982). The impact of a schema on comprehension and memory. In G. H. Bower (Ed.), *The psychology of learning and motivation* (Vol. 16). New York: Academic Press.

Granberg, D., & Brent, E. (1983). When prophecy bends: The preference–expectation link in U.S. presidential elections. *Journal of Personality and Social Psychology, 45,* 477–491.

Grant, I., & Heaton, R. K. (1990). Human immunodeficiency virus-type 1 (HIV-1) and the brain. *Journal of Consulting and Clinical Psychology, 58,* 22–30.

Green, J. A., Jones, L. E., & Gustafson, G. E. (1987). Perception of cries by parents and nonparents: Relation to cry acoustics. *Developmental Psychology, 23,* 370–382.

Green, S. K., Buchanan, D. R., & Heuer, S. K. (1984). Winners, losers, and choosers: A field investigation of dating initiation. *Personality and Social Psychology Bulletin, 10,* 502–511.

Greenberg, J., & Kuczaj, S. A., II. (1982). Towards a theory of substantive word-meaning acquisition. In S. A. Kuczaj, II (Ed.), *Language development: Vol. 1. Syntax and semantics.* Hillsdale, NJ: Erlbaum.

Greenberg, P. D. (1987). Tumor immunology. In D. P. Stites and others (Eds.), *Basic and clinical immunology* (6th ed.). Norwalk, CT: Appleton & Lange.

Greenberg, R., Pearlman, C., Schwartz, W. R., & Grossman, H. Y. (1983). Memory, emotion, and REM sleep. *Journal of Abnormal Psychology, 92,* 378–381.

Greene, A. L., & Grimsley, L. D. (1990). Age and gender differences in adolescents' preferences for parental advice: Mum's the word. *Journal of Adolescent Research, 5,* 396–413.

Greene, A. S., & Saxe, L. (1990). *Tall tales told to teachers.* Unpublished manuscript, Brandeis University.

Greene, B. (1986). When the therapist is White and the patient is Black: Considerations for psychotherapy in the feminist heterosexual and lesbian communities. *Women & Therapy, 5,* 41–65.

Greene, B. (1990). Sturdy Bridges: The role of African American mothers in the socialization of African American children. *Women & Therapy, 10,* 205–225.

Greene, B. (1991). Personal communication.

Greene, B. (1992). Still here: A perspective on psychotherapy with African American women. In J. Chrisler & D. Howard (Eds.), *New directions in feminist psychology.* New York: Springer.

Greene, B. (1993). African American women. In L. Comas-Diaz & B. A. Greene (Eds.), *Women of color and mental health.* New York: Guilford.

Greene, B. (1994). Ethnic-minority lesbians and gay men: Mental health and treatment issues. *Journal of Consulting and Clinical Psychology, 62,* 243–251.

Greene, J. (1982). The gambling trap. *Psychology Today, 16*(9), 50–55.

Greeno, C. G., & Wing, R. R. (1994). Stress-induced eating. *Psychological Bulletin, 115,* 444–464.

Greenwald, A. G. (1992). New Look 3: Unconscious cognition reclaimed. *American Psychologist, 47,* 766–779.

Greist, J. H. (1984). Exercise in the treatment of depression. *Coping with mental stress: The potential and limits of exercise intervention.* Washington, DC: National Institute of Mental Health.

Griffin, E., & Sparks, G. G. (1990). Friends forever: A longitudinal exploration of intimacy in same-sex friends and platonic pairs. *Journal of Social and Personal Relationships, 7,* 29–46.

Grinspoon, L., & Bakalar, J. B. (1994). The war on drugs—A peace proposal. *New England Journal of Medicine, 330,* 357–360.

Grob, G. (1994). *The mad among us: A history of America's care of the mentally ill.* New York: The Free Press.

Gronlund, N. E. (1985). *Measurement and evaluation in teaching* (5th ed.). New York: Macmillan.

Grove, W. M., and others (1991). Familial prevalence and coaggregation of schizotypy indicators: A multitrait family study. *Journal of Abnormal Psychology, 100,* 115–121.

Growdon, J. H. (1992). Treatment for Alzheimer's disease. *New England Journal of Medicine, 327,* 1306–1308.

Gruber, V. A., & Wildman, B. G. (1987). The impact of dysmenorrhea on daily activities. *Behavior Research and Therapy, 25,* 123–128.

Gruber-Baldini, A. L. (1991). *The impact of health and disease on cognitive ability in adulthood and old age in the Seattle Longitudinal Study.* Unpublished doctoral dissertation, Pennsylvania State University.

Gruder, C. L., and others (1993). Effects of social support and relapse prevention training as adjuncts to a televised smoking-cessation intervention. *Journal of Consulting and Clinical Psychology, 61,* 113–120.

Grunberg, N. (1993a). Cited in Adler, T. Gum, patches aren't enough; to quit, counseling is advised. *APA Monitor, 24*(5), 16–17.

Grunberg, N. (1993b). Cited in Adler, T. Nicotine gives mixed results on learning and performance. *APA Monitor, 24*(5), 14–15.

Grush, J. E. (1980). The impact of candidate expenditures, regionality, and prior outcomes on the 1976 Democratic presidential primaries. *Journal of Personality and Social Psychology, 38,* 337–347.

Guilford, J. P. (1967). *The nature of human intelligence.* New York: McGraw–Hill.

Guilford, J. P. (1988). Some changes in the structure-of-intellect model. *Educational and Psychological Measurement, 48,* 1–4.

Guisinger, S., & Blatt, S. J. (1994). Individuality and relatedness: Evolution of a fundamental dialectic. *American Psychologist, 49,* 104–111.

Guralnik, J. M., Land, K. C., Blazer, D., Fillenbaum, G. G., & Branch, L. G. (1993). Educational status and active life expectancy among older Blacks and Whites. *New England Journal of Medicine,* 329, 110-116.

Guthrie, R. V. (1990). Cited in Korn, J. H., Davis, R., & Davis, S. F. (1991). Historians' and chairpersons' judgments of eminence among psychologists. *American Psychologist, 46,* 789–792.

Gutknecht, M. (1992). The "postmodern mind": Hybrid models of cognition. *Connection Science: Journal of Neural Computing, Artificial Intelligence and Cognitive Research, 4,* 339–364.

Haaf, R. A., Smith, P. H., & Smitley, S. (1983). Infant response to facelike patterns under fixed trial and infant-control procedures. *Child Development, 54,* 172–177.

Haaga, D. A. F., & Davison, G. C. (1993). An appraisal of rational-emotive therapy. *Journal of Consulting and Clinical Psychology, 61,* 215–220.

Haaland, K. Y. (1992). Introduction to the special section on the emotional concomitants of brain damage. *Journal of Consulting and Clinical Psychology, 60,* 327–328.

Haber, R. N. (1969). Eidetic images. *Scientific American, 220,* 36–55.

Haber, R. N. (1980). Eidetic images are not just imaginary. *Psychology Today, 14*(11), 72–82.

Hainline, L., & Abramov, I. (1992). Assessing visual development: Is infant vision good enough? In C. Rovee-Collier & L. P. Lipsitt (Eds.), *Advances in Infancy Research* (Vol. 7). Norwood, NJ: Ablex.

Haith, M. M. (1990). Progress in the understanding of sensory and perceptual processes early in infancy. *Merrill–Palmer Quarterly, 36,* 1–26.

Hall, J. (1989). *Learning and memory* (2nd ed.). Boston: Allyn & Bacon.

Hall, J. A., and others (1990). Performance quality, gender, and professional role: A study of physicians and nonphysicians in 16 ambulatory-care practices. *Medical Care, 28,* 489–501.

Hall, S. M., Havassy, B. E., & Wasserman, D. A. (1990). Commitment to abstinence and acute stress in relapse to alcohol, opiates, and nicotine. *Journal of Consulting and Clinical Psychology, 58,* 175–181.

Hall, S. M., Muñoz, R. F., Reus, V. I., & Sees, K. L. (1993). Nicotine, negative affect, and depression. *Journal of Consulting and Clinical Psychology, 61,* 761–767.

Halldin, M. (1985). Alcohol consumption and alcoholism in an urban population in central Sweden. *Acta Psychiatrica Scadinavica, 71,* 128–140.

Halperin, K. M., & Snyder, C. R. (1979). Effects of enhanced psychological test feedback on treatment outcome: Therapeutic implications of the Barnum effect. *Journal of Consulting and Clinical Psychology, 47,* 140–146.

Halpern, D. F. (1986). *Sex differences in cognitive abilities.* Hillsdale, NJ: Erlbaum.

Halpern, D. F. (1989). *Thought and knowledge: An introduction to critical thinking* (2nd ed.). Hillsdale, NJ: Erlbaum.

Halpern, D. F., Hansen, C., & Riefer, D. (1990). Analogies as an aid to understanding and memory. *Journal of Educational Psychology, 82,* 298–305.

Hamer, D., and others. (1993). Cited in Henry, W. A. (1993, July 26). Born gay? *Time,* pp. 36–39.

Hamilton, L. C. (1985). Self-reported and actual savings in a water conservation campaign. *Environment and Behavior, 17,* 315–326.

Hamilton, M., and others (1990). *The Duke University Medical Center book of diet and fitness.* New York: Fawcett Columbine.

Hamilton, R. J. (1985). A framework for the evaluation of the effectiveness of adjunct questions and objectives. *Review of Educational Research, 55,* 47–86.

Hamm, N. M., Baum, M. R., & Nikels, K. W. (1975). Effects of race and exposure on judgments of interpersonal favorability. *Journal of Experimental Social Psychology, 11,* 14–24.

Hammen, C., & Mayol, A. (1982). Depression and cognitive characteristics of stressful life-event types. *Journal of Abnormal Psychology, 91,* 165–174.

Hanson, K. A., & Gidycz, C. A. (1993). Evaluation of a sexual assault prevention program. *Journal of Consulting and Clinical Psychology, 61,* 1046–1052.

Harackiewicz, J. M., Sansone, C., Blair, L. W., Epstein, J. A., & Manderlink, G. (1987). Attributional processes in behavior change and maintenance: Smoking cessation and continued abstinence. *Journal of Consulting and Clinical Psychology, 55,* 372–378.

Hardy, J., and others (1991). *Nature,* February 21.

Hardy-Brown, K., & Plomin, R. (1985). Infant communicative development: Evidence from adoptive and biological families for genetic and environmental influences on rate differences. *Developmental Psychology, 21,* 378–385.

Hare, R. D., Hart, S. D., & Harpur, T. J. (1991). Psychopathy and the *DSM-IV* criteria for antisocial personality disorder. *Journal of Abnormal Psychology, 100,* 391–398.

Hare-Mustin, R. (1983). An appraisal of the relationship between women and psychotherapy: 80 years after the case of Dora. *American Psychologist, 38,* 593–601.

Harkins, S. (1987). Social loafing and social facilitation. *Journal of Experimental Social Psychology, 23,* 1–18.

Harlow, H. F. (1959). Love in infant monkeys. *Scientific American, 200,* 68–86.

Harlow, H. F. (1965). Sexual behavior in the rhesus monkey. In F. A. Beach (Ed.), *Sex and behavior.* New York: Wiley.

Harlow, H. F., Harlow, M. K., & Meyer, D. R. (1950). Learning motivated by a manipulation drive. *Journal of Experimental Psychology, 40,* 228–234.

Harlow, H. F., & Zimmermann, R. R. (1959). Affectional responses in the infant monkey. *Science, 130,* 421–432.

Harlow, M. K., & Harlow, H. F. (1966). Affection in primates. *Discovery, 27,* 11–17.

Harnishfeger, K. K., & Bjorklund, D. F. (1990). Children's strategies: A brief history. In D. F. Bjorklund (Ed.), *Children's strategies: Contemporary views of cognitive development* (pp. 1–184). Hillsdale, NJ: Erlbaum.

Harris, G. T., Rice, M. E., & Quinsey, V. L. (1994). Psychopathy as a taxon: Evidence that psychopaths are a discrete class. *Journal of Consulting and Clinical Psychology, 62,* 387–397.

Harris, T. A. (1967). *I'm OK—You're OK.* New York: Harper & Row.

Hartmann, E. L. (1981). The strangest sleep disorder. *Psychology Today, 15*(4), 14–18.

Hartz, A. J., and others (1984). The association of girth measurements with disease in 32,856 women. *American Journal of Epidemiology, 119,* 71–80.

Harwood, A. (1981). Mainland Puerto Ricans. In A. Harwood (Ed.), *Ethnicity and medical care.* Cambridge, MA: Harvard University Press.

Hashimoto, N. (1991). Memory development in early childhood: Encoding process in a special task. *Journal of Genetic Psychology, 152,* 101–117.

Hasselhorn, M. (1992). Task dependency and the role of typicality and metamemory in the development of an organizational strategy. *Child Development, 63,* 202–214.

Hatfield, M. O. (1990). Stress and the American worker. *American Psychologist, 45,* 1162–1164.

Hatsukami, D., LaBounty, L., Hughes, J., & Laine, D. (1993). Effects of tobacco abstinence on food intake among cigarette smokers. *Health Psychology, 12,* 499–502.

Hauser-Cram, P., Pierson, D. E., Walker, D. K., & Tivnan, T. (1991). *Early education in the public schools.* San Francisco: Jossey–Bass.

Hawkins, S. A., & Hastie, R. (1990). Hindsight: Biased judgments of past events after the outcomes are known. *Psychological Bulletin, 107,* 311–327.

Hayes, P. (1993). Cited in Chartrand, S. (1993, July 18). A split in thinking among keepers of artificial intelligence. *The New York Times,* p. E6.

Hayes, S. C. (Ed.). (1989). *Rule-governed behavior: Cognition, contingencies, and instructional control.* New York: Plenum.

Hayes, S. L. (1981). Single case design and empirical clinical practice. *Journal of Consulting and Clinical Psychology, 49,* 193–211.

Hays, R. B., Turner, H., & Coates, T. J. (1992). Social support, AIDS-related symptoms, and depression among gay men. *Journal of Consulting and Clinical Psychology, 60,* 463–469.

Heaton, R. K., & Victor, R. G. (1976). Personality characteristics associated with psychedelic flashbacks in natural and experimental settings. *Journal of Abnormal Psychology, 85,* 83–90.

Hedge, J. W., & Kavanaugh, M. J. (1988). Improving the accuracy of performance evaluations: Comparison of three methods of performance appraiser training. *Journal of Applied Psychology, 73,* 68–73.

Hefferline, R. F., & Keenan, B. (1963). Amplitude-induction gradient of a small-scale (covert) operant. *Journal of the Experimental Analysis of Behavior, 6,* 307–315.

Heider, F. (1958). *The psychology of interpersonal relations.* New York: Wiley.

Heim, M. (1993). *The metaphysics of virtual reality.* New York: Oxford University Press.

Heingartner, A., & Hall, J. V. (1974). Affective consequences in adults and children of repeated exposure to auditory stimuli. *Journal of Personality and Social Psychology, 29,* 719–723.

Hellams, R. P. (1993). Personal communication.

Heller, D. A., de Faire, U., Pedersen, N. L., Dahlén, G., & McClearn, G. E. (1993). Genetic and environmental influences on serum lipid levels in twins. *New England Journal of Medicine, 328,* 1150–1156.

Hellige, J. B. (1990). Hemispheric assymetry. *Annual Review of Psychology, 41,* 55–80.

Helmes, E., & Reddon, J. R. (1993). A perspective on developments in assessing psychopathology: A critical review of the MMPI and MMPI-2. *Psychological Bulletin, 113,* 453–471.

Helms, J. E. (1992). Why is there no study of cultural equivalence of standardized cognitive ability testing? *American Psychologist, 47,* 1083–1101.

Helson, R., & Moane, G. (1987). Personality change in women from college to midlife. *Journal of Personality and Social Psychology, 53,* 176–186.

Helzer, J. E. (1987). Epidemiology of alcoholism. *Journal of Consulting and Clinical Psychology, 55,* 284–292.

Helzer, J. E., & Schuckit, M. A. (1990, August/September). Substance use disorders. *DSM-IV Update.* Washington, DC: American Psychiatric Association.

Hendrick, C. D., Wells, K. S., & Faletti, M. V. (1982). Social and emotional effects of geographical relocation on elderly retirees. *Journal of Personality and Social Psychology, 42,* 951–962.

Hendrick, S. S., & Hendrick, C. (1977). Aging in mass society: *Myths and realities.* Cambridge, MA: Winthrop.

Hendrick, S. S., Hendrick, C., Slapion-Foote, M. J., & Foote, F. H. (1985). Gender differences in sexual attitudes. *Journal of Personality and Social Psychology, 48,* 1630–1642.

Henkin, W. A. (1985). Toward counseling the Japanese in America: A cross-cultural primer. *Journal of Counseling and Development, 63,* 500–503.

Hennigan, K. M., Cook, T. D., & Gruder, C. L. (1982). Cognitive tuning set, source credibility, and the temporal persistence of attitude change. *Journal of Personality and Social Psychology, 42,* 412–425.

Hensley, W. E. (1981). The effects of attire, location, and sex on aiding behavior: A similarity explanation. *Journal of Nonverbal Behavior, 6,* 3–11.

Hepworth, J. T., & West, S. G. (1988). Lynchings and the economy: A time-series reanalysis of Hovland and Sears (1940). *Journal of Personality and Social Psychology, 55,* 239–247.

Herbert, T. B., & Cohen, S. (1993). Depression and immunity: A meta-analytic review. *Psychological Bulletin, 113,* 472–486.

Herek, G. M. (1993). Sexual orientation and military service: A social science perspective. *American Psychologist, 48,* 538–549.

Herrmann, D. J. (1991). *Super memory.* Emmaus, PA: Rodale.

Hershey, D. A., Walsh, D. A., Read, S. J., & Chulef, A. S. (1990). Relationships between metamemory, memory predictions, and memory task performance in adults. *Psychology and Aging, 5,* 215–227.

Herzog, D. B., Keller, M.B., & Lavori, P.W. (1988). Outcome in anorexia and bulimia nervosa: A review of the literature. The *Journal of Nervous and Mental Disease, 176,* 131–143.

Hewitt, P. L., & Flett, G. L. (1993). Dimensions of perfectionism, daily stress, and depression: A test of the specific vulnerability hypothesis. *Journal of Abnormal Psychology, 102,* 58–65.

Higgins, E. T. (1990). Personality, social psychology, and person-situation relations: Standards and knowledge activation as a common language. In L. A. Pervin (Ed.), *Handbook of personality: Theory and research* (pp. 301–338). New York: Guilford.

Hilgard, E. R. (1977). *Divided consciousness: Multiple controls in human thought and action.* New York: Wiley.

Hilgard, E. R. (1978). Hypnosis and pain. In R. A. Sternbach (Ed.), *The psychology of pain.* New York: Raven Press.

Hill, C. (1987). Affiliation motivation: People who need people . . . but in different ways. *Journal of Personality and Social Psychology, 52,* 1008–1018.

Hiltz, S. R. (1993). Correlates of learning in a virtual classroom. *International Journal of Man-Machine Studies, 39,* 71–98.

Hineline, P. N. (1992). A self-interpretive behavior analysis. *American Psychologist, 47,* 1274–1286.

Hines, C. V., Cruickshank, D. R., & Kennedy, J. (1985). Teacher clarity and its relation to student achievement and satisfaction. *American Educational Research Journal, 22,* 87–99.

Hinton, G. E. (1992). How neural networks learn from experience. *Scientific American, 267*(3), 144–151.

Ho, D. Y. F. (1985). Cultural values and professional issues in clinical psychology: Implications from the Hong Kong experience. *American Psychologist, 40,* 1212–1218.

Hoberman, H. M., Lewinsohn, P. M., & Tilson, M. (1988). Group treatment of depression: Individual predictors of outcome. *Journal of Consulting and Clinical Psychology, 56,* 393–398.

Hobfoll, S. E., Jackson, A. P., Lavin, J., Britton, P. J., & Shepherd, J. B. (1993). Safer sex knowledge, behavior, and attitudes of inner-city women. *Health Psychology, 12,* 481–488.

Hobson, J. A. (1992). Cited in Blakeslee, S. (1992, January 7). Scientists unraveling chemistry of dreams. *The New York Times,* pp. C1, C10.

Hobson, J. A., & McCarley, R. W. (1977). The brain as a dream state generator: An activation-synthesis hypothesis of the dream process. *American Journal of Psychiatry, 134,* 1335–1348.

Hoffman, C., & Hurst, N. (1990). Gender stereotypes: Perception or rationalization? *Journal of Personality and Social Psychology, 58,* 197–208.

Hogan, R., Curphy, G. J., & Hogan, J. (1994). What we know about leadership: Effectiveness and personality. *American Psychologist, 49,* 493–504.

Holahan, C. J., & Moos, R. H. (1990). Life stressors, resistance factors, and psychological health: An extension of the stress-resistance paradigm. *Journal of Personality and Social Psychology, 58,* 909–917.

Holahan, C. J., & Moos, R. H. (1991). Life stressors, personal and social resources, and depression: A 4-year structural model. *Journal of Abnormal Psychology, 100,* 31–38.

Holland, J. (1993). Cited in Rosenthal, E. (1993b, July 20). Listening to the emotional needs of cancer patients. *The New York Times,* pp. C1, C7.

Hollinger, L. M., & Buschmann, M. B. (1993). Factors influencing the perception of touch by elderly nursing home residents and their health caregivers. *International Journal of Nursing Studies, 30,* 445–461.

Hollingshead, A. B., & Redlich, F. C. (1958). *Social class and mental illness: A community study.* New York: Wiley.

Hollon, S. D., & Beck, A. T. (1986). Research on cognitive therapies. In S. L. Garfield & A. E. Bergin (Eds.), *Handbook of psychotherapy and behavior change* (3rd ed.). New York: Wiley.

Hollon, S. D., Shelton, R. C., & Loosen, P. T. (1991). Cognitive therapy and pharmacotherapy for depression. *Journal of Consulting and Clinical Psychology, 59,* 88–99.

Holmes, D. S. (1984). Meditation and somatic arousal reduction: A review of the experimental evidence. *American Psychologist, 39,* 1–10.

Holmes, T. H., & Rahe, R. H. (1967). The social readjustment rating scale. *Journal of Psychosomatic Research, 11,* 213–218.

Holyoak, K., Koh, K., & Nisbett, R. E. (1989). A theory of conditioning: Inductive learning within rule-based default hierarchies. *Psychological Review, 96,* 315–340.

Honorton, C. (1985). Meta-analysis of psi Ganzfeld research: A response to Hyman. *Journal of Parapsychology, 49,* 51–91.

Honorton, C., and others. (1990). Psi communication in the Ganzfeld: Experiments with an automated testing system and a comparison with a meta-analysis of earlier studies. *Journal of Parapsychology, 54,* 99–139.

Honorton, C., Ferrari, D. C., & Bem, D. J. (1992). Extraversion and ESP performance: Meta-analysis and a new confirmation. In L. A. Henkel & G. R. Schmeidler (Eds.), *Research in parapsychology 1990.* Metuchen, NJ: Scarecrow Press.

Honts, C., Hodes, R., & Raskin, D. (1985). *Journal of Applied Psychology, 70*(1).

Hopper, J. L., & Seeman, E. (1994). The bone density of female twins discordant for tobacco use. *New England Journal of Medicine, 330,* 387–392.

Horn, J. M. (1983). The Texas adoption project: Adopted children and their intellectual resemblance to biological and adoptive parents. *Child Development, 54,* 268–275.

Horney, K. (1967). *Feminine psychology.* New York: W. W. Norton.

Horvath, T. (1981). Physical attractiveness: The influence of selected torso parameters. *Archives of Sexual Behavior, 10,* 21–24.

House, J. S., Robbins, C., & Metzner, H. L. (1982). The association of social relationships and activities with mortality: Prospective evidence from the Tecumseh Community Health Study. *American Journal of Epidemiology, 116,* 123–140.

Howard, L., & Polich, J. (1985). P300 latency and memory span development. *Developmental Psychology, 21,* 283–289.

Howard-Pitney, B., LaFramboise, T. D., Basil, M., September, B., & Johnson, M. (1992). Psychological and social indicators of suicide ideation and suicide attempts in Zuni adolescents. *Journal of Consulting and Clinical Psychology, 60,* 473–476.

Hubel, D. H., & Wiesel, T. N. (1979). Brain mechanisms of vision. *Scientific American, 241,* 150–162.

Hudson, J. (1993). Cited in Goleman, D. J. (1993, April 6). Studying the secrets of childhood memory. *The New York Times,* pp. C1, C11.

Huesmann, R. (1993). Cited in DeAngelis, T. (1993b). It's baaack: TV violence, concern for kid viewers. *APA Monitor, 24*(8), 16.

Huesmann, L. R., Eron, L. D., Klein, R., Brice, P., & Fischer, P. (1983). Mitigating the imitation of aggressive behaviors by changing children's attitudes about media violence. *Journal of Personality and Social Psychology, 44,* 899–910.

Huesmann, L. R., & Miller, L. S. (1994). Long-term effects of repeated exposure to media violence in childhood. In L. R. Huesmann (Ed.), *Aggressive behavior: current perspectives.* New York: Plenum.

Hugdahl, K., & Ohman, A. (1977). Effects of instruction on acquisition and extinction of electrodermal response to fear-relevant stimuli. *Journal of Experimental Psychology: Human Learning and Memory, 3,* 608–618.

Hughes, J. R. (1993). Pharmacotherapy for smoking cessation: Unvalidated assumptions, anomalies, and suggestions for future research. *Journal of Consulting and Clinical Psychology, 61,* 751–760.

Hughes, P. L., and others (1986). Treating bulimia with desipramine. *Archives of General Psychiatry, 43,* 182–186.

Hull, J. G., Levenson, R. W., Young, R. D., & Sher, K. J. (1983). Self-awareness-reducing effects of alcohol consumption. *Journal of Personality and Social Psychology, 44,* 461–473.

Humphrey, L. L. (1986). Family dynamics in bulimia. In S. C. Feinstein and others (Eds.), *Adolescent psychiatry.* Chicago: University of Chicago Press.

Hunter, J. E., & Schmidt, F. L. (1983). Quantifying the effects of psychological interventions on employee job performance and work-force productivity. *American Psychologist, 38,* 473–478.

Hurford, J. R. (1991). The evolution of the critical period for language acquisition. *Cognition, 40,* 159–210.

Hurvich, L. M. (1981). *Color vision.* Sunderland, MA: Sinauer Associates.

Huxley, A. (1939). *Brave new world.* New York: Harper & Row.

Hyde, J. S. (1993, August). Teaching the psychology of women and gender for undergraduate and graduate faculty. Workshop of the Psychology of Women Institute presented at the meeting of the American Psychological Association, Toronto, Canada.

Hyde, J. S., Fennema, E., & Lamon, S. J. (1990). Gender differences in mathematics performance: A meta-analysis. *Psychological Bulletin, 107,* 139–155.

Hyde, J. S., & Linn, M. C. (1988). Gender differences in verbal ability: A meta-analysis. *Psychological Bulletin, 104,* 53–69.

Hyman, R. (1994). Anomaly or artifact? Comments on Bem and Honorton. *Psychological Bulletin, 115,* 19–24.

Imber, S. D., and others (1990). Mode-specific effects among three treatments for depression. *Journal of Consulting and Clinical Psychology, 58,* 352–359.

Infant deaths drop but black babies lag. (1993, March 12). *The New York Times,* p. A17.

Insko, C. A. (1985). Balance theory, the Jordan paradigm, and the Wiest tetrahedron. In L. Berkowitz (Ed.), *Advances in experimental social psychology.* New York: Academic Press.

Insko, C. A., Smith, R. H., Alicke, M. D., Wade, J., & Taylor, S. (1985). Conformity and group size: The concern with being right and the concern with being liked. *Personality and Social Psychology Bulletin, 11,* 41–50.

Ironson, G. (1993). Cited in Adler, T. (1993). Men and women affected by stress, but differently. *APA Monitor, 24*(7), 8–9.

Ironson, G., Antoni, M. H., Schneiderman, N., LaPerriere, A., & Fletcher, M. A. (1992, July). *Stress management interventions and psychological predictors in HIV.* Paper presented at the Second International Congress of Behavioral Medicine, Hamburg, Germany.

Isabella, R. A. (1993). Origins of attachment: Maternal interactive behavior across the first year. *Child Development, 64,* 605–621.

Isay, R. A. (1990). Psychoanalytic theory and the therapy of gay men. In D. P. McWhirter, S. A. Sanders, & J. M. Reinisch (Eds.) *Homosexuality/heterosexuality: Concepts of sexual orientation* (pp. 283–303). New York: Oxford University Press.

Isen, A. M., & Baron, R. A. (1990). Positive affect and organizational behavior. In B. M. Staw & L. L. Cummings (Eds.), *Advances in experimental social psychology* (Vol. 12). Greenwich, CT: JAI Press.

Isomura, T., Fine, S., & Lin, T. (1987). Two Japanese families: A cultural perspective. *Canadian Journal of Psychiatry, 32,* 282–286.

Israel, E., and others (1990). The effects of a 5-lipoxygenase inhibitor on asthma induced by cold, dry air. *New England Journal of Medicine, 323,* 1740–1744.

Ivancevich, J. M., Matteson, M. T., Freedman, S. M., & Phillips, J. S. (1990). Worksite stress management interventions. *American Psychologist, 45,* 252–261.

Iversen, I. H. (1992). Skinner's early research: From reflexology to operant conditioning. *American Psychologist, 47,* 1318–1328.

Izard, C. E. (1984). Emotion-cognition relationships and human development. In C. E. Izard, J. Kagan, & R. B. Zajonc (Eds.), *Emotions, Cognition, and behavior.* New York: Cambridge University Press.

Izard, C. E. (1990). Facial expression and the regulation of emotions. *Journal of Personality and Social Psychology, 58,* 487–498.

Izard, C. E. (1992). Basic emotions, relations among emotions, and emotion-cognition relations. *Psychological Review, 99,* 561–565.

Izard, C. E. (1994). Basic emotions, relations among emotions, and emotion-cognition relations. *Psychological Bulletin, 115,* 561–565.

Jackson, J. F. (1993). Human behavioral genetics, Scarr's theory, and her views on interventions: A critical review and commentary on their implications for African American children. *Child Development, 64,* 1318–1332.
Jacob, T., Krahn, G. L., & Leonard, K. (1991). Parent–child interactions in families with alcoholic fathers. *Journal of Consulting and Clinical Psychology, 59,* 176–181.
Jacobs, T. J., & Charles, E. (1980). Life events and the occurrence of cancer in children. *Psychosomatic Medicine, 42,* 11–24.
Jacobson, N. S., & Addis, M. E. (1993). Research on couples and couples therapy: What do we know? Where are we going? *Journal of Consulting and Clinical Psychology, 61,* 85–93.
Jacox, A., Carr, D. B., & Payne, R. (1994). New clinical-practice guidelines for the management of pain in patients with cancer. *New England Journal of Medicine, 330,* 651–655.
James, W. (1890). *The principles of psychology.* New York: Henry Holt.
James, W. (1904). Does "consciousness" exist? *Journal of Philosophy, Psychology, and Scientific Methods, 1,* 477–491.
Jamison, K. K., & Akiskal, H. S. (1983). Medication compliance in patients with bipolar disorder. *Psychiatric Clinics of North America, 6,* 175–192.
Janerich, D. T., and others (1990). Lung cancer and exposure to tobacco smoke in the household. *New England Journal of Medicine, 323,* 632–636.
Janicak, P. G., and others (1985). Efficacy of ECT: A meta-analysis. *American Journal of Psychiatry, 142,* 297–302.
Janis, I. L. (1982). *Groupthink: Psychological studies of policy decisions and fiascoes* (2nd ed.). Boston: Houghton Mifflin.
Janowitz, H. D., & Grossman, M. I. (1949). Effects of variations in nutritive density on intake of food in dogs and cats. *American Journal of Physiology, 158,* 184–193.
Janus, S. S., & Janus, C. L. (1993). *The Janus report on sexual behavior.* New York: Wiley.
Jeavons, C. M., & Taylor, S. P. (1985). The control of alcohol-related aggression: Redirecting the inebriate's attention to socially appropriate conduct. *Aggressive Behavior, 11,* 93–101.
Jeffery, R. W. (1991). Population perspectives on the prevention and treatment of obesity in minority populations. *American Journal of Clinical Nutrition, 53,* 1621S–1624S.
Jellison, J. M., & Green, J. (1981). A self-presentation approach to the fundamental attribution error: The norm of internality. *Journal of Personality and Social Psychology, 40,* 643–649.
Jemmott, J. B., and others (1983). Academic stress, power motivation, and decrease in secretion rate of salivary secretory immunoglobin A. *Lancet, 1,* 1400–1402.
Jemmott, J. B., and others (1990). Motivational syndromes associated with natural killer cell activity. *Journal of Behavioral Medicine, 13,* 53–73.
Jenkins, A. H. (1985). Attending to self-activity in the Afro-American client. *Psychotherapy, 22,* 335–341.
Jenkins, C. D. (1988). Epidemiology of cardiovascular diseases. *Journal of Consulting and Clinical Psychology, 56,* 324–332.
Jensen, M. P., & Karoly, P. (1991). Control beliefs, coping efforts, and adjustment to chronic pain. *Journal of Consulting and Clinical Psychology, 59,* 431–438.
Jensen, M. P., Turner, J. A., & Romano, J. M. (1994). Correlates of improvement in multidisciplinary treatment of chronic pain. *Journal of Consulting and Clinical Psychology, 62,* 172–179.
Jeste, D. V., and others (1992). Cognitive deficits of patients with Alzheimer's disease with and without delusions. *American Journal of Psychiatry, 149,* 184–188.
Johnson, B. T., & Eagly, A. H. (1989). Effects of involvement on persuasion: A meta-analysis. *Psychological Bulletin, 106,* 290–314.
Johnson, C. A., and others (1990). Relative effectiveness of comprehensive community programming for drug abuse prevention with high-risk and low-risk adolescents. *Journal of Consulting and Clinical Psychology, 58,* 447–457.
Johnson, D. (1990, March 8). AIDS clamor at colleges muffling older dangers. *The New York Times,* p. A18.
Johnson, D. J. (1992). Developmental pathways: Toward an ecological theoretical formulation of race identity in Black–White biracial children. In M. P. P. Root (Ed.), *Racially mixed people in America.* Newbury Park, CA: Sage.
Johnson, J. T., & Judd, C. M. (1983). Overlooking the incongruent: Categorization biases in the identification of political statements. *Journal of Personality and Social Psychology, 45,* 978–996.
Johnson, W., Emde, R. N., Pannabecker, B., Stenberg, C., & Davis, M. (1982). Maternal perception of infant emotion from birth to 18 months. *Infant Behavior and Development, 5,* 313–322.
Johnston, L. D., Bachman, J. G., & O'Malley, P. M. (1991, January 23). Monitoring the future: A continuing study of the lifestyles and values of youth. University of Michigan News and Information Services: Ann Arbor.
Johnston, L. D., O'Malley, P. M., & Bachman, J. G. (1993). National survey results on drug use from the Monitoring the Future Study, 1975–1992. The University of Michigan Institute for Social Research; National Institute on Drug Abuse, 5600 Fishers Lane, Rockville, MD 20957; USDHHS, Public Health Service, National Institutes of Health.
Johnston, W., & Dark, V. (1986). Selective attention. *Annual Review of Psychology, 37,* 43–75.
Jones, E. E. (1961). *The life and work of Sigmund Freud.* New York: Basic Books.
Jones, E. E. (1990). *Interpersonal perception.* New York: W. H. Freeman.
Jones, J. (1991). In J. D. Goodchilds (Ed.), *Psychological perspectives on human diversity in America.* Washington, DC: American Psychological Association.
Jones, J. L., & Leary, M. R. (1994). Effects of appearance-based admonitions against sun exposure on tanning intentions in young adults. *Health Psychology, 13,* 86–90.
Jones, M. C. (1924). Elimination of children's fears. *Journal of Experimental Psychology, 7,* 381–390.
Jones, S. L. (1994). A constructive relationship for religion with the science and profession of psychology. *American Psychologist, 49,* 184–199.
Jordan, J. V., Kaplan, A. G., Miller, J. B., Stiver, L. P., & Stiver, J. L. (Eds.). (1991). *Women's growth in connection.* New York: Guilford.
Josephson, W. D. (1987). Television violence and children's aggression: Testing the priming, social script, and disinhibition prediction. *Journal of Personality and Social Psychology, 53,* 882–890.
Juarez, R. (1985). Core issues in psychotherapy with the Hispanic child. *Psychotherapy, 22,* 441–448.
Judd, C. M., & Park, B. (1988). Out-group homogeneity: Judgments of variability at the individual and group levels. *Journal of Personality and Social Psychology, 54,* 778–788.
Julien, R. M. (1988). *A primer of drug action* (2nd ed.). San Francisco: Freeman.

Kahle, L. R., & Beatty, S. E. (1987). Cognitive consequences of post-purchase behavior. *Journal of Applied Social Psychology, 17,* 828–843.
Kail, R. (1990). *The development of memory in children* (3rd ed.). New York: W. H. Freeman.
Kakutani, M. (1992). Is it love, or just the imperatives of reproduction? *The New York Times,* p. C16.
Kamin, L. J. (1982). Mental testing and immigration. *American Psychologist, 37,* 97–98.
Kammeyer, K. C. W., Ritzer, G., & Yetman, N. R. (1990). *Sociology: Experiencing changing societies.* Boston: Allyn & Bacon.
Kandel, E. R., & Hawkins, R. D. (1992). The biological basis of learning and individuality. *Scientific American, 267*(3), 78–86.
Kanner, A. D., Coyne, J. C., Schaefer, C., & Lazarus, R. S. (1981). Comparison of two modes of stress measurement: Daily hassles and uplifts versus major life events. *Journal of Behavioral Medicine, 4,* 1–39.
Kaplan, S. J. (1991). Physical abuse and neglect. In M. Lewis (Ed.), *Child and adolescent psychiatry: A comprehensive textbook* (pp. 1010–1019). Baltimore: Williams & Wilkins.
Karabenick, S. A., & Sharma, R. (1994). Perceived teacher support of student questioning in the college classroom: Its relation to student characteristics and role in the classroom questioning process. *Journal of Educational Psychology, 86,* 90–103.
Karasek, R. A., and others (1982). Job, psychological factors and coronary heart disease. *Advances in Cardiology, 29,* 62–67.
Karasek, R. A., & Theorell, T. (1990). *Healthy work: Stress, productivity, and the reconstruction of working life.* New York: Basic Books.
Kash, K. (1993, March 30.) Paper presented to the American Cancer Society, San Diego, CA. Cited in Friend, T. (1993, March 31). Fear of cancer deters detection. *USA Today,* p. D1.
Kassebaum, N. L. (1994). Head Start: Only the best for America's children. *American Psychologist, 49,* 123–126.
Katzell, R. A., & Thompson, D. E. (1990). Work motivation: Theory and practice. *American Psychologist, 45,* 144–153.
Kaufman, J., & Zigler, E. (1989). The intergenerational transmission of child abuse. In D. Cicchetti & V. Carlson (Eds.), *Child maltreatment: Theory and research on the causes and consequences of child abuse and neglect* (pp. 129–150). Cambridge: Cambridge University Press.
Kazdin, A. E. (1993). Adolescent mental health: Prevention and treatment programs. *American Psychologist, 48,* 127–141.
Keating, C. F., and others (1985). Psychosocial enhancement of immunocompetence in a geriatric population. *Health Psychology, 4,* 25–41.
Keefe, F. J., Dunsmore, J., & Burnett, R. (1992). Behavioral and cognitive-behavioral approaches to chronic pain. *Journal of Consulting and Clinical Psychology, 60,* 528–536.
Keen, S. (1991). *Fire in the belly.* New York: Harper & Row.
Keesey, R. E. (1986). A set-point theory of obesity. In K. D. Brownell & J. P. Foreyt (Eds.), *Handbook of eating disorders: Physiology, psychology, and treatment of obesity, anorexia, and bulimia.* New York: Basic Books.
Keil, J. E., and others (1993). Mortality rates and risk factors for coronary disease in Black as compared with White men and women. *New England Journal of Medicine, 329,* 73–78.
Keinan, G. (1987). Decision making under stress: Scanning of alternatives under controllable and uncontrollable threats. *Journal of Personality and Social Psychology, 52,* 639–644.
Keita, G. P. (1993, February). Presentation to the Fifth Interdisciplinary Congress on Women, University of Costa Rica, San Jose, Costa Rica.
Keita, G. P., & Jones, J. M. (1990). Reducing adverse reaction to stress in the workplace. *American Psychologist, 45,* 1137–1141.
Keller, M. B., First, M., & Koscis, J. H. (1990, August/September). Major depression and dysthymia. *DSM-IV Update.* Washington, DC: American Psychiatric Association.
Kellerman, J., Lewis, J., & Laird, J. D. (1989). Looking and loving: The effects of mutual gaze on feelings of romantic love. *Journal of Research in Personality, 23,* 145–161.
Kelley, H. H., & Michela, J. L. (1980). Attribution theory and research. *Annual Review of Psychology, 31,* 457–501.
Kellman, P. J., & von Hofsetn, C. (1992). The world of the moving infant: Perception of motion, stability, and space. In C. Rovee-Collier & L. P. Lipsitt (Eds.), *Advances in Infancy Research* (Vol. 7). Norwood, NJ: Ablex.
Kelly, G. A. (1955). *The psychology of personal constructs* (Vols. 1 & 2). New York: W. W. Norton.
Kelly, I. W., Culver, R., & Loptson, P. J. (1989). Astrology and science: In S. K. Biswas and others (Eds.), *Cosmoperspectives.* Cambridge: Cambridge University Press.
Kelly, J. A., Murphy, D. A., Sikkema, K. J., & Kalichman, S. C. (1993). Psychological interventions to prevent HIV infection are urgently needed. *American Psychologist, 48,* 1023–1034.
Kemeny, M. E. (1993). Emotions and the immune system. In B. Moyers, *Healing and the mind.* New York: Doubleday.
Kemeny, M. E., Weiner, H., Taylor, S. E., Schneider, S., Visscher, B., & Fahey, J. L. (1994). Repeated bereavement, depressed mood, and immune parameters in HIV seropositive and seronegative gay men. *Health Psychology, 13,* 14–24.
Kemper, P., & Murtaugh, C. M. (1991). Lifetime use of nursing home care. *New England Journal of Medicine, 324,* 595–600.
Kendler, H. H. (1993). Psychology and the ethics of social policy. *American Psychologist, 48,* 1046–1053.
Kenrick, D. T., & MacFarlane, S. W. (1986). Ambient temperature and horn honking: A field study of the heat/aggression relationship. *Environment and Behavior, 18,* 179–191.
Kerr, N. L., & MacCoun, R. J. (1985). The effects of jury size and polling method on the process and product of jury deliberation. *Journal of Personality and Social Psychology, 48,* 349–363.
Kershner, J. R., & Ledger, G. (1985). Effect of sex, intelligence, and style of thinking on creativity: A comparison of gifted and average IQ children. *Journal of Personality and Social Psychology, 48,* 1033–1040.
Kiecolt-Glaser, J. K. (1993). Cited in Adler, T. (1993). Men and women affected by stress, but differently. *APA Monitor, 24*(7), 8–9.
Kiecolt-Glaser, J. K., & Glaser, R. (1992). Psychoneuroimmunology: Can psychological interventions modulate immunity? *Journal of Consulting and Clinical Psychology, 60,* 569–575.
Kihlstrom, J. F. (1980). Posthypnotic amnesia for recently learned material: Interactions with "episodic" and "semantic" memory. *Cognitive Psychology, 12,* 227–251.
Kihlstrom, J. F., Brenneman, H. A., Pistole, D. D., & Shor, R. E. (1985). Hypnosis as a retrieval cue in posthypnotic amnesia. *Journal of Abnormal Psychology, 94,* 264–271.
Kihlstrom, J. F., Glisky, M. L., & Angiulo, M. J. (1994). Dissociative tendencies and dissociative disorders. *Journal of Abnormal Psychology, 103,* 117–124.
Kilborn, P. T. (1995, March 16). Women and minorities still face "glass ceiling." *The New York Times,* p. A22.
Killen, J. D., Fortmann, S. P., Newman, B., & Varady, A. (1990). Evaluation of a treatment approach combining nicotine gum with self-guided behavioral treatments for smoking relapse prevention. *Journal of Consulting and Clinical Psychology, 58,* 85–92.
Kilpatrick, D. (1992). *Rape in America: A report to the nation.* Charleston, SC: Crime Victims Research Center.
Kimble, D. P. (1992). *Biological psychology* (2nd ed.). Fort Worth, TX: Harcourt Brace Jovanovich.
Kimble, G. A. (1989). Psychology from the standpoint of a generalist. *American Psychologist, 44,* 491–499.
Kimble, G. A. (1994). A frame of reference for psychology. *American Psychologist, 49,* 510–519.
Kimerling, R., & Calhoun, K. S. (1994). Somatic symptoms, social support, and treatment seeking among sexual assault victims. *Journal of Consulting and Clinical Psychology, 62,* 333–340.
Kimmel, A. J. (1991). Predictable biases in the ethical decision making of American psychologists. *American Psychologist, 46,* 786–788.
Kimura, D. (1992). Sex differences in the brain. *Scientific American, 267*(3), 118–125.
Kinnunen, T., Zamansky, H. S., & Block, M. L. (1994). Is the hypnotized subject lying? *Journal of Abnormal Psychology, 103,* 184–191.
Kinsey, A. C., Pomeroy, W. B., & Martin, C. E. (1948). *Sexual behavior in the human male.* Philadelphia: W. B. Saunders.

Kinsey, A. C., Pomeroy, W. B., Martin, C. E., & Gebhard, P. H. (1953). *Sexual behavior in the human female.* Philadelphia: W. B. Saunders.

Kintsch, W. (1994). Text comprehension, memory, and learning. *American Psychologist, 49,* 294–303.

Klatzky, R. L. (1980). *Human memory: Structures and processes* (2nd ed.). San Francisco: W. H. Freeman.

Klatzky, R. L. (1983). The icon is dead: Long live the icon. *Behavioral and Brain Sciences, 6,* 27–28.

Klein, D. N., Depue, R. A., & Slater, J. F. (1985). Cyclothymia in the adolescent offspring of parents with bipolar affective disorder. *Journal of Abnormal Psychology, 94,* 115–127.

Kleinke, C. L. (1977). Compliance to requests made by gazing and touching experimenters in field settings. *Journal of Experimental Social Psychology, 13,* 218–223.

Kleinke, C. L. (1986). Gaze and eye contact: A research review. *Psychological Review, 100,* 78–100.

Kleinke, C. L., & Staneski, R. A. (1980). First impressions of female bust size. *Journal of Social Psychology, 110,* 123–134.

Kleinmuntz, B., & Szucko, J. J. (1984). Lie detection in ancient and modern times: A call for contemporary scientific study. *American Psychologist, 39,* 766–776.

Klesges, R. C., Klesges, L. M., & Meyers, A. W. (1991). Relationship of smoking status, energy balance, and body weight: Analysis of the Second National Health and Nutrition Examination Survey. *Journal of Consulting and Clinical Psychology, 59,* 899–905.

Klorman, R., Brumaghim, J. T., Fitzpatrick, P. A., Borgstedt, A. D., & Strauss, J. (1994). Clinical and cognitive effects of methylphenidate on children with attention deficit disorder as a function of aggression/oppositionality and age. *Journal of Abnormal Psychology, 103,* 206–221.

Klosko, J. S., Barlow, D. H., Tassinari, R., & Cerny, J. A. (1990). A comparison of alprazolam and behavior therapy in treatment of panic disorder. *Journal of Consulting and Clinical Psychology, 58,* 77–84.

Kneip, R. C., and others (1993). Self- and spouse ratings of anger and hostility as predictors of coronary heart disease. *Health Psychology, 12,* 301–307.

Knowlton, W. A., Jr., & Mitchell, T. R. (1980). Effects of causal attributions on a supervisor's evaluation of subordinate performance. *Journal of Applied Psychology, 65,* 459–466.

Kobasa, S. C. (1979). Stressful life events, personality, and health: An inquiry into hardiness. *Journal of Personality and Social Psychology, 37,* 1–11.

Kobasa, S. C., Maddi, S. R., & Kahn, S. (1982). Hardiness and health: A prospective study. *Journal of Personality and Social Psychology, 42,* 168–177.

Kobasa, S. C., & Puccetti, M. C. (1983). Personality and social resources in stress resistance. *Journal of Personality and Social Psychology, 45,* 839–850.

Koch, C. (1992). Cited in Blakeslee, S. (1992c, October 27). Nerve cell rhythm may be key to consciousness. *The New York Times,* pp. C1, C10.

Koffka, K. (1925). *The growth of the mind.* New York: Harcourt Brace Jovanovich.

Kohlberg, L. (1969). *Stages in the development of moral thought and action.* New York: Holt, Rinehart and Winston.

Kohlberg, L. (1981). *The philosophy of moral development: Moral stages and the idea of justice.* San Francisco: Harper & Row.

Köhler, W. (1925). *The mentality of apes.* New York: Harcourt Brace Jovanovich.

Kohn, P. M., Barnes, G. E., & Hoffman, F. M. (1979). Drug-use history and experience seeking among adult male correctional inmates. *Journal of Consulting and Clinical Psychology, 47,* 708–715.

Kolata, G. (1991a, February 26). Alzheimer's researchers close in on causes. *The New York Times,* pp. C1, C7.

Kolata, G. (1991b, November 8). Studies cite 10.5 years from infection to illness. *The New York Times,* p. B12.

Kolata, G. (1993a, February 7). AIDS group dismayed by report they see as discounting concern. *The New York Times,* p. 30.

Kolata, G. (1993b, May 6). Cancer-causing gene found with a clue to how it works. *The New York Times,* pp. 1, B15.

Kolata, G. (1993c, October 24). Scientist clones human embryos, and creates an ethical challenge. *The New York Times,* pp. 1, 22.

Kolata, G. (1993d, October 26). The hot debate about cloning human embryo. *The New York Times,* pp. 1, C3.

Kolata, G. (1994, February 16). Debate on using marijuana as medicine turns to question of whether it works. *The New York Times,* p. C12.

Kolko, D. J., & Rickard-Figueroa, J. L. (1985). Effects of video games on the adverse corollaries of chemotherapy in pediatric oncology patients: A single-case analysis. *Journal of Consulting and Clinical Psychology, 53,* 223–228.

Koocher, G. P. (1991). Questionable methods in alcoholism research. *Journal of Consulting and Clinical Psychology, 59,* 246–248.

Korn, J. H., Davis, R., & Davis, S. F. (1991). Historians' and chairpersons' judgments of eminence among psychologists. *American Psychologist, 46,* 789–792.

Koss, M. P. (1993). Rape: Scope, impact, interventions, and public policy responses. *American Psychologist, 48,* 1062–1069.

Koss, M. P., Butcher, J. L., & Strupp, H. H. (1986). Brief psychotherapy methods in clinical research. *Journal of Consulting and Clinical Psychology, 54,* 60–67.

Koss, M. P., Gidycz, C. A., & Wisniewski, N. (1987). The scope of rape: Incidence and prevalence of sexual aggression and victimization in a national sample of higher education students. *Journal of Consulting and Clinical Psychology, 55,* 162–170.

Kosslyn, S. M. (1994). *Image and brain: The resolution of the imagery debate.* Cambridge, MA: The MIT Press, a Bradford Book.

Kramer, P. D. (1993). *Listening to Prozac.* New York: Viking.

Krantz, D. S., Contrada, R. J., Hill, D. R., & Friedler, E. (1988). Environmental stress and biobehavioral antecedents of coronary heart disease. *Journal of Consulting and Clinical Psychology, 56,* 333–341.

Krantz, D. S., Grunberg, N. E., & Baum, A. (1985). Health psychology. *Annual Review of Psychology, 36,* 349–383.

Kring, A. M., Kerr, S. L., Smith, D. A., & Neale, J. M. (1993). Flat affect in schizophrenia does not reflect diminished subjective experience of emotion. *Journal of Abnormal Psychology, 102,* 507–517.

Krosnick, J. A. (1989). Attitude importance and attitude accessibility. *Personality and Social Psychology Bulletin, 15,* 297–308.

Kübler-Ross, E. (1969). *On death and dying.* New York: Macmillan.

Kübler-Ross, E., & Magno, J. B. (1983). *Hospice.* Santa Fe, NM: Bear.

Kuczaj, S. A., II (1982). On the nature of syntactic development. In S. A. Kuczaj, II (Ed.), *Language development: Vol. 1. Syntax and semantics.* Hillsdale, NJ: Erlbaum.

Kuczmarski, R. J. (1992). Prevalence of overweight and weight gain in the United States. *American Journal of Clinical Nutrition, 55*(Suppl.), 495S–502S.

Kushler, M. G. (1989). Use of evaluation to improve energy conservation programs. *Journal of Social Issues, 45,* 153–168.

Lacks, P., & Morin, C. M. (1992). Recent advances in the assessment and treatment of insomnia. *Journal of Consulting and Clinical Psychology, 60,* 586–594.

LaCroix, A. Z., and others (1991). Smoking and mortality among older men and women in three communities. *New England Journal of Medicine, 324,* 1619–1625.

LaFramboise, T. (1994). Cited in DeAngelis, T. (1994). History, culture affect treatment for Indians. *APA Monitor, 27*(10), 36.

LaFramboise, T. D., Coleman, H. L. K., & Gerton, J. (1993). Psychological impact of biculturalism: Evidence and theory. *Psychological Bulletin, 114,* 395–412.

Laguerre, M. S. (1981). Haitian Americans. In A. Harwood (Ed.), *Ethnicity and medical care.* Cambridge, MA: Harvard University Press.

Laird, J. D. (1974). Self-attribution of emotion: The effects of expressive behavior on the quality of emotional experience. *Journal of Personality and Social Psychology, 29,* 475–486.

Lakka, T. A., and others (1994). Relation of leisure-time physical activity and cardiorespiratory fitness to the risk of acute myocardial infarction in men. *New England Journal of Medicine, 330,* 1549–1554.

Lamb, M. E., Sternberg, K. J., & Prodromidis, M. (1992). Nonmaternal care and the security of infant-mother attachment: A reanalysis of the data. *Infant Behavior and Development, 15,* 71–83.

Lambert, W. E. (1990). Persistent issues in bilingualism. In B. Harley and others (Eds.), *The development of second language proficiency.* Cambridge, England: Cambridge University Press.

Lambert, W. E. (1992). Challenging established views on social issues. *American Psychologist, 47,* 533–542.

Lambert, W. E., Genesee, F., Holobow, N., & Chartrand, L. (1991). *Bilingual education for majority English-speaking children.* Montreal: McGill University.

Landy, F. J. (1992, August). The roots of organizational and industrial psychology. Master lecture presented to the annual meeting of the American Psychological Association, Washington, DC.

Lang, A. R., Goeckner, D. J., Adesso, V. J., & Marlatt, G. A. (1975). Effects of alcohol on aggression in male social drinkers. *Journal of Abnormal Psychology, 84,* 508–518.

Lang, P. J., & Melamed, B. B. (1969). Case report: Avoidance conditioning therapy of an infant with chronic ruminative vomiting. *Journal of Abnormal Psychology, 74,* 1–8.

Lang, S. S., & Patt, R. B. (1994). *You don't have to suffer.* New York: Oxford University Press.

Langer, E. J., Rodin, J., Beck, P., Weinan, C., & Spitzer, L. (1979). Environmental determinants of memory improvement in late adulthood. *Journal of Personality and Social Psychology, 37,* 2003–2013.

Langford, H. G., and others (1985). Dietary therapy slows the return of hypertension after stopping prolonged medication. *Journal of the American Medical Association, 253,* 657–664.

Langlois, J. H. (1994). Cited in Brody, J. E. (1994, March 21). Notions of beauty transcend culture, new study suggests. *The New York Times,* p. A14.

Lanzetta, J. T., Cartwright-Smith, J., & Kleck, R. E. (1976). Effects of nonverbal dissimulation on emotional experience and autonomic arousal. *Journal of Personality and Social Psychology, 33,* 354–370.

LaPerriere, A. R., and others (1990). Exercise intervention attenuates emotional distress and natural killer cell decrements following notification of positive serologic status for HIV-1. *Biofeedback and Self-Regulation, 15,* 229–242.

LaPerriere, A. R., and others (1991). Aerobic exercise training in an AIDS risk group. *International Journal of Sports Medicine, 12,* S53–S57.

Laroche, S., & Bloch, V. (1982). Conditioning of hippocampal cells and long-term potentiation: An approach to mechanisms of posttrial memory facilitation. In C. Ajmone Marsan & H. Matthies (Eds.), *Neuronal plasticity and memory formation.* New York: Raven Press.

Larrick, R. P. (1993). Motivational factors in decision theories: The role of self-protection. *Psychological Bulletin, 113,* 440–450.

Larson, R., & Richards, M. H. (1991). Daily companionship in late childhood and early adolescence: Changing developmental contexts. *Child Development, 62,* 284–300.

Larson, R. K. (1990). Semantics. In D. N. Osherson, & H. Lasnik (Eds.), *An invitation to cognitive science: Language* (Vol. 1). Cambridge, MA: The MIT Press, a Bradford Book.

Lashley, K. S. (1950). *In search of the engram. In Symposium of the Society for Experimental Biology* (Vol. 4). New York: Cambridge University Press.

Lasnik, H. (1990). Syntax. In D. N. Osherson, & H. Lasnik (Eds.), *An invitation to cognitive science: Language* (Vol. 1). Cambridge, MA: The MIT Press, a Bradford Book.

Latané B., & Dabbs, J. M. (1975). Sex, group size, and helping in three cities. *Sociometry, 38,* 180–194.

Latané B., & Nida, S. (1981). Ten years of research on group size and helping. *Psychological Bulletin, 89,* 308–324.

Lau, R. R., & Russell, D. (1980). Attributions in the sports pages. *Journal of Personality and Social Psychology, 39,* 29–38.

Laube, D. (1985). Premenstrual syndrome. *The Female Patient, 6,* 50–61.

Laudenslager, M. L., and others (1983). Coping and immunosuppression: Inescapable but not escapable shock suppresses lymphocyte proliferation. *Science, 221,* 568–570.

Laumann, E. O., Gagnon, J. H., Michael, R. T., & Michaels, S. (1994). *The social organization of sexuality.* Chicago: University of Chicago Press.

Lawler, E. E., III. (1985, January/February). Quality circles after the fad. *Harvard Business Review,* pp. 65–71.

Lazar, I., & Darlington, R. (1982). Lasting effects of early education: A report from the Consortium of Longitudinal Studies. *Monographs of the Society for Research in Child Development, 47*(2–3, Serial No. 195).

Lazarus, A. A. (1990). If this be research . . . *American Psychologist, 45,* 670–671.

Lazarus, R. S. (1991a). Cognition and motivation in emotion. *American Psychologist, 46,* 352–367.

Lazarus, R. S. (1991b). *Emotion and adaptation.* New York: Oxford University Press.

Lazarus, R. S., DeLongis, A., Folkman, S., & Gruen, R. (1985). Stress and adaptational outcomes: The problem of confounded measures. *American Psychologist, 40,* 770–779.

Lazarus, R. S., & Folkman, S. (1984). *Stress, appraisal, and coping.* New York: Springer.

Leary, W. E. (1991, October 22). Black hypertension may reflect other ills. *The New York Times,* p. C3.

LeBon, G. (1960). *The crowd.* New York: Viking. (Original work published 1895)

LeBow, M. D., Goldberg, P. S., & Collins, A. (1977). Eating behavior of overweight and nonoverweight persons in the natural environment. *Journal of Consulting and Clinical Psychology, 45,* 1204–1205.

Lederberg, A. R., & Mobley, C. E. (1990). The effect of hearing impairment on the quality of attachment and mother–toddler interaction. *Child Development, 61,* 1596–1604.

LeDoux, J. E. (1986). The neurobiology of emotion. In J. E. LeDoux & W. Hirst (Eds.), *Mind and brain: Dialogues in cognitive neuroscience.* Cambridge: Cambridge University Press.

Lee, C. C., & Richardson, B. L. (1991). *Multicultural issues in counseling: New approaches to diversity.* Alexandria, VA: AACD.

Lee, F. R. (1994, January 5). Grappling with how to teach young speakers of Black dialect. *The New York Times,* pp. A1, D22.

Lefcourt, H. M., & Martin, R. A. (1986). *Humor and life stress: Antidote to adversity.* New York: Springer–Verlag.

Lefcourt, H. M., Miller, R. S., Ware, E. E., & Sherk, D. (1981). Locus of control as a modifier of the relationship between stressors and moods. *Journal of Personality and Social Psychology, 41,* 357–369.

Lefley, H. P. (1990). Culture and chronic mental illness. *Hospital and Community Psychiatry, 41,* 277–286.

Lehrer, P. M., Sargunaraj, D., & Hochron, S. (1992). Psychological approaches to the treatment of asthma. *Journal of Consulting and Clinical Psychology, 60,* 639–643.

Leigh, B. C. (1993). Alcohol consumption and sexual activity as reported with a diary technique. *Journal of Abnormal Psychology, 102*, 490–493.

Leigh, B. C., & Stall, R. (1993). Substance use and risky sexual behavior for exposure to HIV. *American Psychologist, 48*, 1035–1045.

Leippe, M. R. (1985). The influence of eyewitness non-identifications on mock-jurors' judgments of a court case. *Journal of Applied Social Psychology, 15*, 656–672.

Lenneberg, E. H. (1967). *Biological foundations of language.* New York: Wiley.

Lerner, M. J., Miller, D. T., & Holmes, J. G. (1975). Deserving versus justice: A contemporary dilemma. In L. Berkowitz & E. Walster (Eds.), *Advances in experimental social psychology* (Vol. 12). New York: Academic Press.

Lesnik-Oberstein, M., & Cohen, L. (1984). Cognitive style, sensation seeking, and assortive mating. *Journal of Personality and Social Psychology, 46*, 112–117.

Leventhal, H., Watts, J. C., & Paogano, F. (1967). Effects of fear and instructions on how to cope with danger. *Journal of Personality and Social Psychology, 6*, 313–321.

Levi, L. (1990). Occupational stress: Spice of life or kiss of death? *American Psychologist, 45*, 1142–1145.

Levine, I. S., & Rog, D. J. (1990). Mental health services for homeless mentally ill: Federal initiatives and current service trends. *American Psychologist, 45*, 963–968.

Levine, M. P. (1987). *Student eating disorders: Anorexia nervosa and bulimia.* Washington, DC: National Education Association.

Levine, S. R., and others (1990). Cerebrovascular complications of the use of the "crack" form of alkaloidal cocaine. *New England Journal of Medicine, 323*, 699–704.

Levinson, D. J., Darrow, C. N., Klein, E. B., Levinson, M. H., & McKee, B. (1978). *The seasons of a man's life.* New York: Knopf.

Levinson, H. (1994). Why the behemoths fell: Psychological roots of corporate failure. *American Psychologist, 49*, 428–436.

Levy, S. M., Herberman, R. B., Maluish, A. M., Schlien, B., & Lippman, M. (1985). Prognostic risk assessment in the primary breast cancer by behavioral and immunological parameters. *Health Psychology, 4*, 99–113.

Lewinsohn, P. M., Rohde, P., & Seeley, J. R. (1994a). Psychosocial risk factors for future suicide attempts. *Journal of Consulting and Clinical Psychology, 62*, 297–305.

Lewinsohn, P. M., and others (1994b). Adolescent psychopathology: II. Psychosocial risk factors for depression. *Journal of Abnormal Psychology, 103*, 302–315.

Lewis-Fernández, R. & Kleinman, A. (1994). Culture, personality, and psychopathology. *Journal of Abnormal Psychology, 103*, 67–71.

Lex, B. W. (1987). Review of alcohol problems in ethnic minority groups. *Journal of Consulting and Clinical Psychology, 55*, 293–300.

Lichtenstein, E., & Glasgow, R. E. (1992). Smoking cessation: What have we learned in the past decade? *Journal of Consulting and Clinical Psychology, 60*, 518–527.

Lieber, C. S. (1990). Cited in Barroom biology: How alcohol goes to a woman's head (January 14). *The New York Times*, p. E24.

Liebert, R. M., Sprafkin, J. N., & Davidson, E. S. (1989). *The early window: Effects of television on children and youth* (3rd. ed.). New York: Pergamon.

Linden, W., Chambers, L., Maurice, J., & Lenz, J. W. (1993). Sex differences in social support, self-deception, hostility, and ambulatory cardiovascular activity. *Health Psychology, 12*, 376–380.

Lindsay, D. S., & Johnson, M. K. (1989). The reversed eyewitness suggestibility effect. *Bulletin of the Psychonomic Society, 27*, 111–113.

Lindsay, R. C. L., Lim, R., Marando, L., & Culley, D. (1986). Mock-juror evaluations of eyewitness testimony: A test of metamemory hypotheses. *Journal of Applied Social Psychology, 16*, 447–459.

Lindsey, K. P., & Paul, G. L. (1989). Involuntary commitments to public mental institutions: Issues involving the overrepresentation of Blacks and assessment of relevant functioning. *Psychological Bulletin, 106*, 171–183.

Linville, P. W., Fischer, G. W., & Salovey, P. (1989). Perceived distribution of the characteristics of in-group and out-group members. *Journal of Personality and Social Psychology, 57*, 165–188.

Lipsey, M. W., & Wilson, D. B. (1993). The efficacy of psychological, educational, and behavioral treatment: Confirmation from meta-analysis. *American Psychologist, 48*, 1181–1209.

Lipton, D. N., McDonel, E. C., & McFall, R. M. (1987). Heterosocial perception in rapists. *Journal of Consulting and Clinical Psychology, 55*, 17–21.

Llinás, R. (1995). Cited in Blakeslee, S. (1995, March 21). How the brain might work: A new theory of consciousness. *The New York Times*, pp. C1, C10.

Lochman, J. E. (1992). Cognitive-behavioral intervention with aggressive boys: Three-year follow-up and preventive effects. *Journal of Consulting and Clinical Psychology, 60*, 426–432.

Lochman, J. E., Coie, J. D., Underwood, M. K., & Terry, R. (1993). Effectiveness of social relations intervention program for aggressive and nonaggressive, rejected children. *Journal of Consulting and Clinical Psychology, 61*, 1053–1058.

Lochman, J. E., & Dodge, K. A. (1994). Social-cognitive processes of severely violent, moderately aggressive, and nonaggressive boys. *Journal of Consulting and Clinical Psychology, 62*, 366–374.

Locke, E. A., & Latham, G. P. (1990). Work motivation and satisfaction: Light at the end of the tunnel. *Psychological Science, 2*, 131–132.

Loftus, E. F. (1979). *Eyewitness testimony.* Cambridge, MA: Harvard University Press.

Loftus, E. F. (1983). Silence is not golden. *American Psychologist, 38*, 564–572.

Loftus, E. F. (1993a). Psychologists in the eyewitness world. *American Psychologist, 48*, 550–552.

Loftus, E. F. (1993b). The reality of repressed memories. *American Psychologist, 48*, 518–537.

Loftus, E. F. (1994). Conference on memory, Harvard Medical School. Cited in D. Goleman (1994, May 31). Miscoding is seen as the root of false memories. *The New York Times*, pp. C1, C8.

Loftus, E. F., & Burns, T. E. (1982). Mental shock can produce retrograde amnesia. *Memory and Cognition, 10*, 318–323.

Loftus, E. F., & Klinger, M. A. (1992). Is the unconscious smart or dumb? *American Psychologist, 47*, 761–765.

Loftus, E. F., & Loftus, G. R. (1980). On the permanence of stored information in the brain. *American Psychologist, 35*, 409–420.

Loftus, E. F., & Palmer, J. C. (1974). Reconstruction of automobile destruction: An example of interaction between language and memory. *Journal of Verbal Learning and Verbal Behavior, 13*, 585–589.

Loftus, G. R. (1983). The continuing persistence of the icon. *Behavioral and Brain Sciences, 6*, 28.

Loftus, G. R., & Loftus, E. F. (1976). *Human memory: The processing of information.* Hillsdale, NJ: Erlbaum.

Lohr, J. M., & Staats, A. (1973). Attitude conditioning in Sino-Tibetan languages. *Journal of Personality and Social Psychology, 26*, 196–200.

Lonergan, E. T., & Krevans, J. R. (1991). A national agenda for research on aging. *New England Journal of Medicine, 324*, 1825–1828.

Long, G. M., & Beaton, R. J. (1982). The case for peripheral persistence: Effects of target and background luminance on a partial-report task. *Journal of Experimental Psychology: Human Perception and Performance, 8*, 383–391.

Loomis, J. M., & Lederman, S. J. (1986). Tactual perception. In K. Boff, L. Kaufman, & J. Thomas (Eds.), *Handbook of perception and human performance* (Vol. 1). New York: Wiley.

Lopez, S., & Hernandez, P. (1986). How culture is considered in evaluations of psychopathology. *Journal of Nervous and Mental Diseases, 176*, 598–606.

Lore, R. K., & Schultz, L. A. (1993). Control of human aggression: A comparative perspective. *American Psychologist, 48*, 1–25.

Lorenz, K. Z. (1981). *The foundations of ethology.* New York: Springer-Verlag.

Louie, V. (1993, August 8). For Asian-Americans, a way to fight a maddening stereotype. *The New York Times*, p. F9.

Lubin, B., Larsen, R. M., Matarazzo, J. D., & Seever, M. (1985). Psychological test usage patterns in five professional settings. *American Psychologist, 40*, 857–861.

Luborsky, L., Barber, J. P., & Beutler, L. (1993). Introduction to special section: A briefing on curative factors in dynamic psychotherapy. *Journal of Consulting and Clinical Psychology, 61*, 539–541.

Lucariello, J., & Nelson, K. (1985). Slot-filler categories as memory organizers for young children. *Developmental Psychology, 21*, 272–281.

Luchins, A. S. (1957). Primacy–recency in impression formation. In C. I. Hovland (Ed.), *The order of presentation in persuasion.* New Haven, CT: Yale University Press.

Ludwick-Rosenthal, R., & Neufeld, R. W. J. (1993). Preparation for undergoing an invasive medical procedure: Interacting effects of information and coping style. *Journal of Consulting and Clinical Psychology, 61*, 156–164.

Lundeberg, M. A., Fox, P. W., & Puncochar, J. (1994). Highly confident but wrong: Gender differences and similarities in confidence judgments. *Journal of Educational Psychology, 86*, 114–121.

Lurie, N., and others (1993). Preventive care for women: Does the sex of the physician matter? *New England Journal of Medicine, 329*, 478–482.

Lykken, D. T. (1982). Fearlessness: Its carefree charm and deadly risks. *Psychology Today, 16*(9), 20–28.

Lykken, D. T., McGue, M., Tellegen, A., & Bouchard, T. J., Jr. (1992). Emergenesis: Genetic traits that may not run in families. *American Psychologist, 47*, 1565–1577.

Lynn, R. (1982). IQ in Japan and the United States shows a growing disparity. *Nature, 297*, 222–223.

Lynn, R. (1991). Educational achievements of Asian Americans. *American Psychologist, 46*, 875–876.

Lyons, J. S., Rosen, A. J., & Dysken, M. W. (1985). Behavioral effects of tricyclic drugs in depressed patients. *Journal of Consulting and Clinical Psychology, 53*, 17–24.

Lyons-Ruth, K., Alpern, L., & Repacholi, B. (1993). Disorganized infant attachment classification and maternal psychosocial problems as predictors of hostile–aggressive behavior in the preschool classroom. *Child Development, 64*, 572–585.

Maas, J. W., and others. (1993). Studies of catecholamine metabolism in schizophrenia/psychosis—I. *Neuropsychopharmacology, 8*, 97–109.

Maccoby, E. E. (1990). Gender and relationships: A developmental account. *American Psychologist, 45*, 513–520.

Maccoby, E. E., & Jacklin, C. N. (1974). *The psychology of sex differences.* Stanford, CA: Stanford University Press.

Maccoby, E. E., & Jacklin, C. N. (1980). Sex differences in aggression: A rejoinder and reprise. *Child Development, 51*, 964–980.

MacDonald, K. (1992). Warmth as a developmental construct: An evolutionary analysis. *Child Development, 63*, 753–773.

Macfarlane, J. A. (1975). Olfaction in the development of social preferences in the human neonate. In M. A. Hofer (Ed.), *Parent–infant interaction.* Amsterdam: Elsevier.

Mack, D., & Rainey, D. (1990). Female applicants' grooming and personnel selection. *Journal of Social Behavior and Personality, 5*, 399–407.

MacKenzie, T. D., Bartecchi, C. E., & Schrier, R. W. (1994). The human costs of tobacco use. *New England Journal of Medicine, 330*, 975–980.

Mackett-Stout, J., & Dewar, R. (1981). Evaluation of public information signs. *Human Factors, 23*(2), 139–151.

Mackie, D. M., & Worth, L. T. (1989). Processing deficits and the mediation of positive affect in persuasion. *Journal of Personality and Social Psychology, 57*, 27–40.

Mackie, D. M., Worth, L. T., & Asuncion, A. G. (1990). Processing of persuasive in-group messages. *Journal of Personality and Social Psychology, 58*, 812–822.

Macmillan, N. A., & Creelman, C. D. (1991). *Signal detection theory.* New York: Cambridge University Press.

Maddi, S. R., & Kobasa, S. C. (1984). *The hardy executive: Health under stress.* Homewood, IL: Dow Jones-Irwin.

Madigan, S., & O'Hara, R. (1992). Short-term memory at the turn of the century: Mary Whiton Calkin's memory research. *American Psychologist, 47*, 170–174.

Maher, B. A., & Maher, W. B. (1994). Personality and psychopathology: A historical perspective. *Journal of Abnormal Psychology, 103*, 72–77.

Maier, N. R. F., & Schneirla, T. C. (1935). *Principles of animal psychology.* New York: McGraw-Hill.

Malamuth, N. M., Sockloskie, R. J., Koss, M. P., & Tanaka, J. S. (1991). Characteristics of aggressors against women: Testing a model using a national sample of college students. *Journal of Consulting and Clinical Psychology, 59*, 670–681.

Malatesta, V. J., Sutker, P. B., & Treiber, F. A. (1981). Sensation seeking and chronic public drunkenness. *Journal of Consulting and Clinical Psychology, 49*, 282–294.

Malgady, R. G., Rogler, L. H., & Costantino, G. (1990). Hero/heroine modeling for Puerto Rican adolescents: A preventive mental health intervention. *Journal of Consulting and Clinical Psychology, 58*, 469–474.

Malinosky-Rummell, R., & Hansen, D. H. (1993). Long-term consequences of childhood physical abuse. *Psychological Bulletin, 114*, 68–79.

Mann, J. M. (1992). AIDS—The second decade: A global perspective. *Journal of Infectious Diseases, 165*, 245–250.

Mann, L. (1981). The baiting crowd in episodes of threatened suicide. *Journal of Personality and Social Psychology, 41*, 703–709.

Mann, L., Newton, J. W., & Innes, J. M. (1982). A test between deindividuation and emergent norm theories of crowd aggression. *Journal of Personality and Social Psychology, 42*, 260–272.

Manucia, G. K., Baumann, D. J., & Cialdini, R. B. (1984). Mood influences on helping: Direct effects or side effects? *Journal of Personality and Social Psychology, 46*, 357–364.

Manson, J. E., and others (1990). A prospective study of obesity and risk of coronary heart disease in women. *New England Journal of Medicine, 322*, 882–889.

Maratsos, M. (1983). Some current issues in the study of the acquisition of grammar. In J. H. Flavell & E. M. Markman (Eds.), *Handbook of child psychology: Vol. 3. Cognitive development.* New York: Wiley.

Marenberg, M. E. and others (1994). Genetic susceptibility to death from coronary heart disease in a study of twins. *New England Journal of Medicine, 330*, 1041–1046.

Margolick, D. (1994, January 22). Lorena Bobbitt acquitted in mutilation of husband. *The New York Times*, pp. 1, 7.

Margraf, J., and others (1991). How "blind" are double-blind studies? *Journal of Consulting and Clinical Psychology, 59*, 184–187.

Marin, P. (1983). A revolution's broken promises. *Psychology Today, 17*(7), 50–57.

Markman, H. J., Renick, M. J., Floyd, F. J., Stanley, S. M., & Clements, M. (1993). Preventing marital distress through communication and conflict management training: A 4- and 5-year follow-up. *Journal of Consulting and Clinical Psychology, 61,* 70–77.

Marks, G., Miller, N., & Maruyama, G. (1981). Effect of targets' physical attractiveness on assumption of similarity. *Journal of Personality and Social Psychology, 41,* 198–206.

Markstrom-Adams, C. (1992). A consideration of intervening factors in adolescent identity formation. In G. R. Adams, T. P. Gullotta, & R. Montemayor (Eds.), *Adolescent identity formation.* Newbury Park, CA: Sage.

Markus, H., & Kitayama, S. (1991). Culture and the self: Implications for cognition, emotion, and motivation. *Psychological Review, 98*(2), 224–253.

Marriott, M. (1991, June 5). Beyond "yuck" for girls in science. *The New York Times,* p. A26.

Marston, A. R., London, P., Cohen, N., & Cooper, L. M. (1977). In vivo observation of the eating behavior of obese and nonobese subjects. *Journal of Consulting and Clinical Psychology, 45,* 335–336.

Martelli, M. F., Auerbach, S. M., Alexander, J., & Mercuri, L. G. (1987). Stress management in the health care setting: Matching interventions with patient coping styles. *Journal of Consulting and Clinical Psychology, 55,* 201–207.

Martin, R. A., & Lefcourt, H. M. (1983). Sense of humor as a moderator of the relation between stressors and moods. *Journal of Personality and Social Psychology, 45,* 1313–1324.

Martin, R. L., and others (1985). Mortality in a follow-up of 500 psychiatric outpatients: I. Total mortality. *Archives of General Psychiatry, 42,* 47–54.

Martin, S. (1994). Music lessons enhance spatial reasoning skills. *APA Monitor, 27*(10), 5.

Martinez, C. (1986). Hispanics: Psychiatric issues. In C. B. Wilkinson (Ed.), *Ethnic psychiatry.* New York: Academic Press.

Martinez, F. D., Cline, M., & Burrows, B. (1992). Increased incidence of asthma in children of smoking mothers. *Pediatrics, 89,* 21–26.

Martinez, J. (1992). Personal communication.

Maruyama, G., Fraser, S. C., & Miller, N. (1982). Personal responsibility and altruism in children. *Journal of Personality and Social Psychology, 42,* 658–664.

Marx, E. M., Williams, J. M. G., & Claridge, G. C. (1992). Depression and social problem solving. *Journal of Abnormal Psychology, 101,* 78–86.

Maser, J. D., Kaelber, C., & Weise, R. E. (1991). International use and attitudes toward *DSM-III* and *DSM-III-R:* Growing consensus in psychiatric classification. *Journal of Abnormal Psychology, 100,* 271–279.

Maslow, A. H. (1963). The need to know and the fear of knowing. *Journal of General Psychology, 68,* 111–124.

Maslow, A. H. (1970). *Motivation and personality* (2nd ed.). New York: Harper & Row.

Maslow, A. H. (1971). *The farther reaches of human nature.* New York: Viking.

Masters, W. H., & Johnson, V. E. (1970). *Human sexual inadequacy.* Boston: Little, Brown.

Matarazzo, J. D. (1990). Psychological assessment versus psychological testing. *American Psychologist, 45,* 999–1017.

Matarazzo, J. D. (1993). Cited in Michaelson, R. (1993). Behavior gets big billing in medical schools today. *APA Monitor, 24*(8), 56.

Matefy, R. (1980). Role-playing theory of psychedelic flashbacks. *Journal of Consulting and Clinical Psychology, 48,* 551–553.

Matlin, M. (1993). *The psychology of women* (2nd ed.). Fort Worth, TX: Harcourt Brace Jovanovich.

Matlin, M. (1994). *Cognition* (3rd ed.). Fort Worth, TX: Harcourt Brace College Publishers.

Matteson, M. T., & Ivancevich, J. M. (1987). *Controlling work stress.* San Francisco: Jossey–Bass.

Matthews, K. (1994). Cited in Azar, B. (1994). Women are barraged by media on "the change." *APA Monitor, 25*(5), 24–25.

Maugh, T. H. (1982). Marijuana "justifies serious concern." *Science, 215,* 1488–1489.

Maxwell, K. (1994). *The sex imperative: An evolutionary tale of sexual survival.* New York: Plenum.

May, J. L., & Hamilton, P. A. (1980). Effects of musically evoked affect on women's interpersonal attraction toward and perceptual judgments of physical attractiveness of men. *Motivation and Emotion, 4,* 217–228.

Mayer, R., and Goodchild, F. (1990). *The Critical Thinker.* Dubuque, Iowa: Wm. C. Brown.

Mays, V. M. (1985). The Black American and psychotherapy: The dilemma. *Psychotherapy, 22,* 379–388.

McAdoo, H., & McAdoo, J. L. (Eds.) (1985). *Black children.* Beverly Hills, CA: Sage.

McCann, I. L., & Holmes, D. S. (1984). Influence of aerobic exercise on depression. *Journal of Personality and Social Psychology, 46,* 1142–1147.

McCarley, R. W. (1992). Cited in Blakeslee, S. (1992, January 7). Scientists unraveling chemistry of dreams. *The New York Times,* pp. C1, C10.

McCarthy, K. (1993). Research on women's health doesn't show whole picture. *APA Monitor, 24*(7), 14–15.

McCarthy, M. J. (1990, February 26). Anti-smoking groups grow more sophisticated in tactics used to put heat on tobacco firms. *The Wall Street Journal,* pp. B1, B3.

McCartney, K., Harris, M. J., & Bernieri, F. (1990). Growing up and growing apart: A developmental meta-analysis of twin studies. *Psychological Bulletin, 107,* 226–237.

McCaul, K. D., & Haugvedt, C. (1982). Attention, distraction, and cold-pressor pain. *Journal of Personality and Social Psychology, 43,* 154–162.

McCauley, C. (1989). The nature of social influence in groupthink: Compliance and internalization. *Journal of Personality and Social Psychology,* 57, 250–260.

McCauley, C., Woods, K., Coolidge, C., & Kulick, W. (1983). More aggressive cartoons are funnier. *Journal of Personality and Social Psychology, 44,* 817–823.

McClelland, D. C. (1958). Methods of measuring human motivation. In J. W. Atkinson (Ed.), *Motives in fantasy, action, and society.* Princeton, NJ: Van Nostrand.

McClelland, D. C. (1965). Achievement and entrepreneurship: A longitudinal study. *Journal of Personality and Social Psychology, 1,* 389–392.

McConnell, J. V., Shigehisa, T., & Salive, H. (1970). Attempts to transfer approach and avoidance responses by RNA injections in rats. In K. H. Pribram & D. E. Broadbent (Eds.), *Biology of memory.* New York: Academic Press.

McCrae, R. R. (1992). Editor's introduction to Tupes and Christal. *Journal of Personality, 60,* 217–219.

McCrank, E. (1993). Cited in Shuchman, M. (1993, November 3). When a "noninvasive" scan causes panic. *The New York Times,* p. C16.

McDougall, W. (1904). The sensations excited by a single momentary stimulation of the eye. *British Journal of Psychology, 1,* 78–113.

McDougall, W. (1908). *An introduction to social psychology.* London: Methuen.

McFadden, E. R., Jr., & Gilbert, I. A. (1994). Exercise-induced asthma. *New England Journal of Medicine, 330,* 1362–1367.

McGaugh, J. L. (1983). Preserving the presence of the past: Hormonal influences on memory storage. *American Psychologist, 38,* 161–174.

McGaugh, J. L., Martinez, J. L., Jr., Jensen, R. A., Messing, R. B., & Vasquez, B. J. (1980). Central and peripheral catecholamine function in learning and memory processes. In *Neural mechanisms of goal-directed behavior and learning.* New York: Academic Press.

McGovern, T. V., Furumoto, L., Halpern, D. F., Kimble, G. A., & McKeachie, W. J. (1991). Liberal education, study in depth, and the arts and sciences major—psychology. *American Psychologist, 46,* 598–605.

McGowan, R. J., & Johnson, D. L. (1984). The mother-child relationship and other antecedents of childhood intelligence: A causal analysis. *Child Development, 55,* 810–820.

McGrath, E., Keita, G. P., Strickland, B. R., & Russo, N. F. (1990). *Women and depression: Risk factors and treatment issues.* Washington DC: American Psychological Association.

McGregor, D. (1960). *The human side of enterprise.* New York: McGraw–Hill.

McGuffin, P., & Katz, R. (1986). Nature, nurture, and affective disorder. In J. W. W. Deakin (Ed.), *The biology of depression.* Washington, DC: American Psychiatric Press.

McKeachie, W. (1994) Cited in DeAngelis, T. (1994). Educators reveal keys to success in classroom. *APA Monitor, 25*(1), 39–40.

McLeod, J. D., Kessler, R. C., & Landis, K. R. (1992). Speed of recovery from major depressive episodes in a community sample of married men and women. *Journal of Abnormal Psychology, 101,* 277–286.

McNally, R. J. (1990). Psychological approaches to panic disorder: A review. *Psychological Bulletin, 108,* 403–419.

Mead, A., & Drasgow, F. (1993). Equivalence of computerized and paper-and-pencil cognitive ability tests: A meta-analysis. *Psychological Bulletin, 114,* 449–458.

Mead, M. (1935). *Sex and temperament in three primitive societies.* New York: Dell.

Meade, V. (1994). Psychologists forecast future of the profession. *APA Monitor, 25*(5), 14–15.

Medin, D. L., & Ross, B. H. (1992). *Cognitive psychology.* Fort Worth, TX: Harcourt Brace Jovanovich.

Mednick, S. A. (1962). The associative basis of the creative process. *Psychological Review, 69,* 220–232.

Meichenbaum, D. (1993). Changing conceptions of cognitive behavior modification: Retrospect and prospect. *Journal of Consulting and Clinical Psychology, 61,* 202–204.

Meichenbaum, D., & Jaremko, M. E. (Eds.). (1983). *Stress reduction and prevention.* New York: Plenum.

Melzack, R. (1980). Psychological aspects of pain. In J. J. Bonica (Ed.), *Pain.* New York: Raven Press.

Melzack, R. (1990). Phantom limbs and the concept of a neuromatrix. *Trends in Neurosciences, 13,* 88–92.

Mendez, M., and others (1992). Disturbances of person identification in Alzheimer's disease: A retrospective study. *Journal of Nervous & Mental Disease, 180,* 94–96.

Metalsky, G. I., Joiner, T. E., Jr., Hardin, T. S., & Abramson, L. Y. (1993). Depressive reactions to failure in a naturalistic setting: A test of the hopelessness and self-esteem theories of depression. *Journal of Abnormal Psychology, 102,* 101–109.

Metcalfe, J. (1986). Premonitions of insight predict impending error. *Journal of Experimental Psychology: Learning, Memory, and Cognition, 12,* 623–634.

Mevkens, F. L. (1990). Coming of age—The chemoprevention of cancer. *New England Journal of Medicine, 323,* 825–827.

Michaelson, R. (1993a). Behavior gets big billing in medical schools today. *APA Monitor, 24*(8), 56.

Michaelson, R. (1993b). Tug-of-war is developing over defining retardation. *APA Monitor, 24*(5), 34–35.

Michelini, R. L., & Snodgrass, S. R. (1980). Defendant characteristics and juridic decisions. *Journal of Research in Personality, 14,* 340–350.

Michels, R., & Marzuk, P. M. (1993a). Progress in psychiatry. (Part 1). *New England Journal of Medicine, 329,* 552–560.

Michels, R., & Marzuk, P. M. (1993b). Progress in psychiatry. (Part 2). *New England Journal of Medicine, 329,* 628–638.

Mikesell, R. H., Lusterman, D., & McDaniel, S. (Eds.). (1995). *Family psychology and systems therapy.* Washington, DC: American Psychological Association.

Milgram, S. (1963). Behavioral study of obedience. *Journal of Abnormal and Social Psychology, 67,* 371–378.

Milgram, S. (1974). *Obedience to authority.* New York: Harper & Row.

Milgram, S. (1977). *The individual in a social world.* Reading, MA: Addison–Wesley.

Millar, J. D. (1990). Mental health and the workplace. *American Psychologist, 45,* 1165–1166.

Miller, A. G. (1986). *The obedience experiments: A case study of controversy in social science.* New York: Praeger.

Miller, C. A. (1985). Infant mortality in the United States. *Scientific American, 235,* 31–37.

Miller, G. A. (1956). The magical number seven, plus or minus two: Some limits on our capacity for processing information. *Psychological Review, 63,* 81–97.

Miller, J. L. (1990). Speech perception. In D. N. Osherson, & H. Lasnik (Eds.), *An invitation to cognitive science: Language* (Vol. 1). Cambridge, MA: The MIT Press, a Bradford Book.

Miller, J. L. (1992). Trouble in mind. *Scientific American, 267*(3), 180.

Miller, M. E., & Bowers, K. S. (1993). Hypnotic analgesia: Dissociated experience or dissociated control. *Journal of Abnormal Psychology, 102,* 29–38.

Miller, M. F., Barabasz, A. F., & Barabasz, M. (1991). Effects of active alert and relaxation hypnotic inductions on cold pressor pain. *Journal of Abnormal Psychology, 100,* 223–226.

Miller, N. B., Cowan, P. A., Cowan, C. P., Hetherington, E. M., & Clingempeel, W. G. (1993). Externalizing in preschoolers and early adolescents: A cross-study replication of a family model. *Developmental Psychology, 29,* 3–18.

Miller, N. E. (1969). Learning of visceral and glandular responses. *Science, 163,* 434–445.

Miller, N. E., & Dollard, J. (1941). *Social learning and imitation.* New Haven, CT: Yale University Press.

Miller, P. H., Heldmeyer, K. H., & Miller, S. A. (1975). Facilitation of conservation of number in young children. *Developmental Psychology, 11,* 253.

Miller, R. L. (1992). The human ecology of multiracial identity. In M. P. P. Root (Ed.), *Racially mixed people in America.* Newbury Park, CA: Sage.

Miller, W. R. (1982). Treating problem drinkers: What works? *The Behavior Therapist, 5*(1), 15–18.

Millette, B., & Hawkins, J. (1983). *The passage through menopause.* Reston, VA: Reston Publishing.

A million Mrs. Bobbitts. (1994, January 28). *The New York Times,* p. A26.

Millon, T. (1991). Classification in psychopathology: Rationale, alternatives, and standards. *Journal of Abnormal Psychology, 100,* 245–261.

Mills, J., & Harvey, J. (1972). Opinion change as a function of when information about the communicator is received and whether he is attractive or expert. *Journal of Personality and Social Psychology, 21,* 52–55.

Milner, B. R. (1966). Amnesia following operation on temporal lobes. In C. W. M. Whitty & O. L. Zangwill (Eds.), *Amnesia.* London: Butterworth.

Mindell, J. A. (1993). Sleep disorders in children. *Health Psychology, 12,* 151–162.

Mineka, S. (1991, August). Paper presented to the annual meeting of the American Psychological Association, San Francisco. Cited in Turkington, C. (1991). Evolutionary memories may have phobia role. *APA Monitor, 22*(11), 14.

Mischel, W. (1990). Personality dispositions revisited and revised: A view after three decades. In L. A. Pervin (Ed.), *Handbook of personality: Theory and research* (pp. 111–134). New York: Guilford.

Mischel, W. (1993). *Introduction to personality,* (5th ed.). Fort Worth, TX: Harcourt Brace Jovanovich.

Mishkin, M., & Appenzeller, T. (1987). The anatomy of memory. *Scientific American, 256,* 80–89.

Mitchell, J. E., & Eckert, E. D. (1987). Scope and significance of eating disorders. *Journal of Consulting and Clinical Psychology, 55,* 628–634.

Mittelman, M. A., and others (1993). Triggering of acute myocardial infarction by heavy physical exertion—protection against triggering by regular exertion. *New England Journal of Medicine, 329,* 1677–1683.

Mohrman, A. M., Jr., Resnick-West, S. M., & Lawler, E. E., III. (1989). *Designing performance appraisal systems: Aligning appraisals and organizational realities.* San Francisco: Jossey–Bass.

Molfese, D. L., & Molfese, V. J. (1979). Hemisphere and stimulus differences as reflected in the cortical responses of newborn infants to speech stimuli. *Developmental Psychology, 15,* 505–511.

Moliterno, D. J., and others (1994). Coronary-artery vasoconstriction induced by cocaine, cigarette smoking, or both. *New England Journal of Medicine, 330,* 454–459.

Mom blames "Beavis" for 2-year-old's death. (1993, October 9). *Daily News,* p. 4.

Money, J. (1977). Human hermaphroditism. In F. A. Beach (Ed.), *Human sexuality in four perspectives.* Baltimore, MD: The Johns Hopkins University Press.

Money, J. (1987). Sin, sickness, or status? Homosexual gender identity and psychoneuroendocrinology. *American Psychologist, 42,* 384–399.

Montemayor, R., & Flannery, D. J. (1991). Parent–adolescent relations in middle and late adolescence. In R. M. Lerner, A. C. Petersen, & J. Brooks-Gunn (Eds.), *Encyclopedia of adolescence.* New York: Garland.

Monti, P. M., and others (1993). Cue exposure with coping skills treatment for male alcoholics: A preliminary investigation. *Journal of Consulting and Clinical Psychology, 61,* 1011–1019.

Moon, J. R., & Eisler, R. M. (1983). Anger control: An experimental comparison of three behavioral treatments. *Behavior Therapy, 14,* 493–505.

Morales, E. (1992). Latino gays and Latina lesbians. In S. Dworkin & F. Gutierrez (Eds.), *Counseling gay men and lesbians: Journey to the end of the rainbow.* Alexandria, VA: American Association for Counseling and Development.

Moran, D. (1993). Cited in Blakeslee, S. (1993, September 7). Human nose may hold an additional organ for a real sixth sense. *The New York Times,* p. C3.

Moran, J., & Desimone, R. (1985). Selective attention gates visual processing in the extrastriate cortex. *Science, 229,* 782–784.

Moriarty, T. (1975). Crimes, commitment, and the responsive bystander: Two field experiments. *Journal of Personality and Social Psychology, 31,* 370–376.

Morin, C. M., Kowatch, R. A., Barry, T., & Walton, E. (1993). Cognitive-behavior therapy for late-life insomnia. *Journal of Consulting and Clinical Psychology, 61,* 137–146.

Morris, W. N., Miller, R. S., & Spangenberg, S. (1977). The effects of dissenter position and task difficulty on conformity and response conflict. *Journal of Personality, 45,* 251–256.

Morrison, A. M., & Von Glinow, M. A. (1990). Women and minorities in management. *American Psychologist, 45,* 200–209.

Moscovitch, M. (1994). Conference on memory, Harvard Medical School. Cited in Goleman, D. (1994, May 31). Miscoding is seen as the root of false memories. *The New York Times,* pp. C1, C8.

Moser, C. G., & Dyck, D. G. (1989). Type A behavior, uncontrollability, and the activation of hostile self-schema responding. *Journal of Research in Personality, 23,* 248–267.

Mowrer, O. H. (1947). On the dual nature of learning—A reinterpretation of "conditioning" and "problem-solving." *Harvard Educational Review, 17,* 102–148.

Moyers, B. (1993). *Healing and the mind.* New York: Doubleday.

Muehlenhard, C. L., & Falcon, P. L (1990). Men's heterosocial skill and attitudes toward women as predictors of verbal sexual coercion and forceful rape. *Sex Roles, 23,* 241–259.

Mullen, B., and others (1987). Newscasters' facial expressions and voting behavior of viewers: Can a smile elect a president? *Journal of Personality and Social Psychology, 53.*

Murray, E. A., & Mishkin, M. (1985). Amygdalectomy impairs cross-modal association in monkeys. *Science, 228,* 604–606.

Murray, H. A. (1938). *Explorations in personality.* New York: Oxford University Press.

Murstein, B. I., & Fontaine, P. A. (1993). The public's knowledge about psychologists and other mental health professionals. *American Psychologist, 48,* 839–845.

Muslim Women Bridging Culture Gap. (1993, November 8). *The New York Times,* p. B9.

Myers, D. G. (1983). Polarizing effects of social interaction. In H. Brandstatter, J. H. Davis, & G. Stocker-Kreichgauer (Eds.), *Group decision processes.* London: Academic Press.

Myers, L. B., & Brewin, C. R. (1994). Recall of early experience and the repressive coping style. *Journal of Abnormal Psychology, 103,* 288–292.

Nadol, J. B., Jr. (1993). Hearing loss. *New England Journal of Medicine, 329,* 1092–1102.

Nathan, P. (1991). Substance use disorders in the *DSM-IV. Journal of Abnormal Psychology, 100,* 356–361.

Nathans, J., Thomas, D., & Hogness, D. S. (1986). Molecular genetics of human color vision: The genes encoding blue, green, and red pigments. *Science, 232,* 193–202.

National Institute of Mental Health. (1982). *Television and behavior: Ten years of scientific progress and implications for the eighties.* Washington, DC: National Institute of Mental Health.

National Institute of Mental Health. (1985). *Electroconvulsive therapy: Consensus Development Conference statement.* Bethesda, MD: U.S. Department of Health and Human Services.

National Institute of Occupational Safety and Health. (1990). *A proposal: National strategy for the prevention of psychological disorders.* Draft paper provided to the U.S. Senate Appropriations Subcommittee on Labor, Health and Human Services, and Education and Related Agencies by NIOSH.

Neisser, U. (1993). Cited in Goleman, D. J. (1993, April 6). Studying the secrets of childhood memory. *The New York Times,* pp. C1, C11.

Nelson, J. (1990, May 28). Listen to your body for top performance. *The New York Times,* p. A39.

Nelson, K. (1973). Structure and strategy in learning to talk. *Monographs for the Society for Research in Child Development, 38* (Whole No. 149).

Nelson, K., Hampson, J., & Shaw, L. K. (1993). Nouns in early lexicons: Evidence, explanations, and implications. *Journal of Child Language, 20,* 228.

Nelson, M. B. (1994, June 22). Bad sports. *The New York Times,* p. A21.

Nevid, J. S. (1984). Sex differences in factors of romantic attraction. *Sex Roles, 11*(5/6), 401–411.

Nevid, J. S., Rathus, S. A., & Greene, B. A. (1994). *Abnormal psychology in a changing world* (2nd ed.). Englewood Cliffs, NJ: Prentice-Hall.

Newcombe, N., Bandura, M. M., & Taylor, D. G. (1983). Sex differences in spatial ability and spatial activity. *Sex Roles, 9,* 377–386.

Newlin, D. B., & Thomson, J. B. (1990). Alcohol challenge with sons of alcoholics: A critical review and analysis. *Psychological Bulletin, 108,* 383–402.

Newman, F. L., & Howard, K. I. (1991). Introduction to the special section on seeking new clinical research methods. *Journal of Consulting and Clinical Psychology, 59,* 8–11.

Newman, J., & McCauley, C. (1977). Eye contact with strangers in city, suburb, and small town. *Environment and Behavior, 9,* 547–558.

Newman, R. (1994). Prozac: Panacea? Psychological steroid? *APA Monitor, 25*(4), 34.

Newman, R. S. (1990). Children help seeking in the classroom: The role of motivational factors and attitudes. *Journal of Educational Psychology, 82,* 71–80.

Newport, E. L. (1994). Cited in Senior, J. (1994, January 3). Language of the deaf evolves to reflect new sensibilities. *The New York Times,* pp. A1, A12.

Newport, E. L., & Supalla, T. (1993). *Critical period effects in the acquisition of a primary language.* Unpublished manuscript, University of Rochester.

Nezu, A. M., & Ronan, G. F. (1985). Life stress, current problems, problem solving, and depressive symptoms: An integrative model. *Journal of Consulting and Clinical Psychology, 53,* 693–697.

Niaura, R. S., and others (1988). Relevance of cue reactivity to understanding alcohol and smoking relapse. *Journal of Abnormal Psychology, 97,* 133–152.

Nickerson, R. A., & Adams, N. J. (1979). Long-term memory for a common object. *Cognitive Psychology, 11,* 287–307.

Nigg, J. T., & Goldsmith, H. H. (1994). Genetics of personality disorders: Perspectives from personality and psychopathology research. *Psychological Bulletin, 115,* 346–380.

NIMH. See National Institute of Mental Health.

Nisan, M. (1984). Distributive justice and social norms. *Child Development, 55,* 1020–1029.

Nogrady, H., McConkey, K. M., & Perry, C. (1985). Enhancing visual memory: Trying hypnosis, trying imagination, and trying again. *Journal of Abnormal Psychology, 94,* 195–204.

Nolen-Hoeksema, S. (1991). Responses to depression and their effects on the duration of depressive episodes. *Journal of Abnormal Psychology, 100,* 569–582.

Nolen-Hoeksema, S., & Girgus, J. S. (1994). The emergence of gender differences in depression during adolescence. *Psychological Bulletin, 115,* 424–443.

Nolen-Hoeksema, S., Morrow, J., & Fredrickson, B. L. (1993). Response styles and the duration of depressed mood. *Journal of Abnormal Psychology, 102,* 20–28.

Noller, P., & Callan, V. J. (1991). Adolescents' perceptions of the nature of their communication with parents. *Journal of Youth and Adolescence, 19,* 349–362.

Norman, D. A. (1988). *The psychology of everyday things.* New York: Basic Books.

Norris, F. H., & Kaniasty, K. (1994). Psychological distress following criminal victimization in the general population: Cross-sectional, longitudinal, and prospective analyses. *Journal of Consulting and Clinical Psychology, 62,* 111–123.

Northwestern National Life Insurance Company. (1991, July 10). Job stress: Rating your workplace. *The New York Times,* p. C11.

Norvell, N., & Belles, D. (1993). Psychological and physical benefits of circuit weight training in law enforcement personnel. *Journal of Consulting and Clinical Psychology, 61,* 520–527.

Novick, L. R., & Coté N. (1992). The nature of expertise in anagram solution. In *Proceedings of the Fourteenth Annual Conference of the Cognitive Science Society.* Hillsdale, NJ: Erlbaum.

Novick, L. R., & Holyoak, K. J. (1991). Mathematical problem solving by analogy. *Journal of Experimental Psychology: Learning, Memory, and Cognition, 17,* 398–415.

Novin, D., and others (1983). Is there a role for the liver in the control of food intake? *American Journal of Clinical Nutrition, 9,* 233–246.

Nowlis, G. H., & Kessen, W. (1976). Human newborns differentiate differing concentrations of sucrose and glucose. *Science, 191,* 865–866.

ODEER (1994). See Office of Demographic, Employment, and Educational Research.

Offerman, L. R., & Gowing, M. K. (1990). Organizations of the future: Changes and challenges. *American Psychologist, 45,* 95–108.

Office of Demographic, Employment, and Educational Research (1994). Summary report doctorate recipients from United States universities. Washington, DC: American Psychological Association.

Ogbu, J. U. (1993). Differences in cultural frame of reference. *International Journal of Behavioral Development, 16,* 483–506.

Ogden, J. (1994). Effects of smoking cessation, restrained eating, and motivational states on food intake in the laboratory. *Health Psychology, 13,* 114–121.

O'Grady, K. E. (1982). Sex, physical attractiveness, and perceived risk for mental illness. *Journal of Personality and Social Psychology, 43,* 1064–1071.

Ohman, A., Fredrikson, M., Hugdahl, K., & Rimmo, P. (1976). The premise of equipotentiality in human classical conditioning: Conditioned electrodermal responses to potentially phobic stimuli. *Journal of Experimental Psychology: General, 105,* 313–337.

Olds, J. (1969). The central nervous system and the reinforcement of behavior. *American Psychologist, 24,* 114–132.

Olds, J., & Milner, P. (1954). Positive reinforcement produced by electrical stimulation of the septal area and other regions of the rat brain. *Journal of Comparative and Physiological Psychology, 47,* 419–427.

O'Leary, A. (1990). Stress, emotion, and human immune function. *Psychological Bulletin, 108,* 363–382.

Oliver, M. B., & Hyde, J. S. (1993). Gender differences in sexuality: A meta-analysis. *Psychological Bulletin, 114,* 29–51.

Olson, S. L., Bates, J. E., & Kaskie, B. (1992). Caregiver–infant interaction antecedents of children's school-age cognitive ability. *Merrill–Palmer Quarterly, 38,* 309–330.

O'Malley, S. S., and others (1988). Therapist competence and patient outcome in interpersonal psychotherapy of depression. *Journal of Consulting and Clinical Psychology, 56,* 496–501.

Orive, R. (1988). Social projective and social comparison of opinion. *Journal of Personality and Social Psychology, 54,* 953–964.

Orr, S. P., Pitman, R. K., Lasko, N. B., & Herz, L. R. (1993). Psychophysiological assessment of posttraumatic stress disorder imagery in World War II and Korean combat veterans. *Journal of Abnormal Psychology, 102,* 152–159.

Ortega, D. F., & Pipal, J. E. (1984). Challenge seeking and the Type A coronary-prone behavior pattern. *Journal of Personality and Social Psychology, 46,* 1328–1334.

Ouchi, W. (1981). *Theory Z: How American business can meet the Japanese challenge.* Reading, MA: Addison–Wesley.

Outlook, The. (1993, January 6). Positive implications of new population projections. *The Outlook,* pp. 10–11.

Paffenbarger, R. S., Jr., Hyde, R. T., Wing, A. L., & Hsieh, C. C. (1986). Physical activity, all-cause mortality, and longevity of college alumni. *New England Journal of Medicine, 314,* 605–613.

Paffenbarger, R. S., Jr., and others (1993). The association of changes in physical-activity level and other lifestyle characteristics with mortality among men. *New England Journal of Medicine, 328,* 538–545.

Pagan, G., & Aiello, J. R. (1982). Development of personal space among Puerto Ricans. *Journal of Nonverbal Behavior, 7,* 59–68.

Page, R. A. (1977). Noise and helping behavior. *Environment and Behavior, 9,* 311–334.

Paige, K. E. (1971). Effects of oral contraceptives on affective fluctuations associated with the menstrual cycle. *Psychosomatic Medicine, 33,* 515–537.

Paige, K. E. (1973). Women learn to sing the menstrual blues. *Psychology Today, 7,* 41.

Paikoff, R. L., & Brooks-Gunn, J. (1991). Do parent–child relationships change during puberty? *Psychological Bulletin, 110,* 47–66.

Paikoff, R. L., & Collins, A. C. (1991). Editor's notes: Shared views in the family during adolescence. In R. L. Paikoff & A. C. Collins (Eds.), *New Directions for Child Development* (Vol. 51). San Francisco: Jossey–Bass.

Pajares, F., & Miller, M. D. (1994). Role of self-efficacy and self-concept beliefs in mathematical problem solving: A path analysis. *Journal of Educational Psychology, 86,* 193–203.

Palac, L. (1994). Cited in Tierney, J. (1994, January 9). Porn, the low-slung engine of progress. *The New York Times,* pp. H1, H18.

Palladino, J. (1994) Cited in DeAngelis, T. (1994). Educators reveal keys to success in classroom. *APA Monitor, 25*(1), 39–40.

Pandurangi, A. K., and others (1988). Schizophrenic symptoms and deterioration: Relation to computerized tomographic findings. *Journal of Nervous and Mental Disease, 176,* 200–206.

Pantin, H. M., & Carver, C. S. (1982). Induced competence and the bystander effect. *Journal of Applied Social Psychology, 12,* 100–111.

Papini, D. R., & Roggman, L. A. (1992). Adolescent perceived attachment to parents in relation to competence, depression, and anxiety: A longitudinal study. *Journal of Early Adolescence, 12,* 420–440.

Papousek, M., Papousek, H., & Symmes, D. (1991). The meanings of melodies in motherese in tone and stress languages. *Infant Behavior and Development, 14,* 415–440.

Pappas, G., Queen, S., Hadden, W., & Fisher, G. (1993). The increasing disparity of mortality between socioeconomic groups in the United States, 1960 and 1986. *New England Journal of Medicine, 329,* 103–109.

Pardes, H., and others (1991). Physicians and the animal-rights movement. *New England Journal of Medicine, 324,* 1640–1643.

Park, B., & Flink, C. (1989). A social relations analysis of agreement in liking judgments. *Journal of Personality and Social Psychology, 56,* 506–518.

Parkes, C. M., & Weiss, R. S. (1983). *Recovery from bereavement.* New York: Basic Books.

Parron, D. L., Solomon, F., & Jenkins, C. D. (Eds.). (1982). *Behavior, health risks, and social disadvantage.* Washington, DC: National Academy Press.

Parrot, W. G., & Sabini, J. (1990). Mood and memory under natural conditions: Evidence for mood incongruent recall. *Journal of Personality and Social Psychology, 59,* 321–336.

Pascual-Leone, J. (1980). Constructive problems for constructive theories: The current relevance of Piaget's work and a critique of information-processing simulation psychology. In R. H. Kluwe & H. Spada (Eds.), *Developmental models of thinking.* New York: Academic Press.

Patrick, C. J., Bradley, M. M., & Lang, P. J. (1993). Emotion in the criminal psychopath: Startle reflex modulation. *Journal of Abnormal Psychology, 102,* 82–92.

Patterson, C. J., Kupersmidt, J. B., & Vader, N. A. (1990). Income level, gender, ethnicity, and household composition as predictors of children's school-based competence. *Child Development, 61,* 485–494.

Patterson, G. R. (1993). Orderly change in a stable world: The antisocial trait as a chimera. *Journal of Consulting and Clinical Psychology, 61,* 911–919.

Patterson, M. L. (1991). Functions of nonverbal behavior in interpersonal interaction. In R. S. Feldman & B. Rime (Eds.), *Fundamentals of nonverbal behavior.* Cambridge, England: Cambridge University Press.

Patterson, S. J., Sochting, I., & Marcia, J. E. (1992). The inner space and beyond: Women and identity. In G. R. Adama, T. P. Gullotta, & R. Montemayor (Eds.), *Adolescent identity formation.* Newbury Park, CA: Sage.

Pattison, E. M. (1977). *The experience of dying.* Englewood Cliffs, NJ: Prentice-Hall.

Paulus, P. B., & Matthews, R. (1980). Crowding, attribution, and task performance. *Basic and Applied Social Psychology, 1,* 3–13.

Pavlov, I. (1927). *Conditioned reflexes.* London: Oxford University Press.

Pearlman, K., Schmidt, F. L., & Hunter, J. E. (1980). Test of a new model of validity generalization: Results for job proficiency and training criteria in clerical occupations. *Journal of Applied Psychology, 65,* 373–406.

Pedersen, N. L., Plomin, R., McClearn, G. E., & Friberg, L. (1988). Neuroticism, extraversion, and related traits in adult twins reared apart and reared together. *Journal of Personality and Social Psychology, 55,* 950–957.

Pelham, W. E., Jr., and others (1993). Separate and combined effects of methylphenidate and behavior modification on boys with attention deficit-hyperactivity disorder in the classroom. *Journal of Consulting and Clinical Psychology, 61,* 506–515.

Penfield, W. (1969). Consciousness, memory, and man's conditioned reflexes. In K. H. Pribram (Ed.), *On the biology of learning.* New York: Harcourt Brace Jovanovich.

Penner, L. A., Thompson, J. K., & Coovert, D. L. (1991). Size overestimation among anorexics: Much ado about very little? *Journal of Abnormal Psychology, 100,* 90–93.

Perez-Stable, E. (1991, May). *Health promotion among Latinos: What are the priorities?* Chancellor's Distinguished Lecture, University of California, Irvine.

Perkins, D. N. (1993). Teaching for understanding. *American Educator, 17*(3), 8, 28–35.

Perkins, K. (1993a). Cited in Adler, T. (1993). Nicotine gives mixed results on learning and performance. *APA Monitor, 24*(5), 14–15.

Perkins, K. (1993b). Weight gain following smoking cessation. *Journal of Consulting and Clinical Psychology, 61,* 768–777.

Perls, F. S. (1971). *Gestalt therapy verbatim.* New York: Bantam.

Perrett, D. I. (1994). *Nature.* Cited in Brody, J. E. (1994, March 21). Notions of beauty transcend culture, new study suggests. *The New York Times,* p. A14.

Perri, M. G., and others (1988). Effects of four maintenance programs on the long-term management of obesity. *Journal of Consulting and Clinical Psychology, 56,* 529–534.

Perry, D. G., & Bussey, K. (1979). The social learning theory of sex differences: Imitation is alive and well. *Journal of Personality and Social Psychology, 37,* 1699–1712.

Persons, J. B., Burns, D. D., Perloff, J. M., & Miranda, J. (1993). Relationships between symptoms of depression and anxiety and dysfunctional beliefs about achievement and attachment. *Journal of Abnormal Psychology, 102,* 518–524.

A perverse choice. (1993). Cited in Kolata, G. (1993d, October 26). The hot debate about cloning human embryo. *The New York Times,* pp. 1, C3.

Peterson, L. R., & Peterson, M. J. (1959). Short-term retention of individual verbal items. *Journal of Experimental Psychology, 58,* 193–198.

Pettingale, K. W., and others (1985). Mental attitudes to cancer: An additional prognostic factor. *Lancet, 1,* 750.

Petty, R. E., & Cacioppo, J. T. (1986). The elaboration-likelihood model of persuasion. In L. Berkowitz (Ed.), *Advances in experimental social psychology* (Vol. 19). New York: Academic Press.

Petty, R. E., Gleicher, F., & Baker, S. M. (1991). Multiple roles for affect in persuasion. In J. Forgas (Ed.), *Emotion and social judgments.* London: Pergamon.

Phillipson, E. A. (1993). Sleep apnea—A major public health problem. *New England Journal of Medicine, 328,* 1271–1273.

Phinney, J. S., Chavira, V., & Williamson, L. (1992). Acculturation attitudes and self-esteem among high school and college students. *Youth and Society, 23*(3), 299–312.

Phinney, J. S., & Rosenthal, D. A. (1992). Ethnic identity in adolescence: Process, context, and outcome. In G. R. Adams, T. P. Gullotta, & R. Montemayor (Eds.), *Adolescent identity formation.* Newbury Park, CA: Sage.

Piaget, J. (1962). *The moral judgment of the child.* New York: Collier.

Piaget, J. (1963). *The origins of intelligence in children.* New York: W. W. Norton.

Pick, A. D. (1991). Perception. In R. M. Thomas (Ed.), *The encyclopedia of human development and education theory, research, and studies* (pp. 249–254). Oxford, England: Pergamon.

Pihl, R. O., Peterson, J., & Finn, P. (1990). Inherited predisposition to alcoholism: Characteristics of sons of male alcoholics. *Journal of Abnormal Psychology, 99,* 291–301.

Pike, K. M., & Rodin, J. (1991). Mothers, daughters, and disordered eating. *Journal of Abnormal Psychology, 100,* 198–204.

Pillard, R. C. (1990). The Kinsey Scale: Is it familial? In D. P. McWhirter, S. A. Sanders, & J. M. Reinisch (Eds.) *Homosexuality/Heterosexuality: Concepts of sexual orientation* (pp. 88–100). New York: Oxford University Press.

Pillard, R. C., & Weinrich, J. D. (1986). Evidence of familial nature of male homosexuality. *Archives of Sexual Behavior, 43,* 808–812.

Pinderhughes, E. (1989). *Understanding race, ethnicity and power: The key to efficacy in clinical practice.* New York: The Free Press.

Pinker, S. (1990). Language acquisition. In D. N. Osherson, & H. Lasnik (Eds.), *An invitation to cognitive science: Language* (Vol. 1). Cambridge, MA: The MIT Press, a Bradford Book.

Pinker, S. (1994a, June 19). Building a better brain. *The New York Times Book Review,* pp. 13–14.

Pinker, S. (1994b). *The language instinct: How the mind creates language.* New York: William Morrow.

Pinpointing chess moves in the brain. (1994, May 24). *The New York Times,* p. C14.

Pitman, R. K., and others (1990). Psychophysiologic responses to combat imagery of Vietnam veterans with posttraumatic stress disorder versus other anxiety disorders. *Journal of Abnormal Psychology, 99,* 49–54.

Plomin, R. (1989). Environment and genes: Determinants of behavior. *American Psychologist, 44,* 105–111.

Plomin, R., Emde, R. N., Braungart, J. M., Campos, J., and others. (1993). Genetic change and continuity from fourteen to twenty months: The MacArthur Longitudinal Twin Study. *Child Development, 64,* 1354–1376.

Plomin, R., & Rende, R. (1991). Human behavioral genetics. *Annual Review of Psychology, 42,* 161–190.

Plutchik, R. (1984). A general psychoevolutionary theory. In K. Scherer & P. Ekman (Eds.), *Approaches to emotion.* Hillsdale, NJ: Erlbaum.

Polivy, J., & Herman, C. P. (1987). Diagnosis and treatment of normal eating. *Journal of Consulting and Clinical Psychology, 55,* 635–644.

Polivy, J., Zeitlin, S. B., Herman, C. P., & Beal, A. L. (1994). Food restriction and binge eating: A study of former prisoners of war. *Journal of Abnormal Psychology, 103,* 409–411.

Pollack, A. (1991, April 29). Medical technology "arms race" adds billions to the nation's bills. *The New York Times,* pp. A1, B8.

Pomazal, R. J., & Clore, G. L. (1973). Helping on the highway: The effects of dependency and sex. *Journal of Applied Social Psychology, 3,* 150–164.

Pomerleau, O. F., Collins, A. C., Shiffman, S., & Pomerleau, C. S. (1993). Why some people smoke and others do not: New perspectives. *Journal of Consulting and Clinical Psychology, 61,* 723–731.

Porter, R. H., Makin, J. W., Davis, L. B., & Christensen, K. M. (1992). Breast-fed infants respond to olfactory cues from their own mother and unfamiliar lactating females. *Infant Behavior and Development, 15,* 85–93.

Portes, A., & Stepick, A. (1993). *City on the edge: The transformation of Miami.* Berkeley: University of California Press.

Posner, M. I., & Raichle, M. E. (1994). *Images of mind.* New York: W. H. Freeman.

Potter, W. Z., Rudorfer, M. V., & Manji, H. (1991). Drug therapy: The pharmacologic treatment of depression. *New England Journal of Medicine, 325,* 633–642.

Poussaint, A. (1990, September). An honest look at Black gays and lesbians. *Ebony,* pp. 124, 126, 130–131.

Powell, E. (1991). *Talking back to sexual pressure.* Minneapolis: CompCare Publishers.

Pratkanis, A. R., Breckler, S. J., & Greenwald, A. G. (1989). *Attitude structure and function.* Hillsdale, NJ: Erlbaum.

Premack, A. J., & Premack, D. (1975). Teaching language to an ape. In R. C. Atkinson (Ed.), *Psychology in Progress.* San Francisco: W. H. Freeman.

Prentky, R. A., & Knight, R. A. (1991). Identifying critical dimensions for discriminating among rapists. *Journal of Consulting and Clinical Psychology, 59,* 643–661.

Prewett, M. J., van Allen, P. K., & Milner, J. S. (1978). Multiple electroconvulsive shocks and feeding and drinking behavior in the rat. *Bulletin of the Psychonomic Society, 12,* 137–139.

Prigatano, G. P. (1992). Personality disturbances associated with traumatic brain injury. *Journal of Consulting and Clinical Psychology, 60,* 360–368.

Proulx, E. A. (1994, May 26). Books on top. *The New York Times,* p. A23.

Putallaz, M., & Heflin, A. H. (1990). Parent–child interaction. In S. R. Asher & J. D. Coie (Eds.), *Peer rejection in childhood.* New York: Cambridge University Press.

Pyszczynski, T., Holt, K., & Greenberg, J. (1987). Depression, self-focused attention, and expectancies for positive and negative future life events for self and others. *Journal of Personality and Social Psychology, 52,* 994–1001.

Qualls, P. J., & Sheehan, P. W. (1981). Imagery encouragement, absorption capacity, and relaxation during electromyographic feedback. *Journal of Personality and Social Psychology, 41,* 370–379.

Quattrone, G. A. (1982). Overattribution and unit formation: When behavior engulfs the person. *Journal of Personality and Social Psychology, 42,* 593–607.

Quindlen, A. (1993, April 11). The good guys. *The New York Times,* p. E13.

Quinn, J. C., Murphy, L. R., & Hurrell, J. J. (1992). *Stress and well-being at work: Assessments and interventions for occupational mental health.* Washington, DC: American Psychological Association.

Raichle, M. E. (1994). Visualizing the mind. *Scientific American, 270*(4), 58–64.

Rajecki, D. J. (1989). *Attitudes.* Sunderland, MA: Sinauer Associates.

Rao, S. M., Huber, S. J., & Bornstein, R. B. (1992). Emotional changes with multiple sclerosis and Parkinson's disease. *Journal of Consulting and Clinical Psychology, 60,* 369–378.

Rapoport, K., & Burkhart, B. R. (1984). Personality and attitudinal characteristics of sexually coercive college males. *Journal of Abnormal Psychology, 93,* 216–221.

Rappaport, N. B., McAnulty, D. P., & Brantley, P. J. (1988). Exploration of the Type A behavior pattern in chronic headache sufferers. *Journal of Consulting and Clinical Psychology, 56,* 621–623.

Rathus, S. A. (1973). A 30-item schedule for assessing assertive behavior. *Behavior Therapy, 4,* 398–406.

Rathus, S. A., & Boughn, S. (1994). *AIDS—What every student needs to know.* Fort Worth, TX: Harcourt Brace College Publishers.

Rathus, S. A., & Fichner-Rathus, L. (1994). *Making the most of college* (2nd ed.). Englewood Cliffs, NJ: Prentice-Hall.

Rathus, S. A., & Nevid, J. S. (1995). *Adjustment and growth: The challenges of life* (6th ed.). Fort Worth, TX: Harcourt Brace College Publishing.

Rathus, S. A., Nevid, J. S., & Fichner-Rathus, L. (1993). *Human sexuality in a world of diversity.* Boston: Allyn & Bacon.

Ratner, N. B., & Gleason, J. B. (1993). An introduction to psycholinguistics: What do language users know? In J. B. Gleason & N. B. Ratner (Eds.), *Psycholinguistics.* Fort Worth, TX: Harcourt Brace Jovanovich.

Ravo, N., & Nash, E. (1993, August 8). The evolution of cyberpunk. *The New York Times,* p. V9.

Rebok, G. (1987). *Life-span cognitive development.* New York: Holt, Rinehart and Winston.

Redd, W. H., and others (1987). Cognitive/attentional distraction in the control of conditioned nausea in pediatric cancer patients receiving chemotherapy. *Journal of Consulting and Clinical Psychology, 55,* 391–395.

Reeder, G. D., Henderson, D. J., & Sullivan, J. J. (1982). From dispositions to behaviors: The flip side of attribution. *Journal of Research in Personality, 16,* 355–375.

Reeder, G. D., & Spores, J. M. (1983). The attribution of morality. *Journal of Personality and Social Psychology, 44,* 736–745.

Rehm, L. P. (1978). Mood, pleasant events, and unpleasant events. *Journal of Consulting and Clinical Psychology, 46,* 854–859.

Reid, P. T. (1993, August). Teaching the psychology of women and gender for undergraduate and graduate faculty. Workshop of the Psychology of Women Institute presented at the meeting of the American Psychological Association, Toronto, Canada.

Reid, P. T. (1994). The real problem in the study of culture. *American Psychologist, 49,* 524–525.

Reid, T. R. (1990, December 24). Snug in their beds for Christmas Eve: In Japan, December 24th has become the hottest night of the year. *The Washington Post.*

Reinke, B. J., Holmes, D. S., & Harris, R. L. (1985). The timing of psychosocial changes in women's lives. *Journal of Personality and Social Psychology, 48,* 1353–1364.

Reis, H. T., and others. (1990). What is smiling is beautiful and good. *European Journal of Social Psychology, 20,* 259–267.

Reisberg, B., and others (1986). Assessment of presenting symptoms. In L. W. Poon (Ed.), *Handbook for clinical memory assessment of older adults.* Washington, DC: American Psychological Association.

Reiser, M. (1992). *Memory and mind and brain: What dream imagery reveals.* New York: Basic Books.

Reiss, M., Rosenfeld, P., Melburg, V., & Tedeschi, J. T. (1981). Self-serving attributions: Biased private perceptions and distorted public descriptions. *Journal of Personality and Social Psychology, 41,* 224–231.

Remafedi, G. (1990). Study group report on the impact of television portrayals of gender roles on youth. *Journal of Adolescent Health Care, 11*(1), 59–61.

Rempel, J. K., Holmes, J. G., & Zanna, M. P. (1985). Trust in close relationships. *Journal of Personality and Social Psychology, 49,* 95–112.

Renninger, K. A., & Wozniak, R. H. (1985). Effect of interest on attentional shift, recognition, and recall in young children. *Developmental Psychology, 21,* 624–632.

Repetti, R. L. (1993). Short-term effects of occupational stressors on daily mood and health complaints. *Health Psychology, 12,* 125–131.

Reschly, D. J. (1981). Psychological testing in educational testing and placement. *American Psychologist, 36,* 1094–1102.

Rescorla, R. A. (1967). Pavlovian conditioning and its proper control procedures. *Psychological Review, 74,* 71–80.

Rescorla, R. A. (1988). Pavlovian conditioning: It's not what you think it is. *American Psychologist, 43,* 151–160.

Rescorla, R. A., & Holland, P. C. (1982). Behavioral studies of associative learning in animals. *Annual Review of Psychology, 33,* 265–308.

Rescorla, R. A., & Solomon, R. L. (1967). Two-process learning theory: Relationships between Pavlovian conditioning and instrumental learning. *Psychological Review, 74,* 151–182.

Resnick, H. S., Kilpatrick, D. G., Dansky, B. S., Saunders, B. E., & Best, C. L. (1993). Prevalence of civilian trauma and posttraumatic stress disorder in a representative national sample of women. *Journal of Consulting and Clinical Psychology, 61,* 984–991.

Resnick, M., and others (1992, March 24). *Journal of the American Medical Association.* Cited in Young Indians prone to suicide, study finds. *The New York Times,* March 25, 1992, p. D24.

Rest, J. R. (1983). Morality. In P. H. Mussen, J. Flavell, & E. Markman (Eds.), *Handbook of child psychology: Vol. 3. Cognitive development.* New York: Wiley.

Reynolds, A. G. (1991). The cognitive consequences of bilingualism. In A. G. Reynolds (Ed.), *Bilingualism, multiculturalism, and second language learning: The McGill Conference in Honour of Wallace E. Lambert.* Hillsdale, NJ: Erlbaum.

Rhodes, J. E., & Jason, L. A. (1990). A social stress model of substance abuse. *Journal of Consulting and Clinical Psychology, 58,* 395–401.

Rice, M. E., Quinsey, V. L., & Harris, G. T. (1991). Sexual recidivism among child molesters released from a maximum security psychiatric institution. *Journal of Consulting and Clinical Psychology, 59,* 381–386.

Rich, C. L., Ricketts, J. E., Thaler, R. C., & Young, D. (1988). Some differences between men and women who commit suicide. *American Journal of Psychiatry, 145,* 718–722.

Richardson, D. C., Bernstein, S., & Taylor, S. P. (1979). The effect of situational contingencies on female retaliative behavior. *Journal of Personality and Social Psychology, 37,* 2044–2048.

Richardson, P. H., & Vincent, C. A. (1986). Acupuncture for the treatment of pain: A review of evaluative research. *Pain, 24,* 15–40.

Richman, J. (1993). *Preventing elderly suicide.* New York: Springer.

Ridon, J., & Langer, E. J. (1977). Long-term effects of control-relevant intervention with the institutionalized aged. *Journal of Personality and Social Psychology, 35,* 897–902.

Rieff, D. (1993). *Cuba in the heart of Miami.* New York: Simon & Schuster.

Rieser, J., Yonas, A., & Wilkner, K. (1976). Radial localization of odors by human newborns. *Child Development, 47,* 856–859.

Riggio, R. E., & Woll, S. B. (1984). The role of nonverbal cues and physical attractiveness in the selection of dating partners. *Journal of Social and Personal Relationships, 1,* 347–357.

Riley, V. (1981). Psychoneuroendocrine influences on immunocompetence and neoplasia. *Science, 212,* 1100–1109.

Rinn, W. E. (1991). Neuropsychology of facial expression. In R. S. Feldman & B. Rime (Eds.), *Fundamentals of nonverbal behavior.* Cambridge, England: Cambridge University Press.

Riordan, T. (1994, April 18). Patents: Mapping the shape of human emotions to give computers more realistic speaking skills. *The New York Times,* p. D2.

Robberson, M. R., & Rogers, R. W. (1988). Beyond fear appeals: Negative and positive persuasive appeals to health and self-esteem. *Journal of Applied Social Psychology, 18,* 277–287.

Robbins, C., & Ehri, L. C. (1994). Reading storybooks to kindergartners helps them learn new vocabulary words. *Journal of Educational Psychology, 86,* 54–64.

Robbins, S. P. (1989). *Organizational behavior* (4th ed.). Englewood Cliffs, NJ: Prentice-Hall.

Robertson, T. S., Zielinski, J., & Ward, S. (1984). *Consumer behavior.* Glenview, IL: Scott, Foresman.

Robins, C. J., & Hayes, A. M. (1993). An appraisal of cognitive therapy. *Journal of Consulting and Clinical Psychology, 61,* 205–214.

Robinson, L. A., Berman, J. S., & Neimeyer, R. A. (1990). Psychotherapy for the treatment of depression: A comprehensive review of controlled outcome research. *Psychological Bulletin, 108,* 30–49.

Robinson, P. (1993). *Freud and his critics.* Berkeley: University of California Press.

Rodgers, J. L., Billy, J. O., & Udry, J. R. (1984). A model of friendship similarity in mildly deviant behaviors. *Journal of Applied Social Psychology, 14,* 413–425.

Rodin, J. (1986). Aging and health: Effects of the sense of control. *Science, 233,* 1271–1276.

Rogers, C. R. (1951). *Client-centered therapy.* Boston: Houghton Mifflin.

Rogers, C. R. (1959). A theory of therapy, personality and interpersonal relationships, as developed in the client-centered framework. In S. Koch (Ed.), *Psychology: A study of science* (Vol. 3). New York: McGraw-Hill.

Rogers, C. R. (1974). In retrospect: 46 years. *American Psychologist, 29,* 115–123.

Rogers, D. E., & Ginzberg, E. (1993). *Medical care and the health of the poor.* Boulder, CO: Westview Press.

Rohsenow, D. J. (1983). Drinking habits and expectancies about alcohol's effects for self versus others. *Journal of Consulting and Clinical Psychology, 51,* 752–756.

Rosch, E. H. (1978). Principles of categorization. In E. H. Rosch & B. L. Lloyd (Eds.), *Cognition and categorization.* Hillsdale, NJ: Erlbaum.

Rose, S. A. (1983). Differential rates of visual information processing in full-term and preterm infants. *Child Development, 54,* 1189–1198.

Rosenberg, H. (1993). Prediction of controlled drinking by alcoholics and problem drinkers. *Psychological Bulletin, 113,* 129–139.

Rosenberg, J., Perlstadt, H., & Phillips, W. R. (1993). Now that we are here: Discrimination, disparagement, and harassment at work and the experience of women lawyers. *Gender & Society,* 7, 415–433.

Rosenblatt, R. (1994, March 20). How do tobacco executives live with themselves? *The New York Times Magazine,* pp. 34–41, 55, 73–76.

Rosenstock, I. M., & Kirscht, J. P. (1979). Why people seek health care. In G. C. Stone, F. Cohen, & N. E. Adler (Eds.), *Health psychology: A handbook.* San Francisco: Jossey-Bass.

Rosenthal, A. M. (1994, March 15). The way she died. *The New York Times,* p. A23.

Rosenthal, D. M. (1980). The modularity and maturation of cognitive capacities. *Behavior and Brain Science, 3,* 32–34.

Rosenthal, E. (1991, December 3). Study of canine genes seeks hints on behavior. *The New York Times,* pp. C1, C12.

Rosenthal, E. (1993a, March 28). Patients in pain find relief, not addiction, in narcotics. *The New York Times,* pp. A1, A24.

Rosenthal, E. (1993b, July 20). Listening to the emotional needs of cancer patients. *The New York Times,* pp. C1, C7.

Rosenzweig, M. R., Bennett, E. L., & Diamond, M. C. (1972). Brain changes in response to experience. *Scientific American, 226,* 22–29.

Roses, A. D. (1993). Cited in Angier, N. (1993, August 13). Scientists detect a genetic key to Alzheimer's. *The New York Times,* pp. A1, A12.

Roskies, E., and others (1986). The Montreal Type A Intervention Project: Major findings. *Health Psychology, 5,* 45–69.

Ross, C. (1993). Cited in Adler, T. (1993). If parents are unhappy, are children the reason? *APA Monitor, 24*(4), 17.

Ross, L. (1988). Situationist perspectives on the obedience experiments. *Contemporary Psychology, 33,* 101–104.

Ross, L., & Nisbett, R. E. (1991). *The person and the situation.* New York: McGraw-Hill.

Rossouw, J. E., and others (1990). The value of lowering cholesterol after myocardial infarction. *New England Journal of Medicine, 323,* 1112–1119.

Rothbart, M. K., & Ahadi, S. A. (1994). Temperament and the development of personality. *Journal of Abnormal Psychology, 103,* 55–66.

Rothbaum, B. O., Foa, E. B., Riggs, D. S., Murdock, T., & Walsh, W. (1992). A prospective examination of post-traumatic stress disorder in rape victims. *Journal of Traumatic Stress, 5,* 455–475.

Rotheram-Borus, M. J., Koopman, C., & Haignere, C. (1991). Reducing HIV sexual risk behaviors among runaway adolescents. *Journal of the American Medical Association, 266,* 1237–1241.

Rotheram-Borus, M. J., Trautman, P. D., Dopkins, S. C., & Shrout, P. E. (1990). Cognitive style and pleasant activities among female adolescent suicide attempters. *Journal of Consulting and Clinical Psychology, 58,* 554–561.

Rotter, J. B. (1972). Beliefs, social attitudes, and behavior: A social learning analysis. In J. B. Rotter, J. E. Chance, & E. J. Phares (Eds.), *Applications of a social learning theory of personality.* New York: Holt, Rinehart and Winston.

Rotter, J. B. (1975). Some problems and misconceptions related to the construct of internal versus external control of reinforcement. *Journal of Consulting and Clinical Psychology, 43,* 56–67.

Rotter, J. B. (1990). Internal versus external control of reinforcement. *American Psychologist, 45,* 489–493.

Rounsaville, B. J., and others (1987). The relation between specific and general dimensions of the psychotherapy process in interpersonal psychotherapy of depression. *Journal of Consulting and Clinical Psychology, 55,* 379–384.

Rozin, P., & Fallon, A. (1988). Body image, attitudes to weight, and misperceptions of figure preferences of the opposite sex: A comparison of men and women in two generations. *Journal of Abnormal Psychology, 97,* 342–345.

Rudman, D., and others (1990). Effects of human growth hormone in men over 60 years old. *New England Journal of Medicine, 323*(1), 1–6.

Ruiz, P., & Ruiz, P. P. (1983). Treatment compliance among Hispanics. *Journal of Operational Psychiatry, 14,* 112–114.

Ruiz, R. A. (1981). Cultural and historical perspectives in counseling Hipsanics. In D. W. Sue (Ed.), *Counseling the culturally different: Theory and practice* (pp. 186–215). New York: Wiley.

Rule, B. G., Taylor, B. R., & Dobbs, A. R. (1987). Priming effects of heat on aggressive thoughts. *Social Cognition, 5,* 131–143.

Russo, N. F. (1990a). Cited in Korn, J. H., Davis, R., & Davis, S. F. (1991). Historians' and chairpersons' judgments of eminence among psychologists. *American Psychologist, 46,* 789–792.

Russo, N. F. (1990b). Overview: Forging research priorities for women's mental health. *American Psychologist, 45,* 368–373.

Rutkowski, G. K., Gruder, C. L., & Romer, D. (1983). Group cohesiveness, social norms, and bystander intervention. *Journal of Personality and Social Psychology, 44,* 545–552.

Rymer, R. (1993). *Genie: An abused child's flight from silence.* New York: HarperCollins.

Saarni, C. (1990). Emotional competence: How emotions and relationships become integrated. In R. Thompson (Ed.), *Nebraska Symposium on Motivation: Vol. 36. Socioemotional development.* Lincoln: University of Nebraska Press.

Saccuzzo, D. (1994, August). Coping with complexities of contemporary psychological testing: Negotiating shifting sands. G. Stanley Hall lecture presented at the annual meeting of the American Psychological Association, Los Angeles.

Sachs, A. (1994, January 31). Now for the movie. *Time,* p. 99.

Sackheim, H. A. (1990). Cited in Goleman, G. (1990, August 2). The quiet comeback of electroshock therapy. *The New York Times,* p. B5.

Sackheim, H. A., and others (1985). Cognitive consequences of low dosage ECT. In S. Malitz & H. A. Sakheim (Eds.), *Electroconvulsive therapy: Clinical and basic research issues.* New York: Annals of the New York Academy of Science.

Sadalla, E. K., Kenrick, D. T., & Vershure, B. (1987). Dominance and heterosexual attraction. *Journal of Personality and Social Psychology, 52,* 730–738.

Sadalla, E. K., Sheets, V., & McCreath, H. (1990). The cognition of urban tempo. *Environment and Behavior, 22,* 230–254.

Sadker, M., & Sadker, D. (1994). *How America's schools cheat girls.* New York: Scribner's.
Sadowski, C., & Kelley, M. L. (1993). Social problem solving in suicidal adolescents. *Journal of Consulting and Clinical Psychology, 61,* 121–127.
Saegert, S. C., & Jellison, J. M. (1970). Effects of initial level of response competition and frequency of exposure to liking and exploratory behavior. *Journal of Personality and Social Psychology, 16,* 553–558.
Salgado de Snyder, V. N., Cervantes, R. C., & Padilla, A. M. (1990). Gender and ethnic differences in psychosocial stress and generalized distress among Hispanics. *Sex Roles, 22,* 441–453.
Sanchez-Craig, M., Annis, H. M., Bornet, A. R., & MacDonald, K. R. (1984). Random assignment to abstinence or controlled drinking: Evaluation of a cognitive-behavioral program for problem drinkers. *Journal of Consulting and Clinical Psychology, 52,* 390–403.
Sanders, G. S. (1984). Effects of context cues on eyewitness identification responses. *Journal of Applied Social Psychology, 14,* 386–397.
Sanders, G. S., & Chiu, W. (1988). Eyewitness errors in the free recall of actions. *Journal of Applied Social Psychology, 18,* 1241–1259.
Sanna, L. J., & Shotland, R. L. (1990). Valence of anticipated evaluation and social facilitation. *Journal of Experimental Social Psychology, 26,* 82–92.
Santee, R. T., & Maslach, C. (1982). To agree or not to agree: Personal dissent amid social pressure to conform. *Journal of Personality and Social Psychology, 42,* 690–700.
Sarbin, T. R., & Coe, W. C. (1972). *Hypnosis.* New York: Holt, Rinehart and Winston.
Satow, K. L. (1975). Social approval and helping. *Journal of Experimental Social Psychology, 11,* 501–509.
Sattler, J. M. (1988). *Assessment of children.* San Diego, CA: Jerome M. Sattler.
Saunders, C. (1984). St. Christopher's hospice. In E. S. Shneidman (Ed.), *Death: Current perspectives* (3rd ed.). Palo Alto, CA: Mayfield.
Saxe, L. (1991a). Lying. *American Psychologist, 46,* 409–415.
Saxe, L. (1991b). Science and the CQT polygraph: A theoretical critique. *Integration of Physiological and Behavioral Sciences, 26,* 223–231.
Sayette, M. A. (1993). An appraisal-disruption model of alcohol's effects on stress responses in social drinkers. *Psychological Bulletin, 114,* 459–476.
Scarr, S. (1985). An author's frame of mind. [Review of the book *Frames of mind.*] *New Ideas in Psychology, 3,* 95–100.
Scarr, S., & Kidd, K. K. (1983). Developmental behavior genetics. In M. Haith & J. J. Campos (Eds.), *Handbook of child psychology.* New York: Wiley.
Scarr, S., & Weinberg, R. A. (1976). IQ test performance of Black children adopted by White families. *American Psychologist, 31,* 726–739.
Scarr, S., & Weinberg, R. A. (1977). Intellectual similarities within families of both adopted and biological children. *Intelligence, 1,* 170–191.
Scarr, S., & Weinberg, R. A. (1983). The Minnesota adoption studies: Genetic differences and malleability. *Child Development, 54,* 260–267.
Schachter, S. (1959). *The psychology of affiliation.* Stanford, CA: Stanford University Press.
Schachter, S., & Latané, B. (1964). Crime, Cognition, and the autonomic nervous system. In D. Levine (Ed.), *Nebraska Symposium on Motivation.* Lincoln: University of Nebraska Press.
Schachter, S., & Singer, J. E. (1962). Cognitive, social, and physiological determinants of emotional state. *Psychological Review, 69,* 379–399.
Schafer, J., & Brown, S. A. (1991). Marijauana and cocaine effect expectancies and drug use patterns. *Journal of Consulting and Clinical Psychology, 59,* 558–565.
Schafer, R. B., & Keith, P. M. (1990). Matching by weight in married couples: A life cycle perspective. *Journal of Social Psychology, 130,* 657–664.
Schaie, K. W. (1993). The Seattle Longitudinal Studies of adult intelligence. *Current Directions, 2,* 171–175.
Schaie, K. W. (1994). The course of adult intellectual development. *American Psychologist, 49,* 304–313.
Schaie, K. W., & Willis, S. L. (1991). Adult personality and psychomotor performance: Cross-sectional and longitudinal analyses. *Journal of Gerontology: Psychological Sciences, 46,* P275–284.
Schaller, M., & Maas, A. (1989). Illusory correlation and social categorization: Toward an integration of motivational and cognitive factors in stereotype formation. *Journal of Personality and Social Psychology, 56,* 709–721.
Scheier, M. F., & Carver, C. S. (1985). Optimism, coping, and health: Assessment and implications of generalized outcome expectancies. *Health Psychology, 4,* 219–247.
Scheier, M. F., and others (1989). Dispositional optimism and recovery from coronary artery bypass surgery: The beneficial effects on physical and psychological well-being. *Journal of Personality and Social Psychology,* 57, 1024–1040.
Schein, E. H. (1990). Organizational culture. *American Psychologist, 45,* 109–119.
Schenker, M. (1993). Air pollution and mortality. *New England Journal of Medicine, 329,* 1807–1808.
Schiffman, H. (1990). *Sensation and perception.* New York: Wiley.
Schmauk, F. J. (1970). Punishment, arousal, and avoidance learning in sociopaths. *Journal of Abnormal Psychology, 76,* 443–453.
Schmidt, F. L., Hunter, J. E., & Pearlman, K. (1981). Task differences as moderators of aptitude test validity in selection: A red herring. *Journal of Applied Psychology, 66,* 161–185.
Schneider, B. H., & Byrne, B. M. (1987). Individualizing social skills training for behavior-disordered children. *Journal of Consulting and Clinical Psychology, 55,* 444–445.
Schneider, W., & Bjorklund, D. (1992). Expertise, aptitude, and strategic remembering. *Child Development, 63,* 461–473.
Schotte, D. E., Cools, J., & Payvar, S. (1990). Problem-solving deficits in suicidal patients: Trait vulnerability or state phenomenon? *Journal of Consulting and Clinical Psychology, 58,* 562–564.
Schuckit, M. A. (1987). Biological vulnerability to alcoholism. *Journal of Consulting and Clinical Psychology, 55,* 301–309.
Schuckit, M. A. (1990, January/February). Substance use disorders. *DSM-IV update.* Washington, DC: American Psychiatric Association.
Schutte, N. S., Malouff, J. M., Post-Gorden, J. C., & Rodasts, A. L. (1988). Effect of playing videogames on children's aggressive and other behavior. *Journal of Applied Social Psychology, 18,* 454–460.
Schwartz, R. M., & Gottman, J. M. (1976). Toward a task analysis of assertive behavior. *Journal of Consulting and Clinical Psychology, 44,* 910–920.
Schwarz, N., Bless, H., & Bohner, G. (1991). Mood and persuasion: Affective states influence the processing of persuasive communications. In M. Zanna (Ed.), *Advances in experimental social psychology* (Vol. 24). New York: Academic Press.
Schweinhart, L. J., & Weikart, D. P. (Eds). (1993). *Significant benefits: The High/Scope Perry Preschool Study through age 27.* Ypsilanti, MI: High/Scope Press.
Scott, J. (1994, May 9). Multiple-personality cases perplex legal system. *The New York Times,* pp. A1, B10, B11.
Scruggs, T. E., & Mastropieri, M. A. (1992). Remembering the forgotten art of memory. *American Educator, 16*(4), 31–37.
Segal, N. (1993). Twin, sibling, and adoption methods. *American Psychologist, 48,* 943–956.
Seligman, M. E. P., and others (1984). Attributional style and depressive symptoms among children. *Journal of Abnormal Psychology, 93,* 235–238.
Selkoe, D. J. (1992). Aging brain, aging mind. *Scientific American, 267*(3), 134–142.
Selye, H. (1976). *The stress of life* (Rev. ed.). New York: McGraw–Hill.
Selye, H. (1980): The stress concept today. In I. L. Kutash, and others (Eds.), *Handbook on stress and anxiety.* San Francisco: Jossey–Bass.
Senior, J. (1994, January 3). Language of the deaf evolves to reflect new sensibilities. *The New York Times,* pp. A1, A12.
Serlin, E. (1980). Emptying the nest: Women in the launching stage. In D. G. McGuigan (Ed.), *Women's lives: New theory, research, and policy.* Ann Arbor: University of Michigan, Center for Continuing Education of Women.
Seta, J. J. (1982). The impact of comparison processes on coactors' task performance. *Journal of Personality and Social Psychology, 42,* 281–291.
Severn, J., Belch, G. E., & Belch, M. A. (1990). The effects of sexual and non-sexual advertising appeals and information level on cognitive processing and communication effectiveness. *Journal of Advertising, 19,* 14–22.
Shader, R. I., & Greenblatt, D. J. (1993). Drug therapy: Use of benzodiazepines in anxiety disorders. *New England Journal of Medicine, 328,* 1398–1405.
Shadish, W. R., Hickman, D., & Arrick, M. C. (1981). Psychological problems of spinal injury patients: Emotional distress as a function of time and locus of control. *Journal of Consulting and Clinical Psychology, 49,* 297.
Shah, M., & Jeffery, R. W. (1991). Is obesity due to overeating and inactivity or to a defective metabolic rate? A review. *Annals of Behavioral Medicine, 13,* 73–81.
Sham, P. C., and others (1992). Schizophrenia following prenatal exposure to influenza epidemics between 1939 and 1960. *British Journal of Psychiatry, 160,* 461–466.
Shapley, R., & Enroth-Cugell, C. (1984). Visual adaptation and retinal gain controls. In N. Osborne & G. Chaders (Eds.), *Progress in retinal research* (Vol. 3). Oxford: Pergamon.
Shatz, C. J. (1992). The developing brain. *Scientific American, 267*(3), 60–67.
Shavitt, S. (1990). The role of attitude objects in attitude functions. *Journal of Experimental Social Psychology, 26,* 124–148.
Shaw, E. D., Stokes, P. E., Mann, J. J., & Manevitz, A. Z. A. (1987). Effects of lithium carbonate on the memory and motor speed of bipolar patients. *Journal of Abnormal Psychology, 96,* 64–69.
Sheehy, G. (1976). *Passages: Predictable crises of adult life.* New York: Dutton.
Sheehy, G. (1981). *Pathfinders.* New York: Morrow.
Sheehy, G. (1993, April). The unspeakable passage—Is there a male menopause? *Vanity Fair,* pp. 164–167, 218–227.
Sheingold, K., & Tenney, Y. J. (1982). Memory for a salient childhood event. In U. Niesser (Ed.), *Memory observed: Remembering in natural contexts.* San Francisco: Freeman.
Sheppard, J. A., & Strathman, A. J. (1989). Attractiveness and height: The role of stature in dating preference, frequency of dating, and perceptions of attractiveness. *Personality and Social Psychology Bulletin, 15,* 617–627.
Shepperd, J. A. (1993). Productivity loss in performance groups: A motivation analysis. *Psychological Bulletin, 113,* 67–81.
Sher, K. J., & Trull, T. J. (1994). Personality and disinhibitory psychopathology: Alcoholism and antisocial personality disorder. *Journal of Abnormal Psychology, 103,* 92–102.
Sher, K. J., Walitzer, K. S., Wood, P. K., & Brent, E. E. (1991). Characteristics of children of alcoholics: Putative risk factors, substance use and abuse, and psychopathology. *Journal of Abnormal Psychology, 100,* 427–448.
Shiffman, S. (1984). Coping with temptations to smoke. *Journal of Consulting and Clinical Psychology, 52,* 261-267.
Shiffman, S. (1993). Assessing smoking patterns and motives. *Journal of Consulting and Clinical Psychology, 61,* 732–742.
Shinn, M., Rosario, M., Morch, H., & Chestnut, D. E. (1984). Coping with job stress and burnout in the human services. *Journal of Personality and Social Psychology, 46,* 864–876.
Shneidman, E. S. (1985). *Definition of suicide.* New York: Wiley.
Shneidman, E. S. (1987). A psychological approach to suicide. In G. R. VanderBos & B. K. Bryant (Eds.), *Cataclysms, cries, and catastrophes: Psychology in action* (Master Lecture Series, Vol. 6, pp. 151–183). Washington, DC: American Psychological Association.
Shoham-Salomon, V. (1991). Introduction to special section on client-therapy interaction research. *Journal of Consulting and Clinical Psychology, 59,* 203–204.
Shotland, R. L., & Heinold, W. D. (1985). Bystander response to arterial bleeding: Helping skills, the decision-making process, and differentiating the helping response. *Journal of Personality and Social Psychology, 49,* 347–356.
Shuchman, M. (1993, November 3). When a "noninvasive" scan causes panic. *The New York Times,* p. C16.
Shumaker, S. A., & Hill, D. R. (1991). Gender differences in social support and physical health. *Health Psychology, 10,* 102–111.
Shusterman, G., & Saxe, L. (1990). Deception in romantic relationships. Unpublished manuscript. Cited in Saxe, L. (1991). Lying. *American Psychologist, 46,* 409–415.
Siegler, R. S., & Liebert, R. M. (1972). Effects of presenting relevant rules and complete feedback on the conservation of liquid quantity task. *Developmental Psychology,* 7, 133–138.
Signorielli, N. (1990). Children, television, and gender roles: Messages and impact. *Journal of Adolescent Health Care, 11*(1), 50–58.
Silver, E., Cirincione, C., & Steadman, H. J. (1994, February). *Law and Human Behavior.* Cited in DeAngelis, T. (1994). Public's view of insanity plea quite inaccurate, study finds. *APA Monitor, 25*(6), 28.
Silverstein, L. B. (1991). Transforming the debate about child care and maternal employment. *American Psychologist, 46,* 1025–1032.
Simons, A. D., and others (1985). Exercise as a treatment for depression: An update. *Clinical Psychology Review, 5,* 553–568.
Simons, A. D., and others (1986). Cognitive therapy and pharmacotherapy for depression: Sustained improvement over one year. *Archives of General Psychiatry, 43,* 43–48.
Simons, A. D., Angell, K. L., Monroe, S. M., & Thase, M. E. (1993). Cognition and life stress in depression: Cognitive factors and the definition, rating, and generation of negative life events. *Journal of Abnormal Psychology, 102,* 584–591.
Simons, R. L., Whitbeck, L. B., Conger, R. D., & Chyi-In, W. (1991). Intergenerational transmission of harsh parenting. *Developmental Psychology, 27,* 159–171.
Simpson, M., & Perry, J. D. (1990). Crime and climate: A reconsideration. *Environment and Behavior, 22,* 295–300.
Simpson, M. L., Olejnik, S., Tam, A. Y., & Supattathum, S. (1994). Elaborative verbal rehearsals and college students' cognitive performance. *Journal of Educational Psychology, 86,* 267–278.
Sims, C. (1993, December 19). The uncertain promises of interactivity. *The New York Times,* p. F6.
Skinner, B. F. (1938). *The behavior of organisms: An experimental analysis.* New York: Appleton.
Skinner, B. F. (1948). *Walden Two.* New York: Macmillan.
Skinner, B. F. (1957). *Verbal behavior.* New York: Appleton.
Skinner, B. F. (1960). Pigeons in a pelican. *American Psychologist, 15,* 28–37.
Skinner, B. F. (1972). *Beyond freedom and dignity.* New York: Knopf.
Skinner, B. F. (1979). *The shaping of a behaviorist.* New York: Knopf.
Skinner, B. F. (1983). Intellectual self-management in old age. *American Psychologist, 38,* 239–244.

Skinner, B. F. (1987). Whatever happened to psychology as the science of behavior? *American Psychologist, 42,* 780–786.

Sleek, S. (1994). Bilingualism enhances student growth. *APA Monitor, 25*(4), 48.

Sloane, B. (1983). Health care: Physical and mental. In D. S. Woodruff & J. E. Birren (Eds.), *Aging: Scientific perspectives and social issues.* Monterey, CA: Brooks/Cole.

Slobin, D. I. (1973). *Cognitive prerequisites for the development of grammar.* In C. A. Ferguson & D. I. Slobin (Eds.), *Studies of child development.* New York: Holt, Rinehart and Winston.

Slobin, D. I. (1983). Crosslinguistic evidence for basic child grammar. Paper presented to the biennial meeting of the Society for Research in Child Development, Detroit.

Small, M. Y. (1990). *Cognitive development.* San Diego, CA: Harcourt Brace Jovanovich.

Smetana, J. G. (1993, March). *Parenting styles during adolescence: Global or domain-specific?* Paper presented at the biennial meeting of the Society for Research in Child Development, New Orleans.

Smetana, J. G., Yau, J., Restrepo, A., & Braeges, J. L. (1991). Conflict and adaptation in adolescence: Adolescent–parent conflict. In M. E. Colten & S. Gore (Eds.), *Adolescent stress: Causes and consequences.* New York: Aldine deGruyter.

Smith, B., & Sechrest, L. (1991). Treatment of aptitude by treatment interactions. *Journal of Consulting and Clinical Psychology, 59,* 233–244.

Smith, D., King, M., & Hoebel, B. G. (1970). Lateral hypothalamic control of killing: Evidence for a cholinoceptive mechanism. *Science, 167,* 900–901.

Smith, G. F., & Dorfman, D. (1975). The effect of stimulus uncertainty on the relationship between frequency of exposure and liking. *Journal of Personality and Social Psychology, 31,* 150–155.

Smith, M. L., & Glass, G. V. (1977). Meta-analysis of psychotherapy outcome studies. *American Psychologist, 32,* 752–760.

Smith, M. L., Glass, G. V., & Miller, T. I. (1980). *The benefits of psychotherapy.* Baltimore, MD: The Johns Hopkins University Press.

Smith, R. E., Smoll, F. L., & Ptacek, J. T. (1990). Conjunctive moderator variables in vulnerability and resiliency research: Life stress, social support and coping skills, and adolescent sport injuries. *Journal of Personality and Social Psychology, 58,* 360–370.

Smith, S. M., Glenberg, A. M., & Bjork, R. A. (1978). Environmental context and human memory. *Memory and Cognition, 6,* 342–355.

Smith, S. S., & Richardson, D. (1983). Amelioration of deception and harm in psychological research: The important role of debriefing. *Journal of Personality and Social Psychology, 44,* 1075–1082.

Smith, T. W., & Pope, M. K. (1990). Cynical hostility as a health risk: Current status and future directions. *Journal of Social Behavior and Personality, 5,* 77–88.

Smith, T. W., Snyder, C. R., & Perkins, S. C. (1983). The self-serving function of hypochondriacal complaints: Physical symptoms as self-handicapping strategies. *Journal of Personality and Social Psychology, 44,* 787–797.

Smitherman, G. (1994). Cited in Lee, F. R. (1994, January 5). Grappling with how to teach young speakers of Black dialect. *The New York Times,* pp. A1, D22.

Smoke rises. (1993, December 27). *The New York Times,* p. A16.

Smolowe, J. (1993, July 26). Choose your poison. *Time,* pp. 56–57.

Snarey, J. R. (1987). A question of morality. *Psychology Today, 21*(6), 6–8.

Snarey, J. R., Reimer, J., & Kohlberg, L. (1985). Development of social-moral reasoning among kibbutz adolescents: A longitudinal cross-cultural study. *Developmental Psychology, 21,* 3–17.

Snow, C. E. (1993). Bilingualism and second language acquisition. In J. Berko-Gleason & N. B. Ratner (Eds.), *Psycholinguistics.* Fort Worth, TX: Harcourt Brace Jovanovich.

Snow, R. E. (1991). Aptitude-treatment interaction as a framework for research on individual differences in psychotherapy. *Journal of Consulting and Clinical Psychology, 59,* 205–216.

Snyder, M., & DeBono, G. (1989). Understanding the functions of attitudes. In A. R. Pratkanis and others (Eds.), *Attitude structure and function.* Hillsdale, NJ: Erlbaum.

Snyder, M., Grether, J., & Keller, K. (1974). Staring and compliance: A field experiment on hitchhiking. *Journal of Applied Social Psychology, 4,* 165–170.

Snyder, S. H. (1977). Opiate receptors and internal opiates. *Scientific American, 236,* 44–56.

Snyderman, M., & Rothman, S. (1987). Survey of expert opinion on intelligence and aptitude testing. *American Psychologist, 42,* 137–144.

Snyderman, M., & Rothman, S. (1990). *The I.Q. controversy.* New Brunswick, NJ: Transaction Publishers.

Solomon, E. P., Berg, L. R., Martin, D. W., & Villee, C. (1993). *Biology* (3rd ed.). Philadephia: Saunders College Publishing.

Solomon, R. L. (1980). The opponent-process theory of acquired motivation: The costs of pleasure and the benefits of pain. *American Psychologist, 35,* 691–712.

Sommer, R. (1991). James V. McConnell (1925–1990). *American Psychologist, 46,* 650.

Sonstroem, R. J. (1984). Exercise and self-esteem. *Exercise and Sport Sciences Reviews, 12,* 123–155.

Sorce, J. F., Emde, R. N., Campos, J. J., & Klinnert, M. D. (1985). Maternal emotional signaling: Its effect on the visual-cliff behavior of 1-year-olds. *Developmental Psychology, 21,* 195–200.

Sorenson, S. B., & Rutter, C. M. (1991). Transgenerational patterns of suicide attempt. *Journal of Consulting and Clinical Psychology, 59,* 861–866.

Sorrentino, R. M., and others (1988). Uncertainty orientation and persuasion. *Journal of Personality and Social Psychology, 55,* 371– 375.

Spanos, N. P., Jones, B., & Malfara, A. (1982). Hypnotic deafness: Now you hear it—Now you still hear it. *Journal of Abnormal Psychology, 91,* 75–77.

Spanos, N. P., McNeil, C., Gwynn, M. I., & Stam, H. J. (1984). Effects of suggestion and distraction on reported pain in subjects high and low on hypnotic suggestibility. *Journal of Abnormal Psychology, 93,* 277–284.

Spanos, N. P., Radtke, H. L., & Dubreuil, D. L. (1982). Episodic and semantic memory in posthypnotic amnesia: A reevaluation. *Journal of Personality and Social Psychology, 43,* 565–573.

Spanos, N. P., & Radtke-Bodorik, H. L. (1980, April). Integrating hypnotic phenomena with cognitive psychology: An illustration using suggested amnesia. *Bulletin of the British Society for Experimental and Clinical Hypnosis,* pp. 4–7.

Spanos, N. P., Weekes, J. R., & Bertrand, L. D. (1985). Multiple personality: A social psychological perspective. *Journal of Abnormal Psychology, 94,* 362–376.

Sparrow, S. S., Ballo, D. A., & Cicchetti, D. V. (1984). *Vineland Adaptive Behavior Scales.* Circle Pines, MN: American Guidance Service.

Spector, I. P., & Carey, M. P. (1990). Incidence and prevalence of the sexual dysfunctions: A critical review of the empirical literature. *Archives of Sexual Behavior, 19,* 389–408.

Spence, J. T., Helmreich, R., & Stapp, J. (1975). Ratings of self and peers on sex-role attributes and their relation to self-esteem and concepts of masculinity and femininity. *Journal of Personality and Social Psychology, 32,* 29–39.

Spencer, D. D., and others (1992). Unilateral transplantation of human fetal mesencephalic tissue into the caudate nucleus of patients with Parkinson's disease. *New England Journal of Medicine, 327,* 1541–1548.

Spencer, M. B., & Markstrom-Adams, C. (1990). Identity processes among racial and ethnic minority children in America. *Child Development, 61,* 290–310.

Sperling, G. (1960). The information available in brief visual presentations. *Psychological Monographs, 74,* 1–29.

Sperry, R. W. (1993). The impact and promise of the cognitive revolution. *American Psychologist, 48,* 878–885.

Spiegel, D., & Cardeña, E. (1991). Disintegrated experience. The dissociative disorders revisited. *Journal of Abnormal Psychology, 100,* 366–378.

Spielberger, C. D., & Piotrowski, C. (1990). Clinicians' attitudes toward computer-based testing. *The Clinical Psychologist, 43,* 60–63.

Spinhoven, P., and others (1989). Pain coping strategies in a Dutch population of chronic low back pain patients. *Pain, 37,* 77–83.

Spinhoven, P., Labbe, M. R., & Rombouts, R. (1993). Feasibility of computerized psychological testing with psychiatric outpatients. *Journal of Clinical Psychology, 49,* 440–447.

Spitzer, R. L., Forman, J. B. W., & Nee, J. (1979). *DSM-III* field trials: Initial interrater diagnostic reliability. *American Journal of Psychiatry, 136,* 815–817.

Spitzer, R. L., Gibbon, M., Skodol, A. E., Williams, J. B. W., & First, M. B. (1989). *DSM-III-R casebook.* Washington, DC: American Psychiatric Press.

Sporer, S. L. (1991). Deep—deeper—deepest? Encoding strategies and the recognition of human faces. *Journal of Experimental Psychology: Learning, Memory, and Cognition, 17,* 323–333.

Spreat, S., & Behar, D. (1994). Trends in the residential (inpatient) treatment of individuals with a dual diagnosis. *Journal of Consulting and Clinical Psychology, 61,* 43–48.

Squire, L. R. (1986). Mechanisms of memory. *Science, 232,* 1612–1619.

Squire, L. R., Cohen, N. J., & Nadel, L. (1984). The medial temporal region and memory consolidations: A new hypothesis. In H. Weingartner & E. Parker (Eds.), *Memory consolidation.* Hillsdale, NJ: Erlbaum.

Stacy, A. W., Bentler, P. M., & Flay, B. R. (1994). Attitudes and health behavior in diverse populations: Drunk driving, alcohol use, binge eating, marijuana use, and cigarette use. *Health Psychology, 13,* 73–85.

Stacy, A. W., Newcomb, M. D., & Bentler, P. M. (1991). Cognitive motivation and drug use: A 9-year longitudinal study. *Journal of Abnormal Psychology, 100,* 502–515.

Stampfer, M. J., and others (1991). A prospective study of cholesterol, apolipoproteins, and the risk of myocardial infarction. *New England Journal of Medicine, 325,* 373–381.

Stasser, G., Taylor, L. A., & Hanna, C. (1989). Information sampling in structured and unstructured discussion of three- and six-person groups. *Journal of Personality and Social Psychology, 57,* 67–78.

Steck, L., Levitan, D., McLane, D., & Kelley, H. H. (1982). Care, need, and conceptions of love. *Journal of Personality and Social Psychology, 43,* 481–491.

Steele, C. M., & Josephs, R. A. (1990). Alcohol myopia: Its prized and dangerous effects. *American Psychologist, 45,* 921–933.

Steinberg, L. (1991). Parent–adolescent relations. In R. M. Lerner, A. C. Petersen, & J. Brooks-Gunn (Eds.), *Encyclopedia of adolescence.* New York: Garland.

Steinberg, L., Dornbusch, S. M., & Brown, B. B. (1992a). Ethnic differences in adolescent achievement. *American Psychologist, 47,* 723–729.

Steinberg, L., Lamborn, S. D., Dornbusch, S. M., & Darling, N. (1992b). Impact of parenting practices on adolescent achievement: Authoritative parenting, school involvement, and encouragement to succeed. *Child Development, 63,* 1266–1281.

Steinbrook, R. (1992). The polygraph test—A flawed diagnostic method. *New England Journal of Medicine, 327,* 122–123.

Stephan, C. W., & Langlois, J. H. (1984). Baby beautiful: Adult attributions of infant competence as a function of infant attractiveness. *Child Development, 55,* 576–585.

Steriade, M. (1992). Cited in Blakeslee, S. (1992, January 7). Scientists unraveling chemistry of dreams. *The New York Times,* pp. C1, C10.

Stericker, A., & LeVesconte, S. (1982). Effect of brief training on sex-related differences in visual-spatial skill. *Journal of Personality and Social Psychology, 43,* 1018–1029.

Stermac, L. E., Segal, Z. V., & Gillis, R. (1990). Social and cultural factors in sexual assault. In W. L. Marshall and others (Eds.), *Handbook of sexual assault: Issues, theories, and treatment of the offender.* New York: Plenum.

Sternberg, R. J. (1985). *Beyond IQ: A triarchic theory of human intelligence.* New York: Cambridge University Press.

Sternberg, R. J. (1986). A triangular theory of love. *Psychological Review, 93,* 119–135.

Sternberg, R. J. (1988). Triangulating love. In R. J. Sternberg & M. J. Barnes (Eds.), *The psychology of love.* New Haven, CT: Yale University Press.

Sternberg, R. J. (1990). Wisdom and its relations to intelligence and creativity. In R. J. Sternberg (Ed.), *Wisdom: Its nature, origins, and development.* New York: Cambridge University Press.

Sternberg, R. J., & Davidson, J. E. (1994). *The nature of insight.* Cambridge, MA: The MIT Press, a Bradford Book.

Sternberg, R. J. (1995). *In search of the human mind.* Fort Worth: Harcourt Brace.

Stevenson, H. W., Lee, S. Y., & Stigler, J. W. (1986). Mathematics achievement of Chinese, Japanese, and American children. *Science, 231,* 693–699.

Stewart, J. E., II. (1980). Defendant's attractiveness as a factor in the outcome of criminal trials: An observational study. *Journal of Applied Social Psychology, 10,* 348–361.

Stewart, M. W., Knight, R. G., Palmer, D. G., & Highton, J. (1994). Differential relationships between stress and disease activity for immunologically distinct subgroups of people with rheumatoid arthritis. *Journal of Abnormal Psychology, 103,* 251–258.

Stier, D. S., & Hall, J. A. (1984). Gender differences in touch: An empirical and theoretical review. *Journal of Personality and Social Psychology, 47,* 440–459.

St. Lawrence, J. S. (1993). African-American adolescents' knowledge, health-related attitudes, sexual behavior, and contraceptive decisions: Implications for the prevention of adolescent HIV infection. *Journal of Consulting and Clinical Psychology, 61,* 104–112.

Stokols, D. (1992). Establishing and maintaining healthy environments: Toward a social ecology of health promotion. *American Psychologist, 47,* 6–22.

Stone, N. M. (1993). Parental abuse as a precursor to childhood onset depression and suicidality. *Child Psychiatry and Human Development, 24,* 13–24.

Storfer, M. D. (1990). *Intelligence and giftedness: The contributions of heredity and early environment.* San Francisco: Jossey–Bass.

Straube, E. R., & Oades, R. D. (1992). *Schizophrenia: Empirical research and findings.* San Diego, CA: Academic Press.

Stricker, G. (1991). Ethical concerns in alcohol research. *Journal of Consulting and Clinical Psychology, 59,* 256–257.

Strickland, B. (1991). Cited in DeAngelis, T. (1991). Hearing pinpoints gaps in research on women. *APA Monitor, 22*(6), 8.

Strober, M. (1986). Anorexia nervosa: History and psychological concepts. In K. D. Brownell & J. P. Foreyt (Eds.), *Handbook of eating disorders.* New York: Basic Books.

Strom, J. C., & Buck, R. W. (1979). Staring and participants' sex: Physiological and subjective reactions. *Personality and Social Psychology Bulletin, 5,* 114–117.

Strom, S. (1993, April 18). Human pheromones. *The New York Times,* p. V12.

Strupp, H. H. (1990). Rejoinder to Arnold Lazarus. *American Psychologist, 45,* 671–672.

Strupp, H. H. (1992). The future of psychodynamic psychotherapy. *Psychotherapy, 29,* 21–27.

Stunkard, A. J. (1959). Obesity and the denial of hunger. *Psychosomatic Medicine, 1,* 281–289.

Stunkard, A. J., Harris, J. R., Pedersen, N. L., & McLearn, G. E. (1990). A separated twin study of the body mass index. *New England Journal of Medicine, 322,* 1483–1487.

Stunkard, A. J., & Sørensen, T. I. A. (1993). Obesity and socioeconomic status—A complex relation. *New England Journal of Medicine, 329,* 1036–1037.

Suarez, E. C., Harlan, E., Peoples, M. C., & Williams, R. B., Jr. (1993). Cardiovascular and emotional responses in women: The role of hostility and harassment. *Health Psychology, 12,* 459–468.

Sue, S. (1988). Psychotherapeutic services for ethnic minorities: Two decades of research findings. *American Psychologist, 43,* 301–308.

Sue, S. (1991). In J. D. Goodchilds (Ed.), *Psychological perspectives on human diversity in America.* Washington, DC: American Psychological Association.

Sue, S., & Okazaki, S. (1990). Asian-American educational achievements. *American Psychologist, 45,* 913–920.

Suinn, R. A. (1982). Intervention with Type A behaviors. *Journal of Consulting and Clinical Psychology, 50,* 933–949.

Sundstrom, E., De Meuse, K. P., & Futrell, D. (1990). Work teams: Applications and effectiveness. *American Psychologist, 45,* 120–133.

Susser, E. S., & Lin, S. P. (1992). Schizophrenia after prenatal exposure to the Dutch Hunger Winter of 1944–1945. *Archives of General Psychiatry, 49,* 983–988.

Sweeney, P. D., & Gruber, K. L. (1984). Selective exposure: Voter information preferences and the Watergate affair. *Journal of Personality and Social Psychology, 46,* 1208–1221.

Szasz, T. S. (1984). *The therapeutic state: Psychiatry in the mirror of current events.* Buffalo, NY: Prometheus.

Tahka, S., Wood, M., & Loewenthal, K. (1981). Age changes in the ability to replicate foreign pronunciation and intonation. *Language and Speech, 24,* 363–372.

Takaki, R. (1993). *A different mirror: A history of multicultural America.* Boston: Little, Brown.

Talbott, E., and others (1985). Occupational noise exposure, noise-induced hearing loss, and the epidemiology of high blood pressure. *American Journal of Epidemiology, 121,* 501–514.

Tan, L. (1985). Laterality and motor skills in four-year-olds. *Child Development, 56,* 119–124.

Tanford, S., & Penrod, S. (1984). Social influence model: A formal integration of research on majority and minority influence processes. *Psychological Bulletin, 95,* 189–225.

Tangney, J. P. (1990). Assessing individual differences in proneness to shame and guilt: Development of the Self-Conscious Affect and Attribution Inventory. *Journal of Personality and Social Psychology, 59,* 102–111.

Taub, A. (1993, April 8). Narcotics have long been known safe and effective for pain. *The New York Times,* p. A20.

Taylor, H. (1993). Cited in Barringer, F. (1993, April 25). Polling on sexual issues has its drawbacks. *The New York Times,* p. A23.

Taylor, I., & Taylor, M. M. (1990). *Psycholinguistics: Learning and using language.* Englewood Cliffs, NJ: Prentice-Hall.

Taylor, R. C., & Richards, S. B. (1991). Patterns of intellectual differences of Black, Hispanic and White children. *Psychology in the Schools, 28,* 5–9.

Taylor, S. E. (1990). Health psychology: The science and the field. *American Psychologist, 45,* 40–50.

Taylor, S. P., & Sears, J. D. (1988). The effects of alcohol and persuasive social pressure on human physical aggression. *Aggressive Behavior, 14,* 237–243.

Taylor, W. N. (1985). Super athletes made to order. *Psychology Today, 19*(5), 62–66.

Telch, C. F., & Telch, M. J. (1986). Group coping skills instruction and supportive group therapy for cancer patients: A comparison of strategies. *Journal of Consulting and Clinical Psychology, 54,* 802–808.

Télégdy, G. (1977). Prenatal androgenization of primates and humans. In J. Money & H. Musaph (Eds.), *Handbook of sexology.* Amsterdam: Excerpta Medica.

Tellegen, A., and others (1988). Personality similarity in twins reared apart and together. *Journal of Personality and Social Psychology, 54,* 1031–1039.

Teller, D. Y., & Lindsey, D. T. (1993). Motion nulling techniques and infant color vision. In C. E. Granrud (Ed.), *Visual perception and cognition in infancy.* Hillsdale, NJ: Erlbaum.

Teri, L., & Wagner, A. (1992). Alzheimer's disease and depression. *Journal of Consulting and Clinical Psychology, 60,* 379–391.

Terrace, H. S. (1987). *Nim* (2nd ed.). New York: Knopf.

Tesser, A., Campbell, J., & Smith, M. (1984). Friendship choice and performance: Self-evaluation maintenance in children. *Journal of Personality and Social Psychology, 46,* 561–574.

Tetlock, P. E. (1983). Accountability and complexity of thought. *Journal of Personality and Social Psychology, 45,* 74–83.

Tharp, R. G. (1991). Cultural diversity and treatment of children. *Journal of Consulting and Clinical Psychology, 59,* 799–812.

Thigpen, C. H., & Cleckley, H. M. (1984). On the incidence of multiple personality disorder. *International Journal of Clinical and Experimental Hypnosis, 32,* 63–66.

Thompson, C. P., & Cowan, T. (1986). The neurobiology of learning and memory. *Science, 233,* 941–947.

Thompson, L. (1991, January, 15). Health status of Hispanics: Nation's fastest-growing minority lacks access to medical care. *The Washington Post.*

Thompson, L. A., Detterman, D. K., & Plomin, R. (1991). Associations between cognitive abilities and scholastic achievement: Genetic overlap but environmental differences. *Psychological Science, 2,* 158–165.

Thompson, R. A. (1991a). Attachment theory and research. In M. Lewis (Ed.), *Child and adolescent psychiatry: A comprehensive textbook.* Baltimore: Williams & Wilkins.

Thompson, R. A. (1991b). Infant daycare: Concerns, controversies, choices. In J. V. Lerner & N. L. Galambos (Eds.), *Employed mothers and their children* (pp. 9–36). New York: Garland.

Thompson, W. C., Cowan, C. L., & Rosenhan, D. L. (1980). Focus of attention mediates the impact of negative affect on altruism. *Journal of Personality and Social Psychology, 38,* 291–300.

Thoresen, C., & Powell, L. H. (1992). Type A behavior pattern: New perspectives on theory, assessment, and intervention. *Journal of Consulting and Clinical Psychology, 60,* 595–604.

Thurstone, L. L. (1938). Primary mental abilities. *Psychometric Monographs, 1.*

Thurstone, L. L., & Thurstone, T. G. (1963). *SRA primary abilities.* Chicago: SRA.

Tierney, J. (1994, January 9). Porn, the low-slung engine of progress. *The New York Times,* pp. H1, H18.

Timpson, J., and others (1988). Depression in a Native Canadian in Northwestern Ontario: Sadness, grief or spiritual illness? *Canada's Mental Health, 36*(2–3), 5–8.

Tobias, S. (1982). Sexist equations. *Psychology Today, 16*(1), 14–17.

Tolchin, M. (1989, July, 19). When long life is too much: Suicide rises among elderly. *The New York Times,* pp. A1, A15.

Tolman, E. C., & Honzik, C. H. (1930). Introduction and removal of reward, and maze performance in rats. *University of California Publications in Psychology, 4,* 257–275.

Tomes, H. (1993). It's in the nation's interest to break abuse cycle. *APA Monitor, 24*(3), 28.

Topf, M. (1989). Sensitivity to noise, personality hardiness, and noise-induced stress in critical care nurses. *Environment and Behavior, 21,* 717–733.

Torgersen, S. (1983). Genetic factors in anxiety disorders. *Archives of General Psychiatry, 40,* 1085–1089.

Torrey, E. F., Bowler, A. E., & Rawlings, R. (1992). Schizophrenia and the 1957 influenza epidemic. *Schizophrenia Research, 6,* 100.

Trehub, S. E., Schneider, B. A., Thorpe, L. A., & Judge, P. (1991). Observational measures of auditory sensitivity in early infancy. *Developmental Psychology, 27,* 40–49.

Trenton State College. (1991, Spring). Sexual Assault Victim Education and Support-Unit (SAVES-U) Newsletter.

Triandis, H. C. (1990). Cross-cultural studies of individualism and collectivism. In J. J. Berman (Ed.), *Nebraska Symposium on Motivation, 1989. Cross-cultural perspectives.* Lincoln: University of Nebraska Press.

Triandis, H. C. (1994). *Culture and social behavior.* New York: McGraw-Hill.

Trickett, P. K., Aber, J. L., Carlson, V., & Cicchetti, D. (1991). Relationship of socioeconomic status to the etiology and developmental sequelae of physical child abuse. *Developmental Psychology, 27,* 148–158.

Trimble, J. E. (1991). The mental health service and training needs of American Indians. In H. F. Myers and others (Eds.), *Ethnic minority perspectives on clinical training and services in psychology* (pp. 43–48). Washington, DC: American Psychological Association.

Trujillo, C. (Ed.). (1991). *Chicana lesbians: The girls our mothers warned us about.* Berkeley, CA: Third Woman Press.

Trull, T. J. (1992). *DSM-III-R* personality disorders and the five-factor model of personality. *Journal of Abnormal Psychology, 101,* 553–560.

Tryon, R. C. (1940). Genetic differences in maze learning in rats. *Yearbook of the National Society for Studies in Education, 39,* 111–119.

Tsui, A. S., & O'Reilly, C. A., III. (1989). Beyond simple demographic effects. *Academy of Management Journal, 32,* 402–423.

Tulving, E. (1985). How many memory systems are there? *American Psychologist, 40,* 385–398.

Tulving, E. (1991). Memory research is not a zero-sum game. *American Psychologist, 46,* 41–42.

Tupes, E. C., & Christal, R. E. (1992). Recurrent personality factors based on trait ratings. *Journal of Personality, 60,* 225–251.

Turnbull, C. M. (1961). Notes and discussion: Some observations regarding the experiences and behavior of the Bambute pygmies. *American Journal of Psychology, 7,* 304–308.

Turner, A. M., & Greenough, W. T. (1985). Differential rearing effects on rat visual cortex synapses: I. Synaptic and neuronal density and synapses per neuron. *Brain Research, 329,* 195–203.

Turner, J. S., & Helms. D. B. (1991). *Lifespan development* (4th ed.). Fort Worth, TX: Harcourt Brace Jovanovich.

Turner, S. M. (1987). Psychopathology in the offspring of anxiety disorders patients. *Journal of Consulting and Clinical Psychology, 55,* 229–235.

Turner, S. M., Beidel, D. C., & Jacob, R. G. (1994). Social phobia: A comparison of behavior therapy and atenolol. *Journal of Consulting and Clinical Psychology, 62,* 350–358.

Tversky, A., & Kahneman, D. (1982). Judgment under uncertainty: Heuristics and biases. In D. Kahneman, P. Slovic, & A. Tversky (Eds.), *Judgment under uncertainty: Heuristics and biases.* New York: Cambridge University Press.

Ugwuegbu, D. C. E. (1979). Racial and evidential factors in juror attribution of legal responsibility. *Journal of Experimental Social Psychology, 15,* 133–146.

Underwood, B., & Moore, B. S. (1981). Sources of behavioral consistency. *Journal of Personality and Social Psychology, 40,* 780–785.

Unger, R. K., Hilderbrand, M., & Madar, T. (1982). Physical attractiveness and assumptions about social deviance: Some sex-by-sex comparisons. *Personality and Social Psychology Bulletin, 8,* 293–301.

USBC (U.S. Bureau of the Census). (1985). *Statistical abstract of the United States* (105th ed.). Washington, DC: U.S. Government Printing Office.

USBC (U.S. Bureau of the Census). (1990). *Statistical abstract of the United States* (110th ed.). Washington, DC: U.S. Government Printing Office.

USBC (U.S. Bureau of the Census). (1993). *Statistical abstract of the United States* (113th ed.). Washington, DC: U.S. Government Printing Office.

U.S. Congress (1983, November). *Scientific validity of polygraph testing: A research review and evaluation* (OTA-TM-H-15). Washington, DC: Office of Technology Assessment.

USDHHS (U.S. Department of Health and Human Services). (1991, March). *Health United States 1990.* (DHHS Publication No. PHS 91-1232). Hyattsville, MD: Centers for Disease Control, National Center for Health Statistics.

USDHHS (U.S. Department of Health and Human Services). (1992). *For a strong and healthy baby.* (DHHS Publication No. ADM 92-1915). Washington, DC: U.S. Government Printing Office.

USDHHS (U.S. Department of Health and Human Services). (1993, Winter). *Mothers target of passive smoking intervention effort. Heart Memo.* Public Health Service, National Institutes of Health, National Heart, Lung and Blood Institute, Office of Prevention, Education, and Control.

Vachss, A. (1993). *Sex crimes.* New York: Random House.

Vaillant, G. E. (1994). Ego mechanisms of defense and personality psychopathology. *Journal of Abnormal Psychology, 103,* 44–50.

Vaillant, G. E., & Milofsky, E. S. (1982). The etiology of alcoholism. *American Psychologist, 37,* 494–503.

Valenstein, E. S. (1986). *Great and desperate cures: The rise and decline of psychosurgery and other radical treatments for mental illness.* New York: Basic Books.

Van Brunt, L. (1994, March 27). About men: Whites without money. *The New York Times Magazine,* p. 38.

Vandell, D. L., & Corasaniti, M. A. (1990). Child care and the family: Complex contributors to child development. In K. McCartney (Ed.), *New Directions for Child Development* (Vol. 49, pp. 23–37). San Francisco: Jossey-Bass.

Vandenberg, S. G., Singer, S. M., & Pauls, D. L. (1986). *The heredity of behavior disorders in adults and children.* New York: Plenum.

Vandenbergh, J. G. (1993). Cited in Angier, N. (1993, August 24). Female gerbil born with males is found to be begetter of sons. *The New York Times,* p. C4.

Van der Pligt, J., & Eiser, J. R. (1983). Actors' and observers' attributions, self-serving bias, and positivity bias. *European Journal of Social Psychology, 13,* 95–104.

Van der Velde, F. W., van der Pligt, J., & Hooykaas, C. (1994). Perceiving AIDS-related risk: Accuracy as a function of differences in actual risk. *Health Psychology, 13,* 25–33.

Van Kammen, D. P., and others (1990). Norepinephrine in acute exacerbations of chronic schizophrenia. *Archives of General Psychiatry, 47,* 161–168.

Verplanken, B. (1991). Persuasive communication of risk communication: A test of cue versus message processing effects in a field experiment. *Personality and Social Psychology Bulletin, 17,* 188–193.

Visintainer, M. A., Volpicelli, J. R., & Seligman, M. E. P. (1982). Tumor rejection in rats after inescapable or escapable shock. *Science, 216*(23), 437–439.

Vitousek, K., & Manke, F. (1994). Personality variables and disorders in anorexia nervosa and bulimia nervosa. *Journal of Abnormal Psychology, 103,* 137–147.

Volchko, J. (1991). Cited in Celis, W. (1991, January 2). Students trying to draw line between sex and an assault. *The New York Times,* pp. A1, B8.

Von Békésy, G. (1957, August). The ear. *Scientific American,* pp. 66–78.

Wachtel, P. L. (1994). Cyclical processes in personality and psychopathology. *Journal of Abnormal Psychology, 103,* 51–54.

Walker, L. E. A. (1993). Cited in Mednick, A. (1993). Domestic abuse is seen as worldwide "epidemic." *APA Monitor, 24*(5), 33.

Walsh, M. R. (1993, August). Teaching the psychology of women and gender for undergraduate and graduate faculty. Workshop of the Psychology of Women Institute presented at the meeting of the American Psychological Association, Toronto, Canada.

Wardlaw, G. M., & Insel, P. M. (1990). *Perspectives in nutrition.* St. Louis: Times Mirror/Mosby College Publishing.

Wardle, J., & Solomons, W. (1994). Naughty but nice: A laboratory study of health information and food preferences in a community sample. *Health Psychology, 13,* 180–183.

Watkins, M. J., Ho, E., & Tulving, E. (1976). Context effects on recognition memory for faces. *Journal of Verbal Learning and Verbal Behavior, 15,* 505–518.

Watson, J. B. (1913). Psychology as the behaviorist views it. *Psychological Review, 20,* 158–177.

Watson, J. B. (1924). *Behaviorism.* New York: W. W. Norton.

Watson, J. B., & Rayner, R. (1920). Conditioned emotional reactions. *Journal of Experimental Psychology, 3,* 1–14.

Watson, T. J., & Petre, P. (1990). *Father and son.* New York: Bantam.

Webb, W. (1993). Cited in Adler, T. (1993). Sleep loss impairs attention—and more. *APA Monitor, 24*(9), 22–23.

Weber, R., & Crocker, J. (1983). Cognitive processes in the revision of stereotypic beliefs. *Journal of Personality and Social Psychology, 45,* 961–977.

Wechsler, D. (1975). Intelligence defined and undefined: A relativistic appraisal. *American Psychologist, 30,* 135–139.

Weekes, J. R., Lynn, S. J., Green, J. P., & Brentar, J. T. (1992). Pseudomemory in hypnotized and task-motivated subjects. *Journal of Abnormal Psychology, 101,* 356–360.

Wegner, D. M. (1979). Hidden Brain Damage Scale. *American Psychologist, 34,* 192–193.

Weidner, G., Istvan, J., & McKnight, J. D. (1989). Clusters of behavioral coronary risk factors in employed women and men. *Journal of Applied Social Psychology, 19,* 468–480.

Weinberg, J., & Levine, S. (1980). Psychobiology of coping in animals: The effects of predictability. In S. Levine & H. Ursin (Eds.), *Coping and health.* New York: Plenum.

Weinberg, S. L., & Richardson, M. S. (1981). Dimensions of stress in early parenting. *Journal of Consulting and Clinical Psychology, 49,* 688–693.

Weiner, B. (1991). Metaphors in motivation and attribution. *American Psychologist, 46,* 921–930.

Weiner, K. (1992). Cited in Goleman, D. J. (1992, January 8). Heart seizure or panic attack? Disorder is a terrifying mimic. *The New York Times,* p. C12.

Weinraub, M., & Wolf, B. M. (1983). Effects of stress and social supports on mother–child interactions in single- and two-parent families. *Child Development, 54,* 1297–1311.

Weinstein, N. D. (1980). Unrealistic optimism about future life events. *Journal of Personality and Social Psychology, 39,* 806–820.

Weinstein, N. D. (1984). Why it won't happen to me: Perceptions of risk factors and susceptibility. *Health Psychology, 3,* 431–457.

Weinstein, N. D. (1993). Testing four competing theories of health-protective behavior. *Health Psychology, 12,* 324–333.

Weisinger, H. (1990). *The critical edge: How to criticize up and down your organization and make it pay off.* New York: Harper & Row.

Weiss, J. M. (1972). Psychological factors in stress and disease. *Scientific American, 226*(6), 104–113.

Weiss, J. M. (1982, August). A model for the neurochemical study of depression. Paper presented to the American Psychological Association, Washington, DC.

Weisse, C. S. (1992). Depression and immunocompetence: A review of the literature. *Psychological Bulletin, 11,* 475–489.

Weissman, M. M., and others (1991). Affective disorders. In N. L. Robins & D. A. Regier (Eds.), *Psychiatric disorders in America: The Epidemiologic Catchment Area Study.* New York: The Free Press.

Weisz, J. R., Sweeney, L., Proffitt, V., & Carr, T. (1993). Control-related beliefs and self-reported depressive symptoms in late childhood. *Journal of Abnormal Psychology, 102,* 411–418.

Welch, K. M. A. (1993). Drug therapy of migraine. *New England Journal of Medicine, 329,* 1476–1483.

Wells, G. L. (1993). What do we know about eyewitness identification? *American Psychologist, 48,* 553–571.

Wells, G. L., & Luus, C. A. E. (1990). Police lineups as experiments: Social methodology as a framework for properly conducted lineups. *Personality and Social Psychology Bulletin, 16,* 106–117.

Wentzel, K. R. (1994). Relations of social goal pursuit to social acceptance, classroom behavior, and perceived social support. *Journal of Educational Psychology, 86,* 173–182.

Werner, C. M., Brown, B. B., & Damron, G. (1981). Territorial marking in a game arcade. *Journal of Personality and Social Psychology, 41,* 1094–1104.

Westerman, M. A. (1990). Coordination of maternal directives with preschoolers' behavior in compliance-problem and healthy dyads. *Developmental Psychology, 26,* 621–630.

Wetzler, S. E., & Sweeney, J. A. (1986). Childhood amnesia. In D. C. Rubin (Ed.), *Autobiographical memory.* New York: Cambridge University Press.

Wexler, B. E., & Cicchetti, D. V. (1992). The outpatient treatment of depression: Implications of outcome research for clinical practice. *Journal of Nervous and Mental Disease, 180,* 277–286.

Whalen, C. K., & Henler, B. (1991). Therapies for hyperactive children: Comparisons, combinations, and compromises. *Journal of Consulting and Clinical Psychology, 59,* 126–137.

What is sexual harassment? (1993, June 19). *The New York Times,* p. L9.

Whisman, M. A., Miller, I. W., Norman, W. H., & Keitner, G. I. (1991). Cognitive therapy with depressed inpatients: Specific effects on dysfunctional cognitions. *Journal of Consulting and Clinical Psychology, 59,* 282–288.

White, J. L., and others (1994). Measuring impulsivity and examining its relationship to delinquency. *Journal of Abnormal Psychology, 103,* 192–205.

White, J. L., & Nicassio, P. M. (1990, November). The relationship between daily stress, pre-sleep arousal and sleep disturbance in good and poor sleepers. Paper presented at the annual meeting of the Association for the Advancement of Behavior Therapy, San Francisco.

Whitehead, W. E. (1994). Assessing the effects of stress on physical symptoms. *Health Psychology, 13,* 99–102.

Whitten, L. A. (1993). Infusing Black psychology into the introductory psychology course. *Teaching of Psychology, 20*(1), 13–21.

Whittle, J., and others (1993). Racial differences in the use of invasive cardiovascular procedures in the Department of Veteran Affairs medical system. *New England Journal of Medicine, 329,* 621–627.

Whorf, B. (1956). *Language, thought, and reality.* New York: Wiley.

Widiger, T. A. (1990, August/September). Antisocial personality disorder. *DSM-IV update.* Washington, DC: American Psychiatric Association.

Widiger, T. A., and others (1991). Toward an empirical classification for the *DSM-IV. Journal of Abnormal Psychology, 100,* 280–288.

Widiger, T. A., & Costa, P. T., Jr. (1994). Personality and personality disorders. *Journal of Abnormal Psychology, 103,* 78–91.

Widner, H., and others (1992). Bilateral fetal mesencephalic grafting in two patients with Parkinsonism induced by 1-methyl-4-phenyl-1,2,3,6-tetrahydropyridine (MPTP). *New England Journal of Medicine, 327,* 1556–1563.

Wiens, A. N., & Menustik, C. E. (1983). Treatment outcome and patient characteristics in an aversion therapy program for alcoholism. *American Psychologist, 38,* 1089–1096.

Wiggins, J. G., Jr. (1994). Would you want your child to be a psychologist? *American Psychologist, 49,* 485–492.

Wilcox, V. L., Kasl, S. V., & Berkman, L. F. (1994). Social support and physical disability in older people after hospitalization. *Health Psychology, 13,* 170–179.

Wilder, D. A. (1986). Social categorization: Implications for creation and reduction of intergroup bias. In L. Berkowitz (Ed.), *Advances in experimental social psychology.* Orlando, FL: Academic Press.

Wilder, D. A. (1990). Some determinants of the persuasive power of in-groups and out-groups: Organization of information and attribution of independence. *Journal of Personality and Social Psychology, 59,* 1202–1213.

Wildman, B. G., & White, P. A. (1986). Assessment of dysmenorrhea using the Menstrual Symptom Questionnaire: Factor structure and validity. *Behavior Research and Therapy, 24,* 547–551.

Willett, W. C., and others (1990). Relation of meat, fat, and fiber intake to the risk of colon cancer in a prospective study among women. *New England Journal of Medicine, 323,* 1664–1672.

Williams, L. (1992, February 6). Woman's image in a mirror: Who defines what she sees? *The New York Times,* pp. A1, B7.

Williams, R. L. (1974). Scientific racism and IQ: The silent mugging of the Black community. *Psychology Today, 8*(5).

Williamson, D. A., Cubic, B. A., & Gleaves, D. H. (1993). Equivalence of body image disturbances in anorexia and bulimia nervosa. *Journal of Abnormal Psychology, 102,* 177–180.

Willich, S. N., and others (1993). Physical exertion as a trigger of acute myocardial infarction. *New England Journal of Medicine, 329,* 1684–1690.

Willis, S. L., Jay, G. M., Diehl, M., & Marsiske, M. (1992). Longitudinal change and prediction of everyday task competence in the elderly. *Research on Aging, 14,* 68–91.

Willoughby, T., Wood, E., & Khan, M. (1994). Isolating variables that impact on or detract from the effectiveness of elaboration strategies. *Journal of Educational Research, 86,* 279–289.

Wills, T. A. (1986). Stress and coping in adolescence: Relationships to substance use in urban school samples. *Health Psychology, 5,* 503–530.

Wilson, G. L. (1991). Comment: Transgenerational patterns of suicide attempt. *Journal of Consulting and Clinical Psychology, 59,* 869–873.

Wilson, G. T. (1993). Cited in O'Neill, M. (1993, September 29). Diet sabotage: The new battle of the sexes. *The New York Times,* pp. C1, C6.

Wilson, G. T., & Fairburn, C. G. (1993). Cognitive treatments for eating disorders. *Journal of Consulting and Clinical Psychology, 61,* 261–269.

Wilson, G. T., & Walsh, T. (1991). Eating disorders in the *DSM-IV. Journal of Abnormal Psychology, 100,* 362–365.

Wilson, K. G., and others (1991). Effects of instructional set on self-reports of panic attacks. *Journal of Anxiety Disorders, 5,* 43–63.

Wilson, K. G., and others (1992). Panic attacks in the nonclinical population: An empirical approach to case identification. *Journal of Abnormal Psychology, 101,* 460–468.

Wilson, R. S. (1983). The Louisville twin study: Developmental synchronies in behavior. *Child Development, 54,* 298–316.

Wilson, R. S., & Kaszniak, A. W. (1986). Longitudinal changes: Progressive idiopathic dementia. In L. W. Poon (Ed.), *Handbook for clinical memory assessment of older adults* (pp. 285–294). Washington, DC: American Psychological Association.

Wink, P., & Helson, R. (1993). Personality change in women and their partners. *Journal of Personality and Social Psychology, 65,* 597–606.

Winkleby, M., Fortmann, S., & Barrett, D. (1991). Social class disparities in risk factors for disease: Eight-year prevalence patterns by level of education. *Preventive Medicine, 19,* 1–12.

Winson, J. (1992). Cited in Blakeslee, S. (1992, January 7). Scientists unraveling chemistry of dreams. *The New York Times,* pp. C1, C10.

Wirtz, P. W., & Harrell, A. V. (1987). Effects of postassault exposure to attack-similar stimuli on long-term recovery of victims. *Journal of Consulting and Clinical Psychology, 55,* 10–16.

Wlodkowski, R. J. (1982). Making sense out of motivation. *Educational Psychologist, 16,* 101–110.

Wolf, N. (1991). *The beauty myth: How images of beauty are used against women.* New York: Morrow.

Wolf, S., & Bugaj, A. M. (1990). The social impact of courtroom witnesses. *Social Behaviour, 5,* 1–13.

Wolinsky, J. (1982). Responsibility can delay aging. *APA Monitor, 13*(3), 14, 41.

Woloshyn, V. E., Paivio, A., & Pressley, M. (1994). Use of elaborative interrogation to help students acquire information consistent with prior knowledge and information inconsistent with prior knowledge. *Journal of Educational Psychology, 86,* 79–89.

Wolpe, J. (1990). *The practice of behavior therapy* (4th ed.). New York: Pergamon.

Wolraich, M. L., and others (1990). Stimulant medication use by primary care physicians in the treatment of attention-deficit hyperactivity disorder. *Pediatrics, 86,* 95–101.

Women scientists lagging in industry jobs. (1994, January 18). *The New York Times,* p. C5.

Wong, P. K. H. (1991). *Introduction to brain topography.* New York: Plenum.

Wood, J. M., & Bootzin, R. R. (1990). The prevalence of nightmares and their independence from anxiety. *Journal of Abnormal Psychology, 99,* 64–68.

Wood, J. M., Bootzin, R. R., Rosenhan, D., Nolen-Hoeksema, S., & Jourden, F. (1992). Effects of the 1989 San Francisco earthquake on frequency and content of nightmares. *Journal of Abnormal Psychology, 101,* 219–224.

Wood, P. D., and others (1991). The effects on plasma lipoproteins of a prudent weight-reducing diet, with or without exercise, in overweight men and women. *New England Journal of Medicine, 325,* 461–466.

Woods, S. W., and others (1987). Situational panic attacks: Behavioral, physiologic, and biochemical characterization. *Archives of General Psychiatry, 44,* 365–375.

Wood, W. (1982). Retrieval of attitude-relevant information from memory: Effects on susceptibility to persuasion and on intrinsic motivation. *Journal of Personality and Social Psychology, 42,* 798–810.

Woolfolk, A. E. (1995). *Educational psychology,* (6th ed.). Boston: Allyn & Bacon.

Worchel, S., & Brown, E. H. (1984). The role of plausibility in influencing environmental attributions. *Journal of Experimental Social Psychology, 20,* 86–96.

Wu, C., & Shaffer, C. R. (1987). Susceptibility to persuasive appeals as a function of source credibility and prior experience with the attitude object. *Journal of Personality and Social Psychology, 52,* 677–688.

Wulfert, E., & Wan, C. K. (1993). Condom use: A self-efficacy model. *Health Psychology, 12,* 346–353.

Wyatt, G. E. (1989). Reexamining factors predicting Afro-American and White American women's age at first coitus. *Archives of Sexual Behavior, 18,* 271–298.

Wyatt, G. E. (1990). The aftermath of child sexual abuse of African American and White American women: The victim's experience. *Journal of Family Violence, 5,* 61–81.

Wyatt, G. E., Notgrass, C. M., & Newcomb, M. (1990). Internal and external mediators of women's rape experiences. *Psychology of Women Quarterly, 14,* 153–176.

Wyatt, G. E., Peters, S. D., & Guthrie, D. (1988a). Kinsey revisited, Part I: Comparisons of the sexual socialization and sexual behavior of White women over 33 years. *Archives of Sexual Behavior, 17*(3), 201–209.

Wyatt, G. E., Peters, S. D., & Guthrie, D. (1988b). Kinsey revisited, Part II: Comparisons of the sexual socialization and sexual behavior of Black women over 33 years. *Archives of Sexual Behavior, 17*(4), 289–332.

Wyer, R. S., Jr. (1988). Social memory and social judgment. In P. R. Solomon and others (Eds.), *Perspectives on memory research.* New York: Springer–Verlag.

Yamamoto, J. (1986). Therapy for Asian Americans and Pacific Islanders. In C. B. Wilkinson (Ed.), *Ethnic psychiatry.* New York: Academic Press.

Yarmey, D. A. (1986). Verbal, visual, and voice identification of a rape suspect under different levels of illumination. *Journal of Applied Psychology, 71,* 363–370.

Yates, A., and others (1983). Running—An analogue of anorexia? *New England Journal of Medicine, 308,* 251–255.

Yeates, K. O., MacPhee, D., Campbell, F. A., & Ramey, C. T. (1983). Maternal IQ and home environment as determinants of early childhood intellectual competence: A developmental analysis. *Developmental Psychology, 19,* 731–739.

Ying, Y. (1988). Depressive symptomatology among Chinese-Americans as measured by the CES-D. *Journal of Clinical Psychology, 44,* 739–746.

Yoder, J. D., & Kahn, A. S. (1993). Working toward an inclusive psychology of women. *American Psychologist, 48,* 846–850.

Yonas, A., Granrud, C. E., & Pettersen, L. (1985). Infants' sensitivity to relative size information for distance. *Developmental Psychology, 21,* 161–167.

Yoshikawa, H. (1994). Prevention as cumulative protection: Effects of early family support and education on chronic delinquency and its risks. *Psychological Bulletin, 115,* 28–54.

Young, T., and others (1993). The occurrence of sleep-disordered breathing among middle-aged adults. *New England Journal of Medicine, 328,* 1230–1235.

Youngblade, L. M., & Belsky, J. (1992). Parent–child antecedents of 5-year-olds' close friendships: A longitudinal analysis. *Developmental Psychology, 28,* 700–713.

Zahn-Waxler, C., & Kochanska, G. (1990). The origins of guilt. In R. A. Thompson (Ed.), *Nebraska Symposium on Motivation: Vol. 38. Socioemotional development.* Lincoln: University of Nebraska Press.

Zajonc, R. B. (1968). Attitudinal effects of mere exposure. *Journal of Personality and Social Psychology, Monograph Supplement 2*(9) 1–27.

Zajonc, R. B. (1980). Compresence. In P. Paulus (Ed.), *The psychology of group influence.* Hillsdale, NJ: Erlbaum.

Zajonc, R. B. (1984). On the primacy of affect. *American Psychologist, 39,* 117–123.

Zajonc, R. B. (1985). Cited in B. Bower (1985). The face of emotion. *Science News, 128,* 12–13.

Zamansky, H. S., & Bartis, S. P. (1985). The dissociation of an experience. *Journal of Abnormal Psychology, 94,* 243–248.

Zane, N., & Sue, S. (1991). Culturally responsive mental health services for Asian Americans: Treatment and training issues. In H. F. Myers and others (Eds.), *Ethnic minority perspectives on clinical training and services in psychology* (pp. 49–58). Washington, DC: American Psychological Association.

Zeki, S. (1992). The visual image in mind and brain. *Scientific American, 267*(3), 68–76.

Zigler, E. (1993, July 24). Head Start, the whole story. *The New York Times,* p. A19.

Zigler, E., Abelson, W. D., Trickett, P. K., & Seitz, V. (1982). Is an intervention program necessary to improve economically disadvantaged children's IQ scores? *Child Development, 53,* 340–348.

Zigler, E., & Styfco, S. J. (1994). Head Start: Criticisms in a constructive context. *American Psychologist, 49,* 127–132.

Zigler, E., Taussig, C., & Black, K. (1992). Early childhood intervention: A promising preventative for juvenile delinquency. *American Psychologist, 47,* 997–1006.

Zimbardo, P. G., LaBerge, S., & Butler, L. D. (1993). Psychophysiological consequences of unexplained arousal: A posthypnotic suggestion paradigm. *Journal of Abnormal Psychology, 102,* 466–473.

Zuckerman, M. (1980). Sensation seeking. In H. London & J. Exner (Eds.), *Dimensions of personality.* New York: Wiley.

Zuckerman, M. (1992). What is a basic factor and which factors are basic? Tumbles all the way down. *Personality and Individual Differences, 13,* 675–681.

Zuckerman, M., Klorman, R., Larrance, D. T., & Spiegel, N. H. (1981). Facial, autonomic, and subjective components of emotion. *Journal of Personality and Social Psychology, 41,* 929–944.

Zuroff, D. C., & Mongrain, M. (1987). Dependency and self-criticism: Vulnerability factors for depressive affective states. *Journal of Abnormal Psychology, 96,* 14–22.

Zyazema, N. Z. (1984). Toward better patient drug compliance and comprehension: A challenge to medical and pharmaceutical services in Zimbabwe. *Social Science and Medicine, 18,* 551–554.

NAME INDEX

A

Abbey, A., 622
Aber, J. L., 437
Abraham, L. K., 587
Abramov, I., 404
Abramowitz, A. J., 235
Abramson, 104
Abravenel, E., 239
Adair, J. G., 70
Adams, N., 457
Addis, M. E., 545
Adelson, 26
Ader, D. N., 25, 49
Ader, R., 582, 584
Adeyemo, S. A., 294
Adler, A., 446, 529, 531
Adler, N. E., 587
Adler, T., 170, 179, 345
Affleck, G., 170, 171, 577
Agras, W. S., 510, 551, 590, 601
Ahadi, S. A., 108, 437, 499
Ahrens, A. H., 500
Aiello, J. R., 676
Aiken, L. S., 593
Ainsworth, M. D. S., 406, 407, 409
Akhtar, N., 378
Akiskal, H. S., 552
Alagna, 596
Albert, M. S., 430
Aldag, R. J., 643
Alexander, R. A., 661
Alighieri, D., 633
Alkhateeb, M., 424, 639, 640
Alkhateeb, S., 639
Allen, F., 604
Allen, J. P., 437
Allen, L., 20
Allen, M., 450, 474
Allison, K. W., 557
Alloy, L. B., 498, 500, 575
Allport, G. W., 451
Almeida, D. M., 423
Alston, J. H., 27
Altman, J., 623
Altman, L. K., 590
Alzheimer, A., 117
Amabile, T. M., 302, 303
American Association of University Women, 465
American Polygraph Association, 380
American Psychiatric Association, 487, 552
American Psychological Association, 68, 69, 70, 244, 366, 367, 557, 558, 559, 560
Ames, M. A., 368
Anastasi, 58, 342
Anastasiow, N. J., 316
Ancker-Johnson, B., 661, 662
Andersen, B. L., 586, 592
Anderson, C. A., 675
Anderson, J. R., 295
Anderson, R., 564
Andreasen, N. C., 487, 503
Andrews, B., 499
Aneshensel, C. S., 187
Angell, M., 584, 585, 590
Angier, N., 117, 119, 278, 365, 593
Annunziata, J., 546
Antoni, M. H., 591, 595, 605
Arbeit, 594
Archer, R. P., 631
Archer, S. L., 424
Argyris, C., 663, 666
Aristotle, 10–11, 65
Arnold, D. H., 315
Aronson, E., 673
Asarnow, J. R., 499
Asch, S. E., 637–638

Ashe, A., 693
Ashton, R., 182
Aslin, R. N., 405
Astin, A. W., 53, 54
Atkinson, R. C., 254, 273
Ausubel, D., 683
Avis, W. E., 628
Ayanian, J. Z., 586
Ayllon, T., 539
Azar, B., 64, 428, 547

B

Babcock, J. C., 545
Bach, G. R., 610
Bachrach, L. L., 502
Baddeley, 277
Baddeley, A., 258
Baddeley, A. D., 270
Bahr, M., 681
Bahrick, H. P., 272
Bailey, J. M., 64, 368
Baillargeon, R., 417
Baiul, O., 575
Bakalar, J. B., 197
Baker, J., 670
Baker, L. A., 345
Baker, R., 656
Bal, D. G., 586
Baldwin, J., 617
Ballo, D. A., 351
Bandura, A., 20, 52, 239, 245, 360, 420, 454, 457, 477, 493, 537, 538, 574, 596, 694
Bangert, R., 685
Banks, M. S., 404
Banyai, E. I., 202
Baquet, C. R., 586
Barabasz, A., 201
Barbaree, H. E., 690
Barbour, I., 45
Bard, P., 385
Barlow, D. H., 485, 513, 548
Barnes, 632
Barnett, W. S., 346
Barnum, P. T., 73
Baron, R. A., 661, 671, 675, 676
Barr, C. E., 505
Barrett, G. U., 661
Barringer, F., 324
Barsalou, L. W., 291
Bartecchi, C. E., 192, 193, 589, 591
Bartek, S. E., 612
Bartis, S. P., 202
Bashore, T. R., 380, 381
Bates, E., 320
Bates, J. E., 406
Batson, C. D., 645
Bauer, W. D., 437
Baum, A., 492, 577
Baumeister, R. F., 508, 616
Baumgardner, A. H., 622
Baumrind, D., 69–70, 349, 409, 410
Beatty, S. E., 673
Beauchamp, G. K., 162
Beck, A. T., 489, 516, 533, 534, 548
Beck, J., 144
Becker, 499
Becker, K. L., 106
Becker, L. B., 586
Beckman, E. F., 27
Bee, H. L., 346
Beilin, H., 18, 410, 412, 413, 416
Belchetz, P. E., 428
Bell, 429
Bell, A. G., 154
Bell, A. P., 368
Bell, P. A., 675
Belle, D., 499
Belles, D., 606
Belsky, J., 406, 407, 430, 435, 437

Bem, D. J., 75–76
Bem, S. L., 360, 478, 649, 652
Benbow, C. P., 99, 473
Bennett, D., 531
Benson, H., 199, 590
Benson, P. L., 646
Berenbaum, H., 566
Berkman, 579
Berkowitz, L., 246, 478, 536, 645
Berlin, I. N., 561
Berliner, D., 162–163
Berman, J. S., 549
Bernal, M. E., 557, 558
Berne, E., 532
Bernstein, I. L., 593
Bernstein, W. M., 632
Berquier, A., 182
Bersoff, D., 680
Betancourt, H., 22, 25, 586
Beutler, L. E., 68, 549
Bevan, W., 461
Bexton, W. H., 370
Binet, A., 16, 330, 335, 466
Binswanger, L., 459
Birbaumer, N., 171
Birren, J. E., 431
Bishop, J. E., 192, 207
Björklund, D. F., 268, 269, 417
Blake, P., 569
Blakeslee, S., 128, 129, 130, 162, 586
Blanchard, E. B., 549, 565, 588, 601
Blanck, P. D., 69, 70
Blaney, P. H., 575
Blass, E. M., 405
Blass, T., 636
Blatt, S. J., 426, 449, 472, 641
Bloch, V., 278
Bloom, B. L., 466, 489
Bloom, L., 272, 316
Bly, R., 450
Bobbitt, J. W., 679
Bobbitt, L., 679–680
Boden, M. A., 302
Bodenhausen, G. V., 618
Boneau, C. A., 21
Booth-Kewley, S., 575
Bootzin, R. R., 181–182, 207
Bordo, S., 390, 510
Borkovec, T. D., 549
Bornstein, 322
Borod, J. C., 98
Boskind-White, M., 511
Boss, M., 459
Boston Women's Health Book Collective, 691
Bothwell, R. K., 265
Botvin, G. J., 185
Bouchard, C., 389
Bouchard, T. J., Jr., 344, 345
Bower, G. H., 270, 385
Bowers, K. S., 202
Bowlby, J., 406, 407, 409
Bowman, M. L., 466
Boyatzis, R. E., 62, 63
Boyd-Franklin, N., 559
Bracha, H. S., 505
Bradley, E. J., 378
Bradley, R. H., 346
Bransford, J. D., 271
Braun, B. G., 495
Bray, R. M., 641
Breckler, S. J., 611
Brenner, J., 510
Brent, E., 374, 632
Breslow, 579
Breuer, P., 490
Brewer, C. L., 284
Brewin, C. R., 52, 442
Bridges, K., 381
Bridgwater, C. A., 615

Brigham, J. C., 631
Brody, J. E., 119, 162, 164, 310, 390, 428, 586, 588, 592, 593, 596, 597
Brokaw, T., 616
Bronstein, P., 26, 376
Brown, B. B., 623
Brown, D. E., 382
Brown, E. H., 675, 676
Brown, G. W., 499
Brown, L. S., 528
Brown, R., 267, 269, 270
Brown, S. A., 186, 187, 189
Browne, A., 49
Browne, M. A., 682
Brownell, K. D., 103, 390, 391, 590
Brownell, W. E., 157
Brownlee-Duffeck, M., 597
Bruck, M., 264
Bruner, J., 683
Bryant, W. C., 432
Bryden, 475
Buchanan, C. M., 365, 423
Buchanan, R. W., 86, 502, 505, 506, 551
Buck, R. W., 626
Budzynski, T. H., 200
Buffone, G. W., 606
Bugaj, A. M., 679
Burish, T. G., 170, 592, 593
Burkhart, B. R., 690
Burman, B., 578
Burns, D. D., 548, 554
Burns, G., 429
Burns, G. L., 631
Burns, R., 633
Burnstein, E., 619, 642
Burt, M. R., 690, 691
Busch, M. P., 693
Buschmann, M. B., 623
Bush, G., 612
Buss, 632
Buss, D. M., 382, 630, 632
Bussey, K., 476
Butcher, J. N., 467
Buxton, V. M., 660
Byerley, W. F., 206–207
Byrne, B. M., 539
Byrne, D., 671, 675, 676
Byrnes, J., 473
Byron, L., 446

C

Cacioppo, J. T., 383, 611, 613
Calhoun, K. S., 689
Calkins, M. W., 27
Callan, V. J., 423
Campbell, A., 477
Campbell, J., 330
Campbell, N., 627
Campos, J. J., 404, 405
Cannon, W. B., 384, 385, 579
Cantor, N., 454, 455
Cantrell, R. P., 685
Capaldi, E. D., 357
Cappella, J. N., 632
Cardeña, E., 494
Carey, G., 108, 493, 508
Carey, M. P., 512, 593
Carling, P. J., 525
Carlsmith, J. M., 374
Carlson, J. G., 379, 381
Carmichael, L. L., 262
Carpenter, W. T., Jr., 86, 502, 505, 506, 551
Carrere, T., 627
Carroll, K. M., 62, 547
Carter, 106, 337
Carver, C. S., 453, 645
Case, R., 417

Cash, T. F., 631
Cassatt, M., 399
Castelli, W., 565, 589, 590, 605
Castro, F., 24
Castro, F. G., 557, 558
Cattell, R. B., 342, 343, 450, 451, 452, 466
Caulfield, M., 588
Ceci, S. J., 264
Celis, W., 29, 690
Centers for Disease Control (CDC), 192, 207, 516, 586, 594, 693
Cepeda-Benito, A., 209
Cerletti, U., 552
Chadwick, P. D. J., 549
Chagall, M., 180
Chaiken, S., 611, 612, 613, 615
Chan, C., 369
Charles, E., 591
Charles, R., 670
Chartrand, S., 336
Chassin, L., 188
Cher, 629
Chesney, M. A., 594–595, 694
Chesno, F. A., 508
Cheung, F. K., 557
Childs, E. K., 559
Chitayat, D., 49
Chiu, W., 265
Chomsky, N., 319
Christal, R. E., 452
Christiansen, A., 547
Churchill, W., 362
Chwalisz, K., 380
Cicchetti, D., 437
Cicchetti, D. V., 351, 554
Clark, E. V., 320
Clark, K. B., 28
Clark, L. A., 108, 452, 453, 501
Clark, M. S., 633
Clarke, A. C., 102
Clarke-Stewart, K. A., 46, 435
Cleckley, H. M., 497
Clement, J., 297
Clements, C. M., 575
Clinton, W. J., 311
Clkurel, K., 202
Cloninger, C. R., 508
Clore, G. L., 646
Clum, 494, 551
Coates, T. J., 594
Coe, C., 582
Coe, W. C., 203
Cohen, L., 632
Cohen, L. A., 586
Cohen, S., 566, 578, 583, 584, 587, 674
Cohn, E. G., 675
Coie, J. D., 584, 585
Colby, A., 420
Colby, C. Z., 383
Coleman, L., 553
Coleman, M., 652
Collier, G., 58, 343
Collins, A. C., 424
Collins, P. H., 423, 559
Collins, W. A., 423
Colon, A. R., 435
Colon, P. A., 435
Comas-Diaz, L., 529, 558
Condon, J. W., 632
Conn, P. M., 107
Connelly, J., 566
Conrad, P., 596
Cools, J., 390, 392
Coon, H., 112, 345
Cooney, J. L., 573
Cooper, J. R., 501
Cooper, M. L., 187, 196

Copeland, L. J., 120
Corasaniti, M. A., 435
Corkin, S., 276
Corter, J. E., 267
Coryell, W., 528
Costa, P. T., Jr., 452, 506, 508
Costello, E., 549
Costner, K., 627
Coté, N., 297
Cousins, N., 576
Covington, M. V., 616
Cowan, T., 267
Cox, M. J., 406
Coyne, J. C., 578
Crabtree, A., 201
Craighead, L. W., 551
Craik, F. I. M., 265, 271
Cramer, R. E., 646
Crano, W. D., 632
Crawford, C., 342, 367, 632
Crawford, H. J., 201, 202
Creamer, M., 493, 570
Creelman, C. D., 128
Crenshaw, T., 694
Crews, D., 109, 365, 475
Crichton, M., 659
Crick, F., 109, 174, 175
Crick, N. R., 378, 508, 624
Crits-Christoph, P., 548
Crocker, J., 613
Cronbach, L. J., 340
Cross, W., 424
Crowe, R. A., 74–75
Crowley, W. F., Jr., 107
Croyle, R. T., 596
Crusco, A. H., 623
Crystal, A. J., 117
cummings, e. e., 312, 383
Cunningham, M. R., 645
Curb, J. D., 586
Curfman, G. D., 590, 604, 605
Curtis, R. C., 633
Cutler, B. L., 265

D

Da Vinci, L., 99
Dabbs, J. M., 645
Damasio, A. R., 130
Damasio, H., 130
Danforth, J. S., 590
D'Arcangelo, A., 136, 137, 138
Dark, V., 174–175
Darkes, J., 186
Darley, J. M., 646
Darwin, C., 12, 377, 382, 383
Davey, L. F., 424
Davidson, J. E., 298
Davidson, J. R., 492
Davidson, T. M., 202
Davies, P., 117
Davis, J. H., 641, 679
Davis, K. L., 505
Davis, R., 16
Davis, S. F., 16
Davison, G. C., 548
Dawes, R. M., 632
De la Candela, V., 560
De Leon, M. J., 119
De Marchena, M. R., 268
Dean, G., 75
DeAngelis, T., 6, 10, 28, 244, 245, 246, 285, 492, 557, 590, 680, 683
DeBono, G., 612
DeCasper, A. J., 405
DeFries, J. C., 112
DeGroot, G., 196, 311, 678
Delanoy, R. L., 278
Delgado, J., 101
Delgado-Gaitan, C., 325

Delprato, D. J., 454
Dembroski, T. M., 615
Democritus, 11
DeNeve, K. M., 675
DePaulo, B. M., 623
Derryberry, D., 92, 105
Descartes, R., 360
Desimone, R., 175
Deutsch, R. M., 610
DeValois, R. L., 139
Devine, P. G., 618
Dewar, R., 668
Dewey, J., 12
Dewsbury, D. A., 80
Diaz, R. M., 325
Dickinson, E., 65
DiClemente, C. C., 575
Diener, E., 644
Digman, J. M., 452
DiLalla, D. L., 108, 493
DiLalla, L. F., 108
Dill, C. A., 69
DiMatteo, M. R., 596, 597, 598
Dindia, K., 450, 474
DiNicola, D. D., 596
Dinsmoor, J. A., 454
Dix, D., 525
Dix, T., 409
Dockery, D. W., 675
Dodge, K. A., 378, 437, 508, 535, 624
Doherty, W. J., 597
Dollard, J., 221, 643
Domino, F., 549
Donnerstein, E. I., 674
Doob, A. N., 378
Dooley, 171
Dorfman, D., 615
Douglas, M., 507
Dovidio, J. H., 618
Downey, G., 578
Doyle, W., 683
Draguns, J. G., 464
Drasgow, F., 466
Dubbert, P. M., 565, 590
Duckitt, J., 240, 617, 618, 624
Dugan, K. W., 661
Dumas, A., 48
Dumas, J. E., 410
Dunbar-Jacob, J., 596, 598
Dusek, J. B., 652
Duval, T. S., 453
Dweck, C. S., 376, 454
Dwyan, J., 202
Dyck, D. G., 573
Dziuba-Leatherman, J., 436

E

Eagly, A. H., 474, 611, 612, 613, 615, 631, 638, 649
Eastwood, C., 464
Ebbinghaus, H., 16, 272, 273, 274
Eckert, E. D., 510
Eckholm, E., 694
Edgerton, J. W., 677
Edgley, C., 670
Edwards, D. L., 199, 201
Egeth, H. E., 265
Ehlers, A., 490
Ehri, L. C., 315
Einstein, A., 399
Eisenberg, N., 617
Eisenman, R., 632
Eiser, J. R., 622
Ekman, P., 381, 382, 383, 384, 386
Elkins, R. L., 197
Ellickson, P. L., 187
Ellis, A., 38, 171, 533, 534, 572–573, 600, 603

Ellis, L., 368, 513, 690
Ellsworth, P. C., 626
Emde, R., 112, 345
Emery, R. E., 435
Engels, G. I., 548
Epstein, L. H., 391
Erikson, E. H., 19, 424, 425, 427, 431, 432, 446–447, 448, 449, 529
Eron, L. D., 244, 246, 247, 423
Escher, M. C., 141, 142, 146, 151
Escobar, C. M., 346
Espenshade, T., 53
Esterling, B. A., 584
Estes, W. K., 270
Etaugh, C., 233, 475
Etcoff, N. L., 628, 629
Evans, D. A., 117, 118
Evans, G. W., 675
Eysenck, H. J., 31, 451, 451–452, 453, 591
Eysenck, M. W., 451

F

Fairburn, C. G., 536, 552
Fairstein, L. A., 690
Fallon, A. E., 629
Fantz, R. L., 404
Farina, A., 631
Farley, F., 429, 584
Farrell, A. D., 488, 489
Farthing, G. W., 170
Fazio, R. H., 612
Fechner, G. T., 11, 16
Fehr, B., 291
Feingold, A., 630, 631
Ferguson-Peters, M., 559
Ferin, M., 120
Feshbach, S., 378
Festinger, L., 356, 360, 374
Fichner-Rathus, L., 36, 38, 692
Field, S., 496
Field, T. M., 46, 435
Fields, W. C., 617
Finkelhor, D., 436
Fischbach, G. D., 175
Fischer, K. W., 379, 381
Fisher, C. B., 69
Fisher, H. E., 630
Fiske, D., 452
Fiske, S. T., 618, 621, 634, 661
Fitzgibbon, M. L., 389
Flaherty, J. F., 652
Flannery, D. J., 423
Flavell, J. H., 416, 418, 420
Fleming, I., 492
Flett, G. L., 500, 573
Flink, C., 632
Flor, H., 170, 171
Flores, P., 678
Foa, E. B., 491
Foa, E. G., 492
Folkman, S., 577
Fontaine, P. A., 523
Ford, E. S., 587
Fowler, R. D., 70
Frankel, K. A., 406
Franzoi, S. L., 629
Fraser, S. C., 616
Freed, C. R., 93
Freedman, D., 336, 337
Freedman, D. X., 550, 551
Freedman, J. L., 616
Freeman, 586
Freeman, A., 548
Freeman, M. S., 405
Freud, A., 529
Freud, S., 15–16, 18, 19, 20, 31–33, 45, 51, 175–176, 181, 192, 203, 262, 275, 276, 312, 358,

377, 398, 420, 424, 441–445,
446, 447, 448, 449, 450, 451,
453, 459, 475, 486, 525–528,
529
Friedman, H. S., 575
Friedman, L., 680
Friedman, M., 589, 590, 602, 603,
604
Friman, P. C., 21
Frodi, A. M., 437, 474, 477
Fromm, E., 19
Frost, R., 454
Fry, R., 569
Fuller, S. R., 643
Furedy, J. J., 380
Furumoto, L., 27
Fyrberg, D., 69

G
Gable, D., 244
Galambos, N. L., 423
Galanos, A. N., 596
Galanter, E., 126
Galassi, J. P., 537
Galileo, 32
Gallucci, W. T., 580
Gallup, G. H., 74
Galton, F., 451, 466
Galvani, L., 83
Ganellen, R. J., 575
Ganong, L. H., 652
Garcia, A., 627
Garcia, J., 218, 226, 342
Gardner, H., 332, 333, 349
Garland, A. F., 423
Garnets, L., 369
Gastorf, J. W., 596
Gauthier, J., 588
Gayle, H. D., 693
Gaziano, J. M., 188
Gazzaniga, M. S., 100
Geen, R. G., 378
Gekko, G., 507
Gelernter, D., 336, 337
Gelman, R., 417
Genovese, K., 644–645, 646
Gentry, J., 423
Gerstner, L. V., Jr., 310, 311, 664
Gesell, A., 397
Getzels, J. W., 302, 303
Gfeller, J. D., 202
Gibbs, J. T., 425
Gibbs, N., 689, 690
Gibson, 404, 405
Gibson, M., 21, 462
Gidycz, C. A., 692
Gigerenzer, G., 308, 309
Gilbert, I. A., 590
Gilbert, S. J., 636
Gilligan, C., 421, 426, 449, 472
Gillin, J. C., 182, 206, 206–207, 550
Gillis, A. R., 676
Gillis, J. S., 628
Gilman, A. G., 551
Gilmore, G., 507
Gilovich, T., 622
Gingold, H., 239
Ginsburg, G., 376
Ginzberg, E., 587
Giovannoni, J., 435
Girgus, J. S., 499
Glaser, R., 565, 582, 583
Glasgow, R. E., 193, 208, 539
Glasner, P. D., 693
Glass, G. V., 548, 549
Gleason, 321
Gleason, J. B., 312, 314, 318, 320
Gleaves, D. H., 511
Glenn, S. S., 226
Glover, J. A., 238

Gluck, M. A., 267
Goddard, H. H., 342
Godden, D. R., 270
Goelet, P., 278
Gold, J. A., 633
Gold, M. S., 192
Goldberg, L. R., 451, 452, 453
Goldberg, W., 73
Goldman, J. A., 308, 693
Goldman, K., 615
Goldman, M. S., 186
Goldsmith, H. H., 108, 112, 508
Goldstein, I. L., 660
Goldstein, T., 26
Goleman, D., 158
Goleman, D. J., 276, 490
Golledge, R., 158
Gomez, J., 369
Goodall, J., 56, 57
Goodchild, F., 29
Goodchilds, J. D., 22
Goodenough, F., 342
Goodgame, R. W., 694
Goodman, L. A., 49
Goodwin, D. W., 186
Goodwin, F. K., 501
Gortmaker, S. L., 389
Gotlib, 499
Gotlib, I. H., 501
Gottesman, I. I., 108, 505, 506, 508
Gottfried, A. E., 346, 376
Gottman, J. M., 616
Goy, 365
Graf, S., 680
Graham, M., 458
Granberg, D., 374, 632
Grant, I., 693
Green, J., 621
Green, J. A., 437
Green, S. K., 628
Greenbaum, 626
Greenberg, J., 320
Greenberg, P. D., 591
Greenblatt, D. J., 550, 554
Greene, A. L., 423
Greene, A. S., 380
Greene, B., 24, 369, 370, 464, 528,
557, 558, 559, 560
Greene, J., 231
Greeno, C. G., 390
Greenough, W. T., 278
Greenwald, A. G., 174
Greist, J. H., 606
Griffin, E., 632
Grimsley, L. D., 423
Grinspoon, L., 197
Grob, G., 523
Gronlund, N. E., 686
Grossman, M. I., 362
Grove, W. M., 505
Growdon, J. H., 117, 119
Gruber, K. L., 616
Gruber, V. A., 119
Gruber-Baldini, A. L., 347
Gruder, C. L., 579
Grunberg, N., 193, 209
Grush, J. E., 615
Gruzelier, J., 202
Guilford, J. P., 302, 303, 331
Guisinger, S., 426, 449, 472, 641
Guralnik, J. M., 585, 590
Gutenberg, J., 366
Guthrie, R. V., 27
Gutknecht, M., 337
Guzman, L. P., 560

H
Haaf, R. A., 404
Haaga, D. A. F., 548

Haaland, K. Y., 379
Haber, 126, 133, 139
Haber, R. N., 257
Haddad, Y., 639
Hafner, 651
Hagen, J., 417
Hainline, L., 404
Haith, M. M., 404
Hall, 209, 474
Hall, G. S., 12, 16, 423
Hall, J., 218
Hall, J. A., 623
Hall, J. V., 615
Hall, S. M., 193, 587
Halperin, K. M., 72
Halpern, D. F., 294, 296, 473
Halverson, C., 478
Hamer, D., 367, 368
Hamilton, L. C., 673
Hamilton, P. A., 632
Hamilton, R. J., 38
Hamm, N. M., 615
Hammen, C., 499
Hanes, M. L., 316
Hansen, D. H., 437
Hanson, K. A., 692
Hare, R. D., 507
Harkins, S., 641
Harlow, H. F., 373, 407
Harlow, L. L., 308, 693
Harnishfeger, K. K., 417
Harrell, A. V., 493
Harrigan, 598
Harris, G. T., 507
Harris, T., 531
Hartmann, E. L., 183
Harwood, A., 586
Hashimoto, N., 418
Hasselhorn, M., 269
Hastie, R., 308, 309
Hatch, T., 333
Hatfield, E., 379, 381
Hatsukami, D., 193
Haughton, E., 539
Haugvedt, C., 170
Hauser-Cram, P., 346
Hawkins, R. D., 278
Hawkins, S. A., 308, 309
Hayes, A. M., 548
Hayes, P., 336, 337
Hayes, S. C., 238
Haynes, 207
Hays, R. B., 579
Heaton, R. K., 195, 693
Hedge, J. W., 661
Hefferline, R. F., 216
Heflin, A. H., 410
Heidegger, M., 459
Heider, F., 373
Heim, M., 103
Heingartner, A., 615
Heinold, W. D., 645
Hellams, R. P., 183
Heller, D. A., 112
Hellige, J. B., 98–99
Helmes, E., 466, 467
Helmholtz, H. von, 139
Helms, J., 613
Helms, J. E., 340, 342
Helson, R., 426, 428, 429
Helzer, J. E., 184, 185, 187, 487
Hemingway, M., 629
Hendrick, C. D., 431
Henker, B., 197
Henkin, W. A., 560
Hennigan, K. M., 615
Hensley, W. E., 646
Hepworth, J. T., 618
Herbert, T. B., 584

Herek, G. M., 617, 624
Hering, E., 139
Herman, C. P., 392
Hernandez, P., 20, 462
Herrmann, D. J., 284
Hershenson, 126, 133, 139
Hershey, D. A., 297
Herzog, D. B., 510
Herzog, M. E., 629
Hewitt, P. L., 500, 573
Hickey, K., 682
Higan, 661
Higgins, E. T., 454
Hilgard, E. R., 202, 203
Hill, D. R., 529
Hiltz, S. R., 236
Hinckley, J., 482, 679
Hines, C. V., 685
Hippocrates, 450, 452, 482
Hitler, A., 421, 612, 636
Ho, D. Y. F., 557
Hoberman, H. M., 575
Hobfoll, S. E., 693
Hobson, J. A., 179, 181
Hoffman, C., 649
Hogan, H. P., 262
Hogan, R., 664
Hogarth, W., 146, 147
Holahan, C. J., 574, 575, 578
Holland, J., 592
Hollinger, L. M., 623
Hollingshead, A. B., 504
Hollon, S. D., 548, 554
Holmes, D. S., 199, 606
Holmes, T. H., 566, 567
Holyoak, K., 216
Holyoak, K. J., 296
Homer, 464
Honorton, C., 75–76
Honts, C., 380
Honzik, C. H., 239
Hopper, J. L., 193
Horn, J. M., 345
Horney, K., 19, 446, 448, 528, 529
Horvath, T., 629
House, J. S., 579
Howard, 632
Howard, K. I., 547
Howard, L., 273
Howard-Pitney, B., 516
Huba, G. J., 187
Hubel, D. H., 128
Hudson, J., 276
Huesmann, L. R., 244, 246, 247
Huesmann, R., 245, 246
Hugdahl, K., 493
Hughes, J. R., 209
Hull, C., 226, 358
Hull, J. G., 187
Humperdinck, E., 334
Humphrey, L. L., 512
Hunter, J. E., 658
Hurford, J. R., 325
Hurst, N., 649
Hurvich, L. M., 139
Hussein, S., 421, 612
Huston, J., 360
Hutchins, R. M., 31
Huxley, A., 398, 399
Hyde, J. S., 25, 472, 473, 474
Hyman, R., 76

I
Imber, S. D., 554
Insel, 106
Insko, C. A., 638, 640
Ironson, G., 492, 595
Isabella, R. A., 406
Isay, R. A., 368
Isen, A. M., 661

Isomura, T., 559
Israel, E., 590
Izard, C. E., 382, 383

J

Jacklin, C. N., 472, 473, 474, 477
Jackson, J., 613
Jackson, J. F., 349
Jackson, P. W., 302, 303
Jacob, T., 68
Jacobs, G. H., 139
Jacobs, T. J., 591
Jacobson, E., 601
Jacobson, N. S., 545
Jacobson-Kram, P., 546
Jacox, A., 170, 592
James, H., 12
James I., 192
James, W., 12, 16, 17, 27, 29, 33, 174, 233, 254, 258, 266, 358, 361, 384, 386, 404, 440, 450
Jamison, K. K., 552
Jamison, K. R., 501
Janerich, D. T., 193
Janicak, P. G., 554
Janis, I. L., 642
Janowitz, H. D., 362
Janus, C. L., 367
Janus, S. S., 367
Jarenko, M. E., 600
Jason, L. A., 185
Javier, R. A., 649
Jay, 170
Jeavons, C. M., 63
Jeffery, R. W., 390, 589
Jellison, J. M., 615, 621
Jemmott, J. B., 583
Jenkins, C. D., 389, 589
Jensen, M. P., 170, 171
Jeste, D. V., 117
Johnson, B. T., 612
Johnson, C. A., 185
Johnson, D. J., 425
Johnson, D. L., 346
Johnson, J. T., 632
Johnson, M. K., 265
Johnson, S. B., 25, 49
Johnson, V. E., 513
Johnson, W., 382
Johnston, 590
Johnston, L. D., 184, 185, 186, 191, 194, 195, 196
Johnston, W., 174–175
Jones, 533, 534
Jones, E. E., 620
Jones, G. H., 27
Jones, H., 223
Jones, J., 24
Jones, J. L., 615
Jones, M. C., 223
Jones, S. L., 45, 46
Jordan, J. V., 426, 449, 472
Jordan, M., 614, 615
Josephs, R. A., 187
Josephson, W. D., 246
Judd, C. M., 618, 632
Jung, C., 32, 445–446, 451, 529

K

Kahle, L. R., 673
Kahn, A. S., 49
Kahneman, D., 307
Kail, 273
Kail, R., 418
Kakutani, M., 630
Kamin, L. J., 342
Kammeyer, K. C. W., 360, 364
Kandel, E. R., 278
Kaniasty, K., 566
Kanner, A. D., 567

Kaplan, S. J., 437
Karabenick, S. A., 683
Karasek, R. A., 589
Karoly, P., 170, 171
Kash, K., 597
Kaslow, R. A., 693
Kassebaum, N. L., 346
Kaszniak, A. W., 117
Katz, R., 501
Katzell, R. A., 658, 660
Kaufman, J., 437
Kavanaugh, M. J., 661
Kazdin, A. E., 423
Keech, M., 356
Keefe, F. J., 170, 171
Keen, S., 450
Keenan, B., 216
Keesey, R. E., 363, 391
Keil, J. E., 588, 589
Keinan, G., 643
Keita, G. P., 49
Keith, P. M., 632
Keller, M. B., 487
Kellerman, J., 626
Kelley, H. H., 622
Kelley, M. L., 517
Kellman, P. J., 404
Kelly, G. A., 360
Kelly, I. W., 75
Kelly, J. A., 694
Kemeny, M. E., 576, 584
Kemper, P., 430
Kendall, P. C., 68
Kendler, H. H., 30
Kennedy, J. F., 267, 643
Kenrick, D. T., 675
Keown, 596
Kern, 28
Kern, J. H., 16
Kerr, N. L., 641
Kershner, J. R., 302, 303
Kessel, F., 461
Kety, 504
Khan, W., 639
Kidd, K. K., 112
Kiecolt-Glaser, J. K., 565, 570, 582
Kihlstrom, J. F., 203, 273, 497
Kilborn, P. T., 651
Kilmann, P. R., 508
Kilpatrick, D., 436
Kimble, D. P., 162, 166, 167, 177, 179, 363, 365, 368
Kimble, G. A., 29, 74, 108, 174, 209, 330, 335, 357, 359, 452, 621
Kimerling, R., 689
Kimmel, D., 369
Kimura, D., 119
Kinnumen, T., 203
Kinsey, A., 53
Kinsey, A. C., 49, 50
Kintsch, W., 6
Kirkley, B. G., 510
Kirsct, J. P., 652
Kitayama, S., 464
Klatzky, R., 158
Klatzky, R. L., 261
Klein, D. N., 501
Kleinke, C. L., 623, 630
Kleinman, A., 20, 464
Kleinmuntz, 342
Kleinmuntz, B., 380
Klinger, M. A., 441
Klorman, R., 191
Klosko, J. S., 494
Kneip, R. C., 589
Knight, R. A., 690
Knowlton, W. A., Jr., 661
Kobasa, S. C., 575
Koch, C., 130, 174, 175
Kochanska, G., 508

Koelling, R. A., 218
Koffka, K., 14
Kohlberg, L., 418–421, 449
Köhler, W., 14–15, 298–299
Kohn, P. M., 371
Kolata, G., 117, 197, 399, 591, 693, 694
Kolko, D. J., 170, 592
Koocher, G. P., 68
Koop, C. E., 206
Kornblum, W., 619
Koss, M. P., 49, 513, 529, 689, 690
Kosslyn, S. M., 278
Kramer, P. D., 550
Krantz, D. S., 575, 589, 591
Krevans, J. R., 431
Kring, A. M., 503
Krosnick, J. A., 612
Kübler-Ross, E., 431–432
Kuczaj, S. A., II, 316, 320
Kuczmarski, R. J., 389
Kulik, J., 267
Kushler, M. G., 673
Ky, K., 348

L

Lacks, P., 182, 206
LaCroix, A. Z., 207
Ladd-Franklin, C., 27
LaFramboise, T., 557, 561
LaFramboise, T. D., 23, 318
LaFreniere, P. J., 410
Laguerre, M. S., 586
Laird, J. D., 383
Lakka, T. A., 590
Lamb, M. E., 435
Lambert, 548
Lambert, W. E., 324, 325, 327
Landon, A., 47
Landy, F. J., 657
Lang, A. R., 63, 64, 68, 69–70, 547
Lang, P. J., 234
Lang, S. S., 197, 592
Lange, K. G., 384, 486
Langer, E. J., 430
Langford, H. G., 590
Langlois, J. H., 628, 632
Lanzetta, J. T., 383
LaPerriere, A. R., 606
Laroche, S., 278
Larrick, R. P., 642
Larson, R., 423
Larson, R. K., 321, 322
Lashley, K. S., 277
Lasnik, H., 312, 313
Latané, B., 508, 645, 646
Laudenslager, M. L., 583
Laumann, E. O., 367
Laurence, 202
Lazarus, 383, 602
Lazarus, A. A., 549
Lazarus, B., 385
Lazarus, R. S., 566, 567, 570, 577
Le Bon, G., 643
Leary, M. R., 615
Leary, W. E., 389, 586, 588
Lederberg, A. R., 406
Lederman, S. J., 164
Ledger, G., 302, 303
LeDoux, J. E., 379
Lee, C. C., 558
Lee, F. R., 317, 318
Lee, S., 360
Leerhsen, 104
Lefcourt, H. M., 570, 576, 577
Lefley, H. P., 561
Lehrer, P. M., 565, 590
Leigh, B. C., 187
Leiman, 140
Leippe, M. R., 265

Leng, X., 348
Lenneberg, E. H., 320, 325
Lerman, 528
Lerner, M. J., 645
Lesnik-Oberstein, M., 632
Leventhal, H., 615
LeVesconte, S., 474
Levine, I. S., 525
Levine, L., 348
Levine, M. P., 509
Levine, S., 577
Levine, S. R., 191
Levinson, D., 425, 426, 427–428
Levinson, H., 664
Levy, S. M., 593
Lewinsohn, P. M., 516, 517, 579
Lewis, C. E., 389
Lewis-Fernández, R., 20, 464
Lex, B. W., 187
Lichtenstein, E., 193, 539
Lieber, C. S., 187
Liebert, R. M., 244
Lin, S. P., 505
Linden, W., 579
Lindsay, D. S., 265
Lindsay, R. C. L., 265
Lindsey, D. T., 404
Linn, M. C., 472
Linville, P. W., 618
Lipsey, M. W., 548
Lipton, D. N., 378
Liu, H., 301, 463
Lochman, J. E., 378, 508, 536, 624
Lockhart, R. S., 271
Loftus, E. F., 258, 262, 263, 264, 265, 441, 442
Loftus, G. R., 262
Lohr, J. M., 240, 612
Lonergan, E. T., 431
Loomis, J. M., 164
Lopez, S., 20, 462
López, S. R., 22, 25, 586
Lore, R. K., 377
Lorenz, K. Z., 408, 409
Lorion, R., 678
Louie, V., 659
Lowe, C. F., 549
Lubin, B., 466
Luborsky, L., 546, 548
Lucariello, J., 267
Luchins, A. S., 293, 620
Luchins, E. H., 293
Ludwick-Rosenthal, R., 170, 577
Lundeberg, M. A., 308
Lurie, N., 587
Luus, C. A. E., 265
Lykken, D. T., 108, 508
Lynn, R., 341
Lyons, J. S., 552
Lyons-Ruth, K., 407

M

Maas, A., 618
Maas, J. W., 505
Maccoby, E., 417
Maccoby, E. E., 472, 473, 474, 477
MacCoun, R. J., 641
MacDonald, K., 409, 410
Macfarlane, J. A., 405
MacFarlane, S. W., 675
Mack, D., 628, 657
MacKenzie, T. D., 193
Mackett-Stout, J., 668
Mackie, D. M., 615, 616
Macmillan, N. A., 128
Maddi, S. R., 575
Madigan, S., 27
Maher, B. A., 74, 450
Maher, W. B., 74, 450
Mahoney, M. J., 682

Maier, N. R. F., 299
Malamuth, N. M., 378, 690
Malatesta, V. J., 371
Malgady, R. G., 560
Malinosky-Rummell, R., 437
Manke, F., 510
Mann, 188
Mann, J. M., 595
Mann, L., 644
Manson, J. E., 389, 588
Manucia, G. K., 645
Maratsos, M., 313, 319, 320
Marcus, E. B., 586
Marenberg, M. E., 588
Margolin, G., 578
Margraf, J., 547
Markman, H. J., 545
Marks, 322
Marks, G., 632
Markstrom-Adams, C., 424
Markus, H., 464
Marriott, M., 651
Marshall, W. L., 690
Martelli, M. F., 170, 577
Martin, C., 478
Martin, N., 64
Martin, R. A., 576, 577
Martin, R. L., 554
Martin, S., 348
Martinez, C., 557
Martinez, F. D., 590
Martinez, J., 70
Maruyama, G., 645
Marx, E. M., 499
Marx, K., 184
Marzuk, P. M., 493, 494, 501, 506, 516, 551
Maser, J. D., 485
Maslach, C., 616, 638
Maslow, A. H., 19, 359–360, 361, 459, 461, 657
Masry, F., 639–640
Masters, W. H., 513
Mastropieri, M. A., 36, 266
Matarazzo, J. D., 342, 466, 565
Matefy, R., 195
Matlin, M., 25, 290, 296, 304, 306
Matthews, K., 428
Matthews, R., 577
Maugh, T. H., 194
Maxwell, K., 110
May, J. L., 632
May, R., 19
Mayer, R., 29
Mayol, A., 499
Mays, V. M., 559
McAdoo, H., 559
McAdoo, J. L., 559
McCall, 55
McCann, I. L., 606
McCarley, R. W., 179, 181
McCarthy, K., 49
McCarthy, M. J., 584
McCartney, K., 108, 453
McCaul, K. D., 170
McCauley, C., 624, 643, 676
McClelland, D. C., 375
McConnell, J. V., 277
McCrae, R. R., 452
McCrank, E., 170, 596
McDonald, F. J., 420
McDougall, W., 256, 358
McEnroe, J., 681
McEwen, 365
McFadden, E. R., Jr., 590
McGaugh, J. L., 278
McGlone, 475
McGovern, 29
McGovern, T. V., 10, 68
McGowan, R. J., 346

McGrath, E., 529
McGregor, D., 663
McGuffin, P., 501
McKeachie, W., 6
McKeen, J., 466
McLeod, J. D., 579
McNally, R. J., 494
McNeill, D., 269, 270
Mead, A., 466
Mead, M., 360
Meade, V., 32, 624
Medin, D. L., 300, 301
Mednick, 108
Meichenbaum, D., 493, 494, 536, 600
Melamed, B. B., 234
Melzack, R., 166
Mendel, G., 112–113
Mendez, M., 117
Menhardt, H., 681, 682
Menustik, C. E., 539
Mesmer, F., 201
Metalsky, G. I., 501
Metcalfe, J., 298
Mevkens, F. L., 593
Michaelson, R., 351, 565
Michela, J. L., 622
Michelangelo, 99
Michelini, R. L., 631
Michels, R., 493, 494, 501, 506, 516, 551
Midgley, B. D., 454
Mikesell, R. H., 546
Milgram, S., 42–44, 48, 51, 56, 60–61, 63, 68, 69, 70, 477, 635–636, 640, 676
Miller, A. G., 636
Miller, G., 259
Miller, J. L., 174, 175, 321, 322, 425
Miller, K., 633
Miller, L. S., 244, 246
Miller, M. D., 457
Miller, M. E., 202
Miller, M. F., 202, 203
Miller, N. B., 410
Miller, N. E., 200, 643
Miller, W. R., 197
Millon, T., 486
Milner, B. R., 276
Milner, P., 101
Milofsky, E. S., 186
Mindell, J. A., 184
Mineka, S., 493, 500
Mintz, J., 548
Mischel, W., 20, 360, 453, 454, 455
Mishkin, M., 278
Mitchell, J. E., 510
Mitchell, T. R., 661
Mittelman, M. A., 590
M'Naghten, D., 679
Moane, G., 426, 428
Mobley, C. E., 406
Mohrman, A. M., Jr., 661
Molfese, D. L., 97
Molfese, V. J., 97
Molière, J., 360
Moliterno, D. J., 191
Moncher, 187
Mondale, W., 616
Money, J., 367, 368, 475
Mongrain, M., 500
Moniz, A. E., 553
Montemayor, R., 423
Monti, P. M., 187
Moore, B. S., 453
Moore, D., 73
Moos, R. H., 574, 575, 578
Morales, E., 369
Moran, D., 162

Moran, J., 175
Moreland, 615
Morgan, R., 691
Moriarty, T., 645
Morin, C. M., 182, 206, 207
Morris, W. N., 639
Morrison, A. M., 26
Morrison, T., 360, 399
Moscovitch, M., 278
Moser, C. G., 573
Mowrer, O. H., 223, 234
Moyers, B., 167, 170, 564, 596, 597
Mozart, W. A., 348, 399
Mudd, S. A., 272
Mullen, B., 616
Munsterberg, H., 666
Murray, E. A., 278
Murray, H., 469
Murray, H. A., 375
Murstein, B. I., 523
Murtaugh, C. M., 430
Myers, D. G., 642
Myers, L. B., 442

N
Nadol, J. B., Jr., 158, 159
Nash, E., 367
Nathans, J., 140
National Institute of Mental Health, 245, 554
National Institute of Occupational Safety and Health, 649
Neisser, U., 276
Nelson, 320
Nelson, J., 201
Nelson, K., 267, 315, 319, 472
Nelson, M. B., 690
Neuberg, 617
Neufeld, R. W. J., 170, 577
Nevid, J. S., 49, 69, 196, 490, 496, 505, 509, 517, 630
Newlin, D. B., 108, 186
Newman, F. L., 547
Newman, J., 676
Newman, R., 550, 551
Newman, R. S., 683
Newport, E. L., 161, 325
Newport, F., 74
Newton, I., 131
Nezu, A. M., 499
Niaura, R. S., 187
Nicassio, P. M., 182
Nida, S., 646
Nigg, J. T., 508
Nippold, 273
Nisbett, R. E., 457
Nogrady, H., 202
Nolen-Hoeksema, S., 499, 500, 548, 554
Noller, P., 423
Norman, D. A., 668
Norris, F. H., 566
North, O., 643
Norvell, N., 606
Norwood, S., 681
Novick, L. R., 296, 297
Novin, D., 363
Nowicki, 576

O
Oades, R. D., 505
Oberdorfer, M., 158
Oddbert, H. S., 451
Office of Demographic, Employment, and Educational Research, 7, 28
Office of Technology Assessment, 381
Ogbu, J., 21, 462

Ogbu, J. U., 20, 21, 462
Ogden, J., 193
O'Grady, K. E., 631
O'Hara, R., 27
Ohman, A., 493
Okazaki, S., 340, 341
Olds, J., 101
O'Leary, A., 582
O'Leary, S. G., 235
Oliver, M. B., 474
Olivier, L., 244
Olson, G., 64
Olson, K., 437
Olson, S. L., 345, 410
O'Reilly, C. A., II, 657
Orive, R., 374
Orr, S. P., 492
Ortega, D. F., 573
Ouchi, W., 663, 666
Overton, 270

P
Paffenbarger, R. S., Jr., 605
Pagan, G., 676
Page, R. A., 674
Pagel, 499
Paige, K. E., 119, 120
Paikoff, R. L., 424
Pajares, F., 457
Palladino, J., 683
Palmer, J. C., 263, 264
Palmer, M. T., 632
Pantin, H. M., 645
Papini, D. R., 424
Papousek, M., 405
Pappas, G., 585, 590
Pardes, H., 70
Park, B., 618, 632
Parrot, W. G., 500
Pascual-Leone, J., 417
Pasteur, L., 396
Patrick, C. J., 508
Patt, R. B., 197, 592
Patterson, C. J., 340
Patterson, G. R., 246, 507
Patterson, M. L., 623
Patterson, S. J., 424
Paulus, P. B., 577
Pavlov, I., 13, 16, 214–216, 219–221, 228, 238
Pearlman, K., 342
Pedersen, N. L., 108, 493
Peel, R., 679
Pelham, W. E., Jr., 191, 197
Penfield, W., 97, 262
Penner, L. A., 510
Penrod, S., 639
Perez-Stable, E., 587
Perkins, K., 193
Perls, F., 530, 532–533
Perret, D. I., 628
Perri, M. G., 391
Perry, 202
Perry, D. G., 476
Perry, J. D., 675
Persons, J. B., 500, 573
Pesjack, M., 569
Peterson, L. R., 261
Peterson, M. J., 261
Petre, P., 665
Pettingale, K. W., 593
Petty, R. E., 611, 613, 616
Phillipson, E. A., 183
Phinney, J. S., 424, 465
Piaget, J., 16, 18, 252, 263, 264, 320, 321, 360, 398, 410–417, 421, 449
Picasso, P., 81, 99
Pick, A. D., 404
Pihl, R. O., 186

Pike, K. M., 511
Pilac, L., 366
Pillard, R. C., 368
Pinderhughes, E., 558, 559
Pinel, P., 524
Pinker, S., 97–98, 313, 316, 317, 318, 319, 321, 322, 336, 337
Piotrowski, C., 467
Pipal, J. E., 573
Pitman, R. K., 492
Plath, S., 551
Plato, 11
Plomin, R., 108, 345
Plutchik, R., 381
Poe, E. A., 551
Polich, J., 273
Polivy, J., 392, 511
Pollack, A., 67
Pomazal, R. J., 646
Pomerleau, O. F., 186
Porter, 528
Porter, R. H., 405
Portes, A., 23, 462
Posner, M. I., 67
Potter, W. Z., 552
Poussaint, A., 369
Powell, L. H., 573, 589
Pratkanis, A. R., 611
Prentky, R. A., 690
Prescott, P. A., 405
Prigatano, G. P., 440
Proulx, E. A., 236
Pucetti, M. C., 575
Pulos, 533, 534
Putallaz, M., 410
Pyszczynski, T., 500

Q

Quattrone, G. A., 613
Quina, K., 26
Quindlen, A., 690, 691
Quinn, J. C., 529

R

Rahe, R. H., 566, 567
Raichle, M. E., 67–68, 97–98
Rainey, D., 628, 657
Rao, S. M., 93
Rapaport, K., 690
Rapp, P. E., 380, 381
Rappaport, N. B., 588
Rather, D., 565, 616
Rathus, S. A., 36, 38, 50, 90, 120, 233, 364, 365, 369, 428, 475, 541, 630, 692
Ratner, N. B., 312, 314, 318, 320
Rauscher, F., 348, 349
Ravo, N., 367
Ray, M., 141
Rayner, R., 222, 223
Reagan, N., 74
Reagan, R., 74, 616, 641, 679
Rebok, G., 333
Redd, W. H., 170, 592
Reddon, J. R., 466, 467
Reddy, 596
Redlich, F. C., 504
Reese, L., 457
Reid, P. T., 25
Reid, T. R., 364
Reinke, B. J., 426, 428, 429
Reis, H. T., 630
Reisberg, B., 117
Reiser, M., 181
Reiss, M., 622
Rempel, J. K., 622
Rende, R., 345
Renninger, K. A., 258
Repetti, R. L., 566

Reschly, D. J., 340
Rescorla, R. A., 20, 216, 221, 238–239, 360, 373
Resnick, H. S., 492, 493
Resnick, M., 516
Rest, J. R., 420
Reston, J., 167
Reynolds, A. G., 325
Rhine, J. B., 75–76
Rhodes, J. E., 185
Rice, M. E., 539
Rich, C. L., 516
Richards, M. H., 423
Richards, S. B., 340
Richardson, B. L., 558
Richardson, D., 70
Richardson, D. C., 477
Richardson, P. H., 167
Richman, J., 516
Rickard-Figueroa, J. L., 170, 592
Rieff, D., 24
Rieser, J., 405
Riggio, R. E., 630
Riley, V., 591
Ringgold, F., 451
Rinn, W. E., 382
Ritvo, 112
Robberson, M. R., 615
Robbins, C., 315
Robbins, S. P., 640
Robertson, T. S., 670
Robins, C. J., 548
Robinson, F. B., 38
Robinson, L. A., 554
Robinson, P., 448, 528
Rodgers, J. L., 632
Rodin, J., 390, 430, 511
Rog, D. J., 525
Rogers, C. R., 16, 19, 459–461, 464, 530–531, 532, 533, 657
Rogers, D. E., 587
Rogers, R. W., 615
Rogers, W., 613
Roggman, L. A., 424
Rohsenow, D. J., 187
Ronan, G. F., 499
Rook, 171
Rooney, A., 389
Roosevelt, F. D., 47
Rorschach, H., 469
Rosch, E. H., 291
Rosenberg, H., 197
Rosenberg, J., 651
Rosenblatt, R., 192
Rosenfeld, 626
Rosenstock, I. M., 652
Rosenthal, 598
Rosenthal, A. M., 644
Rosenthal, D. A., 424
Rosenthal, E., 114, 188, 197, 592
Rosenzweig, 140
Rosenzweig, M. R., 114, 278
Roses, A. D., 119
Roskies, E., 590
Ross, B. H., 300, 301
Ross, C., 499
Ross, L., 44, 457
Rossouw, J. E., 588
Rothbart, M. K., 108, 437, 499
Rothbaum, B. O., 492
Rotheram-Borus, M. J., 517, 518, 594
Rothko, M., 136, 137, 138
Rothman, S., 341, 347, 348–349
Rotter, J. B., 20, 360, 455, 575
Rounsaville, B. J., 548
Rousseau, J-J., 651
Rovine, M., 435
Rozin, P., 629
Rudman, D., 103

Ruiz, R. A., 560
Rule, B. G., 378
Rundus, 265
Rush, 535
Rushton, 644
Russell, G., 423
Russell, J. A., 291
Russo, N. F., 27, 499, 507
Rüstemli, 474
Rutkowski, G. K., 646
Rutter, C. M., 517
Rymer, R., 52

S

Saarni, C., 623
Sabini, J., 500
Saccuzzo, D., 466
Sachs, A., 680
Sadalla, E. K., 630, 676
Sadker, D., 455, 651
Sadker, M., 455, 651
Sadowski, C., 517
Saegert, S. C., 615
Sakheim, 552, 554
Salgado de Snyder, V. N., 465
Sanchez, J., 28
Sanchez-Craig, M., 197
Sanders, G. S., 264, 265
Sanna, L. J., 641
Santayana, G., 396
Santee, R. T., 616, 638
Sarbin, T. R., 203
Sartre, J.-P., 459
Satow, K. L., 645
Sattler, J. M., 55
Saxe, L., 380, 381
Sayette, M. A., 188
Scarr, 58
Scarr, S., 112, 333, 345, 346, 347
Schachter, S., 376–377, 385, 386, 508
Schafer, J., 186
Schafer, R. B., 632
Schaie, K. W., 347, 348
Schaller, M., 618
Scheier, M. F., 453
Schein, E. H., 662
Schenker, M., 675
Schiffman, H., 165
Schmidt, F. L., 342, 658
Schneider, B. H., 539
Schneider, W., 269
Schneirla, T. C., 299
Schotte, D. E., 517, 518
Schuckit, M. A., 184, 185, 186, 487
Schul, Y., 619
Schultz, L. A., 377
Schutte, N. S., 245
Schwartz, R. M., 616
Schwarz, N., 616
Schwarzenegger, A., 336
Schweinhart, L. J., 196, 346
Scott, J., 482, 679
Scruggs, T. E., 36, 266
Sears, J. D., 63
Sechrest, L., 546
Seeman, J., 193
Segal, N., 70, 112
Seligman, 500, 501
Seligman, M. E. P., 501
Selkoe, D. J., 117
Senior, J., 161
Serlin, E., 429
Seta, J. J., 641
Seurat, G., 137, 138
Seuss, Dr., 440
Severn, J., 670
Shader, R. I., 550, 554
Shaffer, C. R., 612

Shah, M., 390
Shakespeare, W., 4, 5, 32, 73, 179, 251, 380, 382, 431, 502, 522, 526, 533, 551, 570, 686
Sham, P. C., 505
Shannon, E., 404
Sharma, R., 683
Shatz, C. J., 81
Shavitt, S., 612
Shaw, E. D., 552
Shaw, G., 348
Shaw, G. B., 389
Sheehan, 202
Sheehy, G., 425–426, 427, 428, 429
Sheingold, K., 276
Sheldon, W., 450–451
Sheppard, J. A., 628
Shepperd, J. A., 641
Sher, K. J., 108, 185, 186, 507, 508
Shiffman, S., 193, 209
Shiffrin, R. M., 254
Shimomura, R., 241
Shneidman, E., 432
Shneidman, E. S., 516, 518
Shoham-Salomon, V., 549
Shotland, R. L., 641, 645
Shuchman, M., 596
Shumaker, S. A., 529
Shusterman, G., 380
Silver, E., 307, 680
Silverstein, L. B., 435
Simmons, L., 491
Simon, T., 335
Simons, A. D., 499, 548, 570
Simons, R. L., 437
Simpson, M., 675
Simpson, M. L., 39, 266
Simpson, O. J., 267
Sims, C., 236
Singer, J. E., 385, 386
Sizemore, C., 52, 495
Skinner, B. F., 13, 16, 21, 224–227, 229–230, 235, 319, 430, 454
Skoglund, S., 484
Sleek, S., 327
Slobin, D. I., 315
Small, M. Y., 266
Smetana, J. G., 423
Smith, 674
Smith, B., 369, 546
Smith, B. A., 405
Smith, G. F., 615
Smith, M. L., 548, 549
Smith, R. E., 567
Smith, S. M., 270
Smith, S. S., 70
Smitherman, G., 317
Smolowe, J., 190
Snarey, J. R., 420
Snodgrass, S. R., 631
Snow, C. E., 324, 325
Snow, R. E., 549
Snowden, L. R., 557
Snyder, C. R., 72
Snyder, M., 612, 646
Snyder, S. H., 86
Snyderman, M., 341, 347, 348–349
Socrates, 11, 18, 305
Solomon, E. P., 109, 111, 135, 139, 162, 377
Solomon, R. L., 359
Solomons, W., 590
Sommer, R., 278
Sonstroem, R. J., 606
Sorensen, S. B., 517
Sorensen, T. I. A., 389
Sorrentino, R. M., 615
Spanos, N. P., 170, 202, 273, 497
Sparks, G. G., 632
Sparrow, S. S., 351

Spearman, C., 331
Spector, I. P., 512
Spence, J. T., 652
Spencer, D. D., 93
Spencer, M. B., 424
Sperling, G., 256
Sperry, R. W., 18, 66
Spiegel, D., 494
Spielberger, C. D., 467
Spinhoven, P., 171, 489
Spitzer, R. L., 487, 503
Sporer, S. L., 272
Squire, L. R., 92, 276, 278, 279
Staats, A., 240, 612
Stacy, A. W., 186, 612
Stalin, J., 421
Stall, R., 187
Stampfer, M. J., 588
Staneski, R. A., 630
Stanley, J. C., 99, 473
Stansfield, 674
Stasser, G., 641
Stebbins, C., 682
Steck, L., 634
Steele, C. M., 187
Steffen, V. J., 649
Steinberg, L., 341, 345, 423, 424
Steinbrook, R., 380
Steinem, G., 649
Stephan, C. W., 632
Stepick, A., 23, 462
Steriade, M., 181
Stericker, A., 474
Stermac, L. E., 690
Stern, W., 337
Sternberg, R. J., 298, 301, 302, 333, 334, 418, 633, 635
Stevens, A., 644
Stevenson, H. W., 341
Stewart, J. E., II, 631
Stewart, M. W., 567
Stier, D. S., 623
St. Lawrence, J. S., 585, 586
Stokols, D., 584, 585, 673
Stone, N. M., 437
Storfer, M. D., 340
Stoyva, J. M., 200
Strathman, A. J., 628
Straube, E. R., 505
Stricker, G., 68
Strickland, 576
Strickland, B., 49, 529
Strober, M., 509
Strom, J. C., 626
Strom, S., 162
Strupp, H. H., 529
Stunkard, A. J., 389, 390
Styfco, S. J., 346
Suarez, E. C., 589
Sue, S., 24, 28, 340, 341, 557, 558, 559
Sugarman, R., 641
Suinn, R. A., 603
Supalla, T., 325
Susser, E. S., 505
Swayze, P., 73
Sweeney, J. A., 276
Sweeney, P. D., 616
Szasz, T. S., 487
Szucko, J. J., 380

T
Tahka, S., 325
Takahira, S., 473
Takaki, R., 617, 619
Tan, L., 99
Tanford, S., 639
Tangney, J. P., 508
Taub, A., 197
Taylor, H., 53

Taylor, L., 325
Taylor, M. M., 325
Taylor, R. C., 340
Taylor, S. E., 564, 621
Taylor, S. P., 63
Taylor, W. N., 107
Telch, C. F., 593
Telch, M. J., 593
Tellegen, A., 108
Teller, D. Y., 404
Tenney, Y. J., 276
Teri, L., 117
Terman, L., 335
Terrace, H. S., 313
Tesser, A., 632
Tetlock, P. E., 613
Tharp, R. G., 21, 343, 379, 557
Thigpen, C. H., 497
Thompson, C. P., 267
Thompson, D. E., 658, 660
Thompson, L., 587
Thompson, L. A., 345
Thompson, R. A., 406, 435
Thompson, W. C., 645
Thomson, J. B., 108, 186
Thoresen, C., 573, 589
Thorndike, E. L., 16, 224, 226
Thurstone, L., 452
Thurstone, L. L., 331
Thurstone, T. G., 331
Tierney, J., 366
Tilden, 202
Timpson, J., 561
Titchener, E. B., 11
Tobias, S., 474
Tolman, E. C., 239, 299
Tomes, H., 378
Topf, M., 674
Torgersen, S., 493
Torrey, E. F., 505
Toulouse-Lautrec, H. de, 368
Trehub, S. E., 405
Trenton State College, 689, 690
Triandis, H. C., 464
Trickett, P. K., 437
Trimble, J. E., 561
Trujillo, C., 369
Trull, T. J., 108, 452, 507, 508
Tryon, R. C., 114
Tsui, A. S., 657
Tucker, D. M., 92, 105
Tuke, W., 525
Tulving, E., 251
Tupes, E. C., 452
Turnbull, C. M., 149
Turner, A. M., 278
Turner, S. M., 222, 493
Tversky, A., 307
Twain, M., 14, 584
Twentyman, C. T., 437

U
Ulmer, D., 589, 590, 602, 603, 604
Underwood, B., 453
Unger, R. K., 631
U.S. Congress, 381
USBC (U.S. Bureau of the Census), 23, 324, 326, 431, 435
USDHHS (U.S. Department of Health and Human Services), 193, 588

V
Vachss, A., 690
Vaillant, G. E., 186, 496, 570
Valenstein, E. S., 553
Van Brunt, L., 618
Van der Pligt, J., 622
Van der Velde, F. W., 308, 693

Van Gogh, V., 551
Van Kammen, D. P., 505–506
Vandell, D. L., 435
Vandenberg, S. G., 108
Vandenbergh, J. G., 475
Vasarely, V., 146, 147
Verplanken, B., 613
Victor, R. G., 195
Vincent, C. A., 167
Visintainer, M. A., 591
Vitousek, K., 510
Volchko, J., 692
Von Békésy, G., 157
Von Glinow, M. A., 26
Von Hofsten, C., 404

W
Wachtel, P. L., 501
Wadden, T. A., 103, 390, 391, 590
Wagner, A., 117
Walk, 404, 405
Walker, L. E. A., 378
Walsh, M. R., 25
Walsh, T., 511
Walter, A. A., 262
Wan, C. K., 694
Ward, W. S., 170
Wardle, J., 590
Washburn, M. F., 27
Washington, D., 367, 632
Watkins, M. J., 265, 270
Watson, J., 109
Watson, J. B., 13, 16, 19, 20, 33, 174, 222, 223, 284, 381, 397, 454
Watson, T. J., Jr., 664–665
Webb, W., 179
Weber, E., 127
Weber, R., 613
Wechsler, D., 334, 338–339
Weekes, J. R., 202
Wegner, D. M., 72
Weikart, D. P., 196, 346
Weinberg, J., 577
Weinberg, R. A., 345, 346, 347
Weiner, B., 216, 238
Weiner, K., 490
Weinrich, J. D., 368
Weisinger, H., 660
Weiss, J. M., 501, 577, 578, 583
Weisse, C. S., 584
Weissman, M. M., 528
Weisz, J. R., 499
Welch, K. M. A., 588
Welles, O., 244
Wells, G. L., 265
Wentzel, K. R., 234
Werner, C. M., 623
Wertheimer, M., 14, 140
West, S. G., 618
Westerman, M. A., 410
Wetzel, C. G., 623
Wetzler, S. E., 276
Wexler, B. E., 554
Whalen, C. K., 197
Whisman, M. A., 548
White, J. L., 182, 507
White, P. A., 119
White, W. C., 511
Whitehead, W. E., 570
Whitman, W., 83, 374
Whitten, L. A., 23
Whittle, J., 586
Whorf, B., 321
Widiger, T. A., 452, 485, 506, 507, 508
Widner, T. A., 93
Wiens, A. N., 539
Wiesel, E., 617
Wiesel, T. N., 128
Wiggins, E. C., 611

Wiggins, J. G., Jr., 10, 565
Wilcox, V. L., 579
Wilder, D. A., 615, 618
Wildman, B. G., 119
Willett, W. C., 591, 593
Williams, L., 464, 465, 629
Williams, R. L., 341
Williamson, D. A., 510
Williamson, G. M., 578
Willich, S. N., 590
Willis, S. L., 347, 348
Willoughby, T., 6, 284
Wills, T. A., 188
Wilson, D. B., 548
Wilson, D. W., 674
Wilson, E. I., 674
Wilson, G. L., 517
Wilson, G. T., 389, 511, 536, 552
Wilson, K. G., 491
Wilson, R. S., 117, 344
Wing, R. R., 390
Wink, P., 429
Winkleby, M., 587
Winson, J., 179
Wirtz, P. W., 493
Wlodkowski, R. J., 683
Wolf, N., 390, 510
Wolf, S., 679
Wolfe, W. B., 448
Wolinsky, J., 430
Woll, S. B., 630
Woloshyn, V. E., 6, 266
Wolpe, 602
Wolpe, J., 537, 549
Wolraich, M. L., 191
Wong, P. K. H., 66–67
Wood, J. M., 181–182, 182
Wood, L., 378
Wood, P. D., 390, 391, 605
Wood, W., 616
Woodward, J., 495
Woolfolk, A. E., 683
Worchel, S., 675, 676
Worth, L. T., 616
Wozniak, R. H., 258
Wright, E., 348
Wu, C., 612
Wulfert, E., 694
Wundt, W., 11–12, 16
Wyatt, G. E., 50, 51
Wyer, R. S., Jr., 619

Y
Yamamoto, J., 557
Yarmey, D. A., 265
Yashinski, E., 203
Yeates, K. O., 346
Yoder, J. D., 49
Yogi, M. M., 198
Yoshikawa, H., 677
Young, S., 99
Young, T., 137, 139, 183
Youngblade, L. M., 407

Z
Zahn-Waxler, C., 508
Zajonc, 615
Zajonc, R. B., 383, 385, 615, 640
Zamansky, H., 202
Zane, N., 559
Zeichner, A., 573
Zeki, S., 129, 130, 174
Zigler, E., 196, 345, 346, 423, 437
Zimbardo, P. G., 386
Zimmerman, R. R., 407
el-Zoghbi, M., 639, 640
Zuckerman, M., 371, 383, 453
Zuroff, D. C., 500
Zyazema, N. Z., 597

SUBJECT INDEX

A

A–B problem, 612
Abnormal behavior. *See* Psychological disorders
Abreaction, 526, 527
Absolute refractory period, 84–85
Absolute threshold, 126–127
Absolutist thinking, and cognitive therapy, 534
Abstinence syndrome, 184, 185
Accommodation, 410, 411
Acculturation, 464, 465, 650
Acetylcholine
  Alzheimer's disease and, 117, 119
  dreams and, 181
  memory and, 86, 278
  as neurotransmitter, 85–86
ACh. *See* Acetylcholine
Achievement
  definition of, 330, 331
  intelligence and, 57–58
  motivation and, 375–376
Acoustic codes
  definition of, 253
  levels-of-processing model and, 271
  long-term memory and, 269
  nonsense syllables and, 272
Acquired drives, 358
Acquired immune deficiency syndrome. *See* AIDS
Acquisition trial, 219
Acromegaly, 106
Acronyms, 252, 253, 287
Acrophobia, 490
ACTH. *See* Adrenocorticotrophic hormone
Action potential, 84
Activating effects, 365
Activating event, 572
Activation-synthesis model of dreams, 181
Actor–observer effect, 621–622
Acupuncture, 124, 125, 167
Acute stress disorder, 492
Ad baculum arguments, 32
Ad hominem arguments, 31–32
Ad populum arguments, 33–34
Ad verecundiam arguments, 32–33
Additive color mixture, 136, 137
Adenine, 109, 110
ADH. *See* Antidiuretic hormone
Adjustment problems, 523
Adolescence
  alcohol and, 186, 188, 423
  definition of, 420, 421
  depression and, 561
  developmental psychology and, 421–425
  eating disorders and, 509
  ego identity versus role diffusion, 424
  gender and, 424–425
  parenting and, 423–424
  physical development in, 422–423
  social and personality development in, 423–424
  staring and, 626
  substance abuse in, 196–197
Adoptee studies
  anxiety disorders and, 493
  heredity and, 112
  of intelligence, 344, 346–347
  schizophrenia and, 505
Adoption studies, 346–347
Adrenal cortex, 104, 106, 580
Adrenal glands, 104, 106–107, 366
Adrenal medulla, 104, 107, 580
Adrenaline

autonomic arousal and, 385
definition of, 107
endocrine system and, 104
memory and, 278
nicotine and, 193
self-efficacy expectations and, 537–538, 574
sexual orientation and, 368
stress and, 580, 581
Adrenocorticotrophic hormone, 104, 106, 580
Adult, in transactional analysis, 532, 533
Adult development
  developmental psychology and, 396, 425–432
  late adulthood, 429–432
  Levinson's seasons of, 427
  middle adulthood, 427–429
  young adulthood, 425–427
Advertising, 613–615
Aerobic exercise, 604
Afferent neurons, 83, 89, 93
Affiliation, 376
Affiliation need, 376–377
African Americans
  adolescent identity formation and, 425
  aggression and, 378
  aging and, 431
  AIDS and, 585–586
  asthma and, 590
  Black dialect and, 316–318
  cancer and, 586
  cigarette use of, 192
  discrimination and, 617
  education and, 27
  environmental influences and, 345
  health care and, 587
  heart attacks and, 586
  hypertension and, 586
  intelligence tests and, 341, 343, 345
  as involuntary minority group, 21
  IQ scores of, 340, 347, 349
  mortality and, 585
  population of, 23–24
  as psychologists, 27–28
  psychotherapy and, 557–559
  Scholastic Aptitude Test scores and, 341
  self-actualization and, 360
  self-concept and, 465
  sexual orientation and, 369
  sickle cell anemia and, 111
  stereotypes of, 619
  suicide and, 516
  Wyatt survey of, 50–51
Afterimage, 137–139
Age. *See also* Adolescence; Children; Elderly; Infants
  chronological, 335
  discrimination and, 617
  as diversity, 26–27
  eating disorders and, 510
  immune system and, 583
  intellectual functioning and, 347–348
  mental, 335
  second-language learning and, 325
  smoking and, 193
  social support and, 579
  suicide and, 516
Age regression, 202
Age-30 transition, 426
Aggression
  alcohol and, 61–64
  behaviorist theory of, 221

cognitive restructuring and, 535–536
day care and, 435
gender differences and, 474, 477
heredity and, 108
media violence and, 245
motivation and, 377–379
priming of, 246
psychosexual development and, 442
punishment and, 247
social psychology and, 624
sociocultural influences on, 360–361
temperature and, 62, 675
testosterone and, 475
theories of, 377–379
verbal, 378
women and, 48
Aggressive behavior, 540
Aging. *See* Elderly
Agoraphobia, 490, 491
Agreeableness, 452–453
AIDS
  alcohol and, 187
  ethnicity and, 585–586
  health psychology and, 594–595
  heroin and, 190
  prevention of, 678, 689, 693–695
  social support and, 579
Air pollution, 675
Alarm reaction, 579–581, 600
Alcohol and alcoholism
  A–B problem and, 612
  abstinence syndrome and, 185
  aggression and, 61–64, 69
  cancer and, 591
  compliance with medical advice and, 596
  coronary heart disease and, 589
  as depressant, 186–188
  as drug, 184
  effects of, 63, 187–188
  ethics and, 68, 69
  ethnicity and, 186–187
  gender and, 186–187
  gender differences and, 586–587
  genetics and, 186
  heredity and, 108
  pregnancy and, 402
  questionnaire concerning, 189
  reticular activating system (RAS) and, 92
  social class and, 186–187
  treatment of, 197
  use of, 185
Algorithms, 295
All-or-none principle, 84
Alpha waves
  biofeedback training and, 200, 540
  definition of, 178, 179
  meditation and, 199
  operant conditioning, 234
Altered states of consciousness, 176
Altruism, 644–646
Alzheimer's disease, 117–119, 278, 431
Amacrine cells, 133
Ambiguous, 140, 141, 469
Amenorrhea, 510
American Psychological Association, divisions of, 12
American Sign Language
  age of learning and, 325
  chimpanzees and, 5, 108
  deafness and, 158
  diversity and, 161
Amnesia. *See also* Forgetting; Memory
  anterograde, 276–277

dissociative, 275
infantile, 275–276
posthypnotic, 202–204, 273
retrograde, 276–277
Amniotic sac, 400, 401
Amphetamines, 86, 190–191
Amplitude, 154
Amygdala, 92
Anabolic steroids, 106–107
Anaerobic exercise, 604
Anal fixations, 444–445
Anal stage, of psychosexual development, 444–445
Anal-expulsive, 445
Anal-retentive, 445, 451
Analgesia, 188
Analgesic, 166
Analogies, 296
Analogous, 138, 139
Analogous colors, 138
Analytical psychology, 445
Anchoring and adjustment heuristic, 306, 307, 309
Androgens, 365–366, 400, 401, 422
Anger, 379, 386
Animal research
  cancer and, 591
  ethics of, 70–71
  exploration and manipulation, 372–373
  generalizing and, 4–5
  Harlow's attachment study, 407–408
  language and, 5, 108, 313, 315
  naturalistic observation method and, 56–57
  predictability and, 577–578
  symbols and, 310
Animism, 413, 414
Anorexia nervosa, 508, 509–510, 586
Anterograde amnesia, 276–277
Antianxiety drugs, 549–551, 554
Antibodies, 582, 583
Antidepressant, 550–552
Antidiuretic hormone, 104, 106, 278
Antigen, 582
Antipsychotic drugs, 551, 554
Antisocial personality disorder, 507
Anvil, 155
Anxiety
  biofeedback training and, 200
  child abuse and, 437
  heredity and, 108, 112
  psychological disorders and, 483–484
  rational-emotive therapy and, 548
  rebound, 550
Anxiety disorders, 489–494
Apes, language of, 313, 315
Aphagic, 363
Aphasia, 97
Apnea, 183
Applied psychology
  community psychology, 677–678
  consumer psychology, 670–671
  definition of, 656, 657
  educational psychology, 682–686
  environmental psychology, 671–677
  forensic psychology, 679–680
  human factors and, 666–670
  industrial/organizational psychology and, 656–666
  sports psychology, 680–682
Applied research, 6, 7
Appraisal of workers performance, 660–661

Approach-approach conflict, 570, 571
Approach-avoidance conflict, 570, 571
Aptitude, 54, 55, 466
Archetypes, 446
Arguments, fallacies in, 31–34
Armenians, and obedience studies, 42
Aromas, 675. *See also* Smell
Arousal
  autonomic, 380, 381
  bodily, 385
  emotion and, 380–381
  facial-feedback hypothesis and, 383
  group behavior and, 640
  increased, 246
  lowering, 600–602
  motivation and, 357
  parasympathetic, 378–379
  patterns of, 386
  personality disorders and, 508
  sexual, 364
  sympathetic, 378–380
  temperature and, 674
Artificial intelligence, 336–337
Artificialism, 413, 414
Asian Americans
  alcoholism and, 187
  discrimination and, 617
  intelligence tests and, 340
  population of, 23–24
  as psychologists, 28
  psychotherapy and, 557, 559–560
  Scholastic Aptitude Test scores and, 341
  sexual orientation and, 369–370
  sociocultural perspective and, 462
  stereotypes and, 24, 619, 659
  women and, 20
Assertiveness training, 540, 593, 659
Assimilation, 410, 411
Association, 238, 284–285
Association areas, 97
Asthma, 590
Astigmatism, 148, 149
Astrology, 73–76
Asylums, 524–525
Athletes, 680–682
Attachment, 406–409
Attachment-in-the-making phase, 407
Attention-deficit/hyperactivity disorder, 191, 197
Attitude-discrepant behavior, 374
Attitudes
  A–B problem and, 612
  definition of, 612
  origins of, 612–613
  persuasion and, 613–617
  prejudice and, 617–618
  social psychology and, 611–618
Attraction, 626. *See also* Interpersonal attraction
Attribution, 620
Attribution process, 620, 622–623, 625
Attribution theory, 620–625
Attributional styles, 500–501
Auditory, 153. *See also* Hearing
Auditory cortex, 278
Auditory nerve, 157
Authentic, 459
Authoritative, 410
Authority, 419
Authority figures, obedience studies, 42–44, 635–636
Autism, 112
Autobiographical memory, 51–52

Autokinetic effect, 144
Automaticity, 417–418
Autonomic nervous system
  adrenaline and, 385
  alarm reaction and, 580, 581
  anxiety and, 489, 494
  arousal and, 380, 381
  definition of, 93
  generalized anxiety disorder and, 491
  hypothalamus and, 92
Availability heuristic, 306, 307
Average, A1
Aversive conditioning, 538–539
Avoidance learning, 234
Avoidance of powerful stimuli, 542
Avoidance–avoidance conflict, 570
Avoidant personality disorder, 507
Axon, 81

B
Babbling, 314, 315, 319
Babinski reflex, 403
Backward conditioning, 218, 219
Balance theory, 373–374
Barbiturates, 190
Barnum effect, 72–73
Basal ganglia, 92–93
Basic anxiety, 446
Basic hostility, 446
Basilar membrane, 157
Beauty, 628–630
Bed-wetting, 184, 221–222
Bedlam, 524
Behavior
  biological perspective on, 17–18
  cognitive perspective on, 18–19
  as factor in health, 585
  humanistic-existential perspective, 19
  learning and, 20
  learning perspectives on, 20
  observable, 13
  psychodynamic perspective, 19–20
  strategies aimed at, 543
Behavior genetics, 108
Behavior modification. *See* Behavior therapy
Behavior rehearsal, 540
Behavior sociocultural perspective, 20–22
Behavior therapy
  aversive conditioning, 538–539
  cognitive restructuring and, 536
  definition of, 6, 7, 536
  effectiveness of, 549
  fear reduction methods, 537–538
  mental retardation and, 549
  operant conditioning procedures, 539–540
  outcomes and, 547
  schizophrenia and, 549
  self-control methods, 540–544
Behavior-outcome relations, definition of, 457
Behavior-rating scale, definition of, 466
Behaviorism, 12–14, 17
Behaviorist theory
  aggression and, 221
  attachment and, 407
  bedwetting and, 222
  on behavior, 20–21
  classical conditioning and, 215, 238
  cognitive theory and, 19
  continuous development and, 397
  industrial/organizational psychology and, 657, 661

learning and, 213–214
  personality and, 454
  taste aversion and, 218
  weight control and, 390–392
Beliefs, 572
Bell-and-pad method for bedwetting, 221–222
Benzodiazepines, 494, 550
Beta-endorphin, 86
BFT. *See* Biofeedback training
Bias
  in appraisal process, 661
  in intelligence tests, 341
  volunteer, 50, 51
Biculturalism, 22, 23
Big Five personality factors, 452–453
Bilingual education, 324–327
Bilingualism, 24, 324–327, 560
Binding, 129
Binet-Simon scale of intelligence, 335
Binocular cues, 145, 148, 149
Biofeedback training
  altering consciousness through, 199–201
  arousal and, 600
  asthma and, 590
  cancer and, 592
  definition of, 200, 540
  insomnia and, 207
  migraine headaches and, 588
  operant conditioning and, 233–234
  pain and, 171
Biological psychologists, 80
Biological theories
  aggression and, 377
  alcoholism and, 187
  anxiety disorders and, 493
  on behavior, 17–18
  cerebral cortex and, 95–102
  endocrine system and, 102–108
  as factor in health, 585
  gender differences and, 475
  heredity and, 108–115
  interest in, 21
  memory and, 277–282
  mood disorders and, 501
  nervous system and, 87–95
  neurons and, 80–87
  schizophrenia and, 505
  sexual dysfunctions and, 513
  sexual orientation and, 368
  substance abuse and, 186
Biological therapies
  drug therapy, 549–552
  effectiveness of, 548, 554
  electroconvulsive therapy, 552–553
  for personality improvement, 550–551
  psychosurgery, 553
Bimodal, A4
Bipolar cells, 133, 135, 139
Bipolar disorder
  definition of, 498, 499
  heredity and, 108
  lithium and, 550, 552
  psychotherapy effectiveness and, 548
Bisexual, 366
Black dialect, 316–318
Black English Vernacular (BEV), 24, 316–318
Blacks. *See* African Americans
Blind in experimental method, 62–64
Blind navigation system, 158–159
Blind spot, 134, 135

Blood sugar, 363, 390
Body language, 532, 623, 626, 659
Body types, 450–451
Bottom-up processing, definition of, 143–144
Bradykinin, 166
Brain
  accidents and, 66, 119
  binding in, 129–130
  Cannon-Bard theory of emotions and, 385
  central nervous system and, 90–93
  computerized axial tomography (CAT scan) and, 67
  consciousness and, 65–66
  electrical stimulation of, 66
  gender differences in, 475
  hypothalamus experiments and, 363
  mental retardation and, 352
  mind and, 65–66
  nervous system and, 88
  parts of, 91
  positron emission tomography (PET scan) and, 67
  prenatal development of, 368
  research methods and, 65–68
Brain Electrical Activity Mapping, 17
Brain waves, 66–67, 177–178, 207
Brainstorming, 304
Breathalyzer, 70
Breathing reflex, 403
Breeding, selective, 113–115
Brightness constancy, 149
Broca's aphasia, 98, 99
Broca's area, 97–98
Buffers, and obedience, 636
Bulbs, of neurons, 83
Bulimia nervosa, 509–511, 552, 586
Bureaucracy, 663
Buttons, of neurons, 83
Bystander effect, 644–646

C
Cancer, 586, 591–594
Careers, and gender polarization, 651–652
Case study, 51–52, 448, 453
CASPER. *See* Computer Assessment System for Psychotherapy Evaluation and Research (CASPER)
CAT scan. *See* Computerized axial tomography
Catastrophize, 572, 600, 602
Catatonic schizophrenia, 502, 503–504
Catch 30s, 426
Catharsis, 378, 526, 527
Cause and effect
  correlation and, 58, 60, 63
  infants and, 413
  research and, 46–47
Center, 414, 415
Central nervous system
  antianxiety drugs and, 550
  brain and, 90–93
  definition of, 88
  depressants and, 186–190
  schizophrenia and, 505
  spinal cord, 88–90
  stimulants to, 190–194
Central tendency, A2–A4
Cephalocaudal, 400
Cerebellum, 91
Cerebral cortex
  biology and, 95–102

definition of, 80, 92, 93
electrical stimulation of the brain (ESB) and, 101
geography of, 95–97
handedness and, 99
hemispheres of, 95, 97–100
language and, 97–98
memory and, 278
pain and, 166
speech and, 108
split-brain experiments and, 99–100
thought and, 97–98
Cerebrum, 92, 93
Chain breaking, 543
Chemotherapy, 197, 592, 593
Child, in transactional analysis, 532, 533
Child abuse, 377, 436–437
Child psychology, 12
Child rearing, 409–410. *See also* Parenting
Children. *See also* Infants
aggression and, 377
cancer and, 591, 592
day care and, 435–436
emotional development of, 382
exploration and manipulation, 373
eyewitness testimony of, 264
group intelligence tests for, 340
language development and, 314–320
memory development of, 273, 276
memory organization of, 267–268
nervous system development and, 83
phobias and, 490
problem solving and, 310–311
token economies and, 539–540
Chimpanzees, 5, 56–57, 108, 310
Chinese Americans, 619. *See also* Asian Americans
Choice, 11
Choking, and sports psychology, 681–682
Choleric, 450
Cholesterol, 588, 590
Chromosomes, 108–112, 401
Chronic disease, health psychology and, 595
Chronic fatigue, coronary heart disease and, 589
Chronological age, 335
Chunk, 259–260
Cigarettes, 185, 192–194, 207–209. *See also* Nicotine; Smoking
Circadian rhythm, 176, 177
Circular explanation, 453
Cirrhosis of the liver, 188
Clairvoyance, 75
Classic organization theories, 663
Classical conditioning
applications of, 221–224
definition of, 215
discrimination and, 220–221
extinction and, 218–220
generalization and, 220
higher-order conditioning and, 221
as learning, 214–224
Pavlov and, 214–216
spontaneous recovery and, 218–220
stimuli and responses in, 216–217, 223, 225
taste aversion and, 212, 218

types of, 217–218
Classroom management, 8, 234–235, 683–684
Claustrophobia, 490
Clear-cut-attachment phase, 407
Clinical child psychologists, 10
Clinical psychologists, 7–8, 466, 656
Clinical scales, 466, 467
Clitoris, 445
Cloning, 399
Closed captioned, 159
Closure, 139, 141
Cocaine, 86, 184–185, 190–193
Cochlea, 154–157, 160
Cocktail party effect, 175
Codes, in displays, 667–670
Cognitive, 18
Cognitive abilities, and gender, 472–474
Cognitive appraisal, 573, 613
Cognitive appraisal theory of emotions, 385–386
Cognitive behavior theory
cancer and, 593
eating disorders and, 510
Cognitive behavior therapy
antidepressants and, 551–552
attention-deficit/hyperactivity disorder and, 197
cognitive restructuring and, 536
couple therapy and, 545
weight control and, 391–392
Cognitive consistency, 360, 373–374
Cognitive development
developmental psychology and, 410–421
information-processing approaches to, 417–418
in late adulthood, 430
Piaget's cognitive-developmental theory, 410–417
Cognitive-developmental theory, 18
Cognitive factors, in learning, 238–240, 247
Cognitive flexibility, 325
Cognitive learning, 455
Cognitive manipulations, 385
Cognitive map, 298, 299
Cognitive psychologists, 20
Cognitive restructuring
and behavior therapy, 536
cancer and, 593
as cognitive therapy, 535–536
smoking and, 209
Cognitive theories
aggression and, 378
anxiety disorders and, 493
on behavior, 18–19
classical conditioning and, 216, 238
discrimination and, 221
industry and, 657
interest in, 21
language development and, 320
learning and, 213–214
linguistic relativity hypothesis and, 322
mood disorders and, 500–501
motivation and, 360
personality disorders and, 508
schemas and, 238, 262
sexual dysfunctions and, 513
substance abuse and, 186
weight control and, 390–392
Cognitive therapies
cognitive restructuring, 535–536
cognitive therapy, 534–535
definition of, 533

effectiveness of, 548, 554
measuring outcomes and, 547
rational–emotive therapy, 534
schizophrenia and, 548–549
Cognitive–dissonance theory, 75, 356, 357, 374, 673
Collective unconscious, definition of, 446
Collectivists, 464
College students, political views of, 53–54
Color blindness, 139–141
Color constancy, 149
Color vision, 135–139
Color wheel, 136
Comatose, 92
Common fate, 143
Commonsense theory of emotions, 383
Communication styles, gender differences in, 474
Community health, and health psychology, 595
Community mental health centers (CMHCs), 525, 677
Community psychology, 677–679
Competencies, 245, 454, 455
Competing responses, 543
Complementary, 136, 532, 533
Complementary colors, 136
Compliance, with medical advice, 596–598
Componential level, 333
Compulsion, 490, 491
Computer Assessment System for Psychotherapy Evaluation and Research (CASPER), 488–489
Computerized axial tomography, 17, 67, 167
Computers
diagnosis and, 488–489
personality measurement and, 466–467
research methods and, 64–65
Concepts, 290–292
Concordance, 112, 368, 492, 493
Concrete-operational stage, 411, 415–416
Conditional positive regard, 460, 461
Conditioned reinforcer, 228
Conditioned response, 215, 219
Conditioned stimulus, 28, 216, 217
Conditioning
attitudes and, 612–613
definition of, 12, 13
learning and, 20
Conditions of worth, 460, 461
Conductive deafness, 159
Cones, 134, 135, 139
Confidential, 68, 69
Conflict, 570–571
Conform, 637
Conformity
Asch study on, 637–638
factors influencing, 638–639
groupthink and, 643
Muslim women and, 639–640
Congruence, 460, 461, 531
Conscience, 420
Conscientiousness, 452–453
Conscious, 442
Consciousness
biofeedback and, 199–201
brain and, 65–66
definition of, 174–176
depressants and, 186–190
drugs and, 184–186
hallucinogenics and, 194–198

hypnosis and, 201–204
levels of, 176
meditation and, 198–199
sleep and dreams, 176–184
stimulants and, 190–194
Consensus, 622, 622–623, 659, 666
Consequence, 572
Conservation, 414–417
Consistency, 622–623
Consolidation, 276, 277
Consonant, 154
Constructive criticism, 660
Consultation, 6, 7
Consumer behavior, task analysis of, 670
Consumer psychologists, 10
Consumer psychology, 670–671
Consummate love, 634, 635
Consumption patterns, and coronary heart disease, 589
Contact comfort, 407
Context-dependent memory, 270
Contexts, 14
Contextual level, 333
Contiguity, 238
Contiguous, 216
Contingency theories, 238, 663
Continuity, 142, 143
Continuous development, 397–399
Continuous reinforcement, 231
Control, and psychological hardiness, 592
Control groups, 62
Conventional level of moral development, 419–420
Convergence, 148, 149
Convergence zones, 130, 131
Convergent thinking, 302
Conversion disorder, 497
Cooing, 314, 315, 319
Cool colors, 136
Copulate, 372, 373
Cornea, 132
Coronary heart disease, 586, 588–590
Corporations, and psychology, 664–665
Corpus callosum, 92, 93, 99
Correlation coefficient, A6–A7, 56–58
Correlational method, 56–60
Cortical steroids, 106
Corticosteroids, 106, 107, 580, 581
Corticotrophin-releasing hormone, 104, 580
Cortisol, 104, 106, 107, 368
Counseling psychologists, 7–8, 466, 656
Counterconditioning, 222, 223
Couple therapy, 545
Covert reinforcement, 543
Covert sensitization, 543
CR. *See* Conditioned response
Crack, 191
Creative self, 446
Creativity
definition of, 300, 301
factors affecting, 302–304
infinite, 312
intelligence and, 302
thinking and, 301–304
Cretinism, 106, 107
Criminal behavior, and heredity, 108
Criminal-justice system, 10
Criterion-referenced testing, 685
Critical period, 408
Critical period hypothesis, 325
Critical thinking
definition of, 29

fallacies in arguments and, 31–34
principles of, 30–31
psychology and, 29–34
research and, 46–47
Criticism, and workers performance appraisal, 660–661
Cross-cultural perspectives. *See also* Ethnicity
of attachment, 407
on beauty, 628–629
cancer and, 586
individualism and, 463
of learning, 240–241
on menstruation, 120–121
perceptual constancies and, 149
personal space and, 676–677
Crowding, 675–677
CS. *See* Conditioned stimulus
Cuento therapy, 560
Cultural bias, 342
Cultural literacy, 559
Cultural-responsiveness hypothesis, 557
Culture-Fair Intelligence Test, 342–343
Culture-free, 342
Cumulative recorders, 226–227
Cybersex, 367
Cystic fibrosis, 110
Cytosine, 109, 110

D

Daily hassles, 566, 567
Dark adaptation, 135
Date rape, 689, 692–693
Day care, 435–436
Deafness, 158–161. *See also* American Sign Language; Hearing
Death and dying, 431–432
Debrief, 70
Decay, interference theory and, 274
Decays, 256
Decentration, 415
Deception, in research, 69–70
Decibel, 154, 674
Decision making, 306–309, 641–642
Deductive reasoning, 304, 305, 416
Deep structure, 312, 313
Deep-sleep disorders, 183–184
Defense mechanisms, 443, 448
Deindividuation, 643–644
Delayed conditioning, 216–218
Delirium tremens, 184, 185
Delta waves, 178, 179
Delta-9-tetrahydrocannabinol, 194
Delusions, 502
Dendrites, 81, 278
Denial, as defense mechanism, 443
Density, 675, 676
Dependent variables, 61–62
Depersonalization disorder, 496, 497
Depolarize, 84
Depressants, 184, 186–190
Depression
amphetamines and, 191
bipolar disorder and, 108, 498–499, 548, 550, 552
cancer and, 591, 592
child abuse and, 437
components of, 379
drug therapy for, 554
gender differences and, 528
heredity and, 108
in late adulthood, 430
major, 498–499, 548
menopause and, 428
psychological disorders and, 483–484

rational-emotive therapy and, 548
self-serving bias and, 622
women and, 49, 499, 500, 528
Depth perception, 145–148, 404–405
Descriptive statistics
central tendency and, A2–A4
definition of, A1
frequency distribution and, A2
variability and, A4–A5
Desensitization, 130, 131
Destructive criticism, 660
Determinants, 342, 343
Development psychologists, 8
Developmental psychology
adolescence and, 421–425
adult development and, 396, 425–432
cognitive development, 410–421
controversies in, 397–399
goals of, 396–397
moral development, 418–421
physical development, 402–406
prenatal development, 399–402
social development, 406–410
Deviation IQ, 339
Diabetes mellitus, 106
Diagnostic and Statistical Manual (DSM), 485
Dialogue, 532, 533
Dichromat, 140
Dieting, 390, 602
Difference threshold, 127–128
Diffusion of responsibility, 641
Direct inner awareness, 175
Disabled, as diversity, 26–27
Discontinuous development, 397–399, 416
Discovery learning, 683
Discrete behaviors, 226
Discrimination, 220–221, 558–559, 616, 617
Discrimination training, 221
Discriminative stimuli, 230–231
Disease. *See* Health psychology; Illness
Disinhibition, 245–246
Disorganized schizophrenia, 502, 503
Disorientation, 184, 185
Displace, 260, 261
Displaced, 445
Displacement, 274, 312, 443
Dispositional attribution, 620–621, 625
Dissociate amnesia, 494–495
Dissociation, 203–204
Dissociative amnesia, 275
Dissociative disorders, 494–497
Dissociative fugue, 494, 495
Dissociative identity disorder, 482, 483, 495–496
Dissonant, 154
Distinctiveness, 622–623
Divergent thinking, 302
Dizygotic twins, 112
DNA, and chromosomes, 109
Dominant traits, 112–113
Dopamine, 86, 93, 551
Dopamine theory of schizophrenia, 505–506
Double-blind study, 62–64
Down syndrome, 111, 351–352
Dream, 426
Dream analysis, 527
Dreams
activation-synthesis model of, 181
definition of, 179
Freudian view of, 181
nightmares and, 181–182

NREM sleep and, 180
psychoanalysis and, 527
psychodynamic theory and, 20
REM sleep and, 180
sleep and, 176–184
symbols in, 180
theories of content of, 181
Drive for superiority, 446
Drive-reduction theory, 358–359, 361
Drives, 357
Drug therapy
antianxiety drugs, 549–551
antidepressants, 551–552
antipsychotic drugs, 551
lithium, 552
Drugs. *See also* Substance abuse
abuse of, 196–197
altering consciousness through, 184–186
antianxiety, 549
antipsychotic, 551
dependence on, 596
state-dependent memory and, 270
DSM-IV, 485–487
DTs. *See* Delirium tremens
Duchenne smile, 383
Duct, 104
Duncker candle problem, 300
Duplicity theory, 157–158
Dying. *See* Death and dying
Dyspareunia, definition of, 512, 513

E

Ear, 155–157. *See also* Hearing
Eardrum, 154, 155, 159
Eating disorders, 508–512
Echoes, 258, 259
Echoic memory, 258, 259
ECT. *See* Electroconvulsive therapy
Education
bilingual, 324–327
diversity in, 27
ethnicity and, 26
expository teaching, 683
gender polarization and, 650–651
health and, 584
smoking and, 193
socioeconomic status and, 587
Educational psychologists, 8
Educational psychology
applied psychology and, 682–686
classroom management and, 683–684
definition of, 683
exceptional students and, 685
planning and teaching, 684–685
teaching practices and, 683
tests and grades, 685–686
EEG. *See* Electroencephalograph
Efferent neurons, 83, 89, 93
Effort justification, definition of, 374
Ego, 442–443, 446, 526
Ego analysts, 529
Ego identity, 424, 425, 446, 447
Ego integrity versus despair, 430–432
Egocentric, 413
Egocentrism, 414, 416
Eidetic imagery, 256, 257
Elaboration likelihood model, 612, 613
Elaborative rehearsal, 266, 271, 272
Elderly
Alzheimer's disease and, 117–119
cognitive development and, 430
depression and, 430
ego integrity versus despair in, 430–432

late adulthood development and, 429–432
motivation and, 430
physical development in, 430
sensory acuity and, 430
stereotypes of, 431
suicide and, 432
taste and, 164
theories of aging, 430–431
Electra complex, 445, 448
Electrical stimulation of the brain, 66, 101
Electroconvulsive therapy, 552–553
Electroencephalograph (EEG)
biofeedback training and, 200, 234, 540
brain research and, 66–67
definition of, 176, 177
hypnosis and, 201
Electromyograph, 200, 540
Electronic developments, in research methods, 64–65
Electronic memory, 280–281
Embryo, 396, 397
Embryonic stage, 400–402
Emotion
arousal and, 380–381
Cannon-Bard theory of, 385
circle of, 381
components of, 379
definition of, 378, 379
expression of, 382
facial-feedback hypothesis, 383
James-Lange theory of, 384–386
number of, 381–382
theories of, 383–386
Emotional stability, 452–453
Empathic understanding, 531
Empathy, 624
Empirical, 42, 43, 64, 74
Empirically, 228, 229
Employment. *See* Industrial/organizational psychology
Empty-nest syndrome, 429
Encoding
definition of, 253, 454
levels-of-processing model and, 272
short-term memory and, 258–259
social-cognitive theory and, 455–456
Encounter groups, 545
Endocrine system
alarm reaction and, 580
biology of, 102–108
definition of, 80, 104, 105
glands of, 104–108
hypothalamus and, 92
psychoneuroimmunology and, 582
resistance stage and, 581
Endogenous morphine, 86
Endometriosis, 121
Endorphins, 86, 167
Engram, 276, 277
Environment
adult intellectual functioning and, 347–348
aging and, 430
behaviorism and, 454
as factor in health, 585
intelligence and, 345–348
IQ scores and, 345
suicide and, 517
work and, 666–667
Environmental activism, 673
Environmental psychologists, 8–9
Environmental psychology

air pollution and, 675
applied psychology and, 671–677
aromas and, 675
crowding and, 675–677
definition of, 672
environmental activism and, 673
noise and, 673–674
temperature and, 674–675
Epilepsy, 99, 276, 278
Epinephrine, 104, 107
Episodic memory, 251, 269, 276, 279
Epstein-Barr virus, 583
Erogenous zone, 444
Eros, 444
Errors, in measurement, 53
ESP. See Extrasensory perception
Essential hypertension, 588
Esteem needs, 360
Estrogen, 104, 107, 422
Estrus, 365
Ethical, 68
Ethics
    research with animals and, 70–71
    of research methods, 68–71
    research with people and, 68–70
    in vitro fertilization and, 399
Ethics review committee, 68
Ethnic groups, 20, 49
Ethnicity. See also African Americans; Asian Americans; Hispanic Americans; Native Americans
    adolescent identity formation and, 424–425
    aggression and, 378–379
    AIDS and, 585–586
    alcoholism and, 186–187
    compliance with medical advice and, 597
    discrimination and, 617
    eating disorders and, 510
    eyewitness testimony and, 265
    as factor in health, 584, 585
    intelligence and, 340–341, 348–350
    moral development and, 420–421
    postsecondary education and, 26
    psychological disorders and, 21
    psychology and, 22–25
    psychotherapy and, 557–561
    self-concept and, 464
    sexual orientation and, 369–370
    smoking and, 193
    suicide and, 516
Ethologist, 358
Euphoria, 187, 188
Euphoric, 386
Eustress, 565
Evaluation apprehension, 641
Evolution, 12
Exceptional students, 685
Excitatory synapse, 85
Exemplar, 291
Exercise
    behavior modification and, 590
    cancer and, 592
    compliance with medical advice and, 596
    coronary heart disease and, 589
    menstruation and, 121
    physiological benefits of, 604–605
    pregnancy and, 400
    psychological benefits of, 606
    Type A behavior and, 605–606
    weight control and, 391
Exhaustion stage, 581
Existentialism, 18, 19, 459
Expectancies, 454–457

Expectations, 128, 360
Experiential level, 333
Experiment, 60, 61
Experimental groups, 62
Experimental method, 60–64
Experimental psychologists, 9
Experimental scales, 468–469
Expertise, 297
Exploration, and manipulation, 372–373
Expository teaching, 683
Externals, 577
Extinction, 218, 219, 228–229, 319
Extinction trial, 219
Extrasensory perception, 75
Extroversion, 108, 451, 452–453
Eye, 132–135. See also Vision
Eyewitness testimony, 263–265, 679

F

Facial expressions, 382
Facial-feedback hypothesis, 383, 384
Factor analysis, 331, 450, 451
Factor theories, 330–333
Factors, 330, 331
Family therapy, 546, 590
FAP. See Fixed action pattern (FAP)
Farsighted, 148, 149
Fast MRI, 67
Fat cells, 390
Fear, 207, 228, 379, 380
Fear appeal, 615
Fear-reduction methods, 537–538
Feature detectors, 128–129
Feedback, 540
Feeling-of-knowing experience, 269
Female sexual arousal disorder, 512, 513
Fertilization, 396, 398–399
Fetal stage, of prenatal development, 402
Fetus, 398, 399
Fight-or-flight reaction, 579, 580
Figure-ground perception, 140–142
First correct response, 227
Fissures, 92, 93
Fixation, 444
Fixation time, 404, 405
Fixed-action pattern (FAP), 358, 408
Fixed-interval scallop, 231–232
Fixed-interval schedule, 231–232
Fixed-ratio schedule, 232
Flashbacks, 194, 195
Flashbulb memories, 266–267
Flavor, 163, 164. See also Taste
Flooding, 222–223, 537
Follicle-stimulating hormone (FSH), 104, 107
Foot-in-the-door technique, 616, 636
Forced-choice format, 466
Forensic psychologists, 10
Forensic psychology, 678–680
Forgetting. See also Memory
    anterograde and retrograde amnesia, 276–277
    Ebbinghaus's classic curve of, 274
    infantile amnesia, 275–276
    interference theory and, 274–275
    measuring, 272–274
    repression and, 275
Formal-operational stage, 411, 416, 417
Fovea, 135

Frame of reference, 460, 461, 531
Framing effect, 308
Free association, 526, 527
Free will, 11
Frequency distribution, A2
Frequency theory, 157
Frontal lobe, 95, 278–279
Functional analysis, 540
Functional analysis of behavior, 540, 542
Functional fixedness, 300
Functional MRI, 67
Functionalism, 12, 13, 17, 18
Fundamental attribution error, 621, 624

G

"g" factor, 331
GABA. See Gamma-aminobutyric acid
Galvanic skin response (GSR), 199
Gamma-aminobutyric acid, 494
Ganglia, 88
Ganglion cells, 133, 135, 139
Ganzfield procedure, 76
Gate theory, 166–167
Gay males, 366–370, 617. See also Lesbians
Gazing, 623, 626
Gender
    adolescent identity formation and, 424–425
    aggression and, 378–379
    alcoholism and, 186–187
    cognitive abilities and, 472–474
    color blindness and, 139–140
    creativity and, 303
    definition of, 25
    eating disorders and, 510
    gender schema, 360
    generalization and, 49
    health and, 584
    individuality versus relatedness, 449–450
    moral development and, 420–421
    personality development and, 449–450
    polarization and, 649–652
    psychology and, 25–26
    smoking and, 193
    socialization and, 233
    stereotypes of, 649
    suicide and, 516
    young adulthood and, 426
Gender differences
    in aggression, 474
    alcohol and, 586–587
    body shape and, 629–630
    conformity and, 638
    coronary heart disease and, 586
    depression and, 528
    development of, 474–478
    gender-schema theory and, 478
    personality and, 472–474
    physical attractiveness and, 630–631
    physicians and, 587
    psychodynamic theory and, 475
    in self-serving bias, 622
    social-cognitive theory and, 476–477
    in victim helped, 645–646
Gender polarization, 649–652
Gender roles, and sexual orientation, 369
Gender-schema theory, 477, 478
General adaptation syndrome (GAS), 579–581
General medical conditions, 485–486

Generalization, 220, 221
Generalize, 4, 5, 48–50
Generalized anxiety disorder, 490, 491
Generativity versus stagnation, 426, 427
Genes
    chromosomes and, 108–112
    definition of, 16, 17–18, 108
    sexual orientation and, 368
Genetics, definition of, 108. See also Heredity
Genital stage, 445
Genome, 110
Genuineness, 531
German measles, 402
Germinal stage, 399–400
Gestalt, 459
Gestalt psychology, 14–15, 17–18, 140, 299, 308
Gestalt therapy, 532–533, 548
Giftedness, 352
Glial cells, 81, 83
Global assessment of functioning, 486
Glucose, positron emission tomography and, 67, 119
Gonadotropin-releasing hormone (GnRH), 104, 107
Gorillas, 5, 108, 310
Gray matter, 90
Group behavior
    altruism and bystander effect, 644–646
    group decision making, 641–642
    groupthink and, 642–643
    mob behavior and deindividuation, 643–644
    polarization and risk shift, 642
    social facilitation and, 640–641
Group decision making, 641–642
Group therapies, 544–546, 593
Groupthink, 642–643
Growth hormone, 104, 106
Growth-hormone releasing factor (hGRF), 104, 106
Guanine, 109, 110
Guilt, and sympathetic arousal, 380

H

Habit, 12, 228
Habituation, 246
Hallucinations, 184–185, 484–485, 499, 551
Hallucinogenics, 185, 194–198
Halo effect, 660, 661, 686
Hammer, 155
Handedness, 98, 99
Happiness, 386
Hashish, 194
Head start programs, 346, 348
Headaches, 587–588, 600
Health psychologists, 10
Health psychology. See also names of specific illnesses
    compliance with medical advice and, 596–598
    definition of, 564–565
    multifactorial approach and, 584–596
    stress and, 565–584
Hearing
    absolute threshold and, 126
    brain and, 92
    deafness and, 158–160
    ear and, 155–157
    feature detectors and, 129
    locating sounds and, 157
    loudness and, 154
    overtones and timbre, 154–155

perception and, 157–158
perceptual development and, 405
pitch and, 153–154
sensation and, 153–160
temporal lobe and, 95
Weber's constant for, 127
Heart attacks, 586, 605
Heredity
  aging and, 430
  anxiety disorders and, 493–494
  biology of, 108–115
  cancer and, 591
  definition of, 80, 108
  dominant and recessive traits, 112–113
  genes and chromosomes, 108–112
  intelligence and, 344–345
  IQ scores and, 344–345
  kinship studies and, 112
  obesity and, 389–390
  personality disorders and, 508
  schizophrenia and, 108, 112, 505
  selective breeding and, 113–115
  sexual orientation and, 368
  suicide and, 517
  in vitro fertilization and, 398–399
Hering-Helmholtz illusion, 151–152
Heritability, definition of, 345
Heroin, 184–186, 188–190, 193
Hertz, 153
Heterosexual, 366
Heuristics, 295–296, 306–307
hGRF. See Growth-hormone releasing factor
Hierarchical concepts, 291
Hierarchical structure, 268
Hierarchy, 536, 537
Hierarchy of needs, 359, 361, 459
High-density lipoproteins (HDL), 605
Higher-order conditioning, 221
Hippocampus, 86, 276, 278, 279
Hispanic Americans
  aggression and, 378
  AIDS and, 585–586
  compliance with medical advice and, 597
  discrimination and, 617
  health care and, 587
  IQ scores of, 340
  machismo/marianismo stereotypes and, 649–650
  population of, 23
  as psychologists, 28
  psychotherapy and, 557, 560
  Scholastic Aptitude Test scores and, 341
  sexual orientation and, 369
  stereotypes of, 24, 619
  women and, 20
Histogram, A2
Holophrase, 315
Homeless, 525
Homeostasis, 358–359
Homosexual. See Gay males; Lesbians
Homunculus, 65
Horizontal cells, 133
Hormones
  in adolescence, 423
  definition of, 16, 17, 104, 105
  effects of, 104
  hormone-replacement therapy and, 428
  neurotransmitters and, 101
  premenstrual syndrome and, 119
  sex, 365–366, 368, 401, 475
Horoscopes, 74

Hostility, 589, 603–604
Hue, 132, 135
Human diversity
  ethnic diversity, 22–25
  gender and, 25–26
  health and, 584–587
  in higher education, 27
  kinds of, 26–27
  psychologists and, 27–29
  research methods and, 47–50
Human factors
  definition of, 666
  display coding and, 667–670
  person-machine systems and, 666–667
  work environment and, 666–667
Human factors engineering, 656
Human genome project, 110–111
Human iceberg, 441
Human-potential movement, 19, 657
Human-relations movement, 657
Human-relations theories, 663, 666
Humanism, definition of, 18, 19, 459
Humanistic theory, 359–360
Humanistic-existential theories
  behavior and, 19
  evaluation of, 461
  interest in, 21
  Maslow's self-actualization, 459
  of personality, 458–461
  Rogers' self theory, 459–461
Humanistic-existential therapies
  effectiveness of, 549
  gestalt therapy and, 532–533
  person-centered therapy and, 530–531
  transactional analysis and, 531–532
Humor, 576–577
Hunger, 5–6, 362–364, 390
Hunger pangs, 362–363
Hunter's notch, 160
Huntington's chorea, 110
Hydrocarbons, 192, 193, 195
Hyperactivity. See Attention-deficit/hyperactivity disorder
Hyperamnesia, 202
Hyperglycemia, 106
Hyperphagic, 363
Hypertension, 586, 588, 590, 600
Hyperthyroidism, 106, 107
Hypnagogic state, 178, 179
Hypnosis
  altering consciousness through, 201–204
  changes in consciousness and, 202–203
  definition of, 200, 201
  eyewitness testimony and, 264
  Freud's use of, 527
  hypnotic induction, 201–202
  pain and, 170–171
  theories of, 203–204
Hypnotic suggestibility, 202
Hypoactive sexual desire disorder, 512, 513
Hypochondriasis, 498
Hypothalamus
  aggression and, 377
  definition of, 92
  endocrine system and, 104, 105
  experiments with, 363–364
  hunger and, 363, 390
  pheromones and, 162
  pituitary gland and, 106
  pleasure center of, 101, 200
  stress and, 580

Hypothesis, 44, 45, 46
Hypothyroidism, definition of, 106

I

I/O psychology. See Industrial/organizational psychology
Icon, 256
Iconic memory, 256, 257–258
Id, 442, 443, 526
Ideas of persecution, 485
Identification, 443, 476–477
Ill-defined problem, 300, 301
Illness
  asthma, 590
  cancer, 591–594
  compliance and, 596–598
  coronary heart disease, 588–590
  headaches, 587–588
  life changes and, 567, 570
  physician-patient interactions, 597–598
Illusions, 144
Imbalance, 374
Imitation, 318
Immune system
  cancer and, 591, 592
  definition of, 582
  exercise and, 605–606
  nature and functions of, 582
  stress and, 582–584
Imprinting, 408–409
In vitro fertilization, 398–399
In-group
  actor-observer effect and, 621
  peace and, 624
  prejudice and, 618
Incentives, 357
Incest taboo, 364, 445
Incubation, 300
Incubus, 181
Independent variables, 61–62
Indiscriminate attachment, 407
Individual psychology, 446
Individualism, 449
Individualism versus collectivism, 463–464
Individualist, 462, 463
Individuality versus relatedness, 449–450
Individualized instruction, 684–685
Inductive reasoning, 304, 305
Industrial psychologists, 9–10
Industrial psychology, 657
Industrial-engineering movement, 657
Industrial/organizational psychology
  applied psychology and, 656–666
  appraisal of workers performance, 660–661
  and corporations, 664–665
  corporations, 664–665
  currents in, 657
  definition of, 9–10, 657
  organizational theory and, 662–663, 666
  personality and, 453
  recruitment and placement, 657–659
  training and instruction, 660
Infantile amnesia, 275–276, 279
Infants. See also Children
  cause and effect exploration, 413
  day care and, 435
  human face and, 404
  intelligence and, 322
  motor development in, 403
  turn-taking awareness, 314
  visual acuity of, 404

Infer, A7, 49
Inferential statistics, A7–A9
Inferiority complex, 446
Infinite creativity, 312
Inflammation, 166, 580, 582, 583
Inflections, 312
Information processing
  approaches of, 417–418
  cognitive theory and, 18, 238
  definition of, 417
  prejudice and, 618
Information superhighway, and learning, 236–237
Informed consent, 68–69
Inhibitory synapse, 85
Initial-preattachment phase, 407
Injected substances, 385
Innate, definition of, 370, 371
Inner ear, 155–157
Insanity, 482, 483
Insanity plea, 679–680
Insecure detachment, 406
Insight, 14–15, 298–300, 526, 547
Insomnia, 182, 183, 206–207
Instinct, 358
Instinct theory, 358, 361
Instinctive behavior, 212–213
Instruction. See Education; Training and instruction
Instructional objectives, 684, 685
Instrumental conditioning, 224. See also Operant conditioning
Insulin, 104, 106
Intelligence
  achievement and, 57–58
  artificial, 336–337
  creativity and, 302
  definition of, 330, 331
  determinants of, 343–350
  educational psychologists and, 8
  environment and, 345–348
  ethnic differences in, 340–341
  ethnicity and, 348–350
  genetic influences on, 344–345
  giftedness and, 352
  human survival and, 377
  of infants, 322
  measurement of, 336–341
  mental retardation and, 351–353
  nature versus nurture, 114
  Piaget and, 411–412
  socioeconomic differences in, 340–341
  testing controversy, 341–343
  theories of, 330–335
Intelligence quotient (IQ)
  definition of, 335
  deviation IQ, 339
  formula for, 337–338
  heredity and, 344–345
  score distribution, 339
  score variations, 339
Intelligence tests
  bias and, 341
  controversy over, 341–343
  culture-free, 342–343
  group, 339–340
  individual, 335–339
Interest inventories, 658–659
Interference theory, 260–262, 274–275
Internals, 577
Interneuron, 90
Interpersonal attraction
  love and, 633–635
  physical attractiveness and, 626–632
  reciprocity and, 632–633
  similarity and, 632

Interpersonal relationships, and gender polarization, 652
Interposition, 146, 147
Interpretation, 526, 527
Intimacy versus isolation, 424, 425
Introspection, 11, 12, 18
Introversion, 451
Involuntary functions, 200
Involuntary responses, 225
Iris, 132
Irish Americans, 187, 587, 617, 619. *See also* Ethnicity
Irrational beliefs, 572–573, 600–601
Italian Americans, 619. *See also* Ethnicity

J

Japanese Americans, 619. *See also* Asian Americans; Ethnicity
Jewish Americans, 187, 587, 617, 619. *See also* Ethnicity
Jews, and obedience studies, 42
Job strain, and coronary heart disease, 589
Jobs. *See* Industrial/organizational psychology
Judgment, and decision making, 306–309
Just noticeable difference, 127

K

K complex, 178, 179
Kinesthesis, 166–168
Kinsey reports, 50, 53
Kinship studies, 112, 344
Knobs, of neurons, 83
Knowledge-acquisition components, 334, 335

L

L-dopa, and Parkinson's disease, 86, 93
La belle indifférence, 497
Laboratory, 56
Laboratory-observation method, 56–57
Language
    Alzheimer's disease and, 117
    of apes, 313, 315
    bilingualism and, 324–327
    Black dialect and, 316–318
    cerebral cortex and, 97–98
    children and, 314–320
    complex, 315–316
    complex language, 315–316
    concepts of, 312–313
    definition of, 310
    gender differences and, 472–473
    memory and, 276
    mental retardation and, 5
    psychotherapy and, 557
    reading and, 315
    syntax development, 315
    theories of, 318–320
    thinking and, 290, 309–313, 321–322
    vocabulary development and, 314–315
Language acquisition device (LAD), 318, 319–320
Late adulthood, 429–432
Latency, 445, 448
Latent, 238, 239
Latent content, 526, 527
Latent learning, 239
Lateral hypothalamus, 363
Law of continuity, 145
Law of effect, 224

Leadership, and heredity, 108
Learned helplessness, 500, 501
Learning
    avoidance, 234
    behavior and, 20
    behaviorism and, 13
    classical conditioning, 214–224
    cognitive factors in, 238–240
    definition of, 213
    discovery, 683
    effects of media violence and, 244–247
    effects of punishment on, 43
    information superhighway and, 236–237
    latent, 239
    observational, 239–240, 244–245, 247
    operant conditioning as, 224–235
    performance and, 239
    programmed, 234, 235
    punishment and, 224
    random, 227
    school psychologists and, 8
    signal-detection theory and, 128
    social, 239
    sociocultural factors in, 240–241
    two-factor theory of, 223
Learning theories
    aggression and, 378
    anxiety disorders and, 492–493
    behavior and, 20
    cognitive dissonance theory and, 374
    dissociative disorders and, 497
    evaluation of, 458
    hypnosis and, 203
    interest in, 21
    language development and, 318–319
    mood disorders and, 499–500
    personality and, 454–458
    personality disorders and, 508
    schizophrenia and, 504
    sexual orientation and, 368
Least-restrictive placement, 685
Legitimate authority, and obedience, 636
Lens, 133
Lesbians, 366–370, 617
Lesions, 66, 363
Leukocytes, definition of, 582
Levels-of-processing model of memory, 271–272
Lexical hypothesis, 450, 451
Libido, 444
Lie detection, 380–381
Life changes, 566–567, 568–569, 570
Light
    color and, 136
    definition of, 131
    vision and, 131–132
Light adaptation, 135
Limbic system
    definition of, 92
    infantile amnesia and, 276
    lesions of, 66
    memory and, 278, 279
Linguistic-relativity hypothesis, 320, 321–322
Lithium, 501, 550, 552
Liver, and hunger, 363
Lobotomy, prefrontal, 552, 553
Locus of control, 575, 576–577
Long-term memory (LTM)
    accuracy of, 262–263
    capacity of, 265
    context-dependent memory and, 270

definition of, 262
    eyewitness testimony and, 263–265
    hierarchical structure of, 268
    information processing theory and, 18
    interference theory and, 274
    organization in, 267–269
    short-term memory and, 265–266, 278, 284
    as stage of memory, 254–255, 262–271
    state-dependent memory and, 270–271
    tip-of-the-tongue phenomenon and, 269–270
Longevity, 430
Loudness, 154, 157–158
Love
    consummate love, 634–635
    Love scale, 634
    romantic love and, 634–635
    triangular model of love, 633–634
Love and belongingness needs, 360
Low-density lipoproteins, 590, 605
Low-fat diet, 602
LSD, 86, 194, 195, 198
Luteinizing hormone (LH), 104, 107
Lynching, 643–644

M

Machismo, 640
Magnetic resonance imaging (MRI), 67–68, 596
Magnify, 534
Mainstreaming, 351, 685
Maintenance method, 326–327
Maintenance rehearsal
    definition of, 253
    levels-of-processing model and, 271
    memory improvement and, 284
    memory transfer and, 265–266
    nonsense syllables and, 272
Major depression, 498–499, 548
Major tranquilizers, 551
Male erectile disorder, 512, 513
Malingering, 494, 495
Manic, 299, 498
Manifest content, 526, 527
Manipulation, and exploration, 372–373
Manopause, 428–429
Mantras, 198, 199
MAO inhibitors. *See* Monoamine oxidase inhibitors
Marianismo, 650
Marijuana, 162, 184–186, 194–197
Marketing research, 670–671
Marriage, and longevity, 583
Masturbation, 364
Matching hypothesis, 632
Mathematical abilities, 472–473
Maturation, 397
Maturational theory, 397–398
Maze-learning ability, 114–115, 344, 475
Mean, A3
Means-end analysis, 295, 296
Measurement
    errors in, 53
    industrial/organizational psychology and, 657
    of intelligence, 336–341
    interest inventories, 658–659
    methods of, 55
    norm-referenced versus criterion-referenced testing, 685

of personality, 466–469
    psychological tests, 55, 657
    of psychotherapy, 547
Media violence, 244–247
Median, A3
Medical advice, compliance with, 596–598
Meditation, 198–199, 285, 592, 600
Medulla, 91
Melancholic, 450
Memory
    acetylcholine and, 86
    Alzheimer's disease and, 117
    autobiographical, 51–52
    biology of, 277–282
    challenges to, 250–251, 282
    changes at neural level, 278
    changes at structural level, 278–279
    definition of, 254
    electronic, 280–281
    episodic, 251
    flashbulb, 266–267
    forgetting and, 272–277
    kinds of, 251–252
    levels-of-processing model of, 271–272
    long-term, 262–271
    methods for improving, 284–287
    procedural, 251–252
    processes of, 252–254
    as reconstructive, 262–263
    schemas and, 265
    semantic, 251
    sensory, 254–258
    short-term, 258–262
    stages of, 254–271
    storage of, 278–279
Memory trace, 256
Men. *See also* Gender; Gender differences
    antisocial personality disorder and, 507
    compliance with medical advice and, 597
    hormones and, 107
    interpersonal relatedness and, 449–450
    manopause and, 428–429
    research bias and, 49
    sexual behavior and, 365–366
    voice pitch of, 153
Menarche, 422
Menopause, 365, 428, 429
Menstruation
    cross-cultural perspectives on, 120–121
    endocrine system and, 107–108
    premenstrual syndrome and, 119
Mental age, definition of, 335
Mental disorders, 485
Mental processes, 13
Mental retardation, 5, 111, 351–353, 549
Mental set, 297–298
Mental structures, 238
Mescaline, 198, 199
Meta-analysis, 548
Metabolism, 106, 390
Metacomponents, 333
Metamemory, 253, 418, 419
Methadone, 189, 190
Methaqualone, 190
Method of constant stimuli, 126, 127
Method of loci, 285
Method of savings, 274, 275
Mexican Americans, 346, 465, 557. *See also* Hispanic Americans
Microspectrophotometry, 139

Middle adulthood, 427–429
Middle ear, 155, 159
Midlife crisis, 426, 427–428
Midlife transition, 426, 427–428
Migraine headaches, 588
Mind, brain and, 65–66
Minnesota Multiphasic Personality Inventory (MMPI), 466–469
Minor tranquilizers, 549
Minority groups. *See* African Americans; Asian Americans; Ethnicity; Hispanic Americans; Native Americans
MMPI. *See* Minnesota Multiphasic Personality Inventory (MMPI)
Mnemonic, 83
Mnemonic devices, 252, 253, 285–287
Mob behavior, 643–644
Mode, A3–A4
Modeling, 538, 539
Models, 230–231, 240, 245, 318, 454–455
Mongolism. *See* Down syndrome
Monkeys, 372–373, 407–408
Monoamine oxidase inhibitors, 552
Monochromat, 139
Monocular cues, 145–147
Monozygotic twins, 112
Mood disorders, 498–501
Moods, and state-dependent memory, 270
Moral development, 5, 418–421
Moral judgment, and preoperational stage, 415
Moral principle, 443
Moro reflex, 403
Morpheme, 312
Morphine, 188, 190
Morphology, 312
Motion cues, 147
Motion parallax, 146, 147
Motivation
    achievement and, 375–376
    affiliation and, 376–377
    aggression and, 377–379
    Aristotle and, 11
    cognitive consistency and, 373–374
    educational psychologists and, 8
    group behavior and, 640
    hunger and, 362–364
    intelligence tests and, 343
    in late adulthood, 430
    reasons for, 357
    sex and, 364–370
    signal-detection theory and, 128
    stimulus motives, 370–373
    theories of, 357–362
    weight control and, 390
Motives, 357
Motor cortex, 97
Motor development, 403
Movement perception, 144–145
MPD. *See* Multiple personality disorder
MRI. *See* Magnetic resonance imaging (MRI)
Müller-Lyer illusion, 151–152
Multifactorial approach
    human diversity and, 584–587
    to asthma, 590
    to cancer, 591–594
    to coronary heart disease, 588–590
    to headaches, 587–588
Multiple approach–avoidance conflict, 570, 571
Multiple intelligences theory, 332–333, 349

Multiple personality disorder, 482, 483, 495–496
Multiple sclerosis, and myelin, 83
Muscle tension headache, 588
Music, and spatial reasoning, 348–349
Mutism, 504
Myelin, 83
Myelin sheaths, 83, 276

N

Naloxone, 167
Narcolepsy, 182–183
Narcotics, 188, 402
Native Americans
    alcoholism and, 187
    discrimination and, 617
    healing process and, 564
    as involuntary minority group, 21
    IQ scores of, 340
    obedience studies and, 42
    population of, 23–24
    as psychologists, 28
    psychotherapy and, 557, 561
    sexual exclusiveness and, 364
    sexual orientation and, 369–370
    suicide and, 516
Nativist theory, and language development, 319–320
Naturalistic-observation method, 54, 55–57
Nature
    definition of, 110
    developmental psychology and, 397
    importance of, 111–112
Nearsighted, 148, 149
Necker cube, 142–143
Needs
    definition of, 357
    hierarchy of, 359–360, 459
    physiological, 357
    psychological, 357
Negative correlation, 58, 59
Negative feedback, 106
Negative instance, 291
Negative reinforcement, 497
Negative reinforcers, 227–229
Neoanalysts, 18, 19
Neodissociation theory, 202, 203–204
Neonate, 402–405
Nerve, 88
Nervous system
    central nervous system, 88–93
    composition of, 87–88
    definition of, 80
    development of, 402
    divisions of, 88
    maturation of, 398
    parts of, 89
    peripheral nervous system and, 93–95
    psychoneuroimmunology and, 582
    traits and, 451
Neural impulse, 83–85
Neurons
    afferent, 83
    anatomy of, 82
    definition of, 80, 81
    efferent, 83
    electrochemical process of, 84–85
    makeup of, 81–83
    myelin and, 83
    myelinated, 83
    neural impulse and, 83–85
    neurotransmitters and, 85–87
    nonmyelinated, 83

synapse and, 85
    as temperature receptors, 165
Neuroses, psychodynamic perspective of, 486
Neuroticism, 108, 451, 501
Neurotransmitters
    arousal and, 383
    definition of, 81
    dreams and, 181
    electrochemical process and, 84
    hormones and, 101
    mood disorders and, 501
    neurons and, 85–87
Nicotine, 186, 192–194. *See also* Cigarettes; Smoking
Nightmares, 181–182
Nodes of Ranvier, 83
Noise, 128, 129, 155, 258, 673–674
Non-rapid-eye-movement sleep, 178, 179
Nonassertive behavior, 540
Nonbalance, 374
Nonconscious, 175
Nonsense syllables, 272, 273
Nonspecific factors, 548
Noradrenaline
    adrenal medulla and, 107
    antidepressants and, 551–552
    definition of, 86
    endocrine system and, 104
    lithium and, 552
    mood disorders and, 501
    self-efficacy expectations and, 574
    stress and, 580, 581
Norepinephrine, 104, 107, 494
Norm-referenced testing, 685
Normal curve, A5–A6
Normal distribution, A5–A6
Novel stimulation, 372, 373
NREM sleep. *See* Non-rapid-eye-movement sleep
Nuclei, 88
Nurturance, 360–361
Nurture
    definition of, 110
    developmental psychology and, 397
    importance of, 111–112
Nutritional knowledge, 390–391

O

Obedience
    description of, 42–44
    ethics and, 68–70
    experimental method and, 60–61
    gender differences and, 477
    laboratory-observation method and, 56
    Milgram studies on, 42–44, 635–636
    moral development and, 418
    operational definitions and, 63
    replication of, 48
    social psychology and, 624
Obesity, 389–392, 586
Object permanence, 320, 413
Objective, 12
Objective responsibility, 415
Objective tests, 466–469
Observation methods, 51–57
Observational learning
    attitudes and, 613
    cognitive emphasis of, 247
    definition of, 238, 239
    dissociative disorders and, 497
    gender differences in, 476
    modeling and, 538
    prejudices and, 240

social-cognitive theory and, 454–455
    television violence and, 244–245
Obsession, 490, 491
Obsessive-compulsive disorder, 491
Occipital lobe, 95, 139
Odor, 162. *See also* Smell
Oedipus complex, 445, 448, 528
Olfactory, 162. *See also* Smell
Olfactory nerve, 162
Openness to experience, 452–453
Operant behavior, 224, 225
Operant conditioning
    applications of, 233–235
    definition of, 224
    discriminative stimuli, 230–231
    extinction and, 228–229
    law of effect and, 224
    as learning, 224–235
    observational learning, 455
    procedures of, 539–540
    reinforcement and, 224–227
    responses in, 223–224
    rewards and punishments, 229–230
    schedules of reinforcement, 231–233
    spontaneous recovery and, 228–229
    taste aversion and, 212
    types of reinforcers, 227–228
Operants, 224, 225
Operational definition, 46, 63
Opioids, 188–190, 196
Opponent-process theory, 139, 359, 361
Optic nerve, 133, 135
Oral fixation, 444, 445
Oral stage, of psychosexual development, 444
Organ of Corti, 157
Organizational analysis, 660
Organizational psychology, 9–10, 657. *See also* Industrial/organizational psychology
Organizational theory, 662–663, 666
Organizing effect, 365
Orgasmic disorder, 512, 513
Orienting reflex, 216, 217
Out-group
    actor–observer effect and, 621
    peace and, 624
    prejudice and, 618
    stereotyping and, 643
Outer ear, 155
Oval window, 154, 155
Ovaries, 104, 107
Overextension, 315
Overgeneralize, 534
Overregularization, 315–316
Overtones, 154–155
Oxytocin, 104, 106

P

"P", 166
Pacific Islanders. *See* Asian Americans
Pain
    biofeedback and, 171
    cancer and, 592
    endorphins and, 86
    gate theory and, 166–167
    hypnosis and, 170–171
    irrational beliefs, 171
    management of, 170–171
    phantom limb pain, 166
    relaxation training and, 171
    as skin sense, 166–167
    study of, 124

Paired associates, definition of, 273
Pancreas, 104, 106
Panic disorders, 490–491
Paradoxical sleep, 178
Paranoid personality disorder, 506
Paranoid schizophrenia, 502, 503
Parapsychology, 75
Parasympathetic, 93, 378, 379
Parasympathetic branch of autonomic nervous system, 93–95, 581
Parietal lobe, 95
Parent, in transactional analysis, 532, 533
Parental investment model, 630
Parenting
  achievement motivation and, 376
  adolescence and, 423–424
  child rearing and, 409–410
  heredity and, 108
  intelligence and, 345–346, 349
  rejection and, 247
Parents Anonymous, 437, 677
Parkinson's disease, 86, 93
Partial reinforcement, 231
Partial-report procedure, 256
Passive smoking, 193
Pathogens, 565
Pathological gambler, 231
Pattern perception, 143–144
Pavlovian conditioning, 215
Peace, and social psychology, 624–625
Peak performance, and sports psychology, 682
Pelvic inflammatory disease (PID), 121
Pencil electrode, 96
Perception
  definition of, 125
  Gestalt psychology and, 14
  hypnosis and, 202
  measurement of, 11
  sensation and, 126–130
Perceptual constancies, 148–151
Perceptual development, 404–406
Perceptual organization, 140–144
Performance, and learning, 239
Performance anxiety, 513
Performance components, 333
Period of the ovum, 400
Peripheral nervous system, 88, 93–95
Person variables, 454, 455
Person-centered therapy, 530–532, 548
Person-machine systems, 666–667
Personal factors, 303
Personal growth, and psychotherapy, 523
Personal space, 675–677
Personal unconscious, 446
Personal unity, 175
Personality
  Adler's theory of, 446
  Allport's theory of, 451
  Big Five personality factors, 452–453
  Cattell's theory of, 451
  definition of, 441
  employment and, 453
  Erikson's theory of, 446–447
  Eysenck's personality dimensions, 452
  as factor in health, 585
  Freud's psychosexual development, 441–445
  gender differences in, 472–474
  Hippocrates' personality types, 450, 452

humanistic–existential perspective, 458–461
  introduction to, 440
  Jung's theory of, 445–446
  learning perspective, 454–458
  Maslow's self-actualization, 459
  measurement of, 466–469
  psychodynamic perspective, 440–449
  Rogers' self theory, 459–461
  structure of, 442–444
  trait perspective, 450–453
Personality development, 398, 423–424
Personality disorders, 506–508
Personality psychologists, 8–9
Personality tests, 72, 453
Personnel tests, 658
Perspective, 145
Persuasion, 613–617
PET scan. See Positron emission tomography
Phallic stage, of psychosexual development, 445
Phallic symbol, 526, 527
Phantom limb pain, 166
Phencyclidine (PCP), 198, 199
Phenomenological, 459
Phenylketonuria, 352
Pheromones, 162–163, 358
Phi phenomenon, 145
Phlegmatic, 450
Phobias, 490
Phonemes, 312, 314
Phonology, 312
Photoreceptors, 133
Phrenology, 466
Physical attractiveness
  beauty and, 628–630
  behavior and, 630
  gender differences in, 630–631
  hiring practices and, 657
  interpersonal attraction and, 626–632
  matching hypothesis and, 632
  stereotypes of, 631–632
Physical development
  in adolescence, 422–423
  in late adulthood, 430
  perceptual development and, 404–406
  reflexes and, 402–403
  stage theory and, 398
Physical disorders, and heredity, 110
Physician–patient interactions, 597–598
Physicians, authoritarian, 596
Physiological drives, 357
Physiological needs, 357, 360, 362
Pigments, 136
Pitch, 127, 153–154, 157–158
Pituitary gland, 103, 104–106, 580
PKU. See Phenylketonuria
Place theory, 157
Placebo, 62–63, 166, 167
Placebo effect, 167, 201
Placement, 657–659
Placenta, 400, 401–402
Planning and teaching, 8, 684–685
Plaques, 117
Pleasure center, of hypothalamus, 101, 200
Pleasure principle, 442
PMS. See Premenstrual syndrome
Polarization, 642, 649–652
Polarize, 84
Political views, of college students, 53–54
Polygenic, 108–109
Polygon, A2

Polygraphs, 380–381
Pons, 91
Ponzo illusion, 152
Population, A1, A9, 48, 49
Positive correlation, 56, 57, 59
Positive instance, 291
Positive reinforcers, 227–228
Positive visualization, and sports psychology, 682
Positron emission tomography (PET scan), 17, 67, 119
Post-traumatic stress disorder, 492, 493, 510
Postconventional level, 419, 420
Posthypnotic amnesia, 202–203, 204, 273
Posthypnotic suggestion, 203
PQ4R, 38–39
Precedents, 296
Precognition, 75
Preconscious, 175, 442
Preconventional level of moral development, 418–419
Predictability, 577–578, 579, 592
Prefrontal lobotomy, 552, 553
Pregenital, 445
Pregnancy, 400, 402, 505
Prejudice
  attitudes and, 617–618
  definition of, 616, 617
  observational learning and, 240
  peace and, 624
  psychotherapy and, 558
Prelinguistic, 314, 315
Premature ejaculation, 512, 513
Premenstrual syndrome, 119–120
Premises, 204, 305
Prenatal development, 399–402
Preoperational stage, 411, 413–415
Presbyopia, 148, 149
Preschool intervention programs, 346
Prevention, and community psychology, 677–678
Preview, Question, Read, Reflect, Recite, and Review, 38–39
Primacy effect, 259, 619–620
Primary colors, 136, 137
Primary drives, 358, 362
Primary mental abilities, 331
Primary prevention, 677
Primary reinforcer, 228
Primary sex characteristics, 107
Prism, 131
Proactive inhibition, 274
Proactive interference, 275
Problem solving
  Alzheimer's disease and, 117
  approaches to, 293–296
  cancer and, 593
  children and, 310–311
  cognitive restructuring and, 536
  factors affecting, 297–301
  Gestalt psychology and, 14
  thinking and, 292–301
Problems, 293–295, 300–301
Procedural memory, 251–252
Progesterone, 104, 107
Programmed learning, 234, 235
Progressive relaxation, 537, 588, 600–602
Projection, as defense mechanism, 443
Projective test, 469
Prolactin, 17, 104, 106
Prosocial, 454
Prostaglandins, 166, 588
Prototypes, 290–292
Proximity, 142, 143
Proximodistal, 400

Prozac, 550–551
Pseudomemories, 202
Pseudoscience, and science, 72–76
Psi communication, 75
Psychedelic, 194
Psychiatrist, 8
Psychic energy, 358
Psychic structure, 442, 448
Psychics, 73–75
Psychoactive, 184
Psychoanalysis
  definition of, 15, 442, 526
  history of, 15–17
  modern psychodynamic approaches to, 529
  problems in running experiments, 546
  traditional, 526–528
  women and, 528
Psychoanalytically oriented methods, 529
Psychobiologists, 80
Psychodynamic, 16
Psychodynamic theories
  Adler and, 446
  aggression and, 377–378
  anxiety disorders and, 492
  on behavior, 19–20
  case-study method and, 51–52
  definition of, 441
  displacement and, 312
  dissociative disorders and, 496–497
  dream symbols in, 180
  drive-reduction theory and, 358
  eating disorders and, 511–512
  Erikson and, 446–447
  evaluation of, 447–449
  gender differences and, 475
  Horney and, 446
  hypnosis and, 203
  interest in, 21
  Jung and, 445–446
  mood disorders and, 499
  neuroses and, 486
  of personality, 440–449
  personality disorders and, 507–508
  psychoanalysis and, 529
  repression and, 445
  schizophrenia and, 504
  sexual orientation and, 367–368
  somatoform disorders and, 498
  substance abuse and, 185–186
Psychodynamic therapies, 525–529, 548–549
Psychogenic fugue, 494
Psychokinesis, 75
Psycholinguistic theory, 318, 319
Psychological consultation, 52. See also Case-study
Psychological disorders
  anxiety disorders, 489–494
  asylums and, 524
  characteristics of, 483–485
  classification of, 485–488
  community psychology and, 677
  definition of, 4, 5, 482, 483
  demons and, 482–483
  diagnosis of, 466
  dissociative disorders, 494–497
  eating disorders, 508–512
  electroconvulsive therapy and, 552
  ethnicity and, 21
  heredity and, 108, 110, 112
  mood disorders, 498–501
  personality disorders, 506–508
  personality psychologists and, 8
  phobias, 490
  physical attractiveness and, 631

psychotherapy and, 522, 523
psychotherapy effectiveness and, 548
schizophrenia, 501–506
sexual dysfunctions, 512–513
somatoform disorders, 497–498
suicide and, 517
Psychological factors, cancer and, 592–594
Psychological hardiness, 575, 592
Psychological needs, 357
Psychological principles, and psychotherapy, 523
Psychological tests, 55, 657
Psychological theories, and research, 42, 45. *See also* names of specific theories
Psychology. *See also* specific fields such as Social psychology
behaviorism and, 12–14
contemporary perspectives of, 21
corporations and, 664–665
critical thinking and, 29–34
definition of, 4, 5
development in millennium, 32–33
development of, 27–29
as empirical science, 42, 64, 74
ethical issues of, 68–71
functionalism and, 12
Gestalt psychology, 14–15
history of, 10–17
human diversity and, 22–29
important figures in, 16
as laboratory science, 11
psychoanalysis and, 15–17
religion and, 45
research methods in, 42–77
as science, 5–6
structuralism and, 11–12
of studying psychology, 36–39
types of psychologists, 7–10
views of behavior, 17–22
Psychomotor retardation, 498
Psychoneuroimmunology, 582, 583
Psychophysical, 126, 127
Psychophysicists, 126, 127
Psychosexual development, 441–445, 448
Psychosocial development, 446, 447
Psychosocial and environmental problems, 486, 487
Psychosurgery, 552, 553
Psychotherapy
analysis of, 548–549
behavior therapy, 536–544
bilingualism and, 560
biological therapies, 549–554
clinical judgments about, 547–548
cognitive therapies, 533–536
culturally sensitive, 25
definition of, 6, 7, 522–523
discrimination and, 558–559
effectiveness of, 546–549
ethnicity and, 557–561
group therapies, 544–546
history of, 523–525
humanistic–existential therapies, 530–533
measuring outcomes, 547
nonspecific factors and, 548
prejudice and, 558
psychodynamic therapies, 525–530
reasons for using, 523
research problems of, 546–548
women and, 528–529
PTSD. *See* Post-traumatic stress disorder

Puberty, 398, 422
Public health, and health psychology, 595
Punishment
aggression and, 247
definition of, 228, 229
effects of, 43
law of effect and, 224
learning and, 224
moral development and, 418
negative reinforcers and, 229
persuasion and, 613
reinforcers and, 229–230
Pupil, 132, 133
Pupillary reflex, 404, 405
Pure research, 6, 7, 9
Pythagorean Theorem, 295

R

Random learning, 227
Random sample, 49–50
Random trial-and-error behavior, 224
Range, A1, A4
Rape
date rape, 689, 692–693
motivations for, 690
myths of, 690–691
prevention of, 678, 689–693
strategies against, 691–693
Rapid flight of ideas, 498, 499
Rapid smoking, 539
Rapid-eye-movement (REM) sleep, 178, 179, 181
RAS. *See* Reticular activating system
Rathus Assertiveness Schedule, 540, 541
Rational-emotive therapy, 534, 548
Rationalization, as defense mechanism, 443
Re-uptake, 85, 86
Reaction formation, as defense mechanism, 443
Reaction time, 430
Reality principle, 442
Reality testing, 469
Reasoning, 304–306
Rebound anxiety, 550
Recall, 273
Recency effect, 259, 261, 619–620, 620
Receptor site, 85
Recessive traits, 112–113
Reciprocity, 420, 632, 632–633
Recitation, 684, 685
Recognition, 272–273
Recruitment, 657–659
Reflex arc, 90
Reflexes, 215, 402–403, 412
Regression, 202, 433
Rehearsal
elaborative, 266, 271
interference and, 261
levels-of-processing model and, 272
maintenance, 253, 265–266, 271
metamemory and, 418
short-term memory and, 258–259
Reinforce, 224
Reinforcement
cognitive theory and, 238
continuous, 231
definition of, 12, 13
language development and, 318–319
partial, 231
schedules of, 231–233
selective, 319

strategies aimed at, 543
vicarious, 240, 246
Reinforcement of desired behavior, 543
Reinforcers, 227–230
Relatedness versus individuality, 449–450
Relative frequencies, 476
Relative refractory period, 84, 85
Relaxation response, 199
Relaxation training
asthma and, 590
cancer and, 592, 593
insomnia and, 206–207
pain and, 171
progressive relaxation, 537, 588, 600–602
Relearning, 273
Releaser, 358
Reliability, 54, 55
Religion, and psychology, 45
REM sleep. *See* Rapid-eye-movement sleep
REM-rebound, 179
Remote associates test, 304
Repetition, memory and, 284
Replicate, 46, 47
Representativeness heuristic, definition of, 306–307
Repress, 175
Repression
as defense mechanism, 443
definition of, 262, 442
forgetting and, 275
free association and, 527
infantile amnesia and, 276
psychoanalysis and, 526
Research methods. *See also* Statistics
animal research, 4–5, 70–71, 577–578, 591
brain and, 65–68
correlational method, 56–60
deception and, 69
electronic developments in, 64–65
ethical issues of, 68–71
experimental method and, 60–64
generalizing and, 48–50
Milgram studies on obedience, 42–44
observation methods and, 51–57
in psychotherapy, 546–548
samples and population and, 47–50
science versus pseudoscience, 72–76
scientific method and, 44–47
using people, 68–70
Resistance, 442, 526, 527
Resistance stage, 580–581
Respondent conditioning, 215
Response cost, 543
Response prevention, 543
Response set, 466, 467
Responses, 12–13, 216–217
Resting potential, 84
Restriction of stimulus field, 542
Restrictiveness-permissiveness dimension of child rearing, 410
Reticular activating system (RAS), 91, 181
Retina, 133
Retinal disparity, 148, 149
Retrieval, 253–254, 272
Retroactive inhibition, 274
Retroactive interference, 274–275
Retrograde amnesia, 276–277
Reversibility, 415
Rewards, 228–230
Risky shift, 642

Ritalin, and attention-deficit/hyperactivity disorder, 191, 197
RNA, and memory, 277–278
Rods, 134, 135
Role diffusion, 424
Role theory, 202–204
Romantic love, 5, 632
Rooting, 402, 403, 412
Rorschach inkblot test, 469
Rote, 260
Rote learning, 269
Rote repetition, 266, 284
Rubin vase, 142

S

"s" factor, 331
Saccadic eye movements, 256, 257–258
Sadism, 445
Safety needs, 360
Samples, A1, A9, 47–50
Sanguine, 450
Satiety, 362, 363
Saturation, 136
Savings, 274, 275
Schemas, 238, 262–263, 265, 360
Scheme, 410, 411, 412
Schizoid personality disorder, 506
Schizophrenia
antipsychotic drugs and, 554
behavior therapy and, 549
biological perspective on, 17
cognitive therapy and, 548–549
definition of, 482, 483
description of, 501–503
diagnosis of, 487
dopamine and, 86, 551
electroconvulsive therapy and, 552
hallucinations and, 484
heredity and, 108, 112, 505
operant conditioning and, 539
positron emission tomography and, 67
psychotherapy effectiveness and, 548
theoretical views of, 504–506
types of, 503–504
Schizotypal personality disorder, 506
Scholastic Aptitude Test (SAT), A6, 8, 341, 473
School psychologists, as specialty, 8. *See also* Educational psychology
Science, and pseudoscience, 72–76
Scientific method, 44
Sclera, 132
Scoring, computerized, 467
Seattle Longitudinal Study, 347
Second-language learning, and age, 325
Secondary colors, 136–137
Secondary prevention, 677–678
Secondary reinforcer, 228
Secondary sex characteristics, 107, 422
Secure attachment, 406, 435
Security, 409
Sedatives, 185, 186, 552
Selection factor, 46, 246–247
Selective attention, 174–175, 261–262, 417
Selective avoidance, 616
Selective breeding, 113–115
Selective exposure, 616
Selective perception, 534
Selective reinforcement, 319
Self, 175, 446, 464–465
Self-actualization, 359, 360, 459, 530, 547

Self-concept, 460, 464, 478
Self-consciousness, 453
Self-control methods, 540–544
Self-efficacy expectations
  definition of, 457, 574, 575
  irrational beliefs and, 572
  sports psychology and, 681
  stress and, 574–575
  systematic desensitization and, 537–538
Self-esteem
  acculturation and, 465
  definition of, 460, 461
  depression and, 499
  person-centered therapy and, 531
  sociocultural factors and, 464–465
Self-fulfilling prophecy, 683
Self-ideals, 460, 461
Self-insight, 442
Self-monitoring, 540
Self-regulatory systems, 457
Self-serving bias, 622
Semantic codes, 253, 260, 269, 271, 272
Semantic memory, 251, 269
Semanticity, 312–313, 314
Semantics, 312
Semicircular canals, 168
Sensation
  absolute threshold and, 126–127
  binding in brain, 129–130
  definition of, 124, 125
  difference threshold and, 127–128
  feature detectors and, 128–129
  measurement of, 11
  perception and, 126–130
  sensory adaptation and, 130
  signal-detection theory and, 128
Sensation-seeking scale, 371
Sense of humor, 576–577, 602
Sensitive period, 320
Sensitization, 130, 131
Sensorimotor stage, 411, 412–413
Sensorineural deafness, 159, 160
Sensory acuity, in late adulthood, 430
Sensory adaptation, 130, 131
Sensory awareness, 174, 175
Sensory cortex, 278
Sensory deprivation, 370
Sensory memory, 254–258, 274
Sensory receptors, 124–125
Sensory register, 256
Sensory stimulation, 370–372
Septum, 92
Serial-position effect, 259
Serotonin
  antidepressants and, 551–552
  anxiety disorders and, 494
  definition of, 86
  memory and, 278
  mood disorders and, 501
Serotonin-uptake inhibitors, 552
Serum cholesterol, 588, 590
Set point, 363, 390
Settling down, in young adulthood, 427
Sex chromosomes, 108, 109
Sex differences. See Gender differences
Sex hormones
  effects of, 365–366
  gender difference and, 475
  prenatal development and, 401
  sexual orientation and, 368
Sex therapy, 513
Sexual activity, 367

Sexual assault. See Rape
Sexual behavior
  adrenal glands and, 366
  adversarial, 689
  alcohol and, 187
  gender differences in, 474
  hormones and, 365
  Kinsey reports on, 50, 53
  pheromones and, 162–163
  Wyatt survey of, 50–51
Sexual dysfunctions, 512–513
Sexual orientation, 366–369
  definition of, 366
  as diversity, 26–27
  ethnicity and, 369–370
Sexual response, and reflexes, 90
Sexuality
  interactive, 366–367
  motivation and, 364–370
  pleasure in, 364
  psychosexual development and, 442
  sexual orientation, 366–369
Sexually transmitted diseases, 693
Shadowing, 146–147
Shape constancy, 149–151
Shaping, 232–233, 284
Short-term memory (STM)
  chunks of information and, 259–260
  decay and, 274
  definition of, 258, 259
  encoding and, 258–259
  information processing theory and, 18
  interference in, 260–262
  long-term memory and, 265–266, 278, 284
  serial-position effect and, 259
  as stage of memory, 254–255, 258–262
Shyness, and heredity, 108
Sibling rivalry, 446
Siblings, 396, 397
Sickle-cell anemia, 111, 586
Sickness. See Health psychology; Illness
Signal-detection theory, 128, 129, 261
Similarity, 142, 143, 632
Simultaneous conditioning, 216, 217
Single eye fixation, 256
Situational attribution, 620–621, 625
Situational determinants, of helping, 646
Size constancy, 145, 148–149, 152
Skill memory, 251
Skin senses
  pain as, 166–167
  sensation and, 164–168
  somatosensory cortex and, 95
  temperature, 165–166
  touch and pressure, 164–165
Skinner boxes, 225–227
Sleep
  deprivation of, 179
  dreams and, 176–184
  functions of, 179
  paradoxical, 178
  sleep disorders, 182–184, 486
  stages of, 177–178
Sleep paralysis, 183
Sleep spindles, 178, 179
Sleep terrors, 183
Sleepwalking, 184, 486
Smell
  absolute threshold and, 126
  perceptual development of, 405

sensation and, 161–163
  Weber's constant for, 127
Smoking. See also Cigarettes; Nicotine
  A–B problem and, 612
  cancer and, 591
  compliance with medical advice and, 596
  coronary heart disease and, 589–590
  diversity and, 193
  rapid smoking, 539
  socioeconomic status and, 587
  techniques for quitting, 207–209
  Type A behavior and, 602
Snellen chart, 148
Social categorization, and prejudice, 618
Social comparison, and obedience, 636
Social comparison theory, 376, 377
Social conflict, and prejudice, 617–618
Social decision schemes, 641
Social development, 406–410, 423–424
Social dominance, and heredity, 108
Social evaluation, 303–304
Social facilitation, 640–641
Social influence
  conformity and, 637–640
  definition of, 635
  Milgram studies of, 42–44, 635–636
  obedience to authority and, 635–636
Social learning, 239, 618
Social loafing, 641
Social mosaic, 23
Social motives, 375
Social norms, 637
Social perception
  attribution theory and, 620–623
  body language and, 623, 626
  definition of, 619
  primacy and recency effects, 619–620
Social phobia, 490
Social psychologists, 8–9
Social psychology
  attitudes and, 611–618
  consumer psychology and, 670
  definition of, 611
  group behavior and, 640–646
  interpersonal attraction and, 626–635
  peace and, 624–625
  prejudice and, 617–618
  social influence and, 635–640
  social perception and, 619–626
  Socrates and, 11
Social readjustment rating scale, 568–569
Social relationships, 448, 449
Social support, 578–579
Social-cognitive theories
  aggression and, 378
  anxiety disorders and, 493
  of behavior, 20
  behaviorists and, 17
  definition of, 20, 454
  dissociative disorders and, 497
  gender differences and, 476–477
  motivation and, 360
  personality and, 454–457
  substance abuse and, 186
Social-learning theorists, 20
Social-skills training, 540
Socialization
  definition of, 232, 233

gender differences and, 476–477
  obedience and, 636
Sociobiological theory, and physical attractiveness, 630–631
Sociobiology, 377
Sociocultural theories
  aggression and, 378–379
  on behavior, 20–22
  definition of, 20, 462
  individual and, 462–465
  motivation and, 360–361
  of romantic love, 634–635
  schizophrenia and, 504–505
  self-concept and, 478
  social inequality and, 528–529
Socioeconomic status
  alcoholism and, 186–187
  cancer and, 586
  definition of, 587
  depression and, 499
  eating disorders and, 510, 586
  as factor in health, 584, 585
  intelligence and, 340–341, 347–348
  intelligence tests and, 341–342
  smoking and, 193
Soma, 81
Somatic nervous system, 93
Somatoform disorders, 497
Somatosensory cortex, 95
Sounds, locating, 157
Source traits, 451
Spatial reasoning, and music, 348–349
Spatial relations ability, 344–345, 472–473, 475
Specific phobia, 490
Speech, and cerebral cortex, 97, 108
Sphincter, 402, 403
Spinal cord, 88–90, 166
Spinal reflex, 88, 89
Split-brain operation, 99–100
Spontaneous recovery, 218–220, 228–229
Sports psychology, 680–682
Stage, 397
Stage theory, and discontinuous development, 398
Standard deviation, A4
Standardized tests, 466
Stanford Binet Intelligence Scale (SBIS), 335–336, 338–339
Staring, 623, 626
Startle reflex, 403
State-dependent memory, 270–271
Statistically significant differences, A7–A9
Statistics
  correlation coefficient, A6–A7
  definition of, A1
  descriptive, A1–A5
  development of, 11
  inferential, A7–A9
  normal curve and, A5–A6
  statistically significant differences and, A7–A9
STD. See Sexually transmitted diseases
Stereotype, definition of, 8, 612
Stereotypes
  Asian Americans and, 659
  body type and, 451
  definition of, 613
  of elderly, 431
  gender and, 649
  groupthink and, 643
  machismo/marianismo, 649–650
  menstruation and, 119–120

peace and, 624
of physical attractiveness,
631–632
prejudice and, 617
of psychotherapists, 557
of sociocultural groups, 619
Steroids, 104, 583
Stimulants, 184, 185, 190–194, 196
Stimulus
absolute threshold and, 126
in classical conditioning, 216–217
definition of, 12, 13, 215
discriminative, 230–231
self-control methods and,
542–543
Stimulus control, 542–543
Stimulus motives, 370–373
Stimulus-outcome relations, 457
Stirrup, 155
Storage, 18, 253, 272
Strabismus, 148, 149
Stranger anxiety, 407
Stratified sample, 49
Stream of consciousness, 13
Stress
adrenal medulla, 107
alcoholism and, 188
biofeedback training and, 200
cancer and, 591–592, 593
child abuse and, 437
chronic, 593
coping with, 600–606
cortical steroids and, 106
definition of, 565
forensic psychology and, 679
general adaptation syndrome
(GAS) and, 579–581
headaches and, 587–588
immune system and, 582–584
maternal, 368
pain and, 171
premenstrual syndrome and, 120
psychological moderators of,
574–579
socioeconomic status and, 587
sources of, 566–574
sports psychology and, 681
suicide and, 517
Stroboscopic motion, 144–145
Strong/Campbell Interest Inventory, 658
Structuralism, 11–12, 17, 18
Study methods, 36–39
Stupor, 502, 503
Subjective, 12
Subjective moral judgment, 415
Subjective value, 454, 455, 457
Sublimation, as defense mechanism,
443
Subordinate, 269
Substance abuse
in adolescents, 196–197
causal factors, 185–186
definition of, 184
dependence and, 184–185
drugs and, 184–185
kinship studies of, 112
women and, 49
Subtractive color mixture, 136
Successive approximations, 232,
284–285, 540, 543
Succubus, 181
Sucking reflex, 412
Suicide, 432, 499, 516–518,
643–644, 677
Superego, 442, 443, 526
Superordinate, 268, 269
Support groups, 638
Suppression, 175
Surface structure, 312, 313

Surface traits, 451
Survey method, 52–55
Surveys, 53
Symbols, 310
Sympathetic, 93, 378, 379
Sympathetic branch of autonomic
nervous system, 93–95,
378–380, 580, 581
Synapses, 85, 278
Synaptic cleft, 85
Synchrony theory, 129
Syndrome, 106
Syntax, 312–313
Syntax development, 315–316
Syphilis, 402
Systematic desensitization,
222–223, 536, 537
Systematic interactions, 523
Systematic random search, 295

T

TA. *See* Transactional analysis
Tacrine, 119
Tactile, 100
Tangles, 117
Task analysis, 660, 670, 680–681
Taste
absolute threshold and, 126
perceptual development of, 405
sensation and, 163–164
Weber's constant for, 127
Taste aversion, 212, 213, 218
Taste buds, 164
Taste cells, 164
TAT. *See* Thematic Apperception
Test
Taxonomy, 684, 685
Tay-Sachs disease, 586
Teaching practices, 8, 683
Technology, as factor in health,
585
Telegraphic speech, 315
Television, and observational learn-
ing, 244
Temperature, 62, 165–166,
674–675
Templates, 238
Temporal lobe, 95
Terminals, of neurons, 83, 85
Tertiary colors, 136–137
Tertiary prevention, 678
Test-retest reliability, 54, 55
Testes, 104, 107
Testing method, 55
Testosterone
aggression and, 475
definition of, 107, 365
endocrine system and, 104
physical development and, 422
sexual orientation and, 368
Tests. *See* Measurement; and names
of specific tests
Texture gradient, definition of, 146,
147
Thalamus, 92, 139, 166, 279
THC. *See* Delta-9-tetrahydro-
cannabinol
Thematic Apperception Test, 374,
375, 469
Theory, 5, 44, 45. *See also* names of
specific theories
Theory of social comparison, 376,
377
Theory Y, 663
Theory Z, 666
Therapy. *See* Psychotherapy; and
names of specific therapies
Theta waves, 178, 179
Thinking
categorical, 291

cerebral cortex and, 97–98
concepts and prototypes,
290–292
convergent, 302
creativity and, 301–304
definition of, 290, 291
divergent, 302
judgment and decision making,
306–309
language and, 290, 309–313,
321–322
problem solving and, 292–301
reasoning and, 304–306
Thyrotrophin, 104
Thymine, 109, 110
Thyroid gland, 104, 106
Thyrotropin-releasing hormone,
104
Thyroxin, 104, 106
Timbre, 154–155
Time out, 230, 231, 235
Time urgency, 602–604
Tip-of-the-tongue phenomenon,
269–270
TM. *See* Transcendental meditation
Token economy, 234, 539
Tolerance, 184, 185
Top-down processing, 143
Total immersion, 326
Touch
absolute threshold and, 126
body language and, 623
perceptual development of,
405–406
as skin sense, 164–165
Weber's constant for, 127
Trace conditioning, 216, 217
Tracer, 67
Training and instruction, 660
Trait theories
Allport's theory of, 451
Big Five personality factors and,
452–453
Cattell's theory of, 451
Eysenck's theory of, 451–452
Hippocrates' theory, 450–452
personality and, 450–453
personality disorders and, 508
Traits
definition of, 330, 331, 450
dominant, 112–113
genetic influences on, 17
personality psychologists and, 8
recessive, 112–113
Tranquilizers, 184, 402, 549, 551
Transaction, 532, 533
Transactional analysis, 531–532
Transcendental meditation, 198,
199
Transference, 528
Trauma, and amnesia, 276
Treatment, 60, 61
Triangular model of love, 632,
633–634
Triarchic, 333
Triarchic theory of intelligence,
333–334
Trichromat, 139
Trichromatic theory, 139
Tricyclic antidepressants, 552
Trying 20s, 424, 425
Turn-taking, infants' awareness of,
314
Twin studies
anxiety disorders and, 493
heredity and, 112
of intelligence, 344–345
mood disorders and, 501
schizophrenia and, 505
sexual orientation and, 368

Two-factor theory of learning, 223
Two-point threshold, 164, 165
Two-sided arguments, 615
Type A behavior, 573–574
behavior modification and, 590
coronary heart disease and, 589
definition of, 572, 573
migraine headaches and, 588
modifying, 602–603
psychological hardiness and, 575
Type B behavior, 573–574

U

Umbilical cord, definition of, 402
Unconditional positive regard, 460,
461, 531
Unconditioned response, 216
Unconditioned stimulus, 216
Unconscious, 175, 442
Unconscious processes, 16, 20
Understanding, 294, 295
Units of behavior, 225–227
Universal grammar, 319
Unobtrusive, 56
Uplifts, 566
UR. *See* Unconditioned response
US. *See* Unconditioned stimulus
Uterus, 104

V

Vacillate, 570
Vaginismus, 512, 513
Validity, 54, 55
Validity scales, 54, 55, 466, 467
Values, 5, 636
Variability, A4–A5
Variable, 6
Variable-interval schedule, 231,
232
Variable-ratio schedule, 232
Ventromedial nucleus, 363
Verbal ability, 344–345, 472
Verbal aggression, 378
Verbal memory, 279
Vestibular sense, 168
Vicarious reinforcement, 240, 246
Victimization, by prejudice, 618
Vineland Adaptive Behavior Scales,
351
Violence, 244–247, 437. *See also*
Aggression
Virtual reality (VR), 102–103
Virtual sex, 367
Visible light, 131
Visible spectrum, 131
Vision
absolute threshold and, 126
blind navigation system and,
158–159
brain and, 92
color blindness, 139–140
color vision, 135–139
depth perception and, 145–148
eye and, 132–135
feature detectors and, 128
light and, 131–132
movement perception and,
144–145
occipital lobe and, 95
perceptual constancies, 148–151
perceptual development and, 404
perceptual organization and,
140–144
problems in, 148
sensation, 130–140
visual illusions and, 151–152
Weber's constant for, 127
Visual accommodation, 404, 405
Visual acuity, 148, 149, 404
Visual cliff experiment, 404–405

Visual code, 253
Visual cortex, 278
Visual illusions, 151–152
Visual tracking, 405
Vocabulary development, 314–315
Volts, 178, 179
Voluntary functions, 200
Voluntary responses, 225
Volunteer bias, 50, 51
Vomeronasal organ, 162

W

Waking state, 175–176
Warm colors, 136
Warmth-coldness dimension of child rearing, 409–410
Water-jar problems, 293
Waxy flexibility, 504
Weaning, 444
Weber's constant, 127
Wechsler Adult Intelligence Scale, A6, 337–339, 342, 347, 658

Wechsler Intelligence Scale for Children, 348
Weight control, methods of, 390–392
Well-defined problem, definition of, 300
Wernicke-Korsakoff syndrome, definition of, 188
Wernicke's aphasia, 97
Wernicke's area, 97–98
White Anglo-Saxon Protestants, stereotypes of, 619
White matter, 90
White noise, 154, 155
Whole-report procedure, 256
Wish fulfillment, 526, 527
Women. *See also* Gender; Gender differences
   adolescent identity formation and, 424
   aggression and, 48, 378
   careers of, 25–26
   chemical dependence and, 49

cigarette use and, 192–193
compliance with medical advice and, 596–597
date rape and, 378
depression and, 49, 499, 500, 528
discrimination and, 617
eating disorders and, 509, 510
ethnicity and, 369
generalization and, 49
health-related research on, 49
hysterical neuroses and, 498
industry jobs and, 661–662
insomnia and, 182
menstruation and, 107–108
midlife transition and, 428
moral development of, 420–421
Muslim, 639–640
obesity and, 389
post-traumatic stress disorder and, 492, 493
prejudices against, 25

premenstrual syndrome and, 119–120
as psychologists, 27–28
psychotherapy and, 528–529
self-concept and, 464–465
sexual behavior and, 365–366
sociocultural influences on, 360–361
sociocultural perspective of, 20
voice pitch of, 153
weight control and, 390
Wyatt survey of, 50–51
Work. *See* Industrial/organizational psychology
Working memories, 18
Working memory, 258, 259

Y

Young adulthood, 425–427, 509

Z

Zener cards, 75
Zygote, 112, 396, 397, 399

NOTES

NOTES

NOTES

NOTES

NOTES

NOTES

NOTES

NOTES

NOTES